THE OXFORD HANDBOOK OF

INTERNATIONAL LAW IN EUROPE

THE OXFORD HANDBOOK OF

INTERNATIONAL LAW IN EUROPE

Edited by
ANNE VAN AAKEN
PIERRE D'ARGENT
LAURI MÄLKSOO
and
JOHANN JUSTUS VASEL

OXFORD
UNIVERSITY PRESS

OXFORD
UNIVERSITY PRESS

Great Clarendon Street, Oxford, OX2 6DP,
United Kingdom

Oxford University Press is a department of the University of Oxford.
It furthers the University's objective of excellence in research, scholarship,
and education by publishing worldwide. Oxford is a registered trade mark of
Oxford University Press in the UK and in certain other countries

Published in the United States of America by Oxford University Press
198 Madison Avenue, New York, NY 10016, United States of America

British Library Cataloguing in Publication Data
Data available

Library of Congress Control Number: 2024939981

ISBN 978–0–19–886531–5

DOI: 10.1093/oxfordhb/9780198865315.001.0001

Printed and bound by
CPI Group (UK) Ltd, Croydon, CR0 4YY

MIX
Paper | Supporting responsible forestry
FSC® C013604
www.fsc.org

The manufacturer's authorised representative in the EU for product safety is Oxford
University Press España S.A. of el Parque Empresarial San Fernando de Henares, Avenida
de Castilla, 2 – 28830 Madrid (www.oup.es/en).

Preface

'International law and Europe' is a sizeable topic that does not lend itself to easily defined contours. Those contours are of a historical, political, legal, economic, social, or cultural nature and are intrinsically linked to one another. Anne van Aaken, Pierre d'Argent, Lauri Mälksoo, and Johann Justus Vasel, and the numerous authors they have assembled, have conducted their enquiry on international law and Europe with an admirable comprehensiveness, exploring as they do the many nuances that populate the relationship between international law and Europe. Three major themes underlie the handbook. One of these is the diversity of traditions of international law in Europe. The handbook highlights how these traditions can co-exist and can interact with each other, but also lead to fragmentation. Another theme is linked to the fact that the European continent has experienced many conflicts, totalitarian regimes, and much trauma. These have had particular impact on, and resonance in, the legal order both in Europe and at the universal level in the periods of the nineteenth, twentieth, and early part of the twenty-first centuries. Very often there have been attempts to create peace and repair relationships among belligerent parties through the forging of new rules of international law. The quest for new rules, be they of a normative or institutional character, gives rise to many challenges, not least because of the entanglement between law and politics. International law is rather fragile in the face of the greediness of politics. The third theme of the handbook is related to the way in which international law in Europe interacts with other regions of the world, as well as at the universal level. The handbook adeptly shows both the synergies and resistances in these complex interactions. Eurocentrism is referred to often. Its predominance in the development of international law is criticized. Calls are made for a fair acknowledgement of other traditions and approaches to international law. Europe is entangled in the remnants of its past, and most especially the colonial period. There is room for opening new paths of interactions with Asia, Africa, and Latin America by engaging in the effective implementation of core principles of international law such as self-determination and non-discrimination. The shaping of the financial and economic world order is also at stake. That said, Europe is not monolithic. As previously noted, its traditions are diverse and sometimes antagonistic. The 'within' interactions have commonalities with the 'outside' ones. Europe can learn from its own experience.

The editors—correctly—avoid endless discussions about the meaning of Europe. Its geographical extent has been subject to much debate, as have its cultural roots and the values that it promotes. The editors, acknowledging that Europe has various strata, understand it as covering the geographic reach of the Council of Europe. When doing so, Russia's aggression against Ukraine in February 2022 was not foreseen, nor was the ensuing departure of Russia from the Council of Europe. Russia, nonetheless, is part of Europe as emphasized in the various contributions to the handbook.

Europe has had many interactions with international law and has contributed to the shaping of its rules and principles in a political and social environment that has been constantly evolving, quite often through dramatic events. The handbook is replete with fine studies highlighting this contribution in numerous fields involving, *inter alia*, human rights, the rule of law, or solidarity. Europe has also contributed to the shaping of international institutions, demonstrating its preference for cooperation since at least the early nineteenth century. In this context, one can mention the river basin organizations and commissions established following the 1815 Congress of Vienna that promoted the internationalization of the navigation regime on a number of European rivers, as well as the role European countries played in founding the International Office of Public Hygiene and in the subsequent establishment of the World Health Organization with its decentralized governance scheme. In the aftermath of World War II, Europe continued to offer fertile ground for the creation of regional organizations to which substantial responsibilities were delegated. It also played a major role in forging the United Nations and the many specialized organizations.

Paradoxes and ambivalences are nonetheless present in the relationships of Europe with international law. The rule of law, human rights, and democracy are acknowledged by Europe as its core values. In its external relations, however, it has difficulties in these areas. We might think, for example, of migration issues and the various measures of a normative nature (*inter alia* agreements, legislation, EU instruments) which were adopted as well as the implementation mechanisms which have been put in place. These are regularly challenged as falling foul of the values Europe itself promotes.

In its various forms, Europe has different ways of being and provides an interesting laboratory for enhanced cooperation. One of its manifestations is the European Union (EU). The particularity of the EU is difficult to grasp in political and legal terms. Aside from cooperation, the EU is primarily built on a specific integration model, which has not been replicated elsewhere. International law in Europe has been confronted with this phenomenon and has made room for the EU's peculiarities. The handbook highlights this too, not shying away from the exploration and critique of complex approaches, while highlighting once more the plurality of the interactions within Europe and with the other regions of the world.

In sum, the topic of 'International law and Europe' offers us a unique insight into the role international law has played in the past and is playing at present in Europe. It also encourages us to think about how Europe should approach international law in the future.

Laurence Boisson de Chazournes,
Professor of International Law and International Organization
University of Geneva

Acknowledgements

The editors are extremely grateful to Oxford University Press. In particular, we are grateful to Merel Alstein for handling the book proposal so positively and expeditiously. Lisa Butts was an exemplary project editor who was patient with us and the authors and most helpful throughout the process. We are also grateful to Haripriya Soundhariyan and Jaishree from Newgen for the copy-editing and to Christopher Goddard for contributing to the process of language editing.

We are also grateful to our families, bearing with us when we were reading, reviewing, and working on the handbook, often late in the evenings.

Anne van Aaken gratefully acknowledges funding from the Alexander von Humboldt Foundation. Lauri Mälksoo gratefully acknowledges the funding from the Estonian Research Council's grant PRG969.

We mourn the loss of Prof. Dr Ayşe Işıl Karakaş, a valued contributor to this Handbook and co-author of the country chapter on Turkey. In spite of her illness, she wanted to explore Turkey's complex relationship with international law and the editors are highly indebted to her to have taken on that task. Educated in Turkey and France, not only as a lawyer but also as political scientist, she combined to be an academic as well as a practitioner. A true liberal by heart, she served as the first female Turkish Judge at the European Court of Human Rights and later as the Courts Vice President (2008–2019). Lately Işıl Karakaş acted as the Director of the Human Rights Centre and Head of the International Law Department at the Kadir Has University Faculty of Law. Prof. Karakaş regretfully passed away in January 2024 in her hometown of Istanbul at the age of 65.

Contents

PART 4: COUNTRIES AND REGIONS OF EUROPE

Table of Cases

International Jurisdictions

Arbitral Decisions

Benelux Court of Justice

European Council Administrative Tribunal

European Commission of Human Rights

European Court of Human Rights

Courts of Justice of the European Union

International Court of Justice

International Criminal Tribunal for the former Yugoslavia

International Military Tribunal

International Tribunal for the Law of the Sea

Permanent Court of International Justice

National Jurisdictions

Canada

Federal Republic of Germany

French Republic

Hellenic Republic

Italian Republic

Kingdom of Spain

Kingdom of the Netherlands

Republic of Poland

Swiss Confederation

Russian Federation

Конституционный Суд Российской Федерации (Constitutinal Court), N.A. Alekseeva, Ya.N. Evtushenko and D.I. Isakova, Judgment [23 Sep 2014] 735n.38

Конституционный Суд Российской Федерации (Constitutinal Court), Enforceability of the Anchugov and Gladkov v Russia Judgment of the ECtHR of 4 July 2013, Judgment [19 Apr 2016] 741n.126, 793n.129

Конституционный Суд Российской Федерации (Constitutinal Court), Enforceability of the OAO Neftyanaya Kompaniya Yukos v Russia Judgment of the ECtHR of 31 July 2014, Judgment [19 Jan 2017] 741n.126, 793n.129

Конституционный Суд Российской Федерации (Constitutinal Court), Application of the Exemption from Customs Duties during the Import of Selected Products Categories to the Single Customs Territory of the Customs Union, Order [3 Mar 2015] 793n.128

Ukraine

Конституційний Суд України (Constitutional Court of Ukraine), Conformity of the Rome Statute with the Constitution of Ukraine, Opinion [11 Jul 2001], Case N 1-35/2001 .... 837–38n.33

United Kingdom of Great Britain and Northern Ireland

Court of Appeal, Blackburn v Attorney General, [1971] 1 WLR 1037, CA. 853n.67

Court of Appeal, R (Gulf Centre for Human Rights) v Prime Minister, [2018] EWCA Civ 1855 .... 854n.88

Court of Appeal, Trendtex Trading Corporation v Central Bank of Nigeria [1977] 1 QB 529 .... 854n.84

High Court of Justice, R (CND) v The Prime Minister, [2002] EWHC 2777 (Admin) 853n.77

High Court of Justice, R (Freedom and Justice Party) v Secretary of State for Foreign and Commonwealth Affairs, [2016] EWHC 2010 (Admin) 854n.86

High Court of Justice, R (Friends of the Earth and others) v Secretary of State for Business, Energy and Industrial Strategy, [2022] EWHC 1841 (Admin) 853n.79

High Court of Justice, R v Secretary of State for Foreign Affairs, ex parte Rees-Mogg, [1994] QB 552 .... 853n.67

House of Lords, Garland v British Rail Engineering Ltd, [1983] 2 AC 751 .... 853n.69

United States of America

Table of Legislation

International and Regional Instruments

European Union

Directives

Regulations

Resolutions

UN General Assembly (UNGA)

UN Security Council (UNSC)

National Legislation

Algeria

Bosnia and Herzegovina

Croatia

Czech Republic

Estonia

Federal Republic of Yugoslavia

France

Germany

Greece

Serbia

Slovakia

Slovenia

Spain

Switzerland

Turkey

Ukraine

United Kingdom

United States

Contributors

Anne van Aaken, Professor for Law and Economics, Legal Theory, Public International Law and European Law, Faculty of Law, Director, Institute of Law and Economics, University of Hamburg

Olgun Akbulut, Professor of Human Rights and Constitutional Law, Faculty of Law, Kadir Has University

Olabisi D. Akinkugbe, Associate Professor of Law and the Purdy Crawford Chair in Business Law at the Schulich School of Law, Dalhousie University

Antony Anghie, Professor of Law, National University of Singapore and University of Utah

Andreas von Arnauld, Professor of Public Law, Public International and European Law, Director Walther Schücking Institute for International Law, University of Kiel

Veronika Bílková, Head of the Department of Public International Law, Faculty of Law, Charles University

Laurence Boisson de Chazournes, Professor of International Law and International Organization, University of Geneva

Başak Çalı, Professor of International Law, Hertie School

Ludovica Chiussi Curzi, Senior Assistant Professor in Public International Law, University of Bologna, School of Law

Władysław Czapliński, Professor, Institute of Law Studies, Polish Academy of Sciences

Pierre d'Argent, Professor of International Law, Centre Charles De Visscher pour le droit international et européen, University of Louvain (UCLouvain)

Jean d'Aspremont, Professor of International Law, Sciences Po Law School

Anne Dienelt, Senior Research Fellow, University of Hamburg

Carlos Espósito, Professor of Public International Law, Faculty of Law, Universidad Autónoma de Madrid

Hélène Ruiz Fabri, Professor of International Law, Sorbonne Law School, University Paris 1 Panthéon-Sorbonne

Mykola Gnatovskyy, Judge, European Court of Human Rights

Thomas D. Grant, Fellow, University of Cambridge

James Harrison, Professor of Environmental Law, School of Law, University of Edinburgh

Iakovos V. Iakovidis, Deputy Permanent Representative of Greece to the United Nations Office at Geneva, Ministry of Foreign Affairs of Greece

Hent Kalmo, Researcher, Johan Skytte Institute of Political Studies, University of Tartu

Işıl Ergüvenç Karakaş (1958–2024), Professor of International and Human Rights Law, Faculty of Law, Kadir Has University

Helen Keller, Professor of Public Law, European and Public International Law, Institute for International Law and Comparative Constitutional Law, University of Zurich

Astrid Kjeldgaard-Pedersen, Professor, Faculty of Law, University of Copenhagen

Jan Klabbers, Professor of International Law, University of Helsinki

Nicole Lüthi, PhD Candidate, Faculty of Law, University of Zurich

Gail Lythgoe, Lecturer in Global Law, Edinburgh Law School, University of Edinburgh

Sylwia Majkowska-Szulc, Professor of EU Law, University of Gdansk

Lauri Mälksoo, Professor of International Law, University of Tartu

Makane Moïse Mbengue, Professor of International Law, Faculty of Law, Department of Public International Law and International Organization, University of Geneva

Anja Mihr, Programme Director, Center on Governance through Human Rights in Berlin and OSCE Academy in Bishkek

Marko Milanović, Professor of Public International Law, University of Reading

Mary Ellen O'Connell, Robert and Marion Short Professor of Law and Professor of International Peace Studies, University of Notre Dame

Tatjana Papić, Professor of Law, Union University Law School Belgrade

Sevanna Poghosyan, PhD student, School of Law, University of Tartu

Akbar Rasulov, Professor of International Law, University of Glasgow

Vera Rusinova, Professor, Head of the School of International Law, Faculty of Law, Editor-in-Chief of 'Zhurnal VSHÉ po Mezhdunarodnomu Pravu (HSE University Journal of International Law)', National Research University Higher School of Economics

Cedric Ryngaert, Professor of Public International Law, Utrecht University

Sergey Sayapin, Professor and Director of the Centre on International Human Rights Law, School of Law, KIMEP University

Violetta Sefkow-Werner, Research and Teaching Assistant at the Institute for International Law and Comparative Constitutional Law, University of Zurich

Yuval Shany, Hersch Lauterpacht Chair of Public International Law, Hebrew University

Edoardo Stoppioni, Professor of International Law, University of Strasbourg

Pavel Šturma, Professor of Public International Law, Department of International Law, Faculty of Law, Charles University

Attila Tanzi, Professor of Public International Law, Faculty of Law, University of Bologna

Patrícia Galvão Teles, Associate Professor, Autonomous University of Lisbon; Member of the International Law Commission

Antonios Tzanakopoulos, Professor of Public International Law, Faculty of Law, University of Oxford

Vassilis P. Tzevelekos, Reader in Law, School of Law and Social Justice, University of Liverpool

Maria Varaki, Lecturer in International Law, Department of War Studies, King's College London

Johann Justus Vasel, Professor for Public Law and Legal Aspect of Artificial Intelligence, Heinrich-Heine-University Düsseldorf

Christian Walter, Professor of Public International Law and Public Law, Faculty of Law, LMU Munich

Antje Wiener, Professor of Political Science especially Global Governance, Department of Political Science and Faculty of Law, University of Hamburg

Karolina Wierczyńska, Professor of International Law, Department of International Law, Institute of Law Studies, Polish Academy of Sciences

Michael Wood, KC, Twenty Essex Chambers, London

Pål Wrange, Professor, Department of Law, Stockholm University

Ganna Yudkivska, Vice-Chair of the UN Working Group on Arbitrary Detention, Judge of the European Court of Human Rights in 2010–2022

Ineta Ziemele, Judge; Professor of International Law and Human Rights, Court of Justice of the European Union; Riga Graduate School of Law (Latvia)

Editors' Introduction

1. An International Law Handbook about Europe

After handbooks dedicated to Asia and the Pacific,[1] and to the Americas,[2] this handbook focuses on 'international law in Europe'. The focus on regionalism and the role that various regions have been playing in international law touches on something important and has been a pivotal part of the conversation in international law.[3] This regional focus immediately brings to mind the balance between universality and regionalism in international law, as well as whether international law is even international, as Anthea Roberts puts it.[4] Historically, the reach of international law as imagined and discussed in Europe was often intentionally constrained as well.[5] Furthermore, because, in the past, Europe dominated international law so much, other parts of the world represented 'regions' mostly understood as peripheral, for example Latin America.[6] It took time and required critical self-reflection as well as external examination—a kind of Copernican shift—for Europe to realize that it, too, is 'just' a region in the context of international law. In any case, this handbook proceeds from the assumption that regional approaches, histories, and experiences have been central to the historical formation of international law, but also remain important for current understandings and applications of international law. This does not mean abandoning the idea of international law's universality but approaching it in a way that can, in some sense, be called realistic as well as pluralistic.

Thus one may ask: is there something specifically European in how international law manifests itself in Europe? What does it mean to look at international law from European perspectives? What has Europe 'given' to international law? Is international law European? What has international law 'taken' from Europe? Is European law international? How should we evaluate this altogether? By trying to give an overall account of the place and roles of international law in Europe, these are some of the preliminary yet foundational questions that this volume tries to answer. In the context of an international law handbook whose focus is on Europe, the question underlying all these issues is of course: what, after all, is Europe? Indeed, how is Europe defined, given that its contours are contested? Those contours are fuzzy and Europe could be seen as an appendix to the Eurasian continent. Jan Klabbers rightly asks in his chapter 'how Europe sees itself, how others see Europe, and whether it is even possible to see Europe'. His short answer is 'that however Europe is presented, represented, or perceived, none of the images is fully persuasive. Europe is not identical to the European Union (EU); Europe does not fully coincide with the Strasbourg-based Council of Europe (CoE); and Europe is not quite as large as the UN Economic Commission for Europe (UNECE).' Furthermore, different from geographically distinct continents, Europe is also an idea, a feeling, a tradition, something cultural[7]—after all, the name 'Europa' derives from the mythological Phoenician[8] princess who was (somehow voluntarily) kidnapped by Zeus, a Greek god. Yet a choice must be made. For the purposes of this book, when defining 'Europe' we thought primarily of members of the Council of Europe (CoE) at the time when the Russian Federation was still a member of that organization (historically, Russia was a member of the European community of nations at least from the early eighteenth century onwards).

2. 'Zeitenwende' in International Law?

Europe has some claim to being the birthplace of 'classical' international law, with the Westphalian Peace in 1648 being its origin according to the standard narrative. Yet Europe is also the place where the failures of classical international law led to its being replaced by another legal order between the member States of the European Union (EU), which stems from international law but affirms its autonomy therefrom. So is Europe a serial innovator of legal forms of global cooperation which also serve as models for other regions, such as the MERCOSUR,[9] COMESA,[10] and Africa as a whole?[11] Innovators may often fail, and not all destruction is also creative.[12] But it can be, and hitherto the EU has not failed, instead having been an inspiration and a big influence for other regions as well,[13] which is reminiscent of Europe's old claim to view itself as a model for the world. This product of supranationalism, an apparent innovation of Europe, seems to be selling well to neighbouring countries. The EU may be enlarged by nine more countries which currently have candidate status. The architecture, geography, and 'geology'[14] of international law in Europe may well look different twenty years from now. What is certain is that the EU is on its way to discussing a new architecture enabling admission of those new countries, which would significantly enlarge the EU geographically. The long debate over enlargement versus integration and differentiated integration as a possible solution[15] may yet flare up once more.

As already indicated, the national or regional narrative in the context of international law has usually focused on non-European powers such as Latin America,[16] China,[17] or Africa[18] because several powers and regions have historically encountered international law in its European-focused *Gestalt* as 'others'—and were often treated as such. The list of national perspectives on international law from non-Western countries could go on.[19] Politically, these approaches to 'inherited' international law were often most critical when they represented what used to be called the 'Third World' and what nowadays is often called the Global South (whether this semantic shift is helpful remains doubtful—but at least it highlights the problem).[20] Yet over recent years, Europe itself and its constituent countries have also been examined from the perspective of their specific experiences and doctrines in international law, or authors positioning themselves specifically as European.[21] Especially through a historical lens, we keep learning about the depth of international legal traditions in Europe (and beyond).[22] Our edited volume has been written in the same spirit and intellectually builds on these important earlier contributions.

International law has often been built around narratives of progress. So, too, whole generations of international lawyers have been trained and raised with the idea that after World War II, international law changed in a fundamental and positive way—and, in turn, supposedly changed the world.[23] The UN Charter of 1945 (Article 2 para 4) prohibited the threat and use of force in international law; a commitment which was reiterated in Europe in 1975 when the Helsinki Final Act affirmed that the existing borders in Europe would not be changed by military force. The Nuremberg trials of 1945–1946 introduced the principle of individual responsibility for newly defined and already well-established international crimes; in 1948, the Convention on the Prevention and Punishment of the Crime of Genocide was adopted, and it defined the crime of crimes that was supposed never to happen again. These developments later led to adoption of the Rome statute in 1998, after the world experienced two more genocides. So, in principle, international law and the answers in the context of aggression and other major crimes are already there. However, history does not stand still. On 24 February 2022, when our group of authors was in the middle of working on this edited volume, Russia started its full-scale invasion of and—in spite of Putin's semantics—outright war on Ukraine. All the central questions which we wanted to highlight in our volume were suddenly cast in a sharper light and gained definition. Of course, Russia's aggressive moves in its neighbourhood did not start in 2022. The war against Georgia in 2008 and the invasion and annexation of Crimea as well as the war in Donbas since 2014 are major events in this context. What do these wars—and what does Russia's renewed aggression since 2022—tell us about international law in Europe or about international law generally? In international relations and geopolitics, the German chancellor Olaf Scholz called the Russian aggression a *Zeitenwende* (turning point) event.[24] But was it somehow also a *Zeitenwende* event in the context of international law or at least our perception of it?[25] Are we entering a post-post-Cold War era, possibly reanimating a stalemate situation within the United Nations (UN) between the old East (now with changed borders) and the old West, which we had forgotten but that was familiar for some forty years?

In some sense at least, Russia and its current rhetoric on historical spheres of influence, balance of power, and special rights of great powers such as Russia[26] has taken us back to times which many diplomats and international lawyers thought were dead and buried. Yet for several centuries these principles of power were the reality of international law in Europe and beyond;[27] international law and territorial arrangements were nothing more than deals, particularly between great powers. Has Russia's aggression against Ukraine merely been a violation of existing international law or is it also an attempt to make the point that, at the end of the day, the foundations of international law are being (re-)created by great powers; that this will never change due to the nature of power in the world? Even before the start of Russia's war on Ukraine, Russia's practices in international law, for example in the context of international humanitarian law, had come under severe scrutiny.[28] The coming years will give new answers to these questions. However, what is already clear is that the (European) history of international law navigates between the same ideas and sometimes the 'new' is just the forgotten or suppressed 'old'.

3. Three Overarching Questions of this Handbook

The handbook sets out to look at both the theory and practice of international law in Europe through the prism of three overarching themes (or tropes):

- the pacifying role of international law in Europe;
- the diversity of international legal traditions within Europe, often too little understood and appreciated; and
- how European ideas and practices of international law have shaped understandings of universal international law.

The first of these three guiding tropes is the *pacifying function of international law*. The inherent function and feature of law, international or not, is arguably pacification: 'right, not might, shall rule the world'. When it comes to international law, this pacifying function is confronted with challenges. International law has certainly played a pivotal role in restoring peace—think of the Peace of Westphalia (1648) ending the Thirty Years' War in Europe, or the Treaty of Paris (1815). The atrocities of World War I resulted in the Treaty of Versailles (1919) and the Briand-Kellogg Pact, while the terror of the Nazi regime and World War II led to the formation of the UN as well as the most important international treaties tackling 'international crimes' such as crimes against humanity and genocide.[29] Yet 'pacification' is also a term (mis)used by European empires with respect to colonial wars and wars of decolonization. Moreover, even peace treaties may sow the seeds of future wars, as was arguably the case with the Treaty of Versailles. For the greater part of the history of international law, war was a legitimate and legal means to the ends of a sovereign State. Until the Briand-Kellogg Pact of 1928, officially named the General Treaty for Renunciation of War as an Instrument of National Policy, and later Article 2 paragraph 4 of the UN Charter, war was allowed and accepted. To add to this darkness, from a historical perspective Europe seems particularly ill-equipped to bring about peace in the international arena. From time immemorial, the continent's history has been marked by war and bloodshed, devastation and sorrow, which Europe also brought to the rest of the world. European superpowers ruled and dominated the world in a non-peaceful manner (to put it mildly): from the bellicose Roman Empire, through the Crusades, Spain's 'Conquista' and Portugal's 'Coloniaje', the French Époque and its expansionism, the British Empire, Dutch naval pursuits, and the dark German chapter triggering two world wars within half a century, to show only part of the mark Europe has left on the world. This does not mean that violence and domination were uniquely European. Yet, in a dialectical sense, the idea of pacification by and through law has correlated with this abuse of power by European nations. Law, it seems, is often created and shaped reactively. In response to some of the greatest atrocities in human history, we witness a turn to law. It was against the background of Latin American colonization that the Spanish clergyman Bartolomé de Las Casas coined the ideas of 'derechos humanos'. One of the foundational texts of international law, *De iure belli ac pacis* by Hugo Grotius, dealt with the role of law in matters of war while Europe was at war. Samuel von Pufendorf certainly forged his most important work under the impression of the Thirty Years' War. The list is endless.

Over the centuries, the idea emerged that perhaps the most central role of international law was to ensure peace between States and to establish a stable order between them. Yet before World War I the reality of international law was dominated by concepts such as the balance of power and the right of conquest. Full-scale peace remained merely an ideal. After two world wars, new values and institutions emerged to foster cooperation between States and diminish the potential for wars and conflicts. Given the unsuccessful attempt to end wars with a necessary but insufficient prohibition of the use of force, international law was also directed to attack the underlying root causes of wars. Thus ideas such as democracy, human rights, and the rule of law became important landmarks of international law in Europe, being considered critical conditions for upholding peace between nations.[30] With Europe's integration, the understanding of sovereignty has transformed, too. The idea of international law itself was seen to be central for achieving and maintaining peaceful relations between States. The *Institut de Droit International* was established in 1873 and chose as its motto—unsurprisingly—'Justitia et Pace'. This handbook critically explores whether, and to what extent, international law has succeeded in pacifying and ordering Europe (and the world) and, if so, whether it will continue to succeed.

The second guiding trope of this handbook deals with the *diversity of international legal traditions within Europe*. Diversity is, first and foremost, an empirical given: differences in terms of ethnicity, culture, gender, age, religion, and many other features are a fact. The term stemming from the Latin *diversitas* has two different dimensions: difference and contradiction. One of the tasks of law is to guarantee that difference does not turn into contradiction, but is tolerated, accepted, respected, even cherished. Pluralism is enriching by itself, but it also diffuses power and warrants alternatives. Diversity is also indissolubly intertwined with peace: it can be a guarantor of peace by creating mutual tolerance and by diffusing power, but it can also reflect fundamental differences which may result in clash and combat.

Europe has seldom been a unitary actor in the context of international law. It has been marked by considerable diversity, fragmentation, even conflict between different nation-states, alliances, and whole blocs. Diversity has existed between legal and cultural-religious traditions (eg common law and civil law or, in certain respects, Western and Eastern Christianity), between empires with different histories of colonialism (eg France and the UK vis-à-vis countries of the former Austro-Hungarian Empire), between winners and losers of both world wars (eg Great Britain and Germany) as well as the Cold War (the USSR/Russia and Western European countries), between liberal democracies and (reviving) traditions of authoritarianism and illiberal democracy. Europe has had its centres and peripheries, including in the context of international legal thinking and arrangements. Today, Europe—defined in our project as member States of the CoE plus Russia—is still divided between EU and non-EU countries, between NATO members and countries that fundamentally challenge NATO's role in the European security architecture (in particular Russia). In the light of this sub-regional diversity and fragmentation, it is important to explore how international law is understood and implemented in different countries and regions, and how specific traditions of international law have related to overarching ideas, projects, and institutions of international law both in Europe and in the wider world. At the same time, we as editors cannot be certain that after February 2022, it has been possible to write about international law freely and without (self-)censorship in all European countries which are included in this volume.

The third guiding trope of this handbook deals with the *impact of European ideas and practices on the (alleged) universality of international law*. From a historical viewpoint one may question whether universality was born in Europe. The commonly accepted narrative suggests that something that originated from a particular context and cultural tradition (ie Greek philosophy, later joined by religion and Enlightenment concepts of universal history) could result in something global. In this context, the handbook addresses a plethora of questions. How have European ideas and practices influenced international law? Has this changed over time? Are imperialism and universalism mixed up when it comes to Europe? Is Europe obsessed with exclusivity, self-centricity, and regionalism rather than propagating universal ideas and values? Leaving the European dimension aside, does a global or universal legal order even exist? Is there a universal source? Is there universality of common moral values as well as common legal principles?

Most of the principles, of which—at least some—are of universal quality, are not original products of international law but result from continuing comparative interactions between different legal systems. A case in point is Article 38 paragraph 1, *littera* c of the Statute of the International Court of Justice (ICJ) which holds 'the general principles of law recognized by civilized nations' to be a source of public international law. These general principles can only be shaped by the comparative bottom-up approach in which Europe plays a pivotal role—even if the notion of 'civilized nations' has effectively been abandoned in contemporary international law.

At the same time, international law in Europe has seldom been parochial. Its claims and ambitions quite soon went beyond European borders. Up until World War I, European empires used international law to colonize the rest of the world, and what we would nowadays call the Global North 'made' international law.[31] This was not an international law of equal relations but that of the so-called 'civilized' vs the 'non-civilized'; even international law itself was considered primarily a European affair (international law as *jus publicum europaeum* or *droit public de l'Europe*). At some point in the mid-twentieth century, international law was increasingly understood as universal, but of course a global dispute ensued as to what this actually entails. Many Europeans (along with Americans) still instinctively thought that it was *their* historical experiences and progressive ideas that enjoyed universal validity and had to form the foundation of renewed international law, not just in Europe but all over the world, universally. And it may have been used as camouflage for exerting power. Many new States and regimes—actually starting with the Soviet Union, which was formed on the territory of the former Russian Empire in 1922—insisted that the world needed a *new* international law, with different, more progressive principles than what the European-dominated colonial era had to offer. Whether or not they managed to implement any such new principles under their own jurisdiction is a different question. During the twentieth century, the actual universality of international law was often contested from various ideological and regional standpoints. And it is of course contested now—whereas the 'rules-based order' is propagated from the 'West', others, like China and Russia, view the universality of international law as rooted in a different understanding. Often, the very foundational principles of international law are still seen quite differently, even if the universality of international law as such is rarely challenged.

How was this historical jump from unequal relations between European and non-European States to proclaimed universal international law managed—indeed, *was* it managed? Or has international law always been different in various regions *and also* universal? Could the specific international legal ideas and solutions that were promoted in Europe after World War II, in both its Western and Eastern parts (although their ideas differed significantly), be successfully 'transferred' to others universally, or were they doomed to remain primarily regional in terms of values and implementation? Were ideas and values transferred in the opposite direction, into Europe from outside, either before or after World War II? Thus, the second question is whether specific ideas about the direction of international law as promoted in post-World War II liberal (initially 'Western') Europe—such as democracy, human rights, and the rule of law, for example, but also the idea of social justice or even the social State—are constrained regionally as 'international law as understood in Europe' or continue to have universal validity and appeal. How can these ideas be implemented in countries which have been less fortunate than Europe in terms of their economic development, also due to colonialism and other structures of dominance in the past? As the reader will see, these questions are not always open to simple answers which may also differ depending on the specific set of questions explored or the country perspective.

In sum, this handbook uses three overarching organizing themes for approaching international law in Europe—the pacifying function of international law, the often unexplored and downplayed regional diversity and fragmentation of international law within Europe, and the appeal and contestation of European ideas of international law globally/universally. Looking at international law in Europe primarily through these three lenses constitutes one of the novelties of this collaborative project but also makes it realizable—without any substantive starting points, the theme 'international law and Europe' might just be too open-ended and vast.

4. The Different Parts of the Handbook

The *Oxford Handbook of International Law in Europe* is not a modified version of the *Oxford Handbook of the History of International Law* with a focus on Europe. It is primarily meant to cover *contemporary* international law in Europe. That said, historical elements certainly remain indispensable: law being a social phenomenon, history frequently enters our current understandings and helps to explain the present.[32] Thus, the past, legacies, 'dark sides', and traditions are addressed from the point of view of their consequences and how we deal with them now. The history of ideas and values, and the history of countries and international institutions in Europe are thus reflected in many chapters in order to understand the diverse picture of international law in Europe. This should serve European readers but even more so non-European readers in understanding what role international law plays in Europe nowadays, how it was conceived, and how it is contested. Contestation plays along very different lines: legal-theoretical, political, historical, and geographical. The handbook is meant to mirror this diversity and fault lines but still reflects on the core of the significance of international law in Europe and how international law has shaped Europe.

A handbook of international law in Europe can take different forms. It can be descriptive or reflective; it can focus on ideas or on practice. Or it can try to combine these approaches, which indeed is what this handbook aims to do: its target is to provide an in-depth analysis of the state of international law in Europe and thus covers both practice and academia as the two pillars constructing international law in Europe. Even if academics are travellers between countries, nowadays often teaching not in their country of origin, we postulate that certain mainstream traditions or national schools of scholarship exist, and that State practice has developed along features specific to countries and sub-regions of Europe, be it along religious, linguistic, democratic, or power status lines.

The book is divided into four parts: values and ideas, intellectual traditions, the institutional architecture of Europe, as well as country chapters delving into the details of the nation-states of Europe. Yet all those parts are intertwined, so that cross-references are abundant. Furthermore, the unifying threads are the three overarching questions as explained above, which are taken up prominently in many chapters.

Part 1 of the book addresses the special history of international law in Europe and explores some overarching ideas and values of international law in Europe, as they have become an object of international and European law, or at least influenced them. European values and ideas are not always realized progressively but have their variations in time and place. Yet they are closely connected to the pacifying function of international law as Europeans have come to realize that without those values, peace could never be perpetual. The chapters in this and the other parts of the handbook address how and where those values have worked (or not) and discuss the gaps between their promises and their achievements.

This part is meant to capture the (often controversial) history of international law in Europe (Mälksoo), including the influence of religion on international law in Europe (Walter), colonial legacies (Anghie), and the eurocentrism still prevalent in how international law is practised, including in non-European countries and the Global South (Mbengue and Akinkugbe). It specifically analyses the contribution of European ideas and values, as they have become an object of international law, not only in Europe but they are heavily institutionalized in Europe and European law. The history of post-World War II Europe is shaped by values such as human rights (Cali), democracy (Poghosyan), the rule of law (van Aaken), cultural diversity (Bilkova), as well as prosperity and solidarity (Rasulov and Lythgoe) which were made the object of specific international legal rules and institutions in order to promote them and preserve them from the convulsions of domestic politics and prevent new turbulences on the European continent. This has, as we know, only succeeded in parts of the continent. Of course, during the Cold War, the European West and East had different understandings of these foundational ideas, a difference which still plays out today (as reflected upon in the country chapters).

Crucially, Europe entails very different and changing understandings of sovereignty (Kalmo). In this context, not only has Russia, as a power co-determining European history in recent centuries, turned its back on the above-mentioned values, but it also launched the first aggressive war with the goal of territorial conquest in Europe since Hitler's invasion of Poland in 1939. Other countries have also turned their backs on a shared understanding of sovereignty, as is vividly demonstrated by 'Brexit'. Given the central importance of the EU for the European continent, the interaction between classical international law and supranational law as practised in the EU crucial for the role of international law in Europe. Is the EU, as a supranational entity with progressive integration, replacing the classical international law between the member States of the EU? Is a 'new' form of international law emerging from the European continent with a very different understanding of sovereignty (d'Argent)? Can one consider the European continent as a sort of serial inventor of new forms of international law?

Part 2 deals with the most important intellectual traditions originating and practised in Europe. The diverse approaches to international law in Europe can sometimes be traced to intellectual traditions, although a direct translation of an intellectual tradition into a State's international legal policy is difficult. Furthermore, while some intellectual traditions have been universalized, some remain prevalent only in Europe, while still others allow non-Europeans to critically reflect on Europe's attitudes towards international law. The aim of this part is to explore the specific features of legal thinking and schools in Europe, also contrasting them with other regions and powers, such as the US and China. Although many of the intellectual traditions in Europe cannot be said to originate or be prevalent only in Europe, such as Positivism (d'Aspremont) or Realism (Shany/Varaki), others can be found to be mostly prevalent in Europe, such as Constitutionalism (Wiener), perhaps because of (institutional) developments in Europe after World War II, especially the EU. In contrast, Marxism (Tzanakopoulos) as a legal theory of international law has wandered the world from Europe (after all, Marx was a German lawyer) and allowed non-European countries to critically reflect on Europe's international law, first from a Soviet and nowadays from a Third World/Global South perspective. Natural law (O'Connell) has its origin in Europe and deep roots in Christian theology and has influenced the humanitarian tradition in Europe (Dienelt), sometimes culminating in pacifism in particular States.

This brief description about intellectual traditions within and beyond Europe does not do justice to the diversity of intellectual traditions in Europe. And the reader needs to keep in mind that no one of those traditions alone determines international legal policy; rather, they are mixed to various degrees in State practice. Whereas in many States, the study of doctrine remains most important (especially in comparison with the US), in other States European international lawyers attempt to construct and develop a constitutionalized international law, focusing on human rights and the rule of law, as witnessed in some European institutions such as the CoE and the EU. The experiences of slavery and wars have led to humanitarianism and establishing constraints to warfare as witnessed in the International Committee of the Red Cross. Realism has officially gone missing in many States, especially EU States and non-P5 States, although a shift may be diagnosed in States turning mainly against the EU. Realism has been an ingredient of politics and international law in European States to varying degrees and across various times, sometimes with disastrous consequences, including aggressive acts such as invasions. Given the war currently raging in Eastern Europe and recent geopolitical developments more generally, realism has returned to many European capitals. Yet approaches are deeply diverse and at least some European States have been said to be from Venus (in contrast to more realist superpowers, such as the US)[33] after the fall of the iron curtain and as witnessed by the very different attitudes of European States to the war in Iraq in 2003.

Part 3 of this handbook highlights the different institutional layers of international law in Europe, being constructed to deal with all the foundational values described in Part 1. The idea after World War II was to make certain values and ideas part of the international order as a way to prevent the repeat of the horrors of the two world wars and fortify the foundations of peace. This approach was not only meant as a universalist undertaking but was also crucial in terms of building the European order and institutions. First the CoE (Yudkivska) and then the precursors of the EU (Vasel) were created to bring peace to a formerly deeply divided and warring continent—and of course Europe still remained divided during the Cold War. Thus, both the European Communities and the CoE were institutions for those States on the Western side of the iron curtain. The Organization for Security and Co-operation in Europe (OSCE) (Mihr) has played an important role in bringing the divided continent together, even before the end of the Cold War as emerged from the Final Act of Helsinki in 1975. The OSCE continues to play an important role, especially in fostering democracy, human rights, and the rule of law including in many States of the former USSR, and it is now the only organization dealing with democracy and the rule of law as European values including Russia (given that the Russian Federation was excluded from the CoE in 2022). However, at the time of writing, the OSCE also seems to be in crisis in terms of its future, because of controversies between the Western States and Russia.

Yet the EU is not the only regional organization for market integration (although it went furthest). Other European countries have decided to stay out of it (such as Switzerland, Norway, Liechtenstein, Iceland) or left it (the UK). The first four have founded other economic blocs, such as the European Free Trade Association (EFTA, 1960) which is institutionally partially associated with the EU but does not envisage ever-closer integration as the EU does. The UN set up the United Nations Economic Commission for Europe (UNECE) in 1947, which comprised fifty-six members including non-European countries, aiming to promote economic integration, mainly by rule- and standard-setting. Furthermore, there were regional economic and security organizations on the Eastern side of the iron curtain, such as the Council for Mutual Economic Assistance (Comecon, 1949–1991) and the Warsaw Pact (1955–1991) under the leadership of the Soviet Union. Those are not covered by this handbook as they are bygone history. However, the reader should be aware that the institutions covered here are not the only ones existing or having existed in Europe after World War II.

States initially in Western Europe have given more powers to international organizations and courts, such as the CoE and the European Communities, than in any other continent, also influencing their understanding of (shared) sovereignty. That is, the ideas of human rights, democracy, the rule of law, and diversity, as well as prosperity and solidarity inspired the European treaties of the CoE and the European Communities, and they have gradually geographically expanded in the course of time (from the six founding members of the European Communities to twenty-seven in the EU); the CoE has gone from ten to forty-seven, thus making up roughly a quarter of the States in the world. Those were treaties which did not just reflect reality but that have been aspirational as well. Just as the cradle of the welfare state was created in Germany by Chancellor Bismarck to stave off the 'spectre of communism', the existence of the USSR and pressure by socialist countries in the East forced the West to accept important features of worker protection and the social State. The idea of going from contract to constitution has been entrenched in European thought for a long time. This makes it a special case for international law as being witnessed by powerful international and supranational courts in Europe (Ziemele)—Europe is meant to be built on law and not power, with the rule of law embodied by independent (international) courts being seen as an important guarantor of peace in Europe, following Kelsen's ideas. Especially for smaller States, strong international law institutions provide an assurance, since they depend more on law, and their voices are heard in the European institutions. However, nowadays, this sharing of sovereignty is also contested by some major European States (most prominently the UK but also, eg, Hungary and—hitherto—Poland in some EU contexts). Recalling that the ideas as described in Part 1 of this handbook have been viewed as a necessary and sufficient condition for peace in Europe, we describe the main institutions but also shed a critical light on those assumptions.

Europe is not isolated. It has always been part of the geopolitical times—historically as an important player, nowadays often considered to play second fiddle and at times considered to be sitting on the fence in terms of clear positioning in geopolitical constellations. Western European security after World War II and certainly today cannot be understood without NATO (Grant) as the main security guarantor of Western Europe and formerly opposing the Soviet-led Warsaw Pact. Having been declared brain-dead by French President Macron in 2019, calling for Europe to become a great power itself, NATO's role still remains contested, especially by Russia, and, depending on who forms its government, also by the US. Yet NATO has seemingly found a new role (against an old foe) since the 2022 Russian invasion of Ukraine. It has also shifted its geographical limits, expanding after the fall of the Berlin Wall to former Warsaw Pact States and now, after the 2022 invasion of Ukraine, adding formerly neutral countries such as Finland and Sweden. A new East/West European security border has thus emerged. Furthermore, a new value border is also emerging. After the Russian invasion of Ukraine, French President Macron issued a call which may be understood as 'democracies, unite!'. Thus, a European Political Community (EPC), an intergovernmental forum for political and strategic discussions about the future of Europe and based on its values, was established in 2022 with forty-seven participating States.

Europe's peace, security, and prosperity clearly depend on its neighbourhood. The neighbourhood policy of Europe and the EU (Majkowska-Szulc and Wierczyńska) is thus a crucial element for understanding Europe's attitude towards international law, once more reflecting the diversity and mix of intellectual traditions in Europe as well as a healthy dose of realism in EU foreign policy. A clear difference can be distinguished in the treatment of potential accession States (such as Turkey (since 1999), North Macedonia (2005), Montenegro (2010), Serbia (2012), Albania (2014), Moldova (2022), and Ukraine (2022), as well as Bosnia and Herzegovina (2022)) and those States which will not become members of the EU, such as the Maghreb States. Given that we understand Europe to be the CoE member States plus Russia, we have included other economic blocs next to the EU, such as the Eurasian Economic Union (Sayapin), although besides Russia and Armenia this also comprises non-CoE States (current or former) such as Belarus, Kazakhstan, and Kyrgyzstan.

Part 4 reflects the diversity of European States in their attitudes towards international law. No book to date has attempted to map or survey the field of international law across countries and regions in Europe so extensively. As briefly explored above, Europe is a continent of cross-cutting cleavages. How did these fundamentally different experiences of nationhood, of religion and ideology among others, manifest themselves in the role of international law in the different regions of Europe? The country chapters are intended to showcase the diversity of experiences and attitudes towards international law, teasing out the 'international law soul' of each country. The chapters attempt to provide a synergy of national scholarly traditions (to the extent these exist) and tendencies in State practice, often shaped by the history and size of the countries concerned. For example, a commitment to the EU and international law is especially pronounced in those countries transitioning to democracy at any point after World War II, such as Italy, Germany, Spain, Portugal, and Greece, as being on the losing side or associated with the losers. Other countries that had won wars are P5 Members (Russia, the UK, and France) and also former colonizers with their own outlook on and attitude towards the wider world. Yet others, especially smaller States, have very different experiences. Whereas the Benelux countries (Belgium, Netherlands, Luxemburg) have been earlier integrationists in Europe, fighting for the strength of a European international law and relying on international law, other smaller States (eg the three Baltic States) did not find that security until the demise of the iron curtain. Within pockets of Europe, apart from the war in Ukraine, conflicts persist, hopefully to be resolved peacefully, for example between Greece and Turkey. And it could well be that new States emerge in Europe in the future, given the separatist tendencies in some States (eg Catalonia in Spain and Scotland in the UK). Thus, there is no unified Europe from Venus, though some States are more at home on Venus while others are more at home on Mars.

The contribution and relationship to international law of a few major States or regions, in particular the UK (Wood), France (Ruiz Fabri and Stoppioni), Russia (Rusinova), Germany (von Arnauld), as well as the Nordic countries (Wrange and Kjeldgaard-Pedersen), or the intellectual contribution of Spain and the Netherlands (Ryngaert) to international legal thought and practice in the past, are fairly well known. Put simply, some people equate these traditions with 'Europe' generally—perhaps with the exception of Russia, which has had a historically on-off relationship with (the rest of) Europe. However, knowledge about many other regions within Europe, particularly the Eastern European States and other smaller States is much sparser, both in relation to their contribution to and attitudes towards international law, and the place of international law in national law. In addition to the countries mentioned above, the book chapters cover the countries of the former Yugoslavia as a region, still burdened by conflict (Serbia, Croatia, Montenegro, Slovenia, the Republic of North Macedonia, Bosnia and Herzegovina - Milanović and Papić), the Baltic States under Soviet suppression (Estonia, Latvia, and Lithuania - Mälksoo). Both regions have had unique experiences with international law, which allows the countries to be grouped together. Poland (Czapliński), the Czech Republic, and Hungary (Sturma) form the Visegrad countries; they were all part of the Eastern bloc and became members of the EU in 2004. Italy (Chiussi Curzi and Tanzi), Spain, and Portugal (Espósito and Galvão Telles), as well as Greece (Iakovidis and Tzevelekos) as Southern European countries share international law-friendliness after transitioning to democracy. Turkey's (Karakaş and Akbulut) relationship with the EU and NATO remains close but also fraught. Ukraine (Gnatovsky) is still in the process of rediscovering its own history in international law and is currently defending its existence following the imperialist war launched against it by Russia. Switzerland (Keller, Lüthi, and Sefkow-Werner), situated in the middle of Europe, is not an EU member State, although it has close ties and bilateral treaties with the EU and participates in its many activities (eg free movement of persons and scientific cooperation) and is characterized by its long-standing neutrality. Each of these chapters opens a new microcosm of international law and we encourage readers to take time and pay attention to each of them.

The reader will have noticed that not all CoE countries are included. Besides Belarus (as the only certainly European State which was never a member of the CoE, given that its government does not share its values), Andorra, Albania, Armenia, Austria, Azerbaijan, Belgium, Bulgaria, Cyprus, Georgia, Ireland, Iceland, Liechtenstein, Luxemburg, Malta, Moldova, Monaco, Romania, San Marino, Slovakia, and the Vatican are not covered as countries in this handbook. These countries have ever been equally important parts of Europe, however, and we hope that in the future a collection can emerge in which literally all European States are analytically represented with their international law histories and trajectories. Our selection says nothing about the specific experiences, contributions, and attitudes of those countries; it says more about time and other constraints to which we as editors were subject when planning and executing this project. Nevertheless, we believe that the selection of the countries included still allows the reader to capture the diversity and cross-cutting cleavages of European approaches to international law. This matters because the experiences of the 'big players' in the European history of international law—the Western European empires with colonies—were not the only experiences in Europe when one pays attention and zooms in closer.

In Europe, learned societies and the teaching of international law have always enjoyed a prominent role in shaping the international law thinking. For a long time, these remained a national affair with occasional cooperation, and indeed some country chapters in Part 4 refer to the intertwined relationship between national learned societies, and the teaching of international law and its practice at ministries of foreign affairs. Of course, learned societies of international law do not all have national roots, the *Institut de Droit International* and the International Law Association being notable exceptions that predate most national societies of international law as they both celebrated their 150th anniversaries in 2023 in France. The foundation of the European Society of International Law in 2004, thus a relative fledgling, has contributed to an exchange of views and contributes to the mutual understanding of schools of thought in different European countries, simultaneously shedding light on the diversity of intellectual traditions. It also highlights that countries still need to grow closer, including East and West. At the same time, the prominence of EU law as a subject of teaching and research (including in non-EU countries) has brought scholars in Europe together. Undoubtedly, since 1990, European international lawyers and academics have become closer, including young scholars.

5. Outlook

'Each generation imagines it is confronted with stupendous unprecedented novelties', as Philip C. Jessup once put it;[34] and we may indeed be wrong in thinking that the challenges we are facing are novel and unprecedented. However, we do believe that Europe is (again) at a crossroads. Its idea of achieving peace through international law has failed, once again, and on its own soil. At the time of writing, the outcome of the Russian-Ukrainian war is uncertain. Once again, millions of Europeans are refugees and tens of thousands are being killed by massive State violence. At the same time, European values as upheld after World War II are being put into doubt in several European States where populism is on the rise, the rule of law is in decline, and democratic backsliding is being witnessed. Quite apart from the new East/West fault line in Europe, more demarcations may be in the making between autocratic or at least illiberally democratic States and liberal democracies. This has implications for how international law is used in Europe and potentially for the pacifying function of international law.

Furthermore, Europe is closing, certainly to mass migration, being increasingly occupied with its own problems. It has also not yet found its way in the new geopolitical constellations, although the Russian invasion has helped to bring Western and Central European States together. For sure, Europe's role in international law has been changing from a dominant rule-maker to an occasional rule-taker. Europe is trying to keep its head above water in a multipolar world where the security of the West is no longer blindly assured by the US hegemon. It still needs to find its place and strengths, of which there are many. Next to its economic and soft power, the values and ideas on which European institutions were founded have not lost their significance and allure. The editors of this handbook hope that there is no need for another pan-European war to realize that those values are the only ones to keep peace and prosperity in freedom.

We started this introduction with the question whether Europe even existed. After editing this handbook, we believe that it does, in spite of its diversity, which the handbook highlights. Yet diversity is relative—seen from the outside, there is a land called Europe with its own distinctiveness as compared to other parts of the globe.

Notes

1. Simon Chesterman, Hisashi Owada, and Ben Saul (eds), *The Oxford Handbook of International Law in Asia and the Pacific* (OUP 2019).
2. Liliana Obregón Tarazona, Laura Betancur-Restrepo, and Juan Manuel Amaya Castro (eds), *The Oxford Handbook of International Law and the Americas* (OUP 2023).
3. See, eg, Ján Klučka, *Regionalism in International Law* (Routledge 2019).
4. Anthea Roberts, *Is International Law International?* (OUP 2017).
5. See Jennifer Pitts, *Boundaries of the International: Law and Empire* (Harvard UP 2018).

6. See Arnulf Becker Lorca, *Mestizo International Law: A Global Intellectual History 1842–1933* (CUP 2015); Julio A Barberis, 'Les règles spécifiques du droit international en Amérique latine', 235 RCADI 1992, 81; Antônio Augusto Cançado Trindade, 'The Contribution of Latin American Legal Doctrine to the Progressive Development of International Law', 376 RCADI 2015, 9.
7. No one captures this better than Timothy Garten Ash (*Homelands* (Bodley Head 2023), 48) when he says that being European means 'being at home abroad' (citing Kalypso NIcolaidĪs).
8. Which, it should be noted, would lie in the area of modern Israel, Syria, and Lebanon.
9. The founding treaty of MERCOSUR (Treaty of Asunción, signed 26 March 1991) has a common market as its goal, cf Article 1, for which the EU was inspirational. It also has a directly elected parliament, established pursuant to the Constitutive Protocol of the Mercosur Parliament, signed 9 December 2005.
10. The COMESA Treaty of 1993 envisages this treaty as a first step towards the creation of a common market, see Article 1 para 1, and eventually of an economic community for Eastern and Southern Africa. It has a court as established in Article 7 para 1 lit c.
11. In Africa, the development was somewhat different. The African Union, striving for more political integration, has also now launched the African Continental Free Trade Agreement (in 2019), which envisages as long-term objectives: creating a single, liberalized market; reducing barriers to capital and labour to facilitate investment; developing regional infrastructure; and establishing a continental customs union.
12. 'Creative destruction' describes the process that sees new innovations replacing existing ones which are rendered obsolete over time. See Joseph Schumpeter, *Capitalism, Socialism and Democracy* (Harper 1942).
13. See, eg, Anu Bradford, *The Brussels Effect: How the European Union Rules the World* (OUP 2020).
14. Joseph H H Weiler, 'The Geology of International Law—Governance, Democracy and Legitimacy', 64 ZaöRV 2004, 547.
15. Joseph H H Weiler and Johann Justus Vasel, 'The States' Upcoming Choice: Move Ahead All Together, Some Members Only or Alone' in Giuliano Amato et al (eds), *The History of the European Union: Constructing Utopia* (Bloomsbury 2019).
16. Alejandro Alvarez, 'Latin America and International Law', 3 American Journal of International Law 1909, 269.
17. See, eg, Wang Tieya, 'International Law in China: Historical and Contemporary Perspectives', 221 RCADI 1990, 195; Xue Hanqin, 'Chinese Contemporary Perspectives on International Law. History, Culture and International Law', 355 RCADI 2012, 41.
18. See Abdulqawi A Yusuf, 'Pan-Africanism and International Law', 369 RCADI 2014, 165.
19. See, eg, Raul C Pangalangan, *Philippine Materials in International Law* (Brill 2022); Dawood Adesola Hamzah, *International Law and Muslim States: Saudi Arabia in Context* (Routledge 2022); Choung Il Chee, *Korea and International Law* (Seoul Press for the Institute of International Legal Studies, Korea University 1993).
20. See Frederick E Snyder and Surakiart Sathirathai, *Third World Attitudes Towards International Law: An Introduction* (Brill/Nijhoff 1987).
21. See, eg, Peter Hilpold (ed), *European International Law Traditions* (Springer 2021); Jan Wouters et al, *International Law: A European Perspective* (Hart Publishing 2019); Nathalie Clarenc Bicudo et al (eds), *Un droit international français? Pratiques françaises du droit international* (Pedone 2022).

22. See, eg, Martti Koskenniemi, *To the Uttermost Part of the Earth. Legal Imagination and International Power, 1300–1870* (CUP 2021); Natasha Wheatley, *The Life and Death of States: Central Europe and the Transformation of Modern Sovereignty* (Princeton UP 2023).
23. The number of those killed in battle (including civil wars) fell markedly after 1946 and again after 1990. The database is updated to 2008 but presumably numbers have since risen again. See PRIO Battledeaths Dataset – Peace Research Institute Oslo (PRIO).
24. Olaf Scholz, 'The Global Zeitenwende: How to Avoid a New Cold War in a Multipolar Era' (Foreign Affairs, 5 December 2022) <https://www.foreignaffairs.com/germany/olaf-scholz-global-zeitenwende-how-avoid-new-cold-war> accessed 22 October 2023.
25. See also Robert Uerpmann-Wittzack, *Der Angriff auf die Ukraine: Eine Zeitenwende?* (Nomos 2022).
26. Russia's foreign policy concept of 31 March 2023 calls Russia a 'country-civilization' and is full of examples of how Moscow claims special regional influence in the international order, especially in its 'near abroad'. See <https://mid.ru/en/foreign_policy/fundamental_documents/1860586/> accessed 22 October 2023.
27. Seminal for a more realistic perspective are: Hans J Morgenthau, 'Positivism, Functionalism and International Law', 34 American Journal of International Law 1940, 260; Myres S McDougal, 'Some Basic Theoretical Concepts About International Law: A Policy-Oriented Framework of Inquiry', 4 Journal of Conflict Resolution 1960, 337.
28. See Michael Riepl, *Russian Contributions to International Humanitarian Law. A Contrastive Analysis of Russia's Historical Role and Its Current Practice* (Nomos 2022).
29. The architects of these conventions, Hersch Lauterpacht and Raphael Lemkin, were, after all, Europeans who had suffered from the terror regime in Europe and brought to the world concepts to prevent what they had experienced.
30. Important European thinkers pointed out early on the importance of democratic conditions for the maintenance of peace, eg, Alexis de Tocqueville, *Democracy in America* (Harper Perennial 1988) 659–660; see also Immanuel Kant, *Perpetual Peace: A Philosophical Sketch* (Nicolovius 1795), the first definite article on the Perpetual Peace: 'The Civil Constitution of Every State Should Be Republican', in the sense of separation of powers and constitutionalism, though not necessarily in a democratic form.
31. On how one of its legacies was dealt with, see, eg, William A Schabas, *The International Legal Order's Colour Line: Racism, Racial Discrimination, and the Making of International Law* (OUP 2023).
32. See also Bardo Fassbender, Anne Peters, and Simone Peter (eds), *The Oxford Handbook of the History of International Law* (OUP 2014).
33. Robert Kagan, *Of Paradise and Power: America and Europe in the New World Order* (Knopf 2003).
34. Philip C Jessup, 'Diversity and Uniformity in the Law of Nations', 58 American Journal of International Law 1964, 341, 344.

PART 1

HISTORY, IDEAS, AND CURRENT DEVELOPMENTS OF INTERNATIONAL LAW IN EUROPE

CHAPTER 1

A RICH BUT CONTESTED HISTORY

The Role of European States and Lawyers in the History of International Law

LAURI MÄLKSOO

1. Introduction: A Europe Influencing and under the Influence of International Law

International law cannot be understood without understanding its history. The history of international law matters—although it often remains contested what that history was and what it meant. Recently, a lively debate has revolved around whether any accounts of the history of international law could be neutral or objective.[1] Debates about and criticisms of the past of international law are inevitably related to discussions about the contemporary ills of the world, to our sense of justice. The period since the mid-1990s has seen a notable rise of academic interest in the history of international law, the historiographical turn. This focus on the history of international law also reflects sweeping political and economic changes in our world and related redistribution battles. Not surprisingly, the historical legacy of Europe in international law is often at the centre of these contestations.

The current trend of re-evaluating Europe's role in the history of international law is the main starting point for this chapter. The tension seems clear enough. On the one hand, we have inherited great European names and events from the history of international law and still have a scholarly consensus about the predominantly European historical origins of modern international law. On the other hand, many critical questions have been raised and problems spotted, particularly concerning the colonial era in

European history which ended only in the 1950s and 1960s and indeed in some instances has never fully ended.[2]

In this chapter, I have organized the historical discussion around the three main themes that were also identified as common threads for this volume: the impact of European ideas and practices on international law globally; the pacifying effect of international law in European history and beyond; and the diversity of international legal traditions within Europe. However, before tackling these aspects, we should first describe the tension in how Europe's role in the history of international law can be understood.

2. The Janus-Faced Nature of the History of International Law in Europe

European States and lawyers have fulfilled a pivotal role in the history of international law. International law students have been hearing the positive and inspiring aspects of this story since they first engaged with the study of international law and its history.[3] We start with the 'father of international law', the Dutchman Hugo Grotius (1583–1645) and his almost equally acclaimed predecessors the Spaniard Francisco de Vitoria (1483–1546) and the Italian Oxford Professor Alberico Gentili (1552–1608). Moreover, the Peace of Westphalia of 1648 stands as a colloquial symbol for international law of equally sovereign States as opposed to the Holy Roman Empire's previous claim to universal rule in Europe and no acceptance of equal sovereigns. The German Samuel von Pufendorf (1632–1694), the Swiss Emer de Vattel (1714–1767), the Russian Fyodor (Friedrich) Martens (1845–1909), and the Cambridge Professor of East Central European and Jewish origin Hersch Lauterpacht (1897–1960), to name but a few leading scholarly and diplomatic figures, all contributed significantly to the understanding of international law. The Institut de Droit International and the International Law Association, both established in Belgium in 1873, the Hague Peace Conferences of 1899 and 1907, the Paris Pact of 1928, or the Universal Declaration of Human Rights and the Genocide Convention, both adopted in Paris in 1948, a number of important Vienna conventions of the 1960s and beyond—all became landmarks in the history of international law.

Key dates and individuals in the history of international law often read like a dimension of European history at the same time. After all, *ius publicum Europaeum* and *droit public d'Europe* even used to be synonyms for the law of nations until the late 19th century.[4] The Hague and Geneva became central cities in the history of dispute settlement in international law; the first is the seat of the International Court of Justice (ICJ), the Permanent Court of Arbitration (PCA), and the International Criminal Court (ICC) and the latter is where nowadays the UN's International Law Commission (ILC) codification efforts take place. Moreover, the impact of Europe on the development of international law is not only a matter of the past. For example, in the context of international environmental law, we can think of the Aarhus Convention of 1998[5] and the 2015 Paris Agreement[6] as relatively recent notable events. International criminal law started from the Nuremberg trials and the ICC was established with the Rome Statute in 1998. The list of noteworthy international law-related European cities, events, and jurists could go on. Compared to its relative size in the world, Europe has been punching above its weight in the history of international law.

One important caveat needs to be stressed here, namely the role of the US in the more recent history of international law, at least since the Paris Peace Conference of 1919.[7] Initially in 1917 and then in 1944 the US decisively intervened in the European theatre of war during the two World Wars. In 1945, the US became the central pillar of the world order or at least in what became known as the West. The headquarters of the post-World War II universal international organization, the United Nations (UN), were established in Manhattan and the headquarters of the Bretton Woods institutions—the International Monetary Fund (IMF) and the World Bank—in Washington, DC. As a power that was also capable of enforcing its vision of international law, at least to some extent, the US took over from European countries the pole position in the management of international law. At the same time, the US was historically also an outgrowth of European civilization, *inter alia* sharing the same language and legal culture with a leading European power, Great Britain. In that sense, the international rise of the US was also a result of European expansion and heritage. In history, Americans very much appreciated the European tradition of international law. We can see this anecdotally in the fact that George Washington kept a copy of Vattel's 'Law of Nations'[8] and in the enthusiastic interest of American international law scholars such as James Brown Scott (1866–1943) in the European history of international law.[9] In these accounts, Europe was the *alma mater* for America and perhaps for the whole world, in the context of the historical rise of international law.

Of course, what was just presented above is only a part of the picture. Over the last two decades, the historical narrative of international law which highlights the role of Europe and Europeans, briefly sketched above, has come under widespread criticism as being too Eurocentric and West-centric.[10] An increasing amount of critical literature covers the history of international law, often rejecting or at least challenging previous understandings. Instead of endless European 'contributions' to the history of international law, during recent decades we have become ever more aware of the reverse side of the coin: European oppression and abuses in the history of international law, especially during the colonial era. Instead of looking at the history of international law through the eyes of Europeans—as, for example, Carl Schmitt did unapologetically in 1950[11]—today's European researchers on the history of international law tend to look at their subject matter through the eyes of others, or at least take such perspectives extensively into account. This leads to far less celebratory accounts.

During earlier centuries, Europeans were quite ignorant about normative orders in other world regions, dismissing the civilizational features of others and assuming in any case that regional normative ideas and practices elsewhere did not amount to international law, in contrast to Europe.[12] International law belonged only to 'civilized' nations and at least up until the late 19th century 'civilization' meant Christianity and Europe. In this historical understanding, European international law was eventually 'expanded', introduced, and transferred elsewhere as well—starting from acceptance of the Ottoman Empire and Japan as the first non-European members of the 'community of civilized nations' during the second half of the 19th century. This was a process rather than something that happened from one day to another. For example, formally the Ottoman Empire was accepted into the circle of 'civilized nations' with the Paris Peace Treaty of 1856 but even writing in the 1880s, the leading Russian international lawyer Martens denied that Turkey was a full member of the community of 'civilized nations'.[13] In Japan's case, some emphasize the 1894–1895 war with China while others the 1904–1905 war with Russia, in terms of its being fully accepted as member of the family of 'civilized nations'. During the 20th century, the rest of Asia and Africa could finally join in on formally equal terms as well, along with the retreat of the European colonial empires from these territories and the establishment of independent sovereign States there.

What has recently been criticized particularly intensely is (European) international law's complicity in colonization.[14] One of its symbols was the Berlin conference of 1885 when a handful of European empires divided parts of Africa among themselves. Colonialism by European empires meant ruthlessness towards the 'uncivilized' or 'semi-civilized' native peoples, economic exploitation, annexations, unequal treaties, extraterritorial consular jurisdiction, and so on. Up until the early 20th century, leading European international law textbook writers and diplomats were often defenders and enablers of such colonial and discriminatory practices.[15]

In a generation, we have witnessed a re-evaluation of the history of international law. During the Cold War in the West, writings on the history of international law were mostly unapologetically—to an extent even naively—Eurocentric. Nowadays, criticisms of European history in the context of international law has almost become the new mainstream.[16] Upon scrutiny, even the discipline's metaphorical 'father', Hugo Grotius, a lawyer in the service of the Dutch East India Company, does not appear to be the unqualified hero as once celebrated in the past.[17] The establishment of the League of Nations and the emergence of new nation States in 1919 was very important in Central and Eastern Europe but the ideal of self-determination was still denied to other parts of the world living under colonial rule.[18] From today's perspective, there is also the question why so few outstanding women appear in the European history of international law before scholars and practitioners such as Krystyna Marek[19] or Dame Rosalyn Higgins as the first female president of the ICJ made important contributions.

Overall, recent histories of international law make the European heritage of international law look quite problematic. Reading these new accounts, the European-dominated history of international law up until World War II appears primarily as one of European men who were out there for the interests of their privileged nations and classes while at the same time careful to speak the language of international law as the language of progress and even seeing themselves as the 'legal conscience of civilized nations'.[20]

What seems to remain for today's Europeans is to apologize and possibly pay compensation (whatever it is called as the assumption still is that international *law* of the time was technically not violated)—as Germany intends to do for crimes (even genocide) committed against the Herero and Nama peoples in today's Namibia in 1904–1907.[21]

So is it at all possible to reconcile these two approaches, the celebratory and the critical? In this chapter, my argument is that it is possible to both positively recognize, occasionally also celebrate, European contributions to the history of international law as well as at the same time be critical of the darker legacies, especially the colonialism of previous centuries and the totalitarianisms of the 20th century. Europe's role in the history of international law has been complex; it has not been just black or white. We can see this when we examine the European impact on international law globally.

3. The Impact of European Ideas and Practices on International Law Globally, or: Did International Law Ever Become Truly Universal?

A much-debated question in the history of international law has been: since when has this law existed? The Eurocentric view has placed the beginnings of 'modern' international law—usually theorized as being connected to natural law at the time—in the European history of the 16th–17th centuries.[22] Early European authors did not mind seeing some traces of international law in Antiquity,[23] in ancient Greece and Rome, but not necessarily in regions beyond Europe and the Mediterranean basin. At least since the time of decolonization, the traditional Eurocentric position has been challenged and elements of international law have been 'found' in the world's other regions as well.[24] To the extent that the Egyptian–Hittite Peace Treaty of 1280 BC was an expression of international law, it surely was not a European contribution. A copy of that treaty is displayed at the UN headquarters in Manhattan, perhaps also having the subtext that the origin of international law was not exclusively European. In Soviet and post-Soviet Russian scholarship of international law, the established view was that international law has existed ever since several States existed alongside each other which, it was inferred, was already the case in ancient Egypt in 3000 BC.[25]

It has also been argued that different types of international law or at least normative orders existed in East Asia and in the Islamic world.[26] At the same time, it also remains a fact that these regions did not theorize about their respective normative orders (*siyar* in the Islamic world and the Sinocentric tribute system in East Asia) as 'international law'. International/regional 'normative orders' and 'international law' are not identical notions. For example, the Sinocentric tribute system in East Asia explicitly rejected the idea of sovereign equality of States, the possibility that some other territorial entities could have been equal to China and its Emperor.[27] The normative system was theorized as one between the Chinese suzerain, vassal States, and barbarians beyond. Clearly, this thinking had implications for treaty-making, how wars were waged, and so on. Both China and the Europeans saw outsiders as inferior but the difference is that within Europe, a pluralism of competing powers was accepted.

So, if Europeans in the 16th–17th centuries did not invent international law all by themselves, they still promoted or even created a certain new type of international law. This new type of international law came with a theory and philosophy of international law that was preconditioned to a certain level of (admittedly fragile) intellectual freedom and curiosity in Christian West European countries that produced Vitoria, Gentili, Grotius, and other writers. We can speculate about the historical reasons why such writings first appeared in Western and Central Europe, but the fact remains that they did. We can then even postulate that the greatest influence of Europe in the history of international law was in promoting extension of the idea of 'law' to international relations and the international/regional community. This has been considered a Utopian idea even by some positivist European lawyers who looked at law primarily from the perspective of (idealized) domestic law and its centralized sanctions.[28]

The historical importance of the idea of sovereign equality of nations (at least within Europe) should not be underestimated either. The breakthrough of this idea was at least partly due to the Reformation and the subsequent rise of Protestantism in Northern Europe which solidified nation States based on their sovereignty and undermined the idea of a universal (Catholic) empire in Christendom, sometimes also referred to as *respublica Christiana*. The acceptance of formal equality between nations big and small has shaped the understanding of international law globally. Alternatively, we can also postulate that there have been different historical types of international law.[29] But, even so, not every historical regional normative order was firmly based on the idea of *law*—at least not 'international law' in the way that Europeans understood it.

Few European ideas in the history of international law have been criticized and condemned more in recent years than the 'standard of civilization'[30] which during the modern era kept international law exclusively to Europeans and their civilizational offspring such as the US. This has lately been quite unanimously dismissed as a discriminatory and even racist idea.[31] At the same time, note, for example, that in 1882 the leading Russian international lawyer Feodor (Friedrich) Martens (1845–1909) defined the essence of 'civilized States' in the following fashion: civilized States are those which respect the rights of their subjects.[32] If so, then what is so backward about it? The US legal philosopher John Rawls made a comparable argument in the early 21st century, even if using partly different vocabulary.[33] The US human rights scholar Jack Donnelly has argued that Western States made a rhetorical change during the 20th century—instead of the previous 'standard of civilization', they started to emphasize human rights[34] (as an arguably universal and historically less burdened yardstick for 'civilized' behaviour). However, if so then the substantive cultural-normative claim behind the concepts of 'civilization' and 'human rights' may not even have changed so much since the late 19th century. Highlighting the importance of human rights and democracy in the framework of international law is still one of the defining features of how international law is viewed in Europe, especially in the European Union (EU) and the Council of Europe (CoE) countries.[35]

The universalization of international law has been a gradual historical process; it has not happened from one day to another and there have been notable backlashes. For example, when Italy committed aggression against Abyssinia (the Ethiopian Empire) in 1936, one of the reasons why the League of Nations in Geneva was unable to mobilize support for Abyssinia—one of the organization's few African member States—was the purportedly lower civilization of Abyssinia compared to Italy; essentially a direct echo of the earlier European-dominated international law and perceptions.[36]

By the time colonialism collapsed in the 1950s and 1960s, the earlier Eurocentric language of the superiority of the European standard of civilization had already gradually been replaced with the language of the universality of international law. Now all States were equally sovereign and could become members of the UN, whether they were African, American, Asian, or European. In Eastern Europe, it was only in 1991 that a group of nations could liberate themselves from Soviet (but also Russian) imperial domination and become sovereign members of the international community.

Nowadays, it seems realistic to think of the universality of international law as still a work in progress rather than as something already unconditionally achieved. It is noticeable that regionalism and particularism in international law continue to flourish and many applications of core concepts in international law continue to carry national and regional dimensions.[37] Moreover, the criticism of the Western hegemony and 'unipolarity' which is popular in Russia and China advocates multipolarity as essentially co-existence of divergent regional spheres, to an extent at the cost of firm universal rules and standards. Neither globalization nor the usual rhetorical support for the universality of international law has levelled regional and civilizational differences throughout the world, with direct implications for the lived reality of international law.

In a certain sense, elements of the old *ius publicum Europaeum* continue to flourish in the form of the 'supranational' law of the EU as interpreted by the European Court of Justice (ECJ) and in the law of the Council of Europe, especially the European Convention on Human Rights (ECHR) as applied by the European Court of Human Rights (ECtHR) in Strasbourg. When the ECJ decided to resist the UN Security Council (UNSC) in the *Kadi* case,[38] a move which was also criticized by several international and even EU lawyers,[39] this revealed a factual tension between purportedly universal and regional understandings of international law; with the EU's highest court being dissatisfied with how the UNSC as the UN's executive organ had neglected human rights in its international designs against terrorism.

When international law was proclaimed universal through expansion of the international community and decolonization, the understanding of certain key norms and concepts was intriguingly modified according to the new historical and geographic context. For example, the ILC in its draft conclusions on identification and legal consequences on peremptory norms of international law (*jus cogens*) mentions as an example of *jus cogens* norms the right of peoples to self-determination.[40] However, what the right of peoples to self-determination implies in contemporary universal international law remains ambiguous;[41] this right has different connotations in European and African historical contexts. In Central and Eastern Europe in 1917–1920 as endorsed by the Versailles system of treaties and (even more explicitly) the Soviet Russian peace treaties of 1920 with its border States, the right of peoples to self-determination essentially meant the right of compactly living ethnic groups in Central and Eastern Europe to form their own sovereign nation States, the right to secede from the former multinational Empire. In contrast, in Africa in the 1950s–1960s, the right of peoples to self-determination came to mean the right to oust European colonial domination but within previous international or internal colonial borders (thus, either via State succession or *uti possidetis*). These borders often had—and still have—little to do with the actual ethnolinguistic situation on the ground. International law and its fundamental principles such as the right of peoples to self-determination were indeed proclaimed universal and, in a way, gained new life. However, the contours of international law concepts—such as the right of peoples to self-determination—changed in the process.

Today's international law and multilateralism are often seen to be in crisis and underperforming. Russia's aggression against Ukraine since 2022 has also been an attack against the foundational principles of the UN, and this by a permanent member of the UNSC. Calls for multipolarity have (re-)produced autonomous national and regional normative centres such as the US, the EU, China, and Russia, all of which to some extent emphasize different aspects of international law as well,[42] and all of which want to make sure that their understanding of international law will dominate, at least in their immediate neighbourhood. As a rule, Western academic publications on international law often do not sufficiently reflect the reality of international law as interpreted, for example, in China and Russia.[43] Even the US and key EU countries, otherwise historical allies, have at times seen contemporary challenges to international law so differently that we can only conditionally still speak about 'the West' in normative debates on international law.[44] Nevertheless, Russia's aggression against Ukraine has again consolidated the West, also in defence of underlying values and principles of international law.

To conclude the argument in this section, the historical transition from Eurocentric international law to universal international law has not been the unqualified success that we should unreservedly celebrate while criticizing the Eurocentrism of earlier, pre-universal international law. In some ways, significant regional—and probably civilizational—differences still lurk behind the veil of the proclaimed universality of international law. Consider, for example, the many cultural-religious reservations made to key UN human rights treaties, for example the Convention on the Elimination of all Forms of Discrimination Against Women (CEDAW), and generally the—often deficient—implementation of such treaties. Even though 20th-century Europe also produced both Nazism as well as Soviet Communism, two totalitarian challengers to liberalism, the earlier European concept of 'civilized States' to an extent lives on in contemporary ideas of human rights and democracy. Occasionally, the idea that international law would apply exactly in the same way everywhere in the world is little more than a noble fiction addressing a highly complex and bitterly harsh reality in which, for example, a number of sovereign States do not even control their own territory or the world's different regions have not contributed equally to State practice in certain areas of international law. At the same time, Europe has developed significant regional supranational and international law in the form of EU law[45] and the law of the Council of Europe which, in the actual daily practice of the nations concerned, is often at least as important as norms of universal international law which in the European context are in any case primarily based on regional historical-cultural consensuses and understandings.

4. The Pacifying Role of International Law in European and World History

Another question which we can historically tackle is to what extent international law, as it was conceived and practised in Europe, managed to contribute to peace and curb the waging of war.

When nowadays we critically review European use of military force and other violent excesses during the Age of Discovery, settlement of the New World, and the era of colonialism, one thing that needs to be kept in mind for perspective is that before 1928 with the Kellogg-Briand Pact, wars of conquest and annexations were allowed in international law, including within Europe.[46] International law simply had not developed to the point of outlawing conquest. Thus, for example, the three partitions of the Polish-Lithuanian Commonwealth at the end of the 18th century and the liquidation of that State, for centuries a leading power in Central Eastern Europe, were based on treaties between Prussia, Russia, and Austria. Rather than violating international law at the time, the partitions created a new status and boundaries within existing international law. The liquidation of the Polish-Lithuanian Commonwealth in 1795 was discussed from the perspective of morality but not so much international law.[47]

Nowadays, treaties carving up third States would legally be invalid *ex tunc* because the prohibition of aggression against other States is recognized as a *jus cogens* norm in international law.[48] However, this was normal, accepted, and legal back in the 18th century. In other words, while we can condemn past practices morally, when we still try to keep the discussion within the limits of international law, we cannot effectively rewrite past norms and standards of international law. This, however, does not mean that European international law before 1928 was indifferent towards the question of war and conquest.

International law in Europe was developed against a backdrop of the constant reality and threat of war. The Peace of Westphalia in 1648, namely the Treaties of Münster and Osnabrück, concluded the Thirty Years' War, which was one of the most devastating that Central Europe had ever seen. For centuries, the thinking in Europe was that the principle which would diminish the possibility of unnecessary war and conflict would be the balance of power.[49] Ever since, there has been a looming question in the context of international law whether balance of power might still be a sociological precondition for stable and successful functioning of international law in questions important for power.[50] However, the principle of the balance of power historically also justified the occasional use of military force, and not just strictly for self-defence but when other nations teamed up against rising European power(s) that arguably threatened the balance. Smaller nations could arguably be sacrificed for the benefit of others and the overall peace.

For the evolution of *jus ad bellum* rules, the late 19th century and early 20th century were particularly important. At the first Hague Peace Conference in 1899 it was proposed that advancing legally binding dispute settlement procedures, especially international arbitration, would facilitate the cause of international peace. As a result, the PCA came into being. At the second Hague Peace Conference of 1907, which already constituted a leap towards greater universality of participation compared to the first Hague Peace Conference, which was primarily a European event, the Drago-Porter Convention was adopted according to which States agreed not to use armed force for recovery of State debts except in the case of refusal to submit the issue to arbitration. In practice, this had a clear European vis-à-vis non-European connotation in the globalizing international community as it had been the European empires in Latin America which had collected their debts in this way.

One of the issues discussed extensively during and after World War I was how exactly and why it broke out.[51] World War I discredited the idea of the balance of power (the two hostile camps of States in Europe had also been formed and stood against each other according to the logic of the balance of power, the alliance of Britain, France, and Russia on the one hand, and Germany, Austria-Hungary, and the Ottoman Empire on the other). There was a sense that, notwithstanding the achievements of the previous Hague Peace Conferences, there had not been enough available mechanisms for legally binding international dispute settlement. If only the Austro-Hungarian Empire had responded to the assault against its honour that originated from Serbia in legally binding proceedings, then World War I might possibly have been avoided—or such was the thinking.

In the Covenant of the League of Nations adopted at Versailles in 1919, the member States of the League recognized 'that the maintenance of peace requires the reduction of national armaments' and committed 'to undertake to interchange full and frank information as to the scale of their armaments' (Article 8). They undertook to preserve the territorial integrity and existing political independence of all members of the League against external aggression (Article 10). The most immediate lesson that was subsequently learned from the fateful summer of 1914 was in Article 12 of the Covenant, which stipulated that if any dispute should arise between the member States 'likely to lead to a rupture they will submit the matter either to arbitration or judicial settlement or to enquiry by the Council, and they agree in no case to resort to war until three months after the award of the arbitrators, or the report by the Council'. The link between maintenance of peace and peaceful settlement of disputes was once again emphasized in Article 13 of the Covenant.

In 1928, the Paris Pact or the Briand-Kellogg Pact was concluded in which the contracting States solemnly renounced war as a means of national politics.[52] In Eastern Europe in 1929, the Soviet Union initiated a similar treaty called the Litvinov Pact. We can see from these treaties how much international law of the years following 1919 was preoccupied with the Great War and the tragic lessons of 1914. However, we also know that the attempt to curb war via juridical means and international dispute settlement mechanisms during the interwar period failed utterly during the 1930s. In a world of sovereign States, newly available dispute settlement mechanisms and condemnations of war alone could not resolve political and economic rivalries between States, especially as the previous peace settlement was criticized by the losers of World War I as ferociously as were the Versailles, the Saint-Germain, and the Trianon Peace Treaties.

The United Nations Charter adopted at the end of World War II in San Francisco in June 1945 further strengthened the pacifying dimension of the previous League of Nations Covenant. Article 2 paragraph 4 of the UN Charter famously prohibits the threat and use of force in international relations except for the right to self-defence (Article 51) and asserts that the Security Council can authorize the use of military force for the maintenance of international peace and security (Article 42). The UN is already a truly universal organization which the League of Nations—dominated by Great Britain and France, the European winners of World War I, and with a narrower basis of membership—was not. If we also count the Russian Federation as a European power (though more precisely it is a Eurasian power), then at least in terms of their share in the world's population, European States are nowadays overrepresented on the UN SC, with Russia, the UK, and France as permanent members of the SC wielding veto power over resolutions.

Beside Franco-German rivalry in the late 19th and early 20th centuries, wars in Europe have broken out in the context of secessionist activism. In terms of its political map and the number of sovereign States per population, Europe is one of the most politically fragmented regions in the world. The disintegration of the Russian and Austro-Hungarian Empires led to a number of military conflicts in Central and Eastern Europe in 1918–1920. During the 1990s, the secession of Yugoslavia led to civil and international wars in the Western Balkans. The NATO bombing of Yugoslavia because of the situation in Kosovo in 1999, as an example of non-UN sanctioned unilateral humanitarian intervention, led to a violation of rules on the use of force in the UN Charter. The question remains: was it necessary to avoid military intervention at any cost in the absence of consensus in the UNSC, in light of massive human rights violations in a conflict driven by secessionism? The NATO countries and the post-Soviet Russian Federation profoundly disagreed here. Moreover, Moscow later used the 'Kosovo precedent' and the related reference to the right of peoples to self-determination to justify its threat and use of force against Ukraine in 2014 when Russia (illegally) annexed Crimea and its military helped in a covert operation to *de facto* separate most of the region of Donbas from Ukraine.

Russia's war of aggression against Ukraine since 24 February 2022, with numerous war crimes committed, has also awakened old fears about the limits of international law in matters of power politics. As several times before in history, international treaties and agreements promising peace and protection of the equal sovereignty of smaller nations, have not held up.

Thus, the existence of strict international legal rules concerning *jus ad bellum* since the 1920s–1940s has not liquidated all instances of the threat or use of military force in international relations in Europe. Although the basic rules in themselves are quite clear, States have on occasion been quite inventive in circumventing them. What is perhaps most troublesome is that recent examples of the use of force in Europe have had a civilizational dimension and component. The war in Yugoslavia in the 1990s was primarily a war waged around civilizational ideas of distinctness of culture and religion and which piece of land belonged to which people. Moreover, although the Soviet Union disintegrated in 1991, there has been a civilizational component in Russia's wars at its borders since then, against Georgia in 2008 and Ukraine since 2014, in the sense that Orthodox Christianity being the main religion in these countries makes Moscow consider the departure of these countries from its sphere of influence as unnatural. Moscow's aim has been to impose its own regional order which would keep outside Western powers and organizations such as NATO out of these Orthodox Christian territories which have either been historically part of Russia or closely allied to Russia. Yet such civilizational ideas are ideological constructs because Greece, Bulgaria, and Romania are also predominantly Orthodox Christian countries and are members of both NATO and the EU. Security-wise, Europe continues to be divided, as throughout several earlier periods in history, between West and East, the EU and NATO on the one hand and, on the other, Russia, which sees itself as a civilization-State in serious conflict over its security and values with the West.

One lesson which Europe learned from the era of the League of Nations is that solemn declarations and treaties declaring the end of wars alone could not secure peace if political conditions were not right. The Briand-Kellogg Pact alone could not terminate historical Franco-German rivalry for supremacy in the European continent. For this reason, the creation of common regional, even supranational, organizations such as the European Communities (nowadays the EU) but also the CoE, has been first and foremost a successful peace project for the participants. Until February 2022, it was hoped that the CoE and the OSCE would play the same pacifying role vis-à-vis post-Soviet Russia and the country would gradually be integrated into common European structures and projects.[53] In the view of this writer, the main reason why this did not happen successfully is because Russia preferred to maintain its imperial identity, which became incompatible with the post-World War II European values of human rights, democracy, and rule of law. Nevertheless, the pacifying potential of the three values mentioned will also remain appealing in a future Europe. For lack of better criteria, adherence to these values will inevitably help to co-determine which country can politically belong to Europe and which one not.

5. Diversity of International Legal Traditions and Experiences within Europe

In the previous historical section, discussion of Europe and Europeans in the history of international law was conducted as if Europe was a historical monolith of sorts. In reality, however, there have regularly been divisions and sub-regions within Europe in the context of the history of international law. Even nowadays, consider the UN in which the Western European and Others Group and the Eastern European Group still constitute separate regional groups, even many years after the end of the Cold War and after a number of 'East' (in reality, Central and East) European nations became members of the EU in 2004 and 2007, that is, the distinction between the European West and East in the Cold War sense should have become obsolete. But many would argue that the European West and East still continue to exist, at least in people's minds.

The very notion of Europe is historically contested. Up until the early 20th century, Europe included in its people's imagery for centuries only Christian nations; it was the *respublica Christiana*. The Ottoman Empire (Turkey) which was the Islamic power and geographically present in South Eastern Europe was politically—at least during some periods—not seen as part of Europe but in many ways its antipode.[54] On some other occasions, the Ottoman Empire was of course a distinguished treaty partner and finally received the recognition of belonging to the 'international community' with the Paris Peace Treaty of 1856. Furthermore, during the 20th century, the Communist experiment set the Soviet Union and its core country, Russia, apart from the rest of Europe in a number of ways. In addition, Russia had been a latecomer in *jus publicum Europaeum* and joined the system only in the early 18th century, while international law had already been practised in Western and Central Europe for centuries. While this volume takes, as its starting point for understanding what Europe is, membership in the Council of Europe (plus Russia which was a member of the CoE in 1996–2022), it is useful to keep in mind that a culturally and geographically narrower concept of what constitutes Europe was predominant in the past.

If the much-criticized Eurocentrism in international law were a Russian '*matryoshka*' doll, it would also cover another smaller doll: West European centrism. During the Middle Ages, the biggest division within Europe was between Western and Eastern Christendom. This was a consequence of the East-West Schism of 1054 and the resulting two spiritual and power centres, Constantinople and Rome. The European origin of international law is in reality predominantly of West and Central European origin—from the countries that used Latin and afterwards national languages such as French, German, English, Italian, and Spanish. Thus, the reach of Catholic legal cosmology also reached countries that were later temporarily known as part of 'Eastern' Europe during the Cold War. For example, consider the case of the Polish legal scholar Paulus Vladimiri

(Paweł Włodkowic) who in 1414 represented Poland at the Council of Constance and presented legal arguments against the Teutonic Order.[55] Lawyers representing Poland and the Teutonic Order in this dispute were part of the same (Catholic) legal family of nations.

Past historians of international law such as Wilhelm Grewe, Sir Paul Vinogradoff, and Baron Michel de Taube have postulated that during the late Middle Ages, the Catholic and Orthodox Christian parts constituted two different types of legal families, two different spheres of Europe.[56] Unfortunately, the specific understandings of norms and rules in Orthodox Eastern Europe are much less known than those in Western Europe. During the 250 years when the lands of what later became Russia were ruled by the Muslim Tatar Golden Horde (1230–1480) and the subsequent years of Muscovy's relative isolation, voices in Western Europe dismissed Muscovy as not belonging to *respublica Christiana*.[57]

Later, Orthodox Eastern Europe came closer to Western Europe and a more synergetic European civilization and community of nations was forged. Russia, as a gigantic empire, contributed to *jus publicum Europaeum* during the 18th and 19th centuries, as mediator, power broker, and norm-maker.[58] Nevertheless, in most ways Western Europe remained the normative centre in the practice and development of international law in Europe. Typically, it was in Germany and Western Europe where the most influential ideas about international law were born and debated. It was also no historical coincidence that the Russian international lawyer who became most widely known globally was a Protestant from the Baltic provinces, Friedrich (Fyodor Fyodorovich) Martens.[59] It was culturally easier for Martens, as a representative of the Russian Empire and yet originating from the Baltic borderlands, to speak international law as a predominantly West European normative language.

Having highlighted international lawyers with Christian, initially Catholic and later often with Protestant backgrounds, it should also not be forgotten that European Jewish scholars have made important contributions to international law, especially during the 20th century, which turned out so tragically for Jewish people. For example, Jewish scholars were among the main intellectual and spiritual forces who facilitated the human rights revolution in public international law.[60] Usually, they originated from Central or Eastern Europe and later they became influential either in Western Europe (eg Hersch Lauterpacht) or the US (eg Columbia University's famous human rights scholar Louis Henkin was born in present-day Belarus).

The German historian of international law and diplomat Wilhelm Grewe postulated that European international law had its own leading powers during different eras—initially Spain, then France, and finally, partly up until World War II, Great Britain.[61] Today we have almost forgotten how much the rise of international legal arguments and natural law thinking in the 17th century was also connected with religious arguments within Europe, especially between Catholics and Protestants.[62]

When the Bolsheviks came to power in Russia in November 1917, they did not fully recognize the universality of previous 'classic' international law (within its sphere of application: mainly in Europe) and claimed that socialist countries led by Soviet Russia would develop their own type of (initially regional) international law of socialist countries.[63] Thus, only the end of the Cold War, the disintegration of the Soviet Union, and the emergence of the Russian Federation as a sovereign State created hopes for eventual reunification and decline of animosity in wider Europe. In this spirit, Russia became a member of the CoE in 1996 and ratified the ECHR in 1998. However, instead of differences between Communism and the 'free world' during the Cold War, the post-Cold War decades have highlighted different concepts of State sovereignty, collective security, and human rights in the Western part of Europe and in Russia. Over the last two decades, Moscow has endorsed a traditionalist concept of human rights which distances itself in particular from LGBTQ rights but also, in the geopolitical context, challenges NATO's role in the East European security architecture. In 2022, these tendencies, already visible earlier in the minds of Russia's political and spiritual leaders, led to Russia's aggression against Ukraine and Russia's expulsion from the CoE.

In the context of EU countries, a centuries-old debate dates back as far as the times of the Holy Roman Empire during the Middle Ages: what is the proper relationship between a centre with certain unifying tendencies and the constituent units with their emphasis on sovereignty and autonomy?[64] The latter would often like to symbolically maintain their right to have the last word in power struggles with the centre, even if certain solutions within the EU even today are pointing towards *de facto* federation.[65] History teaches us that centrifugal and centripetal forces have often been interlocked in a complex way in Europe and this is not likely to change in the foreseeable future, as the departure of Great Britain from the EU in 2020 (Brexit) has also demonstrated.

A certain awareness of different histories of European countries is needed in order to understand their different behaviour in today's international crises. For example, the countries formerly constituting the Austro-Hungarian Empire did not participate in overseas colonization in the way that the Western European empires did. It is also a different historical experience and legacy that made the successor States of the Habsburg monarchy take more conservative and sovereigntist positions during the refugee and mass migration crisis of 2015. When, on 19 December 2018, the UN General Assembly (UNGA) adopted the 'non-legally binding' Global Compact for Safe, Orderly and Regular Migration,[66] the Czech Republic, Hungary, and Poland voted against it whereas Austria, Bulgaria, Italy, Latvia, Liechtenstein, Romania, and Switzerland abstained and Slovakia did not vote.

Throughout recent centuries, centre and periphery have featured in the international law of Europe. However, what constitutes the centre has been a matter of struggle. While Great Britain, France, and Germany have been the usual suspects in terms of constituting the centre within Europe in the context of international law, today's Moscow remembers with nostalgia and now also revanchism that it, too, constituted a Eurasian regional centre in the international law of the Cold War era. At the same time, several smaller nations within Europe, especially in Eastern Europe, can only with reservations relate to the thesis of Eurocentrism in international law because they too had to struggle for their own right to sovereign existence within Europe in comparable ways to parts of the non-European world.

6. In Conclusion: Europe's Future Role Globally and Regionally

By way of conclusion, we may ask whether Europe's role has been and continues to be moving from former almost absolute cultural-military dominance in the world to further relative decline in the context of international law. Martti Koskenniemi has postulated that international law itself, as a normative language, faced a certain decline of prestige and sense of purpose after World War II, by about 1960.[67] Linking Koskenniemi's assessment with what Carl Schmitt wrote nostalgically about the earlier *jus publicum Europaeum* in 1950, we may wonder whether a certain decline of international law in the public discourse of what used to be called the 'civilized States' of Europe and North America was also due to the fact that international law was made universal in a way that also came with certain costs. It was easier to dismiss international law if its serious and uniform application in the wider world seemed partly like an ideal, often detached from the messy reality on the ground.

From the perspective of old predominantly white, Christian Europe, the enthusiastic doctrine of the universality of international law without regional prerogatives, rights, and reservations may even to a certain extent become dangerous for European interests, at least when these are conservatively defined. Until the 20th century, Europe dominated over and lectured the rest of the world about human rights and the standard of civilization. But now the tides have started to turn and the rhetoric of universal human rights, mixed with post-colonial sentiment and a quest for reparations, is increasingly being used against 'fortress Europe'. In fora such as the UNGA and Human Rights Council in which several European nations have for example not been eager to extend some of the protection foreseen for political refugees to economic migrants, they have faced criticism for their lack of solidarity and for turning inwards. It is a kind of success of European ideas about international law that, historically, Europe was in a position to lecture others about the importance of human rights and the need to emancipate. Nowadays, Europe sometimes gets the same gospel back.

Ideas of global law and extended universal human rights have grown impatient with traditional pillars of international law such as State sovereignty and the right of each State to control migration which follows from it. With global warming and the climate crisis as well as the return of classic threats such as wars of aggression, the world is changing and so are people's expectations towards international law. To be a declining minority in the world, also in the context of international law, this will not be an easy task to manage for European nations. Nevertheless, further emphasis on the development of regional international law in Europe will likely constitute one aspect of the future. Europe's civilization no longer can or needs to dominate globally—or imagine itself as universal—but it will claim its right to exist as a distinct entity and defend its values and identity, at least at home. In other words, no more European-dominated *Nomos der Erde* but still Nomos of Europe.

NOTES

1. Anne Orford, *International Law and the Politics of History* (CUP 2021).
2. See ICJ, Advisory opinion, *Legal Consequences of the Separation of the Chagos Archipelago from Mauritius in 1965*, 25 February 2019, para 177 ('the United Kingdom's continued administration of the Chagos Archipelago constitutes a wrongful act entailing the international responsibility of that State'). See also Philippe Sands, *The Last Colony: A Tale of Exile, Justice and Britain's Colonial Legacy* (Weidenfeld & Nicolson 2022).
3. See generally Bardo Fassbender and Anne Peters (eds), *The Oxford Handbook of the History of International Law* (OUP 2012) and the 26 volumes of the *Journal of the History of International Law* so far at Brill.
4. See, eg, August Wilhelm Heffter, *Das Europäische Völkerrecht der Gegenwart* (Schroeder 1844).
5. The United Nations Economic Commission for Europe (UNECE) Convention on Access to Information, Public Participation in Decision-Making and Access to Justice in Environmental Matters, adopted on 25 June 1998.
6. Paris Agreement, adopted during the Paris Climate Change Conference on 12 December 2015.
7. See generally Mark Weston Janis, *America and the Law of Nations 1776–1939* (OUP 2010).
8. See Stephen C Neff, *Justice among Nations. A History of International Law* (Harvard UP 2014) 1.
9. See Paolo Amorosa, *Rewriting the History of the Law of Nations: How James Brown Scott Made Francisco de Vitoria the Founder of International Law* (OUP 2019).
10. See the chapters by Antony Anghie as well as Makane Moïse Mbengue and Olabisi D. Akinkugbe in this volume. See further also Antony Anghie, *Imperialism, Sovereignty and the Making of International Law* (CUP 2005); Arnulf Becker Lorca, *Mestizo International Law. A Global Intellectual History 1842–1933* (CUP 2014); Luis Eslava, Mikhael Fakhri, and Vasuki Nesiah (eds), *Bandung, Global History, and International Law* (CUP 2017); Jochen von Bernstorff and Philip Dann (eds), *The Battle for International Law. South-North Perspectives on the Decolonization Era* (OUP 2019); Inge van Hulle, *Britain and International Law in West Africa. The Practice of Empire* (OUP 2020); Ntina Tzouvala, *Capitalism as Civilization: A History of International Law* (CUP 2020).
11. Carl Schmitt, *Der Nomos der Erde im Völkerrecht des Jus Publicum Europaeum* (5th edn, Duncker & Humblot 2011; original edn 1950).
12. Onuma Yasuaki, 'When Was the Law of International Society Born?', 2 Journal of the History of International Law 2000, 1–66.
13. See Fedor Fedorovich Martens, *Sovremennoe mezhdunarodnoe pravo tsivilizovannykh narodov* I (Iuridicheski kolledzh MGU 1996; 1st edn 1882) 144. See further in the present volume the chapter on how after World War I, the heartland of the Ottoman Empire was transformed into republican Turkey in the chapter by Işil Ergüvenç Karakaş and Olgun Akbulut.
14. See, eg, Adom Getachew, *Worldmaking after Empire. The Rise and Fall of Self-Determination* (Princeton UP 2019).
15. See L Mälksoo, 'The Legacy of F.F. Martens and the Shadow of Colonialism', 21 Chinese Journal of International Law 2022, 55–77.
16. See references (n 10) but also Martti Koskenniemi, *The Gentle Civilizer of Nations: The Rise and Fall of International Law 1870–1960* (CUP 2001) (hereafter Koskenniemi, *The Gentle Civilizer*).

17. See Martine Julia van Ittersum, 'Hugo Grotius: The Making of a Founding Father of International Law', in Anne Orford and Florian Hoffmann (eds), *The Oxford Handbook of the Theory of International Law* (OUP 2016) 82–100; Oona A Hathaway and Scott J Shapiro, *The Internationalists. How a Radical Plan to Outlaw War Remade the World* (Simon & Schuster 2017) 23–30.
18. Erez Manela, *The Wilsonian Moment: Self Determination and the International Origins of Anticolonial Nationalism* (OUP 2007).
19. See esp Krystyna Marek, *Identity and Continuity of States in International Law* (Droz 1954; 2nd edn 1968.) See further Natasha Wheatley, 'What Can We (She) Know about Sovereignty?: Krystyna Marek and the Worldedness of International Law', in Patricia Owens and Katharina Rietzler (eds), *Women's International Thought: A New History* (CUP 2021) 327–344.
20. Koskenniemi, *The Gentle Civilizer* (n 16) 41.
21. See BBC, 'Germany Officially Recognises Colonial-Era Namibia Genocide', 29 May 2021, https://www.bbc.com/news/world-europe-57279008.
22. However, not all European authors have been 'Eurocentric' in this sense. See Thilo Marauhn and Heinhard Steiger (eds), *Universality and Continuity in International Law* (Eleven 2011); Wolfgang Preiser, *Frühe völkerrechtliche Ordnungen der aussereuropäischen Welt: Ein Beitrag zur Geschichte des Völkerrechts* (Steiner 1976).
23. See David J Bederman, *International Law in Antiquity* (CUP 2009).
24. C H Alexandrowicz, David Armitage, and Jennifer Pitts (eds), *The Law of Nations in Global History* (OUP 2017).
25. See for many A Ya Kapustin (ed), *Mezhdunarodnoe pravo* (Gardariki 2008) 46.
26. Yasuaki Onuma, 'When Was the Law of International Society Born?—An Inquiry of the History of International Law from an Intercivilizational Perspective', Journal of the History of International Law 2000, 1–66.
27. ibid.
28. See John Austin, *The Province of Jurisprudence Determined* (Amherst, NY: Prometheus Books 2000; original 1832); calling international law 'law not properly called so', but rather 'positive morality' as it does not rely on commands of a sovereign. Another famous British legal scholar, H L A Hart (1907–1992), likened international law to a primitive legal order, due to the shortage of secondary rules. See H L A Hart, *The Concept of Law* (2nd edn, OUP 1994) 214.
29. On historical types of international law, see further Sir Paul Vinogradoff, *Historical Types of International Law: Lectures Delivered in the University of Leiden* (Brill 1923); Sir Paul Vinogradoff, *On the History of International Law and International Organization*, ed W E Butler (Lawbook Exchange 2009).
30. On this, see Gerrit W Gong, *The Standard of Civilization in International Society* (Clarendon Press 1984); Gustavo Gozzi, *Rights and Civilizations. A History and Philosophy of International Law* (CUP 2019).
31. See representatively Alexander Orakhelashvili, 'The Idea of European International Law', 17 European Journal of International Law 2006, 315–347.
32. Martens, *Sovremennoe mezhunarodnoe pravo tsivilizovannykh narodov* (n 13) 8.
33. John Rawls, *The Law of Peoples* (Harvard UP 1999); asking 'how far liberal peoples are to tolerate nonliberal peoples', 59.
34. Jack Donnelly, 'Human Rights: A New Standard of Civilization?', 74 International Affairs 1998, 1–23.

35. See the chapters by Basak Cali, Veronika Bilkova, and Justus Vasel in this volume.
36. Schmitt, *Der Nomos der Erde*, 215.
37. See further on regionalism eg in Mariano Aznar and Mary J Footer (eds), *Select Proceedings of the European Society of International Law, Vol 4, 2012* (Hart Publishing 2016); Jan Klučka, *Regionalism in International Law* (Routledge 2018).
38. ECJ, Judgment (Grand Chamber) of 3 September 2008; *Yassin Abdullah Kadi and Al Barakaat International Foundation v Council of the EU and Commission of the European Communities*, European Court Reports 2008 I-06351.
39. See, eg, Jan Klabbers, 'Kadi Justice at the Security Council?', 4 International Organizations Law Review 2007, 293–304; Grainne De Burca, 'The European Court of Justice and the International legal Order After Kadi', 51 *Harvard ILJ* 2010, at 44 et seq.
40. ILC, Draft conclusions on identification and legal consequences of peremptory norms of general international law (*jus cogens*), 2022, conclusion 23 (g) the right to self-determination (hereafter 'ILC, Draft Conclusions').
41. See Jörg Fisch, *The Right of Self-Determination of Peoples. The Domestication of an Illusion*, trans Anita Mage (CUP 2015).
42. See Anu Bradford and Eric A Posner, 'Universal Exceptionalism in International Law', 52 Harvard Journal of International Law 2011, 1–54.
43. The important exception is Anthea Roberts, *Is International Law International?* (OUP 2017).
44. See Chiara Giorgetti and Guglielmo Verdirame (eds), *Whither the West? Concepts of International Law in Europe and the United States* (CUP 2021).
45. For how EU law intends to stand distinct from international law, see the chapter by Pierre d'Argent in this volume.
46. The classic study here is Ian Brownlie, *International Law and the Use of Force by States* (OUP 1963).
47. On hearing that the Austrian Empress Maria Theresia had wept when—with her own approval—the Polish-Lithuanian Commonwealth was destroyed, the Prussian King Frederick II quipped: 'Sie weinte, aber sie nahm' (she cried but she took).
48. See ILC, Draft conclusions (n 40), draft conclusion 23 a (prohibition of aggression).
49. See Detlev Vagts, 'Balance of Power', in *Max Planck Encyclopaedia of Public International Law* (OUP 2007).
50. So suggested, eg, Oppenheim, in his textbook Lassa Oppenheim, *International Law: A Treatise, vol I: Peace* (Longmans, 2nd edn 1912) 80.
51. See, eg, Christopher Clark, *The Sleepwalkers. How Europe Went to War in 1914* (Allen Lane 2012).
52. See further Oona Hathaway and Scott J Shapiro, *The Internationalists: How a Radical Plan to Outlaw War Remade the World* (Simon & Schuster 2017).
53. See further eg Lauri Mälksoo and Wolfgang Benedek (eds), *Russia and the European Court of Human Rights: The Strasbourg Effect* (CUP 2017).
54. On how Russia and the Ottoman Empire worked out their own rules on prisoners of war, see Will Smiley, *From Slaves to Prisoners of War. The Ottoman Empire, Russia, and International Law* (OUP 2018).
55. See Władysław Czapliński, 'Paweł Włodkovic (Paulus Vladimiri) and the Polish International Legal Doctrine of the 15th Century', 7 Baltic Yearbook of International Law 2007, 65–82; Charles H Alexandrowicz, 'Paulus Vladimiri and the Development

of the Doctrine of Coexistence of Christian and Non-Christian Countries', in C H Alexandrowicz, *The Law of Nations in Global History* (OUP 2017) 53–61.

56. Michel de Taube, 'Etudes sur le développement historique du droit international dans l'Europe orientale', Recueil des Cours Vol 11 (1926-I, Leiden) 341 et seq.
57. The first original writing on international law from Muscovy, by Petr Shafirov, from 1716, starts with the complaint that Europeans had talked about Muscovy in the same way as they had about India and Persia, assuming it did not belong to Europe. See P P Shafirov, *A Discourse Concerning the Just Causes of the War Between Sweden and Russia: 1700–1721*, ed W E Butler (Oceana Publications 1973) 2 (the Russian version of Shafirov's text).
58. See, eg, Carl Bergbohm, *Die bewaffnete Neutralität 1780–1783. Eine Entwicklungsphase des Völkerrechts im Seekriege* (Puttkammer & Mühlbrecht 1884) 106 et seq. (discussing the question of armed neutrality proclaimed by the Russian Empress Catherine II).
59. See Edith Sollohub, *The Russian Countess. Escaping Revolutionary Russia* (Impress Books 2010) xiii (memoirs of Martens's daughter, starting with the statement that the parents were Lutheran Protestants, which meant that they did not belong to the established 'state-church').
60. Philippe Sands, *East West Street: On the Origins of Genocide and Crimes against Humanity* (Weidenfeld & Nicolson 2016); James Loeffler, *Rooted Cosmopolitans. Jews and Human Rights in the Twentieth Century* (Yale UP 2018).
61. Wilhelm Grewe, *Epochen der Völkerrechtsgeschichte* (Nomos 1984).
62. See also the chapter on religion in this volume by Christian Walter.
63. See Evgenij A Korovin, *Das Völkerrecht der Übergangszeit. Grundlagen der völkerrechtlichen Beziehungen der Union der Sowjetrepubliken*, trans I Robinson-Kaunas (Walther Rothschild 1929) 6–8.
64. S J Neff, *Justice among Nations. A History of International Law* (Harvard UP 2014) 74 et seq. (discussing the interplay of unity and diversity in mediaeval Christian Europe).
65. See the clash between the German Constitutional Court and the European Court of Justice in BVerfG, *Weiss and Others*, 5 May 2020.
66. A/RES/73/195, *Global Compact for Safe, Orderly and Regular Migration*, 19 December 2018.
67. Koskenniemi, *The Gentle Civilizer* (n 16) 513 et seq.

CHAPTER 2

THE ROLE OF RELIGION IN THE FORMATION OF INTERNATIONAL LAW IN EUROPE

CHRISTIAN WALTER

1. Introduction

Religion has undoubtedly played an important role in the formation and evolution of international law in Europe. This role is complex and may be analysed from quite different angles. Today, we view religion mainly as an object of regulation, which leads to a predominant role of human rights, notably freedom of religion and the prohibition of discrimination on religious grounds. However, from the perspective of the history of ideas, religion may also be viewed as a source of law (natural law in its early, medieval phase understood as divine law) or at least as a formative factor in shaping (international) legal concepts and institutions (eg *bellum iustum* and humanitarian intervention). The reason for this influence of religion is that the relevant international actors each have their own stance on religion. Some are expressly based on certain religious convictions (such as the Holy See or the Islamic Republic of Iran), others base their political authority, contrarily, on secularism (eg Article 1 of the French Constitution of 1958). One possible approach of inquiring into the relationship between international law and religion is thus to try and trace the influence of certain religions on the development of international law.[1]

Yet another approach is to look at individual actors. The influence of individual convictions of lawyers, diplomats, or judges should not be neglected. Their individual convictions may have had a decisive influence on their contribution to the development of international law. The role of Charles H Malik in framing the Universal Declaration of Human Rights (UDHR), and notably its Article 18 on freedom of religion is an illustrative example of the importance of individual religious convictions in the development of international law. Malik was raised in a Greek Orthodox family within the religiously pluralistic environment of the Lebanon in the first half of the 20th century and was strongly influenced by his experience as a foreign student in Germany and the US.[2] His influence is considered decisive for the broad concept of freedom of religion underlying the UDHR.[3]

It is obvious that the present chapter cannot systematically unfold these complex interactions between the development of international law and religion as they have just been alluded to. Notably, it is impossible to enter into biographical details of individual international actors or into a detailed analysis of the various influences from different religions. In a similar manner, it is not possible to disentangle here the complex amalgam of cultural, sociological, and religious factors that frame (international) law in a given period of time. While, for example, a concept such as 'civilized nations' in Article 38 lit c) ICJ-Statute, which was the fruit of a colonialist European perspective on the world, certainly also has a religious background in Christianity, other factors, notably hegemonic or imperialist interests, seem to be predominant.[4] Similarly, the concept of human rights was framed by multiple factors, among them Christian and non-Christian influences, and even anti-clerical and secular forces. An in-depth analysis would require to look at different actors with different agendas in different times. This would go far beyond what can be done in a handbook contribution. For this reason, this chapter does not follow such paths.[5] Instead, in the interest of a coherent approach throughout this handbook, the chapter places emphasis on three different fields which are outlined in the introduction by the editors: the pacifying function of international law; the appeal and contestation of European ideas of international law in the global context; and the intra-regional context of diversity and fragmentation of international law within Europe.[6] In the next section, the overall claim is made that the emancipation of (international) law from religion is a contribution to the pacifying function of international law, which has its roots in the specific European and Western development of the State as international actor and law as a form of exercise (and at the same time: limitation) of public power (Section 2). The following sections are then devoted to an analysis of the treatment of religion in the European regional context as compared to the universal level. Section 3 describes that (and explains why), surprisingly as it may seem at first sight, the prohibition of discrimination on religious grounds has played a rather limited role in the practice of human rights protection. Rather, the focus is on freedom of religion. Section 4 asserts that the European Court of Human Right's (ECtHR) role as a quasi-constitutional court has enabled it to develop a quite unique model of common but differentiated standards for evaluating the treatment of religion within the Contracting States of the European Convention on Human Rights (ECHR). In Section 5 a possible new focus on non-discrimination based on the activities of the European Union (EU) is analysed. Whether this model can serve as a blueprint for other areas of the world is an open question, and this is addressed by way of conclusion in Section 6.

2. Emancipation of Public Authority and Law from Religion

The development of the modern State is the result of a process of secularization.[7] Since international law primarily governs the relations between independent States,[8] the process of secularization, which produced the notion of statehood, necessarily must have had repercussions on the nature of the law that governs the relations between States. This section analyses the development of international law as a process of emancipation from religion, which is closely tied to the process of secularization which generated the State as the central institution for the exercise of public power.[9]

2.1 The notion of 'secularization' as employed here

Whether or not modern societies are necessarily secular is an open and highly disputed question.[10] For that reason, it is important to stress that the term secularization, as used in the following section, does not describe an overall development of modern societies or of the international order as such. The term is merely meant to describe the process by which the legal order gets detached from religion.[11] Thus, the notion of secularization relates to the State and to law as instruments for the exercise of public authority, not to society as such.

2.2 The emergence of the 'Westphalian order' and the secularization of public power

The development of what we call today the Westphalian legal order can only be understood against the background of the religious wars which ravaged Western Europe in the 16th and 17th centuries.[12] These civil wars brought about the notions of sovereignty in the writings of Jean Bodin and of a supremacy of the secular over the ecclesial power in the writings of Thomas Hobbes. In fact, the famous Peace of Westphalia of 1648 provided for a federal solution of religious conflicts. The rulers in the territories acquired a right to decide on the religion of their subjects (*cuius regio, eius religio*). By contrast, the Holy Roman Empire of the German Nation as the federal roof had to remain neutral in religious questions, the Treaty of Westphalia providing for a specific instrument in order to assure consensual decisions on religious questions (*itio in partes*). The construction has rightly been labelled a 'juridification' of the religious schism between Catholics and Protestants.[13] It resulted in a premodern concept of 'neutrality' at the level of the Empire and a 'confessionalization' within the territories.[14] While it is true that the none of the rulers of the time intended to place their territories outside the generally accepted fundaments of Christianity, it should not be overlooked, on a conceptual level, that the religious division created by the reformation changed the foundations of public power fundamentally: True, the rulers factually remained firmly rooted in Christianity, but conceptually the legitimation of public power had been cut from its religious foundations.[15]

It needs to be stressed in this context, that the notions of sovereignty (Bodin) and of supremacy of the secular sovereign (Hobbes) could not in and by themselves avoid religious intolerance and persecution. Basically, they placed the degree of tolerance in the hands of the ruler. This explains why, in all countries concerned, periods of tolerance and periods of religious persecution succeeded intermittently. This shows that the absolutist construction of power as conceived by Bodin and Hobbes—even though it was developed with the aim of overcoming religious fanatism of the religious civil wars—held no guarantee against a religiously fanatic sovereign. In the territories of the German Empire, the federal construction provided for a 'federal outlet' in the sense that migration into a more liberal environment was a (limited) option. Thus, even though ideas of tolerance were developed by leading German proponents of natural law such as Samuel Pufendorf or Christian Thomasius, the relatively tolerant conditions created by enlightened absolutist rulers like Frederick the Great in Prussia (1712–1786) or Joseph II in Austria (1741–1790) did not require revolutionary action against the existing order. It was possible to live in relative peace under the rule of the enlightened patriarchs.

The France of Louis XIV, by contrast, offered conditions of intolerance and suppression that were susceptible of provoking more radical ideas of political and religious freedom. It is, therefore, certainly not by chance that freedom of religion as an individual human right (in contrast to tolerance as an act of grace by the ruler) was developed in the thoughts of French philosophers of the era of enlightenment. The radical and violent revolution against the religiously legitimized order in 1789, its replacement by secular justifications, and a certain hostility of the French State against religion ever since, may be seen as a consequence with effects that last until today.

Another important strand is the liberal concept of tolerance developed by John Locke in his 'Letter concerning Toleration',[16] a concept that was especially influential in North America. For Locke, religion is essentially a matter for each individual,[17] which leads him to develop an early concept of separation of church and State.[18] It should be noted, however, that the situation in North America was fundamentally different from the condition in France mentioned above. In France, especially under the Gallicanism established by Louis XIV, religion was part of public power and controlled by the absolute monarch. Thus, disentanglement was required. In the US, by contrast, the Declaration of Independence and the foundation of a new State, provided for a clean-slate situation allowing the adoption of new forms of interaction between public power and religion.

2.3 Secularization of international law as part of that overall process

This secularization of public power is mirrored in the secularization of international law.[19] The medieval scholastic concept of natural law rested on a close interrelation between law and religion (eg Thomas Aquinas); the law being founded on and shaped by religion. Since then, a process of detaching law from religion has taken place. This process partly operated within the concept of natural law, in that gradually, elements of divine revelation were replaced by reference to reason or the 'nature' of things. In the German terminology this development is reflected by distinguishing between '*Naturrecht*' (natural law) and '*Vernunftrecht*' (law of reason). In addition, positive law acquired the status of a source of law in its own right. Thus, non-religious factors such as treaties and custom gained importance.

As is well known, it was then Hugo Grotius who furnished the theoretical background for severing international law from the theology of a specific confession, thus allowing its application beyond the frontiers of different religions.[20] Obviously, this theoretical leap is a necessary precondition for international law to become truly 'international', that is, a body of law that can also be accepted by actors with different religious backgrounds. For Emer de Vattel, writing in 1758,[21] religion has become an object of law that needs to be regulated, rather than a source of its own or—even less—'the' foundation of international law.

2.4 Interim conclusion—emancipation of international law from religion as a result

In order to summarize this section, two points need to be stressed as decisive contributions to the development of international law. The first concerns the State as the central actor in the international system and the second the legitimation of international law. Both points are, of course, closely interrelated.

With the notion of sovereignty, the religious civil wars brought about a concentration of public power in the State as an abstract legal entity. While there may exist quite different forms of *internal* legitimation of that power (including a strong focus on religion, see, eg, Articles 1 and 2 of the Constitution of the Islamic Republic of Iran), the *external* legitimation of States as sovereign equals (see Article 2, paragraph 1 UN Charter) remains detached from religion and thus secular.

3. Non-Discrimination on Religious Grounds in Modern International Law

Against the backdrop of this historical sketch, discrimination on religious grounds emerges as a major threat to peaceful co-existence in religiously pluralistic societies. A first consequence was the establishment of treaties aiming at the protection of religious and other minorities (Section 3.1). After World War II, this minority-based concept of protection against religious discrimination was replaced by a human rights-based approach (Section 3.2). While most of the human rights treaties concluded after 1945 included provisions against discrimination on religious grounds, freedom of religion as an individual right became far the more important instrument for protection against religious persecution (Section 3.3).

3.1 Treaty-based protection of (religious) minorities in the 18th and 19th centuries and under the League of Nations

The 18th and 19th centuries brought about a limited number of bilateral treaty-based regulations for religious minorities, notably in the context of transfer of territory.[22] After World War I, the issue of minority protection was addressed within the system established by the League of Nations. While minority protection did not, finally, make it into the text of the Covenant, it was present in the first drafts of President Wilson. Notably his third draft is worth being quoted, as it established a clear connection between religious persecution and war, and concluded on the necessity to protect freedom of religion:

> Recognizing religious persecution and intolerance as fertile sources of war, the powers signatory hereto agree, and the League of Nations shall exact from all new States and States seeking admission to it the promise, that they will make no law prohibiting or interfering with the free exercise of religion, and that they will in no way discriminate, either in law or in fact, against those who practice any particular creed, religion or belief whose practices are not inconsistent with public order or public morals.[23]

As mentioned, Wilson's ideas regarding the protection of minorities were not acceptable to the other powers and therefore did not become part of the League of Nations Covenant. Nevertheless, within the framework of the League of Nations, a fairly complex treaty system of minority protection was established. The legal basis of this system rests on identical provisions as those contained in the Treaties of Versailles, Saint-Germain, Neuilly, and Trianon, in which a number of newly founded or territorially reorganized States (Czechoslovakia, Poland, the Serb-Croat-Slovene State, Romania, and Greece) declared that they accepted and agree[d] to embody in a Treaty with the Principal Allied and Associated Powers such provisions as may be deemed necessary by the said Powers to protect the interests of the inhabitants who differ from the majority of the population in race, language or religion'.[24] The major difference of this system with regard to previous treaty guarantees for the protection of religious minorities was its inclusion into the institutional system of the League of Nations which basically implied a procedural framework allowing the Council of the League to address issues relating to alleged infractions.[25] As is well known, this institutional framework was unable to contain the disruptive power of national and religious extremism and hatred.

3.2 A change of paradigm—from minority protection to human rights protection

After World War II, the paradigm shifted from minority protection to human rights protection. Starting with the UDHR of 10 December 1948, the human rights catalogues of the post-World War II era contain provisions on freedom of religion and on the prohibition of discrimination on religious grounds. In contrast to the interwar period, these provisions are based on the concept of individual rights which is fundamental to the entire human rights development since 1945.

These anti-discrimination provisions usually mention a more or less comprehensive list of prohibited grounds of discrimination, all of which include religion.[26] It should be noted that the UN Charter, which does not set out a catalogue of human rights, explicitly mentions the prohibition of (religious) discrimination in its Article 1(3). Interestingly, and in contrast to some other established prohibitions of discrimination on grounds like gender[27] or race,[28] no special convention against religious discrimination was adopted.[29] While some initiatives in that direction were promoted within the UN Human Rights Commission in the 1960s, they never materialized into concrete proposals given strong opposition from two quite different sides: The communist bloc remained critical for fear of discrimination against atheist points of view, and the Islamic world was opposed to any guarantee that would include a right to change one's religion given the prohibition of apostasy in Islam.[30]

3.3 Freedom (rather than non-discrimination) as the paramount focus of the human rights-based approach to religion

In 1981, finally and as a compromise, the General Assembly of the United Nations adopted the 'Declaration on the Elimination of All Forms of Intolerance and of Discrimination Based on Religion or Belief' as a legally non-binding resolution.[31] While the title of this declaration points towards non-discrimination as the primary focus of the declaration, its content reveals a clear focus on freedom of religion. Notably Article 6 contains a number of clarifications regarding practical aspects of free exercise of religion (eg the right to worship or assemble in connection with a religion or belief; the right to establish and maintain appropriate charitable or humanitarian institutions; the right to teach a religion, to write, issue, and disseminate relevant publications, etc). The provisions relating to non-discrimination, by contrast, are of a more programmatic character. A similar focus, freedom of religion rather than non-discrimination, is indicated in the change of the title of the respective UN special rapporteur: Until 2000, he or she was named 'Special Rapporteur on religious intolerance', since then the official title is 'Special Rapporteur on freedom of religion or belief'.[32]

Similarly, a look at the practice of the Human Rights Committee (HRC), the ECtHR and the Special Rapporteur on freedom of religion or belief reveals a strong focus on free exercise of religion rather than non-discrimination.[33] One obvious explanation for these findings must be seen in the fact that, among the usual non-discrimination criteria, religion is the only one which is also protected by a corresponding freedom. Apparently, many of the discrimination issues related to other criteria (like race, gender, ethnicity, etc) can, when it comes to religion, be framed and argued in terms of infringement of freedom of religion, rather than as discrimination. It is noteworthy in that regard, that many of the religion cases decided under the ECHR address the substantive human rights issue under freedom of religion (Article 9 ECHR) with the Court adding that under Article 14, in combination with Article 9, no separate issues arise.[34] This will be examined in more detail in the following section.

4. The Contribution of the ECtHR: Developing Freedom of Religion as an Instrument of Integration for (Religiously) Pluralistic Societies

Since the mid-1990s, the ECtHR has developed a rich jurisprudence on freedom of religion. Among the many facets of that jurisprudence, conceiving freedom of religion as the key instrument for assuring the peaceful co-existence of different faiths in modern societies may be described as the main characteristic. The basis for this jurisprudence was laid down in 1993 in the *Kokkinakis* case, when the Court made use of the individual right to free exercise of religion in order to develop a functional concept that places freedom of religion in the context of pluralism and democracy (Section 4.1). This was later expanded into a corporative direction in order also to cover the rights of religious communities and their legal situation within the secular legal order (Section 4.2). The need to cope with different traditions of church and State relations in the various member States of the Council of Europe led to a reduced standard of review which, relying on the concept of margin of appreciation, aims at assuring a pan-European minimum standard while simultaneously allowing for different approaches based on the respective traditions (Section 4.3). In sum, the Court derives from the individual right to freedom of religion a responsibility of the member States 'to help maintain public order, religious harmony and tolerance in a democratic society'[35] (Section 4.4).

4.1 Individual freedom of religion and its relevance for free and democratic societies

The starting point for the development of the Court's understanding of freedom of religion as a concept, which is of relevance for peaceful co-existence in modern societies, may be seen in the case of *Kokkinakis v Greece*.[36] The case is, on the one hand, a clear case of individual free exercise of religion. Given the Greek prohibition of proselytism applicable at the time, it concerned the right to promote one's own faith, which the applicant had made use of when contacting persons of Greek Orthodox faith.[37] However, beyond that individual aspect, it concerned the treatment of the Jehovah's Witnesses as a religious minority in general. In fact, the applicant had been arrested more than sixty times for prohibited proselytism and imprisoned or interned several times for periods of several months. It is against this background that the—by now—famous formula of the Court must be understood, in which the Court created a clear link between the individual free exercise of religion and the role of that human right in the context of free and democratic societies:

> As enshrined in Article 9 (art. 9), freedom of thought, conscience and religion is one of the foundations of a 'democratic society' within the meaning of the Convention. It is, in its religious dimension, one of the most vital elements that go to make up the identity of believers and their conception of life, but it is also a precious asset for atheists, agnostics, sceptics and the unconcerned. The pluralism indissociable from a democratic society, which has been dearly won over the centuries, depends on it.[38]

The formula continues to be used to describe the function of freedom of religion in the overall concept of human rights protection as it is envisaged by the Court.[39] In this context, it should be noted that at the time when *Kokkinakis* was decided (1993), the ECtHR had not yet established that freedom of religion also included a corporate dimension, that is, a right of religious communities to internal autonomy. The violation of the individual rights of Mr Kokkinakis was thus used to address the broader issue of treatment of religious minorities by the member States. The Court continues to this day to adjudicate along these lines and places the individual case into the overall context of how religion is dealt within the member State concerned.

4.2 Religious communities and their protection under the ECHR

The Court took the opportunity to develop internal autonomy as a corporate right of religious communities when it was confronted with a clear interference by the State into the internal organizational structure of a Muslim community in Bulgaria in the case of *Hasan and Chaush v Bulgaria*.[40] For that purpose, the Court interpreted freedom of religion in the light of the right to freedom of assembly (Article 11 ECHR) and placed its approach, again, into the overall context of free and democratic structures:

> [T]he believers' right to freedom of religion encompasses the expectation that the community will be allowed to function peacefully, free from arbitrary State intervention. Indeed, the autonomous existence of religious communities is indispensable

> for pluralism in a democratic society and is thus an issue at the very heart of the protection which Article 9 affords. It directly concerns not only the organisation of the community as such but also the effective enjoyment of the right to freedom of religion by all its active members. Were the organisational life of the community not protected by Article 9 of the Convention, all other aspects of the individual's freedom of religion would become vulnerable.[41]

In later cases, the corporate dimension of freedom of religion was used in order to establish certain minimum requirements, such as the possibility of acquiring legal personality within a reasonable time and under fair procedural standards in order to function, as a religious association, peacefully and free from arbitrary State intervention.[42] It is against this backdrop that registration requirements have been subject to a rather strict scrutiny and, convincingly, considered to be disproportionate when conceived as a precondition for the free exercise of religion.[43] This jurisprudence concerning the treatment of religious communities is complemented by considerations of non-discrimination under Article 14 ECHR in combination with freedom of religion. In the Austrian case of *Religionsgemeinschaft der Zeugen Jehovas and Others*, the Court held that, where a State 'sets up a framework for conferring legal personality on religious groups to which a specific status is linked, all religious groups which so wish must have a fair opportunity to apply for this status and the criteria established must be applied in a non-discriminatory manner'.[44]

In all cases mentioned, the Court placed its jurisprudence regarding the treatment of religious communities into the overall context of democratic and pluralistic societies. Freedom of religion is thus not only conceived as an instrument for the protection of the rights and freedoms of the individuals or the communities concerned in a given case, but also understood in a broader, functional perspective as a means designed to assure free and pluralistic societies.[45]

4.3 Assuring a common minimum standard and allowing for different approaches based on different historical traditions—the concept of margin of appreciation in the context of freedom of religion

The jurisprudence just described has the potential to interfere with historical traditions regulating the relations between the public authorities and religious communities in the member States. The *Lautsi* case concerning crucifixes in Italian classrooms and the French law banning the concealment of the face in public places, which was the subject of the case of *S.A.S. v France*, are prominent examples of such possible frictions. In both cases the Court reacted by placing a strong emphasis on the concept of margin of appreciation,[46] although in *Lautsi*, only in its Grand Chamber decision after the preceding Chamber judgment had met strong resistance not only from Italy but also from a number of other member States.

4.3.1 *General remarks on the concept of margin of appreciation*

The concept of margin of appreciation is neither new, nor does it only apply in the context of freedom of religion. It was already developed and used by the former European Commission of Human Rights[47] and, today, is firmly anchored in the Court's jurisprudence on most Convention guarantees.[48] In the practice of the Court, the application of the concept of margin of appreciation usually leads to a reduced standard of review when it comes to assessing the proportionality of certain measures or with regard to the determination of a 'legitimate aim' in the context of limitations to the Convention guarantees. Factors determining the width of the margin of appreciation are the nature of the right in question, possible ethical or moral implications, and whether or not there is consensus among the member States on how to deal with the issue.[49] The obvious result of applying the concept is that the member States are granted a 'corridor' of acceptable solutions and will not violate the Convention as long as they remain within that corridor.[50] In its jurisprudence in matters concerning freedom of religion, the ECtHR has made broad use of the concept of margin of appreciation in order to allow different solutions based on quite different religious traditions among its member States. According the Contracting States a rather broad margin of appreciation with respect to restrictions on freedom of religion is thus an instrument in order to deal with regional diversity within Europe.

4.3.2 *Margin of appreciation in the context of freedom of religion*

The Court used the quite different approaches of the member States regarding the relationship between public power and religious communities as an argument for applying a broad margin of appreciation.[51] While the *Lautsi* case concerning the crucifixes in Italian classrooms is probably the most prominent example, given the reversal of the Chamber judgment by the Grand Chamber on the basis of a broad margin of appreciation, the case of *Leyla Sahin* concerning the (at the time existing) ban on headscarves in public universities in Turkey is also an example in point.[52] Here, the ECtHR explicitly acknowledged the different solutions on the relationship between the State and religious communities in the member States and concluded that, as a result, 'the role of the national decision-making body must be given special importance'.[53] On the basis of this approach, the Court accepted the notion of 'secularity' as it had been developed by the Turkish Constitutional Court as being, in principle, compatible with the Convention[54] and, in the end, concluded that there had been no violation of freedom of religion.[55]

As already indicated, the Grand Chamber of the Court used the concept of margin of appreciation in the case of *Lautsi v Italy* in order to reverse the Chamber judgment which had unanimously concluded that the obligation to hang crucifixes in primary school classrooms violated freedom of religion.[56] In its judgment, the Grand Chamber decided that Italy could rely on a broad margin of appreciation not only because of the different traditions regarding the relations between the State and religious communities,[57] but also because the Italian school environment was apparently open towards religion of many kinds and in no way discriminatory against non-Christian religions or against non-believers.[58]

Notably, in the case concerning the French law prohibiting the concealment of one's face in public places, *S.A.S. v France*, the Court used an even broader approach regarding the margin of appreciation of member States. It stressed the subsidiary character of the Convention mechanism and argued that 'national authorities have direct democratic legitimation and are, as the Court has held on many occasions, in principle better placed than an international court to evaluate local needs and conditions'.[59] At the same time, it accepted the French contention that the justification, 'rights and freedoms of others' mentioned in Article 9, paragraph 2 ECHR also covered respect for 'minimum requirements of living together' among which the government had included the possibility to interact openly in the public sphere by seeing the faces of others present.[60] When striking the balance with the individual freedom of religion of the women concerned, the Court, again, stepped back and deferred the decision to the national authorities: 'In such circumstances, the Court has a duty to exercise a degree of restraint in its review of Convention compliance, since such review will lead it to assess a balance that has been struck by means of a democratic process within the society in question. The Court has, moreover, already had occasion to observe that '[i]n matters of general policy, on which opinions within a democratic society may reasonably differ widely, the role of the domestic policy-maker should be given special weight'.[61] It then explicitly explained its restraint as part of 'a wide margin of appreciation'.[62]

It can easily be seen that the democratic legitimacy of the national decision maker adds another layer to the concept of margin of appreciation. In analysing the jurisprudence of the ECtHR on the matter, the literature distinguishes between two main types of margin of appreciation: a substantive and a structural one.[63] The substantive margin of appreciation covers deference on the basis of merits-related reasons, that is, the need to balance the competing rights and the application and interpretation of open concepts, such as notably the legitimate aims for restriction referred to in the limitation clauses (eg 'public order').[64] The structural margin of appreciation, by contrast, addresses the institutional setting of European human rights protection in which the different competences of the ECtHR and domestic institutions need to be coordinated.[65] In the *S.A.S.* case the two types of margin of appreciation are obviously combined: When the Court accepts the broad definition of 'minimum requirements of life in society' or of 'living together' as part of the legitimate aim of protecting rights and freedoms of others and the balancing result against the individual exercise of freedom of religion by the women concerned,[66] this is part of the substantive notion of margin of appreciation. And when it relies on democratic legitimacy of the national decision-making process,[67] this relates to the systemic notion of margin of appreciation.

4.3.3 *Criticism—insufficient minority protection?*

It has been argued by Eyal Benvenisti that the systemic margin of appreciation, notably with the underpinning of respect for the democratically legitimized domestic processes, stands at odds with the idea of minority protection: 'The margin of appreciation doctrine may be theoretically justified as a means to promote democracy within communities. But whenever minorities exist, democracy is prone to undermine their interests. Majorities often monopolize political power with little more than half of the votes and thus use the democratic processes as means to secure their interests at the expense of the minority. In view of this inherent deficiency in the democratic system, national policies warrant no deference when minority rights and interests are implicated.'[68] As the historical analysis has shown, freedom of religion often serves exactly the purpose of minority protection. And, in fact, many of the ECHR cases relate to the protection of minorities (*Lautsi* concerned atheists, *Kokkinakis* Jehovah's Witnesses, and there are, of course, the many cases concerning Islam, *Leyla Sahin*, *S.A.S.*, *Dahlab*, etc). Against this background, the application of a broad concept of margin of appreciation, particularly in the area of religious freedom, has been challenged.[69]

While the criticism is convincing in its structural analysis of the underlying tension between minority protection and majority decision making as part of the democratic process, it nevertheless does not sufficiently take into account the existing mechanisms of minority protection in the domestic systems. The point is mentioned by Benvenisti, but only in passing in the conclusion.[70] However, if one looks at the judgments concerned, the concept of margin of appreciation, even where the Court concludes on a broad margin of appreciation, is always balanced by the insistence of the Court on the fact that it 'goes hand in hand with a European supervision embracing both the law and the decisions applying it. The ECtHR's task is to determine whether the measures taken at national level were justified in principle and proportionate.'[71] The jurisprudence relating to exaggerated registration requirements is a good illustration of the limits of deference based on the concept of margin of appreciation. Here, the Court decided on several occasions that even in view of the State's margin of appreciation either the alleged threat to the public order was not sufficiently plausible (Salvation Army)[72] or that restricting the individual free exercise of religion until registration requirements have been met by the respective community does not meet the requirements of proportionality.[73]

Looked at from this perspective, the concept of margin of appreciation is indeed a flexible instrument in the hands of the Court which allows on the one hand for the necessary flexibility to take into account different religious traditions in the Contracting States, and on the other the necessary European supervision which ensures certain minimum standards to be respected by all. It seems that the concept has, until now, only had a limited impact on the application of freedom of religion and acceptable restrictions at the universal level.[74] Given that the respective domestic backgrounds are even more diverse at the universal level than in the regional context of the Council of Europe ("COE"), pursuing that path also in the context of the ICCPR or the work of the HRC might be an option for future developments at the universal level.[75]

4.4 A positive general obligation—responsibility of States for religious peace

The overall approach of the ECtHR, which becomes apparent behind this analysis, bears close resemblance to the functions of the State as guarantor of peace and stability which was described in the historical part of this chapter. The Court places great emphasis on this role of the State and describes it as a general positive obligation incumbent upon member States. In the case of *Leyla Sahin* this was indicated for the first time, albeit in a descriptive rather than normative manner, when the Court stated that it has 'frequently emphasised the State's role as the neutral and impartial organiser of the exercise of various religions, faiths and beliefs, and stated that this role is conducive to public order, religious harmony and tolerance in a democratic society'.[76] In the *Lautsi* case, the Court went beyond that descriptive assessment and formulated a 'responsibility' of member States for 'ensuring, neutrally and impartially, the exercise of various religions, faiths and beliefs. Their role is to help maintain public order, religious harmony and tolerance in a democratic society, particularly between opposing groups.'[77] Whether or not this 'responsibility' results in concrete positive obligations which may be enforced by the ECtHR is an open question and there may good reasons for the Court to leave the decisions on concrete measures in pursuance of that responsibility with the margin of appreciation of the member States.[78] Irrespective of the concreteness of possible positive obligations, the approach taken by the Court underlines that the pacifying role of the State with regard to possible tensions resulting from religious pluralism is very much present in the judges' minds: Preserving (religious) peace in society is as much a task of the State in the 21st century as it was in the 16th and 17th.

5. An Emerging Role for the EU?

When it comes to the development of human rights in general and freedom of religion more specifically, the predominant international instrument in Europe is certainly the ECHR, along with the rich jurisprudence of the ECtHR. As has already been explained, this jurisprudence focuses strongly on freedom of religion rather than on non-discrimination.[79]

By contrast, up until very recently, religion has played only a minor role in the context of the EU. This is largely due to the fact that the Union only has very limited competencies that may interfere with the exercise of religion. The few early cases concern freedom of religion in the civil service of the Union[80] and possible effects of the data protection directive on the German concept of church taxes in the early 1990s.[81] However, with the adoption and application of the anti-discrimination directives in 2000,[82] the picture gradually started to change. These directives have opened the practically important area of workplace-related aspects of religion for EU law. Since 2017 the ECJ has rendered five judgments relating to that area.[83] More or less at the same time, several cases concerning limitations on ritual slaughter in the interest of animal protection have been decided by the Court.[84] An analysis of these cases reveals that the ECJ is still looking for the best way to include freedom of religion into the interpretation of EU law. Nevertheless, a tendency to take up the approach of the ECtHR based on the concept of margin of appreciation can be detected.

In the area of religious symbols int the workplace the ECJ initially leaned towards finding a balance between freedom of religion on the side of employees and a possible policy of neutrality in the workplace on the part of the employer. Two decisions of 2018 created the impression that, in the Court's view, a policy of religious neutrality pursued by the employer, which is protected by Article 16 CFR, would take precedence over freedom of religion 'provided that that policy is genuinely pursued in a consistent and systematic manner'.[85] In establishing these standards, the ECJ seemed to considerably limit the role of the national courts, even though Advocate General Kokott had expressly referred to the protection of national identities of member States in Article 4, paragraph 2 of the Treaty on European Union (TEU) as an argument in favour of flexible solutions.[86] A similarly harmonizing approach was taken by the ECJ regarding church-related employers and the requirement of church membership or the respect for certain loyalty obligations established by religious communities.[87]

This picture was modified in a decision of July 2021. First, the ECJ placed additional emphasis on the burden of proof of the employer regarding potential conflicts with either customers or other employees and concerning the consistency of a policy of neutrality followed by the employer.[88] Thus, freedom of religion under Article 10 CFR was strengthened in the balancing operation against freedom to conduct a business under Article 16 CFR. And secondly, the ECJ adopted the notion of margin of appreciation into EU law.[89] In fact, this had already been done in late 2020 in the most recent ritual slaughter case, where the ECJ expressly referred to the ECtHR and its decision in *S.A.S. v France*.[90] As a result, also in EU law, different solutions based on different approaches to religion in the public sphere in the member States may be pursued.

The decisions of 2020 in the ritual slaughter case and of 2021 concerning the ban on religious symbols in the workplace have the potential to constitute a turning point in the jurisprudence of the ECJ concerning religion. Until now, the ECJ seemed to follow rather strictly the logic of harmonization which forms part and parcel of the internal market. The most recent decisions, however, indicate that the ECJ is at least in principle prepared to take up the concept of margin of appreciation proved and tested by the ECtHR in the area of religion in order to allow for different solutions in different member States based on their historical and legal traditions. Where the limits of such diversity will be drawn is still an open question.[91] In the ritual slaughter case, the margin of appreciation had the effect of accepting the restrictive Belgian law thus placing animal protection above freedom of religion. In the workplace-related cases, by contrast, the margin of appreciation may well operate in favour of more religion-friendly results. This difference in result may be explained by the nature of the directives in question. In fact, in both decisions the notion of margin of appreciation was applied in the context of directives which provide for minimum harmonization.[92] Under such circumstances the concept allows only for national constitutional traditions to be used in order to go beyond the level of harmonization provided for in the directives. In the ritual slaughter case this was protection of animals at the time of killing. Hence, increased protection at the expense of a fundamental freedom was accepted. In the cases concerning the wearing of headscarves in the workplace, the aim of the directive is equal treatment in employment and occupation. Hence, freedom of religion may be used to reinforce the anti-discrimination objective.

6. Conclusion

The religious civil wars of the 16th and 17th centuries in Europe are not only the cradle of modern statehood. These religious civil wars also stand at the origins of a development of secularization of public power. Thus, religion, which originally served as both purpose and legitimation of the exercise of public power, was gradually transformed into an object to be regulated by that public power. While the internal forms of coordinating the relations between State and religion took quite different forms ranging from strict separation to different types of State-churches, international law was limited to addressing the issue of religion at the level of fundamental rights, that is, freedom of religion and the prohibition of discrimination on religious grounds. In the practice of the ECtHR, a clear focus on freedom of religion has emerged, with non-discrimination usually playing only a minor role, even though many disputes involving religion turn on equal treatment of minority religions. Quite often, one and the same question (eg the prohibition of wearing a headscarf) can be framed as an interference with the free exercise of religion (because it obstructs the observance of a religious duty) or as a factual discrimination on religious grounds (because the prohibition primarily afflicts members of a specific group). In recent years, the anti-discrimination jurisprudence of the EU has become increasingly important in this area. While the ECtHR has a long-standing tradition of using the concept of margin of appreciation in order to accept diverging solutions by the member States, the ECJ only recently steered in this direction. Thus, it remains to be seen where the exact limits to an increased diversity of national solutions in the area of religion will be established.

Generally speaking, it seems doubtful that the subject of religion is suitable for European harmonization. It cannot be overlooked that both the historical traditions and the current changes in the religious landscape are considerably heterogenous even among the twenty-seven members of the EU. For many countries, 'their' way of coordinating State and religion is deeply entrenched in their respective constitutional traditions. As the jurisprudence of the ECtHR shows, European supervision is indispensable in order to guarantee the respect of certain minimum standards. However, this jurisprudence is equally evidence of the need to respect different solutions based on different sociological, historical, and constitutional conditions. Religion continues to be a highly sensitive issue with ambivalent effects on society. It may, on the one hand, provide for 'societal glue' and foster togetherness even in modern societies. But, on the other hand, it also possesses a disruptive potential which may provoke violence and tear societies apart. The pacifying function of (international) law depends on cherishing the first, while fencing in the second. No one-size-fits-all strategy will meet that challenge.

Notes

1. On the influence of Christianity on international law see the various contributions in P Slotte and J D Haskell (eds), *Christianity and International Law—An Introduction* (Cambridge University Press 2021)); P H Kooijmans, *Protestantism and the Development of International Law, Collected Courses of the Hague Academy of International Law*, Vol 52 (1976); on Judaism: G Ben-Nun, 'How Jewish is International Law?', 23(2) Journal of the History of International Law 2021, 249–281; S Rosenne, 'The Influence of Judaism on the Development of International Law: An Assessment' in Janis and Evans (eds), *Religion and International Law* (1999); on Islam: M Berger, 'Islamic Views on International Law' in Meerts (ed), *Culture and International Law* (2008) 105 ff; J Kelsay, *Islam and Christianity in the Works of Gentili, Grotius and Pufendorf, in Hashmi, Just Wars, Holy Wars, and Jihads: Christian, Jewish, Muslim Encounters and Exchanges* (Oxford University Press, 2012) 207 ff; J Allain, 'Acculturation through the Middle Ages: The Islamic Law of Nations and Its Place in the History of International Law' in Orekhelashvili (ed), *Research Handbook on the Theory and History of International Law* (2011) 394 ff.
2. W K Tannous and A Gaffney, 'Charles H. Malik and Religious Freedom: The Influence of Biography on Malik's Contributions to the Drafting of the Universal Declaration of Human Rights', 42(2) Human Rights Quarterly 2020, 817–834 (821 ff, 826 ff).
3. ibid, 829 ff.
4. M Koskenniemi, *The Gentle Civilizer of Nations: The Rise and Fall of International Law 1870–1960* (Cambridge University Press, 2003) 127 ff.
5. For approaches in this direction see Slotte and Haskell (n 1); M Koskenniemi, M García-Salmones Rovira, and P Amorosa (eds), *International Law and Religion* (2017).
6. Introduction.
7. E-W Böckenförde, *Die Entstehung des Staates als Vorgang der Säkularisation, in Böckenförde, Staat, Gesellschaft, Freiheit* (Suhrkamp, 1976) 42 ff.
8. The Case of the S.S. Lotus, judgment of the Permanent Court of International Justice, 7 September 1927, 18.
9. See A von Ungern-Sternberg, 'Religion and Religious Intervention' in Fassbender and Peters (eds), *The History of International Law* (2012) 294 (296 ff).
10. See, eg, J Casanova, 'Rethinking Secularization: A Global Comparative Perspective', *The Hedgehog Review* 2006, 7 ff; H Joas, 'Does Modernisation Lead to Secularisation?' in W Gräb (ed), *Secularization Theories, Religious Identity and Practical Theology* (2009) 25 ff; J C D Clark, 'Secularization and Modernization: The Failure of a "Grand Narrative"', 55(1) The Historical Journal 2012, 161 ff.
11. H Lübbe, *Säkularisierung: Geschichte eines ideenpolitischen Begriffs* (Verlag Karl Alber, 1965) 23; K F Gärditz, 'Säkularität und Verfassung' in Depenheuer and Grabenwarter (eds), *Verfassungstheorie* (2010) 154–155.
12. The following section is set out in much more detail in C Walter, *Religionsverfassungsrecht—in vergleichender und internationaler Perspektive* (Mohr Siebeck, 2006) 23–68.
13. M Heckel, 'Ito in partes. Zur Religionsverfassung des Heiligen Römischen Reiches Deutscher Nation', (95) Zeitschrift der Savigny-Stiftung für Rechtsgeschichte 1978, pp. 188 ff
14. H Dreier, 'Kanonistik und Konfessionalisierung—Marksteine auf dem Weg zum Staat', 57(1) JuristenZeitung 2002, 1–13 (6 ff).

15. E-W Böckenförde, *Die Entstehung des Staates als Vorgang der Säkularisation, in Böckenförde, Staat, Gesellschaft, Freiheit* (Suhrkamp, 1976) 42 ff.
16. J Locke, *A Letter Concerning Toleration and Other Writings* (Liberty Fund Inc. 2010).
17. 'The care of each mans Soul, and of the things of Heaven, which neither does belong to the Commonwealth, nor can be subjected to it, is left entirely to every mans self.' ibid, 48.
18. See J W Tate, *Liberty, Toleration and Equality: John Locke, Jonas Proast and the Letters Concerning Toleration* (2016) 28–31.
19. For the following, see A von Ungern-Sternberg, 'Religion and Religious Intervention' in Fassbender and Peters (eds), *The History of International Law* (2012) 296 ff.
20. See H McCoubrey, 'Natural Law, Religion and the Development of International Law' in Janis and Evans (eds), *Religion and International Law* (1999) 177 (185–186).
21. Emer de Vattel, *Droit des gens, ou principes de la loi naturelle appliqués à la conduite et aux affaires des nations et des souverains* (1758).
22. P Thornberry, *International Law and the Rights of Minorities* (Oxford University Press, 1991) 25–37; W Kymlicka, 'The Internationalization of Minority Rights', 6 International Journal of Constitutional Law 2008, 1–32.
23. D H Miller, *The Drafting of the Covenant*, vol II (Williams, Heins & co1928) 105.
24. Quoted from F Capotorti, 'Study on the Rights of Persons belonging to Ethnic, Religious and Linguistic Minorities', E/CN.4/Sub.2/384/Rev.I, 1979, 17 f (para 94).
25. Thornberry (n 15) 44; R Grote, 'Die Religionsfreiheit im Spiegel völkervertraglicher Vereinbarungen zur politischen und territorialen Neuordnung' in Grote and Marauhn, *Religionsfreiheit zwischen individueller Selbstbestimmung, Minderheitenschutz und Staatskirchenrecht—Völker-und verfassungsrechtliche Perspektiven* (2001) 3 (24 f).
26. See, eg, Article 2 UDHR, Article 14 ECHR, Article 2 (1) ICCPR; Article 1(1) IAHR; Article 2 African Charter; Article 21(1) CFREU, Article 2(1) UNCRC.
27. Convention on the Elimination of All Forms of Discrimination Against Women (CEDAW), UNTS 1249, section 13; BGBl. 1985 II, section 648.
28. International Convention on the Elimination of All Forms of Racial Discrimination (ICERD), UNTS 660, section 195; BGBl. 1969 II, section 961.
29. It should be noted, however, that under certain circumstances religious discrimination may amount to 'racial discrimination' within the meaning of Article 1 CERD (eg antisemitism); this has been confirmed in the practice of the Committee against Racial Discrimination, for details see P Thornberry, *The International Convention on the Elimination of All Forms of Racial Discrimination: A Commentary* (Oxford University Press, 2016) 138; R Wolfrum, *Völkerrechtlicher Schutz religiöser Minderheiten und ihrer Mitglieder, in Grote/Marauhn, Religionsfreiheit zwischen individueller Selbstbestimmung, Minderheitenschutz und Staatskirchenrecht—Völker-und verfassungsrechtliche Perspektiven* (2001) 53 (61 ff).
30. N Lerner, 'The Final Text of the U.N. Declaration Against Intolerance and Discrimination Based on Religion or Belief', 12 Israel Yearbook on Human Rights 1982, 185 (186 f).
31. UN General Assembly, Declaration on the Elimination of All Forms of Intolerance and of Discrimination Based on Religion or Belief, UN GAOR, 36th Sess Sup No 551, section 171, UN Doc A/Res/36/55 (1981).
32. Commission on Human Rights resolution 2001/42, No 11.
33. See the list of Annual Reports available at: https://www.ohchr.org/EN/Issues/FreedomReligion/Pages/Annual.aspx accessed 11 October 2023.
34. Ch Grabenwarter and K Pabel, *Europäische Menschenrechtskonvention* (Beck, 2016) § 26 MN. 2.

35. *Lautsi and Others v Italy* [GC], App no 30814/06, § 60, 18 March 2011.
36. *Kokkinakis v Greece*, App no 14307/88, 25 May 1993; see also B Vermeulen and M van Roosmalen, 'Freedom of Thought, Conscience and Religion' in P van Dijk, F van Hoof, A van Rijn, and L Zwaak (eds), *Theory and Practice of the European Convention on Human Rights* (5th edn, 2018) 735–764.
37. On the facts of the case see also M Hill and K Barnes, 'Limitations on Freedom of Religion and Belief in the Jurisprudence of the European Court of Human Rights in the Quarter Century since Its Judgment in *Kokkinakis v. Greece*', 12 Religion and Human Rights 2017, 174–197 (177 ff).
38. *Kokkinakis v. Greece*, App no 14307/88, § 31, 25 May 1993.
39. *Buscarini and Others v San Marino*[GC], App no 24645/94, § 34, ECHR 1999-I; *Leyla Sahin v Turkey* [GC], App no 4474/98, § 104, ECHR 2005-XI; *S.A.S. v France*[GC], App no 43835/11, § 124, 1 July 2014; see M Evans, 'The Freedom of Religion or Belief in the ECHR since *Kokkinakis*. Or 'Quoting *Kokkinakis*', 12(2–3) Religion & Human Rights 2017, 83–98, who argues that the Kokkinakis 'mantra' should be replaced by a more up-to-date statement.
40. *Hasan and Chaush v Bulgaria*, App no 30985/96, 26 October 2000; see also Vermeulen and van Roosmalen (n 36) 751 ff.
41. *Hasan and Chaush v Bulgaria*, App no 30985/96, § 62, 26 October 2000.
42. *The Moscow Branch of the Salvation Army v Russia*, App no 72881/01, § 71, 5 October 2006.
43. *Masaev v The Republic of Moldova*, App no 6303/05, § 26, 12 August 2009.
44. *Religionsgemeinschaft der Zeugen Jehovas and Others v Austria*, App no 40825/98, § 92, 31 October 2008.
45. C Walter, 'Religions- und Gewissensfreiheit' in Dörr, Grote, and Marauhn (eds), *EMRK/GG Konkordanzkommentar* (3rd edn, 2022) paragraph 115.
46. *Lautsi and Others v Italy* [GC], App no 30814/06, §§ 68 ff, 18 March 2011; *S.A.S. v France* [GC], App no 43835/11, §§ 129 ff, 1 July 2014.
47. ECHR, *X v Germany*, App no 1628/62, 12 December 1963: 'Whereas, in cases in which the rights guaranteed in Articles 8 and/or 10 are at issue, the Commission has the right, and indeed the duty, to appreciate whether or not interference by a public authority fulfils the conditions laid down in paragraph (2) of these Articles (Art. 8-2, 10-2) whereas the Commission has frequently held … that these Articles leave the Contracting Parties a certain margin of appreciation in determining the limits that may be placed on the exercise of the rights in question; … ' (emphasis added).
48. *Engel and Others v The Netherlands*, App no 5100/71 et al., §§ 59, 72, 100, 8 June 1976 (with reference to *De Wilde, Ooms and Versvp v Belgium*, App no 2832/66 a.o., § 93, 18 June 1971 and *Golder v UK*, App no 4451/10, § 45, 21 February 1975, which still refer to 'power of appreciation'; on recent developments see Ch Grabenwarter, Grundrechtsvielfalt und Grundrechtskonflikte im europäischen Mehrebenensystem – Wirkungen von EGMR-Urteilen und der Beurteilungsspielraum der Mitgliedstaaten, Europäische Grundrechte-Zeitschrift 2011, 229 ff; see generally J H Gerards, *General Principles of the European Convention on Human Rights* (Cambridge University Press, 2019) 160 ff. (Chapter 7, The Margin of Appreciation Doctrine); D Spielmann, 'Allowing the Right Margin: The European Court of Human Rights and The National Margin of Appreciation Doctrine: Waiver or Subsidiarity of European Review?' in *Cambridge Yearbook of European Studies*, vol 14 (2012) 381–418; *FC Mayer*, Einleitung Rn. 61, in Karpenstein/ders. (Hrsg.), EMRK-Kommentar, 2012.
49. *Spielmann* (n 48) 392 ff.

50. See *Ch. Grabenwarter*, Grundrechtsvielfalt und Grundrechtskonflikte im europäischen Mehrebenensystem – Wirkungen von EGMR-Urteilen und der Beurteilungsspielraum der Mitgliedstaaten, Europäische Grundrechte-Zeitschrift 2011, 229 (230 ff); G Lübbe-Wolff, 'Der Grundrechtsschutz nach der Europäischen Menschenrechtskonvention bei konfligierenden Individualrechten—Plädoyer für eine Korridorlösung' in Hochhuth (ed), *Nachdenken über Staat und Recht. Kolloquium für D. Murswiek* (2010) 193 ff (esp 199).
51. *S.A.S. v France* [GC], App no 43835/11, § 127 ff, 154 f, 1 July 2014; *Cha'are Schalom Ve Tsedek v France*, App no 27417/95, § 84, 27 June 2000; *Leyla Sahin v Turkey* [GC], App no 4474/98, §§ 109 f, ECHR 2005-XI.
52. *Leyla Sahin v Turkey* [GC], App no 4474/98, ECHR 2005-XI.
53. See *Leyla Sahin v Turkey* [GC], App no 4474/98, §§ 108 f, ECHR 2005-XI.
54. See *Leyla Sahin v Turkey* [GC], App no 4474/98, §§ 30 ff, 114 and 116, ECHR 2005-XI.
55. *Leyla Sahin v Turkey* [GC], App no 4474/98, § 123, ECHR 2005-XI.
56. *Lautsi and Others v Italy* [GC], App no 30814/06, § 77, 18 March 2011 and *Lautsi and Others v Italy*, App no 30814/06, § 58, 3 November 2009; critical of the Chamber judgment, see JHH Weiler, 'Lautsi: Crucifix in the Classroom Redux', 21(1) European Journal of International Law 2010, 1–6.
57. G Itzcovich, 'One, None and One Hundred Thousand Margins of Appreciations: The Lautsi Case', Human Rights Law Review 2013, 287 ff.
58. *Lautsi and Others v Italy* [GC], App no 30814/06, § 74, 18 March 2011.
59. *S.A.S. v France* [GC], App no 43835/11, § 129, 1 July 2014.
60. *S.A.S. v France* [GC], App no 43835/11, § 121 f, 1 July 2014.
61. *S.A.S. v France* [GC], App no 43835/11, § 154, 1 July 2014.
62. *S.A.S. v. France* [GC], App no 43835/11, § 155, 1 July 2014; critical of the wide margin applied, see N Fleming, 'S.A.S. v. France, A Margin of Appreciation Gone Too Far', 52(2) Connecticut Law Review 2000, 917–941 (938 ff).
63. See esp. G Letsas, 'Two Concepts of the Margin of Appreciation', 26 (4) Oxford Journal of Legal Studies 2006, 705–732; Y Arai-Takahashi, *The Margin of Appreciation Doctrine and the Principle of Proportionality in the Jurisprudence of the ECHR* (Cambridge University Press, 2002); O M Arnardóttir, 'Rethinking the Two Margins of Appreciation', 12 European Constitutional Law Review 2016, 27–53.
64. See Letsas (n 63) 709 ff; Arnardóttir (n 63) 29.
65. Letsas (n 63) 720 ff; Arnardóttir (n 63) 29.
66. *S.A.S. v France* [GC], App no 43835/11, § 121, 1 July 2014.
67. *S.A.S. v France* [GC], App no 43835/11, § 129, 1 July 2014.
68. E Benvenisti, 'Margin of Appreciation, Consensus, and Universal Standards', 31 New York Journal of International Law and Policy (1998–1999) 843–854 (849) (footnote omitted).
69. St E Berry, 'Religious Freedom and the European Court of Human Right's Two Margins of Appreciation', 12 (2–3) Religion & Human Rights 2017, 198–209; ibid, 847, 851.
70. Benvenisti (n 68) 853 f.
71. *S.A.S. v France* [GC], App no 43835/11, § 131, 1 July 2014 with reference to *Manoussakis and Others v Greece*, App no 18748/91, § 44, 26 September 1996 and *Leyla Sahin v Turkey* [GC], App no 4474/98, § 44, ECHR 2005-XI.
72. *The Moscow Branch of the Salvation Army v Russia*, App no 72881/01, § 76, 5 October 2006, where the Court states that 'only convincing and compelling reasons can justify restrictions' on the freedom of religion and assembly and §§ 78 ff where the Court examines the arguments put forward in justification of the interference; see also *Church*

of Scientology Moscow v Russia, App no 18147/02, §§ 86 ff, 24 September 2007; Vermeulen and van Roosmalen (n 36) 760.

73. *Metropolitan Church of Bessarabia and Others v Moldova*, App no 45701/99, §§ 119, 128 ff. 27 March 2002.
74. J Crawford, 'Preface' in Y Arai-Takahashi, *The Margin of Appreciation Doctrine and the Principle of Proportionality in the Jurisprudence of the ECHR* (2002) ix; PR Ghandhi, *The Human Rights Committee and the Right of Individual Communication: Law and Practice* (Dartsmouth Publishing, 1998) 312; B Petzhold, *Die 'Auffassungen' des UN-Menschenrechtsausschusses zum Schutze der Religionsfreiheit* (Mohr Siebeck, 2015) 290–295, 298–301, 341–342.
75. Petzhold (n 74) 326.
76. *Leyla Sahin v Turkey* [GC], App no 4474/98, § 107, ECHR 2005-XI.
77. *Lautsi and Others v Italy* [GC], App no 30814/06, § 60, 18 March 2011.
78. See also M Kiviorg, *Religious Autonomy in the ECHR, Derecho y Religión* (2009) 131–142 (142 ff), who assumes a positive obligation in the form of a 'duty to protect'.
79. See Section 2.3.
80. ECJ, *Vivien Prais v Council of the European Communities*, Case 130/75, 27 October 1976; *Emma Mollet*, Case 75/77, 13 April 1977.
81. Article 8(2)(d) Directive 95/46/EC of the European Parliament and of the Council of 24 October 1995 on the protection of individuals with regard to the processing of personal data and on the free movement of such data.
82. Council Directive 2000/43/EC of 29 June 2000 implementing the principle of equal treatment between persons irrespective of racial or ethnic origin and—relevant in the context of religions discrimination—Council Directive 2000/78/EC of 27 November 2000 establishing a general framework for equal treatment in employment and occupation.
83. ECJ, *Achbita*, Case C-157/15, 14 March 2017; *Bougnaoui*, Case C-188/15, 14 March 2017; *Egenberger*, Case C-414/16, 17 April 2018 and *IR v JQ*, Case C-68/17, 11 September 2018; *IX eV* and *MH Müller Handels GmbH*, Joined Cases C-804/18 and C-341/19, 15 July 2021.
84. ECJ, *Liga van Moskeeën en Islamitische Organisaties Provincie Antwerpen VZW and Others*, Case C-426/16, 29 May 2018; *Œuvre d'assistance aux bêtes d'abattoirs (OABA)*, Case C-497/17, 26 February 2019; *Centraal Israëlitisch Consistorie van België and Others*, Case C-336/19, 17 December 2020.
85. ECJ, *Achbita*, Case C-157/15, 14 March 2018, paragraph 40.
86. Opinion of Advocate General Kokott, delivered on 31 May 2016, Case C-157/15, *Achbita*, paragraph 125.
87. ECJ, *Vera Egenberger v Evangelisches Werk für Diakonie und Entwicklung eV*, Case C-414/16, 17 April 2018 and *IR v JQ*, Case C-68/17, 11 September 2018.
88. ECJ, *IX* and *MH Müller Handels GmbH*, Joined Cases C-804/18 and C-341/19, 15 July 2021, paragraphs 64, 67, and 85.
89. ECJ, *IX* and *MH Müller Handels GmbH*, Joined Cases C-804/18 and C-341/19, 15 July 2021, paragraph 86.
90. ECJ, *Centraal Israëlitisch Consistorie van België and Others*, Case C-336/19, 17 December 2020, paragraph 67.
91. For a more detailed analysis of these developments see C Walter and K Tremml, 'Religion und Weltanschauung als Diskriminierungskategorien' in A K Mangold and M Payandeh (eds), *Handbuch Antdiskriminierungsrecht* (2022) 349–385, 363–368, and 368–376.
92. See Article 8(1) of Directive 2000/78 and Article 26 of Regulation No 1099/2009.

CHAPTER 3

EUROPE AND INTERNATIONAL LAW

Colonial Legacies

ANTONY ANGHIE

1. Introduction

JHW Verzijl, in his majestic history of international law, proclaimed that there was one issue beyond any dispute, that the modern law of nations was European.[1] Earlier historians of the discipline, such as Stephan Verosta, had acknowledged the existence of other normative systems that played some role in managing the affairs of certain regions, such as South Asia, the Middle East, and Africa.[2] Indeed, it is noteworthy that one of the first treaties that we know of is an agreement between societies located in Africa and Asia, the Treaty of Kadesh.[3] We might question whether these systems of governance found in Persia or the Middle East qualify as 'international law', as various issues arise as to what might be considered 'international' and 'law'.[4] Nevertheless, the fact remains that the system of international law that eventually became universal, displacing all other versions of regional law, is very much a creation of Europe. Thus, while scholars such as Wolfgang Preiser are notable for pointing out first, that other systems of what might be termed 'international law' existed, and second, that fundamental doctrines of what came to be recognized as 'European international law' were possibly borrowed from and influenced by these other systems, they are also emphatic in affirming that modern international law is essentially European in origin. As Preiser puts it, European achievement is 'secure for all time by reason of the fact that European international law developed into world international law'.[5] In effect, having recognized the existence of these other 'regional' systems of international law, they are then omitted from any further serious consideration.[6] Scholars such as RP Anand[7] and CH Alexandrowicz[8] have attempted to modify this large claim, arguing that international law, while principally European in origin, was influenced by principles that developed in the non-European world, and that Grotius's ideas about the free sea, for instance, were shaped by Asian concepts of trade and navigation.[9]

My purpose in this chapter is to sketch out some of the issues and implications of the European origins of international law. I commence by exploring some of the recent efforts to rethink that legacy by focusing on how the tradition so deeply venerated by scholars such as Verzjil may also have been shaped by its engagement with imperial European practices. Having surveyed the manner in which European international became 'universal', through the process of imperialism and all the factors that drove its expansion, I then trace the complex legacies of this experience for non-European peoples. In this regard, it is possible to identify a number of stages in the response of non-European peoples to the European legacy. I try to present these responses by examining State and diplomatic practice; the larger theorization of the problem by scholars from non-European States grappling with the problem of adapting their own traditions to the new system of power controlled by Europe; the efforts of non-European States to contest some of the fundamental concepts of European international law and, even more concretely, the systems of governance and economic power that had been entrenched by these developments over a long period of history. Needless to say, even if it is accepted that international law is primarily European in its origins, the question of the legacies of this situation is far from easy to identify. My conclusion summarizes some tentative suggestions.

2. The European Legacy as Imperialism

It is hardly contentious that a system of European law, *ius European publicum*, contended with and replaced any regional systems of interaction, which might be considered to be a version of international law in that it sought to order relations among different societies, through the process of imperialism.[10] Beginning in the late 15th century, European States extended into Africa, Asia, and 'the New World'. If we take the inaugural voyage of Columbus as emblematic, the principal reason for this expansion, while presented in many guises and rationalized in different forms, was economic. In the initial phases, this process was animated by the idea of trade which, when the opportunity presented itself, often led to conquest. In the New World, conquest was the immediately employed policy by Spain; in the case of Asia and Africa, a more gradual process of domination unfolded, as local sovereigns were initially treated as equals with whom treaties were negotiated, before those treaties became vehicles of colonialism as European States acquired the military and technological superiority that enabled them to dominate those regions. It is now surely uncontroversial to state that the wealth of imperial European States was significantly based on imperialism and all it involved, the extraction of gold and silver from the mines of the New World, the slave trade and the plantations, and the treasures of Asia. Eric Williams, for instance, in his pathbreaking work, *Capitalism and Slavery*, has traced the ways in which the slave trade contributed to the industrial revolution in Britain[11]—and his insights have now been extensively elaborated in different ways by more detailed research and scholarship that extends our understanding of the operations of slavery in, for instance, North America.[12] Indeed, the further argument might be made that the stability and democracy that emerged in Europe, this in the midst of inter-European rivalries and wars, were products of the exploitation of the non-European world. This claim was soberly articulated, not by critical or dependency theorists but by a scholar who epitomized in so many ways the best qualities of the European intellectual, Max Weber, who broadly asserted:

> The historical origin of modern freedom has had certain unique preconditions which will never repeat themselves. Let us enumerate the most important of these: First, the overseas expansion. In the armies of Cromwell, in the French constituent assembly, in our whole economic life even today this breeze from across the ocean is felt . . . but there is no new continent at our disposal.[13]

The same point is made in a somewhat different form by Carl Schmitt[14] who argued that peace in Europe at the height of Empire was attributable to the availability of land beyond Europe, land that could be seized by European powers within the structure of the Nomos of the Earth as it existed at that time.[15] International law may have been viewed as crucial to the creation of peace in Europe, as exemplified by the defining ending of the Thirty Years war. In the non-European world, however, international law served primarily as a justification for violence and imperialism. The imperial project raised profound moral, religious, and ethical questions at a time when what might be termed 'international law' was inseparable from these other types of discourse. The relationship between international law and imperialism, however, raises important questions about how the 'European' character of international law should be conceptualized. The traditional view, that has prevailed until relatively recently, is that the essential doctrines of international law, and in particular, sovereignty doctrine, were generated by events in Europe. The Peace of Westphalia, then, was based on the idea of the sovereign State. Within this narrative, sovereignty, a uniquely European construct, was then over time transferred to, and indeed embraced by, non-European societies by a complex set of processes driven by a combination of imperial European administrative practices and policies that internally transformed those societies, as well as the efforts of those societies to meet the 'standard of civilization', and thus become sovereign States. Through the campaign for decolonization, non-European countries finally emerged as sovereign States and ostensibly equal States in the community of nations. Seen in this way, international law was a means of progress, a mechanism to create a universal international law, even if non-European States made little contribution to that universal international law.

This narrative supports a traditional view of 'Eurocentrism', the view expressed and indeed celebrated by Verzijl and Preiser. This view has been challenged by non-European lawyers from the 19th century onwards, a challenge that intensified and expanded during the struggle for decolonization. In recent times, inspired by the broader theoretical concerns and strategies of post-colonial scholarship, Third World Approaches to International Law (TWAIL) scholars have offered a different vision of the 'Eurocentric' character of international law. The broad argument here is that doctrines such as sovereignty were not created in Europe and then transferred, even if by imposition, in its pure European form to the non-European world. Rather, crucial doctrines of international law, relating to sovereignty and personality and property and political economy more broadly, were shaped by the imperial encounter, and in particular, the ideas of the 'savage' or 'uncivilized' or 'barbaric' that were fundamental to European means of theorizing that encounter.[16] Sovereignty, rather than a gift bestowed on the non-sovereign world, was rather created initially by a process of excluding and denouncing the non-European entity as barbaric and non-sovereign or imperfectly sovereign, and then engaging in the apparently benevolent and liberal act of transferring sovereignty to this abject entity. In short, sovereignty doctrine is premised on the initial and invariably violent act of exclusion prior to the humanitarian act of inclusion and empowerment, the identity of the barbaric entity having been transformed, notionally or aspirationally in the process, the European model of sovereignty having established itself as the only model by which an entity can achieve personhood—however and invariably imperfectly. The TWAIL argument is basically that sovereignty doctrine cannot be adequately understood by focusing only on the theme of 'sovereignty as liberation'. Rather, sovereignty was also constructed as a process of exclusion, one by which certain peoples could be disempowered and subordinated. This exclusion is a precondition of the operation of sovereignty as liberation, the process of extending sovereignty to those people ostensibly lacking it. Any account of sovereignty must address both these processes, the first of exclusion and then, the ostensibly redeeming project of liberation and inclusion. European norms are, in each case, the basis of the defining test. Societies that do not conform to European norms are excluded; following which, if those societies are to emerge as properly civilized and sovereign States, they must comply with European international law. It is this concept of Eurocentrism, a 'European' international law ineluctably marked and shaped—perhaps one could even say, in keeping with the operative paradigms, disfigured—by the non-European through the colonial encounter that has largely prompted the resurgence of interest in imperial international law. The European legacy cannot be considered to be 'pure' for it was always shaped, since its early modern beginnings as reflected in the writings of Vitoria and Grotius, by its encounter with the non-European world. Further, the TWAIL version of Eurocentrism, then, unsettles in particular the liberal notion that the European legacy, to the extent it was a legacy of colonialism and conquest, has been redeemed and overcome, that imperialism is a practice, a phenomenon of the past. Rather, TWAIL is sensitive to the possibilities that mechanisms of suppression and exclusion that were crucial to the founding of sovereignty as it was shaped by the colonial conflict, may still emerge and assert itself, reproducing violence and dispossession. In short, these two contrasting analytical approaches offer very different understandings of the 'legacy' of European law, its content, and effects.

3. The European Legacy Reconsidered: Origins and an Overview

A broad sense of the character and development of European international law in relation to imperialism is provided by a study of the work of Francisco de Vitoria, the Dominican monk who, in two famous lectures, addressed directly the issue of how European international law applied to non-European peoples.[17] The 'European' character of international law is explicitly manifested in the European sources that Vitoria uses to construct his jurisprudence. What Vitoria's work demonstrates very vividly is how what might be termed 'international law' is very much a product of a rich range of ideas, a particular embodiment of European philosophical and religious traditions. 'International law' was hardly an autonomous discipline; it was integrally connected to the worldviews, debates, and paradigms that were part of a larger European cultural tradition. Indeed, this inevitably continued to be the case even in the 19th century, when jurists were preoccupied with the project of establishing that international law was independent of other disciplines such as philosophy and ethics.[18] International law may have been conceptualized as independent from a disciplinary perspective, but it was inevitably shaped by, and representative of, broader intellectual currents that were also manifested in anthropology, social science, and political philosophy. Vitoria's sources range from St Augustine to Ovid to Aristotle to church teachings and the scriptures. It is out of these materials that Vitoria constructs a far reaching and comprehensive jurisprudence dealing with issues such as the personality of the Indians, the just causes of war, jurisdiction, the relationship between different sources of law (Vitoria distinguishes between man-made and divine law), concepts of ownership, the distinction between the private and public domains, natural rights, etc. It is notable that Vitoria outlines not only particular principles, the law relating to war, for instance, but the armature, the broader conceptual foundations of a system of jurisprudence, the rules about the making of rules. Vitoria makes crucial distinctions, between the private and the public, between dominium and imperium, the rules relating to jurisdiction and the demarcation of the boundaries between the spiritual and civil and temporal realms. Equally important are the doctrines he outlines on trusteeship, governance, the ideal State. Vitoria's work, then, operates on a number of different levels: on one hand, his writings on just war and the laws in war continue to be influential, sometimes because they are actually cited, and others because they have profoundly shaped the development of a particular body of international law even if they are themselves no longer statement of the currently applicable law.

More profoundly perhaps, we see in Vitoria the efforts to fashion a set of approaches to problems and issues that continue to be fundamental to the discipline. Vitoria for instance, directly addresses the crucial task of constructing a 'universal law', one that is applicable to all human beings; universality is key to his account of how Spain exercised sovereignty over the New World. Further, and inseparable from this larger project, are conceptualizations of the universal person, the universal rules relating to acquisition and disposition of property, the rules relating to travel. It is a striking illumination of how 'legacies' work that Vitoria's ideas have in some cases remained dormant for centuries before being recovered and presented as a basis for an entire regime that sought to protect the rights of 'backward peoples'.[19] Quincy Wright, one of the foremost authorities of the Mandate System of the League of Nations, cites Vitoria as an inspiration for the concept of 'trusteeship' that animated that system.[20] The revival of interest in Vitoria's jurisprudence, and the ongoing debate on how we should assess his legacy, reveal startlingly the extent to which initiatives that are presented as new and radical in effect reproduce ideas that were outlined, even if in a somewhat undeveloped form, by Vitoria. This is certainly the case with the 'good governance' initiatives that were begun in the 1990s, for instance, that adopt and elaborate on the basic Vitorian idea of the inferiority of non-European systems that must therefore be reformed. The recent renewed interest in Vitoria's work also attests to the uncertain and fluid character of 'legacies'.

Presented in a nutshell, and returning to the TWAIL perspective, we see in Vitoria's work a series of techniques for constructing a universal law that binds the non-European entity; for presenting that entity as inferior (and this calls for the humanitarian project of transformation to liberate the inferior entity from that condition) and aberrant (which calls for the application of violence, the use of force, to exterminate the Indian and yet resurrect her in the mode of the transformed, now civilized Indian). The different readings of Vitoria, as cosmopolitan and humane on one hand, including the Indians within his universal law, presenting them as beneficiaries of human rights;[21] and a sophisticated advocate of Empire are not amenable to any resolution. But once again, it presents in very vivid terms a version of a debate that we now continue to engage in. If Vitoria's concept of natural rights is in some respects, together with the writings of Bartolome de Las Casas, the foundation of modern human rights law—after all Vitoria presents all human beings, including the Indians, as having natural rights—then can we separate that aspect of his writing from its potentially colonial applications? Or does Vitoria suggest that only particular human beings enjoy rights fully, only certain identities with particular attributes and forms of behaviour and economic characteristics, can be liberated into the realm of the universal as equal, sovereign entities. Vitoria's work is representative of another set of themes. Vitoria himself was a brave defender of the Indians, and Spanish atrocities in the New World affected him deeply.[22] The point is that in seeking to defend the rights of the Indian, he produces a set of ideas that serve as new and ingenious justifications for their conquest. A survey of the writing on imperialism suggests that attempts to refute it instead often produce a more sophisticated justification for it. Imperialism appears so deeply entrenched in the system, both economically and intellectually, that very often even its condemnation is premised in some way on its continuity albeit in some more complex form.

Many of the jurists who wrote on imperial affairs and often justified them in innovative ways, perceived themselves as anti-imperial and indeed, condemned many of their predecessors on this account. Writers who trenchantly condemned colonial practices, sometimes reproduced more ingenious and subtle justifications for them. Grotius denounced the rapacious Portuguese and their exploitation of Asian societies;[23] Vattel denounced the blatant colonial justifications of Grotius himself,[24] and Kant's withering dismissal of all of them could be seen at least in part as motivated by their role in the colonial brutalities that Kant was eloquent in condemning.[25] Each in their different ways, however, reproduced the basic idea that non-European peoples and societies that failed to adhere to universal, idealized European norms—and these varied with the thinkers involved—were inferior even when arguing that in principle all peoples and societies were equal.[26] The fundamental economics of the situation, vividly understood as an economics that ensured the imperial power's preservation and expansion, seemed to ultimately dictate the outcome of any inquiry. Vitoria himself bluntly makes the point. After dismissing many of the arguments made by the more ferocious advocates of Spanish Empire, Vitoria addresses the implications, the stark conclusion that if the Spanish had no proper title to the Indies, then 'all the travel to, and trade with, those parts should be stopped to the loss of the Spaniards and also to the grave hurt of the royal treasury (a thing intolerable)'.[27] The extraction of the riches of the New World, the gold and the silver, were now crucial for the wellbeing of the Spanish State. Having not only thought, but articulated the unthinkable, Vitoria is quick to provide reassurance by stating that trade would still continue, based on the universal principles of political economy that he had outlined. We see in precisely this shift in arguments, the transition from an older and cruder model of conquest based on the idea that the Indians were not human, to the Vitorian argument that because the Indians were human, they were bound by the universal laws of trade and political economy. This may appear a liberal and cosmopolitan response. But it is precisely because of these trade laws, and their inevitable violation by the Indians, that a new and all-encompassing justification for conquest emerges, one which Vitoria outlines in detail in his next lecture, suitably entitled 'On the Indians, Or On the Law of War Made by the Spaniards on the Barbarians'.[28] It is a commonplace argument that trade is the obverse of Empire, that trade benefits all parties as being opposed to the exploitation of inequality and extraction associated with colonialism. However, the writings of Vitoria suggest that at the very moment the lineaments of what might be called international law are articulated, trade and conquest are integrally connected. This surely does not mean that all trade is imperial. But equally, it suggests that intimate relations exist between the two, and this could shape the ways in which trade may be used in international relations and eventually entrench subordination.

Grotius, the younger Grotius of *The Free Sea*, was profoundly influenced by Vitoria and his vision of free trade, and the subordination of sovereignty to that principle.[29] Embedded in this jurisprudence are fundamental and enduring ideas about sovereignty, property, trade, the global commons, and natural rights. Equally importantly, Grotius was constructing his version of international law to vindicate the rights, not of a sovereign, but a corporation, one of the entities that was later to merge into the Dutch East India Corporation.[30] There is an argument to be made then, that the whole system was designed to justify and expand a particular and unique entity, one entirely engineered and dedicated to the making of profit. It was the idea of the corporation as the sovereign actor in the Far East that arguably continued to shape Grotius's later jurisprudence, his great masterpiece, *The Rights of War and Peace*, published in 1625. Thus, TWAIL scholars would argue, these origins are important and must be understood: international law was devised to justify the trade of European empires as conducted by their corporation.[31] A focus on sovereigns as the major actors in international law provides only a limited and distorted means of understanding the imperial engagement in Asia, where much of the interaction took place between companies—the Dutch VOC and the British East India Company—and Asian rulers. The East India Company for instance, created the British Empire in India and extended its influence in China while the Dutch East India company established its Empire in Java and Sumatra and pioneered trade with Japan. Moreover, for Grotius, the 'state of nature' that inspired his thinking of the 'natural rights' found in that condition was the world of the expanding Dutch East India company battling its rivals to acquire the riches of Asia. The non-European world was the 'natural world'. As Martine van Ittersum has shown, Grotius was a loyal servant of the Dutch East India company for many decades. His nephews were employed by the VOC.[32]

It is notable however, that Grotius relies not only on theological sources such as Thomas Aquinas, but very heavily on the Roman traditions—Roman law, and the writings of Ovid, Cicero, and Seneca.[33] Grotius then, was a master of Roman-Dutch law, the law that was used by the Dutch East Indian company in governing their territories in the Cape, Indonesia, and Ceylon. It is notable that both Grotius and Vitoria emphatically assert that Empire is not a justification for war. But what a comparative study of these two major figures in international law demonstrates is the close relationship between trade and Empire, beginning with Vitoria's argument that the right to trade is a fundamental natural right and then expanded by Grotius who draws on Vitoria but elaborates and entrenches the right further by making it central to his concept of self-preservation. For Grotius as with Vitoria, a violation of economic rights was sufficient justification for war. Underlying this jurisprudence is a nascent and yet powerful structure of political economy and all its accompanying ideas of human personality, rights, the State, trade, and property. Altogether, these different doctrines and techniques created a complex and flexible means of control that would enable and support the essential purposes of imperialism. As Robinson and Gallagher point out in their classic article, 'informal Empire', a system that eschewed outright conquest, was very often a more economical and effective mode of imperialism.[34] Recent scholarship elaborating on concepts of 'semi-sovereignty' and 'semi-colonialism' have outlined the legal doctrines and mechanisms, involving for instance, the protectorate and extraterritoriality,[35] that supported this system of informal Empire.

This then is the foundation of the European legacy of international law as it was experienced in the non-European world. The classic and central issue that the most distinguished international lawyers have attempted to resolve is the conundrum that arises from the Westphalian model: how is international law created among equal and sovereign States; or put another way, can there be law in the absence of an overarching sovereign? However, another equally crucial issue arises of how European international law, the *ius publicum* of Europe, became universal. Imperialism was the vehicle for this process. And it is only by appreciating how European international law reconstructed itself to subordinate racially and culturally different entities, to exclude them from the realm of full sovereignty, that we may understand the intimate and formative influence of imperialism and international law; and further, the preconditions for the liberal project of bestowing sovereignty over the benighted uncivilized.

4. The Nineteenth-Century Legacy: Race and Hierarchy

A far reaching jurisprudence of inferiority was constructed by European scholars using concepts of civilization, race, and economic behaviour among other markers.[36] By the 19th century however, all pretence of cosmopolitanism and equality was dispensed with. Non-European peoples were inferior, perhaps irredeemably so, and the category of race became the foundation of the jurisprudence of the time. As James Lorimer, famous for his division of the world into concentric zones, civilized humanity, barbarous humanity, and savage humanity put it, 'No modern contribution to science seems destined to influence international politics and jurisprudence to so great an extent as that which is known as ethnology or the science of races'.[37] As always, there was no single jurisprudence of Empire. As Mohammad Shahabuddin points out in his far reaching study of the different colonial policies of France and Germany, liberal and conservative visions of race and progress, law and order, contended with each other in shaping the policies of the time.[38] In broad terms German colonial policy was generally based on the view that their colonial subjects could never be equal, while France sought to civilize and assimilate their subjects.[39]

In the negotiations surrounding the Treaty of Berlin of 1884–85 European States sought to create a unified jurisprudence on how to acquire territorial sovereignty, this in order to divide up the continent of Africa among themselves without generating the frictions that could result in war. These negotiations proceeded on certain fundamental premises about race and governance. The words of John Westlake, a member of the Institut de Droit and Whewell professor at Cambridge is representative of a general attitude:

> When people of European race come into contact with American or African tribes, the prime necessity is a government under the protection of which the former may carry on the complex life to which they have been accustomed in their homes, which may prevent that life from being disturbed by contests between different European powers for the supremacy on the same soil and which may protect the natives in the enjoyment of a security and well being at least not less than they enjoyed before the arrival of the strangers. In the answer to that question lies, for international law, the difference between civilization and the want of it.[40]

The passage reveals a number of elements of 19th-century jurisprudence, this at the height of Empire. First, it is the category of race that is central to Westlake's system. By now, anthropology and social sciences were preoccupied, if not constructed around, the project of identifying and establishing racial hierarchies, all this influenced by scholars such as Gobineau and Linnaeus amongst a host of others. Race was simultaneously an apparently self-evident attribute[41] as well as the basis for complex and elaborate theories. A number of further disciplines were constructed around race, including craniometry and physical anthropology which studied the skulls and physiognomy of non-European peoples in order to demonstrate how inferiority, lack of intelligence, and morality could manifest themselves physically. Native peoples, from Africa to Australia, were sometimes deprived of proper burial rites as European scientists sent the skeletons, and particularly the skulls of these people, to European centres of learning for study. The efforts of the descendants of some of these people to regain the bodies of their ancestors for proper burial are ongoing.[42] In the 19th century, race is the foundation of the distinction between the 'civilized' and 'uncivilized', and Westlake proceeds to outline further aspects of this difference. In order for a government or, more broadly, a State to win recognition as legitimate under international law it must enable Europeans to enjoy the lifestyle they enjoy in their own home countries. We see here how, despite the many developments that have taken place in international jurisprudence since the time of Vitoria and his naturalist-theological outlook, his central idea that native systems of governance are to be assessed according to European standards remains. The difference, however, is that Westlake presents these standards as explicitly European, whereas Vitoria presents them as 'universal' standards which, on closer inspection and application, reveal themselves as European—indeed, an idealized Europe at that. The point then, is that European international law was, inevitably, inseparable from broader currents of European thinking. And secondly, that despite changes over the centuries, certain fundamental structures relating to the inferiority of the non-European and the use of international law to embark on the imperative and yet impossible task of transforming the native and her systems of governance, persist.

5. Non-European Responses

The trauma of conquest and domination that was experienced by Asian and African countries generated varied responses. Countries such as China and Japan, shaken by their sudden subordination to European countries that they regarded as inferior, attempted to learn the Western traditions of international law. Classic texts such as Vattel's 'Law of Nations' were translated into local languages, and Japan in particular launched a concerted campaign to achieve the difficult task of transforming itself into a Western society that would meet the protean 'standard of civilization', while maintaining their traditions.[43] Japan was especially successful in accomplishing this transition, winning a qualified acceptance into the family of nations, demonstrating its emergence by its famous victory over Russia, a major European power, in the battle of Tsushima in 1905. The first Pan-African congress, organized by a West Indian barrister, Henry Sylvester-Williams, and attended by WE DuBois, took place in London in 1900. The proceedings were dominated by questions of slavery, colonialism, and demands for the respect for the territorial integrity of Abyssinia, Liberia, and Haiti. It was at the Congress that DuBois famously proclaimed that 'The problem of the twentieth century is the problem of the color line', the problem of race determining access to 'the opportunities and privileges of modern civilization'. In warning against a system in which 'the black world is to be exploited and ravished and degraded', DuBois made his appeal to 'the Great Powers of the civilized world, trusting in the wide spirit of humanity and deep sense of justice and of our age'.[44] DuBois, like many others after him, appealed to the ideals of justice and humanity that were proclaimed to be central to the civilization that Western societies were intent on promulgating. The language is moving in its eloquence and its praise of the American Negro for 'the great work he has accomplished in a generation toward raising nine millions of human beings from slavery to manhood'. What is especially poignant is DuBois's simultaneous recognition of the complete devastation suffered by black people, the depredations inflicted by civilization, while appealing to its ideals. It is also notable that DuBois encompasses the plight not only of blacks, but also the 'brown and yellow myriads elsewhere'. Civilization becomes clearly the central controlling preoccupation of blacks, Asians, Africans, and Latin Americans, despite the fact that it was a protean term that lent itself to opportunistic manipulation, its meaning as deployed by Western States continuously shifting and elusive.[45] Later DuBois was to 'urge that the League of Nations take a firm stand on the absolute equality of races'.[46] We might see Japan's effort to transform itself as an attempt to demonstrate that civilization is independent of race, that a non-European society could meet the standards prescribed by Westlake. Despite Japan's major achievements, its emergence as an important industrial power and indeed, its famous victory over a Russia, a great European power, it was still unable to convince the League of Nations to acknowledge the principle of racial equality in 1919.[47] In Latin America, scholars such as Alejandro Alvarez sought to demonstrate that Latin American States embodied the best of the old civilization of Europe together with the innovation of the 'new civilization' emerging in the Americas.[48] Gandhi, however, offered a contrasting vision of European civilization, dismissing it as a ruinous failure rather than seeking to win acceptance within its norms.[49] The slaughter of World War I further diminished Western claims to represent the best of 'civilization'.

6. Some Major Legacies

6.1 Sovereignty and the nation-state

Non-European States responded to this history by asserting the right of self-determination and seeking to ensure their status by acquiring sovereignty. Sovereignty, long denied these societies, became the foundation of their liberation, the legal basis on which they could claim equality, control their own affairs, and protect themselves against the foreign rule and intervention that had defined their immediate history. The powerful promise of sovereignty is suggested by the vehemence with which the 'new States' that had assembled at Bandung in 1955—the largest gathering of non-European States and peoples up to that time—not only asserted sovereignty, but expanded and articulated the many dimensions of it.[50] The doctrine of Pancasila or the 'five principles' were the presented by these States as the defining ideology of the new States. In different ways, each of these principles elaborated on the basic idea of non-intervention. It is not hard to see this proclamation as reinforcing and reaffirming a classic Westphalian notion of territorial sovereignty.

Thus one of the most enduring legacies of European international law is in the universalization of the concept of the 'nation-state' as the central form for the organization of society. This involved a radical transformation for many societies which had established very different systems of governance. As Thongchai Winichakul argues in the case of Thailand, for instance, government was based less on ideas of territorial sovereignty and more on systems of kinship and alliance.[51] The colonial State established itself as the central and dominant political authority. Independence generated many challenges. In ethnically and religiously divided societies, different ethnic groups sought to seize the power of the colonial and now ostensibly post-colonial State. The post-colonial State, despite its supposed foundation on liberal-individualist principles was profoundly shaped by the rise of nationalism which in many ways drove the anti-colonial movement; the same nationalism seemed to suggest that the foundation of the State was an ethnically homogenous entity that would legitimately exercise, and in effect monopolize, State authority, other groups being relegated to 'minorities'. The resulting problems, of course, had already been experienced in Europe, in the Aaland Islands dispute, one of the first to be considered by the newly established League;[52] and the interwar minority treaty system was one attempt to manage the ethno-national State, allowing for its existence while attempting to ensure the rights of ethnic minorities through international protection. The tragedy that accompanied the emergence of India and Pakistan as independent States was surely an important and defining factor for the new States struggling to assert themselves in the external arena while being simultaneously haunted by the spectre of secession from within. The consequences of these tensions are still being played out in many Asian and African countries, where federal and autonomy arrangements attempt, in the lexicon of Western liberal constitutionalism, to manage ethnic relations that had previously in many cases been fluid and adaptable. Needless to say, non-European societies had their own discriminations, divisions, and hierarchies that led to violence. European imperial rule was famously based on the principle of divide and conquer, of setting different ethnic groups against each other. However, even in its innocent form, the European model of the nation-state exacerbated and simplified ethnic identities; and liberal constitutionalism has not always been able to address the problems that have resulted. National politicians and political systems have profoundly exacerbated the situation by making ethnic identity a central and defining feature of politics in post-colonial States.

If anything then, as I have argued elsewhere, the new States embraced the Western idea of the nation-state especially fervently and this is reflected further by the insistence by new States that colonial boundaries had to be respected.[53] Further, these societies have been afflicted by opportunistic racial politics that have often led to civil war and on-going conflict. It is a great irony therefore, that African boundaries established in essence by the Treaty of Berlin of 1884–85, one in which, notoriously, no Africans were present, have been kept in place by the African States that succeeded colonial rule. Ethnic conflict continues to erupt in many developing countries. The causes of such conflict are of course, extremely complex, and the responsibility of national politicians who exacerbate and provoke such conflict should not be underestimated. From the outset, however, the introduction of the nation-state as the one, primary, and authoritative form of internationally recognized sovereignty has been a source of continuing complications. Despite ongoing crises and despite innovations such as the European Union (EU), the nation-state has no real political rival, and plausible alternatives have yet to emerge. Indeed, recent years have witnessed the re-emergence of nationalism and protectionism which have reinforced the power of the nation-state.

6.2 Development and capitalism

As the previous discussion of the founding fathers of international law, Vitoria and Grotius, suggests, the international legal doctrines that animated the whole imperial project developed a particular framework of political economy through their writings on key doctrines relating to legal personality, property, the right to trade, and so forth. While continuities between those ideas and the present systems of political economy raise complex issues, that framework, modified, elaborated, and extended, has basically served to establish the legal foundation of modern capitalism and all this implies. It is in the colonies, constructed after all around the principal ideas of extraction and exploitation, and primitive accumulation, whatever the accompanying humanitarian edifice, that some of the effects of capitalism were seen in their most stark form.

The new States were driven, even defined, by their ambition to achieve economic development. While there are of course significant differences between socialist and capitalist approaches to development, they all had in common the basic idea of extracting and exploiting resources with little regard for environmental consequences. In more recent times, furthermore, it is capitalist development that has come to prevail virtually globally—even if, ironically, in countries such as China, this is a version of development that relies very much on the State for its furtherance. International law, which has in various ways supported and furthered this system of political economy, is another major legacy of European international law. It is the case that the US contributed in many important respects to this body of law—international trade law and international investment law in particular.[54] The US has developed its own distinctive approach to international law, one that is commonly perceived as based on 'policy' and powerfully influenced by realism.[55] It is surely the case that the European and American traditions are distinctive—a distinction usually understood in terms of European formalism and positivism versus American policy science and realism. But at least for Third World scholars, these distinctions, while important, should not conceal the broader fact that both European and US approaches simply added to the arsenal of technologies that could be deployed against them for imperial purposes. Thus, commenting on the impact of the American Declaration of Independence on international law, Bedjaoui argues that what this meant was the replacement of 'the legal system of the European States by that of the States of "Christian civilization"'. And further, that '[f]or Europe, however, the conception of an oligarchic international law was no whit changed because of this geographic enlargement'.[56]

Gandhi observed of the British that '[t]hey wish to convert the whole world into a vast market for their goods'.[57] Accompanying this endeavour was a particular idea of man, as being principally an economic and self-interested actor, a consumer, and a labourer. This powerful idea of a model of man as the property-owning market actor has now been universalized. International law has made and continues to make its own contribution to this idea of man and the broader regime, 'capital's global rule'.[58] Many environmental scholars have pointed out the wide-ranging consequences of this particular legacy for the efforts to protect the environment.[59] Nor has the impact of Europe further ceased in this regard. As Quinn Slobodian has pointed out in his superb book, *The Globalists*, European thinkers such as Hayek and William Rappard were brilliant exponents of the economic system that we now know as 'neo-liberalism'.[60] It is surely no coincidence that the modern beginnings of capitalism were coeval with the modern beginnings of international law. One of the most enduring European legacies, then, a legacy that has been inevitably modified and extended by its various champions including the US, is capitalism. It is a singular irony then, that this legacy is being furthered, albeit in yet another avatar, by China.

7. The Many Legacies of Europe

Imperialism was the subject of ongoing debate within Europe itself. Dramatic differences in thinking about colonial rule and its effects are apparent for instance, in the trial of Warren Hastings and Edmund Burke's famous denunciation of the East Indian company's colonial practices—despite which Hastings was exonerated and the Company's power only increased.[61] As Sankar Muthu has argued, further, Enlightenment thinkers were continuously challenging imperial practices.[62] It is noteworthy for instance, even earlier, that Vitoria was adamant in declaring that 'expansion of empire is no grounds for war'. Within the European tradition itself, then, a whole vocabulary emerged for contesting Empire. Initially developed principally to protect Europeans and European interests against tyranny and arbitrary rule, concepts relating to natural rights presented themselves as universal. Thus anti-colonial resistance could insist on consistency by pointing to the hypocrisy of denying certain peoples supposedly universal rights. The question of how blacks could be deprived of the universal rights so reverently enshrined in the US Constitution was always a source of awkwardness. In many cases, of course, non-European peoples had to demand that certain concepts, such as self-determination be extended to their own societies. When Wilson introduced the concept of self-determination into the realm of international law and relations, he intended it to apply only to European peoples.[63] Non-European peoples then fought to use the language of human rights, self-determination, and equality, that are also an important aspect of Europe's legacy, for their own purposes. Certainly, as we have seen, the anti-slavery and anti-colonial movements relied heavily on these principles. This is evident in the appeals of DuBois to humanity and civilization and the ideals of progress and justice that they were supposed to represent. Anand, like many Third World scholars of his generation, made it clear that he was not seeking to repudiate the whole of international law, despite its European character; instead he sought to excise what he thought of as the 'imperial dimensions' of international law.[64] The new States were emphatic in insisting on equality and the idea of global humanity when arguing for human rights and condemning South Africa for apartheid. All these concepts were an integral part of the vocabulary of the new States. The telling question remains, however, whether these particular approaches to racism and all that followed from them, are capable of addressing the pervasive character of race. As Cedric Robinson argues in his powerful work—which points also to the racism that existed within Europe itself prior to colonialism:

> Racialism insinuated not only medieval, feudal and capitalist social structures, forms of property, and modes of production, but as well the very values and traditions of consciousness through which the peoples of these ages came to understand their worlds and their experiences.[65]

Human rights offers an important means of protecting human dignity. The European origins of international human rights law, extending from the jurisprudence on natural rights, is clear. The traditional genealogy of human rights begins with natural law and extends through the Enlightenment and the French declaration on the rights of man.[66] As Anthony Pagden has argued, human rights were tied 'not only to a specific ethical legal code but also implicitly to a particular type of political system, both of inescapably European origin'.[67] Human rights law has of course been continuously critiqued for this reason. Once again, however, the meaning of this legacy has been interpreted in different ways. The main initial criticism was that human rights are Eurocentric. Two broad versions of this argument are evident. One version could be seen as essentially cultural and political, the argument being that other visions of society, for instance one based on duties rather than rights and that gave priority to the community rather than the individual, had equal validity. The second, and related argument was that economic development and progress had priority over civil and political rights: this was the argument made most prominently by East Asian countries that had been relatively successful in achieving economic growth despite criticisms that individual rights had been sacrificed in the process.[68]

The further question arises about whether that legacy might be amended, and transformed into novel and progressive doctrines that could create new visions of international law and justice. As mentioned, new States were not intent on repudiating international law. Focusing in particular on international human rights law, we might see a spectrum of responses. It is notable that the new States embraced human rights enthusiastically, affirming this in the Bandung declaration. Their specific and explicit concerns, driven largely by the affront of apartheid in South Africa, was to assert the prohibition against racial discrimination, a classic and fundamental right, one that was mentioned in the United Nations Charter itself.[69] More controversially, the developing States combined their demand for self-government and self-determination by asserting it as a right. Although not initially included in the Universal Declaration on International Human Rights, self-determination was mentioned in the United Nations Charter and appears as Article 1 in both the Civil and Political Rights Covenant as well as the International Covenant on Economic and Social Rights. Self-determination has remained a controversial right—although the logic behind its inclusion as a right appears plausible: it is only if a State comes into existence that it is in a position to protect its citizens.[70]

Developing countries and social movements have attempted to expand international human rights law, building on and in some cases departing from its 'European legacy'. This is reflected in the campaign for economic and social rights which in themselves are not entirely foreign to the European tradition, as Susan Marks's important new book points out in its inquiry about alternative visions of rights, one based on 'the rights that needed to be taken away in order that private property could arise'.[71] In each case, however, there was no real attempt to repudiate the very concept of rights. Rather, the new States saw themselves as expanding rights in a manner driven by the basic justification for rights, that is, the protection of human dignity. The African Charter of Human Rights emphasizes the rights of people. The Organization of African Unity definition of refugees affords greater protection to refugees than the 1951 Convention which is based on a set of criteria that were directly shaped by European experience.[72] This attests to the ways in which non-European countries have amended doctrines that could be said to have originated in Europe or else used international law to articulate their own visions of rights and governance. It is through these processes of what might be termed hybridity and adaptation that non-European States sought to extend international law and make their own contribution to the discipline. It is also clear, however, that many of these efforts have been powerfully resisted. This is evident not only in the Western repudiation of the New International Economic Order (NIEO), a topic that is now being explored in great depth, but also in efforts to curtail so-called 'Third Generation' rights, such as the right to peace, the right to development, the right to a healthy environment, and the right to solidarity. What this suggests is the intimate connection between what might be termed a 'classic' vision of human rights, that is, individual civil and political rights and their association with a society based on liberal democracy and market-oriented principles. Europe continues to see itself as the bastion of human rights. The

European Court of Human Rights (ECtHR) is among the most established human rights regimes in the world; and EU policy ties aid and preferential trade arrangements, under its General System of Preferences (GSP) scheme to the adherence by beneficiary States to extensive human rights obligations. Some beneficiary States have signed up to something like twenty human rights treaties in order to qualify for GSP benefits. European States, however, have not been very receptive to the idea of extraterritorial human rights, that is, the rights of people fleeing violence and seeking refuge in the EU. What this suggests is both the potential and the limits of international law, outlining what might be termed 'anti-colonial' international law. And TWAIL scholars such as Upendra Baxi[73] and Balakrishnan Rajagopal[74] have done pioneering work in pointing to the limits of human rights and their inadequacy in preventing the advance of a neo-liberal system of political economy with all the misery and inequality this entails.

The limitations and potentialities of what might be termed 'anti-colonial' international law will be tested in another arena—the current initiative taking place under the auspices of the United Nations (UN), focusing on reparations and restitution for colonialism and slavery. The recent tragic killing of George Floyd in the US and the global protests that followed signify the enduring legacy of racism that afflicts many countries. Even before this event, however, efforts had been made to examine the whole phenomenon of racism and how international law should address it. The report of the Special Rapporteur on racism, Tendayi Achiume, deals with 'Contemporary forms of racism, racial discrimination, xenophobia and racial intolerance'.[75] This wide-ranging report explores questions of reparations for slavery and colonialism, together with a study of the enduring effects, that is, the 'structures of inequality and subordination' that follow from a failure to address these effects. The Special Rapporteur points out that:

> International legal doctrine has a longer history of enabling and justifying colonial domination than it does of guaranteeing equal rights to all human beings. Law that perpetuates neocolonial dynamics—including the failure to eradicate the legacies of slavery and colonialism—must itself be recognized as neocolonial law.[76]

What this particular initiative calls for then, is a complete re-examination of international law and Europe's colonial legacy. What this might also suggest is that we are only beginning to assess the legacies of imperial European international law, and the many ways in which it has transformed itself in order to endure. Clearly, furthermore, each generation understands this legacy differently, as it seeks to understand its own identity and the forces that helped shape that identity.

8. Towards a Conclusion

European thought is so wide-ranging and multifarious that any attempt to speak of a 'European tradition' must inevitably simplify and distort. As Lauri Mälksoo points out in his chapter on the role of European States and lawyers in the history of international law, significant historical and cultural differences separated what might be termed 'Western' and 'Eastern Europe'. While the countries of Asia and Africa have been grappling with the legacies of Europe, a country—indeed Empire—Russia, has engaged in its own complex interaction with Europe.[77] Perhaps then, it is more accurate to speak of a 'Western European' rather than 'European' international law.

Further, the dichotomy between Europe and non-Europe, like the dichotomy between the 'civilized' and the 'uncivilized' and 'black' and 'white' was never coherent, despite the best efforts of jurists, sociologists, and anthropologists to maintain and reinforce such divisions.[78] One of the most significant books to be published in recent years, *The Misery of International Law*,[79] has studied in detail how international law has supported and furthered the system of political economy that has generated ongoing and massive poverty, as the 'law of capital' has extended and expanded. Liberal democracy has failed to prevent growing global poverty and inequality. In simple terms, then, a growing portion of the world's population, including those living in Europe are experiencing unprecedented levels of inequality and social dislocation. Intensifying nationalism and racism have now become a feature of many European societies, raising issues that were previously thought to belong uniquely to non-Western societies. The rise of ethnic politics, that is, the mainstreaming of race as a political strategy, is now a feature of politics in many European countries. How these changing political configurations will affect international law is yet to be seen. The broader question raised by these crises, and the ongoing crisis of the COVID 19 pandemic is whether they might generate alternative ideas of society, of political economy, and governance. It is arguable that capitalism itself may be the most significant creation of Europe, and that all these crises and the impact of these crises are intimately connected to the operations of capitalism. The recent important work of indigenous scholars such as Irene Watson points to alternative visions of society, freedom, and governance that have not as yet been properly engaged with;[80] it offers a radical critique of capitalist society that will only become more relevant as environmental devastation threatens the very existence of the globe.

Burke and liberal critics of imperialism may have feared that colonial abuses would return to the metropolis. Hannah Arendt brilliantly outlined how racial thinking developed through imperial practices before being applied within Europe itself.[81] Broadly, liberal critics of Empire feared that abusive practices in the colonies could be transferred to the imperial centre itself.[82] A version of this has occurred. The 'war on terror' has extended emergency executive powers in the US, for instance, in significant ways.[83] Further examination is needed of the ways in which colonial and neo-colonial technologies of control could themselves become universalized, as it were. Any emerging power may use these technologies, adapted as needed, to pursue their own interests. It is now China that is making large purchases of assets in Europe and elsewhere. And it is surely hardly coincidental that it is precisely at this time that European States, that promoted and developed the regime of foreign investment protection, are suddenly scrutinizing a system that they played such a profound role in shaping. Investor-State dispute settlement is being rethought and the EU has established an entire initiative to look into this system. In this way, Europe might now find itself at the reverse end of a set of doctrines it was instrumental in establishing. Further, perhaps the fluid, contingent character of 'legacies' becomes evident through an exploration of how different generations of international lawyers, both from the developing states and the West, have understood and acted upon this legacy. It is through the exemplary collection of essays focusing on the legacy of an event, not in Europe but in the Third World, that we might appreciate the complex, multifarious ways in which a 'legacy' is understood, how it operates in the world, and the forces that affect all this.[84] Inevitably, each era creates the legacy it believes to be important for its own identity and progress. In this respect we might see the legacy of Europe as consisting not so much in linear terms, as an evolving set of ideas—the tendency to view the history of human rights in this way has recently been subject to ongoing scrutiny and fresh interrogation—so much as a rich repository of ideas and doctrines, many of which lie obscure and fallow until events prompt international lawyers to revive them as responses to urgent contemporary problems. We might see the revival of the doctrine of pre-emptive self-defence to further the war on terror in these terms. Verzijl's assertion as to the primacy of Europe in the making modern international law was right. The urgent task of scholars, regardless of their origins, is to understand this legacy because it has so profoundly shaped the making of our troubled world.

Notes

1. JHW Verzjil, *International Law in Historical Perspective*, vol 1 (AW Sijthoff 1968) 436.
2. Stephan Verosta, 'International Law in Europe and Western Asia Between 100 and 650 A.D', 113 Recueil des Cours 1964, 486.
3. The date of the Treaty is 1269 BCE. For discussion of the Treaty and its broader significance, see Jeremy Levitt, 'The African Origins of International Law: Myth or Reality', 19 UCLA Journal of International Law & Foreign Affairs 2015, 113.
4. This is the point made by Onuma Yasuaki, *A Transcivilizational Perspective on International Law* (Martinus Nijhoff 2010) 715 (hereafter Yasuaki, *Transcivilizational Perspective*).
5. Wolfgang Preiser, 'History of the Law of Nations: Basic Questions and Principles' in Rudolph Bernhardt (ed), *Encyclopedia of Public International Law*, vol 2 (Elsevier Borth-Holland 1995) 824.
6. I would suggest that the commendable efforts made in more recent times to provide some sort of global overview of other regions in the introduction to major textbooks understandably reproduces this structure.
7. RP Anand, *New States and International Law* (Vikas Publishing House 1972).
8. Charles Alexandrowicz, *An Introduction to the Law of Nations in the East Indies* (Clarendon Press 1967).
9. ibid.
10. These forms of interaction might be considered 'law'—but here of course, a great deal depends on how 'law' is to be defined, as alternatives to the European concept of law did exist. The broader question of how we should define 'international law' without simply accepting the European vision of law is explored in Onuma Yasuaki, 'When Was the Law

of International Society Born-An Inquiry of the History of International Law from an Intercivilizational Perspective', 2 Journal of the History of International Law 2000, 1.

11. Eric Williams, *Capitalism and Slavery* (Colin Palmer intro, University of North Carolina Press 1994). The work was also notable for the striking argument that the abolition of the slave trade was driven by economic factors rather than humanitarianism.
12. See Sven Beckert, *Empire of Cotton: A Global History* (First Vintage Books edn, New York Vintage Books 2015).
13. Max Weber, Hans Gerth, and C Mills (eds), *From Max Weber: Essays in Sociology* (Routledge & Kegan Paul 1948) 71.
14. For an account of the complex relationship between Schmitt and Weber, see Kjell Engelbrekt, 'What Carl Schmitt Picked Up in Weber's Seminar: A Historical Controversy', 14 The European Legacy 2009, 667.
15. Carl Schmitt, *The Nomos of the Earth*, trans GL Ulmen (Telos Press Publishing 2006).
16. The concepts of 'civilization' and 'barbarity'—or versions of it—were also of course deployed by non-European States. See Onuma Yasuaki's examination of the Sinocentric tribute system in Yasuaki, *Transcivilizational Perspective* (n 4) 305.
17. Franciscus de Vitoria, *De Indis et de Ivre Belli Relectiones*, ed Ernest Nys; trans John Pawley Bate (Carnegie Institute of Washington 1917) (hereafter Vitoria, *De INdis*).
18. Martti Koskenniemi, *The Gentle Civilizer of Nations* (CUP 2003) (hereafter Koskenniemi, *Gentle Civilizer*).
19. For an insightful exploration of this recovery, see Kojo Koram, 'The Vitorian Recovery and the (Re) Turn Towards a Sacrificial International Law', 6 London Review of International Law 2018, 443.
20. Quincy Wright, *Mandates Under the League of Nations* (University of Chicago Press 1930).
21. Georg Cavallar, 'Vitoria, Grotius, Pufendorf, Wolff and Vattel: Accomplices of European Colonialism and Exploitation or True Cosmopolitans?', 10 Journal of the History of International Law 2008, 181.
22. As he puts it, 'As for the experience of Peru, I must tell you, after a lifetime of studies and long experience, that no business shocks me more than the corrupt profits and affairs of the Indies', Letter to Miguel de Arcos, Salamanca, 8 November 1534 in Anthony Pagden and Jeremy Lawrance (eds), *Vitoria Political Writings* (CUP 1991) 331 (hereafter Pagden and Lawrance, *Vitoria Political Writings*).
23. Hugo Grotius, *The Free Sea*, trans Richard Hakluyt (first published in 1609, Liberty Fund 2004) (hereafter Grotius, *Free Sea*).
24. For this aspect of Vattel's work, see Antony Anghie, 'Vattel and Colonialism: Some Preliminary Observations' in Vincent Chetail and Peter Haggenmacher (eds), *Vattel's International Law from a XXIst Century Perspective* (Martinus Nijhoff 2011) 237 (hereafter Anghie, 'Vattel and Colonialism').
25. Immanual Kant, 'Perpetual Peace' in Hans Reiss (ed), *Kant: Political Writings* (2nd edn, CUP 1991) 103.
26. This is a large topic. Vattel condemned what he saw as Grotius's expansive version of the right to go to war, but then outlined a theory about the cultivation of the soil that was cited as a justification for settlor colonialism. See Anghie, 'Vattel and Colonialism' (n 24); for a study of Kant that explores the racial and colonial dimensions of Kant's work, see Emmanuel Chukwudi Eze, *The Color of Reason: The Idea of 'Race' in Kant's Anthropology in Postcolonial African Philosophy: A Critical Reader* (Blackwell Publishers 1997).
27. Pagden and Lawrance, *Vitoria Political Writings* (n 22) 161.

28. Vitoria, *De INdis* (n 17) 163.
29. Grotius, *Free Sea* (n 23).
30. On the complex character of the 'chartered company' such as the Dutch East India Company and its relationship with the State see Koen Stapelbroek, 'Trade, Chartered Companies, and Mercantile Associations' in Bardo Fassbender and Anne Peters (eds), *The Oxford Handbook of the History of International Law* (OUP 2012) 338 (hereafter Fassbender and Peters, *History of International Law*); see also Philip Stern, *The Company State: Corporate Sovereignty and the Early Modern Foundations of the British Empire in India* (OUP 2012).
31. For a superb study of Grotius in these terms, see José Manuel Barreto, '*Cerberus*: Rethinking Grotius and the Westphalian System' in Martti Koskenniemi et al (eds), *International Law and Empire: Historical Explorations* (OUP 2017) 149. For important recent studies of corporations and international law see Grietje Baars, *The Corporation, Law and Capitalism* (Brill 2019); Doreen Lustig, *Veiled Power: International Law and the Private Corporation* (OUP 2020).
32. Martine Julia van Ittersum, 'The Long Goodbye: Hugo Grotius's Justification for Dutch Expansion Overseas, 1615–1645', 36 History of European Ideas 2010, 386.
33. On Roman influences on the law of nations, see Benedict Kingsbury and Benjamin Straumann, 'Introduction: the Roman Foundations of the Law of Nations' in Benedict Kingsbury and Benjamin Straumann (eds), *The Roman Foundations of the Law of Nations: Alberico Gentili and the Justice of* Empire (OUP 2010); for a detailed study of Grotius see Richard Tuck, *The Rights of War and Peace* (OUP 2000).
34. John Gallagher and Ronald Robinson, 'The Imperialism of Free Trade', 6 Economic History Review 1953, 1.
35. Daniel S. Margolies, Umut Özsu, Maïa Pal, and Ntina Tzouvala (eds), *The Extraterritoriality of Law: History, Theory, Politics* (Routledge 2019).
36. For a detailed analysis of the different deployments of race and civilization see Liliana Obregon Tarazona, 'The Civilized and the Uncivilized' in Fassbender and Peters, *History of International Law* (n 30).
37. James Lorimer, *The Institutes of the Law of Nations: A Treatise of the Jural Relations of the Separate Political Communities* (Blackwood 1883) 101.
38. Mohammad Shahabuddin, *Ethnicity and International Law: Histories, Politics and Practices* (CUP 2016).
39. ibid, 62.
40. John Westlake, *Chapters on the Principles of International Law* (CUP 1894) 151.
41. The complexities of race are evident in the attempts of South African legislation in the time of apartheid to distinguish between white, black, and coloured people.
42. See 'Germany returns skulls of Namibian genocide victims', *BBC* (London, 29 August 2018) <https://www.bbc.com/news/world-africa-45342586>.
43. For a powerful and poignant account of the tensions this created, see Owada Hisashi, 'Asia and International Law The Inaugural Address of the First President of the Asian Society of International Law, Singapore, 7 April 2007', 1 Asian Journal of International Law 2011, 3.
44. W E B DuBois, 'To the Nations of the World, ca' (Pan African Association 1900).
45. For recent studies of the varying uses of 'civilization' see Rose Parfitt, *The Process of International Legal Reproduction: Inequality, History and Resistance* (CUP 2019); Ntina Tzouvala, *Capitalism as Civilization* (CUP 2020).
46. W E B DuBois, 'Manifesto to the League of Nations', 23(1) The Crisis 1921, 18.

47. Kinji Akashi, 'Japan-Europe' in Fassbender and Peters, *History of International Law* (n 30).
48. Alejandro Alvarez, 'Latin America and International Law', 3 Asian Journal of International Law 1909, 269.
49. Mohandas Gandhi and Hind Swaraj in Anthony Parel (ed), *Gandhi: 'Hind Swara' and Other Writings* (CUP 2009) (hereafter Parel, *Hind Swaraj*).
50. Luis Eslava, Michael Fakhri, and Vasuki Nesiah (eds), *Bandung, Global History, and International Law* (CUP 2017) (hereafter Eslava, Fakhri, and Nesiah, *Bandung*).
51. Thongchai Winichakul, *Siam Mapped: A History of a Geo-Body of a Nation* (University of Hawaii Press 1997).
52. League of Nations Doc B7/21/68/106 (1921).
53. Antony Anghie, 'Bandung and the Origins of Third World Sovereignty' in Eslava, Fakhri, and Nesiah, *Bandung* (n 50) 535.
54. Contemporary investment law is profoundly shaped by principles that emerged from claims made by US investors in Mexico and Latin America.
55. The distinction between European positivist approaches that could be theorized in a way that constructed a meaningful international community, and a US approach shaped by realism and policy studies, is one of the major themes in Martti Koskenniemi's work. Koskenniemi, *Gentle Civilizer* (n 18).
56. Mohammed Bedjaoui, *Towards a New International Economic Order* (Holmes and Meier 1979) 51.
57. Parel, *Hind Swaraj* (n 49) 40.
58. Katharina Pistor, 'Capital's Global Rule', 26 Constellations 2019, 430.
59. Karin Mickelson, 'Hope in a TWAIL Register', 1 TWAIL Review 2020, 14; Usha Natarajan and Kishan Koday, 'Locating Nature: Making and Unmaking International Law', 27 Leiden Journal of International Law 2014, 573; Ileana Porras, 'Appropriating Nature: Commerce, Property, and the Commodification of Nature in the Law of Nations', 27 Leiden Journal of International Law 2014, 641.
60. Quinn Slobodian, *Globalists* (Harvard UP 2018).
61. P J Marshall, *The Impeachment of Warren Hastings* (OUP 1965).
62. Sankar Muthu, *Enlightenment Against Empire* (Princeton UP 2003).
63. Erez Manela, *The Wilsonian Moment* (OUP 2007).
64. R P Anand, 'Attitude of the Asian-African States Toward Certain Problems of International Law', 15 International and Comparative Law Quarterly 1966, 55.
65. Cedric Robinson, *Black Marxism: the Making of the Black Radical Tradition* (first published in 1983, University of North Carolina Press 2000) 66.
66. Ed Bates, 'History' in Daniel Moeckli, Sangeeta Shah, and Sandesh Sivakumaran (eds), *International Human Rights Law* (OUP 2017) 17–18.
67. Anthony Pagden, 'Human Rights, Natural Rights and Europe's Imperial Legacy', 31 Political Theory 2003, 171.
68. For an overview of these arguments see Antony Anghie, 'International Human Rights Law and a Developing World Perspective' in Scott Sheeran and Nigel Rodley (eds), *Routledge Handbook of International Human Rights Law* (Routledge 2013) 108.
69. See United Nations, 'United Nations Charter, Articles 1 and 55(c)', 1945, calling for universal respect for human rights and fundamental freedoms 'without distinction as to race, sex. Language or religion'.

70. Samuel Moyn argues that this is a crucial feature of earlier Western thinking about the rights of man. See Samuel Moyn, *The Last Utopia* (Harvard UP 2012) 23.
71. Susan Marks, *A False Tree of Liberty* (OUP 2020) 3.
72. See Article 1(2) of the Convention Governing the Specific Aspects of Refugee Problems in Africa (10 September 1969). Article 1(1) of the Convention outlines the criteria found in the 1951 Refugee Convention, but Article 1(2) provides significant new grounds on which persons can claim refugee status, including 'events seriously disturbing public order in either part or whole of his country'.
73. Upendra Baxi, *The Future of Human Rights* (OUP 2008).
74. Balakrishnan Rajagopal, *International Law From Below: Development, Social Movements and Third World Resistance* (CUP 2003).
75. Tendayi Achiume, 'Contemporary forms of racism, racial discrimination, xenophobia and racial intolerance' (21 August 2019) UN Doc A/74/321.
76. ibid, para 10.
77. See Lauri Malksoo, *Russian Approaches to International Law* (OUP 2015); see also Lauri Malksoo, 'The History of International Legal Theory in Russia: a Civilizational Dialogue with Europe', 19 European Journal of International Law 2008, 211.
78. Liliana Obregon, 'The Civilized and the Uncivilized' in Fassbender and Peters, *History of International Law* (n 30).
79. John Linarelli, Margot Salomon, and Muthucumaraswamy Sornarajah, *The Misery of International Law* (OUP 2018).
80. Irene Watson, *Aboriginal Peoples, Colonialism and International Law* (Routledge 2016).
81. Hannah Arendt, *The Origins of Totalitarianism* (Harcourt 1976).
82. Andrew Fitzmaurice, 'Liberalism and Empire in Nineteenth Century International Law', 117 American Historical Review 2012, 122.
83. Bruce Ackerman, *The Decline and Fall of the American Republic* (Harvard UP 2013).
84. Eslava, Fakhri, and Nesiah, *Bandung* (n 50).

CHAPTER 4

HUMAN RIGHTS IDEAS, LAW, AND INSTITUTIONS IN EUROPE

BAŞAK ÇALI

1. Introduction

Europe, as a political, geographical, and institutional construction, has played, and continues to play, innovative, multi-faceted, but also contradictory roles in the making of human rights ideas, law, and institutions in international law. Europe is the birthplace of the idea of natural rights, which are often seen one of the precursors to universal human rights ideas.[1] Europe is also the birthplace of citizenship rights, embedded in the historically constructed territorial and liberal democratic constitutional traditions of Western European states.[2] Europe has also contributed to canons of human rights critique, most notably developed by the Marxist critique of rights as bourgeois constructs. European States were supporters of the Universal Declaration of Human Rights of 1948. At the same time, European colonial practices have constituted some of the most significant assaults on the universality of human rights.[3] Institutionally, there is more than one Europe, mostly notably the Europe of the European Union (EU) and that of the Council of Europe (CoE). There are also two supranational courts that address questions of human rights law in Europe, namely the European Court of Human Rights (ECtHR) and the Court of Justice of the European Union (CJEU). The geographical boundaries of the human rights-based community of Europe are ever in the making. With the expulsion of the Russian Federation from the Council of Europe in 2022 following its invasion of Ukraine, the Council of Europe now stops at the Ural Mountains, but expands well beyond the Bosporus to the Caspian Sea.

Against this background of Europe's multi-faceted contributions to the ideas and legalization of human rights in international law, this chapter in a spirit of 'provincialising Europe'[4] argues that Europe's contributions to human rights ideas and institutions in international law is both ambivalent and dynamic. Europeans are at once long-time supporters of the universal language of human rights, and proponents of human rights double standards. The latter is best exemplified in Europe's inability to address the harms of its colonial histories[5] and its lax use of human rights to justify unaccountable armed interventions throughout history.[6] Europe's support for human rights also goes hand in hand with human rights minimalism. Europe's post-World War II ambivalence towards the recognition of economic and social rights, the rights of minorities, and migrants,[7] as universal, legally binding and justiciable standards and its resistance towards strong human rights review in the field of civil and political rights,[8] as pioneered by the margin of appreciation and subsidiarity doctrines in international human rights law, are hallmarks of Europe's human rights minimalism.[9]

Human rights ideas in Europe, however, are not static. Like in other regions of the world, they have seen dynamic evolution over time.[10] Human rights ideas in Europe are also influenced by human rights ideas stemming from other regions of the world, and from developments at the level of the United Nations (UN). This can be seen, for example, in the recent integration of the rights of indigenous peoples in EU trade agreements.[11] At certain points, Europe has also acted as a vanguard for human rights ideas and institutions. For example, the emphasis placed on human rights as the 'foundation of justice and peace in the world' (despite Europe's long history of external interventionism) and 'effective political democracy' and 'common understanding' of human rights' as the most effective ways to maintain respect for human rights, as upheld in the preamble of the European Convention on Human Rights (ECHR), have become defining features of international protection of human rights globally. Europe established the world's first regional human rights court. In turn, the ECtHR has advanced pioneering interpretations of human rights law through its application of its living instrument doctrine. For example, the *Soering* judgment of the ECtHR in 1989 was the first decision delivered by an international court on the prohibition of *non-refoulement* beyond the refugee law context under international law.[12]

The ambivalence of Europe's contributions to human rights extends not only to its engagement with human rights from a historical perspective but also to its present. Whilst the ECtHR has been a vanguard of *non-refoulement* since the late 1980s, for example, the other prominent European institution, the EU, has provided a platform for the externalization of migration controls since the 1980s.[13] The EU's accession agreement to the ECHR, concluded in 2013 to create a coherent framework of human rights protection throughout Europe, was unable to address the risk of schism between the EU and Council of Europe's human rights projection regimes. This agreement was found to be incompatible with the autonomy of EU Law by the CJEU in 2014[14] and EU accession negotiations remain ongoing.[15]

In order to unpack the ambivalence of European approaches to human rights in international law, this chapter will first examine natural rights and rights of citizens as twin, but also potentially conflicting, developments in demarcating Europe's contributions to human rights. It will also underline that Europe is historically a home of human rights ideas as well as strong critiques and double standards in the use of these ideas. The chapter will then examine European contributions to the legalization of human rights and will address the ECHR and the ECtHR as critical junctures in Europe's contribution to the legalization of human rights. The differences between the Universal Declaration on Human Rights (UDHR) and the ECHR will also be explored. The chapter will then review the contributions from Europe to the institutionalization of human rights, focusing on the role of the ECtHR alongside those that came much later, particularly the CJEU and the Charter of Fundamental Rights of the European Union (CFEU). Finally, the chapter will consider contemporary debates on human rights in Europe. Needless to say, this chapter takes a broad-strokes approach to the development of ideas, law, and institutions of human rights in Europe. In so doing, it relies on the work of historians, legal scholars, and political theorists who study human rights in Europe and beyond.

2. Europe: Natural Rights and Rights of Citizens

Historians attribute the rise of the linguistic usage of the term 'human rights' to Europe,[16] although the first embrace of the universality of human rights is often traced to the Haitian Revolution of 1791 and its abolishment of slavery and outlawing of colonization of others.[17] Whether that is in the works of academics in the latter half of the 19th century or speeches at the League of Nations, the first utterances of human rights by European powers are vague and do not help us discern, in meaningful ways, what is meant by them. It is clear, however, that prior to the Charter of the United Nations the language of human rights has often been mobilized with reference to universalist general maxims as natural laws that no nation is allowed to violate. This points to strong affinities between human rights and natural law ideas as statements with strong moral appeal, either with reference to Christian traditions or the laws of natural reason.[18]

References to natural law infused human rights ideas by European powers, however, foremost operated as enablers of violence by Europe outside of Europe. The brutality of colonial empires held that despotic governance would improve the capacities of government in non-European lands.[19] At the boundaries of Europe, the ideas around human rights were employed to frequently intervene in the Ottoman Empire for its failings in the treatment of Christian minorities.[20] Whilst the protection of Christian religious minorities as reciprocal obligations in Europe has antecedents going back to the Peace of Westphalia,[21] Europe's focus on human rights in the Ottoman Empire lacked this reciprocity. In particular, it did not include concern for the treatment of Muslim, Jewish or other religious populations in European territories.

Most commentators analyse this violent use of human rights by European powers as flowing from the 'civilizational standard', understood as the right of Europe to colonize and control non-European countries on grounds of its superior qualities.[22] The civilizational standard enabled the use of human rights language to deny equal status to individuals and groups living outside of Europe. This frame further extended to the 20th-century legal texts as manifested in the 'colonial clause' of the ECHR (Article 56).[23] This clause was territorial, allowing for the extension of the application of the ECHR only by way of a formal declaration. Yet, in the absence of such extension, non-European peoples as well as European citizens living in the colonies were deprived of ECHR protection.

The concept of individual rights in modern European constitutionalism, on the other hand, has the rights of citizens, that is, members of European political communities, at its heart. Constitutional rights across Europe share commonalities and diversity, informed by national political and cultural contingencies. The French Declaration of the Rights of Man and of the Citizen in 1789, for example, is well known for its appeal to natural rights. This, however, was received as 'Gallic light-headedness' in England and Germany[24] at the time and spearheaded two famous and longstanding critiques of approaching constitutional rights of citizens as natural rights. Of these, Bentham's well-known critique focused on the act of declaring the rights of man, and held that to say that there exists a set of rights independent of legal enactment and enforcement was nonsense: '... natural and imprescriptible rights, rhetorical nonsense—nonsense upon stilts'.[25] The universal and abstract language employed in the French Declaration was also subject to critique. Burke, for example, insisted that the idea of general rights of man has no meaning, as rights are borne out of particular histories, cultures, and traditions.[26] Real rights of man were wedded closely to a national tradition, which could not have rights rising above that tradition. This historicist insight about the birth and entrenchment of rights was also present in the work of Marx between the 1840s and 1860s. For Marx, however, the problem was not only that rights were historical constructs, but also that the rights found in Europe were ideological constructs that favoured the bourgeoisie class (and their right to property and their religion and political participation) over the concerns of the working class and the true emancipation of human beings.[27] For Marx, rights that were developed in the mirror image of the needs of the bourgeoisie classes were not real rights, but instead a cloaking device for the continuation of the oppression of the working classes.[28]

These foundational critiques of the 'rights of man' by European intellectuals in the eighteenth and nineteenth centuries, underlying the role of power, history, and tradition in the construction of who has what rights, had long lasting effects not only in Europe, but also globally, and acted as precursors to the critiques of modern human rights by feminist, post-colonial, and critical legal scholars.[29] Europe has, therefore, produced two central ideas about human rights: human rights as universal moral ideas and rights of citizens as grounded in history, nation, and tradition, capitalist modes of production, and patriarchal structures. Significantly, the rebellious flair of natural rights doctrines was employed internationally to justify colonial practices and interventions, but not equal rights of non-Europeans. Rights for Europeans have, however, emerged as historically earned rights through long standing political struggles.

Prior to World War II, Europe both exported European rights struggles on to the international law plane and delayed recognition of basic human rights internationally.

For example, the International Labour Organisation (ILO) was created in 1919 as a part of the Versailles Peace Treaty ending World War I. The ILO grew out of 19th-century labour and social movements in Europe, which culminated in widespread demands for social rights and justice.[30] The bilateral minority treaties following World War I aimed to address the specific 'left over populations' of Europe falling on the wrong side of the newly drawn borders after the collapse of the Habsburg and Ottoman Empires. These bilateral minority rights treaties had universal aspirations in terms of the rights assigned by them (ie freedom from discrimination, freedom of religion and the right to education), but were historically grounded in a logic of reciprocity as new States in Europe promised each other to protect the minorities present within the other States.[31] Despite the Europe-wide agreement regarding the immorality of slavery, European States' abolition of slavery was gradual, initially starting with the abolition of the slave trade and later the abolition of slavery itself in the 19th century, culminating in a global ban only in 1926 with the Slavery Convention. Significantly, when the Declaration of the Rights of Man and of the Citizen was promulgated in Paris in 1789, the French bourgeoisie had substantially benefitted from slavery: in the words of C L R James, 'the slave trade and slavery were the economic basis of the French Revolution'.[32]

3. Europe and the Universality of Human Rights in the Post-World War II Period

The adoption of the UDHR and the European States' support for the Declaration may at first sight suggest a victory for the supporters of the natural rights tradition in Europe. It may further suggest that the Western European powers' support for the UDHR had broken the schism between universal human rights and rights of European citizens. After all, the UDHR assigns rights to human beings by virtue of their humanity and it offers an extensive list of rights: civil, social, political, and economic rights. The UDHR also has a decidedly universalistic language, emphasizing that 'everyone' enjoys these rights regardless of nationality, sex, or other social status and promises an international legal order to realize these rights based on a common understanding of what these rights are.

Despite the strong European support for the UDHR as well as the important influence that European jurists had in its drafting,[33] three significant developments, during and after the adoption of the UDHR, point to the fact that the European contributions to the UDHR did not fully resolve the schism between universal rights and European views and critique on rights. First, the Western European States emphasized that the UDHR was not a legally binding instrument and that it did not generate legally binding duties on European States. At the time of drafting, European powers had still colonized much of the world, and the emphasis on the UDHR's lack of enforceability was not merely a legal-technical point. Subsequently, the drafting of a legally binding international bill of rights sprawled over seventeen years and in 1966, two separate covenants were adopted instead of a single treaty.[34] Significantly, when the International Covenant on Civil and Political Rights (ICCPR) and the International Covenant on Economic, Social and Cultural Rights (ICESCR) were finally adopted in 1966, an estimated 50,000 Kenyans were killed in the MauMau Rebellion by British troops, and French use of torture in the Algerian War of Independence was well reported.[35] Second, not all of Europe voted for the UDHR, highlighting the divided and contested nature of Europe as a post-war geopolitical space. The USSR, alongside Czechoslovakia, Poland, Byelorussian Soviet Socialist Republic, Ukrainian Soviet Socialist Republic, and Yugoslavia abstained. The recognition of the right to property in the UDHR was a significant point of disagreement for the Soviet States who, alongside Marx, had argued that the right to property cannot be understood as a human freedom, but as a vehicle that curbs freedoms.[36] The USSR also emphasized that human rights were best realized through governments in a classless society, not by holding rights against governments, the latter seen as characteristics of societies with rival classes.[37] Third, developments soon after the acceptance of the UDHR that led to the adoption of the ECHR show that Western European commitment to human rights as legal rights was notably more minimalist than what was included in the UDHR.

The ECHR's most significant convergence with the UDHR is the emphasis placed on human rights as the foundation of peace and justice in the world and that development of a common understanding of human rights is necessary for their realization. However, the ECHR differs from the UDHR in a number of fundamental ways. The first and the most obvious difference is the discrepancy between the rights recognized in the UDHR and those recognized in the ECHR, originally drafted by a small number of States in Western Europe.[38] Significantly, the ECHR does not include economic, social, and cultural rights or a standalone right to non-discrimination. It also makes no reference to the right to nationality or the universal right to seek asylum, both of which are contained within the UDHR.[39] Whilst the 1951 Geneva Convention on the Status of Refugees is often provided as the reason for this exclusion, it is important to note that the scope of the Refugee Convention allowed States to limit the temporal scope to events around the world before 1 January 1951 and the territorial scope to events occurring in Europe before this date.[40] Instead, the ECHR includes a provision that allows States to restrict the activities of aliens.[41] Thus the ECHR's list of human rights reflected a smaller subset of civil and political rights in Europe and not a universal catalogue of rights to which the European States gave their assent in the form of a universal declaration at the UN. The ECHR's nod to the UDHR in its preamble, therefore, has been just this: a nod to universalism, but without a full commitment to enforce the legalization of all the UDHR rights upon Europe.

Second, whilst the UDHR does not make any reference to the choice of political regime to effectively safeguard rights (it recognizes that everyone is entitled to an international order in which the rights are realized under Article 28), the ECHR is very clear on this when it states in its preamble that human rights and fundamental freedoms can best be safeguarded 'by an effective political democracy'. Such references to democracy are repeated in the formulation of the Convention's substantive provisions as well, when it requires that rights restrictions must be 'necessary in a democratic society' for all of the qualified civil and political rights it enlists.[42]

Third, whilst the UDHR nods to the idea of natural rights and the inherent dignity and equality of human begins as the foundational basis for human rights, the ECHR embeds itself in the historical evolution of rights in Europe with its reference to the 'common heritage of political traditions, ideals, freedom and rule of law' in its preamble. The ECHR, therefore, grounds itself on what the constitutional traditions of Europe had already recognized as fundamental rights rather than what a universal understanding of human rights ought to cover progressively. In this respect, in line with the findings of Duranti on the importance of conservative transnational political forces in shaping the drafting of the ECHR,[43] the text itself also has a conservative flair. It reflects the consensus of what had already been recognized as legal rights in national constitutions in Europe.[44] This is coupled with the drafters' intention to frame the Convention as an 'alarm bell':[45] the Convention is there to protect Europe against what was then understood as forms of totalitarianism in Europe, be it in the form of national socialism or communism, and to act as a force for resistance against attempts to undermine the liberal democratic institutions in Europe.

4. Judicialization of Human Rights in Europe: The European Court of Human Rights

Europe's ideas about human rights, however, do not merely end with the drafting history of the ECHR and its differences from the UDHR. A key and, to some, unexpected,[46] but also outstanding contribution of Europe to international human rights was its vision in creating a European Commission for Human Rights, and more importantly a human rights court providing for individual complaints. This invention of external judicial control as a core feature of human rights in Europe has not only shaped the dynamic interpretation of the ECHR by the Court, but also inspired subsequent institutional developments in the Americas and Africa.[47]

The ECtHR was initially an opt-in and part-time court with few cases in its docket. As well documented by Madsen, the Court had a cautious diplomatic start, through which it enabled the number of European States accepting the right to individual petition before the Court to gradually increase.[48] The cases that started to appear before the Court revealed right from the start, however, that the ECtHR was not seen merely as a line of defence against totalitarianism by those bringing complaints: post-colonial grievances,[49] military operations, minority rights,[50] and women's equal rights[51] all started to appear before the Commission and the Court from the 1960s onwards. By the end of the 1970s and into the early 1980s, the Court departed from its cautious approach to the interpretation of the ECHR by establishing its 'autonomous concepts', 'effective rights', and 'living instrument' doctrines in the cases of *Engel and Others v the Netherlands*,[52] *Airey v Ireland*,[53] *Marcx v Belgium*,[54] *Tyrer v UK*,[55] and *Dudgeon v UK*,[56] which expanded the procedural and substantive scope of the rights protected under the ECHR through dynamic and teleological interpretation. It delivered landmark judgments of global significance on *non-refoulement*[57] and the decriminalization of homosexuality[58] in the 1980s. The ECtHR has not, however, fully abandoned caution. It has also held that European States enjoy a margin of appreciation in the protection of the Convention rights, based on the nature of the right and the absence of a European consensus as well as with due regard to the epistemic and democratic qualities of domestic decision makers in a series of cases, starting from the 1970s.[59] This dual recognition of national courts and decision makers as the primary protectors of human rights and the universal aspirations of human rights interpretation continues to this day in the ECtHR's case law.[60]

Starting from the 1990s, the ECtHR has also played an important role in bringing Western and Eastern Europe together under a reunified Europe and expanding the human rights community of Europe to the Russian Federation and the Caucasus. The significant enlargement of the State parties to the Convention increased to forty-seven State parties by the 2000s, opening up access to approximately 800 million individuals. This enlargement went in hand-in-hand with the establishment of the ECtHR as a full-time human rights court with compulsory jurisdiction for all members of the Council of Europe under Protocol 11 to the ECHR, which came into force in 1998.[61] This dual development, that is, the enlargement of the Council of Europe and the coming into force of Protocol 11, in turn led to an ever-growing number of applications to the Court, making it the international court with the highest number of applications and decided cases.[62]

The ECtHR continues to be the only full-time and compulsory human rights court in the international legal system. It has pronounced on a vast array of pressing human rights questions, at times acting as the *avant-garde* of human rights law interpretation globally. However, the ECtHR has operated, and continues to operate, within the structural constraints facilitated by its doctrine of margin of appreciation. The dual emphasis that the Court places on both the importance of practical and effective protection of rights in the context of changing social, moral, and political conditions, on the one hand, and the subsidiary role of its ECHR supervision, on the other, results in a particularly distinct legacy for this institution. This is also a legacy for which the ECtHR is frequently criticized both by those who advocate the primacy of national rights traditions and those who demand that the Court acts as a trustee for the realization of universal human rights in Europe.[63] This debate has been central to the ECHR reforms in the last two decades, culminating in the insertion of margin of appreciation and subsidiarity into the preamble of the ECHR by Protocol 15 of the Convention.[64] Whether the 'European' approach to human rights interpretation should be exported to other regional systems[65] and the UN system[66] has also engendered debates in international human rights law.

5. Other Council of Europe Human Rights Treaties

Human rights law extends well beyond the ECHR under the auspices of the Council of Europe. Individual treaty regimes other than the ECHR both mirror the content and the monitoring structures found in the UN human rights treaty system and other regional systems, and also incorporate stronger features in terms of institutional design and offering more comprehensive content.

Of these treaty regimes, the European Social Charter (ESC), the counterpart of the ECHR in the sphere of economic and social rights, was adopted some ten years later in 1961, and later revised in 1996. It provides what is called a 'ratification system' whereby States have the ability to choose the provisions that they are willing to accept as binding international legal obligations. This regime is, however, distinct from that of entering reservations at the time of ratification as States are required to accept some part of the Charter in full and can only opt out from a limited number of provisions. The European Committee of Social Rights (ECSR) follows a similar monitoring procedure to that of the UN Committee on Economic Social and Cultural Rights. It departs from the right to individually petition before its UN counterpart, however, as it is the only international committee that allows for a collective complaints procedure through which non-governmental organizations (NGOs) are able to directly apply to the ECSR for decisions on possible non-implementation of the ESC in the States which have accepted its provisions and collective complaint procedure.[67] The European Convention for the Prevention of Torture and Inhuman or Degrading Treatment or Punishment (CPT) was adopted in 1987 (coming into force in 1989),[68] five years after the adoption by the UN General Assembly of the Convention against Torture in 1984, which came into force in 1987. The CPT requires that State parties provide unfettered access to all places of detention, within their jurisdiction, to the Committee on the Prevention of Torture, the body responsible for monitoring compliance with the Convention. It further established that the same Committee can carry out scheduled as well as ad hoc visits to State parties. This institutional model has evidently inspired the creation of the Optional Protocol to the Convention Against Torture at the level of United Nations in 2002.[69]

The European Framework Convention for the Protection of National Minorities which entered into force in 1998 is the most comprehensive multilateral treaty devoted to minority rights in the international system. The same can also be said about the 2014 Council of Europe Convention on Preventing and Combating Violence against Women and Domestic Violence ('Istanbul Convention'), the first legally binding treaty of its kind. In the context of the former, however, it must be noted that the Framework Convention only provides protections to national minorities that European member States officially recognize as such. The term 'national minorities' has a narrow scope, in contrast to, for example, the 1992 UN Declaration on the Rights of Persons Belonging to Minorities, which applies both to 'national' and to 'ethnic, religious and linguistic' minorities.

France and Turkey have not ratified this treaty as they oppose assigning specific rights to minorities in their territories.[70] The Istanbul Convention, the most advanced treaty to combat domestic violence globally, on the other hand, has attracted widespread ratifications alongside a backlash in Europe, on the grounds that even though the treaty is focused on combatting domestic violence, it is also actively promoting LGBTI rights at the expense of traditional family and religious values.[71] In March 2021, Turkey unilaterally withdrew from the Istanbul Convention, becoming the first country to ever withdraw from a Council of Europe human rights treaty.[72]

6. The European Union and Human Rights

Whilst the Council of Europe has been the main European institution driving human rights standard-setting and protection in Europe, protection of human rights under the EU within its member States and in its external relations has emerged as a more prominent debate in Europe in the 1990s, and gained pace in the 2000s and 2010s, in particular with the proclamation of the CFEU in 2012.[73] The reasoning behind the EU playing no role at worst and a peripheral role at best in the development of human rights ideas and institutions in international law from the 1950s until the 1990s has attracted some scholarly attention.[74] In a study that systematically analyses the debates about human rights in the treaties that established the EU from the 1950s, de Burca has argued that the absence of the EU, for the most part of its existence, in the development of human rights ideas can best be traced to the disagreements amongst European States about the form and extent of European political integration.[75]As de Burca notes, the cases brought before the EU courts since the 1960s have also viewed the EU not as a promoter of human rights, but rather as an entity that may encroach upon the fundamental rights of citizens in EU member States protected under national constitutions.[76] This is well reflected in a series of cases brought by German citizens and companies before the CJEU from 1959 onwards, challenging EU actions as a threat to their enjoyment of fundamental rights protected under the German Constitution.[77]

The demand for more human rights in the European integration project has, however, found its reflections in the CJEU case law and EU treaties over time. First, the CJEU developed a body of fundamental rights case law, drawing in particular from the constitutional traditions of its member States and international human rights law, in particular the ECHR.[78] Then the treaties of the EU took more of an initiative in human rights development with the Treaty of Maastricht of 1992, where human rights received formal recognition. In the Treaty of Amsterdam of 1997, the 'Copenhagen criteria' for EU accession required any new member States to respect human rights and introduced a 'suspension of rights' mechanism for member States that engage in serious and persistent violations of human rights. For some commentators, the Treaty of the European

Union (TEU) in 2009 was a critical turning point in the EU becoming a central human rights-oriented institution.[79] This is asserted with reference to the recognition of human rights as a foundational value in Article 2 of the TEU, the treaty's recognition of the legally binding character of the CFEU adopted in 2000, and the EU's commitment to accede to the ECHR.[80]

Whilst the presence of human rights in the internal and external relations of the EU has indeed gained pace in the past decade, this increased emphasis is imbued with multiple tensions. As a matter of EU law, the CFEU, on paper, has consolidated and advanced the European list of human rights for the EU member States by protecting much more specific rights than the 1950s text of the ECHR, notably in the field of asylum, rights of the elderly, rights of disabled people, children's rights, discrimination based on sexual orientation, and data protection. The CFEU also locates the EU within the already existing framework of domestic, EU, and international human rights law by requiring that the Charter cannot be interpreted 'as restricting or adversely affecting human rights and fundamental freedoms as recognised, in their respective fields of application, by Union law and international law and by international agreements to which the Union or all the Member States are party, including the European Convention for the Protection of Human Rights and Fundamental Freedoms, and by the Member States' constitutions'.[81] Yet, in a landmark decision by the CJEU concerning the EU's accession to the ECHR (an aim originally stipulated in the Lisbon Treaty of 2009),[82] the CJEU rejected the accession agreement to the ECHR on the grounds that acceding to the ECHR may adversely affect the autonomy of EU law and the way it protects fundamental rights within the framework of the structure and objectives of the EU.[83] The use of the autonomy of EU law as a resistance to the accession to the ECHR has connotations of States resisting international human rights law on grounds that it would undermine their sovereignty by subjecting them to external control. This decision, therefore, has, perhaps inadvertently, brought the CJEU's concern with the autonomy of EU law closer to States such as the US, that resists the ratification of human rights treaties and refrains from ratifying individual complaint procedures to UN human rights treaties on constitutional autonomy grounds.[84] In the case of the EU, the lack of external human rights oversight has important consequences; particularly, but not only, regarding migration and asylum regulations within the EU borders and in extradition requirements from one EU member country to another. This is because of the EU's principle of mutual trust, which defends the presumption of all EU member States complying with EU law and EU fundamental rights.[85] However, challenges against EU member States before the ECtHR, in particular with regard to the EU's Dublin Regulations, have shown that the presumption of compliance with human rights can lead to human rights violations. Applicants before the ECtHR have relied on the absolute prohibition of torture, and inhuman and degrading treatment, showing that their living conditions and treatment in their first country of entry to the EU violated this absolute protection and that EU member States returning them to the first country of asylum breached their positive human rights obligations to protect them from such inhuman treatment.[86] The ECtHR, in a series of cases, has found that European States sending asylum seekers back to their first country of entry into the EU have violated their obligations under the ECtHR.[87]

As a matter of EU external law, the participation of the EU in the global human rights regime as an actor has also been ambivalent. On the one hand, the EU has become a non-State entity signatory to the UN Convention on the Rights of Persons with Disabilities (CRPD). The EU has also started to integrate labour rights and rights of indigenous peoples in its trade agreements with third party States,[88] thus acting as a model for the mainstreaming of human rights concerns in trade agreements.[89] The CJEU, in its Opinion 2/15 concerning the Singapore trade agreement, further compelled the EU to include sustainable development obligations in its trade agreements and declared that the violation of such obligations in trade agreements constitutes substantive breaches for the purpose of Article 60 of the Vienna Convention on the Law of Treaties (VCLT).[90] On the other hand, the EU's role in the UN-led drafting of a treaty in business and human rights has been cautious: the EU position in this field favours self-regulation of EU-based corporations rather than imposition of hard obligations through international treaty law, a position that it shares with the US.[91]

7. Contemporary Human Rights Struggles and the Future of Human Rights in Europe

Europe in the present day continues to be an important site for multiple struggles in the field of human rights and debates ranging from the role of human rights in the context of armed conflicts, struggles for civil and political rights, to the rights of migrants, and to what may be termed as new human rights,[92] such as human rights in the digital sphere, and human rights in the context of the climate crisis.

The rise of populist authoritarianism in many countries in Europe, both within the EU and the Council of Europe, in contemporary times[93] means that European institutions are under significant stress in upholding or developing human rights standards further in the midst of Europe. The Russo-Georgian War of 2008, the Russian annexation of Crimea in 2014, the ongoing conflict between Armenia and Azerbaijan, and the full scale invasion of Ukraine by the Russian Federation in 2022, further show that the ECHR's vision of human rights as the effective vanguard of peace in wider Europe has ultimately failed.

Europe is currently at the centre of the crisis of liberal democratic constitutionalism, which the ECHR was originally established to safeguard.[94] Populist authoritarian regimes in Europe have led to significant backsliding in the rule of law, particularly with the erosion of the independence of national judiciaries.[95] These regimes also target recent gains in Europe, in particular, in the protection of LGBTI rights, as undermining traditional values, often with reference to Christian religion or, in the case of Turkey,

Islam. Populist far right movements and political groups in Western Europe, too, have targeted migrants as a threat to national European identities and to the social and economic rights of European citizens.[96] These bottom-up populist challenges to human rights in Europe, qualifying them as clashing with or undermining national identities, also target European institutions, both the EU and the CoE and their respective judicial organs, as undermining (illiberal) national constitutional identities in the making. More significantly, European institutions are ill-equipped to address efforts to undermine the consensus regarding human rights in Europe. These political, economic, and social developments unfolding across European States undercut both theses discussed in this chapter as the root causes of Europe's ambivalence towards human rights ideas in international law: Europe as the birthplace of a universalist outlook on human rights and Europe as the home of historically hard-won constitutional rights. The new populist and authoritarian political leaders challenge both of these narratives: Both the universalist outlook and the liberal democratic constitutionalist consensus are under threat.

The rights of migrants or those who wish to seek asylum in Europe has become a crucial site for the battle for European ideas about human rights in contemporary times, where both the EU and individual member States have emulated practices of externalization of migration control originally developed by the US and later by Australia.[97] Whilst social movements and NGOs in Europe challenge and seek to hold the EU and European States accountable for their external migration control practices in the Mediterranean Sea and in Europe's land borders,[98] there are also calls for the CJEU to lower the threshold for EU liability where fundamental rights are concerned.[99] Critical scholars underline that the externalization of migrant controls by the EU echo the long standing colonial European reflex of dehumanizing non-Europeans through international legal techniques.[100]

Whilst populist and authoritarian forces undercut and frustrate the contemporary European human rights project, it is also important to underline that the continuing presence of progressive forces in Europe has influenced human rights ideas in international law in other domains. This is best exemplified in the successful human rights and climate litigation cases across Europe. In the Netherlands, in the case of *Urgenda* in 2019 the Dutch courts found that inadequate mitigating measures undertaken by the Dutch government were in violation of the right to life and right to privacy and family life protections under the ECHR.[101] In 2021, the German Constitutional Court too delivered a seminal judgment holding that future generations have the right to enjoy fundamental rights and the State has a duty to mitigate risks that threaten fundamental freedoms.[102] Similar bottom-up litigation employing human rights law to address the climate crisis is underway across Europe.[103]

Finally, in the field of the unfettered digitalization of the economy, society, and politics, and the human rights risks that these developments have introduced, Europe and its institutions have become important sites for new efforts of standard-setting, particularly in respect of the significant empowerment of corporate actors by the digital turn.[104] In response, the EU General Data Protection Regulation (GDPR), offers EU residents new privacy rights such as the right to be forgotten, the right to access to data, the right to data portability, and the right to explanation of automated decision making.[105] The GDPR has also had effects beyond Europe, forcing non-EU companies operating in the EU to comply with European practices on privacy.[106] Europe is also a major site in the shaping of human rights protections against the risks posed by automated decision making and artificial intelligence (AI) in a wide range of fields, including policing, administration of justice, social benefits, surveillance, and migration.[107]

8. Conclusion

This chapter aimed to discuss the role of Europe in the development of human rights ideas, laws, and institutions in international law over time. It has underlined that Europe is a site of multiple visions and multiple critiques of human rights in international law, which has often led to ambivalent contributions by Europe to human rights. The chapter has argued, in particular, that the tensions in Europe's outlook to human rights can be best understood through the tension between its dual advocacy of human rights as universal ideals and human rights as historical hard-won rights through the establishment of European liberal democracies. The chapter has also shown that human rights as a European project and an international globalist project has located, and continues to locate, Europe both as a progressive site and as a constraining site for the development of human rights ideas.

Institutionally, Europe has led to the establishment of one of the most innovative human rights institutions, a full-time, compulsory human rights court in the form of the ECtHR. Yet, the institutional terrain of human rights in Europe is fragmented due to the tensions between the EU and the Council of Europe human rights regimes, supplemented by the resistance of the former to external accountability under the ECHR and the Council of Europe member States' increasing demands for a wider margin of appreciation, respecting domestic rights traditions in the interpretation of the ECHR.

Finally, the chapter has emphasized the new challenges to human rights ideas and institutions in Europe. The act of aggression committed by the Russian Federation against Ukraine has led to the first ever expulsion of a European State from Europe's central human rights protection institution, the Council of Europe, and has significantly challenged the idea of human rights as a vehicle for lasting peace in Europe. As the geopolitical clout of Europe's human rights law shrinks, the rise of populist and authoritarian governments in Europe also presents a risk to the scope and effectiveness of existing human rights protections in Europe, let alone their progressive development. What is clear, however, is that Europe's ambivalent contributions to human rights ideas and institutions as well as the demand for reimagining human rights in Europe will continue, in particular, to address challenges posed by new technologies, migration, the climate crisis, inequality, and new forms of totalitarianism.

NOTES

1. On the classical beginnings of natural rights as rebellious philosophy in ancient Greece and its influence on the Christian natural rights tradition exemplified in the works of Aquinas, see Costas Douzinas, *The End of Human Rights* (Hart Publishing 2000) 23–45 and 56–61. On human rights as natural rights, see Jack Donnelly, 'Human Rights as Natural Rights', 4(3) Human Rights Quarterly 1982, 391.
2. Thomas Marshall, *Citizenship and Social Class* (CUP 1950) and Chris Thornhill, *A Sociology of Constitutions* (CUP 2013).
3. Alice Conklin, 'Colonialism and Human Rights, A Contradiction in Terms? The Case of France and West Africa, 1895–1914', 103(2) The American Historical Review 1998, 419 and Gurminder Bhambra, 'A Decolonial Project for Europe', 60(2) Journal of Common Market Studies 2022, 229.
4. Dipesh Chakrabarty, *Post-Colonial Thought and Historical Difference* (Princeton UP 2008).
5. Gurminder K Bhambra, 'Postcolonial Europe, or, Understanding Europe in Times of the Postcolonial' in Chris Rumford (ed), *Sage Handbook of European Studies* (Sage 2009) 69.
6. Nigel Rodley and Thomas Franck, 'After Bangladesh: The Law of Humanitarian Intervention by Military Force', 67(2) American Journal of International Law 1997, 275 (hereafter Rodley and Franck, 'The Law of Humanitarian Intervention by Military Force').
7. International Convention on the Protection of the Rights of All Migrant Workers and Members of Their Families (opened for signature 18 December 1990, entered into force 1 July 2003) 2220 UNTS 39481 is the least ratified UN human rights treaty in Europe to date with no ratifications from EU member States and three ratifications from Council of Europe member States, namely Albania, Azerbaijan, and Turkey. For ratification status see <https://indicators.ohchr.org>.
8. Janneke Gerards and Eva Brems, *Procedural Review in European Fundamental Rights Cases* (CUP 2017).
9. See, generally, Yutaka Arai-Takahashi, 'The Margin of Appreciation Doctrine: A Theoretical Analysis of Strasbourg's Variable Geometry' in Andreas Follesdal et al (eds), *Constituting Europe* (CUP 2013) 62; Dean Spielmann, 'Allowing the Right Margin the European Court of Human Rights and the National Margin of Appreciation Doctrine: Waiver or Subsidiarity of European Review?' 14 Cambridge Yearbook of European Legal Studies 2012, 381 and Jan Kratochvíl, 'The Inflation of the Margin of Appreciation by the European Court of Human Rights', 29 Netherlands Quarterly of Human Rights 2011, 324.
10. On a comparative assessment of regional human rights ideas, see Alexandra Huneeus and Mikael Rask Madsen, 'Between Universalism and Regional Law and Politics: A Comparative History of the American, European, and African Human Rights Systems', 16 International Journal of Constitutional Law 2018, 136 (hereafter Huneeus and Madsen, 'Between Universalism and Regional Law and Politics').
11. See, eg, EU-MERCOSUR Trade Agreement (signed on 28 June 2019) <https://policy.trade.ec.europa.eu/eu-trade-relationships-country-and-region/countries-and-regions/mercosur/eu-mercosur-agreement_en> accessed 19 December 2022.
12. *Soering v the United Kingdom*, App no 14038/88, 7 July 1989 (hereafter *Soering v the United Kingdom*).
13. Bhupinder Chimni, 'The Geopolitics of Refugee Studies: A View from the South', 11(4) Journal of Refugee Studies 1998, 350, Carla Ferstman, 'Human Rights Due Diligence Policies Applied to Extraterritorial Cooperation to Prevent "Irregular" Migration:

European Union and United Kingdom Support to Libya', 21(3) German Law Journal 2020, 459. See also Başak Çalı et al, 'Migration and the European Convention on Human Rights' in Başak Çalı et al (eds), *Migration and the European Convention on Human Rights* (OUP 2021) 3, 6.

14. *Opinion 2/13 of the Court* [2014] EU:C:2014:2454 (hereafter *Opinion 2/13*).
15. 'EU Accession to the ECHR'<https://www.coe.int/en/web/human-rights-intergovernmental-cooperation/accession-of-the-european-union-to-the-european-convention-on-human-rights> accessed 16 December 2022.
16. Marco Duranti, *The Conservative Human Rights Revolution: European Identity, Transnational Politics, and the Origins of the European Convention* (OUP 2016) 60 and 68 (hereafter Duranti, *The Conservative Human Rights Revolution*).
17. Franklin Knight, 'The Haitian Revolution on the Notion of Human Rights', 5(3) Journal of the Historical Society 2005, 391.
18. Richard Tuck, *Natural Rights Theories: Their Origin and Development* (CUP 2012).
19. Duranti, *The Conservative Human Rights Revolution* (n 16) 24.
20. Rodley and Franck, 'The Law of Humanitarian Intervention by Military Force' (n 6).
21. Jennifer Jackson-Preece, 'Minority Rights in Europe: From Westphalia to Helsinki', 23(1) Review of International Studies 1997, 75 (hereafter Preece, 'Minority Rights in Europe').
22. Barry Buzan, 'The "Standard of Civilisation" as an English School Concept', 42(3) Millennium 2014, 576; Anthony Anghie, 'The Evolution of International Law: Colonial and Postcolonial Realities', 27(5) Third World Quarterly 2006, 739; Mathew Burrows, '"Mission Civilisatrice": French Cultural Policy in the Middle East, 1860–1914', 29(1) The Historical Journal 1986, 109.
23. *Chagos Islanders v the United Kingdom* (dec), App no 35622/04, 11 December 2012.
24. James Harvey Robinson, 'The French Declaration of the Rights of Man, of 1789', 14(4) Political Studies Quarterly 1899, 653. Robinson, however, finds that this criticism was proven wrong as the French Declaration did indeed ultimately inspire many others.
25. Jeremy Bentham, 'Anarchical Fallacies; Being an Examination of the Declaration of Rights Issued during the French Revolution' in Jeremy Waldron (ed), *Nonsense Upon Stilts: Bentham, Burke and Marx on the Rights of Man* (Methuen 1987) 53.
26. Edmond Burke, *Reflections on the Revolution in France* (1790) <https://socialsciences.mcmaster.ca/econ/ugcm/3ll3/burke/revfrance.pdf> accessed 19 December 2022.
27. Karl Marx, 'On the Jewish Question' in David McLellan (ed), *Karl Marx: Selected Writings* (OUP 2000).
28. Justine Lacroix and Jean Yves Pranchere, 'Was Karl Marx Truly Against Human Rights Individual Emancipation and Human Rights Theory?', 62(3) Revue Française du Science Politique 2012, 433.
29. Catharine MacKinnon, 'Feminism, Marxism, Method, and the State: An Agenda for Theory', 7(3) Signs 1982, 515.
30. Leon Jouhaux, *L'Organisation internationale du Travail* (Les éditions de la Sirène 1921).
31. Preece, 'Minority Rights in Europe' (n 21).
32. Cyril Lionel Robert James, *The Black Jakobins* (Penguin 2001 [1938]) 39.
33. Antoine Prost and Jay Winter, *Rene Cassin and Human Rights: From the Great War to the Universal Declaration* (CUP 2011).
34. Antony Woodiwiss, *Human Rights* (Routledge 2005) 103.
35. Fabian Klose, *Human Rights in the Shadow of Colonial Violence: The Wars of Independence in Kenya and Algeria* (Penn Press 2013). The first ever UN human rights treaty was the

International Convention on All Forms of Racial Discrimination (ICERD, opened for signature 21 December 1965, entered into force 4 January 1969) 660 UNTS 9464. ICERD was adopted on 21 December 1965 and came into force on 12 March 1969. European States supported the adoption of the text of ICERD at the UN General Assembly and subsequently ratified it, albeit, some with reservations.

36. Lauri Mälksoo, 'The Controversy over Human Rights, UN Covenants and the Dissolution of the Soviet Union', 61 Japanese Yearbook of International Law 2018, 260.
37. Johannes Morsink, *The Universal Declaration of Human Rights: Origins, Drafting and Intent* (University of Pennsylvania Press 1999) 22.
38. The original members of the Council of Europe were Belgium, Denmark, France, Ireland, Italy, Luxembourg, the Netherlands, Norway, Sweden, and the UK. Shortly after, Greece (1949), Turkey (1950), Germany (1950), Iceland (1950), and Austria (1956) also become members of the Council of Europe.
39. See Articles 14 and 15 UDHR, respectively.
40. Convention Relating to the Status of Refugees (opened for signature 28 July 1951, entered into force 22 April 1954) 189 UNTS 150. Whilst the 1967 Protocol allowed for the lifting of these restrictions; the Convention still requires individuals to be 'outside the country of nationality' under Article 1(A)(2).
41. See Article 16 ECHR.
42. See, Susan Marks, 'The European Convention on Human Rights and Its "Democratic Society"', 66(1) British Yearbook of International Law 1995, 209.
43. Duranti, *The Conservative Human Rights Revolution* (n 16) 215–321.
44. Michael Rask Madsen, 'From Cold War Instrument to Supreme European Court: The European Court of Human Rights at the Crossroads of International and National Law and Politics', 32(1) Law and Social Inquiry 2007, 137, 144 (hereafter Madsen, 'The European Court of Human Rights at the Crossroads').
45. Ed Bates, *The Evolution of the European Convention on Human Rights: From Its Inception to the Creation of a Permanent Court of Human Rights* (OUP 2010) 74. See also Council of Europe, *Collected Edition of the 'Travaux Préparatoires' of the European Convention on Human Rights Vol. 1* (Martinus Nijhoff 1975) 292.
46. Lauterpacht et al, eg, did not see the establishment of international judicial institutions for the protection of human rights as a likely prospect. Hersch Lauterpacht et al, 'The Proposed European Court of Human Rights', 35 Transactions of the Grotius Society 1949, 25.
47. Huneeus and Madsen, 'Between Universalism and Regional Law and Politics' (n 10).
48. Madsen, 'The European Court of Human Rights at the Crossroads' (n 44) 150.
49. *Greece v the United Kingdom and Northern Ireland*, App no 176/56, Report of the European Commission of Human Rights, 2 October 1958 and *Greece v the United Kingdom and Northern Ireland*, App no 299/57, Report of the European Commission of Human Rights, 8 July 1959.
50. *Ireland v the United Kingdom*, App no 5310/7, 18 January 1978.
51. *Case Relating to Certain Aspects of the Laws on the Use of Languages in Education in Belgium, European Commission of Human Rights v Belgium*, App nos 1474/62, 1677/62, 1691/62, 1769/63, 1994/63 and 2126/64, 23 July 1968.
52. *Engel and Others v the Netherlands*, App nos 5100/71, 5101/71, 5102/71, 5354/72 and 5370/72, 8 June 1976.
53. *Airey v Ireland*, App no 14038/88, 9 October 1979.

54. *Marckx v Belgium*, App no 6833/ 74, 13 June 1979.
55. *Tyrer v the United Kingdom*, App no 5856/72, 25 April 1978.
56. *Dudgeon v the United Kingdom*, App no 7525/ 76, 22 October 1981 (hereafter *Dudgeon v the United Kingdom*).
57. *Soering v the United Kingdom* (n 12). It should, however, be noted that the prohibition of *non-refoulement* does not appear in the judgment itself. Instead the Court held that if substantial grounds are shown for believing that the person concerned, if extradited, faces a real risk of being subjected to torture or to inhuman or degrading treatment or punishment in the requesting country, this would amount to a violation of Article 3 ECHR.
58. *Dudgeon v the United Kingdom* (n 56). See also *Norris v Ireland*, App no 10581/83, 26 October 1988.
59. Dean Spielmann, 'Whither the Margin of Appreciation?', 67 Current Legal Problems 2014, 49, 51.
60. Janneke Gerards, *General Principles of the European Convention on Human Rights* (CUP 2019).
61. Protocol 11 to the European Convention for the Protection of Human Rights and Fundamental Freedoms, Restructuring the Control Machinery Established Thereby (opened for signature 11 May 1994, entered into force 1 November 1998) ETS 155.
62. According to the statistics of the Court, the ECtHR has decided on the examination of around 921,200 applications through a judgment or decision, or by being struck out of the list. See European Court of Human Rights, 'ECHR Overview: 1959–2020' <https://www.echr.coe.int/Documents/Overview_19592020_ENG.pdf> accessed 19 December 2022.
63. Eva Brems (ed), *Diversity and European Rights: Rewriting Judgments of the ECHR* (CUP 2012) and Marie Bénédicte Dembour, *When Humans Become Migrants: Study of the European Court of Human Rights with an Inter-American Counterpoint* (OUP 2015).
64. Protocol No. 15 amending the Convention for the Protection of Human Rights and Fundamental Freedoms (opened for signature 24 June 2013, entry into force 1 August 2021) ETS 213. See also Oddný Mjöll Arnardóttir, 'The Brighton Aftermath and the Changing Role of the European Court of Human Rights', 9 Journal of International Dispute Settlement 2018, 223.
65. Jorge Contesse, 'The International Authority of the Inter-American Court of Human Rights: A Critique of the Conventionality Control Doctrine', 22(9) International Journal of Human Rights 2018, 1168.
66. Yuval Shany, 'All Roads Lead to Strasbourg?: Application of the Margin of Appreciation Doctrine by the European Court of Human Rights and the UN Human Rights Committee', 9(2) Journal of International Dispute Settlement 2018, 180.
67. Holy Cullen, 'The Collective Complaints System of the European Social Charter: Interpretative Methods of the European Committee of Social Rights', (9)1 Human Rights Law Review 2009, 61.
68. European Convention for the Prevention of Torture and Inhuman or Degrading Treatment or Punishment (opened for signature 26 November 1987, 1 February 1989) ETS 126.
69. Optional Protocol to the Convention Against Torture and other Cruel, Inhuman and Degrading Treatment or Punishment (opened for signature 18 December 2002, entered into force 22 June 2006) 2375 UNTS 237.
70. Jeremie Gilbert and David Keane, 'Equality versus Fraternity? Rethinking France and Its Minorities', 14(4) Interational Journal of Constitutional Law 2016, 883.

71. Radosveta Vassileva, 'Bulgaria's Constitutional Troubles with the Istanbul Convention' (*VerfBlog*, 2 August 2 2018), <https://verfassungsblog.de/bulgarias-constitutional-troubles-with-the-istanbul-convention/> accessed 19 December 2022 and 'Istanbul Convention: Poland to leave European treaty on violence against women' (*BBC*, 25 July 2020) <https://www.bbc.co.uk/news/world-europe-53538205> accessed 19 December 2022.
72. Başak Çalı and Larry Helfer, 'The Gender of Treaty Withdrawal: Lessons from the Istanbul Convention', (EJIL Talk! November 28 2022), <https://www.ejiltalk.org/the-gender-of-treaty-withdrawal-lessons-from-the-istanbul-convention/> accessed 20 March 2023.
73. Charter of Fundamental Rights of the European Union [2012] OJ C326/391.
74. Gráinne de Burca, 'The Road not Taken: The European Union as a Global Human Rights Actor', 105(4) American Journal of International Law 2011, 649(hereafter Burca, 'The European Union as a Global Human Rights Actor') August Reinisch, *Essentials of EU Law* (CUP 2012) 99–120.
75. de Burca, 'The European Union as a Global Human Rights Actor' (n 73) 652.
76. ibid, 667.
77. ibid. See also *Stork v High Authority* [1959] ECLI:EU:C:1959:4; *Geitling v High Authority* [1960] ECLI:EU:C:1960:36; *Stauder v City of Ulm* [1969] ECLI:EU:C:1969:57; *Internationale Handelsgesellschaft v Einfuhr und Vorratstelle für Getreide und Futtermittel* [1970] ECLI:EU:C:1970:114.
78. Armin von Bogdandy, 'The European Union as a Human Rights Organisation? Human Rights and the Core of the European Union', 37 Common Market Law Review 2000, 1307.
79. Vasiliki Kosta and Bruno de Witte, 'Human Rights Norms in the Court of Justice of the European Union' in Martin Scheinin (ed), *Human Rights Norms in 'Other' International Courts* (CUP 2019) 263 (hereafter Kosta and de Witte, 'Human Rights Norms in the Court of Justice').
80. Dorota Leczykiewicz, 'Effective Judicial Protection of Human Rights after Lisbon', 35(3) European Law Review 2010, 326, 330.
81. Article 53 CFEU.
82. *Opinion 2/13* (n 14).
83. ibid, para 170.
84. Başak Çalı 'Comparing the Support of the EU and the US to International Human Rights Law: Worlds Too Far Apart?', 13(4) International Journal of Constitutional Law 2015, 901. See also Bruno de Witte, 'The European Union in the International System of Human Rights Protection: Solo Singer or Voice in the Choir? in Emanuelle Bribosia and Isabelle Rorive (eds), *Human Rights Tectonics: Global Dynamics of Integration and Fragmentation* (Intersentia 2018) 225.
85. Kosta and de Witte, 'Human Rights Norms in the Court of Justice' (n 78) 279.
86. *MSS v Belgium* [GC], App no 30696/09, 21 January 2011.
87. *Sharifi and Others v Italy*, App no 16643/09, 21 October 2014; *Tarakhel v Switzerland* [GC], App no 29217/12, 4 November 2014; *AS v Switzerland*, App no 39350/13, 30 June 2015.
88. The EU released its *Trade for All* communication in 2015 to restructure its trade policy in a more progressive dimension. As per the EU's *Trade for All* objective, this 'new approach also involves using trade agreements and trade preference programs as levers to promote, around the world, values like sustainable development, human rights, fair and ethical trade and the fight against corruption'. See European Commission, 'Trade for All: Towards a More Responsible Trade and Investment Policy' (2015) <https://trade.ec.europa.eu/doclib/docs/2015/october/tradoc_153846.pdf> accessed 19 December 2022.

89. Sophie Meunier and Nicolaïdis Kalypso, 'The European Union as a Conflicted Trade Power', 13(6) Journal of European Public Policy 2006, 906.
90. *Opinion 2/15 of the Court* [2017] ECLI:EU:C:2017:376.
91. Jersey Letter Černič, 'European Perspectives on the Business and Human Rights Treaty Initiative' in Jersey Letter Cernic and Nicolás Carrillo-Santarelli (eds), *The Future of Business and Human Rights: Theoretical and Practical Considerations for a UN Treaty* (Intersentia 2018) 229–250.
92. Andreas von Arnauld et al, *The Cambridge Handbook of New Human Rights: Recognition, Novelty, Rhetoric* (CUP 2019).
93. Wojciech Sadurski, *Poland's Constitutional Breakdown* (OUP 2019) and Armin von Bogdandy and Pál Sonnevend (eds), *Constitutional Crisis in the European Constitutional Area* (Hart Publishing 2015).
94. Başak Çalı, 'Coping with Crisis: Whiter the Variable Geometry in the Jurisprudence of the European Court of Human Rights', 35 Wiscosin International Law Journal 2018, 237, 250–253.
95. Laurent Pech and Kim Lane Scheppele, 'Illiberalism within: Rule of Law Backsliding in the EU', 19 Cambridge Yearbook of European Legal Studies 2017, 3.
96. It has been argued, eg, that no far right party in Europe has been 'successful without mobilizing grievances over immigration'. See Elisabeth Ivarsflaten 'What Unites Right-Wing Populists in Western Europe? Re-examining Grievance Mobilization Models in Seven Successful Cases', 41 Comparative Political Studies 2003, 3, 3.
97. Daniel Ghezelbash, *Refuge Lost: Asylum Law in an Interdependent World* (CUP 2015).
98. Moritz Baumgärtel, *Demanding Rights Europe's Supranational Courts and the Dilemma of Migrant Vulnerability* (CUP 2019)
99. Melanie Fink, 'The Action for Damages as a Fundamental Rights Remedy: Holding Frontex Liable', 21(3) German Law Journal 2020, 532.
100. Colin Samson, *The Colonialism of Human Rights: Ongoing Hypocrisies of Western Liberalism* (Polity Press 2020).
101. *The State of the Netherlands v Urgenda Foundation*, Judgment of the Supreme Court of the Netherlands, 20 December 2019.
102. *BvR 2656/18 and Others*, Judgment of the German Constitutional Court, 24 March 2021.
103. Jacqueline Peel and Hari Osofsky, 'Litigation as a Climate Regulatory Tool' in Christine Voigt (ed), *International Judicial Practice on the Environment: Questions of Legitimacy* (CUP 2019) 311–336. See also *Verein KlimaSeniorinnen Schweiz v. Swizerland*, App no 53600/20, 9 April 2024.
104. Dimitri Van Den Meerssche, 'Virtual Borders: International Law and the Elusive Inequalities of Algorithmic Association', 33(1) European Journal of International Law 2022, 171.
105. Regulation (EU) 2016/679 of the European Parliament and of the Council on the protection of natural persons with regard to the processing of personal data and on the free movement of such data, and repealing Directive 95/46/EC (General Data Protection Regulation) OJ L 119/1.
106. He Li et al, 'The Impact of GDPR on Global Technology Development', 22(1) Journal of Global Information Technology Management 2019, 1. See also Anu Bradford, *Brussels Effect: How the European Union Rules the World* (OUP 2020).
107. Regulation (EU) 2024/1689 of the European Parliament and of the Council of 13 June 2024 laying down harmonised rules on artificial intelligence and amending Regulations

(EC) No 300/2008, (EU) No 167/2013, (EU) No 168/2013, (EU) 2018/858, (EU) 2018/1139, and (EU) 2019/2144 and Directives 2014/90/EU, (EU) 2016/797 and (EU) 2020/1828 (Artificial Intelligence Act) Text with EEA relevance and Access Now, 'EU takes minimal steps to regulate harmful AI systems, must go further to protect fundamental rights' (21 April 2022) <https://www.accessnow.org/eu-minimal-steps-to-regulate-harmful-ai-systems> accessed 7 June 2022. See also Giovanni De Gregorio, 'The Rise of Digital Constitutionalism in the European Union', 19(1) International Journal of Constitutional Law 2021, 41.

CHAPTER 5

RULE OF LAW IN EUROPE

A Multi-Layered Network

ANNE VAN AAKEN

1. Introduction

Writing a chapter on the rule of law (RoL) at a time when the RoL is backsliding globally—including in inter-state relations—necessarily involves questioning the progress narrative and enquiring into the effectiveness of the RoL guardian institutions built after World War II. And this chapter meanders between normative ideals and a more sobering reality.

The 'invention' of the RoL can be situated in Europe, starting with Ancient Greece and the writings of Aristotle,[1] diffusing to the Roman Empire, being further developed through medieval times in Europe, and being shaped in its current form in the last 150 years (by then not only in Europe).[2] Europe as understood in this handbook (the Council of Europe (CoE) States plus Russia) and especially the European Union (EU) understand themselves as being built on the RoL as mirrored in diverse institutional arrangements. A chapter on the RoL in Europe has to treat several different meanings and layers of the RoL: the RoL within nations and the RoL among nations (international RoL (IRoL)) as well as the influence of international law on national RoL. The EU is an experiment in 'a Community based on the rule of law'.[3] It has developed a distinct understanding of the RoL, called the European Rule of Law (EURoL),[4] taking the idea of peace through law furthest in its institutional arrangements and being thus distinct from the classic IRoL. Domestic RoL, EURoL, and IRoL are interdependent in Europe. Europe—and the EU to a further degree—can nowadays be understood as a multi-layered network of different rules of law.

Next to other ideas fundamental to international law in Europe treated in this handbook, such as human rights and democracy, the RoL is explicative of two things: the reason for striving for a strong international law in Europe and especially the EU, and the RoL being the very object of international law regulation in Europe in order to have a pacifying function. Europe could only arise from the ashes of World War II with this pacifying function of the RoL:[5] 'The majesty of law is to achieve what centuries of blood and iron were not capable of'.[6] The basis of efforts was the IRoL among the nations of Europe which in turn were deemed difficult to uphold without RoL within States. This very interdependence is still relevant today, including in Europe.

Hans Kelsen and others (see Mälksoo, this volume on the role of the European States and lawyers in the history of international law) early on promoted a formula for international peace guaranteed by compulsory adjudication of international disputes as one of the main elements to shift from a 'primitive legal order'[7] to a complete legal-institutional order to pursue a stable and universal peace among nations (on the landscape of courts in Europe, see Ziemele, this volume);[8] a *desideratum* which had escaped European nations for too long. Thus, in Europe, the RoL was strengthened by delegation to international courts with mandatory adjudication (such as the Court of Justice of the European Union (CJEU) or the European Court of Human Rights (ECtHR)). There is compulsory adjudication between member States of the CoE, but inter-state disputes have for long remained an exception although they are now increasingly adjudicated via the ECtHR. More influential has been direct access by individuals to courts having external control over the EU member States as keepers of specific instruments (EU treaties and the European Convention on Human Rights (ECHR)). Those institutions are unique in the international landscape and have played an important part in attempting to uphold the RoL within and between States.

While there has been a turn to the RoL in the last thirty years in academia and practice, lately, the RoL has become more fragile in Europe, violated in letter or spirit, both within States and between States. Although a convergence of understandings of RoL has been taking place, a huge and growing heterogeneity of RoL understandings is found within different European States, creating tensions, despite margins of appreciation. The (core) EU countries on the one hand and countries such as Russia (former CoE member) and Turkey (CoE member) are starkly diverging in RoL measurement.[9] They also differ in their attitudes towards the IRoL, as lately demonstrated by Russia's illegal invasion of Ukraine. The problem also concerns some formerly Communist EU countries, most notably still Hungary and formerly Poland. Clearly, the IRoL within Europe as well as the national RoL is nowadays no longer a matter of course.

This chapter elaborates briefly on the different notions of national RoL—since they are relevant to understanding how far European countries and institutions have gone in fostering the RoL—before turning to the even more contested notion of the IRoL (Section 2). The chapter then turns to the object of the RoL in Europe with a focus on the most important European international organizations, namely the CoE and the EU. It discusses how national RoL and IRoL are institutionalized, protected, and fostered in Europe and how they are conflicting (Section 3). The concluding outlook speculates whether the institutions built to uphold it are sufficient (Section 4).

2. Concepts of the RoL

The evolution of the RoL was linked to the development of modern statehood[10] and involved a high degree of centralization, institutionalization, and hierarchization but initially served mainly to constrain absolute monarchs.[11] There is a consensus that the RoL is not only a value in itself but also that it fosters values which societies aspire to. After a brief presentation on the different notions of the RoL (Section 2.1), I will turn to the IRoL (Section 2.2).

2.1 The idea of the domestic rule of law

The RoL feeds on the idea of the law's independence; it is based on the assumption of autonomy of the law—law guides the institutions of the legal system in a system of governance. It is a contested concept. Commonly, formal (Section 2.1.1), procedural (Section 2.1.2), and substantive (Section 2.1.3) notions of the RoL are distinguished[12] and those can be based on a continuum which cumulatively entails more elements, from formal to substantive.[13] This distinction is vitally important when considering RoL backsliding and the rise of legalistic autocracies[14] in Europe since those rely on the formal version of the RoL.

2.1.1 *Formal notions*

The formal and thinnest version of the concept of the rule of law is 'rule by law', meaning that any government, whenever it acts, does so through law. Still formal but with minimal moral content is the version best known as the eight formal principles of Lon Fuller's 'inner morality of law':[15] generality; publicity; prospectivity; intelligibility; consistency; practicability; stability; and congruence.[16] As promoted by Dicey,[17] Fuller, and Hayek,[18] formal RoL promotes individual autonomy in that people can plan, and thus it has been justified as containing moral aspects. Yet formal legality is also compatible with ruthless regimes or slavery.[19] Some legal philosophers insist[20] that the RoL must be distinguished from democracy, human rights, and social justice as a matter of analytical clarity. They confine the focus of the RoL to formal and procedural aspects of governmental institutions. This has sparked lively debates, especially after the Nazi regime in Germany.[21]

2.1.2 *Procedural notions*

Others stress that a purely formal RoL is insufficient. Waldron proposes several more criteria, which, if not fulfilled, would be deemed to violate the RoL. The focus here is on the existence of the independence of a legally-trained judiciary acting on the basis of evidence in relation to legal norms[22] and fair procedures.[23] This kind of procedural notion has also found its way into the understanding of RoL as advocated by the CoE and the EU.

2.1.3 *Substantive notions*

Still others, including the EU and the CoE, rely on a substantive definition incorporating human rights aspects. The RoL is then regarded as the 'rule of good law', which is normatively just and fair.[24] This is mostly associated with Ronald Dworkin[25] and Lord Bingham when he included in his list of RoL attributes that the law must afford adequate protection of human rights.[26] Here, two major criticisms arise: the limits imposed on democracy by that definition of the RoL, and the power accorded to (international) judges.[27] Yet, in Europe, in the spirit of Kelsen, the power accorded to judges has not been challenged until recently. Rather, judges at all levels—at least when independent—have been considered as the guardians of the Rol and EURoL.

Moreover, the practice of the main European legal families has turned to a substantive notion of the RoL,[28] although subtle differences still exist between the 'rule of law' and related concepts from other legal systems—'état de droit', 'estado de derecho', 'Rechtsstaat', especially concerning the extent of constitutional review.[29] For many European countries, substantive RoL has become a dominant organizational paradigm of modern constitutional law, in spite of some growing divergences.[30] Although commonalities prevail, it is never precisely or exhaustively defined either by national constitutions or by the courts but is dynamically understood. Yet, they all provide similar answers to similar questions, for example, an independent and effective judiciary with the power of judicial review, the subjection of public power to formal and substantive legal constraints with a view to guaranteeing the primacy of the individual and their protection against arbitrary or unlawful use of public power.[31] Indeed, one major factor explaining this convergence in Europe between national understandings of the RoL appears to be membership of the EU and of the CoE[32]—with some outliers to be discussed below.

2.2 International rule of law

Whereas the Hague Peace Conferences of 1899 and 1907 clearly show that the idea of 'Peace through Law' was nascent in Europe (and beyond) at the beginning of the 20th century, some of the major (European) powers, especially Germany, still opposed it.[33] But there was then a general optimism about the role of international law in pacifying relations between States in the Geneva of the League of Nations;[34] an optimism shattered by World War II and lately by the Russian invasion of Ukraine.

Although the Universal Declaration of Human Rights (UDHR) mentions the RoL in its preamble, the UN Charter does not mention 'rule of law' in its text, and indeed it is questionable whether it is inherent in the Charter,[35] albeit one may argue that recitals 2 and 3 of the preamble refer to respect for international obligations and thus reflect at least a formal understanding of the IRoL. But the UN moved quickly after the end of the

Cold War towards acknowledging the importance of the IRoL on the UN level[36] and reaffirmed that 'the rule of law and democracy are interlinked and mutually reinforcing and that they belong to the universal and indivisible core values and principles of the United Nations'.[37]

Thus, during the last three decades, international practitioners[38] and scholarship[39] have increasingly applied the concept of RoL to the international legal order. For Koskenniemi, '[t]he fight for an international Rule of Law is a fight against politics, understood as a matter of furthering subjective desires, passions, prejudices and leading into an international anarchy'.[40] But this is often 'barely more than a hopeful project in the making'[41] and currently it is ever more unclear whether this belief in progress has been justified,[42] even before the Russian invasion of Ukraine.

Furthermore, whether the content of domestic RoL can be transposed to the IRoL is heavily debated;[43] Philip Allot has called it a category mistake.[44] Scholarship and practice still try to identify the components of the IRoL, mirroring the discussion on the national RoL,[45] centring around two questions.[46] First, where to situate the IRoL on the scale between formal to substantive RoL.[47] It is in this spirit of a very thin notion that the International Law Commission made an indirect reference to the IRoL when it formulated Article 14 of its Declaration on Rights and Duties of States in 1949,[48] connecting it to the principle of *pacta sunt servanda*. In addition, the function of publicity of law could be assigned to the international level since most treaties[49] are freely accessible.[50] Other thin notions reduce the IRoL to (1) the government of laws and the absence of discrimination in the application of international law; (2) the supremacy of law, which comprises recognition of the jurisdiction of the International Court of Justice (ICJ); and (3) equality before the law, which implies the necessity of equality in the decision-making process of international organizations.[51]

Others[52] would formulate a more procedural notion of the IRoL: (1) mandatory jurisdiction; (2) rule-based collective security; (3) formal equality in formalized law-making (codification); and (4) institutionalized implementation. This version goes beyond a 'rule by law' system since IRoL would then mean that legality not only prevails but is also enforced in practice by a centralized adjudicative power. Although international courts and tribunals have proliferated,[53] most international tribunals operate on a consent basis.[54] This is considered to be the biggest obstacle to an IRoL.[55] The ongoing development of holding humans personally accountable for especially egregious conduct, starting with the Nuremberg Trials and 'ending' with the Rome Statute establishing the International Criminal Court (ICC),[56] is surely a development towards a thicker IRoL. Furthermore, given the mandatory court or enforcement system in the EU, parts of Europe have gone a long way from the IRoL to a distinct EURoL.

The second issue resolves around whether States or individuals are meant to be the main beneficiaries of the IRoL. The former seems to be the position of Russia and China.[57] If the latter is the case, the idea of the IRoL seeks to restrain the power of States, to guarantee that they comply with international law, and that they act for the benefit of individuals.[58] This distinction has a clear impact on the way sovereignty is being defined: as protective of States' autonomy and prerogatives for States, or as constraining sovereignty by engendering responsibilities for States (see Kalmo, this volume).[59] Former ICJ President Hisashi Owada envisages an IRoL which 'would serve to constrain states from acting in gross violation of the fundamental principles of justice and human rights that should underpin the contemporary international legal order'.[60] This is echoed by Waldron: individuals' 'well-being, not the well-being of sovereign nation states, is the ultimate end of international law'.[61]

Europe has chosen a substantive version of the IRoL protecting individuals as, for example, envisaged by the ECtHR with mandatory jurisdiction. The EU goes a step further with institutionalizing the RoL not only in its member States but also applying it to the EU itself via its primary treaties and the European Charter of Fundamental Rights (CFR)—in stark contrast to the immunity of international organizations. Although the EU is meant to apply the IRoL in its external relations, arguably, even nowadays (and certainly in the period of colonization—see Anghie, this volume) no full realization of it has been achieved.[62] Furthermore, even within Europe starkly divergent views can be found. Russia envisaged its joint 'Declaration of the Russian Federation and the People's Republic of China on the Promotion of International Law'[63] of 2016 as promoting the IRoL and protecting the UN Charter, condemning unilateral sanctions. In contrast, States adhering to a rules-based order of international liberalism view this position as a hypocritical assertion of non-interference in their territorial claims on Ukraine and the South China Sea including Taiwan. Those conflicting views on the IRoL have since grown more acute. Thus, views on the notion of the IRoL diverge in academia as well as in practice, both in Europe and beyond.

3. The (International) Rule of Law in Europe

One focus of European integration has been the RoL, within and between European States, based on the idea that lasting peace and cooperation can only be built between States which adhere to the RoL. This is considered a necessary—although insufficient—condition for a functioning IRoL as well. The IRoL in Europe, that is, the CoE as well as the EU (less so the OSCE, see Mihr, this volume),[64] certainly entails a thick notion, certainly containing human rights, and most importantly, elements of mandatory jurisdiction of international courts open to individuals and thus allowing for external control of States. Both the CoE and the EU foster—and indeed have as a requirement for entry—adherence to national RoL but at the same time build an IRoL within the respective organizations, certainly within the EU. The deep entanglement of national RoL and IRoL within Europe is evidenced by 'decontextualizing' national RoL so as to become either principles of general application in very different national legal systems (the CoE method) or principles that apply in the distinct EU legal system and are 'recontextualized' when and by becoming part of that system's legal tradition (the Community method). But that should not lead to underestimating the potential frictions between the different layers of the RoL. It can create narrative tensions with democracy and potentially with national constitutions (see Rusinova, this volume),[65] domestic democracy being allegedly hijacked by unaccountable international judges.

3.1 Council of Europe

The CoE is founded on the RoL as one of three core principles as stated in the preamble to its statute[66] and a precondition for accession in its Article 3. If a member State seriously violates respect for the RoL, Article 8 of the Statute provides that it may be suspended from its rights of representation and requested by the Committee of Ministers to withdraw. This happened for the first time after Russia's invasion of Ukraine in 2022,[67] a clear violation of the IRoL; Russia thus ceased to be a member after twenty-six years of membership.[68] After the annexation of Crimea by Russia in 2014 only its voting rights were suspended (restored in 2019). Re-affirmation of the importance of the RoL by the CoE is continuous[69] and it is applied to the CoE itself.[70] Although the CoE's understanding of the RoL is defined, it remains open to contestation, not least due to the diversity of legal traditions and languages in Europe.[71] The decay of RoL in some CoE States remains a huge concern to the CoE.[72]

In the context of the RoL, the CoE operates a range of advisory bodies, monitoring mechanisms and benchmarking institutions that have a particular impact on different aspects of the RoL in member States. The focus here will be on two unique institutions: the Venice Commission and the ECtHR.[73]

3.1.1 *European Commission for Democracy through Law*

The Venice Commission is the CoE's advisory body on constitutional matters, trying to advance the RoL. Article 1(2) of the Statute of the Venice Commission[74] establishes that its work will focus on the 'constitutional, legislative and administrative principles and techniques which serve the efficiency of democratic institutions and their strengthening, as well as the principle of the rule of law'. Interestingly, its sixty-two members are not confined to CoE States but are global (such as the US, Brazil, Israel, and Mexico), thus 'spreading the word' of the RoL universally, and this is often described as one of the great successes of the CoE.

The Venice Commission undertook to find a consensus on the notion of RoL in a Report of 2011[75] where it proposed a functional non-exhaustive definition drawing on a substantive definition first proposed by Lord Bingham.[76] The Commission deemed that there is a consensus on the common features of the RoL within the CoE States, comprising the following components: (1) legality, including a transparent, accountable, and democratic process for enacting law; (2) legal certainty; (3) prohibition of arbitrariness; (4) access to justice before independent and impartial courts, including judicial review of administrative acts; (5) respect for human rights; and (6) non-discrimination and equality before the law.[77] Most notably, it left out Bingham's component dealing with effectiveness and compliance.[78] It thus evaded the problem of (systemic) non-compliance with the RoL by its member States. Yet the Commission went on to draft an operational tool for assessing the level of RoL compliance in any given State, which in turn led to elaboration of the RoL Checklist:[79] thus moving the RoL from political idea to practical implementation.

3.1.2 *European Court of Human Rights*

The ECHR plays a major role in upholding the RoL in Europe (see Çalı, this volume). Its preamble famously positions the RoL as an indispensable part of 'the common heritage' of European countries. The ECtHR has come to regard the RoL as a principle inherent in the whole Convention.[80] In its landmark judgment in *Golder*, the Court underlined the relevance of the RoL for interpreting the ECHR.[81] ECtHR case law offers important guidance on the content of the principle, as it has been interpreted and applied under RoL-related provisions such as Articles 6, 7, and 13 of the Convention, stressing the effectiveness of the individual right to effective judicial protection.[82] The reference to the RoL by the Court as inherent in all articles of the Convention lends it a substantive nature, too.[83] But given the margin of appreciation and the Convention being a minimum standard, the RoL is more decontextualized in the CoE than in the EU. Still, delegation of power to an international human rights court with mandatory jurisdiction is a great achievement for the RoL in many CoE countries (see Ziemele, this volume).

The ECHR allows for inter-state complaints, which used to be rare. This has changed as the Court becomes involved following inter-state conflicts. It thus incidentally may have to take a view on the IRoL between countries on issues of territory, for example, as in the Russian-Ukrainian war,[84] and the Armenian-Azerbaijan conflict.[85] This amounts to mandatorily adjudicating on the IRoL between CoE States.

3.2 European Union

All twenty-seven EU member States (see Vasel, this volume for the EU generally) are simultaneously member States of the CoE and in human rights matters, the CFR refers to the ECHR in Article 52(3), thus creating more uniformity in human rights adjudication within the CoE. In addition, the EU operates an elaborate institutional and procedural system on the RoL—indeed, it may be called the most advanced IRoL system on a regional level giving it a distinct character: a EURoL (see d'Argent in this Handbook). RoL acts as one of the fundamental values of the EU, cross-cutting in both EU internal (Article 2 of the Treaty on European Union (TEU)) and external (Article 21 TEU) policies and being more deeply enshrined in the primary treaties after the end of the Cold War.[86] It is unprecedented in building a spider's web of control of the RoL between the EU, its member States, and their courts. The EU has opened up national legal orders beyond the State to a remarkable extent and replaced the classic principle of reciprocity in international law with the principle of hierarchy,[87] including on issues of national RoL. This of itself is not contentious, but what is contentious are the conditions for opening up and who has the last word on this opening. Positively perceived, this amounts to mutual checks on the RoL; negatively viewed, this spider's web shows ripping. Although the RoL and the EURoL have been mutually interdependent in that national RoL understandings have informed the EURoL and vice versa, the diversity of legal traditions has always been a challenge to its unity, even more so after EU enlargement. Currently, this understanding of an RoL spider's web also leads to a paradox—on the one hand, the EU needs to respect the national constitutional traditions of the member States, whereas on the other hand, it has to remain vigilant with regard to abuses of the RoL, both on the national level as well as on the EURoL level.

While member States have to adhere to the principle of primacy of EU law and do so *inter alia* via the preliminary reference procedure of Article 267 TEU, they also set limits to EU law in two ways. First, by having the possibility of controlling adherence of EU institutions to EU law—for instance, the principle of subsidiarity—through the CJEU. Second, via 'national constitutional resistance'[88] defining the conditions under which national legal orders are opened up to EU law, as for example in Germany.[89]

There are thus many levels on which the RoL plays a role in EU law. First, the RoL on the level of the EU itself (EURoL) (Section 3.2.1), second, in securing national RoL vis-à-vis its members (Section 3.3.2), and third, concerning the IRoL, that is, the relationship between the EURoL and the IRoL (Section 3.3.3).

3.2.1 *RoL as a constitutional principle of the EU*

The European Union's institutions consider the RoL the most fundamental value upon which the Union itself is based:

> While there is no hierarchy among Union values, respect for the rule of law is essential for the protection of the other fundamental values on which the Union is founded, such as freedom, democracy, equality and respect for human rights. Respect for the rule of law is intrinsically linked to respect for democracy and for fundamental rights. There can be no democracy and respect for fundamental rights without respect for the rule of law and vice versa.[90]

The RoL is also the foundation of mutual trust between the member States.[91] This is recalled by the preamble and Article 2 TEU as well as the CFR. The Rome Treaty of 1957 did not contain either an explicit reference to the RoL[92] or to human rights, being focused on economic cooperation. But the end of the Cold War shifted understandings of the common values of Europe, including the EU,[93] and since 1992 the RoL has acquired the status of a foundational value in the EU treaties.

Even before the EURoL was codified, the ECJ recognized in 1986 that the European Communities are a 'Community based on the rule of law'.[94] By using this phrase and its translation as '*Rechtsgemeinschaft*'[95] and '*communauté de droit*' respectively, the Court avoided the vexed questions of statehood of the EC/EU, thereby establishing foundational elements of the EURoL, holding that:

> neither its Member States nor its institutions can avoid a review of the question whether the measures adopted by them are in conformity with the basic constitutional charter, the Treaty.... [T]he Treaty established a complete system of legal remedies and procedures designed to permit the Court of Justice to review the legality of measures adopted by the institutions.[96]

The Court thus established complete judicial review:

> to ensure (i) that its institutions (as well as its Member States where relevant) adopt measures in conformity with the fundamental sources of EC law and (ii) that natural and legal persons are able to challenge the legality of any act which affects their EC rights and obligations.[97]

In short: the Court established the principles of legality and effective judicial protection. With the CFR, substantive elements were added to the EURoL in 2009.[98]

EU institutions are not only entitled, but are also obliged to uphold the EURoL;[99] this precept is meant to permeate the EU's entire legal and institutional structure and all its policies and programmes as well as the EU institutions themselves, including EU agencies with administrative tasks. One problem arose in the context of the European Border and Coast Guard Agency (Frontex), securing the EU's external borders and being bound by the CFR. After instances of illegal pushback of migrants and other incidents, and doubts on the mechanisms of effective redress, the EU Ombudsman opened an inquiry challenging the effectiveness, transparency, and practical accessibility of the Frontex complaint mechanism.[100] In addition, measures taken in the debt crisis of the Euro Area have been criticized as not conforming to the EURoL.[101] Furthermore, the jurisdiction of the CJEU on the treaties constraining the EU is controlled by national courts, as witnessed by the German Constitutional Court's judgment[102] scrutinizing (for better or worse) the acts of the European Central Bank (ECB) as well as the CJEU judgment on the matter. Clearly, a check on the EURoL is exercised by the ECJ but also national courts, with the caveat that the latter may go too far in safeguarding their own and divergent understandings of sovereignty.

3.2.2 *Securing the rule of law in EU member States*

Currently, the most acute danger is RoL backsliding in some member States. To understand the relevance for the EU legal order of the RoL in the member States and why this is a preeminent concern of the EU, basic principles need to be explained in order to understand the spider's web of RoL questions in the EU. First, on the institutional plane, EU law in the member States is implemented by existing national institutions. All the national institutions, be it the executive, the courts, or even the legislator, become *de facto* EU institutions *when acting within the scope of EU law*; they are servants of two masters: the member States and the EU. It is a model of cooperative federalism.[103] Second, EU law has direct effect on member States,[104] in contrast to classic international law, meaning that an EU provision becomes an immediate source of law for the national court or administrator. National courts therefore act as 'EU courts' in the sense that they have to apply EU law and all national bodies have the duty to interpret, as far as possible, all national law in light of and in conformity with EU law, leading to convergence and unity in EU law.[105] Third, EU law enjoys primacy, that is, in the view of the ECJ, *all* EU law prevails over *all* national law.[106] Given those principles and the idea of a community of law, it matters to the EU what happens to the RoL in its member States. Thus, Article 19 TEU, which gives concrete expression to the value of the RoL as stated in Article 2 TEU, requires the member States to provide effective judicial protection in fields covered by Union law.

Although—as compared to the CoE—the EU has no official definition of the RoL, there are now official documents defining how Article 2 TEU has to be understood:

> The rule of law requires that all public powers act within the constraints set out by law, in accordance with the values of democracy and the respect for fundamental rights as stipulated in the Charter of Fundamental Rights of the European Union (the 'Charter') and other applicable instruments, and under the control of independent and impartial courts. It requires, in particular, that the principles of legality, implying a transparent, accountable democratic and pluralistic law-making process; legal certainty; prohibition of arbitrariness of the executive powers; effective judicial protection, including access to justice, by independent and impartial courts; and separation of powers, be respected.[107]

Under Article 49 TEU, respect for the RoL is a precondition for EU membership and heavily monitored in any accession process; indeed, all new member States are screened for it.[108] But that screening mechanism clearly cannot deter backsliding. Given the current problems, in 2014, the EU Commission communicated 'A new EU Framework to strengthen the rule of law',[109] followed by others,[110] including an EU Justice Scoreboard,[111] quantifying RoL realizations and relying on measurement. The goal of the European Rule of Law Mechanism is to promote the rule of law and institute a dialogue between all stakeholders. All those mechanisms testify to the ongoing reflection to answer systemic national RoL crises[112] that have hit several EU member States, most prominently Poland[113] and Hungary.[114]

For a long time, Article 2 TEU seemed rather a mere proclamation of values with only limited direct legal implications and it was argued that a violation of Article 2 TEU cannot in itself be a ground for judicial action.[115] But the EU has several mechanisms at its disposal to enforce the RoL in the member States. In that respect, a distinction can be drawn between EU norms—which are in principle subject to full judicial scrutiny—and EU values, which are subject to political supervision. The latter follows from the procedure under Article 7 TEU, consisting of a preventive arm (Article 7(1) determining a clear risk of breach) and a corrective arm (Article 7(2) determining a serious and persistent breach). Article 7(2) TEU's scope of application is broad and is not limited to member States' actions when implementing EU law, but also covers breaches in areas where they act autonomously. Article 7(2) also provides for sanctions in Article 7(3) TEU: a serious and persistent breach by a member State of the values referred to in Article 2 TEU, might lead to sanctioning the member State concerned and even suspending it from voting at the Council level. However, Article 7(2) and (3) TEU has never been activated in practice due to political obstacles, namely the fact that any member State may veto determination of a breach. This has become a major problem for the EU. In 2023, Poland and Hungary were still subject to Article 7 proceedings before the Council[116] in order to determine the existence of a clear risk of a serious breach by the Polish authorities of the RoL (referred to the Council by the Commission in 2017[117]) and a clear risk of a serious breach by the Hungarian authorities of many of the EU's foundational values (referred to the Council by the Parliament in 2018[118]). But this political process has hitherto not worked: the two countries reassured each other that they would veto a case under Article 7(2) TEU. Whereas Poland tries to restore its national RoL, not an easy task, it remains to be seen whether this mechanism can be effectuated, given the political situation in some EU member states.

Given the institutional design mistake of Article 7(2) TEU, the EU is now attempting to protect the RoL in member States via their budgetary interests, arguing that a deficient RoL endangers those interests and thus EU money should be paid out conditionally on adherence to the RoL.[119] After Hungary and Poland threatened the Budget vote (endangering financial flows to States in times of pandemic), the European Council[120] deferred implementation and asked the EU Commission to draft guidelines on the mechanism subject to review by the ECJ. This has been heavily criticized as delaying enforcement of the Regulation and thus not only being ineffective but also breaking the EURoL for assigning to the Commission legislative competences which belong to the European Parliament and Council.[121] The Parliament and the Council finally approved the new Regulation in December 2020.[122] The legality of the new piece of legislation was challenged in an action for annulment brought by Hungary and Poland but this action was rejected in its entirety by the ECJ.[123] This new budgetary instrument marks an important step in strengthening the Union's toolbox to fight cases of rule-of-law or constitutional backsliding—but its success is not guaranteed.

Yet, despite the political failure to guarantee the RoL in member States, judicial pronouncements on the state of the RoL in member States—a further tool in the RoL toolbox—have been critical in the EU's reaction to RoL backsliding. The ECJ has used Article 2 TEU, in conjunction with Article 19(1) TEU, to ensure respect for the RoL. Starting with the *Portuguese Judges* decision,[124] the ECJ has strongly protected judicial independence and the non-removability of judges, and has continued this in the cases of RoL backsliding by Hungary and Poland.[125] The Court has hitherto used 'the entire procedural toolbox'[126] to defend the RoL, and especially judicial independence, to limited avail. In case C-791/19 of 15 July 2021, the CJEU found that the disciplinary regime for judges in Poland is not compatible with EU law, but one day earlier Poland's Constitutional Court held that the ECJ's previous instruction to halt judicial disciplinary measures was not binding on Poland because it violated Poland's Constitution and national law can take precedence over EU law.[127] This obviously shatters the construct of a community based on law. Furthermore, on 27 October 2021 the ECJ ruled that Poland must pay daily fines of €1 million over its controversial judicial reforms[128] —fines which Poland has not paid. In consequence, the Commission withheld funds from Poland and has only released some funds after Polish adjustments to its laws. As to Hungary, a majority of the European Parliament has published an open letter to withhold funds under the Recovery and Resilience Plan ('Covid' funds)[129] due to its multiple infringements of EU values.

Use of infringement actions under Article 258 of the Treaty on the Functioning of the European Union (TFEU), requests for a preliminary reference under Article 267 TFEU, and use of interim measures under Article 279 TFEU are further significant developments.[130] Thus, the Court cannot be accused of not being inventive in order to protect the RoL, not only institutionally concerning Article 19 TEU but also substantively. ECJ decisions are seconded by those of ECtHR rulings on judicial independence indirectly through Article 6 ECHR on the right to a fair trial[131]—judicial resistance against RoL backsliding is thus a joint endeavour by the EU and the CoE.

Whether the EU's attempt to transcend sovereignty and traditional power politics by establishing a transnational RoL continues and how the institutional structure of the EU is able to deal with RoL backsliding in its own community of law remains an open question. Clearly, institutional tools have not worked, and whether the interaction of the CJEU and withholding of funds (RoL conditionality) can change member States' RoL backsliding is also an open question.[132] Surely, '(i)f it ceases to be a union of Rule-of-Law-abiding democracies, the EU is unthinkable'.[133]

3.2.3 *European RoL and international rule of law*

The relationship between the EURoL and the IRoL involves many facets. In the area of Common Foreign and Security Policy (CFSP), the RoL is set as an essential foreign policy objective. Article 21(1), (2)(b) TEU assigns to the EU's foreign and security policy, its neighbourhood policy,[134] and development cooperation[135] the same objective of developing and consolidating the RoL and respect for fundamental rights as in its internal policies in order to strengthen the international order and the security of EU citizens.[136] This objective thus possesses a universalizing function and is additionally intended as a pacifying means. It has continuously been stressed in various contexts by EU actors,[137] but has also been criticized for the discrepancy between the EU's declared objectives and its concrete actions on the ground, including promoting its own interest at the expense of its partners' particularities.[138] EU foreign policy is surely also guided by realism (see Shany and Varaki, this volume).

The limited jurisdiction of the EU judicature in the area of the CFSP is one of the specific features of EU law, owing to historical reasons.[139] The ECJ has interpreted this exception to its jurisdiction narrowly, arguing, as in *Les Verts*,[140] that the EU treaties offer a complete system of legal remedies and procedures, unleashing a debate as to whether the ECJ has stretched the boundaries of its jurisdiction.[141] By referring to Article 47 CFR (the right to an effective remedy and a fair trial), the Court has emphasized that 'the very existence of effective judicial review designed to ensure compliance with provisions of EU law is of the essence of the rule of law'.[142] Thus, the Court is competent to monitor compliance with Article 40 TEU and to review the legality of decisions providing for restrictive measures against natural or legal persons adopted on the basis of the CFSP provisions in the TEU.

The EU is also an important player in promoting the IRoL, and even considers the IRoL to be under threat. There was thus a French-German initiative on multilateralism, including other countries as well.[143] In 2019, the Foreign Affairs Council adopted Council Conclusions on EU action to strengthen rules-based multilateralism,[144] formulating three strands for action: upholding international norms and agreements, extending multilateralism to new global realities, and reforming multilateral organizations, making them fit for purpose. This has become more urgent with the invasion of Ukraine, bringing a war of aggression back to Europe.

Yet the relation between the EURoL and the IRoL is also not free of tensions. Adherence of the EU to international law was critically questioned in the notorious *Kadi* case.[145] At the end of the day, the ECJ had to remind the Security Council that targeted sanctions against individuals without any fair trial standards contradict fundamental RoL standards.[146] In doing so, the Court created a tension between the IRoL and the EURoL by declaring EU law 'an autonomous legal system which is not to be prejudiced by an international agreement'.[147] The Court somehow emulated the German Federal Constitutional Court with its *Solange* decisions (the FCC still sees EU law as an integral part of German law):[148] opening up to the IRoL but under the condition that it does not endanger the fundamental values on which the EU is based—a decision the ECJ is to make.

The Court also closed the EU legal system to decisions of international investment tribunals—the current way of adjudicating international investment law. In *Achmea*,[149] the Court made clear that it was key that the Union's judicial system remained in full control over the potential interpretation and application of EU law. Given that investment tribunals could interpret or apply EU law under certain formulations of applicable-law clauses in investment treaties, but are not part of the Union's judicial system and thus cannot exploit the preliminary reference procedure, the Court saw the EURoL endangered since it would have lost its role as final arbiter of EU law. In contrast, the EU still tries to uphold multilateralism in the international trading system as witnessed by its initiative on the Multi-Party Interim Appeal arrangement in the World Trade Organization (WTO) to at least temporarily replace the dysfunctional Appellate Body.

4. Outlook

The narrative of Europe's continuous progress towards national RoL, EURoL, and IRoL is evidenced in the institutions having been built in Europe, driven by the idea of the pacifying function of the RoL. According to that narrative, States have been making steady, inexorable progress towards ever more precise, binding, and legally codified international obligations, as well as towards delegating enforcement of those commitments to international and European organizations and courts while protecting individuals. Europe goes further than in other parts of the globe. It is safe to say that a substantive understanding of the RoL holds a central place in European institutions such as the CoE and the EU and their laws, as well as in most member States. Yet this development has been infected with doubts and double standards. And although the IRoL and EuRoL have contributed to convergence in the understanding of the RoL in the different member States, that does not protect against remaining divergence in reality, be it within those institutions or within the member States of the EU and the CoE. And belief in effective IRoL has been shattered by the invasion of Ukraine.

The mandatory courts of Europe have been the guardians of the RoL of their respective constitutional instruments in Europe—on all levels. And this proves Kelsen right—mandatory courts are crucial in terms of upholding not only peace but also the RoL itself. Yet this may be insufficient: the development is open-ended and courts can go only so far. And those courts cover only Europe and thus only regionally substitute for an IRoL. If the narrative of trade-offs between national democracy and domestic RoL, on the one hand, and, on the other, the IRoL or the EURoL become stronger, courts will not be able to stop this development altogether—civil society needs to stand up for the (I/EU)RoL.[150] There is evidence of strong and widespread support for the RoL in every single EU member State, thus representing a solid foundation for the RoL in Europe.[151] Although European political organs are well aware of the additional threats that the Covid-19 pandemic, security concerns, and geopolitical constellations have caused to the (I/EU)RoL, it remains unclear at the time of writing how those threats will play out in the long run. Whether Europe will remain not only the origin but also a standard bearer of the (I/EU)RoL thus remains an open question. Although it is too early to call the RoL an endangered species in Europe, high-alert vigilance and active promotion of the precious and fragile RoL on all levels by citizens and politicians is clearly needed. The original intuition after two World Wars still holds—that is, without the RoL, peace becomes contingent. 'The rule of law is a construct. It was made by people—and is nurtured and preserved by people. It can also be destroyed by people. And unlike the law of gravity, which works everywhere and all the time ... the rule of law is precious and fragile.'[152]

Notes

1. Aristotle, *Politics*, book 3, part XVI, trans B Jowett (Kessinger Publishing 2004): 'And the rule of the law, it is argued, is preferable to that of any individual ... The law is reason unaffected by desire.'
2. Jeremy Waldron, 'The Rule of Law' in Edward N Zalta (ed), *The Stanford Encyclopedia of Philosophy* (2020); Brian Z Tamanaha, *On the Rule of Law: History, Politics, Theory* (CUP 2004) chs 1 and 2 as well as Paul Craig, 'Formal and Substantive Conceptions of the Rule of Law: An Analytical Framework', Public Law 1997, 467. Very convincing now is a definition of the RoL in terms of goals and practices, viewing it as a principle, not a rule. Gregory Shaffer and Wayne Sandholtz, 'The Rule of Law under Challenge: The Enmeshment of National and International Trends' in Gregory Shaffer and Wayne Sandholtz (eds), *The*

Rule of Law under Pressure: A Transnational Challenge (CUP, forthcoming) <https://papers.ssrn.com/sol3/papers.cfm?abstract_id=4617888>.

3. Case 294/83 *Les Verts v Parliament* [1986] ECR 1339, [23]: 'the European Economic Community is a Community based on the rule of law.'
4. Dimitry Kochenov, 'The EU Rule of Law: Cutting Paths through Confusion', 2 Erasmus Law Review 2009, 5, 7.
5. This chapter follows the distinction endorsed by the United Nations (UN) since 2006 between RoL at the national and international level; see UN General Assembly and Security Council, 'Uniting our strengths: enhancing United Nations support for the rule of law', Report of the Secretary-General, a/61/636 and s/2006/980, 14 December 2006 and UNGA, Declaration of the High-level Meeting of the General Assembly on the Rule of Law at the National and International Levels, A/67/L.1, 2012.
6. Walter Hallstein, *Die Europäische Gemeinschaft* (5th edn, Econ Verlag 1979) 53 (own translation).
7. Herbert L A Hart, *The Concept of Law* (3rd edn, OUP 2012) 91–93.
8. Hans Kelsen, *Peace Through Law* (University of North Carolina Press 1944). For Germany's (and other States') reluctant position on compulsory arbitration at the Hague Peace Conference of 1907, see Eugene Fischer, 'Germany at The Hague Peace Conferences', 86(6) Advocate of Peace through Justice 1924, 360–365.
9. Russia is situated in 107th place out of 140 countries worldwide and the constraints of governmental power remain especially poor; Turkey ranked 116th; World Justice Project, *The World Justice Project Rule of Law Index 2022* (World Justice Project 2022) 11.
10. Laura Grenfell, *Promoting the Rule of Law in Post-Conflict States* (CUP 2013) 4.
11. Tamanaha (n 2) 115 et seq.
12. Waldron, 'The Rule of Law' (n 2).
13. Tamanaha (n 2) 91.
14. Kim Lane Scheppele, 'Autocratic Legalism', 85 University of Chicago Law Review 2018, 545.
15. Lon L Fuller, *The Morality of Law* (2nd rev edn, Yale UP 1969).
16. Similarly, John Finnis, *Natural Law and Natural Rights* (Clarendon Press 1980) 270; John Rawls, *A Theory of Justice* (OUP 1971) 236–239.
17. A Venn Dicey, *An Introduction to the Study of the Law of the Constitution* (5th edn, MacMillan 1897) 179, 185, 187. This RoL entails the traditional principles of legality and equality before the law.
18. Friedrich August von Hayek, *The Road to Serfdom* (Routledge 1944) 54.
19. Joseph Raz, *The Authority of Law* (OUP 1979) 214–219 et seq.
20. ibid, 211 et seq.
21. Herbert L A Hart, 'Positivism and the Separation of Law and Morals', 71 Harvard Law Review 1958, 593, answering Gustav Radbruch who, after having lived through the Third Reich, advocated a substantive RoL.
22. Hans Kelsen saw the independence of courts as an element of law, cf for international courts, Jochen von Bernstorff, 'Hans Kelsen on Judicial Law-Making by International Courts and Tribunals: A Theory of Global Judicial Imperialism?', 14 The Law & Practice of International Courts and Tribunals 2015, 35.
23. Jeremy Waldron, 'The Rule of Law and the Importance of Procedure', 50 Nomos 2011, 3.
24. Ronald Dworkin, *Law's Empire* (Harvard UP 1986).
25. Ronald Dworkin, 'Political Judges and the Rule of Law', 64 Proceedings of the British Academy 1978, 259, 262.

26. Thomas H Bingham, *The Rule of Law* (Penguin 2010) 66 et seq.
27. Tamanaha (n 2) 104.
28. Laurent Pech, 'The Rule of Law as a Constitutional Principle of the European Union', Jean Monnet Working Paper 04/09. This paper shows that many newer EU member States entrenched it in their constitutions, often understanding it—as in Germany—as a thick notion of the RoL. This includes Spain and Portugal and the Eastern European States.
29. Instead of many, Rainer Grote, 'Rule of Law, Rechtsstaat and Etat de Droit' in Christian Starck (ed), *Constitutionalism, Universalism and Democracy—A Comparative Analysis* (Nomos 1999) 269; Michel Rosenfeld, 'The Rule of Law and the Legitimacy of Constitutional Democracy', 74 Southern California Law Review 2001, 1307.
30. For the Russian understanding, see G A Gadzhiev, 'The Russian Judicial Doctrine of the Rule of Law: Twenty Years After' in J Silkenat, J Hickey Jr, and P Barenboim (eds), *The Legal Doctrines of the Rule of Law and the Legal State* (Rechtsstaat) (Springer, Cham, 2014) 209–228; Kathryn Hendley, 'Assessing the Rule of Law in Russia', 14 Cardozo Journal of International & Comparative Law 2006, 347; Maria Popova, 'Putin-style "Rule of Law" & the Prospects for Change', 146 Daedalus 2017, 64, 64.
31. Pech (n 28) 70.
32. See Eric Carpano, *État de droit et droits européens: L'évolution du modèle de l'État de droit dans le cadre de l'européanisation des systèmes juridiques* (L'Harmattan 2005).
33. Klaus Schlichtmann, 'Japan, Germany, and the Idea of The Hague Peace Conferences', 40(4) Journal of Peace Research, Special Issue on Peace History 2003, 377–439.
34. Josef Kunz, 'Swing of the Pendulum: From Overestimation to Underestimation of International Law', 44 American Journal of International Law 1950, 135, 137 et seq; Oona A Hathaway and Scott J Shapiro, *The Internationalists* (Simon & Schuster 2017).
35. Bardo Fassbender, 'What's in a Name? The International Rule of Law and the United Nations Charter', 17 Chinese Journal of International Law 2018, 761.
36. At its 60th plenary meeting, 17 November 1989, the UN General Assembly, declared the 'United Nations Decade of International Law' (A/RES/44/23) being 'convinced of the need to strengthen the rule of law in international relations' (preamble); Kofi A Annan, 'We the Peoples': The Role of the United Nations in the 21st Century, UN Doc A/54/2000, UN Sales No E.00.I.16 (2000) N0038897.pdf (un.org) (accessed 30 October 2023); Millennium Declaration in September 2000, GA Res 9758, UN GAOR, 55th Sess, Supp No 49, 3, UN Doc A/55/2 (2000).
37. UN General Assembly, The rule of law at the national and international levels, 18 December 2006, A/RES/61/39: 'Reaffirming further the need for universal adherence to and implementation of the rule of law at both the national and international levels and its solemn commitment to an international order based on the rule of law and international law, which together with the principles of justice, is essential for peaceful coexistence and cooperation among States.'
38. Hans Corell, 'A Challenge to the United Nations and the World: Developing the Rule of Law', 18 Temple International and Comparative Law Journal 2004, 391. For a critical discussion, see Fassbender (n 35).
39. Jeremy Waldron, 'The Rule of International Law', 30 *Harvard Journal of Law & Public Policy* 2006, 15; James Crawford, 'International Law and the Rule of Law', 23 Adelaide Law Review 2003, 3. Simon Chesterman, 'The International Rule of Law', 56 American Journal of Comparative Law 2008, 331.
40. Martti Koskenniemi, *The Politics of International Law* (Hart Publishing 2011) 36.

41. Matthieu Burnay, *Chinese Perspectives on the International Rule of Law* (Edward Elgar 2018) 127.
42. Heike Krieger and Georg Nolte, 'The International Rule of Law— Rise or Decline?—Approaching Current Foundational Challenges' in Heike Krieger, Georg Nolte, and Andreas Zimmermann (eds), *The International Rule of Law: Rise or Decline?* (OUP 2019) 3–30.
43. For an overview on the debate and the argument that only a formal conception of the rule of law can be transposed to the international plane, see Stéphane Beaulac, 'The Rule of Law in International Law Today', in Gianluigi Palombella and Neil Walker (eds), *Relocating the Rule of Law* (Hart Publishing 2009) 197.
44. Philip Allott, 'International Law as True Law: A New Approach to a Perennial Problem', *EJIL:Talk!*, 12 January 2022.
45. Robert McCorquodale, 'Defining the International Rule of Law: Defying Gravity?', 65 International & Comparative Law Quarterly 2016, 277; Leander Beinlich and Anne Peters, 'An International Rule of Law', Oxford Bibliographies, August 2021, DOI: 10.1093/OBO/9780199796953-0222.
46. For a threefold distinction, see Burnay (n 41) 56.
47. Beaulac (n 43) 197 for similar conditions.
48. International Law Commission, Draft Declaration on Rights and Duties of States with Commentaries, Annex to General Assembly Resolution 375 (IV) of 6 December 1949, Article 14 <https://legal.un.org/ilc/texts/instruments/english/commentaries/2_1_1949.pdf> (accessed 30 October 2023).
49. But secret treaties continue to exist. Megan Donaldson, 'The Survival of the Secret Treaty: Publicity, Secrecy, and Legality in the International Order', 111 American Journal of International Law 2017, 575.
50. See generally the depository at the United Nations, Multilateral Treaties Deposited with the Secretary-General, at <http://untreaty.un.org/ENGLISH/bible/englishinternetbible/Bible.asp#partI>.
51. Chesterman (n 39) 359–360.
52. Bernstorff (n 22) 55.
53. Cesare PR Romano, 'The Proliferation of International Judicial Bodies: The Pieces of the Puzzle', 31 New York University Journal of International Law and Politics 1998, 709. Yet, with the exception of the World Trade Organization (WTO) (mandatory), investment tribunals (mandatory), and the ECtHR (mandatory), relatively few cases are brought.
54. Some twenty-five European States have accepted the compulsory jurisdiction of the ICJ (Article 36(2) ICJ Statute) out of forty-six CoE member States; an above-average number globally (seventy-three States).
55. Jean Allain, *A Century of International Adjudication: The Rule of Law and its Limits* (Asser 2000) 7.
56. But the ICC has been contested, first by the US and, since about ten years ago, by African countries, see Kurt Mills and Alan Bloomfield, 'African Resistance to the International Criminal Court: Halting the Advance of the Anti-Impunity Norm', 44 Review of International Studies 2017, 101.
57. See n 63.
58. In this vein, André Nollkaemper, *National Courts and the International Rule of Law* (OUP 2012) 2, 4. See also the preamble of the Universal Declaration of Human Rights (10 December 1948): 'Whereas it is essential, if man is not to be compelled to have recourse,

as a last resort, to rebellion against tyranny and oppression, that human rights should be protected by the rule of law'.

59. Burnay (n 41) 55.
60. Hisashi Owada, 'The Rule of Law in a Globalizing World: An Asian Perspective', 8 Washington University Global Law Studies Review 2006, 187, 193.
61. Waldron, 'The Rule of International Law' (n 39) 24 et seq.
62. The 2003 Iraq war as well as Kosovo 1999 divided Europe, and Russia rather considered those events watershed moments for the IRoL.
63. The Declaration of the People's Republic of China and the Russian Federation on the Promotion of International Law (fmprc.gov.cn) (accessed 30 October 2023).
64. The Organization for Security and Co-operation in Europe (OSCE) has also been a strong supporter of national RoL but will be left out in this chapter.
65. Brexit is one example of that discussion. In Russia, after a long conflict with the ECtHR, the Russian constitutional amendments of 2020 give the Constitutional Court the authority to rule on, and to prohibit, enforcement of a decision by an inter-state mechanism concerning an international treaty that is contrary to the Russian Constitution. See on Poland and Hungary also section 3.2.2. below.
66. 1949, ETS No 001.
67. Parliamentary Assembly, Opinion 300 (2022) of 15 March 2022.
68. On 16 March, the Committee of Ministers (CM) of the Council of Europe decided, 'in the context of the procedure launched under Article 8 of the Statute of the Council of Europe, that the Russian Federation ceases to be a member of the Council of Europe'. This had immediate effect. Resolution CM/Res(2022)2 on the cessation of the membership of the Russian Federation in the Council of Europe.
69. Vienna Declaration (1993), Strasbourg Final Declaration and Action Plan (1997), and the Warsaw Declaration (2005), the latter especially stressing the importance of an independent judiciary.
70. The CoE Administrative Tribunal referred to the internal RoL. In its judgment Appeal no 540/2013, *Staff Committee (XIV) v Secretary General*, 13 March 2014, it recalled that the CoE, by 'its very nature and the values it defends, has a duty to be an organisation upholding the rule of law . . . '.
71. The Parliamentary Assembly of the CoE, PACE Resolution 1594 (2007); cf Jörg Polakiewicz and J Sandvig, 'Council of Europe and the Rule of Law', 4 Journal of Civil & Legal Sciences 2015, 160 for a discussion.
72. Başak Çalı and Esra Demir-Gürsel, 'The Council of Europe's Responses to the Decay of the Rule of Law and Human Rights Protections: A Comparative Appraisal', 2 ECHR Law Review 2021, 165.
73. For others, see only the website of the CoE which lists several issue areas, such as the Group of States against Corruption (GRECO) and money laundering (MoneyVal), European Commission for the Efficiency of Justice (CEPEJ), and the Council of Europe Commissioner for Human Rights.
74. CM Resolution (2002)3 Revised Statute of the European Commission for Democracy through Law.
75. Venice Commission Report on the Rule of Law CDL-AD(2011)003rev.
76. Bingham (n 26).
77. CDL-AD(2011)003rev, paras 37, 41.
78. The principle is described in Bingham (n 26) ch 10.

79. European Commission for Democracy through Law (Venice Commission), 'The rule of law checklist', 18 March 2016.
80. ECtHR, *Stafford v United Kingdom*, App no 46295/99, 28 May 2002, ECHR 2002-IV, [63].
81. *Golder v UK*, App no 4451/70, 21 February 1975 Series A no 18, [34].
82. The case law of the Court was summarized by a report of the Committee of Ministers (CM(2008)170, 21 November 2008), applying the notion of formal and procedural RoL.
83. For a detailed analysis, see Geranne Lautenbach, *The Concept of the Rule of Law and the European Court of Human Rights* (OUP 2013).
84. Philip Leach, 'Ukraine, Russia and Crimea in the European Court of Human Rights', EJIL Talk!, 19 March 2014.
85. See Isabella Risini, 'Armenia v Azerbaijan before the European Court of Human Rights', EJIL Talk!, 1 October 2020.
86. Indeed, the CJEU continues to view the Treaty of the European Communities, albeit formally concluded in the form of a 'mere' international agreement in 1957, as the constitutional document of a polity based on the RoL, see, eg, Joined Cases C-402/05 P and C-415/05 *P Kadi and Al Barakaat* [2008] ECR I- 06351, [281]. And although the treaties speak of 'values', they are considered as being enforceable law: Kim L Scheppele, Dimitry Kochenov, and Barbara Grabowska-Moroz, 'EU Values are Law, after All', 38 Yearbook of European Law 2021, 32–36, arguing that the EU has the institutional mechanisms, namely infringement procedures of Articles 258 and 259 of the Treaty on the Functioning of the Eureopan Union (TFEU) to turn into a 'militant democracy'.
87. cf Case C-5/94, *Hedley Lomas*, ECLI:EU:C:1996:205 ECR 1996, I-02553, Summary: 'Member States are obliged ... to take all measures necessary to guarantee the application and effectiveness of Community law. [They] must rely on trust in each other to carry out inspections on their respective territories and one Member State may not unilaterally adopt, on its own authority, corrective or protective measures designed to obviate any breach by another Member State of rules of Community law.'
88. Mattias Kumm and Victor Ferreres Comella, 'The Primacy Clause of the Constitutional Treaty and the Future of Constitutional Conflict in the European Union', 3 International Journal of Constitutional Law 2005, 473, 474.
89. The Federal Constitutional Court (FCC) has a long tradition of defining the limits for opening up, as witnessed by Judgment no 37, 271 of 29 May 1974 (*Solange I*), Judgment no 73, 339 of 22 October 1986 (*Solange II*), Judgment no 89, 155 of 12 October 1993 (*Maastricht*), and Judgment no 123, 267 of 30 June 2009 (*Lisbon*). For Poland, see Poland section 3.2.2 below.
90. Rec 3, Reg (EU, Euratom) 2020/2092 of the European Parliament and of the Council of 16 December 2020 on a general regime of conditionality for the protection of the Union budget.
91. Witness the discussion on the European Arrest Warrant, Elies van Sliedregt, 'The European Arrest Warrant: Between Trust, Democracy and the Rule of Law', 3 European Constitutional Law Review 2007, 244.
92. Except in Article 173 of the Rome Treaty but using it in a different sense.
93. Charter of Paris on a New Europe, OSCE, 1990, declaring Human Rights, Democracy and Rule of Law as one of the foundations of the 'new Europe'.
94. Case 294/83 *Les Verts* (n 3).
95. 'Rechtsgemeinschaft' was used by the first president of the EC Commission, Walter Hallstein, (n 6) 51.

96. cf (n 3) 23.
97. Pech (n 28) 15.
98. As in ibid, 52–53.
99. Theodore Konstadinides, *The Rule of Law in the European Union. The Internal Dimension* (Hart Publishing 2017).
100. Case OI/5/2020/MHZ. For a discussion, see Luisa Marin, 'Frontex and the Rule of Law Crisis at EU External Borders: A Question of Legal Design?', VerfBlog, 5 September 2022 <https://verfassungsblog.de/frontex-and-the-rule-of-law-crisis-at-eu-external-borders/>, DOI: 10.17176/20220905-230813-0.
101. Claire Kilpatrick, 'On the Rule of Law and Economic Emergency: The Degradation of Basic Legal Values in Europe's Bailouts', 35 Oxford Journal of Legal Studies 2015, 325.
102. BVerfG, 5 May 2020–2 BvR 859/15, paras 1–237 <http://www.bverfg.de/e/rs20200505_2bvr085915en.html> (accessed 30 October 2023).
103. See further Robert Schütze, *From Dual to Cooperative Federalism: The Changing Structure of European Law* (OUP 2009).
104. Although not codified, always confirmed after Case 26/62 *Van Gend en Loos* [1963].
105. The preliminary reference procedure of Article 267 TFEU is vital because it ensures that EU law operates effectively and uniformly throughout the Union through interpretation by the CJEU.
106. Case 6/64 *Costa* [1964] ECR English Special Edition 585.
107. Rec 3, Reg 2020/2092 (n 90) (footnotes omitted).
108. First under the Copenhagen Criteria of 1993, 1993 Copenhagen European Council conclusions, Bull EC, 6-1993, point I.13 and then later via the TEU.
109. Communication from the Commission to the European Parliament and the Council, COM/2014/0158 final.
110. Rule of Law Report, Communication from the Commission to the European Parliament, the Council, the European Economic and Social Committee and the Committee of the Regions, 2020 Rule of Law Report. The rule of law situation in the European Union, COM/2020/580 final. These reports have since been issued annually.
111. Communication from the Commission to the European Parliament, the Council, the European Central Bank, the European Economic and Social Committee and the Committee of the Regions, 2020 EU Justice Scoreboard, COM/2020/306 final.
112. Kim L Scheppele, 'Enforcing the Basic Principles of EU Law through Systemic Infringement Actions' in C Closa and D Kochenov (eds), *Reinforcing the Rule of Law Oversight in the European Union* (CUP 2016) 105; Matthias Schmidt and Piotr Bogdanowicz, 'The Infringement Procedure in the Rule of Law Crisis: How to Make Effective Use of Article 258 TFEU', 55 Common Market Law Review 2018, 1061; Joseph Weiler, 'Epilogue: Living in a Glass House: Europe, Democracy and the Rule of Law' in Closa and Kochenov (n 112); András Sajó, 'The Rule of Law as Legal Despotism: Concerned Remarks on the Use of "Rule of Law" in Illiberal Democracies', 11 Hague Journal on the Rule of Law 2019, 371; for a new book, see Robert Böttner and Hermann-Josef Blanke (eds), *The Rule of Law Under Threat. Eroding Institutions and European Remedies* (Edward Elgar 2024).
113. Wojciech Sadurski, *Poland's Constitutional Breakdown* (OUP 2019). After the latest elections in 2023, a new, more liberal, government will have the problem how to revert to the rule of law, including an independent judiciary within the rule of law. For a proposal, see Kim Scheppele, ASIL Annual meeting 2023, where she argued that "that international

law standards for assessing domestic constitutional institutions are just starting to emerge now, particularly with regard to judicial independence, executive term limits and the operation of independent "fourth branch" institutions. While this new "international law of constitutional democracy" is not yet generally binding on most states and is still tentative in character, its emerging principles can be used by principled democrats inside the new autocracies to guide transitions back to democracy." <https://www.asil.org/events/2023-asil-annual-meeting> (accessed 30 October 2023).

114. Kim L Scheppele, 'Understanding Hungary's Constitutional Revolution' in Armin von Bogdandy and P Sonnevend (eds), *Constitutional Crisis in the European Constitutional Area: Theory, Law and Politics in Hungary and Romania* (Hart Publishing 2015).
115. Peter Van Elsuwege and Femke Gremmelprez, 'Protecting the Rule of Law in the EU Legal Order: A Constitutional Role for the Court of Justice', 16 European Constitutional Law Review 2020, 8.
116. European Parliament resolution of 16 January 2020 on ongoing hearings under Art 7(1) TEU regarding Poland and Hungary (2020/2513(RSP)).
117. Rule of Law: European Commission acts to defend judicial independence in Poland, Rule of Law: European Commission acts to defend judicial independence in Poland (europa.eu).
118. European Parliament resolution of 12 September 2018 on a proposal calling on the Council to determine, pursuant to Article 7(1) of the Treaty on European Union, the existence of a clear risk of a serious breach by Hungary of the values on which the Union is founded (2017/2131(INL)).
119. Proposal for a Regulation of the European Parliament and of the Council on a general regime of conditionality for the protection of the Union budget, intending to condition the distribution of EU money on compliance with the RoL, COM/2018/324 final—2018/0136 (COD).
120. European Council meeting (10 and 11 December 2020), EUCO 22/20.
121. Alberto Alemanno and Merijn Chamon, *To Save the Rule of Law you Must Apparently Break It*, *VerfBlog*, 11 December 2020 <https://verfassungsblog.de/to-save-the-rule-of-law-you-must-apparently-break-it/> DOI: 10.17176/20201212-060201-0; Kim L Scheppele, Laurent Pech, and Sébastien Platon, 'Compromising the Rule of Law while Compromising on the Rule of Law', VerfBlog, 13 December 2020, DOI: 10.17176/20201214-060045-0.
122. Reg 2020/2092, of the European Parliament and of the Council of 16 December 2020 on a General Regime of Conditionality for the Protection of the Union Budget, 2020 OJ (L 433I) 1, 1.
123. C-156/21 (*Hungary v European Parliament and Council*) and C-157/21 (*Poland v European Parliament and Council*).
124. Case C-64/16 *Associação Sindical dos Juízes portugueses v Tribunal de Contas* EU:C:2018:117.
125. Case C-619/18 *Commission v Republic of Poland*, Judgment of the Court (Grand Chamber) of 24 June 2019.
126. Elsuwege and Gremmelprez (n 115) 31.
127. Polish Constitutional Court Judgment of 14 July 2021, case ref P 7/20 and Judgment of 7 October 2021, case ref K 3/21 finding several provisions of EU Law also to be inconsistent with the Polish Constitution. The Court also applied this reasoning to the ECtHR judgments, see extensively Adam Ploszka, 'It Never Rains but it Pours. The

Polish Constitutional Tribunal Declares the European Convention on Human Rights Unconstitutional', 15 Hague Journal on Rule of Law 2023, 51.

128. Order of the Vice-President of the Court in Case C-204/21 R *Commission v Poland*. This case was closed with the Grand Chamber decision in the Case C-204/21 of 5 June 2023, although Poland still needs to pay past dues.
129. Joint open letter of the majority of the European Parliament's political groups of 24 April 2023 EP leaders letter on recent legislative developments in HU <https://app.box.com/s/m37c5v7v41qrmvgy35mxwyyb7ai2p9pa> (accessed 30 October 2023).
130. For suggestions on how to use the existing legal framework to protect or sanction RoL backsliding, see Petra Bárd, Barbara Grabowska-Moroz, and Viktor Zoltán Kazai, 'Rule of Law Backsliding in the European Union Lessons from the Past, Recommendations for the Future', Reconnect Blog, 15 January 2021 and Andras Jakab and Lando Kirchmair, 'How to Develop the EU Justice Scoreboard into a Rule of Law Index: Using an Existing Tool in the EU Rule of Law Crisis in a More Efficient Way', 22 German Law Journal 2021, 936.
131. *Dolińska-Ficek and Ozimek v Poland* (App nos 49868/19 and 57511/19), 8 November 2021.
132. For a discussion, see Sonia Priebus, 'The Commission's Approach to Rule of Law Backsliding: Managing Instead of Enforcing Democratic Values?', 60 Journal of Common Market Studies 2022, 1684.
133. Scheppele et al (n 86).
134. Nicole Wichmann, *Rule of Law Promotion in the European Neighbourhood Policy. Normative or Strategic Power Europe?* (Nomos 2010).
135. The rule of law has been at the core of various EU missions under the European Security and Defence Policy (such as EUJUST Themis in Georgia, EULEX in Kosovo, and EUPOL COPPS in the Occupied Palestinian Territories).
136. Laurent Pech, 'Promoting the Rule of Law Abroad: On the EU's Limited Contribution to the Shaping of an International Understanding of the Rule of Law' in D Kochenov and F Amtenbrink (eds), *The European Union's Shaping of the International Legal Order* (CUP 2013) 108.
137. The importance of promoting the RoL internationally was emphasized, eg, by the Council's Report on the Implementation of the European Security Strategy of 2009 <https://www.consilium.europa.eu/media/30823/qc7809568enc.pdf> (accessed 30 October 2023).
138. See, e.g., on the Western Balkans Isabelle Ioannides and Gemma Collantes-Celador, 'The Internal-External Security Nexus and EU Police/Rule of Law Missions in the Western Balkans', 11 Conflict, Security & Development 2011, 415.
139. Pursuant to Article 24(1)(2) TEU and Article 275(1) TFEU.
140. See n 3.
141. Peter Van Elsuwege, 'Upholding the Rule of Law in the Common Foreign and Security Policy: H v. Council', 54 Common Market Law Review 2017, 841.
142. ECJ 28 March 2017, Case C-72/15, *Rosneft*, EU:C:2017:236, 73 and latest *Bank Refah Kargaran* (T-552/15 and C-134/19 P) 8 October 2020, in which the Grand Chamber of the ECJ rendered judgment in an appeal procedure against the General Court.
143. <Alliance for Multilateralism - Kit Com - Prod (ambafrance.org)> (accessed 30 October 2023).
144. Council conclusions 10341/19 (17 June 2019).

145. Joined Cases C-402/05 P and C- 415/05 P *Kadi et al v Council of the European Union et al* [2008] ECR I-06351.
146. Frederik Stenhammar, 'United Nations Targeted Sanctions, the International Rule of Law and the European Court of Justice's Judgment in Kadi and al- Barakaat', 79 Nordic Journal of International Law 2010, 113.
147. *Kadi* (n 15) 1, 316.
148. See n 89.
149. Case 284/16 *Slovak Republic v Achmea* EU:C:2018:158, [50] et seq. All intra-EU investment treaties have now been terminated, after a long battle with the European Commission on that matter. In Case C-741/19 (Komstroy), the CJEU ruled that the Investor-State Dispute Settlement mechanism provided for by the Energy Charter Treaty is not applicable to intra-EU disputes.
150. Barbara Grabowska-Moroz and Olga Śniadach, 'The Role of Civil Society in Protecting Judicial Independence in Times of Rule of Law Backsliding in Poland', 17 Utrecht Law Review 2021, 59.
151. Eurobarometer 2019, Rule of Law—July 2019—Eurobarometer survey (europa.eu) (accessed 27 April 2023).
152. Chuck Rosenberg, 'This is a revolting assault on the fragile rule of law', Opinions, *Washington Post*, 12 February 2020 <https://www.washingtonpost.com/opinions/2020/02/12/this-is-revolting-assault-fragile-rule-law/> (accessed 30 October 2023).

CHAPTER 6

THE QUESTION OF DEMOCRACY IN INTERNATIONAL LAW IN THE CONTEXT OF EUROPEAN HISTORY

SEVANNA POGHOSYAN

1. Introduction: Democracy as a Multifaceted Discourse

In the context of international law in Europe, few subjects stir as much fascination and contention as the idea of democracy. After all, Europe has been instrumental in shaping Western liberal democratic ideas, human rights, and their critiques (for a detailed overview of the ideas of human rights and institutions in the European legal order see Çalı, this volume). The appeal of liberal democracy is often linked to the 'Democratic Peace' or 'Liberal Peace' thesis, which, in its very simplified form, implies that 'democracies do not fight each other'.[1] 'Liberal Peace' necessitates democracies on both sides to prevent a conflict; as John Rawls articulates in his renowned work *The Law of Peoples*, 'when liberal peoples do go to war, it is only with unsatisfied societies, or outlaw states'.[2] Democracy has indeed played a crucial pacifying role in Europe, notably after World War II and the end of the Cold War, by fostering a shared legal and political framework based on democratic principles. European experiences with democracy, in their turn, have significantly informed and influenced international law's perspective on democracy, albeit with limited effects for universalizing Western liberal ideas of democracy.[3]

While liberal democracy has undeniably played a pacifying role in Europe, its power to ensure lasting peace and stability is limited and subject to internal and external challenges. These issues, deeply resonating with the European context, find echoes across the Atlantic in the global democratic discourse of the United States of America (US). In an essay titled 'How Democracy Can Win: The Right Way to Counter Autocracy', published in *Foreign Affairs* in February 2023, Samantha Power, Administrator of the US Agency for International Development, who also previously served as the US Ambassador to the United Nations (UN), cautioned against the global challenges to (liberal) democracies, highlighting the threats posed by the coordinated efforts of authoritarian regimes and leaders, stating that '[t]o fend off this coordinated assault the world's democracies must also work together'.[4] Considering US foreign policy's historical focus on advancing democracy through soft and hard power, Powers' essay's substance and tone are unsurprising.[5] Nevertheless, they accurately pinpoint a growing sense of alarm and concern regarding the future of Western liberal democracy, long documented by Freedom House reports.[6]

These observations demonstrate that the discourse on democracy is multifaceted and not confined to a single country or region, necessitating an international legal analysis alongside a regional one. Hence, this global perspective will be kept in mind as we examine the evolution of democracy in international law in Europe through the central themes of this handbook: diversity, pacification, and universality. The study does not prescribe a specific definition of democracy. Still, it explores the diversity of definitions proposed in various documents and international legal debates.[7] The study acknowledges its limitations as it cannot cover all aspects of the democracy and international law nexus (such as the democracy of international law; national-level democracy in Europe). Instead, it emphasizes the most pressing issues within international law's European regional context from the author's viewpoint.

The chapter is structured as follows: the initial section (2) examines definition(s) of the idea of democracy in international law. The following section (3), offers an insight into the evolution of the (Western liberal) concept of democracy in Europe that has shaped the current understanding of the concept, focusing on pivotal historical events. In the next section (4) the focus gradually shifts to the current European regional legal order (Council of Europe (CoE) and the European Union (EU)). This section concludes by addressing some of the current challenges to democracy in Europe and the potential remedies. Before conclusions (Section 6), the penultimate section (5) illustrates the challenges to universalizing the Western liberal concept of democracy under contemporary international law. Overall, this chapter argues, and offers evidence to demonstrate, that Europe has played a pivotal role as both the birthplace and the battleground for developing and contesting democratic ideas, which in turn have played a significant role in preserving peace and stability in Europe despite numerous challenges.

2. Definition(s) of Democracy in International Law

The term 'democracy' inherently signifies the principle of governance by the people; nevertheless, its definition elicits fundamental disagreements under international law.[8] While often associated with Western liberal ideals, in fact, international law does not explicitly endorse the Western liberal model of democracy. Instead, it leaves room for interpretations accommodating the diversity of historical, cultural, and political contexts. Still, while doing so, international law clearly upholds certain principles commonly associated with liberal democracy.

Despite variants of definitions of democracy in international law, there is a need to differentiate between '*mala fide* lip service to democracy by authoritarian regimes on the one hand and *bona fide* disagreement about the meaning of democracy on the other'.[9] To illustrate, authoritarian States and leaders often use the conceptual framework of democratic governance to legitimize their otherwise undemocratic rule and practices.[10] Hence, this begs the question: what exactly is democracy? This matter has been extensively examined in international legal scholarship, demonstrating that international law provides helpful insights for addressing this issue.[11]

2.1 Electoral (procedural or thin) definition of democracy

The idea of democracy has had the most extensive interaction with international law within the framework of human rights law.[12] Specifically, Article 21 of the 1948 Universal Declaration of Human Rights (UDHR), which focuses on elections without explicitly naming the concept of democracy, is where the study of the potential status of democracy as a positive human right begins.[13] The provision was subsequently reproduced slightly differently in Article 25 of the 1966 International Covenant on Civil and Political Rights (ICCPR), stating:

> Every citizen shall have the right and the opportunity, without [discrimination] and without unreasonable restrictions:
>
> (a) To take part in the conduct of public affairs, directly or through freely chosen representatives;
> (b) To vote and to be elected at genuine periodic elections which shall be by universal and equal suffrage and shall be held by secret ballot, guaranteeing the free expression of the will of the electors;
> (c) To have access, on general terms of equality, to public service in his country.[14]

In a General Comment from 1996, the UN Human Rights Committee described Article 25 as the fundamental cornerstone of democratic governance supported by popular consent.[15] Furthermore, the concept of 'democracy' is bolstered by Common Article 1 ICCPR and the International Covenant on Economic, Social and Cultural Rights (ICESCR) by asserting the right to self-determination, encompassing peoples' freedom to decide their political status.[16] These documents establish the foundation of the electoral (thin) definition of democracy. However, this view does not explain whether a democratically elected government would still be democratic if it routinely violated human rights.[17]

2.2 Substantive (thick) definition of democracy

A more substantive view on democracy is best exemplified by the 1999 resolution 'Promotion of the Right to Democracy' (legally non-binding), which defines democracy to include *inter alia* the following elements:

> (a) The rights to freedom of opinion and expression, of thought, conscience and religion, and of peaceful association and assembly;
> (b) The right to freedom to seek, receive and impart information and ideas through any media;
> (c) The rule of law, including legal protection of citizens' rights, interests and personal security, and fairness in the administration of justice and independence of the judiciary;
> (d) The right of universal and equal suffrage, as well as free voting procedures and periodic and free elections ...[18]

Thus, the substantive view considers political participation and government accountability unattainable unless other rights are rigorously safeguarded. Meanwhile, it is debatable whether the substantive view adds anything new to existing international law or is purely an analytical category rather than a legally meaningful entitlement in its own right.[19] Furthermore, a middle-ground approach is also discussed. For instance, Tom Ginsburg's definition balances the thick and thin definitions and best informs the perspective of the author of this study. According to this view, democracy entails:

> (1) government characterised by competitive elections, in which the model adult can vote and the losers concede; (2) in which a minimal set of rights to speech, association and the ability to run for office are protected for all on equal basis; and (3) in which the rule of law governs administration.[20]

Regionally, after the Cold War, Europe predominantly embraced the liberal democratic model, characterized by free and fair elections, the rule of law, protection of individual rights, and a clearly defined separation of powers. The European democracy we observe today is the product of centuries of evolution. Therefore, to fully comprehend its place within Europe's current regional legal framework, we must first investigate its complex and rich historical origins. This exploration is the focus of the following section.

3. The Trajectory of Democracy in International Law in Europe—Diversity of Ideas and Histories

3.1 From Ancient Greece to the French Revolution

Democracy, especially in its liberal Western form, was shaped by a complex mix of intellectual traditions and historical events with origins in Europe. The evolution of the concept of democracy over the centuries has an unequivocally 'Western aura'.[21] Ancient Greece is generally considered the birthplace of the concept of democracy in the form commonly understood now as a system where eligible citizens were bestowed participatory rights to form the laws that governed them.[22] While the word 'democracy' came into English in the 16th century from the French *démocratie*, its origins are Greek, and the root meanings are *demos* (people) and *kratos* (rule), which together mean rule by the people.[23] It has been a word signifying conflict since its earliest occurrences.[24] Moreover, early ideas of democracy also developed in ancient Rome. Specifically, concepts with a major impact on current democratic regimes, such as representative democracy and the rule of law, may be traced back to the Roman Republic.[25] Nevertheless, these early systems were inherently selective, excluding key population segments such as slaves and women from political participation.[26] Another important recurring critique of democracy throughout history has been scepticism surrounding its effectiveness as a sustainable form of governance.[27]

During the Middle Ages, democratic ideas significantly retreated. In some locations, however, their basic forms persisted. The English Magna Carta of 1215, which influenced England's political discourse and behaviour for centuries and inspired other nations' constitutions, embodies democratic ideas.[28] Notably, it proclaimed explicitly for the first time in writing that the monarch and his administration were not above the law, thereby limiting the king's authority and strengthening the parliament, albeit without universal suffrage. Ideas of democracy re-emerged and became ingrained in the European consciousness in the 17th and 18th centuries during the Enlightenment era. Through their writings, Enlightenment thinkers such as Rousseau, Voltaire, and Locke established the groundwork for democratic thought, which informed our current understanding of Western ideas of democracy.[29]

Immanuel Kant's legacy deserves special mention regarding the influence of Enlightenment ideas on our current understanding and perception of democratic ideas in international law. Specifically, the 'Democratic Peace' or 'Liberal Peace' thesis, which reflects Kant's notion that democracies do not wage war against one another, is now regarded as one of the most compelling arguments for supporting democracy globally.[30] Nevertheless, it is worth mentioning briefly here that this thesis has its critics, who argue *inter alia* that today's peace is an imperial peace built on American power.[31] Returning to Kant, in particular, he claimed in his 1795 essay 'Perpetual Peace' that 'republics' (now referred to as liberal democracies) are inherently more peaceful than other forms of governance. He argued that 'republics' would avoid wars with other republics because their citizens, who would endure the brunt of war, would prevent their government from engaging in such conflicts.[32] Thus, the influence of Kant's theory on European and international law has been profound, highlighting the significance of democratic governance in ensuring peaceful international relations.[33]

Additionally, the French Revolution of 1789–1799 was another significant historical moment that tested democratic ideas in Europe by turning Enlightenment ideals into a transformative force.[34] According to Melvin Edelstein, while the Greeks developed direct democracy, the American and French Revolutions gave birth to modern representative democracy.[35] The legacy of the French Revolution on the evolution of democratic thought is unmatched as—based on the values of equality, fraternity, and liberty—it attempted to radically alter the relationship between rulers and the governed and reframe the essence of political power by challenging monarchies and questioning aristocratic privileges. Among other things, the French Revolution contributed to the movement towards democratic governance in Europe. However, it was a turbulent and inconsistent process.[36]

As our discussion is primarily about international law, it is worth noting that, overall, democracy held a limited place in the context of European public law or *Ius Publicum Europaeum* from the Peace of Westphalia (1648) until well into the 19th century (see Kalmo, this volume). At the time, sovereign statehood and equality were 'the leading public law paradigm in Europe'.[37] This legal order emphasized the ideas of State sovereignty, diplomatic relations, and the power equilibrium among European States (see Kalmo, this volume). While ideas of governance and political systems were not wholly alien to individual States, the concept of democracy, as we know it today, did not play a prominent role as opposed to the concepts of monarchy or absolute monarchy. Nevertheless, this does not mean that democratic principles and governance discussions were entirely absent. The 'civilised' vs 'uncivilised' dichotomy at the core of *Ius Publicum Europaeum* allows for a cautious inference that 'civilised', in theory, meant honouring basic rights and treaties, something 'savages' were incapable of.[38] While the very idea of 'civilised' vs 'uncivilised' nations and its historical context has sparked heated debates, it emphasizes the relevance of certain values and standards (such as basic human rights and the rule of law) in the European legal order, at least in theory.[39]

3.2 From US Independence to the end of the Cold War

3.2.1 *American democracy: influence and expansion*

Moving forward, while Europe was the birthplace of Western liberal ideas of democracy, the US, a former colony, established the first democratic system, subsequently inspiring the French Revolution. In the succeeding centuries, in Europe and the US, the significance and function of democracy grew substantially. They were manifested at several crucial moments, albeit with little real value for international law at the time. France implicitly cited democratic legitimacy when it recognized the US in 1776, introducing the notion to international affairs. Later, after Louis XVI of France was deposed, the US recognized the new French government, reintroducing democratic legitimacy into foreign affairs. Later this approach was reflected in the so-called Tobar doctrine invoked in the context of The General Treaty of Peace and Amity between the Central American States of 20 December 1907, reaffirmed on 7 February 1923. Nevertheless, from 1930 onwards, the Tobar Doctrine was replaced by the so-called Estrada Doctrine, which recognized a government based on its *de facto* existence rather than its legitimacy.[40]

Nonetheless, the history of democracy during this period is intricately intertwined with Woodrow Wilson's legacy.[41] Specifically, Wilson showed significant readiness to meddle in other nations' affairs for democratic causes, albeit without tangible results in terms of democracy.[42] Notably, he established a well-developed conceptual link between these interventions and the advancement of democracy in international affairs, specifically in the context of World War I.[43] When declaring war on Germany on 2 April 1917, he stated that the world must be made secure for democracy. His 'Fourteen Points' reflected his vision for a peaceful world order based on democratic principles and national sovereignty. Wilson regarded national self-determination as one—albeit limited—method for fostering the conditions required to establish democratic relations between States that would ultimately ensure peace.[44] Nevertheless, the Wilsonian notion of self-determination remained a political concept. It did not recognize all peoples' right to govern their lives without external interference.[45]

3.2.2 *Democracy in international law in the interwar period*

The Covenant of the League of Nations was debated by the proponents of an organization confined to democratic governments and supporters for universal membership.[46] Wilson was the strongest proponent of democratic criteria for League of Nations membership. Nevertheless, the ten-member League of Nations Commission became founding members without evaluating their governments. The Covenant demanded *inter alia* that prospective members be 'fully self-governing', and provide 'effective guarantees of its sincere intention to observe its international obligations'.[47] The League equated 'fully self-governing' with independence and stability when reviewing membership applications, ignoring an applicant's governing system out of respect for State sovereignty.[48] The criteria for admission to the League were not predicated on 'peace through justice' or 'peace through democracy' but instead on the principle of 'peace through universality'.[49]

While Wilsonian ideas did not wholly take root during the interwar period, they significantly impacted the post-World War II order. Meanwhile, parallel to Wilsonian notions of democracy and self-determination, Soviet notions of the same concepts emerged in the 20th century. The Soviets contested the universality of international law and proclaimed the existence of a distinct Soviet or socialist international law based on the premises of Marxist-Leninist thought.[50] They interpreted the practice of self-determination and democracy through the lens of communism's aims, not the ideals of national independence.[51] Even though Western countries did not view the Soviet Union as a democracy, the narrative within the USSR began to assert that it was actually among the foremost democratic nations.[52] The Soviet and socialist positions of democracy and self-determination are significant because they systematically challenged the position of Western liberal notions of democracy and shaped debates on democracy at the UN level after World War II and through the end of the Cold War.[53] These ideological disparities required negotiation and compromise to sustain international cooperation, affecting the understanding and application of democratic ideals in international law.[54]

3.2.3 *Democracy in international law during the Cold War*

3.2.3.1 *Democracy after World War II*

After World War II, democratic norms such as freedom, equality, and the rule of law were held up as the antidote to totalitarian atrocities.[55] The institution of the UN in 1945, which had as its objectives the maintenance of international peace and the promotion of human rights and freedoms—two principles inextricably linked to democracy—paved the way for significant transformations. Thus, the international community had another opportunity to incorporate democracy into international law. Since the term 'democracy' is notably absent from the UN Charter, it is debatable whether it is inherent to the Charter. The Charter mandates that only 'peace-loving states' qualify for membership, a criterion initially designed to prevent governments with a history of fascism from joining the UN. However, 'peace-loving' was not synonymous with 'democratic' because such an assumption would imply intervention in the internal affairs of nations. The criterion for membership in the UN was shaped by a pluralistic standard, mainly due to the UK's insistence that political beliefs should not determine membership.[56] Nevertheless, in international law, the concept of democracy has gained more ground over time.

Defining specific civil and political rights and drafting the founding documents of numerous international organizations were tentative steps towards advancing democracy in international law.[57] For example, the 1948 UDHR (specifically Article 21) paved the way for advancing human rights and democracy.[58] The 1966 Covenants, specifically the ICCPR, were the next significant step in this direction (with Article 25 reflecting the language of Article 21 UDHR).[59] Nevertheless, when evaluating these documents, it is crucial to recall that references to democracy are only implicit, leaving room for multiple interpretations, which reflects the fundamental socio-political and ideological conflict characterizing the Cold War period. During the time of the Cold War the Western bloc, headed by the US, promoted liberal democracy, focusing on political and civil rights, while the Eastern bloc, led by the Soviet Union, promoted an alternative paradigm known as 'people's democracy' or socialist democracy, emphasizing *inter alia* the importance of economic and social rights.[60] Thus, the Cold War era paradigm of democracy was primarily marked by the East/West divide.[61] During this period, State sovereignty and non-interference remained the defining characteristics of international law.[62]

3.2.3.2 *The Organization for Security and Co-operation in Europe (OSCE): efforts to bridge the East/West divide*

Over time, the East-West ideological divide gradually diminished due to complex factors, fostering increased collaboration and understanding. These changes are well captured by the OSCE's (formerly known as Conference on Security and Co-operation in Europe (CSCE)) declarations from the 1990s, which supported the European democratization process following the end of the Cold War, and contributed to a reduction in East-West tensions, thus demonstrating a significant pacifying moment in Europe (see Mihr, this volume). To illustrate, the Copenhagen Document of the CSCE specified the need for pluralistic democracy and the rule of law to safeguard all human rights and fundamental liberties.[63] Furthermore, the Charter of Paris for a New Europe may be regarded as a turning point in the history of Europe, marking an end to 'the era of confrontation and division of Europe' by putting democracy at the centre and stating:

> 'We undertake to build, consolidate and strengthen democracy as the only system of government of our nations.'[64] This passage gives a multi-faceted picture of democracy, including political, legal, social, and ethical components.[65]

The Charter defined the determination of the East and West to transcend their ideological divide and unite based on similar values and principles, thus marking the formal end of the Cold War. The commitment to democracy, human rights, and the rule of law was reiterated in the statement, which served an essential purpose for constructing the post-Cold War European order based on the underlined ideals.[66] The OSCE embarked on this mission, playing a crucial role in advancing democracy in Europe by providing guidance and assistance in upholding human rights, promoting the rule of law, and guaranteeing free and fair elections among its member States by routinely deploying election observation missions to preserve democratic processes.[67]

4. Democracy in the European Regional (International) Legal Order

4.1 The legal-institutional framework

The end of the Cold War marked a fundamental shift in the global political landscape, with the countries of the former Eastern bloc transitioning to liberal democracy. This shift was nuanced and complex, with differing degrees of success and failure. Despite challenges, liberal democracy became vital in the post-Cold War European legal system. While the standard of democracy documented in Europe does not offer a one-size-fits-all definition, it focuses on a substantive view encompassing a right to free and fair elections, liberty for political parties to associate, freedom of political speech, and the right to attempt to shape decisions, among other things.[68]

Currently, a closer look at individual countries reveals a wide variety of democratic structures across Europe, from the direct democracy of Switzerland (where individuals engage in decision-making via referendums) to the representative models of Britain and Germany (where different party systems are prevalent). Traditional values and modernity co-exist in constitutional monarchies like the UK, whereas presidential systems like France's exhibit distinctive executive leadership styles. Europe's dedication to pluralism is on full display in this diverse array of democratic regimes, which also connects to a broader issue of plurality in the European hemisphere.[69]

Furthermore, Europe's internal democratic diversity has not prevented the emergence of a regional standard of democracy. In Europe, democratic governance is administered through the interaction among numerous international treaties and institutions. Specifically, the CoE and the EU are the most important European regional organizations in maintaining and promoting democracy due to their distinct but complementary roles and extensive frameworks for upholding democratic values. Both of them make liberal democracy a precondition for membership, one reason why Belorussia was not a member of the CoE. Considering the leading role of these organizations in shaping Europe's regional international legal standards of democracy, it is vital to examine them closely.

4.1.1 *The Council of Europe*

The CoE was founded on 5 May 1949, to promote greater unity, cooperation, and stability in Europe following the devastation of World War II. For the CoE, promoting and advancing democracy was paramount, together with the rule of law, from the beginning (for more on the CoE see Yudkivska, this volume; for more on the rule of law see van Aaken, this volume). It has played a significant role in the initial stages of democratic transitions, particularly regarding some nations' anticipated and eventual integration. Specifically, Greece's re-entry into the CoE in 1974 following the restoration of democracy in that country and the integration of Portugal in 1976 and Spain in 1977, highlight the considerable contribution of the 1950 European Convention on Human Rights (ECHR) to their democratic consolidation.[70] The impact continued following the end of the Cold War as many newly independent Central and Eastern European countries joined the CoE by agreeing to its standards, despite their different political histories. The flexibility of accession was explained by the CoE's willingness to assist those states in attaining ECHR standards as, according to Ganna Yudkivska, '[t]he fall of the Berlin Wall transformed the "club of democracies" into a "school of democracy"' (see Yudkivska, this volume).

The CoE preamble stresses the fundamental value of democracy to the organization as rooted in spiritual and moral values, individual freedom, and the rule of law.[71] This language later reappeared in the ECHR, which was seen as a significant force driving the concept of democracy forward. The ECHR was intended to function as an 'early warning system' or to protect liberal democracies in the West from backsliding to totalitarianism.[72] It was the first instrument to give effect and binding force to certain rights stated in the UDHR stressing the importance of 'an effective political democracy' to protecting fundamental freedoms.[73] Although, initially, it did not include the right to vote among the protected rights, this was later added through Additional Protocol No 1, Article 3, signifying a limitation in the Convention's original scope regarding voting rights.[74]

The best-known body of the CoE is the European Court of Human Rights (ECtHR), which considers cases alleging violations of civil and political rights outlined in the ECHR. Its binding rulings have shaped the laws and practices of European nations and bolstered democratic governance. The ECtHR has dealt with many significant cases concerning democracy. For instance, criteria for understanding the 'necessary in a democratic society' concept were formulated through *Sunday Times v United Kingdom* (1979).[75] Overall, the ECtHR uses the concept of 'necessary in a democratic society' to balance individual rights and broader societal interests, thereby moulding and bolstering democracy in Europe. This clause is found as a qualification in numerous articles of the ECHR, including but not limited to Article 8 (Right to respect for private and family life), meaning that these rights can be lawfully restricted if it is deemed 'necessary in a democratic society' in order to meet a legitimate aim. Furthermore, *United Communist Party of Turkey v Turkey* (1998) highlighted the significance of political pluralism to democracy.[76] Moreover, in *Hirst v The United Kingdom (No 2)*, the Court ruled that a broad prohibition on voting rights for convicts violated the Convention, highlighting the significance of universal suffrage in a democracy.[77]

The CoE has many democracy-focused documents, some of the most significant examples being the 'Declaration Regarding Intolerance—A Threat to Democracy' of 1981 and the 'Vilnius Declaration on Regional Co-operation and the Consolidation of Democratic Stability in Greater Europe' of 2002.[78] The Parliamentary Assembly of the CoE has also passed important resolutions concerning democracy.[79] The CoE established the European Commission for Democracy through Law, or the Venice Commission, which provides its members with legal advice on constitutional matters, especially fundamental rights and democratic institution-building (see van Aaken, this volume). Venice Commission opinions are not legally binding and amount, at most, to soft law.[80] The Commission has enacted an impressive number of so-called 'main reference documents' addressing the function of parliament in a democracy and topics of fundamental significance to democracy.[81] The significance of the Venice Commission's soft law and soft instruments extends beyond its member States to other States that co-operate informally with the institution, allowing the Commission to extend and universalize the values of democratic norms beyond European borders.[82]

Despite the importance of the CoE in promoting democratic values in Europe, its influence has been extensively questioned over time. Its 'alarm bell' function—a mechanism designed to raise awareness and communicate potential threats to democratic values or instances of human rights violations among its member States—remains the CoE's most significant function. Beyond that function, its impact has been limited, given that it depends on the willingness of its members to adhere to its standards or implement its recommendations.[83] To illustrate, the actual impact of CoE in bringing democracy has been questioned as several member States, such as Russia, Turkey, Azerbaijan, Poland, and Hungary, have become increasingly authoritarian.[84] Moreover, the CoE's inability to prevent inter-state conflicts between its members also highlights its limitations. Specifically, Russia's invasion of Ukraine exemplifies the biggest challenge so far. After a long, complicated history within the framework of the CoE, Russia was expelled following its full-scale invasion of Ukraine in 2022, speaking to the challenges as well as the limitations of the organization in bringing democracy to its member states (see Yudkivska, this volume; for more on the rule of law see van Aaken, this volume).

4.1.2 *The European Union*

While looking at the evolution of European democracy, it becomes clear that establishing the EU, the largest supranational body on the European continent, is one of the most significant milestones in this regard.[85] Born from the ashes of World War II to foster peace and prevent another catastrophe on the continent, the EU's history is deeply tied to, and reflects, the pacifying effect of democracy (for more on the EU see Vasel, this volume). Its roots go back to the European Coal and Steel Community (ECSC) and the European Economic Community (EEC).[86] Both the ECSC and EEC were instrumental in laying the foundation for further cooperation among member States, accomplishing their objectives of economic integration, promoting peaceful relations, and cultivating a sense of European nations' shared interests.[87]

Before the establishment of the ECSC, the transition from fascism to democracy in member States such as Italy and Germany shaped the political context and created the conditions for economic integration and cooperation.[88] In the following years, emphasis on democracy and the rule of law became fundamental to developing European integration, as being democratic was a prerequisite for joining and remaining in the organization. To illustrate: Spain, Portugal, and Greece underwent democratic transitions, which paved the way for their applications to join the EEC. After consolidating democracy and implementing necessary reforms, they became EU members on 1 January 1986.[89]

The EU applies the Copenhagen Criteria for democratic governance as a condition for countries seeking EU membership. To achieve the requirements, a State must have the institutions essential to protect democratic governance and human rights, have a functioning market economy, and embrace the EU's commitments and goals.[90] Post-Cold War European integration placed democracy at its heart, especially when navigating the entry of post-Communist States (see Majkowska-Szulc and Wierczyńska, this volume). The aspirations of these governments to join the EU, partly driven by democratic conditions, significantly influenced their transformation.[91] Thus, the idea of democracy, which had previously served as an ideological dividing line between Eastern and Western Europe, became a unifying marker through EU enlargement.

Democratic ideals were strengthened by the Treaty on European Union (TEU) (Maastricht Treaty), which gave more authority to the European Parliament and established EU citizenship.[92] Democratic conditionality also lies at the core of the EU's

Neighbourhood Policy (ENP), incentivizing states to democratize (see Majkowska-Szulc and Wierczyńska, this volume).[93] Furthermore, the 2009 Treaty of Lisbon established the EU's Charter of Fundamental Rights, which outlines EU citizens' civil, political, and social rights.[94] Moreover, the Charter thoroughly affirms the principles of democratic governance in Europe, emphasizing democratic equality, representative democracy, and participatory democracy.[95]

Despite the EU's reputation as a driver of regional cooperation and development based on democratic values, its influence in this regard is at best questioned or limited. There are debates about the EU's (perceived) democratic deficit, stressing the need for reforms to address transparency, democratic accountability, and sovereignty concerns.[96] In addition, its efforts to promote democracy in the neighbourhood have been interpreted as limited due to factors such as conflicting interests, the complexity of local conditions, the influence of other powers (such as Russia and China), limited resources, and incoherent EU policy.[97] Moreover, the EU's inconsistent engagements with non-democracies explained by economic, political, and security considerations question its credibility as a promoter of democracy and human rights in the region.[98] This has made the EU look more like a 'realist actor in normative clothes'.[99] To illustrate, despite its engagement with Azerbaijan through ENP, the EU has overlooked grave human rights violations and a lack of democratic reforms in Azerbaijan due to its importance as an oil supplier, thus prioritizing energy cooperation over its human rights-based conditionality.[100]

Furthermore, while the EU has processes in place to investigate and redress violations of democratic norms and standards, these measures may not always be successful owing to procedural flaws or the impact of politics. To illustrate, Article 7 TEU is a relevant tool for dealing with concerns about fundamental abuses of democracy in member States, allowing the EU to suspend a member State's rights if it is in continuous and grave breach of EU principles. However, implementing this rule is more difficult than its theoretical underpinnings imply.[101] Due to the flawed institutional design of Article 7(2) TEU, the EU is now seeking to safeguard the rule of law in its member States through budgetary conditionality (see van Aaken, this volume). Nevertheless, as evidenced by the situation in Hungary, the EU's ability to prevent a shift towards authoritarianism or 'non-liberal democracy' is, in reality, somewhat limited.[102]

4.2 Confronting challenges to democracy in Europe: a diversity of perspectives and realities

Despite a well-established regional legal framework for democracy, the political processes of democratization have not been without obstacles in Europe. While each European nation has experienced its unique democratic struggles and crises, specific events and trends have been detrimental to the state of democracy throughout Europe as a whole. While democracy's pacifying role has been well established throughout the history of Europe, these challenges test its actual limits. The global decline of democracy and the rule of law, the rise of populism in Europe, and Russia's war against Ukraine have all posed challenges to the premises of democracy in Europe. A common contributor to this general situation has been dissemination of disinformation and fake news, destabilizing citizens' trust in policies and governments, with the most detrimental adverse effects on liberal democracy.[103]

Specifically, the trend of democratic backsliding, which entails 'the incremental erosion of institutions, rules, and norms that results from the actions of duly elected governments', best encapsulates these challenges.[104] This trend gained momentum in Europe following Brexit and was solidified after the election of Donald Trump as president of the US.[105] In Hungary and Poland, the march of populists appeared almost unstoppable, as they undermined the rule of law and liberal democracy and steered politics in a perilous authoritarian direction.[106] Although they publicly embrace democratic language, they are in fact working to undermine the liberal constitutional foundations of democracy.[107]

Furthermore, the rise of authoritarianism poses a serious threat to Europe's democratic institutions. This is most evident in the development of organizations in the neighbourhood such as the Eurasian Economic Union, the Collective Security Treaty Organization, and the Shanghai Co-Operation Organization. In addition, authoritarian powers like China and Russia are becoming bolder in their pursuit and support of authoritarian allies. To illustrate, the joint statement issued by Russia and China, released in February 2022, clearly outlines their position on various issues related to democracy in international law, effectively challenging Western liberal ideas of democracy.[108] Specifically, Russia, despite formally accepting democratic values and institutions, has challenged democratic principles and institutions while advocating for a multipolar international framework, placing greater emphasis on State sovereignty, hence lessening external pressure to embrace specific political systems. It has contested in particular the genuineness of 'colour revolutions' in post-Soviet space.[109]

According to Rein Müllerson, Russia sees democratization efforts by the West in light of the geopolitical struggle 'between Washington and Moscow, as well as between Washington and Beijing' (for an overview of Russian approaches to international law see Rusinova, this volume).[110] Very recently, Russian Foreign Minister Sergey Lavrov stated that the West's attempts to impose its democratic standards on other nations violate the principle of sovereign equality.[111] Russia's invasion of Ukraine has magnified those challenges and may have profound implications for the future of democracy in Europe. Among many other things, the conflict (particularly if perceived as having a successful outcome for Russia) could serve as a model for other authoritarian regimes to suppress democratic movements in their countries or regions. It may embolden autocratic leaders and sow doubt about the ability of democratic nations to safeguard their sovereignty and maintain peace. The conflict also tests the international community's commitment to protect emerging democracies and uphold the principles of sovereignty and self-determination.

Last but not least, inherent in democracies is the challenge of minority representation, as these groups may never hold power. Thus, democracy alone may struggle to address this; additional methods such as minority protection or regional autonomy are crucial. This issue also rings true for Europe.[112] To illustrate, Anatole Lieven expresses scepticism regarding the efficacy of democracy in resolving ethnic conflicts and emphasizes that this strategy can potentially exacerbate those conflicts. He notes that the recent history of Kosovo demonstrates that forcing contending groups to compete for power during elections may exacerbate ethnic tensions.[113] This observation is particularly interesting if seen in the light of the fact that in the Kosovo case, the 'standards-before-status' policy framework (based on the premises of 'Liberal Peace' theory) required Kosovo to show advancements in several areas, one of them being the creation of functioning democratic institutions, in order to be eligible for independence.[114] Many countries (primarily Western) invoked Kosovo's compliance with democratic norms entailed by the standards-before-status regime among their many arguments.[115]

5. Universalizing (Liberal) Democracy in Contemporary International Law: Challenges and Prospects

The dissolution of the Soviet Union and the subsequent surge of democratization in Eastern Europe repositioned the concept of democracy in international legal discussions, albeit with divergent interpretations and expectations based on diverse ideological, geopolitical, and academic perspectives.[116] In international law, the premature sentiments of the triumph of the Western liberal democratic mode of thought resounded with Thomas M Franck's influential article, where he claimed the emergence of the 'right to democracy' in international law.[117] Franck's assertion was echoed by a number of American scholars, albeit with varying degrees of fervour.[118] Nevertheless, a number of authors have challenged this premise and cautioned against embracing democracy as a means of legitimacy under international law.[119] Meanwhile, European scholars, generally expressing more caution and avoiding full endorsement of the extensive implications voiced by their American counterparts, have gradually recognized the influence of democracy on rules and procedures within the international legal framework.[120]

5.1 Controversies

Samantha Besson best describes the contentious aspects of the claimed right to democracy in international law. First, according to her,whether it is a hard right or a soft-law norm is unclear. Second, it is contested whether democracy is a principle or an individual privilege. Thirdly, the sources of this norm are also debatable; it is not entirely clear whether it stems from international treaties, international customary law, general principles, or the institutional laws of international organizations. Furthermore, one may question whether the standard only protects the right to free and fair elections or a thicker notion of democracy.[121]

This lack of clarity can partially be ascribed to resistance from developing nations, which often perceive efforts to promote global democracy as an extension of Western interests.[122] Furthermore, the idea of State sovereignty raises questions about the existence of the right to democracy as well.[123] In some readings, the modern idea of sovereignty is interpreted as 'popular sovereignty', meaning that sovereignty belongs to citizens rather than the State in which they live.[124] However, this assertion should be treated cautiously.[125] Nevertheless, international law is not indifferent to the concept of democracy. Democracy influences international law and governance by setting the standard for proper and lawful administration, shaping the right of populations to political self-determination, establishing a framework for realizing human rights and fundamental freedoms, and laying the foundation for peaceful and non-violent coexistence.

5.2 Pro-democratic interventions and international law

A key issue that emerges in this discussion is how to enforce a right to democracy universally, if such a right exists at all, especially in the face of denials of this purported right under international law.[126] The most radical interpretation suggests that if a right to democracy is denied, it could justify armed intervention by third-party States or the UN. Proponents of pro-democratic interventions frequently invoke the 'Democratic Peace' theory to support their claim that the spread of democracy contributes to a more peaceful world.[127] Nevertheless, the general consensus in international law is that—in the absence of agreement by a State's government, lawful exercise of the right to self-defence, or authorization by the Security Council (SC) using military force against the territorial integrity or political independence of another State is generally considered a violation of international law.[128]

Consequently, while the concept of democratic peace has certain boundaries in achieving peace within Europe, these limitations are even more pronounced on the global stage.

States can express disapproval of another's undemocratic actions in different ways, commonly by not recognizing a regime's authority or by limiting economic interaction. In exceptional cases where there is comprehensive agreement that enforcement is needed to uphold or restore democracy, collective action through the SC provides a valid legal option to that end.[129] Third World scholars have questioned the modern distinction between democracies and non-democracies, stating that itreproduces the undertone of the infamous 'civilised' versus 'uncivilised' paradigm.[130] Moreover, critics cite the US-led interventions in Iraq and Libya (wars with very distinct *jus ad bellum* grounds) as evidence that removing autocratic leaders can actually undermine democratization efforts and strengthen authoritarianism, prompting further thought and discussion beyond the scope of this chapter.[131]

Although Western liberal ideals have profoundly influenced global perceptions of democracy, these values have not been universally embraced as a standard by all members of the international community. This heterogeneity underscores the challenges to Western liberal democracy. In addition, global challenges such as climate change and the Covid-19 pandemic have widened the gap between the Global North and South on this issue, highlighting the subject's dynamic nature.

6. Outlook: Democracy a Robust Legal Framework but No Magic Potion

This chapter has demonstrated that the concept of democracy, in its Western liberal form, bears a European intellectual and historical imprint. Nevertheless, it has also displayed the universal value of the concept as implied by the international legal framework and its capacity to hold many different meanings and symbolize the diversity of European and global histories, reflecting varied cultural, historical, and political realities. It has also highlighted the diversity of the concept by illustrating how European, American, and Soviet/Russian viewpoints have directly and indirectly shaped the concept of democracy at the heart of Europe by bringing their understanding and concerns to the narrative.

Nonetheless, flexibility is both an advantage and an inconvenience for the idea of democracy. Despite the evident significance of democracy to international law, the assumption of its growth into a fully recognized right under that legal framework, specifically in Western liberal form, is at best premature or flawed. Nonetheless, despite challenges with universalization, the many components of democracy build a robust international legal framework capable of describing what democracy is and what it is not. The chapter also cautions that international law's broad support of democratic rights might be utilized for other than democratic ends. Pro-democratic initiatives, especially military operations, are often criticized based on their history of destabilizing regions, and cast doubt on the participants' intentions. Good intentions are impeded by realities that are often neglected in theory. Despite its limited influence outside its borders, Europe possesses the soft power required to promote democratic values and practices without resorting to hard power. However, for these initiatives to be credible and effective, they must be consistent; otherwise, Europe runs the risk of undermining its own democratic values and its capacity to promote democracy elsewhere.

Furthermore, looking at the history of the evolution of the concept of democracy, specifically in post-World War II developments in Europe, it is possible to conclude that democracy is credited more than any other concept with bringing peace and stability to the continent. Despite this, as illustrated by current challenges, democracy is not a magic potion; its capacity to bring peace and resolve significant domestic and geopolitical challenges is limited, and these limits are constantly being tested. Finally, the chapter also illustrated that while—despite current challenges—Europe remains a regional stronghold of democratic governance, maintaining this status is complex in practice subject to ongoing internal and external challenges. Specifically, Russia's war on Ukraine poses a substantial threat to the democratic future of Europe, with the potential to redefine our perception of the place and role of democracy in Europe as well as worldwide. Future challenges and opportunities will unquestionably influence the development of democracy in international law, with far-reaching consequences for the future of global governance. Europe's response and ability to deal with these challenges will reveal much about democracy's future at both the regional and the global level.

Notes

1. Sid Simpson, 'Making Liberal Use of Kant? Democratic Peace Theory and Perpetual Peace', 33 International Relations 2019, 109, 110; for an international legal perspective see Fernando R Tesón, 'The Kantian Theory of International Law', 92 Columbia Law Review 1992, 53.
2. John Rawls, *The Law of Peoples: With 'The Idea of Public Reason Revisited'* (Harvard UP 2001) 55.
3. For further details see Steven Wheatley, 'Democracy in International Law: A European Perspective', 51 International and Comparative Law Quarterly 2002, 225.
4. Samantha Power, 'How Democracy Can Win | Foreign Affairs' <https://www.foreignaffairs.com/united-states/samantha-power-how-democracy-can-win-counter-autocracy> accessed 22 June 2023.
5. For background on US interventions in international law see Constance G Anthony, 'American Democratic Interventionism: Romancing the Iconic Woodrow Wilson', 9 International Studies Perspectives 2008, 239.
6. The following Freedom House reports summarize and provide an overview for the latest developments on Democratic backslide, 'Marking 50 Years in the Struggle for Democracy | Freedom House' <https://freedomhouse.org/report/freedom-world/2023/marking-50-years> accessed 15 April 2023; Freedom House, 'Freedom in the World 2022: The Global Expansion of Authoritarian Rule' <https://freedomhouse.org/report/freedom-world/2022/global-expansion-authoritarian-rule> accessed 15 April 2023.
7. See, eg, Johannes Fahner, 'Revisiting the Human Right to Democracy: A Positivist Analysis', 21 The International Journal of Human Rights 2017, 321, 323.
8. Armin Von Bogdandy, 'Globalization and Europe: How to Square Democracy, Globalization, and International Law', 15 European Journal of International Law 2004, 885, 889–890.
9. Fahner (n 7) 323.
10. Kim Scheppele refers to this phenomenon as 'Autocratic Legalism', Kim Lane Scheppele, 'Autocratic Legalism', 85 The University of Chicago Law Review 2018, 545.
11. For a brief overview of these discussions, see Jean d'Aspremont, 'The Rise and Fall of Democracy Governance in International Law: A Reply to Susan Marks', 22 European Journal of International Law 2011, 549, 556.

12. For further discussions on a human right to democracy in international law see Thomas Christiano, 'An Instrumental Argument for a Human Right to Democracy: An Instrumental Argument for a Human Right to Democracy', 39 Philosophy & Public Affairs 2011, 142; Christina Cerna, 'Democratic Legitimacy and Respect for Human Rights: The New Gold Standard', 108 American Journal of International Law Unbound 2014, 222; Samantha Besson, 'The Human Right to Democracy in International Law: Coming to Moral Terms with an Equivocal Legal Practice' in Andreas von Arnauld, Kerstin von der Decken, and Mart Susi (eds), *The Cambridge Handbook of New Human Rights: Recognition, Novelty, Rhetoric* (CUP 2020) 481.
13. Universal Declaration of Human Rights (adopted 10 December 1948) UNGA Res 217 A(III) (UDHR), Article 21.
14. International Covenant on Civil and Political Rights, UNTS 999 1966, Article 25.
15. General Comment No 25: The Right to Participate in Public Affairs, Voting Rights and the Right of Equal Access to Public Service (Article 25), UN doc CCPR/C/21/Rev1/Add7, 7 December 1996, para 1.
16. ICCPR (n 14) Article 1.
17. Gregory H. Fox, 'Democracy, Right to, International Protection', in *Wayne State University Law School Research Paper No. 07-22*, 2007, 7.
18. UN Commission on Human Rights, Promotion of the right to democracy, 27 April 1999, E/CN.4/RES/1999/57, para 2.
19. Fox (n 17) 7.
20. Tom Ginsburg, *Democracies and International Law* (1st edn, CUP 2021) 21.
21. Hilary Charlesworth, 'Democracy and International Law' in *Collected Courses of the Hague Academy of International Law*, vol 371 (Brill 2015) 56.
22. John Keane, *The Life and Death of Democracy* (Simon and Schuster 2009) x.
23. David Held, *Models of Democracy* (3rd edn, Stanford UP 2006) 1.
24. Luciano Canfora and Simon Jones, *Democracy in Europe A History of an Ideology* (1st edn, Auflage, John Wiley & Sons 2008) 22.
25. For further details on democracy in the Roman Republic see W Jeffrey Tatum and Ryan K. Ballot, 'Roman Democracy?' in *A Companion to Greek and Roman Political Thought* (Wiley-Blackwell 2009).
26. Keane (n 22) 848.
27. Charlesworth (n 21) 54–56.
28. For further details on the enlightenment ideas please see Edgar Kiser and Yoram Barzel, 'The Origins of Democracy in England', 3 Rationality and Society 1991, 396, 396.
29. For further details on the Enlightenment ideas see James Van Horn Melton, *The Rise of the Public in Enlightenment Europe* (CUP 2001) (online version 2012 <https://doi.org/10.1017/CBO9780511819421>).
30. See more, Michael W Doyle, *Liberal Peace: Selected Essays* (Routledge 2012).
31. Sebastian Rosato, 'The Flawed Logic of Democratic Peace Theory', 97 American Political Science Review 2003, 585, 599.
32. Immanuel Kant, *Toward Perpetual Peace and Other Writings on Politics, Peace, and History* (Pauline Kleingeld ed, David Colclasure trans, Yale UP 2006) 75.
33. See more, Steve Chan, 'In Search of Democratic Peace: Problems and Promise', 41 Mershon International Studies Review 1997, 59; John M Owen, 'International Law and the 'Liberal Peace'' in Brad R Roth and Gregory H Fox (eds), *Democratic Governance and International*

Law (CUP 2000); Azar Gat, 'The Democratic Peace Theory Reframed: The Impact of Modernity', 58 World Politics 2005, 73.

34. Heather M Campbell, *Advances in Democracy: from the French Revolution to the present-day European Union* (1st edn, New Britannica Educational Publishers, in association with Rosen Educational Services 2011) 16.
35. Melvin Allen Edelstein, *The French Revolution and the Birth of Electoral Democracy* (Ashgate 2014) 1. The book was first published in 2014 by Ashgate Publishing, and was later published in 2016 by Routledge.
36. ibid.
37. Juliane Kokott, 'States, Sovereign Equality' in *The Max Planck Encyclopedia of Public International Law*, vol IX (OUP 2012) 571–585, updated by Lauri Mälksoo in March 2023; See more, Derek Croxton, 'The Peace of Westphalia of 1648 and the Origins of Sovereignty', 21 The International History Review 1999, 569, 568.
38. Liliana Obregón Tarazona, 'The Civilized and the Uncivilized' in Bardo Fassbender et al. (eds), *The Oxford Handbook of the History of International Law* (OUP 2012) 684.
39. ibid, 689, 691.
40. Frithjof Ehm and Walter Christian (eds), *International Democracy Documents—A Compilation of Treaties and Other Instruments* (Brill | Nijhof 2015) 4.
41. Roland Rich, 'Bringing Democracy into International Law', 12 Journal of Democracy 2001, 20, 20.
42. Daniel Larsen, 'Abandoning Democracy: Woodrow Wilson and Promoting German Democracy, 1918–1919', 37 Diplomatic History 2013, 476, 477.
43. Anthony (n 5) 239.
44. Trygve Throntveit, 'The Fable of the Fourteen Points: Woodrow Wilson and National Self-Determination', 35 Diplomatic History 2011, 445, 450.
45. Rich (n 41) 22.
46. Alison Duxbury, *The Participation of States in International Organisations: The Role of Human Rights and Democracy*, vol 71 (CUP 2011) 63–72.
47. The Covenant of the League of Nations, Paris 28 April 1919, Article 1.
48. Duxbury (n 46) 74–77.
49. ibid 82.
50. Evgeny Korovin, *Mezhdunarodnoye Pravo Perekhodnoi Vremieni, in English (International Law of the Transition Period)* (Moskva-Petrograd 1924).
51. See more on the Soviet approach, Lauri Mälksoo, 'The Soviet Approach to the Right of Peoples to Self-Determination: Russia's Farewell to Jus Publicum Europaeum', 19(2) Journal of the History of International Law/Revue d'histoire du droit international 2017, 19.
52. This line of argument is explicitly stated throughout the following Soviet legal specialists' writings, Vladimir Guliev and Eduard Kuz'min, *Gosudarstvo i demokratija: kritika antimarksistskih teorij* (Juridicheskaja literatura 1975); Boris Babij (ed), *Demokratija i pravo razvitogo socialisticheskogo obshhestva* (Politizdat Ukrainy 1979); Eduard Kuz'min, *Demokratija i konstitucii dvuh mirov* (Mezhdunorodnye otnoshenija 1981).
53. The socialist perspective has been well captured here, Ned Richardson-Little, 'The Failure of the Socialist Declaration of Human Rights: Ideology, Legitimacy, and Elite Defection at the End of State Socialism', 46 East Central Europe 2019, 318; Jessica Whyte, 'Human Rights, Revolution and the 'Good Society': The Soviet Union and the Universal Declaration of

Human Rights' in Kathryn Greenman et al. (eds), *Revolutions in International Law* (1st edn, CUP 2021); Steven LB Jensen, *The Making of International Human Rights: The 1960s, Decolonization and the Reconstruction of Global Values* (CUP 2016); Ned Richardson-Little, Hella Dietz, and James Mark, 'New Perspectives on Socialism and Human Rights in East Central Europe since 1945: Introduction to the Thematic Issue', 46 East Central Europe 2019, 169.

54. Sevanna Poghosyan, 'The Question of Democracy in the International Legal Theory and Practice of the Soviet Union' in Lauri Mälksoo, Ineta Ziemele, and Dainius Žalimas (eds), *Baltic Yearbook of International Law* (Brill 2023).
55. Marcus Llanque, 'The Edges of Democracy: German, British and American Debates on the Dictatorial Challenges to Democracy in the Interwar Years' in Jussi Kurunmäki, Jeppe Nevers, and Henk Te Velde (eds), *Democracy in Modern Europe: A Conceptual History*, vol 5 (Berghahn Books 2018) 190.
56. For an overview of the relevant documents and further commentary, see Bruno Simma and others, *The Charter of the United Nations: A Commentary* (OUP 2024).
57. Rich (n 41) 21.
58. UDHR (n 13).
59. ICCPR (n 14).
60. Richardson-Little et al., *The Making of International Human Rights* (n 53) 170.
61. Ehm and Christian (n 40) 7.
62. See, eg, UN General Assembly (25th Sess: 1970), 'Declaration on Principles of International Law Concerning Friendly Relations and Cooperation among States in Accordance with the Charter of the United Nations' <https://digitallibrary.un.org/record/202170?ln=en> accessed 20 May 2023.
63. OSCE, 'Document of the Copenhagen meeting of the conference on the human dimension of the CSCE' (2nd Meeting, Copenhagen, 5–29 June 1990).
64. Charter of Paris for a New Europe, Organization for Security and Co-operation in Europe, Second CSCE Summit of Heads of State or Government, Paris, 19–21 November 1990 <https://www.osce.org/mc/39516> accessed 10 June 2023.
65. Organization for Security and Co-operation in Europe (OSCE), *Organization for Co-operation and Security in Europe Charter for European Security*, 19 November 1999.
66. Ibid.
67. For further details see David J Galbreath, *The Organization for Security and Co-Operation in Europe (OSCE)*, vol 14 (Routledge 2007).
68. Wheatley, 'Democracy in International Law' (n 3).
69. For a detailed overview of different systems of democracy within Europe see John Loughlin et al. (eds), *The Oxford Handbook of Local and Regional Democracy in Europe* (OUP 2012).
70. W Sadurski, 'Partnering with Strasbourg: Constitutionalisation of the European Court of Human Rights, the Accession of Central and East European States to the Council of Europe, and the Idea of Pilot Judgments', 9 Human Rights Law Review 2009, 397, 408.
71. Council of Europe 86 Statute of the Council of Europe—Excerpts CETS No: 001, London (Great Britain), 5 May 1949.
72. Esra Demir-Gürsel, '12. The Limits of the European Court of Human Rights Vis-à-Vis Contestation and Authoritarianism: Concluding Observations' in H Aust and E Demir-Gürsel (eds), *The European Court of Human Rights* (Edward Elgar 2021) 245.

73. European Convention for the Protection of Human Rights and Fundamental Freedoms 1950 (ECHR) <https://www.echr.coe.int/documents/d/echr/convention_ENG> accessed 12 June 2023.
74. Javier García Roca, 'From States' International Commitment to Organise Free Elections to the Citizens' Right to Vote and Stand for Election (Art. 3 P1 ECHR)' in Javier García Roca and Pablo Santolaya (eds), *Europe of Rights: A Compendium on the European Convention of Human Rights* (Brill Nijhoff 2012).
75. Wing-wah Mary Wong, 'Sunday Times Case: Freedom of Expression versus English Contempt-of-Court Law in the European Court of Human Rights', 17 NYU Journal of International Law & Policy 1984, 35.
76. *United Communist Party of Turkey and Others v Turkey* (ECtHR, 1998).
77. *Hirst v United Kingdom (No 2)* (ECtHR, 2005); for further details see Buyse, Antoine. 'Dangerous Expressions: The ECHR, Violence and Free Speech', 63(2) International and Comparative Law Quarterly 2014, 491–503; George Letsas, 'The Truth in Autonomous Concepts: How to Interpret the ECHR', 15(2) European Journal of International Law 2004, 279–305; Łącki, Paweł. 'Consensus as a Basis for Dynamic Interpretation of the ECHR—A Critical Assessment', 21(1) Human Rights Law Review 2021, 186–202; Susan Marks, 'The European Convention on Human Rights and its Democratic Society', 66(1) *The British Year Book of International Law* 1996, 209.
78. Committee of Ministers of the Council of Europe, 'Declaration Regarding Intolerance—A Threat to Democracy' (68th Session, 14 May 1981); Committee of Ministers' Deputies, 'Vilnius Declaration on Regional Co-operation and the Consolidation of Democratic Stability in Greater Europe' CM(2002)55.
79. Indicators for Media in a Democracy Resolution 1636 (2008), Adopted by the Assembly, 3 October 2008 (36th Sitting); Abolition of Restrictions on the Right to Vote Resolution 1459 (2005), Adopted by the Assembly, 24 June 2005 (24th Sitting).
80. Wolfgang Hoffmann-Riem, 'Venice Commission of the Council of Europe—Standards and Impact', 25 European Journal of International Law 2014, 579, 580–581.
81. See, eg, Code of Good Practice in Electoral Matters—Guidelines and Explanatory Report Opinion No 190/2002, ACDL-AD (2002) 23 Rev, Adopted by the Venice Commission, Venice (Italy), 18–19 October 2002 (52nd Session).
82. The Commission has sixty-one member States: the forty-six CoE member States (on 17 March 2022 the Committee of Ministers of the CoE decided to suspend the participation of Belarus as associate member in the work of the Venice Commission (Resolution CM/Res(2022)2)), and fifteen other countries (Algeria, Brazil, Canada, Chile, Costa Rica, Israel, Kazakhstan, the Republic of Korea, Kosovo, Kyrgyzstan, Morocco, Mexico, Peru, Tunisia, and the US). Argentina, Japan, the Holy See, and Uruguay are observers.
83. Angelika Nußberger, 'From High Hopes to Scepticism? Human Rights Protection and Rule of Law in Europe in an Ever More Hostile Environment' in Heike Krieger, Georg Nolte, and Andreas Zimmermann (eds), *The International Rule of Law: Rise or Decline?* (OUP 2019) 150.
84. Mikael Madsen, 'From Boom to Backlash? The European Court of Human Rights and the Transformation of Europe' (27 August 2020) 6.
85. For a background on the history of European integration and democracy see Jeppe Nevers, 'Democracy and European Integration: A Transnational History of the Danish Debate 281' in Kurunmäki, Nevers and Te Velde (n 55) 288.
86. For further details see Dermot Hodson et al. (eds), *The Institutions of the European Union* (OUP 2022).

87. For an overview see Jürgen Elvert, 'A Fool's Game or a Comedy of Errors?: EU Enlargements in Comparative Perspective' in Wolfram Kaiser and Jürgen Elvert (eds), *European Union Enlargement* (Routledge 2004) 201–221.
88. See Desmond Dinan, *Europe Recast: A History of European Union* (Palgrave Macmillan 2004).
89. Greece, having restored democracy, applied for EEC membership in 1975 and joined the EU on 1 January 1981, after overcoming challenges. For more on the Greek, Spanish, and Portuguese accessions see Kostas Ifantis, 'State Interests, External Dependency Trajectories and "Europe": Greece' in Kaiser and Elvert (n 87) 75–98; Ricardo Guardia, 'In Search of Lost Europe: Spain' in Kaiser and Elvert (n 87) 93–111; António Costa Pinto and Nuno Severiano Teixeira, 'From Atlantic Past to European Destiny: Portugal' in Kaiser and Elvert (n 87) 119–138.
90. Flamur Mrasori, 'The Role of the Unilateral Harmonization to the EU Integration', 8 Lex Portus 2022, 54, 54.
91. The EU expanded in several rounds to include these States: Austria, Finland, and Sweden in 1995; Cyprus, Czech Republic, Estonia, Hungary, Latvia, Lithuania, Malta, Poland, Slovakia, and Slovenia in 2004; Bulgaria and Romania in 2007; and Croatia in 2013.
92. Consolidated version of the Treaty on European Union [2008] OJ C115/13.
93. Frank Schimmelfennig, 'Rebordering Europe: External Boundaries and Integration in the European Union', 28 Journal of European Public Policy 2021, 311.
94. Treaty of Lisbon amending the Treaty on European Union and the Treaty establishing the European Community [2007] OJ C306/01.
95. Charter of Fundamental Rights of the European Union [2012] OJ C326/02 <https://www.refworld.org/docid/3ae6b3b70.html> accessed 6 August 2023.
96. See, eg, Thomas Jensen, 'The Democratic Deficit of the European Union', 1 Living Reviews in Democracy 2009, 1; Andreas Follesdal and Simon Hix, 'Why There Is a Democratic Deficit in the EU: A Response to Majone and Moravcsik', 44 Journal of Common Market Studies 2006, 533.
97. See more, Michelle Pace, 'Paradoxes and Contradictions in EU Democracy Promotion in the Mediterranean: The Limits of EU Normative Power', 16 Democratization 2009, 39; Elena Baracani, 'The European Neighbourhood Policy and Political Conditionality: Double Standards in EU Democracy Promotion?' in Thierry Balzacq (ed), *The External Dimension of EU Justice and Home Affairs: Governance, Neighbours, Security* (Palgrave Macmillan 2009) 133.
98. See more Richard Youngs et al., 'European Democracy Support Annual Review 2022' (*Carnegie Europe*).
99. Peter Seeberg, 'The EU as a Realist Actor in Normative Clothes: EU Democracy Promotion in Lebanon and the European Neighbourhood Policy', 16 Democratization 2009, 81.
100. Stanislav Secrieru et al., 'The Eastern Partnership a Decade on; Looking Back, Thinking Ahead', European Union Institute for Security Studies 2019, 96.
101. Article 7 TEU (n 92).
102. Bojan Bugaric, 'Protecting Democracy and the Rule of Law in the European Union: The Hungarian Challenge' (29 April 2013).
103. Terry Lee, 'The Global Rise of "Fake News" and the Threat to Democratic Elections in the USA', 22 Public Administration and Policy 2019, 15, 21.

104. Stephan Haggard and Robert Kaufman, 'The Anatomy of Democratic Backsliding', 32 Journal of Democracy 2021, 27, 27.
105. Amir Ali, *Brexit and Liberal Democracy: Populism, Sovereignty, and the Nation-State* (Routledge 2021) 93.
106. Bojan Bugaric and Alenka Kuhelj, 'Varieties of Populism in Europe: Is the Rule of Law in Danger?', 10 Hague Journal on the Rule of Law 2018, 21, 32.
107. ibid, 23.
108. 'Joint Statement of the Russian Federation and the People's Republic of China on the International Relations Entering a New Era and the Global Sustainable Development' (*President of Russia*, 10 April 2023) <http://en.kremlin.ru/supplement/5770> accessed 11 April 2023.
109. Robert Hamilton, 'Russia's Attempts to Undermine Democracy in the West: Effects and Causes', 63 Orbis 2019, 334.
110. Rein Müllerson, *Dawn of a New Order: Geopolitics and the Clash of Ideologies* (IB Tauris 2017) 110.
111. 'Foreign Minister Sergey Lavrov's Answer to a Question from Rossiya 1 Television Channel, June 15, 2023—The Ministry of Foreign Affairs of the Russian Federation' <https://mid.ru/en/press_service/video/view/1888814/> accessed 22 June 2023; Russia's attitude to military interventions is best captured by Roy Allison, *Russia, the West, and Military Intervention* (OUP 2013); Roy Allison, 'Russia and the Post-2014 International Legal Order: Revisionism and Realpolitik', 93 International Affairs 2017, 519.
112. Steven Wheatley, 'Deliberative Democracy and Minorities', 14 European Journal of International Law 507, 2003.
113. Anatol Lieven, 'Ethnic Conflict in Kosovo: Cutting the Gordian Knot' (*Responsible Statecraft*, 2 June 2023) <https://responsiblestatecraft.org/2023/06/02/ethnic-conflict-in-kosovo-cutting-the-gordian-knot/> accessed 22 June 2023.
114. UN, UNMIK: Standards for Kosovo UN/PR/1078 (2003).
115. See more, Sevanna Poghosyan and Eiki Berg, 'When There Is a State? The Politics of Recognition and Kosovo', Diplomacy & Statecraft 2021, 614.
116. See two of the most important collections of articles on the subject, Roth and Fox (n 33); Richard Burchill, *Democracy and International Law* (Ashgate 2006).
117. Thomas Franck, 'The Emerging Right to Democratic Governance', 86 American Journal of International Law 1992, 46.
118. See, eg, Tesón (n 1); Cerna (n 12).
119. Susan Marks, 'What Has Become of the Emerging Right to Democratic Governance?', 22 European Journal of International Law 2011, 507; Euan Macdonald, 'International Law, Democratic Governance and September the 11th', 3 German Law Journal 2002; Thomas Carothers, 'The Backlash against Democracy Promotion', Foreign Affairs 2006, 55; Ruth Hanau Santini and Oz Hassan, 'Transatlantic Democracy Promotion and the Arab Spring', 47 The International Spectator 2012, 65.
120. Niels Petersen, 'The Principle of Democratic Teleology in International Law', 34 Brooklyn Journal of International Law 2008, 33; Pippan Christian, 'International Law, Domestic Political Orders, and the 'Democratic Imperative': Has Democracy Finally Emerged as a Global Legal Entitlement?' (1 October 2010). New York University Jean Monnet Center for International and Regional Economic Law & Justice Working Paper No 02/10; d'Aspremont (n 11).
121. Besson (n 12) 483.

122. Charlesworth (n 21) 108.
123. Samantha Besson, 'Sovereignty, International Law and Democracy', 22.2 European Journal of International Law 2011, 373, 382–383.
124. Michael Reisman, 'Sovereignty and Human Rights in Contemporary International Law' in Roth and Fox (n 33) 252.
125. James Crawford, 'Democracy and the Body of International Law', 91 Democratic Governance and International Law 2000, 107.
126. Michael Byers and Simon Chesterman, '"You, the People"': Pro-Democratic Intervention in International Law' in Roth and Fox (n 33) 260.
127. Owen (n 33) 343.
128. United Nations, 'UN Charter' (*United Nations*) Article 51, 2(4), Ch VII.
129. Byers and Chesterman (n 126) 279–280.
130. BS Chimni, 'Legitimating the International Rule of Law', 290 The Cambridge Companion to International Law 2012, 47.
131. Carothers (n 119); Hanau Santini and Hassan (n 119).

CHAPTER 7

THE IDEA OF EUROPEAN CULTURE(S) AND DIVERSITY

VERONIKA BÍLKOVÁ

1. Introduction

In *varietate Concordia* or *Unity in Diversity*. The official motto of the European Union (EU), introduced in 2000, expresses not only the aspirations of the world's most integrated organization but also the challenge that any project aimed at ensuring normative or institutional integration in Europe is confronted with. How, on the one hand, to promote a common European culture, without, on the other hand, denying and suppressing the vast cultural diversity that exists on the continent? How to ensure that the pursuit of unity and the respect for diversity complement each other rather than rival each other? Should the respect for diversity extend to all cultures in the same way? And what role should international law play in this process? These questions are far from new and far from related to EU integration only. They have, in fact, been asked again and again throughout the European history. Yet, they have recently gained new prominence, mostly due to the creation of, and developments within, new pan-European institutions.

This chapter discusses the way in which the tension between the promotion of a European culture and the need to accommodate cultural diversity in Europe has shaped international law and, vice versa, how international law has helped to strike a balance between the two interests. It shows that rather than adhering to one model and using one specific legal tool, this area itself has been marked by 'cultural diversity'. Three main approaches can be distinguished, each of them reflecting one type of the relationship that exists, or is supposed to exist, between the European culture on the one hand and the specific manifestations of cultural diversity on the other.

The first approach is reserved for cultures that are seen as *indigenous and viable* components of a European culture. This approach dominates at the national level, determining the space that is left to individual States in order to accommodate their national traditions and values. The aim is to ensure that the European culture builds on the plurality of national cultures and gradually contributes to their approximation, without threatening their continued independent existence. The interaction typically takes place in the political and moral areas. The doctrine of the margin of appreciation and the principle of subsidiarity are among the main legal tools used here.

The second approach applies to cultures considered as *indigenous but vulnerable* components of a European culture and of national cultures. This approach manifests itself at the subnational and partly cross-national levels, with respect to national minorities and certain non-territorial groups. The main ambition is to ensure that individuals belonging to such minorities and groups will be able to preserve their culture, if they wish to do so, without at the same time threatening the stability of the host countries. The emphasis is placed on the linguistic and, to a lesser degree, political dimension of the interaction. Legal tools employed here encompass the principle of non-discrimination and various positive measures.

The third approach pertains to cultures that are seen as *exogenous alternatives* to a European culture. This is the case of non-European cultures, whether they are encountered outside Europe or inside it, mostly within migrant communities. Here, the aims are not clearly set. They oscillate between the suppression of cultural diversity (assimilationism), separation of cultures (multiculturalism), and mutual enrichment (interculturalism). In recent times, the last view has taken the upper hand, relying on intercultural dialogue as one of its privileged tools. The religious dimension plays an important role in this dialogue and in the third approach as such.

This chapter discusses the topic from the international law perspective. International law is, obviously, created, implemented, and applied in various settings. The main emphasis in this text is placed on multilateral fora established within Europe (Council of Europe—CoE, EU), though occasionally, the national solutions and the solutions embraced at the universal level (League of Nations, the United Nations—UN) are scrutinized as well. The approaches of the CoE and the EU are used not only to illustrate the three approaches to cultural diversity but also to show that doing the same, and with similar tools, is not necessarily the same. Although 'unity in diversity' is the motto of the EU, it is the CoE which has been more successful in making this motto a reality.

The chapter does not embrace any special definition of culture or cultural diversity. Rather, it uses various definitions embraced by regional organizations and by scholars. A discussion of these definitions, together with an overview of how the relationship between a European culture and cultural diversity has been dealt with throughout history, is presented in Section 2. This section argues that the understanding of culture has been closely linked to normative and political considerations. The next three sections focus on the three approaches identified above. The text shows how the approaches have been applied within the EU, the CoE, and occasionally other organizations, and it demonstrates the role played by the relevant legal tools.

2. European Culture(s): Unity and/or Diversity?

Von Wise once wrote that '/w/e have become accustomed (at least on the continent) to speak of "the European" as a type based on observation; but to define it would be difficult'.[1] He also noted that '/d/espite the uncertainty and vagueness of all these concepts of Europe and the Europeans, we do feel that when we use these words they have a real meaning'.[2] The feeling that, despite our inability to draw clear borders and provide precise definitions, there is an entity called Europe which shares common culture, has prompted debates about European cultural unity and has triggered attempts to promote and protect this unity by legal means. Nowadays, these debates and attempts are most closely associated with the work of the CoE and the EU. Yet, their historical roots can be traced much further back.

The word Europe most probably comes from the ancient Greek terms εὐρύς (*eurús*), that is, wide, broad, and ὤψ (*ōps*), that is, eye, face. It would thus stand for wide-gazing or broad of aspect.[3] In ancient Greek mythology, Europa was a Phoenician princess abducted by Zeus in bull form to the island of Crete. In the classical Greek, the word had a geographical meaning, denoting first mainland Greece and later, the whole continent north of Greece. It also acquired a cultural meaning. Rather than merely describing a region, it referred to an entity that was marked by a common (higher) culture and that, due to its culture, was superior to other regions. This approach has remained relatively constant over time, though the understanding of what exactly is at the root of the so-perceived European superiority, has been gradually changing (Christian religion, higher civilization, white race, adherence to human rights, etc).

The expression 'European culture' has, however, appeared only relatively recently. After scattered uses in the 19th century, the expression gained prominence in the first half of the 20th century. At that time, European culture was mostly being connected with idealism, defined by literature and the arts, and contrasted with the materialist cultures of the US and the Soviet Union.[4] This approach was well captured in the often quoted passage by the French poet Paul Valéry, according to whom '/t/he idea of culture, of intelligence, of great works has for us a very ancient connection with the idea of Europe'.[5] In a less often quoted passage, Valéry added that what made European culture particularly singular was 'the most intense power of radiation combined with an equally intense power of assimilation'.[6] Although assimilation in Valéry's quotation related to the capacity of the continent to creatively absorb external impetuses, it can also be read as referring to the ambition of European culture to become dominant both externally (radiation) and internally (assimilation). As such, European culture was seen as part of a common 'European civilization' which, in addition to 'high culture' would also encompass rationalism, science and technology, and values such as humanism, respect for the rule law, or good administration. The 100th anniversary of the death of the German poet Johann Wolfgang Goethe in 1932 produced a clear image of what an epitome of European culture would look like—a person who is 'cosmopolitan and sophisticated, curious and creative, committed to the highest humane, Christian and Enlightenment values'.[7]

The self-portrait of Europe as a continent of high culture and of humanism was seriously shaken by the horrors of the two world wars and the unprecedented cruelties committed by European totalitarian regimes (Nazi Germany, Fascist Italy, Communist regimes in Central and Eastern Europe, etc). Pre-wars self-confidence was replaced by post-wars self-reflection. The main task for European culture was no longer to show the right way to those outside Europe but, rather, to achieve greater unity within Europe, preventing in that way the repetition of the tragedies of the 1910s–1940s. At the same time, the understanding of 'European culture' as an autonomous, relatively clearly defined, and positive set of values, ideas, and property started to be questioned. The new regional institutions created after World War II in Europe provided a privileged platform for the considerations of the concept of European culture and its relationship to cultural diversity within and outside Europe.[8]

The Council of Europe was established in 1949 'to achieve a greater unity between its members for the purpose of safeguarding and realising the ideals and principles which are their common heritage and facilitating their economic and social progress'.[9] The promotion of cooperation in cultural matters has been part of its agenda since its creation,[10] as has the pursuit of unity in broader, normative matters.

The first legal instrument related to culture, the European Cultural Convention, was adopted in 1954. In force since 1955, the Convention has been ratified by all CoE member States (as well as Belarus, Holy See, and Kazakhstan). By virtue of paragraph 3 of its preamble, it shall help to 'pursue a policy of common action designed to safeguard and encourage the development of European culture'. While it does not contain a definition of European culture or of a more commonly used term, 'common cultural heritage of Europe', the Convention indicates that this heritage is an aggregate of national contributions, which encompass both material objects—so-called objects of European cultural value, and non-material objects—such as languages, history, and civilization. Individual States are guardians of their national contributions to the common cultural heritage of Europe and they shall take appropriate measures to develop and safeguard these contributions. The Convention thus clearly sees no contradiction between cultural unity and cultural diversity—the latter is simply the source of the former.

The 1954 Convention defined culture in terms of artistic, linguistic, and historical heritage. In the following decades, this understanding was gradually, albeit not unambiguously, extended to the idea of culture as 'all of the values that give human beings their reasons for living and doing'.[11] This is reflected in the 2005 Council of Europe Framework Convention on the Value of Cultural Heritage for Society.[12] The Framework Convention introduces a concept of common heritage of Europe which consists of two parts—'all forms of cultural heritage in Europe which together constitute a shared source of remembrance, understanding, identity, cohesion and creativity' (Article 3a) and 'the ideals, principles and values, derived from the experience gained through progress and past conflicts, which foster the development of a peaceful and stable society, founded on respect for human rights, democracy and the rule of law' (Article 3b). The Explanatory Report labels the two parts as cultural heritage and intellectual heritage, stressing the mutually supporting interaction between them. The Framework Convention confirms the importance of cultural diversity, and it conceives of cultural heritage as one of the means to promote this diversity. Finally, the instrument links the protection and promotion of cultural heritage with human rights, recognizing that 'rights relating to cultural heritage are inherent in the right to participate in cultural life / ... /' (Article 1a). Human rights, moreover, make part of the intellectual heritage which is interconnected with cultural heritage.

Other instruments adopted within the CoE pertain to cultural heritage as well. They again seek both to promote cultural unity and to preserve cultural diversity in Europe. These instruments include the 1969 European Convention on the Protection of the Archaeological Heritage, the 1985 Convention for the Protection of the Architectural Heritage of Europe, the 1992 European Charter for Regional or Minority Languages, as well as soft law instruments.[13] Worth mentioning in the last category is the 2000 Declaration on Cultural Diversity.[14] Noting that 'cultural diversity has always been a dominant European characteristic and a fundamental political objective in the process of European construction' (paragraph 2 of the preamble), it calls upon States to 'examine ways of sustaining and promoting cultural and linguistic diversity in the new global environment, at all levels' (paragraph 3.1). The Declaration provides a set of recommendations, related to the use of cultural and audio-visual policies to promote sustainable cultural diversity. Cultural diversity as such is 'expressed in the co-existence and exchange of culturally different practices and in the provision and consumption of culturally different services and products' (paragraph 1.1). Sustainable cultural diversity relates to the need to ensure that technological and other developments do not compromise cultural diversity in future.

The European Union (European Communities (EC)) took a relatively long time to engage in cultural matters. The original Treaty of Rome contained no reference to either culture and/or diversity. It did, however, relate to peoples rather than people, thus aiming at, as Weiler recalls, 'not the creation of one people, but the union of many'.[15] The recognition of political diversity thus lies at the foundations of the European project. The recognition of cultural diversity followed later on. The first step was taken in 1973, when EC leaders adopted the Copenhagen Declaration on European Identity. The Declaration expresses the wish 'to preserve the rich variety of / ... / national cultures' (paragraph 1) and asserts that the European identity takes its originality from 'the diversity of cultures within the framework of a common European civilization, the attachment to common values and principles, the increasing convergence of attitudes to life, the awareness of having specific interests in common and the determination to take part in the construction of a United Europe' (paragraph 3). Similarly as in the CoE, cultural diversity is seen as one of the sources of a common European project, alongside intellectual and normative heritage.

Since the adoption of the Declaration, the debate about European culture(s) has been closely associated with that on the European identity and the construction of the

European *demos*. It is thus not surprising that the EC/EU first gained competences in the cultural area through the same instrument that introduced the European citizenship, namely, the Maastricht Treaty. Amending the Treaty of Rome, the Maastricht Treaty introduced a new Article 128 declaring that:

> The Community shall contribute to the flowering of the cultures of the Member States while respecting their national and regional diversity and at the same time bringing the common cultural heritage to the fore (paragraph 1).

The provision was taken over in the subsequent versions of the Treaty[16] and has finally become, in a slightly modified version, Article 167 of the Treaty on the Functioning of the EU (TFEU). Throughout the years, however, it has attracted criticism not only on account of its vagueness, but also because it invokes cultural unity and cultural diversity without explaining the relation between them, thus giving rise to the question: 'How does one celebrate national and regional cultural diversity while simultaneously "bringing the common cultural heritage to the fore"?'[17] Moreover, Article 6 of the Treaty makes it clear that in the area of culture, the EU role is limited to 'carrying out actions to support, coordinate or supplement the actions of the Member States' (supporting competences).

Since the adoption of the Treaty of Lisbon in 2007, the Treaty on the EU (TEU) has also contained several references to culture and cultural diversity. The preamble refers to 'drawing inspiration from the cultural, religious and humanist inheritance of Europe'. Article 3(3) stresses that the EU 'shall respect its rich cultural and linguistic diversity, and shall ensure that Europe's cultural heritage is safeguarded and enhanced'. That 'the Union shall respect cultural, religious and linguistic diversity' is also confirmed in Article 22 of the Charter of Fundamental Rights of the European Union, which brings the protection of cultural diversity into the ambit of human rights. None of the EU instruments, however, defines what the European culture is, speaking in fact more commonly about European cultural heritage and reserving the word cultures (in plural) for various cultures co-existing within Europe.

The changes in the legal framework have been accompanied by an extended use of the motto 'unity in diversity' which was first invoked in the 1990s and officially embraced by the EU in 2000. According to the official explanation provided on the EU website, the motto 'signifies how Europeans have come together, in the form of the EU, to work for peace and prosperity, while at the same time being enriched by the continent's many different cultures, traditions and languages'.[18] Yet, scholars have argued that the motto, and the EU cultural policy as such, have not struck the right balance between unity and diversity, putting emphasis on the former at the expense of the latter.[19] It has also been suggested that in the construction of the European culture, the EU draws on the pre-wars hegemonic approach.[20]

This section has shown that the idea of a common European culture has been part of the European thinking for centuries. The attempts to provide it with a concrete content, apparent in the early 20th century, have more recently given way to a different perspective. This perspective, marking the policies of the CoE and the EU, seeks to promote European cultural heritage which is defined, rather loosely, as a dynamic set of cultural objects and various values and traditions that stem from contributions by national and other cultures. The understanding of culture is thus not limited to artistic heritage but it closely linked to normative and political considerations as well. The aim of the cultural policy, both in the CoE and the EU, is to ensure the building up of a common European culture while at the same time maintaining and promoting cultural diversity in Europe. Cultural policy should also contribute to peace, security, and prosperity in the continent and outside it. The remaining sections discuss how these aims are pursued through the three approaches introduced above, and what role international law plays in this process.

3. National Diversity—Indigenous and Viable Components of European Culture

Europe is marked by large cultural diversity. Many different cultures co-exist here at the various (national, subnational, and transnational) levels. While all these cultures are supposed to make a unique contribution to a common European culture, they are not necessarily treated in the same way. This section focuses on those cultures that are considered as indigenous and viable components of a European culture. This approach dominates at the national level, with respect to national cultures predominant in individual States, and the emphasis is placed on diversity in the political and moral areas. After decades of European integration, States remain the main political, social, and cultural units in Europe. National cultures thus continue to be seen as the essential building blocks of a common European culture. The latter should complement, rather than replace, the former. While this goal is clear, the way in which it should be achieved is more controversial. How to accommodate national cultural diversity without putting the European integration project into jeopardy? And, vice versa, how to foster European culture without threatening national cultural diversity? The doctrine of the margin of appreciation, introduced by the European Court of Human Rights (ECtHR), and the principle of subsidiarity which, though used in various contexts, has gained special prominence in the EU, have been developed as privileged legal tools that should help to strike the balance between these conflicting interests.

The margin of appreciation concerns 'latitude of deference or error which the Strasbourg organs will allow to national legislative, executive, administrative and judicial bodies'.[21] The doctrine emerged in the late 1950s, when the then European Commission on Human Rights (ECmHR) was asked to assess emergency measures adopted by the UK and Ireland that were justified under the derogation clause enshrined in Article 15 of the European Convention on Human Rights (ECHR). The ECmHR indicated that States resorting to derogation enjoyed 'a certain measure of discretion in assessing the extent strictly required by the exigencies of the situation'.[22] While originally granted only with respect to proportionality of measures, the margin was soon extended to the determination of whether the conditions for derogation (a public emergency threatening the life of the nation) were met.[23] Later on, it was embraced by the ECtHR which has consistently applied it in virtually all cases involving derogation,[24] opting for what has been described as 'deferential attitude towards actions of, and claims made by, a national government that uses its power to derogate'.[25]

From the late 1960s, moreover, the Court has gradually expanded the use of the doctrine to other provisions of the Convention and has started using it 'as one of the / … / primary tools to accommodate diversity within Europe'.[26] In the 1968 Belgian Linguistic Case,[27] the ECtHR applied the doctrine to the principle of non-discrimination, holding that:

> In attempting to find out in a given case, whether or not there has been an arbitrary distinction, the Court cannot disregard those legal and factual features which characterise the life of the society in the State which / … / has to answer for the measure in dispute.[28]

In the 1976 *Handyside* case, the doctrine was used with respect to the right to freedom of expression and associated with the lack of a uniform conception of morals in Europe.[29] The ECtHR however also stressed that States do not have 'an unlimited power of appreciation' and that '/t/he domestic margin of appreciation / … / goes hand in hand with a European supervision'.[30] There is now a rich case law involving the application of the doctrine in cases relating to the rights enshrined in Articles 8–11 ECHR[31] and to certain other provisions (Article 1 of Protocol 1 to the Convention).[32]

The margin of appreciation is a flexible tool. Its extent depends on the nature of the right in question, the aims pursued by limitations imposed on the right, and the presence or absence of a European consensus. The last element merits particular attention, as it reflects the plurality of values and traditions among State Parties to the ECHR. The European consensus relates to 'the level of uniformity present in the legal frameworks of the member States / … / on a particular topic'.[33] It is, as Dzehtsiarou put it, 'a rebuttable presumption in favour of the solution adopted by the majority of the Contracting Parties'.[34] The narrower the degree of consensus, the wider the margin of appreciation left to States.[35]

When applying the doctrine of the margin of appreciation, the ECtHR virtually never refers to cultural diversity explicitly. References to this concept appear more often in connection with the position of minorities.[36] Occasionally, the ECtHR invokes it to describe the general features of a democratic society[37] and to explain the plurality of electoral models in Europe.[38] Implicitly, however, the concept of cultural diversity underpins the Court's case law granting discretion to national authorities in the absence of a common European standard. Cultural diversity, understood as the diversity in the political and moral areas, is presented as one of the features of the European space which, however, may be partly overcome by the gradual normative integration in Europe.

The margin of appreciation may be seen as a special articulation of a more general principle, that of subsidiarity. Subsidiarity, broadly speaking, describes 'a relationship between two institutions or norms, by which one supplements the other in appropriate circumstances'.[39] The word entered the legal dictionary in the 1930s but has only become commonly used in recent decades. Subsidiarity is part of general international law and has even been labelled as one of its constitutional principles.[40] In Europe, it has played a particularly prominent role in human rights law and the EU law.

Human rights law has always, in a way, relied on the principle of subsidiarity. Yet, as noted by Besson, '/f/rom a largely implicit and mainly jurisprudential principle used in discrete guises by international human rights bodies and courts since the 1960s, subsidiarity has become increasingly present and even central in international human rights reasoning'.[41] The ECtHR has invoked the principle in almost 800 cases. It has done so, typically, with a two-fold purpose. On the one hand, it uses the principle to confirm the primacy of the national human rights protection: national authorities are closer to the situation on the ground and better able to assess it and to ensure human rights protection on an everyday basis. On the other hand, the Court also recalls that the protection of human rights is not an internal affair of each State but lends itself to international supervision. The elements of 'the "sanctuarization" of States Parties' interpretation of ECHR rights' and of 'the "constitutionalization" of the ECtHR's control',[42] usually seen as opposites, are thus present at the same time and it is necessary to strike a balance between them. The principle of subsidiarity serves to find this balance and it gives us, as Carozza argues, 'a conceptual tool to mediate the polarity of pluralism and the common good in a globalized world'.[43] The principle is now enshrined in Protocol 15 to the ECHR,[44] which also confirms the close link between subsidiarity and the margin of appreciation.

In recent decades, the principle of subsidiarity has found particularly fertile ground in the EU.[45] Introduced to the EU law by the Maastricht Treaty, it is now laid down in Article 5(3) TEU. The provision stipulates that:

> Under the principle of subsidiarity, in areas which do not fall within its exclusive competence, the Union shall act only if and in so far as the objectives of the proposed action cannot be sufficiently achieved by the Member States, either at central level or at regional and local level, but can rather, by reason of the scale or effects of the proposed action, be better achieved at Union level.

The principle of subsidiarity within EU law applies to areas in which the EU exercises non-exclusive powers. These are areas of shared competences, for example, social policy and the environment, and those where the EU exercises supporting competences, including culture. The principle sets the primacy of the action by the member States in these areas and reserves the intervention of the EU to the situations when the objectives of the action cannot be sufficiently achieved at the national level (necessity) and the action can be implemented more successfully by the EU (added value).

The principle of subsidiarity in EU law is based on somewhat different premises than that applied in human rights law. The aim is not only, and not so much, to safeguard or promote cultural diversity but, rather, to guarantee efficiency by making sure that the relevant actions are taken at the most adequate (national or EU) level. It is open to question whether such a functional approach is sufficient to strike the right balance between EU integration and the preservation of cultural diversity or whether it could in itself, as some have argued,[46] become a threat to the latter. What is, however, shared in the CoE and the EU is an understanding of national cultures as crucial, even indispensable, building blocks of a common European culture, the idea that the pursuit of unity and respect for diversity are not mutually excluding goals and the conviction that legal tools, such as the margin of appreciation and the principle of subsidiarity, may help bring these goals together.

4. Subnational Diversity—Indigenous but Vulnerable Components of European Culture

Cultural diversity in Europe does not exhaust itself at the national level. States are inhabited by groups of people who differ from the majority population by their ethnicity, the language they speak, the religion they profess, their sexual orientation, and many other features. Throughout history, minorities—regardless of the criterion that sets them apart—have been subject to discrimination and even persecution. Law, at the national and international level, has reacted to this phenomenon, seeking to protect persons belonging to non-dominant groups. National minorities have traditionally been paid special attention in this context. Similarly to (dominant) national cultures, cultures of national minorities are seen as indigenous components of a European culture. Unlike them, they are considered vulnerable and in need of protection. The main aim of the legal regimes established in this area is thus to ensure that minorities will be able to preserve their culture, if they wish to do so, without at the same time threatening the stability of the host countries. The emphasis, this time, is placed on the linguistic and, to a lesser extent, political dimensions of the interaction.

The domestic approaches to national minorities in Europe reveal a high degree of 'cultural diversity'. Some countries deny that national minorities exist at all, at least in their territory (France). Other countries provide a list of groups to which they assign the legal status of national minorities (Germany, Sweden) or have a general definition of national minorities (Czech Republic, Switzerland). Still other countries have no list and no definition but leave it up to their inhabitants to decide whether they make up part of a minority (Romania). The domestic definitions of national minorities, where they exist, also show important differences, though they tend to combine objective elements (non-dominant position, permanent settlement, or common language) with subjective ones (will to preserve and promote common identity). Individuals are usually left free to decide whether they want to be considered members of a national minority or not. The domestic legal regulations are not uniform in whether they treat minority rights as individual or collective rights (or a combination of both) and in which rights they accord to the members of national minorities.

In view of such a high degree of diversity, it is not surprising that the international legal regime related to national minorities has not been easily built in Europe. The first provisions on national minorities were included in the peace treaties adopted in the 19th century (Vienna 1814–1815, Paris 1856, Berlin 1878).[47] Yet, they only concerned specific minorities and were relatively vague. A more comprehensive system of the protection of national minorities was construed after World War I, within the League of Nations (LoN).[48] The LoN was not a regional organization but its minority system was almost exclusively designed for Europe or, more exactly, for the new countries established in Central and Eastern Europe after the break-up of multinational empires. The system aimed at ensuring that national minorities, that is, groups founding themselves in a country predominantly inhabited by another nation, would neither be subject to repression, nor would they threaten the stability of the host country.

The minority system of the LoN was based on a series of multilateral[49] and bilateral[50] treaties and unilateral declarations,[51] imposed on the new States as a precondition for their recognition or their admission to the LoN. The treaties and declarations combined the guarantees of non-discrimination for all inhabitants of the new countries, irrespective of their birth, nationality, language, race, or religion, with certain positive rights granted specifically to certain national minorities. Those rights typically encompassed the right to use the minority language in private and public life, including education, the right to political participation, and the right to some minimal degree of cultural autonomy. The rights were granted to the minorities listed in the instruments or meeting the general criterion of substantive territorial representation. Smaller and/or non-territorial minorities, such as the Roma, were left out of the system. There was, moreover, no similar regulation applicable in other regions and no general, universal instrument on minority protection.

The partial and *ad hoc* nature of the minority guarantees together with the inefficiency of the control mechanisms,[52] led to the gradual demise of the system, which was eventually declared defunct in 1950.[53] At the same time, the collectivist approach to national minorities was replaced by an individualist one. Members of national minorities were no longer seen as parts of a collective entity whose special identity had to be preserved and promoted by both negative and positive measures, but as individuals who had to be protected against discrimination. Due to this approach, no special instrument on national minorities was adopted during the Cold War and the general instruments on human rights usually did not contain provisions on minorities.[54] The Consultative Assembly of the CoE sought to change this situation at the turn of the 1950s and 1960s, proposing the adoption of a new protocol to the ECHR on national minorities[55] but the proposal failed to take root.

Another turning point came after 1990, triggered again by the political changes in Central and Eastern Europe. The first institution to engage with the issue of national minorities was the Conference for the Security and Cooperation in Europe (CSCE). In its Copenhagen document, adopted in 1990, the participating States undertook to 'protect the ethnic, cultural, linguistic and religious identity of national minorities on their territory and create conditions for the promotion of that identity' (Article 33). They also recognized that persons belonging to national minorities shall not be discriminated against and shall enjoy various rights that would help them promote their cultural identity. Two years later, the CSCE established the position of the High Commissioner on National Minorities. In the same year, this time within the UN, the Declaration on the Rights of Persons Belonging to National or Ethnic, Religious and Linguistic Minorities,[56] was adopted, confirming the obligation of States to protect national minorities and enshrining various rights that members of such minorities enjoy.

Within the CoE, the idea of adopting a new protocol to the ECHR was shortly resurrected after 1990.[57] However, it encountered opposition among member States, some of which either did not want to have any regulation on national minorities, or favoured regulation that would leave more discretion to national authorities. By means of a compromise, the Framework Convention for the Protection of National Minorities (FCNM) was adopted in 1994 (and entered into force in 1998).[58] The FCNM recognizes that '/t/he protection of national minorities and of the rights and freedoms of persons belonging to those minorities forms an integral part of the international protection of human rights' (Article 1). It also enshrines the principle of non-discrimination and establishes various negative and positive obligations for States (the obligations to guarantee freedom of expression, language rights, educational rights, etc). The text, however, is drafted in a relatively vague and imprecise manner, leaving space for States' discretion. The implementation of the treaty is monitored and assessed by the Committee of Ministers, assisted by the Advisory Committee (ACFC) composed of national experts.

For the EU, the protection of minorities was, for a long time, solely a foreign policy issue. Yet, by first including 'the guarantees for the rights of ethnic and national groups and minorities'[59] among the conditions for the recognition of new States in Central and Eastern Europe and later on admitting some of the States from that region among its members, the EC/EU has gradually internalized the issue, despite the resistance of some of its older members. Nowadays, 'respect for human rights, including the right of persons belonging to minorities' is ranked among the values of the EU enshrined in Article 2 TEU. There is, however, no specific instrument on national minorities adopted within the EU and the Charter of Fundamental Rights and Freedoms refers to national minorities only in its non-discrimination provision.[60]

The overview of the legal regulation applicable to national minorities shows that Europe has treated cultures of such minorities or, more exactly, of some of these minorities, as indigenous but vulnerable component of the European culture. Due to important differences in domestic approaches, the instruments adopted in this area have always been rather general and vague. They have moreover only applied to certain minorities and/or to minorities in certain countries. Today, both the CoE and, to a lesser extent, the EU, following the precedent set by the LoN, seek to protect national minorities through a combination of the principle of non-discrimination and a set of positive rights. These legal tools should help ensure that national minorities will be able to preserve their culture to the extent they wish and in a way that will not threaten the stability of the host country.

5. Cross-National Diversity—Exogenous Alternatives to European Culture

The last level at which cultural diversity manifests itself is the cross-national one. It relates to diversity which is not confined within the borders of one country but transcends these borders. It encompasses such groups as ethnical minorities that spread across various countries with no substantive territorial representation, for example, Roma and Sinti, as well as migrants and refugees. Whereas the former have been treated in a largely similar way as national minorities,[61] the latter have been reserved a different treatment. Their cultures, understood often in religious terms, have been seen as exogenous alternatives to the European culture, giving rise to the dilemma as to how to accommodate them without placing the European culture into jeopardy.

Three main models can be distinguished.[62] The Europocentric (assimilationist) model is based on the conviction that the European culture is superior to other cultures inside or outside Europe. As such, it should be promoted and gradually become the dominant, if not the exclusive culture on the continent or even in the world. The cultural relativist (multiculturalist) model posits that the European culture is just one of many cultures. All cultures, within or outside Europe, are equally valuable and should be free to flourish next to each other. The cultural pluralist (interculturalist) model understands cultures as dynamic sets of values and practices that evolve thanks to interactions with other cultures. Such interactions should be encouraged and should make it possible to identify those values or practices that are more valuable and that should be upheld and supported.

For a long time, the regulation of migration in Europe was left to individual States which were free to choose any of the models. Gradually, however, the migration issues started to be brought to the international level. The prime focus has been on regulating the process of migration to Europe, distinguishing among various categories of persons on the basis of the causes/aims of their move to Europe and establishing minimal rules that should be applied to them. Asylum seekers and refugees, stateless persons, migrant workers and other, lawful or unlawful, migrants are the main categories and, over the years, both the CoE and the EU have adopted instruments regulating the status of those persons. Within the CoE, the European Convention on the Legal Status of Migrant

Workers was enacted in 1977, though with its eleven ratifications, this instrument has not really contributed to the harmonization of the regimes applicable to migrant workers. Moreover, despite the broad title, the instrument applies to migrants from other member States only. The EU has developed a common migration and asylum policy which relies on uniform substantive and procedural rules that the EU States shall apply with respect to migrants and asylum seekers on their territory.[63]

Only relatively recently, after the end of the Cold War, have the two organizations started to pay attention to the migrant communities settled within Europe and to the relationship of their cultures to a European culture and its national components. In the first years, cultural relativism (multiculturalism) was the predominant model, as reflected in the 1990 Declaration on the multicultural society and European cultural identity, adopted by the CoE. Yet, due to its contestation in the academic literature[64] and by politicians (Cameron, Merkel, Sarkozy),[65] multiculturalism gave way, one decade later, to cultural pluralism (interculturalism). This model has found one of the privileged tools for its realization in the intercultural dialogue (ICD).[66]

In the CoE, the concept of ICD was first introduced in 1997, in a report by the European Task Force on Culture and Development.[67] The report noted, in relation to ICD that '/t/he co-existence of different cultures entails dialogue, not confrontation. It is not a matter of delimiting, but of opening up'.[68] The importance of ICD was stressed in the 2004 Opatija Declaration on Intercultural Dialogue and Conflict Prevention, which saw ICD as an instrument to 'preserve the required balance between the safeguarding of cultural diversity and the necessary social cohesion within the various states'. The Declaration also warned against the risks of cultural differences 'resulting in a retreat into identity or community' or 'justifying a policy of forced assimilation stemming from a desire for domination', thus taking a firm stance against both assimilationism and multiculturalism.

The Opatija Declaration was followed by the 2005 Faro Declaration of the CoE's Strategy for Developing Intercultural Dialogue and the 2008 White Paper on Intercultural Dialogue. The latter instrument again contrasts the approach based on ICD which is defined as 'an open and respectful exchange of views between individuals, groups with different ethnic, cultural, religious and linguistic backgrounds and heritage on the basis of mutual understanding and respect',[69] with those used in the past. The new approach, allegedly,

> takes from assimilation the focus on the individual; it takes from multiculturalism the recognition of cultural diversity. And it adds the new element, critical to integration and social cohesion, of dialogue on the basis of equal dignity and shared values.[70]

The White Paper presents ICD as part of a public debate in a free, open, democratic, and culturally diverse international society. Migration is cited as one, albeit not the only, factor making ICD necessary in current European societies.[71] In fact, in a broad understanding, ICD can be applied to any cultural interactions within or outside Europe. Yet, as the programmes on ICD run by the CoE show,[72] it is primarily designed for exchanges with cultures that are not seen as traditional components of a European culture.

Within the EU, ICD started to be mentioned in the early 2000s but it came to the fore only in 2005, when the EU referred to the concept several times and declared 2008 the European Year of Intercultural Dialogue. In 2007, the promotion of cultural diversity and ICD was identified as one of the strategic objectives of the EU.[73] ICD was then described as 'a sustainable process contributing to European identity, citizenship and social cohesion, including by the development of the intercultural competences of citizens'.[74] The updated version of the Agenda, issued in 2018, explicitly links ICD to migration, stressing that:

> Culture promotes active citizenship, common values, inclusion and intercultural dialogue within Europe and across the globe. It brings people together, including newly arrived refugees and other migrants, and helps us feel part of communities.[75]

ICD as an instrument of the construction of the European identity has been invoked in other EU instruments as well. Unlike the CoE, the EU does not introduce any definition of ICD, nor does it explain how a tool, whose primary aim is to contribute to European identity, could be applied without threatening cultural diversity. As Agustin notes, 'ICD seems to legitimize the EU's economic model, adding the cultural dimension rather than proposing an alternative model to deal with cultural diversity'.[76]

Cultural diversity stemming from the presence within Europe of migrant communities, whose cultures are seen as exogenous alternatives to the European culture, has thus been addressed through several approaches. In recent decades, the approach based on cultural pluralism (interculturalism) has prevailed both in the CoE and in the EU, with ICD as one of its privileged tools. Over the years, the CoE has come to a relatively clear vision of how the tool should be used to accommodate cultural diversity and in which way the model based on it is preferable to the assimilationist and multiculturalist models. The EU, on the contrary, seems to give right to Shore who argues that 't/he rationale underlying EU cultural policies appears to be less about celebrating 'difference' / … / than about promoting the idea of Europe's overarching unity through that diversity'.[77]

6. Concluding Remarks

This chapter has considered the ways in which the striving for a common European culture and the efforts to preserve cultural diversity manifesting itself at the national, subnational, and cross-national levels are brought together in Europe. It has shown that three main approaches have been used to strike the balance between the two goals. The first approach is reserved to cultures that are seen as indigenous and viable components of the European culture, the second to those considered as indigenous but vulnerable components of this culture, and the third to those found to be exogenous alternatives to it. The three approaches have different ambitions and use different legal tools. The first approach, applied to national cultures, seeks to ensure that the European culture builds on the plurality of national cultures, without threatening their continued independent existence. The tools used under this approach encompass the doctrine of the margin of appreciation and the principle of subsidiarity. The second approach, used with respect to national minorities, aims at ensuring protection and preservation of vulnerable cultures. It relies on tools such as the principle of non-discrimination and positive measures. The third approach, displayed with regard to migrant communities in Europe, strives to promote integration and social cohesion through an exchange of views based on mutual respect. It has relied on intercultural dialogue as one of its preferred tool.

The chapter has also shown that although the two European regional organizations, the CoE and the EU, both pursue 'unity in diversity' and they do so through similar tools, the former has been so far more successful in establishing rules and designing mechanisms making this pursuit possible. This is not to say that the CoE has a coherent and comprehensive plan as to how to deal with different manifestations of cultural diversity. The CoE initiatives displayed on the three levels in fact have rather loose connections among themselves. Yet, they all seem to reflect the same idea that the construction of a common European culture and the preservation of cultural diversity are mutually complementary projects. The EU, on the contrary, despite having declared 'unity in diversity' its official motto, has fallen behind in elaborating mechanisms that would make this motto a reality. When, moreover, it uses mechanisms similar to those of the CoE, if may do so more for reasons of efficiency or in order to strengthen the common identity rather than to accommodate and/or promote diversity. What is, however, shared by the two organizations is that in their search for a balance between the pursuit of unity and respect for diversity, they have both relied on international legal tools. International law has thus turned out to be indispensable in this search and it has been on its turn, through various new legal instruments and concepts, enriched by it.

Notes

1. Leopold Von Wiese, 'What Is European Culture?', 11(1) The British Journal of Sociology, 1960, 2.
2. ibid, 3.
3. An alternative theory ascribes to the word a Semitic origin, connecting it to the Akkadian word *gharoob* or *erebu*, meaning west or sunset.
4. Benjamin G Martin, *'European Culture' Is an Invented Tradition* https://aeon.co/ideas/european-culture-is-an-invented-tradition accessed 3 March 2020.
5. Paul Valéry, *The Outlook for Intelligence* (Princeton UP 1962) 31.
6. ibid.
7. Martin (n 4).
8. Monica Sassatelli, *Becoming Europeans. Cultural Identity and Cultural Policies* (Palgrave Macmillan 2009).

9. Article 1(1) of the Statute of the Council of Europe.
10. The Statute of the Council of Europe in its Article 1(2) explicitly ranks cultural matters among areas in which agreements and common action should be adopted in order to achieve the aims of the organization.
11. CM(2004)233-Add2, *Report by the Secretary General to the Wroclaw Conference*, Opening conference for the celebrations of the 50th Anniversary of the European Cultural Convention (Wroclaw, 9–10 December 2004), 22 December 2004, point 1.4.
12. The Convention entered into force in 2011 but so far, it has only secured nineteen ratifications (and six signatures).
13. See, for instance, Committee of Ministers' Recommendation No R(98)5 concerning heritage education, 17 March 1998, or Committee of Ministers' Resolution (98) 4 on Cultural Routes, 17 March 1998.
14. Committee of Ministers' Declaration on cultural diversity, 7 December 2000. The text bears resemblance to the Universal Declaration on Cultural Diversity, which was adopted on 2 November 2001 by UNESCO, preceding the adoption of the 2005 Convention on the Protection and Promotion of the Diversity of Cultural Expressions. The Universal Declaration speaks not only about cultural diversity, which is labelled as the common heritage of mankind, to be 'recognized and affirmed for the benefit of present and future generations' (Article 1), but also about cultural pluralism, which 'gives policy expression to the reality of cultural diversity' (Article 2).
15. Joseph H H Weiler, *The Constitution of Europe. 'Do the New Clothes Have an Emperor?' and Other Essays on European Integration* (CUP 1999) 327.
16. The 1997 Amsterdam Treaty added a reference to cultural diversity into Article 128(4) which since then has read as follows: 'The Community shall take cultural aspects into account in its action under other provisions of this Treaty, in particular in order to respect and to promote the diversity of its cultures.' The original version did not contain the second part of the sentence.
17. See also Cris Shore, 'In uno plures' (?). EU Cultural Policy and the Governance of Europe, 5 Cultural Analysis 2006, 16.
18. The EU motto, online at https://europa.eu/european-union/about-eu/symbols/motto_en accessed 3 March 2020.
19. Shore (n 17) 17.
20. Jan Nederveen Pieterse, 'Fictions of Europe', 32(3) Race and Class 1991, 4.
21. Howard C Yourow, *The Margin of Appreciation Doctrine in the Dynamics of European Human Rights Jurisprudence* (Martinus Nijhoff 1996) 13.
22. ECmHR, *Greece v United Kingdom*, App no 176/56, 26 September 1958, 176.
23. ECmHR, *Lawless v Ireland*, App no 332/57, 1 July 1961, §90.
24. See ECtHR, *Ireland v The United Kingdom*, App no 5310/71, 18 January 1978, §§212–214; *Brannigan & McBride v United Kingdom*, App Nos 14553/89 and 14554/89, 26 May 1993, §§41–66.
25. Oren Gross and Fionnuala Ni Aolain, 'From Discretion to Scrutiny: Revisiting the Application of the Margin of Appreciation Doctrine in the Context of Article 15 of the European Convention on Human Rights', 23(3) Human Rights Quarterly 2001, 633.
26. Aaron A Ostrovsky, 'What's So Funny about Peace, Love, and Understanding? How the Margin of Appreciation Doctrine Preserves Core Human Rights within Cultural Diversity and Legitimises International Human Rights Tribunals, 1(1) Hanse Law Review 2005, 48.

27. ECtHR, *Case Relating to Certain Aspects of the Laws on the Use of Languages in Education in Belgium (No. 2)*, App nos 1474/62, 1677/62, 1691/62, 1769/63, 1994/63, 2126/64, 23 July 1968.
28. ibid, §10.
29. ECtHR, *Handyside v The United Kingdom*, App no 5493/72, 7 December 1976.
30. ibid, §49.
31. See Steven Greer, *The Margin of Appreciation: Interpretation and Discretion under the European Convention on Human Right* (Council of Europe 2000) 9–11. See also Yutaka Arai-Takahashi, *The Margin of Appreciation Doctrine and the Principle of Proportionality in the Jurisprudence of the ECHR* (Intersentia 2002).
32. See, for instance, ECtHR, *Sporrong and Lönnroth v Sweden*, App nos 7151/75 and 7152/75, 23 September 1982; *Lithgow and Others v The United Kingdom*, App nos 9006/80, 9262/81, 9263/81, 9265/81, 9266/81, 9313/81, 9405/81, 8 July 1986.
33. Interpretative mechanisms of ECHR case law: the concept of European consensus, online at https://www.coe.int/en/web/help/article-echr-case-law accessed 3 March 2020.
34. Kanstantsin Dzehtsiarou, 'European Consensus and the Evolutive Interpretation of the European Convention on Human Rights', 12 German Law Journal 2011, 1733.
35. 'Where, however, there is no consensus within the Member States of the Council of Europe, either as to the relative importance of the interest at stake or as to how best to protect it, the margin will be wider.' ECtHR, *Dickson v The United Kingdom*, App no 44362/04, 4 December 2007, §78.
36. See, for instance, ECtHR, *Chapman v The United Kingdom*, App no 27238/95, 18 January 2001, §§93–94; *D.H. and Others v. The Czech Republic*, App no 57325/00, 13 November 2007, §181.
37. See, for instance, ECtHR, *İzzettin Doğan and Others v Turkey*, App no 62649/10, 26 April 2016, §182.
38. See, for instance, ECtHR, *Moohan and Gillon v The United Kingdom*, App nos 22962/15 and 23345/15, 13 June 2007, §42.
39. Gerald L Neuman, 'Subsidiarity' in Dinah Shelton (ed), *The Oxford Handbook of International Human Rights Law* (OUP 2013) 361.
40. Andreas Follesdal, 'The Principle of Subsidiarity as a Constitutional Principle in International Law', *Jean Monnet Working Paper 12/11*.
41. Samantha Besson, 'Subsidiarity in International Human Rights Law—What Is Subsidiary about Human Rights?', 61(1) American Journal of Jurisprudence 2016, 70.
42. ibid, 72.
43. Paolo Carozza, 'Subsidiarity as a Structural Principle of International Human Rights Law', 97(1) American Journal of International Law 2003, 38. See also Robert Spano, 'Universality or Diversity of Human Rights? Strasbourg in the Age of Subsidiarity', 14 Human Rights Law Review 2014, 487–502.
44. Protocol 15 to the ECHR was adopted in 2013 but entered into force only in 2021.
45. See also Dieter Fuchs and Hans-Dieter Klingemann, *Cultural Diversity, European Identity and the Legitimacy of the EU* (Edward Elgar 2011).
46. Katharine Sarikakis, 'Cultural Diversity and Subsidiarity: The Case of Cultural Tourism in the European Union' in Elisabeth Dumont and Jacques Teller (eds), *Media and Cultural Policy in the European Union* (Brill 2007) 45–64.
47. Preece J Jackson, 'Minority Rights in Europe: From Westphalia to Helsinki', 23(1) Review of International Studies 1997, 78–81.

48. See H Rosting, 'Protection of Minorities by the League of Nations', 17(4) American Journal of International Law 1923, 641–660; Carole Fink, 'The League of Nations and the Minorities Question' 157(4) World Affairs, Woodrow Wilson and the League of Nations: Part One 1995, 197–205.
49. Multilateral treaties on minorities were concluded between the Principal Allied and Associated Powers on the one hand and Poland (1919), Czechoslovakia (1919), The Kingdom of Serbs, Croats and Slovenes (1919), Romania (1919), and Greece (1920) on the other.
50. Bilateral treaties on minorities were concluded, for instance, between Austria and Czechoslovakia (1920) or Germany and Poland (1922).
51. Unilateral declarations on minorities were issued by Albania (1921), Lithuania (1922), Latvia (1923), Bulgaria (1924), and Greece (1924).
52. The control mechanisms encompassed State complaints and individual petitions to the Council of the League of Nations and the application to the Permanent Court of International Justice.
53. UN Doc E/CN.4/367, *Study of the Legal Validity of the Undertakings Concerning Minorities*, 7 April 1950.
54. One exception to this rule was the 1966 International Covenant on Civil and Political Rights (ICCPR) which, in its Article 27, stipulates: 'In those States in which ethnic, religious or linguistic minorities exist, persons belonging to such minorities shall not be denied the right, in community with the other members of their group, to enjoy their own culture, to profess and practise their own religion, or to use their own language.'
55. Doc 1002, *Position of national minorities in Europe*, 30 April 1959; and Recommendation 285, *Rights of national minorities*, 28 April 1961.
56. UN Doc A/RES/47/135, *Declaration on the Rights of Persons Belonging to National or Ethnic, Religious and Linguistic Minorities*, 3 February 1993.
57. See Florence Benoît-Rohmer (ed), *The Minority Question in Europe: Towards a Coherent System of Protection for National Minorities* (Manhattan Publishing Co 1996).
58. The instrument entered into force in 1998. By July 2024, it had secured thirty-nine ratifications and four more signatures. Among those which have neither signed nor ratified this Convention are France and Turkey.
59. EC, *Declaration on the Guidelines on the Recognition of New States in Eastern Europe and in the Soviet Union*, 16 December 1991.
60. Article 21 of the Charter: 'Any discrimination based on any ground such as sex, race, colour, ethnic or social origin, genetic features, language, religion or belief, political or any other opinion, *membership of a national minority*, property, birth, disability, age or sexual orientation shall be prohibited' (emphasis added).
61. Council of Europe/European Union, 'The Protection of the Rights of Roma People by National Human Rights Structures', Workshop De-Briefing Paper, 24–25 February 2009.
62. Michael Emerson (ed), *Interculturalism Europe and its Muslims in Search of Sound Societal Models* (Centre for European Policy Studies 2011).
63. Kay Hailbronner, *Immigration and Asylum Law and Policy of the European Union* (Brill/Nijhoff 2000).
64. Christian Joppke, 'The Retreat of Multiculturalism in the Liberal State: Theory and Policy', 55(2) The British Journal of Sociology 2004, 237–257.
65. Rita Chin, *The Crisis of Multiculturalism in Europe: A History* (Princeton UP 2017).

66. Oscar Garcia Agustín, 'Intercultural Dialogue: Visions of the Council of Europe and the European Commission for a Post-Multiculturalist Era' Journal of Intercultural Communication 2012, online at https://immi.se/oldwebsite/nr29/garcia.html accessed 21 March 2020.
67. Council of Europe, *In from the Margins: A Contribution to the Debate on Culture and Development in Europe* (European Task Force on Culture and Development 1997).
68. ibid, 47.
69. Council of Europe, *White Paper on Intercultural Dialogue. Living Together as Equals in Dignity*, June 2008, 10.
70. ibid, 19.
71. ibid, 36. See Council of Europe, *Competences For Democratic Culture Living Together as Equals in Culturally Diverse Democratic Societies*, 2016, 17.
72. The programmes focus on topics such as migration, women as agents of change in Mediterranean societies, or the reinforcement of democratic processes and human rights in the Euro-Mediterranean region.
73. Resolution of the Council 2007/C 287/01 of 16 November 2007 on a European Agenda for Culture, paragraph 2(a).
74. ibid, paragraph 3A.
75. COM(2018) 267 final, *A New European Agenda for Culture*, Brussels, 22 May 2018, 1.
76. Agustín (n 66).
77. Shore (n 17) 17.

CHAPTER 8

THE IDEAS OF PROSPERITY AND SOLIDARITY IN EUROPEAN INTERNATIONAL LAW

GAIL LYTHGOE AND AKBAR RASULOV

1. Introduction

Tracing the history of ideas is, by and large, a thankless task. The costs involved are usually too high, the payoff at the end is never certain, and the risk of getting everything wrong is palpable and ever-present.

A large part of what makes the enterprise so difficult comes, of course, from the fundamental uncertainty surrounding its object. Do ideas exist independently of our perceptions of them? If they do, what is the actual mode of that existence? Is it Platonic, Hegelian, Jungian, or something else entirely? If they don't, how can a history of ideas be told separately from that of the people who think them or the language used to express them?

Questions of abstract philosophy aside, an equally important problem that confronts every historian of ideas is the problem of causal inference and proof. If several unconnected scholars over a long enough period of time end up using of the same set of concepts or returning to the same set of themes in their writings, does that mean there was something about these concepts and themes that induced them to do so? What could this something be? And is it the same 'thing' also that pushes us now to recognize this continuity? Do some continuities get recognized more readily than others? Should we be worried about that? How can we know that what we see in other people's discourses is not just a projection of our own bias and prejudices? How can we know that the history we purport to write about other people's ideas does, in fact, reflect something real and true about their actual thoughts and lived experiences? And what place should we assign in all this to all the various mechanisms of repression, denial, foreclosure, and what Gayatri Chakravorty Spivak calls sanctioned ignorance?[1]

If in the late 19th century the concept of the general rate of profit, as Engels claims, was indeed 'completely foreign', in subjective terms, 'to the mind of the individual capitalist', how can we go about testing whether objectively it may, nevertheless, have played a role in shaping the politics and ideology of the capitalist class of the time?[2] If most European international lawyers over the last several decades did not consciously embrace prosperity and solidarity as operatively significant international legal categories, how can we go about seeing if these concepts have, nevertheless, been theoretically and politically active in international law's legal imaginary in Europe?

None of these challenges, of course, is unique to the legal discipline. Recognizing their significance, however, helps highlight the fundamental importance of the question of method. If history is to be regarded as the study of objects in the context of their movement-through-time, what exactly are those objects whose movement-through-time the history of international legal ideas aims to examine? The answer that we propose to give to this question proceeds from a combination of two theses. First, ideas do not 'exist' or 'evolve' in isolation from one another. Every history of an idea, in the final analysis, is the history also of the surrounding *conceptual framework* by which it is structured and contextualized. Secondly, every conceptual framework is a product of its enabling—or as Michel Foucault would say, 'authorising'—discursive *formation*. Concepts, assumptions, beliefs, reasoning protocols do not emerge because they are necessitated into existence by some higher reason or by the semantic demands of objective reality. Rather, they are assembled, constructed, and brought into being partly as functions and building tools of the corresponding field of discourse, partly as side effects of the differentiational dynamics set in motion by its theoretical structure.[3]

Most critically-minded legal scholars today would probably agree that the study of legal discourses, generally, should go beyond surface-level examinations of language-use patterns. Beyond this basic agreement, however, there doesn't seem to be much consensus. If one accepts the view that concepts always exist as part of broader frameworks and that such frameworks in practice may persist or operate not only on the immediately observable surface of our discourse, but also, as it were, 'beneath' or 'behind' it, every attempt to examine the history of a concept inevitably turns into an extension of the decision as to which particular model of the *collective unconscious* one ought to adopt as a working theory.[4] Should one go for the ideology critique of Gyorgy Lukacs, the archaeology of Foucault, the post-colonial critique of Spivak, the mythopoesis of Claude Levi-Strauss?[5] Each of these options presents a viable enough alternative. Yet none of them, at the same time, seems any more obvious or defensible than others.

The compromise solution that we adopt in this chapter seeks to combine a certain form of intertextualist analysis with what one might call politico-cultural contextualism. Unlike the more radical forms of intertextuality studies, the approach we take in these pages stops at a relatively moderate stage of narratological excavations.[6] At most, we seek to proceed only a few modest steps beyond the immediately observable textual surfaces produced within the field of the European international law (EIL) discourse.

A similar preference for restraint characterizes also our approach to identifying what counts as the relevant politico-cultural contexts. Unlike the more sweeping takes on the notion of European legal history that try to trace it back to the Middle Ages,[7] the argument we present in this chapter proceeds from the assumption that the most productive context for examining the operative thought-structure behind contemporary EIL lies much closer to us in time. Seen in this context, the historical horizon of our inquiry one might say does not really extend before the middle of the last century. This is not to imply, of course, that EIL's history begins only at that point. Our claim only says that if we intend to understand the role which the ideas of prosperity and solidarity play in contemporary EIL, it is not, in fact, necessary to go any further back than that.

The theoretical framing we propose will not be to everyone's liking. What we intend to sketch out in these pages is the history of the ideas of prosperity and solidarity taken in the context of the *general legal imaginary* that has come to develop within and around EIL. It is not the only story one might want to tell about these ideas. But it is certainly an important one. The account we present begins with a rather conservative—some might even say, artificially limited—conception of 'Europeanness', at the root of which lies the notion of Europe as an abstract extension or spatial corollary of the European Union (EU). Even so, before too long, the logic of the argument we explore brings us rapidly to the realization that not only does the general vision of Europeanness that underpins EIL actually lack any stable spatial content or boundaries, but also that the question of what these boundaries and content should be is itself, in fact, one of the main objects of anxiety and contestation in the EIL discourse. Given this fact, one may then be tempted to ask what exactly the E in EIL is ultimately meant to represent, and whether the broader idea of EIL, in the end, could ever actually be made intelligible other than in the most superficial and nominalist sense of the term. But that line of inquiry is probably best left for another occasion.

2. The Discourse about Prosperity and Solidarity in EIL: Two Traditions

In the period since the end of World War II, two relatively distinct traditions of thinking and talking about the ideas of prosperity and solidarity have emerged and taken shape within the broader intellectual space of EIL.

The first tradition developed and crystallized primarily in the context of what is known today as European law.[8] Its general evolution has been closely associated with the establishment of the European Economic Community (EEC) and the broader project of European economic integration, and the broader paradigm of thought that underpins it can be best summarized as a mixture of supranational regionalism, transnational technocracy, and neo-liberal economics.

The second tradition, by contrast, has developed mostly in the context of EIL's political and intellectual engagement with what one might call the continuing legacies of European imperialism. Its main ideological thrust, in this sense, has been to situate the European element of EIL much more expressly within its broader global and historical context, rather than importing its meaning from the domain of positive law-making. Spurred on, first, by Soviet and, later, anti-colonialist challenges to what has been variously described as 'bourgeois international law', 'plutocratic international law', and 'the international order of poverty',[9] it finds its main guiding categories—what in French is called *idées forces*—in the concepts of socialist internationalism, economic self-determination, and the law of development. Though its scale of influence was never limited to the European region, its lasting impact on the domain of positive international law has been decidedly quite limited.

For the most part, the two traditions never entered into any form of sustained dialogue with one another. Starting from the 1960s, the first tradition—what we propose to call here the tradition of regionalist thinking in EIL or *European regionalism*—began its steady ascent to dominance, progressively growing in influence and visibility across EIL's internal theoretical space. Its evolution as a practised creed continues to this day and can be readily witnessed in the various developments within the EU institutional order itself—not least in the fields of monetary governance and common foreign policy—and the accompanying scholarly discourses. Russia's aggression against Ukraine and the EU's ongoing response to it have given it a particularly strong impetus.

The second tradition—what we will call here the tradition of post-colonialist reformism in EIL or *European post-coloniality*—has followed a very different historical trajectory. Its fortunes peaked in the second half of the 1970s before declining sharply in the mid- to late 1980s. Geopolitically, the disintegration of the USSR and the demise of the New International Economic Order (NIEO) initiative dealt it a blow from which it has never been able to recover. Legally, the disastrous transformation of the international law of development (*droit du developpement*) into the international right to development (*droit au developpement*), the decline and the subsequent discontinuation of institutional arrangements like the Compensatory Financing Facility (CFF)[10] and Stabex,[11] and the steady withering away of the subject-specific international commodity regimes have meant that European post-coloniality's only enduring legacy in EIL today can be found in the field of legal academia as reflected in the popularization of the so-called Third World Approaches to International Law (TWAIL) project and the revival of Marxist-inspired debates in some segments of contemporary EIL scholarship.[12]

3. The Construction of Ideas of Prosperity and Solidarity in the European Regionalist Tradition

3.1 The place of prosperity and solidarity in European regionalism—general pattern

Even the briefest glance at the official sources of European law shows that, as doctrinal constructs, the concepts of prosperity and solidarity occupy decidedly different positions in the European regionalist discourse. For one thing, the *principle of solidarity* is not only a formally recognized term of art in EU law, while prosperity is not, it is also a subject of extensive academic discussion.[13]

At the same time, from the standpoint of its operative significance in the broader structure of the legal imaginary, the idea of prosperity, quite clearly, seems to play a much more central role in the ideology of European regionalism. The reasons for this are not hard to discern. In terms of its broader politico-cultural genealogy, the European regionalist tradition is essentially a descendant of what one might call the Neoliberal International of the Geneva School.[14] At its root lies a philosophical vision consisting of three basic elements. The first is a *broadly capitalistic view of political economy*: a combination of an explicit commitment to free market policies and a Kantian-style belief in the promotion of commerce as the royal road to peacebuilding.[15] The second element is a conscious endorsement of *supranationalist institutionalism* as the most effective model of regional politics. The project of European federalism, according to this vision, is understood to be both a historically progressive and, if calibrated correctly, institutionally optimal way of tackling most large-scale problems and challenges confronting European States. The third element is an *essentially technocratic attitude towards international law* and a *fundamentally disciplinarian approach to global governance*. The vision of international law that underpins the European regionalist tradition is basically one in which international law is presented as a set of mechanisms and techniques that, on the one hand, serve to stabilize and manage the various political and economic expectations that arise in the process of European integration and, on the other, contain and defuse the excesses of national sovereignty, populism, and regulatory divergence.[16]

The impact each of these elements has had on the way European regionalism approaches the ideas of prosperity and solidarity has been complex, but also deeply consistent. The adoption of an explicitly capitalistic outlook has meant that the general conception of economics that is taken for granted in European regionalism unfailingly tends to construe the economy as a *general equilibrium system*[17] consisting of a relatively decentralized network of markets for capital, labour, services, etc, rather than, say, a planning-and-distribution structure built around an input-output production cycle.[18] Since there exists no reason to think of markets as fundamentally national creatures when it comes to questions of scale and space, and since the market logic generally tends to militate in favour of the broadest possible expansion and integration of supply and distribution chains—which, in turn, requires a systematic harmonization, formalization, and enforcement of the applicable regulatory frameworks—the idea of establishing a strict *rule of international law*, with all the attendant institutional transformations this implies, logically suggests itself to the European regionalist mind as the most self-evident political strategy.[19]

Unsurprisingly, one of the inevitable consequences this legal-political orientation has led to has been a consistent flattening not only of the broader conception of international law adopted in the European regionalist tradition but also, more specifically, of its actual and potential relationship with the politics of prosperity and solidarity.

Starting from the late 1980s, the idea of prosperity in European law has increasingly come to be interpreted in exclusively economic terms. From this point of view, prosperity is essentially a concept that belongs a lot less in conversations about history, ethics, or civic virtue, than it does in discussions of market design, trade, growth, and investment. Put differently, it is a subject that is more 'naturally' linked with the themes of wealth-building, efficiency-generation, and economic integration than justice, 'good life', or freedom from want. Since trade, investment, and integration always require a considerable degree of regulatory harmonization and the systematic removal of bureaucratic barriers and idiosyncrasies, any references to regulatory autonomy, judicial nationalism, or other doctrines traditionally associated with the politics of sovereignty and protectionism have inevitably come to be treated in the European regionalist discourse with a pervading sense of mistrust and apprehension. Given that each of these doctrines is, in large part, a product of *legal* construction—in the sense that there is nothing self-evident about what the concept of regulatory autonomy means, the only meaning one can attribute to it has to be constructed through legal interpretation—the awareness of the general importance of international law in securing the promotion of prosperity has long since become a trademark of European politics.

Crucially, this rise in awareness has not come without a complication. Rather than inspiring a general elevation in legal consciousness, it has led to the entrenchment of a very particular understanding not only of what international law is but also of what it can do. Where classical positivist theory would view international law as a content-free socio-cultural form, the European regionalist tradition has come to treat it as a system of very specific substantive arrangements and institutional apparatuses whose principal value consists in their ability to keep the politics of national sovereignty in check while supporting and enabling the processes of supra- and transnational constitutionalism, thus paving the road for the promotion of growth, efficiency, and ever-deepening economic integration.[20]

In comparison, all engagements with the idea of solidarity in the European regionalist tradition to date have tended to take place within discursive and normative spaces centred around the *themes of macro- and micro-level redistribution* and the *narrative of 'common European identity'*. The ideological grounding for the idea of redistribution comes in this context from the decidedly technocratic doctrine of *market failure*, a trope that in contemporary European practice is applied to issues ranging from social security and labour relations to environmental degradation (but not, crucially, North-South relations). The ideological context that surrounds the narrative of common European identity in the meantime has come in recent times to be mostly grounded in the idea of Europe as a single political space, a regime of common citizenship, and as a distinct legal-cultural Self, finding its voice in the face of adversity arising from the global climate emergency, refugee, food, and energy crises, and military and economic security threats.[21]

FRONTEX, Russian sanctions, Chinese trade policies, refugee burden-sharing schemes, the 'area of freedom, security, and justice', the European arrest warrant, collective bargaining rights, socialized healthcare, the European Stability Mechanism (ESM)—the idea of solidarity in the contemporary European regionalist discourse at first glance seems to serve as a reference point for a wide range of disparate phenomena.[22] What brings all of these different strands together is the fact that in the final analysis they all share the exact same theoretical infrastructure that also underpins European regionalism's approach to thinking about prosperity. This structure, at its root, is essentially a blend of a decidedly cartographic vision of legal geography, an individual rights-centric model of legal imagination, and a quasi-Hegelian theme of supranational-unity-as-a-historical-promise.[23]

3.2 The operative structure of European regionalism as a theory of international law

Starting from the late 1980s, most discussions of the common European identity and intra-European redistributive initiatives, like those about trade liberalization and regional economic integration, have come to be closely associated in the European regionalist practice with the conscious foregrounding of the general idea of *international human rights*—the thesis that certain types of legal entitlements are held by individuals simply by virtue of being human, rather than residents or citizens of a particular State, and can be enjoyed by them directly under international law, rather than via the national legal order—and the closely related tradition of equating the promotion of international human rights with the *pursuit of social justice*.[24]

The process that precipitated this imaginational shift has been well-documented. In a nutshell, what led to it was the emergence and subsequent entrenchment of the idea of the single European space as an area of free movement of capital, labour, and other economic resources,[25] and the structuring of the resulting narratives that grounded the vision of the European legal-political arena in tropes like 'four fundamental freedoms'[26] and the 'principle of direct effect'.[27] By the mid-1990s, as the linkages between the integration processes driven by the EEC and the legal-political systems created by the Council of Europe and the Organization for Security and Cooperation in Europe intensified, what might have seemed initially little more than a mere pattern of historical correlation increasingly came to be perceived as a relationship of structural unity. Just as it became common to think of the European human rights system as an inseparable part of the European political project, so, too, the notion of the European political project became inseparable, in the European regionalist discourse, from the idea of a rights-centred international legal order. Adding to this mix a steadily growing conviction that the path to greater social justice lay through the expansion of individual rights and the corresponding system of supra- and transnational institutional remedies completed the recipe for a full-scale paradigm shift. By the turn of the millennium, the new legal imaginary that grew out of this led to such a fundamental reconfiguration of all the standard—from the traditional international law point of view—assumptions about the presumptive loci of political legitimacy and legal authority and the 'correct' extent and configuration of national sovereignty that what now forms the conventional wisdom on this subject in European law can confidently be said to have no immediate parallels in any other part of the world.

Viewed from this angle, the *spatializing and identity-creating functions* performed by international law's treatment of prosperity and solidarity in the European regionalist context—its centrality to the process of constituting 'Europe' as both a legal-geographical and a politico-identitarian artefact—seems essentially incontestable. What is more, the same can also be said for the deeply political character of the role that has been assigned by European regionalism to international law more generally.[28] Both of these points, however, still seem to remain occluded in European regionalism internal discourse. What might be the reason for that, is unclear. A part of the explanation probably has something to do with the standard tendency to assume that it is legal structures that ultimately follow those of culture and geography, not the other way around. Or one might also point out the general propensity in mainstream EIL circles to combine a fundamentally formalistic approach to the concept of State consent with what the German economist Wilhelm Ropke called the 'liberal principle of separation': the assumption that a strict categorical distinction can be made between the domain of politics (State) and the domain of economics (market).[29] The tendency to view the mechanics of consent through a formalistic lens has created in the European regionalist thought a general predisposition against exploring subjects such as duress, unequal bargaining power, or 'relations of adhesion' when it comes to, for example, relations between EU member States.[30] The tendency to accept uncritically the liberal principle of separation, in turn, has given European regionalism a predisposition towards treating legal regimes traditionally associated with the idea of 'private law' as essentially apolitical.[31] So long, thus, as the international legal structures created in the course of the European integration project, such as the Treaty on the Functioning of the European Union (TFEU), could be plausibly seen as being based on formally valid expressions of state consent or as constructs that focus principally on issues normally allocated to the province of private law, the idea that these structures might be politically biased would tend consistently to escape the reach of one's critical attention.

Significantly, the general approach followed by the European regionalist tradition has been to assign to the province of private law everything relating to the workings of the modern capitalist economy: trade, investment, mergers and acquisitions, payment regulations, interest rates, corporate governance, tax, labour rights, and so on. That this approach is riddled with serious political and theoretical problems, seems beyond doubt. The notion that private law is an intensely political system and few questions in the modern capitalist economy are more deeply politicized than the basic architecture of trade, ownership, and contract, has been recognized in academic legal debates at least since the 1920s.[32] And yet, as Diego Lopez Medina helpfully reminds us, what happens in the domain of academic legal theory often has very little impact on the content of the common juristic sense—what he calls '*pop jurisprudence*'—and it is at the level of pop jurisprudence that international legal traditions such as European regionalism find their source of inspiration, reproduce themselves, and assert their legitimacy.[33]

3.3 The legal politics of 'prosperity' and 'solidarity' in European regionalism

Most ideologies in the neo-liberal age operate, as William Davies puts it, in a zombified manner.[34] European regionalism is not an exception in this regard. Its theoretical foundations offer a textbook example of a postmodernist mashup: a mid-20th-century conception of the political economy combined with elements of an early 20th-century legal-theoretical sensibility and a late-20th-century right-leaning political agenda. Even its official self-image—reflected in statements like that found in Article 3.3 of the Treaty on European Union (TEU): 'The Union shall work for *sustainable development*... based on *balanced economic growth* and *price stability* [and] *social progress*'—seems to be formulated in terms that somehow are meant to invoke simultaneously a 1990s-style technocratic paradigm, a 1950s-style economic programme, and a sociological model the serenely Whiggish language of which unmistakably evokes an image of Victorian-era sensibility.

The underlying *economic model* on which the whole edifice of European regionalism rests is presented as a species of capitalism with a human face. In practice, however, it seems to draw as much inspiration from the intellectual traditions of the Geneva School neo-liberalism as the practical playbook of 'new rentier capitalism'.[35] The *political philosophy* that European regionalism uses for self-rationalization is a blend of an Enlightenment-style conviction in the power of commerce to generate a climate of peace and cooperation[36] and a deep-seated enthusiasm for the kind of supranational juristocracy that scholars like Daniel Tarullo call the 'statutory/adjudicatory model of global governance', a system that, as Tarullo notes, is commonly known to be 'best suited to restraining state action, not to promoting collective or cooperative action'.[37]

The *legal policy vision* that is embraced by European regionalism includes a strong commitment to democracy and the principle of subsidiarity, but is also grounded in an abhorrence of populist politics and local protectionism. It celebrates the idea of human rights, but seems to be deeply wary about the rights of refugees. The temporal concept of Europe that emerges out of all of these aporias projects what looks like a forward-looking temporality of a progressive Self-becoming—Europe as a concrete abstraction, an idea in the process of realizing itself—in which the Self in question just so happens conveniently to seek to construct its area of freedom, security, and justice around the four fundamental freedoms of factor circulation central to free-market economics.

Of course not everything about the European regionalist tradition is mired in this sort of postmodernist contradiction. The macro-level relationship between law and politics that is envisaged by it, in fact, seems rather coherent. Conceptually, it proceeds from *classical voluntarist positivism* and the traditional *liberal distinction* between rule-making (substantive rationality) and rule-application (formal rationality).[38] Where rule-application is imagined to unfold more or less continuously, rule-making is imagined only to play out in bursts. Every now and then European States come together to rethink and adjust Europe's constitutive vision. The pieces of text that are produced in these constitutive moments—the Single European Act (SEA), the Maastricht Treaty, etc—provide the only meaningful source of law for the European regionalist tradition. Whatever authority any element of the European institutional architecture or policy landscape might have, thus, has to be traced directly to these constitutional statements. Outside these moments of periodic constitutional activity, the whole system functions only in the mode of rule-application, that is, subject to the standard principles of textual exegesis, technical legal reasoning, and an extensive set of competence delimitation and legal interpretation doctrines.[39]

Predictably, the general understanding of international law that has grown out of this vision over time has turned out to be both deeply formalist and technocratic in its orientation and deeply apolitical in its self-understanding. The basic function of all legal regimes, according to it, is basically instrumental, technical, and supplementary. International law's role, in effect, is thus limited only to implementing and facilitating the orderly realization of those goals and objectives which have been consecrated by Europe's constitutional documents. The notion that the international legal form itself may carry any ideological or distributional dynamics pre-baked into it that may contaminate this process of actualization and facilitation remains unintelligible, if not fundamentally alien to the whole picture.

Considering such a background, the discourse about prosperity that has evolved in the European regionalist tradition, unsurprisingly, has also developed a strongly pronounced technocratic and apolitical complexion, getting absorbed within a field of debates centred around the themes of market stabilization and trade liberalization on the one hand and the mechanics of regulatory convergence and harmonization on the other. Both of these trope clusters, of course, belong firmly in the standard repertoire of social engineering-style managerialist discourses, and neither of them leaves any scope for any broader moral or ideological reflections, considerations of historical memory, or the politics and ethics of Europe's relationship with the rest of the world.

A broadly similar trend can also be detected in the legal politics that European regionalism assigns to the idea of solidarity. Most engagements with the vocabulary of solidarity in the European regionalist discourse, as noted earlier, tend to take place in the context of debates that focus either on the limits of redistributive adjustments accompanying the process of European integration or the practical implications of the narrative of common European identity that this process is intended to lead to. In the former context, the notion of redistribution is read to address both the question of the *macro-level international burden-sharing arrangements* between EU member States and the question of *micro-level welfare-statist policies* requiring protection through European-level rights-centric international legal structures. In the first case, the general approach is usually to construe solidarity as either a risk management device or an extension of some quasi-federalist idea of unity-through-multilateralism. A typical example can be found in discussions of border policies and security matters, the Dublin system of asylum application processing, as well as the various European financial stability initiatives and responses to the energy crisis.[40] In the second case, the general approach is to conceptualize solidarity as a safety net required to help soften the impact of capitalism's 'creative destruction'. A typical illustration can be found in legal regimes like Title IV ('Solidarity') of the Charter of Fundamental Rights of the European Union (FREU) that covers matters ranging from social security and employment rights to consumer and environmental protection.

The basic relationship which this interpretative trend establishes between the ideas of prosperity and solidarity should not be hard to work out. Formally, the importance of prosperity in the European regionalist segment of EIL is not understood to be greater than that of solidarity. And yet it is the latter that obviously exists within the ideological horizon created by the former, not the other way around. The meaning and content that are ascribed to the idea of solidarity in the European regionalist tradition are defined on the basis of those political and economic realities which the commitment to a policy of prosperity-building implies and, according to the technocratic ethos of neo-liberal philosophy, necessitates.

The pursuit of a solidaristic agenda in European law, to put it differently, does not have any standalone ideological justification, just like the obligation of solidarity in and of itself does not carry any independent normative content. The general endorsement by European regionalism of the legal-political value of pursuing prosperity, thus, is not so much offset or counterbalanced, as only supplemented by, a second-order endorsement of the policies of reciprocal risk-spreading, burden-sharing, and welfare statism.[41] The central theoretical question that shapes the conceptual interplay between the ideas of prosperity and solidarity, thus, is not 'which of these values should have primacy over the other?' but rather, 'how can the pursuit of solidaristic objectives be carried out without upsetting the goal of prosperity-building?'

The spatial formulation that European regionalism assigns to the idea of Europe seems in this context rather symptomatic. On the one hand, it appears to be largely synonymous with what used to be known as the area of the Common Market. On the other hand, it is the cartographic extent of this area that provides the main reference point for the calculation of the limits of solidaristic obligations and, as their flipside, the powers of exclusion. Significantly, the positive-legal framework that underpins the legal reality of the European space is grounded primarily in a network of treaties and institutions deriving from the EU itself: TEU, TFEU, FREU, the ESM, the European Commission, the European Court of Justice (ECJ),[42] and the various structural organs like the European Regional Development Fund (ERDF).[43] Non-EU-related institutions and legal instruments, in comparison, play only a very limited role in the way the European regionalist tradition constructs and executes its understandings of prosperity and solidarity and the related projection of respective spatialities.

3.4 The formal juridical expression of prosperity and solidarity in European regionalism

At the discursive level, the discourse about prosperity and solidarity that has developed in the European regionalist tradition has been structured primarily around a conceptual grid composed of tropes like 'highly competitive social market economy',[44] 'balanced economic growth',[45] 'overall harmonious development',[46] common European citizenship, and the free movement of goods, services, people, and capital.[47] Its supplementary mediating categories include the notion of 'economic, social and territorial cohesion',[48] the concept of socio-economic rights, and the general narrative of 'unity' as the logical corollary and precondition of risk-sharing, freedom, and equality.[49] Outside FREU, TEU, and TFEU, its principal reference points in institutional and formal-juridical terms today are:

(i) the Marshall Plan—the original event that set in motion the European project;[50]
(ii) the SEA—the legal document which represents the turning point in the creation of the internal market and provides an archetypal illustration of how the European regionalist tradition has come to understand the questions of economic integration, regulatory harmonization, and non-tariff barriers;[51]
(iii) the Common Agricultural Policy (CAP)[52] and structural funds like ERDF—an institutional cluster that essentially embodies the legal solution the European regionalist tradition has worked out to the problem of combining the ideology of protectionism and government subsidies with its broader neo-liberal outlook;
(iv) FRONTEX and the Dublin system for the elimination of asylum-shopping;[53] and, last but not least
(v) the Economic and Monetary Union, the ESM, and the European Central Bank (ECB)[54]—a series of institutional expressions of the successive responses generated within the European regionalist tradition to the historical disintegration of the Gold Standard and the resulting attempts to de-politicize the processes of international monetary governance by de-socializing, denationalizing, and de-democratizing its operative institutional structures.

What role, one might ask, does the idea of the European common currency play in all of this? The answer to this is not immediately obvious. It may or may not be true that the introduction of the Euro at the end of the 1990s had rendered the process of European integration politically irreversible.[55] What seems clear, however, is that the Euro's arrival has greatly solidified that general ideological shift which first started with the adoption of CAP and escalated post-Maastricht, with the establishment of the EU itself. The object of this shift, in large part, was the reconfiguration of Europe's self-construction as a legal and political space, and the way the themes of prosperity and solidarity were redefined in this process has certainly played an important role in this transformation. The decoupling of the Euro as an economic and legal regime and the ECB as the relevant decision-making institution from the traditional loci of national sovereignty signalled not only a radical reconfiguration of the broader *institutional framework* surrounding the European monetary space. It also consolidated this space into a single uninterrupted area of wealth-building (prosperity) and risk- and burden-sharing (solidarity), creating in the course of doing so a new form of technocratic governance culture—and, through that, a new model of temporal, spatial, and identitarian imagination.[56]

3.5 The differential status of solidarity and prosperity explained

As noted earlier, while the concept of prosperity does not seem to be invested with any formal connotations in European law, there is undoubtedly meant to exist in European law such a thing as a legally binding 'principle of solidarity'.[57] What exactly the content of this principle might be, is not always made clear.[58] And yet the belief that, unlike the concept of prosperity, the concept of solidarity carries a legally operative meaning certainly remains firm and is rarely put in doubt.[59]

What could be the explanation for this trend? One possible answer is that it may have something to do with the broader evolution of European regionalism as a *system of legal consciousness*.

What we are dealing with here, in basic contours, seems to be in line with what Duncan Kennedy elsewhere calls the *Social paradigm* or *mode of transnational legal consciousness*.[60] An explicit endorsement of the vocabulary of solidarism within law, notes Kennedy, formed a defining ideological feature not only of the abstract legal-philosophical debates that spread across most of European academia in the first half of the 20th century, but also the broader legislative outlook and pop jurisprudence that developed during the same time. The overarching structure that produced this outlook was a mixture of critical and constructive impulses. The critical impulse consisted in the reaction against the arch-formalism of the classical 19th-century science of private law, the constructive impulse in the attempt to rethink law as a 'mechanism that could and should facilitate the evolution of social life in accordance with ever greater perceived social interdependence at every level, from the family to the world of nations'.[61] Though the general popularity of the Social paradigm/mode began to decline after 1960s, its influence, like that of the idea of the welfare state which it helped to legitimize, did not disappear entirely. Seen against this background, one might argue that the European regionalist tradition has inherited the Social paradigm's critical belief that law is not just a series of formally disconnected transactions but also a tool of social engineering, while from its constructive element, it has retained the assumption that law, in addition to everything else, could also be used as a mechanism for producing a shared sense of political identity and social inter-connectedness.

Having said that, it bears noting that an equally significant part of the puzzle can also be found in the fact that the general vision of what has come to count as prosperity and solidarity in the European regionalist tradition appears to be grounded in that long-familiar politico-economic tradition which regards the accumulation of surplus value as a self-evident good that does not require any explicit justification and the promotion of social justice as an essentially palliative process appended to the pursuit of this good. The continuing emphasis on the linkage between solidarity and redistribution that one encounters in the EU legal discourse does not, in this sense, seem at all accidental. As critical scholars have long argued, the project of legally mandated redistribution is essentially a logical extension of the traditional centre-rightwing belief according to which the only permissible species of a social justice agenda can be that which is aimed at *post-hoc intra-systemic adjustments* that would help moderate the excesses of free market capitalism but not challenge its foundations.

Seen from this angle, it certainly seems to make sense that in an ideological environment shaped by the kind of politico-economic worldview that is detailed above one would rarely find the occasion to need to define or legally enshrine the values and ideals of prosperity-building. This part of the programme in a sense is going to take care of itself. But one will certainly repeatedly need to use the help of law to define and implement the programme of solidarity-building.

4. The Construction of Ideas of Prosperity and Solidarity in the European Post-coloniality Tradition

If the European regionalist tradition can be described as EIL's ideological mainstream, European post-coloniality represents its main historical counterpoint, and, as befits a counterpoint, its non-academic impact compared to the mainstream has been, to date, rather modest. The Generalised System of Preferences (GSP) developed under the auspices of the United National Conference on Trade and Development (UNCTAD) in the 1970s and the Lomé-Cotonou system of trade-and-aid arrangements that establishes non-reciprocal trade preferences in favour of developing countries many of which had been European colonies are, by and large, its only surviving representations in the realm of positive international law.[62]

The legacy of legal thought, however, is not limited to its positive-legal implications. A legal tradition that has not succeeded in crossing the gap between theory and practice can still leave a lasting impact at the level of broader disciplinary consciousness. It would hardly be an exaggeration to say in this regard that few theoretical movements over the last half-century have had such a profound influence on the development of EIL's general legal imaginary as European post-coloniality.

Its theoretical origins date back to the work of the early Soviet international lawyers like Evgenii Korovin and Evgenii Pashukanis, who, drawing on Lenin's theory of imperialism, laid down the first foundations of what would later grow into *socialist-internationalist* and *post-colonialist* critiques of mainstream international law.[63] As the two schools evolved, each ended up leaving its own distinct mark on EIL's theoretical and discursive landscapes. The impact of the socialist-internationalist school[64] for the most part manifested itself in helping to decouple the discourse about prosperity from the strictly economic context and link the discourse about solidarity with wider considerations of socio-economic struggle and conflict. The impact of the post-colonialist critique,[65] in turn, can be detected most clearly in helping to bring greater light to the continuing significance of Europe's colonial history and reinserting discussions about prosperity and solidarity within a broader conceptual framework centred around themes like restorative justice, collective bargaining, and 'a historical unearned income'.[66]

Though separated by different intellectual accents, the two sub-strands of the European post-coloniality tradition constantly remained in an active dialogue with one another, often forming a united front in their encounters with the more conservative segments of the discipline.[67] Another factor that brought the two schools together was also their common belief that any systematic reform of the existing international legal system had to start with a fundamental theoretical reconsideration of the concepts of imperialism and exploitation and their relationship to the international legal form.[68] To succeed in this task, the assumption went, international lawyers needed to develop a much deeper understanding of legal history, while also developing basic expertise in subjects like dependency theory and development economics.

What emerged from this intellectual reorientation in the end was a theory of international law as an essentially purposive system (*le droit de finalité*).[69] Unlike classical positivists, socialist internationalists and post-colonial critics viewed international law not just as a historically contingent mode of global governance, but also as a heavily 'viscous' medium that did not easily lend itself to the pursuit of just any political project or agenda.[70] Instead of treating international law as merely a set of technical tools and processes, the European post-coloniality tradition thus sought to impart a vision of law as a 'deeply structurated system' shaped and animated by its own *internal logic* that both limited and constrained its capacity to promote and support particular economic and political values and goals.[71] The inevitable next step that followed from this was to ask whether this logic could ever be changed, and, if it could, what new economic and political values and goals could be imported thus into international law?

The answer which European post-coloniality gave to this question was predictably bold. Of course, it was entirely possible to change the organizing logic of the international legal form, it declared. To achieve that aim, required a process of open theoretical debate, the most immediate goal of which was to demystify international law's traditional thought-structure. The longer-term objective, in turn, was to work out a set of specific legal reform proposals that would help infuse the international legal system with the 'spirit' of *fraternal solidarity*[72] and a structural orientation towards the creation of *equal development opportunities*.[73]

In both cases the way forward lay via a concerted pursuit of the politics of social welfarism at the global and inter-statal level (*le droit social des nations*, *le droit international providence*).[74] The main objective was to enshrine in law the presumption that the rules of formal reciprocity that traditionally governed relations between Western states did not apply in their relations with developing countries, since the latter, as a matter of right, were entitled to a more preferential treatment, even as they enjoyed all the traditional privileges of sovereignty (the so-called *la dualité des normes*).[75] In structural terms, this required rearranging the system of fundamental principles of international law by firstly inserting within it the ideas of compensatory inequality[76] and the generalized system of preferences[77] and, secondly, by giving much greater prominence than before to the principle of economic self-determination[78] and promoting the doctrine of a common technological heritage, to help secure for every former colonial people the ability, without having to rely on the charity of Western States, to pursue its own path to socio-economic development.[79]

In ideological terms, all this implied reconceptualizing the international economic order as a system primarily concerned with matters of *resource circulation*. At the level of legal policy, this involved recognizing international trade law as the principal mechanism by which the international community could increase or decrease the intensity of international solidarity, help redress historical inequalities, and shape the process of prosperity-building,[80] and restructuring international investment law around the doctrines of fair return (*le juste revenu de capital*) and the permanent sovereignty over natural resources.[81] A common theme in both cases was the idea that a central aim of international legal policy was to promote and normalize the process of technology transfers from the developed to the developing world.[82]

At the level of institutional vision, the general trend characteristic of European post-coloniality was to voice active support for the UN and its subsidiary organs, while also trying to shine greater light on their *de facto* operative setup from the standpoint of what needed to be done to make them more democratically inclusive and legitimate.[83] This intense interest in the administrative governance aspects of the UN system betrayed another fundamental feature of the European post-coloniality tradition: a desire to move beyond the standard statocentric ontology of classical international law, without, however, at the same time conflating the impetus for anti-statocentrism with neo-liberal-style individual rights-ism or jeopardizing the normative centrality of the principle of non-intervention in domestic affairs.[84]

Starting from the 1950s onwards, an important component of translating this anti-statist aspiration into legal-political reality was found in the doctrine of the *inter-bloc law*: an approach to thinking about the international legal system that recognized the existence of a certain set of higher-order principles governing relations between large geopolitical constellations.[85] The names assigned to these constellations varied from one phase of the Cold War to another: capitalist versus socialist countries; West versus East; the Global North versus the Global South; First, Second, and Third Worlds.[86] A common theme that remained unchanged, however, was the implicit acceptance that the quickest way to bring about a fundamental reform of the international legal order was for the non-Western States to unite their forces, by consciously adopting a policy of group-voting in international organizations and ensuring every possible 'unity of effort' in multilateral negotiations.[87] Seen in these terms, the whole rationale behind the idea of inter-bloc law, as scholars like Thomas Franck argued, was to learn from the lessons of the organized labour movement so as to produce in the international arena something along the lines of what Bedjaoui would call latter a '*State trade-unionism in action*'.[88]

A direct consequence of this was the quick popularization within the European post-coloniality discourse of a whole raft of topics and doctrines that from today's perspective seem fundamentally alien to the international legal mind: an Integrated Programme for Commodities;[89] export earnings stabilization schemes like Stabex;[90] resource pools, 'common fund', and buffer stock arrangements—a set of legal constructs designed to ensure a stable level of supply for importing countries and revenues for exporting countries in relation to key international commodities, such as tin, cocoa, or rubber.[91]

Compared to European regionalism, European post-coloniality placed an unmistakably stronger emphasis on the theme of solidarity. Not only was the idea of solidarity as a legal doctrine not reduced to a set of palliative measures or supplementary techniques intended to help smoothen the effects of prosperity-building policies, but in some formulations it even went on to be acclaimed as a quasi-constitutional principle of international law.[92]

The end of the Cold War was not kind to the European post-coloniality tradition. The decline in UNCTAD's fortunes and its displacement by the WTO and the OECD as the principal sites of international trade law and policy making over the next decade deprived the European post-coloniality tradition of the first of its two main entry points in the non-academic law-and-policy debate. As the international commodity regimes decayed, programmes like Stabex inevitably followed suit. With them out of the picture, European post-coloniality lost its second main platform.

5. Conclusion

The great contradiction that besets the project of history, argues Jacques Le Goff, derives from the fact that though the object of its inquiry always remains singular, the knowledge it seeks to extract from it mostly aspires to be general.[93] The only solution to that, he goes on to add, rather than casting history as entirely irrational, would be 'to make the historical process [at least partly] intelligible [by] the recognition of regularities in historical evolution'.[94]

There exists a deep and highly regularized pattern of discontinuities separating the legal imaginaries constructed by European regionalism and European post-coloniality. In the former, the theme of solidarity is generally placed in an ideologically subordinated position vis-à-vis that of prosperity; in the latter, this relationship is essentially reversed. In the former, the concept of prosperity seems broadly inseparable from the idea of free markets and capitalist economics; in the latter, from the idea of historical justice and a politics of redistribution and self-determination.

In the European post-coloniality tradition, solidarity was a concept that channelled the hope for 'the triumph of justice over power'[95] and a new international order founded on a 'truly equitable basis'.[96] In the European regionalist context, it became a category deployed mostly in the service of economic safety-net-building and financial burden-sharing politics – but also the politics of humanitarian rationing, deportations, and spatial exclusion. For many around the world today, the most consequential aspect of solidarity produced by European law, when all is said and done, has nothing to do with the ESM or the CAP. Rather, it is the regimes like the Dublin system and the initiatives like 'Operation Themis' that represent the true meaning of solidarity in European law.[97] Reducing the refugees' opportunities to bid for asylum or even to reach European shores may not look like the most obvious way to achieve an 'ever closer union'. But one certainly cannot deny that it has greatly helped solidify EU's external border as a fully integrated legal phenomenon and homogenize its political territory as a single fully operational legal space, 'leading to the strengthening of its economic, social and territorial cohesion'.[98] There is after all nothing, either in logic or in history, that can prevent us from deciding that the real meaning of the solidarity principle has nothing to do with 'altruism', since 'rightly understood, [solidarity] has many egoistic traits' and is 'in many respects a cold and calculating instrument'.[99]

But just as there seems to be a lot that separates the thought-world of European regionalism from that European post-coloniality, there is also a lot that the two of them share in common.

For one thing, the concept of Europeanness constructed in both traditions is, ironically enough, directly predicated on the ontological centrality of the non-European Other. Think of this as an extension of Chantal Mouffe's rule of the primacy of the constitutive outside.[100] It is only after deciding what lies 'outside' Europe—be it in the form of establishing which countries can qualify for the Lomé-Cotonou regime or in the form of determining which groups of economic migrants should be excluded from access to public funds and have to apply for individual work permits—that the legal meaning of Europeanness is fixed and constituted in either of these discourse formations. Whether it is made directly visible, thanks to an open debate about historical reparations and compensatory inequality, or carefully submerged within the opaque interior of a technical discussion of Schengen-style information-sharing systems, the abstract idealized portrait of *Europa* painted by EIL has the non-European Other's fingerprints all over it.

Another important feature that the two traditions seem to have in common is their overall tendency to recruit both the concept of prosperity and the concept of solidarity in the service of temporal and spatial construction. Though the temporal horizons presumed by European post-coloniality differ from those of European regionalism—even if only because in the former case one is actually invited to understand the region's past and its legacy—the temporal structure that is inscribed within the discourses of prosperity and solidarity in both cases seems essentially forward-looking. Both prosperity and solidarity are treated as projects of becoming, a moving target, a future that has to be won over and over again. In a similar sense, although the basic spatial context within which Europe's relationship with these projects of prosperity and solidarity is meant to be actualized differs considerably between the two traditions, in both cases the ultimate effect achieved by both European regionalism and European postcoloniality includes the production of a distinctly non-statal legal space that is at once openly non-Westphalian and explicitly pan-European in its political presentation.

Notes

1. See Zigmund Freud, *Complete Psychological Works*, vol XXII (Vintage Books, 2001) 89–96; Gayatri Chakravorty Spivak, *A Critique of Postcolonial Reason* (Harvard University Press, 1999) 2–5.
2. See 'Letter to W. Sombart' in Karl Marx and Frederick Engels, *Selected Works*, vol III (Progress Publishers, 1976) 504, 505.
3. The idea of concepts as side effects of differentiational dynamics comes from structuralism. For further discussion, see Jonathan Culler, *Structuralist Poetics* (Routledge, 2008) 12–18 (hereafter Culler, *Structuralist Poetics*).
4. In making this claim, we follow Levi-Strauss in holding that one of the most significant lessons modern discourse studies teaches us is the necessity of passing 'from the study of conscious linguistic phenomena to [that] of their unconscious infrastructure'. See Claude Levi-Strauss, *Structural Anthropology* (Basic Books, 1963) 33.
5. For an overview of each of these traditions, see Peter Barry, *Beginning Theory: An Introduction to Literary and Cultural Theory* (4th edn, Manchester University Press, 2017); Terry Eagleton, *Ideology: An Introduction* (Verso, 1991).
6. Further on intertextuality, see Graham Allen, *Intertextuality* (Routledge, 2000); Culler, *Structuralist Poetics* (n 3) 162–164.
7. See, eg, Jacques Le Goff, *The Birth of Europe* (Blackwell, 2005).
8. For an overview and general introduction to European law, see Paul Craig and Grainne de Burca, *EU Law* (7th edn, Oxford University Press, 2020) (hereafter Craig and de Burca, *EU Law*); Robert Schutze, *An Introduction to European Law* (Oxford University Press, 2012) (hereafter Schutze, *An Introduction to European Law*); Damian Chalmers et al, *European Union Law* (2nd edn, Cambridge University Press, 2010) (hereafter Chalmers, *European Union Law*). For a more focussed discussion of European law as an international legal regime, see Bruno de Witte, 'The European Union as an International Legal Experiment' in Grainne de Burca and JHH Weiler (eds), *The Worlds of European Constitutionalism* (Cambridge University Press, 2012) 19.

9. See Mohammed Bedjaoui, *Towards a New International Economic Order* (UNESCO, 1979) 23–24, 59–60 (hereafter Bedjaoui, *Towards a New International Economic Order*).
10. Supported actively by a number of European States, the CFF was a lending programme established by the International Monetary Fund (IMF) in 1963 to help address balance of payment difficulties arising from temporary shortfalls in export revenues and, later, costs of cereal imports. By its design, it was aimed primarily at developing countries, many of which were ex-European colonies. After falling into desuetude in the 1990s, CFF was eliminated in 2009. See 'IMF Overhauls Nonconcessional Lending Facilities and Conditionality', *IMF*, 3 April 2009 <https://www.imf.org/en/News/Articles/2015/09/28/04/53/pn0940> (accessed 6 October 2023); 'Review of the Compensatory Financing Facility', *IMF*, 18 February 2004 <https://www.imf.org/external/np/pdr/ccff/eng/2004/021804.pdf> (accessed 6 October 2023).
11. See n 90.
12. See, eg, Grietje Baars, *The Corporation, Law and Capitalism* (Baars, 2019); Robert Knox, 'Valuing Race? Stretched Marxism and the Logic of Imperialism', 4 London Review of International Law 2016, 81; Susan Marks (ed), *International Law on the Left* (Cambridge University Press, 2008).
13. See nn 57–59.
14. For further background, see Quinn Slobodian, *Globalists* (Harvard University Press, 2018) 5–26, 182–217 (hereafter Slobodian, *Globalists*).
15. See Immanuel Kant, *Perpetual Peace: A Philosophical Essay* (Allen & Unwin, 1903) 157(articulating the idea that since the spirit of commerce is incompatible with war but conducive to the strengthening of mutual cooperation, the surest path to perpetual peace lies through the promotion of trade).
16. See, eg, Robert Schutze, *From Dual to Cooperative Federalism: The Changing Structure of European Law* (Oxford University Press, 2009); Martin Dedman, *The Origins and Development of the European Union 1945–2008* (2nd edn, Routledge, 2010) (hereafter Dedman, *The Origins and Development of the European Union*).
17. See Alessandro Roncaglia, *A Brief History of Economic Thought* (Cambridge University Press, 2017) 167–180.
18. On what is at stake in this distinction and its importance for the neoliberal legal imaginary, see David Kennedy, 'The "Rule of Law", Political Choices, and Development Common Sense' in David Trubek and Alvaro Santos (eds), *The New Law and Economic Development: A Critical Appraisal* (Cambridge University Press, 2006) 95, 129–147 (hereafter Trubek and Santos, *The New Law and Economic Development*).
19. See, eg, Craig and de Burca, *EU Law* (n 8) 690 (noting the centrality of the assumption that 'in economic terms, a properly functioning internal market [is] the key to prosperity').
20. See, eg, Schutze, *An Introduction to European Law* (n 8); Allan Rosas and Lorna Armati, *EU Constitutional Law: An Introduction* (2nd rev edn, Hart Publishing, 2012) (hereafter Roasa and Armati, *EU Constitutional Law*).
21. For various illustrations, see Mario Monti, 'Competition and Solidarity in the European Construct' in Giuliano Amato et al (eds), *The History of the European Union: Constructing Utopia* (Hart Publishing, 2018) 89; Peter Hilpold, 'Understanding Solidarity within EU Law: An Analysis of the 'Islands of Solidarity' with Particular Regard to Monetary Union', 34 Yearbook of European Law 2015, 257.
22. For further discussion see, eg, Pieter van Cleynenbreugel, 'Typologies of Solidarity in EU Law' in Andrea Biondi et al (eds), *Solidarity in EU Law: Legal Principle in the Making*

(Edward Elgar, 2018) 13 (hereafter van Cleynenbreugel, 'Typologies of Solidarity in EU Law'). The reference to Europe as a single 'area of freedom, security, and justice' comes under Article 3(2) of the Treaty on European Union (TEU). See also Title V of the Treaty on the Functioning of the European Union (TFEU).

23. On the Hegelian foundations of EIL imagination, see Peter Swan, 'American Empire or Empires? Alternative Juridifications of the New World Order' in Amy Bartholomew (ed), *Empire's Law* (Pluto Press, 2006) 137, 145–157.
24. David Kennedy discusses the problems raised by this kind of uncritical conflation in David Kennedy, *The Dark Sides of Virtue* (Princeton University Press, 2004) 8–10. See also Andrew Lang, *World Trade Law after Neoliberalism* (Oxford University Press, 2012) 10–11.
25. See Craig and de Burca, *EU Law* (n 8) 810 (noting the 'notion of EU workers as mobile units of production contributing to the economic prosperity of Europe's single market').
26. For background, see Catherine Barnard, *The Substantive Law of the EU: The Four Freedoms* (5th edn, Oxford University Press, 2016).
27. For background, see Alan Dashwood, 'The Principle of Direct Effect in European Community Law', 16 Journal of Common Market Studies 1977, 229; Chalmers, *European Union Law* (n 8) 267–293.
28. See Joseph Weiler, 'The Transformation of Europe', 100 Yale Law Journal 1991, 2403; David Kennedy, 'Turning to Market Democracy: A Tale of Two Architectures', 32 Harvard International Law Journal 1991, 373.
29. See Wilhelm Roepke, 'Economic Order and International Law', 86 Recueil des Cours 1954-II, 203.
30. On duress, unequal bargaining power, and relations of adhesion in the law of voluntary transactions, see generally Robert Hale, 'Bargaining, Duress, and Economic Liberty', 43 Columbia Law Review 1943, 603; Friedrich Kessler, 'Contracts of Adhesion: Some Thoughts about Freedom of Contract', 43 Columbia Law Review 1943, 629.
31. On how and why this is a fiction see, eg, Fabrizio Cafaggi and Horatia Muir Watt (eds), *The Regulatory Function of European Private Law* (Edward Elgar, 2009).
32. See, eg, Morris Cohen, 'Property and Sovereignty', 13 Cornell Law Quarterly 1927, 8.
33. Further on pop jurisprudence, see generally Diego Lopez-Medina, *Teoria Impura del Derecho* (Legis, 2004). See also Akbar Rasulov, 'From Apology to Utopia and the Inner Life of International Law', 29 Leiden Journal of International Law 2016, 641, 646.
34. William Davies, *The Limits of Neoliberalism* (rev edn, SAGE, 2017) 187.
35. Further on the relationship between the Geneva School and the European project, see Slobodian, *Globalists* (n 14) 182–217; Dieter Plehwe et al (eds), *Nine Lives of Neoliberalism* (Verso, 2020) (in particular chapters by Hagen Schulz-Forberg and Stephan Puhringer). On the new rentier capitalism, see generally Brett Christophers, *Rentier Capitalism* (Verso, 2020).
36. But see Edwin van de Haar, 'The Liberal Divide over Trade, Peace and War', 24 International Relations 2010, 132(arguing that the claim that all Enlightenment thinkers accepted, like Kant, the commercial peace thesis is a modern-day myth).
37. Daniel Tarullo, 'Law and Governance in a Global Economy', 93 American Society of International Law Proceedings 1999, 105, 109.
38. On classical positivism, see Richard Collins, 'Classical Legal Positivism in International Law Revisited' in Jorg Kammerhofer and Jean d'Aspremont (eds), *International Legal Positivism in a Post-Modern World* (Cambridge University Press, 2014) 48. On the liberal

distinction, see Duncan Kennedy, 'Legal Formality', 2 Journal of Legal Studies 1973, 351, 355–359.

39. This way of thinking is essentially an echo of Classical Legal Thought. See Duncan Kennedy, 'Three Globalizations of Law and Legal Thought: 1850–2000' in Trubek and Santos, *The New Law and Economic Development* (n 18) 19, 25–37 (hereafter Kennedy, 'Three Globalizations of Law and Legal Thought').
40. See Esin Kuçuk, 'Solidarity in EU Law: An Elusive Political Statement or a Legal Principle', 23 Maastricht Journal of European and Comparative Law 2016, 965 (hereafter Kuçuk, 'Solidarity in EU Law'); Jurgen Bast, 'Deepening Supranational Integration: Interstate Solidarity in EU Migration Law', in Biondi, *Solidarity in EU Law* (n 22) 114; Hilpold, 'Understanding Solidarity within EU Law' (n 21).
41. On the latter theme, see generally Grainne de Burca (ed), *EU Law and the Welfare State: In Search of Solidarity* (Oxford University Press, 2005).
42. See Schutze, *An Introduction to European Law* (n 8) 26–34; Chalmers, *European Union Law* (n 8) 54–67, 143–149.
43. For background, see Paul Craig, *EU Administrative Law* (2nd edn, Oxford University Press, 2012) 90–96 (hereafter Craig, *EU Administrative Law*); Bruno de Witte, 'The Reform of the European Regional Development Fund', 23 Common Market Law Review 1986, 419. See also, more generally, Fernanda Nicola, 'The False Promise of Decentralization in EU Cohesion Policy', 20 Tulane Journal of International and Comparative Law 2011, 65.
44. Article 3.3 TEU.
45. ibid.
46. This language comes from the first paragraph of Article 174 TFEU, which reads: 'In order to promote its overall harmonious development, the Union shall develop and pursue its actions leading to the strengthening of its economic, social and territorial cohesion.'
47. Articles 9 and 10 TEU.
48. Article 3.3 TEU.
49. See, eg, Klaus-Dieter Borchardt, *The ABC of EU Law* (Publications Office of the EU, 2016) 27–29.
50. For background, see Benn Steil, *The Marshall Plan: Dawn of the Cold War* (Simon & Schuster, 2018).
51. See Claus-Dieter Ehlermann, 'The Internal Market Following the Single European Act', 24 Common Market Law Review 1987, 361; Jacques Pelkmans, 'The New Approach to Technical Harmonization and Standardization', 25 Journal of Common Market Studies 1987, 249.
52. For background, see Craig, *EU Administrative Law* (n 43) 80–89; Isabelle Garzon, *Reforming the Common Agricultural Policy: History of a Paradigm Change* (Palgrave Macmillan, 2006).
53. For further background, see 'The European Border and Coast Guard Agency', <http://frontex.europa.eu> (accessed 6 October 2023); 'Country Responsible for Asylum Applications (Dublin)', <https://home-affairs.ec.europa.eu/policies/migration-and-asylum/common-european-asylum-system/country-responsible-asylum-application-dublin-regulation_en> (accessed 6 October 2023); Kuçuk, 'Solidarity in EU Law' (n 40) 971; Hilpold, 'Understanding Solidarity within EU Law' (n 21) 273–274.
54. For background, see Rosas and Armati, *EU Constitutional Law* (n 20) 220–235; Dedman, *The Origins and Development of the European Union* (n 16) 109–165; Chalmers, *European Union Law* (n 8) 714–742.

55. See Stephen Schuker, 'The European Union: From Jean Monnet to the Euro' in Dean Kotlowski (ed), *The European Union: From Jean Monnet to the Euro* (Ohio University Press, 2000) 15, 30.
56. But see also Maria Tzanakopoulou, 'Social Consensus in the EMU: The Constitutional Tenets of a Currency Union' in John Haskell and Akbar Rasulov (eds), *New Voices and New Perspectives in International Economic Law* (Springer, 2020) 195.
57. See discussion in Biondi, *Solidarity in EU Law* (n 22); Hilpold, 'Understanding Solidarity within EU Law' (n 21) 258–261; Craig and de Burca, *EU Law* (n 8) 440.
58. See Kuçuk, 'Solidarity in EU Law' (n 40).
59. See, eg, Hilpold, 'Understanding Solidarity within EU Law' (n 21) 261–265; Kuçuk, 'Solidarity in EU Law' (n 40) 966–967; van Cleynenbreugel, 'Typologies of Solidarity in EU Law' (n 22) 14.
60. See Kennedy, 'Three Globalizations of Law and Legal Thought' (n 39) 38.
61. ibid, 22.
62. See Maurizio Carbone, 'The African, Caribbean, and Pacific (ACP) Group of States: From the Lomé Convention to the Cotonou Agreement and Beyond' in *Oxford Research Encyclopedia* (2020), available at <https://doi.org/10.1093/acrefore/9780190228637.013.1127>; Isabelle Ioannides and Stefano Inama, 'The Generalised Scheme of Preferences Regulation (No 978/2012)' European Parliamentary Research Service 2018.
63. See EA Korovin, *Mezhdunarodnoe parvo perekhodnogo vremeni* (Gosudarstvennoe izdatel'stvo, 1924); EB Pashukanis, 'International Law' [1927] in Piers Beirne and Robert Sharlet (eds), *Pashukanis: Selected Writings on Marxism and Law* (Academic Press, 1980) 168–183 (hereafter Pashukanis, 'International Law').
64. See Manfred Lachs, 'The Development and General Trends of International Law in Our Time', 169 Recueil des Cours 1980, 9 (hereafter Lachs, 'The Development and General Trends of International Law in Our Time'); GI Tunkin, *Theory of International Law* (Harvard University Press, 1974) (hereafter Tunkin, *Theory of International Law*); FI Kozhevnikov et al, *Kurs mezhdunarodnogo prava v shesti tomakh*, vol I (Nauka, 1967).
65. See Bedjaoui, *Towards a New International Economic Order* (n 9); Mohamed Bennouna, *Droit international du développement* (Berger Levrault, 1983) (hereafter Bennouna, *Droit international du développement*); Madjid Benchikh, *Droit International du Sous-Developpement* (Berger-Levrault, 1983) (hereafter Benchikh, *Droit International du Sous-Developpement*); Alain Pellet, *Le Droit International du Developpement* (2nd edn, Presses Universitaires de France, 1987) (hereafter Pellet, *Le Droit International du Developpement*); Maurice Flory, *Le droit international du développement* (Presses Universitaires de France, 1977); Georges Abi-Saab, 'The Newly Independent States and the Rules of International Law: An Outline', 8 Howard Law Journal 1962, 95.
66. See Bedjaoui, *Towards a New International Economic Order* (n 9) 248.
67. See, eg, Tunkin, *Theory of International Law* (n 64) 30–33; Mohammed Bedjaoui, 'Non-Alignement et Droit International', 151 Recueil des Cours 1976, 337, 415–417 (hereafter Bedjaoui, 'Non-Alignement et Droit International').
68. See, eg, Pashukanis, 'International Law' (n 63) 169–171; Bedjaoui, *Towards a New International Economic Order* (n 9) 49–51.
69. See Michel Virally, 'Panorama du droit international contemporain', 183 Recueil des Cours 1983, 9, 320.
70. See, eg, Pashukanis, 'International Law' (n 63) 172–173.

71. See VN Kudriavtsev (ed), *Kurs mezhdunarodnogo prava v semi tomakh*, vol I (Nauka, 1989) 261–271; Maurice Flory, 'Souveraineté des États et coopération pour le développement', 141 Recueil des Cours 1974, 255, 315 (hereafter Flory, 'Souveraineté des États et coopération pour le développement').
72. Tunkin, *Theory of International Law* (n 64) 430–437.
73. Flory, 'Souveraineté des États et coopération pour le développement' (n 71) 305–310.
74. Pellet, *Le Droit International du Developpement* (n 65) 4–5; Emmanuelle Tourme-Jouannet, *Le Droit International* (2nd edn, Presses Universitaires de France, 2016) 73–82.
75. See Benchikh, *Droit International du Sous-Developpement* (n 65), 64–71; Flory, 'Souveraineté des États et coopération pour le développement' (n 71) 320–322.
76. See Guy de Lacharriere, 'L'influence de l'inégalité de développement des Etats sur le droit international', 139 *Recueil des Cours* 227 (1974) 249–260.
77. See Benchikh, *Droit International du Sous-Developpement* (n 65), 72–74; Pellet, *Le Droit International du Developpement* (n 65), 99–101.
78. Lachs, 'The Development and General Trends of International Law in Our Time' (n 64) 53–54.
79. Bedjaoui, *Towards a New International Economic Order* (n 9) 231; Pellet, *Le Droit International du Developpement* (n 65) 103; Flory, 'Souveraineté des États et coopération pour le développement' (n 71) 326.
80. See, eg, Pellet, *Le Droit International du Developpement* (n 65) 90–106.
81. See Claude Imperiali, *Les benefices excessifs, une pratique limitee et controversee*, 24 Annuaire Français de Droit International 1978, 678, 708; Ian Brownlie, 'Legal Status of Natural Resources in International Law (Some Aspects)', 162 Recueil des Cours 1979, 245, 256–271) (hereafter Brownlie, 'Legal Status of Natural Resources in International Law').
82. See Benchikh, *Droit International du Sous-Developpement* (n 65), 218–238.
83. See, eg, NM Minasian, *Pravo mirnogo sosushchestvovaniia* (Rostovskii gosudarstvennii universitet, 1965) 230–235; Tunkin, *Theory of International Law* (n 64) 315–319; Bedjaoui, *Towards a New International Economic Order* (n 9) 256–259.
84. See N Ouchakov, 'La Competence Interne des Etats et la Non-Intervention dans le Droit International Contemporain', 141 Recueil des Cours 1974, 1; VM Shurshalov, 'Ob ob'ekte mezhdunarodnogo prava', 1957/3 Sovetskoe Gosudarstvo i Pravo 1957, 52, 60.
85. On the concept of inter-bloc law, see Edward McWhinney, *Peaceful Coexistence and Soviet-Western International Law* (A.W. Sythoff 1964); Lachs, 'The Development and General Trends of International Law in Our Time' (n 64) 90–91; Tunkin, *Theory of International Law* (n 64) 42–48.
86. See Bedjaoui, 'Non-Alignement et Droit International' (n 67) 380–381; Lachs, 'The Development and General Trends of International Law in Our Time' (n 64) 90–92.
87. Tunkin, *Theory of International Law* (n 64) 40–42.
88. Thomas Franck, 'Minimum Standards of Public Policy and Order Applicable to Collective International Commodity Negotiations', 160 Recueil des Cours 1978, 395, 424–430 (hereafter Franck, 'Minimum Standards of Public Policy'); Bedjaoui, *Towards a New International Economic Order* (n 9) 246.
89. See Franck, 'Minimum Standards of Public Policy' (n 88) 415–423; Dominique Carreau et al, *Droit International Economique* 336–340 (2nd edn, LGDJ, 1980) (hereafter Carreau, *Droit International Economique*).
90. For background, see Carreau, *Droit International Economique* (n 89) 332–335; Roland Herrmann, *On the Economic Evaluation of the Stabex System*, 17 Intereconomics 1982, 7.

91. See J Fawcett, 'Trade and Finance in International Law', 123 Recueil des Cours 1968, 215, 239–240; Carreau, *Droit International Economique* (n 86) 338; Pierre-Michel Eisemann, *Le fonds commun pour les produits de base*, 27 Annuaire Français de Droit International 1981, 568; Brownlie, 'Legal Status of Natural Resources in International Law (n 81) 282–286.
92. See, eg, Michel Virally, 'Le principe de réciprocité dans le droit international contemporain', 122 Recueil des Cours 1967, 1, 101.
93. Jacques Le Goff, *History and Memory* (Columbia University Press, 1992) 115.
94. ibid, 124.
95. René-Jean Dupuy, 'Communauté internationale et disparités de développement', 165 Recueil des Cours 1979, 9, 162.
96. Bennouna, *Droit international du développement* (n 65) 21.
97. For background, see 'Frontex Launches New EU Border Control Mission Operation Themis', *Deutsche Welle*, 2018, <https://www.dw.com/en/frontex-launches-new-eu-border-control-mission-operation-themis/a-42417610> (accessed 6 October 2023).
98. Article 174 (ex Article 158 TEC), Consolidation version of the Treaty on the Functioning of the European Union Official Journal 115, 09/05/2008 P. 0127–0127.
99. Hilpold, 'Understanding Solidarity within EU Law' (n 21) 261–262.
100. Chantal Mouffe, *The Democratic Paradox* (Verso, 2000) 12–13.

CHAPTER 9

SOVEREIGNTY AND EUROPEAN EXCEPTIONALISM

HENT KALMO

1. Introduction

A century ago, Hans Kelsen voiced a sentiment shared by many international lawyers when he augured that the word 'sovereignty' would soon be struck out from the dictionary of international law.[1] This wish is symptomatic of how sovereignty has come to be represented as a foil, an obstacle, a principle of backwardness, and at times even the archenemy of international law, the legacy that must be shed if the latter is to fulfil its vocation. The European Union (EU) has been placed in the vanguard of international law in its efforts to create a post-sovereign condition. Yet its legal order has not sat comfortably in the framework of general international law. EU law's deepening autonomy has led to claims on its behalf that make it so exceptional, so *sui generis*, as to remove it from the purview of international law altogether. To further complicate matters, members of the EU have become champions of sovereignty in the outer domain, defending the rule of non-intervention and territorial integrity in the face of Russian expansionism. While its actions belie this rhetoric, Russia has joined China in foregrounding State sovereignty as the core principle of international law, propounding a version of international order which seems traditional yet also alien in its dependence on 'non-Western agendas'.[2] The idea of sovereignty has thus acquired a curiously ambiguous position in the contemporary European arena where various perspectives co-exist in a state of unresolved tension.

The chapter explores these tensions in the light of Europe's past. Without seeking to downplay the true novelty of the legal configuration embodied in the EU, it shows that the concept of sovereignty is still relevant, indeed pivotal, in Europe, especially if the latter is understood in a wider continental sense. The chapter is organized as follows: Section 2 will outline the position allotted to the concept of sovereignty in the *ius publicum Europaeum* in the 18th and 19th centuries. Its aim is limited to making the essential point that sovereignty was not considered the sole foundation of international law at this time, nor were its implications ever uncontested. Section 3 describes the variability of European exceptionalism by showing how Europe's leadership role in developing international law was redefined in the 20th century as sovereignty became associated with narrow-minded nationalism. Section 4 takes a critical look at various theories which seek to make sense of the unique normative assemblage that has emerged in Europe. Section 5 concludes the chapter.

2. Sovereignty and the *Ius Publicum Europaeum*

The concept of sovereignty has been given pride of place in historical narratives which portray the development of international law as the worldwide expansion of a European archetype.[3] In Carl Schmitt's telling, the story was one of adulteration. Schmitt described how the European law of nations, originally rooted in a 'true community of European princely houses, states and nations', came adrift in a sphere of empty abstraction when, in the process of globalization, it was engulfed in a disorderly mass of 'heterogeneous states, lacking any spatial or spiritual consciousness of what they once had in common, a chaos of reputedly equal and equally sovereign states'.[4] The distinction between a warm, like-minded community and a cold, anonymous society composed of aloof individuals, figured prominently in Nazi scholarship on international law, especially in visions of European unity.[5] Schmitt's picture of the *ius publicum Europaeum* also reflected the mood after World War II when Europe was falling in the shadow of the rivalry between the US and the Soviet Union.[6] The idea of Europe as a political community was already well established, however, by the mid-18th century.[7] In his influential work *The Law of Nations* (1758), Emer de Vattel consecrated the notion that Europe had become 'a kind of republic, of which the members—each independent, but all linked together by the ties of common interest—unite for the maintenance of order and liberty'.[8] The world as a whole was also considered to be a society, governed by *ius gentium* as the common law of humanity.[9] But Europe was described as representing a more close-knit political community where all members had a common interest in preserving their independence by preventing any one ruler from gaining universal monarchy.[10]

The very concept of sovereignty created a kind of imagined universality that extended beyond Europe. Schmitt was wrong in depicting this as a later distortion. The sort of universalizing thinking he deplored was already present in the 16th century. 'Just as a mouse is as much numbered among animals as is the elephant,' wrote Jean Bodin, 'so the rightly ordered government of only three households, provided they are subject to sovereign authority, is just as much a commonwealth as a great empire. The principality of Ragusa, which is one of the smallest in Europe, is no less a commonwealth than the empires of the Turks and the Tartars, which are among the greatest in the world.'[11] The idea of equality encompassed by the sovereign status did not do away with asymmetries of power and dignity. But a crucial characteristic of the language of the law of nations was indifference to some facts and legal relations that were clearly important in other respects. The doctrine of sovereignty regarded all (not merely European) independent political entities as generically akin, entitled to their status as subjects of the law of nations, in spite of even the most glaring differences in size, wealth, dignity, or form of government. San Marino might have been pygmy compared to France, with none of the latter's grandeur, but it was not denied its rightful place in the same category. The assimilation under one heading of the tiniest republic and the most powerful kingdom of Europe was a counterintuitive notion. Gottfried Wilhelm Leibniz took precisely the example of San Marino to argue the point that legal liberty, that is, lack of a superior, was not enough to rise to the kind of sovereignty enjoyed by the King of France. 'For besides freedom and authority over oneself, custom requires something else for [the acquisition of] sovereignty, namely power which wins authority also among foreigners.'[12] Only those political communities could lay claim to sovereignty, Leibniz argued, that have the ability to weigh heavy in international affairs, not simply defend themselves. Merely those with enough power and momentum could 'accede to the privileges of the law of nations'. However commonsensical this view may have appeared at a time when privileges routinely followed rank, it contrasted with the egalitarian orthodoxy of *ius gentium*. Samuel Pufendorf insisted that there is no obligation, no right by which one free and independent State is required to yield precedence to another, for their liberty is equal.[13]

Treatments of the law of nations sought to convey the impression that most, if not all, of what was considered obligatory in international affairs was not accidental but rooted in some fundamental principle. When it came to the discipline as a whole, the *ratio*, the foundation, could be seen as residing in the nature of the sovereign State. Francisco Suarez developed his conception of *ius gentium* as a body of rules binding *between* nations from what he perceived to be the current state of the law.[14] Numerous actual practices, for example the custom of receiving ambassadors under immunity, or that of requiring free commercial intercourse between States, did not spring from natural law, Suarez claimed. They were not 'indispensable by virtue of natural reason' because States might conceivably have refused ambassadors or even avoided any commercial relations among themselves, remaining in complete isolation. What, then, was the rational basis of such customs? It was the fact that States, although each a perfect community in itself, are never self-sufficient. The existence and validity of *ius gentium*, as well as the *raison d'être* of its individual doctrines, were all grounded by Suarez in the ambivalence characterizing the position of sovereign States. The latter are accomplished enough to function as complete political communities, yet not self-sufficient to the extent of being able to stand alone and make do with cooperation. If the first element were absent, a complete political community, a *communitas perfecta*, would only be achieved at some supra-sovereign level, perhaps not before reaching the scale of a world State. By contrast, in the absence of the second element, that is, if sovereign States were able to flourish both materially and morally to the highest degree in isolation, then no sphere of inter-state relations would be required, and hence no scope would exist for a *ius inter gentes* as a separate legal domain.

The law of nations was accordingly considered to have a double foundation. In lieu of a single leviathan, authors such as Wolff and Vattel contrived an equilibrium between two kinds of commonwealths and two corresponding groups of duties owed by a State under natural law: first, to itself, to ensure its own perfection as a political community, and, then, to its fellow States in view of perfecting the larger society established by nature among all nations.[15] A source of permanent tension was thus set within the discipline. The first impression can be one of harmony between the various duties. Consider international trade, for example. It allows a State to obtain what it lacks for the wellbeing of its own citizens while working to the advantage of other communities. Each State should therefore not only engage in foreign trade, argued Vattel, but also protect and foster it. This general precept mandated caring for the safety of foreign travellers, the establishment of ports, admission and favouring of consuls, etc. Yet a State's duty towards itself remained primary. A State was obliged to trade with others only insofar as it did not harm its interests. The reasoning of Wolff and Vattel often has this sort of bitter pill in store for the internationally minded. The requirement of solidarity yields a long list of duties, only to be watered down in the end by the caveat that these duties are imperfect, not collectively enforceable, and subject to the States' own assessment as to whether they are able to fulfil them. The updated impression is thus of State sovereignty winning out at every turn. Yet it would be to miss the character of the whole enterprise to steer it exclusively towards one pole, either the *civitas maxima* or the sovereign State. The task was precisely to show that the two poles could cohabit, in a permanent equilibrium, at the service of mutual perfection.

Besides, the prevailing legal doctrines were formulated in such a way that any single State's sovereignty faced a far greater threat from the freedom of its counterparts than the supremacy of the *civitas maxima*. A perilous excess in freedom resulted from its liberal distribution to all members of the society of nations. The idea of self-protection encompassed not only the right to resist direct military attacks, but also that of standing up against any attempted injury to the 'perfection' of a State. The injury did not have to materialize. As Vattel noted, peace-loving nations could unite and strike a pre-emptive blow against 'a nation of a restless and mischievous disposition, ever ready to injure others, to traverse their designs, and to excite domestic disturbances in their dominions'.[16] This rule acquired great significance in the age of revolutions. In Prince Metternich's vision, the Concert of Europe was called into existence precisely to fulfil a sweeping security mandate.[17] Its role was to identify, as early as possible, without waiting until their hostile temperament had matured, regimes whose very nature made them a threat to other States. The aim was not to create a domineering commonwealth, but rather, in the spirit of Vattel, to protect the common interests of all members of the European republic by preserving their independence.[18] However, it quickly transpired that, for all the talk of European community incessantly flowing from the lips of diplomats, unfailing in their efforts to conjure up an image of unbroken solidarity, there was never going to be any enduring consensus on what the limits of sovereignty were.

Indeed, when the members of the European Concert failed to adhere to the same constitutional principles internally, it is unsurprising that they could not agree on which revolutionary upheavals would justify action abroad, either in general or in view of some concrete proposal of intervention.[19]

This jars with the notion that there was some consensus-producing community underlying the European law of nations, as Carl Schmitt suggested. On the contrary, it was the abstract nature of sovereignty that generated a sense of foundational consensus, whilst rulers were, in fact, continually at odds about the interpretation of the 'public law of Europe'. Sovereignty was taken to be the core of the *ius publicum Europaeum*, but its precise meaning could not be agreed upon even at the time when European rulers did form a kind of extended family in virtue of the long-standing practice of concluding dynastic marriages to strengthen political alliances.[20] Schmitt argued that the common concepts of the *ius publicum Europaeum* became questionable only when they had already been hollowed out by the globalization of the European order. A very different interpretation is also possible, however. The *ius publicum Europaeum* expressed an aspiration, an imagined community, in conditions where there was no real meeting of the minds. As a positive law, it was claimed to offer more precise guidance than universal law of nations in delimiting the rights and duties of States. Georg Friedrich von Martens contrasted the vast corpus of treaties born out of the particular needs of European powers with the merely philosophical *ius Cosmopoliticum*.[21] Yet this historical corpus was condensed into a few fundamental rules which enshrined, on the one hand, the principle of non-intervention and, on the other, an exception allowing other States to intervene all the same if their security was threatened.[22] Although this vague position represented a kind of consensus, its ambiguity was such that the French diplomat Armand Lefebvre was not completely off the mark when he noted in the aftermath of the revolution of 1830 that Europe, in fact, had no public law to serve as a compass.[23]

3. Varieties of European Exceptionalism

The idea that the *ius publicum Europaeum* emanated from something unique to the European continent was itself the result of efforts to rationalize, or read a deeper sense into, a congeries of historical events, treaties, and practices. The 19th century witnessed the heyday of the notion that Europe represents a standard of civilization. An important component of this idea was the belief that history embodies a progress towards an ever more peaceful society as militarism gradually gives way to the spirit of commerce.[24] All actual military conflicts could be dismissed as the last throes of a passing era.[25] The nexus between commerce and peace was taken to be universal, but Europe was portrayed as the site where it was most obviously on display, so that its law naturally appeared as a harbinger of things to come—the future of the law of nations.[26]

On the other hand, when it became accepted that Europe's law was not merely a set of rules but an expression of a particular form of civilization, then its core status, that of sovereignty, ceased to be immediately available to non-European countries. This was made clear when Turkey was 'admitted to participate in the advantages of the public law and the Concert of Europe' (as the Treaty of Paris of 1856 put it). The Turkish government insisted on the removal of foreign nationals' extraterritorial jurisdiction in its territory. If European States failed to accept such limitations upon their sovereignty, why was the Ottoman Empire treated differently? Because of its civilizational backwardness, argued Friedrich Martens. Any restrictions on sovereignty could be abolished only once 'the principles of European civilization and culture' had penetrated 'the inner life of the Ottoman Empire'.[27] Once spelled out, this criterion could also be invoked in support of equal treatment. At the Second Hague Conference (1907), South American States claimed that it is a natural consequence of sovereignty to exclude intervention on the ground that domestic courts are unreliable. 'The states of Europe,' said the Uruguayan representative, 'should not apply to America other rules of conduct than those of international law, which regulates their relations with each other. America has a good right to such treatment, for it is entirely civilized.'[28]

Contrary to the picture of reckless globalization painted by Carl Schmitt, scholars of international law remained unwilling to extend the privileges attached to sovereignty to all States, emphasizing rather the thick cultural underpinnings of the law of civilized nations. The practical consequence of this view was that the rule of non-intervention allowed far more scope for exceptions vis-à-vis non-European States.[29] European powers were not expected to submit to the kind of intervention that was considered legal in the case of the Ottoman Empire.[30] In view of the high value placed on sovereignty as a status, it is something of a paradox that voluntary limitation of sovereignty expanded into a recurring theme in the literature on international law at the turn of the 20th century and started to be acclaimed as a sign of progressive thinking. For example, the International Sugar Union, created by the Brussels Convention of 1902, was described as an historic departure from the prevailing idea of sovereignty, since it included an authority with powers exercised by majority rather than unanimity. This, too, was an intervention of sorts, but the underlying premise was that lost freedom of action was not to be regretted if restricted not by other States but in the form of a common enterprise of international cooperation. Sovereignty had been associated with self-determination as a moral value. It now appeared in a new light: a potentially expendable means for pursuing general welfare.

Gradually, a curious inversion occurred in how Europe's leadership role was perceived with regard to the development of international law. In the 19th century, it was full, unlimited sovereignty that was regarded as a cultural achievement, its qualified versions in the extra-European world being depicted as premodernity. After World War II, by contrast, it was in its efforts to devise unprecedented limitations to sovereignty that Europe suddenly appeared as a pioneer. How did sovereignty, formerly considered as something entirely respectable, come to be vilified as a drag?[31] The answer lies in a changed understanding of the vocation—the *mission pacificatrice*—of international law. Despite the arrival of a new empirical mindset, the second half of the 19th century did not mark the end of the road for the tradition attributing a double foundation to the law of nations. According to Baron de Staal, the President of the First Hague Conference (1899), the work of peace was meant to 'reconcile, while safeguarding, the two principles that lie at the basis of the law of nations, the principle of the sovereignty of States and the principle of a just international solidarity'.[32] The aim of such reconciliation was abandoned when sovereignty began to be seen as irremediably tainted by nationalistic egotism and thus a hindrance to peace. The professional credo of international lawyers became either to condemn sovereignty or to take the sting out of the principle by interpreting it in a community-friendly spirit as a set of competences devolved on States by the higher international legal order. The future was imagined as the gradual dwindling of States' competences until an all-embracing community would establish itself as the sole foundation of international law.

In the post-World War II period, it was in the Western European setting that this argument about the demise of sovereignty was most convincing. It is important to emphasize that the turn to regionalism happened only after a loss of faith in the kind of universalism embodied in the League of Nations. World War I had not exactly nurtured the traditional image of a European republic with common interests, but it did raise the prospect of a world community of States. As years passed, however, it was increasingly felt that the League of Nations was too protective of sovereignty since its universalist ambition was stretching it too thin. Europe began to appear as a more promising terrain for overcoming sovereignty. Hersch Lauterpacht argued that, whilst some basic legal rules favouring peace and communication can develop in the absence of a deep harmony of views and interests, a more substantive and accomplished kind of law—advanced international law, in other words—does presuppose a true community.[33] As Lauterpacht noted, in 1944, there was still little black letter law to undermine the established opinion that only States were subjects of international law. Although many international lawyers deplored this doctrine as retrograde, they had to produce such exotic examples as blockade runners and pirates to dispute it.[34] The future could be different, though, if States were willing to confer direct rights upon individuals.[35] After World War II, Western Europe was held up as the only area where this was practicable and a sincere commitment to human rights could be expected. 'However desirable the conclusion of a general convention regarding the international protection of human rights may appear', wrote Charles de Vischer in 1947, 'it is clear that such a convention would only be effectively applied among States already converted to the ideas incorporated in the proposed Declaration.'[36]

International law became the ground on which European identity was reinvented in the post-war period.[37] The multiplicity of civilizations suddenly loomed large as a topic in the scholarship of international law.[38] All professions of parity aside, the sense that the West was somehow more advanced in its approach to international law was still unmistakably present. The global adoption of the doctrine of sovereignty was offered as 'evidence of the lasting dependence of non-Western nations in the conduct of their international affairs upon fundamental concepts of the Western world'.[39] But Europe itself was moving on. Its civilization was now supposedly best manifested in the capacity to bring forth those elements of international law which had been held back by the absence of worldwide solidarity. The European Convention of Human Rights (ECHR, 1950) and the Treaty establishing the European Coal and Steel Community (1951) represented different strategies of regional integration, but they were seen as driving forward the same tendency: the willingness of enlightened sovereign States to deconstruct sovereignty. The preamble of the ECHR described the treaty as taking first steps for the collective enforcement of universal rights by 'European countries which are like-minded and have a common heritage of political traditions, ideals, freedom and the rule of law'. The rights listed in the ECHR were presented as universal yet they were also narrowly European by their field of application.[40]

The legal instruments used in setting up the European Communities were not unprecedented.[41] The novelty was that supranationality ('an egregious departure from the beaten tracks of international law'[42]), which had already caught the imagination of international lawyers decades ago, was now erected into a routine tool, like a battering ram hitting one sector of State sovereignty after another.[43] As the Court of Justice of the European Union (CJEU) explained, the Community law derived its exceptional penetrative force (which allowed it to confer rights on individuals) from the fact that the EEC Treaty, by contrast with ordinary international treaties, has created its own legal system, one embedded in 'a Community of unlimited duration, having its own institutions, its own personality, its own legal capacity and capacity of representation on the international plane and, more particularly, real powers stemming from a limitation of sovereignty or a transfer of powers from the States to the Community'.[44] In other words, it was left in no doubt that this community was very special indeed. Even so, the European experiment seemed to possess universal relevance. Alf Ross prophesied that the European Communities would be 'a preparatory school for a world federation'.[45] Wolfgang Friedmann described the Communities as 'the world's most important laboratory, in the gradual transition from multinational arrangements to a common constitutional order'.[46]

When these initial hopes are called to mind, it is somewhat ironic that specialists of public international law have later exhibited much annoyance at the talk of European exceptionalism, often despairing of not finding any signs that the prodigal son is about to return to the fold by admitting that it is, after all, a regional organization governed by general international law.[47] Such frustration is understandable in view of the case law of the CJEU which has come to see international law as a threat to specific European rules and values.[48] It has even been suggested that Europe is now developing its own version of the kind of sovereigntist resistance to international law known as American exceptionalism.[49] The issue of exceptionalism appears technical, indeed capable of receiving a definite solution, when tied to specific questions of applicability, for example, as to whether lacunae in EU rules can be filled by falling back on general international law.[50] Yet, in the end, such questions cannot be disentangled from broader ideas about the depth of EU law's autonomy.[51] And then, inevitably, a dilemma emerges. The autonomy of EU law can be construed either as being so deep that the European experiment loses almost any relevance for public international law—it will be simply different, informed by its own values, guided by a logic incapable of replication or even of inspiring by example. Or the legal order of the EU is viewed, more modestly, as a bundle of *leges speciales* in whose absence Member States are thrown back to general international law, with sovereignty at its foundation. But this would be to abandon what has long been considered to be the most pioneering aspect of the European experiment: the ambition to transcend the sovereign State as such.

4. Falling Back on Sovereignty?

The crux of the problem of sovereignty in Europe is that most of the States in this region have a threefold identity, being at once Member States of the EU, subjects of international law, and personifying a domestic legal system. A lawyer's impulse is likely to be to seek to reconcile all these facets, or personas, by merging the three legal systems into one—fashioning a 'unitary legal worldview', to borrow an expression from Alfred Verdross (who invoked, very aptly, the Leibnizian image of *theatrum legale mundi* in this context).[52] Unity can be achieved in various ways, depending on which legal order is placed at the basis. Hans Kelsen argued that there are two equally consistent but radically different perspectives for making sense of legal multiplicity encountered in the world. If any single national legal order is taken as the starting point, then it becomes the mainspring of the whole *theatrum legale mundi*. The sovereignty of other States fades away. The latter are reduced from self-propelling actors to appendages of the one and only sovereign State at the basis of the construction.[53] For Kelsen, debunking the dogma of sovereignty meant choosing the alternative perspective: adopting international law as the basis and reconfiguring all valid law in a grand holistic framework where true plurality is first allowed to arise since not one but multiple sovereign States can then co-exist under the supremacy of international law. This avenue promises a synthesis where sovereignty is not exalted, but rather humanized, cut down to size, tempered with human rights, solidarity, and multilevel governance.[54] In a similar vein, Neil MacCormick has argued that 'pluralism under international law' yields the only fully satisfactory 'theoretical account of the totality of juridical relationships in Europe'.[55]

Many consider that this picture of constitutionalist harmony misrepresents the complexity of legal relationships in Europe. It retains a system of hierarchical ordering, and that in favour of a body of rules which, as actually applied under the Charter of the UN, may not deserve unqualified respect.[56] The reason why Europe has provided 'a kind of regional comfort zone for the ideas of constitutional pluralism'[57] is precisely that it lacks any recognized centre managing its legal diversity from the top down. The idea of European exceptionalism again reveals its ambiguous character at this point. The kind of legal pluralism that has emerged in Europe may be seen as a provincial fact. Or, alternatively, it may be presented as a model for international law more generally, suggesting that there is little reason to feel anxiety about legal fragmentation or regime conflict whenever common cultural sensibilities act as agents of convergence. Bernard Stirn has conjured up the old idea of *ius publicum Europaeum* to describe the symbiotic relationship between the ECHR, EU law, and domestic rules, casting this new version also as a path-breaking achievement. 'By becoming stronger and stronger,' writes Stirn, 'European public law is opening up vistas which—like the genius of Europe—exceed the European continent.'[58] Europe becomes an image of the future, above all, when its legal arrangements are seen as expressions of some ideological leaning, such as democracy or liberalism, something deep enough to be transformative yet potentially universal. The very nature of liberal States is to disaggregate sovereignty, it has been contended.[59]

Some twenty years ago, it could still be argued quite uncontroversially that there exists a peculiar European approach to international law which is destined to become the global future. William W Burke-White and Anne-Marie Slaughter claimed that 'the European way of law' consists in going beyond State-to-State cooperation, and thereby blurring the line between domestic and international realms as traditionally imagined though the lens of Westphalian sovereignty. This model could be expected to be adopted globally, they said, since, in order to deal with new cross-border realities, 'the international legal system must be able to influence the domestic politics of states and harness national institutions in pursuit of global objectives.'[60] The question that is asked now is whether liberal democracies will be able to defend their vision of international law against authoritarian revisionism which precludes any such intervention in domestic politics. In this confrontation, where authoritarian States are thought to favour a sovereigntist downgrading of the current international law, Europe is presented as a liberal region holding out with difficulty in the face of increasing pressure.[61] In fact, within the EU itself, there seems to be opening a rift between liberalism and sovereigntism.[62] Stella Ghervas has described the EU as the latest incarnation of the European idea of perpetual peace. But she offers a bleak assessment of the present situation, decrying the resurgence of ethnonationalism whose purpose, she says, is to revert to the Westphalian model of sovereign States.[63]

It would be incorrect to assume, however, that the EU has ever embodied a project to repudiate sovereignty if the latter is understood in the multifaceted way it operates in public international law. The aspiration to transcend sovereignty within the EU has never been thought to imply a rejection of sovereign statehood as a status enshrined in the UN Charter. This fact has come to the fore with particular clarity when Member States of the EU have positioned themselves as defenders of sovereignty in the international arena. Even before Russia launched an all-out invasion of Ukraine in 2022, the EU adopted sanctions in support of the territorial integrity, sovereignty, and independence of Ukraine.[64] Surely too uncritically, the idea of post-sovereignty has always been associated with peace, in keeping with the dominant image of the EU. But whenever depicting themselves as champions of law against force under the current international legal order, European countries are also indirectly reaffirming the value of sovereignty as protected by international law.

What about the claim that we are witnessing a reversion to the traditional model of sovereignty inside the EU?[65] Europe cannot be experiencing a return of sovereignty for the simple reason that its States have not ceased to enjoy this status under general international law even while experimenting with novel forms of fracturing authority. In this respect at least, Europe is still embedded in the classical tradition of international law. Whilst Europe has been exceptional in creating legal commitments so deep and penetrating that they appear not merely to limit but to erode sovereignty, it is still a state of multi-layered complementarity that has been created, not a world of post-sovereignty. Nor should the important fact be missed that sovereignty is as much an enabler of integration as it is at times an obstacle. Treaty amendments, and thus the expansion of the EU's competences, depend on it.[66] The doctrine of primacy is also underpinned by the treaty-making power that Member States of the EU enjoy under general international law.[67] It has been argued that, within the EU, there 'simply is no nucleus of sovereignty that the Member States can invoke, as such, against the Community'.[68] But what is the meaning of this 'can'? What if a Member State imitates the Russian Constitutional Court which warned in 2015 that Russia was free not to implement a decision of the European Court of Human Rights (ECtHR) should the latter fail to respect 'rights belonging to sovereignty'.[69] The Polish Constitutional Tribunal did just that in 2021 when it declared unconstitutional both the Treaty on European Union (TEU) and the ECHR.[70] It might be said that such invocations of sovereignty are disallowed by EU law. But multiple claims to supreme authority do not cancel each other out.[71] The concept of sovereignty is still pertinent in Europe because it captures the nature of such authority claims.[72]

Europe cannot be identified with the EU, of course. But the latter does exemplify particularly well the problem of multiple legal personas. States outside the EU have multiple identities, too: they appear simultaneously as bearers of a domestic legal system and subjects of international law. This results in what has been called a 'dualistic sovereignty regime' where one, State-centred normative conception is overlain by another which envelops States collectively as addressees of international law.[73] The theory of radical pluralism is certainly correct in foregrounding this normative multiplicity as a problem rather than explaining it away in some all-embracing holistic schema. This is all the more true since the various normative perspectives also represent competing avenues for achieving collective agency. Part of the intellectual background to European integration was the belief that outdated political myths such as sovereignty must be dispelled by aligning them with economic realities.[74] There is nowadays much scepticism about the notion that economic and other cross-border realities must always be accommodated, whatever their consequences. The myth of sovereignty has not gone away, as evidenced by the nearly pan-European wish to 'take back control', stemming from the feeling that control has been lost in a world menacing to become borderless.[75] This feeling is not necessarily isolationist, considering that the ambition to take back control can be pursued not only at the national but also, and today perhaps more credibly, at the European level. The problem for political and legal theory is whether one level of collective agency needs to subsume another or whether they can be thought as co-existing even as ultimate points of reference.

The argument in favour of post-sovereignty is premised on the idea that when States part with their competencies these do not merge into some sort of super-sovereignty higher up. It is thus an intriguing turn of events that there is now much talk of 'European sovereignty'.[76] Whilst this expression may be more metaphoric than strictly legal, it is nonetheless legitimate to ask which tools could serve to create the kind of regional empowerment it suggests. Many of the tools will depend on Member States acting collectively under the aegis of the EU. This does not necessarily involve abandoning their individual sovereignty vis-à-vis the outer world. For example, although the EU-wide investment screening framework is perceived as increasingly important for Europe's 'strategic autonomy', the framework still leaves it to Member States exercising their national sovereignty to protect assets considered to be strategic from the point of view of the EU as a whole.[77] The EU's recently adopted global human rights sanctions regime could be viewed as another step away from the statist paradigm in that it extends the concern with individuals outside the borders of the organization. Yet the targeted measures it foresees also rely on classical acts of sovereignty, such as refusing access into the territory of a State.[78]

It is another question whether State sovereignty is by its very nature retrograde. Contrary to expectations, European integration has not led to federal centralization.[79] The result as it now stands is rather a precariously poised structure of exuberant complexity. The EU's unique pluralist architecture has come to be extolled as 'Europe's *Sonderweg*—its special way and identity'.[80] But the understanding of what is special about it has changed over time. One way to summarize the European experiment is to describe it as being about achieving enhanced collective agency while preserving the international legal sovereignty of participant States, including that of small States. It combines the form of political self-determination realized in a State with the kind of self-determination that can be attained supranationally.[81] As the world changes, the desire to achieve effective control may well require a larger political organization, but this, in itself, does not deprive sovereign statehood of its value. As Benedict Kingsbury has written, sovereign States still 'open the prospect of some autonomy, the possibility for individuals and groups to make a difference in a structured political space whose institutions and community shape their conscious identities'.[82] Perhaps what we have here is evidence for the continuing attractiveness of Francisco Suarez' theory of the nature of international law—that it's a form of community-building for incomplete but still fairly accomplished political communities.

5. Conclusion

Cultural diversity is often explained in two ways. When confronted with differences in behaviour and beliefs, one can either trace them back to disparate cultures, each with its own set of values, or, alternatively, assume that those differences reflect various stages of progress on a universal scale of development.[83] Both perspectives are still discernible in how Europe's relationship to international law is construed. The emerging field of comparative international law has aimed at provincializing the European, or more broadly Western, approach to international law by depicting it as merely one among many national and regional traditions.[84] China and Russia, among others, are said to exemplify a different, authoritarian approach to international law with a preference for State sovereignty.[85] Whatever the global developments happen to be, they always leave scope for the idea of European exceptionalism in some form. If developments outside appear unpleasant and cannot be dismissed as the remnants of a passing era, it can still be argued that Europe rebuffs the general trend and adheres to its unique position as a community of more elevated values. Of course, when Europe itself is witnessing a backlash against supranationality, and the institutions embodying it, then it becomes harder to associate it unambiguously with the ambition to transcend sovereignty. Yet, as history shows, Europe's borders on the mental map can be moved to accommodate a certain idea of international law, just as a certain idea of Europe has often served as a horizon for imagining the character and future of international law.

Carl Schmitt said that Kelsen's fight against sovereignty was the most perfect example of the tendency to let all hard legal problems dissolve into methodology and then into nothingness.[86] Schmitt himself envisaged the return of the classical *ius publicum Europaeum* in a modified, non-Eurocentric form, as a global law governing the relations between the three or four great powers he thought would arise.[87] It might appear this is precisely what is happening now, with the EU seeking an independent standing alongside China, Russia, and the US. There is no return to an imagined past, however, as rightly noted by Tom Ginsburg who argues that 'the future of the international legal order will be determined by how these powerful states, with their different visions for international law, interact in the coming decades'.[88] Such interactions always go beyond legal transfers and acquire a more general symbolic character. Europe was first defined as a political unity by opposition to universal monarchy within and to barbarians outside.[89] Whatever similarities one may find with the present, an important difference is that the security of the European continent and the common interests of its States vis-à-vis the outer world are now framed in terms of general international law, not in terms of some *ius publicum Europaeum*.

Acknowledgements

This work was supported by the Estonian Research Council Grant (PRG942).

Notes

1. It is an ironical fact that he made this remark in his contribution on the topic of sovereignty in a dictionary of international law; Hans Kelsen, 'Souveränität' in Karl Strupp (ed), *Wörterbuch des Völkerrechts und der Diplomatie*, vol 2 (Walter der Gruyter & Co 1925) 555.
2. On Russia and China as representatives of 'non-Western agendas', see Anthea Roberts, *Is International Law International?* (OUP 2017) 306. For the approach of Russian legal scholars to sovereignty, see Lauri Mälksoo, *Russian Approaches to International Law* (OUP 2015) 100.

3. See, eg, Barry Buzan, 'Universal Sovereignty' in Tim Dunne and Christian Reus-Smit (eds), *The Globalization of International Society* (OUP 2017) 230.
4. Carl Schmitt, *The* Nomos *of the Earth* (Telos Press Publishing 1983) 234. This idea has staged something of a comeback in recent historical scholarship which emphasizes the viability of shared moral norms as complements to legal rules in early modern Europe. 'The metavalues of the system', it has been argued, 'impeded the development of institutional forms that subsequently flourished in the modern era. In a world where social hierarchy was the norm, the principle of sovereign equality never took root.' Christian Reus-Smit, *The Moral Purpose of the State. Culture, Social Identity, and Institutional Rationality in International Relations* (Princeton UP 1999) 101.
5. See, eg, Hans Helmut Dietze, 'Europa als Einheit', 20 Zeitschrift für Völkerrecht 1936, 295–296.
6. On the context of Schmitt's post-war conception of Europe, see John P McCormick, 'Carl Schmitt's Europe: Cultural, Imperial and Spatial Proposals for European Integration, 1923–1955' in Christian Joerges and Navraj Singh Ghaleigh (eds), *Darker Legacies of Law in Europe. The Shadow of National Socialism and Fascism over Europe and its Legal Traditions* (Hart Publishing 2003) 139–140.
7. 'The nations of Europe have principles of humanity, which are not to be found in the other quarters of the world', wrote Voltaire. '[T]hey are better united with each other; they have certain laws, which are common to them all; all their royal families are related; the inhabitants of each kingdom travel among their neighbors, and by that means keep up a reciprocal connection with them.' 'Poem upon the battle of Fontenoy, preliminary discourse' in Voltaire, *The Henriade, with the Battle of Fontenoy, Dissertations on Man, Law of Nature, Desctruction of Lisbon, Temple of Taste, and Temple of Friendship* (Derby & Jackson 1859) 253.
8. Emer de Vattel, *The Law of Nations* (Liberty Fund 2008) 496. This idea had appeared earlier, see Martti Koskenniemi, *To the Uttermost Parts of the Earth. Legal Imagination and the International Power, 1300–1870* (CUP 2021) 411.
9. See Ursula Vollerthun, *The Idea of International Society. Erasmus, Vitoria, Gentili and Grotius* (CUP 2017).
10. Wars against powerful rivals were commonly justified as attempts to preserve 'the liberty of Europe'. See H D Schmidt, 'The Establishment of "Europe" as a Political Expression', 9 The Historical Journal 1966, 174.
11. Jean Bodin, *Six Books of the Commonwealth* (Basil Blackwell 1967) 7–8.
12. Gottfried Wilhelm Leibniz, *Tractatus de jure suprematus ac legationis principium Germaniae* (2nd edn, London 1678) 53.
13. Samuel Pufendorf, *On the Law of Nature and Nations* (Oceana Publications 1934) 1253.
14. See Francisco Suarez, *A Treatise on Laws and God the Lawgiver* (Clarendon Press 1944) 347.
15. On moral perfection as a goal in the law of nations, see Emmanuelle Jouannet, *The Liberal-Welfarist Law of Nations. A History of International Law* (CUP 2012) 62.
16. Emer de Vattel, *The Law of Nations* (Liberty Fund 2010) 289.
17. On the kind of European order that participants in the Congress of Vienna were hoping to create, see Matthijs Lok, *Europe against Revolution. Conservatism, Enlightenment, and the Making of the Past* (OUP 2023) 257.
18. See James R Sofka, 'Metternich's Theory of European Order: A Political Agenda for "Perpetual Peace"', 60 The Review of Politics 1998, 136.

19. See Cynthia Weber, *Simulating Sovereignty: Intervention, the State and Symbolic Exchange* (CUP 1995) 48.
20. On familiar ties among European sovereigns, see Lucien Bély, *La société des princes* (Fayard 1999).
21. George Fréderic de Martens, *Du droit des gens moderne de l'Europe fondé sur les traités et l'usage* (Librairie de Dietrich 1821) 14–15.
22. François Guizot, *Mémoires pour servir l'histoire de mon temps*, vol IV (Michel Lévy 1861) 5. See also Wolfram Siemann, *Metternich. Strategist and Visionary* (Harvard UP 2019) 619.
23. See J Schmidt-Funke, 'Imaginaires européens dans les révolutions de 1830' in Sylvie Aprile, Jean-Claude Caron, and Emmanuel Fureix (eds), *La liberté guidant les peuples. Les révolutions de 1830 en Europe* (Champ Vallon 2013) 207.
24. Benjamin Constant, 'De l'esprit de conquête et de l'usurpation dans leur rapports avec la civilisation européenne' [1814] in Benjamin Constant, *Écrits politiques* (Gallimard 1997) 117.
25. Ferdinand Durand, *Des tendances pacifiques de la société européenne, et du rôle des armées dans l'avenir* (J. Dumaine 1844) VII.
26. For the 18th century, see Béla Kapossy, Isaac Nakhimovksy, and Richard Whatmore (eds), *Commerce and Peace in the Enlightenment* (CUP 2017).
27. Friedrich Martens, *Das Consularwesen und die Consularjurisdiction im Orient* (Weidmannsche Buchhandlung 1874) 539. On this work, see Andreas T Müller, 'Friedrich F. Martens on "The Office of Consul and Consular Jurisdiction" in the East', 25 European Journal of International Law 2014.
28. Quoted in William I Hull, *The Two Hague Conferences and their Contributions to International Law* (Ginn & Company 1908) 359.
29. In his widely used textbook, Franz von Liszt described the society of nations as a *Kulturgemeinschaft*: Franz von Liszt, *Völkerrecht systematisch dargestellt* (O. Haering 1902) 2.
30. See Antoine Rougier, 'L'intervention de l'Europe dans la Question de Macédoine', 13 Revue Générale de droit international public 1906, 188. On the Macedonian case, see Mark Swatek-Evenstein, *A History of Humanitarian Intervention* (CUP 2021) 148.
31. 'Whoever takes International Law seriously', wrote Josef Kunz, 'must begin to destroy this false idea of sovereignty which has been, and is, the greatest drag, not only to the development of International Law, but also to the development of the science of International Law.' Josef L Kunz, 'On the Theoretical Basis of the Law of Nations', 10 Transactions of the Grotius Society 1924, 129.
32. *Conférence internationale de la Paix. La Haye 18 mai–29 juillet 1899* (Martinus Nijhoff 1907) 166.
33. Hersch Lauterpacht, 'Règles générales du droit de la paix', 62 Recueil des cours, Académie de droit international 1937, 191–192.
34. See Lauterpacht's remarks in Vladimir L Idelson and others, 'The Law of Nations and the Individual', 30 Transactions of the Grotius Society 1944, 66.
35. This possibility had been pointed out by the Permanent Court of International Justice in *Jurisdiction of the Courts of Danzig* [1928] Permanent Court of International Justice, Series B No 15, 17.
36. Charles de Vischer, 'The Fundamental Rights of Man as the Basis for a Restoration of International Law', 2 International Law Quarterly 1948, 232.

37. On the rearticulation of European identity in the language of human rights, see Marco Turanti, *The Conservative Human Rights Revolution. European Identity, Transnational Politics, and the Origins of the European Convention* (OUP 2017) 326.
38. See, eg, D Schindler, 'Völkerrecht und Zivilisation', 13 Schweizerisches Jahrbuch für internationales Recht 1956, 92.
39. J H W Verzijl, 'Western European Influence on the Foundation of International Law', 1 International Relations 1957, 145.
40. As made clear by the original Article 63, the so-called colonial clause. The group of experts tasked with examining the draft of the Convention offered the following explanation for the clause: 'It is felt that the state of civilization of certain overseas territories does not permit the application of fundamental rights under the same conditions as for European territories. The States concerned have, however, to perform the task of bringing civilization to their overseas territories, a task of which the aim is precisely that of making the human rights applicable to these territories.' Quoted in A W Brian Simpson, *Human Rights and the End of Empire. Britain and the Genesis of the European Convention* (OUP 2001) 697.
41. The European Danube Commission, created by the Treaty of Paris of 1856, was notable for its direct powers over users of the Danube; see Bruno de Witte, 'The European Union as an International Legal Experiment' in Gráinne de Búrca and J H H Weiler (eds), *The Worlds of European Constitutionalism* (CUP 2011) 23.
42. HE Georges Kaeckenbeeck and others, 'The International Authority for the Ruhr and the Schuman Plan', 37 Transactions of the Grotius Society 1951, 11.
43. The distinguishing characteristics of supranationality were considered to be the bypassing of State authority in dealing directly with citizens and the ability to initiate decisions not only on behalf of States but despite them. Nina Heathcote, 'The Crisis of European Supranationality', 5 Journal of Common Market Studies 1966, 141. It should be stressed that there was no consensus among lawyers on the exact nature of supranationality.
44. *Costa v ENEL* [1964] ECLI: EU:C:1964:66. The word 'sovereignty' has been almost completely absent from the case law of the CJEU; see Giulio Itzcovich, 'The European Court of Justice' in András Jakab, Arthur Dyevre, and Giulio Itzcovich (eds), *Comparative Constitutional Reasoning* (CUP 2017) 318.
45. Alf Ross, 'Scandinavian Law' in Arthur Larson and Clarens W Jenks (eds), *Sovereignty within the Law* (Oceana Publications 1965) 120.
46. Wolfgang Friedmann, *The Changing Structure of International Law* (Columbia UP 1964) 114.
47. On diferent views regarding the character of the EU, see Jed Odermatt, *International Law and the European Union* (CUP 2021) 10–22. The CJEU's *Kadi* judgment of 2008, in particular, raised hackles for not being sufficiently *völkerrechtsfreundlich*; see Anthony Aust, 'Kadi: Ignoring International Legal Obligations', 6 International Organizations Law Review 2009, 297; Jan Klabbers, '*Völkerrechtsfreundlich*? International Law and the Union Legal Order' in P Koutrakos (ed), *European Foreign Policy: Legal and Political Perspectives* (Edward Elgar Publishing 2011) 98. For a take on the judgment more favourable to the CJEU's viewpoint, see Mattias Kumm, 'How Does European Union Law Fit into the World of Public Law? Costa, Kadi and the Three Models of Public Law' in Jürgen Neyer and Antje Wiener (eds), *Political Theory of the European Union* (OUP 2011) 125.
48. On the CJEU's use of the concept of autonomy as a defence against international law, see Bruno de Witte, 'The Relative Autonomy of the European Union's Fundamental Rights Regime', 88 Nordic Journal of International Law 2019, 66.

49. Mark A Pollack, 'The New, New Sovereigntism, or How the European Union Became Disenchanted with International Law and Defiantly Protective of Its Domestic Legal Order' in Chiara Giorgetti and Guglielmo Verdirame (eds), *Whither the West? Concepts on International Law in Europe and the United States* (CUP 2021) 75.
50. For a discussion of this topic in relation to EU law as a 'self-contained regime', see Bruno Simma and Dirk Pulkowski, 'Of Planets and the Universe: Self-contained Regimes in International Law', 17 European Journal of International Law 2006, 505.
51. For the question of autonomy as raised in the opinion of the CJEU rejecting the draft agreement providing the EU's accession to the ECHR, see Turkuler Isiksel, 'European Exceptionalism and the EU's Accession to the ECHR', 27 European Journal of International Law 2016, 574
52. Alfred Verdross, *Die Einheit des rechtlichen Weltbildes auf Grundlage der Völkerrechtsverfassung* (J. C. B. Mohr 1923) 104.
53. Hans Kelsen, 'Sovereignty and International Law', 48 Georgetown Law Journal 1960, 638.
54. See Anne Peters, 'Are We Moving Towards Constitutionalization of the World Community' in Antonio Cassese (ed), *Realizing Utopia: The Future of International Law* (OUP 2012) 398–399.
55. Neil MacCormick, *Questioning Sovereignty: Law, State and Practical Reason* (OUP 1999) 118–121.
56. Mattias Kumm, 'Rethinking Constitutional Authority: On the Structure and Limits of Constitutional Pluralism' in Matej Avbelj and Jan Komárek (eds), *Constitutional Pluralism in the European Union and Beyond* (Hart Publishing 2012) 65.
57. Neil Walker, 'Constitutionalism and Pluralism in Global Context' in Matej Avbelj and Jan Komárek (eds), *Constitutional Pluralism in the European Union and Beyond* (Hart Publishing 2012) 23.
58. Bernard Stirn, *Towards a European Public Law* (OUP 2017).
59. Anne-Marie Slaughter, 'International Law in a World of Liberal States', 6 European Journal of International Law 1995, 515.
60. William W Burke-White and Anne-Marie Slaughter, 'The Future of International Law is Domestic (or, the European Way of Law)', 47 Harvard International Law Journal 2006, 328.
61. 'We assume that regional international law in Europe will continue to reflect liberal values. However, the rise of authoritarian international law poses a significant threat to the continued vitality of liberal international law at the global level.' David L Sloss and Laura A Dickinson, 'The Russia-Ukraine War and the Seeds of a New Liberal Plurilateral Order', 116 American Journal of International Law 2022, 799. For the currently popular view that the main ideological divide with regard to international law is the one which puts liberal democracies to one side and authoritarian States to the other, see Tom Ginsburg, *Democracies and International Law* (CUP 2021) 5.
62. On the idea of there being a populist approach to international law which emphasizes State sovereignty, see Heike Krieger, 'Populist Governments and International Law', 30 European Journal of International Law 2019, 978.
63. As a remedy, Ghervas suggests 'yet another peace plan': the creation of a continent-wide European Grand Alliance, both peace-sustaining and sovereignty-protecting, with the means to 'deny any external military intervention or any undue influence from outside powers, whether the United States, Russia, China, or any other'. Stella Ghervas, *Conquering Peace from the Enlightenment to the European Union* (Harvard UP 2021) 371.

64. On the EU's response to the aggression against Ukraine, see Luigi Lonardo, *Russia's 2022 War Against Ukraine and the Foreign Policy Reaction of the EU. Context, Diplomacy, and Law* (Palgrave Macmillan 2022).
65. For the idea of a return of sovereignty, see Stefan Auer, *European Disunion. Democracy, Politics and the Politics of Emergency* (OUP 2022).
66. The rules of revision of the EU treaties are, indeed, especially protective of sovereignty; see Bruno de Witte, 'Rules of Change in International Law: How Special is the European Community', 25 Netherlands Yearbook of International Law 1994, 331–332.
67. See de Witte, 'The European Union as an International Legal Experiment' (n 41) 48–49.
68. Koen Lenaerts, 'Constitutionalism and the Many Faces of Federalism', 38 American Journal of Comparative Law 1990, 220.
69. See Lauri Mälksoo, 'Russia's Constitutional Court Defies the European Court of Human Rights', 12 European Constitutional Law Review 2016, 381.
70. See Adam Ploszka, 'It Never Rains but it Pours. The Polish Constitutional Tribunal Declares the European Convention on Human Rights Unconstitutional', 6 Hague Journal on the Rule of Law 2022, 67.
71. Proponents of radical pluralism lay great emphasis on the point that international law cannot be elevated into the position of a final arbiter of such conflicting claims to supremacy. But the problem with international law is that it is rarely able to serve as the final arbiter of anything. Unlike most domestic systems, it is without a hierarchically organized judiciary (even procedurally final judicial and arbitral pronouncements can be called into question by other international courts and tribunals or by domestic courts; see Stefan Talmon, 'The South China Sea Arbitration and the Finality of "Final" Awards', 8 Journal of International Dispute Settlement 2017, 395). What, then, could be the arbitrating role of international law when a State justifies its refusal to submit to the ECtHR or the CJEU with a claim that these are impinging on its sovereignty? Directly or indirectly, such disputes revolve around the content of international law anyhow. Not much depends on whether we characterize the European legal landscape as decentralized management of pluralism or as decentralized interpretation (autointerpretation) of international law. On the notion of autointerpretation in international law, see Leo Gross, 'States as Organs of International Law and the Problem of Autointerpretation' in G Lipsky (ed), *Law and Politics in the World Community. Essays on Hans Kelsen's Pure Theory and Related Problems in International Law* (University of California Press 1953) 59.
72. For the persistence of sovereignty claims in Europe, see Michael A Wilkinson, *Authoritarian Liberalism and the Transformation of Modern Europe* (OUP 2021) 168; Neil Walker, 'The Sovereignty Surplus', 18 International Journal of Constitutional Law 2020, 402; Bas Leijssenaar and Neil Walker, 'Introduction. Sovereignty in Action' in Bas Leijssenaar and Neil Walker (eds), *Sovereignty in Action* (CUP 2019) 3.
73. See Jean L Cohen, 'Sovereignty in the Context of Globalization: A Constitutional Pluralist Perspective' in Samantha Besson and John Tasioulas (eds), *The Philosophy of International Law* (OUP 2010) 262.
74. See Hent Kalmo, 'The End of Self-fulfilling Europe' in Eva Nanopoulos and Fotis Vergis (eds), *The Crisis behind the Eurocrisis. The Eurocrisis as a Multidimensional Systemic Crisis of the EU* (CUP 2019) 70.
75. On the political consequences of the sense of losing control, see Ivan Krastev, *After Europe* (University of Pennsylvania Press 2017) 41.

76. In the *Van Gend en Loos* decision, the CJEU noted that the EEC Treaty had established institutions 'endowed with sovereign rights'; *Van Gend en Loos* [1963] ECLI: EC:C:1963:1.
77. On this framework, see Bas de Jong and Wolf Zwartkruis, 'The EU Regulation on Screening of Foreign Direct Investment: A Game Changer?', 30 European Business Law Review 2020, 447.
78. Christina Eckes, 'EU Human Rights Sanctions Regime: Striving for Utopia Backed by Sovereign Power', 26 European Foreign Affairs Review 2021, 239.
79. On the expectations of Paul Reuter and his French collegues, see Jean-Michel Guieu, 'State Sovereignty in Question: The French Juristis between the Reorganization of the International System and European Regionalism, 1920–1950' in Julian Wright and HS Jones (eds), *Pluralism and the Idea of the Republic in France* (Palgrave Macmillan 2012) 227.
80. J H H Weiler, 'In defence of the Status Quo: Europe's Constitutional Sonderweg' in J H H Weiler and Marlene Wind (eds), *European Constitutionalism Beyond the State* (CUP 2003) 10.
81. On the link between sovereignty and self-determination, see Martti Kosnenniemi, 'Conclusion: Vocabularies of Sovereignty—Powers of a Paradox' in Hent Kalmo and Quentin Skinner (eds), *Sovereignty in Fragments. The Past, Present and Future of a Contested Concept* (CUP 2010) 239.
82. Benedict Kingsbury, 'Sovereignty and Inequality', 9 European Journal of International Law 1998, 624. Dieter Grimm has argued that '[t]he preconditions for self-determination are still much better in states than in supranational organizations'. Dieter Grimm, 'Post-sovereignty?' in Bas Leijssenaar and Neil Walker (eds), *Sovereignty in Action* (CUP 2019) 30.
83. For such explanations of the fact of diversity, see Anthony Pagden, *The Fall of Natural Man: The American Indian and the Origins of Comparative Ethnology* (CUP 1982) 3–5.
84. Martti Koskenniemi, 'The Case for Comparative International Law', 20 Finnish Yearbook of International Law 2009, 5.
85. On sovereignty as the preferred doctrine of 'authoritarian international law', see Tom Ginsburg, 'Authoritarian International Law', 114 American Journal of International Law 2020, 231.
86. Carl Schmitt, *Tagebücher 1925 bis 1929* (Duncker & Humblot 2018) 348.
87. Carl Schmitt, 'Die Einheit der Welt' in Carl Schmitt, *Frieden oder Pazifismus? Arbeiten zum Völkerrecht und zur internationalen Politik 1924–1978* (Duncker & Humblot 2005) 845.
88. Tom Ginsburg, 'The Future of Liberal Democracy in the International Legal Order' in David L Sloss (ed), *Is the International Legal Order Unraveling?* (OUP 2022) 86.
89. For the emergence of this twofold opposition, see Peter Burke, 'Did Europe Exist before 1700?', 1 History of European Ideas 1980, 25.

CHAPTER 10

THE EUROPEAN UNION

Using International Law to Replace It

PIERRE D'ARGENT

1. Introduction

WHETHER seen from within or from outside, post-Cold War Europe appears to be (one of) the most legally dense or even legally integrated continent in the world. In the first quarter of the 21st century, Europe presents itself as the champion of multilateralism and of a rules-based international order, projecting outside itself the international law recipe of cooperative structures and rules that stabilized its troubled history and allowed for its prosperity. In Europe, international law has been increasingly used in the last seven decades to establish numerous institutions in which many of the States geographically belonging to the European continent participate. Those institutions are generally tasked with supervising compliance with legal obligations common to the States concerned. Often, they are also entrusted with the responsibility of making law and therefore producing new rules and obligations applicable to, or sometimes even directly within, those States. One of the purposes of this handbook is to give an account of this legal reality and variety, and reflect on it. The web of international organizations and institutions addressing issues of common concern is probably nowhere as developed and tight as it is in Europe. Anywhere you look, you'll stumble on international law rules, both substantive and institutional: there is barely an aspect of social life which is not somehow regulated by instruments of international law for most European States.

This legal reality is profoundly transformative of sovereignty understood as a collective freedom for the inhabitants (or rulers, in case of non-democratic institutions) of a State to self-determine and govern themselves within that State, and for the State authorities to make public choices unhindered and unconstrained by legal considerations that do not result solely from their own unilateral will. At the same time, such legal reality also reflects a prior awareness of deep and inescapable interdependence between the peoples of Europe, and the territories where they live. It is not only the need but also the fact, of living together as close neighbours that gives rise to the always expanding organization of the continent through common institutions and law. The reliance on international law as a way to co-exist, if not simply exist, in Europe is undeniable but the perception of such reality may, of course, vary from State to State: as Paul-Henri Spaak, a former Prime Minister of Belgium and Minister of Foreign Affairs who signed the Treaty of Rome in 1957, reportedly said, 'there are only two types of country in Europe: small countries ... and countries which are small, but don't yet know that they are'.[1]

In this respect, the European Union (EU) stands out as one of Europe's most paradigmatic international organizations. The purpose of this chapter is not to give an account of its institutional evolution, nor of the ever-increasing scope of its activities since the European Communities of the late 1950s (see Vasel, this volume), but to reflect on the EU's particular relationship with international law. By this, I do not mean examining whether or to what extent the Union contributes to the strict observance and development of international law as required by Article 3, paragraph 5, of the Treaty on the European Union (TEU).[2] Rather, I intend to question the status and continued relevance of international law for the twenty-seven European countries that participate in the Union and pool together about 450 of the 750 million inhabitants of the European continent.[3] From the outside, that enquiry may seem rather odd as the EU appears to embody the continued relevance of international law in Europe. However, if, as the title of this chapter suggests, the EU is all about using international law in order to replace it, then the place of international law in Europe in the context of the European integration deserves to be (re)examined.

This chapter will first reflect on the classical understanding of the EU as a perfected form of international law (Section 2) before questioning such appraisal in light of the juridical *novatio* at the heart of Union law (Section 3) which results in a substitution of legal subjects on the international plane (Section 4). The chapter then concludes with some questions that international lawyers may find uncomfortable (Section 5).

2. EU Law as (Perfected) International Law

The EU seems to be the perfect fit for the three overarching themes identified by the editors of this volume as guiding questions to help authors think about their respective assignments and to somehow unify the numerous contributions bundled together here.

The first overarching question—that is, the pacifying role of international law in Europe—is probably the most self-evident to any outside observer when it comes to the EU. As often recalled, the three Communities of the late 1950s emerged between former enemies out of the rubble of World War II as an experiment to prevent war from ever occurring again between them. Anchored in, and evidenced by, the vision of the founding fathers, that narrative is taught in schools and easily understood when the institutional machinery aimed at managing together the production and sale of coal and steel—the then indispensable ingredients of any war effort—, and later the single market, is roughly explained. Peace in Europe is thus described both as the purpose and the product of the complex legal arrangements established between the Member States. By creating and solidifying bonds of economic, and therefore political, interdependence, the supporting EU rules created and enforced by the institutions are often presented as the *sine qua non* for continental peace. Along the same lines, the enlargement of the EU—that is, the inclusion of more and more European States and their respective peoples into the Union—is then viewed as an effort to allow all corners of the continent to benefit from *pax europeana*, an invaluable treasure that the peoples of third States and Member States alike are presumed to aspire to. Such understanding is so widely shared that in 2012 the EU was awarded the Nobel Peace Prize because 'for over six decades [it] contributed to the advancement of peace and reconciliation, democracy and human rights in Europe'.[4]

International law in Europe in the form of the European Communities, and later Union, is often viewed as an 'international legal experiment'[5] that has largely succeeded[6]—in other words, as perfected international law. Indeed, while it is obvious that international law of the early 20th century did not protect 'succeeding generations from the scourge of war, which twice in [a] lifetime has brought untold sorrow to mankind'[7], and that such failure was the primary reason for the establishment the United Nations (UN), the success of the UN in delivering peace to humanity remains largely questionable, although there is probably some truth in the oft-heard argument that the world would be a worse place without the world organization. However, one must recognize that—setting aside the very visible work carried out by UN humanitarian agencies—, such an argument remains unproven for lack of a contemporary counterfactual, while scepticism about the alleged virtues of international law abounds.[8] The failures of the universal security architecture have been repeatedly deplored on many continents throughout the last eight decades while the limits of international law under the UN system were suddenly and violently made clear once again in 2022 following the aggression unleashed on Ukraine by the Russian Federation. That aggression exposed the multiple well-known flaws of the UN system, which, despite proclaiming the equal sovereignty of its Member States,[9] entrenches in law the fact that some of them—namely the five permanent members of the UN Security Council—are somehow more equal than others.[10] It is also rather banal to observe that the UN is generally impotent to enforce its own constitutive principles, the treaties negotiated under its auspices, or the rare authoritative pronouncements that it produces, in particular those of its principal judicial organ ruling on a provisional basis.[11] And when the UN enforces its commands, it does so by delegating authority to (some of) its Member States, which has sometimes resulted in divisive accusations of abuse.[12] All those flaws lead to question whether the UN really 'establish[ed] [the] conditions under which justice and respect for the obligations arising from treaties and other sources of international law can be maintained', as the Charter preamble grandly ambitioned.[13]

Be that as it may, all those flaws are presumably cured in Europe by the better EU institutional design based on majority-decision making of democratically appointed and accountable institutions, compulsory judicial control and inclusion of the ultimate beneficiaries of any law—that is, individuals—into the system. In some way: if you want to find international law that effectively works, look no further than to the continent where international law was born and focus on its perfected regional version, that is, the EU and its law.[14]

It is at this juncture that we meet the second overarching theme of this handbook: the fact that the practice of international law in Europe—here, in the form of the EU—shapes understandings of universal international law. As indicated above, this idea appears to be validated by the contrast the EU offers with universal international law. But it is also validated by the fact that, because of its apparent success, the EU constitutes an explicit model for other continents and regions of the world to experiment with enhanced political integration through institutional design of some resemblance, enshrined in international treaties of a particular purpose and character. Regional international organizations with an integrationist agenda are often compared to the EU, which is seen as a model of its kind.[15] In that sense, the EU fits very well with the European tradition of proposing an enlightened model of governance to the rest of the world.

The third overarching theme of this handbook—that is, the often too little explored and understood diversity of international legal traditions within Europe—can also be exemplified by the EU. Because the EU would be a new way of doing international law in Europe, while not all European countries have embraced it and some (the UK) have relinquished it for a more classical form of international law, the EU would constitute a new international legal tradition within Europe, thereby participating in the diversity of such traditions.

All these reflections on the three overarching questions of this handbook applied to the EU are premised on the understanding that the EU and its legal order are of an international law character; in other words, that they are international law, not so much of a different and particular kind, but simply of a perfected type designed for a particular space, that is, between certain sovereign States. Even if EU law were to be viewed as international law of a particular kind,[16] it remains fundamentally (ontologically as it were) international law. This is certainly a fair and rather classical assumption to make. For decades, the European Economic Community (EEC) was indeed presented as just another international organization and European Community law was taught in law faculties around Europe as part of general or specialized courses on public international law.

That assumption is based on a 'normative chain' reasoning according to which, because they are established by treaties between sovereign States under international law, the EEC (later European Community (EC) and later again EU) and its normative production are simply derived from those treaties and therefore share their international law character.[17] The 'normative chain' reasoning was endorsed by the International Court of Justice (ICJ) in its advisory opinion concerning the declaration of independence of Kosovo, the Court finding that, despite its domestic purpose, the Constitutional

Framework for Kosovo was an instrument of international law because it derived from UNSC Resolution 1244 (1999), which itself derived from the UN Charter.[18] Irrespective of the institutional specificities of the EU, the technicalities of its legal order and the abundance of its norms, the normative chain theory links the whole EU legal order to the instruments on which it is based and asserts, as it were, that the international blood from which those basic instruments are made flows down to the tiniest normative extremities that derive from them, making them ultimately part of the international legal order itself, together with the founding treaties. This classical approach allowed, for instance, an investment arbitral tribunal to consider that 'EU law is international law because it is rooted in international treaties; and ... of course ... the EU Treaties are legal instruments under public international law ... Moreover, the Tribunal considers that EU law as a whole is part of the international legal order'.[19] This allowed the tribunal to find that EU law could be taken into account for interpretative purposes of the relevant BIT pursuant to Article 31, paragraph 3, c) of the Vienna Convention on the Law of Treaties (VCLT).

The same arbitral tribunal held that the fact that EU law is an integral part of the domestic law of the Member States does not deprive it of its international legal nature[20] and opined on the 'multiple nature of EU law' in the following terms:

> EU law is a *sui generis* legal order, presenting different facets depending on the perspective from where it is analysed. It can be analysed from the perspectives of the international community, individual Member States and EU institutions. Given those perspectives, EU law has a multiple nature: on the one hand, it is an international legal regime; but on the other hand, once introduced in the national legal orders of EU Member States, it becomes also part of these national legal orders.... In the *Kadi* case, Advocate General Maduro's Opinion also described EU law as a 'municipal legal order of transnational dimension'. It is more accurately expressed in the French version: '*un ordre juridique interne d'origine internationale*'.[21]

While it is certainly true that the relevant 'facet' of EU law is a matter of 'perspective' and that the way in which it is considered in international law essentially depends on the jurisdiction, particularly *ratione personae*, of the judicial body seized and the nature of the dispute brought before it,[22] the internal character of the EU legal order, despite its international origin, deserves closer attention.

3. EU Law Replacing International Law

The classical international law understanding of the EU and of its legal order would be misguided if it were oblivious of the constitutionalist and autonomist turns that the Court of Justice of the European Union (CJEU) imposed[23] on Union law as ultimate reasons for many of its judicial outcomes and which are shaping EU law in ways that have purposely estranged it from international law. In other words, simply considering EU law as *lex specialis* within international law fails to adequately account for what it is (or what it pretends to be, depending on which side of the fence you're on) for itself and its Member States. The classical international law understanding of EU law is profoundly at odds with its own internal self-identification. Taking EU law seriously—or simply, understanding it—requires one to take such self-identification for what it is and recognize that the international law *lex specialis* approach, while apparently logical and straightforward, actually misses what is deeply going on. Worse, the reassuring side of that approach prevents an understanding of the true ambition of the EU and its law vis-à-vis its Member States, the internal legal space it creates between them, and the ensuing reduction of their treaty-making power.

It is certainly a truism to recall that the European Communities—later, the EU—have designed a new and different way of doing politics between, and within, the Member States by establishing institutions and procedures to make laws that are profoundly different, if not alien, to classical international law. The political and legal 'transformation of Europe'[24] is a phenomenon that has long been highlighted and discussed at length by scholars to the point of becoming a distinct field of professional expertise, both in political sciences and in law (see Vasel, this volume).

As is well-known, according to the CJEU, the founding treaties have 'constitute[d] a new legal order of international law for the benefit of which the states have limited their sovereign rights, albeit within limited fields, and the subjects of which comprise not only Member States but also their nationals'.[25] Derived from international law treaties, that legal order has specific characteristics in view of the direct effect of its rules and their primacy over the domestic laws of Member States.[26] Having initially affirmed the affiliation of European law with international law in the landmark *Van Gend & Loos* case recalled above, the CJEU refrained a short year later in the no-less-famous *Costa v Enel* case from mentioning it again. In that case, the Court famously 'contrast[ed]' the EEC Treaty 'with ordinary international treaties' in order to assert that it 'created its own legal system' which 'became an integral part of the legal systems of the Member States' but whose international law pedigree was not recalled.[27] Since then, the Court has rather insisted on the constitutional and 'internal' character of the EU legal order, and on its autonomy from international law.[28] The distinct character of the EU legal order from international law seems to have been accepted by some constitutional courts.[29]

The deliberate estrangement of EU law from international law through the affirmation of the former's autonomy from the latter must be taken seriously, especially by international lawyers who may be less familiar with the EU. Indeed, the foundational paradox, or ontological mystery, of EU law is such that it owes its existence to, and stems from, the most traditional instruments of international law between sovereign States (ie treaties), but that, at the same time, it intends to separate itself from international law by choosing the conditions under which it accepts interaction with the international legal order that gives validity to its *Grundnormen*.[30]

As conceived by the current President of the CJEU, the proclaimed autonomy of EU law defines it 'negatively' in opposition to 'ordinary international law' and 'positively' as 'a legal order that has the capacity to operate as a self-referential system of norms that is both coherent and complete'.[31] By stating in substance that, in the EU legal order, no international obligation can derogate from the founding treaties and their 'constitutional' principles,[32] the CJEU gives to the autonomy of the Union legal order an 'internal' meaning that ultimately underpins its specificity. The affirmation of the 'internality' of the EU legal order explains and supports the position adopted by the Court in the *Kadi* case. Unlike the Court of First Instance, which specifically relied on Article 103 of the UN Charter as a rule governing a conflict between treaties,[33] the CJEU did not regard itself as an international court called upon to arbitrate conflicts of obligations arising for Member States from possibly incompatible international commitments (the UN Charter on the one hand, primary EU law on the other); rather, the Court considered itself to be the guardian of a legal order whose preservation requires a certain degree of non-permeability to international law, despite the fact that international law ultimately provides for its foundation and transformation through successive amendments to the founding treaties. In that sense, the relationship between the international legal order and the EU legal order is, from the point of view of the latter, comparable to that between the former and the domestic laws of the States.[34]

The autonomy so established and understood does not imply, however, that the legal order of the Union would cease, for all intents and purposes, to be dependent on international law insofar as the latter is the ultimate basis of the validity of the founding treaties, irrespective of their proclaimed non-ordinary character. Neither does the autonomy of EU law mean that it does not interact with international law sources and hermetically shuts its door on them—rather, the autonomy of EU law means that the EU may not accede to treaties that would hurt such autonomy, as understood by the CJEU,[35] and that sources of international law binding on the Union will interact with its legal order pursuant to the conditions that it chooses for itself.[36] What one must understand is that the autonomy of EU law from international law results from its founding treaties themselves, which simply derogate from the usual rules of international law governing the relationship between sources and the interpretation of treaties. The founding treaties have not been interpreted by the CJEU pursuant to the customary rules reflected in Articles 31–33 VCLT;[37] in contrast, the Court has developed its own methods for the interpretation of Union law.[38] Under general international law, such derogation from usual conflict or interpretative rules is perfectly possible because its rules in that regard are not mandatory.[39]

The autonomy of EU law from international law, albeit possible under the latter, cannot of course justify, in international law, the violation of international obligations which the Union[40] or its Member States[41] are bound to respect. Furthermore, and as already recalled, such autonomy does not mean that the founding treaties do not derive their legal validity and binding character from international law itself:[42] EU law maybe self-referential, but it is not self-creating.

All this being said, what is paramount to see and crucial to realize is that, across the EU's main areas of competences, EU law is all about (1) replacing domestic law with EU law within each Member State; (2) replacing international law with EU law between the Member States; and, as a result of both, (3) replacing the Member States as subjects of international law by the EU itself vis-à-vis the rest of the world. Phrased differently, the emergence and development of EU law is an experiment in juridical *novatio* of legal orders *and* subjects. Phrased in simple Freudian terms, and because EU law derives from treaties but at the same time aims at getting rid of international law between the Member States and taking over from them internationally, the development of the EU legal order can be likened to the tale of the son (EU law) killing the father (international law). Of course, there is some exaggeration in this claim and analogy, but it remains the case that, overall, the EU experiment is about substituting a pre-existing legal order between the Member States by another one. This does not mean that the former entirely disappears from the picture, but, in the context of the EU, international law will only be used in order to enhance the Union through 'constitutional reform' (ie revision of the TEU and TFEU) or to rescue it, as was done in 2012 with the Treaty on Stability, Coordination and Governance in the Economic and Monetary Union (TSCG).[43]

The fact that the EU is a normative machine designed to replace the domestic law of each Member State with EU law is nothing new. It is very explicitly stated in Article 2, paragraph 1 TFEU as far as all areas falling within the exclusive competence of the EU are concerned: 'When the Treaties confer on the Union exclusive competence in a specific area, only the Union may legislate and adopt legally binding acts, the Member States being able to do so themselves only if so empowered by the Union or for the implementation of Union acts.' The fact for a Member State nevertheless to legislate in an area of EU exclusive competence leads to infringement proceedings under Articles 258–260 TFEU, irrespective of the existence (or not) of a corresponding legally binding act already adopted by the EU. If such EU act exists, the domestic act is moreover rendered inoperative within local law as a result of the well-established doctrine of supremacy of EU law, which is an obligation under that law.[44]

The same applies in all areas of shared competence as defined under Article 2, paragraph 2 TFEU where 'Member States shall exercise their competence to the extent that the Union has not exercised its competence. The Member States shall again exercise their competence to the extent that the Union has decided to cease exercising its competence.'[45] The Union ceases to exercise its shared competence when an EU act is withdrawn and not replaced by another one having the same object: in such a case, the Member States may re-occupy the normative space vacated by EU law. In that sense, shared competences function like communicating vessels: the more EU acts are adopted in areas of shared competence, the less Member States may regulate those same areas and the less their domestic acts remain legally relevant; the EU literally replaces domestic law with its own law and 'pre-empts' the normative space for itself. Naturally, those normative realities translate in, and result from, a substitution of legislators.

The replacement of the Member States' domestic laws by Union law also explains why the latter replaces (and in that sense, gradually excludes) international law between them. Indeed, in areas of EU competences, the Member States may not act jointly outside the procedures and institutions established by the TEU and TFEU.[46] In other words, Member States are prevented from producing law common to them through international treaties in areas of EU competences.

The shift from one legal order (international law) to another (Union law) between Member States for the production of norms common to them is very visible when international treaties binding Member States and concluded by them *qua* sovereign States are replaced by EU acts following the revision of the founding treaties and the conferral on the Union of new areas of competences. This phenomenon is best illustrated by the replacement of the 1968 Brussels Convention on jurisdiction and the enforcement of judgments in civil and commercial matters[47] by the Council Regulation (EC) No 44/2001 of 22 December 2000 on jurisdiction and the recognition and enforcement of judgments in civil and commercial matters.[48] This example is all the more striking in that the content of these two instruments is very similar while the CJEU already had jurisdiction over the Brussels Convention—however, despite these similarities, an EU law instrument displaced and replaced an international treaty between Member States as a result of the EU expanding competences.

The setting aside of international law as a source of rights and obligations in favour of Union law sometimes results from explicit provisions 'disconnecting' the international treaty otherwise applicable between Member States from the 'internal' space where Union law is said to be solely applicable. Such disconnection may result from an agreed provision contained in the international treaty itself,[49] or from a unilateral declaration of the Union when acceding to the said treaty—which amounts to a questionable treaty reservation.[50]

More fundamentally, treaties binding the Union are not considered within the EU legal order as instruments of international law, but rather, 'as far as the European Union is concerned',[51] as 'acts of the institutions',[52] that is, as Union law. Originally designed to justify the interpretative competence of the Court of Justice over normative instruments that cannot be created by the Union unilaterally, such a finding concerning the nature of international treaties within Union law operates like the wave of a magic wand. Some of its apparently logical consequences deserve to be recalled.

For instance, it allowed the Court to consider Ireland in breach of Article 344 TFEU (then Article 292 TEC)—which requires Member States 'not to submit a dispute concerning the interpretation or application' of Union law[53] to any court other than the CJEU—for having initiated international arbitral proceedings against the UK on the basis of the United Nations Convention on the Law of the Sea (UNCLOS). For the CJEU, and because the Union is a party to it, UNCLOS is deemed to be an 'act of the institutions' that is an integral part of Union law, so that its interpretation falls within the exclusive jurisdiction of the CJEU.[54] While the Court's interpretative monopoly over Union law only concerns disputes between Member States,[55] it nevertheless extends to cases in which their settlement requires the interpretation or application of provisions of mixed agreements concluded by the Union and its Member States with third parties, and which bind the Member States in the international legal order, when those provisions fall within the exercise of the Union's external competence, even if it is not exclusive.[56] It must be understood, therefore, that an international treaty concluded by

Member States is at the same time an instrument of international law when it applies in their relations with third States and, if the Union is also party to it, an instrument of EU law when it applies between Member States. In other words, UNCLOS was Union law between Ireland and the UK before Brexit, but regained its international legal character between them following Brexit. The paradoxical result of such legal transubstantiation decreed by the CJEU is that while Ireland was prevented from resorting to the judicial protection afforded under Annex VII UNCLOS when the UK was a Member State, it may now do so. Because the UK exited the Union, Ireland regained procedural rights under UNCLOS *qua* treaty.

In Opinion 1/17 concerning the compatibility of the investor-state dispute settlement (ISDS) mechanism instituted by the EU-Canada Comprehensive Economic and Trade Agreement (CETA) with the autonomy of the EU legal order, the Court affirmed that because the tribunals established by Section F of Part eight of the CETA 'stand outside the EU judicial system, they cannot have the power to interpret or apply *provisions of EU law other than those of the CETA*'.[57] By this strange convolution, the CJEU confirmed that the CETA was to be regarded as EU law, rather than international law, in the EU legal order. However, it is clearly not as Union law, but as international law, that the CETA will be applied by the tribunals established under it. The CJEU's convolution epitomizes its self-referential inner logic.

The *Komstroy* case is also illustrative of the far-reaching and rather paradoxical consequences of considering international treaties binding on the Union and its Member States as acts of Union law within the EU legal order. That case concerned the Energy Charter Treaty (ECT) which, as a mixed agreement, is in principle applicable between Member States *qua* Union law. However, the Court decided nevertheless that the ECT investor–state arbitration provision was not applicable between investors of one Member State and another Member State. The Court reached that outcome as a matter of interpretation, but without actually interpreting any ECT provisions pursuant to the rules on treaty interpretation enshrined in the VCLT that it regularly applies when interpreting treaties in which the EU participates.[58] Rather, in order to find that the investor–state arbitration provision was not applicable between investors of one member State and another Member State, the Court interpreted the ECT in light of the EU principles governing the autonomy of the Union and its legal order. The central reason for such an outcome is that investment arbitral tribunals instituted under the ECT would have to apply substantive ECT provisions to resolve disputes while such provisions are to be considered between Member States as Union law, rather than as international law. According to the Court, it would be contrary to its interpretative monopoly of Union law for investment arbitral tribunals to interpret and apply the ECT, considering that such tribunals may not request preliminary rulings from the Court while the ECT is deemed to be Union law between litigants who, unlike in the contentious configuration of the CETA Tribunal, are both subjects of that law.[59]

The *Achmea* case foreshadowed the *Komstroy* case. However, in the *Achmea* case, the applicable law clause of the Dutch-Slovak BIT referred to the domestic law of the parties, of which secondary Union law became an integral part with Slovakia's accession to the Union.[60] Because Union law is an integral part of the domestic law of Member States, it seems perfectly logical to extend *Achmea* to ECT if ECT is Union law. However, such apparent logic comes with a price: the magical transubstantiation of instruments of international law into acts of Union law, and thereby the replacement of instruments of international law *qua* international law by the same instruments *qua* EU law. As the CETA opinion makes clear, this transubstantiation is however relative in the sense that it only operates with legal (as opposed to rhetorical) effects insofar as the instrument of international origin applies to a situation involving only subjects of the Union's legal order.

4. The EU Replacing Member States Internationally

The replacement of the Member States' domestic laws and of international law between them by EU law entails a further substitution, this time of subjects and on the international plane: the more there is EU law in and between the Member States, the less they are entitled to conclude international treaties, being replaced in that regard by the EU.

When the subject matter of a future treaty falls into an area of EU exclusive competence listed under Article 3, paragraph 1 TFEU, Member States are deprived of their treaty-making power under EU law: in those areas, only the Union may negotiate and conclude treaties with third States or international organizations, irrespective of the development of internal EU regulations, directives, or decisions in those areas.

Pursuant to Article 3, paragraph 2 TFEU which summarized in the Lisbon Treaty decades of incrementally developed case law, the EU is also exclusively competent to conclude an international agreement without its Member States (which are thus prevented from doing so) 'when its conclusion is provided for in a legislative act of the Union or is necessary to enable the Union to exercise its internal competence, or in so far as its conclusion may affect common rules or alter their scope'.

The first hypothesis ('when [the] conclusion [of a treaty] is provided for in a legislative act of the Union') refers to situations of exclusive external competence made explicit in, and as a result of, secondary EU law. In other words, the EU co-legislators may decide to deprive the Member States of their sovereign right to conclude treaties by providing in a regulation, directive, or decision adopted under the ordinary or special legislative procedure[61] that the Union shall conclude a treaty in an area not mentioned under the first paragraph of Article 3.

The second hypothesis ('when [the] conclusion [of a treaty] … is necessary to enable the Union to exercise its internal competence') corresponds to a unique situation where it does not make sense to adopt secondary EU law internally without, at the same time, concluding an international agreement. In other words, situations where the internal and external competences of the Union must be exercised simultaneously, otherwise the internal EU act adopted would fail to be useful or meaningful. The facts that gave rise to Opinion 1/76 provide both an example and a (so far) unique justification for such exclusive external competence, the adoption of a regulation to rationalize the economic situation of the inland waterway transport industry requiring that a third State, namely, Switzerland, participated in such regime through an international agreement.[62]

The third hypothesis of exclusive external competence mentioned under Article 3, paragraph 2 TFEU, is worth a closer look. Under that hypothesis, the Union has exclusive competence to conclude an international agreement 'in so far as its conclusion may affect common rules or alter their scope'. This concise formula originates in the landmark *ERTA* case where the Court affirmed that Member States were deprived of the right to conclude treaties when their subject matter is already regulated under secondary EU law.[63] The reason for such substitution of subjects on the international plane is that if the future treaty overlaps with an already existing internal EU act, amendments to that act might be necessary in order to comply with the treaty. However, only the Union should assess whether it is worth concluding a treaty that could potentially require changes to its laws, since the Union alone may change its own acts. Therefore, only the Union may negotiate and conclude a treaty whose subject matter or provisions are already largely covered by secondary EU law,[64] otherwise Members States concluding treaties with third States could be in a position to request the revision of EU acts, which would endanger the integrity of law-making within the Union. This brings us back to the logic of communicating vessels already mentioned in relation to shared competences: the more EU law expands internally, the more the EU grows as a subject of international law to the detriment of its Member States. In a way, consenting to the adoption of EU internal acts means, for Member States, consenting to a *capitis diminutio* as subjects of international law.[65] By making EU law between themselves, Member States progressively withdraw from the international scene and cede to the Union their age-old sovereign attribute of making treaties with third States and organizations.

In areas of shared competence where pre-emption does not apply for lack of internal EU acts, the Union and their Member States may both conclude treaties. Resorting to a mixed external agreement (ie a treaty concluded by the Union and its Member States, on the one hand, and third parties on the other hand) is, however, optional.[66] The Council may thus mandate the Union to negotiate and conclude a treaty in such shared area, without the participation of the Member States. Here again, and while the internal competence is shared, the Union would displace Member States on the international plane.

5. Conclusion

The EU legal order aims at replacing international law between the Member States by producing law that integrates in their respective legal orders while separating itself from international law. As a result of that process incrementally built by the CJEU through judicial 'coups' that have left Member States stunned but obedient,[67] Member States gradually withdraw from the international stage and increasingly leave it to the Union to exercise 'the right of entering into international engagements'—a right that was famously viewed a century ago as 'an attribute of State sovereignty'.[68]

If the EU legal order is viewed as a perfected form of international law, international lawyers should be ready to face this uncomfortable question: why is it that better and more effective international law (ie Union law) is not universal and that it strives to autonomize itself from international law while displacing States as primary makers of international law?

The extent to which this experiment in the novation of legal orders and subjects, and the ensuing closure to international law between Member States, is sustainable in the long term remains to be seen. It is far from clear that all Member States and their respective peoples understand—let alone desire in the form of a European federation or State—what this chapter has described. Because Article 50 TEU offers Member States a way out from the Union, the revenge of the father (international law) over the son (EU law) will always loom large. However, exiting the Union will obviously never be motivated by the alleged attractiveness of international law—how could international law be attractive in the light of the deep crisis of effectiveness into which it is recurrently plunged?

This leads to another uncomfortable question that international lawyers and EU lawyers alike should perhaps also reflect upon: what if the prospect of the return to international law was the ultimate incentive for keeping the EU and its law?

Notes

1. Although rarely referenced to the writings of Paul-Henri Spaak, the sentence is repeated as oral tradition and used in Belgian politics as a mantra. It is often repeated at the European level to justify European integration and explain the obvious need for States like Belgium to remain unconditionally faithful to it. See, eg, 'Strategic autonomy for Europe—the aim of our generation', speech by President Charles Michel to the Bruegel think tank, 28 September 2020 <https://www.consilium.europa.eu/en/press/press-releases/2020/09/28/l-autonomie-strategique-europeenne-est-l-objectif-de-notre-generation-discours-du-president-charles-michel-au-groupe-de-reflexion-bruegel/> accessed 15 September 2023.
2. See also Article 21 of the Consolidated version of the Treaty on the European Union [2007] OJ C326/01 (TEU).
3. European Union Directorate-General for Communication, 'Facts and figures on life in the European Union' <https://european-union.europa.eu/principles-countries-history/key-facts-and-figures/life-eu_en> accessed 15 September 2023.
4. The Nobel Peace Prize 2012 <http://www.nobelprize.org/prizes/peace/2012/summary> accessed 15 September 2023.
5. Bruno de Witte, 'The European Union as an International Law Experiment' in Gráinne de Burca and Joseph H H Weiler (eds), *The Worlds of European Constitutionalism* (CUP 2012) 19–56.

6. See in this sense Alain Pellet, 'Les fondements juridiques internationaux du droit communautaire', Academy of European Law (ed.), Collected Courses of the Academy of European Law, Vol V, Book 2 (Kluwer 1997) 193–271.
7. UN Charter (opened for signature 26 June 1945, entered into force 24 October 1945), preamble, first recital (hereafter UN Charter).
8. See, eg, 'if we live in a world of chaos and conflict, that is not in spite of international law, it is in part because of it': Susan Marks, 'International Judicial Activism and the Commodity-Form Theory of International Law', 18 European Journal of International Law 2007, 199, 202.
9. Article 2, para 1 UN Charter.
10. Article 27, para 3 UN Charter.
11. While the overall compliance with judgments on the merits delivered by the International Court of Justice (ICJ) is often praised (see, eg, Colter Paulson, 'Compliance with Final Judgments of the International Court of Justice since 1987', 98(3) American Journal of International Law 2004, 434–461; Constanze Schulte, *Compliance with Decisions of the International Court of Justice* (OUP 2004), compliance with binding provisional measures remains highly problematic and corrosive of the Court's authority.
12. This was in particular the case in relation to the way Western Powers implemented the authorization to use force in order to enforce a no-fly zone over Libya pursuant to UN Security Council Resolution 1973 (2011).
13. UN Charter, preamble, third recital.
14. See notably Anne-Marie Slaughter and William Burke-White, 'The Future of International Law Is Domestic (or, the European Way of Law)', 47(2) Harvard International Law Journal 2006, 327.
15. See, eg, Ricardo Martín de la Guardia and Guillermo A Pérez Sánchez (eds), *La integración europea e iberoamericana II: las relaciones de la Unión Europea (UE) y el mercado común del sur (MERCOSUR) con el sistema de integración centroamericano (SICA)* (Thomson Reuters Aranzadi 2021) 564; Maksim Karliuk, *The Emerging Autonomous Legal Order of the Eurasian Economic Union* (CUP 2023) 256.
16. Robert Schütze, *European Constitutional Law* (3rd edn, OUP 2021) 608.
17. See Pierre d'Argent, 'Jusqu'où y a-t-il du droit international? Considérations sur le droit dérivé des organisations internationales et sur le droit de l'Union européenne' in Pierre d'Argent, Béatrice Bonafé, and Jean Cambacau (eds), *Les limites du droit international/ Limits of International Law. Essais en l'honneur de Joe Verhoeven* (Bruylant 2014) 237.
18. Accordance with International Law of the Unilateral Declaration of Independence in Respect of Kosovo (Advisory Opinion) [2010] ICJ Rep 440, para 88. See for a different, ie domestic, appraisal of the Constitutional Framework: Separate Opinion of Judge Yusuf [2010] ICJ Rep 625.
19. *Electrabel SA v The Republic of Hungary*, ICSID case no ARB/07/19, Decision on jurisdiction, applicable law and liability (30 November 2012) (Veeder, Kaufmann-Kohler, Stern) [4.120].
20. ibid, [4.124].
21. ibid, [4.117]–[4.118]. The sentence traces '*ordre juridique interne d'origine internationale*' to the writings of Denis Alland, 'Le juge français et le droit d'origine internationale' in Pierre-Marie Dupuy (ed), *Droit international et droit interne dans la jurisprudence comparée du Conseil Constitutionnel et du Conseil d'Etat* (Panthéon-Assas 2001) 47.
22. For a further elaboration of this point, see d'Argent (n 17) 266.

23. A softer way of saying this would be to assert that the CJEU 'found' those turns in Union law, but this would be a rather naïve account of judicial decision-making in Luxembourg.
24. Joseph HH Weiler, 'The Transformation of Europe', 100(8) The Yale Law Journal 1991, 2403.
25. *van Gend & Loos v Netherlands Inland Revenue Administration* [1963] ECLI:EU:C:1963:1, 12.
26. See notably *Amministrazione delle Finanze dello Stato v Simmenthal SpA* [1978] ECLI:EU:C:1978:49, 629.
27. *Costa v E.N.E.L.* [1964] ECLI:EU:C:1964:66, 1141. In Opinion 2/13 of 18 December 2014 concerning the accession of the EU to the European Convention on Human Rights (ECHR), the CJEU repeated that the founding Treaties are not 'ordinary international treaties' (EU:C:2014:2454, [157]), without again explaining this assertion which seems therefore to be the result of a common-sense observation or belief. Indeed, many international treaties establish institutions, are directly applicable, and concern individuals in domestic legal systems.
28. See not. *P Yassin Abdullah Kadi and Al Barakaat International Foundation v Council and Commission* [2008] ECLI:EU:C:2008:461, [317]. See also Opinion 1/17, ECLI:EU:C:2019:341, [109]–[110].
29. In its Decision no 2004-505 DC of 19 November 2004 on the *Treaty establishing a Constitution for Europe*, the French Constitutional Council held as follows: '*Considering*, secondly, that under the terms of Article 88-1 of the Constitution: "The Republic shall participate in the European Communities and in the European Union, made up of States which have freely chosen, under the Treaties establishing them, to exercise certain of their competences in common"; that the Constitutional Council has thus established the existence of a Community legal order integrated into the internal legal order *and distinct from the international legal order*' (*Rec*, 173, para 11, emphasis added).
30. Opinion of Advocate General M Poiares Maduro delivered on 16 January 2008, in the case *Kadi and Al Barakaat International Foundation v Council and Commission* [2008] EU:C:2008:11.
31. See Koen Lenaerts, José A Gutiérrez-Fons, and Stanislas Adam, 'Exploring the Autonomy of the European Union Legal Order', 81 ZaöRV 2021, 47.
32. *Yassin Abdullah Kadi and Al Barakaat International Foundation v Council and Commission*, 3 September 2008, [285].
33. T-306/01, *Ahmed Ali Yusuf and Al Barakaat International Foundation v. Council and Commission* [2005] ECLI:EU:T:2005:331, [234], [273], and [275].
34. This would appear to be in line with a wish expressed a long time ago by the European Parliament: see Resolution A4- 0278/97 and 20/PE 262-86 on the relationship between public international law, Community law, and the constitutional law of the Member States [1997] and Siegbert Alber, 'Report on the relationships between international law, Community law and the constitutional law of the Member States' [1997] DOC.FR/RR/335/335334.
35. Opinion 2/13, [2014] ECLI:EU:C:2014:2454.
36. Those conditions are not further recalled here; see the substantial case law on the conditions governing the invocation of international law in disputes concerning the validity and legality of EU acts (*International Fruit v Produktschap voor Groenten en Fruit* [1972] ECLI:EU:C:1972:115, 1219; *Germany v Council* [1994] ECLI:EU:C:1994:367, 5039; *Nakajima v Council* [1991] ECLI:EU:C:1991:186, 2169; *Portugal v Council* [1999] ECLI:EU:C:1999:574; *Petrotub SA and Republica SA v Council of the European Union* [2003] ECLI:EU:C:2003:4; *Air Transport Association of America v Secretary of State for Energy and*

Climate Change [2011] ECLI:EU:C:2011:864) or the liability of EU institutions for breach of international law (*Biret International SA contre Conseil de l'Union européenne* [2003] ECLI:EU:C:2003:517; *FIAMM v Council of the European Union and Commission of the European Communities* [2005] ECLI:EU:T:2005:449; *FIAMM v Council of the European Union and Commission of the European Communities* [2008] ECLI:EU:C:2008:476).

37. The invocation of Articles 31–33 VCLT for the interpretation of the TEU and the Treaty on the Functioning of the European Union (TFEU) usually falls on deaf ears before the CJEU (see, eg, *Brussels Capital Region v Commission* [2020] ECLI:EU:C:2020:978, [25]–[27] where the claimant contested the validity of the glyphosate regulation and argued that the admissibility conditions for annulment proceedings under Article 263(4) TFEU had to be interpreted in light of the obligations set out in the Aarhus Convention, which was flatly rejected by the Court for the well-established reason that international treaties binding on the Union could not prevail over nor modify the founding treaties), contrary to their use for the interpretation of external agreements concluded by the EU (see, eg, *Brita GmbH v Hauptzollamt Hamburg-Hafen* [2010] ECLI:EU:C:2010:91, [42]. See also *Western Sahara Campaign UK v Commissioners for Her Majesty's Revenue and Customs and Secretary of State for Environment, Food and Rural Affairs* [2018] ECLI:EU:C:2018:118, [58]).
38. Koen Lenaerts and José A Gutiérrez-Fons, 'To Say What the Law of the EU Is: Methods of Interpretation and the European Court of Justice', 20 Columbia Journal of European Law 2013–2014, 3.
39. This is particularly the case for the rules on treaty interpretation and the other provisions of the VCLT (see Articles 3, 5, and 31 itself which allows for much flexibility and particularization). As far as rules concerning the relationship between sources of international law, *lex specialis* is possible, but Article 103 of the Charter, as a rule of hierarchy between treaty commitments, appears to be a limit to the agreed displacement of the usual rules on conflict between sources.
40. Article 27, para 2 of the Convention on the Law of Treaties between States and International Organisations or between International Organisations (opened for signature 21 March 1986); Article 32 of the Articles on Responsibility of International Organisations, A/RES/66/100, 9 December 2011.
41. See Article 61 of the Articles on the Responsibility of International Organisations, A/RES/66/100, 9 December 2011.
42. However, some scholars maintain all-encompassing doctrinal claims according to which EU law in general (ie including its 'constitutional' instruments) stems independently from international law and 'does not depend for its validity on' it: see Christina Eckes, 'The Autonomy of the EU Legal Order', Europe and the World: A Law Review 2020, 1, 18.
43. In that regard, it is also telling that Article 2 TSCG commands that it be interpreted 'in conformity with the Treaties on which the European Union is founded'—rather than in light of those treaties (Article 31, para 3, c) VCLT) and other customary rules on treaty interpretation—and that it will 'apply insofar as it is compatible with the Treaties on which the European Union is founded and with European Union law'—see <https://www.consilium.europa.eu/media/20399/stootscg26_en12.pdf> accessed 15 September 2023.
44. See *Amministrazione delle Finanze dello Stato v Simmenthal SpA* [1978] ECLI:EU:C:1978:49, 629. On the difference between EU law and international law in that regard, see Pierre d'Argent, 'Remarques sur le conflit en normes de droit interne et de droit international', *Revue belge de droit international*, 2012/2, 355, 357.

45. See also Consolidated version of the Treaty on European Union—Protocol (No 25) on the exercise of shared competence [2008] OJ C115.
46. Opinion 2/13, [2014] ECLI:EU:C:2014:2454, para. 193.
47. Brussels Convention on jurisdiction and the enforcement of judgments in civil and commercial matters [1968] OJ L 299/32, 32–42.
48. Council Regulation (EC) No 44/2001 of 22 December 2000 on jurisdiction and the recognition and enforcement of judgments in civil and commercial matters [2001] OJ L12/1, 1–23.
49. See, eg, the revised Lugano convention: Opinion 1/03, [2006] ECLI:EU:C:2006:81, I-1183, paras 78 ff.
50. This was notably the case of the EU declaration made when concluding the UNESCO convention on cultural diversity; see Pierre d'Argent, 'L'exclusion du droit international dans les relations entre Etats membres de l'UE: à propos de la convention de l'UNESCO sur la diversité culturelle et de la déclaration de 'déconnexion' in Christian Frank and Geneviève Duchenne (eds), *L'action extérieure de l'Union européenne. Rôle global, dimensions matérielles, aspects juridiques, valeurs, Actes de la XIème Chaire AGC – Glaverbel d'études européennes* (Bruylant 2008) 283.
51. *KP v LO* [2018] ECLI:EU:C:2018:408, [24].
52. *R & V Haegeman v Belgian State* [1974] ECLI:EU:C:1974:41.
53. The text of Article 344 TFEU specifically refers to 'disputes concerning the interpretation or application of *the Treaties*' rather than of Union law in general, but the CJEU expanded those words to include all acts of Union law.
54. *Commission v Ireland* [2006] ECLI:EU:C:2006:345 I-04635.
55. Opinion 1/09, [2011] ECLI:EU:C:2011:123, [63].
56. *Commission v Ireland* [2006] ECLI:EU:C:2006:345, [177].
57. Opinion 1/17, [2019], ECLI:EU:C:2019:341, [118]. Emphasis added.
58. *Brita GmbH v Hauptzollamt Hamburg-Hafen* [2010] ECLI:EU:C:2010:91, [42]. See also *Western Sahara Campaign UK v Commissioners for Her Majesty's Revenue and Customs and Secretary of State for Environment, Food and Rural Affairs* [2018] ECLI:EU:C:2018:118, [58].
59. *Republic of Moldova v Komstroy LLC* [2021] ECLI:EU:C:2021:164.
60. *Achmea* [2017] ECLI:EU:C:2017:699.
61. Article 289 of the Consolidated version of the Treaty on the Functioning of the European Union [2007] OJ C326/01.
62. Opinion 1/76, [1977] ECLI:EU:C:1977:63.
63. *Commission v Council* [1971] ECLI:EU:C:1971:32.
64. This issue has been discussed in many cases before the CJEU. The Court has found that 'there is a risk that common EU rules may be adversely affected by international commitments undertaken by the Member States, or that the scope of the rules may be altered, such as to justify an exclusive external competence of the European Union where those commitments fall within the scope of those rules. However, a finding that there is such a risk does not presuppose that the area covered by the international commitments and that covered by the EU rules coincide fully. In particular, the scope of EU rules may be affected or altered by international commitments where the latter fall within an area which is already covered to a large extent by such rules. (Opinion 1/13 (*Accession of third States to the Hague Convention*), [2014] EU:C:2014:2303, paras. 71–73). Furthermore, such a risk of common EU rules being affected may be found to exist where the international commitments at issue, without necessarily conflicting with those rules, may have an

effect on their meaning, scope and effectiveness (see, to that effect *Commission v Council* [2014] ECLI:EU:C:2014:2151, para. 102, and Opinion 1/13, [2014] EU:C:2014:2303, para. 85)' (*Commission v Council (Antarctic MPAS)* [2018] ECLI:EU:C:2018:925, [113]–[114]).

65. One may of course argue that Member States are not deprived of their *capacity* (within the meaning of Article 6 VCLT) to conclude treaties, but only of the *exercise* of such capacity in certain areas. Such an orthodox view is well-founded on paper but is rather beside the point when the CJEU is the ultimate arbitrator of conflicts of competence between the EU and its Member States, and they have always bowed to its rulings in that regard.
66. *Germany v Council of the European Union* [2017] ECLI:EU:C:2017:935; Eleftheria Neframi, 'Article 216(1) TFEU and the Union's Shared Competence in the Light of Mixity', Common Market Law Review 2019, 489; Catherine Flaesch-Mougin, 'La Cour précise la portée de l'article 216§1 TFUE et confirme l'existence d'une compétence externe de l'UE dans un domaine de compétences partagées n'ayant pas fait l'objet d'une réglementation commune', *RTDEur. Revue trimestrielle de droit européen*, 2018, 1, 206.
67. On the evolution of EU law through judicial 'coups', see Perry Anderson, 'The European Coup', 42 London Review of Books 2020, 24 and Perry Anderson, 'Ever Closer Union?', 43 London Review of Books 2021, 1.
68. PCIJ, *Wimbledon*, 17 August 1923, Series A, no 1, 25.

CHAPTER 11

THE CRITICISM OF EUROCENTRISM AND INTERNATIONAL LAW

Countering and Pluralizing the Research, Teaching, and Practice of Eurocentric International Law

MAKANE MOÏSE MBENGUE AND OLABISI D. AKINKUGBE

1. Introduction

SIGNIFICANT scholarly work by critical international law scholarship has illuminated Eurocentrism in international law, its narrow Western origins, colonial legacies,[1] and international law's fraught claims of its universality.[2] The pedagogy of international law is Eurocentric.[3] The literature that is critical of international law's Eurocentricity have thus pinpointed the historical over-representation of Europeans in the institutions of international law, knowledge production, dominance in the syllabi of Global South universities, as well as the hegemonic ideas that animate Eurocentric conceptualizations of international law.[4] In other words, the tenacity of orthodox teaching, practice, and research of international law, especially its subjugation of alternative international law histories, and exclusion of the contemporary international legal knowledge production from the Global South has been subjected to significant critical inquiry by anti-colonial international legal scholarship.[5] Despite the modest progress in illuminating the gap in international law by mainstreaming the other developments in international law across the Global South, the tasks of critically engaging with international law's Eurocentricity and demystifying its contours remain essential. Even more important is the urgency of balancing the critique of Eurocentrism with a compelling account of the growing plurality of international law in the Global South.

Our chapter does not query the different ways that Eurocentrism is interrogated in international legal scholarship nor is the goal to have another analysis of the blind spots of traditional international law. Eurocentric international law effectively occupies the different facets of the fields of international law. From general public international law, international human rights law, international environmental law, international investment law, international courts, to international arbitration, authoritative scholarly works by critically inclined scholars that reveal the duplicity of Eurocentric international law fill the pages of blogs, journals, and textbooks with insights, strategies, and compelling analysis of the blind spots of mainstream international law. Eurocentric international law's challenge criss-crosses both the substantive content and procedural practices of the discipline as well as the theoretical and methodological.[6] As modest gains are recorded by critically minded scholars in these various fields of international law, Eurocentrism is reproduced in other areas. Chapter 2 of this book by Antony Anghie focuses on colonial legacies and other scholarship that have interrogated historical narrowness, universalism, imperialist origins, race, and international law, among others.[7]

This chapter therefore critically engages with contemporary unfair over-representation of Eurocentrism in the (knowledge) production and institutions of international law.[8] As Andrea Bianchi rightly notes, '[p]revailing "discursive policies" grounded in power structures and shaped by epistemic forces determine what is deemed to be an acceptable and competent thing to say about international law'.[9] The ongoing under-representation of international legal knowledge produced by the Global South in mainstream international law illustrates an arena where contemporary international law is distorted. To counter the manifestation of Eurocentrism in the teaching, research, and practice of international law today, we analyse some of the transformative actions that are rooted in the research and teaching of international law which are conceptualized and are being implemented by Global South scholars. As such, this chapter does not problematize European dominance in the research, production, and institutions of 'universal' international law. Likewise, the chapter is not premised on a utopian ideal that the hegemony of international law's Eurocentricity has waned.

African countries, like their counterparts in Asia, Latin America, and the Caribbean did not play a role in the creation of international law.[10] In producing Eurocentrism and globalizing its universalizing claims;[11] international law sanctioned Europe's plunder of the Third World—a stream of virtually all non-European societies who share in a particular voice and form of intellectual and political consciousness. These societies share similar historical experiences of European racism, slavery, and colonization as well as the enduring legacies of these dehumanizing projects.[12]

The ensuing analysis in the chapter therefore focuses on what we describe as the operations or manifestations of and substantive responses to Eurocentric international law in three core areas: research, teaching, and practice. In doing so, we are again not concerned with the blind spots of Eurocentric international law. Significant academic work already exists on this. Our aim is much more modest—to account for the practices (gains and challenges) in the scholarly endeavours of teaching, research, and publication diversity that present useful Global South narratives that pluralize Eurocentrism's narrowness. Pluralizing the epistemic structures that privilege the past and present production and reproduction of Eurocentric international law is not a task that is limited by time.[13] No one piece of research, or body of research will completely realize the transformation that critical scholars of international law seek. Hence, the chapter's analysis in the final section deliberately examines the ways in which various actions at institutional levels, and activities of current Global South scholars, contribute to the pluralizing. The chapter thus evinces the true character of TWAIL: a project rooted in transformative agenda and consciousness in the teaching, research, and practice of the 'other international law' with a view to broadening the narrowness and universality of Eurocentric international law.[14] The chapter focuses on the emergent efforts towards pluralizing the research and the dominance of Eurocentric scholarship and perspectives in the teaching of international law in, by, and from the Global South. The chapter acknowledges that the task of pluralizing international law and centring 'peripheral' perspectives in research and teaching that contrast the logic of Eurocentric international law is an ongoing project.

A core aspect of our argument in this chapter is that scholars of international law—Western and non-Western alike—have not focused enough on the different ways that international legal knowledge is produced and taught. As such, the chapter complements and to some extent balances the scholarly works that continue to criticize international law Eurocentricity in its various guises. While such works are useful, the chapter centres on the other ways in which international law's Eurocentricity in research and teaching are produced and disseminated in the Global South. In this regard, the chapter does not set out 'to strengthen one particular view about what or whose knowledge is real knowledge [among the several critical traditions that question international law's Eurocentricity], but to suggest that alternative forms of knowledge, ways of knowing, or schools of thought do not necessarily fare poorly'[15] once we turn our gaze to the other ways that international law is produced across Global South countries. In the analysis in this chapter, under the broad rubrics of TWAIL, we focus on African and other Global South examples to illustrate the contributions to the scholarship that pluralize and deprovincialize the hegemony of Eurocentric international law.

2. Revisiting Eurocentrism

In this section, we articulate our understanding of Eurocentrism as an important background to the ensuing analysis in the chapter. The social phenomenon of Eurocentrism is amorphous and manifests in multiple ways.[16] According to Samir Amin, Russell Moore, and James Membrez:

> Eurocentrism is now, ..., a social theory, which integrates various elements into a global and coherent vision of society and history. It is rather a prejudice that distorts

> social theories. It draws from its storehouse of components, retaining one or rejecting another according to the ideological needs of the moment . . .[17]

Eurocentric international law is narrow, and ethnocentric.[18]

In our view, unlike the early post-colonization era, contemporary manifestations of Eurocentrism and the universality of international law are multifaceted and difficult to synthesize in a few ideas and in limited spatial contexts as Eurocentric manifestations are uniquely amorphous. The unstructured way Eurocentric international law manifests is one of the defining features of its tenacity in the Global South. For our purposes, the uncritical co-optation and assimilation of Western, and distinctly European, approaches to the teaching of international (economic and human rights) law, domination of Western and European scholarly works in the syllabi of African universities, and the transplantation of European-styled architecture, practice, and assessment of international courts define some of the ways that Eurocentrism continues to be entrenched and reproduced in African societies.[19] The uncritical assimilation of international law in African universities thickens the post-colonial continuities of Western ideas of universality while simultaneously repressing the innovation and knowledge generated by the non-Western Global South. The historical, progressive, and ongoing Europeanization of the discipline of international law marginalizes international legal knowledge production across African and Global South epistemes.[20] Quite against the emerging evidence, this Eurocentric view short circuits the reverse flow of knowledge production by which Europeans and the West can learn about the theory and praxis of international law from Africa and the Global South.[21]

In other words, we push back against the contemporary polarization between centres and peripheries' capacity to generate international legal knowledge by advancing illustrations of the substantive and procedural advancements in international law from Africa—in the fields of international investment law, international human rights law, and international courts—to substantiate our arguments.[22] Eurocentrism remains vibrant as a neo-colonial aperture of continuing the domination of European international law and the over-representation of European (and Western) scholars in institutions of international law. As such, anti-colonial scholarly and practical endeavour in international legal knowledge production (both by scholars, publishers, and Global South international institutions) must be centred, mainstreamed, and understood on their own terms.[23]

Scholarly critiques of Eurocentric international law approach the question from different starting points. Eurocentric international law's deep colonial roots still inform most of the contemporary teaching and practice in the field. It would be naïve to suggest that its heyday is past or that it has been 'gravely weakened'[24] because of the modest pluralization of Global South practices of international law. International legal process, and the production of international legal knowledge are inherently human and social in character.[25] The outcome of our interactions with the research, teaching, and practice of international law is borne out of a unique set of experiences with one version or the other and out of the multiple versions of the dominant Eurocentric international legal knowledge production. In this regard, the chapter echoes James T Gathii's call that Eurocentric international law 'should embrace the practice and scholarship of international and from the Third World as integral to our discipline and practice rather than as destabilizing, irrelevant, and different'.[26]

3. Third World Approaches to International Law and Eurocentrism

Eurocentric international law's fraught history, narrowness, and exclusion of the subaltern has been critically interrogated by a wide spectrum of critical approaches, including most recently, the value of social sciences approaches,[27] behavioural psychology,[28] and Third World Approaches to International Law (TWAIL).[29] TWAIL is both a scholarly enterprise and political project—'it is not fixed and established'.[30] TWAIL pierces the parochialism that characterizes Eurocentric international law in favour of a plural international legal order and international legal knowledge production. It advocates the recognition of radical cultural and civilizational plurality and diversity, rather than a bias for Eurocentrism, in international law.[31] As Obiora Okafor's rightly notes:

> TWAIL scholars (or 'TWAILers') are solidly united by a shared ethical commitment to the intellectual and practical struggle to expose, reform, or even retrench those features of the intellectual legal system that help create or maintain the generally unequal, unfair, or unjust global order ..., a commitment to centre the rest rather than merely the west, thereby taking the lives and experiences of those who have self-identified as Third World much more seriously than has generally been the case.[32]

TWAIL scholarship has unravelled the universality claims that underpin traditional international law by showing that they privilege underlying ideas of the hegemony that characterizes Eurocentrism.[33] In this regard, the term 'Third World' in TWAIL is not necessarily a geographical space that is fixed in time or representing the essence of the Third World.[34] The Third World is an anti-subordination term and an analytical concept. Notably, contemporary Eurocentric international law re-incarnates its domination of the periphery in different ways and spaces.[35] Hence, Antony Anghie invites us to let the 'materials being studies ... speak for themselves, and the task of the scholar is to identify the logic ... that is somehow embodied in those materials'.[36] Similarly, Mohsen al Attar sees TWAIL as the potential and idealism of a youth maturing with each new discovery of where Eurocentrism is hidden in international law.[37] As such, while it is admitted that TWAIL content, strategy, and tactics are characterized by contradictions, incoherencies, and diversity of views, it is argued nonetheless that the approach also offers hope.[38]

Despite the critique by TWAIL scholarship, Eurocentric international law continues to be entrenched, as illustrated by, for example, the over-representation of Western scholarship, scholars, and views of international law in our institutions and the syllabus of Global South universities. In Mohsen al Attar's words, 'TWAIL scholars were optimistic and, perhaps, naïve in presuming that unearthing the biases [of Eurocentric international law] alone would precipitate reform. They disregarded Europe's commitment to securing the advantages its international legal construct affords.'[39] In our view, the naïvety that Attar notes, while true, should not be over-generalized. TWAIL-centric responses to international law's Eurocentricity come with transformative agenda. Addressing the multi-faceted nature of the manifestations of Eurocentrism in contemporary production of international legal knowledge, representation in institutions of international law, and the practice of our discipline, is not going to be resolved by a silver bullet of any one theoretical approach or substantive proposals or institutional diversity. Eurocentric international law indoctrination occurs simultaneously in various spheres, spaces, and arenas that are already captured in academic scholarship.[40] As such, we hope our focus, defined deliberately on the areas of research, teaching, and practice—though broad—offer some coherence in the manifestations of Eurocentric international law in these areas.[41]

4. Re-Orienting the Teaching of Eurocentric International Law for Epistemological Plurality in the Global North and Global South

In both Global North and Global South scholarship, there is a growing desire to teach international law in a more critical way that pluralizes the discipline's Eurocentric and Western origins.[42] Teachers of international law-oriented subjects are committed to diversifying the perspectives on their syllabi by introducing variations in theoretical approaches and scholarly materials.[43] In the Global North, many of the moves to account for critical perspectives in the teaching of international law are dubbed in the language of 'decolonizing the curriculum'.[44] However, the extent to which the move to 'decolonize the curriculum' marks a substantive radical shift in the teaching of international law and the law schools in generally is yet to be seen.[45] Most recently, the impetus to confront the Eurocentricity of international law in Western lecture theatres has been motivated by the increase in racially motivated injustices and the need to remedy them.[46] The teaching of Eurocentric international law is myopic and parochial in its outlook.[47]

With the exception of a handful of institutions, many Global South universities teach international law in an uncritical way.[48] In other words, public (and other) international law courses such as international human rights law, international trade law, and international investment law, to mention a few, are taught and learned through a lens, language, as well as conceptual and theoretical approaches that reinforce Eurocentrism.[49] Thus, the syllabi and curricula of many institutions in the Global South reflect the praxis of the teaching of canonical scholarship from the Global North.[50] Mohammad Shahabuddin locates one source of this uncritical attitude in a 'perception of law as a colonial gift ... '.[51] Scant attention is given to how the teaching and research of international law, especially by many Global South scholars teaching at institutions of higher learning, reinforces how Eurocentric international law is reproduced and entrenched in the Global South today.[52]

As such, Eurocentric international law teaching, even if inadvertently, gatekeeps, regulates, and preserves the agency, power, and structure of the dominant Western approaches.[53] Put differently, Eurocentric teaching of international law affirms the beltways of traditional international legal knowledge production, and simultaneously relegates scholarship from the Global South to the periphery.[54] An instance of the pervasive nature of teaching critically arises from the paucity of scholars and teachers who bring a critical lens to their classrooms and lecture theatres. As Tran Viet Dung notes in the context of Vietnam, the challenges of teaching public international law include: the shortage of lecturers with expertise in international law and the lack of access to good quality textbooks and materials in international law.[55] In the broader Asian context, a recent report from the National University of Singapore's Centre for International Law on 'Teaching and Researching International Law in Asia' presents an empirical survey of the state of international law teaching and research in Asia.[56]

The complexity of mainstream international law, especially, the challenges of agency and authorship that entrench Eurocentricism is not weakened by neutrality claims of the authors. A recent research symposium convened by Fabio Morosini and Luíza Leão Soares Pereira titled 'International Law "in the Palm of our Hand": Reading between the Lines of Brazilian International Law Textbooks'

> explore[s] the tension between the structure of international law that ... textbooks describe, and the agency of their authors and recipients. [The authors] tackle structural questions about international law in Brazil (such as: are there substantive themes of 'national' interest that are repeated in the textbooks? Are there privileged sources among their citations? What are the patterns of nationality and gender among the authors of secondary works cited?) and questions about the agency of the authors of these textbooks (including how do the textbooks reflect professional histories, geographic location, academic background, and positionality?). We embrace in this process the understanding that the power of textbooks and their authors is part of the complex interplay among the mentioned factors, and that their diffused power to produce and reproduce structures and patterns of arguments demands deeper analysis. Thus, we reject the idea that authors can produce a 'neutral' manual or discover international law outside of the tension between structure and agency.[57]

Furthermore, in the broader Latin American context, Amaya Alvez Marin, Laura Betancur Restrepo, Enrique Alberto Prieto-Rios, Daniel Rivas-Ramirez, and Fabia

Veçoso 'found that an uncritical Western perspective is favoured in the teaching of international law in the region'.[58] Amaya et al note further that:

> In many cases, international law is generally presented as a single and objective law that must be applied uniformly in any part of the world and, therefore, leaving no place for regional contextualization or for questioning its premises. Likewise, it is widely preferred to teach it using a bibliography originated in the Global North, despite the substantive contributions of Latin American scholars in International Law and in the Humanities and Social Sciences.[59]

In Africa, despite the growing body of international legal knowledge production by scholars and institutions of international law, similar challenges are replicated regarding the Eurocentric teaching of international law. The international law syllabi in African universities continue to entrench the agency and structure of Eurocentric international law.[60] This unfortunate state of affairs endures because the few scholars who have taken up the challenge of centring 'other' international law remain on the periphery. In teaching Eurocentric international law, following canonical international law textbooks and authors, teachers of international law in the Global South therefore inadvertently validate the manifestation and agency of Eurocentrism.

Capturing the ongoing perpetuation of Eurocentrism in our theatres of learning in the Global South, Mohsen al Attar argues that:

> As TWAIL scholars we must revolutionize our pedagogy, dispossessing ourselves of the epistemological prejudices we maintain through our craft. Critical scholars conceived TWAIL to advance an inclusive and plural international law. Yet, when teaching international law, we show a surprising commitment to the enduring one, always disregarding the regime's obvious antipathy toward epistemological plurality.[61]

In the African context, the paucity in the teaching of critical international law is further highlighted by Babatunde Fagabyibo who argues that: 'At the core of the discourse around the state of international legal scholarship in Africa are two issues: exclusion and relevance.' He goes on:

> Exclusion has both internal and external dimensions. In its internal mode, the concern is about the absence of critical reflection and contexts of non-white ideas and civilizations in the narrative of international law textbooks and practices on the continent. In its external context, exclusion manifests in how global South scholars are excluded from publishing in journals deemed the 'holy grail' of the science of international law.[62]

Outside the traditional theatres of learning, institutional initiatives such as the African Union Commission of International Law (AUCIL) has potential to help African universities in developing an African perspective on international law. Indeed, the mandate of AUCIL is to codify and progressively develop international law on the continent, considering African Union treaties, the decisions of African international courts and policy organs, as well as African state practice. AUCIL is to achieve this by encouraging the codification and progressive development in the teaching, study, publication, and dissemination of literature on international law on the continent.[63] Unfortunately, the work of AUCIL has stalled in this regard, although it has announced new initiatives that could change the direction of its work.

The Eurocentric teaching of international law is path-dependent. Teachers of international law in many parts of the Global South remain indoctrinated in the Eurocentric approaches to international law. In the African context, many of these teachers of international law are pedagogically conservative—formalistic and doctrinal—in their approaches to the subject. In many cases, this is not a deliberate choice.[64] It is simply a reproduction of the ways in which they were taught or happened to have studied. The teaching of international law has thus not centred the contradictions and tensions of international legal scholarship enough in the theatres of learning in Africa.[65]

The near non-existence of critical approaches in the core texts of international law and syllabi on which African teachers and students rely is the very definition of an epistemic wrong—a reincarnation of Eurocentrism. Where then does this leave us? A commitment to a broadly TWAILian style and substance in our work also calls for the recognition of the growing need to reach beyond the typical sites of engagement towards the non-typical sites.

To be clear, our argument is not that the scholarly materials on traditional or mainstream international law should be expunged completely from the syllabi of universities in the Global South. Rather, our core claim is that the scholarly space for critical traditions remains alarmingly small, thus perpetuating the predominance of Eurocentric international law in the higher institutions of the Global South. As such, the plurality of international legal knowledge production as foregrounded by critical theoretical and methodological approaches such as TWAIL, feminism, Marxism, comparative law, and social sciences approaches to international law[66] are not centred in the teaching of international law. There are many opportunities to confront and pluralize Eurocentric international law in the teaching of students in the Global South. We recount, in the next section, some of the initiatives which should be incorporated into the teaching of international law to bring critical perspectives to the lecture theatres of Global South institutions, and at a rate that intensifies the mission to pluralize mainstream international law.

5. Mainstreaming the Production of International Legal Scholarship from and by the Global South

This section examines the production of international legal knowledge from and by the Global South. The Global South is a producer of international legal knowledge. Yet, knowledge about public international law (and its sub-fields such as international investment law and international human rights law, among others)[67] that is produced by Global South scholars has not been centred in the books, journals, blogs, and other associated scholarly materials in a way that would pluralize the dominance of Eurocentric international legal knowledge not only in the Global South but also in the Global North. In our view, what is called for here is a cross-fertilization of the materials that currently exist, and those to be produced in the future.

In essence, confronting the agency and structural power in the Eurocentric teaching of international law in Global South, by pluralizing the reading materials in syllabi, must also take account of the practical reality that the majority of Global South countries are low resource economies. It is important, therefore, that the scholarship generated is made widely available and not locked behind pay walls once they are published in the mainstream.[68] Put differently, important international legal scholarly work that is generated by Global South scholars in public international law[69] (and its sub-fields such as international human rights[70] and international investment law), should be made available via open access, thus ensuring that the cross-fertilization and plurality of Eurocentric international law would no longer remain steeped in the dominant approaches.

Yet, an enduring feature of Eurocentric scholarship is that it is tenacious, resilient, and enduring.[71] While we acknowledge that mainstreaming or centring the 'other' international legal scholarship is an ongoing battle, this chapter argues that the importance of such research must not be measured only by its capacity to 'up-end' or 'undo' Eurocentric international law. This is especially so since the overarching argument in this chapter is one of recognition of the plurality and diversity of voices, places, purpose, producers, and forms of international law beyond Eurocentric tropes. Eurocentric distortions of the history and contemporary practices of international law, while still dominant, are today increasingly challenged by the scholarly work of critical international legal scholars from the Global South and Global North alike. Similarly, scholarly work that pluralizes Eurocentric dominance must display similar resilience, in rigour, scope, and (if possible, open access) publication across diverse areas. In this sense, TWAIL and other critically informed scholarship illustrate the diversity of other practices and this production of international legal knowledge.[72] Their commitment to pluralized thinking and heterogeneity that is grounded in the unique socio-political, economic, historical, and cultural contexts of the region they study has enhanced the utility of their work to pluralize international law.

In the Global North, TWAIL scholarship has been filling the pages of academic journals, blogs, book chapters, and entire books to provide a criticism of international law from different interdisciplinary angles that do address the concerns of African and Third World peoples. TWAIL-oriented scholarship has grown in leaps and bounds and this is evident from the growing bibliography of TWAIL works.[73] Having such a wide range of resources documenting the contributions that Africa and the rest of the Third World is making to international law and its sub-fields is very important to informing the further research, teaching, and practice of international law in ways that do not reproduce the Eurocentricity in the Global South.

In the context of international courts, the potential influence and cross-fertilization of knowledge based on the jurisprudence on international human rights law from African, Latin American, and European courts as well as younger ones in the Caribbean offers an important illustration on decentring and pluralizing Eurocentric international law through the judicial institutions. For example, in the field of international human rights law, the African Court on Human and Peoples' Rights has been at the forefront of cutting-edge advancements of human rights.[74] Our point here is that the European Court of Human Rights, as an institution that embodies and generates a version of Eurocentric— universalized— understanding of international law, can and should be influenced by developments in its African and Latin American counterparts. In this regard, the Joint Law Report of the African Court on Human and People' Rights, European Court of Human Rights, and Inter-American Court of Human Rights is to be commended. The inaugural edition which was published in 2019 with the stated goal, among others, 'to illustrate how the courts are increasingly having regard to each other's approach to human rights protection', is an appropriate example of how the cross-fertilization of knowledge production by institutions of international law across different regions must be pluralized for a more fulsome understanding of international law and its sub-fields.[75] So far, two volumes of the Joint Law Reports have been published. While such an initiative provides an important start, building on and ensuring that the practice thickens and becomes a norm of interaction between the sister courts' jurisprudence remains crucial to pluralizing Eurocentric international law. In other words, beyond being modelled after the European Court of Human Rights, in contemporary times other international courts in marginalized regions offer important sites of production of international legal knowledge that must be centred to pluralize international legal knowledge.[76]

Beyond the courts, TWAIL scholars are now making their scholarship instrumental in the Special Procedures process of the United Nations. Significant, if modest, progress continues to be made by TWAIL scholars who have been appointed to the United Nations' Special Procedures. As at November 2021, there are four TWAIL-oriented mandate holders for the Special Procedures solidarity,[77] racism,[78] food,[79] and housing.[80] In the context of international societies in the Global North, TWAILers continue to serve as Executive Council members and on the board of important international societies around the world—in the US,[81] Canada,[82] Europe,[83] Australia, and elsewhere. Further, a decade after Antony Anghie was invited to deliver the main keynote speech at the ASIL Annual Meeting, the Grotius Lecture, James T Gathii was invited to deliver the same lecture in 2020.

Additionally, academic societies and networks of African scholars play an important complementary role in facilitating the space for the critical analysis of Eurocentrism in international law and its sub-fields. Examples of these societies and networks in Africa include: the African Society of International Law, the African International Economic Law Network, the African Arbitration Association, and the Afronomicslaw Academic

Forum, to mention a few. The cumulative effect of these forums is not only to amplify the voice of Africa and African scholarship in the respective sub-fields, but they have also made substantive proposals towards development in these areas.[84]

The scope for Global South scholarly publication is also on the rise. The open access and substantive quality analysis that these platforms offer are essential to the mission of pluralizing Eurocentric international law. Open access peer-reviewed journals and blogs with an explicit focus on the Global South have been established and are growing in number. TWAIL now has its own journal—the Third World Approaches to International Law Review (TWAILR).[85] Its aim is to provide critical scholars, mainly from the Global South, and their allies, with a space to be active participants in the project of international law in a way that is emancipatory, egalitarian, and truly international.[86] In addition to the journal's annual issue, TWAILR hosts *Dialogues* and *Reflections*. *Dialogues* are often used to gather conference proceedings and interviews with authors and TWAIL scholars while *Reflections* offer the possibility of engaging with a topic via a short, pithy, and crisp analysis of no more 3000 words. There is also Afronomicslaw.org, which, among other things, hosts a blog, a thriving Academic Forum, the African Sovereign Debt Justice Network, and the African Journal of International Economic Law (AfJIEL).[87] Afronomicslaw focuses on international economic law and public international law matters as they (mostly) relate to Africa and the Global South. Afronomicslaw's aim is to amplify those voices and issues that are not often featured in mainstream international scholarship. In terms of research, the pieces that feature on the blog, as one might expect, further the goal of deprovincializing the research and teaching of international law from a non-Eurocentric perspective.[88] In addition, more traditional publication platforms such as regional and national international law journals such as the Asian Journal of International Law, the African Journal of International Law, and the Brazilian Journal of International Law, among others continue to publish essays that challenge the boundaries of Eurocentric international law in important ways.[89]

In terms of substantive principles of international law sub-fields, international investment law represents an area where African state practices in treaty-making and the scholarship on such treaties have introduced innovative provisions and norms that centre the substantive concerns of African peoples with potential ramifications for the Global South and Global North.[90] Although the tendency is to limit these developments to the regional level, this chapter argues that the body of scholarly work by Makane Moïse Mbengue, Won Kidane, Emilia Oyeama, Ibironke Odumosu-Ayanu, Hamed El-Kady, and Kehinde Olaoye, among others illustrate the role Africa is playing in the development of international investment law. This body of scholarship is not monolithic, and their approaches differ. The idea here is that critically-minded scholars are not only questioning the idea that Africa and the Global South are rule-takers in international investment law today, but they foreground aspects where Africa and the Global South are indeed rule-makers.[91] One narrative of the contribution of African states is their role in the generation of international investment law rules and norms through treaty-making. As a result of their more active approach in the formulation of international investment commitments and rule-making at the national, bilateral, and regional levels, a body of contributions that differ from and pluralize the existing types of obligations in the bilateral investment treaties is emerging.[92] The rise of international investment rule-making forms the basis of Hamed El-Kady and Mustaqeem De Gama's argument that African states 'are becoming "investment treaty makers" and are adopting investment policies that reflect primarily their own preferences as opposed to "signing on" to models proposed to them by third parties'.[93] El-Kady and De Gama note further that the reform efforts at the national and regional levels in Africa 'have the strategic objective of supporting structural transformation of African economies while building investment policy frameworks that are development-oriented and establishing a balance between investor and States' rights and obligations'.[94]

While these reform efforts occur in parallel and sometimes overlap with one another, they all converge in their attempt to formulate a new approach to investment policies that aims at safeguarding the right and duty of African countries to regulate and to reflect emerging sustainable development imperatives. These developments, Mbengue argues, make Africa 'an interesting laboratory for the rethinking and reshaping of international investment law'.[95]

6. Conclusion

Our conclusion draws together the thread that connects the arguments in the preceding sections of this chapter. Although African states, like their counterparts in the Global South, were 'rule-takers' in the historical sense of the evolution of international law, today, these 'peripheral players' in the production of international legal knowledge, teaching, and new practices of international law are, in fact, rule-makers in their own rights. In our view, the ongoing contributions of African institutions such as international courts and regional organizations; innovative treaty-making in the areas of international investment law; growing number of African-centred scholarly journals and platforms; as well as casebooks on international law, all point to the emergence of a version of international law as conceptualized by African states, scholars, policy experts, and practitioners.

The chapter illustrates the various ways that the TWAIL scholarship in the research and teaching of international law is pluralizing the narrowness and false claims of universality of international law. The task of centring the 'other' international laws in the areas of research, teaching, and practice remains an urgent one with a multi-layered approach. Yet, despite Eurocentric international law's resilience in contemporary teaching, research, and practice of international law, Global South countries are simultaneously engaged in the making and remaking of international law. The path to mainstreaming Third World scholarship and pluralizing Eurocentrism is certainly clearer today than it was two or three decades ago. There is every reason to hope that such clarity will only increase in the future.

Notes

1. Antony Anghie's contribution to this book focuses on 'Colonial Legacies' (hereafter Anghie). As such we will not explore issues associated with colonial legacies in our chapter.
2. Taslim O Elias, *Africa and the Development of International Law* (AW Sijthoff 1972); Antony Anghie, *Imperialism, Sovereignty and the Making of International Law* (CUP 2005) (hereafter Anghie, *Imperialism*); James Thuo Gathii, 'International Law and Eurocentricity', 9 European Journal of International Law 1998, 184 (hereafter Gathi, 'Eurocentricity'); Arnulf Becker Lorca, 'Eurocentrism in the History of International Law' in Bardo Fassbender and Anne Peters (eds), *The Oxford Handbook of the History of International Law* (OUP 2012) 1034 (hereafter Lorca, 'Eurocentrism'); Martti Koskenniemi, 'Histories of International Law: Dealing with Eurocentrism' (2011) 19 Rechtsgescheichte 2011, 152; Fleur Johns, Thomas Skouteris, and Wouter Werner, 'Editors' Introduction: Taslim Olawale Elias in the Periphery Series', 21 Leiden Journal of International Law 2008, 289 (Special Issue); Oji Umozurike, *International Law and Colonialism in Africa* (Nwamife Publishers 1979).
3. Mohsen Al Attar, 'Must International Legal Pedagogy Remain Eurocentric?', 11 Asian Journal of International Law 2021, 176 (hereafter Al Attar, 'Pedagogy').
4. Makau Mutua, 'Critical Race Theory and International Law: The View of an Insider-Outsider', 45 Villanova Law Review 2000, 851; Sundhya Pahuja, 'The Postcoloniality of International Law', 46 Harvard International Law Journal 2005, 459.
5. See Muthucumaraswamy Sornarajah, 'The Asian Perspective to International Law in the Age of Globalization', 5 Singapore Journal of International and Comparative Law 2001, 284; Anghie, *Imperialism* (n 2); Obiora Cheidu Okafor, 'Newness, Imperialism and International Legal Reform in Our Times: A TWAIL Perspective', 43 Osgoode Hall Law Journal 2005, 171 (hereafter Okafor, 'Imperialism'); Vasuki Nesiah, 'Placing International Law: White Spaces on a Map', 16(1) Leiden Journal of International Law 2003, 1; Liliana Obregon, 'Between Civilization and Barbarism: Creole Interventions' in Richard Falk, Balakrishnan Rajagopal, and Jacqueline Stevens (eds), *International Law and the Third World: Reshaping Justice* (Routledge 2008) 111; Rose Parfitt, *The Process of International Legal Reproduction: Inequality, Historiography, Resistance* (CUP 2019); Hilary Charlesworth, Christine Chinkin, and Shelley Wright, 'Feminist Approaches to International Law', 85 American Journal of International Law 1991, 613 (illustrating international law's blindsight to feminist analysis and illuminating the potential of feminist legal theory to contribute to the progressive development of international law).
6. Ntina Tzouvala, 'The Specter of Eurocentrism in International Legal History', 31(2) Yale Journal of Law & Humanities 2021, 413, 414–415 (Problematizing through the lens of Marxism the emptiness of 'Eurocentrism' and examining the question of Eurocentrism as a result of the 'deep theoretical divisions and the increasingly sour tome of the debate' by 'retrieving the radical potential of early critiques of Eurocentrism, and bringing them to bear on international legal history' and 'arguing that thinking about Eurocentrism as a culturalist distortion that is inextricably linked to global capitalist expansion allows us to discern the role of international law in this irreducibly contradictory process of globalizing capitalism.')
7. Anghie (n 1).
8. cf Andrea Bianchi and Moshe Hirsch (eds), *International Law's Invisible Frames: Social Cognition and Knowledge Production in International Legal Processes* (OUP 2021).

Referring to the social dissonance that constituted the history of international law and its ongoing divergences from contemporary social contexts, notes:

> [W]hat we know as international law is produced by knowledge-production mechanism of a different nature. Social Practices and intellectual processes that are influenced by theories and theoretical discourses shape the social phenomenon we qualify as international law...

Andrea Bianchi, 'Knowledge Production in International Law: Forces and Processes' in Andrea Bianchi and Moshe Hirsch (eds), *International Law's Invisible Frames: Social Cognition and Knowledge Production in International Legal Processes* (OUP 2021) 155.

9. Bianchi, 'Knowledge Production in International Law' (n 10).
10. The question of the 'contribution' of African states to the creation and development of international law has sparked interesting debates among critical international legal scholars. See James Thuo Gathii, 'A Critical Appraisal of the International Legal Tradition of Taslim Olawale Elias', 21 Leiden Journal of International Law 2008, 317; Jeremy I Levitt, 'The African Origins of International Law: Myth or Reality?', 19(113) UCLA Journal of International Law & Foreign Affairs 2015, 114.
11. See for instance Arif Dirlik, 'Is There History after Eurocentrism?: Globalism, Postcolonialism, and the Disavowal of History', 42 Cultural Critique 1999, 1, 8–9, 42.
12. Makau W Mutua, 'What Is TWAIL?', 94 Proceedings of the American Society of International Law Annual Meeting 2000, 31, 35 (hereafter Mutua, 'TWAIL').
13. See generally, Surya Prakash Sinha, *Legal Polycentricity and International Law* (Carolina Academic Press 1996); Siba N'Zatioula Grovogui, *Sovereigns, Quasi-Sovereigns and Africans: Race and Self-Determination in International Law* (University of Minnesota Press 1996). For a review of both books, see Gathii, 'Eurocentricity' (n 2).
14. In this regard, we agree with Karin Mickelson that 'TWAIL can benefit from ways of thinking about hope that have emerged in both scholarship and activism in recent years, and these insights may themselves help calibrate our ongoing engagements with the international legal system'. Karin Mickelson, 'Hope in a TWAIL Register', 1 TWAIL Review 2020, 16 (hereafter Mickelson, 'Hope').
15. Obiora Chiedu Okafor, 'Critical Third World Approaches to International Law (TWAIL): Theory, Methodology, or Both?', 10 International Community Law Review 2008, 371, 372 (hereafter Okafor, 'Critical TWAIL').
16. 'Eurocentrism is, like all dominant social phenomena, easy to grasp in the multiplicity of its daily manifestations but difficult to define precisely. Its manifestations, like those of other prevailing social phenomena, are expressed in the most varied of areas: day-to-day relationships between individuals, political information and opinion, general views concerning society and culture, social science. These expressions are sometimes violent, leading all the way to racism, and sometimes subtle. They express themselves in the idiom of popular opinion as well as in the erudite languages of specialists on politics, the Third World, economics, history, theology, and all the formulations of social science.' Amin Samir, Russell Moore, and James Membrez, *Eurocentrism* (NYU Press 2009) 179 (hereafter Samir et al, *Eurocentrism*).
17. ibid, 166.
18. Lorca, 'Eurocentrism' (n 2) (exploring two moments in the intellectual history of international law in which some, mostly non-Western, international lawyers have dealt with

the problem of Eurocentrism by producing divergent narratives exposing a distortion in conventional histories of international law).

19. Arnulf Becker Lorca echoes a similar point: 'Today, the presence of Eurocentric distortions in the history of international law will depend on the type of history in academic writing. In spite of the intellectual status enjoyed by second-generation TWAIL scholars, the historical introduction of most international law textbooks, and thus arguably the teaching of international law, has not departed from the narrative of progress common in liberal-internationalist histories.' Lorca, 'Eurocentrism' (n 2) 1054.
20. 'For the most optimistic, this Europeanization, which is simply the diffusion of a superior model, functions as a necessary law, imposed by the force of circumstances ... For others, non-European peoples have an alternative choice: either they can accept Europeanization and internalize its demands, or, if they decide against it, they will lead themselves to an impasse that inevitably leads to their decline. The progressive Westernization of the world is nothing more than the expression of the triumph of the humanist universalism invented by Europe.' Samir et al, *Eurocentrism* (n 16) 180.
21. eg the advancements in the field of international human rights law and the African Court on Human and Peoples Rights offers a compelling illustration. We return to this in later sections of this chapter.
22. See generally, James Thuo Gathii, 'The Promise of International Law: A Third World View', 36(3) American University International Law Review 2021, 377, 378–379 (hereafter Gathii, 'Promise of International law') (challenging the limited geography of places and ideas that dominate the beltway of [international law] and arguing that the Third World is an epistemic site of production and not merely a site of reception of international legal knowledge).
23. Our thinking here maps on to James Gathii's characterization that '[t]his *strong* form of international law scholarship self-identifies with group solidarity among less powerful countries. It expresses their desire for self-determination and autonomy from all forms of external or neo-colonial controls. This is opposed to a '*weak* form of anti-colonial scholarship is basically integrationist: meaning that it is largely complimentary of the liberatory claims of principles' [that characterise Eurocentric international law]. Gathii, 'Eurocentricity' (n 2) 187, 189.
24. Malcolm N Shaw, *International Law* (8th edn, CUP 2018) 33.
25. Michel Foucault, *The Archaeology of Knowledge*, trans A M Sheridan (Routledge 2002).
26. Gathii continues, 'By taking this [Third world] scholarship and practice more seriously, we can bother demarginalize this Third world input into international law and learn from the ways that it provides distinctive visions of international law'.
27. Yifeng Chen, 'On Relating Social Sciences to International Law: Three Perspectives', 22(1) Chicago Journal of International Law 2021, Article 6; Daniel Abebe, Adam Chilton, and Tom Ginsburg, 'The Social Science Approach to International Law', 22(1) Chicago Journal of International Law 2021, Article 4 (hereafter Abebe et al, 'Social Science Approach'); James Thuo Gathii, 'Studying Race in International Law Scholarship Using a Social Science Approach', 22 Chicago Journal of International Law 2021, 71 (hereafter Gathii, 'Studying Race'); Hilary Charlesworth, Christine Chinkin, and Shelley Wright, 'Feminist Approaches to International Law', 85 American Journal of International Law 1991, 613.
28. Tomer Broude, 'Behavioural International Law', 163 University of Pennsylvania Law Review 2015, 1100; Anne van Aaken, 'Behavioral International Law and Economics', 55 Harvard Internationall Law Journal 2014, 421.

29. Mutua, 'TWAIL' (n 12) 31. On the question: 'How does TWAIL as scholarship with a focus on peripheral issues forge its ideas within a hegemonic international legal system that continuously re-enacts old challenges and methods in new terms and forms, one of the most recent being the manner in which the war on terror is being implemented?', see Ibironke T Odumosu, 'Challenges for the (Present/) Future of Third World Approaches to International Law', 10 International Community Law Review 2008, 467, 469.
30. Antony Anghie, 'TWAIL: Past and Future', 10 International Community Law Review 2008, 479, 480 (hereafter Anghie, 'TWAIL').
31. See generally, Okafor, 'Critical TWAIL' (n 15); James Thuo Gathii, 'TWAIL: A brief history of its origins, its decentralized network, and a tentative bibliography' (2011) 3(1) Trade, Law & Development 368 (hereafter Gathii, 'TWAIL history').
32. Okafor, 'Imperialism' (n 5) 176–177.
33. 'The Third World ... speaks from a subaltern epistemic location. This means that this Third World approach contests the idea that international law is applicable everywhere and that we should therefore regard it as a view from nowhere ... Third World states and TWAIL scholars have contested this non-situated, universal status of international law in a variety of ways for several generations now.' Gathii, 'Promise of International law' (n 22) 380.
34. Antony Anghie, 'Identifying Regions in the History of international Law' in Bardo Fassbender and Anne Peters (eds), *The Oxford Handbook of the History of International Law* (OUP 2012) 1058.
35. One version of this role is described by Mohammad Shahabuddin who notes,

    'international law, as a core element of the ideology of the postcolonial state, contributes to the marginalisation of minorities. It does so by playing a key role in the ideological making of the postcolonial "national", "liberal", and "developmental" states in relation to: continuation of colonial boundaries in postcolonial states, internal organisation of ethnic relations within the liberal-individualist framework of human rights, and the economic vision of the postcolonial state in the form of "development" that subjugates minority interests.'

    Mohammad Shahabuddin, *Minorities and the Making of Postcolonial States in International Law* (CUP 2021) 3.
36. Anghie, 'TWAIL' (n 30) 481.
37. Mohsen al Attar, 'TWAIL a Paradox within a Paradox', 22 International Community Law Review 2020, 163.
38. 'TWAIL I could be said to have optimism, faith in international law, and hope; TWAIL II lost the optimism but retained a degree of faith in international law as well as a sense of hope; while contemporary TWAIL analysis seems to be skirting the edge of losing faith in international law altogether while still somehow clinging to hope. Hope plays an important role in all three, but arguably is most crucial at the present time, when we can no longer rely on the buoyancy that the other two provide.' Mickelson, 'Hope' (n 14) 17.
39. Al Attar, 'Pedagogy' (n 3) 183.
40. The expansion of international law and artificial intelligence (AI) represents a core example of these new manifestations. See Fleur Johns, 'Data, Detection, and the Redistribution of the Sensible in International Law', 111 American Journal of International Law 2017, 57. Likewise, the burning issues of international law and climate change, as well as racial capitalism, all point to the connections of various strands of law that traffic baked-in Eurocentric logics.

41. We do this, acknowledging:

> that the post-Cold War situation is one characterized by the recognition of multiple identities and heterogeneity, and the rejection of universalist modes of reasoning. Such multiplicity and heterogeneity, in turn, can best be appreciated if seen for what these identities and, indeed, norms and doctrines of international law are: constructed and contingent. The challenge for liberal/conservative approaches to international law, therefore, is to engage this postcolonial predicament rather than to defend international norms in the abstract, . . .

James Thuo Gathii, 'Rejoinder: Twailing International Law', 98 Michigan Law Review 2000, 2066, 2071.

42. For some examples from the Global North, see Christine Schwöbel-Patel, 'Teaching International Law from a Critical Angle', 2 Recht En Methode 2013, 67; Christine Schwöbel-Patel, 'Teaching International Law Critically: Critical Pedagogy and Building as Orientations for Learning and Teaching' in Bart van Klink and Ubaldus de Vries (eds), *Academic Learning in Law: Theoretical Positions, Teaching Experiments and Learning Experiences* (Edward Elgar 2016) 99. See also Christine Schwöbel-Patel, 'Teaching International Law' (*Oxford Bibliographies*, OUP 2018); Anne Orford, 'Embodying Internationalism: The Making of International Lawyers', 19 Australian Yearbook of International Law 1998, 1; Jack L Goldsmith and Eric A Posner, 'The Limits of International Law Fifteen Years Later', 22 Chicago Journal of International Law 2021, 110.

On the Global South, see Mohammad Shahabuddin, 'Teaching and Researching International Law: Some Personal Reflections Via Bangladesh and the UK' (*Afronomicslaw Blog*, 25 September 2020) <https://twitter.com/JTGathii/status/1471565958703636482 accessed 1 May 2023 (hereafter Shahabuddin, 'Personal Reflections').

43. eg Professor Obiora Okafor regularly taught a seminar on 'International Law in the Global South Research Seminar Series' at Osgoode Law School, York University Canada. The 'seminar series focused on international law from a TWAILian perspective, with discussions centred on a work-in-progress presented by younger academics from around the world. An assigned "discussant" led the way during the question-and-answer periods that followed each such seminar.' <https://iligs.osgoode.yorku.ca>

More recently, at the 2022 Loyola University Chicago School of Law International Law Colloquium, Black Traditions in International Law by James T Gathii's focuses on Black Traditions in International Law to 'express and foreground the goals, histories and ideologies of black struggle. Black traditions have long offered visions of global order that challenge the color blindness embedded in accounts of international law. Black traditions counter visions of international law that conceptualize the world in accordance with predominantly European and white conceptions of hierarchy and order.'

See James Thuo Gathii, ' ... The Colloquium will focus on Black Traditions of International Law' (*Twitter*, 16 December 2021) <https://twitter.com/JTGathii/status/1471565958703636482 accessed 22 December 2022; James Thuo Gathii, 'Black Traditions in International Law—Concept Note' (*Afronomicslaw Blog*, 14 December 2021) <https://www.afronomicslaw.org/category/repository/black-traditions-international-law accessed 22 December 2022.

Theoretically, on the continuing rise of social science approach to international law, see Special Issue of the Chicago Journal of International Law on 'The Social Science Approach to international Law', edited by Daniel Abebe, Adam Chilton, and Tom Ginsburg, (2021) 22 Chicago Journal of International Law 1.

44. See generally Folúkẹ́ Adébísí, 'Decolonising the Law School: Presences, Absences, Silences... and Hope', 54 The Law Teacher 2020, 471; Folúkẹ́Adébísí, *Decolonization and Legal Knowledge: Reflections on Power and Possibility* (Bristol University Press 2023); see also Ntando Sindane and Babatunde Fagbayibo, 'Some Thoughts on the Ideational Underpinnings of a Decolonised Pedagogical Approach to International Law in South Africa' (*Afronomicslaw Blog*, 2 October 2020) <https://www.afronomicslaw.org/2020/10/02/some-thoughts-on-the-ideational-underpinnings-of-a-decolonised-pedagogical-approach-to-international-law-in-south-africa/ accessed 22 December 2022.
45. According to Mohammad Shahabuddin:

    The project on 'decolonising the curriculum' has now become almost fashionable so far as higher education institutions in the UK are concerned. While the core philosophy behind the project is praiseworthy, the project is often reduced to a couple of new ornamental modules on decolonisation and race relations without any comprehensive revision of the curriculum as a whole. In this way, the project not only compartmentalises the issue of decolonising knowledge but also offers legitimacy to the prevailing traditional curriculum. It also remains to be seen how these institutions, many of which directly or indirectly benefited from colonialism or even the slave trade, re-engage in radical ways with their own institutional memories and prevalent institutional racism as part of the 'decolonising' project. In the absence of such radical re-engagements at the macro-level, the 'decolonising the curriculum' project will soon prove to be yet another white-washing tool.

    See Shahabuddin, 'Personal Reflections' (n 42).
46. Eg in the European context, see generally the European University Institute's Interdisciplinary Research Cluster titled 'Decentering Eurocentrism', which 'brings together historians, lawyers, political scientists and economists to understand the origins and consequences of an epistemology that places Europe—sometimes explicitly and sometimes implicitly—at the centre of the world'. <https://www.eui.eu/research-hub?id=decentering-eurocentrism-1#:~:text=This%20research%20cluster%20brings%20together,the%20centre%20of%20the%20world> accessed 28 December 2022.
47. See generally Adelle Blackett, 'Follow the Drinking Gourd: Our Road to Teaching Critical Race Theory and Slavery and the Law, Contemplatively, at McGill', 62 McGill Law Journal 2017, 1251; Mohsen Al Attar, '"I Can't Breathe": Confronting the Racism of International Law' (*Afronomicslaw Blog*, 2 October 2020) <https://www.afronomicslaw.org/2020/10/02/i-cant-breathe-confronting-the-racism-of-international-law/> accessed 23 December 2022; Mohsen Al Attar, 'Symposium: Saving Critical International Legal Pedagogy from Formalists, Reactionaries, and Pandemics' (*OpinioJuris*, 30 August 2020) <https://opiniojuris.org/2020/08/31/symposium-saving-critical-international-legal-pedagogy-from-formalists-reactionaries-and-pandemics/> accessed 23 December 2022.
48. Luis Eslava, 'The Teaching of (Another) International Law: Critical Realism and the Question of Agency and Structure', 54 The Law Teacher 2020, 368.
49. See Christian Tomuschat, 'The (Hegemonic?) Role of the English Language', 86 Nordic Journal of International Law 2017, 196; eg in the context of the manifestation and perpetuation of Eurocentric international law's dominance and inequality, Anthea Roberts rightly

argues that 'the common tongue for international education, international conferences, international publications, international meetings, and international dispute resolution' remains English language. Anthea Roberts, *Is International Law International?* (OUP 2017), 3.

The distributional consequences of using the English language are skewed in favour of the speakers and as such deepens a form of Eurocentrism to the detriment of Asian, Latin American, and African non-English native scholars. See generally Alonso Gurmendi and Paula Baldini Miranda da Cruz, 'Writing in International Law and Cultural Barriers' (*OpinioJuris*, 7 August 2020) <http://opiniojuris.org/2020/08/07/writing-in-international-law-and-cultural-barriers-part-i/ accessed 23 December 2022; and Justina Uruburu, 'Between Elitist Conversations and Local Clusters: How Should we Address English-centrism in International Law?' (*OpinioJuris*, 2 November 2020) <http://opiniojuris.org/2020/11/02/between-elitist-conversations-and-local-clusters-how-should-we-address-english-centrism-in-international-law accessed 23 December 2022.

50. As Michelle Burgis-Kasthala and Christine Schwobel-Patel note:

> Syllabi across the Global North and the Global South typically begin with a history section—Grotius as the 'father' of international law and the Treaty of Westphalia in 1648 as the starting point of (European) international law. Teaching outlines then move to the structure of international law, with a teacher's main question seeming to centre on the decision of whether to begin with subjects (such as states, international organisations and individuals) or sources (especially through treaty and customary international law). After such introductory topics, often there will be a few teaching sessions dedicated to the substance and institutions of international law, with international human rights law, aspects of international criminal law and the law of armed conflict all making brief appearances.
>
> Across the board, syllabi tend to follow the structure of the most popular text- books ...

Michelle Burgis-Kasthala and Christine Schwobel-Patel, 'Against Coloniality in the International Law Curriculum: Examining Decoloniality', The Law Teacher 2022, 1, 6.

51. Shahabuddin, 'Personal Reflections' (n 42). Also see, Bhupinder S Chimni, 'Teaching, Research and Promotion of International Law in India: Past, Present and Future', 5 Singapore Journal of International and Comparative Law 2001, 368.
52. Symposium: Teaching and Researching International Law—Global Perspectives (*Afronomicslaw*, 13 September 2020) <https://www.afronomicslaw.org/index.php/2020/09/13/symposium-teaching-and-researching-international-law-global-perspectives accessed 20 April 2021.
53. Luis Eslava, 'The Teaching of (Another) International Law: Critical Realism and the Question of Agency and Structure', 45 The Law Teacher 2020, 368 (making the case that adopting a critical realist approach for the teaching of international law can help teachers create a more emancipatory learning experience for their students in order to face this crucial task).
54. Julia Emtseva, 'Practicing Reflexivity in International Law: Running a Never- Ending Race to Catch Up with the Western International Lawyers' (Max Planck Institute for Comparative Public Law & International Law (MPIL) Research Paper No 2021-11, 30 April 2021) <https://papers.ssrn.com/sol3/papers.cfm?abstract_id=3837283 accessed 23 December 2022; James Thuo Gathii, 'Grotius Lecture: The Promise of International Law: A Third World View' (ASIL 114th Annual Meeting, Virtual, 25 June 2020) <https://www.asil.org/events/2020-grotius-lecture-promise-international-law-third-world-view accessed 23 December 2022.

For a model of the work of re-thinking the teaching and researching of international law from below, see Antony Anghie and J R Robert G Real, 'Teaching and Researching International Law in Asia (TRILA) Project' (National University of Singapore, 2020 Report of the Centre for International Law).

55. Tran Viet Dung, 'Teaching and Researching International Law in Vietnam: An Assessment Based on Ho Chi Minh City University of Law's Experience' (*Afronomicslaw Blog*, 15 September 2020) <https://www.afronomicslaw.org/2020/09/15/teaching-and-researching-international-law-in-vietnam-an-assessment-based-on-ho-chi-minh-city-university-of-laws-experience/ accessed 23 December 2022:

'Lack of qualified resources for teaching international law is probably one of the biggest threats for our faculty and other law schools in Vietnam. We are trying to attract qualified lecturers by engaging more in international research and exchange projects.'

See also Rohini Sen, 'Teaching International Law in Asia: The Predicated Pedagogue' (*Afronomicslaw Blog*, 24 September 2020) <https://www.afronomicslaw.org/2020/09/24/teaching-international-law-in-asia-the-predicated-pedagogue/ accessed 23 December 2022.

56. National University of Singapore's Centre for International Law on 'Teaching and Researching International Law in Asia' <https://cil.nus.edu.sg/trila/ accessed 23 December 2022. The report was the basis of an online Symposium between Afronomicslaw and the National University of Singapore's Centre for International Law in September 2020. The contributions to the Symposium reflect the attitude of the emerging generation of international law teachers, particularly in Asia, Africa, the Caribbean, and Latin America to teach international law in a non-Eurocentric and critical manner that foregrounds the reality of the social, political, economic, and cultural experiences of their regions and nations.

The Symposium by 'Afronomicslaw and NUS Centre for International Law bring together junior and senior scholars and researchers from across the world to critically and comparatively reflect on important issues that we, as academics, face daily, such as teaching approaches and the challenges and opportunities the teaching of international law that technology presents. This rich set of essays also helpfully reflect on ways that we could consider collectively reassessing the international law canon currently centered on the experiences of the Global North. Needless to point out, the essays also take into account the drastic changes that the COVID-19 pandemic has necessitated both in our teaching of international law and in the remaking of institutional priorities.'

See Antony Anghie, James Thuo Gathii, Olabisi D, Akinkugbe, and Titilayo Adebola (Convenors), 'Symposium Introduction: Teaching and Researching International Law—Global Perspectives' (*Afronomcislaw Blog*, 15 September 2020) <https://www.afronomicslaw.org/2020/09/14/symposium-introduction-teaching-and-researching-international-law-global-perspectives/ accessed 23 December 2022.

57. Fabio Costa Morosini, 'International Law "in the Palm of our Hand": Reading between the Lines of Brazilian International Law Textbooks' (*Afronomicslaw Blog*, 12 May 2021) <https://www.afronomicslaw.org/category/analysis/research-symposium-international-law-palm-our-hand-reading-between-lines accessed 23 December 2022.

58. See Amaya Alvez Marin, Laura Betancur Restrepo, Enrique Alberto Prieto-Rios, Daniel Rivas-Ramirez, and Fabia Veçoso, 'Rethinking International Law Education in Latin America' (*Afronomicslaw Blog*, 17 September 2020) <https://www.afronomicslaw.org/2020/09/17/rethinking-international-law-education-in-latin-america/ accessed 23 December 2022.

59. In Colombia, one of the countries they focused on, they 'concluded that international legal education at the undergraduate level, in Bogota's universities, is characterized by a Anglo-Eurocentric bias. This bias creates silences of knowledge (epistemologies of ignorance), preventing students from having a situated and broader understanding of international law. The main silences are related to the absence of historical explorations of international law and a critical understanding of the dynamic relationship between international law and local scenarios.' ibid.
60. See generally Florence Shako, 'Decolonizing the Classroom: Towards Dismantling the Legacies of Colonialism & Incorporating TWAIL into the Teaching of International Law in Kenya, 3(1) Journal of Conflict Management and Sustainable Development 2019, 17–26; Babatunde Fagbayibo, 'A Critical Approach to International Legal Education in Africa: Some Pivotal Considerations', 12 TWAILR: Reflections 2019; Michelle Burgis-Kasthala and Christine Schwobel-Patel, 'Against Coloniality in the International Law Curriculum: Examining Decoloniality', The Law Teacher 2022, 1–22.
61. Al Attar, 'Pedagogy' (n 3) 198.
62. Babatunde Fagbayibo, 'The Future of international Legal Scholarship in Africa: The Trilogy of Agency, Interdisciplinarity and Functionality', 40 TWAILR: Reflections 2021 <https://twailr.com/wp-content/uploads/2021/11/20211101-Fagbayibo-Agency-Interdisciplinarity-Functionality.pdf accessed 23 December 2022; Babatunde Fagabyibo, 'Critical Pedagogy Symposium: "Thus Saith the Euro-America Validation Cathedral"—The Task of Challenging and Changing the Narrative of Eurocentric International Law in Africa' (*OpinioJuris*, 31 August 2020) <http://opiniojuris.org/2020/08/31/critical-pedagogy-symposium-thus-saith-the-euro-america-validation-cathedral-the-task-of-challenging-and-changing-the-narrative-of-eurocentric-international-law-in-africa/ accessed 23 December 2022. See also Florence Shako, 'Teaching and Researching International Law—A Kenyan Perspective' (*Afronomicslaw Blog*, 1 October 2020) <https://www.afronomicslaw.org/2020/10/01/teaching-and-researching-international-law-a-kenyan-perspective/ accessed 23 December 2022; Arnold Nciko Wa Nciko, 'The Hutians—Decolonising the Teaching of Public International Law in African Law School to Address a Real Problem' (*Afronomicslaw Blog*, 17 September 2020) <https://www.afronomicslaw.org/2020/09/17/the-hutians-decolonising-the-teaching-of-public-international-law-in-african-law-schools-to-address-a-real-problem/ accessed 23 December 2022; Suzzie Onyeka Oyakhire, 'Teaching IEL as a Nigerian Teacher in the Era of Decolonisation' (International Economic Law Collective Symposium II, *University of Bristol Law School Blog*, 27 March 2020) <https://legalresearch.blogs.bris.ac.uk/2020/03/teaching-iel-as-a-nigerian-teacher-in-the-era-of-decolonisation/ accessed 23 December 2022.

    An important recent contribution that foregrounds African perspectives on international law and which is published via open access by the Pretoria University Law Press (PULP) is Frans Viljoen, Humphery Sipalla, and Foluso Adegalu, Exploring African Approaches to International Law: Essays in Honour of Kéba Mbaye (PULP 2022).
63. See 'African Union Commission on International Law' <https://au.int/en/aucil/about accessed 16 October 2021.
64. Thanks to Anne van Aaken who pointed out that the same problem characterizes the teaching of international law in Eastern Europe.
65. See generally Anthea Roberts, Is International Law International? (OUP 2017). Also, in this regard, Al Attar has argued that, as much as TWAIL has done a great job in

confronting Eurocentrism in international law through research, it has forgotten that it also has a teaching mission. Al Attar, 'Pedagogy' (n 3) 189.

The authors acknowledge that the inspiration for use of 'theatre' derives from Professor Obiora C Okafor's Guest Lecture titled 'Africa as a "Theatre" of International Law and Development Knowledge, Practice and Resistance'" at the Afronomicslaw.org Academic Forum, 7 August 2022. See https://www.afronomicslaw.org/category/academic-forum/afronomicslaworg-academic-forum-guest-lecture-series-africa-theatre accessed 1 May 2023.

66. Abebe et al, 'Social Science Approach' (n 27); Gathii, 'Studying Race' (n 27).
67. On international human rights law and Africa as human rights norm entrepreneur, see generally Obiora C Okafor, The African Human Rights System, Activist Forces and International Institutions (CUP 2007).
68. The chapter returns to examples of existing and developing open access publications in the Global South in its concluding section.
69. Tiyanjana Maluwa, 'Reassessing Aspects of the Contribution of African States to the Development of International Law Through African Regional Multilateral Treaties', 41 Michigan Journal of International Law 2020, 327 (arguing that in the scheme of modern international law, African states have contributed to the actual practice of international law by highlighting specific examples of their contributions to international legal norms through multilateral treatymaking). See also, generally, Antony Anghie, Bhupinder S Chimni, Karin Mickelson, and Obiora Chinedu Okafor, *The Third World and International Order: Law, Politics, and Globalization* (Martinus Nijhoff 2003).
70. Olabisi D Akinkugbe and Adebayo Majekolagbe, 'The African Court of Human and Peoples' Rights Decision in the Ogiek Case: An Appraisal' in Amissi M Manirabona and Yenny Vega Cardenas (eds), *Extractive Industries and Human Rights in an Era of Global Justice: New Ways of Resolving and Preventing Conflicts* (LexisNexis 2019) 163 <https://ssrn.com/abstract=3307170 accessed 23 December 2022.
71. Anne-Charlotte Martineau, 'Overcoming Eurocentrism? Global History and the Oxford Handbook of the History of International Law', 25 European Journal of International Law 2014, 329;
72. Gathii, 'Promise of International Law' (n 22).
73. Gathii has shared a comprehensive bibliography of about 48 pages covering most, if not all, the TWAIL scholarship between 1996 and 2020. The bibliography covers dozens of journal articles, books, book chapters, book reviews, PhD dissertations, and blog posts; mostly in English and French, with a couple in Spanish. Gathii, 'Promise of International Law' (n 22) (including a TWAIL Bibliography 1996–2019 as an Appendix). See also Gathii, 'TWAIL History' (n 31) 26.
74. See generally Henry Onoria, 'The African Commission on Human and Peoples' Rights and the Exhaustion of Local Remedies under the African Charter', 3 African Human Rights law Journal 2003, 1–24.
75. This inaugural edition of the publication features landmark decisions of the African Court delivered during the year 2019, and from these decisions can be discerned the centrality of the Court in human rights dispute resolutions on the continent. The judgments deal with a wide range of human rights issues shaping the socio-economic and political landscape of the continent, including issues of access to the Court, its jurisdiction and the admissibility of cases before it; fair trial rights, especially the right to be tried by an impartial tribunal;

freedom of movement; right to liberty; right to life and compatibility of mandatory death penalty; legal personality and the right to nationality; the right to participate in government, and related citizenship rights; the right to reparation, including the concept of loss of future opportunities.

See Inter-American Court of Human Rights, *Joint Law Report 2019: African Court on Human and Peoples' Rights, European Court of Human Rights and Inter-American Court of Human Rights / Inter-American Court of Human Rights, African Court on Human and Peoples' Rights and European Court on Human Rights* (San José, 2020) <https://www.echr.coe.int/Documents/Joint_Report_2019_AfCHPR_ECHR_IACHR_ENG.pdf> accessed 23 December 2022. For the 2020 Joint Law Report, see <https://echr.coe.int/Documents/Joint_Report_2020_AfCHPR_ECHR_IACHR_ENG.pdf> accessed 23 December 2022.

76. See generally Ekhator Eghosa, 'Multinational Corporations, Accountability and Environmental Justice: The Move Towards Sub-Regional Litigation in Africa', 12(02) German Journal of Comparative Law 2022, 118–130; Salvatore Caserta and Mikael Rask Madsen, 'The Caribbean Court of Justice: A Regional Integration and Postcolonial Court' in Karen J Alter and Laurence R Helfer (eds), *International Court Authority* (OUP 2018; online edn, Oxford Academic, 20 September 2018); see Alexandra Huneeus, 'Courts Resisting Courts: Lessons from the Inter-American Court's Struggle to Enforce Human Rights', 44 Cornell International Law Journal 2011, 493, 505; Obiora Okafor, Udoka Owie, Okechukwu Effoduh, and Rahina Zarma, 'On the Modest Impact of West Africa's International Human Rights Court on the Executive Branch of Government in Nigeria', 35 Harvard Human Rights Journal 2022, 169.
77. Professor Obiora C Okafor was the Independent Expert on International Solidarity <https://www.ohchr.org/en/issues/solidarity/pages/obioraokafor.aspx> accessed 7 July 2024.
78. Professor Tendayi Achiume was the Special Rapporteur on Contemporary Forms of Racism, Racial Discrimination, Xenophobia, and Related Tolerance <https://www.ohchr.org/EN/Issues/Racism/SRRacism/Pages/CurrentMandateHolder.aspx> accessed 7 July 2024.
79. Professor Michael Fakhri is the Special Rapporteur on Right to Food <https://www.ohchr.org/EN/Issues/Food/Pages/Michael_Fakhri.aspx> accessed 23 December 2022.
80. Professor Balakrishnan Rajagopal is the Special Rapporteur on Adequate Housing <https://www.ohchr.org/EN/Issues/Housing/Pages/BalakrishnanRajagopal.aspx> accessed 23 December 2022.
81. In connection with the American Society of International Law (ASIL), while Antony Anghie, Makau Mutua, and James T. Gathii have all served on the Executive Council, James Gathii was an Executive Vice President and member of the AJIL Board, while Balakrishnan Rajagopal is a Counsellor.
82. Olabisi D Akinkugbe is Editor of the International Decisions section of AJIL, and also serves on the ASIL Executive Council, the AJIL Board, the Canadian Council of International Law, the International Law Association, Canada Branch, and the Society of International Economic Law.
83. Makane Mbengue serves as a Vice-President of the International Academy of Comparative Law and a Member of Council of the French Society of International Law.
84. The African Society of International Law is 'a network of practitioners, scholars, technocrats and students engaging with international law as practiced, implemented, and forged in Africa. The African Society seeks in particular to [among others] amplify the

voice of African states and Africans in international law [and] foster inquiry, exchange of ideas and innovation in international law as it is developed and implemented in Africa.' See <https://www.afsilsadi.org> accessed 23 December 2022; the mission of the African Association of International Law is to 'foster the development and dissemination of African perspectives and practices of international law, in particular through the publication of an African Yearbook of International Law'. <https://aail-aadi.org> accessed 23 December 2022; the African Arbitration Association declares that its 'role is to support the continuing development of international arbitration in Africa and to improve and recognise the international prominence of its members and their activities in international arbitration and international dispute resolution'. See <https://afaa.ngo> accessed 23 December 2022.

85. See generally Third World Approaches to International Law Review (TWAILR) <https://twailr.com> accessed 23 December 2022.

86. Usha Natarajan, Laura Betancur-Restrepo, Amar Bhatia, John Reynolds, Ntina Tzouvala, and Sujith Xavier, 'Third World Approaches to International Law Review: A Journal for a Community', 1 TWAIL Review 2020, 9.

87. See Afronomicslaw <https://www.afronomicslaw.org/about> accessed 16 October 2021. Afronomicslaw.org also has an Academic Forum that is led by Dr Ohio Omiunu.

The Afronomicslaw Academic Forum is founded upon the realization that international (economic) law is usually taught and researched within the Western and/or Anglo-American categories of thought. The core business of the Academic Forum is to give undergraduate students, graduate students, and early career researchers from across the world the critical skills to help them strike a proper balance between international (economic) law and the lived experiences of Third World peoples. To do this, the students develop a list of international topics they intend to cover each year and reach out to critical scholars who will take them through these topics twice a month.

88. ibid. See also James Gathii and Olabisi Akinkugbe, 'Introduction to the Inaugural Issue of the African Journal of International Economic Law', 1 African Journal of International Economic Law 2020, 5.

89. See African Yearbook of International Law <https://brill.com/view/journals/afyo/afyo-overview.xml?language=en> accessed 23 December 2022; African Human Rights Yearbook <https://www.chr.up.ac.za/african-human-rights-yearbook-ahry> accessed 23 December 2022; Asian Journal of International Law <https://www.cambridge.org/core/journals/asian-journal-of-international-law> accessed 23 December 2022; Latin American Journal of International Trade & Policy; Brazilian Journal of International Law.

90. In terms of BITs, the Morocco-Nigeria BIT offers innovative provisions that foreground sustainable development among others.

91. Makane Moïse Mbengue and Stefanie Schacherer, 'Africa as an Investment Rule-Maker: Decrypting the Pan-African Investment Code', 23 Africa Yearbook of International Law 2018, 81.

92. See generally Hamed El-Kady and Mustaqeem De Gama, 'The Reform of the International Investment Regime: An African Perspective', 34 ICSID Review – Foreign Investment Law Journal 2019, 482 (hereafter El-Kady and De Gama, 'The Reform of the International Investment Regime'); Olabisi D Akinkugbe, 'Africanization and the Reform of International Investment Law', 53 Case Western Reserve Journal of International Law 2021, 7. As Fatsah Ouguergouz notes:

For a long time confined to a passive attitude of accepting the rules laid down by the countries of origin of investments, African States have gradually become aware of the need to draw up rules reflecting a balance between, on the one hand, the protection of foreign investments and, on the other, the protection of their fundamental interests in terms of economic development, respect for the environment, protection of human rights, the fight against corruption and the settlement of disputes.

Fatsah Ouguergouz, 'African State and investment Law and Arbitration—Challenges and Opportunities: An Introduction', 23 African Yearbook International Law 2018, 4; see also Mathias G Sahinkuye, 'The Contribution of the African Institute of International Law to the Promotion of Commercial and Investment Arbitration in Africa', 23 African Yearbook International Law 2018, 207.

93. El-Kady and De Gama, 'The Reform of the International Investment Regime' (n 92) 2.
94. ibid, 4.
95. Makane Moïse Mbengue, 'Special Issue: Africa and the Reform of the International Investment Regime', 18 Journal of World Investment & Trade 2017, 371, 376.

PART 2

INTELLECTUAL TRADITIONS OF INTERNATIONAL LAW IN EUROPE

CHAPTER 12

INTERNATIONAL LEGAL POSITIVISM AND THE EUROPEAN QUEST FOR SCIENTIFICITY

JEAN D'ASPREMONT

1. Introduction

It was in the 19th century that references to international legal positivism started to appear in the English- and French-speaking international legal literature, probably reaching a peak shortly before World War I. Or, to put it another way, it was around the end of the 19th century and at the beginning of the 20th century that international lawyers, notwithstanding some occasional dissent,[1] grew inclined to represent their discipline as abiding by a positivist paradigm.[2] It is fair to say that international legal positivism became international law's dominant self-representation in the decades leading up to World War I.[3]

Unsurprisingly, what international lawyers meant by describing their discipline in a positivist fashion was very diverse and sometimes proved highly cacophonic. Whilst there was no consensus as to what the espousal of a positivist paradigm entailed, those 19th-century and early 20th-century descriptions of international law as a positivist discipline were almost all premised on the idea that the positivist tradition of international law had been inherited from those then considered to be international law's forbears, namely Zouche, Bynkershoek, Vattel, etc. This genealogical justification of the positivist attributes of the discipline is noteworthy, because those forebears never actually referred to 'legal positivism' to describe their own theorization of international law, let alone to defend a displacement of natural law by positive law.[4]

Whatever the genealogy of the dominant positivist representation of international law, it is now commonly claimed that international lawyers' attachment to a positivist representation of international law lost its lustre after World War I, Lauterpacht and Brierly often being read as spearheading a revolution against the positivist tradition of international law which they deem to manifest a bygone 19th-century take on international law.[5] Although this historical narrative about the decline of the positivist representation of the international legal discipline has been contested in recent decades,[6] an evaluation of its merits is outwith the scope of this chapter. In the context of this volume, it is more relevant to stress that Europeans—at least those Europeans who wrote in the dominant vernaculars of the discipline, namely the English and French—are those who universalized the representation of international law as a discipline articulated around a positivist paradigm. Even if such representation was quickly embraced and appropriated outside Europe,[7] it is mainly in 19th- and 20th-century European scholarship that international law was first represented as a positivist discipline, such a representation quickly becoming the dominant representation of international law beyond Europe.

Affirming the European pedigree of the positivist representation of international law is of course not a controversial claim to make. In fact, as will be recalled in Section 2, international law being a discipline that, to a large extent, was consolidated in Europe—that is, in European books and academic periodicals, in European institutions, in European voices—it is no coincidence that it can be assumed that it is mainly in Europe that international law came to be represented as following a positivist paradigm. Although it is important to stress again that jurists from semi-peripheral polities appropriated and also contributed to such positivist representation of international law,[8] this chapter does not deem it very relevant to further explore this question of pedigree. After all, the origin of any representation is always caught in that representation itself, thereby making the origin of a representation derived from (and secondary to) that representation itself.[9] Hence, this chapter takes the liberty to leave unquestioned the simplistic premise that the consolidation of a positivist representation of international law took place in Europe before World War I, and zeroes in on the question of *why* these European architects of the international legal discipline sought to shroud the latter with a positivist veil.

This chapter makes the claim that, although the embrace of a scientific project for international law did not systematically translate itself with a representation of international law as a positivist discipline,[10] international legal positivism was most of the time invoked to vindicate the idea of *an international legal science*. In that sense, it is argued that the European portrayal of international law as a positivist discipline mainly boiled down to a project of endowing international law with scientificity, that is, a project to elevate international law into *a discipline grounded in the real and geared towards the real*. It simultaneously shows that, although Europeans themselves later came to contest their earlier project of scientification of international law and even though that project eventually collapsed, the scientistic[11] ambitions that accompanied the positivist representation of international law have proved resilient and still bear important marks on international legal thought and practice today.

This chapter is structured as follows. After a few observations on the professional context in which the project for a scientifization of international law emerged in Europe under the banner of international legal positivism (Section 2), the chapter elaborates on the rise of the European attempt to turn international law into a scientific discipline (Section 3). It subsequently offers a snapshot of the European contestation and subsequent collapse of that European scientistic project which, it will be argued, did not bring an end to the articulation of international law as a discipline grounded in the real and geared towards discoursing the real (Section 4). The chapter ends with a few concluding remarks (Section 5).

2. The Professionalization of International Law in Europe

The rise of a positivist representation of the international legal discipline took place against the backdrop of a professionalization of international law, which is a phenomenon that materialized primarily in Europe in the 19th century. Professionalization refers here to the consolidation of a distinguishable community of mutually recognized professionals devoting their work almost exclusively to international law, the emergence of a distinctly identifiable category of lawyers who engage in the practice of international law as judges, counsel, advisors, or otherwise, the development of specific institutions whose functions are the study, development, or application of international law, the growth of research exclusively focused on international law, and the systematic publication of the results of that research, the inclusion of international law as a self-standing subject in the curriculum of higher education law degrees, etc, a great deal of which first appeared in Europe.

The professionalization of international law can be specifically construed as a product of the second half of the 19th century. Until then, international law—although it was undoubtedly already part of the diplomatic discourse and had been promoted by prominent European statesmen[12]—had been seen as a rather marginal scholarly activity devoted to what some considered a second-order class of law. It was mainly in the second half of the 19th century that international law was turned into a self-standing object of study and practice to which learned societies and scholarly periodicals were devoted.[13] For instance, in Europe,[14] the second half of the 19th century witnessed the development of European publications entirely dedicated to international law and run from Europe. Mention can be made in this respect of the founding of the *Revue Générale de Droit International et de Legislation Comparée* and later the *Revue Générale de Droit International Public* in 1894. The institutionalization of the field came with the creation of the *Institut de Droit international* in 1873. The creation, in Europe, of university professorships specifically dedicated to the teaching of international law also dates back to that time.[15] It has even been claimed that some of these professorships were established as a result of international lawyers' diabolic collaboration with the European colonial project,[16] thereby confirming that, in Europe, the professionalization of international law went hand-in-hand with colonialism.[17]

The foregoing shows that the rise of a representation of international law as a positivist discipline was spearheaded by international lawyers evolving in an increasingly professionalized environment. It was thus at the time of the professionalization of international law in Europe, as it has been understood here, that international legal positivism turned into the dominant representation of the discipline. An elucidation of the precise causality between the professionalization of international law and its positivist representation is outwith the scope of this chapter, for any such finding would inevitably be very precarious.[18] Yet, it is difficult to ignore the idea that the professionalization of international law and the representation of the latter as a positivist discipline entertained some kind of mutual causal relationship. In fact, as is explained in the next section, the professionalization of international law also involved elevating international law into a scientific discipline, that is, one grounded in the real and geared towards the real, with professionalization and scientifization inevitably converging and supporting one another.[19]

3. International Legal Positivism as a Quest for Scientificity

As was noted in the previous section, the professionalization of international law at the end of the 19th and beginning of the 20th century corresponds with the rise of a positivist representation of international law, especially in Europe. This section elaborates on what (European) international lawyers may have meant when they began to represent international law as a positivist discipline. As was also noted, it should be no surprise that what such positivist representation of international law actually entails is rather diverse.[20] Indeed, international legal positivism, back then, came to be associated with a wide range of claims, including the exclusive study of positive law and the displacement of natural law,[21] State-centrism,[22] consensualism, and voluntarism,[23] or even a certain type of economic theory.[24] The representation of the international legal discipline as abiding by a positivist paradigm also included the favouring of a certain type of lawyer's profile in the profession, namely that of the 'technical' international lawyer to the detriment of the idealist international lawyer.[25] Yet, notwithstanding these many claims associated with a positivist representation of international law, it is argued here that international legal positivism primarily functioned as a reference to the scientific character of the international legal discipline. This section starts by substantiating this argument (Section 3.1) before showing how the project of scientifization of international law survived the fall of the positivist representation of international law witnessed in the literature in the wake of World War I (Section 3.2).

3.1 International legal positivism as scientificity: the primacy of the real

It is submitted here that the European positivist representation of international law was geared towards the elevation of international law into a scientific discipline,[26] one that allegedly draws on the scientific positivism of Auguste Comte.[27] This is not a controversial claim given how much these two popular portrayals of international law, namely international law as a positivist discipline and international law as a scientific discipline, were often presented simultaneously in the international legal literature.[28]

Needless to say, the association of the idea of the science of international law with the representation of international law as a positivist discipline remains very polysemic as it can refer to many different meanings. For instance, the idea of legal science can convey an image of scholarship as being rooted in rigorous and systematic methods of investigation which only professionals can possibly master. The reference to the science of international law can also refer to the use of a set of objective methods of inquiry of an inductive nature, meant to acquire proper knowledge of international law.[29] In terms of this chapter, a more generic understanding of the scientificity of international law—and thus of the association of the latter with international legal positivism—is adopted. The elevation of international law into a scientific discipline, and thus its positivist character, are specifically understood here as referring to the necessity to articulate international law around *the real*.[30] This means that international law is both grounded in the real and deployed or invoked to intervene in the real. In a positivist—and thus scientific—discipline like international law, a statement can hardly amount to a truth-claim if, in one way or another, it is not grounded in the real.

In a broad epistemological context, that international law has sought to represent itself, under the banner of positivism, as a discipline about the real should come as no surprise. In fact, in the 19th and 20th centuries, many existing disciplines came to revamp their methods and self-representation with a view to securing the venerated status of discipline about the real.[31] This quest for the venerated status of discipline about the real finds its roots in 18th-century discursive hierarchies that came to dominate the 18th and 19th centuries and whereby the real trumps the narrative, the factual eclipses the literary, and the physical overwrites the metaphysical.[32] As a result, disciplines that produce necessities through realities and facts have enjoyed primacy over those that do not, the latter being marred with suspicion.[33] In the context of the irresistible[34] primacy of disciplines about the real, it is possible to explain why international lawyers became so keen to tap into the discursive hierarchy and came to embrace the self-representation that foregrounds the real both as a foundation and a goal of international law. In that same context, it is no surprise either that, as has been reported, international lawyers at the Hague Peace conferences were called the 'scientific delegates'.[35]

An important nuance is in order. Although international legal positivism became, in the late 19th- and early 20th-century European international legal literature, a shorthand for scientificity, it must be acknowledged that the claim that international law is grounded in the real predated claims that international law is a scientific discipline, let alone that international law is a positivist discipline. In fact, it was in the 18th century that the primacy of the real was elevated into one of international law's most central discursive necessities. Although the necessity to ground international law in the real was not unheard of in pre-classical international legal thought,[36] it was classical international legal thought—and especially the work of Vattel and Martens—that offered the first systematization of such discursive necessity.[37] For those classical international legal thinkers, the real meant the will of States. The primacy of the real, understood as the will of States, gained further currency in the first major treatises of the 19th century,[38] and it was in the following decades that it became one of the most central discursive necessities in international legal thought.[39] It is such primacy of the real that European international legal authors of the 19th and 20th centuries, discussed in this section, tried to capture under the banner of international legal positivism.

3.2 Scientificity short of international legal positivism

It is well known that the positivist representation of international law started to falter in the wake of World War I, a move that consolidated itself throughout the 20th century.[40] Nowadays, few contemporary international lawyers would still describe themselves as international legal positivists.[41] And the few international lawyers that venture to claim some affinity with legal positivism would resort to a wide range of sophisticated nuances and caveats while vindicating a soft or rejuvenated version of this 'school of thought'.[42]

What matters in the context of this chapter is that the demise of the positivist representation of international law, albeit a shorthand for the scientificity in 19th- and early 20th-century literature, did not bring an end to scientistic representation of international law as articulated around the real. Indeed, the primacy of the real continued to dominate in the 20th century and still governs international legal thought and practice today. Although the 20th century upheld the primacy of the real in international law, the way in which the real was understood then underwent significant developments and ceased to be reduced to the will of States as it was in classical international legal thought. In fact, 20th-century international law took issue with the idea that the basis of international law is provided by the will of States.[43] Rather, it reinvented its understanding of the real in which international law ought to be grounded, ceased to reduce it to the will of States, and came to include the words and deeds of a greater variety of actors in understanding the real.[44] It is this expanded and renewed notion of the real that 20th-century international lawyers came to generalize as the idea of *practice* which any international legal claim or argument is now expected to respond to or draw on.

Interestingly, in the 20th century, the primacy of the real—now called 'practice'—was also extended to modes of study of international law and it was made almost a scholarly necessity, a phenomenon that took place especially in the US. For instance, in the 1950s and in the 1960s, the so-called New Haven School can be read as an attempt to ensure that the study of international law was better grounded in the real.[45] Studies on the legitimacy of international law witnessed in the 1990s[46] similarly sought to finetune the focus of international legal studies on the real with a view to better understanding compliance dynamics.[47]

4. The Fall of the Quest for Scientificity

This section briefly depicts how the project of scientifization of international law unravelled in the 20th century, including under the assault of European scholars themselves, thereby showing the demise of what positivist representations of international law had been associated with. It first sheds light on the contestation of the scientistic portrayal of international law (Section 4.1) and then sketches out how the primacy of the real came to be similarly questioned shortly afterwards (Section 4.2). The last subsection will argue that the primacy of the real with which the positivist representation of international law had first been associated is undergoing a revival in most recent international legal thought, this time primarily outside Europe (Section 4.3).

4.1 The primacy of the real short of scientificity

Starting in the second half of the 20th century, the scientifization of international law has come to be subject to intense criticism over recent decades.[48] For instance, the very claim that international legal scholarship constitutes a science was itself discredited in the second half of the 20th century.[49] It has similarly been argued that scientifization brought about other forms of politics.[50] Even the idea of science came to be perceived to be at loggerheads with the dominant pragmatist spirit—embodied by some famous British scholars who claim to favour a practical approach to international law[51]—that came to dominate international legal thought in the second half of the 20th century.[52] The result has been an unravelling of the scientifization of international law.

When did the project of an international legal science collapse under the weight of the abovementioned contestation? There is little agreement on the answer to that.[53] Tracing its demise is probably of little importance. What matters more is that the fall of scientificity as a central feature of international law's self-representation did not do away with the primacy of the real. In other words, although the representation of international law as a scientific discipline faltered, international law has continued, until this day, to foreground its engagement with the real, be it in terms of its origin or of its goals. What the earlier positivist representation of international law pointed to was, once more, salvaged.

4.2 Contemporary contestations of the primacy of the real in Europe and elsewhere

It is important to acknowledge that the primacy of the real—which informed the association of international law with a positivist paradigm and its scientistic ambitions—has not thrived entirely unchallenged in the humanities in the last century. Although some mild contestations were heard as early as the 19th century,[54] it is the 20th century that witnessed the most unprecedented challenges to the primacy of disciplines about the real. For instance, it has been said that disciplines about the real always pre-constitute the real they help give meaning to and always secure confirmations of their claims by virtue of facts which they have themselves created.[55] In the same vein, it has been contended that disciplines about the real do not do away with the metaphysical and the fabulous[56] and fail to meet their own standard of truth.[57] It has even been alleged that disciplines about the real do not allow thinking.[58] And yet, the most severe challenge to the primacy of disciplines about the real probably came in the form of a repudiation of the distinction between disciplines deemed to be about the real and other disciplines.[59] In particular, it has been found that disciplines about the real are as vulnerable and self-referential as other disciplines[60] and that what defines a discipline about the real is not its object or its content but the primacy that is socially awarded to it.[61]

Until recently, international lawyers remained impervious to the abovementioned contestations of the primacy of disciplines about the real and accordingly continued to further international law's engagement with the real. However, in the last two decades, a very rich body of scholarship[62] that questions international law's grounding in the real—and all the universal patterns of arguments that are derived from it—came to be produced by a number of international legal scholars that had been exposed to structuralist and post-structuralist theory[63] as well as findings already made in the 1970s and early 1980s in literary and linguistic studies.[64] These scholars shed light particularly on the constant mediation between the real that is perceived (concreteness) and the real that is wanted (normativity) in the process of delivery of meaning by forms.[65] Such works were later continued and supplemented by an examination of the structural biases, institutional strategies, and special ethos that inform international law's engagement with the real.[66] Others, taking their cue from, for instance, works in literary theory, linguistics, moral theory, and critical sociology,[67] came to acknowledge that the real in which they ground international law does not reveal itself to them, but is always mediated and constructed through a wide range of mental, social, and cultural pre-discursive categories and intelligibility frameworks, which are themselves part of an ideological system of representation.[68] Since then, sophisticated examinations of the ways in which the real is constructed, cognized, captured, and perceived have started to populate the international legal literature.[69] So the end of the 20th century witnessed a serious contestation of the primacy of the real that had dominated international law till then, leaving nothing of the positivist and scientistic representations of international law, and thus of the primacy of the real, that had populated international legal thought at the beginning of the century at the initiative of European international lawyers.

4.3 The reactionary revival of the primacy of the real outside Europe

The abovementioned late 20th-century critical contestation of the articulation of international law around the real spawned, in the 21st century, a strong reactionary reaffirmation of the primacy of the real in methodological[70] or conceptual terms.[71] Severely contested by critical scholarship, the primacy of the real in international law has been reinvigorated in the last decade, especially outside Europe. Indeed, the challenges to the primacy of the real in recent decades that were depicted in the previous section provoked a series of counter-reactions meant to reaffirm the need for studies of international law to be grounded in the real. Mention can be made here of the promotion of a new legal realism in international law,[72] or the vindication, under the banner of a 'new empirical turn', of a more organized and systematized use of empirical data to study the practical conditions under which international law is formed and has effect.[73] In studies of the history of international law, a whole range of scholars, often teaming up with historians interested in international law, similarly came to advocate a return to scientific methods to apprehend the reality of the past of international legal thought and practice.[74] Such reactions indicate that, notwithstanding some serious contestations, the primacy of the real has continued to enjoy some substantial support, thereby perpetuating the central tenet of what was first a primarily European project for the scientifization of the discipline.

5. Concluding Remarks: Legal Positivism, Scientificity, and the Style of Legal Writing

The story told in this chapter is about how, in the 19th and early 20th centuries, international law came to be described mostly by Europeans[75] as a positivist discipline by which they referred to a certain idea of scientificity before references to positivism and scientificity were abandoned altogether in the course of the 20th century. And yet, the legacy of such European representation of the discipline seems to have lingered in the form of a resilient attachment to the primacy of the real in which international law is supposed to be grounded and articulated around.

One dramatic way in which such resilient attachment to the primacy of the real lingers—and which has not been mentioned so far—is the style of academic writing. It is submitted in this final section that international lawyers' attachment to the primacy of the real, notwithstanding the demise of positivism and scienticity discussed in this chapter, has gone as far as infiltrating their writing style and becoming the dominant genre in the international legal literature. By genre, this section means a style of writing, of constructing arguments, and of narrating stories. It is argued here that the primacy of the real, as a literary genre, nowadays manifests itself in a requirement that any claim about the law, the literature, the practice, and the world be *evidenced* through a specific type of referencing. In fact, there is hardly a piece of literature on international law that can evade this requirement. It suffices to mention here the inescapable necessity in the literature to establish the actuality, materiality, and factuality of anything one engages with in a piece of international legal literature through a well-coded system of footnotes and bibliographical references.[76] In that regard, footnoting and referencing can be viewed as a very strong manifestation of such resilient attachment to the primacy of the real. Likewise, as a genre, the primacy of the real today expresses itself through the requirement that one's claims be systematically situated and contextualized against the backdrop of the actual state of the law, of the literature, of the practice, or of the world as they have been evidenced and traced. In the end, by virtue of their continuous attachment to the primacy of the real, international lawyers writing in the English language—like those contributing a chapter to this volume—always feel the necessity to evidence the reality, actuality, and materiality of what they engage with, which in turns translates into a very specific style of writing. In that sense, the European quest for the scientificity of the discipline and its remaining offspring—that is, the primacy of the real, albeit severely and rightly contested—have remained very present in the daily practice of anyone writing about international law. Needless to say that for someone, like the author of this chapter, who feels that the dominant genre of the international legal literature is repressive and detrimental to thinking, such resilience of the attachment to the primacy of the real, even if limited to the style of writing practised in the discipline, is not a joyful state of affairs.[77] Yet, whether the translation into the dominant genre of the discipline of the remnants of the European quest for the scientificity discussed in this chapter is a good or bad thing is too serious a reflection for it to be taken on at this concluding stage. However, it is surely a question that international lawyers, as heirs of the almost defunct European quest for the scientificity of the discipline, should one day seriously confront.[78]

Notes

1. See, eg, on Max Huber's contestation of positivism, Jost Delbrück, 'Max Huber's Sociological Approach to International Law Revisited', 18 The European Journal of International Law 2007, 97–113. On the rejection of positivism by William Whewell, after whom the Chair of Public International Law at the University of Cambridge is named, see Arnaud Dewalque, 'The Reception of Positivism in Whewell, Mill and Brentano', in Ion Tanasescu, Alexandru Bejinariu, Susan Krantz Gabriel, and Constantin Stoenescu (eds), *Brentano and the Positive Philosophy of Comte and Mill* (De Gruyter 2022). See also the 19th-century criticisms of international legal positivism mentioned by Richard Collins, 'Classical Legal Positivism

in International Law Revisited', in J Kammerhofer and J d'Aspremont (eds), *International Legal Positivism in a Post-Modern World* (CUP 2014) 23–49, 30–31 (hereafter Kammerhofer and d'Aspremont, *International Legal Positivism in a Post-Modern World*).

2. See, eg, Hall, Treatise on International Law (3rd edn, Clarendon Press, 1890) 7; L Oppenheim, 'The Science of International Law: Its Task and Method', 2 American Journal of International Law 1908, 313. Another important vindication of international legal positivism is found in the work of Dionisio Anzilotti. See Dionisio Anzilotti 'Trattati generali di diritto internazionale pubblico', 1 RDI 1906, 33 and 166, reprinted in Scritti di diritto internazionale pubblico (1956–1957) 1, 243; D Anzilotti, *Anzilotti' s Corso di diritto intemazionale* (3d edn, 1928) 16. Anzilotti has been hailed as the 'prince of positivism' by Prosper Weil (see P Weil, 'Le droit international en quête de son identité', 237 Collected Course 1992, 3, 77. See also the remarks of Giorgio Gaja, Positivism and Dualism in Dionisio Anzilotti, 3 European Journal of International Law (1992) 123–138.
3. Stefan Neff speaks of the 19th century as the 'positive century'. See S Neff, *Justice Among Nations: A History of International Law* (Harvard UP 2014) 215–340 (hereafter Neff, *Justice Among Nations*).
4. Rousseau sees Moser as the forebear of international legal positivism, especially his 1752 *Eléments de la science du droit des gens*). See Ch Rousseau, *Principes Généraux du Droit International Public*, vol 1 (Pedone 1944) 37) (hereafter Rousseau, *Principes Généraux du Droit International Public*). Brierly sees Richard Zouche (1590–1660) as the forbear of the positivist paradigm in international law (see J L Brierly, *The Law of Nations. An Introduction to the International Law of Peace* (4th edn, Clarendon Press 1949) 35–36) (hereafter, Brierly, *The Law of Nations*). The description of such works as providing a positivist take on international law remains common today. See, eg, Martti Koskenniemi, 'Into Positivism: Georg Friedrich von Martens (1756–1821) and Modern International Law', 15(2) Constellations 2008, 189 (hereafter Koskenniemi, 'Into Positivism'). See also Emmanuelle Jouannet, *Emer de Vattel et l'émergence doctrinale du droit international classique* (Pedone 1998); H Muir-Watt, 'Droit naturel et souveraineté de l'Etat dans la doctrine de Vattel', 32 Archives de Philosophie du Droit 1987, 71. Stefan Neff construes these authors as forerunners of positivism rather than scholars embracing an positivist approach. See Neff, *Justice Among Nations* (n 3) 227.
5. See H Lauterpacht, 'The Grotian Tradition of International Law', 23 British Yearbook of International Law 1946, 1 (who claims that Grotius was not a positivist with a view to reclaiming Grotius as the forefather of a non-positivist tradition); H Lauterpacht, *Private Law Sources and Analogies of International Law* (Longmans 1927) 43–44; J L Brierly, 'The Basis of Obligation in International Law', in Hersch Lauterpacht and C H M Waldock (eds), *The Basis of Obligation in International Law and Other Papers by the Late James Leslie Brierly* (Clarendon Press 1958) 1–67; Brierly, *The Law of Nations* (n 4) 52–53; see also Nicolas Politis, *The New Aspect of International Law* (Carnegie Endowment for International Peace 1928) 5.
6. See David Kennedy, 'International Law and the Nineteenth Century: History of an Illusion', 65 Nordic Journal of International Law 1996, 385–420; Richard Collins, 'Classical Legal Positivism in International Law Revisited', in Kammerhofer and d'Aspremont, *International Legal Positivism in a Post-Modern World* (n 1) 23–49. Even the claim that Oppenheim was a a proponent of a strict positivism has been the subject of some debate. See Benedict Kingsbury, 'Legal Positivism as Normative Politics: International Society, Balance of Power and Lassa Oppenheim's Positive International Law', 13 European Journal of International Law 2002, 401–437.

7. See, eg, Carlos Calvo, *Le droit international théorique et pratique précédé d'un exposé historique des progrès de la science du droit des gens*, vol 1 (2nd edn, Pedone 1870) 104; Carlos Calvo, *Droit international*, vol 1 (3d edn, Pedone-Lauriel 1880) 118; Elihu Root, 'The Sanction of International Law', 2 American Journal of International Law 1908, 451–457. On James Brown Scott's embrace of positivism as the main methodological paradigm for international law, see Christopher Rossi, *Broken Chain of Being. James Brown Scott and the Origins of Modern International Law* (Brill 1998). On Elihu Root's positivism, see Anne-Marie Slaughter, 'Rereading Root', ASIL Proceedings 2006, 203–210. See also Tuomas Lihr, 'Elihu Root and International Legalism: Legalist Remarks on Collective Security and American Realism', 1 Helsinki Law Review 2014, 63–92. See also Arnulf Becker Lorca, 'Universal International Law: Nineteenth-Century Histories of Imposition and Appropriation', 51 Harvard International Law Journal 2010, 475.
8. On the claim that international law, and its main representations, were appropriated and reinforced by jurists from semi-peripheral polities, such as Japan, the Ottoman Empire, and Latin American States rather than being exported by Europeans, see Arnulf Becker Lorca, 'Universal International Law: Nineteenth-Century Histories of Imposition and Appropriation', 51 Harvard International Law Journal 2010, 475.
9. On the idea that writing has no beginning, see Jacques Derrida, *Positions* (Editions de Minuit 1972) 23. See also Jacques Derrida, *Spectres de Marx* (Galilée 1993) 255–256.
10. For the promotion of international law as a science without the resort to the positivist representation, see H Wheaton, *Elements of International Law* (Little, Brown and Company 1866) xv–xvi and xix, 3, 6, 10, 12. T Woolsey, *Introduction to the Study of International Law* (Scribner 1877) 17–20; T J Lawrence, *The Principles of International Law* (7th edn, Macmillan 1923) 1–13; J Lorimer, *Principes de Droit international* (Muquardt 1884) 3–16.
11. In this chapter, 'scienticity' and anything deemed 'scientistic' refer to the belief that scientificity (of a discipline, of a discourse, of a practice, etc) provides discursive superiority to a discipline, as it is the best and most authoritative way to construct epistemology and generate truth-claims.
12. Most famous among them are Hugo Grotius and Friedrich Fromhold von Martens. On Hugo Grotius, see J Haskell, 'Hugo Grotius in the Contemporary Memory of International Law: Secularism, Liberalism, and the Politics of Restatement and Denial', in J M Beneyto, D Kennedy, J Corti Varela, and J Haskell (eds), *New Approaches to International Law: The European and the American Experiences* (Asser Press 2012) 123–150. On Martens, see Koskenniemi, 'Into Positivism' (n 4) 189–207.
13. See generally Neff, *Justice Among Nations* (n 3) 300.
14. For a discussion of some of the manifestations of the professionalization of international law in Latin America and Asia see, eg, Arnulf Becker Lorca, *Mestizo International Law. A Global Intellectual History 1842–1933* (CUP 2014). See also Arnulf Becker, 'Universal International Law: Nineteenth-Century Histories of Imposition and Appropriation', 51 Harvard International Law Journal 2010, 475–552.
15. Neff reports that an early professorship in the subject was established at the University of Turin in 1851. The Chichele Chair of International Law and Diplomacy was established in 1859 at Oxford University, and the Whewell Chair in International Law at Cambridge University in 1867. Although it had tried to appoint Wheaton in the 1840s, Harvard Law School appointed its first international law professors in 1898. See Neff, *Justice Among Nations* (n 3) 304. See also Martti Koskenniemi, 'Nationalism, Universalism, Empire: International Law in 1871 and 1919', talk at Columbia University, April 2005, available at

https://www.scribd.com/document/93419466/Columbia-0405 accessed 4 December 2015. See also the remarks of I de la Rasilia del Moral, 'The Ambivalent Shadow of the Pre-Wilsonian Rise of International Law', 7 Erasmus Law Review 2014, 2 (he argues that in the wake of the independence of the American Republics from Spain, the university teaching of international law emerged comparatively earlier in the US than in Europe, perhaps with the exception of Spain. The first courses in international law in the US were taught in 1846 at Yale, first by Theodore Woosley and later by Francis Lieber).

16. See Vincent Genin, *Le laboratoire belge du droit international: Une communauté épistémique et internationale de juristes (1869–1914)* (with a foreword by Martti Koskenniemi) (Académie Royale des Sciences, des Lettres et des Beaux-Arts de Belgique 2018) 90–94, and 196.
17. See the remarks of Jean d'Aspremont, 'Belgium and the Fabrication of the International Legal Discipline', 31 European Journal of International Law 2020, 1521–1530.
18. On the impossibility of establishing such a causal relationship, see Michel Foucault, *L'archéologie du savoir* (Gallimard 1969) 34; Paul Ricoeur, *Histoire et vérité* (Seuil 1955) 33–34. For an earlier scepticism towards causal laws, see David Hume, *A Treatise of Human Nature* (OUP 2011; original edn 1739–1740).
19. This was examined further in J d'Aspremont, 'The Professionalization of International Law'", Jean d'Aspremont, A Nollkaemper, T Gazzini, and W Werner (eds), *International Law as a Profession* (CUP 2017) (hereafter d'Aspremont et al, *International Law as a Profession*).
20. For a taxonomy of distinct variants of international legal positivism permeating the 19th-century international legal scholarship, see Neff, *Justice Among Nations* (n 3) 226–243 (Neff speaks of international legal positivism as an 'amalgamation', 43). See also Rousseau, *Principes Généraux du Droit International Public* (n 4) 35–37.
21. For a challenge of this traditional dichotomy, see Koskenniemi, 'Into Positivism' (n 4) 190; Martti Koskenniemi, *From Apology to Utopia: The Structure of International Legal Argument* (CUP 2005) 303–387; Emmanuelle Jouannet, *Emer de Vattel et l'émergence doctrinale du droit international classique* (Pedone 1998) esp 142–143; A Carty, 'Conservative and Progressive Visions in French International Legal Doctrine', 16 European Journal of International Law 2005, 525–537, esp 534.
22. This association of legal positivism and State-centricism and voluntarism was central to the criticism of positivism by naturalist international lawyers at the beginning of the 20th century. See, eg, Hersch Lauterpacht, 'Westlake and Present Day International Law', 5 Economica 1925, 307–325, esp 323–324. See also Hersch Lauterpacht, Private Law Sources and Analogies of International Law (Longmans 2927) 43–44. For a genealogy of this criticism, see R Collins, 'Classical Legal Positivism in International Law Revisited', in Kammerhofer and d'Aspremont, *International Legal Positivism in a Post-Modern World* (n 1) 23–49.
23. See, eg, *S.S. 'Lotus' (France v Turkey)*, Judgment of 7 September 1927, PCIJ Series A No 10 (1927) 18. For an overview of this position, see Neff, *Justice Among Nations* (n 3) 236–243. Here too, this association between international legal positivism, consensualism, and voluntarism was found in the criticism of international legal positivism. See, eg, Brierly, *The Law of Nations* (n 4) 53. This association has continued to permeate contemporary criticisms of international legal positivism. See, eg, A Carty, 'Conservative and Progressive Visions in French International Legal Doctrine', 16 European Journal of International Law 2005, 525–537; D Kennedy, 'The Sources of International Law', 2 American University

Journal of International Law and Policy 1987, 1 20. D Kennedy, 'When Renewal Repeats: Thinking Against the Box', 32 New York University Journal of International Law and Politics 1999–2000, 335 355, 366; J Brunnee and S J Toope, 'An Interactional Theory of International Legal Obligation', *University of Toronto Legal Studies Research Series*, No 08–16, July 2008, 31–33, available at http://ssrn.com/abstract=1162882

24. This is the claim made by Monica Garcia-Salmones, *The Project of Positivism in International Law* (OUP 2013).
25. For some critical remarks, see A Carty, *Philosophy of International Law* (Edinburgh UP 2007) 9–14
26. This is a claim also made by Ignacio de la Rasilla del Moral, 'The Ambivalent Shadow of the Pre-Wilsonian Rise of International Law', 7 Erasmus Law Review 2014, 2; Neff, *Justice Among Nations* (n 3) 300; see also J Kammerhofer, 'Hans Kelsen in Today's International Legal Scholarship', in Kammerhofer and d'Aspremont, *International Legal Positivism in a Post-Modern World* (n 1) 81–113.
27. Neff, *Justice Among Nations* (n 3) 222.
28. For some classical expositions of international law as a science, see L Oppenheim, 'The Science of International Law: Its Task and Method', 2 American Journal of International Law 1908, 313; R Ago, 'Science Juridique et Droit International', 90 Collected Courses 1956, 851–958; F Castberg, 'La Méthodologie du droit international public', 43 Collected Courses of the Hague Academy of International Law, 1934. It is Hans Kelsen who was the most explicit on his idea of international legal positivism as a scientific project. For some remarks on that aspect of Kelsen's work, see Anne Orford, 'Scientific Reason and the Discipline of International Law', in J d'Aspremont et al, *International Law as a Profession* (n 19) 93, 103–108.
29. Originally meaning knowledge or skills, it came to mean a whole body of regular or methodological observations and propositions. It was later reserved for the method of natural sciences. The turn to call scientific the sets of methods of social sciences was never self-evident and indeed is still contested. See R Williams, *Keywords: A Vocabulary of Culture and Society* (OUP 2014) 216–218.
30. It is also interesting to note in this respect that the positivist approach is sometimes called the realist approach. See Rousseau, *Principes Généraux du Droit International Public* (n 4) 19. See also Rousseau's ideas that international legal positivism links international law and 'facts', 36.
31. Alasdair MacIntyre, *Three Rival Version of Moral Inquiry. Encyclopaedia, Genealogy, and Tradition* (University of Notre Dame Press 1990) 224.
32. The invocation of 'nature' as the ultimate truth-claiming criteria is a common feature of those discourses about the real. See gen Bruno Latour, *Science in Action: How to Follow Scientists and Engineers Through Society* (Harvard UP 1987).
33. Hayden White, *The Content of the Form. Narrative Discourse and Historical Representation* (John Hopkins UP 1987) 57.
34. Even Hume's famous scepticism towards the possibility of scientific laws about the real (David Hume, *A Treatise of Human Nature* (OUP 2011; originally published in 1739–1740)) and Kant's strong case that we cannot know the real-in-itself (Immanuel Kant, *Critique of Pure Reason* (Hackett Publishing, 1996; originally published in 1781)) proved to be in vain and failed to frustrate the elevation of disciplines about the real at the pinnacle of the discursive universe.

35. Neff, *Justice Among Nations* (n 3) 217; J Kaerhofer, 'Hans Kelsen in Today's International Legal Scholarship', in Kammerhofer and d'Aspremont, *International Legal Positivism in a Post-Modern World* (n 1) 81, esp 83–87.
36. Indeed, authors from the 17th and 18th centuries, while prioritizing moral needs in international legal discourses, recognized that international law could partly be an emanation of the real. See S Pufendorf, *On the Law of Nature and of Nations*, trans C H Oldfather and W A Oldfather (Clarendon Press 1934; originally published 1672).
37. The 1758 work of Emmerich de Vattel, while perpetuating some of the assumptions of his predecessors regarding the necessity of natural law, made the need to ground international law in the real—which he reduced to the will of the States—the main cause of international law. Even more decisive was Georg Friedrich de Martens' radical move away from the moral necessities of natural law and the systematization of international law through treaty and custom *fondé sur les traités et l'usage*. See E de Vattel, *The Law of Nations*, trans Frenwick (Carnegie Institution of Washington. See generally Georg Friedrich von Martens, *Précis du droit des gens moderne de l'Europe fondé sur les traités et l'usage* (Dieterich 1789).
38. See, eg, H Wheaton, *Elements of International Law* (1836); R Phillimore, *Commentaries upon International Law*, 4 vols (AG Benning 1854–1861); T D Woolsey, *Introduction to the Study of International Law* (4th edn, Scribnerm Amstrong & Co 1877). It should be noted that some of them, whilst making the need to ground international law in the real very central, continued to accommodate the idea that the international legal discourse must respond to reason or natural law, or sometimes the will of God.
39. It has been claimed that the necessity to ground international law in the real that arose in the 19th century was part of an overarching dialectical mode of argumentation that simultaneously required the espousal of some utopian principles. It was also said that, for 19th-century authors, responding to the real was a strategy to avoid being utopian. This is the thesis defended by Martti Koskenniemi, *From Apology to Utopia* (CUP 2005) 71–157.
40. For some spectacular exceptions and prominent vindication of international legal positivism in the second half of the 20th century, see Roberto Ago, 'Positive Law and International Law', 51 American Journal of International Law 1957, 691–733; H Kelsen, 'Théorie du droit international public', 84 Recueil des Cours 1953, 1–201; Bruno Simma and Andreas Paulus, 'The Responsibility of Individuals for Human Rights Abuses in Internal Conflicts: A Positivist View', 93 American Journal of International Law 1999, 302–316.
41. For a few exceptions, see J Kammerhofer, 'The Pure Theory of Law and Its "Modern" Positivism: International Legal Uses for Scholarship', 106 Proceedings of the ASIL Annual Meeting 2012, 365–367; T Christakis, 'Human Rights from a Neo-Voluntarist Perspective', in Kammerhofer and d'Aspremont, *International Legal Positivism in a Post-Modern World* (n 1) 421–450; J Hathaway, 'American Defender of Democratic Legitimacy', 11 European Journal of International Law 2000, 121–134; see, eg, C Tomuschat, 'International Law: Ensuring the Survival of Mankind on the Eve of a New Century: General Course on Public International Law', 281 Collected Course 1999, 28; B Fassbender, 'The Meaning of International Constitutional Law', in N Tsagourias (ed), *Transnational Constitutionalism: International and European Perspectives* (CUP 2007) 307, 320. It is interesting to note the extent to which Thirlway balks at calling himself a positivist in H Thirlway, *The Sources of International Law* (OUP 2014) 1–3. And further, it is also interesting to note that despite international lawyers dismissing legal positivism, they have continued to hold that legal positivism informs most of the international legal discourse. In that sense, it is

common for them to say that the patterns of international legal arguments associated with legal positivism continued to be repeatedly taught in the main law schools across the world and featured in the bestselling international law textbooks. See, eg, B S Chimni, *International Law and World Order. A Critique of Contemporary Approaches* (2nd edn, CUP 2017) 10–14; Martti Koskenniemi, 'The Politics of International Law—20 Years Later', 20 European Journal of International Law 2009, 7–8; J Alvarez, *The Impact of International Organizations on International Law* (Brill 2017) 1–52.

42. See, eg, Bruno Simma and Andreas L Paulus, 'The Responsibility of Individuals for Human Rights Abuses in Internal Conflicts: A Positivist View', 93 American Journal of International Law 1999, 302; Olivier Corten, *Le discours du droit international* (Pedone 2009); G J H Van Hoof, *Rethinking the Sources of International Law* (Kluwer Law 1983). Some may be tempted to look at some of the current author's earlier work from this perspective. See Jean d'Aspremont, *Formalism and the Sources of International Law. A Theory of the Ascertainment of Legal Rules* (OUP 2011) (hereafter d'Aspremont, *Formalism and the Sources of International Law*).
43. Twentieth-century international lawyers came to develop a sophisticated doctrine of sources meant to mediate between the will of State and the legal forms by which a rule would be recognized as a legal rule. On the rise of the doctrine of sources, see d'Aspremont, *Formalism and the Sources of International Law* (n 42) 38–82.
44. For a contestation of the 19th-century consensual basis of international obligations, see L Brierly, 'The Basis of Obligation in International Law', in H Lauterpacht (ed), *The Basis of Obligation in International Law and Other Papers* (Scientia Verlag Aalen 1977; originally published OUP 1958) 1–67.
45. See generally M Reisman, 'The View from the New Haven School of International Law', 86 ASIL Proceedings 1992, 118; W Michael Reisman, Siegfried Wiessner, and Andrew Willard, 'The New Haven School: A Brief Introduction', 32 Yale Journal of International Law 2007, 576. For a similar reading of the New Haven approach, see Anne Orford, 'Scientific Reason and the Discipline of International Law', 25 European Journal of International Law 2014, 369–385, 381–382.
46. See Thomas Franck, *Fairness in International Law and Institutions* (Clarendon Press 1995) 6.
47. On this aspect of the turn to legitimacy, see David Bederman, *The Spirit of International Law* (Georgia UP 2002) 3
48. For a criticism of this self-representation see Martti Koskenniemi, 'Letter to the Editors of the Symposium', 93 American Journal of International Law 1999, 351; J Crawford, 'International Law as Discipline and Profession', Proceedings of the American Society of International Law Annual Meeting 2012, 1.
49. Martti Koskenniemi, 'Letter to the Editors of the Symposium', 93 American Journal of International Law 1999, 351; J Crawford, 'International Law as Discipline and Profession', ASILP 2012, 1.
50. For instance, Michael Polanyi has argued that the community of scientists is organized in a way which resembles certain features of a body politic and works according to economic principles similar to those by which the production of material goods is regulated, 'The Republic of Science: Its Political and Economic Theory', in M Polanyi, *Knowing and Being* (Chicago UP) 49.
51. The most famous and archetypical example of such pragmatism is Ian Brownlie. See Ian Brownlie, 'International Law at the Fiftieth Anniversary of the United Nations: General

Course on Public International Law', 255 Collected Courses 1995, 9, 30 (for whom theory provides no real benefit). For some additional reflections on the reasons behind the anti-theoretical stance of mainstream legal scholarship, see J Klabbers, 'Constitutionalism and the Making of International Law', 5 No Foundations: Journal of Extreme Legal Positivism 2008, 84, 95. The famous British aversion of theory is sometimes traced back to Lauterpacht. See A Carty, '"Why Theory"—The Implications for International Law Teaching', in P Allott et al (eds), *Theory and International Law: An Introduction* (British Institute of International and Comparative Law 1991) 75, 77. For a contestation of this contention, see I Scobbie, 'The Theorist as Judge: Hersch Lauterpacht's Concept of the International Judicial Function', 2 European Journal of International Law 1997, 264, 264.

52. A Somek, 'Legal Science as a Source of Law: A Late Reply by Puchta to Kantorowicz', 13-7 University of Iowa Legal Studies Research Paper Series 2012, 4.
53. For Anne Orford, it ended with World War II. See Anne Orford, 'Scientific Reason and the Discipline of International Law', in J d'Aspremont et al, *International Law as a Profession* (n 19) 93, 105–108.
54. On the contestation of modernity by romanticism, see the essays in Thomas Pfau and Robert Mitchell (eds), *Romanticism and Modernity* (Routledge 2015). See also Michael Löwy and Robert Sayre, *Révolte et mélancolie: Le romantisme à contre-courant de la modernité* (Payot and Rivages 2005).
55. Theodor Adorno and Max Horkheimer, *Dialectic of Enlightenment* (Verso 1997) 9; Henri Bergson, *La pensée et le mouvant* (Flammarion 2014) 251; Roland Barthes, *Le bruissement de la langue. Essais critiques IV* (Seuil 1984) 149; Gaston Bachelard, *Le nouvel esprit scientifique* (Presses universitaires de France 1934) 9–18.
56. Theodor Adorno and Max Horkheimer, *Dialectic of Enlightenment* (Verso 1997) xiv.
57. Jean-François Lyotard, *La Condition Postmoderne* (Editions de Minuit 1979) 65.
58. Martin Heidegger, *What is Called Thinking*, trans J Glenn Gray (Harper Perennial 1976) 8.
59. On the idea that scientific modes of inquiry have no distinct superiority over literary ones, even when it comes to engaging with the real, see generally Hayden White, *Tropics of Discourses. Essays in Cultural Criticism* (Johns Hopkins UP 1986) 121–122 and 142–143; Roland Barthes, *L'aventure sémiologique* (Seuil 1985) 14.
60. Jean-François Lyotard, *La Condition Postmoderne* (Editions de Minuit 1979) 11; Roland Barthes, *L'aventure sémiologique* (Seuil 1985) 14. In that regard, it has even been claimed that discourses about the real work as secularized theologies, see Pierre Legendre, *Sur la question dogmatique en Occident. Aspect théoriques* (Fayard 1999) 41.
61. Roland Barthes, *Le bruissement de la langue. Essais critiques IV* (Seuil 1984) 11.
62. For an overview, see Akbar Rasulov, 'What is Critique? Notes Towards a Sociology of Disciplinary Heterodoxy in Contemporary International Law', in J d'Aspremont et al, *International Law as a Profession* (n 19) 189–220 207–219.
63. On the structuralist foundations of Koskenniemi's account of international legal argumentation, see Akbar Rasulov, 'From Apology to Utopia and the Inner Life of International Law', 29 Leiden Journal of International Law 2016, 641–666; Sahib Singh, 'International legal Positivism and New Approaches to International Law', in Kammerhofer and d'Aspremont, *International Legal Positivism in a Post-Modern World* (n 1) 291–316; Justin Desautels-Stein, 'International Legal Structuralism: A Primer' 8 *International Theory* 2016, 201–235; Jouannet comes up with a similar but more nuanced account, see E Jouannet, 'A Critical Introduction', in Martti Koskenniemi, *The Politics of International Law* (Hart Publishing 2011) 2 and 7–12.

64. G Steiner, *After Babel. Aspects of Language and Translation* (OUP 1975)
65. David Kennedy, *International Legal Structures* (Nomos 1987); Martti Koskenniemi, *From Apology to Utopia* (CUP 2005); Martti Koskenniemi, 'The Fate of International Law: Between Technique and Politics', 70 Modern Law Review 2007, 1.
66. David Kennedy, *A World of Struggle: How Power, Law, and Expertise Shape Global Political Economy* (Princeton UP 2016); Martti Koskenniemi, 'The Politics of International Law—20 Years Later', 20 European Journal of International Law 2009, 7–19.
67. Stanley Fish, *Doing What Comes Naturally* (Duke UP 1989) 157; A MacIntyre, *Whose Justice? Which Rationality*? (Duckworth 1988) 352–353 and 367;George Steiner, *Errata. An Examined Life* (Weidenfeld and Nicholson 1997) 86–87; Bourdieu, 'The Force of Law: Toward a Sociology of the juridical Field', 38 Hastings Law Journal 1987, 805; Nelson Goodman, *Ways of Worldmaking* (Hackett Publishing 1978).
68. On ideology as a system of representation, see Louis Althusser, *For Marx*, trans Ben Brewster (Verso 2006). For Paul de Man, the correspondence between linguistic categories and natural reality is what we should construe as the work of ideology. See Paul de Man, *The Resistance to Theory* (University of Minnesota Press 1986) 11.
69. See, eg, Moshe Hirsch, *Invitation to the Sociology of International Law* (OUP 2016); Andrea Bianchi, 'Reflexive Butterfly Catching: Insights from a Situated Catcher', in Joost Pauwelyn et al (eds), *Informal International Lawmaking* (OUP 2012) 200–215; Andrea Bianchi, 'Epistemic Communities', in Jean d'Aspremont and Sahib Singh (eds), *Concepts for International Law—Contributions to Disciplinary Thought* (Edward Elgar 2019) 251–266; Andrea Bianchi, *International Law Theories. An Inquiry into Different Ways of Thinking* (OUP 2016) 7–9 and 17–18.
70. See Section 1.
71. I fear that my earlier work on the social foundations of the sources of international law could be read as constituting such a reactionary rehabilitation of the primacy of the real. See d'Aspremont, *Formalism and the Sources of International Law* (n 42). For a move away from that position, see also Jean d'Aspremont, 'A Worldly Law in a Legal World', in Andrea Bianchi and Moshe Hirsch (eds), *International Law's Invisible Frames* (OUP 2021) 110–123. See generally Jean d'Aspremont, *After Meaning. The Sovereignty of International Legal Forms* (Edward Elgar 2021).
72. See generally G Shaffer, 'A New Legal Realism: Method in International Economic Law Scholarship', in C B Picker, I Bunn, and D Arner (eds), *International Economic Law—The State and Future of the Discipline* (Hart Publishing 2008) 29–42; H Erlanger et al, 'New Legal Realism Symposium: Is it Time for a New Legal Realism?, 2 Wisconsin Law Review 2005, 335; S Macaulay, 'The New Versus the Old Legal Realism: Things Ain't What They Used to Be', Wisconsin Law Review 2005, 365, 375; V Nourse and G Shaffer, 'Varieties of New Legal Realism: Can A New World Order Prompt A New Legal Theory', 95 Cornell Law Review 2009, 61.
73. See, eg, Gregory Shaffer and Tom Ginsburg, 'The Empirical Turn in International Legal Scholarship', 106 American Journal of International Law 2012, 1. For an illustration, see Pierre-Hugues Verdier and Erik Voeten, 'How Does Customary International Law Change? The Case of State Immunity', 59 International Studies Quarterly 2015, 209. See also Jakob V H Holtermann and Mikael Rask Madsen, 'Toleration, Synthesis or Replacement? The "Empirical Turn" and Its Consequences for the Science of International Law', 29 Leiden Journal of International Law 2016, 1001. For a claim about the virtuosity of empirical sensitivity, see Jorge E Vinuales, 'On Legal Inquiry', in Denis Alland et al (eds),

Unity and Diversity of International Law: Essays in Honour of Professor Pierre-Marie Dupuy (Martinus Nijhoff 2014) 72–75.

74. See the account of this return to scientific methods in the study of the history of international law provided by Anne Orford, *International Law and the Politics of History* (CUP 2021) esp chapters 3 and 4. See also Jean d'Aspremont, 'International Law and the Rage against Scienticism', 33 European Journal of International Law 2022, 679–694.
75. See, however, n 8.
76. Vincent Genin recounts how Lieber (who had fought in the Prussian army against Napoleon's troops at Waterloo in 1815) contributed to the import of the German system of referencing to US law schools. See Vincent Genin, *Le laboratoire belge du droit international: Une communauté épistémique et internationale de juristes (1869–1914)* (Académie Royale des Sciences, des Lettres et des Beaux-Arts de Belgique 2018) 55–56. For a famous charge against referencing practices in the US legal academia, see Fred Rodell, 'Goodbye to Law Reviews', 23 Virginia Law Review 1936, 38.
77. I have elaborated on my deep concern with the dominant literary genre practised in international law on various occasions. See Jean d'Aspremont, 'Destination: the Wasteland of Academic Overproduction', Part 1 and Part 2, available at http://www.ejiltalk.org. See also Jean d'Aspremont, 'Wording in International Law', 25 Leiden Journal of International Law 2012, 575–602. More recently, see Jean d'Aspremont, *After Meaning. The Sovereignty of International Legal Forms* (Edward Elgar 2021) 116–118.
78. I have discussed this elsewhere. See Jean d'Aspremont, 'International Law and the Rage against Scienticism', 33 European Journal of International Law 2022, 679–694.

CHAPTER 13

INTERNATIONAL LAW IN EUROPE AND LEGAL REALISM

YUVAL SHANY AND MARIA VARAKI

1. Introduction

International relations in Europe between the Peace of Westphalia and the Peace of Versailles were characterized by intermittent periods of war and peace, the consolidation of new States, the emergence of new international organizations and regimes, and the gradual evolution of new norms and institutions designed to advance humanitarian values, to facilitate international cooperation and, eventually, to achieve long-lasting peace. On the theoretic side of things, international law *as a European tradition*,[1] notwithstanding its diversity,[2] fluctuated during these years between Grotian impulses premised on natural law traditions and humanitarian sensibilities, on the one hand, and positivist tendencies premised on national sovereignty and voluntarism, on the other hand. This duality—an early version of 'from apology to utopia'[3]—has been described by Koskenniemi in one of his other books as underlying the difficulty he experienced in categorizing 'the men of 1873' who established the Institut de Droit International as either positivists or naturalists:

> They were always both at the same time—their arguments about positive law implying loaded assumptions about political worth, and their humanitarian sentiments always receiving expression in the practices of their own states or in some sociological understanding of the fact of European civilization.[4]

A commitment to a hybrid form of international law theory, fusing positive law with notions of justice, seems to continue to have a dominant hold on European international law scholars. For example, the articles of association of the European

Society of International Law from 2012 appear to reflect a belief in the positive effect international law rules can have on the state of the world (the Society strives 'to contribute to the rule of law in international relations'),[5] yet the very first article published in the European Journal of International Law—which is affiliated with the same Society—cautioned against accepting without question any grand design for a world order, as well as the application of legal rules and principles intended to realize such a design.[6]

The difficulty in separating positive law from morality as internal drivers of international law as it developed in Europe invites a consideration of these developments from an external vantage through resorting to other legal theories, which can provide critical insights about the life of international law in the European continent and the role played therein by positivism (see d'Aspremont, this volume) and natural law (see O'Connell, this volume) (and their intellectual progenies).[7] This chapter will review the influence of one key legal theory—realism—on European approaches to international law. Although realism has been traditionally associated in European international law academia with the study of international relations and with American approaches to the study of domestic and international law,[8] at the heart of the chapter is our claim that there has always been a structural undercurrent of realism in European approaches to international law, manifesting itself in the contents of international law which was developed in Europe, the Eurocentrism of international law and the European interest in (if not, obsession with) legal and institutional reforms. Furthermore, the so-called empirical turn in international law scholarship[9] in recent decades further increases the relevance of realism as a framework of analysis for international law practice and scholarship, including in Europe.

At an abstract level, this chapter aims to explore how realism is understood in the European international law tradition both as a tool to understand reality and to construct reality. This requires a discussion both of the meaning of realism and the notion of European international law and its various *kairoi* and *topoi*. Within the relevant space constraints, we will address several dominant aspects of European international law realism throughout key moments in time. Despite the inevitable simplification of engaging in an analysis of this nature and the attendant risk of both over- and under-inclusiveness, we are of the view that a sensibility to realism can accommodate a more nuanced understanding of international law in Europe, its course of development, and the internal contradictions it suffers from.

The next section of this chapter will briefly introduce the realist approach to international law and our understanding of the concept. Section 3 discusses structural features of international law, as it developed in Europe, which can be understood in a new light using realism as a framework of analysis. Section 4 discusses the relationship between realism and the 'empirical turn' in international law scholarship, which helps to flesh out some of the realist sub-structures of international law in Europe, and Section 5 proposes to regard realism as another way of conceptualizing international law in and outside Europe.

2. A Very Short Introduction to Realism and International Law Theory

Political realism, as developed by Hans Morgenthau—who was trained in international law in Germany and Switzerland, and who became, after immigrating to the US in 1937, one of the founding fathers of international relations (IR) studies—constitutes one of three principal schools of IR theory, alongside liberalism and constructivism. Morgenthau's work in the US provided an external perspective on international law, which was critical of narratives of normative impact. This approach, which built on the work of British political scientist, Edward Hallet Carr, seemed to have been influenced by Morgenthau's deep disappointment with the failure of international law norms and institutions to meaningful restrain State power and to prevent the war.[10]

According to Morgenthau in *Politics among Nations*, international relations are premised on the interest of States in accumulating more power or maintaining an existing balance of power. International law plays a useful, albeit limited, role in specific international power configurations—primarily, where there is a community of interests supporting legal regulation, or where regulation is needed to maintain an existing status quo that serves the interests of the most powerful States.[11] Some of the subsequent IR literature has taken an even more dismissive view of international law, qualifying it as epiphenomenal in nature.[12] Still other parts of the literature advanced more nuanced theories of neo-realism and neo-liberal institutionalism, which underscore the influence of the structural contexts in which States exist on the shaping of their national interests,[13] and further developed the English School of IR, which had identified the moderating effects of ideas on international politics.[14]

In parallel, legal realism, as it developed in the US, in the late 19th and early 20th centuries, as a form of rejection of legal formalism, centred around studying the manner in which law is actually applied by judges and other legal decision makers.[15] Underlying the work of legal realists is the then revolutionary assertion that extra-legal dispositions, including sociological, psychological, or ideological considerations, influence the manner in which the law is determined, interpreted, and applied, and that legal texts in and of themselves are too indeterminate or malleable to generate fixed legal outcomes. This approach stood in marked contrast to the self-referential dogma of legal science in Europe, which regarded law as a body of norms with objective contents that can be scientifically deduced and faithfully applied by objective professionals.[16]

In terms of methodology, the realist approach directed the attention of US legal researchers to legal practice (and, in particular, to judicial practice, where debates over the contents of legal norms and their application to real-life situations are most apparent), and to the social sciences as a source of possible explanations and predictions about the actual 'life of the law'.[17] The flip side of the same coin is that extra-legal considerations invite an extra-legal investigation of the potential and actual impact of law on society, including the benefits delivered by legal institutions and their harmful consequences. Through establishing a feedback loop between law and society—an approach first introduced into American jurisprudence in the Brandeis brief submitted to the Supreme Court in 1908 on the impact of long working hours on women—legal realism gave rise to other schools of legal theory focusing on the interplay between law and society, including critical legal studies and economic analysis of the law. By underscoring the importance of actual societal conditions, it also laid the foundations to the introduction into legal scholarship of more radical critical theories, such as radical feminism, Marxism, and critical race theory, which offer new insights on the structural effects of law on society.[18]

It is important to stress that realism in IR and legal realism were developed in the US by separate intellectual communities and focused on different objects of study—the State and decision makers inside the State. They also revolve around different key insights—law as a corollary of power and the epistemic value of observing the actual practice of legal institutions when studying the law. Still, American academy eventually connected the two theoretical frameworks—first, through the work of the New Haven School, and later on, through theories on the disaggregated State and transnational legal process. The New Haven School, also referred to as Policy-Oriented Jurisprudence, proposed a view of international law as a process of authoritative decisions undertaken by global 'actors' or decision makers. According to this theoretical school, law serves as a policy instrument and legal scholarship can explore the changing preferences for specific policies and policy outcomes, decision makers' values, interests, and experiences, and the interplay between different relevant variables.[19] The disaggregated State theory, advanced *inter alia* by Anne-Marie Slaughter, proposes a focus on State organs and agencies operating as *de facto* hubs for creating, interpreting, and applying international law, including through loose international networks bringing different political and professional entities across national borders in contact with one another.[20] In a related manner, the transnational legal process theory, developed by scholars such as Harold Koh, focuses on a rich sets of formal and informal interactions across borders including public and private actors (sometimes referred to as norm entrepreneurs), through which law is developed, internalized, and enforced.[21]

The empirical turn in international law, discussed further below, operates to connect social science theories to legal realism, using international norms and institutions as a principal object of study through methodologies derived from the social sciences. Whereas early forays of international lawyers into empirical research were anecdotal or impressionistic,[22] a rich literature now exists about how law is created, interpreted, and applied. Such literature corroborates a key insight of legal realism—that is, that extra-legal considerations heavily influence the life of the law. At the same time, empirical research shows that the relative pull of legal and extra-legal factors, such as values, interests, social conditions, and ideological dispositions, appear to differ across time, space, and political context.[23]

In a recent publication, Harlan Grant Cohen identifies five common features that underlie American legal realism in its different manifestations, including as applied to international law: (1) empiricism; (2) an orientation towards process, practice, and institutional choice, rather than legal doctrine; (3) anti-formalism; (4) instrumentalism; and (5) pragmaticism.[24] He further explains that these five features interact with four dominant trends in American approaches to international law: focusing on general norms rather than specific rules; focusing on process rather than doctrine; focusing on institutions/power rather than on substantive rules; and embracing pragmaticism and practicality.[25] These four trends are easily mirrored in conceptual undertakings such as works on norm diffusion, the process-oriented work of several schools of legal theory, organizational theories about regime design, and analysis of effectiveness and legitimacy.[26] For Cohen those four trends can be found in diverse school of international law theory, encompassing theories associated both with political conservatives and progressives.[27]

Finally, as Section 3 explains, realism can be conceptualized not only as a theory of international relations or a method for studying the law, but also as a sensibility that can accommodate a host of choices and attitudes, including argumentative strategies,[28] philosophical pragmaticism,[29] and a sense of reality.[30] This sensibility acknowledges the internal limits of legal arguments and reflects expectations that the law should be defined through its relationship to extra-legal concepts such as power or politics.

As the following sections show, the dominant historical approaches to international law in Europe (natural law and legal positivism) traditionally exhibited reluctance to resort to, or acknowledge the relevance of, extra-legal considerations in connection with the application of international law norms.[31] The general reluctance to actively engage with extra-legal factors may provide an explanation for the relative marginality of realism in European international law theory. Another reasons for such relative marginality might be the limited familiarity of many European lawyers with social sciences, at least when compared to their American counterparts. Furthermore, there has been some terminological confusion surrounding the term 'realism' when applied in European international law discussions: Whereas the term 'realism' was occasionally invoked by prominent international law scholars, it tended to be used in order to justify utopian global governance projects, such as 'world federalism', presented as alternatives to a depressing 'reality',[32] or to support positivism as an international law theory engaged with actual law-making and 'real world' conditions.[33] In actuality, these self-described European 'realists' were either full-fledged idealists or positivists.

Still, we argue below that realism, and—in particular—nuanced versions of realistic sensibilities, played an important, albeit largely hidden, role in the development of international law in Europe, and that contemporary developments in research conducted in and around Europe render realism a more prominent theoretical framework than before. Moreover, since realism is a middle-range theory, pointing in the direction of important objects of study—power and practice—but providing limited critical tools to normatively evaluate them, it offers a necessary stepping stone for engagement with specific international law doctrines about power and legal practice, as well as more abstract international law theories which centre around normative commitments to addressing specific forms of injustice.

3. International Law in Europe as a Form of Realism

The main features of international law, as it emerged from the religious wars of the 17th century, and reaffirmed by the order established in the Concert of Europe in the 19th century, were arguably designed to consolidate and legitimize existing political power structures. In fact, the very building blocks of modern international law were built around a European balance of power, whose preservation was deemed a major political objective.[34] This process of convergence between law and power appears to be at odds with traditional European ideas about the separation of law (including international law) from political power. It suggests, by contrast, that a realistic sensibility can be found at the very core of the international legal order, as it developed from the Peace of Westphalia onwards.

Indeed, the notion of State sovereignty and the principle of voluntarism in law-making—both sacrosanct features of the Westphalian order—appear to have been intended to preserve the national interests of existing States, and to protect the coercive powers, political influence, and economic interests of their ruling elites. The gradual move from 17th-century natural law to 19th-century positivism (and, throughout the 20th century, an increased reliance on *lex scripta*)[35] can also be explained by a growing demand for consolidating State power and accepting fewer open-ended and open-sourced constraints on such power.[36] In the same vein, international law rules governing the use of force (*jus ad bellum*), which did not contain until the 20th century a general ban on war, had few if any limits on the conduct of hostilities and recognized a right to self-preservation, as well as a right to violent reprisals and to self-help (see Dienelt, this volume). Such a laissez-faire approach to organized violence corresponded to the Clausowitzian understanding of war as the continuation of policy by other means[37] and to the, by now discredited, 19th-century doctrine of *Kriegsraison* (see Rusinova, this volume).[38]

The strong Eurocentric features of international law during the 17th–19th centuries offers a similar realistic sensibility manifesting itself in a legal architecture that advanced the interests of European powers at the expense of non-European nations. Among these features one may note the institution of State recognition, which placed European countries in the position of gatekeepers for admission to the 'international community',[39] and the notions of civilized nations and *terra nullius* which facilitated the creation of colonial empires and the massive exploitation of vast populations and territories (see Anghie, this volume).[40]

It is perhaps not accidental that the major transition in the early 20th century from a power-based international order into a more rule-based order, constructed less around raw military power and more on universal values, was designed, to a large extent, not by European but rather by US statesmen, such as Presidents Wilson and Roosevelt, Frank Kellogg, and Henry Stimson. The failure to sustain the Wilsonian plan for world peace on the basis of post-World War I legal norms and institutions was indeed explained by IR realists through a reference to its utopian nature[41] and the refusal to acknowledge the 'philosophical anthropology' of national egotism that characterizes international relations.[42] The insight about the importance of acknowledging national interests when creating legal architectures was not lost, arguably, by the drafters of the UN Charter who afforded the P-5 with veto power.[43] The relative success of the UN in reducing the number and frequency of inter-state armed conflicts and in preventing another world war hitherto was indeed attributed by some observers to the alignment between law and the balance of power that was found in the 1945 Charter.[44]

Still, in the post-1945 era, US policies tended to embrace more realistic sensibilities, featuring growing scepticism of international institutions, and invoking American exceptionalism and US interests as justifications for rejecting universal norms.[45] By contrast, European countries have tilted in the same period towards a more legalistic position, embracing sovereignty-limiting norms such as those found in human rights treaties, and the jurisdiction of sovereignty-eroding institutions such as the International Criminal Court (ICC) and the European Court of Human Rights (ECtHR) (see van Aaken, this volume; Çalı, this volume; and Yudkivska, this volume). It may be speculated that realistic sensibilities about the alignment of law and power are themselves found in relation to the geopolitical power held by States, albeit inversely correlated to their political rise or decline.[46] Since international law is increasingly invoked as a counter-hegemonic weapon by the weak against the strong, the declining military power of European countries in the post-World War II era appears to have pushed some of them to adopt an expansive version of international law, so as to limit the ability of other, more militarily powerful countries, to compromise their national and regional interests.[47]

Still, the strong attachment of many European States to international law until this very day, notwithstanding its pro-sovereignty and pro-status quo biases, can also be seen as representing a lingering attachment to realistic sensibilities relating to political power. This is not surprising since under the current world order European countries still occupy key positions of political power, including permanent seats on the UN Security Council. Moreover, even the invocation of more idealistic versions of international law as components of European identity[48] can be understood as reflective of power interests in the sense that such visions promote multilateral economic and diplomatic institutions and processes in which European countries have a prominent voice and considerable influence. In fact, being normative actors and champions of international law has been understood by Europeans policy makers as important sources of their 'soft power'.[49]

One specific area in which contemporary European policies, especially those undertaken under the auspices of the EU, appear to be driven by legal realism is institutional reform, often facilitated by European 'comitology'. Examples of such processes of reform include the significant overhauls of the EU treaties (see Vasel, this volume), from the Single European Act, through the Maastricht and Lisbon Agreements, to the Charter on Fundamental Rights and the Banking Union, major amendments to the European

Convention of Human Rights (especially, Protocols 11 and 14) and the numerous changes in the structure of the OSCE and its substantive competencies (see Mihr, this volume).[50] Underlying many of these changes, no doubt, is a belief in the important role of international institutions and legal processes in giving effect to international co-operation and international law norms and values (this belief is captured by the theory of neo-liberal institutionalism).[51] Still, the said reforms are typically premised upon a careful evaluation of the *de facto* performance of existing international institutions and the actual effectiveness of existing international norms and processes. Such reforms tend to be conservative in nature in that they appear to focus on better implementation of pre-existing standards or fine-tuning them than on engaging in the radical overhaul of the relevant legal regime. The practice of gradual legal reform is closely related to legal realism, as it concentrates on actual law application through institutions, processes, and practices, and on a methodological commitment to investigate law in action (as opposed to law on the books) with a view to improving performance and—through it—actual social conditions.

At the same time, there seems to be deeply-seated resistance in Europe to some key insights found in both IR realism and US legal realism, which perhaps explains the relative marginality of realism in the academic discourse on European approaches to international law. First, IR realism (and its New Haven School offshoots) has been criticized for explicitly or implicitly regarding international law as epiphenomenal and subservient to considerations of raw power and political interest. Such an approach cuts against core liberal values and beliefs considering law and the rule of law as constraints on power and as guarantees of freedom and justice. So while the majority of European international lawyers are likely to acknowledge the role of power and interest in law-making (invoking in us the memory of the proverbial Bismarckian sausage-making process),[52] they are much less keen to concede the continued role of power politics in law-interpretation and application. In other words, the attachment to a separation of powers model in the domestic realm, which facilitates drawing sharp distinctions between stages where politics ends and stages where independent, professional, and 'objective' legal processes begin, appears in the eyes of many Europeans to carry over to the international realm notwithstanding the less-than-well-marked lines of separation between the different stages of operation of the institutional machinery of international governance.

Second, legal realism is premised on recognizing—and implicitly, legitimizing—individual agency and broad discretion in law-interpretation and law-application by judges and other professionals working for State agencies. This, however, goes against dominant myths in European legal culture in which judges are featured as *bouche de la loi*,[53] and where professional expertise is presumed to be scientific and impartial. Here too, domestic perceptions are being projected upon the international realm, notwithstanding the politicized processes which have often been put in place for appointing international judges and other international law-applying officials.[54]

The meta-question that presents itself to us in this regard is whether international law theories are descriptive, providing us with tools to better understand a complicated international reality, or whether they are constitutive of reality and influence public attitudes towards it. In this regard, it has been claimed in the past that European international law scholars tend to be ideologically committed to, and professionally invested in, the success of international law. As a result, they have arguably directed their research towards issues that do not put in question the viability of the international law project and the legitimacy of its main institutional building blocks.[55] Instead of focusing on a middle-range theory like realism that draws attention to actual conditions of work inside the 'sausage-making production line' of legal processes, they focused on specific legal doctrines (law on the books) or on high level theories or utopian projects, which have little bearing to the actual life of international law (such as peace through law or the establishment of world government) (see Wiener, this volume).[56]

The wholesale rejection of realism is clearly no longer the case throughout European international law academia, which, as the next section of this chapter shows, has increasingly embraced the empirical turn in international law scholarship. This turn has been accompanied by a host of other academic projects, addressing *inter alia* the democratic deficit of international institutions, the structural biases of international norms, and the historical wrongs perpetrated through the European-dominated international legal order. The willingness to directly confront through scholarly research the actual weaknesses of, and injustices associated with, international law appears to soften, to a large extent, the traditional objections to realism in Europe and create more hospitable conditions for realistic theories, methodologies, and sensibilities.

4. The Empirical Turn in International Legal Research and Realism

It is against the background of a growing detachment between international law practice and traditional international law theory (natural law or positivism), and a growing, albeit still modest, willingness by European legal researchers to review international law norms and institutions from an external perspective that questions—not assumes—their legitimacy and effectiveness, that the empirical turn in international legal research started to gain traction in Europe. This empirical turn is closely related to realism as it focuses on the actual life of the law, and tends to study the interplay between law and power.

As explained by Shaffer and Ginsburg, empirical studies are not completely new to international law scholarship.[57] International law research has always relied on concrete case studies and on comparative surveys of State practice, *opinio juris* and domestic laws (eg with a view to extrapolating from them general principles of law). Furthermore, international law researchers have often combined their academic work with legal practice, and this combination has allowed them to draw upon their practical experience and first-hand impressions from the life of international law in their academic scholarship.[58] Still, the centrality of empirical research has significantly increased in recent years in international law academia, as did the methodological rigour with which it is now being applied. Researchers resorting to empirical research projects now tend to employ qualitative and/or quantitative methods, including interviews, surveys, statistical analysis, text as data, experiments, observational research, and process-tracing, largely drawn from social sciences research methods.

By and large, the questions explored through empirical research methods can be divided into three main categories: (1) questions relating to the development of international norms and institutions; (2) questions relating to the performance and consequences of international law-application mechanisms; and (3) international law as *explanandum* and *explanans* of real world events.[59] Such questions facilitate the exploration of extra-legal motivations and real-world effects of international law (and vice versa), echoing thereby the insights developed in IR realism and legal realism theories concerning the centrality of interests, values, and actual practices to understanding international relations and for predicting legal outcomes.

Many of the reasons identified by Shaffer and Ginsburg for the empirical turn in international legal scholarship apply *a fortiori* in Europe, and some specific academic traditions (eg the Nordic tradition of legal realism, which developed in the mid-20th century, with a methodological focus on empirical evidence about actual judicial practice)[60] appear particularly receptive to it. First, one may note changes in IR theory itself, which resulted in a rejection of the narrative of international law's epiphenomenality (a narrative which was never endorsed in European mainstream academia, given its ideological attachment to the international rule of law project), in favour of more complex IR theories that factor in ideas and values (eg the English School),[61] legal institutions (eg neo-liberal institutionalism),[62] and social interactions (eg constructivism).[63] In tandem, economists, sociologists, behaviourists, and historians have started to direct their attention towards international law as an arena for producing public goods, transmitting cultural values and practices, taking political decisions, and making policy choices. Whereas much of the relevant scholarship initially produced by such social scientists was published in social science academic outlets, some of their work and the work of international lawyers influenced by them gradually migrated to international law journals, including European-based ones.[64] Such academic research work has sometimes been the fruit of collaborations between international law and social science and humanities researchers, facilitated by the greater focus in European academia and funding institutions on interdisciplinarity.

Second, the proliferation of international law-applying bodies—courts, tribunals and other committees, commissions, etc—in the aftermath of the end of the Cold War, and the sharp increase in their output, has generated considerable academic interest in their work and impact. Not only were there now rich datasets for investigating the intricate operations of legal institutions and studying the implementation of decisions they generate—given the high expectations and public controversies attached to new international mechanisms, researchers increasingly shifted their attention to questions of their cost-effectiveness, efficiency, and effectiveness. Empirical research methods used to measure and evaluate domestic law institutions—as part of the quest for their accountability—were thus gradually extended to international legal institutions. In fact, empirical methods were found to be particularly relevant to the study of international institutions given their novelty (which rendered them 'works in progress'), the extensive public debate over their utility (a debate which does not always have close parallels in domestic settings), and their accessibility to researchers based in different countries (whereas research of domestic institutions is sometimes accessible only to researchers based in the same country).

Nowhere has proliferation of international law-applying bodies been more pronounced than in Europe, given the existence of numerous European-based international and regional organizations and cooperation regimes. European courts (see Ziemele, this volume), such as the Court of Justice of the European Union (CJEU) and the ECtHR, are among the most active judicial bodies in the world; and most other international courts and committees, including ones with a global reach, such as the International Court of Justice, the International Criminal Court, the UN Human Rights Treaty Bodies, and the World Trade Organization Dispute Settlement Mechanism, are also located in Europe. Their geographical location and political centrality in a continent ideologically committed to an international rule of law, has rendered such international institutions particularly visible and accessible to European international law researchers with interdisciplinary training, affiliations, and networks.

Furthermore, the real political power delegated by European governments to regional and global international law-applying bodies, as part of their support for international cooperation and regional harmonization, invites more scrutiny of their performance by scholars interested in conditions in Europe than by scholars specializing in other regions of the world, where international institutions have been, and still are, less influential. Hence, concerns about democratic deficits in the EU, generated by perceptions about the transfer of too much power to EU institutions, or about excessive judicial activism by Strasbourg, are likely to encourage empirical research of the powers held by regional bodies, the actual ways in which they exercise their authority over the European citizenry, and the manner in which they effectuate social, political, and economic conditions in Europe.

The need for evaluating the performance of international institutions and for increasing the democratic legitimacy of their operations has also been felt by European-based regional and international organizations, and underlies extensive processes of review, consultation, and reform, often facilitated by political and expert bodies, such as committees of wise persons, consultative groups, working groups, and groups of experts.[65] The research undertaken by such review bodies interacts with academic research, which is often tasked with assisting such organizational processes and other societal challenges. Hence, for example, the EU's Horizon Europe research support programme 'facilitates collaboration and strengthens the impact of research and innovation in developing, supporting and implementing EU policies while tackling global challenges',[66] and the Social Sciences and Humanities (SSH) component of the programme prioritizes 'the most pressing social, political, economic and cultural concerns and expectations of European citizens'.[67] The strong financial incentives to develop research that is policy-supportive, also explains part of the empirical turn in international legal scholarship in Europe: Empirical research requires more resources and entails the allocation of more resources for European research institutions, such as the European Law Institute.[68]

New developments in the field of technology are also likely to encourage empirical legal research on international law: The growing accessibility of digitalized databases containing information about the operations of international bodies and State practice also opened up new research avenues, which were not available to previous generations of international law researchers. Accessibility to rich international law-related datasets has also attracted the attention of social scientists (including computational social scientists) and digital humanities scholars whose research agenda is often dataset-driven. International law scholars therefore increasingly find themselves participating in interdisciplinary projects on international law datasets, such as compliance data, voting patterns of State representatives in international for a, and litigation rates or treaty-relation networks, often undertaking the role of providing legal context and normative meaning to the data collected and analysed by other scientists.

The upshot of these incentives and background conditions has been increased interest by European-based international law scholars in empirical research. Examples of such research include the work of Sarah Nouwen and Wouter Werner on the domestic impact of international criminal law and transitional justice,[69] Veronika Fikfak's work on the impact of human rights remedies on State compliance,[70] Vera Shikhleman's work on geographical biases in the decisions of UN treaty bodies,[71] Anne van Aaken and Tomer Broude's work on the behavioural turn in international law research,[72] and a research project in which both authors of this chapter have participated aimed at evaluating the effectiveness of international courts.[73]

As Shaffer and Ginsburg note, this empirical turn in international legal scholarship has strong ties to legal realism. It can expose biases in judicial decision making, which could allow for making better predictions about legal outcomes ('the prophecies of what the courts will do in fact, and nothing more pretentious, are what I mean by the law')[74] and facilitate judicial reforms. It also allows scholars to assess 'what works' in international law, in terms of shaping actors' behaviour, and introducing normative or institutional changes.[75] In this latter respect, the new legal realism is often not value-free, but rather tends to embrace ideological positions (informed by neo-liberal institutional considerations), actual beliefs about the ways in which specific legal rules promote public goods,[76] and theories about means-ends relationships. At a practical level, the mapping of real-world consequences of legal interventions by international law researchers is likely to provide decision makers with the ability to make informed and evidence-based policy choices and decisions on institutional or regime design.

Still, like other applications of legal realism, the use of empirical data to predict the outcome of international law-application, and reactions to legal decisions, has been criticized for under-estimating the art of law-interpretation and idiosyncratic aspects of human agency in the life of international law.[77] The notion of path dependency and the 'past projecting into the future' might also be regarded as encouraging technocratic and stagnated visions of international law, which is at odds with actual or necessary societal challenges. This, however, raises once again the aforementioned meta-question: Should international law theory be descriptive or prescriptive; and, at another level, is it worth our while to better understand reality at the price of rendering it harder to imagine another reality?

5. 'Ways of Seeing'

The previous analysis can 'direct' the readers towards different readings of the state of legal realism in the European international law tradition. In any event, it challenges a well-established, yet ultimately simplistic dichotomy regarding the two sides of the Atlantic,[78] which associates Europeans with formalism (and thus, anti-realism) and Americans with rule-scepticism and anti-formalism (and thus, realism). As this chapter hints, this presumption is founded upon various historical, cultural, political, and jurisprudential factors, but ignores many other hidden and not so hidden factors that point in the other direction. Indeed, the traditional dichotomy has been persistently challenged by legal scholars who have offered a more nuanced picture. These include Martti Koskenniemi,[79] Jochen von Bernstorff,[80] Oliver Jütersonke,[81] Benedict Kingsbury,[82] and others. In fact, Jean D'Aspremont has recently claimed that both Americans and Europeans share a common commitment to formalism and reinventing it, although they may be using a different vocabulary to describe their approach.[83]

So where does this leave us? How can we draw some conclusions about a European attitude towards legal realism, if Europeans are not exclusively realists, positivists, or starry-eyed idealists? One possible way to square the circle is to discuss European legal realism as a conceptual tool in the context of the notion of a 'culture of formalism' (a term coined by Martti Koskenniemi).[84] For Koskenniemi, the culture of formalism is a 'culture of resistance to power, a social practice of accountability, openness and equality whose status cannot be reduced to the political positions of any one of the parties whose claims are treated within it'.[85] A formalistic outlook allows us to regard resistance as somewhat of an empty vessel awaiting to be filled by specific contents maintaining thereby a distinctive validity of law without reducing it to something 'else'. At the same time, it acknowledges both the external dimensions and internal contradictions of the law. In other words, the culture of formalism recognizes both the indeterminacy and emancipatory power of law.

Returning back to our own understanding of realism as a sensibility that encompasses a multidimensional conceptual framework, we can reimagine the evolution of a European approach towards international law as a dialectic process, not a linear one, that appears to relate to the external dimensions of legal realism and resist at the same time the absolute reductionism of law to its external points of reference via a culture of formalism. Such an approach offers a nuanced picture of European international law realism and challenges well-established traditional assumptions about it. It also allows for space for the approaches to realism to constantly evolve in different substantive law contexts involving different actors, generating an amalgam of different legal theories and research methods.

6. Conclusion

Although European international law scholars tend to be sceptical of the relevance of realism as an IR and legal theory, international law as it developed in Europe always featured and accommodated relations between law and power, and between law and social reality. Such a relationship has become even more apparent following the empirical turn in international law and the increased interdisciplinary and policy-oriented aspects of international law research.

As a result, we can now speak of a realistic sensibility as part of the European international law mentality. Such as sensibility acknowledges the internal limits of legal arguments and the role that extra-legal considerations play in giving contents and direction to international law. The use of the *Koskenniemic* notion of 'culture of formalism' helps in identifying and conceptualizing the tension between recognizing the role of the extra-legal considerations and resisting the reduction of international law to such considerations. Legal realism is, according to this worldview, a piece that helps us provide meaning and direction to the complex puzzle of international law as developed in Europe.

Notes

1. Martti Koskenniemi, 'International Law in Europe between Tradition and Renewal', 16 European Journal of International Law 2005, 1, 113.
2. See chapters in this volume on approaches to international law theory in Germany, Nordic countries, Russia, and France.
3. Martti Koskenniemi, *From Apology to Utopia: The Structure of International Legal Argument* (Cambridge University Press 2005). Koskenniemi notes that the designation apology/utopia can apply to both naturalism and positivism. ibid, 164.
4. Martti Koskenniemi, *The Gentle Civilizer of Nations: The Rise and Fall of International Law 1870–1960* (Cambridge University Press 2005) 96.
5. https://esil-sedi.eu/wp-content/uploads/2018/04/Articles-of-Association-2012-in-English_0.pdf. Last accessed 19 September 2023.
6. Martti Koskenniemi, 'The Politics of International Law', 1 European Journal of International Law 1990, 4, 31.
7. See Anne Orford and Florian Hofmann (eds), *Oxford Handbook of the Theory of International Law* (Oxford University Press 2016) (esp chapters in Part II).

8. See Gregory Shaffer, 'The New Legal Realist Approach to International Law', 28 Leiden Journal of International Law 2015, 189.
9. Gregory Shaffer and Tom Ginsburg, 'The Empirical Turn in International Legal Scholarship', 106 American Journal of International Law 2012, 1. See also a special issue of the Leiden Journal of International Law (vol 28, 2015) on New Legal Realism, with contributions by Gregory Shaffer, Alexandra Huneeus, Andrew Lang, Daniel M Bodansky, Mikael Rask Madsen and Jakob VH Holtermann, Jan Klabbers, and Ino Augsberg.
10. See, eg, Francis A Boyle, 'The Irrelevance of International Law: The Schism Between International Law and International Politics', 10 California Western International Law Journal 1980, 193, 202–203.
11. Hans J Morgenthau, *Politics among Nations: The Struggle for Power and Peace* (McGraw-Hill Higher Education 2006) (7th edn, revised by Kenneth W Thompson and W David Clinton, 2006) 284–285. See also Richard Goldsmith and Eric Posner, *The Limits of International Law* (Oxford University Press 2006) 13.
12. See, eg, Richard H Steinberg, 'Overview: Realism in International Law', 96 Proceedings of the Annual Meeting of the American Society of International Law 2002, 260, 261.
13. See, eg, Kenneth N Waltz, *Theory of International Politics* (Cambridge University Press 1979); John J Mearsheimer, *The Tragedy of Great Power Politics* (Norton 2001).
14. See, eg, Hedley Bull, *The Anarchical Society: A Study of Order in World Politics* (Bloomsbury Publishing 1977); Adam Watson, *Hegemony & History* (Routledge 2007); Barry Buzan, *From International to World Society: English School Theory and the Social Structure of Globalism* (Cambridge University Press 2004).
15. See, eg, Gregory Shaffer, 'Legal Realism and International Law' in Jeffrey L Dunoff and Mark A Pollack (eds), *International Legal Theory: Foundations and Frontiers* (Cambridge University Press 2022).
16. See, eg, Harm Schepel, 'The European Brotherhood of Lawyers: The Reinvention of Legal Science in the Making of European Private Law', 32 Law and Social Inquiry 2007, 183, 185–187.
17. Anonymous, Book Notices, 14 American Law Review 1880, 233, 234. See also Oliver Wendel Holmes, 'The Path of the Law', 10 Harvard Law Review 1897, 457.
18. For a discussion, see Andrew Altman, 'Legal Realism, Critical Legal Studies and Dworkin', 15 Philosophy & Public Affairs 1986, 205, 216–217.
19. For a discussion of the New Haven School and its relationship to legal realism, see Steven R Ratner, 'Legal Realism School' in *Max Planck Encyclopedia of Public International Law* (online version; last updated in 2007). Ratner notes that the New Haven School was criticized for legitimizing the dilution of the role of the law in decision making and for creating an overly complex model of decision making which rendered predictions of legal outcomes almost impossible.
20. See Anne-Marie Slaughter, 'The Real New World Order', 76 Foreign Affairs 1997, 183. The notion of global networks exercising public authority also underlies the development of Global Administrative Law. See, eg, Andrew D Mitchell and John Farnik, 'Global Administrative Law: Can it Bring Global Governance to Account?', 37 Federal Law Review 2009, 237.
21. See Harold H Koh, 'Transnational Legal Process', 75 Nebraska Law Review 1994, 180. Koh's work is based on the work of New Haven School, as well as on the work of Hart and Sacks on the legal process. See William N Eskridge and Philippe P Frickey, 'The Making of "The Legal Process"', 107 Harvard Law Review 1994, 2031.

22. See, eg, Louis Henkin, *How Nations Behave* (Columbia University Press 1968).
23. See, eg, Mohammed Ayoob, 'Inequality and Theorizing in International Relations: The Case for Subaltern Realism', 4 International Studies Review 2002, 27; Daniel Abebe, Adam Chilton, and Tom Ginsburg, 'The Social Science Approach to International Law', 22 Chicago Journal of International Law 2021, 1.
24. Harlan Grant Cohen, 'Are We (Americans) all International Legal Realists Now?' in Chiara Giorgetti and Guglielmo Verdirame (eds), *Concepts on International Law in Europe and the United States* (Cambridge University Press 2021) 33, 35–36.
25. ibid, 43.
26. ibid, 47.
27. ibid, 49.
28. Oliver Jütersonke, 'Realist Approaches to International Law' in Anne Orford and Florian Hofmann (eds), *The Oxford Handbook of the Theory of International Law* (Oxford University Press 2016) 327, 329.
29. Shaffer and Ginsburg (n 9) 10.
30. cf Pierre Bourdieu, *Outline of a Theory of Practice* (Cambridge University Press 1977) 86.
31. There have been, however, certain notable exceptions to the trend of separating legal from political considerations. See, eg, Pieter H Kooijmans, *The Doctrine of the Legal Equality of States: An Inquiry into the Foundations of International Law*, Leyden : A. W. Sythoff (1964) 2–3.
32. See, eg, Hubert Thierry, 'The Thought of Georges Scelle', 1 European Journal of International Law (1990) 193, 195–196.
33. See d'Aspremont, this volume.
34. Koskenniemi, *The Gentle Civilizer of Nations* (n 4) 189.
35. Bardo Fassbender, 'International Constitutional Law: Written or Unwritten?', 15 Chinese Journal of International Law 2016, 489, 507.
36. See, eg, Antony Anghie, 'Finding the Peripheries: Sovereignty and Colonialism in Nineteenth-Century International Law', 40 Harvard International Law Journal 1999 1, 69.
37. Carl von Clausewitz, *On War*, trans Michael Howard and Peter Paret; Michael Howard, Peter Paret, and Bernard Brodie, eds, (Princeton University Press 1984) 87 (originally published in 1832).
38. Chris af Jochnick and Roger Normand, 'The Legitimation of Violence: A Critical History of the Laws of War', 35 Harvard International Law Journal 1994, 49, 63–65. See also *US v. List*, NMT judgment of 19 February 1948, 11 *TWC* (1950) 1230, 1255–1256. Whereas the rejection of 'hard' realist doctrines has been challenged by the Russian invasion of Ukraine in 2022, it remains to be seen whether this crisis marks a return to stark realist sensibilities in European attitude to international affairs.
39. See, eg, Georges Abi-Saab, 'Wars of National Liberation in the Geneva Conventions and Protocols', 165 Recueil des cours 1979 353, 366.
40. See, eg, Andrew Fitzmaurice, *Sovereignty, Property and Empire, 1500–2000* (Cambridge University Press 2014) 267–268.
41. Norman A Graebner, *The Versailles Treaty and Its Legacy: The Failure of the Wilsonian Vision* (Cambridge University Press 2011) 249.
42. See, eg, Morgenthau (n 11) 266–267.
43. See, eg, Bardo Fasssbender, 'The Security Council: Progress is Possible but Unlikely' in Antonio Cassese (ed), *Realizing Utopia: The Future of International Law* (Oxford University Press 2012) 52, 56.

44. See, eg, Nejat Dogan, *Pragmatic Liberal Approach to World Order: The Scholarship of Inis L. Claude, Jr* (University Press of America 2012) 7.
45. See, eg, Donald E Pease, *The New American Exceptionalism* (University of Minnesota Press 2009) 33.
46. cf Stefano Guzzini, *Power, Realism and Constructivism* (Routledge 2013) 6–7 ('There is a power politics of power analysis').
47. See, eg, Andrew Moravcsik, 'Europe, the Second Superpower', 108 Current History 2010, 91, 94; Nico Krisch, 'International Law in Times of Hegemony: Unequal Power and the Shaping of the International Legal Order', 16 European Journal of International Law 2005, 369, 375.
48. See, eg, Armin von Bogdandy, *International Law in Times of Hegemony: Unequal Power and the Shaping of the International Legal Order*, 3 *I-CON* (2005) 295, 311; Hristina Runcheva Tasev, Milena Apostolovska- Stepanoska, and Leposava Ognjanoska, 'Union Based on the Rule of Law: The Court of Justice of the European Union and the (Future of) European Integration', 11 Eastern Journal of European Studies 2020, 396, 410.
49. See, eg, John McCormick, 'Europe as a Cosmopolitan Global Actor', 77 Il Politico 2012, 32, 40–46; Revecca Pedi, 'The (Small) State of the Union: Assessing the EU's Ability to Implement Its Global Strategy', 27 New Perspectives 2019, 43, 48.
50. See, eg, Wolfgang Zellner, *Using The OSCE More Effectively—Ideas And Recommendations, Institute for Peace Research and Security Policy at the University of Hamburg* (2020).
51. See, eg, Robert O Keohane, 'Twenty Years of Institutional Liberalism', 26 International Relations 2012, 125.
52. The statement that 'laws are like sausages. It is best not to see them being made' is widely attributed to Otto von Bismark, though precise details about when and where it uttered made remain obscure. Steven Luxenberg, 'A Likely Story ... And That's Precisely the Problem', *Washington Post*, 17 April 2005.
53. See Charles-Louis de Secondat de Montesquieu, II *L'esprit des lois—Livre XI* (1803 edn) 57 (originally published in 1748). For a discussion, see Serge Dauchy, 'Le juge, bouche de la loi—A propos de la célèbre métaphore de Montesquieu', Nagoya University Journal of Law and Politics 2014, 325.
54. See generally, Ruth Mackenzie, Kate Malleson, Penny Martin, and Philippe Sands, *Selecting International Judges: Principle, Process, and Politics* (Oxford University Press 2010).
55. See, eg, Jochen von Bernstorff, 'International Legal Scholarship as a Cooling Medium in International Law and Politics', 25 European Journal of International Law 2015, 977, 982–983.
56. See, eg, Martti Koskenniemi, 'The Fate of Public International Law: Between Technique and Politics', 70 Modern Law Review 2007 1, 2–3.
57. Shaffer and Ginsburg (n 9) 2.
58. See, eg, Sara Dezalay (with the contribution of Yves Dezalay), 'Professionals of International Justice from the Shadow of State Diplomacy to the Pull of the Market for Commercial Arbitration' in Jean d'Aspremont, Tarcisio Gazzini, André Nollkaemper, and Wouter Werner (eds), *International Law as a Profession* (Cambridge University Press 2017) 311, 317–323.
59. See Shaffer and Ginsburg (n 9) 5; Anne van Aaken and Joel P Trachtman, 'Political Economy of International Law: Towards a Holistic Model of State Behavior' in Alberta Fabbricotti (ed), *The Political Economy of International Law: A European Perspective* (Edward Elgar Publishing 2016) 9, 12–13.

60. For a discussion of the uneasy relationship between Nordic approaches to international law and to legal realism, see Jakob VH Holtermann, 'Conspicuous Absence and Mistaken Presence: A Note on the Ambiguous Role of Scandinavian Legal Realism in Nordic Approaches to International Law' in Astrid Kjeldgaard-Pedersen (ed), *Nordic Approaches to International Law* (Brill 2017) 214. The Nordic legal realism tradition focuses on studying what judges actually believe constitutes *lex lata*, distinguishing, however, between legal doctrine and legal politics.
61. See Hedley Bull, *The Anarchical Society: A Study of Order in World Politics* (1977); Hedley Bull and Adam Watson, *The Expansion of International Society* (Oxford University Press 1984).
62. See Robert Keohane and Joseph Nye, *Power and Interdependence: World Politics in Transition* (Scott Foresman) (2nd edn, 1989).
63. See Alexander Wendt, *Social Theory of International Politics* (1999); Martha Finnemore and Kathryn Sikkink, 'Taking Stock: The Constructivist Research Program in International Relations and Comparative Politics', 4 Annual Review of Political Science 2001, 391.
64. See, eg, Jeffrey L Dunoff and Mark A Pollack, 'Experimenting with International Law', 28 European Journal of International Law 2018, 1317; Moshe Hirsch, 'Cognitive Sociology, Social Cognition and Coping with Racial Discrimination in International Law', 30 European Journal of International Law 2019, 1319. See also 'Symposium on The Psychology of International Law', co-edited by Anne Van Aaken and Tomer Broude, 30 European Journal of International Law 2019, 1225 et seq.
65. See, eg, Antoine Vauchez, *Brokering Europe* (Cambridge University Press 2015) 192.
66. http://www.ec.europa.eu/info/research-and-innovation/funding/funding-opportunities/funding-programmes-and-open-calls/horizon-europe_en
67. www.ec.europa.eu/info/research-and-innovation/research-area/social-sciences-and-humanities_en
68. https://www.europeanlawinstitute.eu.
69. See Sarah Nouwen, *Complementarity in the Line of Fire: The Catalysing Effect of the International Criminal Court in Uganda and Sudan* (Cambridge University Press 2013); Wouter G Werner and Sarah Nouwen, 'Doing Justice to the Political, The ICC in Uganda and Sudan', 11 European Journal of International Law 2010, 1. A broad EU FP7 empirical research project on the domestic impact of international criminal law was undertaken throughout 2007–2010 by a consortium of European universities including University of Amsterdam, Reykjavik University, Hebrew University, and University College London. https://en.ru.is/domac/.
70. Veronika Fikfak, 'Changing State Behaviour: Damages before the European Court of Human Rights', 29 European Journal of International Law 2019, 1091.
71. Vera Shikhleman, 'Geography, Politics and Culture in the United Nations Human Rights Committee', 28 European Journal of International Law 2017, 845.
72. Anne van Aaken and Tomer Broude, 'The Psychology of International Law: An Introduction', 30 European Journal of International Law 2020, 1225.
73. Yuval Shany, *Assessing the Effectiveness of International Courts* (Oxford University Press 2014).
74. Holmes (n 17) 461.
75. Shaffer and Ginsburg (n 9) 9.

76. On the focus of actual beliefs as part of new realism, see Jakob VH Holtermann and Mikael Rask Madsen, 'European New Legal Realism and International Law: How to Make International Law Intelligible', 28 Leiden Journal of International Law 2015, 211, 221.
77. See, eg, Jan Klabbers, 'Whatever Happened to Gramsci? Some Reflections on New Legal Realism', 28 Leiden Journal of International Law 2015, 469; d'Aspremont, this volume.
78. See Guglielmo Verdirame, '"The Divided West": International Lawyers in Europe and America', 18 European Journal of International Law 2007, 553–580.
79. See Martti Koskenniemi, 'What Is International Law For?' in Malcolm D Evans (ed), *International Law* (Oxford University Press 2011) 57.
80. See Jochen Von Benstorff, *The Public International Law Theory of Hans Kelsen: Believing in Universal Law* (Cambridge University Press 2010).
81. Oliver Jütersonke, *Morgenthau, Law and Realism* (Cambridge University Press 2010).
82. Benedict Kingsbury, 'Legal Positivism as Normative Politics: International Society, Balance of Power and Lassa Oppenheim's Positive International Law', 13 European Journal of International Law 2002, 401.
83. Jean D'Aspremont, 'International Lawyers and Legal Forms: Transatlantic Denials' in Chiara Giorgetti and Guglielmo Verdirame (eds), *Concepts on International Law in Europe and the United States* (Cambridge University Press 2021) 13.
84. For a critical discussion of the 'culture of formalism' notion see, eg, Jochen von Bernstoff, 'Sisyphus was an International Lawyer: On Martti Koskenniemi's "From Apologia to Utopia" and the Place of Law in International Politics', 7 German Law Journal 2006, 1015; Jean d'Aspremont and Martti Koskenniemi, 'The Mainstream, and Self-Reflectivity', 29 Leiden Journal of International Law 2016, 625.
85. Koskenniemi, *The Gentle Civilizer of Nations* (n 4) 500.

CHAPTER 14

CONSTITUTIONALISM

ANTJE WIENER

1. Introduction

In the context of Part II of the handbook and the focus on intellectual traditions in Europe, this chapter recalls key developments of constitutionalism as an emerging concept as political scientists and international and European lawyers sought to explain and understand key principles and terms of the materializing Euro-polity. The chapter especially reflects processes of constitutionalization beyond modern nation-states. Following Ernst B Haas's observation that political processes were not merely driven by States, but also by and through international organizations,[1] notions of constitutionalism 'beyond the State'—including post-national constitutionalism as well as global constitutionalism—gained traction against the background of the European Union (EU)'s novel dynamics of constitution-building in the West, and in parallel, the EU's massive enlargement towards the East.[2] European nation-state building was forged through political processes of locating authority within the organization of the State,[3] the social constitution of the institutions of citizenship rights,[4] and the stipulation of constitutional norms and principles in the written and unwritten constitutions of modern nation-states. By contrast, regional integration and the process of building the European non-State polity was notably driven by what European lawyers dubbed 'integration through law'.[5] In distinction from nation-state building processes and diverse processes of regional integration elsewhere (compare van Aaken, this volume and Vasel, this volume), many political scientists preferred to speak of the EU as an emergent *sui generis* polity.[6]

This model of constitutionalism beyond the State was soon taken beyond the boundaries of the continuously enlarging Euro-polity and used to explain and understand processes of constitutionalization that forged constitutive norms and rules of the international liberal order.[7] While these norms of the liberal international order (LIO) have recently become deeply contested, they were constitutive for ordering global politics and law for the better part of the 20th century. So much so, that constitutionalism developed a global reach and global constitutionalism became a recognized reference concept for international lawyers and International Relations (IR) theorists alike.[8] Typically, the notion of global constitutionalism or its precursors emerges in the environment of international organizations and reflects the need to qualify regulatory practices or to put constitutional principles in place. The EU, the World Trade Organisation (WTO), and the United Nations (UN) have been among the first organizational contexts in which constitutionalization has become a common feature, with the intention of qualifying world trade, environmental, human rights, and post-conflict policies based on constitutional principles.

These changes reflect a shift from globalized towards constitutionalized international relations that accounted for constitutional development through international politics among EU member States and candidate countries[9] as well as through the practices of international relations on a global scale.[10] Politically, this development indicates potential conflict following contested constitutional norms, principles, and procedures—a scenario which gives rise to the question of whether and to what extent the familiar (modern) constitutional reference frame is suitable for assessing and understanding constitutionalism beyond the State?

The remainder of this chapter is organized in three further sections. Section 2 highlights the contested quality and use of constitutionalism as an approach with distinct intellectual traditions and political purposes. The section begins from Weiler and Wind's observation of the process as a European phenomenon[11] and moves on to centre on the emergence of global constitutionalism as an interdisciplinary field. While the former evolved within the interdisciplinary discipline of European integration including probed interdisciplinary conversations and collaborations between law and political science, the latter addresses features and effects of 'unbound' constitutionalism (ie the transfer of constitutional norms, principles, and procedures from domestic into regional and global environments) in a global context.[12] Section 3 recalls scholarly moves towards common conceptual frames for research on constitutionalism beyond the State. Against this backdrop, Section 4 offers an outlook on the developing interdisciplinary field of Global Constitutionalism.

2. Constitutionalism Beyond the State: Contested Meanings, Uses, and Purposes

From the perspective of international lawyers and international relations theorists, contestation of constitutional norms is not surprising. The meanings of norms are always contested outside bounded communities or social groups. In the absence of both, the social recognition of normative meaning differs and becomes contested. These contestations over normative meanings indicate who is jostling over which norm in the 'normative universe' of lawyers[13] or the 'universe of political discourse'.[14] While contestatory practices merely confirm the widely shared view that the purpose and function of global constitutionalization mean different things to different people, they also have a crucial role as indicators of normative conflict. To be sure, under conditions of unequal power relations and socio-cultural diversity that remain a global constant despite advancing economic and financial globalization, contestation of norms in the global realm can be assumed to be the 'default' condition. Outside bounded political communities, international collaboration depends on agreements, treaties, and conventions.[15] While these have traditionally been drawn up by States, the implementation of their norms and regulations depends on the acceptance of a widening State-plus actorship.

As norms research in International Relations (IR) and international law has demonstrated with reference to a plethora of cases, norm implementation that involves transborder practices is never a done deal. Instead, norm following depends on a series of interactions that are qualified by habitual and cognitive elements,[16] a phenomenon also captured in the lawyers' debate on legal tradition.[17] The probability of uncontested compliance with norms grows with iterated international interaction.[18] In turn, this implies that in the absence of common knowledge and shared background experiences, which are defined as individually held normative 'meaning-in-use', norms and their compliance are likely to be contested.[19] While interactively generated, the perception of normative meaning rests with individual actors who carry their 'normative baggage' across borders.[20] It follows that outside bounded communities or social groups, which mark common knowledge, experience, and expectation, normative meanings are less bound by a political community, domestic law, or social groups and, as a consequence, become dispersed and unruly. In the absence of social recognition or doctrinal acceptance, international interaction is therefore subject to the—always latently present—contestation of norms. Speaking more specifically from the perspective of constitutionalism proper, however, the expectation towards the behaviour of the addressees of constitutionalization differs. In the domestic context, a dominant narrative of constitutionalization is expected to forge national unity based on a convincing story about the origin, role, and long-term purpose of a particular constitution.[21] While this does not always work, experience with such successful constitutional narratives does suggest the importance of their role in the domestic context, especially when considering the history of modern state-building. In the global realm, however, it is highly unlikely for the narrative of constitutionalization to be accepted as a convincing story by all stakeholders.

2.1 Constitutionalism unbound

In the absence of established rules of engagement based on modern government institutions, observations of constitutionalization and references to the concept of constitutionalism and related principles such as, for example, in the context of regional integration in (Western) Europe were puzzling at first. As constitutional terms, principles and norms were moved beyond the boundaries of politically constituted nation-states and became 'unbound',[22] as it were, the conceptual meanings and their use were contested. Depending on the distinct intellectual traditions that were brought to bear, the purposes and principles of constitutionalism differed. This contested character of constitutionalism has been coined by debates about the necessity and purpose of constitutionalization, or constitutions, in regional contexts such as the Euro-polity, in global contexts such as the UN setting, and most recently also in national contexts where calls for new constitutions such as in Chile, or the change from an unwritten towards a written constitution in the United Kingdom (UK) were noted.[23]

In light of the contested meaning and purpose of constitutionalism and its increasing interdisciplinary use, the definition of central concepts of constitutionalism and constitutionalization in order to generate a common conceptual language—without oppression or neglecting the rich variety of intellectual traditions underlying constitutional thought—assumes key importance. To provide the means and framework for addressing the phenomenon of constitutionalization and the concept of constitutionalism beyond the State and for purposes of distinction and interdisciplinary recognition elsewhere, we proposed defining 'constitutionalization' as a process by which institutional arrangements in the non-constitutional global realm have taken on a constitutional quality early on.[24]

Notably, as a social process constitutionalization is performed and driven by distinct social, political, and legal practices. Therefore, the emergence and the very constitutional quality of the process remain to be established by empirical research. By contrast, 'constitutionalism' is defined as a theoretical approach which represents a framework for conceiving and conducting research on the phenomenon of constitutionalization. As such, it allows for studying and understanding the phenomenon being observed such as, for example, 'unbound' constitutionalization—the shift from globalized towards constitutionalized international relations. However, as theories are contingent upon their context of emergence (if not necessarily parochial), the distinction between different types of constitutionalism such as ancient, modern, European, Confucian, or late modern is helpful for analytical purposes.[25]

2.2 Intellectual traditions and root disciplines

The intellectual traditions of the root disciplines that carried this debate in Europe to begin with included especially international law, European law, European studies, political theory, and IR theory. The most promising approaches for developing a research programme more specifically on global constitutionalism in conjunction with constitutional theory were the global governance approach, the world society approach, and international law. Each of these three approaches is well equipped to study the emergence and effects of globalization from its own legal, sociological, or political science perspective. However, all are hard-pressed to address the normative challenge that is part of the phenomenon of constitutionalization.[26] Constitutional rules are seen as commonly agreed; constitutional legitimacy follows from the assumption, albeit hypothetical, that the constitution has been put into place by the *pouvoir constituant*, that is, members of a community who are conceptualized as the constitution's constituent power.

Not surprisingly, this concept typically carries greater weight with lawyers than with political scientists and sociologists.[27] However, with the debate turning to constitutional change beyond the State, social scientists are increasingly joining in the discussion.[28] As attention was directed towards global constitutionalism as an approach, constitutionalism beyond the State was further advanced by a vibrant interdisciplinary discussion drawing on international relations[29] as well as transnational interactions.[30] Against this background, global constitutionalisation entails the transfer of fundamental constitutional norms such as the rule of law, human rights, and democracy—as well as adjacent principles and procedures—from the domestic to the global environment. Since 2012, the journal of Global Constitutionalism has facilitated a platform for interdisciplinary debate on the topic. All these developments notwithstanding, to date, the academic literature diverges widely with regard to assessing and evaluating constitutionalization beyond the State and defining global constitutionalism as a concept, a subfield, or simply an 'agora' for debate.[31]

If anything, the phenomenon of constitutionalism beyond the State has been the subject of interdisciplinarity debate. In the process, distinct European intellectual traditions have been brought to bear. Given the range of approaches and meanings and especially the interdisciplinary use of the concept of constitutionalism, conceptual clarifications and definitions that provide a common reference are key. Qualified as a strategy, global constitutionalization stands for multiple normative efforts (predominantly of States advised by learned legal scholars and political experts) to counter the legitimacy deficit in global governance. The latter has been noted as entailing political and legal effects of the ubiquitous process of economic globalization.[32] Sceptical voices regarding both the desirability and the success of global constitutionalization have raised concerns with regard to the future role of international law in light of a scenario of expanding global constitutionalization. The debate about the judgments of the European Court of Justice (now Court of Justice of the European Union (CJEU)) in the *Kadi* case[33] is pertinent here. In a nutshell, the Court objected to the UN's ability to protect fundamental human rights as human rights protector and decided to judge as long as the UN did not perform appropriately, i.e. referring to the Solange norm (Engl.: 'as long as' is translated from the German word: 'solange').[34]

Others wondered, 'why constitutionalize' international institutions in the first place?[35] The global administrative law literature in particular remains highly critical of a constitutional remedy of the legitimacy deficit of Global Governance.[36] Meanwhile, a third group of scholars[37] has been engaged in the project of identifying 'what a constitutional international *legal order* could look like'.[38] Elsewhere, IR scholars pointed to a rising critical view on behalf of non-State actors that defy global constitutionalization because in their perception, it means enhanced Westernization.[39] Emerging regional powers such as the BRICS countries (ie the association of Brazil, Russia, India, China, and South

Africa) have equally raised political concerns about the desirability and purpose of global constitutionalization.[40] Notably, it is increasingly non-'Western' States that advance the position that international agreements are only acceptable as long as they do not threaten to undermine national sovereignty, notwithstanding prior concessions to other institutional arrangements such as, for example, the pooling of sovereignty. Political protest, especially in regions outside Europe, has shed light on non-State actors who equally voice their opposition vis-à-vis the spread of 'Western' principles through global constitutionalization.[41]

These ongoing debates notwithstanding, global constitutionalization has had and continues to have an effect on a range of international institutions of quite distinct size and location.[42] These include, for example, the UN, the EU, the WTO, the African Union (AU), the South African Development Community (SADC), Association of South East Asian Nations (ASEAN) as well as the BRICS. With the increasing reference to and use of global constitutionalization as a strategy to counter the legitimacy deficit in global governance,[43] on the one hand, and contestations of fundamental constitutional norms voiced by State-plus actorship[44] in the global realm on the other, global constitutionalism has gradually carved out an interdisciplinary space—an agora—for addressing matters of constitutionalism beyond the State. Questions which keep this intellectual space alive address the role of global constitutionalism as a reference theory with regard to political and legal strategies or for assessing the normative substance and institutional shape to deliver against the background of previous experience with and expectations towards constitutionalization.

With a view to offering an overview of the emergent field, the following presents three different schools that were perceived as offering a distinct conceptual input often pursuing quite varying normative purposes at the time. Each of these was considered to be of relevance for research on constitutionalism beyond the State.[45]

3. Three Schools of Constitutionalism Beyond the State

This section suggests that contributions to the debate are distinguishable with reference to three schools, which can be roughly classified according to their respective functionalist, normative, or pluralist approaches. Although all the schools share the observation of a qualitative shift from globalized towards constitutionalized relations and take a historically sensitive approach to constitutionalism, the concept of global constitutionalism as applied and developed by the contributors to each school reflects different expectations. A notable quality of global constitutionalism as a field in the social sciences and law is that the distinct perspectives are not informed predominantly by single disciplinary approaches. Instead, the unique characteristic of each school is based on the way the concept is approached and applied and is hence practice-based.

The main features of the schools have developed through a choice of either mapping or shaping the global realm according to constitutional standards. This practice-based distinction of the three schools can be summarized according to the main standpoints, interests, and principles that situate each school within the field of global constitutionalism. Leading questions address the purpose and possibilities of constitutionalism with regard to developing the most feasible approach to justice and legitimacy in the global realm.

Although all three schools generally share the observation of an enhanced constitutional quality beyond the nation or State as a result of a process which can be seen as a major shift from globalized towards constitutionalized international relations and hence agree that global constitutionalism is a social phenomenon, the consequences derived from this observation could hardly be more opposed. The dividing line between the groups emerges according to their answer to the question of whether they consider mapping or shaping the central activity of global constitutionalism. Depending on their respective theoretical standpoints, that is, stressing either a more normative or a more pluralist background, in the 2000s each school harboured different intentions with regard to constitutionalism beyond the State. The debate at the time developed most notably against the background of European integration, hence the reference to predominantly Europe-based scholarship. With the rise of global discipline over time, we witness a much wider range of diverse voices in the now established field of global constitutionalism.[46]

3.1 The normative school

The normative school would view global constitutionalism as a strategic move towards establishing or accommodating a global constitution, or at least towards compensating for constitutional loss at the national or subnational level through purposeful constitutionalization in the global realm. Although its contributors share a common interest in shaping the world order according to modern principles of constitutional law and justice, the normative school is sharply divided between supporters and opponents of a global constitution. In sum, this school engages in the project of shaping the global order according to specific normative principles. The key conceptual approach of this group thus rests on the extension of principles, norms, and rules of modern constitutionalism beyond the modern State with the goal of constructing a global order. Good examples of the approach are included in this section. Habermas[47] puts forward his long-time argument that whereas a global constitution is neither necessary nor desirable, a neo-Kantian, politically constituted world society is. Peters and Armingeon[48] stands out as an interdisciplinary collection of articles edited by a political scientist and a lawyer. As such, it offers a succinct vantage point on the emerging debate about global constitutionalism and constitutionalization. Fassbender[49] represents what might be called a stand-alone perspective in the debate by maintaining the argument that the UN Charter should be seen as a global constitution. Quite the opposite position is expressed by Grimm,[50] who does not consider constitutions other than the modern constitutions of nation-states possible or desirable.

3.2 The pluralist school

The pluralist school emphasizes the importance of distinct ancient, modern, and post-modern eras of constitutionalism. This school takes a critical approach to universalist assumptions and theorizes constitutional change as contextualized, contingent, and constitutive. The school's authors would typically question the uncritical reference to the regulative ideal of neo-Kantian federalism or liberal community ideals as stable regulative frames for constitutional change in the global realm. In sum, this school combines mapping and shaping, taking a reflexive approach that integrates the process of structured observation (mapping) with that of normative construction (shaping). That is, the school takes into account the social practices of constitutionalism as they extend beyond modern State boundaries with the intention of identifying the variety of possible and desired principles, norms, and rules of constitutionalism that are considered appropriate by a plurality of global actors. Accordingly, this group involves mostly pluralists, pragmatists, and critical scholars. Good examples of the school are Krisch[51] and Halberstam and Stein,[52] and Tully who develops a critical approach to democratic constitutionalism and demonstrates its value for the study of real-world politics. This approach is substantiated further by his seminal *Public Philosophy in a New Key* which was published in two volumes.[53]

3.3 Combined perspectives

Despite the distinct standpoints on how to use global constitutionalism (see Section 4), it is important to acknowledge that the boundaries between the schools are fuzzy. Often, a scholarly perspective is developed from a two-tiered perspective that comfortably combines two schools. Examples for this approach are Anne Peters's call for purposeful constitutionalization to compensate for normative deficits following globalization;[54] Mattias Kumm's functionalist distinction between lowercase c and capital C constitutionalism, on the one hand, and his cosmopolitan claim for constitutionalism 'as a jurisprudential account claiming to describe the deep structure of public law',[55] on the other; Jo Shaw's post-national approach to European constitutionalism, which advances a normative argument for responsibility while discarding the modern constitutional architecture favoured by the normative school's main protagonists;[56] and Krisch's combination of the functionalist and pluralist schools when writing on global administrative law[57] and his development of the concept of post-national constitutionalism.[58]

Another way two schools combine is the shared focus of some members of the normative and pluralist schools on the way nonstate actors are able to exercise agency, that is, to shape the development and modification of constitutional norms.[59] There is, in sum, sufficient potential for arguments to be had and positions to be refined. All this should be achieved based on more systematic interdisciplinary research. The scholarship contributing to the interdisciplinary field of global constitutionalism will need to keep its two constitutive dimensions of mapping—describing the shift from globalized towards constitutionalized relations while identifying their constitutional substance and shaping (ie improving) the conditions and substance of this shift according to normative standards—analytically apart. From this background, it will be possible to identify the critical juncture in the relational processes of mapping and shaping constitutional development with global reach. Weiler and Wind[60] demonstrate well that contributions to the pluralist school often draw on studies of regional or subnational processes of constitutionalization beyond the State.

4. Outlook: Global Constitutionalism—A New Interdisciplinary Field

As an interdisciplinary research field, Global Constitutionalism has developed from an earlier literature with a *regional* focus on the phenomenon of 'constitutionalism beyond the State', especially in conjunction with European integration facing various rounds of enlargement.[61] The more recent perspective on global constitutionalization[62] has generated variation with regard to research purpose, approach, and research outcome. While these variations mark the field's interdisciplinary character, they also point towards the advantages and disadvantages of working within a multi-disciplinary setting which is largely demonstrated by 'thin' theoretical frameworks and 'thick' descriptive research methods.[63]

For more than a decade now, Global Constitutionalism has been an emerging interdisciplinary field that draws predominantly, albeit not exclusively, on the literature of international law, IR, and global governance. Notably, the field exists more than an agora, that is, an intellectually conceived place which facilitates interdisciplinary debate (see the journal of *Global Constitutionalism*). While some have remained sceptical about the field's purpose and effect, pointing for example to its 'over-principled approach' with rather 'unspecific demands',[64] some global governance scholars noted the crucial importance of 'emotional' dimensions of democratic global governance which are developed through the identity-forging practices of constitutional democracies (including the singing of national anthems, eg) as quite central when facing the challenge of filling the 'gaps' left by 'nominal global governance'.[65]

The institutional foundations of the academic field of Global Constitutionalism emerged from universities (eg St Andrews, Berlin, Hamburg, Heidelberg, Yale, Berlin, Southampton, Edinburgh among many others) and handbooks,[66] centring on their own flagship journal published with Cambridge University Press and attracting world-renowned interdisciplinary scholarship.

Global constitutionalism should therefore be conceived as both a cutting-edge theory and as the basis for a new research programme with interdisciplinary relevance. Contestations are globally noticeable and much commented upon, whether as a hindrance to smooth policy implementation[67] or as a condition for democratic substance.[68] However, even though political struggle is by now a relatively frequent phenomenon in global law and governance, and access to contestation is no longer under the exclusive control of the State, global constitutionalists still tend to value universal concepts over systematic comparative research or over developing a more methodologically sound interdisciplinary research framework.[69] The latter would, for example, allow for the integration of constitutionalization as a reflexive element in the description of international institutions.

4.1 New places and outlets of constitutional debate

The project of establishing a new journal titled *Global Constitutionalism*[70] providing an agora for discussion about changing norms, rules, and concepts of constitutionalism in the 21st century paved the way towards interdisciplinary discussions including the social sciences and law. Three changes in world politics mattered as well: first, the growing impact of principles of fundamental rights on decision-making processes in international organizations considering, for example, trade policy, climate policy, or security; second, the influence of constitutionalization in the process of European integration; and third, the contested role of the United Nations Security Council (UNSC) with regard to taking decisions about military interventions and the application of smart sanctions that have become almost routine practices following the watershed World Trade Center attacks of 11 September 2001.[71] The latter provided the kick-off of a return to the larger questions in IR theory as well as an enhanced interdisciplinary collaboration that raised awareness about law and politics across disciplinary boundaries.[72]

In the 2020s context, which is marked by multiple crises with global reach including the COVID-19 pandemic, climate change, and the Russian war on Ukraine, the focus on the contested quality of constitutional norms 'beyond the State' in particular has received more urgent attention by scholars and politicians. The repeated Russian aggression against Ukraine in 2022 paired with a rising number of domestic populist uprisings especially has contributed to the concern about the role and effect of international law and the rule of law in a global context.[73] These political events have led to a new discussion about 'deep contestation' of international orders and their fundamental norms.[74]

A number of key articles by renowned academics led the debate by asking big questions which were addressed by a number of seminal articles that have generated key conceptual impact and subsequently triggered often interdisciplinary international debate (compare, eg, the debate between Grimm and Habermas on the question 'Does

Europe Need a Constitution?').[75] Different from international law, in which (global) constitutionalism has been discussed more broadly and intensely since the turn of the 21st century, IR came late to the topic. Yet in light of issues of regulatory governance, politicization, and multilateralism in the increasingly constitutionalized context of the LIO, highlighted the importance of concepts such as accountability and democracy, and with them issues that revealed the shortcomings of governance approaches.[76] Leading up to this wider interdisciplinary discussion included publications which have been particularly vital for defining leading questions about constitutionalism beyond the State.[77] By doing so, these works became instrumental to the development of constitutionalism beyond the State.

Notes

1. Ernst B Haas, *Beyond the Nation State* (Stanford UP 1964).
2. Jo Shaw, 'Post-national Constitutionalism in the European Union', 6(4) Journal of European Public Policy 1999, 579 (hereafter Shaw, 'Post-national Consititutionalism'); Christian Joerges, Yves Meny, and Joseph H Weiler, 'Mountain or Molehill? A Critical Appraisal of the Commission White Paper on Governance' (2001) Jean Monnet Working Papers, Harvard Law School, 2001/06; Neil Walker, 'The EU and the WTO: Constitutionalism in a New Key' in Grainne de Búrca and Joanne Scott (eds), *The EU and the WTO: Legal and Constitutional Aspects* (Hart Publishing 2001).
3. Charles Tilly (ed), *The Formation of National States in Western Europe* (Princeton UP 1975).
4. Thomas H Marshall, *Citizenship and Social Class and Other Essays* (Cambridge UP 1950).
5. Paul Craig and Gráinne de Búrca, *Gráinne EU Law: Text, Cases, and Materials* (6th edn, Oxford 2015); Deirdre Curtin, *Executive Power in the European Union: Law, Practice and Constitutionalism* (OUP 2009).
6. Markus Jachtenfuchs and Beate Kohler-Koch, 'Regieren im dynamischen Mehrebenensystem' in Markus Jachtenfuchs and Beate Kohler-Koch (eds), *Europäische Integration* (Verlag für Sozialwissenschaften 1996).
7. David Lake, Lisa Martin, and Thomas Risse, 'Challenges to the Liberal Order: Reflections on International Organization', 75(2) International Organization 2021, 1.
8. Antje Wiener et al, 'Global Constitutionalism: Human Rights, Democracy and the Rule of Law', 1(1) Global Constitutionalism 2012, 1 (hereafter Wiener et al, 'Global Constitutionalism'); Anthony F. Lang and Antje Wiener (eds), *Handbook on Global Constitutionalism* (Edward Elgar 2017) (hereafter Lang and Wiener, *Handbook 2017*); Anthony F Lang and Antje Wiener (eds), *Handbook on Global Constitutionalism* (Edward Elgar 2023) (hereafter Lang and Wiener, *Handbook 2023*).
9. Joseph H H Weiler and Marlene Wind (eds), *European Constitutionalism beyond the State* (CUP 2003)(hereafter Weiler and Wind, *European Constitutionalism*).
10. Jeffrey L Dunoff and Mark A Pollack (eds), *Interdisciplinary Perspectives on International Law and International Relations: The State of the Art* (Cambridge 2013); Jutta Brunnée and Stephen J Toope, 'Interactional Legal Theory, the International Rule of Law and Global Constitutionalism' in Anthony F Lang and Antje Wiener (eds), *Handbook on Global Constitutionalism* (Edward Elgar 2017).
11. Weiler and Wind, *European Constitutionalism* (n 9).

12. Antje Wiener and Stefan Oeter, 'Introduction: Who Recognizes the Emperor's Clothes Anymore?', 14(3) International Journal of Constitutional Law 2006, 608 (hereafter Wiener and Oeter, 'Introduction'); Wiener et al, 'Global constitutionalism' (n 8).
13. Robert M Cover, 'The Supreme Court 1982, Foreword: Nomos and Narrative', 97 Harvard Law Review 1983, 4; Annelise Riles, 'Anthropology, Human Rights, and Legal Knowledge: Culture in the Iron Cage', 108 American Anthropologist 2006, 52, citing Michael Reisman, 'International incidents: Introduction to a New Genre in the Study of International Law' in Michael Reisman and Andrew R Willard (eds), *International Incidents: The Law that Counts in World Politics* (Princeton UP 1988).
14. Jane Jenson, 'Paradigms and Political Discourse: Protective Legislation in France and the United States before 1914', 22(2) Canadian Journal of Political Science/Revue canadienne de science politique 1989, 235.
15. Abram Chayes and Antonia Handler Chayes, 'On Compliance', 47(2) International Organization 1993, 175 (hereafter Chayes and Chayes, 'On Compliance').
16. Abram Chayes and Antonia Handler Chayes, *The New Sovereignty. Compliance with International Regulatory Regimes* (Harvard UP 1995); Jeffrey T Checkel, 'The Constructivist Turn in International Relations Theory', 50 World Politics 1998, 324; Marta Finnemore and Kathryn Sikkink, 'International Norm Dynamics and Political Change', 52(4) International Organization 1998, 887; Harold Koh, 'Why Do Nations Obey International Law?', 106 Yale Law Journal 1997, 2599 (hereafter Koh, 'Why Do Nations Obey International Law?'); James G March and Johan P Olsen, 'The Institutional Dynamics of International Political Orders', 52(4) International Organization 1998, 943; Thomas Risse, Stephen C Ropp, and Kathryn Sikkink (eds), *The Power of Human Rights: International Norms and Domestic Change* (CUP 1999); Thomas Risse, Stephen C Ropp, and Kathryn Sikkink (eds), *The Persistent Power of Human Rights: From Commitment to Compliance* (CUP 2013).
17. Matthias Ruffert, 'Common Principles and National Traditions—Which Perspective for European Administrative Legal Scholarship?' in Matthias Ruffert (ed), *Administrative Law in Europe: Between Common Principles and National Traditions* (Europa Law Publishing 2013).
18. Stefan Oeter, 'The Legitimacy of Customary International Law' in Thomas Eger, Stefan Oeter, and Stefan Voigt (eds), *Economic Analysis of International Law* (Mohr Siebeck 2014).
19. Nicole Deitelhoff and Lisbeth Zimmermann, 'Things We Lost in the Fire: How Different Types of Contestation Affect the Validity of International Norms' (2013), PRIF Working Paper No 18, Frankfurt/Main, citing Jennifer Milliken, 'The Study of Discourse in International Relations: A Critique of Research and Methods', 5(2) European Journal of International Relations 1999, 225 (hereafter Milliken, 'The Study of Discourse'); Vincent Pouliot, 'The Logic of Practicality: A Theory of Practice of Security Communities', 62(2) International Organization 2008, 257; Antje Wiener, *The Invisible Constitution of Politics: Contested Norms and International Encounters* (CUP 2008), citing Milliken, 'The Study of Discourse' (n 19) 231.
20. Uwe Puetter and Antje Wiener, 'Accommodating Normative Divergence in European Foreign Policy Co-ordination: The Example of the Iraq Crisis', 45(12) Journal of Common Market Studies 2007, 1065; Antje Wiener, 'Normative Baggage in International Encounters: Contestation all the Way' in Oliver Kessler et al (eds), *On Rules, Politics, and Knowledge: Friedrich Kratochwil, International Relations, and Domestic Affairs* (Palgrave Macmillan 2010).

21. Vincent Della Sala Constitutionalising Governance: Democratic Dead End or Dead on Democracy? Constitutionalism Web-Papers, ConWEB No 6/2001; Anthony F Lang Jr, 'From Revolutions to Constitutions: The Case of Egypt', 89(2) International Affairs 2013, 345; Anthony F Lang Jr et al, 'Interdisciplinarity: Challenges and Opportunities', 2(1) Global Constitutionalism 2013, 1; Martin Loughlin and Neil Walker (eds), *The Paradox of Constitutionalism: Constituent Power and Constitutional Form* (Papers presented at a seminar held at the European University Institute, March 2006) (OUP 2007); Ben O'Loughlin, Alister Miskimmon, and Laura Roselle (eds), *Strategic Narratives: Communication Power and the New World Order* (Routledge 2013); Hans Vorländer, *Integration durch Verfassung?* (VS Verlag für Sozialwissenschaften 2022).
22. Wiener and Oeter, 'Introduction' (n 12).
23. Dieter Grimm, 'Does Europe Need a Constitution?' (1995) 1(3) European Law Journal 282 (hereafter Grimm, 'Does Europe Need a Constitution?'); Jürgen Habermas, *Moral Consciousness and Communicative Action* (MIT Press 1995) (hereafter Habermas, *Moral Consciousness*); Bardo Fassbender, 'The Meaning of International Constitutional Law' in Nicholas Tsagourias (ed), *Transnational Constitutionalism: International and European Perspectives* (CUP 2007); Jean L Cohen, *Globalization and Sovereignty: Rethinking Legality, Legitimacy, and Constitutionalism* (CUP 2012); Benjamin Alemparte, 'Towards a Theory of Neoliberal Constitutionalism: Addressing Chile's First Constitution-Making Laboratory', 11(1) Global Constitutionalism 2022, 83 (hereafter Alemparte, 'Towards a Theory of Neoliberal Constitutionalism').
24. Wiener et al, 'Global Constitutionalism' (n 8).
25. James Tully, *Strange Multiplicity: Constitutionalism in an Age of Diversity* (CUP 1995); cf Charles Howard McIllwain, *Constitutionalism Ancient and Modern* (Cornell UP 1947).
26. See Grimm, 'Does Europe Need a Constitution?' (n 23); Jean L Cohen, *Globalization and Sovereignty: Rethinking Legality, Legitimacy, and Constitutionalism* (CUP 2012); Rainer Forst, *The Right to Justification: Elements of a Constructivist Theory of Justice* (Columbia UP 2012) (hereafter Forst, *The Right to Justification*).
27. Joseph H H Weiler, *The Constitution of Europe: 'Do the New Clothes Have an Emperor?' and Other Essays on European Integration* (CUP 1999); Nico Krisch, *Beyond Constitutionalism: The Pluralist Structure of Postnational Law* (OUP 2010) (hereafter Krisch, *Beyond Constitutionalism*); Neil Walker, 'The Idea of Constitutional Pluralism', 65(3) Modern Law Review 2002, 317 (hereafter Walker, 'The Idea of Constitutional Pluralism'); Weiler and Wind, *European Constitutionalism* (n 9).
28. Anne Peters and Klaus Armingeon, 'Introduction: Global Constitutionalism from an Interdisciplinary Perspective' in Anne Peters and Klaus Armingeon (eds), *Special Issue: Symposium; Global Constitutionalism—Process and Substance, Kandersteg, Switzerland, January 2008*. 16(2) Indiana Journal of Global Legal Studies 2009, 385.
29. Jeffrey L Dunoff and Joel P Trachtman (eds), *Ruling the World? Constitutionalism, International Law, and Global Governance* (CUP 2009) (hereafter Dunoff and Trachtman, *Ruling the World?*).
30. Petra Dobner and Martin Loughlin (eds), *The Twilight of Constitutionalism? Oxford Constitutional Theory* (OUP 2010) (hereafter Dobner and Loughlin, *The Twilight of Constitutionalism?*).
31. James Tully et al., 'Introducing global integral constitutionalism', 5(1) Global Constitutionalism 2016, 1–15. doi:10.1017/S2045381715000210.

32. Allen Buchanan and Robert O Keohane, 'The Legitimacy of Global Governance Institutions', 20(4) Ethics & International Affairs 2006, 405; Dunoff and Trachtman, *Ruling the World?* (n 29); G John Ikenberry and Anne-Marie Slaughter, 'Forging a World of Liberty under Law. US National Security in the 21st Century: Final Report of the Princeton Project On National Security.' Woodrow Wilson School of Public and International Affairs (Princeton University 2006) The Princeton Project Papers; Jan Klabbers, *An Introduction to International Institutional Law* (2nd edn, CUP 2009); Anne Peters, 'The Merits of Global Constitutionalism' in Anne Peters and Klaus Armingeon (eds), *Special Issue: Symposium; Global Constitutionalism—Process and Substance, Kandersteg, Switzerland, January 2008.* 16(2) Indiana Journal of Global Legal Studies 2009, 397 (hereafter Peters, 'The Merits of Global Constitutionalism'); Bernhard Zangl and Michael Zürn (eds), *Verrechtlichung—Baustein für Global Governance?* (Dietz 2004).
33. *Yassin Abdullah Kadi and Al-Barakaat International Foundation v Council of the European Union and Commission of the European Communities*, C-402/05 P and C-415/05 P, 3 September 2008, available at <http://eur-lex.europa.eu/LexUriServ/LexUriServ.do?uri=CELEX:62005J0402:EN:HTML> accessed 16 October 2023.
34. Jutta Brunnée and Stephen J Toope, *Legitimacy and Legality in International Interactional Law: An Interactional Account. Cambridge Studies in International and Comparative Law* (CUP 2010) (hereafter Brunnée and Toope, *Legitimacy and Legality in International Interactional Law*); Gráinne de Búrca, 'The EU, the European Court of Justice, and the International Legal Order after Kadi', 51(1) Harvard International Law Journal 2010, 1 (hereafter de Búrca, 'The EU'); Daniel Halberstam and Eric Stein, 'The United Nations, the European Union, and the King of Sweden: Economic Sanctions and Individual Rights in a Plural World Order', 46(1) Common Market Law Review 2009, 13 (hereafter Halberstam and Stein, 'The United Nations'); N Türküler Isiksel, 'Fundamental Rights in the EU after Kadi and Al Barakaat', 16(5) European Law Journal 2010, 551 (hereafter Türküler, 'Fundamental Rights in the EU'); Robert O Keohane, 'Nominal Democracy? Prospects for Democratic Global Governance', 13(2) International Journal of Constitutional Law 2015, 343 (hereafter Keohane, 'Nominal Democracy?'); Mattias Kumm, 'The Idea of Socratic Contestation and the Right to Justification: The Point of Rights-Based Proportionality Review', 4(2) Law & Ethics of Human Rights 2010, 142.
35. Thomas M Franck, 'Preface: International Institutions: Why Constitutionalize? Introduction' in Jeffrey L Dunoff and Joel P Trachtman (eds), *Ruling the World?: Constitutionalism, International Law, and Global Governance* (CUP 2009), citing Philip Allott, *Eunomia: New Order for a New World* (OUP 2001); Martin Loughlin, 'The Concept of Constituent Power', 13(2) European Journal of Political Theory 2014, 218.
36. Krisch, *Beyond Constitutionalism* (n 27); Nico Krisch and Benedict Kingsbury, 'Introduction: Global Governance and Global Administrative Law in the International Legal Order', 17(1) European Journal of International Law 2006, 1.
37. Jürgen Habermas, *Zur Verfassung Europas: Ein Essay* (Suhrkamp 2011) (hereafter Habermas, *Zur Verfassung Europas*); Jan Klabbers, Anne Peters, and Geir Ulfstein (eds), *The Constitutionalization of International Law* (OUP 2011) (hereafter Klabbers, Peters, and Ulfstein, *The Constitutionalization of International Law*); Peters, 'The Merits of Global Constitutionalism' (n 32).
38. Klabbers, Peters, and Ulfstein, *The Constitutionalization of International Law* (n 34) 4.
39. Arshin Adib-Moghaddam, *On the Arab Revolts and the Iranian Revolution: Power and Resistance Today* (A&C Black 2013) (hereafter Adib-Moghaddam, *On the Arab Revolts*);

Robbie Shilliam, *International Relations and Non-Western Thought. Imperialism, Colonialism and Investigations of Global Modernity* (Routledge 2011); Arlene B Tickner, 'Core, Periphery and (Neo)Imperialist International Relations', 19(3) European Journal of International Relations 2013, 627.

40. Andrew Hurrell, *On Global Order: Power, Values, and the Constitution of International Society* (OUP 2007); Nele Noesselt, 'The Rise of China and Chinese International Relations Scholarship', 217(1) China Quarterly 2014, 284; Nele Noesselt, 'Contested Global Order(S): Rising Powers and the Re-legitimation of Global Constitutionalization', 14(3) International Journal of Constitutional Law 2014, 639; Detlef Nolte, 'How to Compare Regional Powers: Analytical Concepts and Research Topics', 36(4) Review of International Studies 2010, 881.
41. Adib-Moghaddam, *On the Arab Revolts* (n 39); Donatella Della Porta, *Mobilizing for Democracy: Comparing 1989 and 2011* (OUP 2014); Donatella Della Porta et al, 'Globalization from Below: Transnational Activists and Protest Networks' (2006) 26 NED-New edition; Donatella Della Porta and Alice Mattoni (eds), *Spreading Protest: Social Movements in Times of Crisis* (ECPR Press 2014); Fawaz A Gerges (ed), *The New Middle East: Protest and Revolution in the Arab World* (CUP 2014); Fawaz A Gerges (ed), *Contentious Politics in the Middle East: Popular Resistance and Marginalized Activism Beyond the Arab Uprisings* (Palgrave Macmillan 2015).
42. Matthias Ruffert and Christian Walter, *Institutionalisiertes Völkerrecht: das Recht der Internationalen Organisationen und seine wichtigsten Anwendungsfelder* (C.H. Beck 2009).
43. Jeffrey L Dunoff and Joel P Trachtman (eds), *Ruling the World? Constitutionalism, International Law, and Global Governance* (CUP 2009.
44. Antje Wiener and Stefan Oeter, 'Constitutionalism Unbound: Introducing Theoretical Triangulation for International Relations' (2011), unpublished research proposal, Science Foundation of the Hamburg Senate, University of Hamburg, Hamburg.
45. Wiener et al, 'Global Constitutionalism' (n 8); Antje Wiener, *Global Constitutionalism* (OUP 2012).
46. cf Alemparte, 'Towards a Theory of Neoliberal Constitutionalism' (n 23); Berihun Adugna Gebeye, *A Theory of African Constitutionalism* (OUP 2021); Luise Wiuff Moe and Anna Geis, 'From Liberal Interventionism to Stabilisation: A New Consensus on Norm-Downsizing in Interventions in Africa, 9(2) Global Constitutionalism 2020, 387–412; Hakeem O Yusuf and Tanzil Chowdhury, 'The Persistence of Colonial Constitutionalism in British Overseas Territories', 8(1) Global Constitutionalism 2019, 157.
47. Habermas, *Zur Verfassung Europas* (n 37).
48. Anne Peters and Klaus Armingeon (eds), Special Issue: Symposium; Global Constitutionalism—Process and Substance, Kandersteg, Switzerland, January 2008. 16(2) Indiana Journal of Global Legal Studies (2009), Article 1. https://www.repository.law.indiana.edu/ijgls/vol16/iss2/1.
49. Bardo Fassbender, *The United Nations Charter as the Constitution of the International Community* (Nijhoff 2009).
50. See Grimm, 'Does Europe Need a Constitution?' (n 23).
51. Krisch, *Beyond Constitutionalism* (n 27).
52. Halberstam and Stein, 'The United Nations' (n 34).
53. James Tully, *Public Philosophy in a New Key* (CUP 2008).
54. Peters, 'The Merits of Global Constitutionalism' (n 32).
55. Mattias Kumm, 'The Cosmopolitan Turn in Constitutionalism: On the Relationship between Constitutionalism in and beyond the State' in Jeffrey L Dunoff and Joel P Trachtman

(eds), *Ruling the World? Constitutionalism, International Law, and Global Governance* (CUP 2009) 262.

56. Shaw, 'Post-national Consititutionalism' (n 2).
57. Benedict Kingsbury, Nico Krisch, and Richard B Stewart, 'The Emergence of Global Administrative Law', 68(3) Law and Contemporary Problems 2005, 15.
58. Krisch, *Beyond Constitutionalism* (n 27).
59. Forst, *The Right to Justification* (n 26).
60. Weiler and Wind, *European Constitutionalism* (n 9).
61. Richard Bellamy and Dario Castiglione, 'Beyond Community and Rights: European Citizenship and the Virtues of Participation', 31(1) Quaderni Fiorentini: Per la storia del pensiero giuridico moderno 2002, 349; Mark Bovens, Deirdre Curtin, and Paul 't Hart, *The Real World of EU Accountability. What Deficit?* (OUP 2010); Dieter Grimm, *Die Verfassung und die Politik* (C.H. Beck 2001); Habermas, *Moral Consciousness* (n 23); Thomas Kleinlein, *Konstitutionalisierung im Völkerrecht. Konstruktion und Elemente einer idealistischen Völkerrechtslehre* (Springer 2012); Bertold Rittberger and Frank Schimmelfennig, 'Explaining the Constitutionalization of the European Union', 13(8) Journal of European Public Policy 2006, 1148; Jo Shaw and Gillian More (eds), *New Legal Dynamics of European Union* (Clarendon Press 1995); Armin von Bogdandy and Jürgen Bast, *Principles of European Constitutional Law* (Hart Publishing 2006); Weiler and Wind, *European Constitutionalism* (n 9); Antje Wiener and Jo Shaw (eds), 'Special Issue: The Evolving Norms of Constitutionalism', 9(1) European Law Journal 2003, 1–126.
62. de Búrca, 'The EU' (n 34); Dunoff and Trachtman, *Ruling the World?* (n 29); Klabbers, Peters, and Ulfstein, *The Constitutionalization of International Law* (n 37); Peters, 'The Merits of Global Constitutionalism' (n 32).
63. Peter A Hall and Rosemary CR Taylor, 'Political Science and the Three New Institutionalisms', 44(5) Political Studies 1996, 936.
64. Möllers, *Die Möglichkeit der Normen* (n 36) 471.
65. Keohane, 'Nominal Democracy?' (n 34).
66. Lang and Wiener, *Handbook 2017* (n 8); Lang and Wiener, *Handbook 2023* (n 8).
67. Chayes and Chayes, 'On Compliance' (n 15); Koh, 'Why Do Nations Obey International Law?' (n 16).
68. Samantha Besson, 'The Extraterritoriality of the European Convention on Human Rights: Why Human Rights Depend on Jurisdiction and What Jurisdiction Amounts to', 25(4) Leiden Journal of International Law 2012, 857; Brunnée and Toope, *Legitimacy and Legality in International Interactional Law* (n 34); James Tully, 'The Unfreedom of the Moderns in Comparison to Their Ideals of Constitutionalism and Democracy', 65(2) Modern Law Review 2002, 204 (hereafter Tully, 'The Unfreedom of the Moderns').
69. Gráinne De Búrca and Joseph HH Weiler, *The Worlds of European Constitutionalism. Contemporary European Politics* (CUP 2011): Dobner and Loughlin, *The Twilight of Constitutionalism?* (n 30); Jeffrey L Dunoff and Mark A Pollack (eds), *Interdisciplinary Perspectives on International Law and International Relations. The State of the Art* (CUP 2012); cf the contributions in Dunoff and Trachtman, *Ruling the World?* (n 29); Martin Loughlin and Neil Walker (eds), *The Paradox of Constitutionalism: Constituent Power and Constitutional Form* (OUP 2007).
70. For the journal which was founded in 2012, see: 'Global Constitutionalism, Cambridge Core' <https://www.cambridge.org/core/journals/global-constitutionalism> accessed 5 May 2023.

71. Jean L Cohen, 'The Role of International Law in Post-Conflict Constitution-Making: Toward a Jus Post Bellum for Interim Occupations', 51(3) New York Law School Law Review 2007, 496; Jean L Cohen, 'Security Council activism in the "war on terror": Legality and legitimacy reconsidered' in *Globalization and Sovereignty: Rethinking Legality, Legitimacy, and Constitutionalism* (CUP 2012) 266–319. doi:10.1017/CBO9780511659041.007.
72. Heike Krieger and Georg Nolte, 'The International Rule of Law—Rise or Decline? Points of Departure' (October 2016) 1 KFG Working Paper Series, Berlin Potsdam Research Group; Heike Krieger and Andrea Liese (eds), *Tracing Value Change in the International Legal Order: Perspectives from Legal and Political Science* (OUP 2023, forthcoming).
73. Heike Krieger, Georg Nolte, and Andreas Zimmermann (eds), *The International Rule of Law: Rise or Decline?* (OUP 2019).
74. David Lake and Antje Wiener, 'Deep Contestation', Paper prepared for presentation at "Deep Contestations of the Liberal International Order", International Studies Association, San Francisco, 6 Apr 2024.
75. See Grimm, 'Does Europe Need a Constitution?' (n 23).
76. Ian Manners, 'Normative Power Europe: A Contradiction in Terms?', 40(2) Journal of Common Market Studies 2002, 235; Tully, 'The Unfreedom of the Moderns' (n 68); Türküler, 'Fundamental Rights in the EU' (n 34); Dobner and Loughlin, *The Twilight of Constitutionalism?* (n 30); Rainer Forst, 'The Basic Right to Justification: Towards a Constructivist Conception of Human Rights', 6(1) Constellations 1999, 35.
77. Walker, 'The Idea of Constitutional Pluralism' (n 27); Jean L Cohen, 'Whose Sovereignty? Empire versus International Law', 18(3) Ethics and International Affairs 2004, 1; de Búrca, 'The EU' (n 34); Anne-Marie Slaughter and William Burke-White, 'An International Constitutional Moment', 43(1) Harvard International Law Journal 2002, 1; Anne-Marie Slaughter, *A New World Order* (Princeton UP 2004).

CHAPTER 15

THE ROLE OF NATURAL LAW IN THE RISE AND DECLINE OF EUROPEAN INTERNATIONAL LAW

MARY ELLEN O'CONNELL

> [I]n the nineteenth century, the law of nations, which had been universal in the sixteenth, seventeenth and eighteenth centuries, abandoned the centuries-old universalist tradition based on natural law theory and 'narrowed' to a regional (purely European) legal system.[1]

1. Introduction

This chapter considers the natural law tradition associated with international law in Europe. Charles Henry Alexandrowicz expresses an enduring view that natural law theory is essential to a persuasive account of international law as universal law.[2] His view was widely shared in Europe until the 19th century. It began to decline for a variety of reasons, including the impact of the scientific revolution and the perception that natural law poses an obstacle to States with imperial ambitions.[3] International law, stripped of natural law, leaves only positive law which can be changed to suit interests in a way natural law cannot. Imperialists used positive law to develop their notion of 'civilizational hierarchy', which restricts participation in positive law-making and other privileges to States with European characteristics. The replacement of natural law with positive law alone also freed imperialists to resort to war at will in defiance of the ancient, natural law prohibition on the use of force.[4]

Despite the advantages in suppressing natural law, natural law has persisted while civilizational hierarchy has faded.[5] Cultural differences among European States accounts for the maintenance of a modicum of natural law scholarship in States with a stronger Roman Catholic influence. In the 21st century, natural law scholarship has reemerged in Europe and beyond as a response to the deficits of positivism, primarily inadequate explanations of core legal precepts, including universality, *pacta sunt servanda*, human dignity, and peace as the purpose of law, as well as the general principles inherent to law and peremptory legal norms known as *jus cogens*.[6]

This chapter will discuss these propositions beginning with early natural law concepts, considering briefly what they held and how they gave rise to international law (Section 2.). The discussion then moves to the 19th-century era of natural law suppression in Europe and the rise of European international law. Scholars from Germany, France, and Great Britain, in particular, contributed to the legal ideas that supported European military, economic, and cultural domination abroad.[7] By the end of the 19th century, however, the contradictions embedded in European international law were becoming plain. Solutions were sought through establishing international and regional organizations, together with variations on positive law theory. These helped, but were insufficient substitutes for natural law[8] (Section 3.). The effort continued to shore up international law, leading to new theories of natural law that were less distinct from positive law. As the final section of the chapter shows, these theories have proven little better than positive law. As a result, classical natural law is re-emerging to pair with positive law for a comprehensive explanation of global law on the basis of equality and universality (Section 4.).

2. Natural Law and the Origins of International Law

The earliest evidence of law at work in human communities points to its role in peacefully settling disputes.[9] Law evolved to become a 'complex, intricate aspect of human culture' and 'normative social practice', providing an alternative to physical force and religion for establishing order among social groups.[10] While law provides an alternative, it also incorporates aspects of both force and religion. Religious teaching is seen in the description of law's purpose as supporting peaceful social order as well as in the understanding of why law has the authority to obligate members of society to comply.[11] The use of limited force is incorporated for purposes of law enforcement in the interest of peace.[12] In Europe two theories of law developed from this early history. Natural law theory emerged first followed by positive law concepts and eventually international law from the natural law premise of law's universality. For the British legal historian, Sir Henry Maine, '"The grandest function of the law of nature ... was discharged in giving birth to modern international law"'.[13]

2.1 The origins and attributes of natural law

Plato and Aristotle contributed foundational ideas about the purpose of law, the features of valid law, and the meaning of legal concepts, such as justice and fairness.[14] The later Stoics 'originated the idea of natural law as such ... '.[15] The Stoics observed that order is pervasive in the natural world and concluded that law as a means of establishing order must also be universal.[16] The Stoics developed a 'radically cosmopolitan, universalist' vision of law.[17] It was the Roman Stoic and jurist Cicero during a period of eclecticism among the philosophical schools in the first and second centuries BCE,[18] who introduced the element of transcendence into Stoic natural law ideas.[19] Cicero taught that contemplation of the divine—in or apart from nature—inspires understanding of the norms that should be observed as legal norms despite any natural human tendencies to breach them.[20] In addition to natural law, Cicero identified two forms of positive law in his day, the *jus civile* governing Romans and the *jus gentium* which applied to the many disparate communities of non-Romans who fell under Roman control. Regardless of category, all positive law had to comply with the standards of natural law to be valid.[21]

Positive law is adopted through accepted processes such as the legislative process or the treaty-making process, as well as practices that culminate in common law and customary international law rules (see d'Aspremont, this volume).[22] These processes provide for expressions of consent, which is the *sine qua non* for positive law and explains why positive law is also known as 'voluntary law'.[23] Positive law is binding because of consent. The reason expressions of consent can yield duties of compliance is found in premises provided in natural law theory (see Walter, this volume).[24]

Natural law has elements in common with positive law. Both categories produce substantive duties.[25] Both require the application of human reason. Natural law requires reasoning about the natural world and human nature, drawing on transcendent sources of knowledge in the discernment of what legal principles are required for supporting the normative end of a peaceful world.[26] Positive law requires reasoning to discern, for example, *opinio juris* as an element of customary international law. Positive law relies on reasoning to interpret and apply law to facts in context and to do so consistently with the objects and purposes of a treaty or statute. Such reasoning with respect to positive law will also take into account human nature and norms.

The essential difference is that natural law does not depend on consent. Classical natural law is not formed through positive, material acts. It is discerned by judges and scholars through their use of reason.[27] Reasoning in contemplation of nature and inspired by transcendent sources of knowledge has led over centuries to the identification of substantive normative principles of law as well as to basic premises about the law.[28] Among the principles discerned in this way are general principles of equality, good faith, due process, and proportionality, and the *jus cogens* prohibitions on the use of force, slavery, torture, genocide, and apartheid.[29] Natural law method has also led to basic legal precepts such as consent to law binds or *pacta sunt servanda*, which provides the basis for holding promisors to their commitments.[30] Natural law method leads to the understanding that international law is universal law. Law requires a normative foundation that is independent from positive law. Natural law fills the role of responding to 'law's dependence upon non-positive normative foundations. Natural Law provides for the fact that the existence and content of positive law depends in some way on normative facts.'[31] These features of natural law explain why natural law yields 'necessary norms'.[32]

Positive law has no inherent screening standard for content.[33] Legislators may apply a personal moral code to their decision making, but if they do not, valid law within the definition of positive law will still result. The popular example is the positive law adopted in Nazi Germany, such as the 'pure Aryan' laws. These laws were invalid under natural law principles.[34] The 18th-century British jurist William Blackstone summarized the role of natural law vis-à-vis positive law as follows: (1) Legally valid principles do not conflict with the natural law; and (2) all law derives its force and authority from the natural law.[35]

The method described above for discerning natural law precepts and principles is divided today into two approaches. One follows the classical method of the medieval cleric and scholar St Thomas Aquinas, who is considered the 'paradigmatic' natural law theorist.[36] Aquinas expanded Cicero's two major categories of law, natural and positive, to four, adding eternal law and divine law. Eternal law is known to God alone and includes God's plans for the universe. Divine law, in contrast to eternal law, is revealed to humanity through sacred texts and other forms of revelation.[37] What is being called 'classical natural law' in this chapter combines Aquinas's natural law category and divine law.

The alternative approach is a variation that arose during the European Enlightenment.[38] It involves a shift from incorporating insights inspired through contemplation of transcendent sources of knowledge to reasoning from nature alone.[39] Proponents of the shift, such as Samuel Pufendorf, argued it placed international law on a firmer scientific footing. It also avoided the theological divides following the Protestant Reformation.[40] Walter explains that 'gradually elements of divine revelation were replaced by reference to reason or the "nature" of things'—a division developed between '*Naturrecht*' and '*Vernuftrecht*'.[41] In English the term 'natural law' continued to be used for both branches, accounting for some of the present-day confusion over what exactly the term 'natural law' means. John Finnis, for example, a prominent natural law scholar of the late 20th and early 21st centuries, describes a form of natural law he developed based on human reasoning alone, a type of *Vernuftrecht*. His approach contrasts with his contemporaries in international law who embraced classical natural law—*Naturrecht*—including Alfred Verdross, Christopher Weeramantry, and Antônio Cançado-Trindade.[42]

During this long evolution, legal scholars continued to invoke natural law even if they no longer adhered to classical natural law. Martti Koskenniemi disputes this evolution in critiquing Alexandrowicz's thesis about the loss of natural law and its impact. Koskenniemi argues that international lawyers, including Grotius and Vattel, identified as natural lawyers well into the 18th century and even lacked the concepts and vocabulary needed to identify as positivists.[43] They were not, however, all identifying with classical natural law. Some were followers of Pufendorf. Vattel, writing a century after Grotius, clearly no longer adhered to classical natural law.[44] Moreover, positivism had been part of legal theory since Cicero labelled the *jus gentium* positivist. Vattel also took the very positivist position that treaties are a sort of superior law, constituting the only real obligation on sovereigns for so long as they consented.[45] By the 19th century, the views of Hobbes, Bodin, and Vattel had produced the positivism that European States used to suppress classical natural law.[46]

2.2 Classical natural law and the origins of international law

By the time Vattel was at work, international law had long been established on the basis of classical natural law.[47] International law is 'as old as the conduct of relations between identifiable independent political entities ... '.[48] Humanity has always 'felt the need of some system of rules, however rudimentary, to regulate their inter-community relations'.[49] These rules evolved into Cicero's dual system of positive law within a normative frame of natural law that applied universally.

Aquinas's natural law theory generally followed Cicero's.[50] Their common view featured, among other principles, regulation of 'destructive armed conflict [that] may be considered, in the middle ages as now, one of the primary "law jobs" of the international community'.[51] Grotius wrote *The Law of War and Peace* for this purpose.[52] It became the blueprint for a new legal order in Europe on the basis of the natural law of Aquinas and the later Scholastics.[53] Grotius also followed Aquinas and Suarez in applying a body of positive law, basically the Roman *jus gentium*, to inter-state relations. He taught that the *jus gentium* was needed for its detail and that it should be interpreted in the light of natural law. Grotius's efforts led to the first 'detailed body of specific rules' for the governing of international relations.[54]

The primary challenge to the Grotian natural law order came first from outside international law. Grotius's British contemporary, the political philosopher Thomas Hobbes, could see no other authority than a State's. Beyond the State is anarchy. He thus rejected the natural law doctrine of law as superior to State will.[55] Hobbes inspired the movement away from the transcendent and universal towards the material and individual, including the concept of absolute sovereignty that is antithetical to natural and positive international law.[56] The secondary challenge came from within international law. Grotius's most prominent successors in the century following him were Pufendorf and Vattel. As mentioned, each rejected classical natural law, one in favor of reason alone, the other in favor of positivism and absolute sovereignty.

International law has survived both challenges. They failed for almost two millennia of natural law thought in Europe, but they did leave international law weakened and open to manipulation in the pursuit of perceived sovereign self-interest.

3. European International Law versus Classical Natural Law

By the 19th century, Europeans had become interested in both legal justification for conquest, as well as the legal tools to aid in controlling conquered peoples.[57] Natural law theory presented obstacles to these aims, so it was replaced by the idea of civilizational hierarchy. This notion conflicted with basic natural law from universality and equality to the prohibition on the use of force. It required reducing international law to reliance on positive law alone but positivism is inadequate to support a full system of law. By the end of the century, the flaws in the new conception of international law were obvious. A first response was to develop a more rational form of positivism through establishing international organizations. These helped but only to an extent. Without natural law, international law became the 'house rules' for the club of 'civilized states'.[58]

3.1 Positivism, absolute sovereignty, and civilizational hierarchy

Classical natural law persisted but among the European States building or expanding empires in the 19th century, the views of Hobbes and Vattel held greater appeal. They promoted the idea of sovereign will as the highest authority. International law was reconceived as rules reflecting the consensus will of States—in other words simple positivism.[59]

This conception inverted the very purpose of law. Instead of a common bond to support peaceful social relations, law was becoming a tool of governments for self-perpetuation and power aggrandizement. It was a State's sovereignty that mattered, not international law. Sovereignty began to be characterized as 'absolute', and, increasingly, only treaties counted as international law. '"[B]etween sovereigns who acknowledge no superior on earth, treaties are the only means of adjusting their various pretensions ... "'.[60] It followed that no positive law existed or could exist to restrict the ultimate sovereign prerogative to resort to war.[61] Law, instituted for peace, no longer prohibited armed conflict.

This meant, of course, that imperial States no longer had the advantage of law to keep the peace in conquered lands. In an attempt to save the law generally while preserving privileges for a few, another idea emerged of a two-class system with some States enjoying full sovereignty and others not—there was European international law and there was international law for others.[62] To justify the two-class legal system, imperial powers adopted a fiction of civilizational hierarchy. Until colonial possessions qualified for the full international legal rights of sovereign States, they needed to comply with the international law imparted to them.[63] Europeans were performing a service in bringing peoples to the higher status.

For this two-class concept to have the desired effect, the system had to apply everywhere. Theorists sought to retain the precept of universality but eliminate the principle of equality. 'The price which the European law of nations had to pay for universality was increasing separation from its Christian foundation and dilution of its ethical contents. It underwent a process of formalization and became a law congenial to the needs of the industrial pioneer and capitalist investor.'[64] Anghie emphasizes how imperialist needs, as well as capitalist ones, drove the idea that European international law applies universally. 'European international law became "universal", through the process of imperialism and all the factors that drove expansion.'[65]

The suppression of classical natural law was necessary for imperialism but left unanswered other foundational theoretical issues. Most critically, without natural law what bound the members of the privileged class of states *inter se*?[66] The influential British legal scholar John Austin, a follower of Hobbes, saw the lack of an answer to this question as proof that international law was not law at all. States might have a moral duty to keep promises or comply with the prohibition on force but international law could not bind co-equal sovereigns. For Austin law is the command of a sovereign—one sovereign—backed by force.[67]

3.2 Attempts to fill the gaps in positive law

Following Austin, positivists have offered various responses to the problem of how to bind sovereign States to law. Some answers reintroduce natural law by other names. One of the more enduring solutions has been the development of international organizations to provide something approximating Austin's national government. Yet, the existence of governments and international organizations do not eliminate the need for natural law. They do, however, serve to obscure the need.

Nineteenth-century German international law scholars seem to have been particularly active in attempting to find explanations of how law binds based on positivism alone. Georg Jellinek developed the idea of 'auto-limitation', arguing that a 'sovereign state, through entering into a legal relation with another state, subjected itself to international law by an act of "self-limitation" ... '.[68] Jellinek admitted, however, that the State could end its 'auto-limitation' at any time.[69] In 1899, Heinrich Triepel argued that when States express their 'common will' in treaties or customary international law, the common will limits the discretion of individual States.[70] Triepel was vague about why the common will could bind individual States. It appears to be a natural law idea, not a positivist one.

A variation on Jellinek's and Triepel's attempts drew on Immanuel Kant's proposal for a federation of States that could mimic a Hobbesian-style State complete with quasi-government.[71] Peace activists showed great enthusiasm for such ideas at the end of the 19th century. They lobbied for domestic-style legal institutions at the international level to satisfy Austin's critique.[72] Government institutions do not, however, remove the need for natural law. Most governments today rely on a fiction of a social contract or agreement between the governed and government in which people hypothetically consent to government's authority to institute positive law and enforce it. At the international level where every State's consent can be registered, 'the consent of every state should be necessary'.[73] In practice, all States do not consent. '[R]egimes of government try to be contractarian, but fall back upon claims of some states to represent all ... '[74] Such assertions of the right to represent perpetuate aspects of civilizational hierarchy. States asserting superior status continue to use armed force in 'civilizing' missions of so-called humanitarian intervention, instituting pro-democratic regimes, or countering terrorism in States deemed 'unable or unwilling' to do so.[75] These are claims to privilege by some States over others, raising once again, 'the specter of imperialism'.[76]

Carty concurs with British moral theologian Oliver O'Donovan '"that the ... idea of the state as moral universe in itself, and of international relations as a morally and legally vacant state of nature, qualified only by particular treaties and conventions" is inadequate'.[77] O'Donovan contrasts this largely Hobbesian picture with '"the Grotian conception that the international sphere is already law-governed, being regulated by the law of God, natural and revealed, as well as by the *ius gentium*, prior to any treaty or custom"'.[78] O'Donovan argues '"the appropriate unifying element in international order is law rather than government"'.[79]

Global institutions succeeded in countering European international law's justification of imperialism as well as in mitigating some deficits of positive law. Organizations cannot underpin the principle of equality, however. A two-tiered system of Western-liberal States versus others has emerged. Moreover, organizations cannot exist without the natural law principle that consent to their constituent treaties binds regardless of sovereign State will to the contrary. For *pacta sunt servanda* and so much else, natural law explanations remain indispensable.

4. Persistent Natural Law over European International Law

Carty sees contemporary international law as so dominated by 'pragmatic positivism', he despairs of progress towards revitalizing international law through a new appreciation of natural law theory.[80] At that same time he shows that natural law principles are found throughout international law, making natural hard to ignore. This section confirms that debates over natural law theory are expanding as the 21st century reaches its middle decades.[81]

4.1 The resolute theory of classical natural law

After World War I, legal theorists turned to critiquing and manipulating 'auto-limitation' and 'State will' concepts. In Germany, Carl Schmitt took State-will positivism to its logical conclusion and argued for giving up 'fictions of legality and to recognize law's dependence on the decisions of the powerful'.[82] Hans Kelsen offered an alternative to State will to explain how law can bind States regardless of their power-ranking on Schmitt's scale.[83] For Kelsen the ultimate source of legal validity is found in the precept he called the *Grundnorm* that conveys society's acceptance or belief in the binding power of law.[84] Kelsen's construct was impressive but for the fact it is a natural law conception, existing as it does outside the processes of positive law-making. Kelsen was, however, an adamant critic of natural law owing to his commitments to science and liberal democracy. He considered that absolute and enduring norms conflict with both. He also argued natural law was prone to dangerously subjective interpretations. 'Kelsen rejected all recourse to natural law as sufficiently vague to legitimise the very horrific crimes against humanity natural law purported to ban . . . '[85]

Alfred Verdross was countering these propositions by his famous professor as early as 1923. Verdross joined others in pointing out that the *Grundnorm* could only be based on natural law.[86] To find that law binds because people accept it as a moral and reasonable means of attaining peaceful, orderly community relies on natural law method. Verdross argued universal moral principles such as the binding quality of consent to law, are accessible to people through the use of reason and openness to divine revelation as indicated by Aristotle and Aquinas.[87] Universal international law is possible owing to the dignity found in all people, in common religious teaching, and in the common purpose of law in creating a peaceful and just world order.[88] Verdross reminded Kelsen that the 'general principles' of the Statute of the Permanent Court of International Justice are natural law principles. Principles such as equality, good faith, *audi alterem partem*, necessity, proportionality, and reasonableness are not subject to change through adoption of new treaties or customary international law. For the same reason, *jus cogens* are also a natural law category. Most trenchantly, Verdross criticized Kelsen's and positivism's acceptance of value neutrality. Law cannot tolerate a majority adopting a statute for the genocide of a minority, and, yet, positivism has no capacity to prevent such law becoming valid and binding.[89]

Germany's Third Reich used positive law against whole classes of human beings. That fact inspired new respect for Verdross's positions and natural law in general.[90] The conclusion, articulated by Radbruch and others, was that suppression of natural law had left lawyers without arguments against to Nazi positivism.[91] The sixth edition of *Brierly's Law of Nations*, published in 1963, warned that 'the result of positivism has been to secularize the whole idea of law and thus to weaken the moral foundation which is essential to the vitality of all legal obligation'.[92] Jacques Maritain, Hersch Lauterpacht, and other architects of the post-war legal order included classic natural law principles as the grounds for positive law mandates. Lauterpacht made an eloquent case in 1946 for the need to expressly acknowledge the role of natural law in international law and warned of the dangers of Machiavellian and Hobbesian realism and positivism.[93] The International Court of Justice's first judgment, the 1949 *Corfu Channel* case, found 'certain general and well recognized principles, namely: elementary considerations of humanity' applicable.[94] The judgment reflected the Court's view that international law is 'an amalgam of naturalist and positivist influences'.[95]

Kelsen was dismayed by the post-war renewal of interest in natural law. He warned of the theological underpinnings of natural law. As European society increasingly rejected a role for theology in public life, Kelsen's position gained hold. Natural law theory would need a secular source of transcendent knowledge to remain more than a vague reference to international law's origins and source of normativity. By the 1960s, legal theorists, perhaps most importantly, HLA Hart, accepted that the concept of law must incorporate natural law but would go no further to elaborate on concept of natural law for the 20th century.[96]

One of Hart's students, John Finnis, did elaborate, however.[97] As mentioned, Finnis's approach departed from classical natural law, employing the sort of pure reason and observation described as *Vernunftrecht* and associated with Pufendorf. The approach followed an earlier one developed at Yale Law School by Myres McDougal.[98] Both Finnis and McDougal developed lists of human goods around which all valid law must be oriented. McDougal's emphasized the good of human dignity attracting adherents to the New Haven School for decades, including Dame Rosalyn Higgins. The approach faded, however, as awareness grew of the method's reliance on subjective personal views, shorn of the external source of transcendent knowledge found in classical natural law.[99] Finnis's work was criticized for the same reason, but in contrast to McDougal, scholarly interest in his work was growing as of 2022.[100]

Meanwhile Verdross worked to answer criticisms of classical *Naturrecht*. He focused on the subjectivity problem as demand grew that all legal theory be wholly secular. Verdross pointed out positivism's own vulnerability to subjectivity. Without natural law, positivism depends on individual subjective interpretation cut off from standards external to the self. Verdross also proposed deriving natural law principles by deduction from widely-held rules of positive international law. These sorts of principles tend to be consistent with diverse cultures and reliably reflect transcendent knowledge.[101] Verdross's method came into wide use though not in the way he intended. The United Nations International Law Commission (UN ILC), for example, uses deduction from positive law to account for *jus cogens*. Peremptory norms are reduced to 'special customary law', not natural law, despite the fact international law has no category of 'special positive law'.[102] The ILC debate over general principles has followed similar lines.[103]

In the 1990s, ICJ Judges Mohammed Bedjaoui, Christopher Weeramantry, and Antonio Cançado-Trindade also wrote of deriving natural law principles through comparative method. Instead of looking to common rules among various domestic legal systems, however, they look to the deeply-held cultural beliefs and practices of diverse communities. They found widespread recognition of enduring, common principles—those unchangeable through treaty and customary law—reflecting moral teaching. It is teaching that reveres the created world and peace over material wealth and violence.

This comparative method links to another secular approach to natural law discernment. Aesthetic philosophy teaches that beauty is a source of knowledge and truth. The human response to beauty leads to the same basic understanding of human nature found by classic natural lawyers from Aquinas and Grotius to Verdross and Cançado-Trindade.[104] Contemplation of beauty in nature gives pleasure and draws people to consider the reaction of others to the same experience. For philosophers Hannah Arendt and Iris Murdoch the reaction to beauty proves that humans are social and need politics and law to support the capacity for selflessness needed for the flourishing of social relations.[105] Arendt more specifically shows how aesthetics provides a secular, compatible approach to divine revelation as a source of transcendent knowledge in the analysis of natural law. Imagination and memory are additional secular sources of transcendent knowledge tied to discernment of natural law.

4.2 Natural law precepts and principles everywhere

The work on natural law theory will continue given that it is essential to a complete theory of law. Improved natural law theory is also needed to account for the natural law precepts and principles that endure throughout the law. As Geoff Gordon has written: 'Natural law has a peculiar way of being everywhere and nowhere in the body of international law.'[106] Natural law has been 'nowhere' to the extent it is excluded from theoretical debate. Substantive natural law is nevertheless everywhere as this section will indicate.

One of the most fundamental premises of law is that consent can bind. It is a quintessential natural law postulate upon which all of positive law depends.[107] Consent is joined by the natural law precept of human dignity that supports the body of international human rights law.[108] The list could continue indefinitely, a fact not well known owing to the suppression of natural law theory. The knowledge deficit respecting natural law has led to the misidentification of general principles and jus cogens as customary international law or not associated with a theory of law at all.[109] More examples of natural law follow, taking up examples from a main theme of this handbook, the promotion of peace.

Certain legal precepts of natural law found in international law have already been discussed, in particular, consent or *pacta sunt servanda*. Positive law is binding because of the consent given to it, and consent binds not as positive law but as natural law. Another legal premise is that the purpose of law is peace. Law provides an alternative to violence and status for the settlement of disputes. Coercion is prohibited except as strictly required for the enforcement of law. Law provides the means of peaceful settlement as an alternative to violence and uniquely provides for the orderly planning of future conduct that prevents conflict. The mechanisms available for peaceful settlement range from negotiation to adjudication. All rely on natural law procedural principles to ensure fair process and the legitimacy of taking coercive measures in cases of failure to comply. Without such principles, including, most importantly, good faith and equal treatment, dispute resolution methods would be no more than political or social exchanges. Thus, dispute resolution depends on natural law process principles to qualify as a legal method. Given the essential role of process principles, they are impervious to change.

Natural law procedural principles are included in Article 38(1)(c) of the Statute of the International Court of Justice. Some of the Statute's drafters proposed adding an express reference to natural law in Article 38 but were opposed by positivists, including Elihu Root of the US. Despite references to natural law in the American Declaration of Independence and throughout US law to the time of the Statute's drafting, Root was a committed positivist. He insisted all general principles are positive law. The drafting conference coincided with the end of World War I and the US's rise as a military and imperial power. The US acquired its first overseas colonies in 1899 after defeating Spain in the Spanish American War. For the same reasons natural law had not appealed to certain European governments as they acquired empires, natural law did not appeal to Root. A compromise was reached in which no reference to either positive or natural law was made.

In his masterful anti-colonial dissenting opinion in the *South West Africa* cases, Judge Kōtorō Tanaka revived the natural law emphasis of Article 38. He made clear that the principle of equality is a natural law norm without which international law cannot attain universality. To apply equality, the ICJ had to be able to point to a provision of Article 38 and that was the provision on general principles:

> The original proposal made by Baron Descamps ... clearly indicated an idea originating in natural law. This proposal met with the opposition of the positivist members of the Committee, represented by Mr. Root. The final draft ... is the product of a compromise between two schools, naturalist and positivist, and therefore the fact that the natural law idea became incorporated therein is not difficult to discover ...[110]

The ICJ today invokes general principles throughout its opinions but rarely identifies them as such. In *Barcelona Traction* the Court cites both the natural law principle that the law must always be applied reasonably and a rule based on the comparative analysis of domestic corporate laws.[111] In the 1974 *Fisheries Jurisdiction* cases between Iceland, the UK, and Germany, the ICJ called on the parties to settle their differences through negotiation conducted in good faith.[112] The source of good faith is not mentioned. The Court does not look to multiple examples in national law or label it customary international law; it simply treats good faith as inherent in law. The ICJ's reference to the Martens' clause has already been mentioned. Natural law was also expressly discussed and is implicitly reflected in the 1969 Vienna Convention on the Law of Treaties. The convention includes both the natural law precept *pacta sunt servanda*[113] and provisions on *jus cogens*. Again, during the negotiations, representatives, including the rapporteur, Sir Gerald Fitzmaurice, took the position that *jus cogens* emanates from natural law.[114]

5. Conclusion

International law in Europe today reflects the scientific and social science conclusions based on material evidence that people have a natural tendency to compete for wealth, status, and physical power. This evidence supports the dominant role that positivism holds in international law. The sciences, however, also provide evidence that the insights of philosophy, theology, the arts, and culture have a role in shaping the law. The insight of greatest importance is that people are 'intrinsically moved by a desire for social life, endowed with an ample measure of goodness, altruism, and morality, and capable of acting on general principle and of learning from experience'.[115] This other reality of humanity accounts for the equally essential natural law component of all law. Without it, arguments in support of imperialism, hegemony, and the unrestricted use of force have all been possible. The 21st century renewal of natural law theory is a return to the precepts of universality, human dignity, and peace.

Notes

1. Charles Henry Alexandrowicz, *An Introduction to the History of the Law of Nations of the East Indies (16th, 17th, and 18th Centuries)* (Clarendon Press 1967) 2.
2. Martti Koskenniemi has contested Alexandrowicz's claim. See nn 43–46 and accompanying text.
3. Antony Anghie, Europe and International Law, Colonial Legacies (this volume)
4. Agatha Verdebout, *Rewriting Histories of the Use of Force, The Narrative of 'Indifference'* (CUP 2022) 1–13.
5. A new theory of civilization emerged after the Cold War, under which certain Western, liberal States claim privileges over others. David P Fidler, 'The Return of the Standard of Civilization', 2 Chicago Journal of International Law 2001, 137–157; G John Ikenberry and Anne-Marie Slaughter, *Forging a World of Liberty Under Law: U.S. National Security Policy in the 21st Century* (Woodrow Wilson School of Public and International Affairs, Princeton University 2006); Department of Defence, Australian Government, *2016 Defence White Paper* (2016); and John Dugard, 'The Choice Before Us: International Law or a "Rule-Based Order"?', Leiden Journal of International Law (online 2023).
6. 'The continuing interest in natural law concepts, now renewed once more, recovers arguments that are otherwise difficult to defend in secularized normative environments.' Stefan Kadelbach, 'Hugo Grotius: On the Conquest of Utopia by Systematic Reasoning' in Stefan Kadelbach, Thomas Kleinlein, and David Roth-Isigkeit (eds), *System, Order, and International Law: The Early History of International Legal Thought from Machiavelli to Hegel* (OUP 2017) 6; Jonathan Crowe and Constance Youngwon Lee, 'The Natural Law Outlook' in Jonathan Crowe and Constance Youngwon Lee (eds), *Research Handbook on Natural Law Theory* (Edward Elgar 2019) 1; Antônio Augusto Cançado-Trindade, *International Law for Humankind: Towards a New* Jus Gentium (Brill Nijhoff 2020); and Arne Føllesdal, 'Current Contributions of the Natural Law Tradition to International Law'

in Jeffrey Dunoff and Mark Pollack (eds), *International Legal Theories: Foundations and Frontiers* (CUP 2022) 39–62.

7. Heike Krieger, 'Of Zombies, Witches and Wizards—Tales of Sovereignty', 33 European Journal of International Law 2022, 275–296.
8. Anthony Carty, 'The Play of Medieval Ghosts and Renaissance Demons in Birth, Death and Rebirth of European International Law' in Thilo Marauhn and Heinhard Steiger (eds), *Universality and Continuity in International Law* (Eleven International Publishing 2011); and Mary Ellen O'Connell, *The Art of Law in the International Community* (CUP 2019) 19–49.
9. The purpose of law is achieving 'order through subjecting people's conduct to the guidance of general rules by which they may themselves orient their behavior'. Lon Fuller, *The Morality of Law* (rev edn, Yale UP 1965) 657.
10. Andrei Marmor and Alexander Sarch, 'The Nature of Law' in Edward N Zalta et al (eds), *The Stanford Encyclopedia of Philosophy* (2019) <https://plato.stanford.edu/entries/lawphil-nature/>.
11. Hilaire McCoubrey, 'Natural Law, Religion and the Development of International Law' in Mark W Janis and Carolyn Evans (eds), *Religion and International Law* (Brill Publishers 2004) 179. See also Michael Stolleis, 'The Legitimation of Law through God, Tradition, Will, Nature and Constitution' in Lorraine Daston and Michael Stolleis (eds), *Natural Laws and Law of Nature in Early Modern Europe* (Ashgate Publishing Ltd 2008).
12. Mary Ellen O'Connell, *The Power and Purpose of International Law* (OUP 2008) 7–16.
13. JL Brierly, *The Law of Nations*, edited by Sir Humphrey Waldock (Clarendon Press 1963) 24, quoting Maine, *Ancient Law*, ch iv.
14. George Duke, 'Aristotle as Natural Law Theorist' in Crowe and Youngwon Lee (n 6) 13–30. The author also mentions Plato (ibid, 17 and 20–21). See also John Tasioulas and Guglielmo Verdirame, 'Philosophy of International Law' in Edward N Zalta et al (eds), *The Stanford Encyclopedia of Philosophy* (2022) https://plato.stanford.edu/entries/international-law/.
15. Anna Taitslin, 'Stoic Natural Law as Right Reason', in Crowe and Youngwon Lee (n 6) 31.
16. Richard Horsley, 'The Law of Nature in Philo and Cicero', 71 The Harvard Theological Review 1978, 42–52, 54–57; and Malcolm Schofield, 'Stoic Ethics' in Brad Inwood (ed), *The Cambridge Companion to the Stoics* (CUP 2006) 233–256.
17. Stephen Neff, *Justice Among Nations: A History of International Law* (Harvard UP 2014) 59–60.
18. Horsley (n 16) 42–50.
19. 'Transcendence' refers to '[e]xistence or experience beyond the normal or physical level'. *Oxford Dictionaries* <https://www.oxforddictionaries.com/us/definition/english/transcendence>. Transcendent knowledge is gained through emotions, aesthetic experience, and memory, in contrast to observation of the material world.
20. Horsley (n 16) 51–57, 58.
21. Brierly (n 13) 18.
22. See also Leslie Green and Tom Adams, 'Legal Positivism' in Edward N Zalta et al (eds), *The Stanford Encyclopedia of Philosophy* (2019) https://leibniz.stanford.edu/friends/members/view/legal-positivism/. Not everyone agrees that customary law is positivist.
23. See the use of this expression in eg Hersch Lauterpacht, 'The Grotian Tradition in International Law', 23 British Year Book of International Law 1946, 1 and Crowe and Lee (n 6) 1.
24. See also McCoubrey (n 11) 185.

25. Crowe and Lee (n 6) 1–6.
26. ibid. On transcendent sources of knowledge, see n 19.
27. O'Connell, *The Art of Law* (n 8) 86–89; and Green and Adams (n 22).
28. John Finnis, 'Natural Law Theories' in Edward N Zalta et al (eds), *The Stanford Encyclopedia of Philosophy* (2020) <https://plato.stanford.edu/entries/natural-law-theories/>.
29. O'Connell, *The Art of Law* (n 8) 86–89.
30. Sir Gerald Fitzmaurice, a rapporteur on the law of treaties for the United Nations International Law Commission, explained that *pacta sunt servanda* is a principle of natural law. Sir Gerald Fitzmaurice, 'The Law and Procedure of the International Court of Justice 1954–1959', 35 British Yearbook of International Law 1959, 183–216, 195. See also Harald Kleinschmidt, 'Naturrecht und Völkerrecht? Beobachtungen zu Wandlungen der Rechts-Quellentheorie seit Ende des 19. Jahrhunderts', 135 Historiches Jahrbuch 2015, 364–411, 371.
31. Duke (n 14) 16, citing M C Murphy, 'Two Unhappy Dilemmas for Natural Law Jurisprudence' in George Duke and Robert P George (eds), *The Cambridge Companion to Natural Law Jurisprudence* (CUP 2017) 354; and McCoubrey (n 11) 185.
32. Jerzy Sztucki, *Jus Cogens and the Vienna Convention on the Law of Treaties, A Critical Appraisal* (Springer 1974) 59.
33. John Gardner, 'Legal Positivism: 51/2 Myths', 46(1) American Journal of Jurisprudence 2001, 199–227; and David Dyzenhaus, 'Why Positivism Is Authoritarian', 37 American Journal of Jurisprudence 1992, 83–112.
34. Gustav Radbruch, *Der Geist des Englischen Rechts* (Adolf Rausch 1947) 49; and nn 89–93 and accompanying text.
35. Sir William Blackstone, 'Of the Nature of Laws in General' in *Commentaries on the Laws of England in Four Books* (J.B. Lippincott Co. 1893, originally published, 1753), online at <https://www.nlnrac.org/node/244>.
36. Duke (n 14) 17, citing MC Murphy, 'Natural Law Jurisprudence', 9 Legal Theory 2003, 241, 244; and Jean Porter, *Nature as Reason: A Thomistic Theory of the Natural Law* (Wm. B. Eerdmans Publishing Co. 2004) 27–8.
37. Porter (n 36).
38. Michael Stolleis and Lorraine Daston, 'Introduction: Nature, Law and Natural Law in Early Modern Europe' in Michael Stolleis and Lorraine Daston (eds), *Natural Law and Laws of Nature in Early Modern Europe, Jurisprudence Theology, Moral and Natural Philosophy* (Routledge 2008) 9–10.
39. Pufendorf attempted to excise consideration of transcendent sources and positive law from the discernment of international law, leaving only reason and observation of nature. Samuel Pufendorf, *Two Books of the Elements of Universal Jurisprudence*, edited by James Brown Scott, trans William Abbott Oldfather (1660) (William S. Hein & Co. 1995) 292–293; Martti Koskenniemi, 'Transformations of Natural Law, Germany 1648–1815' in Anne Orford and Florian Hoffmann (eds), *The Oxford Handbook of the Theory of International Law* (OUP 2016) 59–81; and Verdebout (n 4) 40–41.
40. Marjim Künkler, John Madeley, and S Shankar (eds), *A Secular Age beyond the West: Religion, Law and the State in Asia, the Middle East and North Africa* (CUP 2018); Charles Taylor, *A Secular Age* (Harvard UP 2007); Talal Asad, *Formations of the Secular: Christianity, Islam, Modernity* (Stanford UP 2003); and Harold J Berman, *Law and Revolution, The Formation of the Western Legal Tradition* (Harvard UP 1985).

41. Christian Walter, The Role of Religion in the Formation of International Law (this volume) 27.
42. See nn 83–104 and accompanying text.
43. Martti Koskenniemi, *The Gentle Civilizer of States, The Rise and Fall of International Law 1870–1960* (CUP 2001) 131.
44. Philip Allott, *The Health of Nations: Society and Law beyond the State* (CUP 2002) 56–62.
45. Vattel is a transitional figure moving away from natural law to positivism alone for some tenets of international law while retaining natural law vocabulary and even some natural law principles. See Emmerich de Vattel, *The Law of Nations or the Principles of Natural Law*, trans Charles G Fenwick, 1758 edn (Liberty Fund, Inc 1916) 3–6.
46. 'The separation of naturalism and positivism as mutually exclusive options was ... broadly a product of the 19th century which has retained potent effect throughout the 20th century.' McCoubrey (n 11) 185. This development applied to international law as well. See Alexandrowicz (n 1); Kleinschmidt (n 30); and Patrick Capps, 'Natural Law and the Law of Nations' in Alexander Orakhelashvili (ed), *Research Handbook on the History and Theory of International Law* (Edward Elgar 2020) 58.
47. Brierly (n 13) 43.
48. McCoubrey (n 11) 179.
49. Brierly (n 13) 1.
50. Charles P Nemeth, *A Comparative Analysis of Cicero and Aquinas: Nature and the Natural Law* (Bloomsbury 2017) 135.
51. McCoubrey (n 11) 180.
52. Hugo Grotius, *De Jure Belli ac Pacis* [The Law of War and Peace], trans FW Kelsey (Clarendon Press 1995 [1625]), 'Prolegomena'.
53. Some contest whether Grotius faithfully followed the Scholastics. Capps (n 46) 59 fn 4. He did write that law above nations could be imagined even in a world without God. This hypothetical was presented to bring Catholics and Protestants to look past their theological differences and to law as their common bond. Grotius was indisputably a devout Christian, which shaped his commitment to peace and understanding that law prevails over individual sovereign policy. It was Alberico Gentili who promoted sovereign power over law. Gentili was a humanist, not a Scholastic. Humanists look to human nature rather than transcendent sources. Capps (n 46) 67; Carty (n 8); McCoubrey (n 11) 180; Richard Tuck, *The Rights of War and Peace* (OUP 1999); and Joseph Canning, 'The Universal Rule of Law in the Thought of the Late Medieval Jurists of Roman and Canon Law' in Anthony Carty and Janne Nijman (eds), *Morality and Responsibility of Rulers, European and Chinese Origins of a Rule of Law as Justice for World Order* (OUP 2018) 55–57.
54. Neff (n 17) 141. See also Christoph Stumpf, 'Hugo Grotius and the Universal Rule of Law' in Carty and Nijman (n 52) 186–200.
55. Brierly (n 13) 45–56.
56. Carty (n 8) 67, 173–178, citing, Richard Tuck, *The Rights of War and Peace* (OUP 1999) 130; Brierly (n 13) 25.
57. Fidler (n 5) 140, citing Grewe, *The Epochs of International Law*, 445–458. Barry Buzan, 'The "Standard of Civilisation" as an English School Concept', 42(3) Millenium: Journal of International Studies 2014 <https://journals.sagepub.com/doi/abs/10.1177/0305829814528265?journalCode=mila> (accessed 10 October 2023).
58. Kleinschmidt (n 30) 375.
59. Joachim von Elbe, 'The Evolution of the Concept of the Just War in International Law', 33(4) The American Journal of International Law 1939, 665–688, 682–683.

60. Carty (n 8) 78.
61. ibid, 62.
62. Alexandrowicz (n 1) 2.
63. Fidler (n 5) 137, 140, citing Grewe, *The Epochs of International Law*, 445–458; and Kleinschmidt (n 30) 372–375.
64. Georg Schwarzenberger, 'The Standard of Civilization in International Law', 8(1) Current Legal Problems 1955, 212–234, 220. See also Ntina Tzouvala, *Capitalism as Civilisation: A History of International Law* (CUP 2020).
65. Anghie (n 3) 46.
66. Koskenniemi observes the issue is an 'obvious paradox'. Koskenniemi, *Gentle Civilizer* (n 43) 166.
67. John Austin, *The Province of Jurisprudence Determined* (John Murray 1832) 141–142.
68. Arthur Nussbaum, *A Concise History of the Law of Nations* (rev edn, MacMillan 1962) 234–235; Kleinschmidt (n 30) 376; and Jochen von Bernstorff, 'Georg Jellinek and the Origins of Liberal Constitutionalism in International Law', 4(3) Goettingen Journal of International Law 2012, 659–675.
69. Nussbaum (n 68) 234–235.
70. ibid.
71. Immanuel Kant, *Perpetual Peace, A Philosophic Essay* (The American Peace Society 1897, first published 1795).
72. Carty (n 8) 65.
73. ibid.
74. ibid.
75. For a critique of these claims using positivist analysis of law on the use of force, see Christine Gray, *International Law and the Use of Force* (OUP 2018) and Olivier Corten, *Le droit contre la guerre, L'interdiction du recours à la force en droit international contemporain* (3rd rev edn, Editions Pedone 2020).
76. Carty (n 8) 65.
77. ibid, 66, citing Oliver O'Donovan, *The Ways of Judgement* (2005) 210.
78. ibid, 67, citing Oliver O'Donovan, *The Ways of Judgement* (2005) 210.
79. ibid, 74, citing Oliver O'Donovan, *The Desire of the Nations* (1996) 72.
80. Carty (n 8) 67.
81. Kadelbach (n 6) 6 and Crowe and Lee (n 6) 1.
82. Koskenniemi, *Gentle Civilizer* (n 43) 239.
83. Franz Leander Fillafer and Johannes Feichtinger, 'Natural Law and the Vienna School: Hans Kelsen, Alfred Verdross, and Eric Voegelin' in Peter Lanford, Ian Bryan, and John McGarry (eds), *Hans Kelsen and the Natural Law Tradition* (Brill 2019) 434, 437.
84. Hans Kelsen, *Introduction to the Problems of Legal Theory*, trans Bonnie Litschewski Paulson and Stanley L Paulson; introduced by Stanley L Paulson (OUP 1992, first published 1934) 26.
85. Fillafer and Feichtinger (n 83) 436.
86. ibid, 432 and Kleinschmidt (n 30) 393–398.
87. Fillafer and Feichtinger (n 83) 433.
88. Alfred Verdross, 'Der Einfluß der Naturrechtslehre auf Theorie und Praxis der international Beziehungen' in Franz-Martin Schmölz (ed), *Das Naturrecht in der politischen Theorie* (Springer 1963) 116; and Fillafer and Feichtinger (n 83) 434.
89. Fillafer and Feichtinger (n 83) 434.

90. ibid, 430–431, citing, *inter alia*, Alfred Verdross, *Abendländische Rechtsphilosophie. Ihre Grundlagen und Hauptprobleme in geschichtlicher Schau* (Springer 1958). See also the discussion of Radbruch in Lon L Fuller, 'Positivism and Fidelity to Law—A Reply to Professor Hart', 71 Harvard Law Review 1957, 630–672.
91. Gustav Radbruch, *Der Geist des Englischen Rechts* (Adolf Rausch 1947) 49 and Kleinschmidt (n 30) 384.
92. Brierly (n 13) 44.
93. Lauterpacht (n 23) 23–24.
94. *Corfu Channel (UK v Albania)(Merits)* [1949] ICJ Rep 4, 22.
95. Frauke Lachenmann, 'Legal Positivism' in Rüdiger Wolfrum (ed), *Max Planck Encyclopedias of International Law* (OUP July 2011) para 45. The ICJ incorporated natural law in numerous decisions, eg the Court cited the 1899 Marten's Clause in *Legality of the Threat or Use of Nuclear Weapons* (Advisory Opinion) [1996] 226 ICJ Rep 226, 257. The Martens Clause mandates resort to 'public conscience' in assessing the legality of new weapons and military tactics. Public conscience is a natural law concept. Rupert Ticehurst, 'The Martens Clause and the Laws of Armed Conflict', 37(317) International Review of the Red Cross 1997, 125–134, 125. See also nn 110–112 and accompanying text.
96. HLA Hart, *The Concept of Law* (Clarendon Press, first pub'd 1961, reprinted 1970) 189.
97. John Finnis, *Natural Law, Natural Rights* (OUP 1980). Hart suggested the book's title.
98. Myres S McDougal, *Perspectives for an International Law of Human Dignity*, 53 ASIL Proceedings 1959, 107–136, 108.
99. Oscar Schachter, 'McDougal's Jurisprudence: Utility, Influence, Controversy', 79 ASIL Proceedings 1985, 266–273, 271.
100. Jonathan Crowe, *Natural Law and the Nature of Law* (CUP 2019) 5–6; and Brian Tamanaha 'Beware Illiberal Natural Law', Washington University in St. Louis School of Law Legal Studies Research Paper Series (Paper No 22-05-01, May 2022) <https://papers.ssrn.com/sol3/papers.cfm?abstract_id=4109402>.
101. Alfred Verdross and HF Koeck, 'Natural Law: The Tradition of Universal Reason and Authority' in Ronald St J MacDonald and Donald Johnston (eds), *The Structure and Process of International Law: Essays in Legal Philosophy, Doctrine and Theory* (Martinus Nijhoff 1983) 17–50.
102. André de Hoogh, *Obligations* Erga Omnes *and International Crimes* (Brill 1996) 45 and Conclusion 5 Draft Conclusions on Identification and Legal Consequences of Peremptory Norms of General International Law, referencing customary international law as the 'most common basis' of *jus cogens* and treaties as another basis, UN Doc. A/CN.4/L.967 (11 May 2022), International Law Commission, 73rd Sess. In his Second Report on Peremptory Norms, Dire Tladi states that no attempt would be made to resolve whether *jus cogens* are part of natural law or positive law. Dire Tladi, 'Second Report on *Jus Cogens*', UN Doc A/CN.4/706 (16 March 2017), International Law Commission, 69th Sess.
103. Ample evidence exists that most general principles are based on natural law. Oscar Schachter, *International Law in Theory and Practice* (Kluwer Law International 1995) 49–58. Still, some scholars argue general principles of international law are only principles common in municipal law. This view begs the question of what type of principle they are in municipal law. Equality, good faith, and the like should be found in domestic and international law. In either category they are natural law. To the extent that the US, the Soviet Union, and now Russia object to general principles, it is because natural law

principles cannot be controlled through consent, unlike treaties and customary international law. Michel Virally, 'The Sources of International Law' in Max Sørensen (ed), *Manual of Public International Law* (St Martin's Press 1968) 143–148.

104. O'Connell, *The Art of Law* (n 8) 33–50.
105. Hannah Arendt, *Lectures on Kant's Political Philosophy*, edited by R Beiner (University of Chicago Press 1989).
106. Geoff Gordon, 'Natural Law in International Legal Theory: Linear and Dialectical Presentations' in Orford and Hoffmann (n 39) 279, 279.
107. See nn 5–8, 89–93, and accompanying text.
108. The scholarship on this basic point is extensive. See, eg, Eberhard Schockenhoff, *Natural Law and Human Dignity: Universal Ethics in an Historical World*, trans Brian McNeil (Catholic University of America Press 2003).
109. See nn 102–103 and accompanying text.
110. ICJ, *South West Africa Cases* (*Ethiopia v South Africa*) (*Liberia v South Africa*), Judgment of 18 July 1966, Dissenting opinion, Judge Tanaka, 1966 ICJ Reports, 285–315.
111. ICJ, *Barcelona Traction, Light and Power Co., Ltd.* (*Belgium v Spain*), Judgment of 5 February 1970, ICJ Reports 1970, 48 and 38–39.
112. ICJ, *Fisheries Jurisdiction* (*UK v Iceland*), Judgment of 25 July 1974, ICJ Reports 1974, 3, 7.
113. Martine Julia van Ittersum, 'Global Constitutionalism in the Early Modern Period: The Role of Empires, Treaties and Natural Law' in Anthony F Lang, Jr and Antje Wiener (eds), *Handbook on Global Constitutionalism* (Edward Elgar 2017) 47–59, 56.
114. Jerzy Sztucki, *Jus Cogens and the Vienna Convention on the Law of Treaties, A Critical Appraisal* (Springer 1974) 59. Verdross is credited with promoting natural law in the understanding of *jus cogens*. He 'became the chief theorist of the *jus cogens* in international law . . . '. Fillafer and Feichtinger (n 83) 435 and McCoubrey (n 11) 187.
115. Lauterpacht (n 23) 24.

CHAPTER 16

WHEN HUMANITARIANS GO TO WAR

A European Road to 'Civilized' Warfare?

ANNE DIENELT

1. Introduction

The noble idea of pacifism can fail; past and present show that States will use military force against each other despite a prohibition and criminalization of the use of force. Peace through law has not always been successful:[1] Pacifist attempts in the 19th and 20th centuries to contain force between States did not prevent two world wars. Nevertheless, the idea and hope of pacifism persisted: New wars gave rise to novel initiatives to prohibit the use of force and to regulate warfare. They combined pacifism with humanitarianism, the latter addresses people in distress and aims for their relief. After the devastating human suffering during World War I,[2] the League of Nations was established by States to 'achieve international peace and security'.[3] The League of Nations also assisted refugees of World War I.[4] A few years later, in the 1928 General Treaty for Renunciation of War as an Instrument of National Policy, also known as the Kellogg-Briand Pact, States 'condemn[ed] recourse to war for the solution of international controversies, and renounce[d] it, as an instrument of national policy in their relations with one another'[5] for the first time. Eventually, these attempts also failed, and World War II caused death and suffering among people once again.[6] Post-World War II, States established the United Nations (UN) and adopted the UN Charter to 'maintain international peace and security',[7] which again also included a prohibition of the use of force between States.[8] However, the second half of the 20th century, as well as the beginning of the 21st century, saw renewed severe violence between States with several confirmed genocides[9] and wars, putting humanitarian concerns back on the table despite a prohibition of aggression. Consequently, failed pacifism can result in humanitarianism, sometimes even requiring it. Both are closely related and complement each other in the end.

The continued suffering of people related to military force between States despite prohibitions of the use or threat of force demonstrates that such a prohibition is insufficient to prevent and mitigate human suffering. Pacifists and humanitarians urged States already in the 19th century to adopt principles governing warfare to limit the suffering of innocent people and civilians while campaigning for pacifist aims. Several Europeans played an influential role in the global peace movements and the creation of the *ius in bello*, the laws of war. Additionally, experiences from European wars served as a source of inspiration on how to regulate wars and enhance the protection of innocent people and civilians from the consequences of armed conflict, with lasting impact until today. However, European humanitarianism and law-making is a delicate topic. Many have criticized—with good reason—the Eurocentric narrative of the history of international humanitarian law (IHL), which ignores developments outside of Europe,[10] such as those in Latin America that started even before Franz (Francis) Lieber drafted his Code in 1863 and before States adopted the first Geneva Convention in 1864.[11] Moreover, several humanitarian traditions have evolved over time in different national, religious, and imperial cultures.[12] Nonetheless, in line with the overall topic of the volume, this chapter focuses on European initiatives and legal thoughts and their impact on today's IHL, the *ius in bello*. Other developments and accomplishments beyond Europe will be considered in contrast or support. Issues regarding the *ius ad bellum*, such as the humanitarian intervention (respectively the responsibility to protect),[13] which has not been used by States anymore after the 2011 Libya intervention,[14] are not addressed.

This chapter delves into the history of IHL, and European influences and origins (Sub-section 2.1). At the same time, it contextualizes today's challenges in armed conflicts as well as IHL's claim for universality despite initially being an exclusive European project for 'civilized nations' (Sub-section 2.2). The motivation of pacifist and humanitarian movements from the 19th century, namely preventing and mitigating the suffering of the innocent, has not lost any relevance today; the challenge persists. New developments, such as the urbanization of warfare, new technologies of warfare, or non-State actors,[15] continue to test the existing framework. In light of these challenges, calls for another update to the Geneva Convention and a new Geneva Convention have been voiced. Still, the prospect of a new convention is currently rather poor. The initial European project of pacifists and humanitarians, which resulted in the adoption of several Geneva Conventions, and includes the development of core principles of IHL, might be the best option currently available to address present and future challenges relating to armed conflict.

2. Humanitarianism in Law—A European Project?

To better grasp the dynamic and diverse understandings of humanitarianism and its various facets, as well as the different expressions it can take in law (other fields of public international law, especially human rights law, also contain expressions of humanitarianism; see Çalı, this volume), a look at history is inevitable. This will also shed some light on today's warfare and humanitarianism, which has found an expression in IHL, and is the focus of this chapter. Overall, humanitarianism is always concerned with the suffering of people and aims at reducing and mitigating human distress.

Broadly speaking, humanitarianism dates back several centuries; and it has diverse and multi-layered origins.[16] The protestant Evangelicals in the late 18th century are usually considered among the authors of the first humanitarian movements in European history.[17] But even earlier, in the 16th and 17th centuries, Spanish theologians, jurists, and missionaries followed humanitarian motives when they questioned the legitimacy of enslaving people from the African continent in the Spanish colonial empire.[18] The Spanish humanitarian discourse on anti-slavery is thus older than that of modern American/British abolitionism.[19] Both discourses can be described as a 'long-distance advocacy' of religious actors in light of European imperial expansions.[20] These humanitarians were concerned with the suffering of those far away; they did not address the suffering surrounding them.

Today, suffering represents a universal human experience; it allows people to connect emotionally with strangers, across all differences and divides, near and far.[21] While the European history of humanitarianism cannot be told without reference to European imperialism (see Anghie, this volume, and Shany and Varaki, this volume), history also illustrates the impact of religion on humanitarianism (see Walter, this volume). The Spanish theologians and missionaries, as well as Henry Dunant, one of the co-founders of the International Committee of the Red Cross (ICRC) and one of the 'parents' of the first Geneva Convention of 1864, were influenced by religion in their humanitarian actions.[22] European humanitarianism is often related to Christian humanism and the idea of universal human dignity.[23]

In the 18th and 19th centuries, humanitarianism was in its infancy in Europe and did not have today's contours. Humanitarians and other movements, such as Quaker pacifism or grassroots democratic socialism,[24] were present on the continent. The label 'humanitarian' included various issues, such as social movements dealing with labour protections, prison reform, missionaries, or animal welfare.[25] Over time, humanitarianism found its form in a bourgeois phenomenon that led to the creation of humanitarian associations across Europe (and America) starting in the late 18th century.[26] Some of the humanitarian associations created back then still have a lasting impact today: The ICRC, which was founded in 1863, is still acting as the 'guardian' of IHL, defending humanitarian values, and caring for vulnerable groups in armed conflicts. Likewise, national red cross societies are still doing a tremendous job for people in distress more generally.

In the 19th century, the combined efforts of European pacifists and humanitarians, despite their differences,[27] contributed to what we know today as IHL.[28] In today's international law discourse, the attribute 'humanitarian' is almost omnipresent: the principle of *humanity* and *humanitarian* values are considered a red thread of IHL.[29] Reflections on humanitarian assistance and humanitarian intervention (or the responsibility to protect) have shaped the *ius ad bellum*, which is distinct from IHL. Over the past decades humanitarian considerations have been debated as exceptions to the prohibition of the use of force. In both cases, the attribute usually relates to the prevention and mitigation of human suffering caused by human-induced (international or non-international) conflicts or natural catastrophes. Humanitarianism has also found an expression in human rights law. The perspectives adopted in IHL and human rights law, however, are quite different. On the one hand, humanitarianism in the human rights discourse is based on a rather optimistic promise, while the conflict-related context and IHL take a more pessimistic stance when dealing with the devastating impact of war on civilians and the civilian population. On the other hand, both share many attributes and originate from similar traditions of legal thought, such as liberal political philosophy.[30]

The following section examines how humanitarianism in international law has impacted Europe. Sub-section 2.1 explores the interplay of pacifism and humanitarianism in the 19th century in Europe. The laws of war in the 19th century have been shaped by a range of actors, including individuals who have played an influential role in its creation. Sub-section 2.2 investigates how the 1868 St Petersburg Declaration, which was aimed at a small group of 'civilized' States in Europe, has influenced today's Geneva Conventions and their Additional Protocols with universal aims.

2.1 Peace movements in Europe in the 19th century—hope for the best, prepare for the worst

With combined efforts, pacifists and humanitarians have achieved a long-lasting impact on Europe and beyond since the 19th century, even though there has been a human toll in any conflict ever since. The prohibition of the use of force has been violated several times since its first codification; pacifists have had to accept many setbacks. Nevertheless, IHL, which would not have been the same without the involvement of pacifist and humanitarian movements in Europe, has prevented and mitigated much suffering over the centuries, fulfilling the humanitarian objective of reducing and mitigating human distress.

If we were to tell the history of IHL, we could choose several perspectives and starting dates.[31] In a European context, most would probably refer to some of the 'fathers' of IHL, such as Henry Dunant, a Swiss protestant who co-founded the ICRC in 1863 and lobbied for the adoption of the 'Convention [I] for the Amelioration of the Condition of the Wounded in Armies in the Field' (which was adopted in 1864), or Franz (Francis) Lieber, a German-American legal scholar who drafted the 1863 Lieber Code. Even though the Atlantic separated them, they shared a common origin and similar experiences in Europe: Lieber was born in Berlin, Dunant in Geneva. Both men had suffered on the battlefields in Europe. While Lieber fought in the Napoleonic Wars and in the Battle of Waterloo, Dunant was confronted with suffering on the battlefield in Solferino during one of his business trips to Italy in the Second Italian Independence War. Their individual experiences and conclusions after the events in Europe were similar but different. Lieber emigrated to the US and became a history and political science professor. In the Lieber Code, he codified the first warfare rules during the American Civil War in 1863. Dunant's aim was twofold, he wanted to create a relief organization to care for the wounded, and he campaigned to codify some rules on warfare, such as the impartiality of medical care or the principle of neutrality of medical action. Consequently, he and a small group of Swiss philanthropists started to lobby European governments and monarchs to better protect and care for the wounded on the battlefield. At their initiative, the first Geneva Convention was adopted by twelve States in 1864,[32] in which they codified rules and principles addressing the sick and wounded soldiers on the battlefield. Both documents represent some of the first codifications of the laws of war, grounded in humanitarian motives and based on experiences from European battlefields.

In addition to these prominent men and humanitarians, Bertha von Suttner, an Austrian novelist, suffragette, and pacifist, was one of the leading female protagonists in the European peace movements, in which religious groups, suffrage movements, abolition movements, and political activists came together. She co-founded several peace societies across Europe[33] and became the '*generalissimo* of the peace movement'.[34] She used her impressive network of statesmen, monarchs, and other pacifists as well as humanitarians such as Dunant to campaign for the prevention of wars, international understanding among the people, cooperation between states, and international law more generally.[35] In her writings about peace, militarism, and war, she criticized militarism and advocated for moral peace. She was able to reach a large audience beyond the peace movement with her writings. Von Suttner disapproved of the common opinion of the time that war was inevitable and given by God, and challenged public opinion by questioning the alleged legality of wars. Her bestseller and pacifist novel *Die Waffen nieder!* (*Lay Down Your Arms!*) from 1889, one of the most influential books of the 19th century, is said to have inspired the Russian Tsar Nicholas II to invite her to the first Hague Peace Conference in 1899,[36] at the end of which twenty-seven States adopted the 1899 Hague Regulations.[37] Yet, the 1899/1907 Hague Regulations were disappointing. In retrospect, the first codifications of the laws of war were dominated by Western military needs that trumped humanitarian values in the end. The regulations also exposed civilians to violence, and some argued that it even legalized the suffering and legitimized violent colonial and imperial expansions, disguised as a humanitarian endeavour.[38]

In fact, despite the humanitarian motives of the Tsar when inviting participants to the peace conferences, military considerations prevailed in the legal framework.[39] The outcomes in the 19th century were not yet truly humanitarian.

The combined efforts of pacifists and humanitarians in Europe, such as the Swiss Dunant, the German-American Lieber, and the Austrian von Suttner, together with European statesmen and monarchs resulted in several codifications regarding warfare in the 19th century. Commissions and peace conferences were held in European cities, giving the name to codifications of the laws of war. The impact of individuals on the creation of law was remarkable, even though States dominated the law-making procedure and the content in the end. While private individuals followed humanitarian and pacifist motives and aimed at prohibiting and/or restricting warfare, Statesmen and monarchs as (military) leaders of their nations also wanted to ensure that military considerations were not kept out of the picture. In the end, the combination of pacifist demands to prohibit and abolish war, humanitarian aims to prevent and mitigate human suffering as well as the need to consider military necessities influenced the first codifications to varying degrees.

Over time, pacifist and humanitarian aims have been reconsidered and reevaluated in several new texts and documents in the field of IHL. The most important rules and core principles from the original texts, which go back to Dunant's, Lieber's, and von Suttner's various achievements, have lasted to the present day. They form the 'backbone' of today's IHL. Sub-section 2.2 discusses how the St Petersburg Declaration has influenced today's IHL.

2.2 From St Petersburg to Geneva—a humanitarian history of exclusion?

Despite some disappointment among pacifists and humanitarians, the 1899/1907 Hague Regulations did include humanitarian advances. In the 1899/1907 Hague Regulations, States agreed on limiting the rights of combatants. They included rules regarding the treatment of prisoners of war and the protection of non-combatants.[40] States also agreed on restrictions on injury to the enemy.[41] However, starvation and reprisals were not yet prohibited, even though they caused severe suffering to civilians and the civilian population during conflicts, which explains some of the disappointment within the peace movements. It took two world wars for the laws of war to become more humanitarian, despite their pacifist and humanitarian origins. After the participation of more and more non-European States in the negotiations leading up to the adoption of the 1949 Geneva Convention and, even more importantly, the two 1977 Additional Protocols, today's IHL has become humanitarian, even though every war still takes a human toll. Sub-section 2.2.1 investigates the drafting history of the 1868 St Petersburg Declaration and the humanitarian aims and military purposes of the declaration, while Section 2.2.2 explores the humanitarian evolution from the 1899/1907 Hague Regulations to the 1949 Geneva Convention and the two Additional Protocols.

2.2.1 *The 1868 St Petersburg Declaration—an exclusive humanitarian project?*

Humanitarian movements in the 19th century responded to various calls, from the abolition of slavery in Europe to limiting armament and weapons as an essential issue in the European security system.[42] Almost at the same time, several belligerent States in conflicts on the European continent called for disarmament.[43] The St Petersburg Declaration reflects the spirit of the time in the late imperial era when governments and scholars reflected on ideas of humanity, civilization, and the international community in light of the experiences of the Crimean War.[44] The aim to disarm and restrict warfare was not solely founded on humanitarian considerations, though; tactical and military considerations of the major military powers from the European continent were also involved.[45] Several documents exchanged between military personnel and scholars highlight the mix of rationalism and humanitarianism,[46] as well as realism (see also Shany and Varaki, this volume). In the end, this window in time with pacifists, humanitarians, and State actors facilitated the adoption of the St Petersburg Declaration, balancing military needs with humanitarian aims.

The St Petersburg Declaration was adopted during an international conference on disarmament at the invitation of the Russian Tsar Alexander I.[47] At that point in time, the Russian Tsars initiated several codification procedures; Russia was one of the dominant and effective actors in regulating warfare.[48] The 19th century was a war-driven one, and industrialization and new military technologies promised to make wars even deadlier.[49] There were fears that new technological progress could modify the dynamics of warfare.[50] When Tsar Alexander I called for a simultaneous reduction of armed forces after the Napoleonic Wars, the British Prince Regent and Napoleon III from France supported his initiative. As a result, the 1868 St Petersburg Declaration Renouncing the Use, in Time of War, of Explosive Projectiles Under 400 Grammes Weight established the very basis of modern IHL, namely the limitation of means and methods of warfare.[51] It codified for the first time that warfare should not be unlimited and outlawed the total war, even though the first half of the following century still saw several instances of total war.[52] The Declaration also included several cardinal principles of IHL, such as humanity, distinction, military necessity, and proportionality. Today, they represent the cornerstone of the 1949 Geneva Conventions and their 1977 Additional Protocols.[53]

The Declaration consists of a non-binding preamble,[54] including an introduction[55] and several paragraphs containing restrictions on warfare.[56] It was intended to give adequate weight to the principle of humanity by restricting warfare.[57] In the preamble and introduction, several humanitarian principles, such as the principles of military necessity or proportionality, are introduced. The Declaration concludes by highlighting the balance between the 'necessities of war with the laws of humanity'.[58] The 1868 St Petersburg Declaration turned moral principles, namely the laws of humanity, into positive law, which was fairly unusual in the late 19th century; the rise of positivism only started at the end of the 19th century and beginning of the 20th century (see d'Aspremont, this volume). At the same time, the Declaration was characterized by pragmatism in terms of principles and standards instead of concrete rules.[59]

In this first codification, only a limited number of States participated. Several European statesmen and monarchs in the International Military Commission drafted the St Petersburg Declaration. Spain as a major European State at that time did not attend the conference, neither did the US as an influential Western State. While this highlights the artificial perception of a united or joint European (or Western) humanitarianism, it also illustrates the diversity of views and approaches within Europe at that time. From thirty-two States attending the Commission, only nineteen ratified the final document.[60] A year after the signature in 1869, Brazil, which was considered of European lineage, acceded to the Declaration. Persia (since 1935 known as Iran), another non-European State, had attended the second session of the negotiations in 1868 and also ratified the declaration,[61] which could be interpreted as a first sign of universalization.

The Declaration allowed for States that had not participated in the Commission to accede, which could be read as aiming for universality. The Swiss scholar Bluntschli, for instance, had advocated for a universal membership and application.[62] However, the Tsar had not invited Latin American and Asian States; he did not envisage the Declaration as a universal project. Russia and many others, at that time, did not consider States outside of Europe as true members of the international community,[63] or as 'civilized' States, which referred only to European civilization.[64] The preamble mirrors this perception of that time and generally states that the Declaration only applies to wars between 'civilized' nations. Civilization is mentioned a second time, describing the Declaration and the restrictions on warfare as a consequence of the 'progress of civilization'. Civilization at that time was understood in two ways: First, on an objective basis, civilization was referred to common intellectual and cultural characteristics connecting States;[65] second, in subjective terms, civilization was founded on an expression of community among States that was based on a joint level of intellectual and cultural development.[66] In fact, States who did not grant rights and protection to their citizen were not considered 'civilized'.[67] Several delegations, among them the British, additionally wanted to explicitly exclude an application of the Declaration vis-à-vis Asian or African people.[68] Consequently, the concept of civilization excluded most States and people, especially from the colonial world.[69] In their eurocentric perspective, the then-called 'savages'[70] and 'barbarians'[71] were not supposed to benefit from the humanitarian principles that were codified in Europe.[72] In conflict, these novel principles only applied to State parties to the new codifications, implementing the principle of reciprocity as stated in the preamble.[73] Consequently, according to their understanding, exploding projectiles were considered inhumane and unlawful when deployed against European soldiers, but lawful against anyone else,[74] questioning genuine humanitarian motives of States.

The St Petersburg Declaration illustrates that European States, especially in the context of colonialism, entered into contractual agreements with whom they considered to be 'equal' partners.[75] Their understanding of humanity also only applied reciprocally, unlike the humanitarian movements that cared about the suffering of distant others. Effectively, this resulted in a limited scope of application, excluding 'the mass of humanity'[76] as well as colonial warfare.[77] In fact, it ran contrary to general understandings of humanitarianism but stresses that the European States saw themselves in a central position as the measure of things.[78]

The 'non-civilized' States, however, identified international law and the laws of war as a field in which they could demonstrate they were part of the 'civilized' world. Independent Latin American States, such as Colombia, decided to strengthen their position in the international community by playing by the European rules and principles on warfare.[79] In fact, due to the principle of reciprocity of the St Peterburg Declaration, the only conflict between European and Latin American States in which the Declaration was applied was the war between Colombia and Spain. The other States hence used the European project of the St Petersburg Declaration as a gateway to become part of 'civilization'. As a consequence, the European laws of war were applied more broadly and had an impact beyond the European continent.

The main content of the 1868 St Petersburg Declaration is still found in universal treaties on modern IHL and today's customary law. Current challenges such as the legality of new weapons technologies, for example, autonomous weapons or cyber warfare, are still measured according to the prohibition to cause unnecessary suffering or superfluous injury, which was first codified in the St Petersburg Declaration. Against the backdrop of the prohibition to cause unnecessary suffering or superfluous injury the weapons review according to Article 36 Additional Protocol I (AP I) is conducted. The prohibition is also relevant for the lawfulness of means and methods of warfare, and has impacted the Convention on Certain Conventional Weapons.[80]

Similarly, the idea of laws of humanity, or the principle of humanity, was first codified in the form of the famous Martens Clause of the preamble of the St Petersburg Declaration, and repeated and slightly adjusted in the 1899 Hague Convention II.[81] The clause also found its way in AP I[82] and was included in the Convention on Certain Conventional Weapons[83] as well as in the Convention on Cluster Munitions.[84] The clause goes back to the Russian legal scholar Friedrich (Fyodor Fyodorovich) Martens.[85] The Martens Clause initially stated that '[u]ntil a more complete code of the laws of war has been issued, the High Contracting Parties think it right to declare that in cases not included in the Regulations adopted by them, populations and belligerents remain under the protection and the rule of the principles of the law of nations, as they result from the usages established among civilized peoples, from the laws of humanity, and the requirements of the public conscience'.[86] It is based on the principle that, even in a raging war, the parties to the conflict must respect the inherent dignity of human beings and should not engage in acts that are inherently immoral or that would cause unnecessary suffering, and is thus based on humanitarian motives. It is intended to promote humanitarian aims, such as the protection of the lives, the dignity of individuals affected by armed conflict or the mitigation of the suffering caused by armed conflict. Its gap-filling function is still useful today and has been recalled on several occasions.[87]

Over time, the exclusively European project of the St Petersburg Declaration has created a universal legacy in IHL arguably because of its humanitarian aims and despite its limitations. Notwithstanding the lack of implementation or enforcement provisions, the absence of sanctions for violations, or its limited application between European States, the St Petersburg Declaration contains principles that have endured in the course of time. Several of today's rules and principles in IHL have arguably evolved from this European codification process,[88] eventually becoming universal in the 20th century,[89] despite periods of disrespect for fundamental rules and principles of the laws of war.[90] Over time, the influence of non-European States in the laws of war and IHL has increased, and with the increased participation in the development of IHL the rules and principles became more humanitarian, as will be shown in the following Subsection 2.2.2.

2.2.2 *From The Hague to Geneva—finally a humanitarian story?*

The 1899/1907 Hague Regulations and the 1949 Geneva Conventions represent two separate traditions; together they form today's IHL, the *ius in bello*.[91] The 1899/1907 Hague Regulations are considered to be the 'proper' laws of war, since they regulate the means and methods of the conduct of hostilities and address rights and duties of States.[92] In the run-up to the 1899 Hague Regulation, Tsar Nicholas II of Russia was driven by humanitarian and pacifist motives when he invited fifty-nine heads of State 'with the object of seeking the most effective means of ensuring to all peoples the benefits of a real and lasting peace, and, above all, of limiting the progressive development of existing armaments'.[93] Twenty-six delegations accepted the invitation, only six delegations from outside Europe attended, namely China, Japan, the Islamic Republic of Iran, Mexico, Thailand, and the US.[94] In the end, the Conference failed to agree on the limitation or reduction of armaments, and one of the Tsar's main aims was not fulfilled. Consequently, the peace conference resumed in 1907 when Tsar Nicholas II assembled States for the second Hague International Peace Conference. This time, its purpose was to give 'a fresh development to the humanitarian principles which served as a basis for the work of the First Conference of 1899', which also included agreements on armament.[95] With forty-four States attending, almost half of the attending States came from outside Europe, making the conference as a collective more diverse and less Eurocentric.[96] Among the participants of both peace conferences, in addition to States and military powers peace activists, were humanitarian organizations and arbitration advocates (for more generally on mandatory adjudication and international adjudication, see van Aaken, this volume). In the end, the 1899/1907 Hague Regulations balanced the contradictory principles of humanity and military necessity, meaning a balancing of the needs of war with the standards of civilization.[97] Critics of the 1899/1907 Hague Regulations believed the agreements even facilitated warfare, since in their view only the absence of military imperatives would lead to respect for standards of civilization.[98]

A few decades later, States followed a different approach after the shocking experiences of World Wars I and II, which took place mainly on the European continent. The 1949 Geneva Conventions and their 1977 Additional Protocols addressed shortcomings of the Hague law and focused more on the victims of warfare, such as civilians, the civilian population, prisoners of war, or persons *hors de combat*. The Geneva Conventions thus made the laws of war more 'humanitarian' compared to the 1899/1907 Hague Regulations. The Geneva Conventions cover persons outside the military forces for the first time, who were neither wounded, sick, shipwrecked, nor captives.[99] In general, the Geneva law does not give any rights to States, like the 1899/1907 Hague Regulations initially did. The focus is placed on the protection of civilians and the civilian population as victims of war. The four 1949 Geneva Conventions were signed by fifty-nine States, reaching far beyond the European continent, another step towards universalization.[100] Today, 196 States have signed and ratified the four conventions, resulting in their universal application.

With the adoption of the two Additional Protocols in the 1970s, the *ius in bello* became more humanitarian.[101] Accordingly, a change in title from the laws of war to IHL seemed appropriate, even though the novel designation was criticized for using an oxymoron to describe the laws of war.[102] This change was initiated by Jean Pictet,[103] director general of the ICRC Directorate in the 1960s. The traditional understanding of the laws of war excluded the application of human rights. Based on Pictet's understanding of humanitarianism as a 'universal social doctrine which aims at the good of all mankind',[104] he concluded that human rights were the 'most generous principles in humanitarian law'.[105] Consequently, when Pictet changed the title of the laws of war, he understood IHL in broader terms; he included the Geneva and the Hague law as well as human rights therein.[106] However, some European States did not favour such a merger. The negotiations regarding common Article 3 reveal how decolonization and the Great Powers, as well as the Cold War, shaped the State-led debates at that time, disappointing humanitarians as well as humanitarian organizations including Pictet and the ICRC.[107] Today, even though IHL and human rights law complement each other,[108] both fields are generally understood as separate and distinct fields of public international law.[109] Pictet's idea to extend the laws of war to human rights by changing the title was thus not completely successful, and IHL does not include human rights in today's discourse. A parallel application, or a co-existence, as phrased by the European Court of Human Rights (ECtHR),[110] better describes the current understanding of the relationship between both fields of international law with humanitarian motives.

Even without a merger of human rights law and IHL, the adoption of the four Geneva Conventions and their two Additional Protocols transformed the laws of armed conflict into IHL. Humanitarian aims were taken more seriously than before, and the focus was placed on the protection of civilians and the civilian population. With the Geneva law, the story followed a more humanitarian narrative. At the same time, this turning point correlates with including States beyond the European continent. Ultimately, the European project turned universal, and humanitarian considerations balanced military aims.

3. Conclusions

War has always been part of our world. It has never left, despite a universal prohibition of the threat or use of force in the UN Charter[111] based on pacifist motives, and despite the criminalization of the crime of aggression in the Rome Statute.[112] Humanitarian aims are still as relevant today as they were centuries ago. This lies within the nature of warfare but is partly also due to States that have ignored the *ius ad bellum* and the *ius in bello* in some instances.[113] Especially Russia's behaviour has changed over time, from being an initiator with humanitarian objectives in the 19th century to a lawbreaker without a 'humanitarian conscience' in the 21st century (see Rusinova, this volume). Ignorance of existing rules as well as normative contestation, however, do not *per se* render norms meaningless.[114] Attempts to prevent or at least mitigate human suffering will thus always play an important role, even if rules and principles are ignored.

The combined efforts of pacifists and humanitarians in the 19th century in Europe have achieved several codifications of the laws of war, which still influence today's legal order and current conduct of hostilities. The war-driven 19th and 20th centuries did not result in exasperation and frustration but rather gave rise to important legal texts and documents, initiated by European personalities and States. Diplomatic conferences, as well as peace conferences, took place in Europe, such as the ones in Geneva in 1864 or in The Hague in 1899 and 1907. The various philanthropists in peace movements inspired statesmen and monarchs to regulate warfare. Pacifists like Bertha von Suttner and humanitarians like Henry Dunant lobbied them to first prevent and mitigate human suffering and ultimately to abolish war. Their aim was to codify rules and principles as well as the creations of a relief organization for people in distress. At the same time, States in the Westphalian State order started to believe in the need to adopt joint regulations, like Tsar Alexander I from Russia, who had called for a simultaneous reduction of armed forces after the Napoleonic Wars, or Tsar Alexander II's call to European statesmen and monarchs, which resulted in the adoption of the 1868 St Petersburg Declaration Renouncing the Use, in Time of War, of Explosive Projectiles Under 400 Grammes Weight. The vast majority of the signatory States were European, and the Declaration and its principles were only applied between them, making the initial project an exclusively European one. The exclusion of other States and people from humanitarian protection in war was ended when non-European States started to use this European project to prove their willingness and ability to belong to the 'civilized' world. Consequently, European codifications of the laws of war, together with universal efforts, transformed the regulation of warfare beyond the continent, universally aiming at mitigating human suffering. '[H]umanitarianism begins where the dream of humanity leaves off.'[115]

Acknowledgements

The author would like to thank the editors for their very helpful remarks, as well as Stefan Oeter, Amal Sethi and Franziska Bachmann for taking the time to read and comment on an earlier draft of this chapter.

Notes

1. See Hans Kelsen, *Peace through Law* (first published 1944, The Lawbook Exchange 2000); Cecilia Bailliet and Kjetil Mujezinović Larsen (eds), *Promoting Peace through International Law* (OUP 2015); Robert J Delahunty and John C Yoo, 'Peace through Law—The Failure of a Noble Experiment', 106 Michigan Law Review 2007, 923.

2. There are estimates of 20 million deaths and 21 million wounded during World War I, see, eg, REPERES, Centre Européen Robert Schuman, World War I casualties, as stated here <https://www.census.gov/history/www/homepage_archive/2018/november_2018.html> accessed 1 December 2022.
3. See the preamble of the Covenant of the League of Nations.
4. Based on Article 25 of the Covenant of the League of Nations. On the European tradition of asylum law, see also Atle Grahl-Madsen, '*The League of Nations and the Refugees*' in Peter Macalister-Smith and Gudmundur Alfresson (eds), The Land Beyond (Brill Nijhoff 2001) 126ff.
5. General Treaty for Renunciation of War as an Instrument of National Policy (adopted 27 August 1928, entered into force 25 July 1929) 94 LNTS 57 (Kellogg-Briand Pact) Article I.
6. See, for the fatalities per country during the period of World War II (1939–1945), excluding wounded victims and others suffering, <https://www.statista.com/statistics/1293510/second-world-war-fatalities-per-country/> accessed 1 December 2022.
7. Charter of the United Nations (adopted 26 June 1945, entered into force 24 October 1945), XV UNCIO 335 (UN Charter) Article 1(1).
8. Preamble and Article 2(4) UN Charter.
9. Eg as confirmed by the International Court of Justice (ICJ) and the International Criminal Tribunal for the former Yugoslavia in the case of Srebrenica (Bosnia & Herzegovina) or the Rwandan Genocide's confirmation by the International Criminal Tribunal for Rwanda.
10. For developments beyond Europe and earlier than the 19th century see, eg, Hilaire McCoubrey, *International Humanitarian Law: Modern Developments in the Limitation of Warfare* (2nd edn, Routledge 2019) 8–13.
11. See, eg, Alonso Gurmendi, 'Latin Lieber: Uncovering the History of the Treaty on the Regularisation of War' (*Opinio Juris*, 10 June 2022) <http://opiniojuris.org/2022/06/10/latin-lieber-uncovering-the-history-of-the-treaty-on-the-regularisation-of-war/> accessed 8 October 2022; Tania Atilano, 'The Forgotten Histories of the Codification of International Humanitarian Law in Nineteenth-Century Latin America' (*Opinio Juris*, 7 October 2022) <http://opiniojuris.org/2022/10/07/the-forgotten-histories-of-the-codification-of-international-humanitarian-law-in-nineteenth-century-latin-america/> accessed 8 October 2022.
12. See Abigail Green, 'Humanitarianism in Nineteenth-Century Context: Religious, Gendered, National', 57 The Historical Journal 2014, 1157.
13. See generally on the humanitarian intervention and the related concept of the responsibility to protect, Anne Orford, *Reading Humanitarian Intervention: Human Rights and the Use of Force in International Law* (CUP 2003); Hans-Joachim Heintze, 'Gewalt im Dienste der Menschenrechte?—Von der humanitären Intervention im Kosovo zur Responsibility to Protect' in Ines-Jacqueline Werkner and Ulrike Kronfeld-Goharani (eds), *Der ambivalente Frieden: Die Friedensforschung vor neuen Herausforderungen* (VS Verlag für Sozialwissenschaften 2011) 37ff; Anne Peters, 'The Security Council's Responsibility to Protect', 8 International Organizations Law Review 2011, 15.
14. See Spencer Zifcak, 'The Responsibility to Protect after Libya and Syria', 13 Melbourne Journal of International Law 2012, 59.
15. The International Committee of the Red Cross identified several challenges in its 2019 report on 'International Humanitarian Law and the Challenges of Contemporary Armed Conflicts—Recommitting to Protection in Armed Conflict on the 70th Anniversary of the Geneva Conventions' <https://shop.icrc.org/international-human

itarian-law-and-the-challenges-of-contemporary-armed-conflicts-recommitting-to-protection-in-armed-conflict-on-the-70th-anniversary-of-the-geneva-conventions-pdf-en.html> accessed 1 December 2022.

16. See Thomas Weller, 'Humanitarianism before Humanitarianism?' in Fabian Klose and Mirjam Thulin (eds), *Humanity: A History of European Concepts in Practice from the Sixteenth Century to the Present* (Vandenhoeck & Ruprecht 2016) 168.
17. See ibid, 152ff.
18. See ibid, 151.
19. See ibid, 166.
20. See Peter Stamatov, *The Origins of Global Humanitarianism: Religion, Empires, and Advocacy* (CUP 2013) 1, 12.
21. cf Richard A Wilson and Richard D Brown, *Humanitarianism and Suffering: The Mobilization of Empathy* (CUP 2008) 12.
22. See Michael Barnett and Janice Stein, *Sacred Aid: Faith and Humanitarianism* (OUP 2012). Daniel Warner, 'Henry Dunant's Imagined Community: Humanitarianism and the Tragic', 38 Alternatives 2013, 3, 12ff.
23. See Pedro A de Haro and Davide Mombelli, 'Humanism and Humanitarianism: The Language of the Deaf' in Pedro A de Haro and Davide Mombelli, *Introduction to the Spanish Universalist School* (Brill Nijhoff 2020) 84.
24. See Wilson and Brown (n 21) 4.
25. See Peter J Hoffman and Thomas G Weiss, *Humanitarianism, War, and Politics: Solferino to Syria and Beyond* (Rowman & Littlefield Publishers 2017) 4.
26. See Haro and Mombelli (n 23)84.
27. See eg Samuel Moyn, *Humane: How the United States abandoned Peace and reinvented War* (Verso Books 2022), Chapter 3 describing the reaction of the pacifist von Suttner to Dunant's Nobel price in terms of 'outrage.' Others have interpreted the correspondence von Suttner with and about Dunant differently, Heudtlas, for instance interprets her letter to Rudolf Müller dating 27. June 1897 as proposing to nominate Dunant for the Nobel price, printed in Willy Heudtlas, 'J. Henry Dunant and the events leading to the award of the first Nobel Peace Prize' 4.39 International Review of the Red Cross (1961–1997) (1964) 285–286. On the amicable and appreciative relationship between von Suttner and Dunant and their lasting mutual support as pacifists and humanitarians with joined values (even after he had received the Nobel prize), see André Durand, 'The development of the idea of peace in the thinking of Henry Dunant' 26.250 International Review of the Red Cross (1961–1997) (1986): 16–51.
28. There were earlier expressions of humanitarianism in the laws of armed conflict in Roman and Greek traditions, eg the just war theory in the writings of the 12th/13th century by Gratian or St Thomas Aquinas. For more on this, see McCoubrey (n 10) 11–13.
29. See, eg, Yoram Dinstein, *The Conduct of Hostilities under the Law of International Armed Conflict* (3rd edn, CUP 2016) paras 22–23 + 34–35.
30. See Green (n 12) 5.
31. Some have argued for a more orthodox history of a humanization of war and law, based on compassion and civilization, whilst others give a more negative account of oppression and imperialism. See, for a description of both histories, Amanda Alexander, 'A Short History of International Humanitarian Law', 26 European Journal of International Law 2015, 109, 113.

32. Fifty-seven more States, including many States outside of Europe, acceded to it over time, see <https://ihl-databases.icrc.org/en/ihl-treaties/gc-1864/state-parties?activeTab=historical> accessed 1 December 2022.
33. See, eg, the Austrian Peace Society in 1891, or the German Peace Society in 1892. She also founded the first German pacifist journal 'Die Waffen nieder!'.
34. See Bertha von Suttner—Facts, NobelPrize.org, Nobel Prize Outreach AB 2022 <https://www.nobelprize.org/prizes/peace/1905/suttner/facts/> accessed 1 December 2022.
35. See, eg, United Nations library and Archives, Bertha von Suttners papers, available at https://archives.ungeneva.org/bertha-von-suttner-papers (last visited 5 February 2024; Ulrike Lembke, 'Der Frauenfriedenskongress 1915—Auch ein Beitrag zur Geschichte des Pazifismus als Völkerrechtsidee', 53 Archiv des Völkerrechts 2015, 424.
36. See <https://www.vredespaleis.nl/peace-palace/from-the-archives/bertha-von-suttner/?lang=en> accessed 1 December 2022. Additionally, others, like Friedrich (Fyodor Fyodorovich) Martens who headed the Russian legal team at The Hague in 1899, also influenced the Tsars. For instance, he was also part of the legal delegation to adopt a declaration on the laws of war in Brussels, which was initiated by Tsar Alexander II of Russia. The 1874 Brussels Declaration, however, was never adopted, see <https://ihl-databases.icrc.org/en/ihl-treaties/brussels-decl-1874?activeTab=historical> accessed 15 May 2022.
37. Including non-European States such as China, Islamic Republic of Iran, Japan, Mexico, Thailand, Turkey, and the US, see <https://ihl-databases.icrc.org/en/ihl-treaties/hague-finact-1899/state-parties?activeTab=historical> accessed 1 December 2022. The 1907 final act was signed by forty-four States, including non-European States, see <https://ihl-databases.icrc.org/en/ihl-treaties/hague-finact-1907/state-parties?activeTab=historical> accessed 1 December 2022.
38. Fabian Klose and Mirjam Thulin, 'Introduction: European Concepts and Practices of Humanity in Historical Perspective' in Fabian Klose and Mirjam Thulin (eds), *Humanity: A History of European Concepts in Practice From the Sixteenth Century to the Present* (Vandenhoeck & Ruprecht 2016) 19.
39. See, eg, Boyd van Dijk, *Preparing for War: The Making of the Geneva Conventions* (OUP 2022) 10 citing Pictet and the stopping of 'unbridled humanitarianism', and 320, on the Soviet contribution and US intentions when drafting the convention. See also Eval Benvenisti and Doreen Lustig, 'Monopolizing War: Codifying the Laws of War to Reassert Governmental Authority, 1856–1874', 31 European Journal of International Law 2020, 127.
40. There are earlier examples of the protection of prisoners of war, dating back to the time of the Old Testament, early Indian texts, or ancient Chinese theories. See, for such examples, McCoubrey (n 10) 8–11.
41. See Alexander (n 31) 115 with further references.
42. See Wilson and Brown (n 21) 4. See also Emily Crawford, 'The Enduring Legacy of the St Petersburg Declaration: Distinction, Military Necessity, and the Prohibition of Causing Unnecessary Suffering and Superfluous Injury in IHL', 20 Journal of the History of International Law 2018, 544, at 546f.
43. See Crawford (n 42) 546.
44. See Eric Myles, 'Humanity, Civilization and the International Community in the Late Imperial Russian Mirror: Three Ideas Topical for Our Days', 4 Journal of the History of International Law 2002, 310.
45. See, eg, Scott Keefer, '"Explosive Missals": International Law, Technology, and Security in Nineteenth-Century Disarmament Conferences', 21 War in History 2014, 445, 450.

46. See, eg, the letters exchanged between legal scholar Johann Casper Bluntschli and military chief of staff Helmuth Graf von Moltke, printed in 13 Revue de Droit International et de la Législation Comparé 1881, 79–84. See also Robert Kolb and Momchil Milanov, 'The 1886 St Petersburg Declaration on Explosive Projectiles: A Reappraisal', 20 Journal of the History of International Law 2018, 515, 517.
47. See Crawford (n 42) 546–547.
48. For a more detailed analysis of Russia and IHL, see Michael Riepl, *Russian Contributions to International Humanitarian Law* (Nomos 2022). See also Boyd van Dijk, '"The Great Humanitarian": The Soviet Union, the International Committee of the Red Cross, and the Geneva Conventions of 1949', 37 Law and History Review 2019, 209.
49. See Myles (n 44) 316.
50. See ibid.
51. See Kolb and Milanov (n 46) 515.
52. See, eg, Geoffrey Best, 'Peace Conferences and the Century of Total War: The 1899 Hague Conference and What Came After', 75 International Affairs 1999, 619.
53. Frits Kalshoven, 'The Soldier and His Golf Clubs' in Frits Kalshoven (ed) *Reflections on the Law of War* (Brill Nijhoff 2007) 359, 360.
54. 'On the proposition of the Imperial Cabinet of Russia, an International Military Commission having assembled at St. Petersburg in order to examine the expediency of forbidding the use of certain projectiles in time of war between civilized nations, and that Commission having by common agreement fixed the technical limits at which the necessities of war ought to yield to the requirements of humanity, the Undersigned are authorized by the orders of their Governments to declare as follows:'
55. 'Considering:

    That the progress of civilization should have the effect of alleviating as much as possible the calamities of war;

    That the only legitimate object which States should endeavour to accomplish during war is to weaken the military forces of the enemy; That for this purpose it is sufficient to disable the greatest possible number of men;

    That this object would be exceeded by the employment of arms which uselessly aggravate the sufferings of disabled men, or render their death inevitable;

    That the employment of such arms would, therefore, be contrary to the laws of humanity;'

56. 'The Contracting Parties engage mutually to renounce, in case of war among themselves, the employment by their military or naval troops of any projectile of a weight below 400 grammes, which is either explosive or charged with fulminating or inflammable substances.

    They will invite all the States which have not taken part in the deliberations of the International Military Commission assembled at St. Petersburg by sending Delegates thereto, to accede to the present engagement.

    This engagement is compulsory only upon the Contracting or Acceding Parties thereto in case of war between two or more of themselves; it is not applicable to non-Contracting Parties, or Parties who shall not have acceded to it. It will also cease to be compulsory from the moment when, in a war between Contracting or Acceding Parties, a non-Contracting Party or a non-Acceding Party shall join one of the belligerents.

The Contracting or Acceding Parties reserve to themselves to come hereafter to an understanding whenever a precise proposition shall be drawn up in view of future improvements which science may effect in the armament of troops, in order to maintain the principles which they have established, and to conciliate the necessities of war with the laws of humanity.'

57. See Kolb and Milanov (n 46) 522.
58. See <https://ihl-databases.icrc.org/applic/ihl/ihl.nsf/Article.xsp?action=openDocument&documentId=568842C2B90F4A29C12563CD0051547C> accessed 4 October 2022.
59. See David Kennedy, 'War and International Law: Distinguishing the Military and Humanitarian Professions', 82 International Law Studies 2007, 1, 13.
60. See <https://ihl-databases.icrc.org/en/ihl-treaties/st-petersburg-decl-1868/state-parties?activeTab=undefined> accessed 1 December 2022.
61. For all signatory States and those that have ratified the declaration, see <https://ihl-databases.icrc.org/en/ihl-treaties/st-petersburg-decl-1868/state-parties?activeTab=undefined> accessed 1 December 2022.
62. See Martens who refers to Bluntschli, Fedor F Martens, *Völkerrecht: das internationale Recht der civilisirten Nationen* (Weidmann 1883) 184.
63. See in that sense, eg, ibid, 178. See more specifically on the Russian legal scholar Martens and his colonialist role, Lauri Mälksoo, 'The Legacy of FF Martens and the Shadow of Colonialism', 21 Chinese Journal of International Law 2022, 55.
64. See Martens (n 62) 203; Scott A Keefer, *The Law of Nations and Britain's Quest for Naval Security* (Palgrave Macmillan 2016) 40.
65. See, eg, Myles (n 44) 321. For a general contextualization on Russia, international law, and Martens' contribution, see Lauri Mälksoo, 'FF Martens and his Time: When Russia was an Integral Part of the European Tradition in International Law' 25 European Journal of International Law 2014, 811.
66. See Myles (n 44) 321.
67. See, eg, Martens (n 62) 326: '*Im Schutz der Person gipfelt der Beruf des Staates, er ist auch das höchste Ziel der internationalen Verbindungen. Die Achtung vor der menschlichen Persönlichkeit ist ohne Zweifel dasjenige Kennzeichen, welches ganz besonders scharf die modernen Staaten von den antiken unterscheidet. Während die Sklaverei im Alterthum ein Institut juris gentium war und bei allen Völkern under dem Schutz der Gesetzte und Gerichte stand, verkündet das Völkerrecht es als unumstössliche Wahrheit, dass kein Mensch Eigenthum eines andern sein und die Sklaverei überhaupt nicht bestehen dürfe* [The profession of the state culminates in the protection of the person; it is also the highest goal of international relations. Respect for the human person is undoubtedly the characteristic that distinguishes modern states from ancient ones. Whereas slavery in ancient times was an institute juris gentium and was protected by the laws and courts of all nations, international law proclaims it as an irrevocable truth that no human being may be the property of another and that slavery may not exist at all].'
68. cf Crawford (n 42) 560.
69. Kolb and Milanov (n 46) 525.
70. On the notion of 'savages' in this context see, eg, Frédéric Mégret, 'From "Savages" to "Unlawful Combatants": A Postcolonial Look at International Humanitarian Law's "Other"' in Anne Orford (ed), *International Law and Its Others* (CUP 2006).
71. On notions of 'savage' and 'babarian' in terms of hierarchies of humans, see Francisco Bethencourt, 'Humankind: From Division to Recomposition' in Fabian Klose and

Mirjam Thulin (eds), *Humanity: A History of European Concepts in Practice from the Sixteenth Century to the Present* (Vandenhoeck & Ruprecht 2016) 39.

72. The British legal philosopher James Lorimer had divided humanity into 'civilized' humanity, 'barbarous' humanity, and 'savage' humanity, see James Lorimer, The Institutes of The Law of Nations: A Treatise of the Jural Relations of Separate Political Communities (vol 1, William Blackwood and Sons 1883) 101.
73. States when adopting the 1864 Geneva Convention did not include references to reciprocity, which has been described as a '*nod towards unilateralism*,' see, eg, Crawford (n 42) 561.
74. cf ibid, 560.
75. See Frits Kalshoven, 'Arms, Armaments and International Law', 191 Collected Courses of the Hague Academy of International Law 1985, 213.
76. See Keefer (n 45) 454.
77. See Kolb and Milanov (n 46) 520.
78. ibid.
79. See Gurmendi (n 11). See also Atilano (n 11).
80. Protocol (I) Additional to the Geneva Conventions of 12 August 1949, and relating to the Protection of Victims of International Armed Conflicts (adopted 8 June 1977, entered into force 7 December 1978) (1977) 1125 UNTS 3 (AP I) Article 36; Convention on Prohibitions or Restrictions on the Use of Certain Conventional Weapons which may be deemed to be Excessively Injurious or to have Indiscriminate Effects (with Protocols I, II and III) (adopted 10 October 1980, entered into force 2 December 1983) 1342 UNTS 137 (Convention on Certain Conventional Weapons). On the weapons review more generally, see Alan Backstrom and Ian Henderson, 'New Capabilities in Warfare: An Overview of Contemporary Technological Developments and the Associated Legal and Engineering Issues in Article 36 Weapons Reviews', 94 International Review of the Red Cross 2012, 483; Anne Dienelt, 'The Shadowy Existence of the Weapons Review and Its Impact on Disarmament', 36 Sicherheit und Frieden (S + F)/Security and Peace 2018, 126; Natalia Jevglevskaja, 'Weapons Review Obligation under Customary International Law', 94 International Law Studies 2018, 196; Kathleen Lawand, 'Reviewing the Legality of New Weapons, Means and Methods of Warfare', 88 International Review of the Red Cross 2006, 925; Justin McClelland, 'The Review of Weapons in Accordance with Article 36 of Additional Protocol I', 85 International Review of the Red Cross 2003, 397.
81. See preamble of the 1899 Hague Convention (II) with respect to the laws and customs of war on land: 'Until a more complete code of the laws of war is issued, the High Contracting Parties think it right to declare that in cases not included in the Regulations adopted by them, populations and belligerents remain under the protection and empire of the principles of international law, as they result from the usages established between civilized nations, from the laws of humanity and the requirements of the public conscience.'
82. See the preamble to Additional Protocol I: 'In cases not covered by this Protocol or by other international agreements, civilians and combatants remain under the protection and authority of the principles of international law derived from established custom, from the principles of humanity and from the dictates of public conscience.'
83. 5th preambular paragraph.
84. 11th preambular paragraph.
85. See, eg, Mälksoo (n 63) 814.

86. Available at <https://ihl-databases.icrc.org/en/ihl-treaties/st-petersburg-decl-1868?activeTab=default> accessed 4 October 2022.
87. See, eg, the potential and relevance of the Martens Clause with regard to environmental protection in armed conflict, Dieter Fleck, 'The Martens Clause and Environmental Protection in Relation to Armed Conflicts', 10 Goettingen Journal of International Law 2020, 243. The modern humanitarian discourse also includes the environment, see Michael Barnett, 'Humanitarianism Transformed', 3 Perspectives on Politics 2005, 723, 726.
88. See Crawford (n 42) 557.
89. See Kolb and Milanov (n 46) 525.
90. See Riepl (n 48) 82ff.
91. See Alexander (n 31) 117.
92. See Jean Pictet, 'The Principles of International Humanitarian Law', 6 International Review of the Red Cross (1961–1997) 1966, 455, 458.
93. See Dietrich Schindler and Jiri Toman, *The Laws of Armed Conflicts* (Martinus Nijhoff Publishers 1988) 50.
94. See <https://ihl-databases.icrc.org/applic/ihl/ihl.nsf/States.xsp?xp_viewStates=XPages_NORMStatesSign&xp_treatySelected=145> accessed 4 October 2022.
95. See Schindler and Toman (n 93) 53.
96. Among them Argentina, Bolivia, Brazil, Chile, Colombia, Cuba, Dominican Republic, Guatemala, Haiti, Islamic Republic of Iran, Japan, Mexico, Nicaragua, Panama, Paraguay, Peru, Thailand, United States, Uruguay, and Venezuela, see <https://ihl-databases.icrc.org/applic/ihl/ihl.nsf/States.xsp?xp_viewStates=XPages_NORMStatesSign&xp_treatySelected=185> accessed 4 October 2022.
97. See Georg Schwarzenberger, *International Law and Order* (Praeger Publishers 1971) 172.
98. See Alexander (n 31) 114. For an opposing view, see McCoubrey (n 10) 4–5.
99. See Pictet (n 92) 457.
100. For signatory States and the current ratifications, see <https://ihl-databases.icrc.org/en/ihl-treaties/treaties-and-states-parties> accessed 4 October 2022.
101. Today, 174 States have signed and ratified Additional Protocol I, and 169 States have signed and ratified Additional Protocol II.
102. See, eg, Adams Roberts, 'Humanitarian War: Military Intervention and Human Rights', 69 International Affairs 1993, 429.
103. See, eg, Pictet (n 92) 455; Jean Pictet, *Humanitarian Law and the Protection of War Victims* (Brill 1975).
104. Pictet (n 92) 461.
105. ibid, 458.
106. See ibid.
107. See van Dijk (n 39) 101ff.
108. See, eg, for the continued application of human rights during armed conflict, *Legality of the Threat or Use of Nuclear Weapons* (Advisory Opinion) [1996], ICJ Rep 226, para 25; *Legal Consequences of the Construction of a Wall in the Occupied Palestinian Territories* (Advisory Opinion) [2004] ICJ Rep 136, para 106. For further references and a summary of the current discourse on the interplay between IHL and human rights, see Anne Dienelt, *Armed Conflicts and the Environment: Complementing the Laws of Armed Conflict with Human Rights Law and International Environmental Law* (Springer 2022) 147.

109. See, eg, ILC, 'Fragmentation of International Law: Difficulties Arising From the Diversification and Expansion of International Law, Report of the Study Group of the ILC' (13 April 2006) UN Doc A/CN.4/L.682, paras 129 or 158.
110. See, eg, *Hassan v UK*, App no 29750/09 (ECtHR [Grand Chamber], Judgment of 16 September 2014) paras 104–105.
111. Article 2(4).
112. Article 8 bis. For more on the current discourse on the crime of aggression in the Rome Statute, see Michael L Fremuth, 'The Crime of Aggression and the Prohibition of the Use of Force—Reflections on the Relationship between the Rome Statute and General Public International Law' in Stefanie Bock and Eckart Conze (eds), *Rethinking the Crime of Aggression* (Springer 2022) 171; Kevin J Heller, 'Options for Prosecuting Russian Aggression Against Ukraine: A Critical Analysis', Journal of Genocide Research 2022, 1.
113. Such as the US, see, eg, Brad A Gutierrez, Sarah DeCristofaro, and Michael Woods, 'What Americans Think of International Humanitarian Law', 93 International Review of the Red Cross 2011, 1009, or for Russia, see Riepl (n 48) 82ff.
114. See, eg, Nicole Deitelhoff and Lisbeth Zimmermann, 'Things We Lost in the Fire: How Different Types of Contestation Affect the Robustness of International Norms', 22 International Studies Review 2020, 51; Antje Wiener, *A Theory of Contestation* (Springer 2014).
115. When describing the French title of Finkielkraut's *In the Name of Humanity*, Paul Betts, 'Universalism and Its Discontents: Humanity as a Twentieth-Century Concept', in Fabian Klose and Mirjam Thulin (eds), *Humanity: A History of European Concepts in Practice from the Sixteenth Century to the Present* (Vandenhoeck & Ruprecht 2016) 51, 69.

CHAPTER 17

THE MASTER'S TOOLS AND THE MASTER'S HOUSE

Marxist Insights for International Law

ANTONIOS TZANAKOPOULOS

1. Introduction

AUDRE Lorde wrote a text in 1979 to which she gave the title: 'The Master's Tools Will Never Dismantle the Master's House'.[1] In it, she argued that using the tools of racist patriarchy to examine the fruits of that very same racist patriarchy would only allow the narrowest parameters of change, if any.[2] This is, in a way, the predicament faced by any Marxist, or even Marxian,[3] approach to (international) law. Given that, according to Marx, in communism both law and the State will wither away and disappear,[4] and given that (on a somewhat crude reading) law is part of the superstructure erected to both conceal and justify the economic base,[5] law is but the master's tool.[6] How could it ever really be used to dismantle the master's house?

This puts any Marxist lawyer (in the broadest sense of both these terms) already in some difficulty. The difficulty becomes more pronounced if one were to refer to Marx's eleventh thesis on Feuerbach, the hit thesis on Feuerbach one might say:[7] 'Philosophers have hitherto only *interpreted* the world in various ways; the point is to *change* it'.[8] Alter this slightly to 'Lawyers have hitherto only *interpreted* the law in various ways; the point is to *change* it', and the difficulty becomes apparent.[9] And that is on two levels:

First, while Marxism is generally accepted by both proponents and adversaries as having had a significant impact (though here these will part ways as to whether that is for good or ill) in many disciplines—ranging from economics, history, and sociology to aesthetics and even city planning[10]—law, and especially international law, is not usually counted among them.

Second, is it even up to lawyers to change the law? This depends on how we define lawyers, and what we take their role to be. A more inclusive term would be 'legal actors', including legal scholars, practitioners, judges, as well as officials entrusted with powers of interpretation and application of the law. But let us just call 'lawyers' those with legal training: for a large part, 'lawyers' are responsible for making the law, even if not *qua* lawyers but rather *qua* politicians. More than 200 of the 500-odd members of the US Congress are lawyers by training, more than half of US presidents were lawyers by training, and similar numbers can be found in the parliaments or legislatures of many other 'advanced' capitalist States.[11] So the 'lawyers' *could* in a sense change the law, since they seem to be making it. This is quite unlike philosophers, who rarely seek political office. But lawyers prefer instead to advocate for 'reverence for the law',[12] perhaps because of their *deformation professionnelle*.

If that were not enough, the questions of what is a Marxist approach to (international) law, what is a work in the Marxist tradition, and even what is a Marxist lawyer, are a set of whole other cans of worms, replete with disagreements, accusations, splinter groups, denunciations, and the like.[13] And even if we were to settle these, we would come across another question which divides, creating a whole spectrum of positions, but represented in the extremes by the revolutionaries on one end and the reformists on the other: the question of 'what is to be done'.[14] This translates well in discussing the Marxist tradition of international law (see Anghie, this volume and Mbengue and Akinkugbe, this volume):[15] at one extreme we find those who proclaim the master's tool useless against the master's house, and, having done so, turn to other tools (or just go home), leaving the law behind.[16] At the other extreme, we have those who still believe, beyond the criticism, in the emancipatory potential of international law (at least to some degree).[17] It is difficult to resolve this 'radical's predicament'.[18]

*

A chapter on the influence of Marxist international law in a book on *International Law in Europe* may seem an oddity in more ways than one. Even though Marx(ism) was born in Europe, there is an inescapable orientalist aura around it. The first ones to take Marxism and law seriously were the early Soviet scholars,[19] in particular Pashukanis, a standard point of reference.[20] After Pashukanis's 'liquidation' in 1937 and for many decades, 'Marxist' international law, almost completely bereft of any real emancipatory potential, was pursued by Soviet international legal scholars and those of the then 'Eastern' bloc.[21] I do not engage here with the practice of States that, at least in their own leaders' minds and/or at least to some extent, follow(ed) the Marxist path, but I have focused on theory. Influences of Marxist thought were also evident in proto-TWAIL,[22] and in the attempt of then newly independent States to reshape the international legal order in the 1960s and 1970s, particularly through the attempt to establish a New International Economic Order.[23] After the failure of that attempt, it has been in Europe primarily (though clearly not exclusively) where in the last decades (since the end of the Cold War, and in particular in the new millennium) Marxist approaches to international law have flourished and have thus produced an interesting debate—even if, unfortunately, a slightly esoteric one at times, which, as a consequence, has not had the impact one might have hoped or wished on the wider international legal scholarship.

The first purpose of this chapter is to trace the impact of Marxist thought on international law without following the relatively simplified chronological line of the last paragraph, but rather by focusing on structural aspects of international law, grouping them under the structure of the (international) legal relation, aka 'the legal form' (Section 3); the content of the legal relation with particular emphasis on interpretation (Section 4); and the justification of the legal relation through ideology (Section 5).

A further purpose of this chapter is to do so without necessarily labelling Marxism a European tradition—after all, as already mentioned, it has influenced at least part of TWAIL, which, among others, seeks to not only expose but also to combat the Eurocentrism of international law. Or, if Marxism is to be considered a European tradition in some sense, it is one with a distinctively internationalist and unifying, as well as emancipatory, perspective: 'Workers of the world' are meant to 'unite', after all, having 'nothing to lose but their chains'—but 'a world to win'![24]

The final purpose of the chapter is to trace that impact without aspiring to be comprehensive; but aspiring to avoid as much as possible the jargon that tends to alienate (pun intended) non-specialist (in Marxism!) readers, thereby rendering the debate esoteric. I hope that all comrades with impeccable Marxist credentials will find it in them to excuse me for that latter transgression, and especially for the crash course in Marxism[25] that is about to follow in Section 2, which is to serve as the basis for the rest of the chapter.

2. Marxism 101

This section introduces basic Marxist thought to the reader. It may seem like an impossible task to undertake in a few paragraphs. But it can be done briefly and meaningfully, even if at a cost to nuance and the variety of approaches to and interpretations of Marxist thought, briefly mentioned in the introduction.[26] The best way that this can be done is by emulating Albert Einstein in his 1949 essay 'Why Socialism?' in the first issue of the *Monthly Review*. In that essay, Einstein included short crash course into Marxism.[27]

Einstein describes the basic tenets of the Marxist analysis of the capitalist system in the following simple terms: there are primarily two classes in society, let us call them the workers and the capitalists.[28] The workers only own their own labour power (their power to work and make things), while the capitalists own, well ... everything else. Primarily, though, they own the means of production, that is, those means that are required for production to take place (land, infrastructure, raw materials, capital, etc). These two classes, reduced by the law to abstract and equal individuals, meet in the 'market' and enter 'freely' into agreements, sanctioned by the law,[29] whereby the worker sells their labour power to the capitalist, in exchange for a wage, while the capitalist buys the labour power of the worker and uses it to produce. Whatever is produced becomes the property of the capitalist. The essential point here is that the capitalist does not pay the worker the full value of the final product; what they pay is determined by the costs of the reproduction of the labour force and the balance of coercive power between the worker and the capitalist. The pay is always lower than the value of the final product, with the capitalist in effect pocketing the difference (the surplus value).[30]

This is enabled by the concentration of private capital and ownership of the means of production in the hands of the few, who become very powerful, while the many have no response to that overwhelming power, unless they organize and demand redistribution. Redistribution or radical reform of the ownership of the means of production however is very difficult, and even 'democratic' organization is an insufficient check on the enormous power of private capital. The 'oligarchy of private capital' can (and does) exercise its power to influence political parties, separating the electorate from its representatives, who are supposed to be making the law. The law thus produced not only co-constitutes[31] the system, but also perpetuates it. On top of that, the capitalists are in control of the main sources of information, from the press to education, making it difficult for other individuals to 'make intelligent use' of their political rights.[32]

For Einstein, '[t]he situation prevailing in an economy based on the private ownership of capital is thus characterised by two main principles': first, the private ownership of the means of production (which is possible because of, and sanctioned by, the law); and second, the freedom of (labour) contract (which again is only possible because of, and sanctioned by, the law).[33] As such, the law plays a crucial role in both establishing and perpetuating the prevailing mode of production, that is, the capitalist economic system.

A Marxist theory of law is difficult to pin down, especially since Marx did not directly deal with the issue of law. However, there have been attempts to set out a Marxist theory of law by other thinkers. As mentioned in the introduction, Pashukanis was one of the first to try and do so, and his 'commodity-exchange' theory of the legal form has been influential both at the time of its elaboration in the interwar period, but also in the last decades.[34] According to this theory, the exploitative relationship between capitalist and worker (inherent in an economy based on the commodity) is legally based on the presentation of these two entities as abstract, equal legal subjects with capacity for self-determination.[35] This quality of equal subjects 'specifies' the conditions for exploitation to occur, which takes a particular legal form, the form of 'free contract'.[36] The legal form both structures and perpetuates the exploitative relationship between the two.

This Marxist commodity-exchange theory of the legal form can be juxtaposed to that of Kelsen and his pure theory of law: law is completely removed from the ambit of politics, economics, or morals, and is presented as a self-contained system that can be studied in complete isolation from these other fields of inquiry.

There appears to be a fundamental enmity between Pashukanis and Kelsen, who can be taken to reflect two camps, one representing a Marxist theory of law, and the other representing a mainstream formalist theory of law (see d'Aspremont, this volume). They can thus further be taken to reflect the basic enmity between socialism and capitalism. Both criticize one another and both position one another as the 'arch enemy',[37] occasionally in slightly cartoonish terms.

The reality is that Pashukanis and Kelsen, despite the above, do share a fundamental characteristic—beyond the aspiration of 'purifying' law from ideology.[38] The shared characteristic is that neither theory tells us much about the content of the law. Kelsen, for example, while trying to establish a 'pure theory' of law which divorces law from any social or political influences, fully accepts that beyond the self-contained system that he constructs, politics and society do play a role: not in giving validity to the rules of the system, but definitely in creating and interpreting the rules of the system, acts which he further accepts are political in nature.[39] In that sense, if 'formalist legal thought … call[s] on judges to deduce outcomes from norms "mechanically"',[40] Kelsen is anything *but* a formalist. On the other side, the Kelsenian construction of the pyramidal flow of validity is in no way incompatible with Pashukanis's arguments regarding the structure of legal relations.[41] The two are in effect complementing each other:[42] Pashukanis seeks to read the law as internal to the relation of capitalist production (and thus to find the external source of its *effectiveness*), while Kelsen looks for the internal source of *validity* of the law. The two archenemies are basically just strawpersons for one another: they are answering different questions, focusing on different aspects.

We should in any event heed the warning of Albert Einstein, who cautioned against the overestimation of science and the scientific method in dealing with questions of *human* problems.[43] There is a role for that in law, but it does not exhaust the field. And I would venture a guess that neither Pashukanis nor Kelsen would disagree with that assessment.

3. The Structure of the Legal Relation: Between the Legal and the Real

The impact of Marxist thought can be traced through all aspects of the legal relation: the subject of the legal relation, that is the abstract and formally equal legal subject (Section 3.1); the object of the legal relation, posited here as primarily the sanctioning of property or possession (Section 3.2); and the operation of the legal relation, which requires coercion (Section 3.3). The overarching insight here is the juxtaposition of formal equality in legal reality with the (f)actual inequality in 'real' reality,[44] which pervades the structure of the legal relation.

3.1 The legal subject

Any standard curriculum of a general international law course will include among its first topics that of 'subjecthood' or 'international legal personality'.[45] The idea is to introduce to students the peculiar, fictional entity that is the State, to explain its constitutive elements, and to discuss other potential international legal persons, all the while underlining how these are not States and thus not like States (accordingly, they only have limited international legal personality, even if a 'large measure'[46] of it on occasion). The orthodox understanding of the State as the 'primary' subject of international law, the paradigmatic legal person, rests on the idea of 'sovereignty' (*la plenitude de pouvoir* (see Kalmo, this volume)), which then necessarily produces sovereign equality (a sovereign has no power over another sovereign, thus sovereigns are equals).

This principle of sovereign equality has significant consequences for the international legal order. It sets up the process of production of rules of international law, and it serves as the basis for the elaboration of further principles of substantive international law, such as these of State jurisdiction, sovereign immunity, territorial integrity, non-intervention, and so forth.

The important point here is the establishment of formal equality of legal subjects, the States, against the background of their clear factual inequality.[47] It is the agreement between the States as equal legal subjects that produces international law, it is their consent that subjects them to legal rules, whether that consent is more (treaty) or less (custom, or general principles) explicit.[48] Limiting sovereignty by 'freely' acceding to international obligations is but a function (an 'attribute', as per the Permanent Court of International Justice) of sovereignty.[49] But, 'no one said that freedom's free':[50] factual inequality clearly affects the process of rule-making, with States having different negotiating power, even if they have formally equal status.

International lawyers, like all lawyers, tend to anthropomorphize the State.[51] Marxist insight explains that the legal subject is always a 'reification':[52] the legal form cannot comprehend and deal with actors in their full historical complexity and individuality; it has to flatten them out and then to address itself to, and deal with, these flattened avatars instead of the actual actors, whether people or States. For international lawyers specifically, this tendency of anthropomorphization and reification stems from international law's approach to the State as a unitary actor.[53] But structural Marxism helps to nuance that image of the unitary State, and its exercise of power.[54] It explains that the State and its institutions are not to be understood monolithically as directly controlled by the capitalist in pursuit of short-term interest. Rather, the State functions to protect the long-term interests of capital, thus allowing the occasional blow to the short-term interests of the capitalist class, but stabilizing the system and protecting it from threatening uprisings in the long term.[55] This is replicated to some extent at the international level, not only through the emergence of elements of a global nascent State (especially in areas of economic and financial institutions),[56] but also in terms of how States operate individually at the global level.

With this in mind, let me return to the other important insight from Marxism regarding the subject of the legal relation made in this section: the set-up of equal legal subjects that are factually unequal has consequences both for the object of the legal relation, and for the operation of the legal relation. It is to these two issues to which the following sections now turn, respectively.

3.2 'What is law, if not possession?'

And by 'possession,'[57] let us just agree that we mean property relations and interests in the broadest sense—and by that also sovereignty. Sovereignty, like property, ceases to be 'factual', that is precarious and unstable, capable at being contested at any moment, and needing to be defended, 'weapon in hand'.[58] It becomes 'an absolute, fixed right ... protected the world over' by law.[59] 'To make a thief, make an owner; to create crime, create laws.'[60] Force, once used to determine what is mine to the exclusion of everyone else, has been replaced by 'faithful compliance with legally established rules'.[61] A relation of force has thus been superseded by the legal relation (another relation of force, but under cover). The object of the legal relation, in international law as much as in domestic law, is to sanction possession, property in whatever form, and ultimately power. When it comes to States, this obviously translates quite easily to territory, with a whole set of rules determining title to territory, delimitation of land and maritime boundaries, the principle of *uti possidetis* for the emergence of newly independent States, and so forth. And these rules are complemented by the principle of territorial integrity, which aims to consolidate and stabilize the status quo.

But the object of the legal relation goes beyond possession in that rather obvious sense. It extends to access, including exclusive access, to territory and the natural resources or other resources (including labour power) there available. The law of the sea in large part regulates exclusive rights over natural resources for coastal States in specific maritime zones beyond the territorial sea (which forms part of the State's territory in the strict sense): continental shelf and exclusive economic zone. But it also provides for the 'freedom(s)' of the high seas, freedoms that equally belong to all States, formally, but can actually only be exercised by some. It is easy to say, for example, that (taking the old territorial sea limit of 3 nautical miles (nm)) everyone is 'free' to fish beyond the 3nm limit off the coast of another State, but it is also easy to see how this really only makes sense for a developed, economically and technologically powerful State that can and has invested in long-distance fishing fleets, while it makes little sense for a distant developing State which is only capable of engaging in coastal fishing. This 'freedom' is more meaningful to some than to others, even if it formally belongs equally to all.

This unequal distribution is very difficult to correct, even with significant organization on the part of the less powerful States. During the Third United Nations Conference on the Law of the Sea, the 'coastal', mainly developing States, organized enough to be able to extract some concessions from the developed 'maritime powers'—with the establishment of the exclusive economic zone, for example. But when it came to agreeing on a regime for the exploration and exploitation of the seabed beyond national jurisdiction, things were not as easy. The developing States resisted the establishment of a regime of 'freedom' similar to that applicable to the high seas (the water column above, in rough terms). They pressed for the collective exploration and exploitation of the international seabed, through an international organization, with profit sharing, technology transfers, the works; and all under the new regime of 'common heritage of [human] kind'.[62] This was anathema to the developed States[63]—this was communism!

The developing States had the numbers to push their position through—only for the resulting convention (the 1982 United Nations Convention on the Law of the Sea (UNCLOS)) not to attract *any* ratification by a developed/Western State bar Iceland until the eve of its entry into force. The choice was both clear and stark: either have the Convention enter into force without any participation from the 'first' world, defeating its purpose to serve as a 'constitution of the oceans' and threatening its effectiveness due to the lack of funding for the creation of the various institutions it envisaged (including for the exploration and exploitation of the international seabed); or, simply, make significant concessions to the 'first' world, essentially dismantling the revolutionary regime for the seabed, even if maintaining the moniker of 'common heritage of [human]kind'. You can imagine who won. But if you cannot, have a look at the euphemistically named 'Agreement relating to the *Implementation* of Part IX of the United Nations Convention on the Law of the Sea', adopted on 28 July 1994.[64] The UN Convention on the Law of the Sea entered into force on 16 November of that same year.

Similar examples of attempts to organize and 'correct' rules favouring unequal distribution can be found in other areas of international law, including for example the attempts of newly independent States (emerging from colonial domination, that is) to switch from a rule of 'prompt, adequate, and effective' compensation for expropriation (nationalization) to one of 'fair' compensation, taking into account the effects of colonialism on the natural resources of these States. The outcome of that struggle is portrayed in the so-called 'Libyan arbitrations'.[65]

A struggle over resources is not limited to natural resources; it also includes 'human resources' (a terrifying term), including labour power. When it comes specifically to labour power, one can refer to international migration law, the legal regime that determines which categories of people will be allowed to move freely and which have to either 'stay back' or use illegal migration channels. But the struggle over resources in the broadest sense is apparent in international trade law and in international investment law. These are two areas of international law that mainly involve inward-looking norms, and that are merely a continuation of colonial relationships of domination and subjugation by another means.[66]

Inward-looking norms are norms that require some action at the domestic level in order to be implemented, often through regulatory means. Non-discrimination obligations, such as national treatment and most-favoured-nation treatment, obligations to guarantee fair and equitable treatment or full protection and security, obligations to regulate subsidies or allow access to markets for specific products or investments, are paradigmatic examples of inward-looking obligations (as are human rights obligations, on which see further below). The proliferation of inward-looking norms in international law is a consequence of globalization, understood as the increasing interaction and interdependence of States, which is driven by capital and aims at the globalization of capital. Inward-looking norms are negotiated and adopted between States, but also by special interests that either drive negotiations in specific areas, or at least lobby States hard to affect the negotiating direction.

It is possible, of course, to penetrate the veil of 'the unitary nature' of the State to allow some access to the actual 'struggle within'[67] the State between the 'living forces of production'.[68] The unique tripartite structure of the International Labour Organisation (ILO) is however the only extant example where this has happened formally, with government representation being complemented with independent representation of both employers' and workers' organizations.[69] Even there, the 'new social values' proclaimed in the ILO mandate[70] in the aftermath of the October Revolution, and renewed in the aftermath of the Second World War, have for the most part remained an empty letter:[71] equal distribution of wealth and welfare, extension of social security and guarantee of basic income and comprehensive medical care, adequate nutrition, housing, and recreation, equality of educational and vocational opportunity seem as distant today as at almost any time in the last hundred years.[72] Globalization has been one of capitalist interests and of the legal rules supporting *them*: inward-looking norms either allowing or demanding deregulation,[73] rather than a globalization of 'new social values'. Such 'new social values' might have seemed merely humanitarian (as well as a concession to contain socialism) in the 1920s, or obvious basic rules of coexistence in the 1970s, but have been acquiring an increasingly 'socialist' (or even far-left) whiff in the 2020s, 'socialist' here understood as a derogatory term that is enough to render people 'unelectable' across the world, and a characterization which many politicians will strive to avoid for precisely that reason.

In a more remote manner, almost all areas of (international) legal regulation can be connected to possession and property. This is true even for human rights, the paradigmatic set of inward-looking norms,[74] and one which looks quite innocent, if not outright 'progressive' at first glance. When we talk about the international protection of human rights, however, we are mainly focusing on 'first generation' civil and political rights. These private rights are the only ones considered 'enforceable'. Social, economic, and cultural rights, collective rights to housing, health, food and clean water, work, and what have you, while 'consecrated' in international law,[75] are only loose obligations of best efforts not corresponding to actually enforceable rights.[76] One explanation for this is that 'first generation' private rights impose negative obligations on the State, obligations of abstention which cost nothing—as opposed to socio-economic rights, which require positive action on the part of the State and are thus expensive.[77] This is of course not true: the right to a fair trial very much corresponds to positive obligations, requiring the State to set up and run a justice system to some considerable expense; not to mention the positive aspects of the right to life or of freedom from torture which also require considerable oversight machinery to be in place.[78] All this stuff costs money—it is just a matter of priorities that money is spent primarily on this rather than for the attainment of socio-economic rights. And these priorities are easily explainable on the basis that civil and political rights are quintessentially individual(ist),[79] as opposed to socio-economic rights, which might cultivate solidarity and collectivism and could thus strengthen a counter-hegemonic drive. It is obvious which rights pose no real threat to the system.[80]

Equally importantly, the very basis of civil and political rights is the protection of property,[81] even if the protection of property itself is not included in the International Covenant on Civil and Political Rights (ICCPR).[82] That might as well be, seeing as how every other civil and political right is effectively established to allow one (who has property) to peacefully enjoy it. In order to enjoy your property, you must be alive (right to life), you must remain free (right to liberty and security of the person), you must be assured that nobody is going to take it arbitrarily (right to a fair trial), and so forth. If you think that I am exaggerating (well, perhaps only a bit, but I am trying to make a point here), then please have a look at how the international protection of human rights evolved, in reality, out of the protection of the rights of aliens in international law. The 'basic standards of treatment' (no arbitrary deprivation of life, no arbitrary deprivation of liberty, no denial of justice) were initially consecrated in international law in order to ensure that aliens (from Western, 'civilized' States) would be allowed to fully enjoy their property in the savage lands of the uncivilized States where they would venture in search of fame and fortune.[83]

Surely, you will counter, human rights are a good thing. After all, they include freedom of assembly and freedom of expression and so many other things. Sure they are, in one view. In another, they are nothing but elementary concessions that in the final analysis serve to pacify and thus to further stabilize the system by serving as absorbers of discontent.[84] They are but concessions to avoid rage boiling over into violent uprising.[85]

3.3 What is law, if not coercion?

Taking Kelsen as a starting point, the differentiating factor between law and other systems of rules that regulate the behaviour of any given community is the coercive character of the sanction that forms part of the legal norm.[86] A norm is a command backed by a sanction; a legal norm is a command backed by a *coercive* sanction, and thus it produces a legal relation that is essentially a coercive relation. In domestic legal orders, the application of the coercive sanction has been centralized (or contracted out, to be more provocative) to the State, in particular to its executive branch. In the decentralized international legal order, however, no such contracting out has taken place in favour of some universal, supranational organ. States are left to their own devices to apply coercion in order to enforce legal prescriptions, mainly through the adoption of countermeasures. At an abstract level, a countermeasure is simply a breach of an international obligation by the injured State in response to a previous breach of an international obligation by the responsible State, which refuses to cease the breach and comply with secondary obligations of reparation, and so on.[87]

These countermeasures, these breaches-in-response-to-breaches, tend to be, for the most part, economic in nature, or at least to have economic aspects. And yet there is a long-standing debate in international law, which continues to this day, regarding the prohibition of economic coercion. This debate stems from the customary norm of non-intervention,[88] a norm that prohibits States from 'coercively' intervening into the 'area of freedom', the domestic affairs of other States. The prohibition of intervention consists of, so the orthodox view, two elements: an intervention (a) which is coercive in nature (b) into the area of freedom (or the 'domaine réservé') of another State.[89]

There are numerous international instruments, such as Declarations and other Resolutions of the UN General Assembly, that portray 'economic' coercion as unlawful (and thus as a potential element of prohibited intervention).[90] And yet, in none of these instruments, or in the surrounding debates and practice of States, can this concept of economic coercion (as an element of unlawful intervention) be defined with any certainty.[91] The concept of unlawful economic coercion is proclaimed, but it simply resists definition. The only consensus that can be achieved is that forcible coercion, that is, coercion involving the threat or use of armed force, is definitely unlawful, in view of the prohibition of the threat or use of force in customary law and in Article 2(4) of the UN Charter.[92] But that tells us nothing about 'economic' coercion.

This should not be a surprise. First, as explained above, economic coercion is not some kind of aberration: it is rather a fundamental process for the decentralized enforcement of international law. But it is also, second, a fundamental feature of the prevailing capitalist system and its mode of production. The latter relies on (sometimes not-so-) subtle economic coercion, all the while stressing the equality and freedom (of choice) of economic actors-turned-legal subjects. Both equality and freedom, however, are only formal, not actual. While 'legal' reality treats subjects as free and equal, 'real' reality reveals them to be both unfree and unequal.[93] Of course, a worker is 'free' to sell or not sell their labour power in the market—they are indeed free to choose to die of hunger instead,[94] or to choose to be unable to pay their bills.[95] And a capitalist is 'free' to contract or not contract with that worker—and choose instead some other worker from the extant 'unemployed reserve army of workers', the obligatorily unemployed on which the capitalist system depends.[96] Similarly, a State is legally 'free' to trade or not trade with any other state, and thus its refusal to trade with or to open its market to another state is not in any way prohibited economic coercion.

Factually, however, it is clear that the labourer is coerced—systematically, economically—to sell their labour power to those who own the means of production, just like the economically weaker State is coerced to adopt such conduct as is acceptable to the economically powerful State(s), lest it be devastated. So much for its legal 'freedom' to choose any economic, political, and social system that it wishes.[97]

There is no way out of this 'conundrum'. In fact, this is not a conundrum at all: it is a feature, not a bug![98] Trying to create rules that would prohibit this kind of coercion would amount to questioning the prevailing method of production at its core. It would be an outright revolutionary challenge to the system. The best that can be achieved *within* the system is a rear-guard action. One such has already been fought, and to some extent won, in the sense that recourse to countermeasures, that is, formally lawful economic coercion, has been subjected to conditions and limits.[99] But a whole set of means of economic pressure, even coercion, is still unregulated and available for use: this is retorsion, formally lawful but unfriendly actions, which can be resorted to for any reason, or even for no reason at all.

An example of retorsion as a means for exercising lawful (economic) pressure should suffice to complete the picture. Imagine a State that is economically weak, and that relies heavily on another State (or group of States) for 'voluntary' aid, as well as for 'voluntary' trade relations (ie not trade relations established on the basis of assumed international obligations). That first State, after an election and a change of government, decides to reform its economic system, nationalizing certain industries and services, raising taxes, or whatever. Or simply votes the 'socialists' into power. The second State (or group of States), the one providing 'voluntary' aid and maintaining 'voluntary' trade relations, does not like the socialists. It thus threatens to withdraw (or withdraws) voluntary aid and threatens to cease (or ceases) trade activity. Both these acts are unfriendly, but they are perfectly lawful. They thus require no justification at all. They are retorsion with a clear view to pressuring the first State to think again, appreciate the value of normality, and avoid reformist escapades in the future.[100]

4. The Content of the Legal Relation: The Role of Interpretation

Beyond the structure of the legal relation, there is also the question of its content, or the content of rules. Determination of the content of rules, both at inception, but also during their operation, is itself the outcome of a struggle. This is because legal rules are expressed in words, and words are inherently indeterminate (or underdeterminate) at least to some degree.[101] This applies to domestic law as much as it applies to international law, and is even more prevalent in international law to the extent that part of it consists of customary rules, where even the language (let alone the content) of the rule is not fixed.

Koskenniemi argues that there is something in the structure of the international legal argument itself that allows both sides to a dispute to make plausible claim as to the content of particular rules.[102] Logical claims based on fundamental legitimating concepts of international law, whether ascending (from 'apology' = sovereignty) or descending (from 'utopia' = global order), produce competing plausible interpretations.[103] That much anyone should be ready to concede, and again this is no way unique to international law.[104] Such ascending and descending arguments producing plausible competing interpretations of legal rules are a characteristic of every legal system, of every legal relation even.[105] The important point is who decides between these plausible interpretations, which formally equal legal subjects (in the international legal order, States) have an equal right to make. Even Kelsen concedes that it is power that decides, though power as sanctioned by the legal system.[106] And in that he agrees, in my view, with Pashukanis, in that the determination of the content of the laws is, in the final analysis, a political, coercive determination.[107]

Kelsen argues that between plausible interpretations, the decision is political.[108] Every legal rule (its language, context, object, and purpose, etc) can support a whole range of plausible interpretations.[109] Some may seem more plausible than others—but that is in the eye of the beholder, and it is also (over-) determined by a range of political, ethical, and other conscious or unconscious positions and biases, some of them contradictory.[110] When two formally equal legal subjects, two individuals in one system, two States in another, adopt competing plausible interpretations, then there is no way to choose between them that is imposed by law.

This is quite evident in international law if one looks at, for example, the general 'rule' of interpretation in Article 31 of the Vienna Convention on the Law of Treaties (VCLT). Article 31(1) directs the interpreter to interpret a treaty rule in good faith, in accordance with the ordinary meaning to be given to its terms, in context, and in line with the treaty's object and purpose. Notably, however, it does not guide the interpreter as to how much weight to give to any of these elements (which reflect in reality all standard methods of interpretation in all law: textual, contextual, teleological).[111] The elements are rather to be thrown into a 'crucible',[112] without reference as to how much of each to throw in, or in what order. Whatever comes out is the 'proper' interpretation, though it is quite clear that a number of plausible interpretations may come out, depending on who is doing the interpreting (or the throwing into the crucible). The European Court of Human Rights (ECtHR), for example, is notorious for throwing into the crucible quite a lot of object and purpose,[113] while the World Trade Organization Appellate Body is equally notorious for putting heavy reliance on dictionary definitions.[114]

The 'rule' thus offers no real guidance as to how to select between competing plausible interpretations.[115] At best, what it does is to help draw the circle of plausible interpretations, rejecting some only at the very margins. Everything within the circle though is game, and it is almost unimaginable that there will be only a single *lege artis* plausible interpretation of any given rule. The meaning of a rule is not immanent, there to be discovered by exercise of reason and reflection and interpretation,[116] as Hegel might suggest. Rather, the meaning of a rule is constructed in response to challenges presented in daily life, much like Marx would suggest,[117] inverting Hegel as he does.[118]

So, the crucial question becomes who gets to interpret the rule, who gets to construct its meaning, who gets to determine its content with final authority in each specific case. And it is the law itself, the legal system, that allocates such final authority.[119] In the domestic legal order, for example, final interpretative authority is assigned to domestic courts in the vast majority of cases. These courts will make what is essentially a political[120] decision as to which one among the competing plausible interpretations will be the authoritative one, the one that resolves the specific case. In that, the court will be making the law for the specific case.[121]

In the international legal order, the principle of consensual jurisdiction means that courts will only occasionally be delegated the power by States to make the political determination as to which of the competing plausible interpretations is the authoritative one in each specific case. For the most part, States retain the power to decide for themselves as to the content of each rule: the legal system assigns the power of authoritative interpretation in each specific case to the peculiar 'composite organ'[122] constituted by the two or more States involved in that specific case. In more general terms, it assigns that power to the 'peculiar organ' constituted by all the States that established and are bound by the rule. This power of course requires that the 'peculiar organ' reaches agreement in order to be exercised.

If no agreement is reached between the States constituting the 'peculiar organ' that exercises the political power to finally determine the content of a rule (and we all know how agreement can be reached: horse trading, subtle threats, inducement, and the like), then each State may determine for itself, and at its own risk, the content of the rule and thus its own and any other State's legal position.[123] All such determinations are formally equal: no selection can be made among them until the States either agree ('peculiar organ') or at least agree to delegate the political power to a third party, such as a court or tribunal, as described in the previous paragraph. The determinations remain equal until we reach that final instance. But, to paraphrase Althusser, 'the lonely hour of the "last instance" [may] never come[]'.[124]

We are left then with two or more formally equal, competing, plausible interpretations. And this is where Marx comes in: 'between equal rights, power decides'.[125] What this means, in the particular circumstances, is that each State is entitled to maintain its position in perpetuity unless and until some agreement is reached, as discussed above. This is, as mentioned, 'at its own risk' (of later being found to have engaged its international responsibility),[126] but of course the risk is legal, not actual. When it comes to actual risk, it is obvious that it is much easier for powerful States to maintain a position for far longer and with much more persistence than less powerful States, which can also be subject to all sorts of lawful pressure (described in Section 3.3) to great effect.

5. The Justification of the Legal Relation: The Function of Ideology

The discussion of the structure of the legal relation in Section 3 has shown that the law not only enables, but in fact structures exploitation behind a veneer of legal equality. The political nature of the determination of the content of the legal relation, explored in Section 4, supports this structuring of exploitation provided for by the legal relation in its actual operation. Law also has, however, an ideological function: it justifies and normalizes the exploitation that is structured, enabled, and perpetuated by the legal relation.

Exploitation, in the domestic legal order, is exploitation of one class (the working class) by another (the capitalist class) and one of the roles of the law (and its interpretation) is to 'mask' that exploitation behind the surface of legal relations of exchange.[127] As an apparently 'neutral' system, operating on the basis of abstract rationality,[128] the legal system obfuscates the social relations that 'stand behind' the legal form of those relations.[129] It thus makes factual inequality and exploitation appear natural, inescapable.[130] If the role of law is to both structure and mask exploitation, the function of ideology is to provide justification for, and thus legitimation of, that exploitation. Even when the exploitation at the basis of the capitalist system of production is laid bare for all to see, people will either simply be in denial, not accepting that this is the case; or, if they accept it, they will be made to believe that this is somehow still the best way for everyone to be better off; or, even if they do not believe that, they will (be made to) feel that 'there is no alternative' (TINA), that this is the natural order of things.[131] Political struggle is thus only possible within the bounds prescribed by the dominant ideology, within the 'common sense';[132] people going beyond are simply dismissed as 'loony left'.

Challenging such perceptions, such ideological positions, on the basis of 'justice' presents its own distinct problems. First, the term 'justice' is a 'weasel word' (a word without content, meaning, but with its 'shell' intact),[133] or what George Orwell called a 'meaningless term'.[134] Terms like 'justice', 'democracy' (see Poghosyan, this volume), 'rule of law', and others, are open to private definitions depending on the speaker, and in general do not share a definition acceptable to all or to most. They do, however, evoke a particular feeling and thus agreement with the underlying argument—who does not want 'justice' or 'democracy'? The only thing that we agree on, generally, is that these terms signify something desirable, even if we cannot reach an agreed definition of the term.[135] Because of this, such terms with variable meanings can be used, consciously or unconsciously, to obfuscate, allowing interlocutors to superficially agree, while each of them understands something more or less different to the others.

Second, and because of that feature of variability of meaning, it is open to the dominant class to fill these vessels with meaning,[136] and thus to argue that the current system of distribution is 'just': they are the wealth creators, the job creators, the ones who assume the risk and must also be able to claim (more of) the benefit. And on the basis of the capitalist mode of production, they are of course 'right'—this is in fact the only 'just' distribution.[137] Anything different would require revolutionary change.

The exploitation, and the class 'struggle within' the State,[138] is non-cognizable to, and invisible due to, international law—for which the unitary State is the primary unit of analysis; the primary 'subject'. But it is to some extent replicated at the international level, which results in a 'double masking': not only is the 'struggle within' masked once over due to the now familiar structure of the legal relation as between abstract, formally equal individuals; it is masked twice over with the structure of the international legal relation as between abstract, formally equal States.

During the Cold War one could argue for a 'tripartite' division of States to those belonging to the 'first', the 'second', and the 'third' world—but in reality, the division was between the more powerful but less numerous States on the one hand, and the less powerful but more numerous States on the other. The same is true with the potential divisions both before and after the Cold War, the main division before the Cold War being between 'civilized' and 'semi-civilized' States; and the main division after being between developed and developing States. In both cases there were still further categories in play (uncivilized States, before; least developed States, after). But the point regarding more powerful/less numerous—less powerful/more numerous (and exploited) stands, I think, even if it is somewhat simplistic.

Where does this leave the Marxist lawyer? What emancipatory potential could there be in international law, given the structure and content of the international legal relation (or 'form') and the sugar-coat of ideology designed to justify the exploitation hiding behind the legal relation even when the former is successfully exposed? There seems to be some agreement that, given capitalism, little change can be attained through (or on) international law. The disagreement seems to be over what an international lawyer who 'has seen the Marxist light' ought to do in such circumstances.

At one end of the spectrum, let us call it the revolutionary end, one would argue that one ought then to stop being an international lawyer and rather work for the destruction of capitalism, presumably by agitating and/or writing stunning science fiction novels.[139] At the other end of the spectrum, let us call it the reformist end, one may still somehow believe in the emancipatory potential of the law.[140] Somewhere between these two ends of the spectrum, probably close to the middle, there is one position which seems to make the most sense (to me). This is the position of the pessimistic opportunist. Along the Gramscian lines of 'pessimism of the intellect, optimism of the will',[141] this position advocates for fighting to bring about whatever progressive change is within reach, all the while being painfully aware that the system will simply endure until it is (if it is ever) overthrown. The position of the pessimistic opportunist concedes that the fight for progressive change is only a set of rear-guard actions; rear-guard actions that are fought in an attempt to salvage whatever of the cause of freedom and emancipation is salvageable still, and—in particularly joyous circumstances—to even advance said cause incrementally.

6. Conclusion

The structure of the legal relation embodies coercion through the legal fiction of abstract, equal subjects freely entering into obligations towards one another, when the reality is that of factual inequality, exploitation, and domination. This coercion plays out not only in the establishment of the legal relation, but also in the determination of its content, particularly through the political, coercive act of selecting between formally equal but competing plausible interpretations. Ideology then, including propaganda, always seen as a materially grounded force, serves to justify that entrenchment of coercive relations of domination into law. Law is there to structure, justify, and conserve the 'values' of a ruling class projected upon an imagined 'homogenous' society.[142] And this applies as much to domestic, as it does to international law—where the 'values' of global capital are projected upon an imagined homogenous 'international community'.[143]

What is to be done? Can the master's tools (international law) be used to dismantle the master's house (global capitalism)? Clearly not; but the tools can still be used to alleviate some suffering by defending against unchecked further expansion of the master's house, as much as, in appropriate circumstances, making corrective interventions in the existing structure—or even causing some damage. These are all rear-guard actions: defensive actions carried out by people retreating in the face of expanding global capital.

But within the existing system, they are the best (or: only) option that is available. Nothing stops one from using the law to fight rear-guard actions, while engaging other means in the hope of changing the system as a whole.[144]

Acknowledgements

I thank Anne van Aaken, Miles Jackson, Lauri Mälksoo, Eleni Methymaki, and Christian Tams for helpful comments. Special thanks to Akbar Rasulov and Maria Tzanakopoulou for their deep engagement with the text. All errors, omissions, offensive generalizations, unjust denunciations, and multifarious misconceptions remain my responsibility.

Notes

1. Audre Lorde, 'The Master's Tools Will Never Dismantle the Master's House' in Audre Lorde, *Sister Outsider* ([1984] Penguin 2019) 103.
2. ibid. cf Karl Marx, 'Critique of the Gotha Programme' in Karl Marx, *Later Political Writings* (Terrell Carver ed, CUP 1996) 214–215: 'In a higher phase of communist society ... only then can the limited [narrow, in other translations] horizon of bourgeois right [law, in other translations] be wholly transcended, and society can inscribe on its banner: from each according to [their] abilities, to each according to [their] needs'.
3. There is no consensus that these terms mean the same or different things. For example, some authors use them apparently interchangeably, but Martti Koskenniemi, 'What Should International Lawyers Learn from Karl Marx?', 17 Leiden Journal of International Law 2004, 229, uses exclusively the term 'Marxian', while others use exclusively the term 'Marxist'.
4. Marx, *Later Political Writings* (n 2) 222; Friedrich Engels, *Socialism: Utopian and Scientific* ([1880] Resistance Books 1999) 92; explicitly Evgeny B Pashukanis, *Law and Marxism: A General Theory* ([1924] Chris Arthur ed, Barbara Einhorn trans, Ink Links 1978) 61.
5. Support for this position is usually drawn from Karl Marx, 'Preface to *A Contribution to the Critique of Political Economy*' in Marx, *Later Political Writings* (n 2) 159–160: '[t]he totality of [the] relations of production forms the economic structure of society, the real basis from which rises a *legal* and political superstructure' (emphasis added). In reality, law belongs as much to the base (structuring and enabling the economic base) as to the superstructure (concealing and perpetuating it). In the very same 'Preface', Marx states that 'property relations' are but the 'legal expression' of 'already existing relations of production', thus highlighting how legal relations co-constitute or structure the economic base: ibid, 160. Marx himself later nuanced the determinism of the 'Preface', see Etienne Balibar, *The Philosophy of Marx* ([1993] new ed, Chris Turner and Gregory Elliot trans, Verso 2017) 108–112. See also Pashukanis (n 4) 90–91. Even Kelsen agrees with this position: he notes the reflexivity of the relationship of law to both base and superstructure in Hans Kelsen, *The Communist Theory of Law* (Stevens & Sons 1955) 8–9.
6. As should be clear from the previous footnote, I do not adopt such a purely instrumentalist approach, though of course I fully accept the class-instrumentalist aspect of law (among its other aspects). So does Kelsen, *The Communist Theory of Law* (n 5) 73: 'No serious bourgeois writer who is not a follower of natural-law doctrine excludes from [their] definition of the law a social order which is in the interest of a dominant class'.

7. Other hits include 'the opium of the people' and 'proletarians of the world, unite'. Hits are hits for a reason.
8. Karl Marx, 'Eleven Theses on Feuerbach', available at <http://www.Marxists.org.> accessed 18 August 2023 (original emphasis).
9. Obviously the parallel between 'world' (an entire reality) and 'law' (one very narrow, constructed aspect of it) is a bit strained. The point is that Marx, being himself a lawyer by training, would not have failed to recognize that the same problem that applies to philosophers—only interpreting the world, also applies to the legal profession. I thank Akbar Rasulov for this point.
10. cf Akbar Rasulov, 'A Marxism for International Law: A New Agenda', 29 European Journal of International Law 2018, 631, 634.
11. See, eg, David Podmore, 'Lawyers and Politics', 4 British Journal of Law and Society 1977, 155; Richard Cracknell and Richard Tunnicliffe, 'Social Background of MPs 1979–2019' (House of Commons Library 2022) <https://researchbriefings.files.parliament.uk/documents/CBP-7483/CBP-7483.pdf> accessed 18 August 2023; Devin K Joshi, 'Lawyers and Law Graduates in Parliaments as a Consequence of SMD Electoral Systems: A Comparison of Japan, South Korea, and Germany', 21 Japanese Journal of Political Science 2019, 19.
12. A 28-year-old Abraham Lincoln, a lawyer, famously stated in an 1838 speech: 'Let reverence for the laws … become the *political religion* of the nation'. Abraham Lincoln, *The Perpetuation of Our Political Institutions*, Address before the Young Men's Lyceum of Springfield, Illinois, 27 January 1838 <https://www.abrahamlincolnonline.org/lincoln/speeches/lyceum.htm> accessed 18 August 2023.
13. See Rasulov (n 10) 633–634; Robert Knox, 'Marxist Approaches to International Law' in Anne Orford and Florian Hoffmann (eds), *The Oxford Handbook of the Theory of International Law* (OUP 2016) 306.
14. See Lenin's 1902 pamphlet, available at <http://www.Marxists.org.> accessed 18 August 2023.
15. A similar thing can be said about Third World Approaches to International Law (TWAIL): see Naz K Modirzadeh, '"[L]et Us All Agree to Die a Little": TWAIL's Unfulfilled Promise', forthcoming in 65 Harvard International Law Journal 2023, esp the testimonials in the opening paragraphs and the introduction.
16. See generally China Miéville, *Between Equal Rights: A Marxist Theory of International Law* (Pluto Press 2006) 3, 17–18 and *passim*; Grietje Baars, '"Reform or Revolution"? Polanyian versus Marxian Perspectives on the Regulation of the Economic', 62 Northern Ireland Legal Quarterly 2011, 415.
17. See, eg, Bill Bowring, *The Degradation of the International Legal Order? The Rehabilitation of Law and the Possibility of Politics* (Routledge 2008).
18. See generally Rasulov (n 10). For the term see Hugh Collins, *Marxism and Law* (OUP 1984) 124 ff.
19. Though see for an exception Karl Renner, *Die Rechtsinstitute des Privatrechts und ihre soziale Funktion: ein Beitrag zur Kritik des bürgerlichen Rechts* (Mohr 1929).
20. See n 4. Other important works are by Lenin, Stuchka, Reisner, Vyshinsky, Golunskii, in the volume *Soviet Legal Philosophy* (Hugh Webster Babb trans, Harvard UP 1951), which Kelsen reviews in *The Communist Theory of Law* (n 5).
21. See, eg, Evgeny A Korovin (Korowin), *Das Völkerrecht der Übergangszeit: Grundlagen der völkerrechtlichen Beziehungen der Union der Sowjetrepubliken* ([1923] J Robinson-Kaunas

trans, Rothschild 1929); Nikolai A Ushakov (Ouchakov), 'La compétence interne des États et la non-intervention dans le droit international contemporain', 141 RdC 1974, 1; Grigory I Tunkin, *Theory of International Law* ([1970] William E Butler trans, George Allen & Unwin 1974). For the position that the scholarship emanating from communist States did not contribute significantly see Collins (n 18) 2. On the work of Korovin specifically see Boris N Mamlyuk and Ugo Mattei, 'Comparative International Law', 36 Brooklyn Journal of International Law 2011, 385, 394–406.

22. Or TWAIL I: see further n 15.
23. See generally Mohammed Bedjaoui, *Towards a New International Economic Order* (UNESCO 1979); Robin CA White, 'A New International Economic Order', 24 International and Comparative Law Quarterly 1975, 542; Robert W Cox, 'Ideologies and the New International Economic Order: Reflections on Some Recent Literature', 33 International Organization 1979, 257.
24. Karl Marx and Friedrich Engels, *The Communist Manifesto* ([1848] Verso 1998) 77. See also n 7 re: hits.
25. cf Antony Bourge and John Shelley, 'Crash Course in Brain Surgery' in Budgie, *In for the Kill!* (MCA 1974).
26. See text at n 13.
27. Though nowhere does he actually mention Marx. See Albert Einstein's essay 'Why Socialism', available at https://monthlyreview.org/2009/05/01/why-socialism/ accessed 18 August 2023.
28. It is more complicated than that: on structural overdetermination see generally Nicos Poulantzas, *Political Power and Social Classes* ([1968] Timothy O'Hagan trans, Verso 1978) and Nicos Poulantzas, *State, Power, Socialism* ([1978] Patrick Camiller trans, Verso 2014); for a summary see Akbar Rasulov, '"The Nameless Rapture of the Struggle": Towards a Marxist Class-Theoretic Approach to International Law', 19 Finnish Yearbook of International Law 2008, 243, 259–264.
29. See Pashukanis (n 4) 39 (preface to second Russian edition).
30. See generally Karl Marx, *Capital* ([1867] David McLellan ed, abridg, OUP 1995) 108 ff (ch 6).
31. Or 'overdetermines'.
32. See Einstein (n 27).
33. ibid.
34. For other influential approaches see n 20.
35. See Pashukanis (n 4) 39.
36. ibid. Legal form and legal relation are two terms that I use as meaning the same thing in this text.
37. See Miéville (n 16) 34 ff; and cf Kelsen, *The Communist Theory of Law* (n 5) 89 ff; Pashukanis (n 4) 51 ff.
38. See Kelsen, *The Communist Theory of Law* (n 5) 89; and n 43.
39. See text and references at nn 109–113. See also Kelsen, *The Communist Theory of Law* (n 5) 73, where he accepts that law is 'a social order which is in the interest of the dominant class'. Per Kelsen, ibid, 75, it is the *science* of law that is 'independent of political value judgments', not the *law itself*. This means: Kelsen's limited normative construction of validity flow, not the process of formation and the determination of the content of the law.
40. See Samuel Moyn, 'Reconstructing Critical Legal Studies' 11 <https://papers.ssrn.com/sol3/papers.cfm?abstract_id=4531492> accessed 18 August 2023. Later in ibid, 32, Moyn

aptly characterizes Kelsen's account of norm generation and law application as 'framed "indeterminacy"'.

41. cf Pashukanis (n 4) 51–53. Pashukanis was himself 'accused' of attempting to construct 'a theory of pure jurisprudence' and failing, producing a theory of law 'which is basically sociological', in this case by Ilinsky; Pashukanis was at pains to dispel the accusations: ibid, 106–108.
42. In fact, Kelsen, *The Communist Theory of Law* (n 5) 193, complains precisely about the fact that the Marxian theory of law seeks to substitute its sociological inquiry for the normative theory of law, *instead of 'adding to it'* (emphasis added).
43. See Einstein (n 27) (emphasis added).
44. cf Pashukanis (n 4) 147.
45. Unsurprising: 'Every legal relation is a relation between subjects. The subject is the atom of legal theory, its simplest, irreducible element': ibid, 109. Pashukanis was not up to date on his quantum physics.
46. See *Reparation for Injuries Suffered in the Service of the United Nations* (Advisory Opinion) [1949] ICJ Rep 174, 179.
47. See also Juliane Kokott and Lauri Mälksoo, 'States, Sovereign Equality' in Anne Peters (ed), *MPEPIL* (OUP 2023) MN 2; and further Peter H Kooijmans, *The Doctrine of Legal Equality of States: An Inquiry About the Foundations of International Law* (AW Sythoff 1964).
48. See Article 38(1) Statute of the International Court of Justice. cf Pashukanis (n 4) 113–114 with reference to Marx's *Capital* (n 30). We could even rephrase Marx as follows, positing 'sovereignty' in the place of commodity: The guardians of sovereignty, ie the States, must enter into relations with one another as persons whose will resides in sovereignty and must behave in such a way that each does not appropriate the sovereignty of the other, and alienate its own, *except through an act to which both parties consent*. This explains the reification of sovereignty and its mystification—ie the reasons why we treat sovereignty as a thing, and one we are hardly able to define to boot.
49. *SS 'Wimbledon'* [1923] PCIJ Ser A No 1, 25; cf Pashukanis (n 4) 117: 'The quality of subjecthood is not inherent in humans as animate beings graced with a rational will. It is rather abstracted from the act of exchange, where humans put into practice the formal freedom of self-determination.'
50. Phil Rind and Wiley Arnett, 'The American Way' in Sacred Reich, *The American Way* (Metal Blade 1990).
51. Pashukanis (n 4) 145 (the State exists as an organ of class interests); Hans Kelsen, *Reine Rechtslehre* (2nd edn, Franz Deuticke 1960) 288 ff (the State exists as a closed system of norms). If the law is seen in its class-instrumentalist view, they agree. See further Natasha Wheatley, *The Life and Death of States: Central Europe and the Transformation of Modern Sovereignty* (Princeton UP 2023).
52. On reification see further Georg Lukács, *History and Class Consciousness* ([1923] Rodney Livingston trans, Bibliotech Press 2017) 65 ff.
53. See Emer de Vattel, *Le droit des gens ou Principes de la Loi Naturelle, appliqués à la conduite & aux affaires des Nations & des Souverains* (Tome I, London 1758) 285: 'la Nature a établi une parfaite égalité de Droits entre les Nations indépendantes. Aucune par conséquent ne peut naturellement prétendre de Prérogative. Tout ce que la qualité de Nation libre & souveraine donne à l'une, elle le donne aussi à l'autre'; ibid (Tome II, London 1758) 310: 'la Dignité des Nations indépendantes est essentiellement la même; … un Prince foible, mais

souverain, est aussi bien souverain & indépendant que le plus grand Monarque, *comme un Nain n'est pas moins un homme, qu'un Géant*' (emphasis added).

54. See generally Poulantzas (n 29).
55. See generally Maria Tzanakopoulou, *Reclaiming Constitutionalism: Democracy, Power and the State* (Hart Publishing 2018).
56. See generally Bhupinder S Chimni, 'International Institutions Today: An Imperial Global State in the Making', 15 European Journal of International Law 2004, 1.
57. See Herman Melville, *Moby-Dick; or, The Whale* ([1851] Penguin 2012) 460–462.
58. Pashukanis (n 4) 115.
59. ibid.
60. Ursula K LeGuin, *The Dispossessed* ([1974] Gollanz 2002) 116.
61. Einstein (n 27).
62. For a contemporary view of the negotiations see generally Lawrence Juda, 'UNCLOS III and the New International Economic Order', 7 Ocean Development & International Law 1979, 221.
63. See generally Jonathan L Charney, 'The Law of the Deep Seabed Post UNCLOS III', 63 Oregon Law Review 1984, 19.
64. See generally Edward Duncan Brown, 'The 1994 Agreement on the Implementation of Part XI of the UN Convention on the Law of the Sea: Breakthrough to Universality?', 19 Marine Policy 1995, 5 (emphasis added).
65. For an overview see Gabrielle Marceau, 'Some Evidence of a New International Economic Order in Place', 22 Revue générale de droit 1991, 397.
66. See Nicos Poulantzas, *The Crisis of the Dictatorships: Portugal, Greece, Spain* (David Fernbach trans, NLB 1976) 12–15. See further Bhupinder S Chimni, *International Law and World Order: A Critique of Contemporary Approaches* (2nd edn, CUP 2017) 506 ff.
67. James Hetfield and Lars Ulrich, 'The Struggle Within' in Metallica, *Metallica* (Elektra 1991).
68. Nicos Poulantzas, 'The State and the Transition to Socialism' in T Martin (ed), *The Poulantzas Reader: Marxism, Law and the State* (Verso 2008) 334, 338.
69. See C Wilfred Jenks, *Social Justice in the Law of Nations—The ILO Impact After Fifty Years* (OUP 1970) 16–21. The establishment of the ILO is a consequence of the October Revolution on 1917: the 'major step' of establishing an organization to deal with workers' rights was taken in Versailles in 1919 precisely to 'dampen the attraction of Bolshevism in Western Europe': John Quigley, *Soviet Legal Innovation and the Law of the Western World* (CUP 2007) 77.
70. Jenks (n 69) 14–15.
71. The Soviets criticized the ILO as another instrument of the capitalist class to mask oppression of working people through the making of minor concessions: Quigley (n 69) 78–79.
72. See, eg, Susan Marks and Andrew Clapham, *International Human Rights Lexicon* (OUP 2005) 91, 163. This is not to claim that no 'progress' has been made in some of these areas and at least in some parts of the world. However, the attainment of such goals in the manner proclaimed seems utopian in the current political climate around the globe. As per the World Inequality Database (<https://wid.world/>), eg, the top 1% brought in 24.9% of the world's income in 1920 and 19.2% in 2020. The equivalent numbers for the top 10% are 59.7% in 1920 and 52.5% in 2020.
73. Marks and Clapham (n 72) 181–185.

74. For the feedback loop between domestic and international protection of human rights, starting with the French and American Revolutions, see Antonios Tzanakopoulos, 'Judicial Dialogue in Multi-level Governance: The Impact of the *Solange* Argument' in Ole Kristian Fauchald and André Nollkaemper (eds), *The Practice of International and National Courts and the (De-)Fragmentation of International Law* (Hart Publishing 2012) 185, 210–215.
75. See the International Covenant on Economic, Social, and Cultural Rights 1966.
76. See also Chimni (n 56) 11.
77. See Karel Vasak, 'A 30-Year Struggle: The Sustained Efforts to Give Force of Law to the Universal Declaration of Human Rights', 30 The UNESCO Courier 1977, 29.
78. See generally Sandra Fredman, *Human Rights Transformed: Positive Rights and Positive Duties* (OUP 2008); Stephen Holmes and Cass R Sunstein, *The Cost of Rights: Why Liberty Depends on Taxes* (WW Norton 1999).
79. See Karl Marx, 'On the Jewish Question' in Robert Tucker (ed), *The Marx-Engels Reader* (Norton & Co 1978) 26, 42–43, esp: 'None of the supposed [human] rights, therefore, go beyond the egoistic [human], [human] as [s]he is, as a member of civil society; that is, an individual separated from the community, withdrawn into [her]self, wholly preoccupied with [her] private interest and acting in accordance with [her] private caprice'.
80. But see Margot E Salomon, 'Emancipating Human Rights: Capitalism and the Common Good', 36 Leiden Journal of International Law 2023, 857.
81. cf Marx (n 79) 42–43; Balibar (n 5) 72–75.
82. Though it is included in the Universal Declaration of Human Rights, Article 17.
83. See further Ntina Tzouvala, *Capitalism as Civilisation: A History of International Law* (CUP 2020).
84. See also Marks and Clapham (n 72) 191–192.
85. See the insight from structural Marxism in Section 2.1. But note already the insight from one of the earliest Soviet jurists, Peter I Stuchka (Stučka), 'The Revolutionary Part Played by Law and the State—A General Doctrine of Law in *Soviet Legal Philosophy* (n 20) 17, 51: 'The class exploiters can never aspire to destroy or to exterminate the class which they exploit [or risk their own demise]. From this flows the *adaptability*, the *conciliatory attitude of the class* of oppressors, and its compliance ... as regards the class of the exploited' (original emphasis).
86. Kelsen, *Reine Rechtslehre* (n 51) 34 ff.
87. See Articles on the Responsibility of States for Internationally Wrongful Acts, Part Three, Chapter II [2001] YbkILC (Vol II, Part Two).
88. *Military and Paramilitary Activities In and Against Nicaragua (Nicaragua v United States of America)* (Merits) [1986] ICJ Rep 106 [202].
89. Ibid, 108 [205].
90. See the Declaration on the Inadmissibility of Intervention, UN Doc A/RES/2131(XX) (1965); the Friendly Relations Declaration, UN Doc A/RES/2625(XXV) (1970) annex principle (c); the Charter on the Economic Rights and Duties of States, UN Doc A/RES/3281(XXIX) (1974), Article 32; the Declaration on the Inadmissibility of Intervention and Interference, UN Doc A/RES/36/103 (1981); and the serial resolutions on economic coercion adopted since 1983 (annually between 1983 and 1987, and biennially since).
91. For an overview and an assessment of the practice see Yue Cao, *The Identification of Unilateral Economic Coercion under the Principle of Non-Intervention* (MPhil Thesis, University of Oxford 2023) (on file with author).

92. See generally Antonios Tzanakopoulos, 'The Right to be Free from Economic Coercion', 4 Cambridge International Law Journal 2015, 616.
93. cf Marx, *Later Political Writings* (n 2) 214.
94. Pashukanis (n 4) 157.
95. To use the terms of Oscar Wilde, they are free to 'do uncongenial work'—in other terms they are forced 'by the peremptory, unreasonable, degrading *tyranny of want*': Oscar Wilde, 'The Soul of Man under Socialism' in Linda Dowling (ed), *The Soul of Man under Socialism & Selected Critical Prose* ([1891] Penguin 2001) 125, 129 (emphasis added).
96. See Friedrich Engels, *The Condition of the Working Class in England* ([1845] Penguin 2009) 118. See further Marx, *Capital* (n 30) 350 ff (ch 25, section 3 on 'Progressive Production of a Relative Surplus-Population or Industrial Reserve Army'). See also Einstein (n 27).
97. cf text and nn 88–89.
98. See also generally Miéville (n 16) 117 ff, 140, 151, 289.
99. See Articles on the Responsibility of States for Internationally Wrongful Acts (n 87) Articles 49–53.
100. See Tzanakopoulos, 'The Right to be Free from Economic Coercion' (n 92), eg with respect to Greece during the sovereign debt crisis (2010–2018).
101. See, among many others, Kelsen, *Reine Rechtslehre* (n 51) 348. This is also because law, beyond being 'embodied in language', 'crosses openly into morality or policy': Moyn (n 42) 23. See finally LeGuin (n 60) 29: 'nothing said in words ever came out quite even'.
102. Martti Koskenniemi, *From Apology to Utopia: The Structure of International Legal Argument* ([1989] CUP 2005) 58–69.
103. ibid.
104. Indeed, as per Karl Marx, 'The Eighteenth Brumaire of Louis Bonaparte' in *Later Political Writings* (n 2) 43: 'Consequently both sides can appeal with perfect justice to the constitution, the friends of order, who subverted all those freedoms, just as much as the democrats, who demanded them all outright. Each paragraph of the constitution contains its own antithesis in itself.'
105. See, eg, Mark V Tushnet, 'Marxism as Metaphor', 68 Cornell Law Review 1983, 281, 288–289.
106. Kelsen, *Reine Rechtslehre* (n 51) 245: 'Wenn die generelle Rechtsnorm angewendet werden soll, kann nur *eine* Meinung gelten. Welche, das muß durch die Rechtsordnung bestimmt werden'.
107. Pashukanis (n 4) 134 ff.
108. Kelsen, *Reine Rechtslehre* (n 51) 350: 'Die Frage, welche der im Rahmen des anzuwendenden Rechtes gegebenen Möglichkeiten die "richtige" ist, ist … kein rechtstheoretisches, sondern ein *rechtspolitisches* Problem' (emphasis added). By this term, 'legal policy', Kelsen means political, moral, social, and other considerations, as he clearly states ibid, 351: 'Normen der Moral, der Gerechtigkeit, soziale Werturteile'. He also states, ibid, that the selection among the plausible interpretations is an 'act of will' ('Willensakt'), which can only be a political act.
109. The words Kelsen uses are 'Rahmen', ie 'frame', instead of range, and 'möglich', ie possible, instead of plausible, that I have opted for here. But that this is precisely his point is evident: see ibid, 348–349.
110. The beholder is, after all, inculcated with the dominant ideology—see Section 5. cf generally Louis Althusser, 'Contradiction and Overdetermination' in Louis Althusser, *For Marx* (Ben Brewster trans, Verso 2005) 89 ff. cf Kelsen (n 5) 13: 'it is always some jurist

who presents or interprets the law in a certain way and thus may produce – by his presentation or interpretation—an ideology'.

111. On historical interpretation see Antonios Tzanakopoulos and Anna Ventouratou, 'Nicaragua in the International Court of Justice and the Law of Treaties' in Edgardo Sobenes Obregon and Benjamin Sampson (eds), *Nicaragua before the International Court of Justice: Impacts on International Law* (Springer 2017) 215, 235–236.
112. Draft Articles on the Law of Treaties with Commentaries [1966] YbkILC (Vol II) 219–220.
113. See, eg, *Al-Dulimi and Montana Management Inc v Switzerland* (GC), App no 5809/08 (Judgment of 21 June 2016) [145]: 'In this connection, the Court would emphasise that the *object and purpose of the Convention*, a human rights treaty protecting individuals on an objective basis, require its provisions to be interpreted and applied *in a manner which makes its requirements practical and effective*' (references omitted, emphasis added).
114. See, eg, David Pavot, 'The Use of Dictionary by the WTO Appellate Body: Beyond the Search of Ordinary Meaning', 4 Journal of International Dispute Settlement 2013, 29.
115. cf Kelsen, *Reine Rechtslehre* (n 51) 350: 'Alle bisher entwickelten Interpretationsmethoden führen stets nur zu einem möglichen, niemals zu einem einzig richtigen Resultat'.
116. cf ibid, 349, 350–351, and 353: 'Rechtswissenschaftliche Interpretation muß auf das sorgfältigste die Fiktion vermeiden, daß eine Rechtsnorm stets nur eine, die „richtige" Deutung zuläßt'.
117. 'It is not the consciousness of [humans] that specifies [determines] their being, but on the contrary their social being that specifies [determines] their consciousness': Marx, *Later Political Writings* (n 2) 160.
118. 'With [Hegel, dialectic] is standing on its head. It must be turned right side up again, if you would discover the rational kernel within the mystical shell': Karl Marx, 'Afterword to the Second German Edition [of *Capital Vol I*]' in Marx, *Capital* (n 30) 7, 11. But see further Althusser, *For Marx* (n 110) 89 ff.
119. See n 106.
120. See generally JAG Griffith, *The Politics of the Judiciary* (5th edn, Fontana Press 1997).
121. Kelsen, *Reine Rechtslehre* (n 51) 239 ff (240: 'Rechtsanwendung ist zugleich Rechtserzeugung'), 242 ff ('Der konstitutive Charakter der richtlichen Entscheidung'), 350–352.
122. See Hans Kelsen, *Allgemeine Staatslehre* (Springer 1925) 174–175.
123. *Air Service Agreement of 27 March 1946 between the United States of America and France*, Decision of 9 December 1978, *RIAA*, Vol XVII, 443 [81]; *Lac Lanoux (Espagne, France)*, sentence du 16 novembre 1957, *RIAA*, Vol XII, 310 [16]: 'il appartient à chaque État d'apprécier, raisonnablement et de bonne foi, les situations et les règles qui le mettent en cause'; but: 'en exerçant sa compétence, elle *prend le risque* de voir sa responsabilité internationale mise en cause s'il est établi qu'elle n'a pas agi dans la limite de ses droits' (emphasis added); cf Kelsen, *Reine Rechtslehre* (n 51) 352.
124. Althusser, *For Marx* (n 110) 113. The future, after all, lasts forever: Louis Althusser, *L'avenir dure longtemps* ([1992] Flammarion 2013).
125. 'Zwischen gleichen Rechten entscheidet die Gewalt': Karl Marx, *Das Kapital* (Vol I, 10th edn, Dietz, Berlin 1961) 249, with reference to the struggle between the equal rights of capitalist and worker in order to delimit the working day.
126. See n 106.
127. See Susan Marks, 'Exploitation as an International Legal Concept' in Susan Marks (ed), *International Law on the Left* (CUP 2008) 281, 286.

128. See Hilary Charlesworth, Christine Chinkin, and Shelley Wright, 'Feminist Approaches to International Law', 85 American Journal of International Law 1991, 613, 613.
129. See Roger Cotterrell, 'Review of *Pashukanis: Selected Writings on Marxism and Law*', 7 British Journal of Law and Society 1980, 317, 319.
130. See Charlesworth, Chinkin, and Wright (n 128) 613.
131. Marks (n 127) 291; cf Collins (n 18) 43.
132. 'Common sense' is not that common: it is defined by the dominant ideology.
133. See Merriam-Webster Dictionary, with reference to etymology.
134. See George Orwell, *Politics and the English Language* ([1945] Penguin 2013) 8–9.
135. Equally, per Orwell, ibid, 'fascism' has now 'no meaning except that it signifies something not desirable'.
136. After all, they control the mechanisms for the articulation and dissemination of the dominant ideology, and thus achieve ideological hegemony. See further Louis Althusser, 'Ideology and Ideological State Apparatuses (Notes Towards an Investigation)' in Louis Althusser, *Lenin and Philosophy—and Other Essays* (Ben Brewster trans, Monthly Review Press 2001) 85.
137. Marx, *Later Political Writings* (n 2) 211: 'What is a "just" distribution? Don't the bourgeoisie claim that the present distribution is "just"? And on the basis of the present mode of production, isn't it in fact the only "just" distribution?' cf Marks (n 127) 291; Collins (n 18) 43.
138. See text at nn 70–71.
139. See n 16.
140. See n 17.
141. On the expression, which is not originally Gramsci's, but also on the apparently contradictory predisposition, see generally Francesca Antonini, 'Pessimism of the Intellect, Optimism of the Will: Gramsci's Political Thought in the Last Miscellaneous Notebooks', 31 Rethinking Marxism 2019, 42.
142. See Pashukanis (n 4) 174: '"Society as a whole" does not exist, except in the fantasy of the jurists. In reality, we are faced only with classes, with contradictory, conflicting interests.'
143. Not to mention that 'community' implies a community of purpose that is lacking in society, and thus is a much stronger term. See generally Antonios Tzanakopoulos, 'The Permanent Court of International Justice and the "International Community"' in Christian J Tams and Malgosia Fitzmaurice (eds), *Legacies of the Permanent Court of International Justice* (Martinus Nijhoff 2013) 339.
144. As per Vladimir I Lenin, *'Left-Wing' Communism, An Infantile Disorder* ([1920] International Publishers 1940) 77, 'revolutionaries who are unable to combine illegal forms of struggle with *every* form of legal struggle are poor revolutionaries indeed' (original emphasis). Pashukanis noted that Lenin 'firmly appealed to use those "legal opportunities" which the enemy ... was forced to provide': Evgeny B Pashukanis, 'Lenin and Problems of Law' in Piers Beirne and Robert Sharlet (eds), *Pashukanis: Selected Writings on Marxism and Law* (Peter B Maggs trans, Academic Press 1980) 132, 138.

PART 3

SPECIFIC INSTITUTIONS OF INTERNATIONAL LAW IN EUROPE

CHAPTER 18

THE COUNCIL OF EUROPE

GANNA YUDKIVSKA

> I am convinced that international confidence, ... disarmament, and international security are inconceivable without an open society with freedom of information, freedom of conscience, freedom of speech .... Peace, progress, human rights—these three goals are insolubly linked to one another.
>
> Andrei Sakharov,
> Nobel Lecture, 11 December 1975

1. Introduction

It was in the middle of drafting this chapter when the Council of Europe, that had forty-seven member States in March 2022, lost one of its member States following unprecedented aggression of the latter against another member State.

Seven decades earlier, in 1949, ten Western States being '[c]onvinced that the pursuit of peace based upon justice and international co-operation is vital for the preservation of human society and civilisation ... decided to set up a Council of Europe ... [whose] aim ... [was] to achieve a greater unity between its members for the purpose of safeguarding and realising the ideals and principles which are their common heritage and facilitating their economic and social progress'.[1]

In 1949, this was a great achievement for European diplomacy—just several years earlier the belligerent States were destroying each other in the heat of World War II; and now they were ready to sit together and discuss 'questions of common concern', and to agree and act together 'in economic, social, cultural, scientific, legal and administrative matters and in the maintenance and further realisation of human rights and fundamental freedoms'.[2]

It was a huge step from mutual bombing to joint discussions and common actions; decades later, Europe would observe a step in the opposite direction.

1.1 The pacifying function of international law in Europe—history and the Statute of the Council of Europe

'If Europe were once united in the sharing of its common inheritance—there would be no limit to the happiness, prosperity and glory which its 300 million or 400 million people would enjoy', so began Sir Winston Churchill's famous speech at the University of Zurich, on 19 September 1946. His call to 'build a kind of United States of Europe' and to 'Let Europe arise!' was largely implemented—the city of Strasbourg, that is symbolically situated on the border between Germany and France, became home to the newly created Council of Europe, symbolizing Churchill's dream of 'a partnership between France and Germany' as the 'first step in the re-creation of the European family'.[3]

Thus Europe, scarred by the devastation of World War II, proceeded with creation of the Council of Europe, aiming to ensure peace through justice and international cooperation.

The Council of Europe was set up on 5 May 1949 by ten Western and Northern countries—Belgium, Denmark, France, Ireland, Italy, Luxembourg, the Netherlands, Norway, Sweden, and the UK, joined by Greece[4] and Turkey in August 1949, with Iceland and Germany joining the following year.

The Statute of the organization that was established, declares that 'the aim of the Council of Europe is to achieve a greater unity between its members for the purpose of safeguarding and realising the ideals and principles which are their common heritage and facilitating their economic and social progress ... This aim shall be pursued through the organs of the Council by discussion of questions of common concern and by agreements and common action in economic, social, cultural, scientific, legal and administrative matters and in the maintenance and further realisation of human rights and fundamental freedoms.'

A formidable step from destructive conflicts to harmonious discussions and collective actions, this development transformed the European landscape. The newly created unity of the States that were 'like-minded' and had 'a common heritage of political traditions, ideals, freedom and the rule of law'[5] was given the romantic name of 'club of democracies'

1.2 The appeal and contestation of European ideas of international law—the Council of Europe and global influence

The fall of the Berlin Wall turned the 'club of democracies' into a 'school of democracy', since Central and Eastern European States, that regained their independence, were admitted to the Council of Europe following their ratification of the European

Convention for Human Rights and Fundamental Freedoms (ECHR) (*sine qua non* condition) and other treaties, although they clearly did not share the same 'common heritage of political traditions, ideals, freedom and the rule of law'. These newly admitted member States were immediately offered assistance—different monitoring commissions checked their legal frameworks and administrative practices and advised the most efficient ways to bring them into compliance with the European standards. This process demonstrates the Council's global impact, as its democratic principles continue to inspire and reshape other parts of the world.

But the Council of Europe remains loyal to its principles—it continues to be a platform for exchange of the best practices between European governments and parliaments, for strengthening democracy, rule of law, and respect for human rights. Although the illusionary period of the 'end of history' is over, and it has become clear that the ambitious goal of overcoming the divisions persisting in Europe is now even further from being realized than it was a decade ago, the organization continues to be committed to its Sisyphean task—building a sustainable future for Europe.

It was exactly this loyalty to the goals of the organization that led the Committee of Ministers, in March 2022, to decide that the Russian Federation, after commencing its aggression against Ukraine, had seriously violated its obligations under Article 3 of the Statute of the Council of Europe, and consequently could no longer be a member State of the organization—there is no way that a State that failed its exams at the 'school of democracy' can turn it into what someone might call a 'Titanic of democracies'.

Today the Council of Europe, having lost the Russian Federation in March 2022, consists of forty-six member States. Only two States on the European continent—Belarus and the Vatican—have never been members.

It is important to note that membership in the Council of Europe does not give any privileges, but only obligations that the member States voluntarily undertake. They have each agreed that human life and dignity will be the highest value, and to work together to improve their respective legislation so that human rights (Çalı, this volume), democracy (Poghosyan, this volume), and the rule of law (van Aaken, this volume) are valued and respected, also to learn the best practices, and follow the advice, of their fellow members for the ultimate benefit of all citizens of the European continent.

1.3 The regional diversity and fragmentation of international law within Europe—the Council of Europe, its structure, and its many facets

The three pillars of the Council of Europe are Democracy (Section 2), Human Rights (Section 3), and the Rule of Law (Section 4) which are considered in turn in this chapter. Whilst there are more than 120 Council of Europe conventions and agreements,[6] (doubled by additional protocols) supervised by numerous bodies of the organization, it is fair to say that the most visible and influential instruments within the Council of

Europe are the Parliamentary Assembly, the European Court of Human Rights (ECthR), the Committee for Prevention of Torture, the Commissioner for Human Rights, the European Social Charter, the Congress for Local and Regional Authorities, and the key executive structure—the Committee of Ministers. The limited scope of this chapter allows us to concentrate on the first five of these.

As the organization evolved, growing in both number of the member States and also in accepting new challenges and functions through the adoption of new legal mechanisms, this gave rise to several additional structures dealing with different aspects of the promotion of human rights, in accordance with relevant treaties.

The Group of Experts on Action against Violence against Women and Domestic Violence (GREVIO) monitors the implementation of the Istanbul Convention on preventing and combatting violence against women and domestic violence in accordance with the procedure envisaged in Article 68 of the Convention. The Group of Experts on Action against Trafficking in Human Beings (GRETA) monitors implementation of the Convention of Action against Trafficking in Human Beings. The European Commission against Racism and Intolerance (ECRI) monitors questions related to the fight against racism, discrimination, xenophobia, antisemitism, and intolerance in Europe. The Ad Hoc Committee of Experts on the Rights of Persons with Disabilities (CAHDPH) steers the intergovernmental work in the field of disability rights, giving advice, guidance, and support to other Council of Europe bodies and to member States on disability-related issues, etc.

All of these groups and committees illustrate the multifaceted nature of the organization. While each contributes to the overarching goals of democracy, human rights, and the rule of law, they also highlight the regional diversity and fragmentation within the Council, which is critical to its effectiveness and relevance. As we examine the Council's diverse roles and the unique perspectives of its member States, tools such as the margin of appreciation and reservations become evident as means to facilitate this diversity.

2. Democracy

The ostensible role of the Parliamentary Assembly of the Council of Europe (PACE) is to act as the Council's 'deliberative organ', discussing and making recommendations on any issues falling within the Council's aim and scope. The total number of members of the Assembly is 612 (306 titular members and 306 substitutes); there are also observers (Canada, Israel, and Mexico) as well as 'Partners for democracy' (Jordan, Kyrgyzstan, Morocco, and Palestine), whose MPs participate in the Assembly's meetings. Unlike members of the European Parliament, members of the PACE are not directly elected, it is up to the national parliaments to designate the delegations.

The number of members is proportionate to the population of a member State. However, as it often happens, smaller countries are given a certain bonus: for example

Turkey, with its population of 84 million, has only eighteen deputies in the PACE, whilst San Marino has two, although it has a population of more than two thousand times less.

The PACE meets quarterly in Strasbourg, sitting for a week. It plays an important European role—since, in accordance with the Statute of the Council of Europe, its aim is 'to achieve greater unity between its members' which 'shall be pursued by discussion of questions of common concern and by agreements and common action'. The PACE is an area for public discussion of the major political issues of the day. It has actively sought to promote the notion of parliamentary democracy, and to explore what such a concept means—by engaging with national parliaments and holding 'European parliamentary summits'. It also monitors, through many different procedures, States' compliance with necessary democratic standards.[7]

The PACE has a power to sanction national delegations by suspending them or removing their right voting rights—for serious violations by States of the basic principles upon which the organization is based, or persistent failure to honour their obligations. For example, Russia has been sanctioned twice—in 2000 over the Second Chechen war, and in 2014 following the annexation of Crimea—the PACE noted its condemnation and disapproval of the Russian Federation's actions and suspended the rights of the delegation of the Russian Federation to vote, to be represented in the Bureau of the Assembly, the Presidential Committee, and the Standing Committee, and rights to participate in election observation missions.[8]

The PACE is not the legislative body of the Council of Europe—it is the Committee of Ministers that is responsible for legislative work; however, due to a very particular mission of the Council of Europe, its 'parliamentary dimension' is quite active. Further, if in other intergovernmental organizations (IGOs) only governments have a say, in the PACE the opposition also has a certain influence. Indeed, the work of the PACE is widely covered in the international media and thus is absolutely transparent—it is not possible to make a decision behind-the-scenes, as unsatisfied members can always mobilize the press.

Strictly speaking, the PACE has no real powers, and the member States have no real obligations to this body. Nevertheless, the PACE observes elections, orders different types of investigations, discusses reports, and adopts resolutions, recommendations, and statements that play an important role in international politics and empower different internal and international actors.

Thus, it has adopted resolutions ranging from investigation of allegations of illicit trafficking in human organs in Kosovo,[9] to a situation with detainees with disabilities in Europe,[10] from secret detentions and illegal transfers of detainees,[11] to female genital mutilation in Europe,[12] from the principles and guarantees applicable to advocates,[13] to intellectual property rights in the digital era,[14] and so on.

The PACE further elects the Secretary General of the Council of Europe, the Commissioner for Human Rights, and ECtHR judges—via well-developed and thoughtful procedure. In particular, in the case of ECtHR judges, the process involves two stages: pre-selection by the Committee on the Election of Judges, followed by an election by the PACE. The Committee assesses the candidates' qualifications, experience, and adherence to ECHR principles. It may reject candidates if they do not meet the required criteria or if there are concerns about their independence, impartiality, or integrity. The rejection of candidates is not uncommon in these processes and reflects the rigorous nature of the selection process and the commitment to upholding the highest standards in the Council of Europe—the PACE strives to ensure that only the most qualified and suitable individuals are appointed to these crucial positions.

The democratic dimension of the Council of Europe is also underpinned by the Congress of Local and Regional Authorities, responsible for strengthening local and regional democracy in its member States. It comprises 636 elected representatives representing more than 200,000 local and regional authorities. The Congress is responsible for evaluating the application of the European Charter of Local Self-Government in each member State, it further observes local and regional elections; and supports national authorities in their implementation of the Council of Europe standards in the field of regional democracy.

3. Human Rights

3.1 The European Court of Human Rights

As the author of this chapter served on the Court's bench for about twelve years, it will come as no surprise that the view presented here suggests that the Court is the most efficient structure of the Council of Europe, and the one which has made a great difference for the European continent.

The European Convention on Human Rights and Fundamental Freedoms entered into force in 1953, becoming the first regional system of human rights protection, and the European Court of Human Rights, following entry into force by Protocol No 11 to the Convention, replaced the existing European Commission and Court as the first permanent human rights court in the world. The right of individual petition is at the heart of the Convention system, and it was argued that 'The individual complaints mechanism of the ECtHR is the crown jewel of the world's most advanced international system for protecting civil and political liberties'.[15] Furthermore, the Court's judgments are legally binding on the High Contracting Parties.

The Convention system is subsidiary to national systems for human rights protection: the ECtHR examines a case only after all effective domestic remedies have been exhausted. The very principle of subsidiarity, developed by the Court for decades, was formalized in Protocol No 15 to the Convention, that entered into force in August 2021: it added a new recital to the preamble to the Convention:

> Affirming that the High Contracting Parties, in accordance with the principle of subsidiarity, have the primary responsibility to secure the rights and freedoms defined in

> this Convention and the Protocols thereto, and that in doing so they enjoy a margin of appreciation, subject to the supervisory jurisdiction of the European Court of Human Rights.

The 'margin of appreciation' doctrine, which is at the heart of the principle of subsidiarity, means a certain degree of discretion is afforded to the national authorities, given their better knowledge of their paticular society (see Bílková, this volume). The Court explained this, for example, in its famous judgment in the so-called 'burka case' (on the prohibition in France to fully cover a face in public places): '[T]he national authorities have direct democratic legitimation and are, ... in principle better placed than an international court to evaluate local needs and conditions. In matters of general policy, on which opinions within a democratic society may reasonably differ widely, the role of the domestic policy-maker should be given special weight ... in delimiting the extent of the margin of appreciation in a given case, the Court must also have regard to what is at stake therein.'[16]

'Margin of appreciation' goes hand-in-hand with the 'European consensus'—the concept that reflects the Court's nature as the European supranational judicial body and refers to the level of homogeneousness in the legal frameworks of the member States on a particular legal issue. The Court will restrict the scope of the margin of appreciation afforded to contracting parties if there is an emerging European consensus on the issue and will widen the same scope if there is no uniformity between the member States.[17]

The conventional purpose was to become 'a system of collective guarantee of human rights',[18] thus it guarantees minimum standards—namely, a basic respect for human dignity. Evidently, during decades of interpretation, the Court has expanded the scope of protected rights to a significant degree. The ECHR was born in the aftermath of the atrocities of the Holocaust and World War II; however, today's expansion of human rights has gone far beyond what were believed to constitute fundamental rights when the Convention was drafted. It currently strives to cover almost all aspects of everyday life, dealing with issues both large and small.

It is argued that the founding fathers of the Convention 'saw [it] as more of an inter-state pact against totalitarianism than anything else, with the international system of control unlikely to be invoked other than in extreme cases'.[19] However, long before the post-communist States had joined the Convention back in 1990s, it already proved to have an important instrumental value, capable of making a difference, by effectively combatting, for instance, the discrimination of illegitimate children in the case of *Marckx v Belgium* in 1979, corporal punishments in British schools in the case of *Tyrer v the United Kingdom* in 1978, and criminalization of homosexual relationship in the case of *Dudgeon v the United Kingdom* in 1981, or forbidding the extradition of a suspect to the State where he faced capital punishment in *Soering v the United Kingdom* in 1989.

For citizens of the post-communist States that joined the Council of Europe in the 1990s and early 2000s, whose domestic legal systems suffered from inherited communist corruption and abuses, the Court was the 'last hope for justice'. Unfortunately, any dreams of a quick transformation to democracy and human rights standards met with a sad reality—the way to the rule of law is long, abrupt, and full of obstacles.

It was therefore predictable that the case load of the Court would increase dramatically. Its peak of 160,000 pending cases in 2011 coincided with entry into force of Protocol No 14 to the Convention that allowed a single judge to dispose of clearly inadmissible cases, and also introduced a new ground for inadmissibility—'if the applicant has not suffered a significant disadvantage'[20] as a result of an alleged human rights violation.

It is important to note that there were effectively four High Contracting Parties responsible for this caseload, namely Russia, Turkey, Ukraine, and Romania. A significant number of complaints brought from these States concerned the systemic problems in their domestic legal systems—for example, non-enforcement of their final and binding judgments, appalling detention conditions, long and unjustified pre-trial detention, a number of legislative lacunae, and different shortcomings in the trial proceedings. In addition, a number of cases arose from frozen and pending military conflicts—specifically, Northern Cyprus, Nagorno-Karabakh, Chechnya, Abkhazia, South Ossetia, Crimea, and Donbass.

The Court coped with these challenges by introducing innovative working methods. This included the so-called 'pilot judgments' in which the Court identified a legal problem, suggested a legislative and/or practical solution to a State, and froze similar cases, whilst pending adoption of a domestic reform (these cases were later easily disposed of). For a wider range of persisting issues, the Court utilized the methods of administrative stocktaking of the cases and grouping them in 'projects', adoption of a 'leading judgment' for a persistent legal problem, and disposing of remaining cases as 'follow-up' cases decided by a three-judge formation.

The most exceptional situations required the most pioneering and original approaches: in 2017 the Court, in its *Burmych and Others v Ukraine* judgment dismissed more than 12,000 applications against Ukraine concerning non-enforcement of final domestic judgments, since they were identical to applications covered by a previous pilot judgment that had remained unexecuted by Ukraine for a number of years despite all efforts by the Committee of Ministers.[21]

In 2021, in the case of *Turan and Others v Turkey*, on pre-trial detention of judges and prosecutors in the aftermath of the attempted coup of 15 July 2016, the Court joined 427 applications and found that 'the applicants' detention was not prescribed by law, which runs counter to the fundamental principle of the rule of law and to the purpose of Article 5'. It further had regard 'to the accumulation of thousands of similar applications on its docket ... which puts a considerable strain on its limited resources' and considered 'as a matter of judicial policy—that it is justified in these compelling circumstances to dispense with the separate examination of the admissibility and merits of each remaining complaint raised by each individual applicant'. It pointed out that 'an individualised examination of the remaining complaints brought by each applicant would significantly delay the processing of these cases, without a commensurate benefit to the applicants or contribution to the development of the case-law'. In so doing, the Court was 'guided by the overriding interest to ensure the long-term effectiveness of the Convention system, which is under threat by the constantly growing inflow of applications'.[22]

In parallel with bringing the well-established Convention values to 'new democracies', the Court has faced developing standards of human dignity and social advances, that require evolutive interpretation of the Convention. Obviously, the Court cannot apply the standards from 1950s to the pressing human rights issues some seventy years later—Europe has changed considerably. As the role of the Court is 'to bridge the gap between law and society',[23] the 'living-tree' interpretation of the Convention, that is, judicial modifications of the original meaning of the Convention, is inevitable. Indeed, according to Lech Garlicki, a former ECHR judge, 'the Court has the power to determine the actual meaning of words and phrases which were inserted into the text of the Convention more than fifty years ago'.[24] Technological progress in Europe has been such that strict application of rules existed in the 1950s would render human rights totally ineffective in certain areas. The developments of computers and the Internet—with their advantages and disadvantages for free speech and privacy rights—were simply unimaginable when the founding fathers drafted the Convention. Developments in genetics, cloning, artificial procreation, and new methods of surveillance also have a profound impact on human dignity. As former vice President of the Court, Christos Rozakis, pointed out, a 'failure by the Court to maintain a dynamic and evolutive approach would indeed risk rendering it a bar to reform or improvement'.[25]

A number of 'evolutive' standards in the Court's case law, not clearly stated in the text of the Convention, are either self-evident or constitute a response to natural and predictable evolution of the society—right to respect for one's home and correspondence, guaranteed by Article 8, obviously extends to telephone conversations and e-mail exchange;[26] prohibition of inhuman and degrading treatment under Article 3 presupposes adequate medical care in prisons; human trafficking for the purposes of sexual or other exploitation falls within the scope of 'slavery' forbidden by Article 4.[27]

Some other new standards are much more controversial. It is argued that having ratified the Convention in the 1950s, the Contracting Parties could not imagine that due to the Court's interpretation, the Convention was supposed to protect environmental rights, right to profession, official recognition of same-sex relationships, access to State-held information, the necessity of independent review of life sentences, and so on. Choosing the direction of evolutive interpretation and the right moment for it remains the key challenge which the ECHR faces.

With all the difficulties, challenges, and controversies, for past seven decades the Court has delivered more than 16,000 judgments that—despite many observed failures—have shaped the rule of law in Europe.

3.2 The European Social Charter

As the authors of the ECHR concentrated on civil and political rights only (although the developing practice of the ECHR suggests that there is no longer a clear division between pure 'civil and political rights' and socio-economic rights, especially when it comes to a wide range of social benefits), already in 1951 the Consultative Assembly recommended to the Committee of Ministers 'that a common policy in social matters should be adopted by Member States of the Council of Europe'.

The European Social Charter was adopted in 1961, setting out the main socio-economic guarantees, such as the right to work with adequate working conditions, the right to bargain collectively, the right to health care, and so on. The Charter was revised in 1999 with some developed rights being included, such as the right to take part in the determination and improvement of working conditions and working environment, the right to protection in cases of termination of employment, and the right to protection against poverty and social exclusion.

It is argued that 'despite the desirability of a situation in which economic and social rights are accorded equal importance with civil and political rights, social rights remain the poor step-sister of civil and political rights'.[28] The reference is down to the 'fact that membership of the Council requires ratification of the ECHR but not of the ESC, the discrepancies in staff and resources devoted to the respective supervisory systems, the unequal roles accorded to the different rights within the broad promotional activities of the Council'.[29]

The Fundamental Social Rights of Workers was adopted in 1989 as a non-binding document by the European Council, apparently challenging the leading role of the Council of Europe as the main protector of human rights in Europe. This triggered further discussions in an informal ministerial conference on human rights in Rome on 5 November 1990. As a result, the Committee of Ministers 'was invited to take the necessary steps for a detailed study of the role, contents and functioning of the European Social Charter to be undertaken as soon as possible', that ultimately materialized in the amending Protocol (1991) to clarify the supervisory mechanism. The original version of the Charter contained no complaints procedure but only reporting obligations, with the European Committee on Social Rights assessing compliance with the Social Charter in its Conclusions; the amending Protocol in fact clarified the relations between the Committee of Independent Experts and the Governmental Committee, increased the number of these experts, abolished the role of the PACE, etc. The additional Protocol (1995) provides for a collective complaint procedure as a second supervisory mechanism into the ESC regime; this procedure allowed certain non-governmental organizations (NGOs) and workers' organizations to seek a declaration that certain laws and policies in their respective States are incompatible with their commitments under the Charter, without having to exhaust available domestic remedies, and an updating of the Charter's substantive provisions.

The revised European Social Charter (1996) took into account major developments in labour law, and social and economic standards in Europe. The Charter provides that each of the Contracting Parties undertakes to consider itself bound by at least six of the nine core provisions: the right to work, the right to organize, the right to bargain collectively, the right of children and young persons to protection, the right to social security, the right to social and medical assistance, the right of the family to social, legal, and economic protection, the right of migrant workers and their families to protection and assistance, and the right to equal opportunities and equal treatment in matters of employment and occupation without discrimination on the grounds of sex. Plus, they should consider themselves bound by an additional number of articles or numbered paragraphs at their discretion, provided that the total number of articles or numbered paragraphs by which it is bound is not less than sixteen articles or sixty-three numbered paragraphs.

The supervisory mechanism of the Chapter is a reporting system—States report on the core articles biennially, and on the non-core articles once every four years. Based on these reports, the European Committee on Social Rights—consisting of fifteen independent experts elected by the Committee of Ministers for a six-year term—decides on compliance with provisions of the Charter and adopts relevant conclusions. Then, these experts' conclusions are examined by the governmental committee, composed of representatives of the Contracting States. Finally, the Committee of Ministers decides whether to terminate supervision or to make recommendations for the State to bring its legislation and practice into compliance with the Charter standards.

To date, thirty-five member States of the Council of Europe have ratified the Revised Charter, and only sixteen of these have ratified the Protocol on the collective complaints procedure. The main flaw of this system remains the lack of the right to individual petition.

During its years of work, the European Committee of Social Rights has developed a very wide and progressive jurisprudence, also covering areas of socio-economic policies that were not touched upon by the ECHR. Its impact remains relatively limited—the conclusions to national reports and decisions on the merits to collective complaints do not have the same legally binding nature as the judgments of the Court. However, it fills important gaps in the social and economic rights protection in Europe, and serves as a source of inspiration, both for the domestic authorities, and for the ECtHR, which quite often makes reference to the decisions and conclusions of the European Committee of Social Rights, in its judgments.

3.3 Committee for the Prevention of Torture

Torture is the most serious, brutal, and unjustifiable attack on human dignity. As such, there is no place for torture in a democratic country who is committed to the rule of law. Article 3 ECHR speaks in absolute terms—'No one shall be subjected to torture or to inhuman or degrading treatment or punishment'. Drafters of the Convention deliberately excluded any room for margin of appreciation and relativism; this is the only provision that contains no exception, with no possibility of derogation from this obligation during times of war and emergency.

The prohibition of torture and inhuman or degrading treatment requires that any allegations of such treatment are effectively investigated and perpetrators are made accountable.

This was the idea behind the adoption of the European Convention for the Prevention of Torture in 1987. The Convention established a European Committee for the

Prevention of Torture (CPT) which was set up in 1989—an international independent monitoring body (not an investigative one), that provides a non-judicial preventive mechanism to protect individuals deprived of their liberty against torture and other forms of ill-treatment.

The CPT, to a certain extent, complements the judicial work of the ECtHR on Article 3 ECHR. Similar to other Council of Europe bodies, the CPT consists of independent and impartial experts who serve in their individual capacity, their background being mostly legal or medical.

The CPT is a monitoring body, as provided for in Article 1 CPT Convention: the 'Committee shall, by means of visits, examine the treatment of persons deprived of their liberty with a view to strengthening, if necessary, the protection of such persons from torture and from inhuman or degrading treatment or punishment'. Therefore, the CPT is allowed to visit at any time any place of detention in Europe—including prisons, pre-trial detention facilities, police stations, psychiatric institutions, transit zones in airports, social care homes, etc.[30]

It is worth noting that at the time of the Convention's adoption, the very idea that places of deprivation of liberty could be opened to outside scrutiny by an international body was a truly revolutionary concept. But this very quickly became an absolutely natural part of the democratic accountability for a member State of the Council of Europe. Today the CPT conducts periodic and ad hoc visits to all member States of the Council of Europe. In total, in its roughly thirty years of work, it has carried out just under 500 visits (about 60 per cent of which were periodic, and remainder were ad hoc visits), and published 438 reports,[31] followed by reports and recommendations.

Undoubtedly, monitoring places of detention remains one of the most effective means to prevent torture and other forms of ill-treatment, therefore the CPT was a pioneer in preventing ill-treatment in Europe, bringing transparency to previously closed places.[32]

The role of the CPT is primarily to assess the overall situation of deprivation of liberty in a country in order to identify elements that could potentially lead to violations. Its goal is to intervene *ex ante*, that is, before ill-treatment occurs, by means of recommendations. Consequently, the duty of the Committee is broader than merely reporting on the allegations of torture or inhuman and degrading treatment; rather, it must look into the general conditions surrounding the alleged abuses and, if need be, suggest ways of both stopping the abuses in the near-term and of preventing their recurrence in the future. In order to carry out its work effectively, the CPT has been granted extensive powers to visit any place within a State's jurisdiction where a person is deprived of his or her liberty, at any time, and to be granted access to information it requires to carry out its task. Further, it may interview, in private, persons deprived of their liberty.

Periodic visits are carried out to ensure that at least the majority of High Contracting Parties are visited on average every four years. Ad hoc visits are organized when the Committee decides that 'they are required in the circumstances', in response to some worrying information received concerning certain practices or events in certain countries or places of detention—to allow a rapid and efficient response, and also to prevent the spreading of reproachable practices. The CPT concentrates on both 'active' ill-treatment (deliberate infliction) and 'passive' ill-treatment (conditions of detention, inadequate medical care).

The Committee meets online, and its reports are strictly confidential. On some rare occasions, when a country refuses to cooperate and follow the core recommendations, the CPT may proceed with a public statement. So far, several public statements have been made, in particular in respect of Turkey (1992, 1996), the Russian Federation (2001, 2003, 2007), and Greece (2011).

Country visit reports are mostly published, with the only exception so far being the Russian Federation as it never gave the necessary consent for publication.[33] It is widely accepted that publication of the Committee's materials increases the visibility of the CPT and, consequently, its impact, as these materials and the Committee's proposals and conclusions are instrumental for civil society—the CPT's most important interlocutors to insist upon human rights and to participate in debates on these issues.

The CPT has contributed to substantive improvements in conditions and treatment in places of detention in a plethora of ways. These improvements incorporate key categories—material conditions (eg the removal of shutters on prison windows), procedures, institutional changes (eg prison health services being moved to the Ministry of Health), protection of vulnerable groups, development of safeguards, and legislative changes. The CPT consequently has developed an incredibly important body of standards, which covers a wide range of issues, from policy custody, and women in detention, to migrants. They serve as a reference point for other monitoring bodies and the ECHR.

3.4 The Commissioner for Human Rights

The Commissioner for Human Rights is mandated to 'foster the effective observance of human rights, and assist member states in the implementation of Council of Europe human rights standards; promote education in and awareness of human rights in Council of Europe member states; identify possible shortcomings in the law and practice concerning human rights; facilitate the activities of national ombudsperson institutions and other human rights structures; and provide advice and information regarding the protection of human rights across the region'.[34] In practice this gives the Commissioner quite a wide mandate, allowing him or her to visit all the member States and engage in a dialogue with both national authorities (usually the Commissioner meets the highest officials in governments, parliaments, and the judiciary), and civil society. The Commissioner also visits places—upon receiving relevant information—that are significant to his or her conclusions—like penitentiary institutions, reception centres for refugees, orphanages, etc. If need be, the Commissioners summarizes his or her conclusions from a country visit in a relevant letter to the authorities, that would also include necessary recommendations.

The Commissioner also conducts related work releasing relevant opinions, issue papers, and reports on a variety of issues related to human rights protection—from artificial intelligence to transitional justice, from freedom of expression to LGBTQ+ rights, from environmental issues to economic crises. These papers are the summary of the concerns raised by different actors, examination of relevant domestic and international mechanisms, assessed through the prism of the Commissioner's own experience, wisdom, and vision. Thus, the Commissioner's 'Human Rights Comments' and 'Viewpoints' are regularly published on their webpage, covering a wide range of issues such as artificial intelligence, counter-terrorism, minorities, environmental issues, and many others. These documents serve as a great inspirational tool for anyone working on the topic.

The Commissioner also organizes and takes part in different conferences and seminars on a number of human rights-related issues, together with officials and civil society.

Needless to say, a close cooperation with the national human rights institution (NHRI), including national ombudspersons, is of highest importance for the Commissioner and is indeed advantageous for all parties. Thus, the Commissioner's Office established a Liaison Office for European NHRIs, responsible for their cooperation in promotion and protection of human rights. Furthermore, the Commissioner has a partnership with the United Nations High Commissioner for Human Rights, as well as with relevant specialized officials of the European Union (EU).

Finally, the Commissioner can intervene, at his or her own initiative as a third party in any case pending before the ECtHR.

4. Rule of Law

The 'Venice Commission' is the popular name given to the European Commission for Democracy through Law dealing with constitutional issues and other legal matters related to the rule of law in order to strengthen it in Europe (see van Aaken, this volume). The idea behind its creation reflects the perception of a 'school of democracies' where a 'teacher' for the post-communist States was needed to assist in institutional and constitutional transitions of these States. The idea of creating such a body capable of providing the necessary legal and constitutional support to these new democracies came from the former Italian Minister, Antonio La Pergola, whose proposal was welcomed at the Venice Conference in 1990 and led to the adoption of Resolution 90/6, which provided for the establishment of a European Commission for Democracy through Law.[35] The original 'partial agreement' that meant that the member States of the Council of Europe were free to join, gradually turned into an 'enlarged agreement', which made it possible for non-European States to accede, subsequently opening the door for States from different continents, such as Morocco, Algeria, Tunisia, Israel, Brazil, Chile, Mexico Canada, the US, Kazakhstan and South Korea.[36]

The Venice Commission consists of experts, serving in their individual capacities (albeit appointed by States)—mostly prominent constitutional lawyers, both academic and practitioners, including sitting and former members of the highest courts, and former governmental officials.

The Council of Europe's three pillars—democracy, human rights, and the rule of law—are reflected in three core areas of the Commission's functioning: democratic institutions and fundamental rights; constitutional justice and ordinary justice; elections, referendums, and political parties.[37]

The Venice Commission is primarily concerned with giving legal advice in the form of 'legal opinions' on draft legislation or legislation in force, presented for its examination. The majority of these opinions so far have dealt with the 'new democracies'. It is specified in the Commission's documents that an opinion can be requested by a member State (its head, government, or parliament), different bodies of the Council of Europe (Secretary General, Commissioner for Human Rights, Committee of Ministers, and the PACE—which is the leader of such requests among the Council of Europe bodies) as well as by international organizations. Furthermore, at the request by a constitutional court of a member State or the ECtHR, the Commission may provide amicus curiae.

In recent years, the Venice Commission has had to deal with the constitutional law issues related to political conflicts. Thus, for example, in the opinion on emergency decree laws adopted following the attempted *coup d'état* in Turkey in July 2016, the Commission stressed that:

> the constitutional situation which emerged after the declaration of the state of emergency is a source of concern for the Venice Commission. The declaration itself did not define the scope of the Government's emergency powers. Similarly, Parliament, when approving the declaration, did not circumscribe in any manner the Government's mandate. The Constitution contains certain general principles which should not be contravened even in the times of emergency, but since Parliament did not give general instructions to the Government and did not exercise its controlling functions over specific decree laws until October, the Government, during this period, had unfettered power to rule the country without any checks and balances but its own good will. This situation is dangerous for a democratic legal order, especially in view of the virtually irreversible character of measures taken by the Government.[38]

Addressing the 'Lustration law' introduced in Ukraine after the 'Revolution of Dignity' in 2014, the Commission noted that:

> Applying lustration measures to the period of the Soviet communist rule so many years after the end of that regime and the enactment of a democratic constitution in Ukraine requires cogent reasons justifying the specific threat for democracy which former communists pose nowadays; the Commission finds it difficult to justify such late lustration.... Applying lustration measures in respect of the recent period during which Mr Yanukovych was President of Ukraine would ultimately amount

> to questioning the actual functioning of the constitutional and legal framework of Ukraine as a democratic state governed by the rule of law.

It further underlined some serious shortcomings in the law that would require reconsideration.[39]

Importantly, the Venice Commission is not seeking 'harmonization' of the legislation on constitutional issues in the respective member States—having such a wide range of constitutional systems, it is not possible to advocate any as 'European best practice'. The Commission instead suggests some alternative approaches, explaining their advantages and disadvantages.

One of the priority areas of the Venice Commission's work in recent years has been the judiciary, the importance of which, for the sustainability of democratic institutions, can hardly be overestimated—a truly rule-of-law State is impossible without a strong and independent judicial system. The Venice Commission then was at the forefront when Eastern Europe was gripped by a wave of judicial reforms, apparently conducted for a good cause but potentially capable of undermining judicial independence (see van Aaken, this volume, which deals with Poland and Hungary and the rule of law issues relevant for independence of the judiciary). On the most difficult and painful issue of the accountability of judges, the Venice Commission warned that accountability can naturally lead to interferences with independence:

> The Venice Commission has always stated that the judiciary should not be an entirely self-governing corporation but accountable to the society. However, mechanisms of accountability should not interfere with the independence of the judges, and of the bodies of judicial governance. The judiciary should be insulated from quickly changing political winds. The courts have often to adjudicate on conflicts between individual rights and the State, and that relationship is imperilled when the State takes over the control of judicial functions.[40]

The process of appointing of judges—who are guarantors of the rule of law—also requires strict scrutiny. Thus, in its Report on Judicial Appointments[41] the Commission stated, stressing a particular role of this process for new democracies which still did not share the 'common heritage', that:

> International standards in this respect are more in favour of the extensive depolitisation of the [judicial appointment] process. However no single non-political 'model' of appointment system exists, which could ideally comply with the principle of the separation of powers and secure full independence of the judiciary ... In some older democracies, systems exist in which the executive power has a strong influence on judicial appointments. Such systems may work well in practice and allow for an independent judiciary because the executive is restrained by legal culture and traditions, which have grown over a long time ... New democracies, however, did not yet have a chance to develop these traditions, which can prevent abuse. Therefore, at least in new democracies explicit constitutional provisions

> are needed as a safeguard to prevent political abuse by other state powers in the appointment of judges.

But the Commission's most significant document is its Rule of Law Checklist,[42] in which it assesses the conformity of the legal framework of a State with the Rule of Law's standards in Europe. The Commission presented its practical and inclusive tool to the content of the Rule of Law principle. It created a unique source and collection of standards and best practices that in practice have made the rule of law a 'directly implementable' principle. It is justly argued that nowadays, in asking for the Commission's intervention on its legal provisions, a State acknowledges the value of its approach to the rule of law and manifests its will to conform its legal frameworks to the Commission's understanding.[43]

The Commission has now been operational for approximately thirty years. It has proved to be the best—together with the ECtHR—'professor' of the rule of law and human rights in the 'school of democracy'. Its considerable experience in constitutional assessment has gained ever-increasing importance for the practical implementation of common European standards and values.

5. Conclusion

'Peace, progress, human rights—these three goals are insolubly linked to one another', so said the Soviet Nobel Peace Prize Laureate Andrei Sakharov back in 1975. These goals represent the three pillars of the Council of Europe—Democracy, Human Rights, and the Rule of Law—and underpin every aspect of the Organisation. The same idea—'internal freedom, democracy and the rule of law go hand in hand with countries' peaceful coexistence'—was repeated in 2023, after some lessons learned, by the German Federal Chancellor Olaf Scholz at the Council of Europe Summit.

The Council of Europe has contributed to a plethora of substantial improvements in democratic and human rights standards, alongside maintaining the rule of law across Europe, with all its important bodies analysing and upholding the human rights standards covering a wide range of issues and providing constitutional assistance.

A clear trend in recent years is the transformation of the Council of Europe from a 'club of democracies' with strict membership criteria into a 'round table', at which everyone is invited to sit. This strategy was deliberately chosen in the mid-1990s, when a number of post-communist States were admitted to the Council of Europe, despite a clear inconsistency with the membership criteria.

As with any school, the 'school of democracies' has successfully taught some new member States the key standards of rule of law, whilst others have failed their exams. Forty-six years after Andrei Sakaharov, another Russian Nobel Peace Prize Laureate Dmitry Muratov desperately said from the same floor: 'The world has fallen out of love with democracy ... We've got an illusion that progress can be achieved through technology and violence, not through human rights and freedoms'.[44] This is the same tragic illusion today that the combination of artificial intelligence and flourishing digital connectivity give an advantage to autocratic regimes—with their tendency to concentrate on power—rather than to democratic regimes—who only 'won' in the previous century because they tended to distribute power and were thus more effective. This perception is profoundly wrong—a complex management system can only be achieved by democracy, as this is the only system with a high degree of adaptation. Modern societies are based upon interaction and cooperation, and only democracy allows for the delegation of power and the development of network structures.

The dramatic U-turn of some Council of Europe member States from liberal democracy with its institutions providing checks and balances and its strong essential values—human dignity and individual freedom—cannot but bring injustice to Europe. A member State who engaged in an aggressive war, and thus grossly neglected the underpinning concepts of the organization and ran against its core goals was inevitably expelled from it, however there is an lesson to be learned: keeping States with clear authoritarian regimes within the 'club of democracies' and allowing them an *à la carte* approach to the organization's values not only undermines the authority of the organization,[45] but significantly worsens protection of democracy in a given State by allowing the dictator's appetites to grow unabated.

The Summit of the Council of Europe, held in May 2023, was called to address these key issues, as well as accountability for Russia's actions in Ukraine, reviving commitment to the ECtHR, reinforcing democratic principles, and advancing the agenda of human rights and the environment. The adopted 'Reykjavík Declaration'[46] aimed to strengthen the Council of Europe and the ECtHR, although some language used was criticized for being vague.[47] Its further success will depend on subsequent actions taken by member States, elected representatives, national human rights institutions, and civil society to ensure lasting change and renaissance.

The Russian invasion of Ukraine in February 2022, the first large-scale aggressive war in Europe since World War II, came as a real shock to the organization and to the European continent. But democracy absorbs all shocks—be it a war, Brexit, or neo-authoritarian populists winning elections—it will collect itself, survive, and—it is to be hoped—become even stronger. The fundamental values of liberal democracy, protected and strengthened by different bodies of the Council of Europe, will continue serve as a compass for the European States.

Notes

1. Preamble to the Statute of the Council of Europe.
2. ibid.
3. Winston Churchill, 'Speech in Zurich' (19 September 1946) <https://www.churchill-in-zurich.ch/en/churchill/en-churchills-zurcher-rede/> accessed 28 June 2023.
4. Greece left the Council of Europe in 1969 during the Regime of the Colonels and was readmitted in 1974 after returning to democracy.

5. Preamble to the ECHR.
6. See the full list of the Council of Europe's treaties at <https://www.coe.int/en/web/conventions/full-list> accessed 28 June 2023.
7. Stefanie Schmahl and Marten Breuer, *The Council of Europe: Its Laws and Policies* (OUP 2017).
8. Resolution 1990 (2014).
9. Resolution 1782 (2011).
10. Resolution 2223 (2018).
11. Resolution 1562 (2007).
12. Resolution 2135 (2016).
13. Resolution 2348 (2020).
14. Resolution 2110 (2016).
15. Laurence R Helfer, 'Redesigning the European Court of Human Rights: Embeddedness as a Deep Structural Principle of the European Human Rights Regime', 19 (1) European Journal of International Law 2008, 125–159.
16. *S.A.S. v France* [GC], App no 43835/11, 1 July 2014, § 125.
17. Kanstantsin Dzehtsiarou, *European Consensus and the Legitimacy of the European Court of Human Rights* (CUP 2015) chs 2–4.
18. Michael O'Boyle, 'The Future of the European Court of Human Rights', 12 (10) German Law Journal 2011, 1862–1877.
19. Steven Greer, *The Margin of Appreciation: Interpretation and Discretion under the European Convention on Human Rights* (Council of Europe Publishing 2000) 13.
20. Article 35(3)(b) ECHR.
21. This highly controversial judgment, adopted by ten votes against seven was criticized by legal scholars: see, among many others, Eline Kindt, 'Giving up on Individual Justice? The Effect of State Non-execution of a Pilot Judgment on Victims', 36 (3) Netherlands Quarterly of Human Rights, 175–180.
22. *Turan and Others v Turkey*, App no 75805/16 and 426 others, 23 November 2021, § 98.
23. Aharon Barak, *The Judge in a Democracy* (Princeton UP 2006) 11.
24. *Öcalan v Turkey*, App no 46221/99, 12 May 2005.
25. Alastair Mowbray, 'An Examination of the European Court of Human Rights Approach to Overruling Its Previous Case Law', 9 Human Rights Law Review 2009, 179, 183.
26. *Klass and Others v Germany*, App no 5029/71, 6 September 1978.
27. *Rantsev v Cyprus and Russia*, App no 25965/04, 7 January 2010, §§ 272–282.
28. Philip Alston, 'Assessing the Strengths and Weaknesses of the European Social Charter's Supervisory System' in Grainne de Burca and Bruno de Witte (eds), *Social Rights in Europe* (OUP 2005) 45.
29. ibid.
30. The mandate is thus larger than that of the UNCAT.
31. See the CPT website <https://www.coe.int/en/web/cpt> accessed 28 June 2023.
32. Open Lecture given by the CPT President Latif Huseynov at the Riga Graduate Law School on 10 November 2014.
33. ibid.
34. Resolution (99) 50 on the Council of Europe.
35. Jonida Mehmetaj, 'The Venice Commission and Its Impact on the Justice System', International Conference on Research in Social Sciences and Humanities (Frankfurt/Main, 24–26 October 2019).

36. Cameron, Iain Thorburn, The Role of the Venice Commission in Strengthening the Rule of Law (July 13, 2020). Rule of Law in the EU: 30 Years After the Fall of the Berlin Wall (Forthcoming), Available at SSRN: https://ssrn.com/abstract=3650021 or http://dx.doi.org/10.2139/ssrn.3650021.
37. See the Commission's activities <https://www.venice.coe.int/WebForms/pages/?p=01_activities&lang=EN#:~:text=These%20principles%20have%20their%20expression,of%20action%20of%20the%20Commission%3A&text=democratic%20institutions%20and%20fundamental%20rights%3B&text=constitutional%20justice%20and%20ordinary%20justice%3B&text=elections%2C%20referendums%20and%20political%20parties> accessed 28 June 2023.
38. CDL-AD(2016)037, Opinion no 865/2016 'On Emergency Decree Laws Nos 667–676 adopted following the failed coup of 15 July 2016' adopted by the Venice Commission at its 109th Plenary Session (Venice, 9–10 December 2016).
39. CDL-AD(2014)044, Opinion no 788/2014 'On The Law On Government Cleansing (Lustration Law) Of Ukraine' adopted by the Venice Commission at its 101st Plenary Session (Venice, 12–13 December 2014).
40. CDL-AD(2017)031, Opinion No 904/2017 'On the Draft Act Amending the Act on the National Council of the Judiciary, on the Draft Act Amending the Act on the Supreme Court proposed by the President of Poland and on the Act on the Organisation of Ordinary Courts' adopted by the Venice Commission at its 113th Plenary Session (Venice, 8–9 December 2017).
41. CDL-AD(2007)028, Opinion No 403/2006 'Judicial Appointments', Report by the Venice Commission adopted at its 70th Plenary Session (Venice, 16–17 March 2007).
42. Adopted by the Venice Commission at its 106th Plenary Session (Venice, 11–12 March 2016) <https://www.venice.coe.int/images/SITE%20IMAGES/Publications/Rule_of_Law_Check_List.pdf> accessed 28 June 2023.
43. Francesca Mauri, 'The Contribution of the Venice Commission to the Strengthening of the Rule of Law in Europe' (Université Côte d'Azur; Università degli studi di Milano 2021).
44. Dmitry Muratov, Prize Presentation (The Nobel Peace Prize 2021, 10 December 2021) <https://www.nobelprize.org/prizes/peace/2021/muratov/prize-presentation/> accessed 28 June 2023.
45. K Dzehtsiarou and D K Coffey, 'Suspension and Expulsion of Members of the Council of Europe: Difficult Decisions in Troubled Times', 68 (2) International and Comparative Law Quarterly 2019, 443–476. doi:10.1017/S0020589319000101.
46. Reykjavík Summit, 4th Summit of Heads of State and Government of the Council of Europe 16–17 May 2023 (Council of Europe, 2023) <https://rm.coe.int/4th-summit-of-heads-of-state-and-government-of-the-council-of-europe/1680ab40c1> accessed 28 June 2023.
47. Andrew Forde, 'Summit of Fire and Ice 4th: Council of Europe Summit, Reykjavík' (31 May 2023) EJIL <https://www.ejiltalk.org/summit-of-fire-and-ice-4th-council-of-europe-summit-reykjavik/> accessed 28 June 2023.

CHAPTER 19

THE OSCE

ANJA MIHR

1. Introduction: OSCE and ODIHR as Soft Power Influencers

The Organization for Security and Cooperation in Europe (OSCE) and its fifty-seven participating States can only agree on politically, not legally, binding commitments. These commitments aspire to maintain and enhance international human rights, security, and peace among its participating States through diplomatic means and consensus-building. Established in 1995 as a successor organization to the CSCE (Conference for Security and Cooperation in Europe) and the Helsinki Accord in 1975, the OSCE inherited several politically binding commitments from the Accord. Firstly, to respond to political and military security concerns among its member States; second, to tackle environmental and economic matters; and thirdly, to strengthen democratic institutions, and uphold human rights and the rule of law. The Helsinki Accord was primarily an agreement between the confrontational powers during the Cold War, principally the United States and the Soviet Union, to reduce tensions over security in Central Europe. Over the years, several accords were signed by all the countries of Europe, recognizing the inviolability of post-World War II frontiers in Europe. The signed agreements had no treaty status but enshrined a list of fundamental freedoms and human rights that were later turned into the Human Dimension and became a fundamental part of the OSCE.

Today, upholding democratic institution building and international human rights law are encompassed in the 'Human Dimension' mechanism. A Warsaw-based OSCE office, called the Office for Democratic Institution Building and Human Rights (ODIHR), is responsible for upholding these dimensions. Its key activities range from awareness raising, training, monitoring, reporting, and advising on international law enforcement within the fifty-seven member States. But ODIHR has no explicit OSCE human rights reference document or treaty to monitor or enforce. It refers to international human rights law (IHRL) instruments, the UN core human rights treaties, and the European Convention for Human Rights (ECHR) of 1949. Of its participating States, forty-six are also members of the Council of Europe (CoE) and party to the ECHR, while all fifty-seven member States are also members of the United Nations (UN) and have mostly ratified the UN human rights treaties. This complementary, overlapping, multi-level human rights governance regime poses significant challenges and disadvantages in terms of promoting IHRL, meaning that it lacks accountability, or available enforcement mechanisms in order to intervene in any violation of international law in its member States. The OSCE has no legal personality and no court, while its activities are limited to informal agreements and commitments. For the most part, the OSCE lacks legal and political accountability because it has no constitutive treaty, either for human rights or for observation missions. ODIHR staff on missions and in action can only be held accountable under OSCE's code of conduct. It is entirely up to the member States, the media, and civil society organizations to use ODIHR reports to confront, name, and blame governmental authorities and those responsible for any violation of IHRL.[1]

Over the years, ODIHR has turned into a monitoring organization. Its missions and reports complement the work of UN Treaty Bodies as well as the ECtHR and other CoE commissions and committees, to oversee State obligations that the participating States owe vis-à-vis international obligations. This makes the OSCE-ODIHR an informal yet hybrid organization in terms of IHRL implementation. In this chapter, I will thus focus on how the OSCE as a soft power organization and intermediating actor monitors and implements IHRL among and between its participating States. I will outline how OSCE and ODIHR use their political mechanism to monitor, report, and implement IHRL across the OSCE regions and present the organization's achievements and shortcomings.

2. A Geopolitical Soft Power Mechanism

All fifty-seven participating States agree on the soft and diplomatic power and intermediating character of the OSCE when highlighting that it 'is vital that obligations under both international humanitarian and human rights law are upheld, and civilians are protected from harm during armed conflicts'.[2] Although ODIHR's primary IHRL reference documents are the ECHR and other CoE treaties and framework conventions, some OSCE participating States do not fall under CoE jurisdiction; these include the US, Russia, Mongolia, and Kazakhstan.[3] Hence, the OSCE uses the ECHR only as a reference document to promote these legal human rights standards using soft measures and diplomacy in reminding its member States to comply with those standards when resolving humanitarian and human rights law related conflicts.

The OSCE's other key institutions and structures, such as the Parliamentary Assembly, the Secretariat, and the Commissioner for National Minorities, refer in the same way to the ECHR, and UN treaty law, as indeed does ODIHR.[4] This gives them a neutral, observatory, and pacifistic role, allowing for moderating between conflicting parties, safeguarding border crossings, helping to hold elections and issue reforms, as well as offering advice and recommendations to State parties when other third parties or international organizations are no longer allowed to enter areas of conflict.[5]

The OSCE's structural and legal limitations have earned it the nickname of a 'toothless tiger'. But its mission representatives are in fact among the most visible when monitoring, resolving conflicts, moderating and defending IHRL vis-à-vis participating States. For this reason, the OSCE has turned into a 'de facto legal personality', as Tabassi paraphrases it. For example, if allowed to enter conflict zones, the OSCE can confront State actors on the ground, which can significantly change policies, laws, and behaviour of the member States.[6]

Despite its huge geographical span from Vladivostok via Ulan Bator, Dushanbe, Ankara, and Tirana to Lisbon, Reykjavik to San Francisco and Vancouver, it is primarily a Eurasian organization having long borders with China, Afghanistan, and Syria. This explains the OSCE's activities in the border region of Central Asia, which are often in turmoil and face violent conflicts, infiltration from outside the OSCE region, and civil wars. Its most influential participating States are the Russian Federation, France, the UK, Germany, Turkey, Kazakhstan, and the US, partly because of their large monetary contribution to the OSCE in terms of membership fees, partly because of their geopolitical locations. Indeed, Russia was the former hegemon of half of today's OSCE member States and heads several sub-regional Eurasian organizations among OSCE participating States.

But it is mostly the smaller States such as Norway and Switzerland that fund extrabudgetary programmes to promote IHRL. They often play a moderating role between Eastern and Western participating States in times of conflict. Switzerland, for example, is the fifth largest donor to the OSCE, placing extrabudgetary activities such as promoting human rights and civil society high on the agenda. Confidence and trust-building training activities among local communities and conflicting parties are vital for the OSCE, its legitimacy and credibility.

After the dramatic geopolitical erosion of IHRL—primarily caused by Russia's annexation of Crimea in 2014 and its military invasion of Ukraine in 2022—the OSCE has been the only regional organization in Europe in which Russia and Ukraine both remain permanent participating members. Their State representatives can still informally talk to each other in the corridors of the OSCE headquarters in Vienna and in Warsaw. This is pivotal for the survival of IHRL and its post-war application and adherence after any conflict. Because of its permanent—albeit limited—observer presence on the ground, the OSCE is becoming the main actor in peace negotiations, as seen in the Western Balkans after the end of the war in Former Yugoslavia in 2001.

3. OSCE's Diversity Effect

ODIHR is a norm promoter, and undertakes capacity-building programmes, training, and transnational exchanges of judges and law enforcement personnel. ODIHR representatives monitor and observe, including observations of trials.[7] The main challenge for the office is to safeguard and implement IHRL in member States that are not party to the ECHR and have not ratified specific core UN human rights treaties. It that case, its legal reference tools are scarce, as is the case for member States who have not ratified the 2006 UN Convention for the Protection of All Persons from Enforced Disappearances. That applies to most Central Asian countries. Due to permanent border conflicts and ethnic clashes, people disappear or undergo torture and enforced evictions in the region. States deny any legal obligation to the OSCE or the UN to investigate these cases, and the OSCE has no mechanism to intervene.[8]

Such diversity and different levels of ratification of IHRL treaties and the fact that each member State has different legal traditions make it hard for ODIHR to refer to only one convention or document. Similarly, in many post-Soviet countries, the legacy of top-down legal practice gives little room for a rule of law binding adaptation of IHRL. Fair and free trials and respect for minority or women's rights are often not realized because 'different legal practices and traditional values' prohibit such implementation of IHRL. This also explains why the OSCE has—thus far—restrained itself from having its own human rights convention, which—even if it were established—would be permanently violated by the practice of its member States. Consensus-building efforts to establish such a legally binding document would have little prospect of success. Only forty-six OSCE participating States are party to the 1950 ECHR and the jurisdiction of the European Court of Human Rights (ECtHR), while twenty-seven are party to the EU Fundamental Rights Charter and those courts with their international jurisdictions. Canada and the US, for example, are engaged in the regional inter-American System for human rights. Former Soviet member States such as Armenia, Kazakhstan, and Russia are now members of the Commonwealth of Independent States (CIS) and have their regional human rights convention. Despite their membership in the OSCE and UN, they all follow different legal traditions and adhere to other international legal frameworks, too.

Even though the ECHR is the prime guiding IHRL treaty for the OSCE, others also apply when OSCE monitors compliance in the field. In addition, a plethora of Memoranda of Understandings (MoU) exists between the OSCE, the CoE, and the European Union (EU), for example, that allow for the OSCE to draw attention to their norms and standards when monitoring human rights compliance. For instance, the CoE and OSCE MoU of 2012 underlines that:

> especially the [OSCE's] human dimension overlaps with the work of the Council, since it aims to ensure full respect for human rights and fundamental freedoms;

> to abide by the rule of law; to promote the principles of democracy by building, strengthening and protecting democratic institutions; and to promote tolerance throughout the OSCE region.[9]

The MoU enhance and manifest institutional collaboration, mutual memberships, and consultations on institutional levels. They do not, however, imply mutual acceptance of legal norms or laws between member States, for example, between CIS and EU countries.

In this vein, other regional organizations such as the EU call the OSCE the 'Pillar of the European Security Order', because of its collaborative agreements, for example in the field of democratic institution building and support for its Election Observation Missions (EOMs). The OSCE Representative on Freedom of the Media, and the High Commissioner on National Minorities are vital for peace and security in Eurasia, but are most effective when collaborating with other regional organizations on the ground.[10] In fact, the EU co-finances most OSCE field missions. ODIHR's soft law and soft power approach to human rights should enhance:

> respect for all human rights and fundamental freedoms, the development of human contacts and the resolution of other issues of a related humanitarian character, … by international human rights standards, their political, social, economic and cultural systems. In exercising this right, they will ensure that their laws, regulations, practices, and policies conform with their obligations under international law and are brought into harmony with the provisions of the Declaration on Principles and other CSCE commitments.[11]

No more, no less.

ODIHR's geographical stretch and collaboration with participating States and other organizations, such as the UN, the EU, and CIS, in terms of EOMs to build and strengthen democratic institutions through international election laws and standards, has increased massively since the early 1990s.[12] In thirty years, ODIHR conducted over 400 EOMs in the OSCE participating States, often in collaboration with EU institutions and according to EU election laws and standards. ODIHR also refers to the 2007 Convention for Democratic Election by the CIS, and standards set by the Council of Europe's Venice Commission, stating that the:

> importance of the Universal Declaration of Human Rights and the International Covenant on Civil and Political Rights, which have established that empowerment to rule should rely on the nation's will expressed in authentic and periodical elections, as well as of documents of the Organization for Security and Co-operation in Europe, of the Council of Europe and other international organizations on conducting free and fair elections . . . .[13]

But legal mechanisms to hold CIS countries accountable for electoral fraud or violation of electoral standards are absent. Only those participating States that are also members of the CoE or the EU can be held legally accountable. ODIHR is not equipped to intervene in electoral fraud. But even for members such as Hungary and Poland, which are members of the EU and the CoE, the organization cannot stop them from democratic backsliding and violating the rule of law. That said, however, ODIHR reports on these cases can be used by other CoE or EU bodies to confront these members about their backsliding tendencies. Therefore, the main OSCE-ODIHR caveat is that it lacks a legal framework and personality which would allow it to hold its participating States accountable for any misconduct or violation of IHRL. And so far, none of the participating States has ever faced severe consequences from the OSCE for any of its violations of IHRL, such as being expelled from ODIHR meetings or paying penalties.

It could be argued that accountability measures, such as a court of arbitration, would make the organization more credible but at the same time would also turn it into a potential competitor with the Strasbourg ECtHR and the European Court of Justice (ECJ) in Luxemburg. Its member States would also compete with each other, unless a potential human rights treaty orchestrated by the OSCE adds any value and nuances to existing legal frameworks by the CoE or the UN.[14] Whereas the CoE, for example, focuses on law enforcement personnel and legal reforms approved by national parliaments to meet ECHR standards, the EU has direct jurisdiction over its member States' compliance with EU Charter law. Therefore, the EU also promotes Charter awareness by financing ODIHR training and capacity-building programmes outside the EU, so that EU member States do not see the need for a third regional human rights convention on the continent (see Majkowska-Szulc and Karolina Wierczyńska, this volume).

Jóźwicki and Kędzia illustrate how political interactions between the EU, the CoE, and the OSCE on different, mostly informal-level work, through co-financing monitoring operations, for example, give the OSCE legitimacy and credibility on the ground. Informal agreements, MoU, and mutual participation between the OSCE, the CoE, and the EU entangle them even more strongly.[15] In this way, the OSCE has turned into a quasi-hybrid or multi-level organization promoting IHRL in fifty-seven participating States. Nevertheless, the closer the CoE, the EU, and the OSCE work together, the more exclusive they become vis-à-vis non-EU and CoE countries, such as CIS countries and new member States like Mongolia. Upholding coherence among the OSCE States becomes more problematic. To avoid exclusiveness and cleavages between Western European and CIS States within the OSCE and thus *de facto* two different levels and pace of compliance towards human rights, the CoE and the CIS countries need to find cooperative alliances—the more so after Russia left the CoE in 2022. And if that were already not challenging enough, in the CIS countries overall in Central Asia, anti-Western propaganda is deepening, along with norm violation.[16] OSCE's weakness as a soft law 'norm-creator'[17] is increasing because of the dramatic political and legal divide among its participating States.[18]

4. ODIHR's Human Dimension

Once a year, ODIHR holds its Human Dimension Implementation Meetings (HDIMs) at its headquarters in Warsaw for all its fifty-seven participating States to report their human rights and democratic achievements, improvements, misconduct, or failures during the past year. In 2020 the meeting was cancelled because of the Covid pandemic, and again in 2021 after Russia vetoed the conference, accusing the Western States of political bias. In 2022, it was not even on the agenda since the OSCE was already torn apart over Russia's aggression in Ukraine. In 2022, its only aim was not to fall apart and keep the organization's momentum going as much as possible. Even diplomatic confrontations between its members were strictly avoided. However, in July 2022 it launched a vital report on 'violations of international humanitarian and human rights law, war crimes and crimes against humanity committed in Ukraine'. The report had the sole purpose of providing other international and European actors, organizations and member States, and the UN with the opportunity to use the report for further follow-up and potential international legal investigations and potential war crimes trials.[19]

But even before 2022, the political and personal tensions among representatives in the meeting rooms and corridors in Warsaw have often undermined the collaborative and consensus-building purpose and ultimately the confidence-building purpose of ODIHR,[20] in particular that of the informal and political arrangement towards peace and security in Eurasia, namely the 1992-established Minsk Group. This was first set up to coordinate activities to find a peaceful solution to the Nagorno-Karabakh conflict between Armenia and Azerbaijan that lasted until 1994 and has re-emerged many times since. Yet, after Russia annexed Crimea and the conflict in Donbas (Ukraine) escalated in 2014, this group established a crisis response mechanism under the Minsk Agreement to monitor the security and IHRL situation in Donbas. But neither of the participating States involved complied with the agreement or led by example. This ultimately led to the war in Ukraine starting in 2022. Mackiewicz argues that the lack of permanent and independent human rights officers or rapporteurs who could have monitored IHRL compliance on both sides and reported to the HDM was partly responsible for escalation in 2022.[21] But any such direct intervention in conflict has thus far never been part of any mandate.[22] Even during the plethora of anti-terrorism training in Uzbekistan, rule of law training in Mongolia, border control and monitoring missions in Georgia and Ukraine, peacebuilding training in Armenia, law enforcement training in Albania, and Special Missions to Kosovo or Bosnia Herzegovina and EOMs, the OSCE kept to its non-interference clause.[23]

Nevertheless, on many occasions, the OSCE's soft power strength shows when its field operations reports are published and cited during UN Human Rights Council meetings or at CoE parliamentary assemblies. For instance, for years, during the HDIMs in Warsaw, Tajikistan's delegates were confronted with allegations of severe human rights violations, such as torture, disappearances, and suppression of political and religious groups. During these meetings, ODIHR referred to the UN Universal Periodic Review (UPR) process and its reports on Tajikistan. And in response the UN Human Rights monitoring and treaty bodies referred to the ODIHR report on these matters. Points of concern were upholding religious freedom rights and branding Islamic groups and parties as terrorist organizations without public trial or hearing.[24] Then, ahead of the OSCE conference in Warsaw in 2015, Tajikistan pushed back on less-than-favourable assessments of its human rights compliance when the ambassador rejected any recommendations before and during the meeting, indicating that free press and other political freedoms and fundamental rights enshrined both in the UN treaties and in the ECHR would shortly be introduced in Tajikistan.[25] This was not an unusual manner for participating States to respond to allegations of violations of IHRL before HDIMs.

But despite the HDIM's incentivizing effects, such as increasing transparency over human rights (non-)compliance on the ground, the HDIMs have become a friction point of frustration for some governments and civil society representatives and were *de facto* suspended over recent years. As the case of Tajikistan illustrates, some diplomats felt 'trapped' when confronted with criticisms and assailed by accusations from civil society representatives in the meeting room. The meetings have been accused of being 'led by Western values and standards only' to which representatives from authoritarian States, predominantly CIS States, could not respond properly. For this and other reasons, in 2021, Russia blocked the meeting from taking place, fearing ODIHR criticisms of its electoral process and upcoming Duma elections that year, which turned out to be in violation of CIS electoral laws and IHRL.[26] This blockade and *de facto* dissolution of the HDIM and Russia's subsequent withdrawal from the Council of Europe and the ECHR in 2022 led to the deepest fragmentation that OSCE has so far experienced.

The fact that these meetings depend on consensus among all participating States is often seen as their main weakness. But the fact that ODIHR is often the only player (left) in a region to deliver reliable data on violations of human rights remains its strongest asset in times of 'fake news' over contested territorial disputes and random counter-terrorism measures. Wouters adds that OSCE's lack of democratic accountability can only be compensated by the transparency and credibility of its actions, such as the HDIM.[27] Thus, if the HDIM is permanently abandoned, a reliable source of human rights situations and violations in a quarter of all the world's countries ceases to exist, and the century-grown method of 'naming and shaming' comes to an end in the OSCE region if governments ignore, boycott, falsify, block, or otherwise undermine ODIHRs efforts and decisions because they fear legal or other direct repercussions.[28]

The fragmentation of the OSCE resulted from a chain of events cumulating over the years and dividing Eurasia and the OSCE into two opposing sides, not least over different interpretation and implementation of IHRL. One group of member States emphasizes 'Western norms', democratic institution building, and human rights more than ever. The other group, mostly CIS countries, is led predominantly by anti-democratic and nationalistic rhetoric, with its leaders calling upon the issue of so-called traditional values and norms. Today, this divide within the OSCE region also reflects the global divide in the New Cold War era between autocracies and democracies, most strongly seen in the OSCE region and among those countries in the East that rely heavily on China and Russia, and those in the West moving closer to the EU and even with NATO as a security actor.

For its part, the government of the Russian Federation instead stresses the principle of the obligation not to strengthen security at the expense of the security of other States, and therefore condemns the expansion of NATO within the OSCE as a security actor.[29] It seems likely that the OSCE will only survive this severe violation of IHRL and takeover by other actors in the region if it reforms itself. Long-time OSCE observer, Bloed, commented a day after the Russian aggression against Ukraine on 24 February 2022 that 'IHRL and security ... has been fatally affected to the extent that it could mean the end of it'.[30] Since Russia's war against Georgia over Abkhazia and South Ossetia in 2008, and the annexation of Crimea in 2014, the CIS countries—of which none has ever officially condemned Russia's aggressions—have been slowly drifting away from European-friendly norms and legal practices, while others in Central and South Eastern Europe have been drawn towards the EU.[31] Instead, many CIS governments joined Russia's strike against IHRL even before 2014; branding human rights promotion such as gender equality, gay and lesbian and other minority rights, as 'non-traditional', and not compatible with their legal and political culture.[32]

This prevailing post-Soviet legacy in Eastern Europe and Central Asia, paired with failed political and legal reforms, not only led many CIS countries to violate the rule of law IHRL, but even 'traditionalize' their constitutions, penal codes, and legal practices in the same way as the Russian Federation maintained from the Soviet period. Wars and civil unrest were often ongoing in CIS countries, such as Tajikistan, between 1991 and 1997, or every so often these States turn violent against each other in the Ferghana Valley between Tajikistan, Uzbekistan, and Kyrgyzstan. Since 1991, most of them have been trapped in permanent conflicts over territorial issues and self-determination, and with direct military involvement by Russia for separatists in these regions, as indeed the example of Abkhazia and Ossetia in Georgia in the years up to 2008 clearly illustrates. These disputes and conflicts have justified martial law and anti-terror measures in these participating States, which in turn has seriously undermined IHRL, and often OSCE representatives are only allowed to remain in the conflict zones as observers.

For OSCE field missions in Central Asia, one way of adapting to permanent political tensions was to conduct transnational meetings to allow for national law-makers to harmonize, modernize, and adapt national penal codes and procedures according to IHRL—if the political situation allowed it.[33] But OSCE's efforts and joint responsibilities, in terms of territorial integrity, peace, and security, are at stake, partly due to its weak mandate and lack of resources, but most of all due to governments' lack of political will to strengthen democratic institutions in the first place.[34] Many of these CIS countries depend heavily on Russia as a former hegemon for their security matters, and therefore cannot introduce any significant legal reforms without the consent of the Moscow government.[35]

5. OSCE Peace and Security Policies

The downward spiral of IHRL violations dramatically affects the soft power and informal approach of some participating States and erodes the ODIHR in the same way. It has, at the same time, given its representatives access to situations in the furthest corners of the region, observing and reporting on the violent conflicts in the Pamir Mountains in Tajikistan, into the territories of Abkhazia, and moderating among ethnic rivalries in Albania. The OSCE is often the only actor left in a conflict region that gets access to villages, prisons, border checkpoints, and disputed territory. For example, OSCE mediators, diplomats, and special envoys talk to warlords and tribal leaders, help to reallocate displaced people in Armenia, introduce gender rights in enclaves in Tajikistan, run border crossing points between Uzbekistan and Kyrgyzstan, and support governmental activities in the State of Kosovo.[36]

It is one thing whether the OSCE withdraws from a mission since it can no longer meet its standards, as in the case of the declined EOM in Russia in 2021, but quite another when it unsuccessfully attempts to ease a conflict situation but must withdraw for security reasons, such as in the Donbas in 2022.

Another controversial matter is whether OSCE missions have, over the years, often taken up governmental tasks but without any enforcing instruments or a clear mandate, such as in Kosovo. The CSCE 1990 Copenhagen document leaves little doubt about how the organization should operate. It states that the 'full range of human rights, democracy and the rule of law' tools and means must be applied to enhance peace and security.[37] Although it focuses on conflict prevention through inter-state conflict resolution mechanisms such as the Minsk Group, it understands that this cannot be achieved without building solid democratic institutions and the rule of law in its participating States—and hence it not only recommends building and monitors institutions but also enforces democratic institution building, for example, when OSCE officials nominate judges or prepare for elections. This makes States more dependent and the OSCE more biased and may jeopardize its neutral character.[38]

A similar trap for OSCE missions can be seen in the cases of the non-recognized territories of South Ossetia and Abkhazia (Georgia) and Transdnistria (Moldova). Gawrich argues that diplomatic and informal efforts by the OSCE, together with the CoE—of which Georgia and Moldova are members—had come to an end in 2020 due to a lack of accountability and compliance with agreed norms by both governments. The parliamentary assemblies of the OSCE and the CoE had, since the early 2000s, aimed to reach a confidence-building mechanism in both countries. But territorial disputes increased and the soft power of the OSCE vanished, turning the regions into 'frozen' secessionist conflicts.[39] Instead, the former regional hegemon, Russia, re-emerged yet again, to secure peace or at least ceasefires for the time being.

But due to a lack of economic and political incentives by the 'West', principally by the EU, the OSCE did not have the leverage to negotiate and keep the territories as an integrated part of Georgia and Moldova. Russia saw the opportunity to act as a unilateral peacemaker in the area and resume its hegemonic control while widely blocking any further OSCE initiatives in these regions and other CIS countries.[40] As one of the consequences, violent and deadly disputes occurred, so that thousands have to be evacuated and resettled every year, for example, in the Ferghana Valley, starting with deadly clashes between Uzbek and Kyrgyz clans in 2010 in Kyrgyzstan. The OSCE was sending observers and rapporteurs, which were later followed up by UN missions.[41] The region has been a tension triangle for decades, with intensified human rights violations at the very periphery of the OSCE.[42] Nevertheless, it has been one of the regions with the strongest OSCE presence, including the fact that the participating States in Central Asia border with Afghanistan and are under constant threat from their neighbours.[43] Money laundering, human and drug trafficking (80 per cent of the world market), organized crime and bribery of politicians and security guards have become chronic and cannot be resolved through capacity-building programmes or by a handful of OSCE observers on a mission.[44] This and other violent ongoing crises within the OSCE regions emphasize the urgent need for political and legal reforms if the organization wants to survive.[45]

6. OSCE's Informal and Pacifying Impact

The informal and pacifying character of the OSCE started with its long-term mission to former Yugoslavian countries in the Western Balkans. In particular, its missions to Bosnia and Herzegovina and Croatia as early as 1995 were the first stress tests for young organizations aiming to fulfil the principles laid out in the OSCE Copenhagen Agreement in 1990. At that time, OSCE membership required significant statehood reorganization as well as political (democratic) and legal reforms in line with IHRLs. For many new participating States, that meant building democratic institutions from scratch, such as in Kosovo.[46] It was in this way that the informal and rather pacifying character of the OSCE was shaped. This informal method to help participating States reform and consolidate their democratic institutions turned 'informality' into the way to be for the OSCE. For example, the 1995 UN Dayton Peace Agreement for Bosnia and Herzegovina[47] mandated the OSCE and other international actors to monitor the peace agreement and process, even if that meant taking up governmental tasks in the country—without any formal legitimation. The OSCE installed and built a unique structure of transitional administration to install institutions. The OSCE was explicitly entrusted with various tasks to democratize the country, such as the smooth running of the first elections and the training of lawyers.[48] The country became a quasi-protectorate of the OSCE. To introduce necessary legal reforms, the heads of the OSCE Mission drew for the first time on ECHR standards and UN treaties, asking the Bosnian government to introduce them into their national legislation. The OSCE even appointed judges and prosecutors, an intervention that came close to interfering in State sovereignty. The OSCE even referred criminal cases from the region to the International Criminal Tribunal for the Former Yugoslavia (ICTY) in The Hague, with which the organization collaborated closely. This gave the OSCE in Bosnia-Herzegovina and later in Kosovo in 1999 an interventionist—albeit informal—flavour, replacing *de facto* governmental duties without the possibility to be held accountable for its actions inside these countries. Instead, in most post-Yugoslavian countries, contestation of European ideas and IHRL has not been much of an issue during OSCE missions and operations, primarily because they were desperately seeking membership in the CoE with the incentive to later qualify to become members of the EU.[49] To take that path, the new States and governments in the Western Balkans had first to become diligent members of the OSCE, and comply with its standards before filling in a membership application to the CoE, let alone to the EU. This has changed over recent years for Serbia, which has turned its back on the OSCE and the CoE and allies itself more with Russia, joining its anti-democratic and anti-human rights rhetoric.

These cases illustrate that even though almost all countries emerging out of the Cold War and the Soviet Union's grip have signed and ratified most of the core UN treaties, and even completed UN Universal Periodic Review (UPR) cycles after joining the UN Human Rights Council, they have still not fully embraced IHRL norms and practices.[50] Firstly, many post-Soviet countries are still bound to old penal codes as well as Soviet hierarchical traditions and legal education systems. Golkovo has called these Soviet legacies a 'fundamental deformation' of legal systems prohibiting practical adaptation of IHRL into domestic jurisdiction and counteracting OSCE informal and promotional work to install IHRL in domestic legislation. Secondly, law-makers lack the confidence to emancipate themselves from Soviet penal codes and legal practices and move to modern, international ones. The Soviet penal system is primarily based on punishment, fear, and intimidation, not on amends, rehabilitation, and remorse. Constitutional reforms do not automatically turn into the transformation of penal codes and criminal law, let alone practice. It not only requires, as Golkovo phrases it, a 'long-term plan of legislative measures but also long-lasting doctrinal and educational efforts' that subsequently enhance the enforcement of IHRL.[51] The Soviet legal and political heritage, for example in Central Asian countries, has not only slowed down the process of democratic transition and transformation, but instead (re-)produced dysfunctional, corrupt, and authoritarian regimes, which became an obstacle for OSCE pacifying methods. In 2011, the Kyrgyz government even degraded the OSCE mission offices to the Program Offices after the OSCE and UN expressed open criticism of how the government dealt with the trials of ethnic minorities after violent clashes in the Ferghana Valley in 2010 that left hundreds of dead and injured.[52]

For CIS countries to adapt to IHRL practices, Sayapin sees the most effective way only in a new generation of law-makers and members of law enforcement agencies to overcome Soviet legal traditions and heritage. Only they can seriously institutionalize

IHRL into new policies, because it would require a paradigm shift towards a more constructive, realistic, and practical understanding of the phenomenology of international law, to which senior law-makers, educated under the Soviet regime, are not willing to adhere.[53] The Council of Europe's Venice Commission, together with the EU, started a new Central Asia Rule of Law Programme in 2020 until 2023, aiming to reinforce human rights, the rule of law, and democracy in Central Asian partner countries following European and other IHRL standards. The Venice Commission—a close ally of the OSCE in the region—is aiding reform processes and fostering a demand-driven approach that would benefit from the CoE's expertise in implementing IHRL.[54]

7. Conclusion: Challenges to the Soft Power Influence of OSCE and ODIHR

Efforts by the OSCE and ODIHR in promoting and enhancing IHRL among its fifty-seven participating States have undergone paradigm shifts since 1995, firstly during missions in former Yugoslavia and secondly after 2014, when one of its founding members, the Russian Federation, annexed Crimea. These situations have together shaped both the current policies and fragmentation of the OSCE. Over the past thirty years the OSCE has become an informal and pacifying organization focusing on capacity building, awareness, and reporting mechanisms. However, these can only safeguard or enforce IHRL norm compliance through close collaboration with other international organizations and governments in its areas of operation.

Whilst western European countries have become closer allies with the OSCE, CIS States have been drifting increasingly apart from the OSCE, highlighting 'traditional and anti-western values, norms and standards'; even though in light of the tightening grip of Russia in Central and Eastern Europe and Central Asia, in 2012, the OSCE and the CoE intensified their collaboration, emphasizing the complementary role of both organizations in IHRL promotion. In its statement, the CoE stressed that the field presence of the OSCE, predominantly in the member States that are not members of the EU it is important in building national capacity for the implementation of the standards. On the other hand, the legal standards of the Council of Europe have the advantage of being subject to formal monitoring and dispute settlement through judgments by the Court. In addition, the Venice Commission provides expert advice to be used by all organizations, letting EU, CoE, and OSCE merge closer together.[55] Although the OSCE-ODIHR, together with the EU and the CoE, have intensified their efforts to promote European legal provisions and best practices, such as the ECHR and the EU Fundamental Rights Charter, in the CIS countries the OSCE has been facing significant resistance by law-makers among those States, which has eventually led to fragmentation of the organization.

Notes

1. Nathalie Ebead and Thomas Vennen, 'Rechtsstaatsförderung durch die OSZE' in M Kötter et al (eds), *Rechtsstaatsförderung, Handbuch für Forschung und Praxis*, Rechtswissenschaften und Verwaltung (Kohlammer 2022) 21–127.
2. OSCE, 'Preventing violations of international humanitarian law and protecting civilians require closer cooperation', 28 March 2022, Vienna/Warsaw, Press Release <https://www.osce.org/odihr/514789> accessed January 2023.
3. The Russian Federation, as the 47th member, left the Council of Europe in March 2022.
4. Most of the OSCE'S fifty-seven participating States have signed and ratified the UN core human rights treaties and are members of the UN, see UN Office of the High Commissioner for Human Rights <https://www.ohchr.org/en/what-are-human-rights/international-bill-human-rights>. Of these, forty-six are members of the Council of Europe and party to the 1949 European Convention for Human Rights and Fundamental Freedoms <https://www.echr.coe.int/Pages/home.aspx?p=basictexts&c>.
5. On 1 January 1995, it emerged from the Conference on Security and Cooperation in Europe (CSCE), which was founded twenty years earlier at the height of the Cold War, on 1 August 1975 after the Helsinki Final Act and Accords had been signed.
6. Lisa Tabassi, 'The Role of the Organization in Asserting Legal Personality. The Position of the OSCE Secretariat on the OSCE's Legal Status' in M Steinbrück Platise, C Moser, and A Peters (eds), *The Legal Framework of the OSCE* (CUP 2019) 48–81.
7. Ebead and Vennen (n 2).
8. FIDH, Resolution to end impunity and enforced disappearances of citizens in Central Asian countries, 2019 https://www.fidh.org/en/region/europe-central-asia/turkmenistan/resolution-to-end-impunity-and-enforced-disappearances-of-citizens-in> accessed 10 September 2022.
9. eg Council of Europe, 2012, Directorate of Policy Planning, September 2012, 'The Council of Europe and the OSCE: Enhancing Co-operation and Complementarity through Greater Coherence' (Strasbourg) para 3.
10. European Parliament, 2021, 'The Organization for Security and Co-operation in Europe (OSCE), A pillar of the European security order', Briefing European Parliament Research Service (Brussels).
11. CSCE-OSCE, 1990, Copenhagen Document of the Copenhagen Meeting of the Conference on the Human Dimension of the CSCE, 29 June 1990.
12. Rick Fawn, 'European-Central Asian International Election Observation Cooperation' in Mihr and Hasan (eds), *Europe-Central Asia Relations—A New Connectivity Framework* (Palgrave 2023) 32–67.
13. Council of Europe, Venice Commissions, Opinion No 399/2006 'European Commission for Democracy Convention and the Standard of Democratic Elections, Electoral Rights and Freedoms in the Member States of the Commonwealth of Independent States' (Strasbourg, 22 January 2007).
14. Catherine Barnard (ed), *European Union Law* (3rd edn, OUP 2020).
15. Wolfgang Zellner, 'Adapting to a Changed World: The CSCE/OSCE in 1990 and Today' in IFSH (ed), *OSCE Yearbook 2018*, No 24 (Nomos 2019) 53–78.
16. Jakub Jaraczewski, Wladyslaw Jóźwicki, and Kędzia Zdzislaw, 'The EU's Engagement with the Council of Europe and the OSCE on Human Rights' in Jan Wouters et al (eds),

The European Union and Human Rights: Law and Policy (Oxford Scholarship Online: February 2021).

17. Eric Manton, 'The OSCE Human Dimension Process and the Process of Customary International Law Formation' in IFSH (ed), *OSCE Yearbook 2004*, No 11 (Nomos 2005) 1–20.
18. Olivia Herman and Jan Wouters, 'The OSCE as a Case of Informal International Lawmaking?' in M Steinbrück-Platise, C Moser, and A Peters (eds), *The Legal Framework of the OSCE* (CUP 2019) 241–272; Tanja Börzel and Ingo Take, '"It's Politics, Stupid": An International Relations Perspective and Strengthening the Legal Framework of the OSCE' in M Steinbrück-Platise, C Moser, and A Peters (eds), *The Legal Frameworks of the OSCE* (CUP 2019) 95–118.
19. OSCE, 'Report on Violations of International Humanitarian and Human Rights Law, War Crimes and Crimes against Humanity, Committed in Ukraine, 1 April–25 June 2022' (Warsaw, 11 July 2022).
20. Georg Nolte, 'The Contribution of the ECtHR to the Development of Public International Law, The European Court of Human Rights and the Sources of International Law', Seminar, Ministry of Foreign Affairs of the Czech Republic in connection with the 59th Meeting of CAHDI, Prague (23 September 2020).
21. Lukasz Mackiewicz, 'More than Countering Ceasefire Violations—The Human Dimension within the OSCE Special Monitoring Mission to Ukraine' in ISFH (ed), *OSCE Yearbook 2018*, No 24 (Nomos 2019) 181–192.
22. Thomas Greminger, 'Sustaining Peace, Sustaining Development—The Role of the OSCE' in ISFH (ed), *OSCE Yearbook 2019*, No 25 (Nomos 2020) 27–39.
23. See OSCE, What we do <https://www.osce.org/what-we-do>.
24. Dastan Aleef, 'Identity and Power—The Discursive Transformation of the Former Islamic Revival Party of Tajikistan' in A Mihr (ed), *Between Peace and Conflict in the East and the West* (Springer 2021) 175–193, <https://doi.org/10.1007/978-3-030-77489-9_9> accessed December 2022.
25. UN GA-Doc A/HRC/33/11, Human Rights Council Thirty-third Session Agenda item 6, Universal periodic review, Report of the Working Group on the Universal Periodic Review—Tajikistan (14 July 2016).
26. Civic Solidarity Platform Europe, 'Russia is Blocking Europe's Largest Human Rights Conference' (27 September 2021) <https://civicsolidarity.org/article/1828/russia-blocking-europes-largest-human-rights-conference> accessed December 2022.
27. Olivia Herman and Jan Wouters, 'The OSCE as a Case of Informal International Lawmaking?' in M Steinbrück-Platise, C Moser, and A Peters (eds), *The Legal Framework of the OSCE* (CUP 2019) 268.
28. Carolyn Moser, 'Conceptualizing Accountability in the Legal and Institutional Framework of the OSCE' in M Steinbrück-Platise, C Moser, and A Peters (eds), *The Legal Framework of the OSCE* (CUP 2019) 273–330.
29. Alexander Graef and Ukrich Kuehn, 'A Letter from Moscow: (In)divisible Security and Helsinki 2.0', Commentary, Texas National Security Review (14 February 2022) <https://warontherocks.com/2022/02/a-letter-from-moscow-indivisible-security-and-helsinki-2-0/> accessed 10 September 2022.
30. Arie Bloed, 'Is this the death of the OSCE Decalogue', Security and Human Rights Monitor (25 February 2022) <https://www.shrmonitor.org/is-this-the-death-of-the-osce-decalogue/> accessed December 2022.

31. CIS member States: Azerbaijan, Armenia, Belarus, Kazakhstan, Kyrgyzstan, Moldova, Tajikistan, Turkmenistan, and Uzbekistan. Ukraine left the CIS in 2022 due to the Russian war of aggression on its territory.
32. Dimitri Bartemev, 'LGBT Rights in Russia and the European Human Rights Standards' in L Malksoo and W Benedek (eds), *Russia and the European Court of Human Rights* (CUP 2017) 326.
33. Ebead and Vennen (n 2).
34. Bloed (n 31).
35. Francesco Marchesano, 'Election Observation as a Point of Contention between the Russian Federation and ODIHR' in IFSH (ed), *OSCE Yearbook 2014* (Nomos 2015) 263–274.
36. Claudio Formisano and Georgia Tasiopoulou, 'The OSCE Mission in Kosovo: A Performance Appraisal Yesterday, Today, and Tomorrow: A Play in Three Acts' in IFSH (ed), *OSCE Yearbook 2011* (Nomos 2012) 127–135.
37. Conference for Security and Cooperation (CSCE) Copenhagen Document of the Copenhagen Meeting of the Conference on the Human Dimension of the CSCE, 29 June 1990.
38. Frederic Oberson, 'OSCE Special Monitoring in Ukraine' in Mihr (ed), *Between Peace and Conflict in the East and the West* (Springer 2021) 47–76. Cham. <https://doi.org/10.1007/978-3-030-77489-9_3>.
39. Andrea Gawrich, 'Conflict Management, International Parliamentary Assemblies and Small States: The Cases of Georgia and Moldova' in A Mihr (ed), *Between Peace and Conflict in the East and the West* (Springer 2021) 3–32. Cham. <https://doi.org/10.1007/978-3-030-77489-9> accessed December 2022.
40. Tim Epkenhans, 'The OSCE's Dilemma in Central Asia' in IFSH (ed), *OSCE Yearbook 2006* (Nomos 2007) 211–222. See also: Conflict Prevention Center, ODIHR, the Representative on Freedom of the Media, the Transnational Threats Department, and the Programme Office in Bishkek, Tashkent, and Dushanbe in 2021.
41. OSCE, Annual Report on OSCE Activities 2010, The Secretary General Organization for Security and Co-operation in Europe (Vienna 2011).
42. Anja Mihr, 'Human Rights in Central Asian States and European Initiatives' in A Mihr and K Hasan (eds), *Europe-Central Asia Relations—A New Connectivity Framework* (Palgrave 2023) 106–134.
43. Anastasiya Bayok, Frank Evers, and Stefan Wolff, 'The OSCE's Afghanistan Challenge, The Foreign Policy Center' (8 September 2021) <https://fpc.org.uk/the-osces-afghanistan-challenge/> accessed December 2022.
44. Sharibek Juraev and Eric McGlinchey, 'What Drives Border Conflicts in Central Asia? Roots of the Deadly Violence on the Kyrgyz-Tajik Border' (Ponars, January 2022) <https://www.ponarseurasia.org/what-drives-border-conflicts-in-central-asia-roots-of-the-deadly-violence-on-the-kyrgyz-tajik-border/> accessed December 2022.
45. Niels Blokker and Rameses Wessel, 'Revisiting Questions of Organisationhood, Legal Personality and Membership in the OSCE' in M Steinbrück Platise, C Moser, and A Peters (eds), *The Legal Framework of the OSCE* (CUP 2019) 135–164.
46. Solveig Richter, 'Wie effektiv fördert die OSZE Demokratie? Ein analytischer Streifzug zur Wirkung der Langzeitmissionen in Suedosteuropa' in IFSH (ed), *OSZE Jahrbuch 2008* (Nomos 2009) 211–228.

47. UN Doc, General Framework Agreement for Peace in Bosnia and Herzegovina (Dayton Agreement) 1995, General Assembly Security Council, Fiftieth session Fiftieth year, Agenda item 28, The Situation in Bosnia and Herzegovina <https://peacemaker.un.org/bosniadaytonagreement95>.
48. The General Framework Agreement for Peace in Bosnia and Herzegovina. Initialled in Dayton on 21 November 1996 and signed in Paris on 14 December 1995 <https://www.osce.org/mission-to-bosnia-and-herzegovina> in IFSH (ed), *OSCE Yearbook 2008* (Baden-Baden 2009) 211–228.
49. Martina Huber, 'The Effectiveness of OSCE Missions: Synthesis Report' in Martina Huber et al (eds), *The Effectiveness of OSCE Missions: The Cases of Uzbekistan, Ukraine and Bosnia and Herzegovina* (Den Haag 2002) 13–38.
50. Since the establishment of the UN Human Rights Council in 2006, the following post-Soviet Central Asian and Caucasus countries have become elected members to the Council: Armenia, Azerbaijan, Georgia, Kyrgyzstan, Kazakhstan, Mongolia, and Uzbekistan.
51. Leonid Golkovo, 'The Space for Legal Reform in Central Asia: Between Political Limits and Theoretical Deformations' in IFSH (ed), *OSCE Yearbook 2010* (Nomos 2011) 105–115.
52. UNRCCA, 2010, 22 Nov 2010, Statement by UN, OSCE and EU Special Envoys on the situation in Kyrgyzstan <https://unrcca.unmissions.org/statement-un-osce-and-eu-special-envoys-situation-kyrgyzstan-1> accessed December 2022.
53. Sergey Sayapin, 'The Post-Soviet Central Asia and International Law: Practice, Research and Teaching' in Seokwoo Lee (ed), *Encyclopedia of Public International Law in Asia* (Brill 2020) 1–4.
54. See <https://pjp-eu.coe.int/en/web/central-asia> accessed December 2022.
55. Council of Europe, Directorate of Policy Planning, 'The Council of Europe and the OSCE: Enhancing Co-Operation and Complementary through Greater Coherence', by Geir Ulfstein, University of Oslo, Strasbourg (2012) 8.

CHAPTER 20

THE EUROPEAN UNION

Silent Superpower or Noah's Ark

JOHANN JUSTUS VASEL

1. Introduction—The EU and Its Uncertain Nature in a Nutshell

2022 marked the 70th anniversary of the European Union (EU), which everyone knows, yet nobody really knows what exactly it is. Born out of the unparalleled atrocities of World War II and the alleged decline of the nation-state,[1] the core idea was to secure peace through prosperity and prosperity through peace.[2] To this end, State sovereignty and nationalism pictured as the cause of war and bloodshed needed to be deconstructed,[3] or 'shared'[4] and replaced by 'governance without a center'.[5] Initially, the predominant concept was (neo)functionalism: economic integration would cause spillover effects and lead to political integration. Accordingly, the European project—or rather the process—in its early stages is typically described as political through economic integration,[6] which entails power-diffusion to form 'an ever-closer Union' among the Member States. First, a single market, later a single currency, and even a single army were envisioned, reflecting the deconstruction of national symbols as well as a new form of 'supranational' integration. Yet, the underlying and fundamental cultures behind the nation and the State (and ultimately law itself)[7] were meant to be preserved. The aspiration was a Europe made of and in plurality and diversity. Hence, *in varietate concordia* (united in diversity) became the official motto of the EU. Enlargement—from originally six Member States to twenty-eight (post-Brexit, twenty-seven)—and deepening—from import restrictions to artificial intelligence (AI) regulation and a banking Union—developed asymmetrically in profundity and speed. This *Ungleichzeitigkeit*[8]—in EU terms known as *differentiated integration* and *géométrie variable*[9]—added tensions and fissures but also allowed flexibility and dynamism. The foundational *trias* of prosperity, peace, and pluralism later became galvanized by an aim to promote universal values such as human rights or the rule of law. Therefore, by and large, the European integration project appears to be a paragon of pacification, diversity, and universality, which constitute the three overarching topics of this handbook. However, these ideals, hopes, ambitions, and agendas are—at times—in conflict with one another. 'Singularization', reflected in a single market and a single currency, points in the opposite direction of 'pluralization'. Heterogeneity can be a strength but may also hamper growth in a market economy based on scaling effects which precondition a certain level of homogeneity. Diversity may serve democracy and provide checks and balances, but too much division and diffusion can endanger basic democratic consensus and circumvent power, let alone permit the rise to global superpower status in the international arena. To some, these variegated cornerstones result in an aslant house instead of a both welcoming and protective European 'oikos'. Leaving normative judgements aside, it remains a matter of fact that the EU is marked by certain innate antagonisms and has been pulled and is still being pulled in different directions, which has caused diverse developments as well as populist counter-narratives to the grand integration story.

Formally, the EU is an international organization. However, until the transforming Maastricht Treaty it was labelled as the European *Communit(ies)* and the EU nowadays pictures itself as a *Union*, occasionally speaking of a 'unique partnership'. Creative lawyers have coined the term *supranational*[10] to pronounce EU law's hierarchical superiority with respect to national, even constitutional, law and its direct and immediate application, so as to create rights and obligations not only for but within the Member States. For the German Federal Constitutional Court as one of the powerful national (veto)players[11] co-shaping or at least escorting the European integration process—hand in hand with the reconstruction and rehabilitation of Germany—the Union qualifies as a morphydite, something between a *Bundesstaat* and a *Staatenbund* creating a category *sui generis* called Staaten*ver*bund.[12]

These labels in a way reflect the two conflicting camps on how to look at the EU: Broad brush 'realists' or 'neo-realists' including 'liberal intergovernmentalists' stress the role of the Member States and their bargaining power to instrumentalize the Union for maximizing national interests. (Neo-)Functionalists and federalists focus on the European institutions and their aspirations towards an EU built on fundamental principles such as human rights, democracy, and the rule of law.[13]

Some theorists see the Union as the very epitome of constitutionalization *of*, *within* or *by* international law (see Wiener, this volume),[14] for in the beginning it was founded by and shaped with instruments of international law. No matter if one is a constitutionalist or not, the EU has certainly emancipated itself from its foundations in international law. To Eurosceptics, European integration is at worst an undemocratic, overly Court-centric creation or a Commission-centric bureaucratic monster—at best a regulatory superpower. From an international viewpoint, 'strategic unconsciousness', 'normative hubris', and 'existential doubts' have been attested, making the Union a confusing and contradictory international actor.[15] In harsh contrast to this assessment the EU is also frequently pictured as a 'sound' or 'quiet superpower'[16] given its economic capacity, aggregated military power, and influence abroad—an image well-liked and cultivated by the Union—that will be subject to further examination.

Europe's multiple dimensions and diversity are so deeply embedded and engrained in the Union's genesis that it escapes any definitional attempts. The understandings, narratives, and framings of the European Union are so multifaceted and its fields of action so diverse that it is possible to pinpoint certain aspects, but impossible to grasp the whole. Thus, it is reminiscent of *Werner Heisenberg*'s famous uncertainty principle:[17] A static analysis will certainly and correctly tell you *something* about the Union, allow you to 'measure' an ensemble of the European endeavour, but it can neither understand nor explain it in its complexity. Any attempt to capture the EU is limited to statements of probability and approximations. Mindful of this, this chapter is neither meant to provide a brief overview of the Union,[18] how it was forged[19] and transformed,[20] what it does and how it functions,[21] nor is it a summary of the EU as an international actor and its international relations.[22] Rather, it looks at the EU from a tripartite viewpoint: diversity, universality, and pacification—both *within* and fostered *by* the EU. Accordingly, the chapter is divided into three major sections, with two subsections respectively focusing on the *internal* and *external* dimensions. The ultimate section deals with the overarching question of whether the claim of universality, the practice of diversity, and the promotion of pacification warrant the image of the EU as a silent superpower[23] or whether this is merely self-aggrandizement.

2. Pacification—European Exceptionalism?

2.1 Internal

Almost 2,000 years of war and seventy years of peace—this, in essence, is the history of this part of Europe that now forms the European Union. Pacification is possibly not just one but *the* core narrative of European integration, its largest driver and greatest success. As with every narration, counter-narratives exist, questioning the peacebuilding role of the former European Community (EC) as a mere beneficiary of reconciliation, or limiting the merit to delivering social peace and cultivating a culture of compromise.[24] However, *pacification by Europeanization* remains the dominant perspective,[25] an almost DNA-like, deeply engrained notion of the Union. Accordingly, the European Union received the Nobel Peace Prize in 2012. The Norwegian Nobel Committee justified this prestigious accolade by stating: 'The union and its forerunners have for over six decades contributed to the advancement of peace and reconciliation, democracy and human rights in Europe'.[26] The preposition 'in' is of utmost importance: It is not Europe's outreach, its international diplomatic endeavours, partnerships, alliances, and neighbourhood policy (see Majkowska-Szulc and Wierczyńska, this volume) or humanitarian aid and civil protection action. Rather, it is the introspective, successful story of pacification by integration, a 'tale' from 'war to peace'[27] *within* the Union and especially the reconciliation of the Franco-German-enmity that allowed this success.[28] When praising this achievement one should also be aware that the peace finally brought under the auspices of the EU marks not the beginning but rather the end of more than 200 years of political and intellectual endeavours to construct stability in Europe by some form of integration or institution building.[29] The dominant image, alas, of the 'pax Europaea' would be incomplete without mentioning inter- and intra-state clashes within the Union and with neighbouring states, betraying its core purpose. They range from the unresolved conflicts between Catalonia and Spain (see Espósito and Galvão Teles, this volume) and between Northern Ireland and the UK (no longer a member of the Union) to the dispute between Greece (see Iakovidis and Tzevelekos, this volume) and Turkey (the latter not being a member of the Union) regarding Cyprus.[30] Nevertheless, the brightening achievement of 'warlessness' within the formal borders of the EU overshadows these lamentable conditions. In light of the almost unquestioned notion of pacified and pacifying Europe, also enshrined in positive law (eg Articles 3 I, V; 8 I; 21 II c; 42 I; 43 I of the Treaty on European Union (TEU) and the preamble of the Treaty on the Functioning of the European Union (TFEU)), the major focus under this heading shall be on external pacification—the ideas and instruments the Union provides for fostering peace outside Europe.

2.2 External

As often with respect to the EU, myths, stereotypes, and false impressions last when it comes to its peacebuilding capabilities and achievements as well as its military strength. Although the Union is held to be a peaceful if not impotent military behemoth, largely pictured or perceived as a mere soft power,[31] this is true as much as it is false.

The EU has no armed forces—although historically it was supposed to be armed. The proposal to create a European Defence Community (EDC) can be traced back to 1950—with the Pleven Plan as a forerunner—even coming into existence before the signing of the European Coal and Steel Community (ECSC) Treaty in 1951. The Treaty comprised the creation of joint forces, a common budget, and institutions. In 1952 the EDC-Treaty was even signed by the six ECSC States. However, the *spiritus rector* of the plan—France—failed to ratify it in 1954 when the French National Assembly did not let it pass because it would have granted the 'Feindstaat', freshly freed Germany, equal rights. It would also have triggered the US to remove troops from Europe, shifting the burden of protection against Soviet pressure to Europe. JHH Weiler has called this failure a 'childhood trauma', creating 'wasteful replications of the defence efforts of the Member States coupled with a total reliance on American force' and even stating that 'it became part of European faith that defence, security and military matters had to be kept separate from the European construct'.[32]

Initiatives to reanimate this idea reoccur periodically but have never gained the momentum needed to establish immanent military power at the EU level. However, some cooperation by twenty-five out of the twenty-seven Member States was established under the Permanent Structured Cooperation (PESCO). Founded in 2017 to enhance and foster the dialogue on defence matters, twenty agreements on future cooperation from training troops to developing equipment and forty-seven joint projects have been realized so far.[33] In addition, the reporting mechanism Coordinated Annual Review of Defence (CARD) was created and the European Defence Fund (EDF) established in 2017. The effort may be laudable, but against the backdrop of Russia's invasion of Ukraine and the military support provided by the US and NATO remains rather farcical (see Grant, this volume). The picture looks quite different when viewed from a different angle: The aggregated forces of the Member States constituting the EU arguably decree large military power.[34] Collectively, the EU is the second largest military spender[35] and—at least until Brexit as well as depending on the metrics—ranked second with respect to firepower worldwide.[36] Yet, this power and its impact must certainly be attributed to the (militarily sovereign) Member States of the Union. In addition, cultural and political ramparts remain. After all, the saying 'Europeans Have Weapons but Aren't Warriors'[37] bears some truth to capture the status quo.

It would be a misunderstanding, however, to equate missing military capacity with missing pacification power. In the absence of unified military power, the EU has embarked on different paths and strategies to pacify other parts of the world in its own way. Four of those shall be highlighted: its merits as a *diplomatic actor*, its role in *UN politics*, its *peacebuilding capacities* and its '*economic warfare*'.

First, the EU has over time become an important diplomatic actor.[38] Early on, the European Communities featured a mere 'emerging "diplomatic persona" distinct from their own member states'.[39] In the late 1990s and early 2000s, action, perception, and language shifted. The EU became a 'diplomatic actor' in its own right, *inter alia* due to the newly created Common Foreign and Security Policy (CFSP). The Lisbon Treaty and the founding of the European External Action Service (EEAS) in 2011 further increased its—potential or actual—influence. In this respect, some see the establishment of the High Representative of the Union for Foreign Affairs and Security Policy as an achievement, while others see *Trumpf*, *Solana*, *Ashton*, *Mogherini*, and *Borrell* as faces of failure.[40]

Second, the EU has also played a vital role in United Nations (UN) politics, ranging from contributions to environmental issues to disarmament, from its influence in the UN General Assembly (UNGA) and the UN Security Council (UNSC) to special agencies and agreements such as the International Labour Organization (ILO) or UNESCO.[41] When it comes to the UNSC, the EU itself obviously has no permanent seat. However, in the past, two EU Member States were permanent members, whereas after Brexit, one remains. In addition, three to five EU member States have consistently been among the fifteen permanent and non-permanent UNSC members making up one third of the Council.[42] Thus, both input and output exist by sharing information with other EU Member States and institutions and representing EU positions in this forum (Article 34 I and II TEU).[43]

Third, the EU has played a pivotal role over the last two decades when it comes to conflict prevention and peacebuilding. Although significant challenges and limitations remain,[44] the Union has moved away from its 'hyperliberal idealist approach' using 'conditionality, social learning, and passive enforcement' to a more 'pragmatic, bottom-up' approach supporting 'states' resilience'.[45] Some studies suggest that Europe-led peacekeeping operations are more efficiently and effectively run than American operations.[46] In total, the Union's experience in military operations comprises more than twenty missions, nine of which are still ongoing,[47] spanning geographically from Macedonia to Congo.[48]

Besides these military attempts and ambitions, arguably at the cusp between soft power and hard power, the Union has largely tried to mitigate conflicts and pacify the world through 'economic warfare'.[49] Due to the EU's economic power, sanctions—at times coined the most successful tool of 'liberal internationalism'—have been front and centre.[50] Although until 2004 a particular legal regime was not in place, the Union has made use of this tool for more than forty years.[51] Facing Russia's attack on Ukraine, the EU for the first time even considered placing third-party sanctions—a measure hitherto used by the US and until now considered by the Union to be in violation of international law.[52]

The Russian attack on Ukraine beginning in February 2022 certainly creates a litmus test for the EU with respect to its pacifying role and capacity. Russia's invasion exposed how militarily weak and vulnerable the Union is beyond NATO's protective shield. Some fear that without US military supremacy, Russian revisionism might not stop in Ukraine. Next to and besides the US, the pivotal role was taken up by NATO (see Grant, this volume). The actions and omissions of the Union reflect traditional behaviour and showcase the strengths and character traits just examined: Besides 'a collective responsibility to act'[53] it is first and foremost the sovereign Member States that provide military support and intelligence. Government-to-government transfers remain key.[54] At the same time, the EU is active as a diplomatic actor and provides financial and civil support—although the EU Military Assistance Measures (EUMAM) including training missions and support for border management under the newly created European Peace Facility worth €4.6 billion deserves mention.[55] The EU has also passed—at fast pace—multiple comprehensive sanction packages 'attacking' Russia's economy. Finally, this 'Zeitenwende' (as coined by German Chancellor Olaf Scholz[56]) has predictably once again reanimated and galvanized the spirit to forge a European Defence Union. It remains to be seen if the 'childhood trauma' (JHH Weiler) can be overcome.

This overall observation of predominantly economic and technocratic responses at the EU level, be it in Syria, Sudan, or Ukraine, while military action rests and remains largely vested within the Member States and even more so with the US, implies a rather silent, all too silent, superpower. This allows the Union to keep its image of innocence and create a kind of European exceptionalism, leaving the dirty and dangerous work to Member States, to NATO, and the US. Whether a 'postimperial empire' can be established in this fashion is doubtful. It seems as if the Union is still in search of its own identity amidst new geopolitical constellations.[57]

3. Diversity

3.1 Internal

Diversity is first and foremost an actual feature of the EU. Consisting of twenty-seven States, with twenty-four official languages and three working languages, countless dialects, prior to the introduction of the Euro at least thirty different currencies and remaining ten working currencies, a uniquely rich set of cultures and sub-cultures as well as religions, more than 300 regions[58] and almost 100 administrative divisions (NUTS),[59] we unquestionably witness shades of factual diversity in the Union (the diversity of the EU is also embedded in the diversity of the Council of Europe (CoE); see Bílková, this volume). In the words of Romano Prodi: The Union is 'a union of minorities'[60] and hence of diversity. Second, diversity and—arguably not congruent but related—pluralism are also enshrined in positive EU law. Diversity and plurality are mentioned in Articles 2 and 3 TEU as well as in the preamble,[61] and in Articles 152, 165(1), 167, 207(4) TFEU, setting up an entire system of 'diversity management' to maintain this richness with respect to language, heritage and other forms of cultural diversity.[62] This is also reflected in the stars of the European flag and in the European Union's motto 'United in Diversity'.[63] The *legal* reality is, however, rather intricate. Diversity exists and endures since the Union also acts as a guardian of factual national diversity, for example by funding certain programmes. It is however also contested, of heated debate,[64] and under pressure due to the Union's own integrational success which ultimately results in a certain level of homogeneity. The integrative intent becomes evident at the very start as reflected in the Copenhagen criteria, which establish a necessary common ground for States to join the EU.[65] Moreover, the wide spectrum of harmonization activities ranging from transport to health and from consumer protection to AI regulation further align and constrict the variety within national standards inside the Union. Heterogeneity and homogeneity are in conflict and the European integration project is a constant balancing act oscillating between mutual recognition (allowing diversity) and harmonization (undermining diversity). The reasons for this are at least two-fold: First, homogeneity is an inherent consequence of law, since law requires to be applied to everyone equally (regarding Lon Fuller, see van Aaken, this volume). Second, it is a common market precondition as much as it is its consequence. The fundamental freedoms constituting the European common market aim for an opening and thus a blending of goods, services, and citizens, yet ultimately levelling out significant protective and protected differences. Once a product is allowed anywhere, it is allowed everywhere within the Union. Since products and services need to meet certain standards, this convergence and standardization—although in a limited sense—undermine diversity.[66] Yet, legal regimes and safeguards such as the principle of non-discrimination, EU citizenship, and the right to free movement reduce the 'pressure of assimilation' and 'contribute to the cultural diversification of the Member States'.[67] In short, '[t]he single European market is a force of cultural convergence as well as of cultural diversity'.[68]

3.2 External

What is true for the single market also impacts the rest of the world. According to Anu Bradford's ground-breaking scholarship, the EU is a 'regulatory superpower' due to the so-called 'Brussels effect'. In this respect, Europe arguably 'rules the world'[69] and lives up to the 'superpower'-(self)image exporting both the enhancement and limitations of diversity—whereas the latter may even preponderate due to the regulation's homogenization tendency.

But the Union also reaches beyond economic power and regulatory capacity to enhance diversity globally. In a seminal article, Armin von Bogdandy identified three practices and activities boosting diversity.[70] The first results from the nexus between human rights, diversity, and the protection of minorities. Consequently, the human rights conditionality supposedly insisted on by the Union in international agreements functions as an active diversity protection.[71] Second, the EU is prone to recognize newly created States and by this caters to diversity.[72] Third, the Union plays an active role when it comes to the UNESCO Convention on the Protection and Promotion of the Diversity of Cultural Expressions.

In principle, all these findings are convincing. However, a closer analysis raises some doubts as to whether the trajectory is as glorious as it seems. With respect to the 'Brussels effect', reservations have been voiced whether this verdict is overly optimistic if not seductive.[73] One may also wonder if it is continuous in the 'digital economy' or whether it has passed its zenith.[74] A stronger caveat also stems from the fact that the 'Brussels effect' is neither caused by nor the consequence of inherent EU powers but has its roots in companies freely deciding to comply with EU law out of self-interest. Hence, the EU is object, not subject, passive, not active, when it comes to this sway. The practice of the human rights conditionality also looks more gloomy than glary. Many loopholes remain, only very serious violations trigger appropriate measures, they are less frequent in contemporary agreements and in general seem underutilized[75]—even more so with respect to minority protection. The recognition and respect of newly created States is also marked by limitations, exceptions, and derogations. A case in point is the independence of Kosovo (accepted by twenty-two EU Member States), and the Union remains split regarding the recognition of Palestine. Finally, and with respect to the UNESCO Convention on cultural diversity, reservations remain—quite literally. It is quizzical that the EU, the alleged promoter of diversity, made a unilateral declaration of disconnection when acceding to the Convention since it proved impossible to have a disconnection clause within the Convention.[76] The EU considers that the Convention does not apply towards its relations to its Member States. While this may seem rather technical, it indicates limitation with respect to international law fostering diversity.

Once again, the depth and reach of 'diversity governance' differ significantly within the Union when compared to action abroad. While, within the Union, 'diversity' is ennobled as a legal principle with concrete mechanisms and procedures for its protection and promotion, it remains more of a trope than actionable legal reality for foreign affairs.

4. Universality

4.1 Internal

To examine universality with respect to the European Union encounters profound paradoxes and difficulties—starting with the sheer fact that the Union is geographically, historically, culturally, and legally a *regional* entity whereas universality in its most abstract sense represents the validity of something on a *global* scale.

Secondly, the Union was famously described by one of its founding fathers, Walter Hallstein, as a 'Rechtsgemeinschaft' (legal community).[77] Law, however, is by its very nature typically created or set, applied, and enforced within a limited territorial context—for the last centuries primarily within a nation-state, or within a community. In other words, law is limited and limiting. It has a predominant inward dimension. Universality, by contrast, is characterized by an 'everywhere' and 'everyone' lacking the codicil 'within the Community' or 'Union'. And yet the very epitome of universality might be the foundation of the UN and the emergence of internationally widely accepted human rights since World War II. The turn to 'universal' institutions, rights, and values, however, must be seen in the context of the international liberal world order's still relatively short lifespan, processes of fragmentation[78] as well as a diverging understanding and practice of human rights.[79]

Third, the European process of integration is arguably marked by (neo-)functional or technical integration. The dominant and driving idea, already reflected in the famous Schuman Declaration, was to integrate economic sectors to secure peace and prosperity. Political integration—understood to be the promotion of normative ideas and values—was marginalized as a 'spill-over' effect. The core 'value' of the European Communities was—and maybe even remains—the common market. Market ideology, in turn, may have a universal tendency but is not *stricto sensu* universal and remains far from the goals and objectives typically discussed when it comes to universality. Put differently, the 'valuearization' or 'universalization' of the European Union started much later and was neither quintessential for its foundation nor its development. Although early development to create and shape fundamental rights within the Union can be traced back to the 1970s and earlier, this finding is *inter alia* reflected in the Charter of Fundamental Rights of the European Union, declared in 2000, which came into force only in 2009.

All three aspects—the Union's territorial regionality, the inherent legal limitations, and the late and lacking 'valuearization' of the EU—put stronger universal aspirations into question. Nevertheless, these days the EU has emphatically endorsed values and fundamental or human rights that are typically seen as universal. From a positivistic perspective Articles 2, 3, 6, and 7 TEU are front and centre (although Article 7 proved to be rather dysfunctional in practice). However, this dedication is marked by several serious issues.

One of these could be labelled the 'Paradox of European Universality', shimmering through in Article 3(5), and renders evident in the second paragraph of the preamble to the TEU which reads: 'DRAWING INSPIRATION from the cultural, religious and humanist inheritance of Europe, from which have developed the universal values of the inviolable and inalienable rights of the human person, freedom, democracy, equality and the rule of law'. The EU receives its universal values from the international level, yet it understands them as their own creation-kind of turning 'DC' into 'AC'.

A second paradox or at least a grievance is the gap between preaching and practising, declaration and implementation regarding these values. Although Article 2 TEU holds that the *Union* is founded on these values, and that these 'values are common to the *Member States*,[80] the EU neither has a specific competence or power to enforce this and enact rules on human rights with respect to the Member States, nor is there explicit commitment across the EU's internal policies.[81] While the deeper reason for this might be an intrinsic conflict between avowal to universality and a commitment to pluralism as well as the fear to overstretch the integration-willingness of the Member States, this results in the criticism of double standards when it comes to human rights between the inward and the outward dimension.

All in all, the EU attempts to cultivate a certain 'ethos' when it comes to values[82] and their enforcement,[83] trying to become a 'just institution',[84] but the three-dimensionality consisting of the national, the European, and the international levels engenders some sombre theoretical and practical 'AC/DC'-problems regarding the genesis, enforcement, and review of universal values. The current 'rule of law' crisis[85] (see van Aaken, this volume) displays how constitutionally weak and fragile the setup remains. Ultimately, ideas of universality—or rather universalization understood as a process—may have their origin within Europe as a continent, but less so within Europe understood as a legal construct.

4.2 External

While the role of universality within the Union is rather limited and the very nature of the EU being a regional actor points towards limitations, it would be a fundamental mistake to think an external dimension is inexistent. Hence, a short overview of the Union's *agenda*, *instruments*, and *achievements* to foster universal values and rights shall be provided.

From the very beginning, Europe attempted to 'universalize' and promote its own values and rights elsewhere. Already the Schuman Declaration, as a founding document, somewhat surprisingly qualified the 'development of the African continent' as an 'essential task', showing a hint of proselytism and universalization. In the 1970s, the idea of the EU as a 'civilian' global actor occurred.[86] In the 1980s Hedley Bull famously questioned Europe's 'civilian' role in international affairs amidst the background of power politics.[87] The end of the Cold War led to a vibrant discourse at the latest since Ian Manners' concept of a 'normative power' in the early 2000s.[88] An increased focus on values[89] and external human rights policy[90] with respect to the EU's actions is certainly noticeable. From a legal and positivistic perspective, however, the paradigmatic shift arguably came with the Lisbon Treaty in 2009 creating an entirely new architecture and agenda for Europe's outreach. Although some voices remained pessimistic since foreign policy remained largely within the purview of the Member States,[91] Article 21 TEU forms the bedrock for exporting and promoting universal rights and values.[92] This norm with its messianic traits is prima vista of exhilarating utopianism, but on sober second thought of almost astonishing hubris: 'inspired by its own creation, development and enlargement' the Union reaches out to the 'wider world' to bring no less than 'democracy, rule of law, the universality and indivisibility of human rights[[93]] and fundamental freedoms, respect for human dignity, the principles of equality and solidarity' to the world (on democracy, see Poghosyan, this volume; on the rule of law, see van Aaken, this volume; on human rights, see Çalı, this volume). The rather pretentious agenda does not stop here. The EU also seeks to foster the 'development of developing countries', to 'eradicate poverty', and to preserve the environment and global natural resources as well as confront 'man-made disasters' (Article 21 II D, F, G TEU). In other words, the EU aims to become the saviour of the world—fighting global problems globally.

The *instruments* to implement what is nowadays often coined the 'Global Reach'[94] of the EU with respect to universal goals and beyond its inverted market power are manifold and have been the object of much study. *Inter alia* the 'global reach' factors, instruments, and phenomena include the extraterritorial application of EU law, the so-called 'Brussels Effect', the bilateral relationships of the EU, for example in trade[95] and development, its engagement with multilateral fora, and the negotiation of international legal instruments[96] as well as funding certain projects and its enlargement policy. Even the jurisprudence of the Court is—to a certain degree—'exported' to neighbouring countries.[97] With respect to external relations, however, the non-judicial interactions remain key and can be divided into the *formation* of universal norms and the *application* of universal norms.[98]

With respect to the *accomplishments* of the EU as a 'good global actor'[99] fostering universal norms and solving eminent global issues, the attempts are certainly laudable, but the results appear mixed. The focus and major achievements lie in the sector of human rights with the EU's human rights conditionality as a classical instrument.[100] A prime example for the formation of human rights treaties is the EU's effort to negotiate and ratify the UN Disability Convention adopted in 2006.[101] Another huge success can be seen in the negotiation of the Paris climate agreement, in which the EU played a pivotal role.[102] Yet, endeavours and attainments like this remain a rarity since traditional international treaties do not allow regional organizations, but only States to join. Another example of participation in the formation of universal law can be identified in the Union's input, negotiation, and goal achievement in the UN Human Rights Council.[103]

While the overall trajectory may be remarkable, some misgivings remain. The starting point is the significant gap between 'self-aggrandizing rhetoric' causing unrealistic expectations and the actual practice,[104] rendering the high human rights agenda at times farcical. Some brief examples illustrate that this wide-ranging European ambition is not only marked by hubris but is also—at times—hypocritical: As JHH Weiler puts it, there is a 'shameful European lack . . . to defend and protect the values it professes to hold most dear'[105] reflected in Srebrenica, as this genocide on European soil in 1995 was not averted.

With respect to the thwarted accession to the European Convention on Human Rights (ECHR), the law is clear. Article 6 II TEU reads: 'The Union shall accede the European Convention for the Protection of Human Rights and Fundamental Freedoms'. Yet, the judges of the Court ignored this imperative in their Opinion 2/13, in 'defending the EU legal order against a Foreign Human Rights Court'.[106] By this, they arguably protected autonomy or autarky,[107] saving EU exceptionalism.[108] Ultimately, the impeded accession to the ECHR creates not only an illegal (Article 6 II TEU) and unresolvable paradox—to become a member of the Union one has to join the ECHR, but the Union is reluctant to join itself—but undermines the credibility of human rights commitment more generally. Accordingly, it damages the internal as well as the external dimension of human rights.

While some picture the infamous *Kadi* case as a trade-off between the rule of law and fragmenting the international order[109] or see it as a balancing exercise,[110] it also had to do with autonomy[111] and revealed how 'constitutionally narcissistic' (JHH Weiler) or 'Triepelesk'[112] the EU can be, reflecting the struggle of the EU with international law.[113] However, one should remember that this questionable move had positive repercussions: It reminded the UNSC of its human rights obligations and led to a refined approach when it comes to sanctions. In other words, while the impeded accession shows the ignorance of its own law, *Kadi* reflects the ignorance of international legal obligations.[114]

In addition, the Turkey Refugee Deal also darkens the Union's image of fostering universal rights, values, and goals for multiple reasons.[115]

A final, more contemporary case in point is the Union's relationship and policy with China regarding human rights.[116] It lamentably shows that the values are certainly important for the Union's self-perception, less so for its self-projection.[117]

In a very abstract sense, all these examples have in common that they deal with human rights and showcase a rather harsh impact of the insider-outsider phenomenon. The picture becomes brighter, however, when one moves from 'subjects' to 'objects'. As mentioned, the commitments regarding the protection of the environment and fighting climate change seem to be less hypocritical—from fighting the unregulated emission of chlorofluorocarbons and protecting the ozone layer in the 1980s to the 2015 Paris Agreement.

In conclusion, the EU certainly is a protagonist co-shaping the international legal order[118] and could be pictured as 'a Voice in the Choir in the International System of Human Rights Protection'.[119] However, the discrepancy between ambition and reality regarding EU policy is eminent, the aspiration problematic, and the track record mixed. While there is what JHH Weiler calls the mobilizing 'destiny legitimation', or 'political messianism'[120] written in the Treaties, one can but only find it there—it never gained enough traction. The comparison with other regional superpowers is also telling. Besides a messianic demeanour, neither China nor the US forthrightly *formally declare* such strong visions on how to change the world holistically on almost every spectrum of global policy. Yet both do have a fundamental and arguably greater impact than the EU—for worse, not for better.

5. Conclusion: The EU as Noah's Ark?

In the end, we witness a structural disparity concerning the EU's track record internally and externally. Jean Monnet's vision presented in 1954 at Columbia University that the European Community could be an example of how 'to create a more prosperous and peaceful world'[121] has come true for EU Europeans but remains an unfulfilled dream for the rest of the world.

Internally the Union remains powerful and is widely seen as a success with respect to the three overarching themes of this handbook. For more than seventy years Europe has created peace by prosperity and prosperity by peace, while being an unattainable paragon for other regional integration efforts such as Mercosur and COMESA. In line with Walter Hallstein's famous metaphor of the bicycle (keep moving or fall), the integration process steadily continues and results not necessarily in an ever closer but ever more pluralistic Union comprising twenty-seven diverse Member States and possibly more to come. The values *inter alia* engraved in Articles 2, 6, and 7 TEU are by and large not dreamed but lived reality in most Member States. In particular, the level of realization of these respected values in the relatively new Member States has increased significantly for joining and through joining the elitist 'club'. As Timothy Garton Ash puts it: 'From Helsinki to Athens and Tallinn to Lisbon, you'll find yourself in the largest area of relative freedom, prosperity and security achieved in European history.'[122]

Externally, however, the power to pacify, to foster universal values and rights, and to promote diversity is relatively limited. Although the Union's activities have significantly increased, structures and institutions were built, and an almost messianic mission enshrined in the Treaty (Article 21 TEU), the overall achievements remain limited when compared to the high self-set standards and the impact of other superpowers. The war in Ukraine lamentably spotlighted the weakness from a security angle. In this respect the Union looks particularly frail and unsuccessful—although this is by design, not by default.[123]

This allows for three concluding remarks:

First, the gulf between the inner and the outer leaves us with a certain allegory of the Union. *In a nutshell* the EU may be seen *as a nutshell*. Within it, Europe has remarkably successfully preached and practised diversity, pacification, and universality. A shell, however, certainly takes effect both ways: It may be hard to crack and is resistant—protective and promising for those inside. Yet any outreach or spill-over effect is restricted all the same. During the refugee crisis a similar allegory was fashionable, the one of Europe being a fortress,[124] a kind of 'fortress of the privileged'.[125] To put it more positively: The EU is a kind of Noah's Ark for Europeans. An Ark, however, is not quite a superpower.

Second, the great success *within* the Union combined with a prevailing two-dimensionality may provide an explanation why the Union is often perceived, and likes to portray itself, as a silent superpower. Irrespective of the jarring rhetoric of sovereignty transfer constantly lamented by national constitutional courts, the integration process can be understood as a *dédoublement* (although not in the sense of George Scelle[126]) of everything: The twenty-seven self-standing Member States still exist *and* have forged the Union. Arguably this dédoublement that differentiates the Union from other regional powers creates the impression—to a certain degree the illusion—of being a superpower and skews deficiencies.

Third, the future of the EU is unknown, and prognosis is a difficult subject.[127] But in the past, the Union has proved to be remarkably resilient and typically turns weaknesses into strengths. It has not only survived but surpassed the 'seemingly insurmountable polycrisis'.[128] Although crisis-ridden it has grown bigger and stronger. And while there are hopes that the war in Ukraine will push forward the denationalization of 'Defence Policy'[129] and accelerate as well as substantiate its Europeanization, gnawing questions remain. A proactive role when it comes to belligerent action, even with the intent to foster peace on earth, would certainly run counter to its very founding ideas and legacy of pacification by economic integration. Since the 'Zeitenwende', however, is most likely not confined to questions of war and peace,[130] and as we are witnessing the slow decline of American supremacy and the rise of China as well as India as regional superpowers, the chances for the EU to remain one out of many regional powers in a 'multipolar' world are high. Most likely diplomatic action, UN politics, peacebuilding, and economic warfare will remain its methods of choice. Ultimately, the Union will most likely remain softer and more silent since it is the only giant to be based exclusively on law, not on power.[131]

Notes

1. Alan Milward, *The European Rescue of the Nation State* (2nd edn, Routledge 1999) 4.
2. See the famous founding document, the Schuman declaration of 1950.
3. Harry Anastasiou, 'The EU as a Peace Building System: Deconstructing Nationalism in an era of Globalization', 12(2) International Journal of Peace Studies 2007, 31.
4. John McCormick, *Understanding the European Union: A Concise Introduction* (Bloomsbury 2020).

5. Jeremy Rifkin, *The European Dream: How Europe's Vision of the Future is Quietly Eclipsing the American Dream* (Polity 2004) 220.
6. See the self-description of the EU, eg Publications Office of the European Union, 'The European Union: What it is and what it does' <https://op.europa.eu/webpub/com/eu-what-it-is/en/> accessed 14 May 2023. For a rich perspective and characterization, see Joseph H H Weiler, *The Constitution of Europe* (CUP 1999).
7. Peter Häberle, 'The Jurisprudence of European Law – viewed as a Cultural Study' in Markus Kotzur (ed), *Peter Häberle on Constitutional Theory* (Nomos 2018) 303, 323.
8. Daniel Thym, *Ungleichzeitigkeit und europäisches Verfassungsrecht* (Nomos 2004).
9. See Joseph H H Weiler and Johann Justus Vasel, 'The States' Upcoming Choice: Move Ahead All Together, Some Members Only or Alone?' in Giuliano Amato et al (eds), *The History of the European Union: Constructing Utopia* (Hart Publishing 2018) 535, 549.
10. The term was invented by Hugo Krabbe, *Die moderne Staatsidee* (2nd edn, Scientia 1919).
11. See generally George Tsebelis, *Veto Players: How Political Institutions Work* (Princeton UP 2003).
12. BVerfGE 123, 267.
13. For an overview on this topic and divide see Andrew Moravcsik, 'Federalism in the European Union: Rhetoric and Reality' in Kalypso Nicolaidis and Robert Howse (eds), *The Federal Vision: Legitimacy and Levels of Governance in the United States and the European Union* (OUP 2001) 161.
14. See also Thomas Kleinlein, *Konstitutionalisierung im Völkerrecht: Konstruktion und Elemente einer idealistischen Völkerrechtslehre* (Springer 2011); Jan Klabbers, Anne Peters, and Geir Ulfstein, *The Constitutionalization of International Law* (OUP 2011). See also Johann Justus Vasel, *Regionaler Menschenrechtsschutz als Emanzipationsprozess: Grundlagen, Strukturen und Eigenarten des europäischen und interamerikanischen Menschenrechtsschutzsystems* (Duncker & Humblot 2017) 192.
15. Simon Duke, *Europe as a Stronger Global Actor* (Palgrave Macmillan 2017) 15–62.
16. Andrew Moravcsik, 'Europe: The Quiet Superpower', 7(3) French Politics 2009, 403; Thomas R Reid, *The United States of Europe: The New Superpower and the End of American Supremacy* (Penguin Press 2005); Mark Leonard, *Why the European Union will Run the 21st Century* (Public Affairs 2005); Enrique Baròn Crespo and Pelayo Castro Zuzuárreguie, 'The European Union: A Sound Superpower in a Multipolar World' in Francisco Rojas Aravena (ed), *The Difficult Task of Peace* (Palgrave Macmillan 2020) 171.
17. Werner Heisenberg, *Der Teil und das Ganze* (R. Piper & Co. Verlag 1969).
18. See Simon Usherwood and John Pinder, *The European Union: A Very Short Introduction* (4th edn, OUP 2018).
19. See Luuk van Middelaar, *The Passage to Europe: How a Continent Became a Union* (Yale UP 2013).
20. Joseph H H Weiler, 'The Transformation of Europe', 100(8) Yale Law Journal 1991, 2403.
21. See Paul Craig and Gráinne de Búrca, *EU Law: Text, Cases, and Materials* (7th edn, OUP 2020); Damian Chalmers and Anthony Arnull (eds), *The Oxford Handbook of European Union Law* (OUP 2015).
22. See Christopher Hill, Michael Smith, and Sophie Vanhoonacker (eds), *International Relations and the European Union* (4th edn, OUP 2023); Jan Klabbers, *The European Union in International Law* (Editions Pedone 2012); Enzo Cannizzaro, Paolo Palchetti, and Ramses A Wessel (eds), *International Law as Law of the European Union* (Brill 2011); Jed Odermatt, *International Law and the European Union* (CUP 2021); Marise Cremona

and Joanne Scott (eds), *EU Law Beyond EU Borders: The Extraterritorial Reach of EU Law* (OUP 2019).

23. See for this thesis Moravcsik, 'Quiet Superpower' (n 16) 403.
24. Kiran Klaus Patel, *Project Europe: A History* (CUP 2020) 52. For a neorealist view focusing on the US and NATO see John Mearsheimer, 'Why Is Europe Peaceful Today?', 9(3) European Political Science 2010, 387.
25. Anastasiou, 'EU as a Peace Building System' (n 3) 34.
26. Press release, Nobel Prize Outreach AB 2023, 'The Nobel Peace Prize 2012' <https://www.nobelprize.org/prizes/peace/2012/press-release/> accessed 2 August 2023.
27. See the self-image of the EU, eg in Herman Van Rompuy and José Manuel Durão Barroso, 'From war to peace: a European tale' (Acceptance of the Nobel Peace Prize Award to the European Union, Oslo, 10 December 2012, SPEECH/12/930).
28. The committee suggested: 'In the inter-war years, the Norwegian Nobel Committee made several awards to persons who were seeking reconciliation between Germany and France. Since 1945, that reconciliation has become a reality. The dreadful suffering in World War II demonstrated the need for a new Europe. Over a seventy-year period, Germany and France had fought three wars. Today war between Germany and France is unthinkable. This shows how, through well-aimed efforts and by building up mutual confidence, historical enemies can become close partners.' (n 26).
29. Stella Ghervas, *Conquering Peace: From the Enlightenment to the European Union* (Harvard UP 2021) 348–349.
30. Angela K Bourne, 'European Integration and Conflict Resolution in the Basque Country, Northern Ireland and Cyprus', 4(3) Perspectives on European Politics and Society 2003, 391, 410–411.
31. Seminal Joseph S Nye, Jr, *Soft Power: The Means to Success in World Politics* (Public Affairs 2004); see also Anna Michalski, 'The EU as a Soft Power: the Force of Persuasion' in Jan Melissen (ed), *The New Public Diplomacy: Soft Power in International Relations* (Palgrave Macmillan 2005) 124.
32. Joseph H H Weiler, '60 Years since the First European Community—Reflections on Political Messianism', 22(2) European Journal of International Law 2011, 303, 308.
33. See PESCO Secretariat, 'Projects' <https://www.pesco.europa.eu> accessed 23 May 2023.
34. See Moravcsik, 'Quiet Superpower' (n 16); Andrew Moravcsik, 'Europe Is Still a Superpower' (*Foreign Policy*, 13 April 2017). Also: Global Firepower Index, 'European Union Military Strength (2023)' <https://www.globalfirepower.com/countries-listing-european-union.php> accessed 7 May 2023.
35. European External Action Service, 'A stronger EU on security and defence' (19 November 2018) <https://www.eeas.europa.eu/eeas/stronger-eu-security-and-defence_en> accessed 2 August 2023.
36. Moravcsik, 'Quiet Superpower' (n 16); Rajan Menon, 'Europe Doesn't Need the United States Anymore' (*Foreign Policy*, 30 January 2023).
37. Alexis Carré, 'Europeans Have Weapons but Aren't Warriors' (*Foreign Policy*, 4 December 2022).
38. See broad analysis in Joachim A Koops and Gjovalin Macaj (eds), *The European Union as a Diplomatic Actor* (Palgrave Macmillan 2015).
39. Joachim A Koops and Gjovalin Macaj, 'Introduction: The European Union as a Diplomatic Actor' in Koops and Macaj, *Diplomatic Actor* (n 38) 1; Christopher Hill and William Wallace, 'Diplomatic Trends in the European Community' 55(1) International Affairs 1979,

47; see also Carol Ann Cosgrove and Kenneth J Twitchett (eds), *The New International Actors: The UN and the EEC* (Macmillan 1970).

40. See generally Niklas Helwig, *The High Representative of the Union: The Constrained Agent of Europe's Foreign Policy* (PhD Cologne 2014); Christine Kaddous, 'Role and Position of the High Representative of the Union for Foreign Affairs and Security Policy under the Lisbon Treaty' in Stefan Griller and Jacques Ziller (eds), *The Lisbon Treaty: EU Constitutionalism without a Constitutional Treaty?* (Springer 2008) 205.
41. For an overview, see Spyros Blavoukos and Dimitrios Bourantonis (eds), *The EU in UN Politics: Actors, Processes and Performances* (Palgrave Macmillan 2017); Katie Verlin Laatikainen and Karen E Smith (eds), *The European Union at the United Nations: Intersecting Multilateralisms* (Palgrave Macmillan 2006).
42. Thomas Mayr-Harting, 'Representing the European Union at the United Nations: The Security Council Dimension' in Nico J Schrijver and Niels M Blokker (eds), *Elected Members of the Security Council: Lame Ducks or Key Players?* (Brill Nijhoff 2019) 153.
43. Johan Verbeke, 'EU Coordination on UN Security Council Matters' in Jan Wouters et al (eds), *The United Nations and the European Union: An Ever Stronger Partnership* (T.M.C. Asser Press 2006) 49; Christopher Hill, 'The European Powers in the Security Council: Differing Interests, Differing Arenas' in Laatikainen and Smith, *EU at the UN* (n 41) 49.
44. Ana E Juncos and Steven Blockmans, 'The EU's role in conflict prevention and peacebuilding: four key challenges', 4(2–3) Global Affairs 2018, 131, 133–136.
45. Nathalie Tocci, 'The European Union and Peacebuilding' in Oliver P Richmond and Gëzim Visoka (eds), *The Oxford Handbook of Peacebuilding, Statebuilding, and Peace Formation* (OUP 2021) 288.
46. James Dobbins et al, *Europe's Role in Nation-Building: From the Balkans to the Congo* (RAND 2008) 214–226.
47. European External Action Service, 'EU Missions and Operations' (20 March 2023) <https://www.eeas.europa.eu/eeas/eu-missions-and-operations_en> accessed 23 May 2023.
48. Steven Blockmans et al (eds), *The European Union and Peacebuilding. Policy and Legal Aspects* (T.M.C. Asser Press 2010); Annemarie Peen Rodt, *The European Union and Military Conflict Management. Defining, evaluating and achieving success* (Routledge 2014) 3.
49. See generally Nicholas Mulder, *The Economic Weapon: The Rise of Sanctions as a Tool of Modern War* (Yale UP 2022).
50. See historically ibid; with respect to the sanctioning packets and its impact Johann Justus Vasel, 'De Bello Oeconomico', Europäische Zeitschrift für Wirtschaftsrecht 2022, 541. According to Barry E Carter, the EU has been '[t]he most frequent regional entity to invoke economic sanctions', Barry E Carter, 'Economic Sanctions', *Max Planck Encyclopedia of Public International Law* (April 2011) <https://opil.ouplaw.com/display/10.1093/law:epil/9780199231690/law-9780199231690-e1521?prd=OPIL> accessed 2 August 2023.
51. For a retrospect see Joakim Kreutz, 'Hard Measures by a Soft Power? Sanctions Policy of the European Union 1981–2004' (2005) BICC Working Paper 45, <https://www.bicc.de/uploads/tx_bicctools/paper45.pdf> accessed 23 May 2023, 7–14; for an overview see Jan Wouters, Frank Hoffmeister, and Geert De Baere, *The Law of EU External Relations: Cases, Materials, and Commentary on the EU as an International Legal Actor* (3rd edn, OUP 2021) 177–229; Piet Eckhout, *EU External Relations Law* (2nd edn, OUP 2011) 501–548.

52. Tom Ruys and Cedric Ryngaert, 'Secondary Sanctions: A Weapon out of Control? The International Legality of, and European Responses to, US Secondary Sanctions', British Yearbook of International Law 2020, 1, 30.
53. Heidi Maurer et al, 'The EU and the invasion of Ukraine: a collective responsibility to act?', 99(1) International Affairs 2023, 219, 230–236.
54. The multitude of activities are continuously tracked by the IfW, see Kiel Institute for the World Economy, 'Ukraine Support Tracker' <https://www.ifw-kiel.de/topics/war-against-ukraine/ukraine-support-tracker/> accessed 7 May 2023; Trebesch et al, The Ukraine Support Tracker: Which countries help Ukraine and how? (2023) Kiel Working Paper 2218 <https://www.ifw-kiel.de/publications/kiel-working-papers/2022/the-ukraine-support-tracker-which-countries-help-ukraine-and-how-17204/> accessed 7 May 2023.
55. European Commission, 'EU assistance to Ukraine' <https://eu-solidarity-ukraine.ec.europa.eu/eu-assistance-ukraine_en> accessed 7 May 2023; for a timeline of EU actions see: European Council, 'Timeline—EU response to Russia's invasion of Ukraine' <https://www.consilium.europa.eu/en/policies/eu-response-ukraine-invasion/timeline-eu-response-ukraine-invasion/> accessed 7 May 2023.
56. Olaf Scholz, 'The Global Zeitenwende' (*Foreign Affairs*, 5 December 2022).
57. See, eg, 'This is the moment for the European Union to discuss what it wants to be. To face the challenges of the future, we have a lot of things to review. About our procedures, our methods, putting more attention on our capacity to act than on internal discussions. The pandemic pushed us down the path of coming closer together, especially with Next Generation EU. The current tragic moment must spur us to go further on this path to protect the lives, security and prosperity of all. That's the real challenge we have to face in the next weeks and months. In that regard, the Conference on the Future of Europe can play an important role', Josep Borrell, 'The future of Europe is being defined now' (The Diplomatic Service of the European Union, 3 March 2022) <https://www.eeas.europa.eu/eeas/future-europe-being-defined-now-0_en> accessed 7 May 2023.
58. See Council Decision (EU) 2019/852 of 21 May 2019 determining the composition of the Committee of the Regions OJ L139/13.
59. NUTS stands for Nomenclature of Territorial Units for Statistics; Europe consists of around ninety-six NUTS-1 regions.
60. cf Armin von Bogdandy, 'The European Union as Situation, Executive, and Promoter of the International Law of Cultural Diversity—Elements of a Beautiful Friendship', 19(2) EJIL 2008, 241, 255.
61. See para 2 of the preamble: 'DRAWING INSPIRATION from the cultural, religious and humanist inheritance of Europe, from which have developed the universal values of the inviolable and inalienable rights of the human person, freedom, democracy, equality and the rule of law'. The (ultimately rejected) Treaty establishing a Constitution for Europe (TCE) from 2004 was much more foundational: 'CONVINCED that, while remaining proud of their own national identities and history, the peoples of Europe are determined to transcend their former divisions and, united ever more closely, to forge a common destiny, CONVINCED that, thus "United in diversity", Europe offers them the best chance of pursuing, with due regard for the rights of each individual and in awareness of their responsibilities towards future generations and the Earth, the great venture which makes of it a special area of human hope.'
62. von Bogdandy, 'The European Union as Situation' (n 60) 270.

63. Gabriel N Toggenburg, 'Unity in Diversity: Searching for the Regional Dimension in the Context of a Someway Foggy Constitutional Credo' in Roberto Toniatti, Marco Dani, and Francesco Palermo (eds), *An Ever More Complex Union* (Nomos 2004) 27.
64. Ulrich Haltern, 'Europäischer Kulturkampf', 37(4) Der Staat 1998, 591; Peter A Kraus, 'Cultural Pluralism and European Polity-Building', 41(4) JCMS 2003, 665.
65. European Council, 'European Council in Copenhagen 21–22 June 1993. Conclusions of the Presidency' SN 180/93. See also Ronald Janse, 'Is the European Commission a Credible Guardian of the Values? A Revisionist Account of the Copenhagen Political Criteria during the Big Bang Enlargement', 17(1) International Journal of Constitutional Law 2019, 43.
66. von Bogdandy, 'The European Union as Situation' (n 60) 248.
67. ibid, 249.
68. ibid, 248.
69. Anu Bradford, *The Brussels Effect: How the European Union Rules the World* (OUP 2019).
70. von Bogdandy, 'The European Union as Situation' (n 60) 272.
71. See ibid, in particular n 178 with further references.
72. ibid, 272.
73. Peter L Lindseth, 'The Brussels Effect: How the European Union Rules the World', 70(3) American Journal of Comparative Law 2022, 641, 644–645.
74. Jens Frankenreiter, 'Cost-Based California Effects', 39(3) Yale Journal on Regulation 2022, 1155, 1216–1217.
75. Lorand Bartels, 'Assessment of the implementation of the human rights clause in international and sectoral agreements' (Paper requested by the European Parliament's Subcommittee on Human Rights, EP/EXPO/DROI/2022/01 2023) 21–23.
76. Magdalena Ličková, 'European Exceptionalism in International Law', 19(3) EJIL 2008, 463, 484.
77. Seminal: Walter Hallstein, *Der unvollendete Bundesstaat: Europäische Erfahrungen und Erkenntnisse* (Econ 1969); Michael Stolleis, 'Europa als Rechtsgemeinschaft' in Stefan Kadelbach (ed), *Europa als kulturelle Idee: Symposion für Claudio Magris* (Nomos 2010) 71; Manfed Zuleeg, 'Die Europäische Gemeinschaft als Rechtsgemeinschaft', Neue Juristische Wochenschrift 1994, 545.
78. See Study Group of the International Law Commission, *Fragmentation of International Law: Difficulties Arising from the Diversification and Expansion of International Law* (A/CN.4/L.682 2006).
79. See Nick Goetschalckx, 'The Mythic Universality of the Universal Declaration on Human Rights: Revisiting the Drafting History of the UDHR in Search for a Foundational Theory' in Jan Wouters et al (eds), *Can We Still Afford Human Rights? Critical Reflections on Universality, Proliferation and Costs* (Edward Elgar 2020) 27; Paul Lemmens, 'The Universality of Human Rights: A European Perspective' in Jan Wouters et al (eds), *Can We Still Afford Human Rights? Critical Reflections on Universality, Proliferation and Costs* (Edward Elgar 2020) 69; classical Jack Donnelly, 'Cultural Relativism and Universal Human Rights', 6(4) Human Rights Quarterly 1984, 400.
80. Manuel Kellerbauer, Marcus Klamert, and Jonathan Tomkin (eds), *The Treaties and the Charter of Fundamental Rights—A Commentary* (2nd edn, OUP 2023) Article 2 (forthcoming). Article 2 TEU has in fact been activated by the Court of Justice ever since its ruling in Associação Sindical dos Juízes Portugueses, see Luke Dimitrios Spieker, *EU*

Values Before the Court of Justice: Foundations, Potential, Risks (OUP 2023) 11. However, this transformation of Article 2 TEU into an operational and judicially applicable provision to hold the Member States accountable firstly does not come without certain risks and, secondly, underlines again the two dimensions with respect to the Union as well as the Member States lacking universal outreach.

81. Gráinne de Búrca and Paul Craig, *EU Law: Text, Cases, and Materials* (6th edn, OUP 2015) 392–393.
82. Andrew Williams, *The Ethos of Europe: Values, Law and Justice in the EU* (CUP 2012).
83. András Jakab and Dimitry V Kochenov (eds), *The Enforcement of EU Law and Values: Ensuring Member States' Compliance* (OUP 2017).
84. Andrew Williams, *The Ethos of Europe: Values, Law and Justice in the EU* (CUP 2012) 283.
85. Regarding this conflict: Kim Lane Scheppele, Dimitry V Kochenov, and Barbara Grabowska-Moroz, 'EU Values Are Law, after All: Enforcing EU Values through Systemic Infringement Actions by the European Commission and the Member States of the European Union', 39 Yearbook of European Law 2020, 3, 10.
86. See François Duchêne, 'Europe's Role in World Peace' in Richard Mayne (ed), *Europe Tomorrow: Sixteen Europeans Look Ahead* (Fontana 1973) 32–47.
87. Hedley Bull, 'Civilian Power Europe: A Contradiction in Terms?', 21(2) JCMS 1982, 151.
88. Ian Manners, 'Normative Power Europe: A Contradiction in Terms?', 40(2) JCMS 2002, 235.
89. See generally Sonia Lucarelli and Ian Manners (eds), *Values and Principles in European Union Foreign Policy* (Routledge 2007); François Foret and Oriane Calligaro (eds), *European Values. Challenges and Opportunities for EU Governance* (Routledge 2018); Stephen Weatherill, *Law and Values in the European Union* (OUP 2016) 393.
90. Marise Cremona, 'The EU and the External Dimension of Human Rights Policy' in Stratos V Konstadinidis (ed), *A People's Europe. Turning a Concept into Content* (Routledge 1999) 155.
91. In this sense see Jan Zielonka, *Europe as Empire: The Nature of the Enlarged European Union* (OUP 2006) 140 holding that the EU is more like a 'neo-medieval empire' than a 'Westphalian state'.
92. Vivian Kube, 'The European Union's External Human Rights Commitment: What is the Legal Value of Article 21 TEU?' (2016) EUI Working Paper LAW 2016/10 <https://cadmus.eui.eu/handle/1814/40426> accessed 23 May 2023 10–24.
93. For an analysis of the 'export' of human rights Jan Wouters et al (eds), *The European Union and Human Rights: Law and Policy* (OUP 2020); Jan Wouters and Michal Ovádek, *The European Union and Human Rights: Analysis, Cases, and Materials* (OUP 2021); critical with respect to the implementation: Maria Torres Pérez, 'The European Union Protection of Human Rights through its Global Policy: The Implementation of the Regime of Restrictive Measures Against Serious Violations and Abuses of Human Rights', 19 The Age of Human Rights Journal 2022, 255.
94. Elaine Fahey, *The Global Reach of EU Law* (Routledge 2018); see earlier Joanne Scott, 'Extraterritoriality and Territorial Extension in EU Law', 62(1) American Journal of Comparative Law 2014, 87.
95. Samatha Velluti, *The Role of the EU in the Promotion of Human Rights and International Labour Standards in Its External Trade Relations* (Springer 2020).
96. For an in-depth study of these see Marise Cremona and Joanne Scott (eds), *EU Law Beyond EU Borders: The Extraterritorial Reach of EU Law* (OUP 2019).

97. Arie Reich and Hans-Wolfgang (eds), *The Impact of the European Court of Justice on Neighbouring Countries* (OUP 2020).
98. See for this division regarding human rights norms Bruno de Witte, 'The European Union in the International System of Human Rights Protection: Solo Singer or Voice in the Choir?' in Emmanuelle Bribosia and Isabelle Rorive (eds), *Human Rights Tectonics: Global Dynamics of Integration and Fragmentation* (Intersentia 2019) 235.
99. For a recent analysis of many fields see Elaine Fahey and Isabella Mancini (eds), *Understanding the EU as a Good Global Actor* (Edward Elgar 2022).
100. Rather critical Elena Fierro, *The EU's Approach to Human Rights Conditionality in Practice* (Brill 2002); Päivi Leino, 'European Universalism?—The EU and Human Rights Conditionality', 24(1) Yearbook of European Law 2005, 329.
101. Gráinne de Búrca, The EU in the Negotiation of the UN Disability Convention, 35(2) European Law Review 2010, 174.
102. See generally Pete Betts, 'The EU's Role in the Paris Agreement' in Henrik Jepsen et al (eds), *Negotiating the Paris Agreement: The Insider Stories* (CUP 2021); see also Clara Brandi, 'EU Climate Leadership? Europe's Role in Global Climate Negotiations' in Claus Leggewie and Franz Mauelshagen (eds), *Climate Change and Cultural Transition in Europe* (Brill 2018); Stefanos Matthaios Minas and Vassilis Ntousas (eds), *EU Climate Diplomacy: Politics, Law and Negotiations* (Routledge 2018).
103. Hanna Touminen, 'Effective Human Rights Promotion and Protection? The EU and its Member States at the UN Human Rights Council', 61(4) JCMS 2023, 935, 945–948.
104. Raja Noureddine, 'Normative Power Europe and in Field of Human Rights: Is the EU a Force for Good in the World?', 8(2) Australia and New Zealand Journal of European Studies 2016, 111, 117; see also Toby King, 'The European Union As A Human Rights Actor' in Michael O'Flaherty et al (eds), *Human Rights Diplomacy: Contemporary Perspectives* (Brill 2011) 97–100.
105. Weiler, 'Reflections on Political Messianism' (n 32) 304.
106. Bruno de Witte and Šejla Imamović, 'Opinion 2/13 on Accession to the ECHR: Defending the EU Legal Order against a Foreign Human Rights Court', 40(5) European Law Review 2015, 683.
107. Piet Eeckhout, 'Opinion 2/13 on EU Accession to the ECHR and Judicial Dialogue: Autonomy or Autarky', 38(4) Fordham International Law Journal 2015, 955; Daniel Halberstam, '"It's the Autonomy, Stupid!" A Modest Defense of Opinion 2/13 on EU Accession to the ECHR, and the Way Forward', 16(1) German Law Journal 2015, 105; Adam Łazowski and Ramses A Wessel, 'When Caveats Turn into Locks: Opinion 2/13 on Accession of the European Union to the ECHR', 16(1) German Law Journal 2019, 179.
108. Turkuler Isiksel, 'European Exceptionalism and the EU's Accession to the ECHR', 27(3) European Journal of International Law 2016, 565.
109. Katja S Ziegler, 'Strengthening the Rule of Law, but Fragmenting International Law: The Kadi Decision of the ECJ from the Perspective of Human Rights', 9(2) Human Rights Law Review 2009, 288.
110. Juliane Kokott and Christoph Sobotta, 'The Kadi Case—Constitutional Core Values and International Law—Finding the Balance?', 23(4) European Journal of International Law 2012, 1015.
111. Bruno de Witte, 'European Union Law: How Autonomous is its Legal Order?', 65 Zeitschrift für öffentliches Recht 2010, 141.

112. Bardo Fassbender, 'Triepel in Luxemburg—Die dualistische Sicht des Verhältnisses zwischen Europa- und Völkerrecht in der „Kadi-Rechtsprechung" des EuGH als Problem des Selbstverständnisses der Europäischen Union', 8 Die Öffentliche Verwaltung 2010, 333.
113. Samantha Besson, 'How international is the European Legal Order? Retracing Tuori's steps in the exploration of European legal pluralism', 5 No Foundations 2008, 51.
114. Anthony Aust, 'Kadi: Ignoring International Legal Obligations', 6(1) International Organizations Law Review 2009, 293; see also Veronika Fikfak, 'Kadi and the Role of the Court of Justice of the European Union in the International Legal Order', 15 Cambridge Yearbook of European Legal Studies 2013, 587; Gráinne de Búrca, 'The European Court of Justice and the International Legal Order after *Kadi*' (2009) Jean Monnet Working Paper 01/09; Samantha Besson, 'European Legal Pluralism after Kadi', 5(2) European Constitutional Law Review 2009, 237; Turkuler Isiksel, 'Fundamental Rights in the EU after Kadi and Al Barakaat', 16(5) European Law Journal 2010, 551.
115. Sergio Carrera et al (eds), *Constitutionalising the External Dimensions of EU Migration Policies in Times of Crisis: Legality, Rule of Law and Fundamental Rights Reconsidered* (Edward Elgar 2019); UNHCR, 'Legal considerations on returning asylum seekers & refugees from Greece to Turkey under safe third country & first country of asylum concepts' (23 March 2016); Hakkı Onur Arıner and Yiğit Kader, 'On the Removal of Asylum Seekers to Third Countries and the Scope of the EU–Turkey Readmission Agreement', 34(3–4) International Journal of Refugee Law 2022, 416.
116. Sara Kahn-Nisser, 'The EU, China, trade dependence and human rights', 35(4) Cambridge Review of International Affairs 2022, 545; earlier also Elena Fierro, *The EU's Approach to Human Rights Conditionality in Practice* (Brill 2002) 379.
117. See early on Marise Cremona, 'Values in EU Foreign Policy' in Malcolm Evans and Panos Koutrakos (eds), *Beyond the Established Legal Orders: Policy Interconnections between the EU and the Rest of the World* (Hart Publishing 2011) 275.
118. See generally Dimitry V Kochenov and Fabian Amtenbrink (eds), *The European Union's Shaping of the International Legal Order* (CUP 2013).
119. de Witte, 'Choir' (n 98).
120. ibid.
121. See Jean Monnet, *Les États-Unis d'Europe ont commencé* (Robert Laffont 1955) 128.
122. Timothy Garton Ash, *Homelands: A Personal History of Europe* (Bodley Head 2023) 337.
123. The now reanimated attempts to become a military power by finally building a Defence Union prove extremely difficult to realize, since there is an institutional lock-in as a silent superpower, maybe even 'traumata' (JHH Weiler), killing any deeper desire to move into this direction.
124. David Scott FitzGerald, *Refuge beyond Reach: How Rich Democracies Repel Asylum Seekers* (OUP 2019), in particular ch 8 'Building Fortress Europe'; more recently John Reynolds, 'Fortress Europe, Global Migration & the Global Pandemic', 114 AJIL Unbound 2020, 342.
125. Ash, *Homelands* (n 122) 338.
126. With respect to this see Antonio Cassese, 'Remarks on Scelle's Theory of "Role Splitting" (*dédoublement fonctionnel*) in International Law', 1(1) EJIL 1990, 210.
127. Reinhart Koselleck, 'The Unknown Future and the Art of Prognosis' in Reinhart Koselleck, *The Practice of Conceptual History: Timing History, Spacing Concepts* (Stanford UP 2002) 131.

128. Luca Argenta, *The Seemingly Insurmountable Polycrisis of the European Union* (Villa Vigoni 2022).
129. Frédéric Mérand, *European Defence Policy: Beyond the Nation State* (OUP 2008).
130. Daniel S Hamilton, Gregor Kirchhof, and Andreas Rödder (eds), *Zeitenwende? Zur Selbstbehauptung der Europäischen Union in einer neuen Welt* (Mohr Siebeck 2022).
131. Former Advocate General Sir Francis G. Jacobs, Foreword to Robert Schütze and Takis Tridimas (eds), *Oxford Principles of European Union Law, Volume 1: The European Union Legal Order* (OUP 2018) viii.

CHAPTER 21

EUROPEAN NEIGHBOURHOOD POLICY AND EU ENLARGEMENT

SYLWIA MAJKOWSKA-SZULC AND KAROLINA WIERCZYŃSKA

1. Introduction

THE European Union (EU) cooperates with third countries and organizations from all over the world, but the EU's relations with its neighbours are of a special nature. The aim of close neighbourly relations is to prevent the emergence of new dividing lines between the enlarged EU and its neighbours. It is worth emphasizing that neighbourhood policy as promoted by the United Nations (UN) is not characterized by setting up any privileged relation among neighbouring countries. In contrast to the neighbourhood policy introduced by the EU, which tends to enhance political and economic interdependence among 'the ring of friends',[1] the UN is focused on promoting universal ideas such as peace, tolerance and sovereign equality among all States. The policy of the EU has developed, regionalized, but also limited its perception of good neighbourhood solely to those States embraced by the European Neighbourhood Policy (ENP), which includes close relations not necessarily leading to membership in the EU. While UN policy is universal and open in scope, EU policy develops within the borders of States engaged in the ENP and within those borders involves certain universal rules and values. It should be highlighted that becoming a member of the EU is a complex procedure, separate from the neighbourhood policy framework, concentrated on implementation of EU law and rules in all areas (the whole *acquis communautaire*). That is why States participating in the ENP are not necessarily candidate States and not all candidate States participate in the ENP.[2]

The general objective of the ENP and its instruments is to promote the Union's values, principles, and fundamental interests worldwide, but regionally rather than universally as it refers to the EU's closest neighbours: six Eastern countries (Armenia, Azerbaijan, Belarus, Georgia, Moldova, and Ukraine) and ten countries in the South (Algeria, Egypt, Israel, Jordan, Lebanon, Libya, Morocco, Palestine,[3] Syria, Tunisia). The list of countries engaged in the ENP differs from the list of candidate countries because not all countries involved in the ENP are candidates for the EU. Moreover, some countries engaged in the ENP will by design never become candidate countries for the EU. The list of candidate countries includes Albania, Macedonia, Moldova, North Montenegro, Serbia, Turkey, and Ukraine. As expressed in the communication by the Commission,[4] the ENP tends to fulfil a rather pacifying and controlling role, and—beside the fact that all States engaged in the ENP should universally and effectively share European common values—it is mostly focused on peace, stability, sharing common universal values, and friendly relations within the borders of the States concerned. The Communication mentioned above underlines that enhanced political and economic interdependence can itself be a means to promote stability, security, and sustainable development both within and outside the EU. The ENP does not include the Russian Federation. Relations between the EU and Russia have been tense ever since Russia's illegal annexation of Crimea in 2014 and its destabilizing actions in eastern Ukraine. After Russia launched its invasion of Ukraine on 24 February 2022, further political, cultural, and scientific co-operation was suspended.

The most tempting goal for States, such as future membership or a complete waiver of visa regimes, are not the principal aims of the ENP. The question of membership was left to agreements between the EU and States, with the result that engagement in the ENP requiring certain convergence with EU values is not very attractive for third countries. Some European States intentionally decided not to join the EU, but have chosen other ways of economic cooperation with EU member States. Some European States do not participate in the ENP and do not intend to join the EU, but maintain particularly close relations with the EU. On the one hand, three countries from the European Free Trade Association (EFTA) (Iceland, Liechtenstein, and Norway) form the European Economic Area (EEA) along with all EU member States. The Agreement on the EEA entered into force on 1 January 1994[5] and is principally concerned with the four EU fundamental freedoms of the internal market (free movement of goods, people, services, and capital). On the other hand, Switzerland fosters close relations with EU member States in the fields of politics, trade, and science by way of bilateral agreements in particular matters. It should be highlighted that Iceland, Liechtenstein, Norway, and Switzerland respect the case law of the Court of Justice of the European Union (CJEU) interpreting legal provisions underlying their relations with the EU. Finally, one country—the United Kingdom (UK)—carried out its decision to withdraw from the EU and from the European Atomic Energy Community ('Euratom').

Setting aside the obligations put on States that want to join the EU, other political reasons might seem discouraging for potential candidates. Looking at the practice in the States engaged in the ENP, it is evident that the idea standing behind the ENP to 'create an area of shared prosperity and values based on deeper economic integration, intensified political and cultural relations, enhanced cross-border cooperation and shared responsibility for conflict prevention between the EU and its neighbours'[6] has not prevented armed conflicts and political turbulence in those States. Territorial disputes involve Moldova (over Transnistria), the dispute between Armenia and Azerbaijan over the status of the Republic of Nagorno Karabakh, the Georgian-Russian armed conflict, or the Russian annexation of Ukrainian Crimea or, finally, Russia's large-scale invasion of Ukraine in 2022—all directly indicate the low effectiveness of the ENP's 'mission' in terms of stability and peaceful relations. Although the EU is not directly involved in those events, the States directly concerned are engaged in the ENP (excluding Russia) which allows us to assume that limiting this policy only to the borders of States engaged in the ENP is a rather short-sighted solution, not necessarily reflecting the aspirations of States (on peaceful relations and stability). Since neither the ENP nor any international dialogue provided an opportunity to stop Russia from attacking Ukraine, on 23 June 2022 EU leaders gathered at the European Council summit granted Ukraine candidate status for EU membership, laying the groundwork for even closer cooperation with Ukraine.

This chapter aims at a thorough analysis of the ENP, its achievements, and challenges. The introduction (in this Section 1) sketches some general problems referring to different statuses of States. Taking into account the principles of neighbourhood policy (Section 2), the legal grounds of the ENP (Section 3), and its genesis (Section 4), the chapter will critically analyse and assess the ideals of the ENP, the underlying successes and failures of the policy, and its prospects (see Conclusions, Section 5).

2. Principles of European Neighbourhood Policy

The basic rule is that the Union's actions on the international scene will be guided by the same principles which inspired its own creation, development, and enlargement. Simultaneously, since its launch in 2004, the ENP has constituted a crucial aspect of EU foreign policy. In turn, the EU seeks to advance the following ideals and principles in the wider world: democracy, the rule of law, the universality and indivisibility of human rights and fundamental freedoms, respect for human dignity, the principles of equality and solidarity, and respect for the principles of the United Nations Charter (UN Charter) and international law. Simultaneously, the EU will promote multilateral solutions to common problems, in particular in the framework of the UN (Article 21.1 of the Treaty on European Union (TEU)). The basic principles of the ENP are the principle of cooperation and the principle of respect for EU fundamental values.

2.1 The principle of cooperation

The ENP constitutes an element of international relations and should be analysed in the light of international law. According to Article 3.5 TEU the Union will contribute, for example, to strict observance and development of international law, including respect for the principles of the UN Charter. Since its creation in 1945, the UN has emphasized the development of cooperation between States, their peaceful relations, and good neighbourliness between States as provided in the preamble of the Charter 'to practice tolerance and live together in peace with one another as good neighbours'.[7] Article 74 developed this preambular declaration, referring to the policy of member States which 'must be based on the general principle of good-neighbourliness, due account being taken of the interests and well-being of the rest of the world, in social, economic, and commercial matters'.

The drafters of the UN Charter introduced a new scale of values as this principle was neglected in the statute of the League of Nations, where the emphasis was put on prevention of future wars rather than development of good neighbourly relations. According to Article 2, the UN is 'based on the principle of the sovereign equality of all its Members' and adds that 'members shall refrain in their international relations from the threat or use of force against the territorial integrity or political independence of any state'. Universal respect for these principles lies precisely in the principle of good neighbourliness, although its content is not defined in the Charter nor indeed in any document existing at the time. The situation did not change after adoption of Resolution 2625 by the General Assembly in 1970 titled 'The Declaration on Principles of International Law concerning Friendly Relations and Co-operation among States',[8] which recalled the provisions of the Charter in this regard. For some years, the question of good neighbourliness was on the UN agenda. Consequently, the UN General Assembly emphasized the importance of promoting good neighbourliness for peace, security, and friendly cooperation between States.[9] The Sub-Committee on Good-Neighbourliness—created within the UN to identify and clarify the elements of good neighbourliness—in a few reports presented its findings referring to existing and accepted principles of international law such as: 'universal applicability of the concept of good-neighbourliness between neighbouring States; observance of generally accepted principles and norms of international law as a basic requirement of good-neighbourliness and mutual tolerance'.[10] This demonstrates a strong link between the principle of good neighbourliness and recognition of traditional concepts of international law such as sovereignty, territorial integrity, or political independence on which the system of the UN is based. In that context, good neighbourliness is called the 'key principle underpinning the peaceful coexistence between states'.[11] It is worth observing the principle in the context of the dictum from the *Lotus* case and 'every State's obligation not to knowingly allow its territory to be used for acts contrary to the rights of other States'[12] as mirroring the idea of the responsibility of States not to allow their territory to be used for acts of war and aggression against other States.

But the functioning of this principle in EU law has been modified and differs from classic international law.[13] As noted, it was traditionally bound up with the sovereign equality of States and the enjoyment of their traditional rights within State borders. The EU, with its shift from classic recognition of territorial sovereignty and traditionally perceived legal borders and political independence, has undoubtedly introduced a new context for the development of good neighbourliness. The ENP is clearly marking a shift from good neighbourliness between neighbours to good neighbourliness between all member States of the EU and other States, from good neighbourliness referring only to good relations, cooperation, and protecting borders to good neighbourliness based on possible future membership of those States in the EU, which in turn is equated with exporting some normative preferences into the domestic systems of potential EU candidates.[14]

2.2 The principles of respect for EU fundamental values

The standards defining the values on which the EU is based were laid down in primary EU law, in particular in the TEU. The fact that EU values are enshrined in the TEU means that they have been signed by the heads of State or government of all the member States and have been ratified by all the member States in line with their constitutional requirements. When adopting the TEU, the leaders of the member States acted under the influence of the 'cultural, religious and humanist inheritance of Europe, from which have developed the universal values of the inviolable and inalienable rights of the human person, freedom, democracy, equality and the rule of law'.[15] Specifically, the EU is founded on the values of respect for human dignity, freedom, democracy, equality, the rule of law, and respect for human rights, including the rights of persons belonging to minorities (see Çalı, this volume).[16] The content-related fundamentality is confirmed in the universality of the values of the EU treaties because they do not relate to specific areas of law but appear in all areas of EU law. Both candidate countries and those involved in the ENP must share the same values that the EU is founded on. Article 2 TEU contains legal principles which are detailed in different treaty provisions such as Article 19 TEU, which gives concrete expression to the value of the rule of law (see van Aaken, this volume).[17] Simultaneously, these values are common to the member States in a society in which pluralism, non-discrimination, tolerance, justice, solidarity, and equality between women and men prevail.[18] Firstly, this means that mutual trust between the member States, including their courts and tribunals, is based on the fundamental premise that member States share a set of common values on which the EU is founded.[19] Secondly, compliance by a member State with the values enumerated in Article 2 TEU is a condition for enjoyment of all the rights deriving from application of the treaties to that member State. Simultaneously, a member State cannot amend its legislation in such a way as to bring about a reduction in protection of one of those shared values.[20] Moreover, any European State which respects the values referred to in Article 2 TEU may apply to become a member of the Union.[21] In this way, respect for Union values is a precondition for membership in the EU.[22] Finally, respect for shared values is one of the aims of the Union's external action,[23] including its neighbourhood policy. Once a candidate country becomes a member State of the EU, it will be responsible for breach of the values the EU is founded on, because violation of the Union's values is backed up by certain sanctions indicated in Article 7 TEU.[24] To conclude, even if the mechanisms set out in Article 7 TEU cannot be applied to third countries, they still play a role in the case of countries seeking EU membership.

3. Legal Basis for European Neighbourhood Policy

The ENP is governed by Article 8 TEU.[25] From a systemic point of view, this provision forms part of Title I 'Common Provisions' of the TEU, alongside provisions relating to the values the EU is founded on (Article 2 TEU) and objectives of the EU (Article 3 TEU). Article 8 TEU, introduced by the Lisbon Treaty as a new provision,[26] requires the Union to develop a special relationship with neighbouring countries, aiming to establish an area of prosperity and good neighbourliness, founded on the values of the Union and characterized by close and peaceful relations based on cooperation.[27] For this purpose, the Union may conclude specific agreements with the countries concerned. These agreements may contain reciprocal rights and obligations as well as the possibility of undertaking activities jointly. Their implementation is the subject of periodic consultation.[28] It was noted in the doctrine that the ENP started in 2004 with the idea of a 'Wider Europe', but over time the EU set out to create 'a ring of friends' to ensure stability, prosperity, and peace.[29]

Moreover, Article 37 TEU may serve as the legal basis for neighbourhood relations in the area of Common Foreign and Security Policy. Specifically, the Union may conclude agreements with one or more States or international organizations in the abovementioned area governed by Chapter 2 of Title V TEU.[30] As far as trade relations with neighbouring countries are concerned, Articles 206 and 207 of the Treaty on Functioning of the European Union (TFEU) constitutes the legal basis. By establishing a customs union, the EU should contribute to the harmonious development of world trade, progressive abolition of restrictions on international trade and on foreign direct investment, and lowering of customs and other barriers.[31] Furthermore, the common commercial policy should be based on:

> uniform principles, particularly with regard to changes in tariff rates, the conclusion of tariff and trade agreements relating to trade in goods and services, and the commercial aspects of intellectual property, foreign direct investment, the achievement of uniformity in measures of liberalisation, export policy and measures to protect trade such as those to be taken in the event of dumping or subsidies.[32]

All the treaty provisions presented above constitute the substantive basis for relations between the EU and third countries. Simultaneously, from a formal point of view, the basis of relations with third countries are international agreements concluded by the EU on the terms set out in Articles 216–219 TFEU. These agreements are binding upon EU institutions and on EU member States.[33] Bilateral relations are carried out between the EU and its sixteen ENP partners. Multilateral relations consist of ENP regional and multilateral cooperation initiatives. These initiatives include the Eastern Partnership, the Renewed Partnership with the Southern Neighbourhood, the New Agenda for the Mediterranean, the Union for the Mediterranean, the Black Sea Synergy, the Northern Dimension, the EU Arctic Policy, and Cross Border Cooperation (CBC). Over the period 2021–2027, the EU has been supporting implementation of ENP policy through the Neighbourhood, Development and International Cooperation Instrument (NDICI—Global Europe).[34]

Hypothetically, Article 8 TEU could have been used within Brexit negotiations on the future relationship between the EU and the UK. The key question was whether the EU was obliged to negotiate a reasonable deal for the UK based on Article 8 TEU. On the one hand, the UK has become a neighbouring country and, as a rule, the EU develops a special relationship with its neighbours. To that end, the EU may conclude specific agreements with the countries concerned. Catherine Barnard and Emilija Leinarte presented five reasons why Article 8 TEU did not oblige the EU to negotiate a future deal which would have been favourable to the UK.[35] Firstly, Article 8 forms part of the Union treaty, so it is an 'internal' rule but does not create an international obligation. This means that it applies exclusively to the EU and its member States and, what is more, it probably cannot be enforced by a non-EU country. It has always been clear that Article 265 TFEU allows EU member States to bring an action before the Court of Justice against EU institutions for failure to act. However, the UK is not able to bring such an action as it is no longer a member State since 29 March 2019. Secondly, Article 8 aims at establishing an express Union 'neighbourhood competence' as part of the EU's 2003 ENP. In this context, Barnard and Leinarte emphasize that the ENP has always been focused on integrating the economically least developed neighbouring countries and encouraging political and economic reforms within those countries, in particular following the Arab Spring. Therefore, it does not seem that Article 8 TEU justifies preferential trade agreements with trading partners such as the UK. Thirdly, Article 8 TEU neither specifies the content of the given 'special relationship' nor obliges the EU to provide any specific model for the future UK-EU relationship, and in particular it did not oblige the EU to prevent a 'no deal' Brexit. The fourth reason is that Article 8 TEU has never been used as a typical 'legal basis' as special relationships between the EU and its neighbours are commonly concluded in the form of international agreements indicated in specific treaty provisions. Concurrently, association agreements (AAs) and free trade agreements are governed by Article 217 TFEU and Article 207 TFEU, respectively. Finally, the decision on the content of the UK-EU relationship might have to have been approved not only by the EU but also by the national and regional parliaments of the twenty-seven States. Consequently, these constitutional dependencies suggest that the EU could not be obliged to grant a good deal to the UK.[36]

The reality has shown that these assessments were justified because Article 8 has not in fact been used in any of the agreements concluded between the EU and the UK, including the EU-UK Withdrawal Agreement, the EU-UK Trade and Cooperation Agreement, the EU-UK Security of Information Agreement, and the EU-UK Agreement for Cooperation on the Safe and Peaceful Uses of Nuclear Energy. This solution should not be surprising as significant differences exist between third countries and a country which was a member of the EU over several decades. As rightly emphasized by Thomas Streinz, determining the terms for withdrawal and the nature of the future relationship between the EU and a leaving member State is fundamentally different from the conduct of negotiations between the EU and third countries, because all parties are operating within the EU legal framework during the withdrawal process. In this case, the principle of sincere cooperation, which forms an integral part of a 'supranational law of Brexit', provides the legal foundation for a 'cooperative Brexit'.[37]

4. Genesis of the European Neighbourhood Policy and EU Enlargement

The ENP was formally launched in 2004 based on a Communication entitled 'Wider Europe—Neighbourhood' adopted by the European Commission one year earlier.[38] The aim of the framework policy was to govern the EU's relations with sixteen of the EU's Eastern and Southern Neighbours (as mentioned in Section 1). The genesis of the EU's neighbourhood policy is closely related to EU enlargement. In the short-term perspective its aim undoubtedly includes legal 'pacification' of the EU's surroundings, including regulation of migration flows. The EU and its ENP have faced many challenges with regard to migration. It should be highlighted that it is hard to stabilize third countries acting from the outside in times of crisis.[39] In November 2002, the General Affairs and External Relations Council noted the situation of new neighbours on the Union's land border since 2004: Ukraine, Moldova, and Belarus. In December 2002, the Copenhagen European Council confirmed that the Union should take the opportunity offered by enlargement to enhance relations with its neighbours based on shared values. Simultaneously, the Copenhagen European Council reaffirmed that the enlargement concerned would serve to strengthen relations with Russia, at the same time calling for enhanced relations with Ukraine, Moldova, Belarus, and the Southern Mediterranean countries, all to be based on a long-term approach promoting reform, sustainable development, and trade. The Council also reaffirmed the European perspective of the countries of the Western Balkans in the Stabilization and Association Process.[40]

Then, in 2003, the European Commission officially noted that over the coming decade and beyond, the Union's capacity to provide security, stability, and sustainable development to its citizens would no longer be distinguishable from its interest in close cooperation with neighbours. The accession of new member States in 2004 constituted the biggest enlargement in the history of the EU and significantly changed the shape of the EU's political and economic relations with other parts of the world. As a result, on 1 May 2004, the EU entered a new and historic phase. This presented a unique chance to strengthen the Union's interest in enhancing relations with new neighbours. At that time, political and economic interdependence with the Union's neighbourhood was already a reality as closer geographical proximity meant common interests in working together to tackle transboundary threats—from terrorism to airborne pollution. It became clear that neighbouring countries are the EU's essential partners. Consequently, the whole range of Union policies, such as foreign affairs, security, trade, development, the environment, and others met the challenge of interdependence with the EU's world partners.[41]

In its Communication of March 2003 the European Commission considered how to strengthen the framework for the Union's relations with those neighbouring countries which did not have the prospect of membership in the EU. In the view of the European Commission, the EU's neighbourhood should benefit from the prospect of closer economic integration with the EU in order to achieve concrete progress. In 2003 it seemed that, to this end, Russia—along with the countries of the Western newly independent States and the Southern Mediterranean (Algeria, Egypt, Israel, Jordan, Lebanon, Libya, Morocco, the Palestinian Authority, Syria, and Tunisia)—should have been offered the prospect of a stake in the EU's Internal Market and further integration and liberalization to promote the four EU economic fundamental freedoms. This New Neighbourhood Policy (NNP) therefore proposed further measures, such as:

(1) Extension of the internal market and regulatory structures.
(2) Preferential trading relations and market opening.
(3) Perspectives for lawful migration and movement of persons.
(4) Intensified co-operation to prevent and combat common security threats.
(5) Greater EU political involvement in conflict prevention and crisis management.
(6) Greater efforts to promote human rights, further cultural co-operation, and enhance mutual understanding.
(7) Integration into transport, energy and telecommunications networks and the European Research Area.
(8) New instruments for investment promotion and protection.
(9) Support for integration into the Global Trading System.
(10) Enhanced assistance, better tailored to needs.
(11) New sources of finance.[42]

It was decided that the NNP would be taken forward via country and/or regional strategic action plans developed by the Commission in partnership with neighbouring countries. Once these action plans were agreed, they could supersede common strategies to become the Union's main policy document for relations with neighbouring countries over the medium term. Moreover, the Communication also opened the prospect of new neighbourhood agreements, supplementing existing partnership and cooperation agreements, as well as AAs. The Commission's intention to develop proposals for enhancing the Union's relations with Russia, Ukraine, Moldova, Belarus, and the Southern Mediterranean countries were welcomed by the European Council in Copenhagen on 12 and 13 December 2003.[43]

Eighteen months after implementation of the ENP, the Commission took stock of the results of the NNP. The assessment showed that the ENP required strengthening because of the numerous problems the partner countries were facing, such as poverty, unemployment, mixed economic performance, corruption, weak governance, as well as frozen conflicts in certain regions. The challenges mentioned had gone beyond their borders and, as a result, also concerned the EU. It became clear that the EU and its partners had a mutual interest in stability to help combat illegal immigration, environmental degradation, and terrorism and to ensure reliable energy supplies. Therefore, the EU has supported and encouraged reforms in partner countries since the beginning of the ENP.[44] In answer to the needs listed above, the European Commission proposed a package of means by which the various Community agencies and programmes could be opened to neighbouring countries.[45] The Commission's proposal was accepted by the General Affairs and External Relations Council in its conclusions of March 2007.[46] On the one hand, the Council encouraged stakeholders to explore their potential to this end. On the other hand, the Council recalled the need for it to approve individual agreements on participation in any Community agency on a case-by-case basis. In the period 2007–2013, the European Neighbourhood and Partnership Instrument (ENPI) aimed at supporting achievement of ENP objectives with a view to establishing an area of prosperity and good neighbourhood relations between and with ENP partner countries and Russia. In the same period, the budget for the ENPI amounted to some €11 billion, of which 95 per cent was for national and multi-country programmes and 5 per cent for cross-border cooperation programmes.[47]

In 2011, following the 'Arab Spring' uprisings, the ENP was broadly reviewed.[48] In these new circumstances, the Commission aimed to improve its support for the processes of reform undertaken by its partner countries, so proposed a new strategy for the ENP. The new approach was based on greater differentiation by country of cooperation objectives (the principle of flexibility). The so-called more for more principle was introduced, according to which partner countries' efforts towards additional reforms were to be rewarded with additional support, in particular financial support. As a consequence, the strategy adopted in 2011 aimed to increase the conditionality of financial assistance, which could be increased or restricted depending on progress made in terms of democracy and human rights. Moreover, the strategy aimed to support inclusive economic development, promoting trade, investment, sustainable development, and reducing unemployment. Finally, the new strategy was focused on strengthening regional synergies between the partners, within the Eastern Partnership—a specific

Eastern dimension of the ENP, and the Union for the Mediterranean—an intergovernmental institution bringing together the EU member States and fifteen countries from the southern and eastern shores of the Mediterranean, especially in the areas of trade, energy, transport, migration, and mobility.[49]

On the one hand, 2014 was a year of challenges in EU neighbourhood policy. The Russian invasion of Crimea (Ukraine) in 2014 and increasing Russian pressure on other eastern partners constituted major challenges in the EU's neighbourhood. In addition, both inside and outside Syria, millions of people were fleeing because of actions by the Assad regime. Concurrently, Gaza was still a fragile region. As a rule, the EU has always been involved in the Israeli-Palestinian conflict and has supported and kept alive the prospects of a two-State solution through its promotion of the Palestinian State-building process.[50] Moreover, lack of control over migratory flows to and from Libya in 2014 created favourable conditions for criminal networks engaged in irregular migration and trafficking in human beings to Europe.[51]

On the other hand, some successes were also noted. An example of success of the neighbourhood policy in 2014 was the signature of three AAs: with Georgia, Moldova, and Ukraine.[52] This was a new generation of agreements which includes provisions on a Deep and Comprehensive Free Trade Area (AAs/DCFTAs), putting in place the most ambitious contractual relations (third-generation AAs). Moreover, relations with Morocco and Tunisia were strengthened and continued to reflect the depth and breadth of reform efforts in these countries. Moldova successfully implemented all the benchmarks set in its Visa Liberalization Action Plan (VLAP), so that Moldovan citizens could enjoy visa-free travel to the Schengen countries as of spring 2014. Tunisia and Jordan also signed a Mobility Partnership with the EU in 2014. Finally, the instruments offered by the ENP played a central part as the new European Neighbourhood Instrument (ENI), adopted in 2014,[53] provided €15.4 billion for the period 2014–2020.[54]

Given all these developments in the neighbourhood, in March 2015 the EU launched a consultation on the future of the ENP.[55] Stakeholders were invited to react to the consultation. The review, proposed by President of the European Commission, Jean-Claude Juncker and requested by the EU member States, brought over 250 responses from member States, partner governments, EU institutions, international organizations, social partners, civil society, business, think tanks, academia, and members of the public, which as a whole largely confirmed the need for change in the ENP in both substance and in methodology. This demonstrated that, on the one hand, the offer of a closer relationship with the EU for those countries which have undertaken governance reforms has encouraged change in some countries, but on the other hand, practice and policy has been regarded by other partners as too prescriptive, and as not sufficiently reflecting their own aspirations. In addition, responses to the consultation indicated that greater flexibility must be sought to enable the EU and its partners to respond to ever-changing needs and circumstances. The response to the consultation was adopted on 18 November 2015.[56]

The main purpose of the 2015 ENP review was to propose how the EU and its neighbours could build more effective partnerships in the neighbourhood. Actually, the revision of the ENP resulted from the failure of the uniform 'one size fits all' approach. That explains why the revision was aimed at making the ENP more flexible. It was emphasized that the new ENP had to be designed in a spirit of inclusiveness to keep on board those countries which were unable or unwilling to meet all the requirements of the *acquis communautaire*.[57] This is the way of exporting the EU *acquis*, which contributes to establishing a friendly legal environment between the EU and third countries.[58] It was highlighted that the EU's own stability has always been built on democracy, human rights, the rule of law, and economic openness and, consequently, the new ENP should take stabilization as its main political priority in this mandate. A new transformative political framework was provided via adoption by the UN General Assembly of the 2030 Agenda for Sustainable Development and its Sustainable Development Goals (SDGs). The EU strongly supported its implementation. Four main areas formed the heart of the new ENP:

(1) good governance, democracy, rule of law, and human rights;
(2) economic development for stabilization;
(3) security; and
(4) migration and mobility.

The 2015 Review reinforced the principle of flexibility in order to ensure it is better adapted to rapidly evolving political circumstances and priorities. Furthermore, the review was closely coordinated as part of broader work on the EU Global Strategy on Foreign and Security Policy.[59] To sum up, differentiated partnerships and the tailor-made approach have been the hallmarks of the revised ENP.

Since adoption of the 2015 Review, substantial steps have been taken to deliver on those commitments. A report on implementation of the ENP Review, published in 2017, contained some positive conclusions. Firstly, even though the challenges in the region remained immense, the EU was acting with more flexibility and sensitivity towards its partners, deploying limited resources but with more impact. Secondly, the key principles of the policy, such as a differentiated approach and greater ownership, were to continue to guide its implementation in the upcoming years through diplomatic action, trade and investment relations, financial assistance, and long-term regional frameworks. Moreover, in a process of continuous engagement with EU citizens and citizens in partner countries, the EU decided to continue to enhance the visibility of the ENP, notably through highlighting the short-term, medium-term, and long-term benefits of cooperation with its neighbours. Finally, the report reconfirmed the broad engagement of all relevant stakeholders in implementing the 2015 Review.[60]

4.1 Candidate countries and EU enlargement

The EU's enlargement policy, along with the ENP, enhances the EU's presence in the global arena. Simultaneously, it has become one of the most successful European policies in promoting political, economic, and societal reforms, as well as in achieving EU goals, which consist in consolidating peace, stability, and democracy across the continent. Currently the EU numbers twenty-seven European States that together cover much of the continent.[61] Accession of new member States to the EU is governed by Article 49 TEU. A State that wishes to apply for EU membership must satisfy two basic preconditions. Firstly, it must be a European State. Secondly, it must respect and undertake to promote EU common values as defined in Article 2 TEU. As far as the procedure is concerned, the European Parliament and national parliaments are notified of an application by the given State. Then, that State addresses its application to the Council, which consults the Commission and obtains the consent of the European Parliament. In the meantime, the conditions of eligibility are agreed upon by the European Council. Finally, the Council acts unanimously in considering the conditions of eligibility agreed before. The conditions of admission are the subject of an agreement between all member States and the applicant State. This agreement must be submitted for ratification by all contracting States in accordance with its constitutional requirements.[62]

Candidate country status does not give a right to join the EU automatically. The criteria that must be met for accession are known as the Copenhagen criteria because they were established by the Copenhagen European Council in 1993. Then, they were strengthened by the Madrid European Council in 1995. The Copenhagen criteria were prepared in view of accession to the EU of the associated countries in Central and Eastern Europe, but the criteria so far still apply today. Accession of a new member State takes place as soon as an associated country can assume the obligations of membership by satisfying the economic and political conditions required. Simultaneously, membership requires from the candidate country the following:

> stability of institutions guaranteeing democracy, the rule of law, human rights, and respect for and protection of minorities, the existence of a functioning market economy as well as the capacity to cope with competitive pressure and market forces within the Union.[63] Moreover, membership presupposes the candidate's ability to take on the obligations of membership including adherence to the aims of political, economic and monetary union.[64]

Current candidate countries are: Albania (since 2014), Georgia (since 2022), Moldova (since 2022), North Macedonia (since 2005), Montenegro (since 2010), Serbia (since 2012), Turkey (since 1999; see Karakaş and Akbulut, this volume) and Ukraine (since 2022).

The evolution of the ENP shows that it draws considerably on the EU's enlargement policy and its 'Europeanization beyond Europe' logic.[65] One of the key factors determining the shape of the EU's eastern policy has become aggression by the Russian Federation towards Ukraine. The first invasion took place in February 2014, taking the form of a hybrid war. A month later the political chapters of the EU-Ukraine AA were signed, and then in June 2014 the rest of the agreement. As of 1 November 2014, provisional application of several important parts of the agreement started, including sectoral and economic cooperation involving the energy sector. In turn, the DCFTA was applied provisionally from 1 January 2016, lifting most customs tariffs regarding trade in goods. The entire EU-Ukraine AA entered into force on 1 September 2017. As late as December 2021, at the Eastern Partnership summit, the heads of State discussed the importance of energy resilience so that, less than a month after the Russian invasion, namely on 16 March 2022, the power grids of Ukraine and Moldova had successfully been synchronized with the European continental network. Escalation of the war that started in 2014 took place on 24 February 2022 when the Russian Federation launched a full-scale military invasion of Ukraine. The European Council and the Council of the EU have been meeting regularly to discuss the situation in Ukraine from different perspectives. One of the key actions taken by the European Council was conclusion of an agreement on the sixth package of sanctions against Russia on 30 May 2022.[66] The sanctions were intended to weaken Russia economically, including depriving it of access to critical technologies and markets, in order to significantly reduce Russia's combat capability. In the face of the Russian invasion, Ukraine has started negotiations to implement the 'fast track' for EU membership. This was a clear political signal. On 23 June 2022, the European Council decided to grant the status of candidate country to Ukraine as well as to Moldova.

Consequently, the Russian invasion accelerated political and social integration between the EU and Ukraine, but simultaneously disrupted world markets, causing a sharp rise in world prices of key commodities, including fuel and food. The war created uncertainty about security of energy supply, prompting the EU to take immediate action to ensure supply in all possible countries. The DCFTA opened up markets for goods and services on both sides but based on predictable and enforceable trade rules. In May 2022, the EU temporarily liberalized trade with Ukraine, but controls at the EU's external borders remained crucial. The treaty provision according to which the Union defines and conducts common policies and activities and works towards a high level of cooperation in all areas of international relations[67] takes on greater importance.

4.2 Who does not want to join the EU and who withdrew?

Among European States which have not joined the EU, the majority have the status of candidate country. As already mentioned, Iceland, Liechtenstein, Norway, and Switzerland do not intend to join the EU at the moment because they do not want to be bound by all areas of EU law. At the same time, they benefit from special economic cooperation with the EU and visa-free transfer. All four countries form part of the border-free Schengen Area,[68] even though only twenty-three of the twenty-seven Member States of the EU form part of the Area. One State—the UK—decided to withdraw and finished the procedure with conclusion of the Withdrawal Agreement.[69]

The withdrawal procedure is based on Article 50 TEU on the internal constitutional requirements of the withdrawing State.[70] Firstly, the member State concerned notifies the European Council of its intention to withdraw from the EU. Secondly, the Union negotiates and concludes an agreement with that State. The agreement is concluded by the Council acting on behalf of the Union by a qualified majority after obtaining the consent of the European Parliament.[71] From the date of entry into force of the withdrawal agreement or, failing that, two years after notification of intention to withdraw, the Treaties cease to apply to the withdrawing State. However, the possibility to extend this period is available if the European Council, in agreement with the withdrawing State, acting unanimously decides to extend the period.[72] Finally, if a State that has withdrawn from the EU wishes to rejoin the EU, its request will have to follow the procedure referred to in Article 49 TEU,[73] namely the standard accession procedure. The first application of Article 50 TEU in practice was Brexit.

In 2016, after forty-four years of membership, the British decided to withdraw from the EU. The UK formally notified its intention to the European Council in 2017.[74] As a result, an extraordinary European Council adopted guidelines defining the framework for negotiations.[75] On the one hand, all member States expressed their wish to retain close partnership with the UK, but on the other hand, it was clearly noted that any agreement with the UK should be based on a balance of rights and obligations, and non-EU countries could not have the same rights or enjoy the same benefits as its members. In January 2020, the House of Commons approved the Withdrawal Agreement Bill (WAB).[76] Subsequently, the Withdrawal Agreement (WA) was signed by President of the European Council, Charles Michel, and President of the European Commission, Ursula von der Leyen—both acting on behalf of the EU—and by Prime Minister Boris Johnson acting on behalf of the UK.[77] Ultimately, the WA entered into force at midnight on 31 January 2020, which is also the end of the period referred to in Article 50 paragraph 3 TEU.

As the UK has withdrawn from the EU it is no longer an EU member State and is considered a third country from the perspective of EU law. The transition period ended on 31 December 2020. Negotiations on a future partnership with the UK began in early March 2020, but talks were delayed due to the outbreak of the Covid-19 pandemic. Finally, the Trade and Cooperation Agreement was signed on 30 December 2020, applied provisionally as of 1 January 2021, and entered into force on 1 May 2021.[78] The UK's decision was perceived by European leaders as a threat to the unity of the EU. The fragmentation caused by Brexit required adoption of legal solutions guaranteeing protection of the rights and status of Union citizens in the UK and British citizens in the EU.[79]

5. Conclusions: Achievements and Challenges of Close Neighbourhood

The main purpose of the ENP has always been promotion of the Union's values, principles, and fundamental interests worldwide. Simultaneously, the ENP pursues the objectives and principles of the Union's external action, as laid down in Articles 3(5), 8, and 21 TEU.

All Union actions should promote respect for human rights, including the Universal Declaration of Human Rights. In recent years, the ENP and the EU as such have faced many challenges not only in relation with third countries, but also inside the EU. The experience of Brexit and the fact that a long-lasting member of the European Union decided to withdraw from the EU is probably the most tragic failure among the political and institutional failures of Brexit-related campaigning. Brexit-related data-driven campaigns were marked by undemocratic practices based on disinformation.[80] Among other failures, the lack of stability or shortcoming of democracy could be pointed out among close neighbours. Even the Russian invasions could be seen as a failure of the ENP. However, firstly Russia only pretended to cooperate, but in fact was never taking part in this policy, and secondly the EU had tried to engage Russia in some processes fostering democracy, human rights, and the rule of law in the past, for example in 2002 and 2003 as noted above, but to no avail. It is hard to believe that any European strategy (pacification) could have prevented current Russian aggressive policies.

Undoubtedly, due to Russia's invasion of Ukraine, the EU's enlargement policy needed to be adapted to a new geopolitical situation. As a rule, the EU integrates new member States through the enlargement process once they meet the political and economic conditions. The process encourages democratic and economic reforms in candidate countries and as a consequence promotes greater stability and prosperity in Europe. In the current situation, the EU is making extraordinary efforts to clarify its engagement with Ukraine, Moldova, and Georgia by moving them from the neighbourhood to the enlargement policy framework. This delivers a strong political message to Russia that the EU is committed to restoring peace on the European continent.[81]

As far as EU-UK relations are concerned, the UK has become a third country, which means that it is no longer a 'friend from a ring' or 'privileged country'. On the contrary, the UK is—legally speaking—now a much more distant State for the EU than its southern or eastern neighbours engaged in the ENP. From the first circle of closeness the UK has become a State with which the EU shares universal values, a desire for peace and stability like never before, but is no longer engaged in economic or political relations comparable to membership or even to participation in the ENP. Today voices are being raised among British politicians that Brexit was a mistake.[82] In a sense, recognizing Brexit as a mistake can be considered a success, but it is a pity that such conclusions came when the United Kingdom is no longer on board. At least this can be seen as reflecting the UK's wish to build a new, close relationship with the EU. Undoubtedly, the ENP and EU enlargement policy face further serious challenges related to multiple regional and global peace, health, climate, and economic crises.

Notes

1. Communication from the Commission to the Council and the European Parliament, 11.3.2003, COM(2003) 104 final <https://eur-lex.europa.eu/LexUriServ/LexUriServ.do?uri=COM:2003:0104:FIN:EN:PDF> accessed 11 July 2024, 5.

2. Currently, among the candidate countries, only Moldova and Ukraine take part in the ENP while Georgia, another participant of the ENP, has the status of potential candidate. Candidate status will be granted once Georgia addresses some key priorities reflected in the Commission's opinion—Commission Opinion on Georgia's application for membership of the European Union, COM/2022/405 final, Brussels, 17 June 2022.
3. The designation of Palestine shall not be construed as recognition of a State of Palestine and is without prejudice to the individual positions of the member States on this issue.
4. Communication from the Commission to the Council and the European Parliament, 11.3.2003, COM(2003) 104 final <https://eur-lex.europa.eu/LexUriServ/LexUriServ.do?uri=COM:2003:0104:FIN:EN:PDF> accessed 11 July 2024, 5.
5. OJ L 1, 3 January 1994, 3–522.
6. Communication from the Commission to the Council and the European Parliament, 11.3.2003, COM(2003) 104 final <https://eur-lex.europa.eu/LexUriServ/LexUriServ.do?uri=COM:2003:0104:FIN:EN:PDF> 9.
7. Preamble of the Charter of the United Nations, San Francisco, 26 June 1945.
8. GA Res 2625 (XXV).
9. See, eg, GA Res 37/117; GA Res 34/99.
10. Report of the Sub-Committee on Good Neighbourliness, A/C.6/42/L.6, 12 November 1987 <https://digitallibrary.un.org/record/148847/files/A_C.6_42_L.6-EN.pdf> accessed 11 July 2024.
11. Elena Basheska, 'The Position of Good Neighbourliness Principle in International and EU Law' in Dimitry Kochenov and Elena Basheska (eds), *Good Neighbourliness in the European Legal Context* (Brill Nijhoff 2015) 24.
12. Corfu Channel case (*UK v Albania*), ICJ Reports 1949, P. 4, 22.
13. For a broad analysis see also Dimitri Kochenov, 'The Internal Aspects of Good Neighbourliness in the EU: Loyalty and Values' in Kochenov and Basheska (n 11) 57 et seq.
14. Broadly on Europeanization see Jan Wouters, Andree Nollkaemper, and Erika de Wet (eds), *The Europeanisation of International Law: The Status of International Law in the EU and its Member States* (TMC Asser Press 2008).
15. Recital 2 of the Preamble to the Treaty on European Union, OJ C 202, 7 June 2016, 15–16.
16. Article 2 TEU.
17. See also Judgment of the Court (Grand Chamber) of 2 March 2021 in case C-824/18 *A.B. and Others v Krajowa Rada Sądownictwa and Others*, point 108, ECLI:EU:C:2021:153.
18. Article 2 TEU.
19. Judgment of the Court (Grand Chamber) of 27 February 2018 in case C-64/16 *Associação Sindical dos Juízes Portugueses v Tribunal de Contas*, point 30, ECLI:EU:C:2018:117.
20. Judgment of the Court (Grand Chamber) of 2 March 2021 in case C-824/18 *A.B. and Others v Krajowa Rada Sądownictwa and Others*, point 108, ECLI:EU:C:2021:153.
21. Article 49 TEU.
22. Andreas Haratsch, 'Democracy—A Value Common to the Member States of the European Union' in Armin Hatje and Lubos Tichý (eds), *Liability of Member States for the Violation of Fundamental Values of the European Union* (Nomos 2018) 74. Moreover Bruno de Witte and Gabriel N Toggenburg, 'Respect for Human Rights as a Condition for Membership of the European Union' in Steve Peers and Angela Ward (eds), *The European Union Charter of Fundamental Rights* (Hart Publishing 2004) 72.
23. Article 21(2)(a) TEU.

24. Article 7(3) TEU last sentence. For more on Article 7 TEU see Ewa Bagińska and Sylwia Majkowska-Szulc, 'Causation as a Requirement for the Member State Liability under Art. 7 TEU in Conjunction with Art. 2 TEU' in Hatje and Tichý (n 22) 130–140.
25. Consolidated version of the Treaty on European Union, OJ C 202, 7 June 2016.
26. Article 1 point 10 of the Treaty of Lisbon amending the Treaty on European Union and the Treaty establishing the European Community, signed at Lisbon, 13 December 2007, OJ C 306, 17 December 2007.
27. Article 8(1) TEU.
28. Article 8(2) TEU.
29. Dimitri Kochenov and Elena Basheska, 'The European Neighbouring Policy's Value Conditionality: From Enlargements to post-Crimea' in Sara Poli (ed), *The European Neighbourhood Policy—Values and Principles* (Routledge 2016).
30. Article 37 TEU.
31. Article 206 TFEU.
32. Article 207(1) TFEU.
33. Article 216(2) TFEU.
34. Regulation (EU) 2021/947 of the European Parliament and of the Council of 9 June 2021 establishing the Neighbourhood, Development and International Cooperation Instrument—Global Europe, amending and repealing Decision No 466/2014/EU of the European Parliament and of the Council and repealing Regulation (EU) 2017/1601 of the European Parliament and of the Council and Council Regulation (EC, Euratom) No 480/2009 (Text with EEA relevance), PE/41/2021/INIT, OJ L 209, 14 June 2021, 1–78.
35. Catherine Barnard and Emilija Leinarte, Is the EU obliged to prevent a 'bad Brexit'? <https://ukandeu.ac.uk/is-the-eu-obliged-to-prevent-a-bad-brexit/> accessed 11 July 2024.
36. ibid.
37. Thomas Streinz, 'Cooperative Brexit: Giving Back Control over Trade Policy', 15(2) International Journal of Constitutional Law 2017, 271.
38. Communication from the Commission to the Council and the European Parliament, Wider Europe—Neighbourhood: A New Framework for Relations with our Eastern and Southern Neighbours, Brussels, 11 March 2003, COM(2003) 104 final.
39. Margaret Walton-Roberts and Jenna Hennebry, *Territoriality and Migration in the E.U. Neighbourhood: Spilling over the Wall* (Springer Science & Business Media 2013) 205.
40. Communication from the Commission to the Council and the European Parliament, Wider Europe—Neighbourhood: A New Framework for Relations with our Eastern and Southern Neighbours, Brussels, 11 March 2003, COM(2003) 104 final, 3–4.
41. ibid.
42. ibid, 10–14.
43. Communication from the Commission to the Council and the European Parliament, Wider Europe—Neighbourhood: A New Framework for Relations with our Eastern and Southern Neighbours, Brussels, 11 March 2003, COM(2003) 104 final, 15–18.
44. Communication from the Commission to the Council and the European Parliament on strengthening the European neighbourhood policy, COM/2006/0726 final.
45. Communication from the Commission to the Council and to the European Parliament on the general approach to enable ENP partner countries to participate in Community agencies and Community programmes, COM/2006/0724 final.
46. The General Affairs and External Relations Council's Conclusions of 5 March 2007, 2788th Council meeting, 6755/07 (Presse 38), 9.

47. Regulation (EC) No 1638/2006 of the European Parliament and of the Council of 24 October 2006 laying down general provisions establishing a European Neighbourhood and Partnership Instrument, OJ L 310, 9 November 2006, 1–14.
48. Joint Communication to the European Parliament, the Council, the European Economic and Social Committee and the Committee of the Regions of 25 May 2011—A new response to a changing Neighbourhood COM(2011) 303 final.
49. ibid.
50. For more on this topic see Anders Persson, *The EU and the Israeli–Palestinian Conflict 1971–2013: In Pursuit of a Just Peace* (Lexington Books 2015).
51. Idil Atak and James C Simeon, *The Criminalization of Migration: Context and Consequences* (McGill-Queen's UP 2018) 367–388.
52. For more on this topic see Naděžda Šišková, *From Eastern Partnership to the Association: A Legal and Political Analysis* (Cambridge Scholars Publishing 2014).
53. Regulation (EU) No 232/2014 of the European Parliament and of the Council of 11 March 2014 establishing a European Neighbourhood Instrument, OJ L 77, 15 March 2014, 27–43.
54. Joint Communication to the European Parliament, the Council, The European Economic and Social Committee and the Committee of the Regions, Implementation of the European Neighbourhood Policy in 2014, JOIN/2015/0009 final.
55. European Commission, *Towards a new European Neighbourhood Policy: the EU launches a consultation on the future of its relations with neighbouring countries*, Brussels 4 March 2015, IP/15/4548.
56. Joint Communication to the European Parliament, the Council, The European Economic and Social Committee and the Committee of the Regions, Review of the European Neighbourhood Policy, Brussels, 18 November 2015, JOIN(2015) 50 final.
57. Opinion of the European Economic and Social Committee on the Joint communication to the European Parliament, the Council, the European Economic and Social Committee and the Committee of the Regions 'Review of the European Neighbourhood Policy' (JOIN(2015) 50-final), points 1.2–1.4, OJ C 303, 19 August 2016, 138–146.
58. Roman Petrov, 'Means to Promote EU Values into the Legal Systems of Ukraine, Moldova and Georgia via Association Agreements' in Poli (n 29) 104.
59. Joint Communication to the European Parliament, the Council, The European Economic and Social Committee and the Committee of the Regions, Review of the European Neighbourhood Policy, Brussels 18 November 2015, JOIN(2015) 50 final.
60. Joint Communication to the European Parliament, the Council, The European Economic and Social Committee and the Committee of the Regions, Report on the Implementation of the European Neighbourhood Policy Review, Brussels 18 May 2017, JOIN(2017) 18 final.
61. 'Founding fathers' in 1951 and 1957: Belgium, Germany, France, Italy, Luxembourg, the Netherlands; 1973: Denmark, Ireland, and the UK; 1981: Greece; 1986: Spain and Portugal; 1995: Austria, Finland, and Sweden; 2004: Czech Republic, Estonia, Cyprus, Latvia, Lithuania, Hungary, Malta, Poland, Slovakia, and Slovenia; 2007: Romania and Bulgaria; 2013: Croatia.
62. Article 49 TEU.
63. Conclusions of the Presidency—Copenhagen, 21–21 June 1993, SN 180/1/93 REV 1, 13.
64. ibid.
65. Tobias Schumacher, Andreas Marchetti, and Thomas Demmelhuber (eds), *The Routledge Handbook on the European Neighbourhood Policy* (Routledge 2018) 4.

66. European Council conclusions on Ukraine, 30 May 2022, EUCO 21/22, CO EUR 19 CONCL 4, Brussels, 31 May 2022.
67. Article 21(2) TEU.
68. The Schengen acquis—Agreement between the Governments of the States of the Benelux Economic Union, the Federal Republic of Germany and the French Republic on the gradual abolition of checks at their common borders, OJ L 239, 22 September 2000, 13–18.
69. OJ L 29, 31 January 2020, 7–187.
70. Article 50(1) TEU.
71. Article 50(2) TEU.
72. Article 50(3) TEU.
73. Article 50(5) TEU.
74. United Kingdom notification under Article 50 TEU—A letter of 29 March 2017 from the Prime Minister of the UK to the President of the European Council, Brussels, 29 March 2017, BXT 1, XT 20001/17.
75. Special meeting of the European Council (Article 50) (29 April 2017)—Guidelines, EUCO XT 20004/17, Brussels, 29 April 2017.
76. Bill stages—European Union (Withdrawal Agreement) Bill 2019–2020 <https://bills.parliament.uk/bills/2517/stages> accessed 11 July 2024.
77. Agreement on the withdrawal of the United Kingdom of Great Britain and Northern Ireland from the European Union and the European Atomic Energy Community, 2019/C 384 I/01, OJ C 384I, 12 November 2019, 1–177.
78. Trade and Cooperation Agreement between the European Union and the European Atomic Energy Community, of the one part, and the United Kingdom of Great Britain and Northern Ireland, of the other part, OJ L 149, 30 April 2021, 10–2539.
79. Oliver Garner, *After Brexit: Protecting European Citizens and Citizenship from Fragmentation*, EUI Department of Law Working Paper No 2016/22 <http://hdl.handle.net/1814/44004> accessed 11 July 2024.
80. Julia Rone, 'Beyond Brexit? Public Participation in Decision-Making on Campaign Data During and After Referendum Campaigns', 11(1) Media and Communication 2023, 69–80; Online, 4 February 2023, 76–77.
81. Tinatin Akhvlediani, 'Geopolitical and Security Concerns of the EU's Enlargement to the East: The Case of Ukraine, Moldova and Georgia', 57 Intereconomics 2022, 225–228, 227.
82. See *The Financial Times* <https://www.ft.com/content/a13f684f-f55c-4e83-b5ee-55bb3ce55712>accessed 24 February 2023; *The Guardian* <https://www.theguardian.com/commentisfree/2023/jan/13/brexit-mistake-northern-ireland-protocol> accessed 11 July 2024.

CHAPTER 22

EUROPEAN JUDICIARY (ECtHR, ECJ, NATIONAL COURTS)

INETA ZIEMELE

1. Introduction

The chapter introduces the concept of a European judiciary, and its origins. The concept denotes that all the courts in Europe that form a web of judicial interrelations within a common European legal space. It describes European courts and the relations between all courts in Europe. It shows that the value of the rule of law, as it materializes, *inter alia*, through the functioning of independent and impartial courts at national and European levels, has become an inalienable feature of European culture. Europeans believe that an independent judiciary has a pacifying function in that such judiciary plays a crucial role in restraining power. Especially since the 20th century, European States have brought to international relations the principle of rule of law, of which the notion of independent and impartial courts forms a crucial element. This is part of Europe's universalist vision.

The chapter consists of four sections: the concept of a European judiciary; its development; the courts; and the future challenges.

2. The Concept of a European Judiciary and Its Origins

For the purposes of this chapter, several concepts will be used that, although bearing similarities, nevertheless differ in scope and substance. The concept of the European judiciary denotes all the courts in Europe that form a web of judicial interrelations within a common European legal space.[1] The phrase, European courts, refers to international or supranational courts in Europe. And the term, courts in Europe, refers to the numerous individual and specialized courts that are essential to the functioning of the European system of governance.

The idea of dispute resolution by an independent, authoritative party accompanies the development of Europe itself. However, submitting modern States to permanent international courts is to be seen as an ultimate achievement in the evolution of these ideas and a counterpoint to the idea of absolute sovereignty, especially insofar as such management of disputes is considered essential for the maintenance of peace. It is important to realize that the view taken on the role of courts in Europe reflects an integral part of philosophical theories, political thinking, and legal imagination in European societies.[2] For the first time in human history, European States agreed that their citizens will have the right to challenge internal actions and decisions of the governments in an international court rendering binding judgments. This is undoubtedly an achievement even for broader international law since it contributes to its more democratic and legitimate character.[3]

3. The Development of a European Judiciary

Europe's development of a modern judiciary and its system of fundamental rights protection has been referenced as a 'crowded house'.[4] The creation of strong European courts reflects the evolution of values and the impacts of power therein.

Following World War II, the Western European governments realized that another lapse into totalitarianism and resistance to communism, which had already overwhelmed Eastern Europe, could only be prevented through joint action. This realization led to the establishment of the Council of Europe (CoE) in 1949 and the European Coal and Steel Community (ECSC) in 1951.

As a result, there are two central systems of law at a European level with their respective courts, which by now have their respective bill of rights, namely, the European Convention on Human Rights (ECHR) system and the European Union (EU) law with the Charter of Fundamental Rights. However, the European legal space includes other sub-systems and special tribunals, courts performing constitutional adjudication, and all the courts applying European law.[5] Among them, special mention should also be made of so-called internationalized constitutional courts.

The European Court of Human Rights (ECtHR), based in Strasbourg, France, having jurisdiction over forty-six European States and almost 800 million Europeans,[6] is the world's best-known international human rights court.[7] Over the years, however, the ECtHR has developed an important dialogue with other regional courts in Americas and Africa and one can speak about a process of mutual inspiration among these courts.[8]

The judiciary of the EU—the Court of Justice of the European Union (CJEU)—comprises the Court of Justice and the General Court, both based in Luxembourg, and is the first truly supranational judiciary in the world. The twenty-seven member States of the EU depend on these courts to ensure the rule of law and facilitate the integration process, which goes much further than the traditional intergovernmental cooperation.[9] These States have willingly given up some of their sovereignty to become part of a greater supranational legal order with common institutions that facilitate economic, political, and legal integration for the benefit of the Union as a whole.[10]

The EU courts are not the only supranational courts in Europe. The European Free Trade Association (EFTA) Court and the Benelux Court of Justice also belong in this category of courts. These two courts represent an interesting dynamic within the European system. The EFTA Court deals with four countries external to the EU, and the Benelux Court deals with three countries within the EU.

As part of the peace settlement in Bosnia and Herzegovina in 1995, the Constitutional Court was set up to include nine judges, three of whom were nominated by the President of the ECtHR. Similarly, following the end of the war in 1999, the Kosovo Constitutional Court and other courts were formed as internationalized national courts during a period of post-war settlement and transition to the formation of a State. These two cases reflect the constitutional role of the ECHR in post-war European settlement contexts and continue to reflect the European view that an independent judiciary is an essential means to ensure peace and stability.

Another layer of courts belonging to this crowded house of the European judiciary is the national constitutional and supreme courts. The Court of Justice's interpretation of Article 267 of the Treaty on European Union (TEU), which enshrines the preliminary reference procedure, and Article 19, 'which gives concrete expression to the value of the rule of law stated in Article 2 TEU, entrusts the responsibility for ensuring judicial review in the EU legal order not only to the Court of Justice but also to national courts and tribunals'.[11] Consequently, the courts can 'no longer operate in isolation but carry a common legal responsibility for the European legal space'.[12] For that reason, the principles and standards applicable to the functioning and composition of the courts have gained preeminent importance. Their independence and impartiality have become vital elements of European judicial architecture. Through mutual support and inspiration among European courts and courts of the European States, a common standard of independence and impartiality of the judiciary has been reinforced.[13]

At the same time, the regional courts' role and their interaction with national courts have reached another level in Europe; it can indeed be designated as a union of 'courts that perform constitutional adjudication', or *Verfassungsgerichtsverbund*, as well as the courts with legal responsibility for European legal space, especially among those applying the EU law.[14] Because of these developments, we can now talk about a web of close mutual relations through formal and informal procedures and communications, that is, judicial dialogue among courts in Europe, which forms a real and complex architecture of what can be termed the European judiciary, which has the primary aims of protecting individuals against abuses of power and protecting individuals from each other to ensure long-term peace and development.

4. European Courts and Courts in Europe

Within a European judiciary, there are 'supranational' European courts, such as the ECtHR, the CJEU, the EFTA Court, and the Benelux Court of Justice; and there are national courts, which include internationalized courts, such as the Bosnia-Herzegovina Constitutional Court and the post-war Kosovo courts. For formal interactions of these courts, the scope of their competence and their admissibility rules are particularly relevant since they determine the scope and procedural ways of a so-called formal judicial dialogue within the European judiciary. This section of the chapter therefore highlights the main elements of the competences of European courts and the main features of their admissibility criteria. It must be stressed that the European judiciary is characterized by a constantly growing informal dialogue among the courts. They are bilateral and multilateral within a single or multiple language groups. Both European courts have become focal points for respective networks of courts in Europe.[15] The ever-growing density of exchanges among courts in Europe builds a special kind of judicial culture on the continent.

4.1 European Court of Human Rights

Western European States ratified the ECHR, including a two-tier control mechanism over the compliance with the Convention and the right to individual petition, relatively quickly, with the exception of France (ratified in 1974) and the UK (which did not accept the right to individual complaint or the jurisdiction of the ECtHR until 1966).[16] On 18 May 1954, the Committee of Ministers of the Council of Europe elected the first members to the Commission. The Court, which then operated on a part-time basis, was set up in 1959.

Following the fall of the Berlin Wall, Eastern European nations, with few exceptions, embraced the Convention mechanism, which for them symbolized freedom and belonging to the club of free and developed nations. In 1989 the Council of Europe had twenty-two States; twenty years later, it had forty-seven States (in 2023, forty-six). The doubling of its membership, and the expansion of the Convention system's reach, brought new challenges to the functioning of the ECtHR. Individual applications continue to overburden the Court, and all the mechanism's reforms have not been able to solve the problem of the length of proceedings in the Court. The Court now on average delivers dozens judgments per week, which is a radical change as compared with its early years; the Court rendered its first judgment in *Lawless v Ireland* (1961) and its second seven years later in the *Belgian Linguistic* case (1968).[17] This surge in the number of cases reflects the Court's growing role in European social and political processes.

It is crucial to remember that the rationale of different States for accepting the jurisdiction of the ECHR control mechanism and their different national historical narratives did not disappear with the joining of the mechanism.[18] Western European States, which acted upon the idea of a human rights bill for Europe to counter threats of communism and thus created a Convention system with its control mechanism, had time to grow into this idea on their own terms. This process was different for Eastern European States. Having liberated themselves from non-democratic regimes, they immediately had to comply with the Convention standards concretized through the Court's case law. The Convention was of great symbolic importance. The Convention and the ECtHR played a critical legitimizing function in internal democratic change.[19] This membership was also seen in security terms, which is especially evident for the Baltic States and the new States in the territory of the ex-USSR.[20] These States, even though they had just become independent from a totalitarian power, did not particularly question external judicial control of their internal actions since their sovereignty could only function if their security was guaranteed. It could also be argued that at the time Eastern Europe joined the Convention system, they could not fully appreciate the role that the ECtHR was going to play in their internal matters.

It is true that these States brought forth different pressures on the Court and new expectations, something the system's founders had certainly not anticipated.[21] Although the realization that the mechanism would need serious reforms came about in the 1990s—in the expectation that the expansion of the Council of Europe would bring about a totally new epoch for the organization—it is doubtful that there was a true understanding of what was to come once the Court had jurisdiction over forty-seven States, including the Russian Federation until September 2022.[22] The most significant change in the ECtHR was its confrontation with cases caused by wide systemic problems in legal systems in the Easter European States and therefore different than those that the Court had dealt with in its first four decades. It should be noted that, in the view of some Western European States, these developments have backfired, as they argue that the Court has gone too far in interpreting the Convention when placing Convention standards in the specific context of new democracies.[23]

However, two early judgments remain a paradigm for what was to become the undeniable identity of the Strasbourg Court: *Golder v the United Kingdom* (1979–80) and *Tyrer v the United Kingdom* (1978). In the *Golder* case, the Court declared that it interprets Article 6 ECHR, which guarantees the right to a fair trial, in accordance with Articles 31 to 33 of the Vienna Convention on the Law of Treaties (VCLT), which requires to look at the subsequent practice of States and other rules of international law, including the relevant general principles of law.[24] One of these principles is the rule of law, which recognizes the right to access the courts.[25]

The *Tyrer* case grounded the Court's reliance on dynamic interpretation meaning that the Convention rules evolve alongside the evolution of society and its values.[26]

4.1.1 *Competence and admissibility*

Article 1 ECHR determines that 'The High Contracting Parties shall secure to everyone within their jurisdiction the rights and freedoms defined' in the Convention. In the *Bankovic and Others v Belgium and Others* (1999) case, the Court clarified that in its interpretation, the term 'jurisdiction' has the same meaning as that attributed to it in international law, that is, it is presumed to be 'essentially territorial'.[27] Case law confirms that States exercise their jurisdiction not only within their territory but may also exercise effective control outside their territory. This means that the jurisdiction of the Court goes where the Contracting Party exercises effective control over a territory or a people.[28]

It has been generally recognized that the main contribution of the ECHR system lies with the individual complaint to the Court. At a practical level, each application must meet admissibility requirements set out in Article 35 of the Convention. This principle serves multiple purposes, and the approach to these requirements is carefully tailored to balance several interests. First, the Convention control mechanism is a judicial mechanism, therefore, like all judicial mechanisms, it lays down strict conditions for access to the mechanism to avoid its use for purposes other than those provided for in the Convention. Secondly, it sorts unmeritorious applications from those that *prima facia* have some merit and attempts to prevent the mechanism from being submerged by applications.

The Court has been instrumental to the advancement of democracy, accountability, and human rights in Europe but has also suffered from its success since the number of applications has constantly been too high for the Court to be able to render justice on time in every case. This has led the Court to review its working methods from the moment a single full-time Court was put in place following the entry into force of Protocol 11 on 1 November 1998. On the one hand, the fusion of the European Commission of Human Rights and the Court, replacing them with a single full-time judicial institution clearly strengthened independent and impartial adjudication of human rights violations in Europe by placing a full-time court in the middle of the system. On the other hand, since the Court now deals with all the matters of international adjudication, such as filtering, fact-finding, determining admissibility, and negotiating settlements, in addition to providing binding rulings in admissible cases, the task of rendering individual justice by a regional international court has become monumental and remains unique in modern human history.[29]

In this context Protocol 16 was adopted to enable the 'highest courts and tribunals' of States parties to request an advisory opinion from the Court on interpretation of the Convention. These developments ensure and assist States in their compliance with the Convention at a domestic level with the aim to strengthen protection of human rights at national levels.[30] Finally, following the entry into force on 1 August 2021 of Protocol 15, which reiterates the principle of subsidiarity, the delay for submission of applications to the Court following the final national decision has been reduced from six months to four months with effect from 2022; the measure is geared towards focusing on really burning matters of Convention violations. These reforms have raised concerns about the future of the individual complaint as it had evolved since the early days of the

Convention system. At the same time, it is true that the responsibility for the maintenance of peace and European public order through the protection of human rights should be shared by national and European courts. Regional courts, such as the ECtHR, cannot exercise their functions without proper exercise of the functions by the national courts in protecting the rights and freedoms of the individuals. This is a fundamental foundational element of the philosophy underlying the European judiciary.

For the purposes of a procedural dialogue within a European judiciary, two legal mechanisms are of particular relevance and will be addressed for the purposes of this chapter. First, the mechanism of the exhaustion of domestic remedies and, second, Protocol 16 to the Convention.

4.1.2 *Exhaustion of domestic remedies*

One of the admissibility requirements of Article 35, point 1, is the exhaustion of domestic remedies which embodies the idea of the subsidiary character of the Convention mechanism. It is only when the national courts have not been able to remedy the violation that Europeans can go to the Strasbourg Court. In other words, 'the crux of the rule on exhaustion is that the complaint made to the Court must first have been made: (a) at least in substance; (b) to the appropriate domestic body; (c) and in compliance with the formal requirements and time limits laid down in domestic law'.[31] The rule on exhaustion of domestic remedies forms part of the formal elements of the judicial dialogue within the European judiciary which entrusts the primary responsibility for the compliance with the ECHR to national courts.

4.1.3 *Protocol 16*

Protocol 16 follows the same line of thought. The highest national court or tribunal can now request a non-binding advisory opinion on an important question of the interpretation of the Convention only in a case pending in front of such court.[32] To enable the effectiveness of the formal dialogue set forth by Protocol 16, the national court has to provide details of the legal and factual background of the case and to explain the reasons for asking the advisory opinion. The Strasbourg Court decides on the admissibility of such a request in a panel of five judges of the Grand Chamber. In case of a refusal, the reasons must be provided. Evidently, the individuals in such a case are not prevented from bringing an application to the Court. However, there is a certain shift from individual action towards a judicial role and initiative in upholding European values.

The developments in and around the ECtHR show that international protection of human rights can only really work if the States, and especially the domestic judiciary, do their share. The system of the protection and enforcement of the Convention is therefore premised on the ideas of subsidiarity, the margin of appreciation, effective domestic remedies, judicial dialogue, as strengthened through the advisory procedure, and effective execution of judgments. These notions and procedures are part of formal procedural relationships within the European judiciary.

4.2 Court of Justice of the European Union

The Treaties on the European Union and the Functioning of the European Union (the Treaties) entrust the CJEU (the Court of Justice and the General Court) to ensure that the rules of EU law are upheld and applied uniformly throughout the Union.

The first landmark decision of the Court of Justice was adopted in 1963 in the *Van Gend en Loos* case. In the words of Joseph HH Weiler: '*Van Gend en Loos* not only shaped the legal order; it constituted that order'.[33] It did so in the following manner: The judgment conceptualized the legal order of the Communities as 'a new legal order of international law' and ever since, the Court of Justice has attempted to live up to this definition. It is probably true to say that at the centre of this new legal order are a few key elements, such as a preliminary reference procedure and the principles of direct effect and primacy of EU law, verbalized in the *Van Gend en Loos* case. This legal order has been consolidated with the adoption of the Lisbon Treaty on 1 December 2009, giving the EU full legal personality.[34] Article 2 TEU now reflects the shared values of the Members of the European Union:

> The Union is founded on the values of respect for human dignity, freedom, democracy, equality, the rule of law and respect for human rights, including the rights of persons belonging to minorities. These values are common to the Member States in a society in which pluralism, non-discrimination, tolerance, justice, solidarity and equality between women and men prevail.[35]

The institutionalization of these values has given rise to important case law holding the EU institutions and States accountable for non-compliance with Article 2 values.[36] This accountability process both increases the rights of individuals and improves the rule of law in Europe. Along with the Lisbon Treaty, the Charter of Fundamental Rights became legally binding.[37] With this development, it was clearly and formally acknowledged that economic integration also requires common values that are legally binding and transcend common economic solutions.

Article 19(1) TEU entrusts national courts, together with the CJEU, with the responsibility for ensuring the full application of Union law in the member States and the judicial protection of natural and legal persons provided for in the EU law. In fact, the main philosophy of the application of the EU law, including subjective rights that it may provide, is that it rests primarily with national courts. It is therefore the case that all judges in the EU member States are also European judges. The special character of the EU legal order, which includes its autonomy, primacy, and effectiveness, among other elements, has enabled the kind of integration through law that was not known in human history before. It is a constitutional legal order common to all Member States in which a shared responsibility for the application and compliance with the principles and rules of the EU law is carried out in a particularly intertwined manner on an equal rather than hierarchical footing among all the relevant institutions, including the courts.[38]

4.2.1 *Competence and admissibility*

4.2.1.1 *Court of Justice*

The Court of Justice (also ECJ) today has one judge per member State and eleven Advocate Generals. The Court interprets all primary Union law, including the EU Charter of Fundamental Rights,[39] and secondary Union law provisions, as well as international agreements concluded by the European Union that therefore become sources of EU law. General principles of law, as identified and interpreted by the Court, transcend the EU legal system. A particularly important source of the general principles of law is the common constitutional traditions of EU member States which potential might not yet be fully explored for the purposes of a more integrated and intertwined functioning of the European judiciary.[40] In this regard and within the limits of its competence, the Court leads an important dialogue with national constitutional courts which is part of a general constitutional process of the EU.

Article 267 TFEU establishes a mechanism of judicial cooperation between the Court of Justice and national courts. By means of reference for a preliminary ruling, a national court may obtain from the Court of Justice, before ruling (ie preliminary), the necessary guidance as to the interpretation which it must give to Union law in the proceedings before it ('the main proceedings'). Preliminary reference procedure should be seen as one of the core elements and a building block of the reality of European judiciary.

It follows that an important feature of the competence of the Court of Justice lies in the fact that it does not have the right to determine how to apply national law in a manner compatible with EU law. That is the responsibility of a national court, which relies on the interpretation of the relevant EU law provided for by the Court.

Another important element of the competence of the Court of Justice is the determination of the validity of Union acts.

4.2.1.2 *General Court*

Since 2019 there have been two judges from each EU member State in the General Court. Article 256 TFEU delimits the competence of the court. The General Court is particularly important in the CJEU system because under Article 263 TFEU, natural and moral persons can bring proceedings to the General Court if the EU legal act is addressed directly to the person concerned, or directly and personally affects the person concerned, or where a regulatory act is of direct concern to that person. [41] The Court of Justice serves as the appeals court in such instances on points of law only.

Addressees of a EU legal act can bring proceedings if they feel that the EU institutions have exceeded their competence, have not complied with the essential requirements of the procedure, have violated primary law, or have misused their power in any other manner. As can be seen, these are essential elements of the rule of law aimed at preventing the abuse of power by the EU institutions in their exercise of legislative or administrative powers.

4.3 EFTA Court of Justice

The EFTA Surveillance Authority and the EFTA Court are charged with overseeing compliance with EEA regulations. The latter is made up of three judges from the EFTA countries party to the EEA, and functions to adjudicate cases brought forth by the EFTA Surveillance Authority against an EFTA country for discordance with EEA, hear appeals between these two parties, and clarify EEA regulations for national courts. On the EU side, the Court of Justice is responsible for interpreting and applying EEA obligations. Switzerland is neither in the EU nor the EEA, but operates on a series of bilateral agreements with the EU that allows it access to the European Single Market.

The EFTA Court must follow the case law of the EU courts in the areas of EEA law that are identical to, or correspond to, EU law. Article 6 of the EEA Agreement provides that insofar as the EEA Treaty rules are identical or corresponding to EU law, they shall be interpreted in conformity with Court of Justice case law. At the same time, the Court admitted that EFTA States are free to establish the mechanism of control that aims to ensure the objective of homogeneous application of the EEA rules throughout their territories.[42]

There is also a close judicial dialogue between the EFTA Court and the national courts. The EEA law which is sufficiently precise can be invoked directly in the national courts of the EFTA States. However, primarily the formal dialogue is ensured by the advisory procedure to the EFTA Court. There is no doubt that the EEA Agreement in terms of its domestic legal impact has gone beyond 'what is usual for an agreement under public international law. [It] is characterised by the creation of an internal market ... the protection of the rights of individuals and economic operators and an institutional framework providing for effective surveillance and judicial review.'[43] The synergies between the EU and the EFTA in the area of internal market, which also include applying fundamental rights as an integral part of the 'day-to-day activities' of all the courts active within these legal systems, is an important element of what makes the European judiciary.[44]

4.4 Benelux Court of Justice

This Court is also a supranational court. Three States, Belgium, the Netherlands, and Luxembourg, came together and established their own Court of Justice in 1965. The ECJ accepted the Benelux Court in its *Opinion 1/09*, stating that it fits within the homogeneity framework previously discussed in *Opinion 1/91*. This is because the three States party to the Benelux Agreement are also member States of the EU, meaning that 'its decisions are subject to mechanisms capable of ensuring the full effectiveness of the rules of the European Union'.[45] The point of the EU is to decrease barriers between EU nations, but this does not prevent member States from creating Unions that are even more liberal. On that note, the Benelux Court of Justice's role is to provide interpretations of common regulations in the areas where the three States have agreed to harmonize their legislation.[46] The Court has three types of competence which are carried out by three Chambers. The first judgment in the case of *Colgate v Palmolive/Bols* was handed down in 1975.[47]

4.5 Bosnia and Herzegovina Constitutional Court

While the Constitutional Court of Bosnia and Herzegovina marks the establishment of constitutional jurisdiction in the country going back to 1964, the current Court was established by the 1995 Constitution, which was Annex 4 of the General Framework Agreement for Peace in Bosnia and Herzegovina, the so-called Dayton Agreement.[48] The Constitutional Court began to function in 1997, and Article VI(3) outlines the competence of the Court. Its primary function is to uphold the Constitution and settle disputes between Entities. Based on the principle of power-sharing between the Entities and the three main communities (Croats, Bosniacs, and Serbs), the country's constitutional structure was the compromise that helped end the war in Bosnia and Herzegovina.[49] The same article of the Constitution determines that the Court has nine judges, and three among them are selected by the President of the ECtHR. These three judges do not have citizenship of Bosnia and Herzegovina. Another particularity of the work of the Court relates to the fact that, per Article II(2) of the Constitution, it directly applies the ECHR and the case law of the Strasbourg Court when adjudicating cases.[50] Moreover, in cases of conflict between national norms and the ECHR, the latter prevails.

The constitutional outlook of Bosnia and Herzegovina is unique in this regard. It attests to the idea that has emerged as central to the European judiciary, in that different kinds of closer synergies and dialogue within this web of judicial relations serve the interests of peace on the continent.

4.6 Kosovo judiciary

Following the 1999 NATO military campaign in the Federal Republic of Yugoslavia, the United Nations Security Council (UNSC) adopted Resolution 1244, establishing an 'international civil presence' for the 'interim administration' of Kosovo.[51] This led to the internationalization of Kosovo domestic courts as part of the comprehensive United Nations Interim Administration Mission in Kosovo (UNMIK). In particular, Regulation 1999/1 regarding the authority of UNMIK in Kosovo provided that "the administration of the judiciary [was] vested in UNMIK and [was] exercised by the SRSG, who could appoint 'any person to ... the judiciary' ".[52] Subsequently, a series of regulations were adopted, 'which increasingly introduced international personnel into the legal system of Kosovo', culminating with Regulation 2000/64, which permitted the creation of three-judge panels within the District Courts and the Supreme Court of Kosovo that included 'at least two international judges' (Regulation 64 Panels).[53] As Zane Ratniece explains in her comprehensive study on the Kosovo judiciary, the deployment of international judges and prosecutors in Kosovo courts 'was deemed necessary in order to preserve the independence and impartiality of the judiciary' in the adjudication of 'serious crimes, including cases of war and inter-ethnic crimes'.[54]

Similar to UNMIK, EULEX appointed international judges to the Kosovo domestic courts to work with local judges. However, unlike with UNMIK international judges, EULEX judges were governed by a law adopted by the Kosovo Assembly based on the Kosovo Constitution. In particular, the 'Law on Jurisdiction' regulated their integration and jurisdiction in Kosovo's judicial system. In addition to the courts of general jurisdiction, international judges were appointed to the Constitutional Court of Kosovo. Such initial composition of the Constitutional Court was based on transitory provisions of the Constitution, which provided that three out of nine judges must be international. The International Civilian Representative (ICR) appointed the international judges after consulting the President of the ECtHR. The ICR was responsible for supervising the implementation of the Comprehensive Proposal for the Kosovo Status Settlement. According to its author, the UN Special Envoy for Settling Kosovo's Status, Martti Ahtisaari, the Comprehensive Proposal '[provided] the foundations for a future independent Kosovo'. Unlike UNSC Resolution 1244, the Comprehensive Proposal was initially integrated into the Kosovo Constitution, which afforded superiority to the Comprehensive Proposal 'over all other legal provisions in Kosovo'.[55] Therefore, the mandate of the international judges in the Constitutional Court emanated from a framework receptive to Kosovo's independence. The international judges' mandate expired in 2018.

While the formation and functioning of the Kosovo judiciary are specific to the particular character of Kosovo's status in international law following the war in former Yugoslavia, it should be seen as a post-war transitory solution until proper civilian governance in Kosovo was formed. Nevertheless, even in such a context the formation and functioning of the Kosovo judiciary reflects several important lessons. First, it portrays the importance of the independent judiciary for the purposes of post-war settlements and bringing about lasting peace. Second, this can be achieved by forming a national judiciary deeply integrated into the European judiciary and with the assistance of the European judiciary. It is in this perspective that the presence of international judges and their appointment to the domestic (internationalized) courts attests to yet another dimension of the European judiciary, that is, its pacifying function.

4.7 Constitutional courts and the national judiciary

The special cases of Kosovo and Bosnia and Herzegovina are examples of the evolutionary process that has taken place in Europe and contributed to the formation of what is described in this chapter as the European judiciary. The domestic judiciary is increasingly part of a broader concept of the European judiciary. As was described above, formal procedures shape the dialogue of all the courts in Europe, and there are plenty of informal dialogues too among the courts within different constellations. It has been rightly pointed out that:

> Europeanization has reshaped courts performing constitutional adjudication and continues to do so. Today, these courts are not only responsible for securing the respect for the domestic constitution within their own legal order—though this remains their main task and the basis of their legitimacy—but are also called upon to contribute to the orderly functioning of the European legal space as a whole.[56]

Considering that any national court may refer questions about the interpretation of an EU legal act to the Court of Justice, and the national courts may be called to settle the dispute in front of them while also taking into account the case law of the ECtHR, it is fair to say that Europeanization, a shared responsibility for a common European legal space, has affected national courts of all levels and competencies.

Constitutional courts and supreme courts, performing constitutional adjudication, have a particular responsibility within, and in the name of, the European judiciary, since they have the final say in triggering the dialogue mechanisms therein. That is of crucial importance for the development and viability of the European judiciary. Armin von Bogdandy has conceptualized this role to imply four specific and discernible functions.[57]

'First, a system-generating function of connection, transformation, and translation.' This function refers to the maintenance of a two-way street between European law and jurisprudence, and the national implementation and tradition contributing to European jurisprudence. 'Second, constitutional courts (in a broader sense) carry out a function of legitimation.' The European experience shows that the acceptance of national courts and their decisions to the European courts has paved a way at a national level for the openness by national judiciaries to European law,[58] as well as comparative law, since, as explained earlier, horizontal synergies do not stop with the European courts. 'Third, courts performing constitutional adjudication have a function of providing integrated legal protection by filling the lacunae in the protection that European courts offer.' In other words, neither the EU law nor the ECHR, or even the Council of Europe law, offers the protection of all legal relations between individuals. Moreover, each European nation has its own historical past, and therefore there are different approaches to different legal manifestations. As noted above, it is the case, therefore, that principles such as subsidiarity and margin of appreciation, as well as the limits of the competence conferred on the EU institutions, leave plenty of room for national courts to ensure effective protection of rights within the national law. 'Fourth, . . . a specific function of control at the interface between different systems.' It has been noted that this function may compromise constitutional identity, *ultra vires*, and possibly common values control.[59] National doctrines and practices vary in this regard. Nevertheless, the stronger the pull towards a more centralized political integration in Europe, the more the need for the protection of national constitutional identities will be underlined, even if Article 4 TEU makes national identity part of the EU's identity in the sense that the ultimate goal is to avoid conflicts between these social phenomena.[60]

It is in this context that the idea that courts, performing constitutional adjudication both at European and national levels, should engage properly with the protection of Article 2 TEU values as well as the minimum human rights standards, as set forth in the ECHR, will require further elaboration. The Court of Justice in cases C-156/21 and C-157/21, the so-called conditionality cases, explained that the protection of the rule of law, as one of the common values enshrined in Article 2 TEU, permits the Commission to suggest other measures alongside the procedures of Article 7 TEU. While setting strict requirements for the resort to such measures, the Court explained that the foundation for its analysis lies in the very concept of the EU identity, that is, 'The shared values, as stated under Article 2 TEU, define and layout the very identity of the European Union as a common legal order'.[61] In its reasoning, the Court stated that the EU, in case of breach, should be able to defend these values. This is the basis for the proposition that constitutional courts and other national courts also have the competence to ensure that foundational EU values are respected if the case in front of a court raises that issue. The idea of a shared responsibility for the implementation of common European values emanating from the EU Treaties and the ECHR is in fact the core function of the European judiciary and the necessary substantive element in addition to the above-mentioned procedural elements that consolidate the close web of courts in Europe.

5. The Role and Future Challenges for a European Judiciary

Europe shows how the evolution of ideas about better ways of governance to ensure peace between nations materializes in several key concepts, such as human rights, the rule of law, and separation of powers, implementation of which requires an independent and impartial judiciary.[62] Moreover the European legal space has responded to historical challenges by creating a house with several supreme courts which overlap in their jurisdiction. This has given ground to arguments that '[t]he mutual relationships among these courts are not satisfactorily, clearly, and convincingly established, as each of them belongs to a different legal order and system'.[63] Indeed, in principle, none of the courts is a supreme court of Europe. That is not the idea characterizing European legal space. Rather, Article 267 TFEU, as well as the principle of subsidiarity which transcends both the Convention system and the EU legal system, make all courts in Europe responsible for upholding common values. Europe's foundational idea of unity in diversity is the balance that each court must strive to achieve when carrying out its respective competence. This is both a challenge at a technical level of adjudication of a dispute, but it is also a unique opportunity because for the first time in Europe the centuries-old idea of unity of European States takes place in reality and the courts have been elevated to play a major role. The European judiciary has taken centre stage along with political and legislative processes in Europe in substantiating and implementing the idea of

Europe as a space of peace, prosperity, and values. This takes place through the search and deduction of general principles of law. It can be argued that the EU law principle of mutual trust, which requires further conceptualization, has the potential to explain the relations within a European judiciary, as well as EU member States, and to impact wider Europe in ways that bring forward the construction of Europe more than ever before.[64] If we accept that mutual trust derives from 'the foundations of the EU legal structure',[65] then we can see that the EU has added a new layer to the principle of State consent as the basis for the construction of international law.[66] Europe constructs common rules not only because it is in the self-interest of each State to do so but also because there is mutual trust in each other in that they share a common view of how the rights of citizens should be protected and mutual interactions strengthened. Formal and informal dialogues within a European judiciary is therefore required to adapt to this new paradigm. A mutual trust paradigm cannot be achieved without strong national courts protecting human rights and rule of law as well as the ECtHR which ensures that a minimum common European human rights standard is observed. These are the foundation blocks for the new kind of legal space in Europe in which a new kind of legal order of the EU is a key element. The leap from cooperation to mutual trust, as experienced by the EU, is not easy; it requires a considerable evolution of culture of true belief in equality among States irrespective of their size or history as well as a fundamental acceptance that there will be important differences, but they should not affect mutual trust.

The challenges are numerous. Following *Opinion 2/13* of the Court of Justice which considered that Protocol of EU Accession to the ECHR did not comply with several basic principles of the EU legal order, such as primacy and autonomy, as well as the principle of mutual trust among the EU member States, the question of coherence and harmony in upholding the key principles within European legal space remains open.[67] The Strasbourg Court's position in *Avotiņš v Latvia* was a reply giving the ECtHR's stance on the position adopted by the Court of Justice in *Opinion 2/13*. The ECtHR upheld the Bosphorus doctrine, which assumes that the EU ensures a level of human rights protection equivalent to that offered by the Convention. However, the ECtHR should be viewed as walking '"right up to the edge of finding that a manifest deficiency in the protection of fundamental rights has occurred," but then back[ing] off at the last second due to the specific features of this case'.[68] In *Avotiņš*, Strasbourg reiterates that the Bosphorus presumption does not preclude the ECtHR from evaluating a 'complaint on the sole ground that [the domestic courts] are applying EU law,' meaning that there are limits to blanket 'mutual trust in the area of human rights protection'.[69] Thus, the ECtHR maintains that the presumption of compliance is to be verified.[70]

One should keep in mind that mutual trust is an idea which serves the purpose of EU integration, however the Court of Justice has recognized that in practice it does not mean blind trust. For example, serious reasons to doubt independence and impartiality of courts in a member State may trigger a more substantial examination of the European Arrest Warrant requesting to surrender a person to that State.[71] Mutual trust is certainly a forward-looking idea but also one that requires constant work and review.

In Europe the ideas of external control of the actions of the State as well as the principles underlying the functioning of such control mechanisms have taken a long time to materialize. Today they are an essential part of the way European citizens see the achievement of peace and prosperity. Moreover Europe has, over centuries, influenced the construction of the world order and has always taken the universalist worldview. At the same time, it has been overshadowed by the European so-called civilizing mission in the other continents over these centuries which is one of the reasons that impacts the spread of European ideas today. Nevertheless, the ECHR and the EU, with the functioning and synergies among its institutions, are interesting ideas to the other continents. It is doubtful that the notion of mutual trust and its normative effects are fully known outside Europe, but the concepts of regional human rights protection and regional economic union are examples that generate interest outside Europe to follow them.

While multiple avenues and formal procedures of judicial dialogue are established among courts in Europe, the main challenge lies in their further strengthening and fine tuning. In that regard, digitalization is conducive to further consolidation of a European judiciary, since it allows for more immediate communication among the courts, and that communication should be put to better use. The next stage of the European judiciary's evolution would be to fully accept that it is a single and unique web of different but interlinked courts with the same purpose to ensure peace, protection of human rights, and prosperity in a common European legal space.

Notes

1. The notion of 'a common European legal space' refers, first, to the Council of Europe (CoE) standards as a common minimum denominator for rule of law and human rights among forty-six member States of the organization and, second, to the European Union (EU) law applicable in twenty-seven member States of the Union which are also members of the Council of Europe. Moreover, some treaties concluded within the Council of Europe are the minimum legal standard within the EU legal order.
2. Martti Koskenniemi, *To the Uttermost Parts of the Earth: Legal Imagination and International Power, 1300–1870* (CUP 2021).
3. James Crawford, *Chance, Order, Change: The Course of International Law, General Course on Public International Law* (Brill Nijhoff 2014) 380.
4. Pedro Cruz Villalón, 'Rights in Europe. The Crowded House' King's College Working Paper 1 (2012) available at kcl.ac.uk/research/centres/European/research.
5. Armin von Bogdandy, Christophe Grabenwarter, and Peter M Huber, 'Constitutional Adjudication in the European Legal Space' in Armin von Bogdandy, Christophe Grabenwarter, and Peter M Huber (eds), *Max Planck Handbooks in European Public Law*, vol 3 (OUP 2020) 4.
6. In 2022, the Russian Federation was expelled from the Council of Europe as a result of its waging a war in Ukraine. Until then the ECtHR had jurisdiction over forty-seven States in Europe. The only other State not a member of the Council of Europe and thus of the ECHR is Belarus.

7. For instance, only nineteen out of the thirty-five countries in the Americas (not including Canada and the US) act under the jurisdiction of the Inter-American Court of Human Rights (IACtHR), which does not have nearly the amount of international judicial influence as the ECtHR. Nicolas A Croquet, 'The International Criminal Court and the Treatment of Defence Rights: A mirror of the European Court of Human Rights' Jurisprudence?', Human Rights Law Review 2011, 91, 125.
8. The IACtHR has been considered more 'progressive' in some areas of human rights law. The ECtHR has taken note from the IACtHR and has been inspired by its case law in areas such as disappearance cases. However, the other courts absorb the ECtHR's jurisprudence and the African Court 'refers explicitly to the idea of margin of appreciation'. See Angelika Nussberger, *The European Court of Human Rights* (Elements of International Law series in Mark Janis et al (eds), 1st edn, OUP 2020) 107.
9. *Opinion 2/13* EU:C:2014:2454 [2014] OJ C 260/19 (Request for an opinion submitted by the European Commission pursuant to Article 218(11) TFEU) para 157.
10. ibid.
11. Case C-64/16 *Associação Sindical dos Juízes Portugueses* EU:C:2018:117 [2018] OJ C 142/2.
12. von Bogdandy et al (n 5) 4.
13. Among the judgments with regard to the situation in Poland, see, eg, Case C-791/19 *Commission v Poland* [2021] OJ C 413/36 (on Disciplinary Chamber of the Supreme Court), also: Case C-157/21 *Poland v Parliament and Council* EU:C:2022:98 [2022] OJ C148/8, para 150. Generally, Case 11/70 *Internationale Handelsgesellschaft mbH v Einfuhr- und Vorratsstelle für Getreide und Futtermittel* EU:C:1970:114 [1970].
14. von Bogdandy et al (n 5) 8. This concept was developed by Professor Andreas Voßkuhle, former President of the German Constitutional Court.
15. Since 2018, the CJEU and the presidents of the Constitutional and Supreme Courts of the Member States have participated in the Judicial Network of the EU (RJUE). The RJUE provides for increased cooperation between the Court and the national courts through greater centralization of court documents and information regarding the application of CJEU rulings; the ability to informally consult the CJEU on national cases with specific EU law concerns; direct access to preliminary rulings on a shared, private database. (For more information see <http://www.curia.europa.eu/jcms/jcms/p1_2170157/en/>.) On the other hand, the ECtHR launched the Superior Courts Network (SCN) and the SCN Intranet in 2015 and 2016 'to enrich dialogue', facilitate 'the implementation of the Convention', and 'create a practical and useful means of exchanging relevant information on Convention case-law and related matters'. (For more information see <http://www.echr.coe.int/Pages/home.aspx?p=court/dialoguecourts/network&c=>.)
16. The right to individual petition is unique to the ECtHR. In comparison, the Inter-American Court's 'Executive Secretariat ... is in charge of carrying out the initial sifting of the petitions'. Françoise Hampson, Claudia Martin, and Frans Viljoen, 'Inaccessible Apexes: Comparing Access to Regional Human Rights Courts and Commissions in Europe, the Americas, and Africa', 16(1) International Journal of Constitutional Law 2018 <http://www.doi.org/10.1093/icon/moy007> accessed 10 October 2022. See also Nussberger (n 8) 7. As pointed out by Nussberger, the States were not united in their vision for the Convention and the control mechanism and 'the debate was based on the assumption that democratic States did not have to fear to be accused before the new Court as only truly abusive human rights restrictions would be sanctioned'. ibid.

17. *Case of Lawless v Ireland (No 3)* App no 332/57 (Commission Report, 19 December 1959) (*Lawless v Ireland*) was also the first case against a country concerning the interpretation of human rights law; *Relating to Certain Aspects of the Laws on the Use of Languages in Education in Belgium v Belgium (Merits)*(1968) 1 EHRR 252 (the *Belgian Linguistic* case (No 2)).
18. Wojciech Sadurski, 'Enlargement of the Council of Europe and Constitutionalization of the European Court of Human Rights' in *Constitutionalism and the Enlargement of Europe* (OUP 2012) 49 et seq.
19. Ineta Ziemele, 'Conclusions' in Iulia Motoc and Ineta Ziemele (eds), *The Impact of the ECHR on Democratic Change in Central and Eastern Europe: Judicial Perspectives* (CUP 2016) 495.
20. Mārtiņš Mits, 'The European Convention on Human Rights and Democratisation of Latvia' RGSL Research Paper (2016) <http://www.rgsl.edu.lv/uploads/research-papers-list/6/mits-4-final.pdf> accessed 9 October 2022.

    Michal Bobek, 'The Court of Justice of the European Union', European Legal Studies Research Papers in Law 2014, 9 <http://www.ssrn.com/abstract=2445422> accessed 10 October 2022.
21. With the expansion of the 1990s, the Council had ballooned from a 'rather homogenous' association to one that included a range of sizes, different levels of democratization and development and rich and poor countries. According to Nussberger, '[t]he task of not only setting, but also implementing common human rights standards for all of them seemed Herculean, if not utopian'. It was around this time that the European Commission of Human Rights, integral to the Court's filtration system, was abolished, and people gained much greater access to the Court. See Nussberger (n 8) 27. 'It is therefore no surprise that after the enlargement the Court rendered judgments that went rather boldly into the substance of the matter without a dialogue with the national authorities because there was none possible in the given context or at the given time.' See Ziemele (n 20) 501. The need to protect Convention standards firmly in new Contracting Parties also had the effect of creating precedents that had not been anticipated by the founders of the system.
22. The Committee of Ministers suspended Russia from representation in the Committee and the Parliamentary Assembly in February, and the Council of Europe in March (<http://www.eeas.europa.eu/node/411049_it?s=51>). Russia formally withdrew from the ECHR on 16 September 2022 <http://www.coe.int/en/web/portal/-/russia-ceases-to-be-party-to-the-european-convention-on-human-rights>.
23. It should be noted that the system has kept this reticence or self-imposed bias of the Western European States throughout the functioning of the Council of Europe and the ECHR. Following the judgment in *Hirst v the United Kingdom* of 2005, the UK government harshly criticized the Court for having gone beyond its competence. Moreover, the Court was not internally unanimous as to the outcome in *Hirst*. However, later case law, which seems to have departed from *Hirst*, has not settled the matter within the Court either. See Nussberger (n 8) 82–83. *Hirst v the United Kingdom (No 2)* ECHR [GC], 2005-IX 681.
24. See *Golder v the United Kingdom* (1975) Series A no 18, §29.
25. Lord Jonathan PC Sumption, 'The Right to a Court: Article 6 of the Human Rights Convention' (James Wood Lecture, University of Glasgow, 13 November 2015) 4–5.
26. ibid 6. See *Tyrer v the United Kingdom* (1978) Series A no 26, 15–16 § 31.
27. *Banković and Others v Belgium and Others* App no 52207/99 (ECtHR, 12 December 2001).
28. *Al-Skeini and Others v the United Kingdom* App no 55721/07 (ECtHR, 7 July 2011).

29. David Harris et al, *Harris, O'Boyle, and Warbrick: Law of the European Convention on Human Rights* (4th edn, OUP 2018) 103.
30. Protocol 16 entered into force on 1 August 2018.
31. Harris et al (n 30) 47.
32. In 2019, the first request for an advisory opinion was submitted by the French Court of Cassation regarding *Mennesson v France*, which concerned parental rights in cases of surrogacy. In *Mennesson* and a parallel case, *Labasee v France*, the parents had their children via surrogate in the US and were declared their legal parents there. However, France did not recognize this 'parent-child relationship legally established between them in the United States'. The Court ruled that France had violated the children's Article 8 right to private life, since this lack of recognition under French law would negatively affect them throughout their lives. Nussberger (n 8) 52, 174.
33. Joseph HH Weiler, 'Revisiting Van Gend en Loos: Subjectifying and Objectifying the Individual' (Conference Proceedings, 50th Anniversary of the Judgment in *Van Gend en Loos*: 1963–2013, Luxembourg, 13 May 2013).
34. Treaty on European Union (TEU), Article 47.
35. ibid, Article 2.
36. See C-156/21 *Hungary v Parliament and Council* [2022] OJ C 148, para 127. The Court held that: 'The values contained in Article 2 TEU have been identified and are shared by the Member States. They define the very identity of the European Union as a common legal order. Thus, the European Union must be able to defend those values, within the limits of its powers as laid down by the Treaties.'
37. Article 6(1) TEU.
38. Koen Lenaerts, 'Concluding Remarks' (Conference Proceedings, EUnited in diversity: between common constitutional traditions and national identities, Riga, 2–3 September 2021) 231–232.
39. Charter of Fundamental Rights of the European Union (adopted 2000, entered into force 2009) (Charter).
40. Ineta Ziemele, 'Common constitutional traditions as a means of legitimacy and coherence of the EU legal order' (Conference Proceedings, EUnited in diversity: between common constitutional traditions and national identities, Riga, 2–3 September 2021) 45–52.
41. Two cases that showcase the importance of the General Court are Case T-604/18 *Google and Alphabet v Commission (Google Android)* (2022) and Case T-125/22 *RT France v Council* (2022). In *Google*, the Court fined the company and its parent company, Alphabet, €4.125 billion for skirting antitrust regulations by limiting people's ability to switch over to rivals and forcing manufacturers and mobile networks to use Google-approved operating systems and apps. The fine is the third one imposed by the Court, making the total fines Google has accrued €8.25 billion over a decade. This illustrates the Court's effectiveness as an antitrust enforcer. In the latter case, the European Council enacted restrictions on Russian state-owned media companies and their ability to broadcast in the EU in light of the war in Ukraine. The Court dismissed RT France's claims that the Council had discriminated against RT France on the grounds of nationality, and violated its right to defence, freedom of expression, and ability to conduct business.
42. *Opinion 1/09* EU:C:2011:123 [2011] ECR I-01137 (Opinion pursuant to Article 218(11) TFEU).
43. See Hans Peter Graver, 'The Effects of EFTA Court Jurisprudence on Legal Orders of the EFTA States' (2004) ARENA Working Papers 18, 91–92 <http://www.econpapers.repec.org/paper/erparenax/p0035.htm> accessed 10 October 2022.

44. Allan Rosas, 'Fundamental Rights in the Luxembourg and Strasbourg Courts' in Carl Baudenbacher, Per Tresselt, and Thorgeir Orlygsson (eds), *The EFTA Court: Ten Years On* (Hart Publishing 2005) 167.
45. *Opinion 1/09* EU:C:2011:123 [2011] ECR I-01137 (Opinion pursuant to Article 218(11) TFEU), para 82.
46. The seat of the Court was originally in Brussels, but it has now moved to Luxembourg. The seat of the EFTA Court was originally in Geneva and then it was also moved to Luxembourg.
47. *Colgate-Palmolive BV v Koninklijke Distilleerderijen Erven Lucas Bols NV* Affaire no A 74/1 (Benelux Court of Justice, 1 March 1975). The case concerned the resemblance of the Colgate patented product with the Palmolive/Bols patented product. The Court has adopted judgments in such domains as trademarks, intellectual property, car insurance, civil responsibility, assistance in tax declaration matters, and bird protection, etc.
48. Dayton Peace Agreement, General Framework Agreement for Peace in Bosnia and Herzegovina (14 December 1995).
49. In *Sejdić and Finci v Bosnia and Herzegovina* Apps nos 27996/06 and 34836/06 (ECtHR, 22 December 2009), the Court ruled that Bosnia and Herzegovina must allow other minority groups access to the Presidency and the House of Peoples, eg people of Roma and Jewish ethnicities, which counters the Dayton Agreement's outlines for three presidents. Three judges dissented, holding that, in some cases, lasting stability is more important than human rights.
50. For the case law, see 'Bulletin of the Constitutional Court of Bosnia and Herzegovina No. 3' (Constitutional Court of Bosnia and Herzegovina 2016).
51. UNSC Res 1244 (10 June 1999) UN Doc S/RES/1244, paras 5, 10.
52. UNMIK Regulation 1999/1 'On the Authority of the Interim Administration in Kosovo' (25 July 1999) UNMIK/REG/1999/1, sections 1.1–2.
53. See further for a detailed study, Zane Ratniece, 'Engagement of Kosovo's Domestic (Internationalised) Courts with International Law' in Andre Nollkaemper, Yuval Shany, and Antonios Tzanakopoulos (eds), *Engagement of Domestic Courts with International Law* (OUP 2024).
54. ibid, and the footnotes therein.
55. 'Art 143: Comprehensive Proposal for the Kosovo Status Settlement', Constitution of the Republic of Kosovo [2008].
56. von Bogdandy et al (n 5) 4.
57. These functions have been conceptualized by von Bogdandy et al (n 5) 4–6.
58. Ziemele (n 20) 494 ff.
59. von Bogdandy et al (n 5) 6.
60. Ziemele, 'Common constitutional traditions' (n 41).
61. Case C-156/21 *Hungary v Parliament and Council*, ECLI:EU:C:2022:97, para 127. Also: Case C-157/21 *Poland v Parliament and Council*, ECLI:EU:C:2022:98
62. See further Koskenniemi (n 2).
63. David Sehnálek, 'Normative Approach to the Interplay between the CCC and the CJEU/ECTHR: Judicial Dialogue or a Dictate?', 1 Law, Identity and Values 2022, 204 <http://www.doi.org/10.55073/2022.1.203-223> accessed 11 October 2022.
64. Koen Lenaerts et al (eds), *An Ever-Changing Union? Perspectives on the Future of EU Law in Honour of Allan Rosas* (Hart Publishing 2019).

65. Christiaan Timmermans, 'How Trustworthy is Mutual Trust? Opinion 2/13 Revisited' in Koen Lenaerts et al (eds), *An Ever-Changing Union? Perspectives on the Future of EU Law in Honour of Allan Rosas* (Hart Publishing 2019) 27.
66. According to Timmermans, mutual trust 'has a special dimension .... It has a certain emotional connotation, which fits well in a constitutional language attempting to qualify the implications of the interrelationships between the Member States in the EU legal order.' Christiaan Timmermans, 'How Trustworthy is Mutual Trust? Opinion 2/13 Revisited' in Koen Lenaerts et al (eds), *An Ever-Changing Union? Perspectives on the Future of EU Law in Honour of Allan Rosas* (Hart Publishing 2019) 29.
67. *Opinion 2/13* (n 9).
68. Paul Gragl, 'An Olive Branch from Strasbourg? Interpreting the European Court of Human Rights' Resurrection of Bosphorus and Reaction to *Opinion 2/13* in the Avotins Case', 13(3) European Constitutional Law Review 2017, 6.
69. ibid, 7.
70. *Avotiņš v Latvia*, App no 17502/07 (ECtHR, 23 May 2016).
71. See Joined Cases C-354/20 PPU AND C-412/20 PPU *Openbaar Ministerie (Indépendance de l'autorité judiciaire d'émission)* EU:C:2020:1033 [2020] OJ C 62/10 relating to the Dutch court's response to the Polish Arrest Warrant Order.

CHAPTER 23

EUROPE'S INTERACTION WITH THE REST OF THE WORLD

JAN KLABBERS

1. Introduction

This chapter asks how Europe sees itself, how others see Europe, and whether it is even possible to see Europe. The short answer will be that however Europe is presented, represented, or perceived, none of the images is fully persuasive. Europe is not identical to the European Union (EU); Europe does not fully coincide with the Strasbourg-based Council of Europe; and Europe is not quite as large as the UN Economic Commission for Europe (UNECE). For reasons unrelated to geography, what are ostensibly European cultural events and sports competitions tend to include non-European States, so these too are not a reliable guide, and the geographical boundaries are likewise not very firmly settled. This is mainly because metropolitan Europe (Russia, Turkey) extends into Asia, but beyond this, there are also European outposts, residues of earlier times, located outside Europe: Spanish enclaves in Northern Africa; Dutch islands in the Caribbean; and French and British territories all over the world, really.

There may be a widespread consensus that international law, for much of its recorded existence, has been a European project, but to think of Europe as an actor speaking with a single voice in international law is not very compelling. For much of modern international law's recorded history, from the sixteenth and seventeenth centuries onwards, there can be little doubt that Europe was the dominant force, but this meant effectively that the world was governed by a succession of competing European States, rather than by some entity called 'Europe'. The colonial adventures of Spain and Portugal, with approval from the Pope, were European ventures, and so were those of the Dutch, the French, the Belgians, the Germans, and the English—assuming the English qualify as part of Europe, something they themselves might take issue with. Non-Europeans may have had their own interpretations and sometimes could take credit for inventing new doctrines that have made it to the general international law canon (the Calvo doctrine comes to mind),[1] but by and large international law was a European product, made by Europeans and for the greater benefit of Europeans, whether operating in Europe, the Americas, Africa, Asia, or elsewhere. Except, those people from Europe never acted as 'Europeans', except perhaps in sharing the idea of having a civilizing mission or, more accurately perhaps, presenting imperial expansion as a civilizing mission.

Many of the well-known peace settlements too tended to be European. This is not something to take particular pride in, if only because the familiarity of these settlements is largely the result of European discourse dominance. Moreover, and more perniciously perhaps, such settlements tend to come at the end of warfare and may often in turn contain the seeds of new conflicts. The Westphalia settlement of 1648 may have marked the birth of modern international law, but could only do so by institutionalizing the idea of sovereignty, providing States with legal cover to treat their own citizens miserably. The Versailles settlement, in turn, may have marked the end of World War I, but many would agree that the imposition of unfavourable terms on Germany played some role in fomenting World War II.[2] The redrawn boundaries of Eastern Europe and the Balkans imploded or exploded in the 1990s, when Czechoslovakia and the Socialist Federal Republic of Yugoslavia dissolved, and the territorial re-shufflings of the 1815 Congress of Vienna had likewise proved less than durable.[3]

The picture emerges of a Europe dominated by European States and European thinkers, but it is probably useful to point out that this was possible partly because there was a considerable overlap between the academy and diplomacy. This is no longer the case, at least not to the same extent. There are, so to speak, two versions of international law these days: an international law practised at Foreign Offices and within multilateral fora; and an international law studied at universities. These used to go hand in hand, but no more. In what follows I shall mainly address the former; it is no doubt true that academic insights (and influence) may come to inform practice, but these days the connection is no longer quite as direct as it was until the beginning of the 21st century.[4]

The broad picture of an international law dominated by European States (though not 'Europe') only started to change in the second half of the 19th century when the US entered the global scene and started to come into its own as a colonial power, with European States and the US vying for prominence, and memorably symbolized through the *Island of Palmas* arbitration.[5] If the International Telegraphic Union, set up in 1865, was still made in Europe, the creation of the Universal Postal Union (UPU) a decade later already owed much to the US and its Postmaster General, Montgomery Blair.[6] The law of state responsibility developed through arbitrations and mixed commissions resulting from US investments and conquests in Mexico, Venezuela, and elsewhere.[7] Where the League of Nations, US absenteeism notwithstanding, owed much to US President Woodrow Wilson, the simultaneously created International Labour Organization (ILO) was set up to mimic British corporatism and regulate worker protection so as to fend off the communist threat in Western Europe and protect industries relying on cheap labour from the colonies—in particular the colonies of Western Europe.[8] And while the codification work was done in the US by individuals, sometimes with European roots (think of the Lieber Code[9]) or institutions of higher learning, such as the Harvard Draft Conventions, much of its took place in a very European professional association, the Institut de Droit International.[10]

In other words, roughly until World War II, it is clear that international law was mostly a European international law—or rather, a product stemming from and influenced by competing European States—albeit interlaced with US contributions and the odd contribution from elsewhere. Things get more interesting after World War II though: can post-war international law meaningfully be said to have grown out of Europe's interactions with the world? In what follows, I will first aim to delimit the notion of Europe (Section 2), followed by a discussion on how international organizations elsewhere tend to see Europe and its representatives (Section 3). This will be followed by two sections outlining the work of two of the most comprehensive manifestations of Europe: the Council of Europe (Section 4) and the lesser-known United Nations Economic Commission for Europe (Section 5). Section 6 concludes. For the record, I will not examine the role of the EU or perceptions of the EU except in passing—the EU will be scrutinized in the dedicated chapter in this volume by Justus Vasel.[11]

2. Europe versus the United States, and Not Much Else

It is one thing to say that international law was mostly a European creation, but what does that signify, really? A first factor to look at is to figure out what exactly is meant by 'Europe' and 'European'. Obviously, Europe is a geographical notion, but that is not a very useful starting point, if only since it comes riddled with exceptions in many contexts. Israel and even Australia these days take part in the annual pop music extravaganza known as the Eurovision Song Contest, and football teams from Israel take part in European competitions, as do teams located in the Asian parts of Turkey and Russia.[12]

Far more interesting is whether there exists a particular sensibility which may be called European and which differs in relevant respects from other sensibilities that may or may not demand a geographically inspired label. This is something historians too have struggled with. Some of the first histories of Europe (as opposed to some national history or other) were written by Benedetto Croce and Henri Pirenne less than a century ago,[13] and as recently as the early 2000s Tony Judt's magisterial *Postwar* was still rather special in covering Europe as a whole, and not just its eastern or just its western parts.[14] There were precedents, but these were relatively few and relatively far between.[15]

Two answers are often provided to the question of whether Europe marks a specific sensibility, both of them a little facile, and both of them pitting Europe against the US, without paying much attention to the rest of the world. The first of these often suggests, in very broad strokes, that Americans are keen on creating dispute settlement mechanisms, whereas the Europeans are more interested in establishing mechanisms for cooperation.[16] And if pressed, protagonists can even present something of a beginning of an explanation. This can be an explanation in cultural terms (the US is a litigious society, so it stands to reason that in foreign relations too, dispute settlement quickly comes to mind) or an explanation in materialist terms. On the latter line of thought, dispute settlement is about the application of existing rules, and since existing rules tend to favour powerful interests, and since no interests are as powerful as those of the US, therefore it goes without saying that the US favours dispute settlement. Europe, on the other hand, having forever been divided, is well aware of the need to cooperate, and therefore much more in tune with cooperative schemes and devices, with building institutions.

One major problem with this thesis, as alluded to above, is that it lacks unequivocal empirical support, at least in state-centric terms.[17] It was the US which was behind the League of Nations, the UPU, and many, many other international institutions and, lest it be forgotten, the US itself is likewise the product of cooperation between States.[18] Moreover, the same materialist explanation that would help to explain the American predilection for litigation can serve to elucidate the creation of international institutions by powerful interests instead of the endorsement of mere dispute settlement mechanisms: institutions help to cement current power configurations, and this can serve the hegemon's interests. This was already observed by US international lawyers in the beginning of the 20th century, when the influential Paul Reinsch told his audiences that US membership of the Pan American Union was just as effective for US interests as occupying Latin America would be, but considerably easier and cheaper.[19] And it was observed by US international relations scholars towards the closing of the 20th century, when some of them realized that the hegemon's interest could be protected by international institutions long after the hegemon had stopped being a hegemon.[20]

The second facile position sometimes provided holds that where Americans instrumentalize the law, for Europeans law is a cultural achievement in its own right, deserving to be appreciated as a cultural achievement, on a par with the symphonies of Beethoven, the operas of Puccini, or the writings of Goethe. Notions such as *Rechtsstaat* or the Rule of Law, on such a view, could only come from Europe. Americans would be too busy choosing between the instrumental use of law, or morality, or legitimacy, or naked power, perhaps grounded in such *topoi* as 'rugged individualism' and the 'frontier mentality', to allow themselves such vaguely romantic sensibilities.[21]

This distinction between law as cultural achievement and law as instrument is by no means an eccentric proposition. It mirrors, by and large, a distinction also found in the neighbouring academic discipline of International Relations, where it can be (and has been) summarized as a distinction between American rationalism and European reflectivism, with further national or regional traditions within Europe. German, British, and French traditions are distinguished, all of them captured by the reflectivist label, but nonetheless quite different from each other.[22]

This points to a pressing issue for international lawyers: to what extent can one even think of Europe as having a separate tradition?[23] The founding fathers of the US (disabusing the native population, obviously) were all of European descent, sometimes not all that many generations ago, and many of the international lawyers who have been recently or are currently influential at US universities tend to come from Europe. There are actually surprisingly few leading US international lawyers, given the size of the country, the size of its academic industry, and the global role of the US. And if those who engage in 'foreign relations law' rather than inter-State international law are excluded, the number of leading American scholars dwindles even further. And the numbers go down even further if one discounts those American international lawyers who have adopted the methodologies of the social sciences or economics: there are not that many prominent American international lawyers whose work can mostly be seen as 'doctrinal' in a manner immediately recognizable to German, French, or Italian international lawyers.[24] Regardless of causation, likely to be of the chicken-and-egg variety at any rate, there would seem to be clear cultural differences between American and European conceptions of what international law is, and what it is for.

That said, it is not at all clear that one can think of European international law as a single tradition. There are worlds of difference between the Germans and the French in terms of historical development of legal thought and cultural sensibilities attached to the law; likewise between the Spanish and the English, or the Italians and the Russians, never mind the many smaller legal cultures: the Greeks, the Dutch, the Swedes, and the Romanians. This still presupposes that 'nationality' is somehow of relevance, but there seem to be relevant differences in approach and conception between Dutch-speaking and French-speaking Belgian international lawyers, or between international lawyers in the various language parts of Switzerland: perhaps the relevant factor is not nationality, but language and its *accoutrements*. Focusing on nationality only strengthens, ironically enough, the State-centric nature of much thinking about 'the international'. So the question remains: where does Europe begin and end for purposes of identifying a European tradition? And does this remain constant over time?

Making things even more complicated is the awkward circumstance that for almost half of the 20th century, Europe was divided (literally) into two parts with opposing ideologies and sensibilities, and while that Cold War division has been formally lifted, its effects linger. There is the geopolitical reality, in early 2022, of Russia forcibly claiming Ukraine as its backyard. And leaving the geopolitics aside, this is a matter of violently attacking not just Ukraine, but also the underlying liberal global order, something that right-wing populists welcoming Putin's invasion have intuitively realized. In an important sense, Ukraine may be Russia's target of opportunity (because it is next door, because there have been historical connections, because Ukraine is home to a sizeable amount of Russian-speakers), but the real conflict is between an autocratic style of politics and the liberal post-World War II order. And it plays out within Europe, involving two States seen as European, and is thus far removed from anything like speaking with one voice. The extreme right understands that the attack on Ukraine is an attack on the liberal order (the extreme right, informed mostly by the gut, is usually quicker to grasp seismic shifts). The left, by contrast, often hindered by too much cerebral activity and too much self-righteousness, fails to see any difference between Russia's invasion of

Ukraine and the US/UK invasion of Iraq two decades earlier, or Saudi Arabia's ongoing misadventures in Yemen.

Finally, in addition to the international law made by States and their leaders, there is the international law made by individual thinkers. The latter is not, of course, to be taken literally: individuals rarely create specific legal rules, even if the recognized catalogue of sources of international law (Article 38 ICJ Statute) keeps that option open. Much more plausible is it to say that through thought patterns, ways of arranging materials, and conceptualization, individual thinkers influence the way we think about international law.[25] John Maynard Keynes, rather influential himself, knew this quite well: witness the closing pages of his two main and best-known works, both of them overtly striving towards influencing public opinion.[26]

It is at least arguably the case that this form of influence through the exercise of epistemic authority by individuals ought not to be under-estimated. By this measure, there can be little doubt that international law has always been, and continues to be, a largely European affair: the individuals influencing how we think about international law tend to be mostly Europeans. If that was not surprising in the 16th and 17th centuries, when the likes of Vitoria and Grotius helped explain, justify, and legitimize the policies of Spain and Holland, it has nonetheless persisted to this day. Few theorists have been as influential in the 20th century as Kelsen, Austrian by birth and vocation. The Realist tradition in International Relations was inspired by yet another Austrian lawyer, Hans Morgenthau, while Vienna-trained Hersch Lauterpacht was surely the most influential international lawyer of the first half of the 20th century. And even the critical tradition in international law owes much to Europe, both in drawing inspiration from French philosophy and in its leading scholar, Martti Koskenniemi, being from Finland.

Regardless of their individual merits, it is difficult to think of counterparts from elsewhere. Some Americans may have been somewhat influential around the turn of the 20th century and a little later (James Brown Scott, Manley Hudson, Quincy Wright),[27] but nowhere near as influential as Hans Kelsen or Hersch Lauterpacht; and it is difficult even to think of international lawyers from other parts of the world, let alone to consider them influential. Partly, no doubt, this is the result of European empire: with Europe ruling much of the world, it cannot come as much of a surprise that the world came to be influenced by European thought. Partly also there may be other factors at play. It is at least arguable that freedom of thought and expression in Western Europe helps to generate influential thinkers, who can become influential precisely because they are relatively autonomous—they need not follow instructions from autocratic governments or, these days, take sides in the culture wars prevailing at US colleges (not yet, and not completely, at any rate). Instead, they are allowed the space to think for themselves. That does not mean they are not 'situated' in a relevant sense: all of us are products of our environment to a greater or lesser degree. But it does mean that the environment in Western Europe may be more conducive to stimulating the sort of pathbreaking work that becomes influential.

There are several ways to illustrate the point that much influence can be epistemic in nature and does not merely reflect other forms of power. One way would be to trace the influence of particular writings on everyday practice, for instance the invention, in the literature, of the idea that some agreements between States can be something other than treaties.[28] By the same token, it could be of interest to analyse in some depth the work of the International Law Commission (ILC), a geographically (though not gender-wise) more or less representative body, part of the United Nations (UN), tasked with the codification and development of international law. It is at least arguable, for example, that the preparation of the Vienna Convention on the Law of Treaties (VCLT) owes much to the English roots of the special rapporteurs appointed by the ILC. Just imagine a VCLT prepared by a succession of German law professors instead, and the point will become obvious. Additionally, doing so would underline, yet again, that to think of 'Europe' as speaking with one voice would be problematic.

And some epistemic influence[29] can emanate from the work of European international organizations, as will be indicated below. European organizations engage in experiments with legal techniques that inspire repetition and mimicry; they set Europe-wide standards that, being the first of their kind, tend to become global standards. And none of this even needs to involve the EU, although the EU is probably best known for this.[30]

3. Europe Perceived from the Outside

If Europe-based organizations are either too limited (Council of Europe, the Organization for Security and Co-operation in Europe (OSCE), Benelux, etc) or too encompassing (the North Atlantic Treaty Organization (NATO), the Organization for Economic Cooperation and Development (OECD)), then perhaps it pays to have a look at how the non-European world views Europe. The UN, with 193 member States, is divided into a number of regional groups for purposes of, for instance, elections to organs and bodies. In this setting, Europe is effectively divided in two, reflecting mostly the former Cold War division. The Eastern European group contains, for example, Poland, Estonia, and a few other States nowadays members of the decidedly Western EU. The Western European and Others Group contains States geographically located towards the east (think of Finland), and yet another EU member State, Cyprus, is part of the Asia-Pacific group.

In other universal organizations, the picture that emerges is reasonably similar. The ILO, for instance, uses international organizations as reflecting 'country groupings', and along these lines lists the EU and the OECD, the latter also comprising non-European States.[31] The World Trade Organization (WTO) has separate observer status for its various councils, negotiating groups, and working parties, but Europe is not represented other than in the form of the OECD—bearing in mind that the EU is a full member of the WTO. This should come as no surprise, as the mandates of other European organizations, such as the Council of Europe, hardly cover trade-related matters, and most of the observers to the WTO tend to be economic organizations, some even sector-specific, such as the International Vine and Wine Office (OIV). That said, though, there are general regional organizations which do have some observer status with the WTO, such as the Organization of Islamic Countries, the Pacific Islands Forum and the African Union. In this light, the absence of the Council of Europe is perhaps a little more surprising.[32]

Other international organizations, if they accept and recognize observers, tend to think mostly of the EU as the embodiment of something European, without covering the eastern part of the continent. This makes sense. The EU, after all, is almost like a State; it is the only international organization with anything coming close to a State-like foreign policy, with its own economic and security interests. Others may have external relations, but lack what is traditionally referred to as a foreign policy. Hence, it is no surprise that the Organization of American States (OAS), for instance, accepts the EU as a permanent observer, in addition to 71 States (including all 27 EU member States).[33] Likewise, the EU is unique in being the only international organization to have a permanent mission to the Association of South East Asian Nations (ASEAN).[34] Intriguingly, the little known Economic Cooperation Organization[35] lists as one of its three observers the International Energy Charter, itself the institutionalization of the Energy Charter Treaty, with mostly European member States as well as the EU.[36] Other regional organizations either have no observers, or at least do not appear to refer to them on their websites. And yet others, such as the Shanghai Cooperation Organization (SCO), boast cooperation with a number of others, but not within Europe. Even this is complicated of course, as the largest member State (Russia) of the SCO is itself partly located in Europe.

Either way, what is clear from this—rather incomplete but not unrepresentative—overview is that Europe is not seen as a monolithic entity in the rest of the world. To the extent that Europe as a whole (or almost whole) has an institutional version, in the form of the Council of Europe, this is rarely tapped into, rarely seen as speaking for Europe. In a subtle way, to the extent the Council of Europe has observer status elsewhere, it has it as one of many international organizations, one that just happens to be composed of European States. The more current and more often acknowledged embodiment of Europe is the EU, and for all sorts of reasons that is no surprise: it has its own policies, and it encompasses all former European colonial powers[37]—or did so until the UK withdrew in early 2021.

The same applies *a fortiori* to membership of international organizations. The starting point for any conversation is the position that many international organizations only accept States as members. There may be some uncertainty as to what that entails with respect to entities such as Kosovo or Palestine, but few would argue that the EU currently must be seen as a State. Consequently, it is only on rare occasions that an international organization joins another one. Perhaps the best-known example is that the EU helped to found the WTO and a little earlier had joined the Food and Agricultural

Organization (FAO)—the latter, however, had to formally change its constitution to make this possible.[38] In addition, the FAO had to re-think its internal rules about voting in plenary, representation in its organs, financial contribution, etc to accommodate EU membership.

Beyond this, there are few examples of international organizations having joined other organizations, although what does occur from time to time is participation in loose networks which have no strict rules on membership. One example is that the EU, NATO, and the International Maritime Organization all at some point participated, alongside private actors and civil society organizations, in the Contact Group on Piracy off the Coast of Somalia, a 'governance mechanism' rather than formal international organization, for those who see such distinctions as relevant.[39]

Likewise, it is solely the EU, as an international organization, that is a party to any treaty aimed at protecting global community interests. Not a single international organization has ever joined any convention on international humanitarian law, although the UN already under Secretary-General U Thant announced that it would respect the principles of humanitarian law in its military and peacekeeping operations.[40] The EU is the only international organization to have joined a number of environmental treaties, such as the Convention on Persistent Organic Pollutants,[41] and is the only international organization to have joined a human rights regime: the Convention on the Rights of Persons with Disabilities.[42] While the EU is under a legal obligation to accede to the European Convention on Human Rights (ECHR) (Article 6, paragraph 2 of the Treaty on European Union (TEU) leaves little wriggle room), this has hitherto not happened.[43]

If there is a point emerging from the above overview, it is that for the world at large, 'Europe' tends to mean the EU. It is the EU, if anyone, that can (sometimes ...) speak with one voice, joins treaty regimes and international organizations, and has observer status with other international organizations. Other European organizations are considerably less actively engaged in international affairs. But as a geographical matter, this entails at best an incomplete representation of Europe: without Norway, without Switzerland, without some smaller States, without most of the former Yugoslav and USSR republics, and for the foreseeable future also without the UK.

4. Legal Technique at the Council of Europe

It is not immediately self-evident that the Council of Europe should be seen as the best possible embodiment of the European continent. Partly this is because its membership has never comprised all States recognized as being located in Europe: Belarus has never been a member State, and the Russian Federation was expelled in the Spring of 2022 after it invaded Ukraine. More importantly though, while the Council of Europe was envisaged as a pan-European creature by its *auctor intellectualis*, Winston Churchill,

Churchill himself never thought it should include the UK: 'We British have our own Commonwealth of Nations', he noted in his famous 1946 Zurich speech. By implication, he also left out the USSR, noting that he hoped it would become 'one of the friends and sponsors of the new Europe', alongside the UK, the Commonwealth, and the US.[44] And as a matter of fact, the Council, created in the early years of the Cold War, was a solidly Western European organization from the moment of inception, in 1949, until the beginning of the 1990s. Its membership comprised the States of Western Europe, although Greece was absent for a few years;[45] it is only for the last three decades or so that the Council can plausibly be considered pan-European.

Still, the Council of Europe is interesting for present purposes—summarized under the heading of Europe's impact on international law—for at least three reasons.[46] The first and most obvious of these is that it is the institutional home of the ECHR, which has served as a model for other continents. In particular the Inter-American convention system, concluded in the late 1960s, owes much to the European Convention, both in terms of substance and in terms of institutionalization: its structure with a Commission and a Court[47] was first pioneered in the ECHR. In Europe it was later replaced when the need for a court in permanent session arose; the development has yet to happen in the Americas and elsewhere.[48]

Second, the Council of Europe has sponsored the conclusion of a considerable amount of treaties in the more than seventy years of its existence. Mostly, these do not aspire to reach States that are not member States of the Council of Europe, but some of them are open to non-member States, and have accordingly attracted ratifications by those non-member States. Typically, it concerns fairly 'technical' conventions, such as the Convention on Mutual Assistance in Tax Matters which, since 2010, has been opened up to third parties. The facility has been used by some seventy-five third parties to date.[49] Likewise, the Convention on Cybercrime has been acceded to by a significant number of non-member States of the Council of Europe, including Australia, Canada, Japan, and the US. Less spectacular, a handful of third States has joined the Convention on Counterfeiting Medical Products,[50] while the Convention on Manipulation of Sports Competitions has been signed by two non-member States (Australia and Morocco) but not yet ratified by them.

But more interesting still is a third aspect, highly technical perhaps and mostly invisible, but all the more important as an exercise in epistemic influence. The Council of Europe has been a sometime laboratory for experimentation with legal techniques, a role that goes back to the 1950s. One example, perhaps less-known than it should be, is how the European Social Charter, as revised in 1996, offers a menu for choice to State parties.[51] It starts, in Part I, by listing a number of social policy objectives, but Article 1 only follows thereafter—Part I therewith finds itself in the no-man's land between the traditional preamble, and the operative terms of the Charter. Interesting as this is, as a matter of drafting technique, even more interesting is that Part III, Article A, allows the parties to pick and choose from a number of concrete social rights those which they undertake to respect. The result is an intriguing legal edifice, a smorgasbord where the menu can be customized. Where traditionally treaty drafters resort to reservations, the European Social Charter is set up differently.

Even more intriguing, aiming to reconcile the conflicting (perceived) interests of particularism and universalism, is the pioneering work of the Council of Europe on grafting universal regimes onto bilateral treaty relations. The standard-bearer is the European Convention on Extradition,[52] which most likely has the distinction of being the first multilateral convention concluded in order to amend a series of pre-existing bilateral agreements. Traditionally, extradition is a bilateral affair, with State A and State B concluding an agreement to extradite criminal suspects should the occasion arise.[53] While this has the advantage of facilitating tailor-made arrangements, it has the disadvantage of fragmentation: it might entail that State A's extradition relations with State B are different from those it has with States C, D, and E, leading to different treatment of criminal suspects and, potentially leading to unequal treatment of criminal suspects. As a result, the 1957 Convention now supersedes earlier bilateral agreements, and only allows for further bilateralism between its parties if this is supplementary in nature.[54] The regime has been joined by three non-member States (Israel, South Korea, and South Africa), but its true relevance resides in its technique: turning a web of bilateral agreements into a single multilateral regime.

Similar techniques have been used later, in similar circumstances. For instance, the idea of creating a global tax regime as free as possible from loopholes, sponsored by the Organization for European Cooperation and Development in 2014–2015, likewise involved concluding a multilateral treaty to supplement a multitude of bilateral tax treaties in one fell swoop. At the time of writing (Spring 2022) there are discussions ongoing in UNCITRAL to use the same technique to come to a multilateral investment dispute settlement convention, replacing or complementing a multitude of existing bilateral agreements. And the EU similarly 'multilateralized' the bilateral extradition treaties and mutual legal assistance treaties its individual member States had concluded, after extradition and legal assistance had come to be subsumed under EU competences.[55]

5. Mundane Matters at the UN Economic Commission for Europe

The Council of Europe only became pan-European with the end of the Cold War. The OSCE owed its very existence to the same Cold War: it was conceptualized first as a conference where East and West could meet (in Helsinki, in 1975), and further institutionalized also only once the Cold War had come to an end. It was not the only place where East and West could meet: the Vienna-based International Institute for Applied Systems Analysis (IIASA) has been a common venture of Western and Eastern scientists since 1972, though it never encompassed all of Europe. That means, effectively, that the only pan-European entity in existence for much of the Cold War was the UN Economic Commission for Europe: even Switzerland participated long before it joined the UN, as did a number of East European States well before they would join the UN proper. Only the German Democratic Republic (GDR) stayed outside until it received general recognition in 1973.

The UNECE operated—and operates—mostly below the radar, but did a lot of work on very mundane but important matters. Travellers through Europe may notice, for example, that most traffic signs in Europe look similar or identical, whether one drives through Italy, the Netherlands, or Finland. This owes much to the work of the UNECE, which sponsored all sorts of conventions on such matters.[56]

Especially in its early years, the late 1940s and 1950s, the UNECE was well aware of its function as a possible bridge-builder between East and West Europe.[57] Under the direction of Nobel laureate Gunnar Myrdal, it aspired to create something of a European-wide welfare project. Myrdal was a trained economist and a social-democrat by vocation, cut from much the same cloth as UN Secretary-General and fellow-Swede Dag Hammarskjöld, and well-aware of the powers of *episteme*. If the UNECE was not all that influential in terms of sponsoring high-profile exercises of statesmanship, it derived much influence from such things as gathering statistics: its *Economic Survey of Europe* had an unparalleled reputation as a reliable source of economic information concerning Europe. And this, in turn, was of obvious relevance when the continent was divided and reliable statistics were otherwise difficult to come by.[58]

The UNECE may be best-known for the pioneering Aarhus Convention of 1998, concerning access to information and transparency in environmental decision making. In fact, the UNECE has been pioneering more generally when it comes to environmental protection: the first convention concluded under its auspices addressed long-range transboundary pollution, and goes back to the late 1970s. It has also realized that as environmental protection is difficult to regulate for a variety of reasons, there may be merit in creating procedures: the above-mentioned Aarhus Convention is an example of a largely procedural device, as is the convention on environmental impact assessment in transboundary contexts.

Apart from this visible focus on environmental matters, the UNECE also engages in much technical, low-profile work. It is active in adopting agricultural standards, adopting standards on meat, potatoes, eggs, and cut flowers, amongst others. It adopts standards on the quality of timber, sometimes paving the way for the better-known standards of the International Organization for Standardization (ISO). It addresses the steadily growing problem of ageing, and addresses issues of land governance, ranging from energy-efficient housing standards to proper ways of cadaster services. It develops trade facilitation standards on such wonderfully mundane but sometimes pivotal matters as how to represent dates (8/5/2001 or 5/8/2001, eg), how to abbreviate currencies, how the layout of trade documents should ideally look, etc. Mundane this may be, but it should be obvious that doing so facilitates trade and commerce. The harmonization thus accomplished is never politically innocent: it will benefit some more than others, and perhaps even at the expense of those others, but is nonetheless possibly of great utility in the service of dreams of eternal peace.[59]

Standards on trade facilitation, agricultural products, and timber strength are most likely at their most useful when universally shared. Being developed in Europe, these standards may then need to radiate southward, westward, and eastward, and thus come to resemble yet another way of exercising some kind of domination. This need not be malevolent or the result of evil intentions—far from it, and if standards are deemed desirable to begin with (as is likely to be the case) then someone will have to make the first move at any rate. But the possibility remains that European standards reflect European priorities, creating adaptation hurdles and additional costs in other parts of the world.

6. Final Remarks

Europe is, and always has been, far too divided to be considered to speak with one voice in global affairs. There is considerable sense in suggesting that with the disappearance of European-led empires and the end of World War II, the 'post-European age' had arrived,[60] but only on the understanding that the preceding 'European age' always was a label of convenience rather than precision. Europe has never spoken with one voice in global affairs—although it may sometimes have seemed that way to others, when the globe was divided between Spain and Portugal, for example, in the 15th century, or when a number of European States decided to sublimate their continental rivalries by engaging in what became known as the scramble for Africa.[61] And yet, while there has never been a single European voice, the multiple European voices have been, and continue to be, highly influential. This is an interesting phenomenon in its own right, something for International Relations scholars to reflect upon perhaps: like the smile of the Cheshire cat, the influence of individual European States, and even individual European international lawyers, lingers on long after the basis for power has disappeared.[62]

Europe's influence on international law does not reflect military strength for, by most standards, Europe simply lacks military strength. Nor does it reflect political or economic power *simpliciter*, if only because Europe's States are much too divided, even when assembled together within the EU. Instead, Europe's influence is largely epistemic in nature: it follows from concentrating on the mundane, from experimenting with legal forms and methods, and generally from using the strengths of international law. International law is not terribly good at handling crisis situations (neither is domestic law, for that matter). It cannot prevent tin pot dictators from invading neighbouring countries if they are so inclined, in much the same way that domestic law cannot prevent spouses from murdering each other or prevent seriously rich people from evading their tax obligations. But law, including international law, is very good at handling everyday matters, facilitating, streamlining, and channelling the everyday lives of people. It is here that Europe, in its many manifestations, leaves a mark.

Notes

1. See, eg, Arnulf Becker Lorca, *Mestizo International Law: A Global Intellectual History 1842–1933* (CUP 2014).
2. As contemporary observers already realized all too well: see, eg, Harold Nicolson, *Versailles 1919* (Methuen 1964 [1933]). French Marshall Foch reportedly noted in 1919, with an admirable eye for the temporal dimension: 'This is not peace. It is an armistice for twenty years.' Quoted in George Lichtheim, *Europe in the Twentieth Century* (Cardinal 1972) 292.
3. There is the further consideration, as Kratochwil has it, that settlements 'are never just past events but rather emerge from what subsequent generations make of them'. See Friedrich Kratochwil, *After Theory, Before Big Data: Thinking about Praxis, Politics and International Affairs* (Routledge 2022) 58.
4. I discuss this in more detail in Jan Klabbers, 'On Epistemic Universalism and the Melancholy of International Law', 29 European Journal of International Law 2018, 1057.
5. *Island of Palmas (Miangas) (USA v Netherlands)*, 2 Reports of International Arbitral Awards 829. On the rise of the US, see Walter LaFeber, *The New Empire: An Interpretation of American Expansion, 1860–1898* (Cornell UP 1963).
6. John F Sly, 'The Genesis of the Universal Postal Union', 233 International Conciliation 1927, 393.
7. Alan Tzvika Nissel, *A History of State Responsibility* (doctoral thesis, University of Helsinki, 2016).
8. George N Barnes, *History of the International Labour Office* (Williams and Norgate 1926).
9. Lieber also left his mark on political science, and has been called 'the founder of systematic political studies in the United States'. See John Gunnell, *The Descent of Political Theory: The Genealogy of an American Vocation* (University of Chicago Press 1993) 25.
10. Martti Koskenniemi, *The Gentle Civilizer of Nations: The Rise and Fall of International Law 1870–1960* (CUP 2001)It is no coincidence that in Koskenniemi's history of 19th- and 20th-century international law, the US is by and large absent.
11. Justus Vasel, 'The European Union' in this volume.
12. Journalist Geert Mak's easternmost ports of call are Istanbul and Stalingrad (now Volgograd), still considered to be located in the European parts of Turkey and Russia, respectively. See Geert Mak, *In Europe: Travels Through the Twentieth Century* (Pantheon 2007).
13. Benedetto Croce, *History of Europe in the Nineteenth Century* (Allen and Unwin 1934); Henri Pirenne, *A History of Europe* (Allen and Unwin 1939).
14. Tony Judt, *Postwar: A History of Europe since 1945* (Penguin 2005).
15. For instance, the excellent study by Lichtheim, *Europe in the Twentieth Century*.
16. While it must have been tempting to draw parallels with common law thinking, Janis attributes an American predilection for dispute settlement to American religious thought. See Mark W Janis, *The American Tradition of International Law: Great Expectations 1789–1914* (Clarendon Press 2004).
17. This might suggest that the problem resides with the state-centric nature of the investigation: perhaps it makes more sense to think of the creation of the World Intellectual Property Organization (WIPO) not so much in terms of the interests of Denmark or France, but rather of those of authors and inventors.
18. See also Hatsue Shinohara, *US International Lawyers in the Interwar Years: A Forgotten Crusade* (CUP 2012).

19. Jan Klabbers, 'The Emergence of Functionalism in International Institutional Law: Colonial Inspirations', 25 European Journal of International Law 2014, 645.
20. Robert O Keohane, *After Hegemony: Cooperation and Discord in the World Political Economy* (Princeton UP 1984).
21. Useful is Brian Tamanaha, *On the Rule of Law: History, Politics, Theory* (CUP 2004).
22. Ole Waever, 'The Sociology of a Not So International Discipline: American and European Developments in International Relations', 52 International Organization 1998, 687.
23. The question also underlies Anthea Roberts, *Is International Law International?* (OUP 2017), who distinguishes between (in Europe) the French, British, and Russian traditions—to say nothing of other traditions. The same problem of delimitation also plagues other academic disciplines: see, eg, Benjamin J Cohen, *Advanced Introduction to International Political Economy* (Edward Elgar 2014).
24. And conversely, there are not that many Europeans who do mostly 'law and economics', or 'law as IR'.
25. See also Luiza Leao Soares Pereira, *International Lawyers as Lawmakers* (doctoral thesis, Cambridge University, 2022).
26. See, for instance, John Maynard Keynes, *Economic Consequences of the Peace* (MacMillan 1920) 279: '... the true voice of the new generation has not yet spoken, and silent opinion is not yet formed. To the formation of the general opinion of the future I dedicate this book.' Some treat him as a forerunner when it comes to endorsing expert governance: see Richard Davenport-Hines, *Universal Man: The Seven Lives of John Maynard Keynes* (Basic Books 2015).
27. Benjamin Coates, *Legalist Empire: International Law and American Foreign Relations in the Early Twentieth Century* (OUP 2016); Paolo Amorosa, *Rewriting the History of the Law of Nations: How James Brown Scott Made Francisco de Vitoria the Founder of International Law* (OUP 2019).
28. This refers to James Fawcett, 'The Legal Character of International Agreements', 30 British Yearbook of International Law 1953, 381; for critical reflection, see Jan Klabbers, 'Governance by Academics: The Invention of Memoranda of Understanding', 80 Zeitschrift für ausländisches öffentliches Recht und Völkerrecht 2020, 35.
29. See generally Pertti Alasuutari and Ali Qadir, *Epistemic Governance: Social Change in the Modern World* (Palgrave MacMillan 2019).
30. Anu Bradford, *The Brussels Effect: How the European Union Rules the World* (OUP 2020).
31. United Nations Treaty Collection, Status of Treaties, The Convention on the Rights of Persons with Disabilities, <https://treaties.un.org/Pages/ViewDetails.aspx?src=TREATY&mtdsg_no=IV-15&chapter=4&clang=_en> accessed 29 March 2022.
32. World Trade Organization, International Intergovernmental Organizations Granted Observer Status to WTO Bodies, <https://www.wto.org/english/thewto_e/igo_obs_e.htm> accessed 29 March 2022.
33. Organization of American States, Permanent Observers, <https://www.oas.org/en/ser/dia/perm_observers/countries.asp> accessed 20 March 2022.
34. Association of Southeast Asian Nations, Non-ASEAN Member States Ambassadors to ASEAN (NAAAS), <https://asean.org/our-communities/asean-political-security-community/outward-looking-community/external-relations/non-asean-member-states-ambassadors-to-asean-naaas/> accessed 20 March 2022.
35. It comprises ten states in roughly the western part of Asia, including Turkey, Pakistan, Afghanistan, and Iran.

36. Economic Cooperation Organization, Observers, <https://www.eco.int/general_content/85362-Observers.html?t=General-content> accessed 20 March 2022.
37. Unless one were to consider also Russia and Turkey as former colonial powers—which would not at all be unreasonable.
38. See generally Rachel Frid, *The Relations between the EC and International Organizations: Legal Theory and Practice* (Martinus Nijhoff 1995).
39. Its website has an outdated feel, and may not have been updated since 2018: Contact group on Piracy off the Somali Coast, Lessons from Piracy, <http://www.lessonsfrompiracy.net> accessed 29 March 2022.
40. See Hilaire McCoubrey and Nigel D White, *The Blue Helmets: Legal Regulation of UN Military Operations* (Dartmouth 1996) 156.
41. Stockholm Convention, Status of Ratifications, <http://www.pops.int/Countries/StatusofRatifications/Overview/tabid/3484/Default.aspx> accessed 29 March 2022.
42. United Nations Treaty Series, Status of Treaties, Convention on the Rights of Persons with Disabilities, <https://treaties.un.org/Pages/ViewDetails.aspx?src=TREATY&mtdsg_no=IV-15&chapter=4&clang=_en> accessed 29 March 2022.
43. Article 6, paragraph 2 TEU reads in relevant part: 'The Union shall accede to the European Convention on Fundamental Rights and Freedoms'. For further discussion, see Jan Klabbers, 'On Myths and Miracles: The EU and its Possible Accession to the ECHR', 1 Hungarian Yearbook of International and European Law 2013, 45.
44. Churchill's speech is reproduced in David Cannadine (ed), *The Speeches of Winston Churchill* (Penguin 1989). Nevertheless, the UK became one of the founding members of the Council of Europe. The pan-European movement also owed much to individual thinkers such as Count Richard von Coudenhove-Kalergi.
45. Greece originally was the first State to join the Council (apart from its founding members) in 1949. It left the Council in 1969, after its military government had come under fire over human rights violations, but joined again in 1974. Intriguingly, the website of the Council still lists 1949 as the year in which Greece joined.
46. See also 'The Council of Europe' by Ganna Yudkivska in this volume.
47. See further 'European Courts' by Ineta Ziemele in this volume.
48. Likewise of course, the EU has been a source of inspiration for other regional economic integration organizations: see, eg, David S Berry, *Caribbean Integration Law* (OUP 2014).
49. European Treaty Series, Chart of Signatures and Ratifications of Treaty 127, Convention on Mutual Administrative Assistance in Tax Matters, <https://www.coe.int/en/web/conventions/full-list?module=signatures-by-treaty&treatynum=127> accessed 20 March 2022.
50. European Treaty Series, Chart of Signatures and Ratifications of Treaty 211, Council of Europe Convention on the Counterfeiting of Medical Products and Similar Crimes Involving Threats to Public Health, <https://www.coe.int/en/web/conventions/full-list?module=signatures-by-treaty&treatynum=211> accessed 20 March 2022.
51. European Treaty Series, no. 163.
52. European Treaty Series, no. 24.
53. Seminal is Ivan Shearer, *Extradition in International Law* (Manchester UP 1971).
54. Article 28, paragraphs 1 and 2.
55. Agreement on Extradition between the European Union and the United States of America, Official Journal of the European Union, L/ 181/27, 19 July 2003, <https://eur-lex.europa.eu/legal-content/EN/TXT/PDF/?uri=CELEX:22003A0719(01)&from=EN> accessed 6 May 2022.

56. Students of EU law may recall that one of the seminal cases in EU external relations (case 22/70, *Commission v Council* [*ERTA*]) relates to an agreement negotiated under the auspices of the UNECE: the European Road Transport Agreement.
57. UNECE's former Executive Secretary, Yves Berthelot, observed that perhaps the 'major achievement' of the UNECE 'was to keep alive the idea of a larger and older Europe' transcending the EU. See Yves Berthelot and Paul Rayment, 'The ECE: A Bridge between East and West' in Yves Berthelot (ed), *Unity and Diversity in Development Ideas: Perspectives from the UN Regional Commissions* (University of Indiana Press 2004) 63.
58. See further Jan Klabbers, 'Rival Systems: European Law' in Matt Craven, Sundhya Pahuja, and Gerry Simpson (eds), *Cambridge History of International Law, volume 11: The Cold War* (CUP forthcoming).
59. See in a similar vein Alex Wright, *Cataloging the World: Paul Otlet and the Birth of the Information Age* (OUP 2014).
60. Lichtheim, *Europe in the Twentieth Century* (n 2) 417.
61. H L Wesseling, *Verdeel en heers: de deling van Afrika 1880–1914* (Bert Bakker 1991).
62. And sometimes there seems to be no relationship whatsoever: surely, Martti Koskenniemi's influence on the academic discipline of international law is unrelated to Finland's position in the global order.

CHAPTER 24

NATO

THOMAS D. GRANT

1. Introduction

THE North Atlantic Treaty Organization (NATO) is the principal security organization for the Euro-Atlantic world and the longest-lasting organxization of its kind anywhere in the world. The 'closest and most institutionalized political-military alliance' in history,[1] NATO more than any other organization realizes the concept of 'the inherent right of individual or collective self-defence' that Article 51 of the United Nations Charter envisaged.[2] NATO has, for nearly eighty years, maintained peace across a region that was the scene of catastrophic destruction in two World Wars and the launch point of world-ranging violence and conquest for centuries before. While the proposition is by no means universally accepted, it is to be entertained that the unprecedented legal and institutional integration of Europe from 1945 to the present is owed to the security that NATO created and preserved.

This chapter will briefly relate the history of NATO from its founding through several enlargements both during and after the Cold War (Section 2). It then will turn to Article 5 of the North Atlantic Treaty—the collective defence provision without which, arguably, the other legal and institutional projects that emerged in Europe in the decades after World War II would not have come to fruition (Section 3).

Deterrence of an adversary through military means is NATO's most obvious mission. At the same time, it would not be accurate to say that military preparedness is NATO's only mission. The Allies were joined from the start by shared values, and, though some Allies were less than perfect exemplars of the values professed,[3] they embodied this connection in the North Atlantic Treaty, under Article 2 (Section 4). Meanwhile, the interest of the European Union (EU) in defence and security has increased, and this adds saliency to the rules and mechanisms by which NATO and the EU interact (Section 5).

Few governments treated the recrudescence of armed aggression in Europe in 2014 as an urgent concern. This changed with Russia's all-out invasion of Ukraine in February 2022, which has invited fresh reflection on NATO enlargement (Section 6).

Furnishing security in Europe, NATO has fostered an environment in which rules and institutions have flourished. Moreover, NATO has been a subject of legal rules and a relevant actor in proceedings before institutions that apply legal rules. The main multilateral courts with jurisdiction in Europe, as well as the constitutional court of Germany, the most powerful State in Europe, have adjudicated disputes concerning NATO. Less often remarked, NATO has contributed to the resolution of disputes among its members and aspiring members and in its own internal procedures has joined a trend toward accountability and due process (Section 7).

The chapter closes by considering the possible future of NATO in a period in which some writers and policy makers say that it is the Asia-Pacific world, not the Euro-Atlantic, that will play the leading role (Section 8).

2. Founding of the Alliance and Its Enlargement

A train of events after 1945 convinced the US that its security depended on Europe's security and that only a significant, long-term commitment would guarantee the latter. The US, apprehensive that Greece and Turkey would fall into the USSR's sphere of influence following the cessation of British support,[4] indicated that henceforward it would be US policy to defend democratic countries against Soviet expansion. President Harry S Truman articulated the policy in a speech to Congress on 12 March 1947.[5] Some three months later, the US Secretary of State, George C Marshall, announced a programme of economic reconstruction in Europe, to be funded by the US.[6]

The liquidation of the democratic government of Czechoslovakia early in 1948, and then the USSR's blockade of West Berlin, imposed from 24 June 1948, reinforced the conclusion that a significant US commitment to Europe's defence was necessary. US Senator Arthur H Vandenburg, in May 1948, advanced a resolution proposing a security treaty for Western Europe. The US Senate adopted the Vandenburg Resolution in June 1948, and negotiations on what became the North Atlantic Treaty ensued.[7] Twelve States—the founding members[8]—signed the Treaty on 4 April 1949 at Washington.[9]

Under Article 10 of the North Atlantic Treaty, NATO's members, by unanimous agreement, may invite 'any other European State in a position to further the principles of the Treaty and to contribute to the security of the North Atlantic area to accede' to the Treaty.[10] Greece and Turkey acceded to the Treaty in 1952 and the Federal Republic of Germany (FRG) in 1955. The USSR referred to the FRG's accession as cause for the USSR to establish the Warsaw Pact. From its formation until its dissolution in February 1991, the Warsaw Pact would see two countries withdraw permanently (Albania in 1961, East Germany in 1990); one temporarily (Hungary in 1956); two invaded by the USSR in order to reverse or prevent withdrawal (respectively, Hungary in 1956; and Czechoslovakia in 1968); and one threatened with invasion (Poland in 1980–1981). No country has yet withdrawn from NATO;[11] and no NATO country has invaded or threatened to invade another in order to keep it from withdrawing.

NATO admitted Poland, Hungary, and the Czech Republic as members in 1999;[12] Bulgaria, Estonia, Latvia, Lithuania, Romania, Slovakia, and Slovenia in 2004;[13] Albania and Croatia in 2009;[14] Montenegro in 2017;[15] and North Macedonia in 2020.[16] In 2022, the Organisation had thirty members.[17] In addition to its members, the Alliance has invited Bosnia and Herzegovina to join the Membership Action Plan, in anticipation of that State's accession; and at its 2008 Bucharest Summit agreed to the eventual accession of both Georgia and Ukraine.

Responding to the threat that Russia will pursue further aggression still, Finland and Sweden on 18 May 2022 formally signified their wish to join NATO. The Allies concluded Accession Protocols for Finland and Sweden on 5 July 2022, the fastest any NATO candidate had moved to that advanced stage.[18] Every Ally having completed its national ratification procedure for the Accession Protocols,[19] Finland acceded to NATO on 4 April 2023; Sweden, on 7 March 2024.

3. Article 5 and Effective Security

Central to the Atlantic Alliance is the legal commitment its members express in Article 5 of their Treaty. A provision of constitutional importance to Europe, Article 5 merits recalling in full:

> The Parties agree that an armed attack against one or more of them in Europe or North America shall be considered an attack against them all and consequently they agree that, if such an armed attack occurs, each of them, in exercise of the right of individual or collective self-defence recognised by Article 51 of the Charter of the United Nations, will assist the Party or Parties so attacked by taking forthwith, individually and in concert with the other Parties, such action as it deems necessary, including the use of armed force, to restore and maintain the security of the North Atlantic area.
>
> Any such armed attack and all measures taken as a result thereof shall immediately be reported to the Security Council. Such measures shall be terminated when the Security Council has taken the measures necessary to restore and maintain international peace and security.[20]

Article 5's opening clause, equating 'an attack against one' to 'an attack against them all', establishes a legal identity of security interest and commitment. It also joins Europe to a larger Atlantic region and the security of both to the legal framework of the UN Charter. The significance of Article 5 is obscured, however, if one reads the text as a purely formal expression of legal relations. An operational reality, consisting of military commitments on the ground lends the text its practical efficacy.

Treaties to limit war as an instrument of international relations, or eliminate it altogether, were not a novelty in 1949. The UN Charter was fresh in the minds of policy makers. The Covenant of the League and the Kellogg-Briand Pact were not far in the past. As for mutual defence commitments, the drafters of the North Atlantic Treaty knew that allies, whatever their treaties might stipulate, did not always come to one another's defence in time of need.[21] The plain text of Article 5 of the North Atlantic Treaty suggested no reason that the new instrument would achieve more than had earlier attempts to build a general security architecture for Europe. To understand why NATO worked, one needs to look in the Treaty beyond Article 5—and in State practice beyond the Treaty.

In the Treaty, crucial struts to Article 5 are contained in Articles 3 and 9. Article 3 commits the Allies, 'separately and jointly, by means of continuous and effective self-help and mutual aid' to 'maintain and develop their individual and collective capacity to resist armed attack'.[22] Article 9 constitutes the North Atlantic Council (NAC) which is empowered to 'set up such subsidiary bodies as may be necessary' and to 'establish ... a defence committee which shall recommend measures for the implementation of Articles 3 and 5'.[23]

Beyond the Treaty, NATO's success has owed to the material commitment of the Allies to its formal provisions and the credibility of the deterrent that that commitment engendered. Indispensable here has been the generations-long investment by the US in the security of Europe. Though other Allies at times contributed substantial resources, the contributions of the US were unique in quantity and kind. The US, by implementing Article 5, and moreover, Articles 3 and 9 which buttress Article 5, brought to NATO, and thus to Europe, what the Military Staff Committee provisions of the UN Charter[24] failed to bring to the United Nations (UN) and thus to the world at large—an apparatus with the functional capability to supply collective defence.

It is doubtful whether a functional capability with no legal framework would have achieved long-term security in the Euro-Atlantic region. But a legal framework without a functional capability almost surely would have failed. The effective commitment of the US to Europe's security and the embedding of that commitment in a legal framework mutually reinforced security and law.[25]

If a virtuous cycle emerged under the aegis of NATO, then what, after the many centuries of war in Europe, had set the cycle in motion? Perhaps the World Wars subjected the Continent to a kind of moral shock therapy: so sanguinary had the years between 1914 and 1945 been that Europeans no longer could countenance violence as an extension of statecraft. Under that thesis, the rules and institutions now prevailing in Europe came to be thanks to changes in how Europeans think and how they organize their political and social life. Without deprecating the achievements of Europe since 1945, however, one might ask whether changes such as these are all there was to it.

Europe in the second half of the 20th century did not exist in a geopolitical vacuum. The threat of Nazi tyranny had brought the US on the scene; but the advance of the USSR to the middle of Europe and the threat of further encroachment helped keep it there. One may posit that, if the US had not remained in Europe, either the USSR would have prevailed; or efforts to build and maintain a purely European defence would have given rise once again to the kinds of frictions among European States that often before had led to war. Whether or not the American security commitment *alone* was enough to foster Europe's long peace, the US had the largest economy and most advanced military in the world, and it was relatively aloof from Europe's inter-sovereign rivalries. As such, the US supplied material support to Europe's defence and cohesion among Allies, contributions that no single Western European State or grouping of States was likely to have matched. Article 5 constituted a legal structure suitable to the collective security of Europe. Articles 3 and 9 committed the Allies to give that structure effective substance. Foremost among the Allies, the US fulfilled the commitment.[26]

4. Values

Article 10 of the North Atlantic Treaty, as noted, refers to the 'principles of the Treaty'. Article 2 elaborates on those principles. In accordance with Article 2, the Allies 'seek to eliminate conflict in their international economic policies' and to 'encourage economic collaboration between any or all of them'. While obligations of best efforts, these obligations to 'seek' and 'encourage' outcomes in the economic sphere go well beyond the bare necessities of a military-operational treaty. Article 2 reflects the intention of NATO's founders that the Alliance be more than a defence pact in a narrow sense. The European Communities and their Single Market, which emerged in the ensuing decades, bear a natural relationship to the ambitions expressed in Article 2.

Also of interest in Article 2 is the clause obliging each Ally to 'contribute to the further development of peaceful and friendly international relations ... by bringing about a better understanding of principles upon which these institutions are founded'. A resemblance may be detected here to the contemporaneous Geneva Conventions, for example Article 47 of the First Geneva Convention,[27] obliging the study of the Conventions in military and, 'if possible', civil curricula, 'so that the principles [of the Conventions] may become known to the entire population, in particular to the armed fighting forces'. The 'understanding' clause of Article 2 of the North Atlantic Treaty is neither as clear nor as specific as the 'may become known' clause of the Geneva Conventions, but Article 2 arguably reaches further, requiring as it does that the Allies promote 'conditions of stability and well-being'. Reading it in context, the parties could readily interpret this clause to apply to domestic governance and overall welfare, as indeed they have.[28]

In NATO's fifth decade, the Alliance confirmed the wider aims that Article 2 suggests. The 1995 Study on Enlargement stated that 'NATO views security as a broad concept embracing political and economic, as well as defence, components'.[29] The Study referred to an 'interplay' among multilateral institutions in Europe and referred, by way of example, to the EU, the Western European Union (WEU), and the Organization for Security and Co-operation in Europe (OSCE).[30] The Study identified the 'benefits of common defence' as conducive to 'the further democratic development of new members' and to an 'existing community of values and institutions'.[31]

The 1995 Study envisaged NATO's enlargement as 'complement[ing]' that of the EU, which the Study described as a 'parallel process'.[32] By no means as exacting as the process through which an EU aspirant comes to accede to the Union, NATO's process for aspirants nevertheless has a broadly similar shape to the EU's. When seeking to accede to either organization, a State must undertake steps to bring its own rules and practices into alignment with those of the organization before accession is completed. NATO's accession process is a 'graduated process of integration and dialogue' designed to ready an aspirant State to 'further the principles of the Treaty and to contribute to the security of the North Atlantic Area'.[33]

The most recent NATO Strategic Concept confirms that values continue to be a NATO concern. The 2022 Strategic Concept states that the Alliance 'will continue to safeguard the freedom and security of all Allies, as well as [their] shared democratic values'[34] and that the Allies 'are united in [their] commitment to democracy, individual liberty, human rights, and the rule of law'.[35]

5. From the WEU to the CSDP

NATO has proved the most enduring of the post-1945 multilateral defence institutions, but it was not the first. The Western Union, constituted in 1948 by France, the UK, Belgium, the Netherlands, and Luxembourg, addressed its parties' concern that Germany might again embark upon aggression in Europe. The USSR, however, rapidly emerged as the chief threat.

Reorganized in 1954 as the WEU,[36] the organization continued to function, and from time to time European policy makers suggested that it would be the kernel for a European defence distinct from NATO and integrated into the new European Communities under their European Political Cooperation (EPC). Steps in that direction were unsteady, and no European army came to be during the Cold War or in the several decades after. Even in 2003, when the US-led coalition war in Iraq heightened transatlantic differences, an attempt to create an EU 'defence union' did not succeed.[37] The WEU was at last dissolved in 2011.[38] By then certain WEU functions had been integrated into the EU as part of the Common Security and Defence Policy (CSDP).[39]

Overlap in the functions of the Alliance and the CSDP raises questions as to possible redundancies between the two, or cross-purposes. The EU eventually perhaps will supply an organizational framework for a more robust European defence.[40] Whether in an EU framework or elsewhere, it is difficult to see how European States will ensure their own security without larger expenditures on defence if the US re-directs its strategic focus to East Asia. This chapter will reflect, in closing, on the possible role of Europe and NATO in the Pacific century that some say we now have entered.

The EU today takes formal account of NATO and the legal commitments NATO entails for its members. The Treaty on European Union (TEU), as amended by the Treaty of Lisbon of 13 December 2009, provides in Article 42(2) that the 'common security and defence policy shall include the progressive framing of a common Union defence policy ... lead[ing] to a common defence' subject to unanimity in the European Council.[41] Article 42(2) also contains a savings clause, which reads as follows:

> The policy of the Union in accordance with this Section shall not prejudice the specific character of the security and defence policy of certain Member States and shall respect the obligations of certain Member States, which see their common defence realized in the North Atlantic Treaty Organisation (NATO), under the North Atlantic Treaty and be compatible with the common security and defence policy established within that framework.

Article 42(7) goes on to affirm NATO's role in stronger terms:

> Commitments and cooperation in this area shall be consistent with commitments under the North Atlantic Treaty Organisation, which, for those States which are members of it, remains the foundation of their collective defence and the forum for its implementation.[42]

As this chapter has noted, NATO not only sets out a legal 'foundation' for collective defence. It also implements defence through operational integration. The TEU commits the EU member States to a 'progressive' development of EU military capabilities (Article 42(3)) but in definite and present terms acknowledges the priority of NATO commitments for those member States that belong to the Alliance.[43]

In the Washington Summit Declaration of 10 July 2024, NATO's members referred to their 'unprecedented levels' of cooperation with the EU and indicated 'respect for the organisations' different mandates, decision-making autonomy, and institutional integrity.[44]

6. The Russo-Ukrainian War and NATO Enlargement

Russia, having begun an all-out invasion of Ukraine on 24 February 2022, visited upon Europe over the ensuing months the worst atrocities and most costly war the Continent had seen since 1945. A Russo-Ukrainian war had begun already in 2014, when Russia annexed Ukraine's Crimean peninsula[45] and took hold Ukraine's provinces of Donetsk and Luhansk by force.[46] However, it was in 2022 that policy makers seemed at last to acknowledge that Russia's geopolitical aims are a threat to general public order.[47]

The Secretary General of NATO on 27 June 2022, presaging the Alliance's Madrid Summit, indicated that NATO will undertake a significant increase in the Alliance's military preparedness and that more Allies than at any time since the Cold War meet, will soon meet, or pledge to meet, the NATO defence expenditure target of 2 per cent of GDP.[48] The Secretary General added that '[t]wo percent is increasingly considered a floor, not a ceiling'.[49] The Summit Declaration noted 'common resolve' between NATO and the EU 'in responding to Russia's war against Ukraine'.[50]

Separately, the heads of State and government of the EU member States met at Versailles on 10–11 March 2022 and adopted a Declaration calling for their countries 'resolutely [to] invest' in defence, including 'innovative technologies', and to foster a 'stronger and more capable EU in the field of security and defence ... complementary to NATO'.[51] This was not the first time that NATO Allies and others in Europe made commitments to increase defence spending. Not all in the past met the commitments that they made. It bears observing that the contribution of European NATO Allies to Europe's collective defence was at its height in the Cold War years when the threat from the USSR was at its height.[52] It remains to be seen whether European NATO Allies restore their defence contribution to a level commensurate with the threat that Russia presents today.

NATO has indicated a long-term plan to assist Ukraine in equipping its armed forces with NATO equipment.[53] Ukraine's adoption of NATO-standard arms, and also of certain theories and practices of command structure and operational method,[54] is likely to affect legal relations. Rein Müllerson observed in the late 1990s that NATO's relations with both its members and other States 'inevitably bring ... about direct legal consequences' and have impact upon the 'entire political and military-strategic environment' in which legal concepts are interpreted and applied.[55] Ironically, Müllerson at that time had in mind relations between NATO and Russia; one might well observe the same today about relations between NATO and Ukraine.

For sake of completeness, the present chapter must mention Russia's occasional complaints about NATO enlargement. Russia alludes to NATO enlargement as a supposed justification for the use of force and for increasingly profligate threats of force, including nuclear force, against numerous countries in Europe and elsewhere. This is not to suggest that Russia identifies any single coherent justification for the war it started in 2014 and escalated in 2022: Russia has gyrated between one pretext and another.[56] However, Russia's official and semi-official narratives about Ukraine from time to time have portrayed NATO as the main protagonist.[57]

Curiously, Russia's antecedent diplomatic practice contains little if anything that precisely anticipates Russia declaring NATO enlargement a *casus belli*. In March 1999, the accession of Poland, Hungary, and the Czech Republic to NATO occasioned Russia's Foreign Ministry to say that enlargement 'will not promote a strengthening of trust and stability in international relations'.[58] This was a vague and rather muted response, if Russia in truth understood enlargement to have infringed a legal right. No more indication of a legal claim can be discerned in Russia's suggestion that accession to NATO of Estonia, Latvia, and Lithuania would be a 'red line':[59] talk of red lines might (or might not) serve as a signal in geopolitical or military settings, but without more they carry no legal consequence. Nor do policy papers or legal writings.[60] There were many forums and channels that Russia could have used to place on record a view that NATO's enlargement was a breach of legal commitment, the possible starting point for an international dispute.[61] Russia used none of them. Russia expressed no such view in the formal way one would have expected a State to have done if it believed its legal rights were under threat. The NATO pretext—i.e., the proposition that NATO enlargement provoked Russia to resort to war—in this regard resembles Russia's allegations of genocide: in forums where Russia might have alleged human rights violations in the years immediately before the invasion of Ukraine in 2014, Russia said nothing about genocide in Ukraine, or anything even close to it.[62] Much the same way, the diplomatic practice of the Russian Federation does not contain the clear, specific, and timely protests that one would have expected if NATO enlargement had indeed been a concern.

Writers on geopolitics occasionally speculate what, precisely, NATO told Mikhail Gorbachev and members of his government in the final days of the USSR about NATO's intentions with regard to enlargement, and what the USSR's leaders thought what NATO told them meant.[63] Thus, the discourse around this matter reduces to speculation whether even an informal commitment existed, and the evidence that it might have is so thin that even those individuals whom the matter most concerned were, at best, unsure. To argue that the largest invasion in Europe since 1945 finds justification in a putative NATO pledge about enlargement is unconvincing if measured against basic standards of legal plausibility.

It is a principle of international law that each sovereign chooses which, if any, alliances it might seek to join. NATO affirms that principle.[64] The International Court of Justice (ICJ) does too.[65] Under Article 50 TEU, any member State may conduct a voluntary and unilateral withdrawal from the Union. The UK's exit from the EU illustrates that Article 50 is no mere window dressing; the principle that it embodies has real effect. Under general international law, a country is free to remain outside NATO and, if NATO invites it, free to join; and no conventional undertaking limits that freedom. Even if Russia had protested NATO's enlargement, Russia did not have a veto over the security policies of other States, nor does it have such a veto today.

7. NATO and the Legal Systems It Secures

Even where not impleaded as a party, NATO has been relevant in a number of well-known cases before national and international courts. NATO's conduct has contributed to the formation of international law in Europe and beyond. NATO also has played a role, less frequently remarked, in resolving disputes among States in Europe. Finally, fulfilling the needs of an intergovernmental organization with a large civil service of its own, NATO has a tribunal for administrative dispute settlement, and this has adapted in line with the larger trend towards due process in international organizations.

7.1 NATO at the ICJ: extramural commitments and accountability of the international security organization

Greece and the former Yugoslavia Republic of Macedonia (as North Macedonia then was called) adopted an Interim Accord in 1995 under which Greece agreed, *inter alia*, 'not to object to the application by or the membership of' North Macedonia in 'international, multilateral and regional organizations and institutions of which [Greece] is a member'.[66] Greece was already at that time a member of NATO; North Macedonia was not. At the NATO Bucharest Summit in April 2008, Greece did not lend its support to North Macedonia's application for membership,[67] and NATO, requiring consensus (ie unanimity),[68] did not invite North Macedonia to begin accession talks.[69] North Macedonia, on grounds that Greece had breached the commitment not to object to North Macedonia's NATO application, in November 2008 instituted proceedings against Greece at the ICJ.[70] The ICJ concluded that Greece indeed was in breach.[71] The Court restricted the remedy to a declaration to that effect.[72]

The Court, in its judgment, did not address Greece's argument that the commitment in the Interim Accord, because it imposed on Greece a particular course of action in NATO (ie withholding objection to North Macedonia's accession), was not one that the Court could adjudicate, the Court having 'so far been exceptionally careful to respect' the 'general legal relation between the Court and international organisations'.[73] It could be that the Court had that argument in mind, when it restricted the remedy and denied North Macedonia's request for a direction to Greece to refrain from objecting in the future. The Court also took care to note that its judgment did not concern the conduct of NATO or of other NATO member States.[74] Thus, the judgment avoided any trespass against the legal interests of NATO.

Earlier, Serbia and Montenegro[75] had instituted proceedings at the ICJ against nine individual NATO members. The applicant State alleged that the NATO member-respondents had breached the obligation against use of force against another State[76] when they had participated in the NATO military campaign to stop Serbia's atrocities against the people of Kosovo and prevent an exodus of refugees that threatened to destabilize Southeastern Europe.[77] Serbia and Montenegro, however, in the judgment of the Court, at the time it instituted proceedings (29 April 1999) was not a member of the UN; thus not in a position to avail itself of Article 35, paragraph 1 of the Statute of the Court. In result, the Court had no jurisdiction to address the merits of Serbia and Montenegro's claim.[78]

In an oft-remarked *dictum* in the *NATO* cases, the Court recalled 'the fundamental distinction between the existence of the Court's jurisdiction over a dispute, and the compatibility with international law of the particular acts which are the subject of the dispute'.[79] The Court further recalled that whether or not it has jurisdiction over a dispute, parties to the dispute 'remain in all cases responsible for acts attributable to them that violate the rights of other States'.[80] The Court recalled the 'special responsibilities' of the UN Security Council under Chapter VII of the Charter when a dispute concerns a threat to the peace, a breach of the peace, or an act of aggression.[81] In light of the procedural posture of Serbia and Montenegro's claims, none of which advanced to the merits, the Court did not say anything more about these matters, including the matter of attribution and accountability to which it had alluded.[82]

7.2 NATO at the ECtHR: accountability redux

In *Bankovic v Belgium et al*, Serbian citizens, invoking the European Convention on Human Rights (ECHR), brought claims against NATO member States for damages in connection with the death of the claimants' family members during the Kosovo campaign. The difficulty for the claimants was that the Federal Republic of Yugoslavia (FRY) was not a party to the Convention at the relevant time. 'The Convention,' the European Court of Human Rights (ECtHR) reasoned, 'is a multi-lateral treaty operating ... in an essentially regional context and notably in the legal space ... of the Contracting States. The FRY clearly does not fall within this legal space.'[83] Writers widely criticized the *Bankovic* judgment.[84]

The NATO campaign of 1999 gave rise to further litigation at the ECtHR. The joined *Behrami* and *Saramati* cases concerned, respectively, (i) death and injuries resulting when a group of young boys in Mitrovika, Kosovo came upon unexploded bombs that had been dropped during the campaign and one of the bombs exploded; and (ii) the arrest and detention by the NATO Kosovo Force (KFOR) of a suspect, Mr Saramati, on suspicion of attempted murder and illegal weapon possession. The Behrami claimants instituted proceedings against France; Saramati against France, Germany, and Norway. Saramati's claims against Germany were withdrawn during the proceedings.

France and Norway argued, *inter alia*, that conduct of KFOR was not to be attributed to States whose forces comprised KFOR, because this was an integrated mission having independent command and control and acting under a mandate that the UN Security Council had conferred in Resolution 1244 (1999).[85] Attribution, according to France and Norway, was either to KFOR or to the UN itself.[86] The respondent States also argued, as a matter of policy, that it would deter States from contributing to international peacekeeping, if the Court were to attribute the conduct concerned in these claims to constituent States of KFOR.[87]

The ECtHR concluded that the unexploded ordnance had been the responsibility of UNMIK at the time of the injuries concerned; and that issuing detention orders fell within KFOR's mandate.[88] As for the States contributing personnel to KFOR, the ECtHR concluded that these did not have such involvement with KFOR as to interfere with NATO's operational command: KFOR officers were answerable to NATO, and KFOR was exercising 'lawfully delegated Chapter VII powers of the UNSC', from which delegation the ECtHR further concluded that the impugned conduct 'was, in principle, attributable to the UN',[89] not to the respondent States.[90]

Turning to consider jurisdiction, the ECtHR observed that 'the primary objective of the UN is the maintenance of international peace and security' and that '[w]hile it is equally clear that ensuring respect for human rights represents an important contribution to achieving international peace ... the fact remains that the UNSC has primary responsibility, as well as extensive means under Chapter VII, to fulfil this objective, notably through the use of coercive measures'.[91] Getting to the heart of the matter, the ECtHR then said as follows:

> Since operations established by UNSC Resolutions under Chapter VII of the UN Charter are fundamental to the mission of the UN to secure international peace and security and since they rely for their effectiveness on support from member states, the Convention cannot be interpreted in a manner which would subject the acts and omissions of Contracting Parties which are covered by UNSC Resolutions ... to the scrutiny of the Court. To do so would be to interfere with the fulfilment of the UN's key mission in this field ...[92]

In thus holding that it could not reach the merits of the applicants' complaints, the ECtHR, interestingly, also affirmed the autonomy of each member State when participating in the parliamentary procedures of an international organization: the respondent States did not attract legal responsibility for their votes in favour of the Chapter VII resolution that had authorized KFOR.[93] It might be asked how to reconcile this conclusionwith that in the *North Macedonia* NATO case, where Greece *was* responsible for its intramural conduct in NATO.

Much as the *Banković* judgment had done, the judgment in *Behrami and Saramati* provoked a sharp reaction from legal writers.[94] Writers' disquiet again arose from the seeming gaps in the coverage of the European human rights regime. Less widely observed in either case, however, was the dependency of that regime upon the collective security of Europe, which the ECtHR, it may be submitted, rightly identified as 'imperative'.[95]

7.3 NATO in German constitutional law

While canvassing the jurisprudence of some thirty countries would exceed the scope of a chapter on NATO and international law in Europe, a brief word is in order about Germany's constitution.

The German Constitutional Court draws attention to the special role that collective security plays in German constitutional law. The Court explains that the relevant provisions of the German Basic Law relating to the armed forces were intended to 'integrate [the armed forces] as a "parliamentary army" into the constitutional system of a democratic state under the rule of law'.[96] Article 24.2 of the Basic Law, the Court recalls, applies to 'deployments in systems of mutual collective security'.[97] Article 24.2 authorizes the Federal Republic to join 'a system of mutual collective security for the maintenance of peace'. The Court noted that, '[i]n addition to the United Nations, NATO, as a defensive alliance, constitutes such a system'.[98]

The Court thus highlights the integration of Germany's armed forces within Germany's democratic political system; and the integration of Germany within NATO's collective security system.[99] Clarity about these relationships, it is submitted, is welcome in light of Germany's history and present-day importance to Europe.

7.4 NATO's conduct and the formation of international law

From time to time, NATO adopts statements that express the views of the Alliance in regard to legal issues. For example, the NATO foreign ministers in November 2022 stated that 'Russia bears full responsibility for [the] war [against Ukraine]', a war that is 'a blatant violation of international law and the principles of the UN Charter'.[100] NATO has stated that the conduct of Russia and China threatens the 'rules-based international order', a point to which this chapter will return. In regard to nuclear deterrence (which remains a core component of NATO doctrine), the North Atlantic Council in its Brussels Communiqué of June 2021, indicated that the Alliance does not accept 'any argument that the [Treaty on the Prohibition of Nuclear Weapons] reflects or in any way contributes to the development of customary international law'.[101] Such statements, being a form of conduct for purposes of identifying customary international law,[102] are a further way in which NATO has participated in the modern international law of Europe.

NATO's 'conduct on the ground'[103] is, similarly, relevant to customary international law.[104] As NATO of course concludes a wide range of international agreements, NATO also has been an active participant in the creation of conventional international law rules.

7.5 NATO membership as incentive to resolve disputes

Not as a party, nor as a mediator; and not in any formal good offices role as such, NATO nevertheless has facilitated the settlement of a number of disputes between European States. This chiefly has been through the process of accession of new members.

The 1995 Study on NATO Enlargement indicated that 'States which have ethnic disputes or external territorial disputes, including irredentist claims, or internal jurisdictional disputes must settle those disputes by peaceful means in accordance with OSCE principles'.[105] The Study identified '[r]esolution of such disputes' to be a 'factor in determining whether to invite a state to join the Alliance'.[106] The Alliance thus connected dispute resolution expressly to the accession process, which, in turn, has given aspirants an incentive to resolve disputes. The incentive appears to have led Hungary and Romania to resolve differences concerning ethnic minority rights at the time of their candidacy to NATO,[107] Hungary eventually being admitted in 1999, Romania in 2004.

The incentive was visible again in June 2022, when Turkey, Finland, and Sweden adopted a Trilateral Memorandum addressing Turkish complaints regarding the presence of certain groups in Finland and Sweden that Turkey understood to pose a threat to the latter's national security.[108] Turkey, a NATO member, had expressed misgivings about the applications of Finland and Sweden for NATO membership. Under the Trilateral Memorandum, both Finland and Sweden undertook not to support the groups; confirmed that the Kurdish group PKK is a 'proscribed terrorist organization', and, among further steps, agreed to establish a Permanent Joint Mechanism with Turkey.[109]

For its part, Turkey committed 'to support ... the invitation of Finland and Sweden to become members of NATO'—and the two NATO aspirants, which were already EU member States for their part, committed 'to support the fullest possible involvement of Turkiye and other non-EU Allies in the existing and prospective initiatives of the European Union's Common Security and Defence Policy'. Thus, the NATO accession process for Finland and Sweden, as accession for other aspirant States in the past had done, addressed the settlement of outstanding issues between States in the European area and involved an exchange of commitments relating to one or more parties' quest for further integration. One might detect an echo in the Trilateral Memorandum of the Greece-North Macedonia commitments, about which those States litigated after the 2008 Bucharest Summit.

7.6 Administrative law of the international organization

Article XXIV of the Agreement on the Status of the North Atlantic Treaty Organization, National Representatives and International Staff, authorizes the North Atlantic Council (NAC) to 'make provision for appropriate modes of settlement' of disputes involving NATO officials or experts.[110] A NATO Appeals Board operated under Article XXIV from 1965 until the NAC replaced it in 2013 with the NATO Administrative Tribunal (AT).[111]

A NATO senior legal officer observed not long ago that 'NATO has been poorly—or not at all—studied under international institutional law'.[112] Serving some 6,000 civilian NATO staff, the NATO AT's caseload is modest in comparison, for example, to that of the United Nations Dispute Tribunal which serves the considerably larger UN staff system.[113] Nevertheless, motivated by the interest in assuring due process for its personnel, NATO has pursued a course of institutional development in recent years similar to other international organizations.[114]

8. NATO and Europe in a Pacific (?) Century

In recent years, the US has contemplated a turn in security strategy towards the Pacific.[115] Some defence intellectuals argue that the Pacific is so important, and that defending the Pacific will place such a burden on American resources, that a corresponding turn *away* from Europe is required.[116] As NATO now appears to affirm, the challenge in the Pacific is China.

On the eve of the June 2022 Madrid Summit, the Secretary General of NATO said that NATO will 'for the first time' take into account the rise of China as a source of challenge to the 'security, interests, and values' of the Atlantic area. In its Summit Declaration, NATO referred to China as a source of 'systemic competition', 'challeng[ing] our interests, security, and values and seek[ing] to undermine the rules-based international order'.[117] The phrase 'rules-based international order' appears often enough in academic writings and in the pronouncements of governments to have become hackneyed. NATO's 2022 Strategic Concept evinces no apprehension in that regard on NATO's part, however. The Strategic Concept uses the phrase 'rules-based international order' five times.[118] In respect of China, the Strategic Concept says that China 'strives to subvert the rules-based international order, including the space, cyber and maritime domains', and that the 'deepening strategic partnership between [China] and the Russian Federation and their mutually reinforcing attempts to undercut the rules-based international order run counter to our values and interests'.[119]

'Rules-based' or otherwise, international order now involves more than one continent or region. Reflecting the new scope of NATO's strategic awareness, the Madrid Summit was the first that Australia, Japan, New Zealand, and the Republic of Korea attended. True, the pursuit by European States of geopolitical interests outside Europe has well-known antecedents. It is in the wake of that pursuit that international law, as it emerged in Europe, came to apply to the world at large;[120] the 'rules-based international order' to which NATO refers was in large part that which emanated centuries before from Europe.[121] A remarkable aspect of the 2022 Strategic Concept is the seeming return to a far-reaching perspective on the geography of Europe's collective defence.

It was in the frame of NATO that European States and the US coordinated to deter the USSR from attempting to impose hegemony on Europe. If they had not, then a very different kind of legal order likely would have resulted in Europe. What kind of legal order exists among States in the Pacific, and what might it develop over time to be?

International lawyers note that East Asia, though home to the world's fastest-growing economies, has the least effective intergovernmental institutions of any major region.[122] Yet, in recent years, the US and several countries in Asia have come closer together on international security. The Quad Powers—Australia, India, Japan, and the US—do not constitute a standing international organization, and defence policy thinkers in these countries have judged it better to keep their security relations on less formal lines than NATO.[123] Nevertheless, in the Quad States' growing proximity on security might be discerned at least a glimmer of Europe's post-1945 development.[124] To be sure, it is hard to imagine today such a divergent group of States embarking on a project such as the European Communities or even the Council of Europe. And yet, those European institutions in time embraced dozens of countries across the full diversity of the Continent. As this chapter has suggested, a reliable security apparatus was their precursor.

Institutional forms seldom replicate themselves precisely in different places at different times. Patterns nevertheless exist that have recurred in multiple settings.[125] Observers of new security initiatives in the Pacific naturally ask whether NATO provides a relevant institutional pattern. It remains to be seen whether, and if so to what degree, the Pacific will reprise the experience of Europe that the chapters of this volume have addressed.

Notes

1. Stephan Frühling, '"Key to the Defense of the Free World": The Past, Present and Future Relevance of NATO for US Allies in the Asia-Pacific', 17 Journal of Transatlantic Studies 2019, 238–254.
2. As to the somewhat otiose debate whether NATO is also a *regional* organization, in the sense of Article 52 UN Charter, see Nigel D White, 'The EU as a Regional Security Actor within the International Legal Order,' in Martin Trybus and Nigel White (eds), *European Security Law* (OUP 2007) 329, 332–333 (hereafter Trybus and White, *European Security Law*) and works cited therein.
3. See Ruud van Dijk and Stanley R Sloan, 'NATO's Inherent Dilemma: Strategic Imperatives vs. Value Foundations', in Sergey Radchenko, Timothy Andrews Sayle, and Christian F Ostermann (eds), *NATO in the Cold War and After. Contested Histories and Future Directions* (Routledge 2021) 251.
4. See Bruce R Kuniholm, *The Origins of the Cold War in the Near East: Great Power Conflict and Diplomacy in Iran, Turkey, and Greece* (Princeton UP 1980); Wilson D Miscamble, 'The Foreign Policy of the Truman Administration: A Post-Cold War Appraisal', 24(3) Presidential Studies Quarterly 1994, 479–494. See also John Kent, 'The British Empire and the Origins of the Cold War, 1944–1949,' in Anne Deighton (ed), *Britain and the First Cold War* (St Martin's Press 1990).
5. See https://history.state.gov/milestones/1945-1952/truman-doctrine
6. See https://history.state.gov/milestones/1945-1952/marshall-plan
7. For a contemporary summary of the transactions leading to the Treaty, see 'Consultative Council of Western Powers', 3(1) International Organization 1949, 166–169. See also Timothy Andrews Sayle, *Enduring Alliance. A History of NATO and the Postwar Global Order* (Cornell UP 2019) 12–17 (hereafter Sayle, *Enduring Alliance*); Lawrence S Kaplan, *The US and NATO: The Formative Years* (University Press of Kentucky 2014) 93–120.
8. Belgium, Canada, Denmark, France, Iceland, Italy, Luxembourg, the Netherlands, Norway, Portugal, the UK, and the US.

9. North Atlantic Treaty (Washington Treaty), signed 4 April 1949; entered into force 24 August 1949: 34 UNTS 243.
10. 34 UNTS 248. Further to Article 10, see Nick Minogue, 'The North Atlantic Treaty at 70—Article 10', 34 Emory International Law Review 2019, 165–180 (hereafter Minogue, 'The North Atlantic Treaty at 70—Article 10').
11. France's break with the US led in 1966 to France discontinuing its participation in NATO military command but not its formal withdrawal from the Alliance. Regarding the episode generally, see Sayle, *Enduring Alliance* (n 7) 50–75; Andreas Wenger, 'Crisis and Opportunity: NATO's Transformation and the Multilateralization of Détente, 1966–1968', 6(1) Journal of Cold War Studies 2004, 22–74.
12. https://www.nato.int/docu/comm/1999/9904-wsh/pres-eng/03acce.pdf
13. https://www.nato.int/docu/update/2004/03-march/e0329a.htm
14. https://www.france24.com/en/20090401-croatia-albania-join-nato-
15. https://www.nato.int/cps/en/natohq/news_144647.htm
16. https://www.nato.int/cps/en/natohq/news_174589.htm
17. The twelve founding members (see n 8), plus Albania, Lithuania, Bulgaria, Montenegro, Croatia, the Czech Republic, Poland, Estonia, Romania, Germany, Slovakia, Greece, Slovenia, Hungary, Spain, Turkey, Latvia, and North Macedonia.
18. https://www.nato.int/cps/en/natohq/news_197763.htm
19. See, eg, Latvia's Instrument of Acceptance: https://twitter.com/Flash43191300/status/1548206985689976832/photo/1 As of December 2022, for a list of ratifying States see https://www.nato-pa.int/content/finland-sweden-accession
20. 34 UNTS 246–248.
21. Inter-European treaties before the World Wars are well-known examples, but there were other failures too, eg alliance treaties between European States and indigenous polities in the Americas: Ken Coates, 'North American Indigenous Peoples' Encounters', Bardo Fassbender and Anne Peters, 'Introduction: Towards a Global History of International Law', in Bardo Fassbender and Anne Peters (eds), *The Oxford Handbook of the History of International Law* (OUP 2012) 797–798 (hereafter Fassbender and Peters, *The Oxford Handbook of the History of International Law*). The practice of ignoring such treaties extended well past the age of imperialism: see *Land and Maritime Boundary between Cameroon and Nigeria (Cameroon v. Nigeria: Equatorial Guinea intervening)*, Judgment, 10 October 2002, ICJ Rep 2002, 303, 405–407, paras 206–209.
22. Further to Article 3, see Matjaž Kačič, 'Commentary on Articles 2 and 3 of the Washington Treaty', 34 Emory International Law Review 2019, 53, 57–70 (hereafter Kačič, 'Commentary on Articles 2 and 3 of the Washington Treaty').
23. Further to Article 9, see Andrés B. Muñoz Mosquera, 'The North Atlantic Treaty: Article 9 and NATO's Institutionalization', 34 Emory International Law Review 2019, 149–164 (hereafter Mosquera, 'The North Atlantic Treaty: Article 9 and NATO's Institutionalization').
24. Article 47 UN Charter (and Articles 26, 45, and 46).
25. International relations writers have made similar observations. See, eg, John S Duffield, 'Explaining the Long Peace in Europe: The Contributions of Regional Security Regimes', 20(4) Review of International Studies 1994, 369, 381.
26. Further to Article 5, see Michael N Schmitt, 'NATO Collective Defense at 70: Confession and Response Revisited', 34 Emory International Law Review 2019, 85–120.

27. Geneva Convention for the amelioration of the condition of the wounded and sick in armed forces in the field, signed 12 August 1949, entered into force 21 October 1950: 75 UNTS 30, 62.
28. Further to Article 2, see Kačič, 'Commentary on Articles 2 and 3 of the Washington Treaty' (n 22) 53–56. See also John C Milloy, *The North Atlantic Treaty Organization, 1948–1957: Community or Alliance*? (McGill-Queen's UP 2006) 35–66.
29. Study on NATO Enlargement, 3 September 1995, para 1, available at https://www.nato.int/cps/en/natohq/official_texts_24733.htm (hereafter 'Study on NATO Enlargement'). For comment, see John Woodliffe, 'The Evolution of NATO for a New Europe', 47(1) ICLQ 1998, 174, 180–183 (hereafter Woodliffe, 'The Evolution of NATO for a New Europe').
30. Study on NATO Enlargement, para 1.
31. ibid, para 2.
32. ibid, para 4.
33. Minogue, 'The North Atlantic Treaty at 70—Article 10' (n 10) 174. For some observations regarding, eg, legal reforms in connection with Ukraine's earlier efforts towards possible future accession under the 2008 NATO–Ukraine Annual Target Plans and Action Plan, see Kate Klunk, 'Ukraine: Not Putting Itself on the Right Track for MAP?', 28 Penn State International Law Review 2010, 755, 773–774.
34. NATO Madrid Summit Declaration, 29 June 2022, para 22.
35. ibid, para 2.
36. Anne Deighton, 'The Last Piece of the Jigsaw: Britain and the Creation of the Western European Union, 1954', 7(2) Contemporary European History 1998, 181–196.
37. Giandomenico Majone, 'Unity in Diversity: European Integration and the Enlargement Process', 33(4) European Law Review 2008, 457, 479–480. See further Fiona Schnell, 'Member States Resistance to the EU Operations Centre', 20 European Foreign Affairs Review 2015, 63–82.
38. See Alyson J K Bailes and Graham Messervy-Whiting, *Death of an Institution: The End for Western European Union, a Future for European Defence?* (Egmont Institute 2011). For observations by several speakers about the relations between the WEU, the EC, and NATO at the end of the Cold War, see (1991) 85 ASIL Proc. 277–302. See also Woodliffe, 'The Evolution of NATO for a New Europe' (n 29) 187–192.
39. Jo Coelmon, *European Strategic Autonomy: Which Military Level of Ambition?* (Egmont Institute 2019) at 2.
40. For some of the range of opinion, see Max Bergmann, James Lamond, and Siena Cicarelli, 'The Case for EU Defense. A New Way Forward for Trans-Atlantic Security Relations' (1 June 2021), available at https://www.americanprogress.org/article/case-eu-defense/ and Raluca Csernatoni, 'EU Security and Defense Challenges: Toward a European Defense Winter?' (11 June 2020), Carnegie Europe, available at https://carnegieeurope.eu/2020/06/11/eu-security-and-defense-challenges-toward-european-defense-winter-pub-82032 For an assessment of *why* European States have pursued a security arrangement despite it having 'no functional need' see Stephanie C Hofmann, *European Security in NATO's Shadow: Party Ideologies and Institution Building* (Cambridge UP 2013) 122.
41. See Ratification of the Treaty of Lisbon, 2 BvE 2/08, Judgment of 30 June 2009 [2010] 3 CMLR 13, 377.
42. Regarding the relation between this provision and Article 5 of the North Atlantic Treaty, seeElie Perot, 'The Art of Commitments: NATO, the EU, and the Interplay between Law

and Politics within Europe's Collective Defence Architecture', 28(1) European Security 2019, 40–65.

43. For detailed consideration of the relation between NATO and the EU, see Heike Krieger, 'Common European Defence: Competition or Compatibility with NATO?', in Trybus and White, *European Security Law* (n 2) 174–197; Fabien Terpan, 'EU-NATO Relations: Consistency as a Strategic Consideration and a Legal Requirement', in Trybus and White, *European Security Law* (n 2) 270–294. See also Károly Végh, 'The North Atlantic Treaty and Its Relationship to Other "Engagements" of Its Parties—A Commentary on Article 8', 34 Emory International Law Review 2019, 135–148; and, for comparison between Lisbon Treaty defence obligations and NATO obligations, Alfred Grosser, 'The Federal Constitution Court's Lisbon Case: Germany's "Sonderweg"—An Outsider's Perspective', 10 German Law Journal 2009, 1263, 1264–1265.
44. Washington Summit Declaration, 10 July 2024, para 29.
45. See Thomas D Grant, 'Annexation of Crimea', 109(1) American Journal of International Law 2015, 68–95 (hereafter Grant, 'Annexation of Crimea').
46. See Brad Roth, 'The Virtues of Bright Lines: Self-Determination, Secession, and External Intervention', 16 German Law Journal 2015, 384, 387. cfRobert Heinsch, 'Conflict Classification in Ukraine: The Return of the "Proxy War"?', 91 International Law Studies 2015, 323, 354–360.
47. Earlier suggestions that Russia presented a threat did not significantly affect policy. See, eg, the exchange on 22 October 2012 between US President Barack Obama and Republican presidential nominee Mitt Romney: https://www.cbsnews.com/news/transcript-of-final-2012-presidential-debate/ (NB the author of the present chapter served on the working group that advised the Republican presidential nominee's campaign on defence policy.)
48. https://www.nato.int/cps/en/natohq/opinions_197080.htm
49. ibid.
50. Madrid Summit Declaration, 29 June 2022, para 15. See also Statement by NATO Foreign Ministers, Bucharest, 29–30 November 2022, paras 1–2: https://www.nato.int/cps/en/natohq/official_texts_209531.htm
51. See Alicia Hinarejos, 'Responding to Russia's Invasion of Ukraine', 47(2) European Law Review 2022, 151–152.
52. Though even then, concerns arose that the European Allies did not invest enough in their armed forces. See the remark by US Chairman of the Joint Chiefs of Staff in the early 1970s, quoted in Sayle, *Enduring Alliance* (n 7) 172.
53. Press conference (16 June 2022): https://www.nato.int/cps/en/natohq/opinions_196623.htm
54. See, eg, Taras Kuzio, 'Nato training: How Ukraine is actually winning against Russia', EU Observer (5 July 2022), available at https://euobserver.com/opinion/154763
55. Rein Müllerson, 'NATO Enlargement and the NATO-Russian Founding Act: The Interplay of Law and Politics', 47(1) International and Comparative Law Quarterly 1998, 192, 194 (hereafter Müllerson, 'NATO Enlargement and the NATO-Russian Founding Act').
56. See https://www.thedailybeast.com/vladimir-putins-ukraine-lies-have-russian-state-tv-flailing-and-fighting-on-air?ref=author
57. That is to say, when Russian leaders were not *embracing* NATO. See the friendly statements from 1997 to 2010 at Robert Person and Michael McFaul, 'What Putin Fears Most', 33(2) Journal of Democracy 2022, 20–21.

58. https://www.rferl.org/a/1090795.html
59. F Stephen Larrabee, 'The Baltic States and NATO Membership,' Testimony to the U.S. Senate Committee on Foreign Relations (3 April 2003), available at https://www.rand.org/content/dam/rand/pubs/testimonies/2005/CT204.pdf
60. See, eg, materials referenced in Müllerson, 'NATO Enlargement and the NATO-Russian Founding Act' (n 55) 193–195.
61. See especially Articles 34 and 35 UN Charter. The Russian Federation knows how to bring matters to the attention of the Security Council. See, eg, in connection with Kosovo: *Repertoire of the Practice of the Security Council, 1996–1999*, 1075, citing S/1999/320 (24 March 1999). Russia did nothing of that kind at the time NATO invited Bulgaria, Estonia, Latvia, Lithuania, Romania, Slovakia, and Slovenia to commence the move towards NATO membership via the Membership Action Plan in 2002 or when they eventually acceded to the Alliance in March 2004. While there is no obligation on a State to notify the Security Council at every juncture when the State believes trouble might arise, it is striking that, in connection with NATO enlargement, Russia confined itself to expressions of vague displeasure and diplomatic pique.
62. Grant, *Aggression Against Ukraine: Territory, Responsibility, and International Law* (2015) 32, 48–49.
63. See Liviu Horovitz, 'A "Great Prize," But Not the Main Prize. British Internal Deliberations on Not-Losing Russia, 1993–1995', in Oxana Schmies (ed), *NATO's Enlargement and Russia: A Strategic Challenge in the Past and Future* (Ibidem 2021) 86; and works cited in n 2.
64. cf NATO Madrid Summit Declaration, 29 June 2022, para 4 ('support[ing] Ukraine's inherent right . . . to choose its own security arrangements').
65. *Military and Paramilitary Activities in and against Nicaragua (Nicaragua v. United States of America)*, Judgment, 27 June 1986, 1986 ICJ Rep 14, 133, para 265.
66. Article 11(1) Interim Accord, concluded 13 September 1995, entered into force 13 October 1995: 1891 UNTS 3, 7.
67. *Application of the Interim Accord of 13 September 1995 (the former Yugoslav Republic of Macedonia v. Greece)*, Judgment, 5 December 2011, ICJ Rep 2011 644, 670, paras 81–83.
68. See Press Conference, NATO Secretary General, Lord Robertson, 16 February 2003, available at https://www.nato.int/cps/en/natohq/opinions_20380.htm Further to NATO's consensus decision making, see Aaron D Lindstrom, 'Consensus Decisionmaking in NATO: French Unilateralism and the Decision to Defend Turkey', 4 Chicago Journal of International Law 2003, 579–585
69. ICJ Rep 2011 644, 655, para 22 (5 December 2011).
70. See Application Instituting Proceedings, 17 November 2008.
71. ICJ Rep 2011 679–680, para 113.
72. ibid, 692–693, para 168.
73. Counter-Memorial of Greece, 10 January 2010, para 1.3.
74. ICJ Rep 2011 660, para 42. For comment, see Filippo Fontanelli and Eirik Bjorge, 'Current Developments', 61(3) International and Comparative Law Quarterly 2012, 775–784; Francesco Messineo, 'Maps of Ephemeral Empires: The ICJ and the Macedonian Name Dispute', 1(1) Cambridge Journal of International and Comparative Law 2012, 169–190.
75. The State was titled 'Federal Republic of Yugoslavia' (FRY) from 1992 to 2006, then reconstituted as the 'State Union of Serbia and Montenegro', which form it maintained until the independence of Montenegro in 2006.

76. See Application Instituting Proceedings (29 April 1999), eg against Germany, available at https://icj-cij.org/public/files/case-related/108/7161.pdf
77. See Michael J Matheson, 'Justification for the NATO Air Campaign in Kosovo', 94 American Journal of International Law 2000, 301; Dino Kritsiotis, 'The Kosovo Crisis and NATO's Application of Armed Force Against the Federal Republic of Yugoslavia', 49(2) International and Comparative Law Quarterly 2000, 330–359; Ian Johnstone, 'Security Council Deliberations: The Power of the Better Argument', 14 European Journal of International Law 2003, 437, 465–475. See also the Memorandum of Christopher Greenwood to the Parliamentary Foreign Affairs Committee, reprinted at 49(4) International and Comparative Law Quarterly 2000, 926–934.
78. See, eg, *Legality of Use of Force (Serbia and Montenegro v. Germany)*, ICJ Rep 2004 720, 754, para 89 (15 December 2004). The Court found that Serbia and Montenegro's invocation of the compromissory clauses of the Genocide Convention and other treaties was also unavailing.
79. ICJ Rep 2004 764, para 114.
80. ibid, quoting *Fisheries Jurisdiction (Spain v. Canada)*, Jurisdiction, ICJ Rep 1998 456, paras 55–56; *Aerial Incident of 10 August 1999 (Pakistan v. India)*, Jurisdiction, ICJ Rep 2000 33, para 51.
81. *Legality of Use of Force (Yugoslavia v. United States of America)*, Order of 2 June 1999, ICJ Rep 1999 916, 925, para 33.
82. Among writers who doubted the 'compatibility with international law' of the Kosovo intervention, see Aaron Schwabach, 'The Legality of the NATO Bombing Operation in the Federal Republic of Yugoslavia', 11(2) Pace International Law Review 1999, 405–418; David Wippman, 'Kosovo and the Limits of International Law', 25(1) Fordham International Law Journal 2001, 129–150. cf Bruno Simma, 'NATO, the UN and the Use of Force: Legal Aspects', 10 European Journal of International Law 1999, 1, 12; Michael Wood, 'International Law and the Use of Force: What Happens in Practice?', 53 Indian Journal of International Law 2013, 345, 350.
83. *Banković v Belgium, et al*, Appl no 52207/99, Decision as to Admissibility (12 December 2001) para 80.
84. See Marko Milanovic, 'Al-Skeini and Al-Jedda in Strasbourg', 23(1) European Journal of International Law 2012, 121 and works cited therein at 123 fn 12. See also for criticism of the UK House of Lords' later reliance on *Banković* in *Al-Skeini*, Ralph Wilde, 'R (on the Application of Al-Skeini) v. Secretary of State for Defence (Redress Trust Intervening),' 102 American Journal of International Law 2008, 628, 630–634.
85. SCR 1244 (1999), 10 June 1999.
86. *Behrami and Behrami v France; Saramati v France, Germany and Norway*, 71412/01; 78166/01, Decision, Grand Chamber, 2 May 2007, 91–95. Respondents in *Bankovic* had made similar arguments: see *Bankovic* at paras 31–32.
87. *Behrami and Saramati* at para 94.
88. ibid, para. 127.
89. ibid, para 141.
90. ibid, para 151.
91. ibid, para 148.
92. ibid, para 149.
93. ibid. cf *Questions of Interpretation and Application of the 1971 Montreal Convention arising from the Aerial Incident at Lockerbie (Libya v. United Kingdom)*, Provisional Measures, Order of 14 April 1992, ICJ Rep 1992 3, 15, paras 39–42.

94. See, eg, Marko Milanović and Tatjana Papić, 'As Bad as it Gets: The European Court of Human Right's *Behrami and Saramati* Decision and General International Law', 58 International and Comparative Law Quarterly 2009, 267–296; Bernard Knoll, 'Rights Without Remedies: The European Court's Failure to Close the Human Rights Gap in Kosovo', 68 Zeitschrift für ausländisches öffentliches Recht und Völkerrecht 2008, 421–451; Kjetil Mujezinović Larsen, 'Attribution of Conduct in Peace Operations: The "Ultimate Authority and Control" Test', 19 European Journal of International Law 2008, 509–531.
95. *Behrami and Saramati*, Judgment, para 151. Further to attribution and NATO, see David Nauta, *The International Responsibility of NATO and Its Personnel During Military Operations* (Brill/Nijhoff 2018) 152–167. And, in a sort of coda to the human rights scrutiny that followed the Kosovo intervention, see, following the Libya intervention, Human Rights Council, *Report of the International Commission of Inquiry on Libya*, UN Doc A/HRC/19/68, annex II (8 March 2012).
96. *FDP Parliamentary Group v Federal Government of Germany*, Judgment of the Second Senate of 7 May 2008, 2 BvE 1/03, para 57, citing BVerfGE 90, 286 (381–382).
97. ibid.
98. ibid, para 62, citing BVerfGE 90, 286 (350–351); 104, 151 (209); 118, 244 (261–262).
99. cf 2 BvE 2/08, Judgment of 30 June 2009 [2010] 3 CMLR 13, 334. See generally Volker Roeben, *Außenverfassungsrecht: Eine Untersuchung zur auswärtigen Gewalt des offenen Staates* (Mohr Siebeck 2007).
100. Statement by NATO Foreign Ministers, Bucharest, 29–30 November 2022, para 1.
101. North Atlantic Council, Brussels Communiqué, 14 June 2021, https:/www.nato.int/cps/en/natohq/news_185000.htm, as to which see Thomas D Grant, 'The ILC's Draft Conclusions on Customary International Law and the Treaty on the Prohibition of Nuclear Weapons (TPNW): Lawmaking and Its Limits in a Nuclear Age', 13(1) George Mason International Law Journal 2022, 45–49.
102. See ILC Draft conclusions on identification of customary international law with commentaries (2018), Draft Conclusion 6(1), and Comment (2): A/73/10, 133.
103. The ILC's term. See Draft Conclusion 6(2) and Comment (5): A/73/10, 133, 134.
104. For the example of the Kosovo campaign, see Michael P Scharf, *Customary International Law in Times of Fundamental Change. Recognizing Grotian Moments* (Cambridge University Press: 2013) 157–182.
105. 1995 NATO Enlargement Study, para 6.
106. ibid. See also ibid, para 72.
107. Andrew Cottey, 'Central Europe After NATO Enlargement' (June 1998) 20: available at https://www.nato.int/acad/fellow/96-98/cottey.pdf
108. Dated 28 June 2022: https://www.nato.int/nato_static_fl2014/assets/pdf/2022/6/pdf/220628-trilat-memo.pdf. See also Madrid Summit Declaration, 29 June 2022, para 18.
109. The NATO foreign ministers, following a terror bombing in Istanbul on 13 November 2022, condemned terrorism and expressed solidarity with Turkey: Statement by NATO Foreign Ministers, Bucharest, 29–30 November 2022, para 5.
110. https://www.nato.int/cps/en/natohq/official_texts_17248.htm
111. See Article 62 NATO Civilian Personnel Regulations.
112. Mosquera, 'The North Atlantic Treaty: Article 9 and NATO's Institutionalization' (n 23) 163.

113. For 2021, the NATO AT reports having rendered twenty-two judgments: AT(TRI)(2021)0002, 4, available at https://www.nato.int/nato_static_fl2014/assets/pdf/2022/5/pdf/220516-2021_EN_Annual_Report.pdf; for 2018 (the most recent year for a case count is available), the UN DT disposed of 285 cases: UN Office of Administration of Justice, 2018 Activity Report, 6, available at https://www.un.org/en/internaljustice/oaj/reports/OAJ_Activity_Report_2018_E.pdf
114. See generally Abdelaziz Megzari, *The Internal Justice of the United Nations. A Critical History 1945–2015* (Brill/Nijhoff 2015) 420–449.
115. *National Security Strategy of the United States of America* (December 2017) 45–47; *Interim National Security Strategic Guidance* (March 2021), *passim.*
116. See esp Elbridge Colby, *The Strategy of Denial. American Defense in an Age of Great Power Conflict* (Yale UP 2021).
117. NATO Heads of State and Government, North Atlantic Council Meeting, Madrid Summit Declaration, 29 June 2022, para 6.
118. ibid At fourth prefatory paragraph; twice at para 13; once each at paras 42 and 44.
119. ibid At para 13. At the NATO foreign ministers' meeting in Bucharest, 29–30 November 2022, the Secretary General expressed NATO's concern over 'our dependencies on ... authoritarian regimes, not least China, for our supply chains, technology, or infrastructure'. See https://www.nato.int/cps/en/natohq/news_209493.htm?selectedLocale=en
120. As to the European origins of international law, see Fassbender and Peters, 'Introduction' in Fassbender and Peters, *The Oxford Handbook of the History of International Law* (n 21) 4–7; Matthew Craven, 'Colonialism and Domination', in Fassbender and Peters, *The Oxford Handbook of the History of International Law* (n 21) 862–886.
121. See Miloš Vec, 'From the Congress of Vienna to the Paris Peace Treaties of 1919', in Fassbender and Peters, *The Oxford Handbook of the History of International Law* (n 21) 654–677; Peter Krüger, 'From the Paris Peace Treaties to the End of the Second World War', in Fassbender and Peters, *The Oxford Handbook of the History of International Law* (n 21) 679–697.
122. Or at least 'ambivalence' about international law and institutions: Simon Chesterman, 'Asia's Ambivalence about International Law and Institutions: Past, Present and Futures,' 27(4) European Journal of International Law 2016, 945–978.
123. See generally Tanvi Madan, 'The Rise, Fall, and Rebirth of the "Quad"', *War on the Rocks* (16 November 2017), available at https://warontherocks.com/2017/11/rise-fall-rebirth-quad/; Patrick Gerard Buchan and Benjamin Rimland, 'Defining the Diamond. The Past, Present, and Future of the Quadrilateral Security Dialogue', *CSIS Briefs* (March 2020), available at https://csis-website-prod.s3.amazonaws.com/s3fs-public/publication/200312_BuchanRimland_QuadReport_v2%5B6%5D.pdf?fuRA6mwjWYKqROtSmJD4u5ct.vijdkZv; Susannah Patton, 'The Uses and the Limits of the Quad', Lowy Institute Commentary (27 May 2022, available at https://www.lowyinstitute.org/publications/uses-and-limits-quad
124. Rory Medcalf, 'The Quad has seen off the sceptics and it's here to stay', National Security College, Crawford School of Public Policy (16 March 2021), available at https://nsc.crawford.anu.edu.au/department-news/18586/quad-has-seen-sceptics-and-its-here-stay
125. Addressing patterns of governmental administration and policy at national (but not intergovernmental) level, see Ryan Goodman and Derek Jinks, *Socializing States: Promoting Human Rights through International Law* (OUP 2013).

CHAPTER 25

THE EURASIAN ECONOMIC UNION

SERGEY SAYAPIN

1. Introduction

Founded on 1 January 2015, the Eurasian Economic Union (EAEU) is a regional trade organization currently uniting five post-Soviet nations—Armenia, Belarus, Kazakhstan, Kyrgyzstan, and the Russian Federation. Three more States—Cuba, Moldova, and Uzbekistan—currently have the Observer State status at the EAEU. As promising as this regional integration project was at its early stages,[1] it was later complicated by Russia's attempts to 're-establish the Russian sphere of influence lost by the dissolution of the Soviet Union',[2] and by external factors such as international sanctions introduced in response to Russia's continued aggression against Ukraine.[3]

This chapter provides an overview of the EAEU structure, law, and practice, and considers the EAEU law and practice in the context of their relationship with other relevant institutions such as the European Union (EU),[4] whose unique integration experience reportedly inspired the EAEU founders,[5] and the World Trade Organisation (WTO).[6] This section (Section 1) offers a brief historical introduction to the EAEU, its membership, and some key statistical data. Sections 2–5 generally follow the structure of the Treaty on the Eurasian Economic Union (EAEU Treaty) of 29 March 2014.[7] Section 2 describes the structure of the EAEU, and the functions of its main organs. Section 3 outlines the hierarchy of the sources of the EAEU law, and Section 4 deals with the legal foundations of the EAEU Customs Union. Section 5 discusses the key parameters of the EAEU Common Economic Space, the basics of their legal regulation, and controversies in their practical application. Section 6 discusses conceivable prospects for the EAEU, and is followed by a Conclusion with policy recommendations (Section 7).

1.1 Background

After the dissolution of the Soviet Union in December 1991, economic cooperation between the newly independent post-Soviet States took place within the framework of the Commonwealth of Independent States (CIS).[8] The CIS States undertook, 'by mutual efforts, to ensure the economic and social progress of their peoples',[9] to carry out 'cooperation in the political, economic, ecological, humanitarian, cultural, and other areas',[10] and to cooperate 'in the formation and development of a common economic space, the pan-European and Eurasian markets, [and] customs policy'.[11] Article 19 of the CIS Statute provided more specifically:

> Member States shall cooperate in the economic and social fields in the following areas:
>
> formation of a common economic space based on market relations and free movement of goods, services, capital and labour;
>
> coordination of social policy, development of joint social programs and measures to reduce social tension in connection with the implementation of economic reforms;
>
> development of transport and communication systems, as well as energy systems;
>
> coordination of credit and financial policy;
>
> assistance in the development of trade and economic relations of the Member States;
>
> encouragement and mutual protection of investments;
>
> promotion of standardization and certification of industrial products and goods;
>
> legal protection of intellectual property;
>
> promoting the development of a common information space;
>
> implementation of joint environmental protection measures, provision of mutual assistance in eliminating the consequences of environmental disasters and other emergencies;
>
> implementation of joint projects and programmes in the field of science and technology, education, healthcare, culture and sports.

As a next step, on 24 September 1993, the CIS member States concluded a Treaty on the Economic Union.[12] In accordance with Article 30 of the Treaty, Ukraine declared it would cooperate with the Economic Union as an associate member.[13] Further, on 29 March 1994, in a speech delivered at the Moscow State University, the first President of Kazakhstan, Nursultan Nazarbayev, proposed the concept of a more inclusive Eurasian integration:

> God Himself ordered us, the states of the former USSR, to trust each other. We see that there are forces that want to separate us to the end, weaken everyone, sow distrust and enmity. But it will only make things worse for the people. Look: the countries of Western Europe with centuries-old statehood are moving towards unification. They are well aware that the world market is severely polarised: North America, Japan, and finally, the Asian 'young tigers'. We, the republics of the former

> Soviet Union, have been prepared by history and fate for a single community. I have long proposed to remove all customs barriers, to open borders.[14]

On 20 January 1995, Belarus and Russia, on one side, and Kazakhstan, on the other side, concluded an Agreement on the Customs Union.[15] Next, on 10 October 2000, Belarus, Kazakhstan, Kyrgyzstan, Russia, and Tajikistan founded the Eurasian Economic Community.[16] The Customs Union became operational on 1 January 2010, with the entry into force of the Common Customs Tariff (for more details on the Tariff, see Section 4).[17] In 2014–2015, these legal regimes were consolidated within a single framework of the EAEU (see Section 4).

1.2 Members

The founding members of the EAEU are Belarus, Kazakhstan, and Russia who signed the EAEU Treaty on 29 May 2014. The Treaty entered into force for them on 1 January 2015.[18] The EAEU Treaty was subsequently signed by Armenia (on 10 October 2014) and Kyrgyzstan (on 23 December 2014). Armenia became an EAEU Member on 2 January 2015, and Kyrgyzstan on 12 August 2015. The total area of the EAEU is 20.26 million km^2, with the total population of about 181.45 million people.[19] In 2021, the total nominal GDP of the EAEU was US$1.74 trillion (3.2 per cent of world GDP),[20] with the nominal GDP per capita of about US$9,600.

1.3 Observer States

On 14 May 2018, the Supreme Eurasian Economic Council approved the Regulation 'On the Observer State Status at the Eurasian Economic Union'.[21] The Regulation builds on the provisions of Article 109 of the EAEU Treaty, and expounds, in seventeen paragraphs, the substantive and procedural rights of the observer States at the EAEU. Article 109(1) of the EAEU Treaty provides that the observer status may be requested by any state. In accordance with Article 109(2), '[t]he decision to grant or refuse the observer status within the Union is made by the Supreme Council'. The statutory functions of the authorized representatives of an observer State are limited to being present at meetings of the Organs of the Union by invitation, and obtaining non-confidential documents adopted by the Union (Article 109(3)). The observer States do not participate in the decision-making processes within the EAEU (Article 109(4)). With due regard to paragraph 17 of the Regulation, the Supreme Council may annul the observer status, if an observer State infringes on the interests of the Union and its member States, or if an observer State expresses its intention to terminate the status.

As of November 2022, the EAEU granted the observer State status to Moldova (on 14 May 2018), Cuba, and Uzbekistan (on 11 December 2020). The latter development was in contrast to a statement made on 2 October 2019 by Valentina Matviyenko, Chair of the Federation Council of the Federal Assembly of the Russian Federation, to the effect that 'the President of Uzbekistan [had] made a decision', and 'now [the] issue on the accession of Uzbekistan to the Eurasian Economic Union [was] being worked out'.[22] The authorities of Uzbekistan 'clarified later that Uzbekistan [was] merely exploring the option of joining the EAEU'.[23]

1.4 Free trade agreements with the EAEU

To facilitate free trade with external partners, the EAEU has concluded four free trade agreements (FTA) since 2015. The first FTA was concluded with Vietnam on 29 May 2015. Iran concluded an FTA with the EAEU on 17 May 2018. The FTA with Singapore was concluded on 1 October 2019, and with Serbia on 25 October 2019.[24] On 18 May 2018, an agreement on trade and economic cooperation with China was concluded.[25] It is not equivalent to a free trade agreement but aims 'to further reduce the non-tariff trade barrier[s], improve the trade facilitation and create sound environment for industrial development so as to promote trade and economic relations between China and the union and its member countries, bring real benefits to business and people of both sides and provide system guarantee for bilateral trade and economic cooperation'.[26] Negotiations on the conclusion of FTAs commenced with Egypt (in May 2015), Thailand (in April 2016), Mongolia (in June 2017), India (in June 2017), and Israel (in September 2019).[27] Several nations—including Argentina, Indonesia, Cambodia, Chile, Laos, Pakistan, Peru, South Korea, Syria, and Tunisia—expressed an interest in cooperating with the EAEU.[28] Given the regime of comprehensive international sanctions introduced against Russia for its aggression against Ukraine, progress in this dialogue remains to be seen.

2. Structure of the EAEU

In accordance with Article 8 of the EAEU Treaty, the EAEU consists of four main organs—the Supreme Eurasian Economic Council, the Eurasian Intergovernmental Council, the Eurasian Economic Commission, and the Court of the Eurasian Economic Union—which exercise the powers accorded to them by the EAEU Treaty and other treaties concluded within the Union. Simultaneous chairmanship of the Supreme Council, the Intergovernmental Council, and the Commission rotates in the Russian alphabetic order, and is for one calendar year, with no right of extension (Article 8(4) of the EAEU Treaty).

2.1 Supreme Eurasian Economic Council

The Supreme Eurasian Economic Council (also referred to as the Supreme Council) is the supreme organ of the EAEU. It appears to have been largely modelled after the European Council, with the notable difference that the EAEU Supreme Council consists only of the Heads of all EAEU member States (Article 10 of the EAEU Treaty), whereas the European Council includes 'the heads of state or government of the 27 EU member states, the European Council President and the President of the European Commission'.[29] The EAEU Supreme Council meets in regular sessions at least once a year, and extraordinary sessions may be convened, in order to solve urgent issues (Article 11(1) of the EAEU Treaty). The agenda for the meetings of the Supreme Council is arranged by the Commission based on proposals made by the member States (Article 11(3), third paragraph). The Supreme Council considers the main issues of the Union's activities, defines the strategy, directions, and prospects of the integration development, and makes decisions aimed at implementing the objectives of the Union (Article 12(1)). Article 12(2) lists twenty-two main functions of the Supreme Council pertaining to the staffing, budget, procedures, and the overall direction of the Union, and provides that the Council exercises 'other powers provided for by this Treaty and treaties concluded within the Union'. The Supreme Council's decisions and dispositions are made by consensus, except those pertaining to the termination of membership whereby the member State declaring its intent to terminate its membership in the Union should refrain from voting (Article 13(2)).

2.2 Eurasian Intergovernmental Council

The Eurasian Intergovernmental Council (or the Intergovernmental Council) consists of the Heads of Governments of all member States (Article 14 of the EAEU Treaty). Its functions and membership are not equivalent to those of the Council of the European Union, for the latter 'meets in 10 different configurations, each corresponding to the policy area being discussed. Depending on the configuration, each country sends their minister responsible for that policy area'.[30] The EAEU Intergovernmental Council convenes as necessary but at least twice a year (Article 15(1)). The agenda for the meetings of the Intergovernmental Council is arranged by the Commission based on proposals made by the member States (Article 15(3), third paragraph). Article 16 lays down nine main functions of the Intergovernmental Council in the enforcement of the EAEU law, provision of support to the Supreme Council, and the issuance of instructions to the Commission, making it an intermediary organ between the Supreme Council and the Commission. The decisions and dispositions of the Intergovernmental Council are adopted by consensus (Article 17(2) of the EAEU Treaty).

2.3 Eurasian Economic Commission

The Eurasian Economic Commission (also known as the Commission) is a permanent governing organ of the EAEU. It consists of a Council and a Board (Article 18(1) of the EAEU Treaty). The Council makes its decisions, dispositions, and recommendations by consensus, whereas decisions, dispositions, and recommendations of the Board are made by a qualified majority (two-thirds of all members of the Board), or by consensus (Article 18(2)). The status, tasks, composition, functions, powers, and procedures of the Commission are laid down in Annex 1 to the EAEU Treaty. The seat of the Commission is in Moscow (Russian Federation).

Although the Eurasian Economic Commission was allegedly modelled after the European Commission, Chatham House notes with respect to the former that its 'power is limited. Member states disagreeing with its judgements can appeal to other bodies, and the Commission has no power to bring a member state before the Court [of the Eurasian Economic Union] in a case of non-compliance. Disputes are often resolved bilaterally rather than via [EAEU] institutions'.[31] The European Commission is more powerful than its EAEU counterpart in that '[i]t is alone responsible for drawing up proposals for new European legislation',[32] 'together with the Court of Justice, ensures that EU law is properly applied in all the member countries',[33] and 'represents the EU internationally'.[34]

2.4 Court of the Eurasian Economic Union

In accordance with Article 19(1) of the EAEU Treaty, the Court of the Eurasian Economic Union (or the Court of the Union) is a permanent judicial organ of the EAEU. The status, composition, jurisdiction, functioning, and formation procedures of the Court are regulated by its Statute annexed to the EAEU Treaty (Article 19(2)). The Court includes two judges from each member State (para 7 of the Statute). The judges are appointed by the Supreme Council for nine years (paras 8, 10 of the Statute). In accordance with paragraph 9 of the Statute, '[a]ll judges shall be of high moral character, highly qualified in the field of international and domestic law, and shall usually meet the requirements applicable to judges of the highest judicial authorities of the Member States'. The seat of the Court is at Minsk (Belarus).

The jurisdiction of the Court may be triggered at the request of a member State (para 39(1) of the Statute), or at the request of an economic entity (para 39(2)). For the purpose of the Statute, economic entities include legal entities registered under the law of the member States or third States, or natural persons registered as individual entrepreneurs registered under the law of the member States or third States (cf the concluding provision in para 39 of the Statute). The jurisdiction of the Court is not automatic, and may only be triggered 'following a prior appeal of an applicant to a Member State or the Commission to address the issue in the pretrial order through consultation, negotiation or other means provided for by the [EAEU] Treaty and treaties concluded within the Union, except as expressly provided for by the [EAEU] Treaty' (para 43). Notably, in addition to the sources of the EAEU law listed in Article 6 of the EAEU Treaty (see Section 3), the Court may also apply 'the generally recognised principles and norms of international law' (para 50(1) of the Statute), and 'international custom as evidence of the general practice accepted as law' (para 50(4)). In contrast to Article 38 of the Statute of the International Court of Justice (ICJ), paragraph 50 of the Statute of the EAEU Court makes no mention of the general principles of law,[35] or judicial decisions and the teachings of the most highly qualified publicists of the various nations, as subsidiary means for the determination of rules of law.[36]

3. EAEU Law

The scope of the EAEU law is determined by Article 6 of the EAEU Treaty. In accordance with Article 6(1), the EAEU law includes:

- the EAEU Treaty;
- other treaties concluded within the Union;
- treaties of the Union with a third party;
- decisions and dispositions of the Supreme Eurasian Economic Council, the Eurasian Intergovernmental Council, and the Eurasian Economic Commission adopted within the powers provided for by the EAEU Treaty and treaties concluded within the Union.

The EAEU Treaty was concluded in Astana (Kazakhstan) on 29 May 2014. It is a comprehensive document consisting of 118 Articles grouped in four Parts and twenty-eight sections, with thirty-three Annexes. The EAEU Treaty was concluded in Belarusian, Kazakh, and Russian languages but the text in the Russian language prevails in case of divergence of interpretations of the Treaty. Part One (Articles 1–22) contains general and structural provisions pertaining to the establishment of the EAEU. Part Two (Articles 23–61) lays down the legal regime of the EAEU Customs Union, and largely builds on the law of the WTO. Part Three (Articles 62–98) is devoted to the EAEU Common Economic Space, and includes specific regulations on macroeconomic policy; monetary policy; trade in services, incorporations, activities and investments; financial markets; taxes and taxation; competition; natural monopolies; energy industry; transport; public procurement; intellectual property; manufacturing industry; agriculture; labour migration; and other matters.[37] Part Four (Articles 99–118) contains transitional and final provisions.

In accordance with Article 6(3) of the EAEU Treaty, the Treaty has superior legal force in the Union. The Treaty prevails in case of its conflict with other treaties concluded within the Union. Decisions and dispositions of the Union may not be inconsistent with the Treaty (Article 6(3)). Article 6(2) emphasizes that the EAEU Treaties with a third party may not contradict the main objectives,[38] principles, and rules of the Union.[39]

Decisions of the Supreme Eurasian Economic Council and Eurasian Intergovernmental Council are enforceable by the member States in accordance with the procedures provided for by their national legislation.[40] The legal force of the EAEU organs is determined by their respective rank in the EAEU structure: Article 6(4) of the EAEU Treaty provides that decisions of the Supreme Eurasian Economic Council prevail over decisions of the Eurasian Intergovernmental Council and the Eurasian Economic Commission, and decisions of the Eurasian Intergovernmental Council prevail over decisions of the Eurasian Economic Commission.

4. Customs Union

Technically, the EAEU is a customs union.[41] It is a successor to the Eurasian Customs Union, which included Belarus, Kazakhstan, and Russia, and operated between 1 January 2010 and 31 December 2014, until the EAEU Treaty entered into force on 1 January 2015, and the Customs Union was integrated in the EAEU, in accordance with Part Two of the EAEU Treaty.

Article 25(1) of the EAEU Treaty stipulates the following functional principles of the EAEU Customs Union:

1) an internal market for goods shall be in place;
2) the Common Customs Tariff of the Eurasian Economic Union and other common measures regulating foreign trade with third parties shall be applied;
3) a common trade regime shall be applied to relations with third parties;
4) Common customs regulations shall be applied;
5) free movement of goods between the territories of the Member States shall be ensured without the use of customs declarations and state control (transport, sanitary, veterinary-sanitary, phytosanitary quarantine), except as provided for by this Treaty.

Article 25(1) and related provisions are instrumental in that they bring together various legal regimes, which were in force before the establishment of the EAEU. Article 28(2) specifies further that the internal market includes an economic space with free movement of goods, persons, services, and capital ensured under the provisions of the EAEU Treaty. Formally, these 'Four Freedoms' mirror the EU philosophy of trade liberalization, in that the member States should not apply import and export customs duties (other duties, taxes, and fees having equivalent effect), non-tariff regulatory measures, safeguard, anti-dumping and countervailing measures in mutual trade, except as provided for by the EAEU Treaty (Article 28(3)). However, the member States may introduce lawful restrictions on the freedom of trade in accordance with Article

29(1), provided that such measures are not a means of unjustifiable discrimination or a disguised restriction on trade, if required for:

1) protection of human life and health;
2) protection of public morals and public order;
3) environmental protection;
4) protection of animals, plants, or cultural values;
5) fulfilment of international obligations;
6) national defence and security of a Member State.[42]

In turn, Article 42(1) of the EAEU Treaty stipulates that the EAEU Single Commodity Nomenclature of Foreign Economic Activity and the EAEU Common Customs Tariff,[43] as approved by the Commission, apply on the customs territory of the Union and represent the trade policy instruments of the Union. In accordance with Article 42(2), the main objectives of the application of the EAEU Common Customs Tariff are as follows:

1) enabling efficient integration of the Union into the global economy;
2) streamlining the commodity structure for goods imported into the customs territory of the Union;
3) maintaining a rational correlation between export and import of goods on the customs territory of the Union;
4) enabling progressive changes in the structure of production and consumption of goods within the Union;
5) support for various economy sectors of the Union.

Pursuant to Article 45(1) of the EAEU Treaty, the Common customs regulations are within the competence of a Commission on Customs Tariff Regulation.[44]

In accordance with Article 33(3) of the EAEU Treaty, the Union's foreign trade policy is regulated through the conclusion by the Union, independently or jointly with the member States, of treaties with third parties. Such cooperation with third parties is subject to the most favoured nation treatment principle.[45] Given that all EAEU member States, except Belarus, are also WTO members,[46] the EAEU law should be in harmony with the WTO treaties. Notably, Article 46 provides that trade with third countries may be affected by non-tariff regulatory measures such as quantitative restrictions, export and import licences, etc, and pursuant to Article 47, the EAEU may determine and introduce such measures unilaterally.

Section XI of the EAEU Treaty lays down regulations on sanitary, veterinary-sanitary, and phytosanitary quarantine measures. Article 56(1) provides generally that '[s]anitary, veterinary-sanitary and phytosanitary quarantine measures shall be applied based on scientifically justified principles and only to the extent required to protect life and health of humans, animals and plants'. This rule is in general conformity with the WTO Agreement on the Application of Sanitary and Phytosanitary Measures (SPS Agreement).[47] Articles 57–59 contain more detailed provisions on sanitary, veterinary-sanitary, and phytosanitary quarantine measures applicable, respectively, to persons, vehicles, products, and goods (including goods for personal use). The development of common requirements and procedures pertaining to the respective State controls is within the competence of the Commission.

5. Common Economic Space

Part Three of the EAEU Treaty lays down regulations for a few key parameters of the EAEU Common Economic Space. In fact, the overall success of the EAEU may be assessed by these very parameters.

5.1 Macroeconomic policy

In accordance with Annex 14 to the EAEU Treaty, the Commission carries out coordination of the implementation of an agreed macroeconomic policy, for the purpose of achieving the member States' 'balanced economic development' (cf Article 62(1) of the EAEU Treaty). Article 62(3) further stipulates the main directions of the agreed macroeconomic policy:

1) ensuring sustainable development of the economies of the Member States using the integration potential of the Union and competitive advantages of each Member State;
2) establishing common operation principles for the economies of the Member States and ensuring their effective interaction;
3) creating conditions to increase internal sustainability of the economies of the Member States, including their macroeconomic stability and resistance to external influences;
4) development of common principles and guidelines to predict social and economic development of the Member States.

These principles appear to be somewhat internally inconsistent. The first principle contradicts the second in that it may be difficult to exploit the member States' individual competitive advantages while establishing 'common' operation principles for their economies. In turn, 'resistance to external influences' in the third principle sounds quite isolationist, and the development of 'common principles and guidelines' for the purpose of 'predict[ing] social and economic development' in the fourth principle sounds reminiscent of planned economies. Finally, 'common principles and guidelines' may be detrimental to the member States' competitive advantages, which are individual to each EAEU member State, and are conditioned by such objective factors as geography, size, population, and resources. In addition, two of the three main macroeconomic indicators determining the sustainability of economic development under Article 63 of the EAEU Treaty are State-centric,[48] and raise questions about their inclusivity.

5.2 Monetary policy

It follows from Article 64(1) of the EAEU Treaty that the coordinated EAEU monetary policy has five main objectives: (1) to deepen economic integration between the member States; (2) to develop their cooperation in the monetary sphere; (3) to ensure free movement of goods, services, and capital on the territories of the member States; (4) to enhance the role of national currencies of the member States in foreign trade and investment operations; and (5) to ensure mutual convertibility of their currencies. In practical terms, though, the EAEU monetary policy has resulted in detrimental effects since 2015. Since the Russian ruble dominates the EAEU financial market, international sanctions introduced against the Russian Federation and its banking system since 2014—and especially in 2022[49]—also had powerful secondary effects against the other EAEU currencies. In August 2015, the Kazakh tenge (KZT) lost about 23 per cent of its value overnight,[50] and in 2022, the KZT fluctuations were significant.[51] The other EAEU currencies have experienced similar effects.[52] Since the beginning of Russia's full-scale invasion of Ukraine in February 2022, 'tens of thousands of Russian citizens' were reported to arrive in Kazakhstan, in order to transfer their personal funds to commercial banks in those countries, and to obtain internationally acceptable debit or credit cards issued by local banks.[53] As reported by The Astana Times, the amount of personal funds transferred from Russia to Kazakhstan between January and May 2022 reached '72.3 billion tenge (US$149.9 million), reflecting an increase of 3.1 times over the year'.[54]

5.3 Energy industry

Article 79(1) of the EAEU Treaty provides that '[i]n order to effectively utilise the potential of the fuel and energy complex of the Member States, as well as to provide national economies with the main types of energy resources (electricity, gas, oil and petroleum products), the Member States shall develop long-term mutually beneficial cooperation in the energy sphere, conduct coordinated energy policy and *gradually* create common energy markets ... with due account for ensuring energy security ... ' (emphasis added). It appears that the qualification 'gradually' is key in this context, since it is repeated in Articles 81(1) (on a common electric power market), 83(1) (on a common gas market), and 84(1) (on common markets of oil and petroleum products). Whereas it does make sense that relevant developments depend, to a decisive extent, on the 'existing technical capabilities',[55] and on the conclusion of treaties regulating the markets in question,[56] one may call into question whether some decisions pertaining to the EAEU energy market were made in good faith. For example, on 19 June 2022, just two days after the President of Kazakhstan Kassym-Jomart Tokayev had stated at the 2022 St-Petersburg

Economic Forum that Kazakhstan would not recognize the so-called Donetsk and Luhansk 'People's Republics',[57] Russia stopped the transit of oil from Kazakhstan via the Novorossiysk port, the official reason being 'mines from the Second World War, which were suddenly discovered in the port waters'.[58] After a brief resumption, the transit was blocked again on 5 July 2022, after the President of Kazakhstan, on 4 July 2022, in a discussion with the President of the European Council, Charles Michel, expressed his readiness to help Europe overcome the energy crisis.[59]

5.4 Transport

Article 86(1) of the EAEU Treaty stipulates that the coordinated transport policy of the EAEU aims at 'ensuring economic integration, consistent and gradual formation of a common transport space based on the principles of competition, transparency, security, reliability, availability and sustainability'. The types of transport covered by the EAEU Treaty and its Annex 24 are road, air, water, and rail transport (Article 87(1) of the EAEU Treaty). In the years preceding 2022, there were some notable developments relative to the construction and renovation of roads, the role of the Caspian Sea in the international transport networks,[60] and the ambitious Belt and Road project.[61] According to Nurlanova and Kaliyeva, modernization of the transport system was 'one of the main goals', because the transport infrastructure was seen as a 'catalyst for [the] social and economic development of Kazakhstan' in the long term.[62] However, in 2022, as a result of new sanctions introduced in response to Russia's invasion of Ukraine, a few threats to the integrity of the EAEU transport system became apparent.

For example, it was reported that China was seeking alternative rail routes to the West through the territories of Kyrgyzstan and Uzbekistan, so that the territory of the Russia could be bypassed.[63] Also, the sanctions affected more than 500 aircraft—mostly, Boeing and Airbus—used by Russian airlines in that the aircraft are no longer allowed to use the airspace of most countries in Europe and North America,[64] and they may not, at this time, land abroad except in a few 'friendly nations' where there is currently no threat of their impending arrest on the ground of termination of lease agreements.[65] The need for Western spare parts is also becoming acute.[66] As far as the maritime transport is concerned, in 2022, more than a dozen luxury yachts reportedly belonging to Russian oligarchs were seized or identified for seizure.[67]

5.5 Intellectual property

The legal basis for the protection of intellectual property (IP) in the EAEU is Article 89(1) of the EAEU Treaty, which provides that '[t]he Member States shall cooperate in the sphere of protection and enforcement of intellectual property rights and ensure in their territories the protection and safeguarding of these rights in accordance with international law, international treaties and acts constituting the law of the Union and the legislation of the Member States', and Annex 26 to the EAEU Treaty. Article 90(1) provides further that nationals of the EAEU member States are granted national treatment in the protection of intellectual property. Article 90(3) lists the key treaties on the international protection of IP rights, and stipulates specifically that 'Member States, which are not parties to these agreements, shall be obliged to accede thereto'. Domestic legislation on the protection of IP rights is also in place.[68] However, in 2022, Russia took wide-ranging measures in breach of its obligations under international IP law, in order to attempt circumventing restrictive measures affecting various sectors of Russian economy, and to deal with the unfavourable effects of such measures. While, for example, the rebranding of the McDonalds food chain[69] and the attempts to put in place what the Russian authorities call the 'import replacement' were not technically unlawful, the taking of measures to legalize a 'parallel import' of goods and technologies affected by sanctions most certainly was,[70] and the holders of respective IP rights might contemplate some remedial action.

5.6 Manufacturing industry

Unlike in most sectors of the EAEU economy discussed above where coordinated action is required, in accordance with Article 92(1) of the EAEU Treaty, national industrial development programmes and other measures of industrial policy are to be developed by the member States 'independently', and coordination through the Commission and, as the case may be, the Intergovernmental Council is encouraged (cf Annex 27 to the EAEU Treaty). This must be due to the EAEU member States' unequal industrial potential. Further, unlike the WTO law, which generally discourages subsidies, Article 93 of the EAEU Treaty contains 'common rules for granting subsidies for industrial goods', subject to Annex 28 to the EAEU Treaty. With the reinforcement of sanctions against Russia, reliance of businesses on State subsidies has noticeably increased.[71] In 2022, after many foreign businesses had withdrawn from Russia, it was reported that some of them were negotiating the possibility of relocation with the governments of Kazakhstan and Uzbekistan.[72] Such relocation may well benefit the economies of the latter countries, provided it would not be used to circumvent anti-Russian sanctions.

5.7 Labour migration

The freedom of internal and external labour migration is essential to national economies. It is therefore commendable that pursuant to the second sentence of Article 97(1) of the EAEU Treaty, workers who are nationals of the member States are not required to obtain work permits in the State where they seek employment. Accordingly, Article 97(3) stipulates that education certificates issued by educational institutions of the member States—except in the subject areas of education, law, medicine, and pharmacy—are to be recognized automatically. The higher education degree certificates in these four areas are subject to the regular recognition procedures established by law. It is also helpful that, in accordance with Article 97(6), nationals of the member States entering the territory of another member State for employment and their family members are exempt from the obligation to register with the migration authorities within thirty days from the date of entry. A comprehensive catalogue of the rights and obligations of workers is included in Article 98 of the EAEU Treaty.

In 2021, labour migration to Russia from the other EAEU member States reportedly tripled compared to 2020.[73] However, 2022 saw two large and spontaneous waves of migration of the labour force from Russia itself to Central Asia, the Caucasus, Turkey, the United Arab Emirates, and other countries, which remained open to Russian nationals.[74] Whereas the 'first wave' (February–August 2022) were predominantly 'economic migrants' seeking to save their personal funds (see Section 5.2), the 'second wave' (since September 2022) were men of military age fleeing the 'partial mobilisation' announced by Vladimir Putin on 21 September 2022, and their immediate family members. No fewer than 700,000 Russian citizens were reported to have left Russia since September 2022.[75] Since the new migrants are mostly men of economically active age, often with higher education and useful qualifications, their migration can reasonably be expected to have adverse effects on Russia's economy, even from a mid-term perspective, and to add value to the economies of their new host States. The overall effect of these factors should also be detrimental to Russia's war effort.

6. Prospects

Probably the biggest problem of the EAEU so far is that Russia has repeatedly tried to use the essentially economic union as a political tool for consolidating its influence in the post-Soviet space. At times, statements by some Russian politicians appeared to be in plain violation of Article 3 of the EAEU Treaty pertaining to 'universally recognised principles of international law, including the principles of sovereign equality of the Member States and their territorial integrity'.[76] Such attempts have led politicians in the EAEU States to recall the economic nature of the Union, and some civil society actors to call for withdrawal from the EAEU.[77] Given that the start of Russia's use of force against Ukraine in February 2014 was in response to Ukraine's renewed Euro-integration course, instead of rapprochement with the prospective EAEU, it is unlikely that any EAEU member States would attempt to leave the Union at this stage, at the risk of irritating the Russian leadership. Yet, Russia too ought to cease using the language of threats in communication with its EAEU allies, if the Union is to be sustainable.

From a mid-term perspective, the EAEU could experience a higher education crisis. On 24 May 2022, the Russian Minister of Science and Higher Education Valery Falkov announced that Russia would pull out of the Bologna System.[78] The significance of this decision is that workers from all EAEU member States, including the Russian Federation, who are holders of non-EAEU higher education degrees might not have their degrees recognized in Russia. This would be a significant blow to the quality of the labour market in Russia, and would cause further brain-drain from the country.

Given the scale of sanctions introduced against Russia since February 2022, and the departure of major businesses from the Russian market, the prospects of foreign direct investment (FDI) in the country are not promising. It is likely that some of the EAEU dialogue partners (see Section 1.4) will reconsider the level and quality of their cooperation with the EAEU, since doing business with Russia will not be fashionable in the foreseeable future. A statement made by the Belarusian leader Alexander Lukashenko on 11 November 2022 on the effect of possible nationalization of foreign businesses in Belarus will not make the EAEU more attractive either.[79]

Overall, the EAEU is not likely to live up to its full potential without a genuine democratization of its member States' political systems,[80] embracing freedom,[81] and respect for the rule of law,[82] including international law beyond the EAEU legal framework. 'No one pours new wine into old wineskins.'[83] Sustainable economic prosperity is impossible where economies are still State-centric, investors have little faith in their counterparts, courts are not independent, and where the leading economy in the Union is under a comprehensive regime of international sanctions for waging a war of aggression. The EAEU is in urgent need of internal reform if its progress is to be meaningful.

7. Conclusion

After eight years in existence, the EAEU seems to be at a crossroads. On the one hand, contemporary realities do beg for a closer economic integration in the post-Soviet space, if the experience of some of the most successful economic integration projects elsewhere—such as the EU, NAFTA, ASEAN, and others—is any guide. Objectively, the individual EAEU economies are not among the strongest, and a more intensive economic cooperation with neighbours, with due regard to the international distribution of resources, and division of labour, should help to improve the quality of life in the EAEU member States. On the other hand, one should bear in mind that regional economic organizations are still parts of the world economic system, and a regional project will only be successful if it is properly integrated with the other components of the overall network.

It appears that currently, in addition to the significant internal issues discussed above, the EAEU lacks the necessary external outlook. The EAEU approach to energy focuses predominantly on non-renewable sources, and the concept of 'green energy' does not at all feature in the EAEU Treaty. The Energy Charter Treaty (ECT) is of limited significance within the EAEU, since it is secondary to the EAEU law (see Section 3). Besides, on 20 August 2009, Russia informed the ECT depositary of its decision not to ratify the ECT.[84] Developments in 2022—triggered by Russia's full-scale invasion of Ukraine—have shown that the traditional consumers of the EAEU energy resources—such as the EU—are working with alternative suppliers, and the perception of the EU dependence on Russian oil and gas was significantly exaggerated. The EAEU should therefore urgently reconsider its energy strategy, and contemplate ways to increase the role of 'green energy'.

Notably, ecology does not feature prominently in the EAEU documentation. The concept is explicitly mentioned only once in the EAEU Treaty (in Article 86(1), in connection with the transport policy), and is referred to only on two occasions in Annex 20 to the EAEU Treaty.[85] 'Environment' is mentioned in the EAEU Treaty no more than four times.[86] Given the impact of the Aral Sea disaster on economies and livelihood especially in Central Asia,[87] and the ever-growing climate change concerns, much more attention should now be paid to the EAEU's environmental policies.

For years, energy resources were central to the EAEU economy, and diversification of the economy is an unresolved issue. As of 2022, the share of energy resources in the GDP of Russia[88] and Kazakhstan[89] is overwhelming. For the sake of ensuring the sustainability of the EAEU member States' national economies in the long run, reliance on energy resources should be reconsidered. This major reform will not be easy, given that technology transfers from developed nations will be required, but the expected result is worth the effort.

Corruption is another major issue in all EAEU member States.[90] Unless genuine and sufficient efforts are made to combat it, chances for real progress in the economy and other areas are very low. Among others, the digitalization of State services is a major factor in reducing corruption-related risks. The EAEU member States should invest, as a matter of urgency, in developing efficient and transparent digital platforms for the provision of State services with a minimum involvement of the human factor. The experience of Kazakhstan may be useful in this regard.[91]

Importantly, the rule of law and the quality of justice will be important factors for the future sustainability of the EAEU. The independence of domestic judges,[92] and the quality of their understanding of the EAEU law and international law, will be crucial for the protection of lawful interests of the domestic and international economic actors, and the role of arbitration in the protection of investments will be key. Measures should therefore be taken to provide regular in-service training on international law to judges in the EAEU member States,[93] and to continue building local expertise in international investment arbitration.[94]

Last but not least, a few more general comments are in order. Unlike in Europe, where integration was based on a common set of fundamental legal and political values—such as democracy, the proximity of continental legal systems based on Roman law, and the market economy—in the EAEU, respect for these same values is rather weak. Interference of the State in the economy is strong, democratic successes are not obvious, and the quality of the rule of law requires improvement. Since the foundation of the EAEU in 2015, each of its members was involved in armed conflicts with neighbours, or experienced situations of violence, which testify to internal instability within the EAEU. Probably as a result of its protracted conflict with Azerbaijan, Armenia announced, at the end of 2022, its intention to ratify the Rome Statute of the International Criminal Court (ICC).[95] This decision may, within the foreseeable future, lead to Armenia's alienation from Russia, which 'unsigned' the Rome Statute in November 2016,[96] and now is a determined opponent of the Court. Belarus experienced large-scale protests in 2020, and has been providing political, military, and logistical support to Russia's invasion of Ukraine since February 2022. In early January 2022, Kazakhstan was shattered by internal violence,[97] and in 2021 and 2022, unresolved border issues led to armed conflicts between Kyrgyzstan and Tajikistan. This picture appears to suggest that economic cooperation is not engendering peace in the EAEU region, and the potential for conflict is likely to persist.

Given the current confrontation between Russia and the Global West, it is now premature to contemplate a rapprochement—let alone, unification—between the EU and the EAEU.[98] With the reinforcement of authoritarian trends throughout the EAEU space, it appears to be drifting away—in geopolitical and geoeconomic terms—from Europe, and getting closer to Asia (see Sections 1.3–1.4). As desirable as a single economic—and political —space from Lisbon to Vladivostok might be, coordination (instead of unification) among multiple regional organizations, and their economic actors, is a more likely scenario for the next few years.[99] With Russia's departure from the Council of Europe in 2022, the role of the Organization for Security and Co-operation in Europe (OSCE) in promoting democracy, respect for human rights, and the rule of law in the EAEU space should grow (see Mihr, this volume).

Acknowledgements

This chapter was completed during the author's fellowship at the Asian Law Institute (ASLI), Faculty of Law, National University of Singapore (NUS) in October–November 2022. The author gratefully acknowledges support from NUS Law and ASLI.

Notes

1. See Andrew Gardner, 'Putin praises Eurasian Economic Union: Kazakhstan and Belarus agree to unite labour, capital and services markets with Russia' <https://www.politico.eu/article/putin-praises-eurasian-economic-union/> accessed 17 November 2022.
2. See Chatham House, 'What is the Eurasian Economic Union? Explaining the history, purpose, and political background to the Eurasian Economic Union' <https://www.chathamhouse.org/2022/07/what-eurasian-economic-union> accessed 17 November 2022.
3. See generally Sergey Sayapin and Evhen Tsybulenko (eds), *The Use of Force against Ukraine and International Law: Jus Ad Bellum, Jus In Bello, Jus Post Bellum* (T. M. C. Asser Press/Springer 2018).
4. On the EU law, see generally Elspeth Berry et al, *Complete EU Law: Text, Cases, and Materials* (5th edn, OUP 2022).
5. See Alexander M Libman, 'Learning from the European Union? Eurasian Regionalism and the "Global Script"', 12 Outlines of Global Transformations: Politics, Economics, Law 2019, 247–268, 247.

6. On the law of the WTO, see generally Peter Van den Bossche and Werner Zdouc, *The Law and Policy of the World Trade Organization* (5th edn, CUP 2021).
7. For the text of the EAEU Treaty (in English), see <https://www.un.org/en/ga/sixth/70/docs/treaty_on_eeu.pdf> accessed 19 November 2022.
8. For the text of the CIS Statute of 22 January 1993 (in Russian), see <https://cis.minsk.by/page/180/ustav-sodruzestva-nezavisimyh-gosudarstv-g-minsk-22-anvara-1993-goda> accessed 19 November 2022.
9. CIS Statute, fourth preambular paragraph.
10. ibid, Article 2, second paragraph.
11. ibid, Article 4, fourth paragraph.
12. For the text (in Russian), see <http://www.consultant.ru/document/cons_doc_LAW_5465/> accessed 12 November 2022.
13. For the text of the Declaration (in Russian), see <http://www.consultant.ru/document/cons_doc_LAW_5465/a1e8ecc193d65376f21aba6148ae81b0400ad6dd/> accessed 12 November 2022.
14. Quoted in: 'Pod Nazarbayeva v EAES uchredyat dolzhnost pochetnogo predsedatelya' [The EAEU will establish the position of Honorary Chairman for Nazarbayev] <https://fergana.agency/news/106717/> accessed 12 November 2022.
15. For the text (in English), see <http://evrazes.com/docs/view/118> accessed 12 November 2022.
16. For the text of the Treaty on the Establishment of the Eurasian Economic Community (in Russian), see <http://evrazes.com/docs/view/3> accessed 12 November 2022.
17. See 'Dossier: Tamozhennyy Soyuz i Edinoye ekonomicheskoye prostranstvo Rossii, Byelorussii i Kazakhstana' [Dossier: The Customs Union and Single Economic Space of Russia, Belorussia and Kazakhstan] <https://tass.ru/info/853189> accessed 12 November 2022.
18. For an overview of the establishment of the EAEU, see Maksim Karliuk, *The Emerging Autonomous Legal Order of the Eurasian Economic Union* (CUP 2023) 51–74.
19. The data for the Russian Federation includes only the area and population within its internationally recognized borders. See WorldData.Info <https://www.worlddata.info/trade-agreements/eeu-eurasian-economic-union.php#:~:text=The%20EEU%20is%20a%20trade,and%20about%20181.45%20million%20people> accessed 17 November 2022.
20. See Evgeny Gontmakher, 'A closer look at the Eurasian Economic Union' <https://www.gisreportsonline.com/r/eurasian-economic-union/> accessed 17 November 2022.
21. The text of the Regulation (in Russian) is available at <https://docs.eaeunion.org/docs/ru-ru/01417792/scd_16052018> accessed 4 November 2022.
22. See 'Uzbekistan prorabatyvayet vopros o prisoyedinenii k EAES, zayavila Matviyenko' [Uzbekistan is considering the issue of joining the EAEU, said Matviyenko] <https://ria.ru/20191002/1559343154.html> accessed 17 November 2022.
23. Umida Hashimova, 'Not So Fast: Will Uzbekistan Join the Eurasian Economic Union? In Russian framing, the Uzbek decision to join the EAEU has already been made. But Tashkent is still exploring its options' <https://thediplomat.com/2019/10/not-so-fast-will-uzbekistan-join-the-eurasian-economic-union/> accessed 17 November 2022.
24. See Chris Devonshire-Ellis, 'Eurasian Economic Union Plans for More Free Trade Agreements' <https://www.russia-briefing.com/news/eurasian-economic-union-plans-for-more-free-trade-agreements.html/#:~:text=To%20date%2C%20the%20EAEU%20has,reductions%20have%20yet%20been%20agreed> accessed 18 November 2022.

25. See PRC Ministry of Commerce, 'China and Eurasian Economic Union Officially Sign Trade and Economic Cooperation Agreement' <http://english.mofcom.gov.cn/article/newsrelease/significantnews/201805/20180502746079.shtml> accessed 18 November 2022. The Asia Regional Integration Center observes that the Agreement is not yet in force <https://aric.adb.org/fta/peoples-republic-of-china-eurasian-economic-union-free-trade-agreement> accessed 18 November 2022.
26. See PRC Ministry of Commerce (n 25).
27. See Evgeny Vinokurov, 'The free trade agreements of the Eurasian Economic Union' <https://sites.utu.fi/bre/the-free-trade-agreements-of-the-eurasian-economic-union/> accessed 18 November 2022.
28. See Devonshire-Ellis (n 24).
29. See European Union, 'European Council' <https://www.consilium.europa.eu/en/european-council/> accessed 18 November 2022.
30. See European Union, 'Council of the European Union' <https://european-union.europa.eu/institutions-law-budget/institutions-and-bodies/institutions-and-bodies-profiles/council-european-union_en> accessed 18 November 2022.
31. See Chatham House (n 2).
32. See European Union, 'European Commission' <https://european-union.europa.eu/institutions-law-budget/institutions-and-bodies/institutions-and-bodies-profiles/european-commission_en> accessed 18 November 2022.
33. ibid.
34. ibid.
35. cf Article 38(1)(c) of the ICJ Statute.
36. cf Article 38(1)(d) of the ICJ Statute. On the Court of the EAEU, see Karliuk (n 18) 176–218.
37. The regulatory basis for some of these areas is considered in Section 5.
38. cf Article 4 of the EAEU Treaty.
39. cf Article 3 of the EAEU Treaty.
40. cf Article 6(1) of the EAEU Treaty, second paragraph.
41. See WTO, 'Regionalism: friends or rivals?' <https://www.wto.org/english/thewto_e/whatis_e/tif_e/bey1_e.htm> accessed 19 November 2022. Chatham House noted, however, that 'The EEU can only be said to be a partial customs union as member states so often behave unilaterally. Russia has acted without consulting the union on critical economic points … In 2014, Russia blocked agricultural imports from the EU and trade with Ukraine in retaliation for the imposition of financial and economic sanctions. Other EEU member states did not support or implement the ban. Instead, Belarus, Armenia and other nations attempted to profit from it'. See Chatham House (n 2).
42. cf Article XX of the General Agreement on Tariffs and Trade (GATT).
43. In accordance with Article 42(3) of the EAEU Treaty, the EAEU Common Customs Tariff applies the following types of import customs duty rates:
    1) ad valorem rates expressed as a percentage of the customs value of goods;
    2) specific rates determined depending on the physical characteristics in kind of taxable goods (quantity, weight, volume or other characteristics);
    3) combined rates having the features of both types specified in sub-paragraphs 1 and 2 of this paragraph.
44. cf Article 45 of the EAEU Treaty ('Powers of the Commission on Customs Tariff Regulation').

45. cf Article 34 of the EAEU Treaty ('Most Favoured Nation Treatment'): 'With regard to foreign trade, most favoured nation treatment shall be applied within the meaning of the General Agreement on Tariffs and Trade of 1994 (GATT 1994) in cases and under the conditions where the use of most favoured nation treatment is provided for by international treaties of the Union with a third party, as well as by international treaties of the Member States with a third party.'
46. For a current list of the WTO Members, see <https://www.wto.org/english/thewto_e/whatis_e/tif_e/org6_e.htm> accessed 7 November 2022.
47. For the text of the SPS Agreement, see <https://www.wto.org/english/tratop_e/sps_e/spsagr_e.htm> accessed 19 November 2022.
48. ie the annual deficit of the consolidated budget of the State-controlled sector, and the correlation between the debt of the State-controlled sector and the gross domestic product (GDP). The third indicator—inflation rate per annum—is characteristic of a State's economy as a whole.
49. As observed by Russia Briefing, '[t]he Russian Ruble accounted for 74% of the total volume of settlements in EAEU currencies, up from 71.5% in 2021. These reasons are logical, because during 2022, Russia found itself under very tough Western sanctions, and foreign currency transactions through the SWIFT system were banned, meaning it was to be expected that Russian authorities would make efforts to normalize foreign trade with other countries using national currencies.' See Russia Briefing, 'Eurasian Economic Union Dedollarizes: Emphasis Now On Increasing Use Of Mutual Currencies & China Yuan Trade' <https://www.russia-briefing.com/news/eurasian-economic-union-dedollarizes-emphasis-now-on-increasing-use-of-mutual-currencies-china-yuan-trade.html/> accessed 18 November 2022.
50. See Andrew E Kramer, 'Kazakhstan's Currency Plunges' <https://www.nytimes.com/2015/08/21/business/international/kazakhstans-currency-plunges.html> accessed 18 November 2022.
51. See Trading Economics, 'Kazakh Tenge' <https://tradingeconomics.com/kazakhstan/currency> accessed 18 November 2022.
52. See the country-by-country overviews of the main economic indicators at <https://tradingeconomics.com/countries> accessed 18 November 2022.
53. See Radio Free Europe/Radio Liberty, 'Kazakh Banks Tighten Process of Payment Card Issuance to Russians' <https://www.rferl.org/a/kazakhstan-payment-cards-procedures-tightened-russians/31867119.html> accessed 18 November 2022.
54. Dana Omirgazy, 'Sanctions, Migration of Russian Citizens to Kazakhstan Boost Popularity of Money Transfer Systems' <https://astanatimes.com/2022/07/sanctions-migration-of-russian-citizens-to-kazakhstan-boost-popularity-of-money-transfer-systems/> accessed 18 November 2022.
55. cf Articles 83(4) and 84(4) of the EAEU Treaty.
56. cf Articles 81(3), 83(3), and 84(3) of the EAEU Treaty.
57. See Radio Liberty, 'Tokayev: Kazakhstan ne priznayet "kvazigosudarstvennye" "DNR" i "LNR"' [Tokayev: Kazakhstan will not recognize the 'quasi-State' 'DPR' and 'LPR'] <https://rus.azattyq.org/a/tokaev-o-priznanii-lnr-i-dnr/31903400.html> accessed 22 November 2022.
58. See 'Rossiya priostanovila otgruzku kazakhstanskoy nefti iz Novorossiyska' [Russia suspended the shipment of Kazakh oil from Novorossiysk] <https://eadaily.com/ru/news/

2022/06/19/rossiya-priostanovila-otgruzku-kazahstanskoy-nefti-iz-novorossiyska> accessed 19 November 2022.

59. See 'Otvet na shag Moskvy: Kazakhstan hochet transportirovat neft v Evropu v obkhod RF' [Response to Moscow's move: Kazakhstan wants to transport oil to Europe bypassing the Russian Federation] <https://www.epravda.com.ua/rus/news/2022/07/7/688954/> accessed 19 November 2022.
60. cf Articles 10 and 11 of the Convention on the Legal Status of the Caspian Sea of 12 August 2018. See also Sergey Sayapin, 'Convention on the Legal Status of the Caspian Sea' in Seokwoo Lee et al (eds), *Encyclopedia of Public International Law in Asia*, Vol III: Central & South Asia (Brill 2021) 200–201.
61. See Gaziza Shakhanova and Jeremy Garlick, 'The Belt and Road Initiative and the Eurasian Economic Union: Exploring the "Greater Eurasian Partnership"', 49 Journal of Current Chinese Affairs 2020, 33–57.
62. See N K Nurlanova and A B Kaliyeva, 'The Eurasian Economic Community is a New Opportunity to Develop Transit Potential of Kazakhstan', 2(70) KazNU Bulletin. International Relations and International Law Series 2015, 207–2011, 207.
63. See 'China Signs Major Railroad Deal with Uzbekistan And Kyrgyzstan, Bypassing Russia' <https://oilprice.com/Geopolitics/International/China-Signs-Major-Railroad-Deal-With-Uzbekistan-And-Kyrgyzstan-Bypassing-Russia.html> accessed 20 November 2022.
64. See BBC News, 'Ukraine invasion: EU shuts airspace to Russian planes' <https://www.bbc.com/news/world-europe-60539303> accessed 20 November 2022; David Schaper, 'A ban of Russian aircraft from U.S. airspace has gone into effect' <https://www.npr.org/2022/03/02/1084101038/ban-of-russian-aircraft-from-u-s-airspace-has-gone-into-effect#:~:text=According%20to%20a%20statement%20from,is%20a%20citizen%20of%20Russia.%22> accessed 20 November 2022.
65. S Pfeifer, 'Russia's aviation industry defies sanctions to remain airborne' <https://www.ft.com/content/0adc01f3-f87e-4ab2-9dc6-96a472f09435> accessed 20 November 2022.
66. See Reuters, 'Exclusive: Russia starts stripping jetliners for parts as sanctions bite' <https://www.reuters.com/business/aerospace-defense/exclusive-russia-starts-stripping-jetliners-parts-sanctions-bite-2022-08-08/> accessed 20 November 2022.
67. See 'How many Russian oligarchs' yachts have been seized so far' <https://www.axios.com/2022/04/13/stranding-russian-oligarchs-yachts> accessed 20 November 2022.
68. At the domestic level, IP rights are regulated in the EAEU Member States by the Civil Codes and IP laws.
69. See 'What's in a name? Russia rebrands McDonald's restaurant chain' <https://www.aljazeera.com/news/2022/6/12/whats-in-a-name-russia-rebrands-mcdonalds-restaurant-chain> accessed 20 November 2022.
70. Denis Khabarov et al, 'Russia partially legalizes parallel imports' <https://sanctionsnews.bakermckenzie.com/russia-partially-legalizes-parallel-imports/> accessed 20 November 2022.
71. See 'Na kakuyu podderzhku mozhet rasschityvat malyy i sredniy biznes v period sanktsiy?' [What kind of support can small and medium businesses count on during the sanctions period?] <https://fincult.info/article/na-kakuyu-podderzhku-mozhet-rasschityvat-malyy-i-sredniy-biznes-v-period-sanktsiy/> accessed 20 November 2022.
72. See, eg, 'Relotsirovat biznes iz Rossii v Kazakhstan gotovy 56 mezhdunarodnyh kompaniy—Smailov' [56 international companies are ready to relocate business from

Russia to Kazakhstan] <https://vlast.kz/novosti/52184-relocirovat-biznes-iz-rossii-v-kazahstan-gotovy-56-mezdunarodnyh-kompanij-smailov.html> accessed 20 November 2022.

73. See 'Potok trudovoy migratsii iz stran EAES v Rossiyu za god vyros v tri raza' [The flow of labour migration from the EAEU countries to Russia tripled over the year] <https://tass.ru/ekonomika/13106201> accessed 20 November 2022.
74. Due to the visa restrictions introduced by the Baltic States and Poland, the labour migration to the EU was less significant.
75. See Elena Tofanyuk and Yyulya Sapronova, 'Rossiyu posle 21 sentyabrya pokinuli okolo 700000 grazhdan' [About 700000 citizens left Russia after 21 September] <https://www.forbes.ru/society/478827-rossiu-posle-21-sentabra-pokinuli-okolo-700-000-grazdan> accessed 20 November 2022.
76. See Bruce Pannier, 'An Old Refrain: Russian Lawmakers Question Kazakhstan's Territorial Integrity, Statehood' <https://www.rferl.org/a/russia-lawmakers-question-kazakhstan-territorial-integrity-statehood/31003732.html> accessed 20 November 2022.
77. See 'Dossym Satpayev: EAES predstavlyayev ugrozu natsionalnoy bezopasnosti RK' [Dossym Satpayev: The Eurasian Economic Union poses a threat to the national security of the Republic of Kazakhstan] <https://ulysmedia.kz/news/13191-vygodno-li-kazakhstanu-byt-v-eaes-otvetil-sagintaev/> accessed 20 November 2022.
78. See 'Glava Minobrnauki raskryl detali otkaza Rossii ot Bolonskoy sistemy' [The head of the Ministry of Education and Science revealed the details of Russia's rejection of the Bologna system] <https://www.forbes.ru/society/467539-glava-minobrnauki-raskryl-detali-otkaza-rossii-ot-bolonskoj-sistemy> accessed 20 November 2022.
79. See 'Lukashenko zayavil o nastionalizatsii "nedobrosovestnyh" kompaniy s inostrannym kapitalom' [Lukashenko announced the nationalisation of 'unscrupulous' companies with foreign capital] <https://www.vedomosti.ru/economics/news/2022/11/11/949973-lukashenko-zayavil-o-natsionalizatsii> accessed 20 November 2022.
80. On the relationship between democracy and international law, see Jan Wouters et al, 'Democracy and International Law', 34 Netherlands Yearbook of International Law 2003, 139–197.
81. See Freedom House's annual Freedom in the World Report at <https://freedomhouse.org/countries/freedom-world/scores> accessed 20 November 2022.
82. See The World Justice Project Rule of Law Index 2022 at <https://worldjusticeproject.org/rule-of-law-index/> accessed 20 November 2022.
83. cf Gospel according to Mark, 2:22.
84. See Tania Voon and Andrew D. Mitchell, 'Ending International Investment Agreements: Russia's Withdrawal from Participation in the Energy Charter Treaty', 111 AJIL Unbound 2017, 461–466, 463.
85. cf Annex 20 (Protocol on Common Regulation Principles and Rules for Activities of Natural Monopoly Entities), paras 9(6) and 20(4).
86. cf Articles 29(1)(3), 52(1), 68(5), and 86(2)(7) of the EAEU Treaty.
87. See Sergey Sayapin, 'The Aral Sea' in Seokwoo Lee et al (n 60) 198–199.
88. See Angelina Davydova, 'Will Russia ever leave fossil fuels behind?' <https://www.bbc.com/future/article/20211115-climate-change-can-russia-leave-fossil-fuels-behind> accessed 20 November 2022.

89. See ADB, 'Kazakhstan Country Diagnostic Study—Highlights', 1 <https://www.adb.org/sites/default/files/publication/445446/kazakhstan-diagnostic-study-highlights.pdf> accessed 20 November 2022.
90. See Transparency International's Corruption Perception Index 2021 <https://www.transparency.org/en/cpi/2021> accessed 20 November 2022.
91. For the electronic government of the Republic of Kazakhstan, see <https://egov.kz/cms/en> accessed 20 November 2022.
92. See Sergey Sayapin, 'Critical Analysis, Strict Discipline and Personal Responsibility: Some Reflections on Strengthening the Independence of the Judiciary in Central Asia', 3(84) Law and State 2019, 18–27; Sergey Sayapin, 'Réflexions sur le renforcement de l'indépendance de la magistrature en Asie centrale' [Reflections on the Reinforcement of the Independence of the Judiciary in Central Asia], 14(4) Les Cahiers de la justice 2019, 655–665.
93. See Sergey Sayapin, 'Mezhdunarodnoye pravo v Tsentralnoy Azii: teoriya i praktika' [International Law in Central Asia: Theory and Practice], 2(95) Law and State 2022, 31–54, 46.
94. ibid, 46–47. See also Sergey Sayapin, 'International Law in Central Asia: Practices and Doctrines', 47 Review of Central and East European Law 2022, 322–351, 349.
95. See News.Am, 'Armenia to ratify the Rome Statute of the International Criminal Court' <https://news.am/eng/news/737552.html> accessed 13 January 2023.
96. See Sergey Sayapin, 'Russia's Withdrawal of Signature from the Rome Statute Would Not Shield its Nationals from Potential Prosecution at the ICC' <http://www.ejiltalk.org/russias-withdrawal-of-signature-from-the-rome-statute-would-not-shield-its-nationals-from-potential-prosecution-at-the-icc/#more-14774> accessed 13 January 2023.
97. See Human Rights Watch, 'Kazakhstan; Joint Statement on January 2022 events' <https://www.hrw.org/news/2022/07/29/kazakhstan-joint-statement-january-2022-events> accessed 13 January 2023.
98. cf a statement made by the first President of Kazakhstan, Nursultan Nazarbayev, in a documentary aired in December 2021: '[I]n the future, for example, I would expect the Eurasian Union and the Shanghai [Cooperation Organisation] to unite but ideally it would be for the European Union and the Eurasian Union to unite and create one single entity. But when it will be, I don't know ....' See Ria.Ru, 'Nazarbayev dopustil obyedineniye v budushchem ES i EAES' [Nazarbayev Supposed the EU and the EAEU Could Unite in the Future] <https://ria.ru/20211207/obedinenie-1762608420.html> accessed 11 January 2023.
99. See Sergey Sayapin, 'Institutional Attitudes Towards Acts of Aggression' in Stefanie Bock and Eckart Conze (eds), *Rethinking the Crime of Aggression: International and Interdisciplinary Perspectives* (T. M. C. Asser Press/Springer 2022) 139-151, 147.

PART 4

COUNTRIES AND REGIONS OF EUROPE

CHAPTER 26

THE BALTIC STATES

LAURI MÄLKSOO

1. Introduction

INTERNATIONAL law has been a source of both euphoria and desperation for the three Baltic States: The Republics of Estonia, Latvia, and Lithuania. We can see this anecdotally in stories related to two Estonian statesmen, Lennart Meri and Antonius (Ants) Piip. When President Lennart Meri (1929–2006), himself an historian by education, was asked in 1998 what he thought of the successful nuclear tests by India and Pakistan—big news at the time—he responded: 'The nuclear weapon of small States is international law'.[1]

Leaving aside the possibility that this comment was made ironically, what was the source of Meri's enthusiasm about the role of international law? Presumably, it was the experience of how the 1991 restoration of independence of the three Baltic States materialized, some months before the disintegration of the Soviet Union. In this process, many Baltic people and politicians had the feeling that international law as applied to the history of their States was a powerful tool; international law carried weight. So, Meri's metaphor of international law as a powerful weapon for small States in international relations was based on recent Baltic experience. Later on, too—for example when they were candidates for United Nations Security Council (UNSC) membership[2]—the Baltic States referred to the importance of international law in world affairs.

However, Meri's attitude towards international law is not the only defining story which we can think of when contemplating the historical experience of the three Baltic States. During the interwar period, one of Estonia's leading politicians was Antonius (Ants) Piip (1884–1942), an international lawyer. Educated in international law at St Petersburg Imperial University and Berlin, he worked towards recognition of Estonia at the Paris Peace Conference in 1919 and was a member of the Estonian delegation when the Tartu Peace Treaty between Soviet Russia and Estonia was signed on 2 February 1920. During the interwar period, Piip was several times Estonia's Foreign Minister and also worked as Professor of International Law at the University of Tartu. In the latter capacity, Piip published the first textbook on international law in the Estonian language,[3] a language spoken by only a million people. Essentially, Piip's life work was to introduce Estonia to international law and international law to Estonia.

Piip was also Foreign Minister when the Soviet Union presented an ultimatum to the Estonian government on 16 June 1940. In June 1941, immediately after the outbreak of the German-Soviet war, Piip was arrested and sent to a Soviet camp in Siberia, where he would die a year later. Eyewitnesses have recorded that Piip had taken with him to Siberia a photograph with a dedication which Soviet leader Joseph Stalin had presented to him during treaty negotiations in Moscow in September 1939.[4] Probably Piip hoped that the Soviet dictator's photograph might save his life in the Soviet camp. A learned man who had practised and taught treaties and other concepts of international law throughout his life had to resort to Stalin's photo as his last desperate plea. In a way, a foreign dictator's photo in the hands of an international law professor was also a symbolic humiliation for international law which, at least in the Soviet camp of Nyrob in 1941–1942, did not turn out to be a 'nuclear weapon' for either Piip or his country.

This explains why, in the Baltic States, international law has been a source of both euphoria and disappointment, winning and losing. Small States in challenging geopolitical neighbourhoods occupy a particularly precarious situation in international law. In their background is always the echo of the realist words of Athenians to the Melian negotiators in the famous Melian dialogue of Thucydides: '... since you know as well as we do that right, as the world goes, is only in question between equals in power, while the strong do what they can and the weak suffer what they must'.[5] Can international law mitigate vast differences in power, not only on paper but also in real life? For small States, the existence of international law invokes the possibility of sovereign equality; their right to exist.

In the following, I will proceed chronologically and discuss how international law was relevant before the emergence of the Baltic States in 1918 and then also how experience during more than one hundred years of statehood have shaped Baltic perceptions of international law.

2. The Baltic Lands Before the Beginning of Their Modern Statehood in 1918

Estonia, Latvia, and Lithuania have had almost identical histories since 1918. However, before that there were significant differences between them. Today's Latvia and Estonia was a territory conquered by German (and partly also Danish) crusaders in the early 13th century. The fact that the Livi (a people who have almost died out), the Latvian, and Estonian peoples who inhabited these territories had not yet adopted Christianity was used as the rationale for conquest. German nobility took control over the land and until 1919 remained the ruling minority in what historically used to be called Livonia (much of today's Latvia and Estonia). Thus, colonization happened not only outside Europe but also inside Europe; at the same time, Livonia was made part of Europe through this act of conquest. The political identity of medieval Livonia was determined by the German language and the Christianity of the Baltic German nobility, first Catholicism and then, after the Reformation, Lutheranism. Since then, many have seen in the Estonian-Russian border—symbolically, for example, in the city of Narva, where two mediaeval castles face each other across the river, one built by the Teutonic Order and the other by Muscovy (Ivangorod)—as a civilizational border,[6] the border where (Western) Europe and Russia face each other.

Lithuania's trajectory was different during the Middle Ages. In the 13th century, the Lithuanians managed to withstand Teutonic attempts to conquer their territory, established their own kingdom with Vilnius as its capital, and in the 14th century adopted Christianity on their own initiative. At that time, the territory of the Lithuanian Kingdom also included much of what would be today's Belarus. After 1385, Poland and Lithuania were under the same sovereign and in 1569 the two countries merged and formed the single Polish-Lithuanian Kingdom. The Polish-Lithuanian Kingdom was itself incorporated into the Russian Empire in 1795, as a consequence of the third partition of Poland between Russia, Prussia, and Austria. The partitions of the Polish-Lithuanian Kingdom were completed using treaties between the annexing empires and thus formalized with an instrument of international law.

Since when have international treaties and arguments related to international law been at work in Livonia (today's Estonia and Latvia)? Baron Taube (1869–1961), an exiled Russian international lawyer, highlighted that the Teutonic Order, the Danish knights in Estonia, and two other local States concluded the Treaty of Dorpat (Tartu) in 1304 to form an alliance. They agreed to decide their mutual differences by arbitration, and in conflicts with mediaeval Russia the arbitral commission also would decide on justness of cause in war.[7] The Livonian crusader States and Lithuania also concluded treaties of commerce with Russian principalities such as Novgorod.[8] Further arbitration agreements were concluded by the mediaeval Livonian States, for example in Walk (Valga) in 1435.[9] The Lithuanian Grand Duke Vytautas was a driving force behind the congress of Lutsk in 1429, where a number of European monarchs gathered and discussed a variety of regional and international issues.[10]

In the 16th century, the territories of the German crusader States in Livonia became interesting for outside powers, especially Muscovy in the East. Muscovy started the Livonian War (1558–1583) but eventually Sweden, which also intervened, emerged as the victorious power in the war and annexed the Livonian territories. Nevertheless, the beginning of the Livonian War was the first Livonian encounter with Muscovy's territorial claims and interpretation of treaties as well as its own ancient chronicles. In particular, Ivan Grozny, the Tsar of Muscovy, claimed that in the past, before the 13th century, Livonia had paid tribute to Rus'; now it was time to repay the 'tax of Dorpat (Tartu)'.[11] The Livonians had not heard of such a tax, not even from their history books. In the experience of the Livonian negotiators, Muscovy was in possession of different facts and had a different interpretation of earlier agreements.

After more than a century of Swedish rule in Livonia, Muscovy started another campaign to conquer the territory. This finally happened in the Great Nordic War (1700–1721), as a result of which, sovereignty over Livonia went to Russia by the Russian-Swedish Treaty of Nystad (Uusikaupunki) in 1721. A further relevant aspect to this transfer of sovereignty was that the representatives of the Baltic German nobility achieved recognition of their privileges from Russia's Tsar Peter I and respect for internal autonomy in the affairs of Livonia (1710, the so-called *Accord Punkten*). As a result, even though being now part of the Russian Empire, Livonia's language of administration and education remained German and the predominant religion, Lutheranism, was protected.

Just as in the earlier Livonian War (1558–1583), debates about previous treaty commitments played a significant role in disputes about the justness of Muscovy's launch of the Great Nordic War (1700–1721). Former professor at the University of Dorpat (Tartu) and later Sweden's state historian, Olof Hermelin (1658–1709), presented the arguments for Sweden, claiming that Muscovy had violated various agreements and promises when launching the war, especially the Treaty of Stolbova (Stolbovo) of 1617 in which Muscovy had recognized the Swedish sovereignty over the Baltic provinces.[12] 'Barbarian' and 'violators of the law of all nations' were some of the epithets with which Hermelin described Muscovy's war. Also from the time of the Great Nordic War stems Muscovy's first writing related to international law, written by Tsar Peter I's diplomat Petr Shafirov.[13] Shafirov's treatise (which can be understood as a response to Hermelin and other Swedish accusations) has been highly appreciated in the historiography of international law in Russia.[14] In the end, the question of transfer of sovereignty over the Eastern Baltic shores was decided on the battlefield. Nevertheless, it is important that Muscovy/Russia first seriously encounters *jus publicum europaeum* in lands which later become the Baltic States.

In addition, the question of the legal meaning of the 1710 *Accord Punkten* (conditions based on which the Baltic nobility recognized the authority of the Russian Tsar) became an issue in the late 19th century when the Russian central government started to curb the administrative rights and autonomy of the Baltic German nobility in the provinces of Estonia and Livonia.[15] Was the *Accord Punkten* a gift from the Tsar which could be revoked if circumstances changed, or was it a binding agreement?[16] Baltic German authors argued that there had been a contract (if not a treaty) and trying to Russianize the Baltic provinces, as Tsar Alexander III did, would violate it.[17] This debate, too, belonged to the long lineage of Baltic debates with Russia over historical agreements, which formed a large part of how the Baltic territories experienced international law.

The reason why this earlier history of the Baltic territories is presented here relatively extensively is because patterns of international law in the territories of the three Baltic States go further back in time than the creation of the three nation-states in 1918. The three Baltic States may be relatively young but the role of international law in their territories is not. Moreover, old history apparently continues to matter. On 15 September

2022, the Twitter account of the Russian Ministry of Foreign Affairs (MFA) announced, citing the Ministry's spokesperson Maria Zakharova: 'The Battle of Orsha of 1522 between Muscovy & the then Lithuania is glorified in Lithuania & Ukraine on an annual basis. Russophobes can manipulate history as much as they want, in the end it all comes down to peace treaties, which fixed Moscow achieving its goals.'[18] On 9 June 2022, when celebrating the legacy of Tsar Peter I in the context of Russia's war against Ukraine, Russia's President Vladimir Putin made the following comment about the Great Nordic War: 'During the war with Sweden, Peter the Great did not conquer anything, he took back what had always belonged to us, even though all of Europe recognized it as Sweden's. It seems now it's our turn to get our lands back.'[19]

In a certain sense then, not much has changed on the Eastern shores of the Baltic Sea. The Baltic States have experienced international law as Western border States neighbouring Russia, which in turn has its own interpretation of treaties and international law. They are also the archetypical small States having as their neighbour an ambitious and occasionally aggressive great power. When the geopolitical situation between Russia and the West worsens, international law becomes part of ontological attacks and interpretations, more so than in other European regions where the neighbourhood has become peaceful and history less relevant.

3. 1918–1921: The Rise of Baltic Self-Determination

In the 19th century, Livonia produced several well-known international lawyers. For example, two Baltic German international law professors, August von Bulmerincq (1822–1890) and Carl Bergbohm (1849–1927), were leading legal positivists in their time. After his professorship at Tartu (Dorpat), Bulmerincq became a professor at Heidelberg and in this capacity organized the 1887 conference of the Institut de Droit International. The biggest Baltic name in international law, Friedrich (Fyodor Fyodorovich) Martens (1845–1909), who was born in Livonia's Pärnu (Pernau), worked for the Russian imperial MFA, besides his professorship at St Petersburg University. When Martens published his famous Russian textbook of international law in 1882, he made the following comment about the rising claims of peoples to self-determination in Europe (or as he called it, 'principle of nationality'): many European intellectuals had started to think that the principle of nationality was a panacea of sorts, while in reality this principle could destroy a great deal.[20] Martens realized correctly that what became known as the right of peoples to self-determination would undermine old European Empires, inevitably including the Russian Empire.

The 1917 February revolution in the Russian Empire brought down the Romanov dynasty. The provisional government made concessions to the right of peoples to self-determination. For example, they agreed to redraw the borders of the provinces of

Estonia and Livonia based on the ethnic principle; the borders of the now enlarged province of Estonia started to follow the contours of the ethnic border between the Latvians and Estonians. The territory of the province of Livonia was diminished accordingly. The Baltic provinces received autonomy within republican Russia but this was no longer the autonomy led by the previously dominant Baltic German minority but by the ethnic Estonian and Latvian majorities. On 22 April 1917, the Minister of Justice of the Russian provisional government, Alexander Kerensky, visited Estonia's capital Tallinn and was celebrated by local crowds. In his speech, Kerensky said: 'We look peacefully towards the future and won't believe those who declare that the freedom of Russia means the beginning of disintegration of the State. Bravely and with pure hearts we come to you and say: if you want, come with us, if you don't want—you are free. And if you don't want to join us, it would hurt us but we can live with this undeserved injury.'[21] Prospects of freedom in Russia and for the peoples of the Russian Empire were connected with conflicting emotions.

The 1917 October revolution in Russia brought into power the Bolsheviks led by Vladimir Lenin. They proclaimed that they were willing to give to the peoples of the Russian Empire self-determination, and even allow secession from Russia. At the same time, there was an angle to the Leninist concept of self-determination—the Bolsheviks thought that while the Baltic provinces would gain independence, they would be ruled by local Bolsheviks. Thus, notwithstanding the formal proclamation of support for self-determination, Soviet Russia still got into a war with secessionist forces in the Baltics; a war which the Bolsheviks interpreted as a class war but for the majority of the local population was a war of national liberation.

In 1920, Soviet Russia recognized the independence of the three Baltic States and concluded peace treaties with them.[22] Each of these peace treaties (and also the one with Georgia) had an identical article which stipulated that the new States were born based on the right of peoples to self-determination and that Russia renounced its former rights over these territories 'for ever'. This is important because sometimes the story of self-determination in international law is primarily told in the context of decolonization in the 1960s.[23] However, the right of peoples to self-determination up to the point of secession had already entered at least regional international law in Eastern Europe via Soviet Russian peace treaties with its border States in 1920. This was not a Soviet gift but a demand by the peoples of those countries.

What would the borders of the newly formed Baltic States be? Lithuania claimed its historical capital Vilnius but Poland had claims over the same city (Wilno in Polish); a Polish general occupied the city and it remained *de facto* part of Poland until 1939. The status of Vilnius preoccupied international lawyers during the interwar period.[24] Moreover, Germany and Lithuania were in dispute over the former East Prussian town of Klaipeda (Memel). The disputed town of Valga/Valka on the Estonian-Latvian border was split in two halves, one to Estonia and the other to Latvia, by an arbitrator sent by the League of Nations, the British Colonel Sir Stephen Tallents.

One fascinating aspect about the Baltic States in 1918–1921 was how difficult it was to gain full recognition of their sovereignty from existing European powers. Baltic envoys—including Antonius Piip—were actively lobbying at the Paris Peace Conference in 1919.[25] The West European powers did not want to give *de jure* recognition to the Baltic States before the future of Russia was certain, especially while in 1919 the White Admiral Kolchak still seemed to have prospects of coming to power in Russia. It did not help that top lawyers from the Russian provisional government, now already in exile, such as André Mandelstam (1869–1949), still argued in 1919 against the independence of Estonia and Latvia *inter alia* because these territories would be vitally important for Russia.[26] Essentially, the representatives of the Baltic States had to argue that their nations had a high enough civilizational level (they liked to emphasize that the literacy level was considerably higher than in Russia proper); that they would manage to be viable States, despite their small size.[27] Thus, civilizational arguments had to be made not only by extra-European nations but also by emerging smaller States in the already centuries-old international community in Europe.[28] In addition, Baltic international lawyers claimed that the independence of the Baltic States was not only due to the temporary weakness of Russia and Germany but that already in the distant past, before the crusades in the 13th century, the Baltic peoples had formed independent States.[29] In a sense, then, these diplomats and professors claimed that Estonia and Latvia, re-born in 1918, were not *new* States. The argument was similar to that which several countries outside Europe which freed themselves from decolonization put forward in the 1950s and 1960s.[30] The Baltic representatives also emphasized that historical development determined that the countries could belong neither to Russia nor to Germany but deserved independence by maintaining independent languages and cultures between these two Eastern and Central European great powers.[31]

The politics of the newly created Baltic States involved elements resembling decolonization as well. Thus, Estonia and Latvia carried out land reforms in 1919 in which the estates of the Baltic German nobility were expropriated, without full compensation. This policy was justified by rhetoric presenting the Baltic Germans as having for centuries been colonizers in the lands of the Estonians and the Latvians. As a result, some German authors stemming from the former Baltic provinces thought that the rights of ethnic minorities, particularly of the German minority, were violated in the nascent Baltic States.[32]

Because of the territorial dispute over Vilnius between Poland and Lithuania, the Allied powers recognized Lithuania *de jure* later than they recognized Estonia and Latvia. The Allied Council recognized Estonia and Latvia *de jure* in January 1921 and Lithuania in December 1922. The US recognized the Baltic States *de jure* only in July 1922[33] when it had become clear that the Bolsheviks would remain in power in Russia. At the time, countries such as the US did not deem it right to dismember old Russia without the consent of the rightful inheritors of power in the country, because imperial Russia had been an ally in World War I. Nevertheless, independent Estonia and Latvia were to play a role in future US-Soviet relations as the leading American diplomat on issues related to the Soviet Union, George F Kennan, started his consular career in Tallinn and Riga in the late 1920s and *inter alia* used his time there to study Russian language, history, and culture,[34] something which became very useful after the US established diplomatic relations with the Soviet Union in 1933. It was clear enough, though, that in Kennan's mind, the Baltic States were first and foremost successor States of (imperial) Russia.[35]

The accession of the three Baltic States to the League of Nations was a somewhat awkward affair. Their first bid to become members of the League of Nations in December 1920 failed but the three States (and Georgia) were allowed to join work in the League's 'technical organizations'.[36] Contemporary authors commented that the Baltic States were first admitted to the League of Nations *de facto* and only later, in 1921, *de jure*.[37] Already during the Paris Peace Conference in 1919, the Baltic diplomatic representatives had learned that the creation of new (and small) States in Europe was not an easy matter at all; one had to spend considerable time waiting in the antechambers of more powerful actors.

What matters in our context is that international law—or rather, arguments drawn from international law—played a central role in these processes and decisions concerning statehood. This also explains the centrality of international legal expertise for the Baltic States during the interwar period. This is particularly marked for Estonia—with the personalities of Antonius (Ants) Piip and Kaarel Robert Pusta. Both were leading Estonian voices in Paris in 1919 and they continued to work with international law during the interwar period, as foreign ministers, ambassadors, and international law experts. While Piip was more active as Professor of International Law in Estonia, Kaarel Robert Pusta, Estonia's ambassador in Paris, became a member of the Institut de Droit International and lectured at The Hague Academy of International Law.[38] In Latvia, a somewhat similar role was played by Hermanis Albats (1879–1942), who also combined teaching international law in Riga with diplomacy and foreign policy.

The minority situation differed somewhat in the three Baltic States; interwar Lithuania had a considerable Jewish minority whereas in Latvia and Estonia the most relevant minority were the Baltic Germans. Responding to the expectations of the League of Nations, Estonia adopted a progressive Act on Cultural Autonomy in 1925 which recognized widespread minority rights. One of the leading defenders of minority rights in the League of Nations era,[39] Jacob Robinson (1889–1977), worked in Kaunas (the temporary capital of Lithuania) and at the end of World War II became an influential adviser when the UN Commission of Human Rights was created and when the State of Israel was born.[40] During the interwar period, Robinson also represented Lithuania's interests in the debate over the Klaipeda (Memel) region.[41] Britain, France, Italy, and Japan sued Lithuania in the Permanent Court of International Justice (PCIJ) over interpretation of the Statute of the Memel Territory,[42] the governance of which was internationalized. At the end of the interwar period, Estonia and Lithuania also had an investment dispute in the PCIJ.[43]

4. Soviet Occupation and the Continuity of the Baltic States in International Law

We can now turn to the biggest trauma in the history of the three Baltic States, namely their *de facto* loss of independence during World War II, a situation which lasted from 1940 until 1991. While the circumstances of this story, like those of all stories, are particular, this one raises important universal questions about the role of international law, particularly at a time of geopolitical cataclysms. The main question is the extent to which the international community, with the help of international law, is capable of protecting its smaller and thus more vulnerable member States. Between the big and the small, will things be decided by force or based on international law? After all, the Melian dialogue of Thucydides is not only of historical interest.

The interwar order in Central and Eastern Europe was created in particular by two powers, Britain and France. By the 1930s, two revisionist powers emerged in Eastern and Central Europe, both dissatisfied with how World War I ended for them: (from 1933 Nazi) Germany and the Soviet Union. Germany's grievance was that, according to the Versailles Peace Treaty of 1919, it had to accept whatever territorial arrangements were agreed upon by the Allied powers in Central Eastern Europe. For the Soviet Union, even if it had concluded a number of reassuring treaties with its new border States, the grievance which remained was that these territories separated from Russia at the time of the latter's internal weakness. Moreover, the Soviet communists were also expansionist in the sense that they wanted to see their ideology come to power in other countries, starting with their neighbours.

On 23 August 1939, Nazi Germany and the Soviet Union concluded a non-aggression pact which had a secret protocol based on which Berlin and Moscow divided States between them into spheres of influence. Finland, Estonia, and Latvia were allocated to the Soviet sphere of influence and Lithuania to the German sphere of influence; Poland was divided between Germany and the Soviet Union. This is how World War II broke out in Europe; Germany attacked Poland on 1 September and the Soviet Union invaded Eastern Poland on 17 September 1939. Later, Lithuania too was transferred to the Soviet sphere of influence, by an additional secret protocol between Nazi Germany and the Soviet Union.

Stalin promised the Baltic States that, if they allowed Soviet military bases to be temporarily established in their territories, their independence would remain intact. Agreements for the introduction of those military bases were concluded in Moscow in September 1939; the Soviet government had already threatened to use military force if the Baltic governments refused. Finland resisted the Soviet push for military bases, as a result of which the Soviet Union attacked Finland under false pretexts on 30 November 1939 and the Soviet-Finnish Winter War broke out. The Soviet Union was expelled from the League of Nations at the end of 1939.

In violation of bilateral and regional treaties, the Soviet Union created a blockade and presented ultimatums to the Baltic States in June 1940, then Sovietized and later in August 1940 annexed those States. A Soviet regime of terror was created in the Baltic States, in particular targeting the previous ('bourgeois') political elite. On 14 June 1941, tens of thousands of individuals were deported from Soviet-annexed Estonia, Latvia, and Lithuania as well as Bukovina (formerly part of Romania; another victim of the Molotov-Ribbentrop Pact) to Soviet Russia;[44] many of these individuals perished in Soviet Russia. Later, at the Nuremberg trials in 1945, Soviet prosecutors and judges participated in condemning Nazi deportations of civilians during World War II as crimes against humanity.[45]

During World War II, the fate of the Baltic States was discussed several times by the Allied powers.[46] The Atlantic Charter of 14 August 1941, agreed upon by the leaders of the US and the UK, proclaimed that the two powers 'desire to seek no territorial changes that do not accord with the freely expressed wishes of the peoples concerned' and that 'they respect the right of all peoples to choose the form of government under which they will live; and they wish to see sovereign rights and self-government restored to those who have been forcibly deprived of them'. During World War II, the Baltic peoples pinned their hopes on these aims even if Nazi Germany (which was the occupying power in 1941–1944) said in its propaganda that the Allies would not defend the Baltic States against Stalin. In 1944, surviving Estonian and Latvian pre-World War II leaders—such as Jüri Uluots, the last Estonian prime minister before June 1940 and also a history of law professor—called on their peoples to fight against the Soviet invasion, even in German uniform; tens of thousands of Balts recruited into the German army did so.

In the end, the three Baltic States were the only European States which *de facto* lost their independence as a consequence of World War II. A whole group of Central and East European countries fell under Soviet domination in or after 1944 but did not lose their statehood. Of course, one confusing aspect of this was the Soviet constitutional claim that the Soviet republics would be independent, sovereign States. In 1945, Moscow even had an initiative that all fifteen Soviet republics would become members of the UN. However, the Western powers did not accept the claim that the Soviet republics were sovereign States; in the end, only Soviet Belarus and Ukraine were accepted as UN members, besides the Soviet Union itself; an awkward compromise. Moreover, the Soviet Union claimed that it was a democracy, indeed a much more perfect democracy than the bourgeois democracies in the West. Moscow also claimed that the Baltic States had joined the Soviet Union of their own free will. Most people in the annexed Baltic States saw it differently; one expression of this was the guerrilla war against the Soviets ('the forest brothers') which was particularly intense in Lithuania and lasted until the 1950s.

The US and the UK, as well as a number of other mostly Western States, did not recognize *de jure* the incorporation of the Baltic States in the USSR.[47] As early as 23 July 1940, with the Sumner Welles declaration in the US, the policy of non-recognition of the Soviet annexation of the Baltic States started to take shape. After World War II and when the Cold War broke out, diplomats in Baltic legations in the US and elsewhere were allowed to continue to further represent their annexed countries. For example, Kaarel Robert Pusta, the Estonian diplomat who was present at the Paris Peace Conference in 1919 and remained active as a member of the Institut de Droit International, continued to represent independent Estonia in Madrid and Paris until his death in 1964. Former politicians, diplomats, and scholars who had managed to escape from the Soviet-annexed Baltic States, continued to speak out and write about the illegality of the Soviet occupation and annexation of the Baltic States, and the repressions the Soviet government carried out afterwards.[48] International lawyers in the West such as Boris Meissner (a Baltic German and graduate of the University of Tartu) and Krystyna Marek (an international law scholar of Polish origin and working in Switzerland) explained in their writings that due to the illegality of the Soviet annexation of the Baltic States in 1940, the Baltic States had not disappeared as subjects of international law.[49] In 1955, the US Congress produced a report by the so-called Kersten committee on the illegality of the Soviet annexation of the Baltic States.[50] In the words of Lennart Meri, the first president of the restored Republic of Estonia in the 1990s: the Baltic States found their 'last refuge' in international law.

Nevertheless, this remained a somewhat weak consolation because, just as for Antonius Piip in the Soviet camp in 1942, international law was put on hold for the Baltic nations after World War II. Soviet mass repressions also continued. For example, on 25 March 1949, another mass deportation of tens of thousands of people to Siberia was organized by the Soviet government in the annexed Baltic States, this time to carry out collectivization.

In August 1991, against the backdrop of a Soviet hardliner *coup d'état* in Moscow, the Baltic States proclaimed the restoration of their independence. This was soon recognized by Western nations and eventually also by the Soviet government in Moscow. In December 1991, the Soviet Union disintegrated and other Soviet republics also became sovereign States. Vis-à-vis other Western nations, the Baltic governments were altogether successful in their claim that their sovereignty since August 1991 was based on State continuity with the pre-World War II Baltic republics. However, the Russian Federation which emerged from the Soviet Union did not recognize the Baltic State claim of continuity. The post-Soviet Russian government continued to insist that the three Baltic States joined the Soviet Union in a legally acceptable manner in 1940. In turn, the Russian government blamed Latvia and Estonia for discriminating against ethnic Russians who had settled in the republics during the Soviet period. Based on the State continuity doctrine, the Soviet-era settlers did not receive the citizenship of restored Latvia and Estonia automatically but had to go through naturalization, including demonstrating a knowledge of the official language. The Conference on Security and Cooperation in Europe's (CSCE) High Commissioner on National Minorities, Mr Max van der Stoel from The Netherlands, was working intensively with the Baltic States in the 1990s, perhaps unintentionally also invoking the League of Nations minority disputes concerning the new East and Central European 'border States' in the 1920s. The European Court of Human Rights (ECtHR) has also dealt with the question of whether applications of the State continuity doctrine are compatible with the rights of individuals in specific circumstances.[51]

After 1991, one way in which the Baltic States dealt with the trauma of Soviet annexation was to become integrated as much as possible with the Western world and Western institutions. Estonia and Lithuania joined the Council of Europe (CoE) in 1993 and Latvia in 1995. In 2004, the three Baltic States were invited to join the European Union (EU) and NATO.[52] Unlike for the Baltic States in 1920, neutrality was no longer an option. It was the experience of the Baltic States that Russia's peacefulness and acceptance of Baltic independence may be a merely cyclical phenomenon: another tsar, secretary general, or president could come along and dismiss previous solemn treaties and agreements out of hand. When speaking in 1994 in Hamburg, Estonia's President Lennart Meri warned that even though the Soviet Union was gone, Russian imperialism had not disappeared; his remarks triggered a demonstrative walk-out by the Russian delegation led by the then St Petersburg city official Vladimir Putin.[53]

Several European traumas are related to World War II and not all of them have been successfully dealt with. However, a fundamental difference exists between the attitudes of Germany and Russia concerning World War II. Post-World War II Germany, even if it does not for its own legal reasons accept, for example, Poland's recent reparations claims, does not deny that heinous Nazi crimes were perpetrated against neighbouring States. Democratic Germany's leaders have repeatedly apologized for Nazi crimes and Germany has also paid compensation to individual victims and victim groups. In contrast, the Russian government has rejected any serious *Vergangenheitsaufarbeitung* and under President Putin has even retracted 'historical concessions' made in the 1990s. The process started with a denial of Stalinist crimes committed against the Balts and the Poles and has now deepened further in the downplaying of crimes committed against Soviet citizens and Russians as well, as demonstrated *inter alia* by the shutting down of the Memorial non-governmental organization in Russia.[54] It is important to understand why this has been so—it is because the imperial idea has dominated over all else in Russian (including post-Soviet) political practices. If the historical truth collides with imperial interests, the truth must retreat.

One of the places in which the Baltic States have found recognition for their story is in European institutions. For example, the European Parliament has repeatedly acknowledged that Soviet totalitarian power committed crimes under international law in the Baltic States. Another institution where the Baltic States have been able to find recognition for atrocities committed by the Soviet Union is the ECtHR in Strasbourg. The Court has repeatedly acknowledged the illegality of the Soviet occupation and annexation of the Baltic States as well as the fact that crimes against humanity, war crimes, and even acts of genocide were committed in the Soviet-annexed Baltic States.[55] For example, in the cases of Penart as well as Kolk and Kislyiy, the ECtHR acknowledged that 'after the German occupation in 1941–1944, Estonia remained occupied by the Soviet Union until the restoration of its independence in 1991'.[56]

But acknowledgement of the continuator State of the Soviet Union is absent; the Russian President has said that it was a good thing that Russia parted ways with the ECtHR in 2022 because the Court had become too 'politicized'.[57] Of course, the Russian people have their own major legitimate trauma related to World War II; nevertheless, the Russian government and society have apparently decided to deal with this trauma by denying any Soviet wrongdoing between 23 August 1939 and 22 June 1941, an approach which the independent Baltic States (and Poland) will not accept.

5. Conclusion: On Small States and International Law

This chapter has turned out to be quite historical. There are reasons for this. One is that while the Baltic States were annexed by the Soviet Union, the interwar history of the Baltic States was put aside as being temporary and of little relevance (as their *de facto* independence did not survive World War II). However, history and violations of fundamental norms in international law of States cannot be put aside like this; if they are, they can come back to haunt the peoples concerned. During the Cold War, the sovereignty of the Baltic States could only be suppressed, but could not be eradicated under international law. Quite aptly, one of the exhibitions of the Estonian History Museum in Tallinn summed up the last thousand years of Estonian history with the title (and cultural reference to Hollywood) 'die hard'; certainly, a resurrection of statehood after occupation must also be an example when nations refuse to die. Perhaps, as such, the Baltic story can serve as a positive example for other nations whose rights are violated; restoration of rights may take time but eventually it may happen. At least it did happen in the case of the Baltic States in August 1991.

Small States can also play a role in the knowledge production and progressive development of international law. After the 2007 cyberattacks against Estonian websites, Estonia launched, and has ever since supported, the international Tallinn Manual process on the study of how international law applies to conflicts carried out in cyberspace.[58] International lawyers from the Baltic States have organized major international law conferences such as the 2015 biannual conference of the IDI in Tallinn or several annual conferences of the ESIL, for example in 2011 in Tallinn, in 2016 in Riga, and the 2024 conference in Vilnius. The common Baltic Yearbook of International Law (at Brill) has already reached its 22nd volume, demonstrating that by pulling together intellectual and other resources, the critical mass and visibility of the three Baltic States in the context of international law can be enhanced. In 2021, a representative of the Baltic States was for the first time elected a member of the ILC—Martins Paparinskis of Latvia.

The three Baltic States of Estonia, Latvia, and Lithuania are archetypical small States. For small States, the functioning of international law—which also supports the equal right of smaller States to exist—is an existential matter. In a certain sense, in their history the Baltic States have fulfilled a 'Western' cultural-political agenda—the equivalent of individual freedom in international relations is the freedom of peoples. When already endorsing the self-determination of peoples in international affairs, numerically smaller nations also have the right to claim and exercise that very self-determination. Clearly, this agenda of 'small but beautiful' goes ontologically against the imperial ideal for which no replacement has apparently been found in Russia. For example, Igor I Lukashuk, once Russia's member of the ILC (and with family roots in Ukraine), criticized the 'psychology of a small State, egoism of the weak, its irresponsibility'.[59] However, most people in the Baltic States tend to think that small States express something positive and enriching in the world. In a way, they contribute to the political diversity of the world, not mere fragmentation.

Notes

1. Cited in Paavo Palk, 'Eesti: väikeriigist advokaat' (Estonia: Small State Attorney), *Postimees*, 12 February 1998 <https://arvamus.postimees.ee/2535661/eesti-vaikeriigist-advokaat> accessed 26 October 2023.
2. Lithuania joined the UNSC in 2014–2015, Estonia in 2020–2021, while Latvia is currently a candidate for membership in 2026–2027.
3. Ants Piip, *Rahvusvaheline õigus* (International Law) (Akadeemiline Kooperatiiv 1936).
4. Lembit Lauri, *Kirjutamata memuaare VI* (Unwritten Memoirs) (Memoir of Tamara Kask-Skolimowska on her service in the Estonian MFA and then as a deportee to Siberia) (Perioodika 1991) 176.
5. Robert B. Strassler (ed.) *The Landmark Thucydides. A Comprehensive Guide to the Peloponnesian War* (Free Press 1996) 352.
6. Samuel P Huntington, *The Clash of Civilizations and the Remaking of World Order* (Simon & Schuster 1996) 159 (map 'The Eastern boundary of Western civilization'). In the 19th century, books which emphasized Russia's cultural and political differences from Western Europe were widespread. See, eg, Victor Hehn, *De moribus Ruthenorum. Zur Charakteristik der russischen Volksseele. Herausgegeben von Theodor Schiemann* (Stuttgart Cotta 1892).
7. Baron Michel de Taube, 'Études sur le développement historique du droit international dans l'Europe orientale', 11 *RCADI (Recueil des cours de l'Académie de La Haye)* 452.
8. ibid, 462.
9. ibid, 466.
10. ibid, 468.
11. Balthasar Russow, *Liivimaa provintsi kroonika* (Chronicle of the Province of Livonia), trans Jüri Kivimäe (Tallinn Tänapäev 2022) 126 et seq. See further Margus Laidre, *Dorpat 1558–1708. Linn väe ja vaenu vahel* (Dorpat 1558–1708. City between Army and Animosity) (Tallinn Argo 2008) 38 et seq.
12. Olaus Hermelin, *Gerechte Ablehnung derer lassterhafften Beschuldigungen, womit der Moscowitische Czar seinen Krieg damit er Schweden wieder Eyd und noch neulich versicherte Treu und Glauben angegriffen zu beschönigen gesuchet hat* (Just Rejection of Vicious Accusations with which the Muscovite Tsar Has Attempted to Gloss Over Its War Attacking Sweden against Oath and Recently Assured Good Faith) Nach dem Lateinischen Original ins Deutsche übersetzt (Stockholm 1701).
13. P P Shafirov, *A Discourse Concerning the Just Causes of the War between Sweden and Russia: 1700–1721*, with an introduction by W E Butler (Dobbs Ferry, NY Oceana Publications 1973).

14. V E Grabar, *The History of International Law in Russia 1647–1917. A Bio-Bibliographical Study*, trans and ed WE Butler (Clarendon Press 1990) 76 et seq.
15. Karsten Brüggemann, Mati Laur, and Pärtel Piirimäe (eds), *Die baltischen Kapitulationen von 1710. Kontext—Wirkungen—Interpretationen* (Wien Böhlau 2014).
16. See further Boris E Nolde, *Ocherki Russkago Gosudarstvennago Prava* (St Petersburg Pravda 1911), 331–410.
17. Carl Schirren, *Livländische Antwort an Herrn Juri Samarin* (Leipzig Duncker & Humblot 1869); Anonymous, *Rechtskraft und Rechtsbruch der liv- und estländischen Privilegien* (Leipzig Duncker & Humblot 1887) 7.
18. MFA Russia (@mfa_russia) Twitter account, 15 September 2022.
19. See TASS (Russian news agency), 'Estonian Foreign Ministry Summons Russian Ambassador Over Putin's Comments on Narva', 10 June 2022 <https://tass.com/world/1463735> accessed 26 October 2023.
20. F F Martens, *Sovremennoe mezhdunarodnoe pravo tsivilizovannykh narodov*, Vol I (1st edn 1882, St Petersburg; Moscow Iuridicehskii kolledzh MGU 1996) 121.
21. Pekka Erelt, 'Eesti vabadust kuulutanud Vene ministrit kanti Tallinnas kätel' (The Russian Minister Who Proclaimed Estonia's Freedom Was Carried on People's Hands in Tallinn), *Eesti Ekspress*, 12 April 2017 <https://ekspress.delfi.ee/artikkel/77815440/eestile-vabadust-kuulutanud-vene-ministrit-kanti-tallinnas-katel> accessed 26 October 2023.
22. Esthonia and the Soviet Republic of Russia; Peace Treaty, signed at Tartu, 2 February 1920, XI LNTS 1922, No 289, 29–71; Lithuania and Soviet government of Russia, Peace Treaty and protocol, signed at Moscow, 12 July 1920, LNTS 1921, No 94, 106–137; Latvia and Russia; Treaty of Peace, done at Moscow, and completed and signed at Riga, 11 August 1920, LNTS 1920–1921, No 67, 195–231.
23. The advisory opinion of the ICJ on the status of the Chagos islands discusses the customary international law status of the right of peoples to self-determination in the 1960s but does not mention even in passing the earlier East European treaties recognizing this right. See ICJ, *Legal Consequences of the Separation of the Chagos Archipelago from Mauritius in 1965*, advisory opinion of 25 February 2019, 142 et seq.
24. See, eg, *Question de Vilna. Consultations de MM A. de Lapradelle, Louis le Fur et André N. Mandelstam concernant la force obligatoire de la décision de la Conférence des Ambassadeurs du 15 Mars 1923* (Paris Jouve 1928).
25. See Charlotte Alston, *Antonius Piip, Zigfrīds Meierovics and Augustinas Voldemaras. The Baltic States* (Haus Publishing Ltd 2010).
26. André N Mandelstam, *Mémoire sur la délimitation des droits de l'État et de la nation d'après la doctrine du Président Wilson* (Paris Imprimerie Polyglotte Hugonis 1919), 48–67.
27. A Piip, 'Esthonia and the League of Nations' in *Transactions of the Grotius Society*, Vol VI (London British Institute of International and Comparative Law 1920) 35–44.
28. See, eg, *Latvie (Lettonie). Mémoire presenté par la délégation latvienne à l'Assamblée de la Société de Nations* (Riga 1921), arguing *inter alia* that the country was 'peuplé par une race aryenne très pure', 3.
29. Piip (n 3) 40–41. See also Jüri Uluots, *Die Verträge der Esten mit den Fremden im XIII. Jahrhundert* (Tartu Akadeemiline Kooperatiiv 1937).
30. Mohammed Bedjaoui, 'Problèmes récents de succession d'états dans les états nouveaux', 130 RCADI 1970, 467.

31. *La Lettonie. État actuel et possibilités d'avenir d'une des républiques baltiques. Manuel pour les économistes, les diplomates et les journalistes composé par les soins de la délégation lettonne à la conférence de Génes* (Riga Imprimerie d'Etat 1922) 17.
32. Baron A Heyking, *The Main Issues Confronting the Minorities of Latvia and Eesti* (London PS King & Son 1922).
33. See Malborne W Graham, 'The Diplomatic Recognition of the Border States. Part II: Estonia', 3 *Publications of the University of California at Los Angeles in Social Sciences* 1939, 231–398.
34. George F Kennan, *Memoirs (1925–1950)* (Boston Little, Brown 1967) 25 et seq.
35. eg Kennan thought that in post-1917 Estonia and Latvia, because of the Bolshevik transformation of Russia 'more of pre-revolutionary Russia was still present than in Russia proper', ibid, 50.
36. Gregor Rutenberg, *Die baltischen Staaten und das Völkerrecht. Die Entstehungspobleme Litauens, Letlands u. Estlands im Lichte des Völkerrechts* (Riga Loeffler 1928) 115.
37. ibid.
38. C R Pusta, 'Le statut juridique de la mer baltique a partir du XIXe siècle', 52 RCADI 1935, 106–188.
39. Jacob Robinson, *Das Minoritätenproblem und seine Literatur. Kritische Einführung in die Quellen und die Literatur der europäischen Nationalitätenfrage der Nachkriegszeit, unter besonderer Berücksichtigung des völkerrchtlichen Minderheitenschutzes. Allgemeiner Teil* (Berlin Duncker & Humblot 1928); Jacob Robinson, *Minorities and the League of Nations* (American Council of Public Affairs 1941).
40. See Omry Kaplan-Feuereisen, 'Jacob Robinson', *The YIVO Encyclopedia of Jews in Eastern Europe* <https://yivoencyclopedia.org/article.aspx/robinson_jacob> accessed 26 October 2023.
41. See also Jacob Robinson, *Kommentar der Konvention über das Memelgebiet vom 8. Mai 1924*, 2 vols (Kaunas Spaudos Fondas 1924).
42. PCIJ, *Interpretation of the Statute of the Memel Territory*; *Britain, France, Italy, Japan v Lithuania*, General list No 50, Judgment of 11 August 1932.
43. PCIJ, *Panevezys-Saldutiskis Railway Case, Estonia v Lithuania*, Judgment of 28 February 1939, Series A/B No 76.
44. The approximate numbers are 10,000 for Estonia, 15,000 for Latvia, and 17,500 for Lithuania.
45. See further Francine Hirsch, *Soviet Judgment at Nuremberg. A New History of the International Military Tribunal after World War II* (OUP 2020).
46. Kaarel Piirimäe, *Roosevelt, Churchill, and the Baltic Question. Allied Relations During the Second World War* (Palgrave Macmillan 2014).
47. William JH Hough, III, 'The Annexation of the Baltic States and Its Effect on the Development of Law Prohibiting Forcible Seizure of Territory', 6 New York Law School Journal of International and Comparative Law 1985, 301–533.
48. See, eg, August Rei (ed), *Nazi-Soviet Conspiracy and the Baltic States. Diplomatic Documents and Other Evidence* (London Boreas Publishing Co 1948); Aleksander Kaelas, *Human Rights and Genocide in the Baltic States* (Stockholm Estonian Information Centre 1950).
49. Krystyna Marek, *Identity and Continuity of States in Public International Law* (Geneva Librairie E Droz 1954); Boris Meissner, *Die Sowjetunion, die baltischen Staaten und das Völkerrecht* (Verlag für Politik und Wirtschaft 1956).

50. Communist Takeover and Occupation of Estonia. Special Report No 3 of the Select Committee on Communist Aggression. H Res 346 and H Res 438, Washington, DC: 1955 (House select committee to investigate communist aggression and the forced incorporation of the Baltic States into the USSR (Charles J Kersten, Chairman)).
51. See, eg, ECtHR, Grand chamber, *Case of Savickis and Others v Latvia* (App no 49270/11), Judgment, 9 June 2022 (giving the right to the Latvian government but with several dissenting opinions). See also Grand Chamber, *Case of Andrejeva v Latvia* (App no 55707/00), Judgment, 18 February 2009 (another case concerning the interaction of the pension system with the State continuity claim; here violations of the ECHR were found). On the language of education, see Valiullina and Others v Latvia (Application no 56928/19 and 2 others), judgment, 14.09.2023. (Confirming that Latvia had not violated rights of Russian-speaking individuals when reforming the school education so that it would predominantly be in the Latvian language.)
52. See also Peter van Elsuwege, *From Soviet Republics to EU Member States. A Legal and Political Assessment of the Baltic States' Accession to the EU*, 2 vols (Brill 2008). (Note, however, that in their self-understanding, the Baltic States were never 'Soviet republics'; these were more like a camouflage by the Soviet occupation authorities.)
53. See, eg, Roman Goncharenko, 'Putin's Infamous History in Hamburg', DW, 7 March 2017 <https://www.dw.com/en/vladimir-putins-infamous-history-in-hamburg/a-39529602> accessed 26 October 2023.
54. See, eg, Andres Roth, 'Russian Court Orders Closure of Country's Oldest Human Rights Group', *Guardian*, 28 December 2021 <https://www.theguardian.com/world/2021/dec/28/russian-court-memorial-human-rights-group-closure> accessed 26 October 2023.
55. See, eg, ECtHR, Grand Chamber judgment of 17 May 2010, *Kononov v Latvia* (App no 36376/04); *Drelingas v Lithuania* (App no 28859/16), judgment of 12 March 2009.
56. ECtHR, Chamber decision of 24 January 2006, *Vladimir Penart v Estonia* (App no 14685/04); Chamber decision of 17 January 2006, joined applications of *August Kolk v Estonia* (App no 23052/04) and *Petr Kislyiy v Estonia* (App no 24018/04).
57. 'Putin: rossiiskie sudy i posle vykhoda iz ESPCh sposobny nadezhno zashchishchat' prava rossiian', *Kommersant*, 14 February 2023 <https://www.kommersant.ru/doc/5826146?query=%D0%95%D0%A1%D0%9F%D0%A7%20%D0%9F%D1%83%D1%82%D0%B8%D0%BD> accessed 26 October 2023.
58. Michael N Schmitt (ed), *Tallinn Manual 2.0 on the International Law Applicable to Cyber Operations* (CUP 2017).
59. Igor I Lukashuk, *Mezhdunarodnoe pravo. Obshtshaia chast'* (2nd edn, Moscow Beck 2001) 323.

CHAPTER 27

FRANCE

HÉLÈNE RUIZ FABRI AND EDOARDO STOPPIONI

1. Introduction

The role of international law in France today is torn between two poles. On the one hand, international law is perceived as a universal language French lawyers need to speak fluently, all the more so as globalizing trends are increasingly pervading domestic systems. On the other hand, as with any language, international law comes with its traditions and cultural connotations: French is no longer the *lingua franca* of international law, and France's colonial past of France is processed.

Understanding what 'international law in France' represents today requires, first, recollection of the fundamental historical role that France played in forming international law as a power able to shape it according to its own political needs at certain periods in time (Section 2). Indeed, the role of international law in the French legal system is closely tied to France's historical role in international law (Section 3). Last, but not least, we need to grasp the particular understanding of international law that has shaped the way lawyers are educated in international law in France and, therefore, a certain French vision of international law (Section 4).

2. France in the History of International Law

2.1 Ancien Régime

The history of the emergence of an international legal language in the late Middle Ages in Europe reveals a complex power struggle. Sovereignty was crafted as a tool to empower some political entities and reject claims of domination from others. During the 13th century, the Burgundian jurist Jean de Blanot claimed that '*Rex Franciae in regno suo princeps est*' (the King of France is sovereign in his kingdom). The intention is clear: 'to be the emperor in his reign therefore made the King of France equal to the emperor' of the Holy Roman Empire and empowered him against the Pope.[1] Yet this equality remained theoretical as it was not conceived as being either reciprocal or mutual, as attested by the failure of the international court set up to mediate peace among European kings. 'A sovereign king like the King of France, Louis XI (1423–83), nominated as the president of the international court, was by no means willing to accept equality if it meant that he himself was to be part of a group of others.'[2]

The concept of sovereignty was first and foremost used as a basis for expansion. For a long time, historians of diplomacy saw the French invasions of Northern Italy in 1494, with the establishment of the first formal embassies, as a turning point. Similarly, Francis I's opposition to the Treaty of Tordesillas, which had left the domination of South American lands to Spain and Portugal only, epitomized the French colonization launched at that time.[3]

According to Grewe, the Peace of Westphalia (1648) strengthened the influence of its two guarantors, France and Sweden, against the Holy Roman Empire. Instead of bringing in an era of peace, it reinforced Louis XIV's position to embark on wars of expansion. Grewe defines this period as the 'French Age', where the French Empire launched aggressive acts against all its neighbours.[4] Networks of diplomats constituted yet another major instrument of this hegemonic expansion strategy, as witnessed by the *Recueil des instructions données aux ambassadeurs de France*: 'unlike many other States, France also dispatched diplomats to smaller courts, courts that it considered important for political or strategic reasons. It was a policy most other States could not afford.'[5]

According to historians, this balance of powers shifted with the Seven Years' War (1756–1763), which some identify as the fundamental cause of the French Revolution. Revolutionaries (generally invoking Vattel's scholarship[6]) used international law to advance France's influence: together with concluding neutrality treaties to allow their troops to cross neutral territories and defending the idea of 'natural borders', they 'took an active interest in the right to intervention, arguably to ensure freedom and human rights, in reality, to extend French hegemony'.[7]

The Revolution transformed progressively into Napoleonic hegemony, which ended in 1815 with the Congress of Vienna, dramatically reducing the hegemonic stance of France. Widespread political instability characterized the period between 1815 and the Third Republic. Historians commonly described it as a dark moment in French history, with profound changes and the slow metabolization of a democratic spirit that would flourish only with the coming of the Third Republic. As far as external relations were concerned, Napoleon III started a paradigm shift (known as the *Empire libéral*), pushing for the reconsideration of trade protectionism and mercantilism, favouring the conclusion of international free-trade agreements.[8] Colonial expansion and military activism led to the Paris Treaty of 1856 and Napoleon III claiming he had restored France to the great European powers.

2.2 Third Republic (1870–1940) and Fourth Republic (1944–1958)

In the fourth chapter of his *Gentle Civilizer*, Martti Koskenniemi underlined that a 'striking aspect of French international law towards the end of the nineteenth century was its ability to connect a cosmopolitan outlook with an impeccably patriotic alignment behind French interests', given that the political attitude at the time was to 'identify the French nation through the universal principles of the Revolution'.[9]

Historians have shown that international lawyers' discourse at the end of the 19th and beginning of the 20th century centred around the transposition of the pacifists of the *Belle époque*'s ideas on law.[10] The emergence of this notion of *paix par le droit* remained limited in scope, as the colonial appetite of the Third Republic shows. Moreover, a certain reluctance hampered a general pacifist engagement in international law. Louis Renault, who together with Léon Bourgeois played a central role in the development of international humanitarian law and rules for international dispute settlement mechanisms during the Hague Conferences of 1899 and 1907, expressed reticence towards a '*société de la paix*'.[11] Renault was one of the recipients of the 1907 Nobel Peace Prize.

The French approach to creating the League of Nations evolved dramatically in a short period of time. Initially, although France was one of the worst affected countries at the end of World War I, the French government was highly sceptical about the idea of an international organization such as the League. Aristide Briand, for instance, increased war censorship concerning all 'peace through law' initiatives.[12] It was only in 1915–1916 that the Socialist party advanced the founding ideas of the League of Nations, together with non-governmental organizations (NGOs) like the *Ligue des droits de l'homme*.[13] Prime Minister Ribot appointed Léon Bourgeois to the French committee considering setting up the League. In 1918, France submitted a draft Covenant establishing the architecture of the international organization to the American president Woodrow Wilson. Thanks to his activism during the peace conferences, Bourgeois received the Nobel Peace Prize in 1920,[14] although, curiously enough, his name is no longer significant to French international lawyers. Because France eventually played such a vital role advocating in favour of the League, it was able to secure the participation of one of its representatives in the Committee of Jurists who drafted the Statute of the Permanent Court of International Justice: Albert de Geouffre de La Pradelle, who had inherited Renault's chair at the University of Paris, participated in the drafting of the Statute, defending his rather positivist positions.[15]

The political evolutions of the inter-war period greatly influenced France's stance in the international arena. In the area of peace and security, France was initially excluded from the UN negotiation process despite its role in establishing the League of Nations. Several political reasons explained this initial absence: France's complicated military situation, its defeat by Germany starting in 1940, and the suspicions that the 'Big Three' nurtured against the directive figure of Charles de Gaulle. With the establishment of a new government and the 'Fourth Republic', Churchill convinced the other powers, the

US and USSR, to restore France's role within the UN process, hence its permanent seat on the United Nations Security Council (UNSC) today.[16]

In the specific area of international trade, the figure of Alexandre Kojève is somewhat emblematic. A Hegelian philosopher and civil servant, he played a central role in the negotiations of the European Communities treaties as well as the GATT. Initially, 'colonialism, if appropriately reformed, was touted by Kojève as the wave of the future' to shape French trade policy. However, in time, he adapted to the decolonization processes and 'spent his last years calling for a more equitable global trade architecture, collaborating with noted dependency theorists and siding at the GATT Kennedy negotiations (1964–1967) with developing nations'.[17]

2.3 Fifth Republic (from 1958 to today)

The Constitution of the Fifth Republic of 1958 resulted directly from the colonial war in Algeria. The chronic governmental instability that characterized the Fourth Republic made it impossible to settle such crises, as the war in Indochina had already shown. De Gaulle's ideas greatly influenced the new constitutional text, reinstating a robust executive power with a President of the Republic at its head. This led to the core decisions concerning foreign policy, as a '*domaine réservé*' at the margins of the Constitution, being assigned to the president. In sum, the political vision of the President of the Republic became a fundamental factor that influenced the evolution of French positions in international law. It might also explain the rather paternalistic approach to decolonization, which was viewed as a difficult process.[18]

De Gaulle is well known for his defence of French sovereignty, which translated into the vision of a '*Europe des Nations*' as opposed to a more federalist approach towards European integration. This turned into the '*politique de la chaise vide*' when more integration of the European Economic Community (EEC) was discussed, and France's repeated use of the veto regarding the UK's accession because of the British conception of the EEC as a market rather than a political project. De Gaulle is also remembered for the 'cold' relationship between France and the United Nations. In the same spirit, in 1969, France was the only State of the 120 negotiating the Vienna Convention on the Law of Treaties (VCLT) that refused to sign it.[19] The uncertainty surrounding the concept of *ius cogens* that the Convention consecrates as positive law lies at the heart of this rejection, which still holds today. Even in 2000, an advisory opinion of the *Conseil d'État* to the government reaffirmed the concerns that the French delegation had already voiced during the *travaux préparatoires*.[20]

De Gaulle's approach faded as time passed. President Valéry Giscard d'Estaing ended the cold approach towards the UN, heralding a new era in the relationship. This also translated into a push for a 'reasonable use' of the power of the veto and contested the use of the Acheson resolution transferring the power to decide peacekeeping operations from the UNSC to the General Assembly.[21] France's stance continued along these lines, most notably with Dominique de Villepin's famous speech concerning Iraq in 2003, asking the UN to resist the American push for unilateral action and recalling the importance of multilateralism. Accordingly, the UNSC should maintain its powers to evaluate the need for a proportionate response and not become an *ex-post* validator of unilateral actions.[22] This position led to criticism of France's hypocritical attitude, which had not opposed the legality of the Acheson resolution strongly enough but avoided mentioning it in later resolutions, or claiming the need to prevent unilateralism but intervening unilaterally in Mali in 2013 at the request of this State.

The fact that France is a country which believes in international law has been part and parcel of the mainstream discourse of French diplomacy since the 1970s. Thus, France, the second maritime power in the world thanks to its overseas territories, claims to have been at the forefront of the preparatory work on the UN Convention of the Law of the Sea (UNCLOS) (1982–1994). The Convention is seen as allowing mining and fishing interests to flourish while striking a balance between the appropriation of oceans and the protection of fundamental freedoms within them.[23] In the 1980–1990s, a robust French-led campaign defended the idea of an obligation to intervene in cases of catastrophe with the well-known '*droit d'ingérence*', the predecessor of the responsibility to protect (R2P). Just as it had strongly supported the establishment of ad hoc criminal tribunals by the UNSC, France also supported the 1998 Rome Statute establishing the International Criminal Court, even though it used the opt-out clause for war crimes under Article 124 of the Statute and the fact that the ratification process of the Statute was slowed down by the need to modify the 1958 French Constitution.[24] Later, France was among the first States to ratify the 2004 United Nations Convention on Jurisdictional Immunities of States and Their Property, which the Court of cassation had already started to apply even before its entry into force.[25]

A large number of scholars believe in the French influence on international law and consistently hold the view that France believes in international law, largely participates in international conventions, and applies them in national law: 'France is a *status quo* power, satisfied with the whole current state of international law, that preserves its interests and role'.[26]

3. International Law in the French Legal Order

The relationship between the international and national legal systems has long been considered a central issue in French academia.[27] From an historical perspective, a dual movement stands out: the French constitutional framework evolved from strong dualism towards nuanced monism, whereas the national judges' approach to international law evolved from their reluctance to adopt a more open position.

3.1 From dualism to monism: the constitutional attitude towards international law

In a well-known article published in 1964, Virally denounced what he considered a dialogue of the deaf as a response to the heated debates opposing dualism and monism. Instead of looking at the pluralist evolutions of the interactions between international and national law, these debates resulted in an exaggerated opposition between the two approaches and transformed into a *pons asinorum* ('bridge of asses').[28]

During the Third Republic (1870–1940), French foreign policy was mostly focused on its colonial objectives, as evidenced by the first issues of the *Revue générale de droit international public* where 'it almost seems as if international law's field of application was between European powers acting *outside* Europe—as if intra-European questions concerned policy and commerce, but not of law'.[29] This general atmosphere may explain why the French legal system envisaged international law in terms of pure dualism, with international treaties having no direct effect.[30] The Constitutional Laws of 1875 invested the President of the Republic with the exclusive power to conduct international negotiations and conclude treaties.

This dualist stance was reversed with the Fourth Republic (1944–1958), which introduced a rather generalized monist approach towards international norms, as manifested in paragraph 14 of the Preamble[31] and Article 26 of the 1946 Constitution.[32] In this context, the *Conseil d'État* (the Administrative Supreme Court) evolved and admitted the invocability of an extradition treaty against an administrative act breaching its provisions, even though the national measure conformed with national law.[33] In parallel, the constitution allotted the power to conclude treaties to the prime minister in conformity with the general spirit of reducing the powers of the President of the Republic.[34]

The stance of the 1958 Constitution towards international law results from this historical evolution. Meant to restore the stability that the previous Constitution had failed to provide, especially when facing colonial wars, the new Constitution gave back to the President of the Republic the core of treaty-making power (Article 52) while foreseeing the case of 'agreements not submitted to ratification' to the Minister of Foreign Affairs. All the same, the 1958 Constitution is said to perpetuate the monist choice through its Article 55: 'Treaties or agreements duly ratified or approved shall, upon publication, prevail over Acts of Parliament, subject, with respect to each agreement or treaty, to its application by the other party'. However, to a certain extent, Article 54 indirectly maintains the primacy of the constitution[35] by foreseeing a mechanism to prevent conflicts between the constitution and international treaties. This provision allows the *Conseil constitutionnel* (Constitutional Council) to be seized to assess the compatibility of an international agreement with the constitution before its ratification or approbation. In case of incompatibility, the agreement can be ratified or approved only after a constitutional revision, which practice shows is kept to the minimum required level, for example, by introducing an exception covering the agreement (as was the case for ratifying the Statute of the International Criminal Court). Article 54 case law has changed considerably over time. A first, highly criticized approach consisted in distinguishing authorized 'sovereignty limitations' from prohibited 'sovereignty transfers'.[36] However, today, the *Conseil constitutionnel* seeks to verify whether the international agreement infringes 'essential conditions for the exercise of sovereignty'.[37]

3.2 From rejection to acceptance: the international legal argument in national courts

The issue of the application of international norms by national courts is a fundamental part of the discussion. In his theory of *dédoublement fonctionnel* (role splitting), Georges Scelle famously underlined how the function of the national judge is fundamental in applying international law, with account taken of the particularism of the international legal order.[38]

French authors generally depict the evolution of the a posteriori control of conformity of internal law with international law norms as moving from reluctance to progressive acceptance. This shift is less visible for non-written international norms, which are still subject to some rejection, than for treaties.

As far as the traditional French discourse on international customary law goes, despite the lack of clarity of the constitutional framework, customary rules can produce some effects in the domestic legal order, but their hierarchical position is not as solidly grounded as it is for treaties.[39] The *Conseil constitutionnel* declined to incorporate international customary law into the '*bloc de constitutionnalité*' (ie all norms of constitutional value) in 1975. Only customary rules codified in the constitution would be a parameter of constitutionality control of French laws (eg the right to self-determination).[40] The *Conseil d'État* followed suit, clarifying in its 1997 *Aquarone* decision[41] that Article 55 of the Constitution does not encompass international customary law. The latter is nevertheless part of the legality parameters that the administrative judge must consider. The case law of the Court of cassation does not follow such a clear-cut line. The Court has applied international customary law (concerning crimes against humanity) at least since the *Barbie* case in 1983.[42] Still, the limitation that unwritten law cannot be the sole legal basis for criminal charges derives from the principle of strict interpretation of criminal law.[43]

Regarding treaty law, the abovementioned Article 55 clearly establishes the primacy of treaty norms over sub-constitutional national norms, which triggered friction regarding the integration of European Union (EU) law. Admittedly, the primacy doctrine obliged the French legal order to open up. Still, national courts followed a relatively minimalist approach which also had some bearing on the opening up to international law. The milestone decision framing the judges' role in applying the so-called '*contrôle de conventionnalité*' (conventionality control) is the 1975 *IVG* decision of the *Conseil constitutionnel*.[44] The latter opted for self-restraint and considered it to be up to the judiciary to verify the conformity of national laws with international treaties (mainly because of the structural difference between constitutionality and conventionality control). The *Cour de cassation* immediately followed suit with its 1975 *Jacques Vabre* decision,[45] while the *Conseil d'État* was more reluctant and waited until the 1989 *Nicolo* decision[46] to do the same. Generally speaking, this entailed a progressive empowerment of the judiciary concerning the application of international law. Following in the footsteps of the *Cour de cassation*, which had linked treaty interpretation to its judicial function,[47] the administrative judge stopped deferring to the Ministry of Foreign Affairs to interpret treaties and began to accept its own role as treaty interpreter,[48] clearly stating that it would follow the rules of public international law.[49] Both courts also progressively agreed to verify the formal regularity of treaty incorporation.[50] However, despite this continuous opening up of the French legal order to conventionality control, both courts recalled the superiority of the constitution in the domestic order.[51]

This evolution shows how national judges shaped and transformed constitutional choices. They introduced nuances in the constitutional text's option for monism with international law primacy, either by way of reluctance as shown by the *Conseil constitutionnel* (explicit in *IVG* or *Autodétermination des Comores*) or through the reassertion of the constitution's primacy.[52] Following this line of reasoning, national judges developed a certain dualist attitude to accommodate the primacy of the constitution in the national order with the primacy of EU law in the supranational order, building a subtle test based on the presumption of equivalent protection.[53] For that reason, instead of blindly following the simple story of progressive judicial opening up towards international law, it is far more interesting to highlight the political choices of national judges, making the reading of the constitution evolve and constructing theories to adjust their point of view in a context of increasingly multi-level constitutionalism. In light of this, it is interesting to note that there was no particular resistance towards the European Convention on Human Rights (ECHR) or any singling out of this instrument in the context of the conventionality control.[54]

4. International Law in French Legal Academia

Understanding a particular area requires figuring out how the people working within it form their opinions and what their cultural imprinting is. French sociologists like Pierre Bourdieu[55] and Bruno Latour[56] carried out a remarkable such investigation in the legal field.

4.1 French international law tradition

Distilling the characteristics of a national tradition is an arduous task. Emmanuelle Jouannet's work richly contributes to it.[57] In her view, because of the important scepticism regarding the very existence of an 'international law' (as witnessed in the writings of Raymond Aron[58]), the need for justification translated into the construction of a highly technical approach to the science of international law and the consequent generalization of positivism. From this point on, French doctrinal positions tend to marginalize alternative theoretical approaches and prefer technical to highly theoretical debates. Methodologically speaking, a certain 'pragmatism' (in the sense of interest to discuss international law as it is or of fidelity to what is real) stands out. Therefore, the core of the theoretical debates is how to conceive international law as a system and its functioning.[59]

Martti Koskenniemi also identifies positivism as a common feature of renowned French international lawyers, which started to become hegemonic in academia from the Renault era.[60] Even though harshly challenged in the 1940–1960s, it survived and was vigorously reaffirmed by Charles Rousseau and Suzanne Bastid.

This feature is not specific to the international law field. Even today, it characterizes all French legal academia: more than 'positivism' as the dominant, if not sole, approach to law, the particular trait of (most) French academics is the attention they devote exclusively to positive and black letter law. This trend has increasingly obscured the prestige of legal philosophy and theory to the point where 'the very expression "French philosophy of law" has long sounded like an oxymoron, and it still does'.[61]

During the first macro-phase of French international legal tradition, Renault managed to raise a cohort of disciples who strictly followed the vision of their master: Albert de Geouffre de La Pradelle inherited Renault's chair, Renault asked Paul Fauchille to edit a new edition of Henri Bonfils' textbook, Jules Basdevant replicated the pragmatic approach of his master, and Gilbert Gidel carried on this trend regarding the law of the sea. Together they represent what can be called the 'Renault era'.[62]

Nevertheless, prominent alternative visions arose. This dominant positivism was challenged by Duguit's sociological approach, as well as by Georges Scelle's doctrine or Louis Le Fur's natural law approach. The latter's work evolved at the margins of the positivist approach to international law. He did not deny the importance of positivism as a method but highlighted the limits of this widespread vision. He considered that equating it with a sole and ineluctable key to thinking the international legal system transformed positivism into a 'philosophy for the short-sighted'.[63] His proposal for the revival of a natural law understanding of the international order was anchored in some fundamental principles of law and morality: *neminem laedere*, *honeste vivere*, *suum cuique tribuere*, and *pacta sunt servanda*. But this vision, together with his solid Catholic faith and political beliefs, led him to refute the merits of a republican regime, and to support the Nazi Germany and Franco's regimes for the birth of a new Europe.

At the University of Paris, Le Fur was preferred to his contemporary Georges Scelle, who had developed a very personal understanding of international law, questioning the dogma of its inter-State nature to see it instead as a tool at the service of the human being. Having taught labour law and agricultural law for several years, Scelle looked at international law from below and questioned the sharp distinction between the international and the national legal order. His theory of *dédoublement fonctionnel* or his criticisms of the obnoxious nature of the law of State immunities are milestones for international legal theory.[64] The beauty of a refined and sharp style is also part of Scelle's appeal to numerous French international lawyers, even though his theories were received very harshly at that time.

A second macro-phase opened up with the creation of the *Annuaire français de droit international* by Charles Rousseau in 1955 and of the *Société française pour le droit international* by Suzanne Bastid in 1967. Hereafter, publications and conferences tended to privilege the positive method to which these lawyers adhered. Indeed, Rousseau's textbook clearly defended a 'strictly positive method purged of all naturalism—if not of all theory'.[65] Similarly, the pride with which her students praise Suzanne Bastid's unwillingness to engage in theoretical quarrels or to attempt to shape the international legal system is noticeable.[66]

International lawyers at that time (eg Paul Reuter, Michel Virally, and Prosper Weil) adhered to this general doctrinal posture. What Robert Kolb called Reuter's love for the 'small detail',[67] Virally's focus on distinguishing between law and non-law, *lex lata* and *lex ferenda*,[68] or Prosper Weil's theory of relative normativity in international law, all bear witness to this.[69]

The exceptions are in the minority, be it the approach of the *Ecole de Reims* or the humanist approach of René-Jean Dupuy. Dupuy was a student of Scelle, from whom he inherited a strong affinity with the ideas of humanity and community in international law.[70] In Reims, Charles Chaumont built a circle of intellectuals who explored international law with a materialist analysis inspired by the writings of Marx and Hegel and aimed at demystifying international norms and their concrete functioning. In so doing, Chaumont most notably highlighted a paradigmatic shift in contemporary international law, no longer being a law between governing powers but including the emergence of peoples, of the dominated and of the subjugated, who might progressively question the existing balances in international society.[71] These approaches nevertheless remained in a minority, and today's academia is solidly grounded on a deep belief in the ineluctability of the positivist dogma. Trends of thought associated with an interdisciplinary 'Law and … '-approach (be it culture, society, gender, etc) have only a marginal echo in France, and significantly few legal academics would openly associate themselves with such trends. Critical Legal Studies and their international law sequels are known and have few experts, but authors like Derrida or Bourdieu are barely studied and even less cited by French lawyers. This also explains a somewhat fragmented approach to epistemic communities, with lawyers showing more reluctance than others to engage with their political science colleagues.

4.2 Doctrinal trends in French textbooks

As the means by which each generation of students first comes into contact with the discipline, textbooks are a powerful tool to convey a certain vision or approach to international law to a broader audience. Because of this generational effect, the influence of textbooks tends to evolve rapidly over time. For instance, the book *La politique juridique extérieure* by former *Conseil d'État* and International Court of Justice (ICJ) judge Guy de Lacharrière[72] played a fundamental role in shaping the vision of international law in France in the 1980s: its idea to describe how the politics of international relations shape international law (rather than the more common opposite approach) had a great impact on French scholarship even if it is a rather neglected work nowadays, although it has recently been re-edited.[73]

In 1994, a Canadian observer described the French textbook market as follows:

> The two most widely used general texts (précis) are those published by Dalloz and the Presses Universitaires de France. Under the pen of two great scholars, Charles Rousseau and Paul Reuter, these texts on the general principles of public international law have provided the first (and often the only) access to the discipline for many thousands of students and practitioners of public international law in France during the last fifty years.[74]

The textbook by Rousseau was passed on to Pierre-Marie Dupuy, who was later joined by Yann Kerbrat, and is still widely used, while the one by Paul Reuter was passed on to Jean Touscoz and finished with him. Other books emerged at that time, which became the mainstream references: the textbook co-authored by Hubert Thierry, Serge Sur, Jean Combacau, and Charles Vallée, whose later editions were authored by Combacau and Sur, on the one hand, and, on the other, the international law treaty by Nguyen Quoc Dinh which was passed on to Patrick Daillier and Alain Pellet, who were later joined by Mathias Forteau and Alina Miron.

Anthony Carty, who has worked extensively on the view conveyed in French international law publications, suggests a kind of *summa divisio*. He presents the work by Combacau and Sur as depicting a 'conservative' vision of international law. In this vision, States remain the centre of gravity of the study, following in the footsteps of a cultural approach dating back to Jean Bodin. Secondly, Carty identifies opposing strands of French international legal thinking. In his view, the treatise by Daillier, Forteau, and Pellet carries the 'implicit ambition of offering an alternative vision of France in the world' and of the 'realization of integration of each state in the objective world of an international community', even though this ambition is limited as the authors show several 'reservations about both Le Fur and Scelle' and 'conclude on a rather amorphous note that law has to be understood in its political, economic and social context'.[75] Carty also includes the works by Pierre-Marie Dupuy in the 'progressive' approach.

From the perspective of textbooks, a peculiar trend is revealed in the teaching of international law in France, which is the generalized attention paid to State practice in the presentation of the discipline. Meanwhile, marginal importance is paid to the history or philosophy of international law or the presentation of different approaches to international law.

4.3 Contemporary French academia

In her book on parochial approaches to international law, Anthea Roberts defined a sort of 'nationalized French approach' in international law academia that she opposes (in quite a caricatural way) to the much more internationalized and open posture of Sciences Po Paris. The latter is presented as a hub of openness and internationalism compared to closed and old-fashioned ordinary law schools.

Some factors play a significant role in the construction of such a nationalized approach: (1) the modalities of access to the academic profession; (2) the national tropism in publications ('the French international law academics published approximately 88 per cent of their articles in domestic French-language journals. Within this group, about 65 per cent of the papers appeared in specialist international law journals'[76]); (3) the number of foreigners recruited to academic posts; and (4) the role played by the French language.

Concerning access to academic positions, it should be stressed that French international lawyers are traditionally public lawyers and do not have a thorough knowledge of private international law for instance, which is the domain of private lawyers. Even if the disciplinary barriers are progressively readjusting (notably concerning arbitration in economic matters), the public/private law divide is a strong tenet for understanding the discipline in France from a sociological perspective. International lawyers have to show more knowledge or interest in other public law topics for both the national competition to become a full professor (*concours d'agrégation*) or to be qualified as an assistant professor (*maître de conférences*). In this context, it is true that publications submitted in support of an application for a professorial position should generally be in French (or at least supported by a substantial summary in French). The situation is less closed-off than the book by Roberts seems to maintain: young international lawyers are increasingly active in English-speaking contexts and there is a growing awareness of the prestige of foreign journals or internationally well-known fora. It is nevertheless true, and very problematic, that many French international lawyers are not yet comfortable using English as a working language. It is clear that the requirement to speak French fluently discourages foreigners from applying for academic positions in France, but this seems less a peculiar feature of the French system than a basic necessity, which also exists in many other countries (UK or US universities would hardly welcome foreigners who are not proficient in their working language). Nevertheless, French universities are slowly introducing—and not without some resistance—law courses in English.

In addition, there is a significant number of foreigners among the young generation of international lawyers in French academia, many from other EU member States. Citizenship is irrelevant when compared to academic nationality: what is important is that they received at least part of their legal education in a French (more than a French-speaking) university. To be awarded a fully-funded PhD scholarship in France, an applicant usually needs to possess a top-ranking Master's degree with a research focus.

Only a dozen universities appear to be 'competitive' for international legal studies, at least in terms of critical mass. Generally, there is a clear-cut dichotomy in the minds of students and professors between the Parisian main universities (the '*Sorbonne*', ie the University of Paris 1 Panthéon-Sorbonne, '*Assas*', ie the University of Paris II Panthéon-Assas, and '*Nanterre*', ie the University of Paris X Nanterre La Défense), and '*la province*', an approach which matches the very centralized nature of the French State. Even though less evident today, undertaking legal research in international law is not always easy outside Paris in terms of access to bibliographical resources. This also explains the sociology of 'French international law', revolving around professors with chairs in the capital city or having contacts with the Ministry of Foreign affairs.

4.4 The influence of French academia abroad

Now that French is no longer the language of diplomacy, the *grandeur* that this entailed is no longer felt abroad. However, the domestic academic field seems willing to be convinced of the opposite and to function in a sometimes very self-contained fashion.

First, French international law journals do not generally use the method of blind peer-reviews and prefer to commission articles on topics selected by their editorial board or editor in chief. This is especially true for the *Annuaire français de droit international*, where the influence of the Ministry of Foreign Affairs on the editorial board is astonishingly strong, intervening even in the selection of topics. As a result, such topics are often strongly practice-oriented, normally based on recent decisions or events. This tendency is less true for the *Revue Générale de Droit International Public* or the *Journal du Droit International*, which accept spontaneous submissions but where peer-review, when it exists, is generally done internally within the board. Therefore, bibliometrics and impact factors remain foreign to the field.

Second, for the foreign observer, the intelligibility of French writings is not a given. One of the most striking features of the French approach towards law in general is the methodological customary rule of '*le plan en deux parties et deux sous-parties*': scholars present their reasoning (orally or in writing) in two parts, each being divided into two sub-parts (to a point which can look like systematic binarism to some eyes). This tradition seems to date back to the distant past, when lawyers had to write a dissertation on Roman law, in the first part and local *droit commun* in the second. Nevertheless, this methodological particularism today appears as a hurdle to foreigners, and this barrier is particularly strong concerning PhD theses.

Third, although the situation is changing, mastering English is not a requirement, and university classes in English are quite rare. Mastering French is an asset for EU lawyers because it remains the working language of the Court of Justice of the EU, but the ICJ and other international courts value the mastering of English, which means that clerkship opportunities for French academics are becoming less abundant.

Sociologically, a peculiar feature of French international law academics is their relatively scarce participation as judges in international courts and tribunals, investment arbitration seemingly being the only remaining open field. For a long time, the French Ministry of Foreign Affairs (the '*Quai d'Orsay*') appointed its civil servants to international delegations or courts, but the *Conseil d'État* took progressive control of positions as legal advisors, especially at ministries involved in international relations. The same holds true for international courts and tribunals, be it the ICJ, the European Court of Human Rights (ECtHR), the Court of Justice of the European Union (CJEU), and even the ICC, although a member of the *Cour de cassation* is from time to time elected to the ECtHR, and the French Advocate General at the Court of Justice is generally from the *Cour de cassation*.

In such a context, it is mainly through the role of counsel that French academic traditions can still shine bright in international dispute settlement arenas. However, at a time of increasing claims for more diversity, no historical position may be taken for granted. Even though there had always been a French member of the International Law Commission (ILC), traditionally an academic, this longstanding occurrence was recently interrupted before being reinstated.

Oscillating between the strong homeostatic reflex of tradition and the aspiration to universality, international law in France results from a mixture of different melodies playing together. There are several possible paths to harmony. French international lawyers should be eager to learn more about the tradition that preceded them: they should read it, question it, criticize it. However, and inevitably, they also have to deal with how international law is seen abroad, and the positions taken in the rest of the world—not necessarily to embrace them but not to be completely isolated from what happens elsewhere in dealing with the 'same' object. Awareness of this complexity constitutes fertile ground for useful new ideas.

Notes

1. M Kintzinger, 'From the Late Middle Ages to the Peace of Westphalia' in B Fassbender and A Peters (eds), *The Oxford Handbook of the History of International Law* (OUP 2012) 624.
2. ibid, 625.
3. J-F Haas, *Le Testament d'Adam* (Seuil 2017).
4. W G Grewe, *Epochen der Völkerrechtsgeschichte* (Nomos 1984) (hereafter Grewe, *Epochen der Völkerrechtsgeschichte*).
5. H Duchhardt, 'From the Peace of Westphalia to the Congress of Vienna' in B Fassbender and A Peters (eds), *The Oxford Handbook of the History of International Law* (OUP 2012) 647.
6. Grewe, *Epochen der Völkerrechtsgeschichte* (n 4) 381.
7. H Duchhardt, 'From the Peace of Westphalia to the Congress of Vienna' in B Fassbender and A Peters (eds), *The Oxford Handbook of the History of International Law* (OUP 2012) 649.

8. F Saint-Bonnet, 'Le combat pour les libertés publiques à la fin du Second Empire', 5 Jus Politicum 2010, at <http://juspoliticum.com/article/Le-combat-pour-les-libertes-publiques-a-la-fin-du-Second-Empire-288.html>
9. M Koskenniemi, *The Gentle Civilizer of Nations—The Rise and Fall of International Law 1870–1960* (CUP 2001) 270–271 (hereafter Koskenniemi, *The Gentle Civilizer of Nations*).
10. J-M Guieu, 'Les juristes internationalistes français, l'Europe et la paix à la Belle Époque', 1 Relations internationales 2012, 27–41.
11. Conférence de Louis Renault published in *Annales des sciences politiques*, 1908, 432.
12. Scott G Blair, *La France et le pacte de la Société des Nations (1914–1919* (doctoral thesis, Université Paris 1 Panthéon-Sorbonne, 1992) 24.
13. J-M Guieu, 'Pour la paix par la Société Des Nations', 2 Guerres mondiales et conflits contemporains 2006, 89–102.
14. Koskenniemi, *The Gentle Civilizer of Nations* (n 9) 294–295.
15. C Rousseau, 'Albert de Geouffre de La Pradelle', 7(2) Revue internationale de droit comparé, 1955, 383–384.
16. A Williams, 'France and the Origins of the United Nations, 1944–1945: Si La France ne compte plus, qu'on nous le dise', 28 Diplomacy & Statecraft 2017, 215–234.
17. D Scholz, 'From Colonialism to Third Worldism? Alexandre Kojève and the Developing Nations (1945–1968)', <https://rhetoric.berkeley.edu/events/from-colonialism-to-third-worldism-alexandre-kojeve-and-the-developing-nations-1945-1968/>; R Howse, 'Europe and the New World Order: Lessons from Alexandre Kojève's Engagement with Schmitt's "Nomos der Erde"', 19(1) Leiden Journal of International Law 2006, 93–103.
18. See De Gaulle's expression: 'la décolonisation est notre intérêt, et par consequent notre politique' (J Rioux, 'Point de vue–La décolonisation, cette histoire sans fin', 96 *Vingtième Siècle* 2007, 225–234). More broadly on French decolonization, see M M Mbengue, 'Decolonization: French Territories', MPEPIL, 2011.
19. H Ruiz Fabri, 'La France et la Convention de Vienne sur le droit des traités' in G Cahin, F Poirat, and S Szurek (eds), *La France et le droit international* (Pedone 2007), 137–167.
20. H Ruiz Fabri and E Stoppioni, 'Jus Cogens Before International Courts: The Mega-Political Side of the Story', 84 Law & Contemporary Problems 2021, 153.
21. T Tardy, 'La France et l'ONU, entre singularité et ambivalence', (4) Politique Étrangère., 2002, 942.
22. Y Daudet, 'La France et la cohérence du système des Nations Unies ;: bilan et perspectives', in G Cahin, F Poirat, S Szurek (eds), *La France et les organisations internationales*, Pedone, 2023, 222–227.
23. See the *travaux préparatoires* of the French law of ratification of UNCLOS. Senate, 'La France et la Convention des Nations Unies sur le droit de la mer', <https://www.senat.fr/rap/l95-021/l95-0211.html#fn4>
24. H Ruiz Fabri, 'La convention de Rome créant la Cour pénale internationale. Questions de ratification', 54 Revue internationale de droit comparé 2002, 441.
25. In the *NML* case, the Court of cassation used it as a justification for its requirement of a 'special' renunciation to the immunity of execution (even though the Convention only requires an explicit one): Civ. 1, 28 mars 2013, no 10-25.938; R Bismuth, in A Pellet and A Miron (eds), *Les grandes décisions de la jurisprudence française de droit international public* (Dalloz 2015) esp. 648 § 33 ff.
26. S Sur, 'L'influence française sur le droit international', discours prononcé devant l'Académie des sciences morales et politiques le lundi 7 octobre 2019, <https://www.afri-ct.org/2019/linfluence-francaise-sur-le-droit-international-par-serge-sur/>

27. See B Bonnet (ed), *Traité des rapports entre ordres juridiques* (LGDJ, Lextenso éditions 2016).
28. M Virally, 'Sur un pont-aux-ânes: les rapports entre droit international et droits internes' in Henri Rolin (ed), *Mélanges offerts à Henri Rolin: Problèmes de droit des gens* (Pedone 1964) 488 ff.
29. Koskenniemi, *The Gentle Civilizer of Nations* (n 9) 279.
30. See, eg, the seminal decision of the Conseil d'État, Assemblée, 28 May 1937, *Decerf*, requête numéro 54631, rec. p. 534.
31. 'La République française, fidèle à ses traditions, se conforme aux règles du droit public international. Elle n'entreprendra aucune guerre dans des vues de conquête et n'emploiera jamais ses forces contre la liberté d'aucun peuple.'
32. 'Les traités diplomatiques régulièrement ratifiés et publiés ont force de loi dans le cas même où ils seraient contraires à des lois françaises, sans qu'il soit besoin pour en assurer l'application d'autres dispositions législatives que celles qui auraient été nécessaires pour assurer leur ratification.'
33. Conseil d'État, Assemblée, 30 May 1952, *Dame Kirkwood*, requête numéro 16690, rec. p. 291.
34. Article 31 of the 1946 Constitution.
35. 'If the Constitutional Council, on a referral from the President of the Republic, from the Prime Minister, from the President of one or the other Houses, or from sixty Members of the National Assembly or sixty Senators, has held that an international undertaking contains a clause contrary to the Constitution, authorization to ratify or approve the international undertaking involved may be given only after amending the Constitution.'
36. Décision no 76-71 DC, 30 December 1976, *Décision du Conseil des communautés européennes relative à l'élection de l'Assemblée des Communautés au suffrage universel direct.*
37. Décision no 85-188 DC, 22 May 1985, *Protocole no 6 additionnel à la Convention européenne de sauvegarde des Droits de l'homme et des libertés fondamentales concernant l'abolition de la peine de mort, signé par la France le 28 avril 1983.*
38. G Scelle, '*Précis de droit des gens*', 43(I) Principes et systématique 1932, 54–56, 217; 'La doctrine de Léon Duguit et les fondements du droit des gens', *Archives de philosophie du droit et de sociologie juridique*, 1932, 83–119.
39. B Stirn, 'La place de la coutume internationale en droit public français', Colloque organisé le 21 septembre 2012 au Ministère des affaires étrangères sur *Le juge et la coutume internationale*, <https://www.conseil-etat.fr/actualites/discours-et-interventions/la-place-de-la-coutume-internationale-en-droit-public-francais>
40. Décision no 75-59 DC, 30 December 1975, *Loi relative aux conséquences de l'autodétermination des îles des Comores.*
41. Conseil d'État, Assemblée, 6 June 1997, 148683, published in *recueil Lebon*.
42. Cour de cassation, Chambre criminelle, 6 October 1983, 83-93.194, published in Bulletin.
43. Cour de cassation, Chambre criminelle, 17 June 2003, 02-80.719, *Aussaresses* published in Bulletin.
44. Décision no 74-54 DC, 15 January 1975, *Loi relative à l'interruption volontaire de la grossesse.*
45. Cour de cassation, Chambre mixte, 24 May 1975, 73-13.556, published in Bulletin.
46. Conseil d'État, Assemblée, 20 October 1989, 108243, published in *recueil Lebon*.
47. Cour de cassation, Chambre civile 1, 19 December 1995, 93-20.424, *Banque africaine de développement*, published in Bulletin.

48. Conseil d'État, Assemblée, 29 June 1990, 78519, *GISTI*, published in *recueil Lebon*.
49. Conseil d'État, Assemblée, 23 December 2011, 303678, *Kandyrine de Brito Pavia*, published in *recueil Lebon*.
50. Cour de cassation, Chambre civile 1, 29 May 2001, 99-16.673, *M N'Doye*, published in Bulletin; Conseil d'État, Assemblée, 18 December 1998, 181249, *Blotzheim*, published in *recueil Lebon*.
51. Conseil d'État, Assemblée, 30 October 1998, 200286 200287, *Sarran*, published in *recueil Lebon*; Cour de cassation, Assemblée plénière, 2 June 2000, 99-60.274, *Pauline Fresse*, published in Bulletin.
52. D Alland, 'Consécration d'un paradoxe: primauté du droit interne sur le droit international', *Revue française de droit administratif* 1998, 1094.
53. Décision no 2004-496 DC, 10 June 2004, *Loi pour la confiance dans l'économie numérique*; Conseil d'État, Assemblée, 8 February 2007, 287110, *Société Arcelor*, published in *recueil Lebon* (see the conclusions of the rapporteur public M Guyomar).
54. The *IVG* decision of the *Conseil constitutionnel* concerned the ECHR. Quite rapidly, French courts recognized the *res interpretata* value of the case law of the Court (see the conclusions of the *Commissaire du Gouvernement* Labetoulle under the *Debout* case of the *Conseil d'Etat*, 27 October 1978, 07103, published in *recueil Lebon*; or the *Dentico* case of the Court of cassation, 2 March 2001, 00-81.388, published in Bulletin).
55. P Bourdieu, 'La force du droit. Pour une sociologie du champ juridique', 64 Actes de la recherche en sciences sociales 1986, 6.
56. B Latour, *The Making of Law: An Ethnography of the Conseil d'État* (Polity 2010).
57. E Jouannet, 'French and American Perspectives on International Law: Legal Cultures and International Law', 58 Maine Law Review 2006, 292.
58. R Aron, *Paix et guerre entre les Nations* (Calman-Lévy 1961).
59. E Jouannet, 'Regards sur un siècle de doctrine française du droit international', 46 Annuaire français de droit international 2000, 1–57.
60. Koskenniemi, *The Gentle Civilizer of Nations* (n 9) 277.
61. P Brunet, V Champeil-Desplats, E Millard, C Miguel Herrera, J L Halpérin, and A J Arnaud, '20th-century Legal Philosophy in France' in E Pattaro (ed), *A Treatise of Legal Philosophy and General Jurisprudence* (Springer 2016) 411.
62. A Hamann, 'The French Tradition of International Law' in P Hilphold (ed), *European International Law Traditions* (Springer 2021) 137.
63. L Le Fur, 'La théorie du droit naturel depuis le XVIIIe siècle et la doctrine moderne', 18 Hague Academy Collected Courses 1927, 259–442.
64. G Scelle, *Précis de droit des gens—Principes et systématique*, vol I (Sirey 1932); G Scelle, *Précis de droit des gens–Principes et systématique*, vol II (Sirey 1934).
65. Koskenniemi, *The Gentle Civilizer of Nations* (n 9) 348.
66. A Pellet, 'Suzanne Bastid', at <http://www.sfdi.org/internationalistes/bastid/>
67. R Kolb, *Les cours généraux de droit international public de l'Académie de la Haye* (Bruylant 2003) 368.
68. D Bardonnet, 'In Memoriam: Michel Virally 1922–1989', 34 Annuaire français de droit international 1988, 11.
69. P Weil, 'Vers une normativité relative en droit international?', 86 Revue générale de droit international public 1982, 5–47.
70. R-J Dupuy, *L'Humanité dans l'imaginaire des nations* (Julliard 1991); R-J Dupuy, *La communauté internationale entre mythe et histoire* (Economica 1986).

71. Ch Apostolidis, *Doctrines juridiques et droit international* (Eyrolles 1991) 256–270; E Jouannet, 'La pensée juridique de Charles Chaumont', 1 RBDI 2004, 259–289.
72. G Ladreit de Lacharrière, *La Politique juridique extérieure* (Economica 1983) reedited by Bruylant in 2023 with a presentation by F Coulée..
73. D Alland, 'Quelques observations sur la notion de politique juridique de l'Etat', xiii Annuaire français de relations internationales 2012, 555–563.
74. A de Mestral, 'Droit international. By Jean Touscoz. Paris: Presses Universitaires de France, 1993. Pp. 411. Index. F 188', 88(3) American Journal of International Law 1994, 553–555.
75. A Carty, 'Conservative and Progressive Visions in French International Legal Doctrine', 16(3) European Journal of International Law 2005, 525–537, 528.
76. A Roberts, *Is International Law International?* (OUP 2017) 95.

CHAPTER 28

GERMANY

ANDREAS VON ARNAULD

1. *Vergangenheitsbewältigung*: Coming to Terms with a Violent Recent Past

1.1 Taking responsibility for crimes against humanity

Germany's stance towards international law today cannot be understood without the context of her violent recent past. World War II, the Holocaust, and other atrocious crimes against humanity committed by Germany and Germans have shaped German politics and policies to this day.[1] Having been given the chance of a 'rebirth' by the Allied Powers after 1945, the Western German State, the Federal Republic of Germany (FRG), considered itself to be identical with the defeated *Reich* and accepted responsibility for crimes committed under the National Socialist (NS) regime between 1933 and 1945. The responsibility the FRG assumed and still assumes is primarily a moral and political one, but also includes considerable financial engagement. From 1956 to the end of 2013 only, Germany paid a total of €71 billion in reparations to surviving NS victims.[2] However, Germany has always been watchful to keep her past out of international—and, of course, foreign—courts. This is one of the reasons why Germany submitted to the compulsory jurisdiction of the International Court of Justice (ICJ) as late as 2008, limited to 'disputes arising after the present declaration'.[3]

The special case of the Luxemburg Agreement of 10 September 1952[4] excepted, which dealt with German reparations to Israel and compensation for losses of Jewish lives and property via the Jewish Claims Conference, foreign NS victims were largely excluded from compensation. Here, reparation was paid on the basis of lump-sum agreements on inter-state level (in the 1960s with Western European, in the 1990s with Eastern European States), but the money was rarely forwarded to the victims. In recent years, due to political and lobby pressure, individual compensation schemes have been set up for forced labourers in World War II and for former Russian prisoners of war. Groups not included in such schemes—such as the so-called Italian military internees—have been suing Germany unsuccessfully in German courts and then turned to appeal to their respective national courts.[5] Court rulings in Greece and Italy which denied Germany immunity for war crimes eventually led to the ICJ's *Jurisdictional Immunities* judgment in 2012, affirming Germany's entitlement to sovereign immunity before Italian courts.[6] The 2014 judgment of the Italian *Corte Costituzionale* which declared a statute incorporating the ICJ's judgment unconstitutional,[7] has caused a deadlock situation[8] which even prompted a second application to the ICJ in April 2022.[9] Whether the fund aiming at a settlement of reparation claims set up by the Italian government (and confirmed by the Italian legislator on 29 June 2022)[10] will finally resolve the dispute, remains to be seen. In its July 2023 judgment the *Corte Costituzionale* considered this fund an 'adequate alternative safeguard' compatible with the Italian Constitution, but upheld its previous finding that Germany could not claim immunity from Italian jurisdiction in cases of violation of international *jus cogens* norms.[11]

While *Vergangenheitsbewältigung* was for decades almost synonymous with coming to terms with NS, only recently Germany has been reminded of her brief but brutal colonial past. Especially the 1904 massacre against the Herero and Nama peoples in 'German South-West Africa' (today's Namibia) has prompted legal action more than once, though ultimately unsuccessfully.[12] In May 2021, the Namibian and German governments issued a joint declaration,[13] in which Germany for the first time qualifies the massacre as a genocide in terms of current international law while denying retroactivity of that concept and any international legal responsibility. Instead, Germany pledged to pay an exceptional development aid of €1.1 billion which is to be used for the particularly affected communities and allocated in close cooperation with their representatives. A further 'postcolonial' issue that has gained more attention recently is the return of objects from colonial times.[14]

1.2 Overcoming the division of Germany

Another consequence of World War II was the division of Germany, into four zones of occupation at first, then, in 1949, with the Cold War defining politics between the Western and Eastern blocs, into two States, the Federal Republic of Germany (FRG) and the German Democratic Republic (GDR). The gradual retransfer of sovereign powers by the Western Allies to the FRG, with the end of the occupation regime in 1955, on the one hand, and the integration of the GDR into the Soviet sphere of hegemony on the other, further entrenched the division, as did, physically, the building of the Berlin Wall in 1961 and the installation of border fences between the two Germanys.

At the beginning, reunification was a political imperative on both sides, however, the official GDR policy changed in the 1950s. It portrayed the GDR as an independent State in the Eastern bloc, the 'first workers' and farmers' state on German soil', a new creation without any ties to the old *Reich*.[15] The FRG, on the other hand, claimed the sole right to represent Germany internationally and refrained from diplomatic relations with States that recognized the GDR (Hallstein Doctrine). This strict position was abandoned under the impression of the general *détente* in East-West relations in the 1960s and 1970s and a change of government in the FRG. Chancellor Willy Brandt and his social-liberal coalition government pursued a new *Ostpolitik* and concluded treaties with the Soviet Union (1970), Poland (1970), the GDR (1972), and Czechoslovakia (1973). The constitutionality of these treaties was affirmed by the Federal Constitutional Court (FCC) which paved the way for a more cohabitation-friendly policy, identifying the *Reich* as the 'roof' under which two German States had been formed whose relations to one another were *sui generis* and not international or inter-state relations.[16] The GDR was still not considered a sovereign State, but a stabilized *de facto* regime.[17]

The fall of the Berlin Wall and the scurry of events of 1989–1990 led to an unexpected dynamic where the briefly pursued idea of a close association of two German States gave way to German reunification. This was implemented by an accession of the GDR to the FRG (a rare case of state succession by incorporation[18]) on 3 October 1990.[19] The conditions for the former Allied Powers' agreement to this were laid out in the '2+4 Treaty'[20] which, *inter alia*, demanded the conclusion of a treaty of amity and good neighbourly relations with Poland to confirm the border between the two States which had been drawn by the Allied Powers in 1945. While the treaty concluded between Germany and Poland on 17 June 1991[21] settled the issue of the German 'Eastern territories' unequivocally, the legal conflicts arising after the unification were, *inter alia*, whether the German government was under an obligation to undo or compensate for the expropriation of landowners in the former Soviet zone of occupation,[22] and whether criminal prosecution related to the shooting of 'illegal emigrants' ('*Republikflüchtlinge*') by GDR border patrols was compatible with the German Constitution and international human rights law.[23]

2. *Offener Verfassungsstaat*: Constitutionally Integrating National and International Law

2.1 'Open constitutional State'—situating Germany within the international community

The FRG was founded on 23 May 1949 as a democratic State based on the rule of law. To underline the rejection of the law and policies of the NS era, its constitution, the Basic Law, was deliberately drafted for an 'open constitutional state' (*offener Verfassungsstaat*),[24] '[i]nspired by the determination to promote world peace as an equal partner in a united Europe' (preamble).[25] A programmatic reference is made in Article 1(2) to 'inviolable and inalienable human rights', as they had just recently been proclaimed in the Universal Declaration of Human Rights (UDHR). Another, more indirect, reference is made to human rights and to the Nuremberg principles in Article 25,[26] which acknowledges the 'general rules of international law' as an integral part of federal law with precedence over statutory law, by adding that they 'directly create rights and duties for the inhabitants of the federal territory'. Wars of aggression and other '[a]cts tending to and undertaken with the intent to disturb the peaceful relations between nations' are being outlawed in Article 26 which also calls for an arms export control mechanism.[27]

A central provision for the development of the 'open constitutional state' would become Article 24. This allows for the integration into the international society of States by accession to international organizations (paragraph 1), to join alliances of collective security (paragraph 2), and to submit to international arbitration and adjudication (paragraph 3). On the basis of Article 24(2), the FRG joined the North-Atlantic Treaty Organization (NATO) (1950), and the United Nations Organization (UNO) (1973), on the basis of Article 24(1), among many others, the Council of Europe (CoE) (1950). Article 24(1) also formed the constitutional basis for the European integration. Its unprecedented dynamic, however, made more specific rules necessary which were introduced in the wake of the Maastricht Treaty in 1993 in a revised Article 23.[28]

2.2 'Openness to international law'—foundations and limits

2.2.1 *'Moderate dualism' as the conceptual backbone*

In the reading of the FCC, the Basic Law adopts a dualist conception of the relationship between national and international law and does not formally grant precedence to international law; however, in a holistic interpretation of the Basic Law as a whole, the FCC has proclaimed a constitutional principle of *Völkerrechtsfreundlichkeit* ('openness towards international law')[29] which helps to overcome problems of direct applicability and hierarchy of norms and allows to align the whole body of national law to Germany's international legal obligations.[30] Thus, the underlying constitutional concept is usually termed as 'moderate dualism' (*gemäßigter Dualismus*).[31]

There is some ambivalence in the concept of the 'open constitutional State' as developed in the jurisprudence of the FCC, however, as it is hinged on the idea of sovereign statehood. According to the FCC, '[t]he openness to international law of the Basic Law is ... the expression of an understanding of sovereignty which is not only not in conflict with an integration into international and supranational contexts and their further development, but actively presumes and expects them. Against this background, even the "last word" of the German constitution is not opposed to an international and European dialogue of courts, but is the normative basis for this.'[32] Thus, sovereignty serves both as the basis for and as limitation to international and European integration. One might discern in this conception vestiges of the old, Hegel-inspired view which considered international law as 'äußeres Staatsrecht' ('external law of the State'),[33] albeit, today, with a constitutional hue.[34]

2.2.2 *Judicial dialogue between cooperation and conflict*

In recent years, the FCC has become somewhat notorious for its involvement in battles over 'last words'.[35] With the European Court of Human Rights (ECtHR), the battle was mainly fought over balancing privacy rights of celebrities with the freedom of the press;[36] more recently, the Court has found a way to 'contextualize', that is, to distinguish (though in a defeasible manner), ECtHR judgments in cases involving Turkey to save the general ban on strikes for German civil servants.[37] The confrontation is more open, however, when it comes to the relationship with the European Court of Justice (ECJ). In May 2020, the FCC for the first time declared an European Union (EU) legal act (the European System of Central Bank's decision on the Private Sector Purchase Programme) as *ultra vires* and attested the ECJ's judgment on this matter to be 'not comprehensible' and 'arbitrary from an objective perspective'.[38] Already in its 2009 judgment on the compatibility of the ratification of the Treaty of Lisbon with the Basic Law,[39] 'sovereignty/sovereign' had been mentioned no less than seventy-five times in the merits alone, and the commitment to *Europarechtsfreundlichkeit* there[40] clearly grounded EU law in international law, challenging the ECJ's claim of a legal order *sui generis*.[41]

That 'judicial dialogue' over EU matters is more prone to conflict than elsewhere, is certainly due to the wide-ranging transfer of competences to the EU which is as much perceived by the FCC as a latent challenge to Germany's sovereign statehood (and the FCC's own position as guarantor of the German constitution) as it pushes into an area close to the fundamental tenets of the Basic Law. Article 79(3) declares these as inviolable, and Article 23(1) clause 3 makes it clear that they are also to remain unaffected by any transfer of sovereign powers to the EU. One of those fundamental tenets being the principle of democracy, the FCC has effectively turned the right to vote in federal elections, Article 38(1) clause 1, into a catch-all clause to invite proceedings for checking measures of European integration.[42] By interpreting any such measure as encroachment upon the powers and competences of the *Bundestag*, these become actionable by every voter or group of voters.

While there are good reasons to criticize some of the more recent 'Eurosceptic' decisions of the FCC, especially its Second Senate (the 'international and EU law Senate'), one should not forget this Senate's lasting contribution to the constitutionalization of the EU in terms of fundamental rights. With its 'Solange I' judgment of 1974,[43] it pushed the ECJ to develop its fundamental rights jurisprudence; with the 'Solange II' reversal in 1986,[44] it accepted the ECJ's precedence in principle, while reserving a right to apply the Basic Law's fundamental rights when reviewing acts of German public authorities implementing EU law, as far as these acts are not fully determined by Union law.[45] It was the ECJ which, with the rather unfortunate *Åkerberg Fransson* judgment of 2013,[46] challenged these terms of cooperation. After a phase of some irritation, in November 2019 the FCC's First Senate (the 'fundamental rights Senate') established a new framework of cooperation in two decisions on the 'right to be forgotten':[47] While in matters which are fully determined by EU law, the FCC will apply only the EU's Charter of Fundamental Rights (CFR) (and eventually refer to the ECJ for decisions on interpretation), in matters not fully determined by EU law it will continue to apply the Basic Law—if it is not established in a given case that either the EU legislator deliberately referred to a harmonized fundamental rights standard or the CFR provides a higher level of protection than the Basic Law. The Second Senate seems to have acceded to this new line of jurisprudence, at least for the time being.[48]

Turning away from the FCC, international law has become more and more important for the practice of German courts over the last years.[49] For a long time, whether international law was being applied depended on a number of factors, 'inter alia on specialization, express reference or on a more or less aleatory "awareness by contact"'.[50] While this most certainly still holds true, contacts have become more frequent, not least through the involvement of the FCC which obliges courts to take relevant international law into account[51] (and even demands consultation of non-binding recommendations of the CoE's Council of Ministers[52]). Especially elaborate is the FCC's jurisprudence when it comes to the duty to interpret the fundamental rights of the Basic Law in the light of the European Convention on Human Rights (ECHR) and the jurisprudence of the ECtHR, either by harmonizing the respective concepts and principles or by achieving ECHR-compatible results in the proportionality stage of rights review.[53] The practical importance that international law in general, and the ECHR in particular, have for the everyday legal practice makes it all the more regrettable that the German law school syllabus (which is defined by the ministers of justice of the Federation and the States on the basis of interfederal coordination) is still all-too introverted.[54]

2.2.3 *The constitutional framework for international law and foreign policy*

Further limits to *Völkerrechtsfreundlichkeit* follow from the FCC's jurisprudence concerning the division of treaty-making powers between the executive and legislative branches of government. Since Parliament can only assent to the ratification of a treaty concluded by the government, whereas the question of suspension or renunciation of a treaty lies solely with the government, the Court's Second Senate in 2015 decided that the *Bundestag* is constitutionally entitled to 'override' treaty obligations by way of (express) counter-legislation.[55] Instances in practice are rare, however, and the Court made an exception for human rights treaties which attain a quasi-constitutional status as points of reference for the interpretation of the Basic Law's fundamental rights.

The FCC does not only stress the preponderance of the executive branch in the conduct of foreign policy vis-à-vis the *Bundestag* but also in relation to judicial oversight. Thus, FCC and Federal Administrative Court (FAC) generally apply a restricted standard of judicial review here. There is no political questions doctrine, though. In principle, external actions of executive organs are subject to law and to judicial review; the review standard is defined by recourse to executive discretion and margins of appreciation instead.[56] With regard to the functions of the judiciary and the *Völkerrechtsfreundlichkeit* of the German constitutional order, it is not wholly convincing when the FCC accords a primacy to the Federal government also in the interpretation of international law and the assessment of the legality of their own actions.[57] While the judiciary is traditionally rather generous towards the Federal government in its review of policy decisions, more recent cases show a more stringent standard of review with regard to external operations of executive organs below the 'political' level. Thus, the FCC has declared the extraterritorial bulk surveillance programme of the Federal Intelligence Service (*Bundesnachrichtendienst*) as partly unconstitutional[58] and confirmed the Federal Court of Justice's (FCJ) jurisprudence applying international humanitarian law and international criminal law to actions of members of the German armed forces abroad.[59] Nevertheless, the FCJ remains reluctant to award compensation in cases of violations of humanitarian law.[60]

3. *Normbasierte Aussenpolitik?* International Law in German Foreign Policy

3.1 Germany's credo—promoting the international rule of law and multilateralism

With some good reason, Germany prides herself on a generally good track record in respecting and promoting the international rule of law and multilateralism.[61] Germany is a member of some 120 international organizations, among them UNO, EU, CoE, OECD (Organisation for Economic Co-operation and Development), NATO, WTO (World Trade Organization). A member of UNO since 1973 (the two German States had been admitted at the same time), four Germans have served as judges at the ICJ since (Hermann Mosler, 1976–1985, Carl-August Fleischhauer, 1994–2003, Bruno Simma, 2003–2012, Georg Nolte, since 2021). German members of the International Law Commission (ILC) were Christian Tomuschat (1985–1996), Bruno Simma (1997–2002), and Georg Nolte (2007–2021); the sole member of the ILC from the GDR having been Bernhard Graefrath (1987–1991). The FRG held a non-permanent seat in the Security Council six times (1977/78, 1987/88, 1995/96, 2003/04, 2011/12, 2019/20; the GDR was a member in 1980/81). Add to this membership of German experts in other UN bodies, especially the UN human rights committees, and a strong German commitment to UNO, and to international law especially, becomes palpable. Germany hosts a large number of UN offices and institutions, the most prominent being the International Tribunal of the Law of the Sea (ITLOS) in Hamburg. To underline the importance of multilateralism in times of 'my country first' rhetoric, in February 2019, the foreign ministers of Germany and France jointly initiated an 'Alliance for Multilateralism' to cooperatively address major global challenges, among them the COVID-19 pandemic.[62]

Germany is committed to fostering peace and security globally, especially in its wider neighbourhood, for example the Middle East and Northern Africa. As such, side by side with the P5 and the EU, she played a pivotal role in the negotiations leading up to the 2015 Joint Comprehensive Plan of Action concerning the Iranian nuclear programme, and several times offered good offices in post-civil war transition processes, such as the Petersberg process for Afghanistan (2001–2006) and the Berlin process for Libya (since 2019). The general outline of German engagement for peacebuilding was laid down 2017 in the 'Guidelines on Preventing Crises, Resolving Conflicts, Building Peace',[63] supplemented in December 2022 by a 'Foreign and security policy concept for an integrated action for peace.'[64] October 2021 saw the release of Germany's first Cyber Security Strategy.[65] Since German foreign policy is generally characterized by great constancy, regardless of the coalition in power, these guidelines and strategies are also likely to be indicative for Germany's future foreign policy. In line with this, Germany's first ever National Security Strategy, adopted in June 2023 against the backdrop of the Russian war of aggression against Ukraine, does not mark a radical departure but rather appears as an attempt to redefine Germany's traditional foreign policy objectives in a new geopolitical context.[66]

Other fields in which Germany is striving for a leading role are human rights, protection of the environment, and the fight against climate change,[67] though critics will argue that Germany's policies sometimes fall short of her own aspirations.[68] Germany has been an especially fervent supporter of the International Criminal Court since its inception and continues to work with like-minded States to overcome blockades at meetings of the member States. To make the crimes in the Rome Statute punishable offences under German law, the German legislator enacted a Code of Crimes against International Law (*Völkerstrafgesetzbuch*) which was amended in 2016 so as to include the newly defined crime of aggression.[69] However, for a long time the German government maintained a cautiously critical stand towards exceptions to the immunity of State officials from foreign criminal jurisdiction, which was only modified after a seminal judgment of the FCJ in January 2021[70] sentencing a former officer of the Afghan army for war crimes committed in his official capacity.[71]

Germany is a dedicated member of the EU. In fact, membership in the Union can be seen as a guiding reason of state to which all Federal governments have been and still are committed. Demands to leave the EU, unlike in other member States, find favour at best with only a small fraction of the population[72] and have been championed only by the political fringes. Germany appears to be aware of her special status as the largest member State (in terms of population) and the largest economy within the Union and generally is watchful not to be perceived as a dominating force. That Ursula von der Leyen ran in 2019 as the first German President of the Commission since Walter Hallstein headed the EEC Commission (1958–1967) can be seen as indicative of this approach. However, Germany's role in the Greek government debt crisis and Chancellor Merkel's unilateral promise to open the borders for Syrian refugees in August 2015, have contributed to a critical view of the German position within the EU among some of the smaller member States.[73] Outside the institutional structures of the EU, Germany sees herself as having a special guarantor duty for the European integration process, together first and foremost with France, but also with Poland as its most important eastern neighbour.[74]

The FRG is not only a country with a mission when it comes to the development of the EU. After the end of the East-West conflict 1989/90, Germany actively—and successfully—promoted its constitution as a model for the emerging democracies in Eastern Europe (and also, eventually, for South Africa after the end of the Apartheid regime in 1994).[75] German constitutional solutions (primacy of the constitution, enforceable individual constitutional rights, and a strong independent constitutional court) were imported by most of the former communist States, 'partly because they were specifically designed for post-authoritarian situations, and partly because many of the Eastern European lawyers who wrote the new constitutions ... had actually spent one or two years as guest researchers in Germany in the 1980s'.[76] For a considerable period, this secured the FCC an almost hegemonic position among the constitutional courts in Europe. Over the years, however, this influence has faded. In terms of human rights jurisprudence the ECtHR has taken over the mantle,[77] and when it comes to citations of foreign judgments in general, there is a trend towards a 'normalisation', with the FCC citing foreign jurisprudence more and more often itself.[78] Unfortunately, it seems that it is the FCC's *ultra vires* jurisprudence which has proven most successful in terms of precedent, having been cited as a model recently by the Polish constitutional tribunal in its notorious decision of 7 October 2021 on the primacy of the Polish Constitution before EU law.[79]

3.2 Exceptions to the rule—of special relations and national interest

As stated, German foreign policy traditionally (and independently of the ruling coalition or party) is rule-based, favouring international law, multilateralism, and international institutions. This is as much the result of lessons learned from Germany's recent past as it is a natural and sensible strategy for an intermediate power with strong economic and limited military capabilities. These underlying causes also explain why Germany sometimes does not live up to her rule-based and multilateral credo.

3.2.1 *Special relations as limits to the international rule of law*

The 2021 coalition agreement between Social Democrats, Green Party, and Liberal Democrats explicitly calls Israel's security a 'reason of state' (*Staatsräson*),[80] thus subscribing to a leitmotif of German foreign policy. Aware of the special relationship between both States forged by the Holocaust, Germany generally refrains from harsh criticism of Israel's occupation policies in West Bank and Gaza. German governments have, however, consistently refused to recognize Israeli annexations and have referred to Israel's settlement policy as illegal under international law. In such criticism, Germany is usually careful to flag it as the consensus position of the international community.[81]

After the attack by Hamas on Israel on 7 October 2023 and in the subsequent armed conflict in Gaza, Germany declared its 'unconditional solidarity' with Israel and criticized South Africa's lawsuit against Israel on the basis of the UN Genocide Convention. This prompted Nicaragua to sue Germany before the ICJ for supplying military equipment to Israel and defunding the UN Relief and Works Agency for Palestine Refugees in the Near East (UNRWA). In the proceedings for the adoption of provisional measures, Germany emphasized (successfully) that it was not practicing blind solidarity, had supplied virtually no war weapons to Israel since the start of the armed conflict, and was also supporting the Palestinian side with humanitarian aid.[82]

With the exception of France, the other country to which Germany is bound by special relations is the US. German transatlantic loyalty is owed as much to the post-war experience, with the Marshall Plan as stepping stone for West Germany's *Wirtschaftswunder*, as to the US being, via NATO, the main guarantor for Germany's security. Apart from frosty relations during the Trump administration, the most distancing of Germany from US foreign and security policy occurred during the invasion of Iraq in 2003. Though Germany did not join the invasion, the German government refrained from calling it illegal.[83] Furthermore, Germany gave indirect support by, *inter alia*, substituting for US personnel in guarding US bases and establishments in Germany, or by military cooperation on a technical and on intelligence level.[84] These special relations, as well as a general opposition to the Assad regime in Damascus, also explain Germany's reaction to the US- and UK-led airstrikes against Syria after the use of chemical weapons which the Federal government at the time called 'understandable' and 'necessary and appropriate',[85] thus deliberately eschewing the language of international law, given the at best shaky legal basis for these strikes.[86] As partner in NATO's Nuclear Sharing Programme (with US nuclear weapons stored in Büchel Air Base), Germany also kept a critical distance from the 2017 Treaty on the Prohibition of Nuclear Weapons (TPNW). The new German government announced that it would 'constructively accompany' the TPNW as an observer State, 'in close consultation with our allies'.[87] Nuclear threats by the Russian government in the context of its still ongoing military aggression against Ukraine might contribute to a change of priorities in this respect, however.

3.2.2 *Handelsstaat: economic interests as limits to multilateralism*

Some twenty years ago, the FRG was aptly characterized as a 'mercantile state' (*Handelsstaat*).[88] Even though Germany pursues other State interests as well (cf Section 3.2.3), economic interests certainly define German foreign policy and policy preferences to a significant degree. When it comes to projects of major significance for her economy, Germany is even prepared to bypass multilateral networks and put security concerns of her allies and neighbours aside. This is well illustrated by the rather belated suspension of the controversial Nord Stream 2 pipeline project between Russia and Germany[89] after the Russian invasion of Ukraine on 24 February 2022, as well as by Germany's reluctance to broaden the scope of the cut-off of Russian financial institutions from the SWIFT payment system by the EU in reaction to that invasion, at least in the early stages of the conflict.

With a notoriously large trade surplus, the German economy relies to a large extent on the export of goods 'made in Germany'.[90] To facilitate their distribution, Germany has a clear preference for free access to international markets. The fact that this is not primarily about reciprocal market opening but first and foremost about opening up sales markets for German companies becomes clear, for example, when Germany, together with the EU, protects the export interests of her farmers even against developing countries within the WTO.[91] Within the EU's internal market, too, Germany strives to protect her economic interests.[92] Germany has also traditionally been an exporter of capital with an innate interest in secure environments for German investments abroad. Thus, Germany can claim to be the inventor of bilateral investment treaties (BIT), the BIT between Germany and Pakistan, concluded in 1959, being the first of its kind worldwide.[93] Since then, Germany has concluded more than 130 such treaties. However, the transfer of competence for foreign direct investments to the EU has heralded the end of BITs between EU member States and third countries.

In recent years, Germany had had to realize that she can herself be a target country for investments and a defendant in investment arbitration proceedings. For example, Germany was sued before an arbitration tribunal by the Swedish Vattenfall Group, among others, because of the nuclear phase-out announced in 2011.[94] In March 2021, the German government agreed with Vattenfall and other energy suppliers on compensation totalling €2.4 billion.[95] These developments have raised awareness in Germany of the importance of the 'right to regulate', which is also reflected in the new generation of EU trade and investment agreements.[96] A comparable learning process has also heightened sensibility for responsible trading. This is witnessed by a new supply chain due diligence law which was enacted in 2021.[97] If prospective EU legislation does not supersede it, this law requires large companies to take responsibility for the observance of human rights also in their supply chains.

3.3 Civilian power? Searching for a more involved international role

These basic coordinates of (Western) German foreign policy since the regaining of full sovereignty in 1955 have sometimes been challenged by the ongoing search for a more active and visible international role after German reunification in 1990. This search sometimes produces tensions with the FRG's self-conception as a champion of European integration and as a civilian, as opposed to a military, power. An expression of this ambition can be seen in Germany's campaigning for a permanent seat on the UN Security Council in the context of a reform of its composition.[98] The competing proposal of a joint EU seat in the Council suggested by staunch integrationists never really found favour with the German government.

While the Federal army, the *Bundeswehr*, had been a standing army tasked only with defence of the FRG against a potential intrusion from the East before 1990, after the end of the East-West conflict the *Bundeswehr* underwent a transformation into an army deployed abroad.[99] Unlike in 1955, when West Germany rearmed herself and the *Bundeswehr* was founded, and in 1968, when the deployment of the army at home became possible in the event of an emergency, there was no broad public discussion this time. The Basic Law was not changed either, but rather reinterpreted according to the new world situation.[100] The same happened when compulsory military service was suspended in 2011 as part of a professionalization strategy of the then governing conservative-liberal coalition. The mixture of a somewhat half-hearted new self-image, a reaction to more or less unspoken expectations of the allies, and the will to participate internationally 'somehow', may have contributed to the fact that Germany is still trying to work out what role she wants to play militarily.

1993 saw the first deployment of *Bundeswehr* soldiers abroad, as part of the UN 'blue helmet' operation UNOSOM II, which did not stir a debate at the time. This was different with the first participation in a combat operation, the NATO air raids against Serbia in the Kosovo conflict 1998–1999. These put the Green Party in particular to the test, which on the one hand had emerged from the peace movement and on the other, provided a foreign minister who had agreed to humanitarian intervention without a UN mandate.[101] At the time, however, the public discussion in Germany was more about the moral legitimacy of humanitarian interventions than about the role of the *Bundeswehr*. This briefly became an issue when, in 2004, the Federal Defence Minister justified the military participation in the International Security Assistance Force (ISAF) in Afghanistan by saying that Germany's security was being defended in the Hindu Kush.[102]

Germany engages militarily only as part of multilateral forces, primarily under the roof of UNO, NATO, or the EU. Within the framework of the division of labour, German units rarely take on active combat functions. The German Navy has been active in operations against pirates in the Gulf of Aden or against human trafficking and smuggling in the Mediterranean in the context of EUNAVFOR operations, the Air Force usually participates in the form of AWACS air reconnaissance. On land, the *Bundeswehr* participates in humanitarian aid through medical units, in training missions, and in UN peacekeeping missions, to name the most frequent. Precisely because German soldiers are usually rarely directly involved in combat, an incident in Kunduz on 4 September 2009 attracted a great deal of attention when the German commander on the ground ordered the dropping of bombs on two tankers hijacked by the Taliban, resulting in the deaths of an indeterminable number of people.[103] The incident triggered a flood of criminal, civil, and administrative court cases in Germany which absolved the responsible officers from any legal responsibility. In a judgment of 16 February 2021, the ECtHR found that Germany had fulfilled her positive obligations under Article 2 ECHR to investigate the case.[104]

While the German public does not seem to be keen to more adventurous military engagements and does not cultivate hero worship, there have been demands from NATO and the US for an increased military commitment from Germany. These demands have been met with more robust aspirations in parts of the military elite and a wish 'to be out there with the others'. Examples of this attitude are Germany's participation in the Western coalition fighting the so-called 'Islamic State' in Syria (ISIS). Rather than subscribing to the problematic standard of 'unwilling or unable'[105] favoured by the US, Germany preferred to base its contribution on a combination of two half-convincing arguments: collective self-defence for France, and the ambiguous[106] Security Council Resolution 2249 (2015).[107] Even after the defeat of ISIS, German troops remain deployed on Syrian territory, with reference to underground networks which work towards a return of ISIS to power in parts of Syria.[108] Russia's war of aggression against Ukraine could prove a game-changer, though, and bring about a reorientation of Germany's military policy: In his speech of 27 February 2022, Chancellor Scholz announced a *Zeitenwende* (turning point)—more investment in military equipment and infrastructure for collective defence, less orientation towards participation in extraterritorial operations. In reaction to the invasion of Ukraine the German government announced a plan for a long-term strengthening of military capabilities in order to contribute to a European security architecture which, as long as Putin's system persists, will be mainly oriented towards containing potential threats from Russia. Accordingly, the new National Security Strategy of June 2023 identifies Russia 'for now' as 'the most significant threat to peace and security in the Euro-Atlantic area' and commits to a 'robust' (*wehrhaft*) national and collective defence.[109]

4. The Position(s) of German International Lawyers

4.1 The role of international lawyers in Germany

As Christian Tomuschat has pointed out, '[i]n the German Foreign Office, the question as to whether a planned action is compatible with international law is invariably taken very seriously and not dealt with as an inconvenient or annoying formality. International law is observed as a truly binding normative proviso for external action.'[110] While in the 1950s, the German Foreign Office employed established scholars of international law as legal advisers (Wilhelm G Grewe, Erich Kaufmann), the office of legal adviser to the Foreign Minister is since entrusted—on a rotating basis—to a career diplomat who serves as head of the Foreign Office's Legal Department.[111] The international law advisers meet regularly with their counterparts in other States with which there are close ties for an exchange of views and opinions. Direct contact with German international law scholarship is mainly channelled through an advisory council, presently consisting of seven academic members. While these members are formally appointed, the work of the council is rather informal. It is convened by the legal adviser and their staff two to three times a year to discuss topical questions of international law; the advisory function is limited to those meetings and does not include written statements or opinions. Probably more influential for the day-to-day work of the foreign office are scholarly publications which are regularly consulted by its legal staff, thus guaranteeing an indirect contact with international law scholarship. Individual scholars will also be hired to represent Germany before international courts and draft declarations and memorials in cooperation with the Foreign Office.

Turning to German international law scholars, there is one peculiarity which distinguishes Germany from most other countries: In Germany, it is virtually impossible to build an academic career based on international law alone.[112] The law school syllabus being geared to a (first) state examination in which the candidates have to show their acquaintance with almost the whole body of German civil, public, and criminal law, international law plays but a small part in the curriculum and is mainly reserved to a one-year period of specialization (during which usually other courses have to be taken as well). From the teachers' perspective this means that at most Law Faculties less than half of the teaching will be devoted to international law. Professors of international law in Germany are therefore in practically every case first and foremost hired as professors of public law—and by committees dominated by other professors of public law.

This accounts as much for the almost complete lack of international law professors without a German law degree as it explains why German international law scholars might often seem, in Nico Krisch's words, 'not so international'.[113] The field in which they have to gain reputation in order to get hired or to move on to the more prestigious Law Faculties is—at least at the outset—the field of German public law (constitutional law and, usually to a lesser degree, administrative law). Add to this an academic linguistic community that is large enough to conduct a discourse on international law in the vernacular and has established journals (*Zeitschrift für ausländisches öffentliches Recht und Völkerrecht, Archiv des Völkerrechts*)[114] and textbooks[115] in German, as well as its own professional organization (*Deutsche Gesellschaft für internationales Recht*), and it becomes clear why Krisch writes: 'The German model certainly does not encourage specialization or a sustained presence in the transnational discourse of international law.'[116]

4.2 'Typisch Deutsch'—is there a German approach to international law?

Given that international law scholarship in Germany is, naturally, diverse in its topics and approaches, any attempt to pin down a typically 'German' way[117] with international law has to be taken with a pinch of salt.[118] That said, the fact that most international lawyers in German academia are also public lawyers, does seem to influence the general approach to international law, in terms of perspective and methodology.[119]

It might account for a way of thinking that takes the State as point of departure[120:121] While in the generation of Jellinek and Triepel international law was mostly characterized as Hegel's 'äußeres Staatsrecht',[122] theorizing about a constitutionalization of international law became something of a trademark of German scholarship from the 1980s onwards.[123] As Andreas Paulus puts it, with the constitutionalization thesis, 'German international law scholarship transfers the experiences with its own constitution and with European law to the sphere of international law'.[124]

In terms of methodology, the German approach has been characterized as relying on doctrine and system.[125] The doctrinal approach is aptly summarized by Lauri Hannikainen thus: 'German experts of international law are competent lawyers whose analyses are juridically of high quality. They are careful not to express political or polemic opinions. Sometimes their analyses are so exhaustive that the reader has difficulty maintaining his/her interest.'[126] Characteristic is a clear separation of law and politics (with law providing a framework for politics), and thus also between legal scholarship and political science.[127] Even if a brush with postmodernism might have dispelled 18th-century dreams of perfect coherence in law, legal analysis 'German style' still presupposes law, including international law, as a system.[128] Within this system, order is created by recourse to general concepts and principles which inform the interpretation of more specific rules.[129] As Nico Krisch has remarked, this method shapes a preference for certain forms of publication: encyclopaedias,[130] commentaries, and handbooks.[131] That leading international academic publishing houses like OUP and CUP are heavily invested in the production of commentaries on international treaties and conventions and of handbooks on diverse topics of international law these days might speak for a certain appeal of the 'systematic' approach also beyond the confines of the German-speaking world.

The systematization of international law is not just an ordering exercise, but—through the reliance on principles such as rule of law, human rights, self-determination, and the like—represents an ethical endeavour as well; this also explains an enduring fascination with larger-than-life concepts like *jus cogens* and *erga omnes*, which some might find overly idealistic or even outright naive.[132] Not without a hint of mockery, Jan Klabbers wrote: '[T]here is probably not a country in the world where the concept of *erga omnes* obligations has received such a warm welcome as precisely in Germany; there is hardly a country in the world more jubilant about the *jus cogens* concept than Germany; and there is not a country in the world where the UN Charter is so steadfastly and seriously regarded as a constitution for the international community as Germany.'[133] In a more generous tone, Fred L Morrison has contrasted the topics that attract German international law scholars with those which attract their US colleagues: 'German scholarship concentrates on the centripetal forces that hold nations together. It tends to focus on treaties, international organization, and other forms of international cooperation. Thus, it frequently concentrates on international institutions, and on regimes that pull the various states into concerted common action. American scholarship, in contrast, seems to emphasize the centrifugal forces of the international order. It tends to focus on state sovereignty, international conflict, and the legitimacy of independent state actions.... Germans think in social contract terms like *John Locke*. Americans think like *Thomas Hobbes*, who dealt in a mean, nasty, and brutish state of nature.'[134] Given the mean, nasty, and brutish state of Germany herself just eighty years ago, this shows how much the NS experience has contributed to shaping the approach of Germany and German scholars to international law in a globalized world.

Notes

1. cf Pierre-Marie Dupuy, 'Taking International Law Seriously: The German Approach to International Law', 50 German Yearbook of International Law 2007, 375, 376–382. On international law and legal scholarship in Nazi Germany, see Rüdiger Wolfrum, 'Nationalsozialismus und Völkerrecht' in Franz Jürgen Säcker (ed), *Recht und Rechtslehre im Nationalsozialismus* (Nomos 1992) 89–101; Michael Stolleis, 'Against Universalism—German International Law under the Swastika: Some Contributions to the History of Jurisprudence 1933–1945', 50 German Yearbook of International Law 2007, 91–110.
2. For further details, see Andreas von Arnauld, 'Damages for the Infringement of Human Rights in Germany' in Ewa Baginska (ed), *Damages for Violations of Human Rights: A Comparative Study of Domestic Legal Systems* (Springer 2015) 101–135, 121–124.
3. On this declaration and its limitations, see Christophe Eick, 'Die Anerkennung der obligatorischen Gerichtsbarkeit des Internationalen Gerichtshofs durch Deutschland', 68 Zeitschrift für ausländisches öffentliches Recht und Völkerrecht/Heidelberg Journal of International Law 2008, 763–777. Another important limitation refers to any dispute that 'relates to, arises from or is connected with the use for military purposes of the territory of the Federal Republic of Germany, including its airspace, as well as maritime areas subject to German sovereign rights and jurisdiction'.
4. United Nations Treaty Series (UNTS) 162, 205.
5. For a closer analysis, see Andreas von Arnauld, 'Deadlocked in Dualism: Negotiating for a Final Settlement' in Valentina Volpe, Anne Peters, and Stefano Battini (eds), *Remedies against Immunity? Reconciling International and Domestic Law after Italian Constitutional Court's Sentenza 238/2014* (Springer 2021) 313–329, 318–323.
6. *Jurisdictional Immunities of the State (Germany v Italy: Greece intervening)*, Judgment, ICJ Reports 2012, 99.
7. Corte Costituzionale, Judgment of 22 October 2014, No 238/2014, English translation under https://www.cortecostituzionale.it/documenti/download/doc/recent_judgments/S238_2013_en.pdf (all websites last accessed 18 March 2022).
8. On this, see contributions in Volpe, Peters, and Battini (n 5).
9. cf https://www.icj-cij.org/en/case/183.
10. See Gazzetta Ufficiale, Serie Generale no150 del 29-06-2022, Article 43.
11. Corte Costituzionale, Judgment of 4 July 2023, No 159/2023. For an analysis, see Andrea Maria Pelliconi, 'The Italian Constitutional Court's new decision on state immunity and the ICJ Germany vs Italy No. 2' https://www.ejiltalk.org/the-italian-constitutional-courts-new-decision-on-state-immunity-and-the-icj-germany-vs-italy-no-2/ (28 July 2023).
12. Latest in the line is *Rukoro et al v Federal Republic of* Germany, US District Court, Southern District of New York, No 17-00062, Judgment of 24 September 2020.
13. See https://www.parliament.na/wp-content/uploads/2021/09/Joint-Declaration-Document-Genocide-rt.pdf.
14. Recently, the German Digital Library has launched an online portal listing such objects in public collections: https://ccc.deutsche-digitale-bibliothek.de/.
15. On international law scholarship in the GDR, see Theodor Schweisfurth, 'The Science of Public International Law in the German Democratic Republic', 50 German Yearbook of International Law 2007, 149–200.

16. FCC, 7 July 1975, BVerfGE (= Collected Decisions of the FCC) 40, 141. See further Knut Ipsen, 'International Legal Scholarship in West Germany after World War II', 50 German Yearbook of International Law 2007, 111–137, 112, 127.
17. As drafted conceptually already by Jochen Abr Frowein, *Das de-facto-Regime im Völkerrecht: eine Untersuchung zur Rechtsstellung 'nichtanerkannter Staaten' und ähnlicher Gebilde* (Heymanns 1968).
18. Oliver Dörr, *Die Inkorporation als Tatbestand der Staatensukzession* (Duncker & Humblot 1995).
19. Article 1, Treaty of Unification of 31 August 1990, reprinted 30 International Legal Materials (ILM) (1991) 457.
20. Treaty on the Final Settlement with Respect to Germany, 12 September 1990, UNTS 1696, 115.
21. Treaty on Good Neighbourliness and Friendly Co-Operation, 17 June 1991, UNTS 1708, 502.
22. FCC, 23 April 1991, BVerfGE 84, 90; 18 April 1996, BVerfGE 94, 12.
23. FCC, 24 October 1996, BVerfGE 95, 96. Confirmed by ECtHR, 22 March 2001, no 34044/96 ao, *Krenz, Streletz and Kessler v Germany*.
24. On this concept, see Klaus Vogel, *Die Verfassungsentscheidung des Grundgesetzes für eine internationale Zusammenarbeit: ein Diskussionsbeitrag zu einer Frage der Staatstheorie sowie des geltenden deutschen Staatsrechts* (Mohr 1964); Stephan Hobe, *Der offene Verfassungsstaat zwischen Souveränität und Interdependenz: eine Studie zur Wandlung des Staatsbegriffs der deutschsprachigen Staatslehre im Kontext internationaler institutionalisierter Kooperation* (Duncker & Humblot 1998).
25. For contextualization, see Christian Tomuschat, 'The Concept of International Law: The German Perspective' in Peter Hilpold (ed), *European International Law Traditions* (Springer 2021) 19–59, 28–29.
26. On Article 25, see ibid, 29–36. See also, more generally, Rüdiger Wolfrum, Holger Hestermeyer, and Silja Vöneky, 'The Reception of International Law in the German Legal Order: An Introduction' in Erika de Wet, Holger Hestermeyer, and Rüdiger Wolfrum (eds), *The Implementation of International Law in Germany and South Africa* (PULP 2015) 2–21.
27. For further information on this mechanism and its relation to Germany's international legal obligations, see ICJ, *Alleged Breaches of Certain International Obligations in Respect of the Occupied Palestinian Territory (Nicaragua v. Germany)*, Request for the indication of provisional measures, order of 30 April 2024, para 16–17.
28. For details, see Tomuschat (n 24) 39–41.
29. In more depth, see Mehrdad Payandeh, 'Völkerrechtsfreundlichkeit als Verfassungsprinzip—Ein Beitrag des Grundgesetzes zur Einheit von Völkerrecht und nationalem Recht', 57 Jahrbuch des öffentlichen Rechts der Gegenwart 2009, 465–502.
30. cf only, FCC, 14 October 2004, BVerfGE 111, 307, 316–319; 15 December 2015.
31. Andreas von Arnauld, *Völkerrecht* (5th edn, C.F. Müller 2023) 218–223, paras 524–533.
32. FCC, 4 May 2011, BVerfGE 128, 326, paragraph 90. English translation https://www.bundesverfassungsgericht.de/SharedDocs/Entscheidungen/EN/2011/05/rs20110504_2bvr236509en.html.
33. cf Georg Wilhelm Friedrich Hegel, *Grundlinien der Philosophie des Rechts* (Nicolai 1820/21), paragraphs 330–340.

34. In this sense, Luzius Wildhaber, 'A Sensible and Serious Approach to International Law', 50 German Yearbook of International Law 2007, 415–418, 417–418.
35. Tomuschat (n 24) 45.
36. FCC, 15 December 1999, BVerfGE 101, 361; ECtHR, 24 June 2004, no 59320/00, *von Hannover v Germany*.
37. FCC, 12 June 2018, BVerfGE 148, 296, summary statement no 3(b). English translation https://www.bundesverfassungsgericht.de/SharedDocs/Entscheidungen/EN/2018/06/rs20180612_2bvr173812en.html. Critically discussed by Matthias Jacobs and Mehrdad Payandeh, 'The Ban on Strike Action by Career Civil Servants under the German Basic Law: How the Federal Constitutional Court Constitutionally Immunized the German Legal Order Against the European Convention on Human Rights', 21 German Law Journal 2020, 223–239. The ECtHR endorsed the FCC's position and found no violation of Convention rights: judgment of 14 December 2023 (Grand Chamber), *Humpert and Others v Germany*, no 59433/18 et al.
38. FCC, 5 May 2020, BVerfGE 154, 17, summary statement no 2. English translation https://www.bundesverfassungsgericht.de/SharedDocs/Entscheidungen/EN/2020/05/rs20200505_2bvr085915en.html.
39. FCC, 30 June 2009, BVerfGE 123, 267. English translation https://www.bundesverfassungsgericht.de/SharedDocs/Entscheidungen/EN/2009/06/es20090630_2bve000208en.html.
40. ibid, summary statement no 4.
41. cf ECJ, 15 July 1964, 6/64, *Costa v ENEL* [1964] ECR 585.
42. See, eg, FCC, 21 June 2016, BVerfGE 142, 123, 173–175, paragraphs 80–84. English translation https://www.bundesverfassungsgericht.de/SharedDocs/Entscheidungen/EN/2016/06/rs20160621_2bvr272813en.html.
43. FCC, 29 May 1974, BVerfGE 37, 271 – *Solange I*.
44. FCC, 22 October 1986, BVerfGE 73, 339 – *Solange II*.
45. FCC, 2 March 2010, BVerfGE 125, 260, 306–307, paragraphs 180–182 – *Data Retention*. English translation https://www.bundesverfassungsgericht.de/SharedDocs/Entscheidungen/EN/2010/03/rs20100302_1bvr025608en.html.
46. ECJ, 26 February 2013, C-617/10, *Åklagaren v Hans Åkerberg Fransson* [2013] ECR 105.
47. FCC, 6 November 2019, BVerfGE 152, 152 – *Right to be Forgotten I*; English translation https://www.bundesverfassungsgericht.de/SharedDocs/Entscheidungen/EN/2019/11/rs20191106_1bvr001613en.html; 6 November 2019, BVerfGE 152, 216 – *Right to be Forgotten II*; English translation https://www.bundesverfassungsgericht.de/SharedDocs/Entscheidungen/EN/2019/11/rs20191106_1bvr027617en.html.
48. FCC, 1 December 2020, BVerfGE 156, 182 – *European Arrest Warrant III*; English translation https://www.bundesverfassungsgericht.de/SharedDocs/Entscheidungen/EN/2020/12/rs20201201_2bvr184518en.html.
49. A query in the 'International Law' section of the jurisprudence database *juris*, adjusted for decisions of international or foreign courts, yields the following numbers of hits: 1950–1959: 34; 1960–1969: 128; 1970–1979: 265; 1980–1989: 362; after reunification (which was accompanied by a rise in the number of courts): 1990–1999: 631; 2000–2010: 900; 2010–2019: 2004; 2020–2023: 766.
50. Andreas von Arnauld, 'Public International Law and the Role of Federal Courts in Germany' in Christian Tomuschat and Joe Verhoeven (eds), *Les pratiques comparées du droit international en France et en Allemagne* (Pedone 2011) 12–25, 24.

51. eg FCC, 19 September 2006, ECLI:DE:BVerfG:2006:rk20060919.2bvr211501, paragraphs 58–62 (right to consular assistance). English abstract https://www.bundesverfassungsgericht.de/SharedDocs/Entscheidungen/EN/2006/09/rk20060919_2bvr211501en.html.
52. FCC, 31 May 2006, BVerfGE 116, 69, 90. On this, see Katharina Reiling, 'Die Anwendung des Grundsatzes der Völkerrechtsfreundlichkeit auf rechtsunverbindliche internationale Standards', 78 Zeitschrift für ausländisches öffentliches Recht und Völkerrecht/Heidelberg Journal of International Law 2018, 311–338.
53. FCC, 4 May 2011, BVerfGE 128, 326, paragraphs 91–94; English translation https://www.bundesverfassungsgericht.de/SharedDocs/Entscheidungen/EN/2011/05/rs20110504_2bvr236509en.html.
54. For a critical assessment, see Wissenschaftsrat ([German] Council of Science and Humanities), *Prospects of Legal Scholarship in Germany: Current Situation, Analyses, Recommendations* (2012), English translation https://www.wissenschaftsrat.de/download/archiv/2558-12_engl.html.
55. FCC, 15 December 2015, BVerfGE 141, 1, 26, summary statements no 3–5; English translation https://www.bundesverfassungsgericht.de/SharedDocs/Entscheidungen/EN/2015/12/ls20151215_2bvl000112en.html.
56. cf, eg, FAC, 25 November 2020, ECLI:DE:BVerwG:2020:251120U6C7.19.0 (US Air Base Ramstein).
57. FCC, 3 July 2007, BVerfGE 118, 244, 268–269, paragraphs 66–68; English translation https://www.bundesverfassungsgericht.de/SharedDocs/Entscheidungen/EN/2007/07/es20070703_2bve000207en.html; 17 September 2019, BVerfGE 152, 8, paragraphs 46–51; English translation https://www.bundesverfassungsgericht.de/SharedDocs/Entscheidungen/EN/2019/09/es20190917_2bve000216en.html.
58. FCC, 19 May 2020, BVerfGE 154, 152; English translation https://www.bundesverfassungsgericht.de/SharedDocs/Entscheidungen/EN/2020/05/rs20200519_1bvr283517en.html.
59. cf FCC, 18 November 2020, ECLI:DE:BVerfG:2020:rk20201118.2bvr047717; English abstract https://www.bundesverfassungsgericht.de/SharedDocs/Entscheidungen/EN/2020/11/rk20201118_2bvr047717en.html.
60. FCJ, 2 November 2006, BGHZ (= Collected Decisions of the FCJ in Civil Matters) 169, 348 (Vavarin); 6 October 2016, BGHZ 212, 173 (Kunduz). For a closer analysis, see von Arnauld, 'Damages for the Infringement of Human Rights in Germany' (n 2) 128–130.
61. Tomuschat (n 24) 54.
62. Mirjam Reiter, 'Germany champions "Alliance for Multilateralism" ' https://gpil.jura.uni-bonn.de/2021/02/germany-champions-alliance-for-multilateralism/ (2 February 2021).
63. https://www.auswaertiges-amt.de/blob/1214246/057f794cd3593763ea556897972574fd/preventing-crises-data.pdf.
64. https://www.auswaertiges-amt.de/blob/2586726/4810ccbbc8aa4d2140817311f68afe74/aussen--und-sicherheitspolitisches-konzept-fuer-ein-integriertes-friedensengagement-data.pdf.
65. https://www.bmi.bund.de/SharedDocs/downloads/EN/themen/it-digital-policy/cyber-security-strategy-for-germany2021.pdf.
66. cf https://www.nationalesicherheitsstrategie.de/en.html.
67. Tomuschat (n 24) 46–49.
68. Criticism comes not only from activists and civil society groups. In a March 2021 landmark decision, the FCC ordered the Federal legislator to introduce more impactful strategies in the fight against climate change, arguing on the basis of positive human rights obligations

towards future generations, cf FCC, 24 March 2021, BVerfGE 157, 30, English translation https://www.bundesverfassungsgericht.de/SharedDocs/Entscheidungen/EN/2021/03/rs20210324_1bvr265618en.html.

69. English translation https://www.gesetze-im-internet.de/englisch_vstgb/index.html.
70. FCJ, 28 January 2021, ECLI:DE:BGH:2021:280121U3STR564.19.0. Report in English: Tom Syring 'Judgment on Foreign Soldiers' Immunity for War Crimes Committed Abroad (BGH)', 60 ILM 2021, 1–7, doi:10.1017/ilm.2021.44.
71. See letter (October/November 2021, not dated) to the Sixth Committee, https://www.un.org/en/ga/sixth/76/pdfs/statements/ilc/21mtg_germany_2.pdf.
72. In recent years, between 7 and11 per cent in opinion polls: https://de.statista.com/statistik/daten/studie/271580/umfrage/einschaetzung--bessere-zukunft-fuer-deutschland-ohne-europaeische-union-eu/.
73. cf Beverly Crawford, 'Moral Leadership or Moral Hazard? Germany's Response to the Refugee Crisis and Its Impact on European Solidarity' in Marianne Riddervold, Jarle Trondal, and Akasemi Newsome (eds), *The Palgrave Handbook of EU Crises* (Palgrave Macmillan 2021) 489–505.
74. With France and Poland there are regular joint consultations in the context of the so-called 'Weimar Triangle' which have been taken up again in 2020 after a break of four years.
75. On this phenomenon, see Till Patrik Holterhus, *Der extrovertierte Rechtsstaat* (Mohr Siebeck 2024, in preparation). cf Also, Matthias Kötter et al (eds), *Rechtsstaatsförderung. Handbuch für Forschung und Praxis* (Kohlhammer 2022).
76. András Jakab, 'The Fading International Influence of German Constitutional Thinking', *Verfassungsblog* (9 October 2020), https://verfassungsblog.de/the-fading-international-influence-of-german-constitutional-thinking/.
77. ibid.
78. cf contributions in Tania Groppi and Marie-Claire Ponthoreau (eds), *The Use of Foreign Precedents by Constitutional Judges* (Hart Publishing 2013); András Jakab, Arthur Dyevre, and Giulio Itzcovich (eds), *Comparative Constitutional Reasoning* (CUP 2017). Especially on the changing practice of the FCC, see Stefan Martini, *Vergleichende Verfassungsrechtsprechung. Praxis, Viabilität und Begründung rechtsvergleichender Argumentation durch Verfassungsgerichte* (Duncker&Humblot 2018).
79. For a brief analysis of that decision, see Adam Łazowski and Michał Ziółkowski 'Knocking on Polexit's door? Poland, the Constitutional Tribunal and the battle over the primacy of EU law' (21 October 2021) https://www.ceps.eu/knocking-on-polexits-door/.
80. Coalition agreement 2021–2025, between SPD, Bündnis 90/Die Grünen, and FDP, at 155. https://www.bundesregierung.de/breg-de/aktuelles/koalitionsvertrag-2021-1990800.
81. cf, eg, Stefan Talmon, 'Non-recognition of Israeli annexation of the occupied Syrian Golan' https://gpil.jura.uni-bonn.de/2019/04/non-recognition-of-israeli-annexation-of-the-occupied-syrian-golan/ (1 April 2019); Tomuschat (n 24) 49.
82. ICJ, *Alleged Breaches of Certain International Obligations in Respect of the Occupied Palestinian Territory (Nicaragua v. Germany)*, Request for the indication of provisional measures, Order of 30 April 2024.
83. Tomuschat (n 24) 48, with further references.
84. On the ambiguous position of the German government at the time, see Matthias Herdegen and Thilo Rensmann, 'Is There a Specific German Approach to the Prohibition of the Use of Force', 50 German Yearbook of International Law 2007, 349, 372–373.

85. For a critical discussion, see Helmut Philipp Aust and Mehrdad Payandeh, 'German Practice with regard to the Use of Force in Syria', 61 German Yearbook of International Law 2019, 451–463.
86. See Marko Milanovic, 'The Clearly Illegal US Missile Strike in Syria' https://www.ejiltalk.org/the-clearly-illegal-us-missile-strike-in-syria/ (7 April 2017); 'The Syria Strikes: Still Clearly Illegal' https://www.ejiltalk.org/the-syria-strikes-still-clearly-illegal/ (15 April 2018).
87. Coalition agreement 2021–2025, between SPD, Bündnis 90/Die Grünen, and FDP, at 145.
88. Michael Staack, *Handelsstaat Deutschland: Außenpolitik in einem neuen internationalen System* (Ferdinand Schöningh 2000).
89. Bjorn Gens, 'Germany's Russia Policy and Geo-economics: Nord Stream 2, Sanctions and the Question of EU Leadership towards Russia', 5 Global Affairs 2019, 315–334.
90. cf Joachim Becker, 'The German Political Economy Today' in Brigitte Unger (ed), *The German Model—Seen by its Neighbours* (SE Publishing 2015) 237–249.
91. See, *inter alia*, Simon Lester, 'Is the Doha Round Over? The WTO's Negotiating Agenda for 2016 and Beyond', 64 Cato Institute Free Trade Bulletin, available at SSRN: https://ssrn.com/abstract=2784917 (11 February 2016).
92. cf, eg, Jeffrey J Anderson, 'Hard Interests, Soft Power, and Germany's Changing Role in Europe' in Peter J Katzenstein (ed), *Tamed Power: Germany in Europe* (Cornell University Press 1997) 1–48.
93. Treaty for the Promotion and Protection of Investments, 25 November 1959, UNTS 457, 63.
94. For an overview, see Markus Ludwigs, 'Germany's Nuclear Phase-out and the Right to Property' in 4 *European Networks Law & Regulation Quarterly* 2016, 43–47.
95. Rhea Tamara Hoffmann, 'Über Richten und Schlichten: Einigung der Bundesregierung mit den Energieversorgern zum Atomausstieg' https://verfassungsblog.de/uber-richten-und-schlichten/ (10 March 2021).
96. For a differentiated analysis, see Jessica C Lawrence, 'The EU in the Mirror of NPE: Normative Power Europe in the EU's New Generation Trade and Investment Agreements' in Csongor István Nagy (ed), *World Trade and Local Public Interest* (Springer 2020) 33–50.
97. English translation https://www.bmas.de/SharedDocs/Downloads/DE/Internationales/act-corporate-due-diligence-obligations-supply-chains.pdf.
98. On this campaign, see Tomuschat (n 24) 41–42; Stefan Talmon, https://gpil.jura.uni-bonn.de/2021/09/un-security-council-reform-a-story-of-growing-german-frustration/ (30 September 2021).
99. Heiko Borchert, 'The Rocky Road to Networked and Effects-Based Expeditionary Forces: Military Transformation in the Bundeswehr' in Theo Farrell, Terriff Terry, and Osinga Frans (eds), *A Transformation Gap? American Innovations and European Military Change* (Stanford University Press 2010) 83–107.
100. FCC, 12 July 1994, BVerfGE 90, 286 – *AWACS/UNOSOM II.*
101. On the illegality of NATO's Kosovo operation, see, from a sympathizing perspective, Antonio Cassese, 'Ex iniuria ius oritur: Are We Moving towards International Legitimation of Forcible Humanitarian Countermeasures in the World Community?', 10 European Journal of International Law 1999, 23–30.
102. Egbert Jahn, *German Domestic and Foreign Policy: Political Issues Under Debate*, vol 2 (Springer 2015) 209–224.

103. On this incident, see Emma J Marchant, 'Insufficient Knowledge in Kunduz: The Precautionary Principle and International Humanitarian Law', 25 Journal of Conflict and Security Law 2020, 53–79.
104. ECtHR, *Hanan v Germany*, App no 4871/16, 16 February 2021.
105. For a thorough critique, see Dire Tladi, 'The Nonconsenting Innocent State: The Problem with Bethlehem's Principle', 107 American Journal of International Law 2013, 570–576; Paulina Starski, 'Right to Self-Defense, Attribution and the Non-State Actor—Birth of the "Unable or Unwilling" Standard?', 75 Zeitschrift für ausländisches öffentliches Recht und Völkerrecht/Heidelberg Journal of International Law 2015, 455–501; Olivier Corten, 'The "Unwilling or Unable" Test: Has it Been, and Could it be, Accepted?', 29 Leiden Journal of International Law 2016, 777–799.
106. See Dapo Akande and Marko Milanovic https://www.ejiltalk.org/the-constructive-ambiguity-of-the-security-councils-isis-resolution/.
107. For a critique, see von Arnauld, *Völkerrecht* (n 29) 496–497, paragraph 1135; Mehrdad Payandeh and Heiko Sauer, 'Die Beteiligung der Bundeswehr am Antiterroreinsatz in Syrien: Völker- und Verfassungsrechtliche Rahmenbedingungen', Zeitschrift für Rechtspolitik 2016, 34–37.
108. cf Stefan Talmon https://gpil.jura.uni-bonn.de/2020/02/german-government-on-foreign-troop-presence-in-syria/ (17 February 2020).
109. National Security Strategy (n 69) 22, 30.
110. Tomuschat (n 24) 53.
111. On the practice, see Gerd Westdickenberg 'The Role of the Legal Adviser in the German Federal Foreign Office in Comparison to some Other Aspects of the Role of Legal Adviser in Other Countries' in Tomuschat and Verhoeven (n 49) 35–50.
112. For a closer analysis, see Nico Krisch, 'The Many Fields of (German) International Law', in Anthea Roberts et al (eds), *Comparative International Law* (OUP 2018) 91–109, 100–106.
113. ibid, 100.
114. Both journals are bilingual today and publish articles in German and English. The Kiel-based *German Yearbook of International Law*, in contrast, became an English-only periodical in 2009. On this development and its ramifications, also in comparison with the other two periodicals, see Andreas von Arnauld and Daley J Birkett, 'The German Yearbook of International Law: Origins, Development, Prospects', 50 Netherlands Yearbook of International Law 2019, 149–168.
115. To name but only the regularly updated, there are currently textbooks available by Andreas von Arnauld; Matthias Herdegen; Stephan Hobe (founded by Otto Kimminich); Knut Ipsen (editor, founded by Eberhard Menzel); Markus Krajewski; Torsten Stein, Christian von Buttlar and Markus Kotzur (founded by Ignaz Seidl-Hohenveldern); Wolfgang Graf Vitzthum and Alexander Proelss (editors). A textbook by Anne Peters and Anna Petrig is devoted to 'General International Law' only. Finally, mention must also be made of the monumental rewriting of Georg Dahm's classic textbook by Jost Delbrück and Rüdiger Wolfrum which was discontinued in 2002 after three instalments of the first volume.
116. Krisch (n 112) 101.
117. This section borrows its title from the focus section of the 50th volume of the *German Yearbook of International Law* (2007), conceived and edited by Thomas Giegerich and Andreas Zimmermann.

118. See also Krisch (n 112) 99; Tomuschat (n 24) 20–23. Developed in a programmatic manner by Anne Peters, 'Die Zukunft der Völkerrechtswissenschaft: Wider den epistemischen Nationalismus', 67 Zeitschrift für ausländisches öffentliches Recht und Völkerrecht/ Heidelberg Journal of International Law 2007, 721–776, 747–764.
119. Such imprints can be traced even further back, to the 17th and 18th centuries where at German universities the law of nations was academically wedded to legal philosophy. The resulting *ius naturae et gentium* has recently been called by Martti Koskenniemi, *To the Uttermost Parts of the Earth: Legal Imagination and International Power 1300–1870* (CUP 2021) 797, a 'German discipline'.
120. Paraphrasing the title of the study by Frieder Günther, *Denken vom Staat her: Die bundesdeutsche Staatsrechtslehre zwischen Dezision und Integration 1949–1970* (Oldenbourg 2004) on German public lawyers' approach to law between 1949 and 1970.
121. In this sense, see Krisch (n 112) 98–99, 107.
122. Stephan Hobe and Karsten Nowrot, 'Whither the Sovereign State?', 50 German Yearbook of International Law 2007, 243–302, 250–262. On Hegel's influence on proponents of the 'Machtsstaat' around 1900, see Anthony Carty, 'The Evolution of International Legal Scholarship in Germany during the Kaiserreich and the Weimarer Republik (1871–1933)', 50 German Yearbook of International Law 2007, 29–90.
123. Dupuy (n 1) 386–390; Tomuschat (n 24) 49. See, *inter alia*, Hermann Mosler, *The International Society as a Legal Community* (Sijthoff & Noordhoff 1980); Bruno Simma, 'From Bilateralism to Community Interest in International Law', 250 Recueil des cours de l'Académie de Droit International de La Haye 1994, 217–384; Anne Peters, 'The Merits of Global Constitutionalism', 16 Indiana Journal of Global Legal Studies 2009, 397–411. On the German debate about 'constitutionalism beyond the state', see Stefan Kadelbach and Thomas Kleinlein, 'International Law—A Constitution for Mankind? An Attempt at a Re-appraisal with an Analysis of Constitutional Principles', 50 German Yearbook of International Law 2007, 303–347.
124. Andreas Paulus, 'Zur Zukunft der Völkerrechtswissenschaft in Deutschland: Zwischen Konstitutionalisierung und Fragmentierung des Völkerrechts', 67 Zeitschrift für ausländisches öffentliches Recht und Völkerrecht/Heidelberg Journal of International Law 2007, 695–719, 701.
125. Krisch (n 112) 96.
126. Lauri Hannikainen, 'Juridically Solid, Politically—What: Personal Reflections on the German Approach to International Law', 50 German Yearbook of International Law 2007, 431–444, 437.
127. Krisch (n 112) 106.
128. Eyal Benvenisti, 'The Future of International Law Scholarship in Germany: The Tension Between Interpretation and Change', 67 Zeitschrift für ausländisches öffentliches Recht und Völkerrecht/Heidelberg Journal of International Law 2007, 585–598, 588–589; Eyal Benvenisti, 'The Conception of International Law as a Legal System', 50 German Yearbook of International Law 2007, 393–405; Dupuy (n 1) 382–386.
129. Andreas Zimmermann, 'Zur Zukunft der Völkerrechtswissenschaft in Deutschland', 67 Zeitschrift für ausländisches öffentliches Recht und Völkerrecht/Heidelberg Journal of International Law 2007, 799–824, 805; Armin von Bogdandy, 'Wissenschaft vom Verfassungsrecht: Vergleich' in Armin von Bogdandy, Pedro Cruz Villalón, and Peter M Huber (eds), *Handbuch Ius Publicum Europaeum*, vol II (C.F. Müller 2008) § 39, 807–842, 817, as translated by Krisch (n 112) 106.

130. The first post-war encyclopaedia was a new edition of Karl Strupp's *Wörterbuch des Völkerrechts und der Diplomatie* (de Gruyter 1924–1929), edited by Hans-Jürgen Schlochauer (de Gruyter 1960–1962). This was followed by a modernized version in English, the *Encyclopaedia of Public International Law* (Elsevier 1981–2003), edited by the then director of the Heidelberg Max Planck Institute, Rudolf Bernhardt, which has been updated and transported into the digital age by his successors at the Institute, Rüdiger Wolfrum and Anne Peters, as the *Max Planck Encyclopaedia of Public International Law* (OUP, since 2008).
131. Krisch (n 112) 97.
132. Tomuschat (n 24) 49.
133. Jan Klabbers, 'Book Review', 16 Leiden Journal of International Law 2003, 201–207, 202–203.
134. Fred L Morrison, 'German Scholars in the Invisible College of International Lawyers', 50 German Yearbook of International Law 2007, 445–455, 445, 447.

CHAPTER 29

GREECE

IAKOVOS V. IAKOVIDIS AND
VASSILIS P. TZEVELEKOS

1. Introduction: (Self-)Perceptions

Public international law (PIL) is a rather popular concept in Greece that occupies a prominent position in the public discourse. Greece's self-image is that of a law-abiding nation that relies on PIL and its membership of international organizations, such as the United Nations (UN), the North Atlantic Treaty Organisation (NATO), and the European Union (EU), as a 'shield' to protect itself and as a medium to peacefully promote its national interests. Another (self-)perception is that, unlike the important contributions of Ancient Greece to areas such as philosophy, science, and the arts, modern Greece's footprint is fairly limited. This also applies to PIL. Indeed, mathematics and philosophy are rich in the Greek terms they contain; PIL being significantly 'younger', it only contains a few and not particularly prevalent Greek terms and concepts. For instance, the Olympic Truce replicates the ancient tradition of '*εκεχειρία*' (*ekecheiria*), in terms of which, to ensure the safety of the Olympic Games, hostilities were to cease.[1] 'Synallagmatic' is another term for reciprocal obligations, but how many (non-Greek) PIL lawyers use this jargon? A third example is the Aristotelian concepts of 'equity' and 'equitable', which have been 'absorbed' by (international) law, to 'return' to Greek literature and practice as a 'loan', translated *inter alia* as 'equal'[2] or 'fair',[3] which are terms different to the one (ie *ἐπιείκεια*, *epieikeia*) employed by Aristotle.[4] Thus, Greece may be seen as 'importing' PIL. Our impression is that this is related to another popular perception in Greece about PIL: when PIL is not understood in the public opinion (ie by non-experts) as coinciding with a natural law-stemming conception of fairness (which 'naturally' favours Greek interests), it is perceived as a 'made not-in-Greece' construct, mostly shaped by the 'powerful ones' to serve their interests. However, oxymoronic as this may be, the Greek public sphere and collective imagination have also developed a (quite selective) sense of 'ownership' of PIL. Thus, be it 'exotic', PIL is also appreciated as an 'enlightened' area of law of higher authority and value that Greece can strategically use to defend itself and to equip its claims and interests with legal foundations, particularly in areas that are important to it because of the country's particular features, such as its geography (eg law of the sea, maritime delimitation) or history (eg cultural heritage and the reunification of the Parthenon sculptures through their return to Greece from the UK[5]).

In this chapter we endeavour to offer an inevitably brief and selective, albeit—we trust or, at least, this is our ambition—fair account of modern Greece's contribution to PIL. Indeed, Greece's impact—both directly and indirectly—on PIL is not negligible, which means that the noted perception of Greece as a mostly passive recipient of PIL or even on the receiving end of PIL is fairly inaccurate. Besides, as all nations do, Greece contributes to PIL simply by being a member of the international community of states and by interacting with other actors. Greece declared its independence from the Ottoman Empire on 1 January 1822.[6] In these 201 years, the encounters between the modern Greek state and PIL have been frequent and wide-ranging. Indeed, Greek history offers an abundancy of PIL 'case studies', spanning from an early instance of forcible intervention possibly qualifying as humanitarian,[7] that is, the 1827 Navarino naval battle, where the fleets of France, Great Britain, and Russia defeated the forces of Ottoman Empire, paving the way for the independence of Greece, to the 1923 Convention Concerning the Exchange of Greek and Turkish Populations Between Turkey and Greece,[8] which led to the denaturalization and compulsory displacement from their homelands of over 1.6 million people—a controversial arrangement that raises delicate issues pertaining to the balance to be maintained between, on the one hand, the protection of human life through the prevention of atrocities and ethnic cleansing and, on the other, uprooting, compulsory expulsion, and respect for rights such as home and family life.

Overall, as this chapter will seek to demonstrate, Greece's direct and indirect contribution to PIL is not insignificant. The role of individuals coming from Greece who, acting as scholars and/or practitioners, have left their mark on PIL has also been considerable. Considering the scope of the volume that hosts this chapter, but also the chapter's confines, we are mostly limiting our discussion here to the contribution of Greece and of Greeks to PIL in the more recent decades and, in any case, after World War I. Section 2 examines how PIL is received by the Greek legal order, highlighting Greece's openness to rules pertaining to European integration. It also provides a characteristic example showing how PIL rules received in the municipal order may 'bounce back' to and impact the international order, as state practice, for instance. Section 3 discusses the direct contribution of the Greek state to PIL, giving select examples of international rules and standards aiming at protecting, not only Greece's individual interests, but also the international community's collective interests. Section 4 turns to indirect contribution through, first, PIL case law concerning Greece and, second, the international reach of Greek PIL scholarship. Section 5 briefly discusses pacific dispute settlement, exploring how Greek foreign policy employs PIL to that end and to advance, outside of national interests, international peace. Section 6 concludes by bringing together the pieces in the analysis contained in the previous sections to draw the broader picture of Greece's contribution to PIL. Conclusions also connect the discussion in this chapter with the three key questions raised in their introduction by the volume's editors.

2. The Domestic Legal Order and PIL: Not Just a Passive Recipient of PIL

2.1 Beyond formalism—unconditional openness?

Article 28(1) of the 1975 Greek Constitution (GC) sets a framework for international conventional law that is dualist in principle, as treaties are transformed into municipal law through ratification.[9] Under that Article, both customary and conventional international law are granted infra-constitutional, but supra-legislative power.[10] That is, formally at least, in case of conflict between domestic law and PIL, the latter prevails as long as the municipal rule is not of constitutional calibre.

This is the framework set by the GC. But to better understand and assess the stance of the Greek legal order vis-à-vis PIL, one needs to look beyond formalism and situate this framework within its broader political and historical context. Article 28 GC was enacted after the collapse of the seven-year dictatorship. This era coincides with Greece's efforts to join the European institutions. Article 28 GC also provides the requirements (such as the requisite number of Members of Parliament (MP) votes) for Greece to become a member of international organizations.[11] The 2001 constitutional revision added an interpretative note under the text of Article 28 GC explaining that said Article 'constitutes the foundation' for Greece's participation in the European integration process.[12] This chapter is not the place to discuss the expediency of such interpretive notes complementing the text of the (Basic) law or what legal effects they may produce. Yet, this particular note can also be read as a declaration attesting to the Greek polity's commitment to European integration, which—being associated with democracy, political stability, prosperity, and security—amounts to a wider socio-legal goal of higher *gravitas*.

Perhaps this offers an explanation as to why, although, formally, under Article 28 GC, in case of conflict, EU law and the European Convention on Human Rights (ECHR) do not prevail over the GC, in practice, the latter has proven to recede in favour of these two areas of law. This is evidenced by the fact that the GC has consistently been interpreted and applied in a manner that favours harmony, and even amended to align its provisions with EU and ECHR law. To give just a few examples, Article 4(4) GC provides that '[o]nly Greek citizens shall be eligible for public service, except as otherwise provided by special laws'.[13] According to Article 110(1) GC, Article 4(4) is non-amendable.[14] This led to harmonization being pursued through the special law complementing Article 4(4) GC, that is, through ordinary legislation that defines the term 'public service' in conformity with the relevant Court of Justice of the European

Union (CJEU) case law.[15] Another example is Article 14(9) GC, which was revised in 2011 to establish an incompatibility between the sectors of public works and media.[16] Among other persons, the owner, partner, major shareholder, or managing director of a media company cannot be contractors for public works or provide goods/services to the public sector. After the CJEU held that Article 14(9) GC fails to respect proportionality and that EU law cannot tolerate an irrebuttable presumption of incompatibility between persons involved in public works and media,[17] the Greek courts departed from their previous case law[18] and deferentially aligned their interpretation of the GC with that of the CJEU.[19] Moving to the ECHR, a characteristic example is Article 57(1) GC, which was amended in 2001 to prohibit the exercise of any profession during an MP's tenure in office.[20] The European Court of Human Rights (ECtHR) found Greece to be in breach of Article 3 Protocol No 1 ECHR because an MP who was elected before the entry into force of revised Article 57 GC forfeited their seat.[21] In 2008, Article 57 GC was amended and the prohibition on MPs' exercise of professional activities was removed.[22]

The list with examples showing the openness of the Greek legal system vis-à-vis the ECHR and the EU orders is rather long. In this way, the Greek legal order complies with its supranational obligations under EU law and with the ECHR, whilst also contributing to European integration through the approximation of the legal systems and rules of the European nations. The Greek order thereby co-shapes European integration. This is also made possible because, *en fait*, the municipal system of Greece is much more porous and open to international rules than the law (ie Article 28 GC) formally provides. One of us has described this as a 'meta-positivist' reality, in terms of which, in principle, European integration through the EU and the Council of Europe (CoE) supersedes *de facto* the Greek municipal order in its entirety.[23] That is, domestic law, including the GC, recedes in favour of political projects, goals, and processes, such as European integration, that are perceived as beneficial.

Yet, the picture drawn above needs to be complemented and fine-tuned. First, the openness, both legally and politically, of the Greek legal system mostly concerns European integration rules, not necessarily PIL more generally. Second, openness is neither unlimited, nor unconditional. Indeed, there are instances of what could be described as judicial 'resistance'. Without commenting here on the rationale behind these instances or their legitimacy, we could give examples of case law challenging standards set by the ECtHR or of more 'principled' conditionality set by the Greek courts for them to align their decisions with ECtHR case law. For instance, the highest administrative court, the Council of State, has established a 'test' for judicial process before it to be repeated in cases where its first decision led to a finding by the ECtHR of an ECHR violation.[24] Accordingly, among other conditions that ought to be met, the Council of State shall ensure that compliance with an ECtHR judgment against Greece through a new judicial decision rectifying the problem(s) identified by the ECtHR does not result in the violation of other PIL rules and does not infringe the GC.[25] This shows that the judiciary may occasionally (attempt to) set certain 'red lines', 'vetoing/obstructing' the alignment of the Greek legal order with European/international (human rights) standards. Yet, the Council of State has also highlighted that it shall strive to harmonize the GC with the ECHR.[26]

2.2 The complexity of the domestic legal system rendering state practice ambiguous

This sort of *Solange*[27] by the Council of State—which is willing to enable compliance with ECtHR judgments *as long as* certain (judge-made) conditions have been met—is also revelatory of the complexity of the legal system. By no means is this a particularity of the Greek legal order. Quite the opposite, complexity is inherent to municipal orders. This applies even more so to democracies, where separation of powers and the involvement of different national authorities in decision making over an issue can render the identification of state practice contributing to customary international law quite difficult.

An apposite example to illustrate this point is the *Distomo* 'saga' concerning the decline of state jurisdictional immunity in favour of access to justice as a means to remedy World War II crimes.[28] In the *Distomo* case law lie the roots of the *Jurisdictional Immunities of the State* judgment of the International Court of Justice (ICJ).[29] The long line of case law and state practice that connects *Distomo* with the ICJ judgment raises some very interesting PIL issues, concerning, for instance, the identification of state practice for the purposes of customary international law,[30] the effects of *jus cogens* rules,[31] the normative conflict between access to justice and sovereign immunity,[32] and, ultimately, the clash between the so-called 'humanization' of PIL and a more traditional, state-centric approach that emphasizes sovereignty and tends to prioritize state rights over human rights. Accordingly, *Distomo* could have also been included in Section 4 of this chapter, which discusses Greece's indirect impact on PIL. Yet, we decided to discuss this set of case law here because it shows how the complexity of its municipal system can blur Greece's practice, thereby making it difficult to appraise how it influences PIL rules and standards.

In *Jurisdictional Immunities of the State*, the ICJ allowed Greece to intervene as a non-party 'in so far as [its] intervention was limited to the decisions of Greek courts which were declared by Italian courts as enforceable in Italy'.[33] The Greek courts that adjudicated the *Distomo* case set aside Germany's jurisdictional immunity and awarded damages to the relatives and successors of the victims of the World War II Distomo village massacre.[34] However, according to Article 923 of the Code of Civil Procedure, to enforce judgments against foreign states, authorization by the Minister of Justice is required.[35] The Greek government refused to grant such authorization. It then successfully defended its refusal to grant such authorization before the ECtHR, which was invited by the claimants in *Distomo* to hold that this refusal amounted to a violation of their rights to a fair trial and property.[36] The ECtHR declared this complaint inadmissible and refrained from examining it on the merits.

The trajectory of the *Distomo* case shows that the Greek state was essentially ambivalent. The judiciary favoured the claimants' (human) rights and their reparation, whereas the executive favoured state immunity. Yet, the picture is even more complex. Proceedings that successors of victims of World War II crimes in another Greek village, Lidoriki, brought before domestic courts resulted in the Greek Special Supreme Court ultimately and authoritatively confirming the prevalence of state immunity.[37] One may wonder why after all these 'back and forths' resulting in both the judiciary and the executive branches eventually favouring state immunity, the Greek government decided to intervene in the dispute between Germany and Italy regarding the former's jurisdictional immunities to support the latter and the case law produced by some, but not all, relevant Greek courts. The ICJ's well-justified answer came with its conclusion that 'Greek State practice *taken as a whole* actually contradicts, rather than supports, Italy's argument'.[38]

The signalling of different messages or even inconsistency in state practice can stem from the involvement of different authorities or governments of different colour in the development of state practice. Therefore, the complexity of the legal system, particularly in pluralistic democracies relying on separation of powers and on judicial independence, can obscure state practice and render the identification of the direction in which such fuzzy practice points a delicate intellectual exercise. Greece is not an exception to this, and the *Distomo* family of cases—outside of their broader impact on the PIL order regarding the (still unsettled) issue of the decline of sovereign immunities as a means to hold states and their agents accountable for serious human rights violations—is quite a telling example. However, this does not mean that states can never speak with one voice or that their will and practice cannot be clear and directly impact on PIL. The next section gives examples of Greece's direct impact on PIL.

3. Greece's Direct Impact on PIL

Greece systematically endeavours to contribute to the development of PIL rules, such as through proactive participation in international conferences codifying key PIL areas and various standard-setting institutional forums. The first part of this section gives illustrative examples[39] pertaining to general international law in the areas of the law of the sea and of treaty law. The second part gives select instances of soft law and standards of smaller magnitude. The topics discussed below have been chosen as examples of direct contribution to PIL, but also to evidence that Greece moves beyond areas that are of special interest to it and/or concern its self-interest, also seeking to promote rules and standards pertaining to the protection of the international community's collective interests.

3.1 Hard law—the regime of islands, underwater cultural heritage, and *jus cogens*

Starting with the law of the sea, Greece is a nation of seafarers with a coastline of over 13,000 kilometres consisting of continental seashores and the shoreline of over 6,000 islands, islets, and sea rocks. Thus, it comes as no surprise that Greece sought to be influential in the development of the law of the sea throughout all stages of its evolution. It also proactively participated in the Third UN Conference on the Law of the Sea, thereby contributing to the shaping of 'a legal order for the seas and oceans', as a means to 'strengthen ... peace, security ... [and] cooperation'—some of the aims of the 1982 UN Convention on the Law of the Sea (UNCLOS), as they figure in its preamble.[40]

An UNCLOS provision of particular interest to Greece is Article 121 on the '[r]egime of islands'.[41] In the 1970s, customary international law had already moved in the direction of endowing islands with maritime zones, including the continental shelf. However, Greece was concerned as various aspects (eg 12 nautical miles territorial sea and continental shelf of islands) of this evolution were still challenged.[42] Greece's position was that 'islands were as much a part of the territory of a State as its principal territory, and were therefore entitled to the same treatment under international law',[43] so 'that insular populations ... [can] be on an equal footing with others'.[44] To that end, Greece presented in the Third UN Conference on the Law of the Sea, among other versions,[45] the following proposed text, which starts by reproducing the definition of an island of Article 10(1) of the 1958 Convention on the Territorial Sea and the Contiguous Zone,[46] and continues as follows:

> ... 2. An island forms an integral part of the territory of the State to which it belongs. The territorial sovereignty over the island extends to its territorial sea, to the air space over the island and its territorial sea to its sea-bed and subsoil thereof and to its continental shelf for the purpose of exploiting its natural resources. 3. The maritime zones of the island are determined in accordance with the same provisions applicable for the measurements of the territorial sea of the continental part of the territory of the State...[47]

The amendment proposed by Greece has been influential in that, in terms of Article 121(2) UNCLOS, islands have all maritime zones, and these are determined in the same way as the maritime zones of the continental part of a state's land territory.[48] Moreover, in terms of Article 77(1) UNCLOS, states do not have full sovereignty over their continental shelf, but they exercise sovereign rights for the purpose of exploiting their natural resources,[49] which is close to Greece's proposed amendment. For Greece, the PIL rules on the regime of islands are 'universally accepted ... under existing international customary ... law'.[50]

Moving to another UNCLOS provision, Article 303 is titled '[a]rchaeological and historical objects found at sea', and establishes an obligation of means for states 'to protect objects of an archaeological and historical nature found at sea'.[51] Before UNCLOS, a gap existed in PIL as to the protection of underwater cultural heritage.[52] A question that dominated the debates in the last sessions of the Third UN Conference on the Law of the Sea was that of jurisdiction for the purposes of underwater cultural heritage protection. Greece, along with Cape Verde, Italy, Malta, Portugal, Tunisia, and Yugoslavia, proposed that the sovereign rights of coastal states be recognized over archaeological objects on their continental shelf.[53] This arrangement was opposed by, among others, the Netherlands, the UK, and the US.[54] Beyond the contiguous zone, which is regulated in respect of underwater cultural heritage by Article 303(2) UNCLOS,[55] states shall cooperate. This rather 'soft' and far from perfect[56] arrangement is the product of compromise, towards which Greece contributed with a proposal, in terms of which 'all states have the duty to protect in a spirit of cooperation objects of archaeological or historical value found in the marine environment'.[57] Accordingly, read together with Article 149 UNCLOS, which deals with underwater cultural heritage found in the area,[58] Article 303(1) establishes a positive duty for states to cooperate to protect underwater cultural heritage.[59]

Moving to treaty law and, more specifically, to peremptory norms, in its 1966 commentaries on the law of treaties draft articles, the International Law Commission (ILC) expressed the following concern regarding what was at the time draft Article 50 on the invalidity of an international treaty that conflicts with a peremptory norm of general international law: '... there is no simple criterion by which to identify a general rule of international law, as having the character of *jus cogens*'.[60] In the first session of the UN Conference on the Law of Treaties—Vienna conference, held between March–May 1968—this Article was abundantly discussed over five consecutive meetings.[61] Greece contributed significantly to the final wording of this Article—which became Article 53 of the Vienna Convention on the Law of Treaties (VCLT)[62]—concerning both the criteria for identifying a rule as peremptory and the nullity effects generated by *jus cogens* rules in case of normative conflict. As far as the identification of *jus cogens* is concerned, Greece and Finland, joined by Spain, proposed inserting '[b]etween the words "general international law" and "from which no derogation" ... the words "recognized by the international community as a norm" '.[63] Professor Dimitrios Evrigenis, member of the Greek delegation to the Vienna conference, explained the rationale of this amendment, noting that '[t]he essential element of international *jus cogens* ... lay in the universality of its acceptance by the international community. Peremptory international law was expressed in rules from which by general consent no derogation was permitted'.[64] This is reflected in the text of Article 53 VCLT, in terms of which, a key criterion for a PIL rule to qualify as *jus cogens* is that it is accepted and recognized by the international community of states as a whole.[65] As far as the nullity effects of *jus cogens* rules are concerned, the Vienna conference's *travaux* reveal that academic consensus as to the point that treaties conflicting with *jus cogens* norms shall be void *ab initio* was also built thanks to an academic PIL conference held in Greece in April 1966.[66]

3.2 Soft law—the safety of journalists, illicit trafficking of cultural property, and neurotechnology and human rights

Until November 2013, the UN General Assembly (UNGA) had never truly dealt with the issue of the safety of journalists.[67] In September 2012, following the launch by the UN Educational, Scientific and Cultural Organization (UNESCO) in April 2012 of the UN Plan of Action on the Safety of Journalists,[68] the UN Human Right Council (HRC) adopted resolution 21/12 on the same issue.[69] Transforming this HRC resolution into a UNGA resolution was considered almost impossible at that time, as this would require support by the majority of all UN member states, as opposed to support by the majority of the forty-seven HRC member states that was required for resolution 21/12. Nevertheless, on 18 December 2013, the UNGA managed to adopt resolution 68/163 on this topic,[70] with Greece's role being instrumental in this respect.

In the past, Greece had already played a leading role on the topic of the safety of journalists in situations of armed conflict, when, in 2006, acting within the framework of the UN Security Council (UNSC), it had put forth resolution 1738 in cooperation with France.[71] However, given the confines of the UNSC's competence, this resolution's ambit was limited to armed conflict. Considering the loss of many journalists over the years, and in particular, in 2011, of Greek-American Chris Hondros in Libya and, in 2012, of the US national, Marie Colvin, in Syria, Greece decided to put the topic in the UNGA's agenda. The initiative was initially met with scepticism or even opposition. The exponential multiplication of initiatives before various institutions and the possible overlap with the HRC resolution on the same topic were two of the reasons explaining initial lack of support. However, the tragic event of the killing in Northern Mali of two French journalists, Claude Verlon and Ghislaine Dupont, on 2 November 2013, reversed the course of the negotiations. As an immediate reaction, the then French Foreign Minister instructed France's Mission to the UN to support the Greek initiative.[72] Credit is also due to the civil society organizations, particularly to the Committee to Protect Journalists. Greece also closely cooperated with UNESCO. Joint efforts resulted in resolution 68/163 being adopted by consensus and co-sponsored by seventy-eight States.

Upon agreement, resolution 68/163 established 2 November, the day the two French journalists were killed, as the 'International Day to End Impunity of Crimes Against Journalists'.[73] Building upon Article 19 of the International Covenant on Civil and Political Rights (ICCPR),[74] which enshrines freedom of expression and the right to hold opinions, resolution 68/163 is the first UNGA document safeguarding the rights of journalists in non-conflict situations. It contributes significantly by establishing soft law standards of protection. Resolution 68/163 has also proven to be quite impactful. For instance, it has been followed by UNGA resolutions adopted on a biennial basis that enable discussion of the challenges faced by journalists and those working in the media.[75] Moreover, resolution 68/163 initiated a process that led to proposals to develop tools furthering protection, such as the idea of the elaboration of an international instrument on the safety of journalists.[76] Finally, although we are of course unable to evidence causality, UNESCO reports that crimes against journalists and impunity for such crimes have decreased since the adoption of resolution 68/163.[77]

Moving to another area, because of its rich cultural heritage, Greece, almost since the inception of the modern Greek state, has made the international protection of cultural heritage a priority. Greece has placed emphasis on the 1970 Convention on the Means of Prohibiting and Preventing the Illicit Import, Export and Transfer of Ownership of Cultural Property[78] and on the work of the UNESCO Intergovernmental Committee for Promoting the Return of Cultural Property to its Countries of Origin or its Restitution in Case of Illicit Appropriation (ICPRCP). Greece presents a triannual resolution to the UNGA, the last of which was resolution A/76/16.[79] Outside of raising awareness about the illicit import, export, and transfer of ownership of cultural property, the resolution's most important contribution is that it identifies standards of conduct. For instance, the UNGA calls on states to train police and border officials and to criminalize trafficking in cultural property in their domestic orders.[80]

The final example concerns a very recent initiative led by Greece in the area of human rights law. Mindful of the challenges that new technologies pose for human rights, acting in cooperation with Chile, Singapore, and Switzerland, in 2022, Greece included in the agenda of the HRC the question of the impact of neurotechnology on human rights. The High Commissioner for Human Rights recognized this issue as one of the forward-looking topics that the HRC has started to venture into.[81] The Greek initiative led to HRC resolution 51/3 in October 2022,[82] which recognizes in its preamble that, whilst neurotechnology can be beneficial for human health, it also raises ethical and legal questions. To study further the impact of neurotechnology on human rights and to initiate a process that may result in standard-setting in this field, the resolution requests the HRC Advisory Committee to produce a study on the impacts, opportunities, and challenges of neurotechnology with regard to human rights.[83]

4. The Indirect Contribution of Greece and of Greek Scholarship to PIL

We now turn to what may be described as 'indirect contribution'. Advisory opinions and judicial decisions involving Greece, either as a party to a dispute or even more generally, because, for instance, they concern its nationals, have made contributions to various PIL areas. Below, we give a few relevant examples highlighting the impact of the jurisprudence at issue on PIL. Then, we briefly turn to another type of indirect contribution to PIL through the works of Greek scholars and practitioners.

4.1 Case law

Starting with more recent times, we have already discussed Greece's intervention in the *Germany v Italy* dispute on jurisdictional immunities and the impact of Greek (judicial) practice on the question of the gradual erosion of sovereign immunities as a means to grant human rights victims access to justice. Other instances where Greece has appeared before the ICJ have also enabled this Court to shed light on important PIL issues. In the *Application of the Interim Accord of 13 September 1995*, the ICJ rejected Greece's 'defences' on the basis of countermeasures,[84] *exceptio non adimpleti contractus*,[85] and response to a material breach of a treaty,[86] largely because of the absence of a breach by the applicant state that would trigger the application of such defences. Moving to the *Aegean Sea Continental Shelf* case, this instance enabled the ICJ to elaborate on the criteria for determining the existence of a binding inter-state agreement, such as the terms it contains, the 'context in which it was agreed and issued', and the parties' intention.[87]

The ICJ's predecessor, the Permanent Court of International Justice (PCIJ), had also delivered important jurisprudence involving Greece that contributed significantly to the evolution of PIL.[88] *Mavrommatis* is a point of reference, *inter alia*, for the definition of 'dispute',[89] and the legal fiction of diplomatic protection that 'transforms' injury to individuals into injury to their state of nationality.[90] But other PCIJ judgments involving Greece—possibly less well-known than *Mavrommatis*—have also added to PIL. To give just a few examples, it is interesting that in its *Minority Schools in Albania* opinion, the PCIJ applies teleological interpretation on the basis of the 'object and effect' of the provision that it interprets.[91] Most importantly, this opinion provides for positive discrimination for the protection of minority rights, holding that 'equality in fact may involve the necessity of different treatment in order to attain a result which re-establishes an equilibrium between different situations'.[92] With regard to minority protection, another weighty contribution of the PCIJ had already been made before *Minority Schools in Albania*, when the Court delivered its *Greco-Bulgarian 'Communities'* opinion, where it defined the term 'community'.[93] It is notable that, apart from offering a very influential basis for the definition of the term 'minority', the *Greco-Bulgarian 'Communities'* opinion also affirms the 'generally accepted principle of international law that in the relations between … contracting Parties to a treaty, the provisions of municipal law cannot prevail over those of the treaty'.[94]

The list of similar examples is long and reaches beyond the ICJ and the PCIJ. However, given the confines of this chapter, we shall limit our discussion to one more example, which—we think—stands apart. Out of all the cases against Greece within the ECHR system, we distinguish the *Greek Case*[95] as an act of genuine solidarity towards the Greek people by Denmark, Norway, Sweden, and the Netherlands, which sued Greece on the basis of the ECHR for serious human rights violations by the dictatorial regime that ruled Greece at the time, thereby giving effect to the provisions of the ECHR framework for inter-state applications that enables non-injured (or, better, not directly injured) states to invoke the responsibility of a state allegedly violating human rights rules and thereby collectively enforce them. This reflects the *erga omnes partes* nature of the ECHR substantive provisions, which is just one among other contributions of the *Greek Case* in important areas and topics, such as emergency human rights derogations and the prohibition of torture.

4.2 The contribution of Greek scholars and practitioners

Another type of indirect impact is the one stemming from PIL scholars and practitioners. We are cognizant of the fact that we can only discuss this question here very superficially, and that this, inevitably, results in abstraction in our reasoning and omitting important figures. Having said that, we can make the following key point. With the exception of certain Greek scholars at the beginning of the 20th century, it is difficult to discern an utterly distinctive or 'stand-alone' school of thought (such as critical legal studies or feminist approaches to PIL) that Greek scholarship has exclusively or originally developed. However, we can safely argue that several leading PIL Greek scholars and practitioners fall within what has been described as 'enlightened positivism',[96] which recognizes and preserves the key PIL positivist tenets, features, and principles, whilst promoting a more cosmopolitan, liberal, and even democratic perception of and vision for the international legal system that mitigates state will.

To unpack and evidence this point, we shall begin with early 20th-century Greeks, whose scholarship (in particular in the interwar period) occupies a central place within a—rather forgotten nowadays, but prominent at that time—school of thought, namely sociological objectivism, which situated itself within legal positivism, professing that *lax lata* exists and is socially constructed, but rejected the voluntarist premises of positive law that attribute the legal force of PIL rules to state will.[97] Indeed, sociological objectivism went as far as entirely negating state sovereignty. Next to Duguit and Scelle, the 'founding fathers' of this school of thought, we can situate Politis, who maintained that '[b]ehind the vain fiction of the state, there is only one real person: that of the individual'.[98] Over time, this rigid and contemptuous for sovereignty 'aphorism' has clearly been mitigated and diluted. Yet, although sovereignty remains a basic PIL principle, ever since, the state and human rights 'negotiate' an equilibrium between them. This more 'anthropo-centric' and *pro homine* approach to PIL can be an almost invisible 'thread' that connects (as also evidenced by their respective teachings at the Hague Academy of International Law) Politis,[99] Seferiades,[100] and Spiropoulos[101] with nowadays renowned jurisconsults and scholars, such as Roucounas[102] and Sicilianos,[103] and earlier, Eustathiades,[104] Valticos,[105] and Tenekides.[106] The same 'thread' almost imperceptibly connects the past and present Greek PIL practitioners (and scholars), from the ICJ Judge Spiropoulos to the ECtHR Vice-President Rozakis, the President of the same court, Sicilianos, the sitting ECtHR Judge, Ktistakis, and the CJEU President, Skouris, through to several other important contributions by distinguished Greek lawyers to various UN institutions[107]—such as the ILC[108] or the former UN Sub-Commission on the Promotion and Protection of Human Rights[109]—and other international organizations,[110] or even as defenders of the most fundamental values of humanity.[111]

5. Settling Disputes Peacefully and Spreading Peace

Having concluded this brief and, inescapably, incomplete *tour d'horizon* on the indirect impact of Greece and Greeks on PIL, this section moves to international peace. Greece, a founding member of the UN and the League of Nations, was also one of the twenty-six states that signed the Convention on the Pacific Settlement of International Disputes at the first Hague Peace Conference in 1899, which introduced the homonymous principle to PIL,[112] providing for mediation, good offices, commissions of inquiry, and arbitration as means to settle disputes peacefully,[113] and establishing the Permanent Court of Arbitration.[114] The lines that follow discuss Greek foreign policy and provide select examples showing that Greece systematically uses PIL means to peacefully settle its disputes and protect its national interests, but also to promote international peace.

Starting with disputes and/or issues pertaining to its individual interests, Greece signed a continental shelf delimitation agreement with Italy in 1977.[115] Over forty years later, in 2020, the two parties complemented their 1977 agreement with another on the delimitation of their respective maritime zones.[116] In similar terms, in 2020, Egypt and Greece signed an exclusive economic zone delimitation agreement in Cairo.[117] Thus far, negotiations between Greece and Albania over maritime delimitation issues have been fruitless.[118] Following a political agreement in October 2020, the two states are currently envisaging the possibility of assigning this task to the ICJ through a special agreement to that end.[119] Greece's wish is that a mutually acceptable agreement can also be reached with Turkey over the delimitation of the continental shelf in the Aegean and in the Eastern Mediterranean Sea (see Karakaş and Akbulut, this volume).

PIL means have also been employed to solve the dispute between Greece and North Macedonia over the latter's name. The confines of this chapter do not allow us to discuss this issue in detail. Suffice it to note that this dispute led to the involvement of the UNSC.[120] The two states negotiated an interim agreement[121] that remained in force for over twenty years, serving also as a basis for a contentious case that North Macedonia brought against Greece before the ICJ.[122] In 2018, the two countries reached a mutually acceptable agreement solving the naming dispute through the so-called Prespa treaty.[123]

Moving to another family of disputes, one might be tempted to think that Greece is a 'third' state to the (diachronically very complex) Cyprus issue. Technically, to an extent,[124] this is correct. Yet, this approach overlooks the shared common ethnic identity of Greek-Cypriots and Greeks. This explains Greek foreign policy's systematic and painstaking efforts to peacefully solve the Cyprus issue as this evolved, first as a problem of decolonization from British rule, and then as a problem of unlawful military intervention and foreign occupation by Turkey. This might also explain, without however justifying, past instances of interferences by Greece within the domestic affairs of Cyprus, such as the 1974 *coup d'état* that the dictatorial regime that ruled Greece at the time sponsored and presumably even directed.[125] The limited confines of this chapter prevent us from discussing in detail the use of PIL as a foreign policy tool to peacefully solve the Cyprus issue. Therefore, we limit analysis here to two notable 'avenues' that Greece took when Cyprus was still a British colony. The first concerns the protection of human rights in Cyprus through Greece's two inter-state applications in the 1950s against the UK on the basis of the ECHR.[126] The second avenue is the UNGA as a vehicle for the internationalization of the Cyprus issue towards self-determination and, ideally at that time for Greece, *enosis*, that is, union of Cyprus with Greece. In August 1954, Greece requested the UNGA to redress the situation in Cyprus. The title of the document submitted by Greece is self-explanatory: 'Application, under the auspices of the United Nations, of the principle of equal rights and self-determination of peoples in the case of the population of the island of Cyprus'.[127] This was the first of five recourses that Greece tabled to the UN from 1954 to 1958.[128] *Prima facie*, resolutions adopted as part of this process contribute little to Cyprus' self-determination.[129] Yet, what should be borne in mind is that these resolutions predate seminal resolution 1514 (XV),[130] which was undoubtedly a milestone for the development of self-determination as a right. Be they cautiously 'pale' and 'bystanding', the UNGA resolutions on the Cyprus issue in the 1950s still contributed by internationally registering the Cypriot claim for self-determination, recalling its foundations in the UN Charter and calling for negotiations towards a 'just solution'[131] against the backdrop of previous failed diplomatic initiatives outside the UN that had fuelled anticolonial paramilitary liberation resistance in Cyprus.[132] Negotiations between Greece, Turkey, the UK, and Cypriot community leaders led to Cyprus becoming an independent nation in 1960.[133] Alas, this was not the end of the Cyprus issue.

Beyond self-interest, Greek diplomacy systematically serves international peace. Greece's geographical position, diaspora, and history—that dissociates it from other nations' colonial or totalitarian past—enable it to act as a 'bridge'. During the 1982 Lebanon War, a Greek merchant vessel evacuated the Palestine Liberation Organization (PLO) leader to Athens, a destination of his choice.[134] A few weeks later, incorporating Greek, French, and Irish amendments,[135] the European Economic Community Foreign Ministers' statement called for a peace settlement based on Israel's right to exist and Palestinian self-determination.[136] During the Chadian-Libyan war, in 1984, Greece facilitated a meeting between the French and Libyan leaders on their armies' presence in Chad—a peace initiative greeted as 'a "foundation stone" … in Franco-Libyan relations'.[137] As to the 1992–1993 Abkhazia conflict in Georgia, the UN Secretary General praised the first 'confidence-building' conference that was held in Athens, in October 1998.[138] With Greece acting as an intermediary, a set of (unfortunately short-lived) measures were agreed involving non-resumption of hostilities and direct economic/ commercial activity between the parties.[139]

6. Closing Observations

In this chapter, we endeavoured to evidence and assess Greece's direct and indirect impact on PIL. Greece employs PIL to protect and promote its interests, but also to protect collective interests, including international peace, that are the concern of all members of the international community broadly conceived. Depending on the circumstances, the Greek state wilfully and directly contributes to law-making and to the elaboration of PIL rules and standards. But Greece's contribution to PIL can also be occasional and incidental when, for instance, it employs PIL means to peacefully solve its disputes or safeguard its interests. Such uses of PIL can take many 'faces' and 'nurture' PIL through, for instance, state practice or by stimulating the reaction of authorities, such as international courts and tribunals, which, by exercising their jurisdiction, contribute to the interpretation and identification of PIL rules and standards. Another key dimension concerning the interrelationship between Greece and PIL is that the latter is employed as an avenue to solve disputes peacefully. Greece is deeply committed to international peace and strives to proactively foster peace in its own affairs and by acting as an intermediate party that facilitates the peaceful settlement of disputes between third parties. Last but not least, Greece as a state, and Greek academia, have significantly contributed to the shifting of the international legal order from bilateralism and horizontality to the development of a 'vertical' dimension within that legal system that sets 'red lines' to the omnipotence of state sovereignty and will, whilst moving beyond state-centrism by paying due attention to human rights and other areas, such as cultural heritage, that are the common concern of humankind in its entirety and, for that very reason, also collectively enforceable. That is, Greece as a state, and Greek academics, diplomats, and practitioners, have been conducive to the surfacing and forging of an international *ordre public*.

Finally, as to the connection between this chapter and the three strands of analysis set by this volume's editors, our discussion supports the argument that the Greek 'case study' confirms and reinforces the pacifying function of PIL. Admittedly, it is difficult to discern a particular approach or even a 'school of thought' pertaining to PIL to which Greece as a state or even Greek scholars and practitioners subscribe or have advanced that would be distinctive enough or that could claim to radically contribute to diversity within Europe. Nevertheless, Greece and Greeks have tangibly contributed to the development of rules, standards, and features of PIL that are—or which at least aspire to be—truly universal, either in the sense of being general international law or because they reflect common interests, values, and concerns of humankind.

Acknowledgements

We are thankful for their comments to the editors, Professor Linos-Alexander Sicilianos, Dr Antal Berkes, and Ms Demi-Lee Franklin. The opinions expressed in this publication are those of the authors.

Notes

1. In 1993, the UN General Assembly (UNGA) adopted its first resolution on the 'Observance of the Olympic Truce' (2 November 1993, UN Doc A/RES/48/11). Upon a Greek proposal, 6 April, the date when, in 1896, the first modern Olympic Games started in Athens, has been set by the UNGA as the 'International Day of Sport for Development and Peace' (18 September 2013, UN Doc A/RES/67/296).
2. 'Fair and equitable treatment' in investment law is translated as 'fair and equal treatment'. See, eg, Case C-284/16 *Slowakische Republik v Achmea BV* [2018] OJ C 161/7, ECLI:EU:C:2018:158. The term 'just and equitable' in the preamble of the United Nations Convention on the Law of the Sea (UNCLOS) (adopted 10 December 1982, entered into force 16 November 1994) 1833 UNTS 3, 1834 UNTS 3, and 1835 UNTS 3 has been officially translated as 'just/fair and egalitarian'. Law 2321/1995 (transforming UNCLOS into municipal law), Official Government Gazette (OGG) of the Hellenic Republic, 136 A/23-06-1995.
3. 'Equitable solution', concerning the delimitation of the continental shelf provided by Article 83(1) UNCLOS (n 2), has been officially translated as 'fair solution'. 'Equity' in Article 59 UNCLOS has been translated as 'equidistance' (*ευθυδικία, eythidikia*), which in Greek means 'fair decision'. See Law 2321/1995, OGG, 136 A/23-06-1995.
4. Aristotle, *Nicomachean Ethics* (Book V, 1137a32–1138a3). However, we acknowledge that in ancient Greek, as compared to modern Greek, the term '*ἐπιείκεια*' (equity) had a broader meaning.
5. Catherine Titi, *The Parthenon Marbles and International Law* (Springer 2023), in particular Chapter 10, discussing the possible emergence of a customary rule in favour of the repatriation of unlawfully removed cultural property and Greece's contribution in this development.
6. Preamble of the 1822 GC adopted by the First National Assembly of Epidaurus on 1 January 1822 <http://www.hellenicparliament.gr/UserFiles/f3c70a23-7696-49db-9148-f24dce6a27c8/syn06.pdf> accessed 11 April 2023.
7. Simon Chesterman, *Just War or Just Peace? Humanitarian Intervention and International Law* (OUP 2001) 28–33.
8. Convention Concerning the Exchange of Greek and Turkish Populations Between Turkey and Greece (adopted 30 January 1923, entered into force 25 August 1923) 32 LNTS 76. The implementation of the Convention was facilitated by two advisory opinions by the Permanent Court of International Justice (PCIJ). The first concerned the meaning of the term 'established' as a precondition for the 'Greek inhabitants of Constantinople' to be exempted from the compulsory exchange (*Exchange of Greek and Turkish Populations (Lausanne Convention VI, January 30th, 1923, Article 2)* (Advisory Opinion) PCIJ Rep Series B No 10). The second concerned the Mixed Commission for the Exchange of Greek and Turkish Populations on property disputes and, in particular, the conditions that ought to be met for reference to 'arbitration' regarding a difference of opinion between the members of the Mixed Commission. This opinion made an important contribution to PIL as it defines 'arbitration' (*Interpretation of the Greco-Turkish Agreement of December 1st 1926 (Final Protocol, Article IV)* (Advisory Opinion) PCIJ Rep Series B No 16).
9. Article 28(1) GC. For the latest version of the GC, OGG, 2011 A/24-12-2019; a translation in English is available at the Hellenic Parliament's website <http://www.hellenicparliament.gr/en/Vouli-ton-Ellinon/To-Politevma/Syntagma/> accessed 11 April 2023.
10. ibid.

11. ibid, Article 28(2) and (3).
12. ibid, Article 28.
13. ibid, Article 4(4).
14. ibid, Article 110(1).
15. Article 1 of Law 2431/1996 (OGG, 175 A/30-07-1996) reproduces *verbatim* the CJEU definition of 'public service'. eg Case C-290/94 *Commission of the European Communities v Hellenic Republic* [1996] ECR I-03285, paragraph 2, ECLI:EU:C:1996:265.
16. GC (n 9) Article 14(9).
17. Case C-213/07 *Michaniki AE v Ethniko Simvoulio Radiotileorasis and Ipourgos Epikratias* [2008] ECR I-09999, paragraphs 60–69, ECLI:EU:C:2008:731.
18. Council of State, 3670/2006, 08-12-2006, paragraph 14, ECLI:EL:COS:2006:1208A3670.02E7710, holding that the incompatibility between public works and media is absolute.
19. Council of State, 3470/2011, 04-11-2011, ECLI:EL:COS:2011:1104A3470.02E7710.
20. *Lykourezos v Greece*, App no 33554/03, 15 June 2006, paragraph 15.
21. *Lykourezos v Greece* (n 20).
22. Committee of Ministers, 'Execution of the Judgment of the European Court of Human Rights Lykourezos Against Greece' (2 December 2012) CM/ResDH(2010)171; GC (n 9), Article 57.
23. Vassilis P Tzevelekos and S Vetsika, 'Report on Greece' in Giuseppe Martinico and Oreste Pollicino (eds), *The National Judicial Treatment of the ECHR and EU Laws: A Constitutional Comparative Perspective* (Europa Law Publishing 2010) 225.
24. eg Council of State, 1993/2016, 19 October 2016, ECLI:EL:COS:2016:1019A1993.15E2419. Process reopening is possible under Article 105A(1) of the Code of Administrative Procedure, as amended by Article 23 of Law 3900/2010, OGG, 213 A/17-12-2010.
25. 1993/2016 (n 24).
26. ibid.
27. German Federal Constitutional Court, *Internationale Handelsgesellchaft mbH v Einfuhr- und Vorratsstelle fur Getreide und Futtermittel*, BVerfG (2 BvL 52/71) of 29 May 1974, [1974] 2 CMLR 540 (*Solange I*).
28. Court of Cassation, 11/2000, 04 May 2000, known as '*Prefecture of Voiotia v Federal Republic of Germany*' (2007) 129 International Law Reports 513.
29. Jurisdictional Immunities of the State *(Germany v Italy: Greece Intervening)* (Judgment) [2012] ICJ Rep 99, paragraphs 30–36.
30. ibid, paragraph 76.
31. ibid, paragraphs 92–97.
32. eg *Al-Adsani v The United Kingdom*, App no 35763/97, 21 November 2001, paragraph 56.
33. *Jurisdictional Immunities of the State* (n 29) paragraph 10.
34. ibid, paragraph 30.
35. Article 923 of Code of Civil Procedure, Presidential Decree 503, OGG, 182 A/24-10-1985.
36. *Kalogeropoulou and Others v Greece and Germany*, App no 59021/00, 12 December 2002.
37. Special Supreme Court, 6/2002,17 September 2002, known as '*Margellos and Others v Federal Republic of Germany*' (2007) 129 International Law Reports 525.
38. *Jurisdictional Immunities of the State* (n 29) paragraph 76 (emphasis added).
39. When selecting the examples to include in this section, we could not imagine that one instance of Greek contribution to PIL would become very topical after the International Criminal Court (ICC) issued an arrest warrant against the President of the Russian Federation on the basis of Article 8(2)(a)(vii) and (b)(viii) of the Rome Statute of the

International Criminal Court (adopted 17 July 1998, entered into force 1 July 2002) 2187 UNTS 3. Article 8(2)(b)(viii) was introduced to the Rome Statute through a proposal by Greece, in co-operation with Cyprus, Egypt, and Switzerland. UNGA, 'Preparatory Committee on the Establishment of an International Criminal Court, Working Group on Definitions and Elements of Crimes' (11 December 1997) UN Doc A/AC.249/1997/WG.I/DP.22.

40. UNCLOS (n 2) preamble.
41. ibid, Article 121.
42. Office for Ocean Affairs and the Law of the Sea, *The Law of the Sea: Regime of Islands: Legislative History of Part VIII (Article 121) of the United Nations Convention on the Law of the Sea* (United Nations Publications 1988) 33 http://www.un.org/depts/los/doalos_publications/publicationstexts/E_87_V_11_e.pdf accessed 11 April 2023.
43. ibid, 53.
44. ibid, 34.
45. ibid, 17–18 and 31–32. See also UNGA, 'Committee on the Peaceful Uses of the Sea-Bed and the Ocean Floor Beyond the Limits of National Jurisdiction, Sub-Committee II' (16 July 1973) A/AC.138/SC.II/L.37.
46. Article 10(1) of the Convention on the Territorial Sea and the Contiguous Zone (adopted 29 April 1958, entered into force 10 September 1964) 516 UNTS 205.
47. *The Law of the Sea* (n 42) 31.
48. UNCLOS (n 2) Article 121(2).
49. ibid, Article 77(1).
50. *The Law of the Sea* (n 42) 32.
51. UNCLOS (n 2) Article 303(1).
52. Alexander K Altes, 'Submarine Antiquities: A Legal Labyrinth', 4 Syracuse Journal of International Law & Commerce 1976–1977, 77, 79, 94, and, regarding Greece's contribution, 82.
53. Emmanuel Roucounas, 'Greece and the Law of the Sea' in Laura Pineschi and Tullio Treves (eds), *The Law of the Sea: The European Union and its Member States* (Brill 1997) 225, 251.
54. ibid. States were also divided over the same issue when negotiating the UNESCO Convention on the Protection of Underwater Cultural Heritage (adopted 2 November 2001, entered into force 2 January 2009) 2562 UNTS 3. Anastasia Strati, 'Protection of the Underwater Cultural Heritage: From the Shortcomings of the UN Convention of the Law of the Sea to the Compromises of the UNESCO Convention' in Anastasia Strati, Maria Gavouneli, and Nikolaos Skourtos (eds), *Unresolved Issues and New Challenges to the Law of the Sea: Time Before and Time After* (Brill 2006) 21, 46.
55. UNCLOS (n 2) Article 303(2).
56. Michail Risvas, 'The Duty to Cooperate and the Protection of Underwater Cultural Heritage', 2 Cambridge Journal of International and Comparative Law 2013, 562.
57. ibid, 566, citing UN Doc A/CONF.62/GP/10.
58. UNCLOS (n 2) Article 149.
59. ibid, Article 303(1).
60. ILC, 'Documents of the Second Part of the Seventeenth Session and of the Eighteenth Session Including the Reports of the Commission to the General Assembly' (1966) II Yearbook of the International Law Commission 1, 247–248 (A/CN.4/SER.A/1966/Add.l).

61. 52nd to 57th meeting of the United Nations Conference on the Law of Treaties, 4–7 May 1968. The summary records of the meetings are available at <https://legal.un.org/diplomaticconferences/1968_lot/sess1.shtml> accessed 11 April 2021.
62. Article 53 VCLT (adopted 23 May 1969, entered into force 27 January 1980) 1155 UNTS 331.
63. United Nations, 'United Nations Conference on the Law of the Treaties, First and Second Sessions, Vienna, 26 March–24 May 1968 and 9 April–22 May 1969' (1971) UN Doc A/CONF.39/11/Add.2, 174 (citing A/CONF.39/C.l/L.306 and Add.l and 2). See also ILC, 'Report of the International Law Commission Seventy-Third Session' (18 April–3 June and 4 July–5 August 2022) UN Doc A/77/10, 35.
64. United Nations, 'United Nations Conference on the Law of Treaties: 52nd Meeting of the Committee of the Whole' (4 May 1968) UN Doc A/CONF.39/C.1/SR.52, 295.
65. VCLT (n 62) Article 53.
66. A/CONF.39/C.1/SR.52 (n 64) 294.
67. But see the 1974 UNGA resolution on 'Human Rights in Armed Conflicts: Protection of Journalists Engaged in Dangerous Missions in Areas of Armed Conflict', which was mostly of procedural nature (29 November 1974, UN Doc A/RES/3245 (XXIX)).
68. UNESCO, 'UN Plan of Action on the Safety of Journalists and the Issue of Impunity, International Programme for the Development of Communication' (12 April 2012) UN Doc CI-12/CONF.202/6.
69. United Nations Human Rights Council, 'Safety of Journalists' (27 September 2012) UN Doc A/HRC/RES/21/12.
70. UNGA, 'The Safety of Journalists and the Issue of Impunity' (18 December 2013) UN Doc A/RES/68/163.
71. UNSC, Res 1738 (23 September 2006) UN Doc S/RES/1738.
72. Some details come from the personal experience of one of the authors in leading the negotiations on behalf of Greece within the UNGA.
73. A/RES/68/163 (n 70) paragraph 3.
74. Article 19 of the International Covenant on Civil and Political Rights (adopted 16 December 1966, entered into force 23 March 1976) 999 UNTS 171.
75. eg UNGA, 'The Safety of Journalists and the Issue of Impunity' (19 December 2017) UN Doc A/RES/72/175; UNGA, 'The Safety of Journalists and the Issue of Impunity' (18 December 2019) UN Doc A/RES/74/157.
76. eg the International Federation of Journalists is lobbying for an international treaty <https://www.ifj.org/fileadmin/user_upload/Draft_Convention_Journalists_E.pdf> accessed 11 April 2021.
77. UNESCO, 'Director General's Report on the Safety of Journalists and the Danger of Impunity' (8 November 2022) UN Doc CI-22/COUNCIL.33/6 Rev.
78. Convention on the Means of Prohibiting and Preventing the Illicit Import, Export and Transfer of Ownership of Cultural Property (adopted 14 November 1970, entered into force 24 April 1972) 823 UNTS 231.
79. UNGA, 'Return or Restitution of Cultural Property to the Countries of Origin' (6 December 2021) UN Doc A/RES/76/16 (co-sponsored by 110 states <https://en.unesco.org/news/general-assembly-urges-continued-action-stop-illicit-trafficking-cultural-property> accessed 11 April 2023).
80. ibid, paragraph 18.

81. See Volker Türk, 'Statement of the United Nations High Commissioner for Human Rights at the Organisational Session of the Human Rights Council' (*Office of the United Nations High Commissioner for Human Rights*, 9 December 2022) <https://www.ohchr.org/en/statements/2022/12/statement-united-nations-high-commissioner-human-rights-volker-turk> accessed 11 April 2023.
82. United Nations Human Rights Council, 'Neurotechnology and Human Rights' (6 October 2022) UN Doc A/HRC/RES/51/3.
83. ibid, paragraph 1.
84. Application of the Interim Accord of 13 September 1995 *(the former Yugoslav Republic of Macedonia v Greece)* (Judgment) [2011] ICJ Rep 664, paragraph 164.
85. ibid, paragraph 161. See also the separate opinion of Judge Simma and paragraph 66 of the dissenting opinion of the ad hoc Judge Roucounas.
86. ibid, paragraph 162.
87. Aegean Sea Continental Shelf *(Greece v Turkey)* (Judgment) [1978] ICJ Rep 3, paragraph 107. cf Maritime Delimitation and Territorial Questions Between Qatar and Bahrain *(Qatar v Bahrain)* (Jurisdiction and Admissibility) [1994] ICJ Rep 112, paragraphs 25–30.
88. See also n 8.
89. *Mavrommatis Palestine Concessions (Greece v the United Kingdom)* PCIJ Rep Series A No 2, 11.
90. ibid, 12.
91. *Minority Schools in Albania* (Advisory Opinion) PCIJ Series A/B No 64, 20.
92. ibid, 19.
93. *The Greco-Bulgarian 'Communities'* (Advisory Opinion) PCIJ Rep Series B No 17, 21.
94. ibid, 32.
95. *Denmark, Norway, Sweden and the Netherlands v Greece*, App nos 3321/67 and others, 5 November 1969. James Becket, 'The Greek Case Before the European Human Rights Commission', 1(1) Human Rights 1970, 91. Because of the *Greek Case*, Greece was going to be expelled from the CoE in December 1969. The colonels' regime decided Greece's withdrawal to 'save face'. Following the regime's collapse in 1974, Greece immediately re-joined the CoE.
96. Bruno Simma and Andreas L Paulus, 'The Responsibility of Individuals for Human Rights Abuses in Internal Conflicts: A Positivist View', 93(2) American Journal of International Law 1999, 302, 303–308.
97. Vassilis P Tzevelekos and Antal Berkes, 'Sociological Objectivism: Still Relevant?' in Rossana Deplano and Nicholas Tsagourias (eds), *Research Methods in International Law: A Handbook* (Edward Elgar 2021) 436.
98. Nicolas Politis, 'Le problème des limitations de la souveraineté et la théorie de l'abus des droits dans les rapports internationaux', 6 Collected Courses of The Hague Academy of International Law 1925, 1, 6 (authors' translation).
99. ibid. See also the papers on Politis in the (2012) 23(1) European Journal of International Law <https://www.sfdi.org/internationalistes/politis/> accessed 11 April 2023.
100. Stelio Séfériadès, 'L'échange des populations', 24 Collected Courses of the Hague Academy of International Law 1929, 307; Stelio Séfériadès, 'Le problème de l'accès des particuliers a des juridictions internationales', 51 Collected Courses of the Hague Academy of International Law 1935, 1.
101. Jean Spiropoulos, 'L'individu et le droit international', 30 Collected Courses of the Hague Academy of International Law 1929, 192.

102. Emmanuel Roucounas, 'Facteurs privés et droit international public', 299 Collected Courses of the Hague Academy of International Law 2002, 9.
103. Linos-Alexander Sicilianos' general course at the Hague Academy of International Law in summer 2023 is titled the 'Human Dimension of International Law'.
104. Constantin Eustathiades, 'Les sujets du droit international et la responsabilité internationale. Nouvelles tendances', 84 Collected Courses of the Hague Academy of International Law 1953, 397.
105. Nicolas Valticos, 'Les méthodes de la protection internationale de la liberté syndicale', 144 Collected Courses of the Hague Academy of International Law 1975, 77.
106. Georges Ténékidès, 'L'action des Nations Unies contre la discrimination raciale', Collected Courses of the Hague Academy of International Law 1980, 269.
107. eg Constantin Stavropoulos served as the UN's Under-Secretary-General and Chief Legal Counsel, and Sotiris Mousouris as Assistant Secretary General.
108. Constantine Economides, Constantin Eustathiades, Emmanuel Roucounas, Jean Spiropoulos, and Constantin Stavropoulos. eg ILC, 'Formulation of the Nürnberg Principles' (1950) II Yearbook of the International Law Commission 1, containing the report of the ILC Special Rapporteur, Jean Spiropoulos, endowing the Nürnberg principles that underpin individual criminal accountability for international crimes with universal applicability beyond the Nazi regime (181–195).
109. See, eg, UN Economic and Social Council, 'Specific Human Rights Issues: New Priorities, in Particular Terrorism and Counter-Terrorism. Terrorism and Human Rights' (22 June 2015) UN Doc E/CN.4/Sub.2/2004/40, with the final report of Special Rapporteur, Kalliopi Koufa.
110. eg Nicolas Valticos and his work at the International Labour Organization (ILO). See <https://www.sfdi.org/internationalistes/nicolas-valticos/> accessed 11 April 2023.
111. eg George Bizos, campaigning against apartheid and defending Nelson Mandela.
112. Article 1 of the Convention on the Pacific Settlement of International Disputes (adopted 22 July 1899, entered into force 4 September 1900) 1 Treaties and Other International Agreements of the United States of America 1776–1949 (Bevans) 230.
113. ibid, Titles II–IV (Chapter I).
114. ibid, Title IV (Chapter II).
115. Agreement Between the Hellenic Republic and the Italian Republic on the Delimitation of the Respective Continental Shelf Areas of the Two States (adopted 24 May 1977, entered into force 12 November 1980) 1275 UNTS 425.
116. Agreement Between the Hellenic Republic and the Italian Republic on the Delimitation of Their Respective Maritime Zones (adopted 9 June 2020, entered into force 8 November 2021) UN Registration no 57024.
117. Agreement between the Government of the Hellenic Republic and the Government of the Arab Republic of Egypt on the Delimitation of the Exclusive Economic Zone Between the Two Countries (adopted 6 August 2020, entered into force 2 September 2020) UN Registration no 56237.
118. The agreement of 27 April 2009 between Albania and Greece on the delimitation of the continental shelf and their maritime borders was declared unconstitutional by the Albanian Constitutional Court in 2010, 'vetoing' essentially its entry into force. Kyriaki Noussia, 'Current Legal Developments: Albania: The Decision of the Albanian Supreme Court Annulling the 2009 Maritime Delimitation Agreement between Albania and Greece', 25(4) The International Journal of Marine and Coastal Law 2010, 601.

119. See <https://www.dw.com/en/albania-and-greece-seek-joint-maritime-border-resolution-from-the-hague/a-55343112> accessed 11 April 2023, and the Greek Foreign Affairs Minister's statement of 21 December 2022 <https://www.mfa.gr/en/current-affairs/top-story/minister-of-foreign-affairs-nikos-dendias-statements-following-the-talks-with-the-foreign-minister-of-albania-olta-xhacka-tirana-21122022.html> accessed 11 April 2023.
120. UNSC, Res 817 (7 April 1993) UN Doc S/RES/817; UNSC, Res 845 (18 June 1993) UN Doc S/RES/845.
121. Interim Accord (adopted 13 September 1995, entered into force 13 December 1995) 1891 UNTS 3.
122. *Application of the Interim Accord* (n 84). The ICJ found that Greece has breached Article 11(1) of the Interim Accord.
123. Final Agreement for the Settlement of the Differences as Described in the United Nations Security Council Resolutions 817 (1993) and 845 (1993), the Termination of the Interim Accord of 1995, and the Establishment of a Strategic Partnership Between the Parties (adopted 17 June 2018, entered into force 12 February 2019) UN Registration no 55707. The Prespa Agreement raises very interesting questions from the perspectives of PIL, eg under the Prespa Agreement, North Macedonia undertook the obligation to (and indeed it did) amend its national Constitution, the content of which can never change in the future with respect to the relevant issues regulated by the Prespa Agreement. Another example is the meaning and effects of the term '*erga omnes*' regarding the use of the agreed name 'North Macedonia'. Ioannis Prezas, 'A Bilateral Treaty Developing Legal Effects *Erga Omnes*? Reflections on the Prespa Agreement Between Greece and North Macedonia Settling the Name Dispute', 65 Questions of International Law 2020, 21; Vassilis Pergantis, 'The Prespa Agreement Between Greece and North Macedonia and the Settlement of the Name Dispute: Of Objective Regimes, *Erga Omnes* Obligations and Treaty Effects on Third Parties', 65 Questions of International Law 2020, 63.
124. Greece is one of the guarantors of the independence, territorial integrity, and security of Cyprus. Treaty of Guarantee (adopted 16 August 1960, entered into force 16 August 1960) 382 UNTS 3.
125. Edward Collins Jr and Timothy M Cole, 'Regime Legitimation in Instances of Coup-Caused Governments-in-Exile: The Cases of Presidents Makarios and Aristide', 5 Journal of International Law and Practice 1996, 199, 203–207.
126. *Greece v The United Kingdom (I)*, App no 176/56, 2 June 1956; *Greece v The United Kingdom (II)*, App no 299/57, 12 October 1957. These were the first ever inter-state complaints in the ECHR framework.
127. Stephen G Xydis, 'The UN General Assembly as an Instrument of Greek Policy: Cyprus, 1954–58', 12(2) The Journal of Conflict Resolution 1968, 141, 141. The UNGA refrained from considering the issue raised by Greece: 'Application, Under the Auspices of the United Nations, of the Principle of Equal Rights and Self-Determination of Peoples in the Case of the Population of the Island of Cyprus' (17 December 1954) UN Doc A/RES/814 (IX).
128. Xydis (n 127) 141–158.
129. UNGA, 'Question of Cyprus' (26 December 1957) UN Doc A/RES/1013 (XI).
130. UNGA, 'Declaration on the Granting of Independence to Colonial Countries and Peoples' (14 December 1960) UN Doc A/RES/1514 (XV).

131. A/RES/1013 (XI) (n 129); UNGA, 'Question of Cyprus' (5 December 1958) UN Doc A/RES/1287 (XIII). For a discussion on the creation, uses, and impact of these resolutions, see Xydis (n 127) 144–156.
132. The Tripartite London Conference on the Eastern Mediterranean and Cyprus (29 August–6 September 1955) was inconclusive.
133. Treaty Concerning the Establishment of the Republic of Cyprus (adopted 16 August 1960, entered into force 16 August 1960) 382 UNTS 8.
134. Sofia Papastamkou, 'Greece Between Europe and the Mediterranean, 1981–1986: The Israeli–Palestinian Conflict and the Greek-Libyan Relations as Case Studies', 21(1) Journal of European Integration History 2015, 49, 54.
135. ibid, 55.
136. Secretariat-General of the Commission of the European Communities, *Bulletin of the European Communities*, no 9, vol 15 (European Communities 1982) 53.
137. Michael Dobbs, 'France-Libya Talks Said to Reaffirm Chad Pullout Pact' (*The Washington Post*, 16 November 1984) <https://www.washingtonpost.com/archive/politics/1984/11/16/france-libya-talks-said-to-reaffirm-chad-pullout-pact/8ca5b82b-50b8-4b89-8705-2b2e3ddd406f/> accessed 11 April 2023.
138. UNSC, 'Report of the Secretary-General Concerning the Situation in Abkhazia, Georgia' (29 October 2018) UN Doc S/1998/1012, paragraph 11.
139. ibid.

CHAPTER 30

ITALY

LUDOVICA CHIUSSI CURZI AND ATTILA TANZI

1. Introductory Remarks: Distilling Italy's Approach to International Law

It is no wonder that Italy's history, legal tradition, and political path are crucial to grasp the country's stance towards international law. The complex environment that preceded and followed Italy's birth as a nation-state, makes the task of identifying its 'soul' vis-à-vis international law, a daunting one.

It is not the aim of this contribution to provide an exhaustive analysis of the historical roots of the discipline of international law in Italy, a topic which has been thoroughly covered by academic works.[1] This chapter will provide some distinguishing features of the Italian outlook to international law, arguing that such approach can be framed in terms of 'moderation'. Following this introduction, Section 2 illustrates the openness to international law of the 1948 Constitution. Section 3 shows how such permeability has been tempered by elements of legal protectionism, especially by the domestic judiciary acting as guardian of the axiological values of the domestic legal order.[2] Section 4 addresses Italy's commitment to multilateralism at the policy-making level. The attitude of the country is characterized by a faithful attachment to the transatlantic alliance and by compromising positions driven by the priorities set by the European Union (EU). As to the Italian international law scholarship, Section 5 takes stock of the key stages of its development, as well as of its underlying features, which include tendency towards systematization, a prevalence of positivism in formal terms, and an increasingly internationalized outreach. The sixth and final section wraps up the stance of international law in Italy, singling out elements of policy continuity despite the numerous changes in governmental representation.

2. The 'Resistance' Constitution: Openness to International Law

Just like in Germany, World War II profoundly shaped Italy's approach to international law.[3] Yet, differently from the German context, the Italian totalitarian period was not strongly characterized by a 'fascist' doctrine of international law.[4] The reason for this can be found in the lack of a consistent foreign policy strategy, as well as in the absence of leading scholars who would put their theories at the service of the political project of the regime.[5] This, however, did not prevent *in toto* the pursuit of a foreign policy in line with the Regime's priorities, such as war intended as a means of dispute settlement, the trivialization of *pacta sunt servanda*, and a dismissive attitude towards international organizations.[6] Indeed, whilst after World War I Italy had taken an active role in the development of internationalism as a member of the League of Nations, it withdrew from the organization in 1937, after the unfortunate invasion of Ethiopia.[7]

The post-World War II Constitution – authoritatively defined as an 'ambitious one'–,[8] was adopted in 1948. It was a period fraught with changes and challenges: a lost war, the end of the monarchy, the losses suffered during the civil strife at the end of the War and an entire country to rebuild.[9] The 'Resistance' Constitution, to borrow the expression by one of the most influential members of the Constituent Assembly,[10] intended to mark the end of two decades of totalitarian experience, ushering the country into a new era of multilateralism.[11]

In the words of the President of the Republic and former Judge of the Constitutional Court, Sergio Mattarella:

> Such new era had been prepared in the darkest years, by the women and men who had shown the courage to resist and fight. And who had begun, at the same time, to think about how to shape a liberated Italy. Where to start again, to put a torn, wounded country, until then isolated in the eyes of the international community, back on its feet.... We have been supported by the mutual values and perspectives of the many nations with which we have cooperated. It is this dimension of multilateralism—rooted in our Constitution—that expresses our country's true vocation: to contribute to the creation of a peaceful world, in which the rights of individuals and peoples are fully realized, in accordance with rules established by the international community.[12]

The main political forces involved in the drafting of the 1948 Constitution (the Catholics, the Liberals, and the Social communists), converged on the idea that the new Constitution had to be as open as possible to international law.[13] This openness was perceived as a passport to restore the country's credibility vis-à-vis the international community, and a way to secure democracy by 'deference of the newly reconstituted Italian State to the general standards of behaviour agreed by the majority of member States of the international community'.[14] And yet such openness was also meant to allow Italy to actively contribute to the internationalization of the rule of law and of human rights.[15]

A key legal gate to international law is notably represented by Article 10(1) of the Constitution, which provides that the 'Italian legal system shall conform to the generally recognised principles of international law'.[16] Such provision, drafted with the active contribution of international lawyers,[17] was intended to operate as a 'permanent converter' of customary international law into domestic law.[18] Given the constant evolution of customary international law, the Constitution provided the Italian legal system with a decisive tool to adapt to its transformations automatically.[19]

It might be argued that this approach was already implicitly envisaged by the Statuto Albertino, a predecessor of the 1948 Constitution. Yet an explicit recognition of the openness to international law should not be underestimated, especially in the light of the nationalist turn of the early 1920s.[20] Such proclaimed openness was also the product of the political involvement of the catholic forces in the country, which brought their ecumenical views encompassing what were perceived as universal principles of mankind.[21]

Under Article 10(1) of the Constitution, once a customary rule of international law enters the Italian legal system, it assumes constitutional rank. Therefore, the entire legal order—through its organs—has to conform with it. This includes first and foremost the legislature, which is precluded from adopting laws or approving agreements at variance with customary international law. In the same vein, the judiciary has in principle to interpret and apply domestic rules in conformity with general international law. When a conflict emerges between an ordinary domestic provision and an international customary rule, the former should be quashed by the Constitutional Court.[22]

As put by the Constitutional Court in 2008, 'the observance that the international legal system as a whole pays to [customary] norms' requires that the domestic legal order has to conform to them, in order to avoid 'an intolerable discrepancy with respect to the "domestic" implementation of universally affirmed principles which are the common heritage of peoples'.[23]

While Article 80 of the Constitution recognizes a decisive role for the Parliament when it comes to authorizing the ratification of certain categories of treaties (but not their withdrawal, which is a prerogative of the executive),[24] there is no express constitutional provision addressing the implementation of treaties in the domestic legal order. The proposal of the internationalists Roberto Ago and Gaetano Morelli to extend to treaty implementation the automatic mechanism of adaptation provided for customary rules, was not followed by the Constitutional Assembly.[25] While it has been argued that the customary rule *pacta sunt servanda* might open the door to automatic incorporation of treaties too,[26] such argument is neither supported by the wording of the Constitution, nor followed by the case law of the Constitutional Court.[27]

Treaties are by constitutional practice implemented through the adoption of legislation which replicates the text of the treaty, or by a '*renvoi*' to the treaty itself, through the so-called '*ordine di esecuzione*'. According to the Italian Court of Cassation, even when the treaty has not been ratified, but the Parliament has already authorized the ratification, the instrument may in any event play a role in the interpretation of domestic provisions.[28]

As to the rank of international treaty obligations in the Italian legal order, differently from international customary rules, treaties were initially considered to have the same rank of ordinary domestic laws. Interestingly, in 2001 the openness of the system towards treaty law has been strengthened by the amended Article 117(1) of the Constitution, which provides that '[l]egislative powers shall be vested in the State and the Regions in compliance with the Constitution and with the constraints deriving from Community and international obligations'.[29]

Based on new constitutional Article 117, the Constitutional Court recognized, in the famous 'twin judgments' 348 and 349 of 2007, that treaties (in the specific case, the European Convention on Human Rights (ECHR)) are hierarchically superior to ordinary domestic laws. Yet the Court also specified that, for treaties to be recognized such status, they must conform to the basic domestic constitutional norms. In other words, treaties have an 'intermediate' ranking between ordinary law and the Constitution.[30] In principle, a domestic provision at variance with the ECHR would be incompatible with Article 117(1) of the Constitution. Domestic courts must interpret domestic provisions in line with the construction of the ECHR given by the Strasbourg Court, and, more generally, domestic legislation is to be interpreted in conformity with international treaties in force for Italy.[31]

However, if a domestic judge finds that a conflict arises between domestic law and the ECHR, or any other binding international instrument, the case must be referred to the Constitutional Court. Accordingly, domestic legislation believed to be in conflict with international treaties, differently from a case of conflict with EU law, cannot be automatically disapplied by domestic judges.[32] This renders the domestic system theoretically open to international law, while preserving the 'judicial monopoly' of the Italian Constitutional Court.[33]

In the words of Sabino Cassese, a public law scholar and a former constitutional judge:

> [W]e had to open the Italian legal order to the ECHR, and [...] the best way was to accept judicial pluralism. At the same time, we accepted the principle that parliamentary legislation must respect Italy's international obligations. Stating clearly that Italian law must comply with the ECHR or itself be unconstitutional was the best way to do so, while also preparing the way for a continuous conversation with the Strasbourg Court.[34]

As we shall see in the following section, the judicial dialogue between the Italian Constitutional Court and the European Court of Human Rights (ECtHR), as well as with other international courts such as the International Court of Justice (ICJ), has sometimes proved a complex one.[35]

Finally, Article 11 of the Constitution represents another milestone marking Italy's intentional break from the past, shifting from a nationalist regime to a fully integrated member of the international community. While the original wording of Article 11 was split in two articles, the final version contains a comprehensive statement:

> Italy rejects war as an instrument of aggression against the freedom of other peoples and as a means for the settlement of international disputes; Italy agrees, on conditions of equality with other States, to the limitations of sovereignty that may be necessary to a world order ensuring peace and justice among the Nations; Italy promotes and encourages international organizations furthering such ends.[36]

The very structure of Article 11 sets out the principles which must inspire Italy's foreign policy.[37] It provides that in order to effectively repudiate war, sovereignty needs to be limited, and that this must be done through the participation in international organizations.[38] Whilst the term 'international organisations' was intended primarily to cover the United Nations (UN) and the European Community, such a general expression left the door open to other intergovernmental forums. The limitation of sovereignty doctrine under Article 11 of the Constitution, soon provided the legal basis to grant EU law prevalence over Italian domestic law.

Unambiguous repudiation of war represented a way for Italy to silence the ghosts of its totalitarian and belligerent past during fascism. It was also a key tool for a renewed multilateral outlook on international politics, based on peaceful settlement of disputes.[39]

The compatibility with Article 11 of Italy's governmental choices of foreign policy has been called into question throughout the years, including with respect to Italy's participation in the Gulf War, NATO's operations in Kosovo, and, more recently, its support to Ukraine in the Russian-Ukraine conflict.[40] In this respect, it is worth recalling that the repudiation of the use of force is not expressed in absolute terms under the Italian Constitution. Article 78(9) of the Constitution states that 'the Parliament has the authority to declare a state of war and vest the necessary powers into the Government', while Article 87(9) establishes that the President of the Republic 'shall make declarations of war as have been agreed by Parliament'. The reasonable person reading of the above provisions is to the effect that the repudiation of war is without prejudice to the exceptions set out in the UN Charter.

Having regard to the ongoing conflict in Ukraine, in the recent parliamentary debate concerning continuous supply of military equipment to Ukraine, the Undersecretary of State for Defence stressed that 'the Government is acting according to Article 51 of the UN Charter, which recognizes the right to individual and collective self-defence'.[41]

3. A Moderate Openness: Shadows of Legal Protectionism

The constitutional architecture of a country cannot alone capture its stance towards international law. For a more accurate picture, one has to look at the pivotal and inevitably unpredictable enforcers of international rules, with special regard to national courts.[42]

As Benedetto Conforti, one of the leading 20th-century scholars of international law in Italy, used to emphasise, 'respect for international law is guaranteed to the extent that national judicial and enforcement agencies … pay heed to that international solidarity which is often lacking at government level'.[43] In this respect, the openness of the Italian legal system to international law has not been immune from shadows of legal protectionism.

In the abovementioned 2007 decision on the legal status of the ECHR in the Italian domestic system, the Constitutional Court found that the Convention 'does not set up a supranational legal order, thus it does not produce norms that have a direct applicability in State parties'.[44] It follows that, as already noted, when a conflict arises between a norm of the Convention and a domestic provision, the Italian judge will not be entitled to disapply the conflicting domestic legislation, but will have to refer the issue to the Constitutional Court.

In the same vein, the Constitutional Court had already underscored that 'the tendency of the Italian system to be open to generally recognized international rules and to international treaties is limited by the necessity to preserve its identity; thus, first of all, by the values enshrined in the Constitution'.[45] The Court later recognized that while 'it certainly cannot replace its own interpretation of the ECHR for that of the Strasbourg Court', it may, however, assess how and to what extent the results of the interpretation of the European Court interact or clash with the Italian constitutional order.[46] Against similar premises, the Court has invited Italian judges not to be 'passive recipients' of the interpretation provided by the ECtHR, but to engage in an autonomous interpretative process.[47] This proactive attitude does not come without risks, the main one being that of jeopardizing the Strasbourg Court's authority in the name of domestic law.

Signs of legal protectionism seem to be complemented by Italy's lack of ratification of Protocol 16 to the ECHR.[48] The latter recognizes the possibility for the highest courts of member States to request from the ECtHR 'advisory opinions on questions of principle relating to the interpretation or application of the rights and freedoms' protected under the Convention. The Protocol was adopted based on the acknowledgement of the need to foster the judicial dialogue between the ECtHR and the courts of the member States.[49] In 2020, during the Italian parliamentary discussion on Protocol 16, the Rapporteur on Foreign Affairs and EU Relations affirmed that the ratification of the Protocol had been postponed due to concerns of a 'possible erosion' of the role of the highest courts in Italy and the 'fundamental principles of the Italian legal order'.[50] However, it is interesting to note that advisory opinions issued by the ECtHR upon request of French judges within the Protocol 16 procedure, have been referred to by both the Italian Constitutional Court[51] and the Italian Court of Cassation.[52]

On a positive note, in 2023 a new ground for revocation of judgments was added to the Italian Code of Civil Procedure. Article 391 *quater* provides that when domestic courts' final decisions are found by the ECtHR to be in violation of the Convention, they can be revoked. The new legislative measure, which follows a recommendation issued over twenty years back by the Committee of Ministers of the Council of Europe,[53] is key to ensuring effective implementation to the Court's judgments in the Italian legal order. This is all the more so given that the Italian Constitutional Court had previously dismissed referrals concerning the constitutional legitimacy of Articles 395 and 396 of the Code of Civil Procedure, for failing to recognise revocation in tort and administrative law proceedings.[54]

The dark shadow cast over Italy's openness to international law remains the twenty-year-old dispute with Germany over claims of compensation before Italian domestic courts for Nazi war crimes.[55]

The first episode of this jurisprudential saga was marked by the 2004 judgment of the Italian Court of Cassation which disregarded Germany's sovereign immunity from civil jurisdiction with respect to the international crimes committed in Italy during World War II.[56] In an unprecedented balancing exercise between international rules, the Court found that the rights protected by international criminal and human rights law 'lie at the heart of the international order and prevail over other conventional and customary norms, including those relating to State immunity'.[57] Therefore, according to the Italian Court of Cassation, Germany was not entitled to sovereign immunity. This was notwithstanding the fact that the Italian government, who had intervened in the case through the Attorney General's Office, had upheld Germany's immunity in the proceedings.

As is well known, once vested with the dispute, the ICJ relied on the distinction between procedural and substantive norms, concluding that there could be no conflict between the procedural rule on immunity and substantive *jus cogens* rules.[58] The absolute character of immunity for acts *jure imperii* was confirmed by the ICJ, which ordered Italy to abstain from exercising its jurisdiction over Germany.[59]

The matter ended at the doorstep of the Italian Constitutional Court, which was asked by the Tribunal of Florence to ascertain whether compliance with the 2012 ICJ Judgment was compatible with Articles 2 and 24 of the Italian Constitution, which protect inviolable rights and the right to access to justice.[60]

The Italian Constitutional Court had already had occasion to assess the relationship between the right to access to justice and international jurisdictional immunities, upholding the latter without undermining the former. While in principle confirming the compatibility between the two rules in question, the Court distinguished between customary rules predating the Constitution, and those formed after 1948.[61] Such temporal approach was later dismissed by the same Court, as well as by the Court of Cassation.[62] By way of *obiter*, the Court noted that 'as regards international norms enjoying general recognition that entered into force after the Constitution, the mechanism of automatic incorporation ... cannot in any way permit breach of the fundamental principles of our constitutional order'.[63]

In Judgment 238 of 2014 on the issue of the recognition and enforcement of the 2012 ICJ Judgment on Jurisdictional Immunities, the Constitutional Court acknowledged that the ICJ Judgment represents a 'particularly qualified interpretation [of international rules], which does not allow further examination by governments and/or national judges'.[64] And yet the Court concluded that the customary rule on immunity could not override Articles 2 and 24 of the Constitution, as the latter belong to the fundamental principles of the Italian constitutional order. Such principles would represent 'counter-limits' to the reception of general international law, otherwise incorporated into the Italian legal order under Article 10(1) of the Constitution. Therefore, lacking any alternative remedy for victims, the customary rule on immunity was found by the Court non-transposable into the Italian legal order under Article 10.

The doctrine of "counter-limits"—which was originally devised in the context of the relationship between EU law and Italian domestic law[65]—is based on the assumption that international norms cannot be granted absolute prevalence over fundamental constitutional principles. On such basis, the Constitutional Court monitors the entrance of external rules into the domestic legal order.[66] Yet before Judgment 238, the Constitutional Court had hardly really addressed the constitutionality of a customary international rule. This is also because, under Article 134 of the Constitution, the Court decides on the constitutionality of laws and other legislative acts, with the consequence that the actual object of its assessment is not the international rule as such, but the domestic act giving effect to it.

Interestingly, the Constitutional Court did not ignore the effects of its decision on the international legal order, acknowledging being in breach of Article 94 of the UN Charter. And yet, after recalling the role played in the past by Italian and Belgian courts in limiting immunity to *acta iure imperii*, the Court concluded that the 'reduction of immunity for the purposes of a fuller protection of individual rights ... may also contribute to a desirable – and desired by many – evolution of [customary] international law itself'. [67] With hindsight, international practice shows that a similar evolution has not occurred to date.

The 238 Constitutional judgment, which has been defined as a 'sort of murder of international law through municipal law',[68] and a retrograde proclamation of 'provinciality'[69] has been harshly criticized by many internationalists in Italy and abroad.[70] It has rightly been argued that the Court targeted only the role of international law with respect to State immunity, forgetting to address the role of Italian political organs in ensuring alternative forms of redress for the victims.[71]

Judgment 238 has become an exemplary breach of international law by the Italian judiciary, providing constitutional ground for the continuation of that internationally wrongful attitude by lower courts.[72] Once, by 2022, certain claims for compensation before Italian Courts reached the enforcement stage over Germany's immovable assets in Italian territory, Germany brought the matter before the ICJ, once again, with a request for provisional measures.[73] Meanwhile, the Italian government had just passed legislation establishing a compensation fund for the victims of war crimes and crimes against humanity on Italian territory. This legislative move would shield Germany and its assets from execution, and prompted Germany's withdrawal of its request for provisional measures to the ICJ, but not of its Application.[74] At the time of this chapter the case was before the ICJ is still pending. Shortly later, the Italian Constitutional Court recognised the constitutional compatibility of the law establishing the Fund, thus mitigating the 238/2014 judgment, at least for purposes of immunity from execution.[75]

4. Moderate Positions in Multilateral Forums

The change of government sixty-eight times in seventy-six years may make it difficult to identify the distinguishing features of Italian foreign policy and its attitude towards international law-making and implementation.[76] However, elements of continuity are unquestionably recognizable. The red thread seems to be moderation and compromise, so much so that Italy's stance has been considered by some to have informed some kind of a "passive" role in the field.[77]

Italy is among the funding members of the Council of Europe and of the EU. It joined the UN in 1955, after a decade-long diplomatic journey that ended once the Kremlin lifted its veto to the membership of the former 'enemy States' under Article 107 of the Charter.

Since then, Italy has been an active player in multilateral forums. Seven times Member of the UNSC,[78] Italy has repeatedly carried out peace support operations under the aegis of the UN, EU, and NATO, earning the respect of the international peacekeeping community, being one of the main peacekeeping contributors.[79]

As to international treaty commitments, Italy is a party to all the major human rights treaties within the UN framework and has accepted the great majority of the individual complaints procedures thereto.[80] The same goes for the main multilateral environmental agreements,[81] and for the approximately 200 international investment agreements to which Italy is a party.[82] Italy's initial—and for more than two decades around the turn of the century—enthusiastic partnership in investment agreements has been gradually reversed, starting from the decision, in 2015, to quit the Energy Charter Treaty. This decision and the following reversal of its stand on the investment law process, with special regard to investor-State dispute settlement, faithfully reflects the EU strategy in the field.[83]

Throughout the 1990s, Italy was at the forefront of the process for the establishment of an international criminal court. This is epitomized by its hosting of the 1998 Rome Conference on the Establishment of an International Criminal Court and by the prompt signature and ratification of the ICC Statute in 1999. However, the passing of the necessary implementing legislation, required by the Rome Statute, took more than a decade to be completed.[84]

While being a party to multiple international treaties whose compromissory clause would afford jurisdiction to the ICJ, Italy's Declaration of Acceptance of the Jurisdiction of the Court under Article 36(2) of its Statute was filed in 2014.[85]

Since the 1970s, Italian judges have significantly contributed to the ICJ,[86] in continuity with the Permanent Court of International Justice (PCIJ).[87] The same applies to the International Tribunal on the Law of the Sea,[88] to ad hoc criminal tribunals,[89] and to the International Criminal Court (ICC).[90] Italy's contribution to the International Law Commission (ILC) has also been a central one since its early days.[91]

Italy has been significantly involved in contentious or advisory cases before international courts and tribunals.[92] Recently it has intervened as a third party in the proceedings before the ECtHR concerning Ukraine's allegations of mass and gross human rights violations committed by the Russian Federation in its military operations,[93] as well as in the case brough by Ukraine before the ICJ, under the Genocide Convention.[94] Most recently, Italy has co-sponsored the request for advisory opinions on climate change before both the ICJ and ITLOS.[95] In the first climate case before the ECtHR, characterized by an extraordinarily high number of co-defendants,[96] Italy has put in place its best efforts at coordination, exercising a proactive role in mediating between the different positions expressed by the various governmental agents involved.

While Italy's position in the majority of multilateral forums tends to follow the line dictated by the EU and by its transatlantic partnership, there are two particular issues where Italy has been in the front line: the moratorium on the death penalty and the reform of the UN Security Council. As to the former, on Italy's initiative, in 2007 the EU and eight member States presented a draft resolution for a UN moratorium on the death penalty. The resolution was passed with 104 votes in favour.[97] The resolution is routinely re-submitted every two years by Italy and a coalition of member States, reaching 127 votes in 2022.[98]

As to the Security Council reform, since 1993 Italy has been vocal in its criticism of what it views as the dysfunctional composition of the Council, all too often paralysed by crossed vetoes and in any event at risk of losing legitimacy in the light of an ever increasing need for international governance in meeting threats to the general interests of the international community.[99] A Memorandum on the issue in point was sent to the then UN Secretary General Boutros Boutros Ghali by Foreign Minister at the time, Beniamino Andreatta, calling for a permanent seat for the EU. The Memorandum suggested correcting the principle of regional representation with further qualitative criteria based on the conduct and behaviour of candidates especially with respect to UN principles and resolutions.[100]

In the second half of the 1990s, Italy ceased its efforts to promote a common European approach and avoided attempts to increase the number of permanent seats. To that end, a group of States, known as the 'Coffee Club', coalesced around Italy and grew to more than fifty member States. In 2005, the Coffee Club, still upon Italy's input, evolved in the so-called Uniting for Consensus (UfC) movement, which gathers countries aiming at reforming the Security Council with a view to making its composition and functioning more efficient. Italy's position within the UfC is inspired by its opposition to an increase in the number of permanent seats, while favouring the enlargement of non-permanent members.[101]

Concurrently, Italy has advocated a reform of the Security Council's methods and procedures aimed at enhancing efficiency and the principle of fairness in the functioning of the UN. To that end, Italy has co-sponsored the so-called 'Veto-Initiative'. Under this initiative, following the blocking of the Security Council by the veto of a permanent member, the General Assembly would be automatically convened within ten days,[102] in terms reminiscent of the long obsolete Uniting for Peace precedent.[103]

Finally, still on Italy's attitude on the international political scenario, one may wonder whether Italy's vote against the requests of an advisory opinion from the ICJ on the legal consequences arising from policies and practices of Israel in the Occupied Palestinian Territory,[104] as well its abstention in the resolution calling for a ceasefire in the ongoing dramatic conflict, may mark some kind of distancing from its traditional attitude of informal mediation.[105]

5. International Law Scholarship in Italy

The doctrinal approach of Italian scholars to international law appears diverse and is inevitably shaped by its deep-rooted tradition of legal 'science', based on a strong inclination towards systematization.[106] When embarking on a survey of international legal studies in the Italian context, it is easy to find oneself wandering in a vast doctrinal space between the re-discovered and sometimes distorted Roman law, as it was employed during the Middle Ages to address external relations of war and peace between the communes,[107] and a new conception of *ius gentium* as a tool allowing law to prevail over force.[108]

At the same time, also the Italian international law scholarship appears to be characterized from its inception by moderation on the substantive side and a sense of methodological compromise. Alberico Gentili, who sought to develop *ius gentium* as a reliable and just system of laws applicable to international relations, seemed to combine the natural law approach with pragmatism and realism.[109] The substance of his theories could be traced to some middle ground between Hobbes' bellicose doctrine and Erasmus' pacifism.[110]

The process of political unification of Italy throughout the 19th century marked a turning point in the study of international law.[111] The unification process developed through a series of breaches of international law, starting from the use of force.[112] The spirit of the *Risorgimento*, inspired by Giuseppe Mazzini[113] and fed by the urge to drive out the Austrian-Hungarian domination, created a fertile environment for the development of international law scholarship in Italy. The patriotic theories on unlawful foreign domination of Terenzio Mamiani were the typical product of his time. He strongly rejected humanitarian intervention, conceiving two exceptions: the case of a war waged by a subject people, and the opposition to wrongful intervention of others.[114]

It is no coincidence that one of the first chairs in international law in Europe was established at the University of Turin in 1851. It was entrusted to Pasquale Stanislao Mancini, a jurist and Minister of Foreign Affairs, as well as the first President of the Institut de droit international.[115] Mancini's theory on nationality, echoing the basic pillar of the Westphalian paradigm, was put at the service of the process of unification of Italy.[116] At the same time, such principles were considered by Mancini to be applicable only to 'civilised peoples',[117] in order to justify the colonial policy of the newly born nation state.[118]

Pasquale Fiore shifted the focus from a conception of international law merely as a set of rules on the protection of State interests to some kind of law of humankind. He argued for the existence of a *magna civitas* whereby individuals and entities other than States were entitled to autonomous rights directly under international law.[119]

The revival of nationalism through voluntarism characterized the origin of Italy's tradition of legal positivism spread at the end of the 19th century.[120] From a methodological perspective, Dionisio Anzilotti theorized a conception of positivism aimed at strengthening the normative dimension of international law, while preserving its independence from domestic law,[121] in stark contrast to German scholarly positions based on Jellinek's theory of state. Alongside the positions of Santi Romano, Anzilotti aimed at building an autonomous place for international law, one which could guarantee its effectivity in the social realm.[122] His configuration of positivism was also aimed at defending international law from abuses of power.[123]

Anzilotti's theories had the methodological merit of conjugating formalism with a solid and meticulous reference to practice, contributing to the modern thinking of international law, not only in the Italian context. His rigorous systematization of the law of international State responsibility and his contribution on attribution and reparation remain at the core of the International Law Commission Draft Articles on the Responsibility of States for Internationally Wrongful Acts.[124] Its masterpiece of theoretical elaboration in this field has been widely referred to by Roberto Ago in his studies on the subject, as a scholar and as a special rapporteur of the ILC on the topic.[125]

The legacy of Anzilotti was continued by Tomaso Perassi and later, in formalistic terms, by Gaetano Morelli who was largely informed by elements of Kelsenian abstract systematization approaches.[126] The highly deductive approach of Italian scholarship of the mid-20th century clearly emerges by comparing British Ian Brownlie's 1966 seminal treatise on international law, heavily substantiated by practice and case law, and the second edition of Morelli's treatise published in 1967, which relied almost exclusively on abstract legal reasoning.[127]

The 1970s were characterized by increased attention paid by Italian legal scholars to diplomatic practice and domestic case law relevant to international law. Positivism was resorted to in combination with pragmatic and realist modulations. The Foreword to the first volume of the Italian Yearbook of International Law announced that 'articles and comments relating to present and actual situations will have priority over studies of a predominantly theoretical nature', stressing that 'this should also help to confute the belief that the Italian doctrine on international law has a leaning towards abstract subjects (a belief which, today at least, is incorrect)'.[128] The Italian Yearbook of International Law was also the first Italian journal of international law to be published in English.[129]

The 1980s were characterized by idealistic and yet never utopian stances, as emerges from the works of Antonio Cassese. Thanks to his polyhedric role (professor, judge of the ICTY and the Special Tribunal for Lebanon, President of the Council of Europe

Committee Against Torture) Cassese's scholarship, aimed at pursuing values and change in international law, was combined with a fair dose of realism.[130] Cassese's interview with Sir Robert Jennings confirms two important and innovative priorities for Cassese: international lawyers' engagement in public life, and integrating the academic activity and legal practice.[131]

These two aspects are perhaps still underdeveloped in the Italian context. With respect to the former, this is partly because of the inadequate attention to foreign policy and issues of international law in the media, and to the scant presence of international lawyers in governmental positions. It is regrettable that international lawyers have hardly ever had a seat in Parliament, while few have been appointed to the Constitutional Court.[132] Given the ubiquity of international law in domestic legal systems, Italy would highly benefit from a stronger presence of international lawyers where law is made and enforced.

In this respect, it should be noted that for a number of years, the role of Head of the Service for Legal Affairs, Diplomatic Disputes and International Agreements of the Italian Ministry of Foreign Affairs was assigned to a scholar of international law. This is regrettably no longer the case.[133] The position of legal adviser to the Permanent Mission of Italy to the United Nations in New York, has also been traditionally performed by a scholar, and still is today.[134]

As to the relationship between scholarship and practice, as already mentioned, Italian international scholars have made, and continue to make, an important contribution both to the ILC[135] and to the ICJ.[136]

More generally, it may be noted that the involvement of Italian international lawyers in advocacy before international courts and tribunals remains scant when compared to other European countries. The gap becomes even wider if one looks at Italian female scholars.

As to present days scholarly features, by and large, elements of positivism with a 'scientific' inclination towards systematization have never been lost, where theoretical themes of international law still retain a prominent place in the choice of research topics.[137] While the inclination towards systematization is shown by the publication in Italy of a high number of international law textbooks published both in Italian and English,[138] the methodology of the legal analysis is becoming less and less dogmatic, and is increasingly based on legal authorities, with a significant level of engagement in legal and judicial policy elaborations.

Interdisciplinary studies remain limited compared to other countries, although the new generation of Italian international lawyers is increasingly focusing on the intersection between international law and other disciplines. Publications in English are continually increasing, although many Italian scholars still publish prevailingly in Italian. This may reduce the impact of the Italian scholarship both among foreign scholars and before international courts and tribunals. And although we are witnessing an increasing number of law programmes taught in English, language barriers still reduce the number of foreign scholars enrolling in Italian universities for long-term programmes.

6. Concluding Remarks: Moderation as an Element of Continuity

This chapter has aimed to provide a bird's eye overview of Italy's stance on international law. While on paper the Italian legal order appears to be open to international law, a closer look reveals signs of legal protectionism, and a certain mistrust by the judiciary towards the international law perspective of prevalence of international rules over domestic legislation. Accordingly, while domestic judges are inevitably increasingly dealing with issues pertaining to the interpretation and application of international rules, the dialogue between domestic and international courts is not immune from elements of controversy.

A concurrent collegial and compromising attitude in multilateral forums has remained a constant feature of the Italian foreign policy. While it may seem that the country is sometimes sitting on the fence in international policy-making venues, its moderate stance has contributed to a high degree of stability in Italy's foreign policy and, thus, in its foreign relations. At the time of writing, almost a year has passed since a right-wing coalition, the first of its kind since World War II, has won general election and formed a government. Despite the fact that during the electoral campaign of 2022, the parties making up the coalition now in power strongly criticized a number of key EU policy strategies and depicted themselves as the guardians of the 'national interest' over multilateralism, moderation has prevailed yet again. Aside from a degree of protectionist rhetoric by the current government on issues such as migrants' rights or the ratification of the European Stability Mechanism, overall, Italy does not seem to be shifting away from its traditional line of European and trans-Atlantic cooperation. By way of example, it is telling that Italy's traditionally moderate and compromising attitude resurfaced in the EU Council of 30 June 2023, when the Italian Prime Minister tried to cajole—albeit unsuccessfully—recalcitrant Hungary and Poland to join the other twenty-five member States in a statement on allocation of migrants.[139]

As to the Italian scholarship of international law, it has not lost its traditional keenness on systematization. However, the purely positivist, and often formalistic, approaches to legal analysis, which were predominant during a large part of the last century, have given way to case law and practice-based legal research. More often than not, such methodology is put at the service of international social engagement through proactive interpretive and law-making policy arguments.

Authors' Note

This chapter is the result of a joint effort by the authors. Sections 1 and 6 were jointly drafted. Sections 2 and 4 were drafted by Ludovica Chiussi Curzi, whilst Sections 3 and 5 were drafted by Attila Tanzi.

NOTES

1. See, among others, Angelo Piero Sereni, *The Italian Conception of International Law* (Columbia UP 1943); Francesco Messineo, 'Is there an Italian Conception of International Law?', 2 Cambridge Journal of International and Comparative Law 2013, 879; Giulio Bartolini (ed), *A History of International Law in Italy* (OUP 2020); Antonio Cassese, *Il diritto internazionale in Italia* (Il Mulino 2021).
2. See Giuseppe Martinico, 'Constitutions, Openness and Comparative Law', 67 Estudios de Deusto 2019, 111.
3. See Antonio La Pergola and Patrick del Duca, 'Community Law, International Law and the Italian Constitution', 79 American Journal of International Law 1985, 598.
4. Sereni (n 1) 277; among the rare exceptions, see Serena Forlati, 'Lea Meriggi: A Fighter—For the Wrong Cause' in Immi Tallgren (ed), *Portraits of Women in International Law* (OUP 2023) 338.
5. See Bartolini, 'Italian Legal Scholarship of International Law in the Early Decades of the Twentieth Century' in Bartolini (n 1) 165; Giulio Bartolini, 'The Impact of Fascism on the Italian Doctrine of International Law', 14 Journal of the History of International Law 2012, 237.
6. See Giambattista Mazzoleni, 'Il Diritto internazionale secondo la Dottrina Fascista', 12 Annali di Scienze politiche 1939, 77.
7. See Madeleine Herren, 'Fascist Internationalism' in Glenda Sluga and Patricia Clavin (eds), *Internationalisms: A Twenty-Century History* (CUP 2017) 191.
8. Antonio Cassese, 'Lo Stato e la Comunità internazionale' in Giuseppe Branca (ed), *Commentario della Costituzione: Principi Fondamentali* (Zanichelli 1975) 461.
9. See Diletta Tega, 'The Constitution of the Italian Republic: Not Revolution but Principled Liberation', 17 International Journal of Constitutional Law 2019, 690; Giuliano Amato, 'The Constitution' in Erik Jones and Gianfranco Pasquino (eds), *The Oxford Handbook of Italian Politics* (OUP 2016).
10. Costantino Mortati, *Le forme di governo. Lezioni* (Cedam 1973) 222.
11. See Giuseppe Martinico, Barbara Guastaferro, and Oreste Pollicino, 'The Constitution of Italy: Axiological Continuity Between the Domestic and International Level of Governance?' in Anneli Albi and Samo Bardutzky (eds), *National Constitutions in European and Global Governance: Democracy, Rights, the Rule of Law* (Springer 2019) 495.
12. President Sergio Mattarella, Speech of 2 June 2021, available in Italian at <https://www.quirinale.it/elementi/56979> (free translation), accessed 2 November 2023.
13. Cassese, 'Lo Stato e la Comunità internazionale' (n 8) 464 ff.
14. Antonio Cassese, 'Modern Constitutions and International Law', 192 Recueil des Cours 1985, 370; Antonio Cassese, 'Politica estera e relazioni internazionali nel disegno emerso alla Assemblea Costituente' in Ugo de Siervo (ed), *Scelte della Costituente e cultura giuridica. I: Costituzione italiana e modelli stranieri* (Il Mulino 1980) 505.
15. Cassese, 'Lo Stato e la Comunità internazionale' (n 8) 472.
16. An official translation of the Constitution is available at https://www.senato.it/sites/default/files/media-documents/COST_INGLESE.pdf, accessed 2 November 2023.
17. See Roberto Virzo 'The Influence of Italian International Scholars on the Crafting of the 1948 Constitution' in Bartolini (n 1) 390.
18. Tomaso Perassi, *Lezioni di diritto internazionale* (CEDAM 1957) 29.

19. Luigi Condorelli, 'Il riconoscimento generale delle consuetudini internazionali nella costituzione italiana', 62 Rivista di diritto internazionale 1979, 5; Augusto Barbera and Carlo Fusaro, *Diritto Costituzionale* (6th edn, Il Mulino 2022) 61 ff.
20. See Condorelli (n 19).
21. Cassese, 'Modern Constitutions and International Law' (n 14) 371.
22. Judgment 278/1992 (1992), [2] (Italian Constitutional Court); Judgment 131/2001 (2001), [23] (Italian Constitutional Court). All the decisions of the Italian Constitutional Court are available at http://www.cortecostituzionale.it, accessed 2 November 2023.
23. Decision 129/2008, [4.2] (Italian Constitutional Court).
24. According to Article 80 of the Italian Constitution, 'The Chambers shall authorize by law the ratification of international treaties of a political nature, or which call for arbitration or legal settlements, or which entail changes to the national territory or financial burdens or changes to legislation'.
25. Gaetano Morelli, 'L'adattamento del diritto interno al diritto internazionale in alcune recenti costituzioni', 25 Rivista di diritto internazionale 1933, 3.
26. Rolando Quadri, *Diritto internazionale pubblico* (Liguori Editore 1968) 64–68.
27. Enzo Cannizzaro, *Diritto Internazionale* (5th edn, Giappichelli 2022) 478.
28. Decision 21748/2007 (Italian Court of Cassation), [7.2].
29. Article 117(1), as amended by Constitutional Law no 3 of 2001. See Enzo Cannizzaro, 'La riforma "federalista" della Costituzione e gli obblighi internazionali' 84 Rivista di diritto internazionale 2001, 921.
30. Decisions 348/2007 and 349/2007 (Italian Constitutional Court). See Francesca Biondi Dal Monte and Filippo Fontanelli, 'The Decisions No. 348 and 349/2007 of the Italian Constitutional Court: The Efficacy of the European Convention in the Italian Legal System', 9 German Law Journal 2008, 889.
31. See Decision 239/2009, [3] and Decision 43/2017, [2] (Italian Constitutional Court). See Giorgio Gaja, 'Il limite costituzionale del rispetto degli "obblighi internazionali": un parametro definito solo parzialmente' 91 Rivista di diritto internazionale 2008, 136.
32. See Ugo Villani, 'Sul valore della Convenzione europea dei diritti dell'uomo nell'ordinamento italiano', 1 Studi sull'integrazione europea 2008, 7.
33. See Giuseppe Martinico, 'Is the European Convention Going to be "Supreme"? A Comparative-Constitutional Overview of the ECHR and EU Law Before National Courts', 23 European Journal of International Law 2012, 401.
34. Alec Stone Sweet and Giacinto della Cananea, 'A Conversation with Sabino Cassese', 22 German Law Journal 2022, 1526, 1536.
35. See Iulia Motoc and Markos Valikos, 'The Dialogue Between the ECHR and the Italian Constitutional Court' in Linos-Alexandre Sicilianos et al (eds), *Intersecting Views on National and International Human Rights Protection* (Wolf Legal Publishers 2019) 603. With regard to the ICJ, see Section 3.
36. Italian Constitution, Article 11.
37. See Luigi Bonanate, *Costituzione italiana: articolo 11* (Carocci Editore 2018) 24.
38. See Natalino Ronzitti (ed), *L'articolo 11 della Costituzione. Baluardo della vocazione internazionale dell'Italia* (Editoriale Scientifica 2013).
39. See Palmiro Togliatti, 'Speech at the Session of the 1st Subcommittee' (3 December 1946); Fulvio Palombino, *In difesa del diritto internazionale* (Zanichelli 2023) 39.
40. See Laura Cappuccio, 'Article 11 of the Italian Constitution Between Text and Context', 1 Italian Review of International and Comparative Law 2021, 188, 195; Andrea Spagnolo, 'The

Armed Attack Against Ukraine and the Italian Reaction from a Ius ad bellum Perspective', 2 Italian Review of International and Comparative Law 2022, 443; Paolo Zichittu, 'Article 11 of the Italian Constitution and the War in Ukraine: The Constant Dialogue Between Constitutional and International Law', 99 Questions of International Law 2023, 23.

41. For an overview of the parliamentary debate, see https://www.senato.it/japp/bgt/showdoc/19/Resaula/0/1365979/index.html?part=doc_dc-ressten_rs-ddltit_ddddl389pcmmau, accessed 3 November 2023. See Spagnolo (n 40); Pierfrancesco Rossi, 'La compatibilità con la Costituzione italiana e il diritto internazionale dell'invio di armi all'Ucraina', Blog of the Italian Society of International Law (8 March 2022) http://www.sidiblog.org/2022/03/08/la-compatibilita-con-la-costituzione-italiana-e-il-diritto-internazionale-dellinvio-di-armi-allucraina/, accessed 2 November 2023.
42. See Daniele Amoroso, 'Italy' in Fulvio Maria Palombino (ed), *Duelling for Supremacy* (CUP 2019) 184.
43. Benedetto Conforti, *Lezioni di diritto internazionale* (Editoriale Scientifica 1982) 8.
44. Decision 348/2007, [3.3] (Italian Constitutional Court). See Diletta Tega, 'The Constitutional Background of the 2007 Revolution. The Jurisprudence of the Constitutional Court' in Giorgio Repetto (ed), *An Italian Perspective* (Intersentia 2013) 25; see also Luca Mezzetti and Francesca Polacchini, 'Primacy of Supranational Law and the Supremacy of the Constitution in the Italian Legal System', in Luca Mezzetti (ed), International Constitutional Law (Giappichelli 2014) 141.
45. Decision 73/2001, [3.1] (Italian Constitutional Court).
46. Decision 236/2011, [9.7] (Italian Constitutional Court), quoting Decision 317 of 2009. See Raffaele Sabato, 'Judicial Dialogue: The Experience of Italy', in Amrei Müller (ed), *Judicial Dialogue and Human Rights* (CUP 2017) 267.
47. Decision 49/2015, [7.3, 7.4] (Italian Constitutional Court).
48. See Elisabetta Lamarque, 'The Failure by Italy to Ratify Protocol No. 16 to the ECHR', Italian Review of International and Comparative Law 2021, 159.
49. See Christos Giannopolous, 'Considerations on Protocol 16: Can the New Advisory Competence of the European Court of Human Rights Breathe Life into the European Convention on Human Rights', 16 German Law Journal 2019, 337.
50. See Session no 399 of 28 September 2020, Intervention of Ms Ehm, 36 (in Italian) https://www.camera.it/leg18/410?idSeduta=0399&tipo=stenografico#sed0399.stenografico.tit00190.sub00010.int00020, accessed 2 November 2023.
51. See Antonello Tancredi, 'I pareri resi dalla Corte europea dei diritti dell'uomo ai sensi del Protocollo 16 nella recente giurisprudenza costituzionale' in Alessandra Annoni et al (eds), *Il diritto internazionale come sistema di valori: Scritti in onore di Francesco Salerno* (Jovene editore 2021) 589.
52. Decision 8325/2020 (Italian Court of Cassation); Decision 38162/2022 (Italian Court of Cassation).
53. Council of Europe, Recommendation 2 of 19 January 2000.
54. Decision 123/2017, Decision 93/2018 (Italian Constitutional Court). The Court had recognized the necessity to reopen domestic proceedings only in criminal law cases.
55. See Andreas Paulus, 'Between a Rock and a Hard Place: Italian Concerns Between Constitutional Rights and International Law' in Valentina Volpe et al (eds), *Reconciling International and Domestic Law After the Italian Constitutional Court's Sentenza 238/2014* (Springer 2021) 337.

56. Decision 5044/2003 (Italian Court of Cassation). See Pasquale De Sena and Francesca De Vittor, 'State Immunity and Human Rights: The Italian Supreme Court Decision on the Ferrini Case', 16 European Journal of International Law 2005, 89.
57. *Ferrini* (n 56) [9].
58. *Jurisdictional Immunities of the State* (*Germany v Italy: Greece intervening*) [2012] ICJ Rep 99. See Stefan Talmon, 'Jus Cogens After Germany v. Italy: Substantive and Procedural Rules Distinguished', 25 LJIL 2012, 979.
59. See Attila Tanzi and Lorenzo Gradoni, 'Immunità dello Stato e crimini internazionali tra consuetudine e bilanciamento: note critiche a margine della sentenza della Corte Internazionale di Giustizia del 3 febbraio 2012', 67 La comunità internazionale 2012, 203.
60. Decision 238/2014 (Italian Constitutional Court). See Riccardo Pavoni, 'Simoncioni v. Germany' 109 American Journal of International Law 2015, 400.
61. Decision 48/1979, [3] (Italian Constitutional Court).
62. Decision 73/2001, [3.1] (Italian Constitutional Court); Decision 1072/2009 (Italian Court of Cassation).
63. Decision 48/1979, [3.4] (Italian Constitutional Court).
64. Decision 238/2014, [3.1] (Italian Constitutional Court).
65. See Decisions 98/1965, 183/1973, and 170/1984 (Italian Constitutional Court).
66. See Decision 73/2001 (Italian Constitutional Court); Paolo Palchetti, 'Conformità dell'ordinamento italiano alle norme del diritto internazionale generalmente riconosciute e controlimiti: problemi aperti', in Giuseppe Palmisano (ed), *Il diritto internazionale ed europeo nei diritti interni* (Editoriale Scientifica 2020) 371.
67. Decision 238/2014, [3.3] (Italian Constitutional Court).
68. See Robert Kolb, 'The Relationship Between the International and the Municipal Legal Order: Reflections on the Decision No 238/2014 of the Italian Constitutional Court', Questions of International Law 2014, 5.
69. Filippo Fontanelli, 'I know it's wrong but just can't do right: First impressions on Judgment no. 238 of 2014 of the Italian Constitutional Court', Verfassungsblog (27 October 2014), available at https://verfassungsblog.de/know-wrong-just-cant-right-first-impressions-judgment-238-2014-italian-constitutional-court/ (accessed 2 November 2023).
70. See, among others, Attila Tanzi, 'Un difficile dialogo tra Corte internazionale di giustizia e Corte costituzionale', 50 La comunità internazionale 2015, 13; Enzo Cannizzaro, 'Judicial Immunity and Judicial Protection: The Decision of the Italian Constitutional Court No. 38 of 2014', 48 Rivista di diritto internazionale 2015, 126; for a different view, see Benedetto Conforti, 'La Court constitutionnelle italienne et le droits de l'homme méconnus sur le plan international', 119 RGDIP 2015, 253; Massimo Lando, 'Intimations of Unconstitutionality: The Supremacy of International Law and Judgment 238/2014 of the Italian Constitutional Court', 78 Modern Law Review 2015, 1028.
71. Paolo Palchetti, 'Right of Access to (Italian) Courts über alles? Legal Implications Beyond Germany's Jurisdictional Immunity' in Valentina Volpe et al (eds), *Remedied Against Immunity?* (Springer 2021) 39. On the asymmetry between rights and remedies and the consequences of immunity, see Beatrice Bonafé and Enzo Cannizzaro, 'Of Rights and Remedies: Sovereign Immunity and Fundamental Rights' in Ulrich Fastenrath et al (eds), *From Bilateralism to Community Interests: Essays in Honour of Bruno Simma* (OUP 2011) 825.

72. Carlo Focarelli, 'State Immunity and Serious Violations of Human Rights: Judgment No. 238 of 2014 of the Italian Constitutional Court Seven Years on', Italian Review of International and Comparative Law 2021, 29.
73. *Questions of jurisdictional immunities of the State and measures of constraint against State-owned property (Germany v. Italy)* <https://www.icj-cij.org/case/183>.
74. See Decree Law No 36/2022, converted into Law 79 of 29 June 2022.
75. Decision 159/2023 (Italian Constitutional Court); See Donato Greco, 'Jurisdictional Immunities and Reparation for WWII Crimes: The Impact of the Italian Constitutional Court's Judgement No. 159/2023 on Greek Victims' Claims', EJIL: Talk! (15 August 2023); Francesco Salerno, 'Il contenzioso italo-tedesco dopo la sentenza n. 159/2023 della Corte costituzionale', Giurisprudenza Italiana, October 2023, 2073; Pierfrancesco Rossi, 'Truce or Settlement? The Dispute Over Germany's Immunity From Wartime Reparations Claims After Judgment No. 159/2023 of the Italian Constitutional Court', 33 Italian Yearbook of International Law 2023.
76. See Pierangelo Isernia and Francesca Longo, 'The Italian Foreign Policy: Changes and Continuities', 47 Italian Foreign Policy Review 2017, 107.
77. Alain Posner, 'Italy: Dependence and Political Fragmentation', 31 International Organization 1977, 808, 812.
78. 1959–1960; 1971–1972; 1975–1976, 1987–1988, 1995–1996, 2007–2008, 2017.
79. Gabriele Abbondanza, 'Italian Peacekeeping Missions: Vast, Praised, Underused' Istituto Affari Internazionali (2020) https://www.iai.it/sites/default/files/iaip2020.pdf, accessed 2 November 2023.
80. Except from the individual complaints procedure under the International Convention for the Protection of All Persons from Enforced Disappearance and the Individual Complaints Procedures under the International Convention on the Protection of the Rights of All Migrant Workers and Members of their Families.
81. See https://www.informea.org/en/countries/it/party-status, accessed 3 November 2023.
82. See https://investmentpolicy.unctad.org/international-investment-agreements/countries/103/italy, accessed 3 November 2023.
83. See Johannes Tropper, 'Withdrawing from the Energy Charter Treaty: The End is (not) Near', Kluwer Arbitration Blog (4 November 2022). See Francesco Montanaro, *The European Union and International Investment Law* (Bloomsbury 2023).
84. See Emanuela Fronza and Chantal Meloni, 'The Draft Italian Code of International Crimes', Journal of international Criminal Justice 2022, 1027; Florian Jeßberger et al (eds), *Domesticating International Criminal Law: Reflections on the Italian and German Experiences* (Routledge 2023).
85. See https://www.icj-cij.org/declarations/it, accessed 3 November 2023.
86. Gaetano Morelli (1961–1970); Roberto Ago (1979–1995); Luigi Ferrari Bravo (1995–1997); Giorgio Gaja (2012–2021).
87. Judge Dionisio Anzilotti was a member of the Committee of Jurists that drafted the Statute of the PCIJ and Judge of the Court through its existence (1922–1946).
88. Tullio Treves (1996–2011); Ida Caracciolo (2020–).
89. Antonio Cassese was Judge and President of the ICTY (1993–2000) and of the Special Tribunal for Lebanon (2009–2011); Fausto Pocar was a Judge (2001–2015) and President of the ICTY (2015–2017) and Member of the Court of Appeal of the ICTR; Flavia Lattanzi was Judge *ad litem* at the ICTR (2003–2007).
90. Mauro Politi (2003–2006); Cuno Tarfusser (2009–2018); Rosario Salvatore Aitala (2018–).

91. Roberto Ago (1957–1978); Gaetano Arangio Ruiz (1985–1986); Giorgio Gaja (1999–2011); Giuseppe Nesi (2023–).
92. See, in particular, *Case of the Monetary Gold Removed from Rome* in 1943 (*Italy v France*) (Preliminary Question) [1954] ICJ Rep 19; *Continental Shelf (Libyan Arab Jarnahiriya/ Malta)* (Application to Intervene) [1984] ICJ Rep 3; *Elettronica Sicula S.p.A. (ELSI) (United States of America v Italy)* (Judgment) [1989] ICJ Rep 15; *Loan Agreement Between Italy and Costa Rica*, Ad hoc arbitration, Award (26 June 1998); *Jurisdictional Immunities of the State (Germany v Italy: Greece intervening)* [2012] ICJ Rep 99; *'Enrica Lexie' Incident (Italy v India)* PCA Case no 2015-28 [2020] Final Award; *The M/V 'Norstar' Case (Panama v Italy)* (10 April 2019); *Questions of jurisdictional immunities of the State and measures of constraint against State-owned property (Germany v Italy)* [2023].
93. *Ukraine and the Netherlands v Russia* (App nos 8019/16, 43800/14, 28525/20, and 11055/ 22); see Council of Europe Press Release, 'Update on Third Party Intervention Requests Granted in Inter-State Case (*Ukraine and the Netherlands v. Russia*)' (17 March 2023).
94. *Allegations of Genocide Under the Convention on the Prevention and Punishment of the Crime of Genocide* (*Ukraine v Russian Federation*), Declaration of Intervention of Italy <https://www.icj-cij.org/node/106219>.
95. *Request for an Advisory Opinion submitted by the Commission of Small Island States on Climate Change and International Law (Request for Advisory Opinion submitted to the Tribunal)* [2022]; *Obligations of States in respect of climate change (Request for Advisory Opinion submitted to the ICJ)* [2023].
96. See, eg, the pending case *Duarte Agostinho and Others v Portugal and Others* (App no 39371/20), which concerns the greenhouse gas emissions from thirty-three countries that, according to the applicants, are contributing to the global warming and result in the violation of a number of rights of the ECHR.
97. 'Moratorium on the Use of Death Penalty' UN Doc A/RES/62/149 (18 December 2007).
98. 'Moratorium on the Use of Death Penalty' UN Doc A/RES/77/222 (15 December 2022).
99. See Attila Tanzi, 'Prospects of Revision of the United Nations Charter' in SIOI (ed), *Prospects for Reform of the United Nations System* (CEDAM 1993) 455; Attila Tanzi, 'Notes on the "Permanent Conference of 78 Revision" of the United Nations Charter at the 50th Anniversary of the Organization', Rivista di diritto internazionale 1995, 723. Francesco Paolo Fulci, 'Italy and the Reform of the UN Security Council, 34 Italian Journal of International Affairs 1999, 7; Nico Schrijver, 'Reforming the UN Security Council in Pursuance of Collective Security', 12 Journal of Conflict & Security Law, 2007, 127; Giuseppe Nesi, 'La riforma del Consiglio di sicurezza delle Nazioni Unite tra politica e diritto' in Pietro Gargiulo, Ivan Ingravallo and Pierfrancesco (eds), *L'ONU nei nuovi assetti sistemici internazionali: le riforme necessarie-Pace e sicurezza internazionali, sviluppo sostenibile, tutela dei diritti umani* (Editoriale Scientifica 2023) 19.
100. 'Testi e documenti sulla politica estera dell'Italia' (1993) Ufficio Studi Roma <https:// www.farnesina.ipzs.it/>.
101. See Joint Press Release of the Uniting for Consensus Group (27 March 2023) <https://italyun.esteri.it/en/news/dalla_rappresentanza/2023/03/joint-press-release-of-the-uniting-for-consensus-group/>.
102. 'Standing Mandate for a General Assembly debate when a Veto is Cast in the Security Council', UN Doc A/RES/76/262 (28 April 2022).
103. See Michael Scharf, 'Power Shift: The Return of the Uniting for Peace Resolution', 55 Case Western Reserve Journal of International Law 2023, 217.

104. 'Israeli practices affecting the human rights of the Palestinian people in the Occupied Palestinian Territory, including East Jerusalem, UN Doc A/RES/77/247 (9 January 2023).
105. 'Protection of civilians and upholding legal and humanitarian obligations', UN Doc A/RES/ES-10/21 (27 October 2023).
106. See John Henry Merryman, 'The Italian Style I: Doctrine', 18 Stanford Law Review 1965, 39; Enzo Cannizzaro, 'Il mutamento dei paradigmi della scienza giuridica internazionalista e la dottrina italiana', Annuario di diritto comparato 2014, 77.
107. See Claudia Storti, 'Early "Italian" Scholars of Ius Gentium' in Bartolini (n 1) 19; Susanne Lepsius, 'The Legal System among City Republics' in Helmut P Aust and Janne E Nijman (eds), *Research Handbook of International Law and Cities* (Edward Elgar 2021) 44.
108. Storti (n 107) 31; Orazio Condorelli, 'Bartolo da Sassoferrato 1313/14-1357' in Orazio Condorelli and Rafael Domingo (eds), *Law and Christian Tradition in Italy* (Routledge 2020) 160 ff.
109. Alberico Gentili, *De iure belli* (1612); see Peter Haggenmacher, 'Grotius and Gentili: A Reassessment of Thomas E. Holland's Inaugural Lecture' in Hedley Bul et al (eds), *Hugo Grotius and International Relations* (OUP 1992) 133; Carlo Focarelli, '*Jus gentium* in Alberico Gentili: A Call for Prudence and the Common Sense of Humanity', 100 Rivista di diritto internazionale 2017, 329.
110. See Ursula Vollerthun, *The Idea of International Society: Erasmus, Vitoria, Gentili and* Grotius (CUP 2017).
111. See Edoardo Greppi, 'The *Risorgimento* and the "Birth" of International Law in Italy' in Bartolini (n 1).
112. See Sergio Marchisio, 'L'utilizzo delle categorie giuridiche del diritto internazionale nel processo di unificazione italiana', Nomos 2017, 1; Sergio Marchisio, 'The Unification of Italy and International Law' in Bartolini' (n 1) 285.
113. See Stefano Recchia and Nadia Urbinati (eds), *A Cosmopolitanism of Nations: Giuseppe Mazzini's Writing on Democracy, Nation Building and International Relations* (Princeton UP 2010). See also the writings of the internationalist Augusto Pierantoni, *Storia degli studi del diritto internazionale in Italia* (Vincenzi 1869).
114. Terenzio Mamiani, *Rights of Nations, or the New Law of European States Applied to the Affairs of Italy* (W Jeffs 1860) 177.
115. Pasquale Stanislao Mancini then became Professor of International Law in Rome, at La Sapienza University. See Elisabetta Fiocchi Malaspina, '"Toil of the Noble World": Pasquale Stanislao Mancini, Augusto Pierantoni and the International Legal Discourse of 19th Century Italy', 18 Clio Themis (Online) 2020, 1.
116. Pasquale Stanislao Mancini, *Della nazionalità come fondamento del diritto delle genti* (Tipografia Eredi Botta 1854).
117. Pasquale Stanislao Mancini, 'Discorso pronunciato alla Camera dei Deputati' (27 January 1885) Atti Parlamentari, Legislatura XV, Discussioni, Roma, Tipografia Camera dei Deputati, 1886, 1086.
118. See Tullio Scovazzi, 'The Italian Approach to Colonialism' in Bartolini (n 1) 334.
119. Pasquale Fiore was Professor of International Law at the University of Turin, then of Naples. See Pasquale Fiore, 'La veritable mission de la science du droit international pour donner à la société internationale son organisation juridique', 12 Révue de droit international et de legislation comparé 1912, 169; Pasquale Fiore, *International Law Codified and its Legal Sanction* (trans 5th edn, Baker Voorhis and Company 1918).

120. See Riccardo Guastini, 'The Italian Tradition of Legal Positivism' in Torben Spaak and Patricia Mindus (eds), *The Cambridge Companion to Legal Positivism* (CUP 2021) 152.
121. Dionisio Anzilotti was Professor of International Law at the University of Rome La Sapienza, as well as Judge (1921–1946) and President (1928–1939) of the Permanent Court of International Justice. See Dionisio Anzilotti, *Teoria generale della responsabilità dello Stato in diritto internazionale* (Lumachi 1902).
122. See Francesco Salerno, 'L'influenza di Santi Romano sulla dottrina e la prassi italiana di diritto internazionale', 101 Rivista di diritto internazionale 2018, 357, 359.
123. Dionisio Anzilotti, *Corso di diritto internazionale* (3rd edn, Athenaeum 1927); see Paolo Palchetti, 'Coerenza del diritto interno al diritto internazionale in Anzilotti' in Alessandra Annoni et al (n 51) 449.
124. Pierre Marie Dupuy, 'Dioniso Anzilotti and the Law of International Responsibility of States', 3 European Journal of International Law 1992, 139.
125. See Roberto Ago, *Scritti sulla responsabilità internazionale degli Stati* (Jovene Editore 1986).
126. Tomaso Perassi was Professor of International Law at the Univeristy of Rome La Sapienza. See Tomaso Perassi, *Lezioni di diritto internazionale* (Foro Italiano 1939).
127. Compare Ian Brownlie, *Principles of Public International Law* (Clarendon Press 1966) with Gaetano Morelli, *Nozioni di diritto internazionale* (CEDAM 1967).
128. Foreword to 1 Italian Yearbook of International Law 1975.
129. See Riccardo Pavoni, 'Italian Yearbook of International Law: Genesis, Development and Prospects', 50 Netherlands Yearbook of International Law 2019, 195.
130. See Antonio Cassese (ed), *Realizing Utopia: The Future of International Law* (OUP 2012).
131. Rosalyn Higgins, 'Anthony Cassese, Interview with Sir Robert Jennings' in Jill Barret and Jean-Pierre Gauci (eds), *British Contribution to International Law* (Brill Nijhoff 2019) 1797.
132. Among the exceptions, see Maria Rita Saulle, Professor of International Law at the University of Rome La Sapienza, Judge of the Italian Constitutional Court from 2005 to 2011, and Giuseppe Tesauro, Professor of EU Law at the University of Naples and Judge of the Italian Constitutional Court from 2005 to 2014.
133. Such position was held by Riccardo Monaco, then by Luigi Ferrari Bravo, and by Umberto Leanza. Today, the role is no longer filled by a scholar.
134. Enrico Milano, current legal adviser to the Permanent Mission, was preceded by Salvatore Zappalà, Giuseppe Nesi, Mauro Politi, Tullio Treves, and Luigi Ferrari Bravo.
135. Gaetano Morelli (1961–1971); Roberto Ago (1957–1978); Gaetano Arangio Ruiz (1985–1996); Luigi Ferrari Bravo (1997–1998); Giorgio Gaja (1999–2011); Giuseppe Nesi (2023–).
136. Roberto Ago (1979–1995); Luigi Ferrari Bravo (1995–1997); Giorgio Gaja (2012–2021).
137. Paolo Palchetti and Maurizio Arcari, 'International Law in Italian' *Oxford Bibliographies* (OUP 2022).
138. ibid.
139. <https://www.politico.eu/article/giorgia-meloni-italy-eu-migration-mediation-cant-save-eu-summit-talks/> accessed 5 July 2023.

CHAPTER 31

THE NETHERLANDS

CEDRIC RYNGAERT

1. Introduction

Despite its small size, the Netherlands may be boxing above its weight in the international law league. It is considered as one of the birthplaces of modern international law, its capital, The Hague hosts a large number of international judicial institutions and is termed the 'legal capital of the world', and it actively promotes international law in its foreign policy.

A brief contribution like this one can only fail to do justice to the rich Dutch *palette* of international law contributions. Choices are therefore called for. The author has opted not to provide biographies of the international law scholars of the Dutch 'Golden Age' (17th century), like Grotius, Bynkershoek, or Voet.[1] Instead, the emphasis has been placed on Dutch contributions to international law after the liberal '*esprit de l'internationalité*' came to animate European and American legal and diplomatic circles in the second half of the 19th century.[2] The Netherlands jumped on the bandwagon of these developments, of which The Hague became the epicentre.

Drawing on recent methodological turns in international legal history and theory—the turns to legal materiality, biographies, and cities in particular—this chapter opens in Section 2 with a brief reflection on the ascendancy of The Hague, paying particular attention to the role of one exceptional lawyer, T M C Asser. In the central Section 3, the chapter goes on to uncover the international law soul of the Netherlands. It contrasts the country's active promotion of international law in foreign affairs, its advisory culture, and vibrant scholarship on the one hand, with its darker colonial legacy and its occasional pursuit of narrow national interests on the other. Section 4 turns its gaze to the role of international law in Dutch courts. It foregrounds how Dutch court judgments have shaped international legal discourse, while sometimes creating tensions with the political branches, especially where the Dutch government or a foreign State is directly or indirectly in the dock. Section 5 concludes.

2. The Hague's Ascendancy to the Legal Capital of the World

The current pre-eminence of the Netherlands in international law, and especially the place occupied by its capital, The Hague, in international dispute-settlement, was not pre-ordained. In fact, by the mid-19th century, characterized by the balance of power between Europe's great powers, the small country of the Netherlands pursued a policy of neutrality, given its precarious geographic position between Germany and Britain. This neutrality yielded a passive attitude of the Netherlands towards international relations and international law. While the Netherlands also remained politically neutral in World War I,[3] by the turn of the century, neutrality no longer meant that the Netherlands simply stood aside. In fact, The Hague started to brim with international legal and diplomatic activity.

The Hague seemed a logical location for such activity. In the second half of the 19th century, due to improved railway connections, The Hague had been able to establish itself as a leading seaside resort in northwestern Europe. It attracted the upper classes, in particular of neighbouring Germany, to its Scheveningen *Kurhaus*, established in 1884.[4] Interdisciplinary scholarship has recently foregrounded how materiality can make legal difference,[5] and how objects and infrastructures have been instrumental in global regulation and governance.[6] Applying these insights, it can be posited that the new material conditions in the Netherlands, coupled with the country's relatively central geographical location, were instrumental in The Hague becoming a diplomatic conference centre, and subsequently the seat of the leading international judicial institutions.

However, cities do not become knowledge centres simply because of beneficial material conditions: human agency is also required. In this respect, a recent turn in international legal history has drawn attention to the role historically played by (well-connected) sub-State actors rather than States themselves in the construction and development of modern international law.[7] As far as The Hague is concerned, the envelope was very much pushed by the lawyer Tobias (T M C) Asser (1838–1913).[8] Without his tireless efforts, The Hague may never have become the world's legal capital. Asser convened and chaired conferences on private international law in 1893, 1894, and 1904, which resulted in the adoption of a number of treaties on issues of private international law. Asser also chaired an international peace conference, which was organized in The Hague in 1899 on the initiative of the Russian czar, after his delegate Fedor de Martens was so impressed by the 1894 conference.[9] For all these efforts, Asser received the Nobel Peace Prize in 1911.[10] He was also one of the founding fathers of the Institut de Droit International and the International Law Association, and the Hague Academy of International Law was his brainchild.[11] In 1965, the renowned Asser Institute was named after him.[12]

The international legal discipline's turn to the history of international law has been characterized by an interest in the biographies of prominent international lawyers.[13] The animating idea of this methodological approach is that legal initiatives taken by these lawyers should be understood against a particular personal, political, and social background. As far as Asser is concerned, it could be argued that his more cosmopolitan Jewish upbringing and his connections to similarly internationally-oriented Amsterdam-based Jewish lawyers—some of whom also went on to occupy prominent positions in the burgeoning international law field—may have served as factors which explain, at least in part, his devotion to international law.[14] This devotion was obviously also kindled by the dissemination of anti-discrimination-based liberal ideologies in the 19th century, to which wealthier Dutch Jews, especially lawyers and doctors, became attracted.[15]

On a more general note, the role of Jewish lawyers in the development of international law in specific countries in Europe, may deserve further scrutiny,[16] even if there is already considerable literature on the general contribution of Judaism and Jewish lawyers to the development of international law.[17] That being said, it is not unlikely that Jewish lawyers in the Netherlands may have had a larger impact on (international) legal development than their counterparts in other countries. Dutch antisemitism in the 19th century was, after all, relatively subdued compared to other European countries, and Jews were considered as an integral part of a pluriform Dutch society, even if antisemitic incidents did occur.[18]

Asser's conference efforts were the crucible in which more permanent Hague-based international legal institutions were established. The international law conferences planted the seeds for the Hague Conference on Private International Law (HCCH: *Hague Conference/ Conférence de La Haye*), which was established as an intergovernmental organization in 1951,[19] the Permanent Court of Arbitration (PCA),[20] and the Permanent Court of International Justice (PCIJ),[21] subsequently the International Court of Justice (ICJ).[22] The presence of the PCA and the ICJ in The Hague was a pull factor for the establishment of other international legal institutions in the 'legal capital of the world' (dixit former UN Secretary General Boutros-Ghali in 1993),[23] or the 'city of peace and justice', as The Hague smartly started to brand itself.[24] One can refer in this respect to the Iran-US Claims Tribunal, the International Criminal Tribunal for the former Yugoslavia, the International Criminal Court, the Special Court for Sierra Leone, the Special Tribunal for Lebanon, and the Kosovo Tribunal. Not only international tribunals, but also other international organizations are headquartered in the Netherlands, most notably the Organization for the Prohibition of Chemical Weapons.[25] This central role of the city of The Hague in international law, and especially international dispute-settlement, may have paved the way for the discipline's recent scientific interest in the role of cities more generally in international law. Lately indeed, 'cities and international law' has become a research field of its own.[26] Not surprisingly, one of its pioneers was the chair of the Asser Institute.[27] It appears as if, from his grave, Tobias Asser continues to cast his shadow on the scholarly development of our discipline.

3. Teasing out the Dutch 'International Law Soul'

The Netherlands is not just the home base of a large number of international tribunals and organizations which have gone on to develop international law, but it has also contributed to the development of international law in its own right. This section aims to answer one of the guiding questions of this volume, namely what impact European—in our case Dutch—ideas and practices had on the universality of international law. More fundamentally, it teases out the international law soul of the Netherlands.

The Netherlands has a self-professed 'historical call' and constitutional duty to develop international law. We will highlight that international law indeed plays a major role in contemporary Dutch foreign policy, supported by a strong advisory culture and active legal scholarship. It will be noted, however, that the credibility of Dutch promotion of international law, in particular human rights, is somewhat dented by its incomplete *Vergangenheitsbewältigung* of colonial legacy, as well as by its occasional selective application of international law.

3.1 The 'historic call' of the Netherlands

Our point of departure is that the development of international law is, somewhat unusually, a *constitutional duty* for the Dutch government: Article 90 of the Dutch Constitution, as introduced during the revision in 1983, provides that 'the Government shall promote the development of the international legal order'.[28] A similar provision featured in the Constitutions of 1922 and 1953, but this focused only on the duty to promote the peaceful settlement of disputes. Article 90 of the Constitution conveys a strong Dutch belief in the international rule of law.[29] This provision finds its historical roots in a mission on which the Dutch branch of the International Law Association (ILA), the *Nederlandse Vereniging voor Internationaal Recht* (NVIR, since 2010 KNVIR), the very first national branch of the ILA, embarked as early as 1910. During the first NVIR meeting in 1910, the association's first president characterized international lawyers as 'formalizers of international relations', and called on 'Grotius' Country' to accept 'its historic call'.[30] This 'historic call', which was later also described as the '(missionary) burden' of the Netherlands to promote international law,[31] was a direct reference to an article titled 'The Vocation of Holland' (*De roeping van Holland*), also published in 1910, by Cornelis van Vollenhoven, Professor of International Law at Leiden University.[32] The aim of the NVIR would be 'to finally bring Holland out of its introspection and isolation, and help it start thinking internationally',[33] a repudiation of its 19th-century stance of passive neutrality. Similar rousing words could be found in subsequent communications of the NVIR during World War I (when the Netherlands also remained neutral). Reference was made to the 'special mission' of the Netherlands, 'that small nation, sympathetic to all and cherishing its unblemished, wise and true neutrality', a nation that should 'make its voice heard, advocate mutual respect and calm to the warring nations, insist on respect for the laws of neutrality and commerce at sea, and enhance its beneficial influence on international affairs'.[34] The NVIR hoped that 'in peace to come our country with its colonies may rise to become the global centre of international law and commerce, the world's staple market, to which position its geography and historical antecedents have eminently predestined our nation'.[35] Soon after this clarion call, the first chairs exclusively for international law were established at Dutch universities.[36]

The historic call of the Netherlands should not be overstated, however: the heralds of the NVIR did not conceive of international law as a cosmopolitan construct, but rather as *ius publicum Europaeum*,[37] that is, as an instrument serving the more immediate interests of the Netherlands as a small nation sandwiched between larger European powers. This clearly builds on the approach of Grotius to international law in *De Mare Liberum* (1609), in which he advocated the freedom of the high seas with a view to breaking up the maritime monopolies of Spain and Portugal and thereby enabling the Dutch Republic to take part in the East Indian trade.[38]

Even if the Netherlands has, at least officially, abandoned the limited *ius publicum Europaeum* conception of international law (as will be discussed in Section 3.3), the latter continues to inform contemporary Dutch positions. This is notably exemplified by the contrast between, on the one hand, the vigorous Dutch *condemnation* of the illegal Russian invasion of Ukraine (2022), which was accompanied by military assistance to Ukraine and economic sanctions against Russia,[39] and on the other hand, the Dutch political and logistical *support* given to the equally illegal UK/US invasion of Iraq (2003).[40] It is undeniable that the Dutch response to Russia's actions is not only informed by their blatant illegality but also by geopolitical concerns over a broader war in Europe in which the position of the Netherlands could be affected.[41]

3.2 The Dutch colonial legacy

The original conception of international law as *ius publicum Europaeum* also meant that the Netherlands did not pay any attention to the injustices of colonialism. This was indeed *l'esprit du temps*, characterized by the position that matters internal to a Western State and its colonies were the State's *domaine réservé*, not subject to international regulation, and largely impervious to international criticism.[42] Thus, just a few years before the first NVIR meeting, Dutch *marechaussee* units could deploy scorched earth tactics in the Aceh war (Dutch East Indies), killing thousands of civilians, without a major outcry in the Netherlands or elsewhere.[43]

It is undeniable, however, that the dark sides of the Netherlands' colonial past are incompatible with its curated self-image of, on the one hand, promoter of international law and justice, and on the other hand, victim of the unconscionable manoeuvres of the great powers.[44] Somewhat belatedly, the Netherlands is currently reckoning with this past. Court cases recently brought by surviving victims or relatives of Dutch police actions in the East Indies (Indonesia) have raised awareness of colonial atrocities.[45] In addition, the Netherlands is in the process of revisiting racist stereotypes that have their origins in colonial times. A focal point of discussion has been the figure of *Zwarte Piet*, the blackface folkloristic assistant of *Sinterklaas* (Saint Nicholas). It is striking that Dutch support for this character significantly decreased in the wake of its condemnation by a UN Special Rapporteur and the UN Committee on the Elimination of Racial Discrimination,[46] a shift that is largely explained by the presence of vocal minority communities of colour in the Netherlands,[47] and the influence of the US-origin Black Lives Matter (BLM) Movement. Relatedly, in the last few years, the Netherlands is increasingly coming to terms with its role in the transatlantic slave trade and slavery in the colonies. In 2021, an advisory panel recommended that the Netherlands adopt a law recognizing these practices as crimes against humanity, and urged the government to offer an apology and, to the extent possible, provide reparations.[48] Concomitantly, a 2021 exhibition on slavery in the Rijksmuseum raised major awareness among the wider public of the dark sides of the Dutch 'Golden Age'.[49]

Such introspection is long overdue and may pay both moral and strategic dividends. Indeed, for the Netherlands to own up to its past 'mistakes'—which would, under current classifications, qualify as internationally wrongful acts—may allow it to more credibly defend international law on the global stage. In particular, it would undercut the force of *tu quoque* arguments advanced by the foreign addressees of Dutch criticism, notably in the human rights field.[50]

3.3 Contemporary Dutch foreign policy and international law

The Netherlands is a middle power, that is, a State that is 'neither great nor small in terms of international power, capacity and influence', and 'demonstrates a propensity to promote cohesion and stability in the world system'.[51] Because of its relatively small size, the Netherlands opts to pursue its interests first and foremost through multilateral institutions. Thus, the December 2021 Dutch coalition agreement lists as the first foreign policy priority the promotion of international cooperation through a leading role played by the Netherlands in the European Union (EU) and multilateral organizations, such as NATO.[52] By joining NATO as a founding member in 1949, the Netherlands gave up its traditional position of neutrality.[53] NATO membership, which constitutes the cornerstone of Dutch collective self-defence, has cemented a staunch transatlantic (pro-US) attitude of the Netherlands. Recently, Dutch public opinion, especially since the Trump presidency, may be gravitating away from the US in favour of more European strategic autonomy,[54] although the election of President Biden and the reinvigoration of NATO since the Ukraine war have strengthened Dutch transatlantic attitudes, at least for the time being.

In terms of legal areas of interest, historically, the Netherlands has focused primarily on the procedural dimension and the codification of international law.[55] Ever since the 1970s, and especially thanks to the efforts of the idealistic Minister of Foreign Affairs Max van der Stoel (who was later appointed High Commissioner on National Minorities of the Organisation for Security and Cooperation in Europe),[56] the promotion of human rights abroad has assumed a prominent place in Dutch foreign policy.[57] These days, the Netherlands is also a leading advocate of sanctions as a foreign (including human rights) policy tool.[58] It is of note in this respect that the adoption of the EU Global Human Rights Sanctions regime, adopted in 2020,[59] finds its origins in a 2018 proposal of the Netherlands.[60] As regards sanctions, the Netherlands currently strives to replace unanimous EU decision making with a qualified majority voting system,[61] although it is rather unlikely that other member States will go along with this given national sensitivities.[62]

The Netherlands reckons that putting a high premium on the rule of law in international relations will pay dividends for its own stability and export-oriented economy. What is good for the world, is also good for the Netherlands.[63] In official parlance, a realistic foreign policy does not imply a principled opposition between interest-based policy on the one hand, and law and morality on the other.[64] Nevertheless, the wish to uphold and defend the international rule of law sometimes clashes with *Realpolitik* and economic considerations. In fact, there is an oft-used and quite revealing Dutch expression which characterizes Dutch foreign policy as navigating between the commercial interests of the 'merchant' (*koopman*) and the missionary ideals of the 'reverend' (*dominee*).[65] The subtext of this expression is that the Netherlands may well pay lip-service to grand legal ideals, such as the promotion of human rights, freedom, and solidarity, but that, when push comes to shove, it prioritizes its national, often economic interests. For instance, in the 2010s, the Dutch government was reluctant to come to the rescue of southern European countries hit hard by the financial crisis, or at least demanded strict loan conditions.[66] Also, the Netherlands, fearful that large-scale migration may erode its economic base, has an asylum procedure that is arguably among the strictest in Europe,[67] and Dutch scholars and civil society have vigorously criticized Dutch treatment of aliens for its purported injustices and insufficient judicial control.[68]

Governmental prioritization of national interests over international law and solidarity may at times be supported by—and even take their cue from—conservative-leaning media.[69] However, the media may also take up the mantle of defending the (international) rule of law against governmental inertia informed by short-sighted parochial or commercial interests. For example, after Dutch media exposed the fact that, compared to other countries, the Netherlands had only frozen few Russian assets under the EU sanctions regime imposed after the 2022 invasion of Ukraine, law-makers put significant pressure on the government to do more to protect the international legal order, a move which had as its immediate result the appointment of a national sanctions coordinator.[70]

3.4 Dutch advisory practice in international law

Because of the importance it attaches to international law, over the years the Dutch government has established various bodies tasked with providing advisory opinions on issues of international law, most notably the standing advisory committee for public international law questions (*Commissie Advies Volkenrechtelijke Vraagstukken* (CAVV)). This body was created in 1953 to assist J P A Francois, then legal adviser to the Foreign Ministry,[71] in his ILC activities,[72] although an earlier advisory body had been active since 1921. Initially, the CAVV was composed of government officials, but by 1981, it had become an external body consisting of international law professors.[73] These days, legal practitioners from outside academia can also become members.[74] The CAVV is a unique entity that does not appear to have a counterpart in other countries. It comments on ILC drafts and gives advisory opinions to the Dutch government and parliament on a wide range of international law questions.[75] The CAVV normally advises by invitation, but it has also, although rarely, advised *proprio motu*. Where the government asks the CAVV for an advisory opinion, it is under a legal duty to react to the opinion.[76] The activities of the CAVV arguably increase the quality of the ILC's codification work and promote an international law-based Dutch foreign policy. Sometimes, the CAVV writes joint opinions with the Advisory Council on International Affairs (*Adviesraad Internationale Vraagstukken* (AIV)),[77] which also produces separate reports that are relevant to international relations and international law.[78]

Occasionally, the Dutch government requests advisory opinions on international law from other bodies, or creates ad hoc commissions for that purpose. Ad hoc commissions are typically set up to assess the government's engagement with international law in respect of a particular incident, and to draw lessons for the future. Thus, the government recently set up commissions to study the legality of humanitarian intervention,[79] and to investigate the Dutch aerial bombardment of an alleged Islamic State target in Hawija (Iraq), in which seventy civilians died.[80]

In 2011, after a government-appointed commission had uncovered that the Foreign Ministry's legal advisers' opinion on the illegality of Dutch participation in the 'illegal' US-UK invasion of Iraq (2003) had been overruled,[81] the government appointed an external international law adviser on a contractual basis.[82] The authority of the independent adviser's opinions would arguably have ensured better respect for international law by the government. However, the function of external adviser was abolished in 2021, as his role vis-à-vis the internal legal adviser and the CAVV never became fully clear.

3.5 Contemporary Dutch international law scholarship

Dutch international legal scholarship oscillates between idealism and pragmatism. This tension between idealists, who may tend to naturalism, and pragmatists, who stick to legal positivism, already came to the fore in the writings of the first generation of

Dutch international lawyers in the interbellum.[83] Also currently, it appears that pragmatism tends to guide many Dutch(-based) international lawyers, possibly because they are part-time legal practitioners or (government) advisers.[84] As André Nollkaemper observed in the 2015 *Liber Amicorum* for Professor A H A Soons (Utrecht University), Dutch pragmatist international lawyers tend to believe 'that international law cannot save the world, but it can make small differences, and should be studied in order to improve it, in small steps, so that these differences can indeed materialize'.[85]

Especially these days, however, it is difficult to capture the 'soul' of Dutch international law scholarship. Owing to the openness of Dutch universities, coupled with rising student numbers,[86] foreign scholars are increasingly filling the academic ranks of international law chairs. While affiliated with Dutch universities, these scholars may have little affinity with any perceived 'Dutch tradition'.[87] Rather, eclecticism may characterize the current state of international law scholarship at Dutch universities. What is striking, nevertheless, is the strong influence wielded by evolutions in English-speaking countries, which is in part a consequence of English having become the *lingua franca* of Dutch academic teaching and scholarship pertaining to international law.[88] Thus, we see a surge in interest in interdisciplinary scholarship (which is also partly driven by funding opportunities) and critical studies, which expose the biases of our discipline (eg decolonizing the legal curriculum).[89]

4. International Law in Dutch Courts

As regards the relationship between international and domestic law, the Netherlands boasts a *monist* system, at least in theory.[90] This means that international law need not be transformed into domestic law to have effect in the Dutch legal order. Until 1953, monism was based on unwritten constitutional law, as identified by the courts.[91] In 1953, it was laid down in the Dutch Constitution, which provided (at the time) that treaties were binding on persons insofar as such treaties had been published, and that domestic legislation did not apply if inconsistent with treaties to which the Netherlands was a party.[92] In 1956, the Constitution was amended once more in order to introduce a mitigated version of monism: only the self-executing provisions of treaties ratified by the Netherlands were henceforth considered as having (direct) effect in the Dutch legal order.[93] This restriction aimed to prevent a legal vacuum in which national law was absent or inapplicable, without there being clear provisions of international law that could be applied instead.[94] The Dutch Supreme Court held that for a treaty provision to be self-executing, it must be of such a nature that it can be directly applied in the national legal order.[95] In more recent case law, the Court has considered treaty provisions to be self-executing even if domestic implementing legislation was necessary, provided that the provisions were 'unconditional and sufficiently precise' in the results that they aim to achieve.[96] Pursuant to the supremacy clause laid down in the Dutch Constitution (Article 94 Dutch Constitution), self-executing treaty provisions prevail over inconsistent Dutch law. The supremacy of international legal norms takes on particular relevance in Dutch legal practice, as Dutch courts are constitutionally precluded from reviewing Dutch statutory law in light of constitutional norms.[97] Especially the directly applicable provisions of the European Convention on Human Rights (ECHR), as interpreted by the European Court of Human Rights (ECtHR), have had a major impact on Dutch legal practice.[98] Apart from treaties, other sources of international law can also have effect in the Dutch legal order. Under Dutch law, binding resolutions of international organizations can have direct effect, and prevail over inconsistent domestic law, under the same conditions as treaties (Article 93 Dutch Constitution).[99] Customary international law, for its part, can be directly applied in the Dutch legal order, but courts are precluded from reviewing Dutch statutory law in light of customary international law, that is, customary law does not enjoy supremacy.[100] Any source of international law can also have *indirect* effect in the Dutch legal order via the technique of consistent interpretation. Pursuant to this technique, domestic law provisions are construed in such a way that they not conflict with international law.[101] For consistent interpretation under Dutch law, international law provisions need not be self-executing;[102] it suffices that they contribute to a legal solution.[103] Finally, it is of note that Dutch law may authorize judges to directly apply relevant international law, in particular international immunities.[104] In this respect, there is an ever-growing body of Dutch case law concerning immunities of both States and international organizations.[105]

Recently, the Netherlands has offered fertile ground for global public interest litigation, which is largely tort-based, but relies on international law to draw the contours of the standard of care expected from tortfeasors.[106] The *Mothers of Srebrenica*, *Urgenda*, and *Shell* cases deserve specific mention here, as they have had a major international impact on international discussions on domestic courts' roles in addressing global governance challenges, such as climate change and human rights accountability. In *Mothers of Srebrenica*, the Supreme Court (2019) held the State partly liable, *inter alia* on the basis of the international law of State responsibility and European human rights law, for the cooperation of the Dutchbat peacekeeping contingent with the Bosnian Serbs at the time of the Srebrenica genocide in 1995.[107] In *Urgenda*, the Supreme Court (2019) ordered the State to reduce greenhouse emissions by at least 25 per cent compared to 1990 levels—citing *inter alia* the ECHR.[108] In *Shell*, the Hague District Court (2021) ordered the Anglo-Dutch energy giant Royal Dutch Shell to reduce the CO_2 emissions of the Shell group by 45 per cent net in 2030 compared to 2019 levels—citing the ECHR as well as the UN Guiding Principles on Business and Human Rights.[109] These cases were procedurally facilitated by a unique provision in the Dutch Civil Code that allows foundations protecting the public interest, for example, in relation to the environment or human rights, to start legal proceedings before Dutch courts, including against the State itself.[110] The judgments in these three cases, all of which were translated into English, have had a major impact internationally, as they demonstrated the ways in which governments and large corporations implicated in global harm could be held accountable.[111] In the Netherlands itself, the judgments sparked a heated domestic debate on the appropriateness of courts' powers to legally review complex political and business decisions.[112] One political party on the far-right of the political spectrum even proposed to end 'dikastocracy' ('government by judges') by means of a repeal of the aforementioned Articles 93 and 94 of the Dutch Constitution (on monism) as well as an amendment of the provision on public interest litigation.[113]

At times, the openness of Dutch courts to litigation that is (at least partly) based on international law may cause inter-State tensions to flare. By way of example, three Dutch court cases involving Russia can be mentioned. First and foremost among these cases is the Dutch prosecution of three Russian nationals and one pro-Russian Ukrainian national accused of involvement in bringing down Malaysia Airlines flight MH17 in eastern Ukraine in 2014,[114] a national trauma for the Netherlands due to the large number of Dutch victims. Russia rejected the Dutch District Court's conviction in 2022 of two of its citizens as politically motivated,[115] and attempted to discredit the proceedings by spreading misinformation.[116] The criminal case concerning the downing of the MH17 has been accompanied, for that matter, by an inter-State case filed by the Netherlands against Russia before the ECtHR and the International Civil Aviation Organization.[117] A second case involves the return of treasures which the Amsterdam-based Allard Pierson Museum had borrowed from Crimea-based museums before Crimea's annexation by Russia in 2014, which led to two Dutch court decisions, largely based on private international law, ordering the Dutch museum to return the treasures to Ukraine rather than Crimea (Russia).[118] Unsurprisingly, Russia subsequently threatened to no longer cooperate with Dutch museums.[119] A third case concerns Dutch courts' review, at the very request of Russia, of the international arbitral tribunal's Yukos award, in which the international tribunal had ordered Russia to pay around US$50 billion in damages to several shareholders of Yukos.[120] At the time of writing, Dutch court proceedings were still ongoing, although it is not unlikely that Russia's claim will eventually be dismissed, in the wake of the Supreme Court's *Yukos* ruling of 2021, which rejected all but one of Russia's arguments.[121] So far, Russia has largely refrained from criticizing Dutch courts' decisions in *Yukos*, rather on the contrary: the chief prosecutor's office of Russia, probably hoping that the case might still go Russia's way, even stated that the Supreme Court's decision 'reaffirms the principles of the rule of law and the independence of the judiciary'.[122] Russia's reaction is likely to be different, however, if the Dutch courts eventually rule against Russia, and authorize Yukos shareholders to seize Russian assets in the Netherlands.[123]

It can be gleaned from these 'Russian' *vignettes* that Dutch court decisions adversely affecting foreign States may well cause diplomatic headaches for the political branches of the Netherlands. However, this appears to be a price worth paying. While in the short term, such decisions may be politically inconvenient, over a longer term horizon, an independent judiciary may be a key foreign policy asset that allows the Dutch government to credibly take autocratic regimes to task.[124] Obviously, insofar as diplomatic relations between the Netherlands and a foreign State are already at a low, the political branches can directly draw foreign policy benefits from favourable Dutch court decisions. This is arguably the case with respect to Russia.

5. Final Observations

The Netherlands is one of the cradles of modern international law. This is not just because its capital, The Hague is also dubbed the 'legal capital of the world', boasting a large number of international judicial institutions. It is also because, since Dutch independence from Spain in the late 16th century, as a small or at most middle power,[125] the Netherlands has put a high premium on international law. Initially, it saw international law as an insurance policy against the scheming of the larger, especially European powers. Especially since the 1970s, however, it has staked out a more universalist position, in particular by actively promoting human rights in its foreign policy. The Dutch self-image of a champion of international law is not free of contradictions, however. The Netherlands is only slowly coming to terms with its colonial past and legacy. Also, its reliance on international law is at times selective and self-serving. Its independent courts, vibrant media, advisory bodies, and academic institutions may, however, prevent its international law confidence from turning into smugness.

Notes

1. See, for short biographies, J Wouters and N Pineau, 'Exploring Belgian and Dutch "Traditions" in International Law' in P Hilpold (ed), *The European International Law Tradition* (Springer 2020). See, for longer contributions, K Akashi, 'Cornelius Van Bynkershoek (1673–1743)'; P Haggenmacher, 'Hugo Grotius (1583–1645)' in B Fassbender and A Peters (eds), *The Oxford Handbook of the History of International Law* (OUP 2012).
2. See M Koskenniemi, *The Gentle Civilizer of Nations* (OUP 2002) especially Chapter 1. The Dutch lawyer Asser, whose contributions will be discussed below, was a key contributor to this international spirit, which led, *inter alia*, to the establishment of the Institut de Droit International, the International Law Association, and the *Revue de droit international et de législation compare*, the first international law journal.
3. M M Abbenhuis, *The Art of Staying Neutral. The Netherlands in the First World War, 1914–1918* (Amsterdam UP 2006)
4. See A Eyffinger, 'Tobias Asser's Legacy: The Pertinence of the *Institut de Droit International* to The Hague', 66 Netherlands International Law Review 2019, 313, 326.
5. See, eg, H Yoon Kang and S Kendall, 'Legal Materiality' in S Stern, M Del Mar, and B Meyler (eds), *The Oxford Handbook of Law and Humanities* (OUP 2020).
6. D R Quiroga-Villamarín, 'Beyond Texts? Towards a Material Turn in the Theory and History of International Law', 23(3) Journal of the History of International Law 2020, 466–500; J Hohmann and D Joyce (eds), *International Law's Objects* (OUP 2018).
7. See, eg, M Pal, *Jurisdictional Accumulation* (CUP 2020) (discussing how sub-sovereign consuls, ambassadors, merchants, and lawyers drove European imperial expansion); I van Hulle, *Britain and International Law in West Africa* (OUP 2020) (discussing how 'men on the spot' such as governors, merchants, and military men developed British 19th-century imperial international law in Africa).

8. See, on the life and legacy of T M C Asser, G De Baere and A Mills, 'T.M.C. Asser and Public and Private International Law: The Life and Legacy of "a Practical Legal Statesman"', 42 Netherlands Yearbook of International Law 2011, 3.
9. H van Loon, 'The Hague Conference on Private International Law', 21 Hague Justice Journal 2007, 75, 76. The 1899 conference led to the adoption of four conventions, mostly on international humanitarian law, and a number of declarations on the use of weapons. Another conference held in The Hague in 1907 led to the adoption of thirteen other conventions on international humanitarian law. The body of humanitarian law norms adopted at these Hague conferences gave rise to the term 'Hague law', a colloquial term still in use which denotes the rules on the conduct of hostilities and on the specific means and methods of warfare.
10. 'Tobias Asser—Biographical' (*The Nobel Prize*) <http://www.nobelprize.org/prizes/peace/1911/asser/biographical/> accessed 3 May 2022.
11. At the 1907 Hague Conference, Asser raised the idea of organizing courses on international law in The Hague. Funding for the Academy was provided by Asser himself, who donated a part of his Nobel Peace prize money, and by the Carnegie Endowment for Peace. The first courses at the Academy took place in 1923. The venerable Academy is best known for its summer courses on both public and private international law. See: 'History' (*The Hague Academy of International Law*) <http://www.hagueacademy.nl/about/history/> accessed 18 April 2023. These courses are published as the 'Collected Courses of the Hague Academy of International Law' (in French: *Recueil des cours de l'Académie de droit international de La Haye*). At the time of writing, almost 400 volumes had been published.
12. 'About the Asser Institute' (*Asser Institute*) <http://www.asser.nl/about-the-institute> accessed 3 May 2022.
13. I De la Rasilla, 'Biographical Approaches to the History of International Law' in *International Law and History: Modern Interfaces* (CUP 2021) 308–338.
14. A Eyffinger, *T.M.C. Asser (1838–1913), In Quest of Liberty, Justice and Peace* (2 vols, Brill 2019)Chapter 6.
15. I Schöffer, 'The Jew in the Netherlands: The Position of a Minority Through Three Centuries', 15(1) Studia Rosenthaliana 1981, 85, 93 (hereafter Schöffer, 'The Jew in the Netherlands').
16. But see C Walter, 'The Role of Religion in the Formation of International Law in Europe' in this volume, fn 1, in which the author mentions the influence of Judaism on international law, even if his approach is a different one.
17. S Rosenne, 'The Influence of Judaism on the Development of International Law', 5(2) Nederlands Tijdschrift voor Internationaal Recht 1958, 119–149; J Loeffler and M Paz (eds), *The Law of Strangers: Jewish Lawyers and International Law in the Twentieth Century* (CUP 2019).
18. Schöffer, 'The Jew in the Netherlands' (n 15) 96, 99.
19. The Hague Conference, obviously based in The Hague, works for the progressive unification of private international law, and, at the time of writing, counted eighty-five members. See 'About the HCCH' (*HCCH*) <http://www.hcch.net/en/about> accessed 3 May 2022.
20. See Article 20 of the 1899 Convention: 'With the object of facilitating an immediate recourse to arbitration for international differences which it has not been possible to settle by diplomacy, the signatory Powers undertake to organize a Permanent Court of Arbitration, accessible at all times and operating, unless otherwise stipulated by the

parties, in accordance with the rules of procedure inserted in the present Convention.' The ground for the PCA had been prepared by a number of successful inter-State arbitrations between the US and the UK (see notably the Treaty of Amity, Commerce, and Navigation, Between His Britannic Majesty and the United States of America (the 'Jay Treaty', 1795) which established claims commissions to handle outstanding disputes between Britain and the US in the aftermath of the American Revolutionary War) and the adoption of a draft procedural code by the Institut de Droit International ('Project de Règlement pour la Procédure Arbitrale Internationale', Session de La Haye, 1875). In 1902, the first case was submitted to the PCA.

21. Article 14 of the Covenant on the League of Nations had envisaged the creation of such a court.
22. In the history of the ICJ, one Dutch national served on the bench, between 1997 and 2006: Peter Kooijmans, former Minister of Foreign Affairs and Professor of International Law at Leiden University. See, on Peter Kooijmans, J G Lammers, 'Peter Kooijmans: Minister for Foreign Affairs', 10(1) Leiden Journal of International Law 1997, 121; C Flinterman, 'Peter Kooijmans and Human Rights', 10(1) Leiden Journal of International Law 1997, 126; M Brus, 'Peter Kooijmans: Professor of Public International Law', 10(1) Leiden Journal of International Law 1997, 132; M Brus, 'Judge Peter Kooijmans Retires from the International Court of Justice', 19(3) Leiden Journal of International Law 2006, 699; N J Schrijver, 'In Memoriam: Professor P.H. Kooijmans (1933–2013)', 60 Netherlands International Law Review 2013, 161.
23. P van Krieken and D McKay (eds), *The Hague: Legal Capital of the World* (TMC Asser Press 2005).
24. See, for an academic analysis of actions to exploit the unique identity of the city of The Hague, B A B F Hulleman and R Govers 'The Hague, International City of Peace and Justice' in K Dinnie (ed), *City Branding* (Palgrave Macmillan 2011).
25. See, for an overview of all international organizations established in The Netherlands, 'Lijst van Internationale Organisaties in Nederland' (*Rijksoverheid*) <http://www.rijksoverheid.nl/onderwerpen/internationale-organisaties-in-nederland/lijst-van-internationale-organisaties-in-nederland> accessed 3 May 2022.
26. See notably H P Aust and J E Nijman (eds), *International Law and Cities* (Edward Elgar 2021).
27. 'Prof. Mr. Dr. Janne Nijman' (*Asser Institute*) <http://www.asser.nl/about-the-asser-institute/whos-who/JanneNijman> accessed 18 April 2023.
28. This provision is concerned with the government's execution of foreign policy, but is not justiciable, however, meaning that it does not allow for review of governmental acts before Dutch courts. L Besselink, 'The Constitutional Duty to Promote the Development of the International Legal Order: The Significance and Meaning of article 90 of the Netherlands Constitution', 34 Netherlands Yearbook of International Law 2003, 89, 136.
29. See also, on the rule of law, A van Aaken, 'Rule of Law in Europe: A Multi-Layered Network' in this volume.
30. 'Het pleit van het Internationalisme' ('The Plea of Internationalism') in *Mededelingen NVIR* (No 1) 12, 13, 19, cited in A Eyffinger, ' "A Caravan Passes By . . . " The Centenary of the Netherlands Society of International Law', 57 Netherlands International Law Review 2010, 143, 147 (hereafter Eyffinger, ' "A Caravan Passes By" ').
31. N Schrijver, 'A Missionary Burden or Enlightened Self-Interest? International Law in Dutch Foreign Policy', 57 Netherlands International Law Review 2010, 209 (hereafter

Schrijver, 'A Missionary Burden'); P Malcontent and F Baudet, 'The Dutchman's Burden? Nederland en de internationale rechtsorde in de twintigste eeuw' ('The Dutchman's Burden? The Netherlands and the International Legal Order in the 20th Century') in B de Graaff, D Hellema, and B van der Zwan (eds), *De Nederlandse Buitenlandse Politiek in de Twintigste Eeuw* (The Dutch Foreign Policy in the Twentieth Century) (Boom 2003).

32. C van Vollenhoven, 'De Roeping van Holland' ('Holland's Vocation'), 74 De Gids 1910, 185, republished in C van Vollenhoven, *Verspreide Geschriften* (C van Vollenhoven's Collected Writings) vol 2: International Law (Tjeenk Willink 1934) 157; C van Vollenhoven, *The Three Stages in the Evolution of the Law of Nations* (Martinus Nijhoff 1919). See also, on Van Vollenhoven, J K Oudendijk, 'Van Vollenhoven's "The Three Stages in the Evolution of the Law of Nations". A Case of Wishful Thinking', 48 Tijdschrift voor Rechtsgeschiedenis 1980, 3; P H Kooijmans, 'How to Handle the Grotian Heritage: Grotius and Van Vollenhoven', 30 Netherlands International Law Review 1983, 81.
33. 'Het pleit van het Internationalisme' ('The Plea of Internationalism') in *Mededelingen NVIR* (No 1) 29–30, cited in Eyffinger, ' "A Caravan Passes By" ' (n 30) 147.
34. *Mededelingen NVIR* (No 7) 10–19, cited in Eyffinger, ' "A Caravan Passes By" ' (n 30) 150.
35. *Mededelingen NVIR* (No 8) 11, cited in Eyffinger, ' "A Caravan Passes By" ' (n 30) 151.
36. H de Waele, 'A New League of Extraordinary Gentlemen? The Professionalization of International Law Scholarship in the Netherlands, 1919–1940', 31(3) EJIL 2020, 1005, 1010–1011 (hereafter De Waele, 'A New League of Extraordinary Gentlemen?').
37. See also on this, L Mälksoo, 'The Role of European States and Lawyers in the History of International Law' in this volume.
38. H Grotius, *The Freedom of the Sea, or the Right Which Belongs to the Dutch To Take Part in the East Indian Trade* (OUP 2016).
39. Dutch government, Kamerbrief stand van zaken ontwikkelingen in en rondom Oekraïne, 26 February 2022.
40. Dutch participation in the illegal US-UK invasion of Iraq in 2003 was later condemned by an ad hoc Dutch government commission: W Davids, *Rapport Commissie van onderzoek besluitvorming Irak* (Boom 2010).
41. Dutch government, Kamerbrief over het beleid van Buitenlandse Zaken, 8 March 2022.
42. See also on European colonialism, A Anghie, 'Europe and International Law: Colonial Legacies' in this volume; see also on how a 'civilisational standard operated to deny equal status to individuals and groups living in the colonies', B Cali, 'Human Rights Ideas: Europe' in this volume. Like other colonial powers, the Netherlands developed a separate—and discriminatory—legal system for the colonies. Notably on law and jurisprudence in the Dutch East Indies, see N S Efthymiou, *Recht en rechtspraak in Nederlands-Indië* (Wolf 2013).
43. A Stolwijk, *Atjeh: het verhaal van de bloedigste strijd uit de Nederlandse koloniale geschiedenis* (Prometheus 2016).
44. O Tasevski, 'The Dutch Are Uncomfortable With Being History's Villains, Not Victims' in *Foreign Policy* (Melbourne, 10 August 2020).
45. Most cases relate to Dutch police actions in Indonesia in the late 1940s, on the eve of Indonesia's independence in 1948. See L van den Herik, 'Addressing Colonial Crimes through Reparations?', 10 Journal of International Criminal Justice 2012, 693–705. Some of these cases have been successful (eg District Court The Hague, 25 March 2020, ECLI:NL:RBDHA:2020:2584), while others were not (eg District Court The Hague, 23 January 2019, ECLI:NL:RBDHA:2019:500).

46. Concluding observations on the 19th to 21st periodic reports of the Netherlands, CERD/C/NLD/CO/19-21 (2015); J Fontein, 'Hoofd VN-onderzoek: Zwarte Piet is terugkeer slavernij', *De Volkskrant* (22 October 2013).
47. See on subnational cultural diversity in Europe notably V Bilkova, 'Idea of European Culture(s) and Diversity' in this volume.
48. Adviescollege Dialooggroep Slavernijverleden, *Ketenen van het verleden* (2021).
49. D Boffey, 'Rijksmuseum slavery exhibition confronts cruelty of Dutch trade' *The Guardian* (Amsterdam, 18 May 2021).
50. More generally, indeed, the Netherlands has a tendency to lecture others on their human rights record, whereas human rights hardly play a role in domestic Dutch discourse. See B Oomen, 'The Rights for Others: The Contested Homecoming of Human Rights in the Netherlands', 31(1) Netherlands Quarterly of Human Rights 2013, 41–73.
51. E Jordaan, 'The Concept of a Middle Power in International Relations: Distinguishing between Emerging and Traditional Middle Powers', 30 Politikon 2003, 165.
52. Coalitieakkoord, 'Omzien naar elkaar, vooruitkijken naar de toekomst' (15 December 2021) 38.
53. See, on various legal aspects of Dutch membership of NATO, R A Wessel, 'The Netherlands and NATO' in J Raine (ed), *Legal Implications of NATO Membership: Focus on Finland and Five Allied States* (Erik Castrén Institute 2008) 137–161.
54. R Korteweg, C Houtkamp, and M Sie Dhian Ho, 'Dutch Views on Transatlantic Ties and European Security Cooperation in Times of Geopolitical Rivalry' (research report, Clingendael 2020).
55. Schrijver, 'A Missionary Burden' (n 31) 217–236. See, for an overview of Dutch contributions to international law up to the 1970s, H F van Panhuys et al (eds), *International Law in the Netherlands*, vols I–III (Sijthoff 1979).
56. A Bleich, *De stille diplomaat: Max van der Stoel, 1924–2011* (Balans 2018).
57. Each year, the Ministry of Foreign Affairs publishes a lengthy report on the use of human rights in Dutch foreign policy, and its results. See, for the latest report, Ministry of Foreign Affairs, *Mensenrechtenrapportage 2020. Inzet en resultaten Nederlands buitenlands mensenrechtenbeleid* (2021).
58. Coalitieakkoord (2021) (n 52) 38.
59. Council Regulation (EU) 2020/1998 of 7 December 2020 concerning restrictive measures against serious human rights violations and abuses [2020] OJ L410I, 1–12.
60. Dutch Human Rights report 2018, Parliamentary Paper 22 112, no 2529 (2019).
61. Coalitieakkoord (2021) (n 52) 37.
62. L Schuette, 'Should the EU Make Foreign Policy Decisions by Majority Voting?' (policy brief Centre for European Reform, Brussels 2019).
63. See, eg, the title of this policy document of the Dutch Foreign Ministry (2018): 'Investeren in Perspectief. Goed voor de wereld, goed voor Nederland' (*Investment in perspective. Good for the world, good for the Netherlands*).
64. J Voorhoeve, 'Het gaat om de gevolgen: elf aandachtspunten', 70 Internationale Spectator 2016, special issue 'Een realistisch buitenlands beleid', item 7 (former Dutch Foreign Minister Voorhoeve suggesting instead that the relevant questions should be what could be done, and for whom); Regeerakkoord, 'Vertrouwen in de toekomst', Rijksoverheid 2017, part 4.1 (stating that a realistic foreign policy serves both Dutch interests and the international legal order, and calling in this context for more focus and effectiveness).

65. See, eg, in the context of the Dutch development cooperation, P Hoebink, 'Hoe de dominee de koopman versloeg. Nederlandse ontwikkelingssamenwerking gewogen', 60 Internationale Spectator 2006, 578.
66. See, for instance, the Dutch Finance Minister's infamous remark that southern European countries may spend northern European aid on 'booze and women'. See W Mussler, 'Nach Interview in der F.A.Z. Dijsselbloem: "Ich bedauere, dass es als ‚Nord gegen Süd' aufgefasst wurde" ', *Frankfurter Allgemeine Zeitung* (22 March 2017).
67. W Boersema, E Huisman, and A Kootstra, 'Nederland heeft een van de strengste asielprocedures van Europa', *Trouw* (27 November 2019).
68. SVMA, VAJN, *Ongehoord onrecht in het vreemdelingenrecht* (report, April 2021); K Geertsema et al, 'Ongezien onrecht in het vreemdelingenrecht' Nederlands Juristenblad 2021, 1046–1053.
69. S Bout, 'De Griekse schuldencrisis. Een frame analyse van berichtgeving in de Nederlandse media' (Thesis, University of Amsterdam 2015).
70. Letter of the Minister of Foreign Affairs to Parliament (Tweede Kamer), no 36045-60, 4 April 2022.
71. A Dutch international law prize was named after Francois: <http://www.knvir.org/francois-prize/francois-prize/> accessed 3 May 2022.
72. Speech by P Kooijmans, 'De Rol van het Volkenrecht in het Nederlands Buitenlands Beleid' (CAVV symposium 1993) 8 (on file with the author). A predecessor of this CAVV had already been active after World War I—a body that was in turn the successor of the Commission for the Preparation of the Third Peace Conference in The Hague, a conference that eventually did not take place due to the war. A H A Soons, Introductory Remarks, 'De rol van het Volkenrecht in het Nederlands Buitenlands Beleid' (CAVV symposium 1993) 1 (on file with the author) (hereafter Soons, 'Introductory Remarks').
73. Soons, 'Introductory Remarks' (n 72) 2.
74. For the current membership: <https://www.advisorycommitteeinternationallaw.nl/about-the-cavv/advisory-committee> accessed 18 April 2023. The author of this contribution is the chair of the CAVV.
75. See for an overview: <https://www.advisorycommitteeinternationallaw.nl> accessed 18 April 2023.
76. See, on the impact of the CAVV's opinions on the work of the parliament, L van den Herik, 'Checks and balances and the role of international law in foreign policy discussions: parliamentarian condemnations of genocide and crimes against humanity', draft paper for European Society of International Law conference (Stockholm, September 2021) (discussing these condemnations against the background of a CAVV opinion on the use of the genocide label by politicians, issued in 2017) (paper on file with the author).
77. eg Advisory Council on International Affairs 'Advisory Report 97: Autonomous Weapon Systems: The Need for Meaningful Human Control' (October 2015).
78. For instance, the AIV has a commission on human rights, which also produces reports relevant to international human rights law. See 'Over de AIV. Organisatie en samenstelling' *(Adviesraad Internationale Vraagstukken)* <http://www.adviesraadinternationalevraagstukken.nl/over-de-aiv/organisatie> accessed 18 April 2023.
79. Report of the Expert Group Established by the Minister of Foreign Affairs of the Netherlands, 'Political Support for Interstate Use of Force and on Humanitarian Intervention' (December 2019) https://zoek.officielebekendmakingen.nl/blg-917814.pdf accessed 18 April 2023.

80. Instellingsbesluit Commissie van onderzoek wapeninzet Hawija, 27 November 2020.
81. W Davids, *Rapport Commissie van onderzoek besluitvorming Irak* (Boom 2010) (concerning Dutch participation in the 'illegal' US-UK invasion of Iraq in 2003).
82. Kamerstukken II 2010/11, 32 635, n 3. The first (and only) external adviser was André Nollkaemper, Professor of International Law at the University of Amsterdam.
83. See De Waele, 'A New League of Extraordinary Gentlemen? (n 36) 1011–1014.
84. See also, on the devotion to public service of the first Dutch international law scholars, ibid, 1017–1019.
85. P A Nollkaemper, 'Fred Soons: A Pragmatic Trust in International Law' in C Ryngaert, E J Molenaar, and S Nouwen (eds), *What's Wrong with International Law? Liber Amicorum Professor A.H.A. Soons* (Brill 2015) 6. Note that Nollkaemper is nevertheless of the view that the idealist stream may 'perhaps' be 'dominant' in the Netherlands. According to him, this stream includes 'international lawyers who profess international law in the pursuit and support of some grander ideals [relating to] human rights, international criminal justice or a fair division of wealth in the world'.
86. Dutch universities offer a strong international law curriculum in English, thereby attracting a seemingly ever-increasing number of foreign students and foreign staff, including from outside Europe. International law is taught as a compulsory course at the undergraduate level, and many universities offer English-language master degrees in international law. The explosive growth in (international) students at Dutch universities has led them to stop actively recruiting students abroad. See 'Dutch universities less eager for international students' *NL Times* (6 August 2021).
87. *Vice versa*, originally Dutch scholars have moved abroad, and may show little inclination to act as heralds of a 'Dutch tradition'.
88. Dutch masters programmes in international law are offered in English. Also, the Royal Netherlands Society of International Law (KNVIR) organizes most of its activities in English, but its board still meets in Dutch.
89. eg A L Fischer, 'Colonialism, Context and Critical Thinking: First Steps Toward Decolonizing Dutch Legal Curriculum' 18 Utrecht Law Review 2022, 14–28.
90. The author wishes to thank Anouk van Midden for her research assistance in this respect.
91. Leading cases in this respect are Supreme Court 25 May 1906, W (*Weekblad van het Recht*) 8383; Supreme Court 3 March 1919, NJ 1919, 371 *(Grenstractaat Aken)*.
92. Then Articles 65 and 66 of the Dutch Constitution. For an overview of the 1953 amendments of the Dutch Constitution, see H F van Panhuys, 'The Netherlands Constitution and International Law', 47 American Journal of International Law 1953, 537.
93. See (current) Article 93 of the Dutch Constitution (previously Article 66). The supremacy clause of Article 65 became (current) Article 94 of the Constitution. In 1983, the Constitution was revised once more, but there were no major changes regarding the role of international law.
94. J Fleuren, 'Application of Public International Law by Dutch Courts', 57 Netherlands International Law Review 2010, 245, 253 (hereafter Fleuren, 'Application of Public International Law').
95. Supreme Court 30 May 1986, NJ 1986, 688; 18 NYIL (1987) 389–397 (*Spoorwegstaking*). To determine the self-executive nature of a treaty provision, courts are supposed to objectively look at the *content* (formulation) of the provision. However, a subjective approach, based on the intent of the contracting parties, is not precluded altogether. See Supreme Court 18 April 1995, NJ 1995, 619 (ruling that the content of the provision can be disregarded where the parties explicitly intended a provision to have (or to not have) direct effect.

96. District Court The Hague 16 May 2012, ECLI:NL:RBSGR:2012:BW6789 (*Nietrokersvereniging CAN v Staat der Nederlanden*) 386–387. The aim of these provisions should be ascertained in accordance with Articles 31–33 of the Vienna Convention on the Law of Treaties (VCLT) 1969. See for a discussion of the recent approach J Fleuren, 'Recent Developments Regarding the Direct and Indirect Application of Treaties by Dutch Courts: Fresh Approaches to Self-Executing, Non-Self-Executing and Non-Binding International Law', 47 Netherlands Yearbook of International Law 2016, 377 (arguing that Dutch domestic courts increasingly move from a 'binary' approach to a 'contextual' approach in determining the self-executing character of treaty provisions).
97. Article 120 Dutch Constitution. As a result, unlike in many other countries, there is no constitutional court in the Netherlands. See also on this issue, Fleuren, 'Application of Public International Law' (n 94) 258.
98. N S Efthymiou and J C de Wit, 'The Role of Dutch Courts in the Protection of Fundamental Rights', 7 Utrecht Law Review 2013, 75–88.
99. Article 93 Dutch Constitution.
100. *Nyugat* doctrine (Supreme Court 6 March 1959, NJ 1962, 2; 10 NILR (1963) 82 (Nyugat II), confirmed in *Bouterse* (Supreme Court 18 September 2001, LJN AB1471, NJ 2002, 559; ILDC 80 (NL 2001).
101. Supreme Court 19 November 1990, NJ 1992, 107, (*T.S.M. Compagnie d'Assurance Transports v Geiseller Transport A.G)* 3.2.3. In the US, this is known as the *Charming Betsy* doctrine. See *Murray v The Schooner Charming Betsy* 6 US 64 (US 1804). See, on consistent interpretation, G Betlem and P A Nollkaemper, 'Giving Effect to Public International Law and European Community Law in Front of Domestic Courts. A Comparative Analysis of the Practice of Consistent Interpretation', 14 European Journal of International Law 2003, 569 (hereafter Betlem and Nollkaemper, 'Giving Effect to Public International Law').
102. Supreme Court 2 May 1995, NJ 1995, 621.
103. Supreme Court 12 May 1999, NJ 2000, 170. In practice, consistent interpretation can create the same results as direct effect. See Betlem and Nollkaemper, 'Giving Effect to Public International Law' (n 101) 583.
104. Article 13a *Wet Algemene Bepalingen*.
105. See, for recent decisions of the Supreme Court, Supreme Court 18 December 2020, ECLI:NL:HR:2020:2103; Supreme Court 14 October 2016, ECLI:NL:HR:2016:2354 (concerning State immunity from execution); Supreme Court 24 December 2021, ECLI:NL:HR:2021:1956 (concerning the immunity of international organizations).
106. eg J van Zeben, 'Establishing a Governmental Duty of Care for Climate Change Mitigation: Will Urgenda Turn the Tide?', Transnational Environmental Law 2015, 339–357.
107. Supreme Court 19 July 2019, ECLI:NL:HR:2019:1223.
108. Supreme Court 20 December 2019, ECLI:NL:HR:2019:2006.
109. District Court The Hague 26 May 2021, ECLI:NL:RBDHA:2021:5339.
110. Article 3:305a Dutch Civil Code. See, for a discussion, O Spijkers and J Zheng, 'Public Interest Litigation Before Domestic Courts in the Netherlands on the Basis of International Law: Article 3:305a Dutch Civil Code' (*EJIL:Talk!*, 6 March 2020), <http://www.ejiltalk.org/public-interest-litigation-before-domestic-courts-in-the-netherlands-on-the-basis-of-international-law-article-3305a-dutch-civil-code/> accessed 3 May 2022.

111. See, for international news items, eg, I Kaminski, 'Dutch supreme court upholds landmark ruling demanding climate action', *The Guardian* (The Hague, 20 December 2019); 'Srebrenica massacre: Dutch state "10% liable" for 350 deaths', *BBC News* (19 July 2019). See, for scholarly publications, eg, B Mayer, 'The State of the Netherlands v. Urgenda Foundation: Ruling of the Court of Appeal of The Hague (9 October 2018)', 8(1) Transnational Environmental Law 2019, 167–192. See, on the impact of the *Srebrenica* cases in the Netherlands, special issue of the Netherlands International Law Review 62(2), 2015.
112. See, eg, J C A de Poorter, 'Is Nederland verworden tot een dikastocratie?', 49 Nederlands Tijdschrift voor Bestuursrecht 2020, 105–113.
113. Tweede Kamer, Rondetafelgesprek: 'Dikastocratie?', 9 March 2020, <https://www.tweedekamer.nl/debat_en_vergadering/commissievergaderingen/details?id=2020A00508> accessed 18 April 2023.
114. 'MH17 plane crash. Prosecution and trial' (*Netherlands public prosecution service*) <http://www.prosecutionservice.nl/topics/mh17-plane-crash/prosecution-and-trial> accessed 3 May 2022.
115. 'Russia says it rejects "scandalous" Dutch MH 17 verdict', *Reuters* 17 November 2022.
116. G Kent, 'Russia's MH17 Web of Lies Looks Set to Unravel in Court' *The Atlantic Council* (22 July 2020).
117. 'The Netherlands brings MH17 case against Russia before European Court of Human Rights (*Government of the Netherlands* (10 July 2020)); 'The Netherlands and Australia submit complaint against Russia to the International Civil Aviation Organization', *Government of the Netherlands* (14 March 2022).
118. Court of Appeal of Amsterdam 26 October 2021, ECLI:NL:GHAMS:2021:3201 (*Crimean Museums v Ukraine and the University of Amsterdam*).
119. M Back, 'Rusland dreigt museale samenwerking Nederland op te zeggen', *NRC* (16 November 2017).
120. *Yukos Universal Limited (Isle of Man) v The Russian Federation*, UNCITRAL, PCA Case No AA 227, Final Award (18 July 2014).
121. Supreme Court 5 November 2021, ECLI:NL:HR:2021:1645 (*Russian Federation v Yukos et al*).
122. D Kemp, 'Russia Wins Latest Round of $50-Bln Yukos Case', *Moscow Times* (5 November 2021).
123. In this phase, the shareholders appear to be focusing on vodka brands linked to the Russian State. See R Baurichter, 'Aandeelhouders oliegigant Yukos hervatten jacht op miljardencompensatie', *Het Financieele Dagblad* (13 February 2022).
124. Strikingly, strengthening the democratic legal order is the top priority of the Dutch government. See Coalitieakkoord (2021) (n 52) 5. This priority can be linked to the government's foreign policy priority to take action against EU member States which undermine democracy and the rule of law. ibid, 39.
125. A middle power is a State that is 'neither great nor small in terms of international power, capacity and influence', and 'demonstrates a propensity to promote cohesion and stability in the world system'. See E Jordaan, 'The Concept of a Middle Power in International Relations: Distinguishing between Emerging and Traditional Middle Powers', 30 Politikon 2003, 165.

CHAPTER 32

THE NORDIC STATES

PÅL WRANGE AND
ASTRID KJELDGAARD-PEDERSEN

1. Introduction

Is the Nordic perspective on international law different from traditions in other regions of the world? Judging from the presentations of the 2015 conference *A Nordic Approach to International Law?*, most Nordic international lawyers believe that if there is a distinct Nordic perspective, it is manifested in substantive areas like human rights or international environmental law or in a common approach to key international organizations such as the United Nations (UN). None of the conference participants suggested a Nordic tradition with regard to general issues such as State responsibility, State immunity, or the sources of international law. To the extent that a sense of a shared identity exists among Nordic international lawyers, it seemingly revolves around ethics and policy in relation to the development and enforcement of particular international legal norms. In the Nordic countries, both governments and academics care about human dignity, the environment, and collective security—or so we think of ourselves.

Upon closer scrutiny, however, a remarkable interplay—or dichotomy perhaps—appears between substantive idealism and the profound scepticism towards utopian natural law, which lies at the core of the school of thought within legal philosophy for which the Nordics are most famous: 'Scandinavian legal realism'.

This chapter begins by briefly outlining in Section 2 some relevant aspects of the history—domestic as well as international—of the Nordic region. Section 3 then turns to the general attitude in the Nordics (mostly from a government perspective) towards international law and the extensive inter-Nordic collaboration in the field. Section 4 addresses the Nordic Sstates and selected areas of international law, specifically international security law (Section 4.1) and human rights law (Section 4.2), whilst Section 5 discusses historic and current Nordic trends in international legal scholarship. Section 6 concludes the chapter with some reflections on the notion of 'a Nordic approach to international law'.

2. History

2.1 Domestic

The Nordic region consists of the Scandinavian countries Denmark, Norway, and Sweden, as well as of Iceland and Finland. The first four countries speak related languages and consolidated themselves in kingdoms towards the end of the Viking age—with borders shifting back and forth until the 20th century. Finland, dominated by the totally different Finnish language (most closely related to Estonian) had a different early history, before it came under the dominance of its Western neighbour. Sweden ruled over Finland from the late Middle Ages until 1809, when Sweden lost Finland to Russia, but then gained Norway in 1814. Between 1536 and 1814, Norway had been a part of the Danish realm following the dissolution of the Kalmar Union.[1] The union between Norway and Sweden was dissolved in 1905, in 1917 Finland declared independence, and in 1944 the Icelanders voted to leave the union with Denmark to create the fully independent republic of Iceland. Denmark's other former colonies, Greenland and the Faroe Islands, remain a part of the Danish realm, but enjoy extensive self-government.[2]

Denmark and Sweden have sometimes exercised considerable power internationally. Sweden, for example, was a Scandinavian great power during the Thirty Years' War and exerted significant influence on the Peace of Westphalia in 1648. Nevertheless, the Nordic countries have usually been importers of cultural influences: most strongly from Germany during the Middle Ages, from France during the 17th and 18th centuries, again from Germany during the 19th century and early 20th century and then from the Anglo-American countries after World War II.

In the north, there is a small but important Sami indigenous people, and the Danish autonomous region of Greenland is mainly populated by Inuit.[3] There are Finnish-speaking groups in Sweden and Norway and a Swedish-speaking minority in Finland. For the most part, however, the Nordic populations were ethnically and religiously homogenous well into the post-war years. Since then, all of the Nordics—with Sweden in front—have received significant groups of immigrants (both labour immigrants and refugees).

There is less of a feudal heritage in the Nordic region than on the continent, and historically the peasantry could sometimes exercise considerable political power. Even though the Nordic countries are now characteristically secular,[4] they share a Lutheran heritage, which according to many observers constitutes a fundamental explanation for the generally high levels of trust in the State and the law.[5]

This history has fed into what is often called the Nordic model. Even though its essential characteristics are disputed, it is generally agreed that a vital aspect of this model is the institutionalized welfare state,[6] with a high degree of equality,[7] and the goal to provide equal opportunities for all.[8] This is coupled with a strong and well-functioning administration as well as a faith in the rule of law, which is guaranteed by fairly stable political systems rather than by constitutional courts. According to some observers, the Nordic model is a 'combination of extreme individualism and a strong state that has shaped the fertile ground for an efficient market economy'.[9] All in all, although marred by their share of problems, the Nordic countries are comparably peaceful, incorrupt, and egalitarian.

2.2 International

After having participated in European wars 1500–1815, the Nordic countries receded into a more secluded existence between 1815 and 1940.[10] Sweden has remained at peace since 1814, while Norway and Denmark were victims of German aggression in 1940. Finland was born in the turmoil of a divisive civil war and thereafter fought two wars with the Soviet Union (1939–1940, 1941–1944). After World War II, Finland had to sign an onerous peace treaty with the Soviet Union, and the term Finlandization was coined to denote the way that its government had to always consider the views of its mighty neighbour. Hence, the Nordic countries have different experiences of foreign and security policy, and they chose different paths during the Cold War. Norway and Denmark were (and remain) members of NATO while Finland and Sweden pursued policies of neutrality (though with important shades of difference between them) and remained not aligned until their application for NATO membership in 2022 following the Russian aggression against Ukraine. Despite these different paths in security policy, the Nordic region has often been held up as a paradigmatic example of what Karl Deutsch called a security community.[11] The Nordics have all been active participants in the Conference and later Organization for Security and Cooperation in Europe (OSCE), with the two neutrals playing special roles, including Finland's hosting of the groundbreaking Helsinki conference in 1973–1975. At any rate, all the Nordics have benefitted (sometimes uneasily) from the US nuclear umbrella, and they are firmly anchored in the West.

Though profiting from—and sometimes being complicit in—European colonialism, the Nordic countries were generally not a part of the scrambles for Africa, Asia, or Latin America,[12] which means that the Nordic countries do not have 'client states' in the Global South. In an increasingly internationalized world after World War II, the Nordics have generally been fairly supportive of third world positions, though not uniformly so.[13] Through their often active and vocal stances, as well as their comparatively generous development cooperation programmes, the Nordic States have been branded as 'Global Good Samaritans' and 'moral superpowers'. Being self-consciously aware of their consistent ranking in the top 5 or top 10 of almost every global index (from happiness to gender equality[14] to the rule of law), the Nordics are often keen to export their model.[15]

The Nordic countries have a history of close cooperation based on a sense of trust.[16] After the Napoleonic wars, rivalry between Sweden and Denmark was replaced by Scandinavianism and cooperation began in many fields, including several projects for common Nordic legal codes. The Nordic Council of 1952, was complemented by the Nordic Council of Ministers in 1971. The Nordic countries have had a passport union and a common labour market since the 1950s, and they continue to cooperate in all policy areas, including military security.[17] The border agreements between Finland, Sweden, and Norway include joint regimes for their common waterways and other issues, while Denmark and Sweden agreed to build a bridge across Öresund—the approximately 8-kilometre wide strait that separates the two countries.

Nordic cooperation has been affected—but not substantially hampered—by their different relations with the European Union (EU). Denmark joined what is now the EU in 1973, Sweden and Finland in 1995, while Norway and Iceland have remained outside, though with a close relationship with the EU (*inter alia* through the EEA Agreement, which entered into force in 1994).[18]

3. Attitude to International Law

3.1 In general

Nordic lawyers and politicians routinely emphasize the importance of international law, especially for small States. Foreign ministers and other politicians talk about international law as a 'cornerstone' of foreign policy, to cite a regular expression in Swedish foreign policy declarations. The Nordic countries, as well as Nordic international lawyers, generally also show strong faith in international institutions and mechanisms as the only alternative to geopolitics.[19] They support international mediation and other forms of conflict resolution, manifested most prominently in Norway's strong position as an international peacemaker (and the home of the Nobel Peace Prize),[20] consistent and visible participation in peace missions, the first two Secretary-Generals of the UN (Trygve Lie and Dag Hammarskjöld), and the Helsinki accords (1975). International law is also important in public debate. It is generally considered highly relevant whether a certain event—be it the US invasion of Iraq, the Russian annexation of Crimea, or the Israeli occupation of Palestine—is legal or not.

Nordic international lawyers, like their governments, have always been intensely interested in issues to do with conflicts, sovereignty, and borders, and in particular for Finland, international law has often been an existential matter.[21] It has been assumed that international law provides valuable support for national sovereignty against hegemonic great powers, but in a wider international context of peaceful settlement of disputes.

Often, Nordic governments have submitted such disputes to legal settlement. After the dissolution in 1905 of the union between Norway and Sweden, the maritime borders between the two States were settled in the Permanent Court of Arbitration in 1909.[22] The Dispute between Sweden and Finland over the Aaland Islands was referred to a committee of legal rapporteurs (at the initiative of Great Britain), which recommended that the islands would belong to Finland under an autonomy regime. That decision formed the basis for a decision by the Council of Ministers of the League of Nations, and the ensuing Åland Agreement between the Finnish and Swedish delegations.[23] In 1923, the Permanent Court of International Justice (PCIJ) ended a Finnish claim that the Soviet Union had not honoured the peace agreement in Dorpat (nowadays: Tartu) regarding the Finnish-related population in Eastern Carelia, since the Soviet Union refused to participate in the process.[24] The *Eastern Greenland* case, which incidentally has become a landmark case on unilateral declarations, was settled in the PCIJ in 1933. A promise by the Norwegian Foreign Minister Nils Claus Ihlen that Danish plans for Greenland 'shall not face any difficulties on the part of Norway' meant that Erik den Røde land was awarded to Denmark.[25] Norway successfully defended itself against France before the International Court of Justice (ICJ) in the *Certain Norwegian Loans case* in 1957.[26] Sweden had a dispute over international family law with the Netherlands decided by the ICJ in 1958.[27]

The Nordic countries all have long coastlines, and it is not surprising that many disputes have concerned the law of the sea. Three oft-cited cases on law of the sea issues (and the formation of customary international law) which involved Nordic countries have been adjudicated by the ICJ: the *Fisheries* case (*United Kingdom v Norway*),[28] one of the two *North Sea Continental Shelf* cases (*Germany v Denmark*),[29] and the *Fisheries Jurisdiction* case (*United Kingdom and Germany v Iceland*).[30] In 1992, Denmark and Finland amicably settled a case before the ICJ on passage through the Great Belt,[31] and the year after, the ICJ adjudged a case filed by Denmark against Norway, the *Maritime Delimitation in the Area between Greenland and Jan Mayen* case.[32]

It is fair to say that the Nordic countries have a very positive attitude to legal settlement and regulations in general. With the exception of Iceland, the Nordic countries have accepted the optional clause in the ICJ Statute, all of them have accepted the optional protocol to the ICCPR on individual complaints as well as the competence of the Fact-Finding Commission under the First Additional Protocol to the Geneva Conventions. The OSCE Court of Conciliation and Arbitration was created in 1992 partly at Swedish initiative. This positive attitude towards international law and international legal mechanisms may be explained as a mix of self-interest, idealism, and trust in the rule of law, but it is sometimes tempered by political realism or external constraints. The Nordic countries are located close to Russia and its access routes to the oceans, and they are more or less dependent on US military backup.[33] This location prevented Finland from joining the Council of Europe during the Cold War, while realist calculations have contributed to preventing any of the Nordic countries from ratifying the Treaty on the Prohibition of Nuclear Weapons. Further, being a part of the economic Global North and being very confident in the excellence of their political, economic, and legal systems, the Nordics have sometimes allowed economic self-interest or domestic sovereignty to prevent them from joining some international projects. For instance, only Finland has accepted individual complaints to the International Covenant on Economic, Social and Cultural Rights (ICESCR), and only Denmark and Norway have ratified the ILO Convention No 169 on Indigenous and Tribal Peoples.

Being small States the Nordics have good incentives to pool their domestic resources. The foreign services in the Nordic capitals are as full of academics as the Law Faculties are crowded with former foreign policy practitioners, and the services of academics are regularly used in government committees and the like. To be an academic in international law has not been an obstacle to a political career. Two of the most high-profile Swedish foreign ministers were former academics and had both been legal advisers to the minister for foreign affairs (Östen Undén, 1945–1962; Hans Blix 1978–1979), the first Finnish professor of international law, Rafael Erich, became Prime Minister and Minister of Foreign Affairs, while the Prime Minister of Norway during the breakup negotiations with Sweden, Professor Francis Hagerup, was one of the first Nordic members of the Institut de droit international.[34] Nordic lawyers have always been active in the League of Nations and in the UN, including as judges in the World Court (Didrik Nyholm, Åke Hammarskjöld, Rafael Erich, Helge Klaestad, Sture Petrén, Jens Evensen),[35] and as legal counsels to the UN Secretary-General, like Hans Corell (1939–) or Edvard Hambro, who, soon after his short stay at the UN, wrote the first commentary on the UN Charter.[36] Francis Hagerup, the Norwegian, even participated in the Advisory Committee of Jurists that drafted the Statute of the Permanent Court of International Justice.[37]

3.2 Inter-Nordic cooperation concerning international law

The Nordics cooperate to a large degree, perhaps more so than in any other subregion in Europe. The Nordic countries present common candidates to positions in institutions like the ICJ, the International Criminal Court (ICC), and the International Law Commission (ILC), and they hold joint Nordic speeches on international law topics in the sixth committee of the UN General Assembly. Even when they take different positions, they often consult, and Nordic diplomats and lawyers can usually talk to one another in a more relaxed manner than with colleagues from other parts of the world. When different stances are taken, that is usually so for 'realist' reasons, such as the very long border to Russia (Finland has not joined the ban on anti-personal landmines) or military integration with NATO. The close Nordic collaboration is a procedural matter, but it presupposes substantive commonality.

4. The Nordics and Selected Areas of International Law

Historically, the Nordic countries have generally been active in all areas of international law-making. In addition to the law of the sea and polar law, the Nordic brand has been deeply imprinted in international environmental law ever since the Stockholm Conference on the Environment in 1972 and the Brundtland Commission's report 'Our Common Future' on sustainable development in 1987. The latter has been followed up by all the Nordic countries and their international lawyers, with names like the Espoo Convention on Environmental Impact Assessments (1991) and the Aarhus Convention on Access to Information, Public Participation in Decision-Making and Access to Justice in Environmental Matters (1998). In international economic law, in marked contrast, the Nordic countries have been less conspicuous, though generally taking free trade positions.[38]

In the remainder of this section, we will focus our attention on two selected (partly overlapping) clusters of legal regimes of general importance to the Nordic region: international security law and human rights.

4.1 International security law

As mentioned, the Nordic countries are small States, who were long on the periphery of power politics, and then found themselves in between great powers. With limited military strength, the Nordics have little opportunity to bend or breach international law and a strong interest in the effective regulation of international security.

Sweden (with Finland) and Denmark-Norway (with Iceland) inaugurated the first alliance of armed neutrality in 1780 together with Russia, and the doctrine was underpinned by writings of the Danish scholar Martin Hübner.[39] With the important exception of two Danish-German/Prussian wars, the Nordic countries generally tried to stay out of belligerent affairs on the continent during the 19th century and gradually became accustomed to pursuing a policy of neutrality. It was natural for the Nordic countries to apply to seek membership in the League of Nations, though as neutral powers. The compatibility between neutrality and the sanctions system was, however, not a given, and this was the subject of a heated debate in the Swedish Parliament.[40] After the Abyssinian (Ethiopian) crisis, and the failed sanctions against Italy, the then four Nordic States in 1938 issued a common declaration of intended neutrality and enacted similar neutrality laws to that effect.[41]

Even though the Nordic countries chose different approaches to alliances after the war, they generally find that security must be collective, because they cannot rely on their own military means. Denmark and Norway were among the founding members of the UN, Iceland and Sweden joined in 1946, while Finland was allowed to become a member only in 1955, due to the Cold War. Their aforementioned engagement in the OSCE is also a reflection of this attitude.

Nordic governments (and international lawyers) generally favour a fairly extensive interpretation of the prohibition of the use of force. For example, Ove Bring, legal adviser at the Swedish Ministry for Foreign Affairs subscribed to the interpretation of Article 2(4), which claims that the words 'the territorial integrity or political independence of any state, or in any other manner inconsistent with the Purposes of the United Nations' do not limit the scope of the prohibition, and he also finds that there is no right to anticipatory self-defence.[42] But there is also a widely-shared feeling among the Nordics that there needs to be a way to handle mass atrocities, as discussed in a nuanced report from the Danish Institute of International Affairs, commissioned by the Danish government.[43] In 2013, for example, the Danish government expressed support for the controversial position put forward by the British government that humanitarian intervention (absent Security Council mandate) in Syria was permissible under international law.[44]

During the 'war on terror' after the September 11 attacks, Nordic governments and scholars usually found the US counterattacks in Afghanistan justified. The invasion of Iraq in 2003 was more divisive. Though held to be illegal by an almost unanimous Nordic international law expertise, the Danish government decided, controversially, to participate in Operation Iraqi Freedom. Another, and unusual, example of Nordic State practice was provided during the Swedish submarine hunt in its territorial and internal waters against real or presumed Soviet intruders during the 1980s. Sweden did not refer to Article 51 of the UN Charter, but instead justified the operations with the right to protect sovereignty; in addition to the legal arguments for this view it was also understood that it would not be advantageous to imply a state of armed conflict with the Soviet Union.[45]

The Nordic countries have generally been careful about the implementation of UN sanctions and other measures and they have enthusiastically cooperated with the UN and with each other in peace missions.[46] Moreover, the Nordic countries have generally been very supportive of international humanitarian law. The Red Cross Conference in 1948, which prepared the diplomatic conference in 1949, was chaired by the Swedish count Folke Bernadotte (assassinated later that year on a mission as the UN mediator in Palestine).[47] During the Diplomatic Conference in 1974–1977, which resulted in the two additional protocols to the 1949 Geneva Conventions, the Norwegian delegate Hans Wilhelm Longva was a leading negotiator, often speaking in favour of proposals promoted by G77 delegations, while Sweden, under the leadership of Hans Blix (later foreign minister, director general of IAEA, and weapons inspector in Iraq), pushed for provisions on conventional weapons, which eventually led to the adoption of the Convention on Conventional Weapons in 1980.

Notably, the Nordics are currently divided on the question of the meaning of the 'duty to ensure respect' under Common Article 1 of the Geneva Conventions. At the Nordic launch of the Updated Commentary to the Third Geneva Convention held at the University of Copenhagen in September 2021, the representative from the Finnish Ministry of Foreign Affairs expressed support for the ICRC's interpretation that States are obliged to ensure, for example, their military partners' respect for international humanitarian law,[48] while her Danish counterpart overtly opposed this view arguing that it might have a 'chilling effect' on the willingness of States to cooperate.[49] One might speculate that this difference of opinion has to do with Denmark's relatively more recent engagements in offensive military operations, not least in Afghanistan and Iraq.

Finally, it bears mentioning that the Nordic countries are active and strong supporters of the ICC, not least during the negotiations leading up to the adoption of the Rome Statute.[50]

4.2 Human rights

Among the general public in the Nordic region, there is a significant interest in the application of human rights, both at home and globally. All of the Nordic countries except Iceland have national human rights institutions, and—to name an example—the annual National Human Rights Forum in Sweden gathers up to 5,000 participants from civil society, public administration, and the academy.

4.2.1 *The Nordics and global human rights conventions*

The Nordic countries have ratified almost all global human rights conventions, with the important exception of the International Convention on Migrant Workers, and they are active members or observers of the UN Human Rights Council.[51]

The Nordics have a history of protesting jointly against 'general' reservations to human rights conventions, and they have influenced the approach to such reservations, including in the International Law Commission's Guide to Practice on Reservations to Treaties.[52] All of the Nordics have given a prominent place to human rights in general in their foreign relations, though not always without consideration of bilateral consequences.

While being firm supporters of the UN's and other multilateral efforts to combat terrorism, the Nordic countries have been careful to note the human rights implications of such measures, and this issue has also been widely commented on in Nordic academia.[53] The Finnish professor Martin Scheinin was the Human Rights Council's first Special Rapporteur on human rights and counter-terrorism. After having found six Swedish individuals and private entities on one of the UN Security Council's sanctions lists, Sweden joined Germany and Switzerland in a long-standing and partially successful campaign for more legal security regarding targeted sanctions against individuals.[54]

4.2.2 *The Nordics and the ECHR*

Denmark, Iceland, Norway, and Sweden joined the ECHR in 1953, while Finland had to wait until 1990, due to resistance from its Soviet neighbour.[55] There was initial reluctance about the role of human rights conventions in domestic law, partly because of a sense of already having superior legal systems, partly because of the dominant doctrine of dualism in Nordic constitutional law. To the surprise of Nordic countries, the European Court of Human Rights (ECtHR) began handing down judgments against them in the 1980s, starting with *Sporrong-Lönnroth v Sweden* concerning the right to property.[56] While the Nordic States have generally complied with decisions of the ECtHR (as well as with decisions by the UN human rights committees on individual complaints), the political attitude has not been consistently favourable. In fact, overt resistance towards the Court has played an important role in domestic Danish politics, and this was a key factor in the process that led to the adoption of the Copenhagen Declaration in 2018.[57]

There are interesting differences between the Nordics when it comes to the attitudes of judges towards international law. In a recent study, Marlene Wind argues that the approach of the Supreme Courts of Denmark and Sweden is considerably less friendly to international law than that of the Supreme Court of Norway.[58] Remarkably, however, another recent study shows that the voting patterns of the Nordic judges of the ECtHR to some degree evidence a distinctive Nordic trait when it comes to treaty interpretation. Based on an examination of dissenting opinions joined by all of the Nordic judges (who took part in deciding that particular case), Jens Elo Rytter draws contours of a Nordic approach to the interpretation of the ECHR, which is characterized by an 'insistence that some basis in the ordinary meaning of the text is required', 'reliance on preparatory works rather than on more autonomous and free considerations', and 'resistance towards imposing (without a solid legal basis) obligations on the national political organs, notably in the field of economic and social policy'.[59] Interestingly, both Wind and Rytter refer—as a possible explanation for their respective findings—to the relatively weak constitutional role of courts in the Nordic countries as well as to the strand of legal philosophy for which the Nordic region is arguably most famous—Scandinavian legal realism (which will be discussed in Section 5.1).

This apparent contradiction between the Nordic States acting as 'moral superpowers' in relation to international human rights while being reluctant to fully embrace those same conventions at home has sometimes been labelled the 'Nordic human rights paradox'.[60] In fact, as noted by four commentators, 'human rights are virtually absent from standard accounts of the history of the Nordic model'.[61] It is beyond the scope of this chapter to elaborate on the causes of this paradox, but it is relevant to point out that the welfare state in its formative years was based on other ideas.

5. International Legal Scholarship in the Nordics

5.1 Scandinavian legal realism—theory

A few notes on Scandinavian legal realism seem pertinent in the present context, not least because many contemporary Nordic scholars share the belief of Wind and Rytter that this school of thought informs the way that Nordic lawyers take account of international law.

Scandinavian legal realism—which is not to be confused with American legal realism or realism in the academic study of international relations—of course consists of many different ideas given that it is a movement comprising more than a handful of authors and their writings over the course of at least fifty years.[62] If we were, as Jakob v. H. Holtermann notes, to summarize their scholarly endeavours in one main message, it would be the importance of securing the foundations of legal science. The Scandinavian legal realists were all devoted to—some would even say obsessed with—the project of ensuring that the doctrinal study of law is feasible '*as a respectable science*.'[63] Among the basic propositions to that end was the notion that legal science must be separated from morality. The only purpose of legal *science* was to deal with the description of objectively valid law. Hence—in order to avoid collapsing into metaphysics—legal science should completely refrain from making assessments of the moral value of the law in question and should certainly steer clear of proposing changes to it. This brought the realists to draw a categorical distinction between the—scientifically sound—doctrinal study of law (*retsdogmatik*) on the one hand and legal politics (*retspolitik*) on the other.[64]

In Sweden, Scandinavian legal realism is known as the Uppsala school, but from an international point of view, the most significant proponent was the Dane, Alf Ross. In Ross's specific theory, the crux was the distinction between norm-expressively valid law (in Danish: *gyldig ret*) and norm-descriptively valid law (in Danish: *gældende ret*). While the Scandinavian legal realists have consistently attracted substantial criticism, most legal scholars seem to agree (albeit many regretfully) that their ideas have had a significant influence on Nordic intellectual history as well as on the practice of law, including international law, in the Nordic countries, as will be discussed in the next section.[65]

5.2 International legal scholars

Two of the most celebrated forefathers of international law, Hugo Grotius and Samuel Pufendorf, were both employed by Sweden—Grotius as the Swedish Ambassador to France and Pufendorf as professor in Lund (where he published *De jure naturae et gentium* in 1672). The first Nordic writer (though born in Hannover) of any importance was the aforementioned Martin Hübner, whose *De la saisie des bâtiments neutres* (1759) was very influential in his time.[66] Richard Kleen, a Swede, wrote an oft-cited treatise on the law of neutrality in 1898 and 1900.[67]

This is not the place to define the criteria for a putative Nordic tradition (nationality, education, professional situs, etc) and it has always been the case that writers from the Nordic countries, as of any region, also belong to different transnational traditions. Nevertheless, it is reasonable to hold that there are certain common traits that make it possible to speak of 'Nordic doctrine', perhaps as a matter of family resemblance (Wittgenstein) rather than a category. Jaakko Husa and others have found a Nordic tradition in constitutional law, perhaps divided into West and East Nordic.[68] The founding of the *Nordic Journal of International Law/ Acta scandinavica juris gentium*[69] in 1930 suggests a self-identification of the founders (and the many succeeding editors) as 'Nordic'.[70]

When international law matured into an academic topic and universities started to appoint chairs on the subject (often in conjunction with constitutional law), Nordic international law academics, like legal academics in general, were heavily dependent on the German (often Hegelian) tradition. Francis Hagerup, for instance, translated Franz von Holzendorff's *Das europäische Völkerrecht* into Norwegian in 1885 and he was very influenced by Georg Jellinek's *Die Lehre von Staatenverbindungen*.[71] Echoes of Jellinek's concept of *Selbstverpflichtung* (autolimitation) and Paul Laband's theory of the state were heard as late as 1950, when the Swedish professor Halvar Sundberg (1894-1973) declared that each state has its own international law.[72]

During the interwar years, Nordic international lawyers debated the reality of international law, partly as a reaction to the faith that Nordic governments seemed to invest in this law and in the League of Nations. Scandinavian legal realists played significant but not identical roles in that debate. Vilhelm Lundstedt, one of the most vocal members of the Uppsala school, claimed that states follow rules of international law only if it is in their interest in a book of 1937 entitled *The law of nations—a mortal danger for the nations*. His fellow Uppsala scholar (and student of Hägerström) Östen Undén, however, described neutrality as completely appropriate for a member of the League[73] and proposed, in his later position as foreign minister, that Sweden join the UN (though without any illusions that the Charter would be a sufficient protection[74]). Alf Ross (Copenhagen) and his former student and subsequent counterpart at Aarhus University, Max Sørensen, spent substantive parts of their careers as academic and practising international lawyers, including as judges. Ross, who defended his dissertation under the supervision of the founder of the Uppsala school, Axel Hägerström, engaged in a significant debate about the character of international law with the legal idealist and rector of Oslo University, Frede Castberg, who defended the idea of human rights.[75] One common criticism—mentioned above—is that Scandinavian legal realism contributed to the formation of an 'excessively majoritarian conception of democracy' and the corresponding sceptical view of judicial review and human rights.[76] While this may be true, it should also be mentioned that leading Scandinavian legal realists had a more nuanced view. Ross, for instance, thought that even though rights could not be based on natural law and though the term 'rights' lacked a 'semantic reference', the concept could still have a legitimate function in legal language.[77]

While a certain degree of 'realism' is necessary in the foreign service, there are very few hard-nosed political realists in Nordic academic international law circles. Theoretically, contemporary Nordic international lawyers are generally 'soft positivists'.[78] Hence, although the legacy of Scandinavian legal realism is not carried forward directly, it is surely felt indirectly in certain prevailing attitudes, like the scepticism of both natural law and absolute sovereignty and the belief in (positive) law-making as a tool for progress.

There are also certain distinct strands of theoretical thinking in Nordic international law that seem hard to imagine without that sceptical undertone. Undoubtedly the most internationally influential strand of thinking in Nordic international law in recent decades is the body of work produced by Martti Koskenniemi, with colleagues and collaborators in Helsinki and beyond. Koskenniemi took over the chair from Bengt Broms—who led the UN working group that drafted the 1974 definition of aggression—and named the newly founded Erik Castrén Institute (ECI) after another eminent predecessor. The cosmopolitan cohort gathered at the ECI points to another trend in Nordic scholarship, the formation of large, internationalized and interdisciplinary research centres. iCourts in Copenhagen and PluriCourts in Oslo, which both focus on international courts, are two prominent examples.[79]

Both Copenhagen and Oslo are also home to significant centres on academic research in human rights, as is Lund, with its Raoul Wallenberg Institute (RWI). The *Nordic*

Journal of Human Rights, based in Oslo, was already founded in 1982 as a Scandinavian language journal, while RWI publishes a significant book series.

Although international law is fairly marginal in legal culture in the Nordic countries—as in many other places—all law students in the Nordic countries have to study public international law as a compulsory subject, and these students have a growing number of elective international law courses from which to choose. A significant driver of this development is that the Nordic Law Faculties have been internationalized to a very large extent as concerns both education and research. Today, English is the working language of several Nordic research groups in international law.

6. Concluding Reflections: A Nordic Approach to International Law?

While Nordic scholars and professionals—like others—take part in global or regional networks of likeminded people, there is no escaping geography. However, despite the unavoidable backdrop of its perilous geopolitical location, the Nordic region has become a fairly safe cocoon, created by a mix of cautious foreign policy, fortunate economics, and level-headed domestic politics. Nordic international lawyers share domestic experiences of functional and relatively well-meaning legislatures combined with black-letter legal practice, faithful to the intentions of the elected law-makers. From this comfortable position, post-war Nordic international lawyers have had the luxury to engage with global issues, often with an altruistic (and sometimes self-righteous) bent. The overall positive outlook on international law and trust in international institutions in the Nordics thus seems to rest on a combination of idealism and a foundational belief in the rule of law—which is, granted, from time to time set aside by political pragmatism or simply to promote self-interest.

Against this background, outsiders—non-Nordics as well as non-lawyers—may reasonably wonder whether the fact that Nordic international lawyers intuitively dismiss the idea of 'a Nordic approach to international law' is indeed an expression of what Freud referred to as the 'narcissism of small differences'.[80] All things considered, the longstanding inter-Nordic collaboration on a wide range of international legal questions—including, to mention just one example, the tradition of selecting Nordic candidates to important international organs such as the ILC—would seem to indicate at least some degree of Nordic unity in relation to international law.

Acknowledgements

The two authors are grateful for the comments provided by the editors on an earlier draft. Pål Wrange wishes to thank the participants of the SCILJ BBL weekly seminar series, and in particular Sia Spiliopoulou Åkermark and Mark Klamberg, for very useful comments on an earlier draft. Astrid Kjeldgaard-Pedersen wishes to thank Jakob v.H. Holtermann for his comments and insights concerning Scandinavian legal realism. The authors also wish to acknowledge that the lecture 'Folkrätten i de nordiska länderna på 1900-talet' by Martti Koskenniemi at the Nordic Lawyers meeting (Nordiska juristdagarna) in 2017 provided a very useful springboard for this article. As mentioned in the text, the 2015 conference *A Nordic Approach to International Law?*, organized by Astrid Kjeldgaard-Pedersen, was an important gathering of reflections on international law in the Nordic countries. The edited volume with contributions from the conference, which was published in 2017, is cited throughout the chapter. Much information about international law in Sweden is provided in Ove Bring, Mark Klamberg, Said Mahmoudi and Pål Wrange, *Sverige och folkrätten* (6th edn, Norstedts juridik 2021).

Notes

1. The Kalmar Union brought Denmark, Norway, and Sweden together under a single monarch from 1397 to 1523.
2. Some important areas, including eg foreign affairs as well as defence and national security, are, however, still under Denmark's jurisdiction.
3. In addition to Greenland and the Faroe Islands (located between Scotland and Iceland and with a distinct Scandinavian language), the Åland islands (with a Swedish speaking population) enjoys far-reaching territorial autonomy within Finland. The Sami groups in Finland, Norway, and Sweden can exercise a limited non-territorial autonomy. See further Markku Suksi, 'Territorial Autonomy: The Åland Islands in Comparison with Other Sub-State Entities' in Zoltán Kántor (ed), *Autonomies in Europe: Solutions and Challenges* (NPKI, Research Institute for Hungarian Communities Abroad 2014) 37–58.
4. In fact, the Nordic States are consistently placed in the upper right-hand corner of the Inglehart-Weizel World Cultural Map 2022, at <https://www.worldvaluessurvey.org/WVSContents.jsp> accessed 8 July 2022.
5. Mikko Kuisma, 'Social Democratic Internationalism and the Welfare State After the "Golden Age"', 42 Cooperation and Conflict 2007, 9, 15; Johan Strang, 'Nordic Political and Economic Cooperation', Conference paper, 2016, 3. <http://www.asean-aemi.org/energy-security-and-connectivity-the-nordic-and-european-union-approaches/> accessed 8 July 2022.
6. Kuisma (n 5), 12; Strang, 'Nordic Political' (n 5) 3.
7. However, there may be a growing trend towards inequality. See, eg, Erling Barth, Kalle Moene, and Axel West Pedersen, 'Rising Inequality in the Egalitarian Nordics' in Georg Fischer and Robert Strauss (eds), *Europe's Income, Wealth, Consumption, and Inequality* (OUP 2021) 219–246.
8. Kuisma (n 5) 16.
9. Anu Koivunen, Anu, Jari Ojala, and Janne Holmén, 'Always in Crisis, Always a Solution? The Nordic Model as a Political and Scholarly Concept' in Anu Koivunen, Jari Ojala, and Janne Holmén (eds), *The Nordic Economic, Social and Political Model: Challenges in the 21st Century* (Routledge 2021) 1–19, 2.
10. A notable exception is the border dispute between Denmark and Germany in Southern Jutland. In 1864, Denmark lost one third of its territory and 40 per cent of its population to Prussia and Austria in the Second Schleswig War. This turn of events is considered a national trauma as well as the birth of modern-day Denmark. See further Rasmus Glenthøj, 'The meaning of the Second Schleswig War ("1864") in Denmark', 1 May 2019, available at

<https://nordics.info/show/artikel/the-meaning-of-the-second-schleswig-war-in-denmark> accessed 18 September 2023. Following the German defeat in World War I, the reunification of Southern Jutland with Denmark was brought about by a referendum in the relevant areas. See further Jørgen Fink, 'The Reunification of Denmark in 1920', 5 May 2019, available at <https://nordics.info/show/artikel/the-reunification-of-denmark-in-1920 accessed 18> September 2023. In spite of widespread disappointment among the Danes that the southern parts of Schleswig did not become a part of Danish territory as well, the solution to the German-Danish border dispute and the minority issues along the border is generally considered to be a success story.

11. Strang, 'Nordic Political' (n 5) 4.
12. Denmark and Sweden made feeble colonial efforts in the 1600s and 1700s, including slave trading and the brief New Sweden colony (now Delaware) in North America, but they were quickly marginalized. Remarkably, the Danish West Indies (now Virgin Islands) were sold to the US as late as 1917.
13. To take an example: Finland, Iceland, and Sweden voted yes to the Charter on Economic Rights and Duties of States (UN A/RES/3281(XXIX)), whereas Norway abstained and Denmark voted no.
14. Kuisma (n 5) 14 Hanne Hagtvedt Vik, Steven LB Jensen, Linde Lindkvist, and Johan Strang, 'Histories of Human Rights in the Nordic Countries', 36 Nordic Journal of Human Rights 2018, 189–201. Gender equality has also been a feature in the branding of the Nordics, even as 'gender superpowers'. See Eirinn Larsen, Sigrun Marie Moss, and Inger Skjelsbaek Larsen, 'Introduction', in Eirinn Larsen, Sigrun Marie Moss, and Inger Skjelsbæk (eds), *Gender Equality and Nation Branding in the Nordic Region* (Routledge 2021) 1, 1.
15. For a nuanced view of this phenomenon, see Sunniva Engh, 'The "Nordic Model" in International Development Aid' in Haldor Byrkjeflot, Lars Mjøset, Mads Mordhorst, and Klaus Petersen (eds), *The Making and Circulation of Nordic Models, Ideas and Images* (Routledge 2021) 124–142.
16. Strang, 'Nordic Political' (n 5) 2.
17. The Helsinki Convention of 1962 is often referred to as a Basic Law of Nordic Cooperation. See Strang, 'Nordic Political' (n 5) 2.
18. The Norwegian people has twice rejected membership of the EU (1994) and its predecessor the European Community (1972), though both times with slim margins.
19. A famous example is Dag Hammarskjöld's last public lecture held in Oxford on 30 May 1961, 'The International Civil Servant—In Law and in Fact', <https://www.daghammarskjold.se/wp-content/uploads/2021/05/international-civil-servant-in-law-and-in-fact.pdf> accessed 20 July 2022.
20. In recent years, Swedish diplomat and politician Alva Myrdal (together with Alfonso García Robles) won the Nobel Peace Prize in 1982 for 'for their work for disarmament and nuclear and weapon-free zones'. Finnish diplomat and politician Martti Ahtisaari won the prize in 2008 'for his important efforts, on several continents and over more than three decades, to resolve international conflicts'.
21. Martti Koskenniemi, 'Diplomats, Professors, and Then Some: Notes for a History of International Law in 20th Century Finland' in Astrid Kjeldgaard-Pedersen (ed), *Nordic Approaches to International Law* (Brill 2017) 22–32.
22. Permanent Court of Arbitration, *The Grisbådarna Case*, Award, 23 October 1909 (available at <https://pcacases.com/web/sendAttach/508> accessed 18 September 2023).

23. See Sten Harck, 'Åland Islands', Max Planck Encyclopedias of International Law, 2008. <https://opil.ouplaw.com/display/10.1093/law:epil/9780199231690/law-9780199231690-e1884?prd=MPIL> accessed 18 September 2023. See further Sia Spiliopoulou Åkermark, Saila Heinikoski, Pirjo Kleemola-Juntunen, *Demilitarization and International Law in Context: The Åland Islands* (Routledge 2018).
24. *Status of Eastern Carelia*, Advisory Opinion, 23 July 1923, PCIJ Series B no 5.
25. *Legal Status of Eastern Greenland, Denmark v Norway*, Judgment, 5 April 1933, PCIJ Series A/B no 53.
26. *Case of Certain Norwegian Loans*, Judgment, 6 July 1957, ICJ Reports 1957, 9.
27. *Case concerning the application of the convention of 1902 governing the guardianship of infants, Netherlands v Sweden*, Judgment, 28 November 1958, ICJ Reports 1958, 55.
28. *Fisheries* case (*United Kingdom v Norway*), Judgment, 18 December 1951, ICJ Reports 1951, 116.
29. *North Sea Continental Shelf* cases (*Germany v Denmark*), 20 February 1969, ICJ Reports 1969, 3.
30. *Fisheries Jurisdiction* case (*United Kingdom v Iceland*), 25 July 1974, ICJ Reports 1974, 3.
31. *Passage through the Great Belt* (*Finland v Denmark*), Order, 10 September 1992, ICJ Reports 1992, 348.
32. *Maritime Delimitation in the Area between Greenland and Jan Mayen*, Judgment, 14 June 1993, ICJ Reports 1993, 38.
33. Notably, Norway has recently entered into a bilateral defence agreement with the US (Supplementary Defence Cooperation Agreement signed in April 2021, currently awaits approval by the Norwegian Parliament). The Danish government announced in February 2022 that negotiations have been opened for a similar agreement between the US and Denmark, thus breaking with the decade-long tradition of not allowing foreign troops on Danish territory.
34. Koskenniemi (n 21).
35. Astrid Kjeldgaard-Pedersen, 'Nordic Judges of the Permanent Court of International Justice and International Court of Justice' in Kjeldgaard-Pedersen (ed) (n 21) 49–62.
36. Leland M Goodrich and Edvard Hambro, *Charter of the United Nations: Commentary and Documents* (1st edn, World Peace Foundation 1946).
37. Advisory Committee of Jurists: Proces-Verbaux of the Proceedings of the Committee, League of Nations Council June 16–24 July (1920), <https://www.icj-cij.org/public/files/permanent-court-of-international-justice/serie_D/D_proceedings_of_committee_annexes_16june_24july_1920.pdf> accessed 8 July 2022. As is well known, the PCIJ Statute was transferred almost verbatim to the current Statute of International Court of Justice.
38. Since the EU has exclusive competence for trade and investment, Denmark, Finland, and Sweden cannot pursue independent policies in these fields.
39. Thorvald Boye, 'Quelques aspects du développement des règles de la neutralité', 64 RdC 1938, 157–231, 179.
40. Per Ahlin, *Folkrätten i svensk säkerhetspolitik* (Juristförlaget 1993) 48–50; Pasi Ihalainen, 'Internationalization and Democratization Interconnected: The Swedish and Finnish Parliaments Debating Membership in the League of Nations in 1920', 39 *Parliaments, Estates and Representation* 2019, 11–31.
41. 'Denmark-Finland-Iceland-Norway-Sweden: Declaration Regarding Similar Rules of Neutrality', 27 May 1938, reprinted in English in *American Journal of International Law*,

32(4), Supplement: Official Documents (October 1938) 141–163. Iceland was at this time under the sovereignty of Denmark. See also Ove Bring, *Neutralitetens uppgång och fall—eller den gemensamma säkerhetens historia* (Atlantis 2008).

42. Ove Bring, *Aggression Självförsvar Och Non-Intervention: Tre Studier i Internationell Rätt* (Iustus 1982) 28 and 60.
43. Danish Institute of International Affairs, *Humanitarian Intervention Legal and Political Aspects* (Danish Institute of International Affairs 1999).
44. Anders Henriksen and Marc Schack, 'Lovligheden af en humanitær intervention i Syrien', 147 *Ugeskrift for Retsvæsen, Den litterære Afdeling* 2013, 393–399.
45. Ahlin (n 41) 67–70.
46. Notably, the first peacekeeping missions of UNEF in 1956 and UNOC in 1960 were undertaken under Secretary-General Dag Hammarskjöld, a Swede.
47. The assassination gave rise to the seminal *Reparation for injuries suffered in the service of the United Nations*, Advisory Opinion, ICJ Reports 1949, 174.
48. See, eg, ICRC, *Commentary on the First Geneva Convention* (CUP 2016), also available at https://ihl-databases.icrc.org/ihl/full/GCI-commentary) Article 1, paragraph 120.
49. See further Cornelius Wiesener and Astrid Kjeldgaard-Pedersen, 'Ensuring Respect by Partners—Revisiting the Debate on Common Article 1', 27 Journal of Conflict and Security Law 2022, 135–157, 139.
50. So far, however, only Sweden, Finland, and Iceland have ratified the 2010 Kampala amendments to the Rome Statute on the crime of aggression. In Sweden there have been a significant number of cases of prosecutions for international crimes since the mid-2000s, partly due to the large number of refugees.
51. The Council was created under the active General Assembly Presidency of Jan Eliasson (Sweden), who later became the fourth Deputy Secretary-General of the UN.
52. Adopted by the International Law Commission at its sixty-third session, in 2011, and submitted to the General Assembly as a part of the Commission's report covering the work of that session (A/66/10, paragraph 75). The report appears in *Yearbook of the International Law Commission*, 2011, vol II, Part Two.
53. See, eg, Iain Cameron, 'UN Targeted Sanctions, Legal Safeguards and the European Convention on Human Rights', 72 *Nordic Journal of International Law* 2003, 159–214.
54. See the Swedish government's dedicated web-page on sanctions, under the rubric 'Initiative for increasing due process protection' <https://www.government.se/government-policy/foreign-and-security-policy/international-sanctions/> accessed 8 July 2022.
55. The ECHR is incorporated into the domestic legislation of all of the Nordic countries since the 1990s: Finland 1990, Denmark 1992, Iceland 1994, Sweden 1994, Norway 1999. Norway and Finland have also incorporated a number of UN human rights conventions while Sweden and Iceland have incorporated the Convention on the Rights of the Child. Kjetil Mujezinović Larsen, 'Konventionsorganens generella kommentarer till barnkonventionen och andra människorättskonventioner – vilken betydelse har kommentarerna i nordisk rätt? in *Det 41 Nordiska Juristmötet* (conference proceedings) (Helsinki: Stiftelsen för de nordiska juristmötena, 2018) 641–655 <https://nordisktjuristmote.fi/wp-content/uploads/njm41_web9449585.1.pdf> accessed 8 July 2022.
56. *Sporrong and Lönnroth v Sweden*, Judgment, Merits, App no 7151/75 (A/52), 23 September 1982.
57. In 2017, warming up to the Danish Presidency of the Committee of Ministers of the Council of Europe, then Danish Prime Minister Lars Løkke Rasmussen confronted the

ECtHR, and especially its dynamic and expansive interpretation of the Convention, an explicit priority of the Danish government. See Mikael Rask Madsen, 'Two Level Politics and Backlash against International Courts: Evidence from the Politicisation of the European Court of Human Rights', 22 *The British Journal of Politics and International Relations* 2020, 728–738. See also Jacques Hartmann, 'A Danish Crusade for the Reform of the European Court of Human Rights', *EJIL Talk!*, 14 November 2017.

58. Specifically, Wind's study documents *inter alia* that the Supreme Court in Norway referred to international agreements 1,285 times between 1961 and 2014, while its Scandinavian counterparts made only 291 (Denmark) and 169 (Sweden) references respectively. Marlene Wind, 'Who Cares about International Law? A Study of How Scandinavian Judges Cite International Law and Courts' in Kjeldgaard-Pedersen (ed) (n 21) 76–96, 90.
59. Jens Elo Rytter, 'A Nordic Approach to the Interpretation of the European Convention on Human Rights?' in A Kjeldgaard-Pedersen (ed) (n 21) 63–75. On the voting patterns of Nordic judges of the PCIJ and ICJ, see A Kjeldgaard-Pedersen, 'Nordic Judges of the Permanent Court of International Justice and International Court of Justice' in A Kjeldgaard-Pedersen (ed), *Nordic Approaches to International Law* (Brill 2017) 49–62. Given that only seven Nordic judges have sat on the PCIJ and the ICJ—and not at the same time—it is inherently difficult to determine on the basis of their voting patterns whether it makes sense to speak of a Nordic approach to international law. The available material does, however, indicate that Nordic judges of the World Court are inclined to favour objective and effective treaty interpretation over restrictive interpretation and judicial restraint.
60. For a nuanced analysis, see Malcolm Langford and Johan Karlsson Schaffer, 'The Nordic Human Rights Paradox: Moving Beyond Exceptionalism', University of Oslo Faculty of Law Research Paper No 2013-25 (2015). See also Hanne Hagtvedt Vik, Steven LB Jensen, Linde Lindkvist, and Johan Strang, 'Histories of Human Rights in the Nordic Countries', 36 *Nordic Journal of Human Rights* 2018, 189, 193–194.
61. Vik et al (n 60) 195.
62. The movement's founding father was Axel Hägerström (1868–1939), whose main works include Axel Hägerström, *Stat och rätt. En rättsfilosofisk undersökning* (Almqvist & Wiksell 1904), and Axel Hägerström, *Der römische Obligationsbegriff im Lichte der allgemeinen römischen Rectsanschauung* (Kungl. Humanistiska Vetenskaps-Samfundet 1941). Other well-known members include Karl Olivecrona (1897–1980), who authored *Law as Fact* (OUP 1939), and Alf Ross (1899–1979), whose seminal work, *Om ret og retfærdighed*, appeared in Danish in 1953 (*Nyt nordisk forlag*). The latter has recently been published in a new English translation in Jakob v.H. Holtermann (ed), *On Law and Justice*, trans Uta Bindreiter (OUP 2019).
63. Jakob v.H. Holtermann, 'Conspicuous Absence and Mistaken Presence. A Note on the Ambiguous Role of Scandinavian Legal Realism in Nordic Approaches to International Law' in Kjeldgaard-Pedersen (ed) (n 21) 214–237, 220.
64. Ibid., 221.
65. Ibid. See also Jakob v.H. Holtermann and Astrid Kjeldgaard-Pedersen, 'International Law from a Nordic Perspective' in Peter Hilpold (ed), *European International Law Traditions* (Springer 2020) 245–259.
66. Koen Stapelbroek, 'Universal Society, Commerce and the Rights of Neutral Trade: Martin Hübner, Emer de Vattel and Ferdinando Galiani' in Petter Korkman and Virpi Mäkinen

(eds), *Universalism in International Law and Political Philosophy* (Helsinki Collegium for Advanced Studies 2008) 63, 72.

67. *Lois et Usages de la Neutralité*, vols I and II (A. Chevalier-Marescq 1898 and 1900).
68. Jaakko Husa, 'Guarding the Constitutionality of Laws in the Nordic Countries: A Comparative Perspective', 48 *The American Journal of Comparative Law* 2000, 345.
69. Originally *Nordisk Tidsskrift for International Ret/Acta scandinavica juris gentium*. The Latin translation remains a part of the journal's title.
70. The Editorial and Advisory Boards are composed of scholars and expert practitioners from the Nordic countries. Since its foundation, one of the declared purposes of the journal has been to publish regular 'updates on Nordic state practice', which are typically authored by civil servants from the Nordic foreign ministries.
71. Koskenniemi (n 21).
72. Halvar Sundberg, *Folkrätt* (2nd edn, Institutet för offentlig och internationell rätt 1950) 2–4.
73. Östen Undén, *Neutralitet och folkrätt* (Albert Bonniers förlag 1939)45 et seq.
74. See Östen Undén, 'Den Kollektiva Säkerhetens Filosofi', 25 *Nordic Journal of International Law* 1955, 11, 24.
75. Johan Strang, 'Scandinavian Legal Realism and Human Rights: Axel Hägerström, Alf Ross and the Persistent Attack on Natural Law' (2018) 36 Nordic Journal of Human Rights 202, 208 and 210.
76. ibid, 213.
77. ibid, 209. Hägerström stressed that human rights was 'a mantle in which both the bourgeoisie and the proletariat, both a Rockefeller and a Marat, can dress their social ideas'.
78. See, eg, Ove Bring, Mark Klamberg, Said Mahmoudi, and Pål Wrange, *Sverige och folkrätten* (6th edn, Norstedts juridik 2020) 26.
79. It is pertinent to mention that the director of iCourts, Mikael Rask Madsen, with Jakob Holtermann, has suggested a new European legal realism which builds partly on Scandinavian legal realism. Jakob Holtermann and Mikael Rask Madsen, 'European New Legal Realism: Towards a Basic Science of Law' in Shauhin Talesh, Elizabeth Mertz and Heinz Klug, *Research Handbook on Modern Legal Realism* (Edward Elgar Publishing 2021) 67.
80. Holtermann (n 63) 217.

CHAPTER 33

POLAND

WŁADYSŁAW CZAPLIŃSKI

1. Introduction: Scope of this Research

The primary intention of the editors of the volume was that the development of international law in Central Europe (or rather that part of it, which today is sometimes referred to as the Visegrad Group) should be presented in a common chapter. Finally, however, Poland was separated from the other three countries (Czechia, Slovakia, and Hungary). This was determined by a number of factors: the international legal traditions in Poland; its contribution to the development of the science of international law; historical reasons (legal doctrine in Poland was shaped at the crossroads between Russia, Prussia, and Austria); the specific role of Poland in the democratic changes of 1989; but also, the special position of Poland as the largest and most populous country in the region. This chapter tries to highlight the most outstanding figures who had a significant impact on the development of international law in Europe and worldwide, including Polish judges in the World Court, but also the place of international law in the Polish legal order and the principles of its application. The discussion also covers current contentious issues (crossroads of Polish foreign policy), especially in Poland's relations with the Council of Europe (CoE). However, politics in relations with the European Union (EU) are omitted, even if the present author is a supporter of the concept of the unity of international law, which also includes the EU legal system.

2. Origins of the Law of Nations in Poland

The story of Poland and international law started in the Middle Ages. Two Polish scholars influenced European law of nations. The first of these was Stanisław ze

Skalbmierza (Scarbimiri) (died 1431) who is known as one of the first rectors of the University of Kraków. From 1422, he represented the Polish king in negotiations with the Teutonic Order. One of his sermons, De bellis iustis, was written shortly before the 1409–1411 war against the Teutonic Order. It was a so-called academic sermon, a strictly-defined form of academic teaching addressed to the academic community, the royal court, and noble knights (*szlachta*). It reflected the Polish legal position, according to which all peoples (including Christians and pagans) had the right to their own States, subject to the same law. Wars of aggression should be forbidden. A just war should meet five criteria—relating to the subject of launching, object, cause, spirit (*animus*), and authorization (by the Pope, or by a sovereign ruler).

The second important Polish scholar of the medieval period was Paweł Włodkowic (or Paulus Vladimiri), who was born between 1365–1370, and died in 1431. In 1414–1415 he became rector of Kraków University. Subsequently (1415–1418) he was an important member of the Polish delegation at the Council of Constance, where he gained international recognition and respect. He published a number of texts relating to the dispute between Poland and the Teutonic Order. Włodkowic discussed the authority and jurisdiction of the Pope and the Emperor with respect to infidels who should have the right to establish their own State structures. Paulus constructed a coherent system of international law, based on the Ten Commandments, natural law, canon law, and Roman law. All the power existing in the world finds its source either in divine law, or in the will of the people. State authority is bound by the rule of law. A ban on war was the cornerstone of the law of nations. Paulus supported human rights being granted also to Saracens, Jews, infidels, and pagans.

During the Renaissance, a number of authors dealt with political issues including the interactions between, and mutual influence of, international and domestic politics. For instance, Stanisław Orzechowski (1513–1566), a clergyman and political writer, discussed aspects of Polish-Turkish relations (the Ottoman Empire was at that time the principal enemy of Poland). Orzechowski pointed to the differences between the State systems of Poland and Turkey, the latter threatening the nobility's freedom and democracy, and warned against the dangers to Christianity from militant Islam (calling Poland a 'bulwark of Christianity').[1]

Several authors published manuals for candidates to the diplomatic service, confirming an interest in the consular and diplomatic profession among young noblemen. Reinhold Heidenstein (1553–1620) described[2] the diplomatic functions of the royal chancellery, organization of the foreign service, diplomatic correspondence and tasks, personal characteristics (such as honesty, discretion, diligence, and prudence), and skills (including knowledge of history, domestic and foreign law, as well as the law of nations, and international agreements) expected from diplomats. Krzysztof Warszewicki (1543–1603) remained in royal service for some time. He was regarded as extremely conservative, and wrote several political and theological treatises of varying quality, including his most important book: De legato legationeque liber (1595). This contained practical advice on how to select which diplomats to send to particular countries, based upon psychological and sociological analyses of the respective nations.[3]

The Enlightenment brought an enormous interest in the law of nations across the whole of Europe, including Poland. Polish authors were aware of threats to the sovereignty of the country, so they argued for the survival of the State and the illegality of annexation of territory. These arguments were based on notions of equity and justice, natural law, and the doctrine of mutual rights and obligations between nations. Apart from theoretical dissertations, international law was discussed through speeches in the parliamentary forum.

In 1768–1773, Karol Wyrwicz published three editions of his *Political Geography*, which also contained a short description of the law of nations. In 1773, Wincenty Skrzetuski (1745–1791) published collected essays on aspects of dealings in public life[4] such as the law of treaties, rights of States, equality of States, colonies, and the law of peace and war. These were influenced by writings by Emer de Vattel, who spent two years at the royal court in Warsaw. Antoni Popławski (1739–1799) was professor of the law of nations and natural law at the Jagellonian University of Kraków. He dealt with external relations of the State including laws of war, diplomacy, treaties, and the principles of international trade. Konstanty Święcicki published the first Polish systemic treatise on international law: De jure naturae et gentium in genere; et de jure belli et pacis in specie (1763). The book was based on writings by Grotius, Gentilis, and Pufendorf, and stated that the law of nations should be based on agreement between States (conventional or customary). Feliks Słotwiński (1788–1863) published Prawo narodów naturalne, połączone z praktyką państw europejskich (1822). He tried to reconcile natural law with the law of nations, and concentrated on international customary law as the main source of the law of nations. Polish authors also published collections of international treaties in the second half of the 18th century. Some of these contained commentaries on particular treaties.

Polish authors of the Enlightenment era widely accepted natural law, and were quite sceptical about international agreements. They were critical of diplomats, probably because of the deeply unfriendly role played by the ambassadors of the neighbouring powers at that time in Poland. In turn, much attention was devoted to consuls, recognizing their importance for international trade. Finally, a surprisingly large discrepancy exists between political journalism—which generally condemned war, especially unfair wars—and legal doctrine, which analysed detailed legal issues related to wars to a very limited extent.

3. Modern International Law in Poland

Franciszek Ksawery Kasparek (1844–1903) was the first Polish author who referred to the notion of 'public international law' at the end of the 19th century. From 1872 Kasparek was professor of the chair of philosophy of law and law of nations in Kraków.

In 1873, he was elected as a member of the Institut de Droit International (IDI). His most important book dealt with the input of Polish lawyers to public international law. Kasparek criticized the positivist approach to the law of nations. Both nations and individuals should enjoy external freedom and freedom to act. The conduct of all subjects (individuals and rulers) should be guided by a moral order.

3.1 Polish judges at the World Court

The successor to Kasparek in Kraków was Michał Rostworowski (1864–1940), the first Polish judge at the World Court. He studied law under the guidance of Martens and Karrev. He was nominated professor of political law and the law of nations (1903). In 1898 he was elected to the IDI. He wrote extensively on the law of nations, constitutional law, and conflict of laws. After 1918 he concentrated on a new field: the law of international organizations (including the League of Nations). He sat as a judge ad hoc on behalf of Poland at the PCIJ (Permanent Court of International Justice) (in the cases of certain German interests in Upper Silesia and minority schools in Upper Silesia). In 1930, he was elected a regular judge. He was a conservative lawyer, strongly emphasizing the key importance of protecting the interests of States. Rostworowski strongly opted for the primacy of the constitution over international obligations of the State. Interestingly, while Rostworowski was highly regarded as a scholar, he failed to win respect as a university lecturer.

Ludwik Ehrlich (1889–1968) lectured in political science at the University of California, Berkeley, in 1917–1920. Subsequently he worked as a Polish diplomatic representative in New York. He returned to Poland in 1923 and was appointed professor and chairholder of constitutional law at the university of Lwów (Lviv, Lemberg, Львов). In 1929 he was nominated ordinarius of the law of nations. In his work, he combined interest in theory and practice, in particular for interactions between international law and international relations. Ehrlich served as a judge ad hoc at the PCIJ (1927–1928), including in the Chorzów factory case. He achieved great merit as he popularized writings by Polish medieval scholars. He wrote the first modern Polish manual of public international law (several editions published between 1927 and 1958). His fields of interest were: the law of treaties, sovereignty, and the law of the sea.

Bogdan Winiarski (1884–1969) started his career in Kraków (as research assistant to Rostworowski). In 1921, he moved to Poznań, where he was a professor at the Law Faculty until the end of his life. He spent World War II in the West as, *inter alia*, president of the Bank of Poland in London. After the war, he worked on revision of the ICJ Statute, and in 1946 was elected judge at the Hague Tribunal. He served at the International Court of Justice (ICJ) until 1967, as its president in 1961–1964. In 1947, he was elected a member of the IDI, and in 1965 became its president. His activities covered Polish and French constitutional law, and the law of nations. In particular, he was an outstanding expert in the law of international rivers, and published two important monographs on international security (1928) and on self-defence in the law of nations (1935). In his judicial activity at the ICJ, he repeatedly emphasized the dominant role of State sovereignty in international law.

Manfred Lachs (1914–1993) was one of the most distinguished international lawyers in the global history of international law. During World War II he stayed in London, where he was involved in diplomatic activities. After returning to Poland, he combined holding high positions within the Ministry of Foreign Affairs (in 1947–1960 he was the chief legal adviser) with teaching international law at the University of Warsaw in 1952–1984. He became a member of the International Law Commission (ILC), and in 1962–1967 he served as chairman of the UN Subcommittee on Peaceful Use of Outer Space. In 1967, he was elected as a judge at the ICJ, and remained in office until his death.

Krzysztof Skubiszewski (1926–2010) was a judge ad hoc in the East Timor and Gabčikovo-Nagymaros cases, and his dissenting opinion in the former case is of great significance for the development of international law. He also served as president of the US-Iran Claims Tribunal (1994–2010). Skubiszewski worked at the Law Faculty of Poznań until 1968, when he was dismissed because of his critical opinion of the invasion of Czechoslovakia by Warsaw Pact armed forces. He joined the Institute of Law Studies of the Polish Academy of Sciences in 1973 and worked there until his retirement in 1996. He wrote extensively on the relationship between municipal law and domestic law, Polish-German relations, and the law of international organizations. He was appointed first minister of foreign affairs of sovereign Poland (1989–1993). He was an old-fashioned person, always elegant, brilliant, a man of deep knowledge and principles. He enjoyed great authority and respect among politicians all over the world, and among the general public.

3.2 Teaching international law in Polish law schools

In 1364, the first university in the territory of Poland was established in Kraków by Kazimierz Wielki (Casimir the Great), one of the most famous rulers in Polish history. After his death in 1370, the Academy fell into decline. However, it was re-established in 1400 and granted important donations and subsidies by Jadwiga d'Anjou, the wife of another important Polish king, Wladyslaw Jagello. There were eight professors at the juridical faculty (in canon and Roman law). Over the years, one of these positions covered the law of nations (probably in 1749). At least since that time, international law has continued to be practised at the Jagellonian University of Kraków.[5]

Professors of the law of nations were nominated at various universities from the mid-19th century, under both Austrian and Russian domination. Public international law teaching was mandatory in the interwar period, a practice that continued after World War II. Compared to the other States of the Eastern bloc, Poland under communist rule was a (relatively) liberal country, in particular when considering academic life and legal research. Polish scholars actively participated in different programmes, and published with Western publishers and law journals.

In the part of Polish territories under Russian rule, Antoni Białecki (1836–1912) was the first professor of international law at the Imperial University of Warsaw in 1865. His thesis on international law and its sources was published in both Russian and Polish in 1872, and can be regarded as the first Polish academic manual of international law. He retired in 1887, after which lectures on international law were given by Russian professors. After the creation of the independent Polish State in 1918, international law was lectured by Zygmunt Cybichowski (1879–1946), followed by Cezary Berezowski (1898–1970), who was chairholder from 1937 until 1968. Berezowski published several important books dealing with the creation of States in international law, the restitution of the Polish State after World War I, air law, and protection of cultural property during armed conflict. Berezowski was highly respected as the Nestor of Polish international lawyers.

Under Austrian rule, the University of Lwów played a leading role in teaching and research on the law of nations. The first professor was Gustaw Roszkowski (1847–1915), nominated in 1878, the author of numerous works on diplomatic law, international organizations, codification of international law, the law of war, and the philosophy of law. In 1923 L Ehrlich was appointed as chairholder in international law, and extraordinary professor of constitutional law. He continued teaching until December 1939, when he was dismissed by the Soviet occupiers of Lwów. He managed to escape to the German occupation zone, saving his life. After the war, he settled in Kraków and was nominated as head of the chair of international law. He was dismissed again under the framework of Stalinist political cleansing. He eventually returned to the faculty in 1956, and taught until his retirement in 1961. He always promoted young scholars, and appointed numerous assistant professors (according to rumour, he was very efficient at arranging funding); among those he selected, Stanisław Hubert, Stanisław E Nahlik, and Raphael (Rafał) Lemkin all had outstanding careers. As an academic, he was a man of principle, highly demanding of himself and others, which did not always bring him popularity among students and other professors.

Karol Wolfke (1915–2015) devoted his entire life and scientific career to the Law Faculty of the University of Wrocław, where he was appointed as a full professor (1946). Jan Kolasa (1926–2016) prepared a thesis at the University of Princeton, and from 1960 for his whole life remained connected with Wrocław Law School. For more than twenty years, he held the chair of public international law. He focused on different aspects of the law of international organizations, the law of the international judiciary, including procedural law, and international environmental law. He was a brilliant teacher, a gentle and erudite scholar.

Stanisław E Nahlik (1911–1991) started his career as an assistant to Ehrlich in Lwów. He entered the diplomatic service in 1936 and worked with the MFA until 1949 when he was dismissed under Stalinist rule. He then moved to the Ministry of Culture, where he dealt with the issue of restitution of works of art plundered in Poland by Nazi Germany and the Soviet Union. In 1962 (relatively late in life) he started his research work at the Jagellonian University in Kraków, mostly in the area of international protection of cultural, artistic, and historic property. He was renowned as a great teacher (the fame of his postgraduate seminars was widespread); he was also known as the character of numerous anecdotes.

4. International Law and the Polish Legal Order

Since regaining independence in 1918, the Polish constitutional and legal system has been open to international law. In the pre-war era, Polish courts played an important role in constructing the Polish legal position. The domestic courts applied international law even under communist rule, though the earlier constitutions (of 1921 and 1952) did not contain provisions concerning the position of international law in the municipal legal order. The Supreme Court adopted the view that international treaties duly ratified should be applied in the Polish domestic legal order.[6] International agreements were valid in municipal law *ex proprio vigore*, due to their validity in international law. The courts also accepted the concept of self-executing norms, in some very sensitive jurisprudence concerning registration of the independent and free trade union Solidarność,[7] and the non-conformity of the decree on martial law of 13 December 1981 with Article 15 International Covenant on Civil and Political Rights (ICCPR) (the non-retroactivity rule). The jurisprudence was relatively coherent and confirmed the primacy of ratified international treaties over domestic statutes.

The Polish Constitution of 2 April 1997 contains regulations on the position of international law in domestic law. According to Article 8, the Constitution is the supreme law of the Republic of Poland. However, Article 9 (often intentionally neglected) provides that the Republic of Poland must respect international law binding upon it. Chapter 3 of the Constitution defines sources of law of general application. Article 87 includes ratified international agreements in the sources of universally binding law in Poland. The following provisions define the modality of introducing international law in the domestic legal order, as well as the modalities of its application. A ratified international agreement constitutes part of the domestic legal order and is applied directly. In the case of a conflict between a statute and an international agreement ratified upon prior consent granted by statute (ie consent by both chambers of Parliament), the treaty takes precedence over statutes. Ratification of international agreements belongs to the prerogative of the president. The Constitution exhaustively enumerates treaties requiring the consent of Parliament for ratification. However, it does not contain any provision concerning the position of non-ratified agreements or customary international law (or other possible sources of international law). Constitutional regulation is completed by a statute of 14 April 2000 on international treaties.[8] We find frequent references to international law in numerous provisions of the Constitution, concerning, for example, foreign relations power, extradition, and refugees.

In practice, Polish courts at different levels apply international agreements, including EU law. Moreover, the judiciary also applies international customary law. The Natoniewski case is the most widely known decision of the Polish Supreme Court involving customary international law.[9] The case concerned a claim brought before a Polish court by a Mr Natoniewski, a Polish national who claimed damages from the German government for injuries suffered during the Nazi occupation of Poland. The Supreme Court rejected the claim, invoking international customary law on State immunity. The decision was somehow controversial as the Constitution requires application of international treaties as the basis for individual decisions, but not international custom.

Looking from the standpoint of classic international law, we should classify the Polish legal system as monist or dualist. The present author is not convinced that this issue still plays an important role. Taking into account the wording of the Constitution and the jurisprudence of the Constitutional Court,[10] the Polish legal order is rather based on monism. Polish authors referred to the notion of 'multicentrism' to describe the essence of law-making in Poland.

5. Crucial International Legal Issues of Interest to Poland

The contribution of Polish legal thought to international law has primarily been related to historical events including the Polish-Teutonic Order wars, and subsequently Polish-Turkish relations, as well as the law of war and State security. Religious issues, and then the partitions of Poland as well as the need to deal with their consequences, had a significant impact on the approach of Polish authors to international law.

The attitude of Polish lawyers to the Catholic religion and the institutional church, especially in the Middle Ages and the Renaissance, was relatively distant, even though most lawyers were clergymen. The Reformation in Poland was quite gentle, and religious tolerance prevailed throughout the 16th century, which was expressed in the parliamentary declaration of one of the Polish kings, Sigismund Augustus: I will not be the king of your consciences. The situation changed in the 17th century, when the Counter-reformation began to dominate the country. This tendency was exacerbated by the Swedish invasions of the Polish-Lithuanian Commonwealth, after which the Roman Catholic Church gained a dominant position in the country. This domination continued until the third decade of the 18th century, when the progressive Piarist order gained significant influence on education in Poland.

During Poland's partitions, the Catholic Church made a significant contribution to the preservation of Polish tradition, culture, and language. After the regaining of independence in 1918, the Roman Catholic Church gained a dominant position in the State, becoming the State religion. This situation was upheld by the 1925 concordat, but the

Church has never had a decisive influence on international law doctrine. After World War II, the communist authorities did not feel strong enough to attack the Church, further strengthened by the election of the Bishop of Kraków as Pope John Paul II. After 1989, the role of the Catholic Church was so powerful that it was able to take advantage of the State's weakness to protect its own interests. The new concordat of 1993 confirmed the position of the Church in the country. This was not reflected in Polish foreign policy, and thus in Poland's international legal position. In recent years, after the death of John Paul II and the exposure of numerous sexual abuse and property scandals, the Church is no longer so important, and public opinion increasingly often favours denunciation of the concordat.

After Poland regained independence in 1918, the main issue was to merge the three parts (ex-Russian, Austrian, and Prussian) of the new Republic into one uniform state. The newly created Polish army succeeded in resisting the Soviet invasion (1920). Over the following years, the State consolidated. With regard to international law, the attention of the new State focused on the consequences of State succession, property matters, occupation of foreign territory, State and diplomatic immunity, as well as citizenship and statelessness. The Polish-German neighbourhood had a significant impact on the development of Polish international legal tradition. In the interwar period, Polish-German disputes were often dealt with by the PCIJ, and its decisions (in matters resulting from the Treaty of Versailles, like the effect of treaties, boundary and property issues, minority rights, and the like) were important for the development of international law. Poland participated in seven disputes (out of thirty-five decided by the court before 1939) and was involved in ten advisory opinions (out of twenty-seven delivered).

5.1 A dispute concerning the Morskie Oko Lake

Although Poland did not exist as a sovereign State in 1795–1918, she still had a certain input to the law of nations. The long-lasting dispute between Galicia (annexed by the Austrian Empire in 1772) and the Kingdom of Hungary, both parts of the Austro-Hungarian Monarchy, concerning the situation of the beautiful mountain lake Morskie Oko, was finally decided by an arbitral award pronounced in Graz (1902). From the international legal perspective, the dispute was interesting, as it concerned the delimitation of two properties situated in two neighbouring States: in Galicia (Austria) and in Hungary. The demarcation line between the two estates also constituted the international boundary between the two States. After 1880 the Hungarian and Galician courts passed several judgments concerning the ownership rights to the disputed area, so that Emperor Franz Josef II ordered the parties to submit the dispute to arbitration, which was decided in favour of Galicia. The dispute played a vital role in maintaining the patriotic spirit in the divided Polish territories, as it demonstrated the unity of the Polish people.

5.2 Discussion concerning the rebirth of Poland after World War I

The Polish State was (re-)created after World War I. Polish authors have proposed various dates for its creation (mostly in November 1918) which were important from the domestic point of view. The first instrument of the Polish State was a declaration by Józef Piłsudski, nominated as head of State, issued on 16 November 1918 and addressed to the major world powers, which informed the world about the creation of the State of Poland, composed of all united Polish territories. Credentials issued by the Polish authorities were recognized at the Paris peace conference in 1919, and Poland was accepted as a founding member of the League of Nations. In 1922–1923 Poland was recognized by twenty-three States.

A dispute arose as to the continuity and identity of Polish statehood,[11] and the status of the Polish State created in 1918. Two conflicting approaches were formulated. Some eminent professors supported the concept of restitution of the 'First Commonwealth',[12] while others—equally respected—presented the stance that Poland was a new State. The first group included W Komarnicki, L Ehrlich, and S Hubert; the most important backer of the latter concept was C Berezowski. Komarnicki[13] declared simply that the liberation of territories annexed by Prussia and Austria was equivalent per se to restitution of Polish statehood. Ehrlich referred to the concept of ius postliminii known in Roman law. He wrote that by obtaining independence in 1918, Poland had regained her fully-fledged position as a subject of international law which had been enjoyed for many centuries, and this was not the creation of a new State. Hubert[14] presented several arguments in favour of the concept of restitution, the main one being that the collapse of Poland at the end of the 18th century was contrary to international law, as the three powers concerned had violated a number of principles of international law; the international community had never recognized the occupation of Poland as a permanent and final solution.[15] On the other hand, Berezowski[16] simply considered the annexation of parts of Polish territory to be lawful under 18th-century international law (although he modified his position after World War II). Z Cybichowski attempted to combine both positions mentioned above, speaking about the continuity of the 'idea of Polish statehood', although Poland as created in 1918 was a new State. Discussion continued after World War II. New arguments in favour of and against the new State theory were presented by K Dembski and S Krukowski. Dembski[17] referred to the theory of Cybichowski. He stated that the Polish nation existed as a subject of the right to self-determination, but there was no continuity of the Polish State as a legal entity. Krukowski[18] based his position on the alleged illegality of the subjugation of Poland in the 18th century, and on the resistance of the Polish nation to the occupying powers. The judicial practice of the Supreme Court and administrative courts before World War II, and the legislation and political practice of Polish State agencies were coherent and promoted the idea of restitution. The status of the Polish People's Republic was less important, as the continuity of statehood was essentially not questioned.

From its very creation, Poland was confronted with territorial disputes. Indeed, Poland was a textbook example of a State which existed for several years after World War I without fixed international boundaries. Some disputes continued after World War II. Polish authors have concentrated on analysing and resolving territorial conflicts with nearly all the country's neighbours. We concentrate here on the most important elements.

5.3 Boundary between Poland and Lithuania

The dispute with Lithuania concerning Vilna (Polish Wilno, Lithuanian Vilnius) was crucial, because of the historical importance of the capital of the Grand Duchy of Lithuania, which for centuries formed a part of the Polish-Lithuanian Commonwealth. The alliance and then union with Lithuania was concluded against the Teutonic Order, but also reoriented Polish foreign policy and led to conflicts and wars with Moscow (as Russia and the USSR). In summer 1920, Soviet Russia occupied Vilna and ceded it to the newly established State of Lithuania. Soviet troops were defeated by the Polish army at the battle of Warsaw in August 1920, and Poland started a counter-offensive. Vilna was occupied by allegedly rebellious Polish troops in October 1920. The Polish military authorities organized local legislative elections, and the newly elected representative organ applied for incorporation into Poland. This happened in March 1922. The League of Nations accepted the situation in 1923. After the invasion of Poland by the USSR in 1939, the Soviet government ceded Vilna to Lithuania, although the price was the annexation of Lithuania by the USSR in 1940. Poland confirmed the territorial status quo in a treaty concluded with independent Lithuania in 1994.

5.4 Eastern boundary of Poland

Nazi Germany and the USSR invaded Poland in September 1939, implementing the Hitler-Stalin (Ribbentrop-Molotov) pact. The Soviet action was preceded by a declaration by the Soviet Ministry of Foreign Affairs falsely proclaiming the collapse of the Polish State. Polish territory was divided in accordance with a secret German-Soviet protocol on delimitation of respective zones of influence.[19] The annexation of eastern Polish territories took place in November 1939, preceded by requests allegedly presented by local assemblies elected under the Soviet occupation.[20] Mass persecutions, deportations, and killings followed the annexation.

The situation changed radically following German aggression against the USSR in June 1941. Under British pressure, the Polish government concluded the so-called Sikorski-Maysky[21] treaty, which left certain problems (such as territorial problems and property issues) unresolved. The Soviets rejected further negotiations. In spring 1943, the graves of 25,000 Polish officers—captured by the Red Army in September 1939 and murdered by the Soviets in 1940—were found close to the small village of Katyn, which remains a symbol of Soviet crimes against Polish nationals during World War II. Stalin decided to break contact with the Polish government in exile. When Soviet troops entered Polish territories (westwards of the so-called Curzon line), a puppet government was established.[22] It concluded an agreement with the USSR, and ceded former eastern Polish territories to the USSR. The boundary agreement—first published in 1974 in a collection of historical documents—was contrary to the Polish Constitution of 1921 and therefore invalid.

The eastern boundary of Poland was fixed by the treaty of 17 August 1945 concluded by the Provisional Government of National Unity[23] just after the Potsdam conference. The Polish Constitutional Court confirmed in its jurisprudence that the entry into force of the treaty (on 6 February 1946) meant transfer of sovereignty. The boundary was confirmed by the treaty of 22 May 1992 on Friendly Cooperation and Good Neighbourhood between Poland and the Russian Federation. Issues of responsibility and reparations for violations of international law committed by the USSR during the war against Poland and her nationals were never addressed and the discussion first started in 2022.

5.5 Western boundary of Poland

A political territorial decision was taken during the conference between the heads of the allied States at Yalta in February 1945. The boundary was established by the Potsdam agreement of 2 August 1945, which provided that former German territories should be placed under Polish administration. A final territorial decision should be taken, however, in the framework of a future peace settlement with Germany.

This short passage from the protocol of the Potsdam conference reflected the difficulties connected with the long-lasting boundary dispute between Poland and Germany (or: the Federal Republic of Germany (FRG)). The FRG claimed that it was absent from the Potsdam conference. Any territorial decision could only be taken by the future government of a re-united Germany. Poland, in contrast, consistently insisted that the decision on the border line was final. Adjudication by the Great Powers was lawful, as the Allied powers were competent to take any decisions concerning German borders.[24]

On 6 July 1950, Poland and the German Democratic Republic (GDR) concluded a boundary treaty in Görlitz. This was followed by another agreement concerning delimitation of the boundary between Poland and the GDR (acting on behalf of the German State). Delimitation of a frontier should be decided by the neighbouring States as directly concerned (in this case Poland and the GDR). Boundary treaties enjoy an erga omnes status, as an exception to the pacta tertiis rule.[25] However, Western States (including the FRG) did not recognize the GDR.

The West German government appointed in 1969 started a new eastern policy, which included new relations between East and West. The Treaty of 7 December 1970 on the basis of normalization of relations between Poland and the FRG played a crucial role. In

Article I, both parties declared that the existing boundary line as laid down in Chapter IX of the Potsdam Agreement should constitute the western frontier of Poland. Poland considered the 1970 treaty as formal recognition of the western boundary. However, West Germany still emphasized that the boundary had to be confirmed by the future united German State.

Political changes in Europe after 1989 allowed the (re-)unification of Germany. The 1990 Two Plus Four Treaty between the two German States and the former Allied powers confirmed the territorial shape of the united Germany and her external borders. The treaty concluded between Poland and the new/old FRG on 14 November 1990 confirmed the existing boundary referred to in the Potsdam Agreement, the Treaty of Görlitz of 1950, and the Warsaw Treaty of 1970.

5.6 Minority issues

Pre-war Poland was a multi-ethnic State. Her population consisted of some 35 million inhabitants, of which 68 per cent were ethnic Poles. The Ukrainian minority amounted to 15 per cent, Jewish—8.5 per cent, Ruthenian—3 per cent, and German—2 per cent. Relations with the minorities (in particular Ukrainian, Jewish, and German) remained tense.

World War II changed the ethnic composition of Poland radically. Approximately 50 per cent of the 6 million Jews killed in Nazi concentration camps were Polish nationals. Germans residing in Poland (but also in Czechoslovakia and Hungary) were resettled to Germany in accordance with a decision taken at the Potsdam conference. In September 1944, the pro-Soviet Polish puppet government concluded agreements on exchange of the population with three Soviet Republics: Lithuanian, Belorussian, and Ukrainian. A similar agreement was concluded by Poland with the USSR in 1957. The rights of minorities remaining in Poland under communist rule were not respected.

Attitudes towards protection of human rights were a symbol of change. In November 1991, Poland joined the Council of Europe. The country also acceded to the 1950 European Convention on Protection of Human Rights and Fundamental Freedoms (ECHR). Democratic Poland was heavily involved in protection of minorities, in particular in the framework of the CSCE (Copenhagen Document on Human Dimension, 1990, and Geneva Meeting of Experts of 1991) and the Council of Europe (Poland ratified the 1995 Framework Convention for the Protection of National Minorities).

Poland concluded a number of bilateral agreements regulating issues of minority protection, primarily with neighbouring countries. All these bilateral treaties were constructed according to a similar pattern: they contain a catalogue of minority rights, a list of State obligations towards minority groups, and a so-called loyalty clause. Some treaties, like the Polish-Lithuanian Treaty of 1994[26] and the Polish-German Treaty of 1991, contain a definition of protected minorities. Other agreements (with Belarus, Czechia, and Slovakia) contain provisions relating to minorities without defining them. The Treaty between Poland and Russia (as well as those concluded with Bulgaria,

Georgia, Moldova, and Uzbekistan) adopted a standard formula: Citizens of Poland of Russian origin, and citizens of the Russian Federation of Polish origin. Finally, in some instruments, the subjective scope of the minority clauses was asymmetrical. Under the Polish-German Treaty, the right to a protected identity is granted to members of the German minority in the Republic of Poland, and—on the other hand—to persons in the FRG who are German nationals but are of Polish origin, language, culture, and tradition. Poles do not enjoy minority status in Germany, due to specific German regulations on national minorities.

Polish domestic law on protecting minorities was less consistent. Article 35 of the Constitution of Poland of 2 April 1997 provides that Polish citizens belonging to national or ethnic minorities enjoy important rights, including protection of ethnic identity, and cultural and educational rights. The crucial legislative act in that domain is the law on national and ethnic minorities, and on regional language, passed on 6 January 2005. A national minority is defined as a group of Polish citizens who jointly meet the following criteria: is numerically smaller than the rest of the population; significantly differs from other citizens in its language, culture, or tradition; its ancestors have been living on the present territory of Poland for at least 100 years; and identifies itself with a nation organized in its own State. An ethnic minority is defined as a group of Polish citizens who meet the same conditions, except that it does not identify itself with a nation organized in its own State (as there is no such State). Some groups are recognized as national minorities (for instance, Belarusian, Ukrainian, German, Lithuanian, Jewish), while others have the status of ethnic minorities (Karaims, Lemkos, Roma). Belonging to a minority is a matter of free decision by the person concerned.

5.7 Current issues: Poland and the ECHR, and protection of refugees

Appointment of an authoritarian and nationalist government in 2015 led to difficulties in fulfilling international obligations by Poland.[27] These concern the rule of law in connection with alleged judicial reform, and policy towards refugees.

Poland is party to the ECHR and five protocols, though excluding recent protocols 12 and 16. Since the accession of Poland, the Court has received 75,579 complaints from Poland, of which 1,247 have been issued judgments. Some of these were of a pilot nature (a novelty in the practice of the Tribunal), that is, they concerned problems of a systemic nature, requiring changes in legislation, which were the subject of numerous complaints to the Tribunal. All similar cases would be settled in the same way. The first pilot judgment in the case of Broniowski v Poland (App no 31443/96, 22 June 2004) concerned protection of property rights in the context of ineffective compensation mechanisms for property left by Polish citizens in areas lost to the USSR after World War II. In Kudła v Poland (App no 30210/96, 26 October 2000) the Court presented a new interpretation of the right to an effective remedy as an additional guarantee of the rights of the individual under the Convention.

Judgments concerning moral matters in Poland are spectacular. Tysiąc v Poland case (App no 5410/03, 20 March 2007) concerned the consequences of making legal abortion impossible in practice. The case of Bączkowski et al. v Poland (App no 1543/06, 3 May 2007) condemned a restriction of the right to peaceful demonstrations, which also covered the organization of the Equality Parade in Warsaw. Several applications concern lack of regulation of the legal status of same-sex relationships: for example, Przybyszewska and Others v Poland (App no 11454/17, communicated in June 2020).

Two judgments, namely *Al-Nashiri v Poland* (28761/11) and *Abu-Zubaydah v Poland* (7511/13), both of 24 July 2014, declared a violation of the ECHR in connection with participation of the Polish authorities in the so-called CIA secret detention prisons, and unwillingness to investigate the cases.

A number of cases in recent years concerned protection of the rule of law. In Xero Flor w Polsce sp. z o.o. v Poland (App no 4907/18, 7 May 2021) the Tribunal found a violation of the right to a fair trial due to irregularities in nominating judges of the Constitutional Tribunal (infringement of judicial independence and impartiality). The judgment in the case of Reczkowicz v Poland (App no 43447/19, 22 July 2021) questioned the systemic position of the Disciplinary Chamber of the Supreme Court as a court established by law.

The Constitutional Court, now dominated by judges nominated by politicians of the until 2023 governing party, recently passed two judgments in which it rejected the binding force of certain judicial decisions of the Strasbourg court, and declared Article 6 ECHR allegedly contrary to the Constitution, which enjoys priority before international law (cases 6/21 of 24 November 2021, and K7/21 of 10 March 2022). The practice of the Constitutional Court is astounding, as the wording of the Constitution on the point of the right to judicial review is the same as that of the ECHR and EU Charter of Fundamental Rights.

Contemporary Poland has never been unequivocally open to accepting people seeking international protection there. The wave of refugees from 2015–2016 led to a conflict between Poland, Hungary, and Slovakia, and the EU over the provisions on relocation of refugees. In proceedings before the European Court of Justice (ECJ), a violation of EU law—the principle of solidarity in migration and asylum policy—was found as a result of Poland's rejection of relocation.[28]

From July 2021 a massive influx of refugees occurred along the eastern border of Poland, probably supported by the State of Belarus. The Polish authorities introduced a state of emergency in the border areas in violation of the Constitution, limiting the flow of information. However, it can be confirmed from reliable sources (non-governmental organizations (NGOs)) that the acts of the State were racist and hostile towards aliens, and violated the Geneva Convention of 1951 as well as human rights and EU law. By preventing refugees from entering Poland, many people, including children, died while illegally crossing the border via forests and swamps, and pushbacks were common.[29] Individuals and NGOs assisting the refugees were prosecuted, including criminally.

The situation on the Polish-Belarusian border is fundamentally different from that on the Polish-Ukrainian border after Russia's aggression against Ukraine, where services (army, border guards, police) have supported refugees. The reason is embarrassing for the Polish government: Ukrainian refugees are mainly white women with children, of Slavonic origin, as opposed to Asians and Africans coming from Belarus.

6. The Most Important Theoretical Input by Polish Lawyers into International Law

The notion of genocide was introduced by Raphael Lemkin, professor of criminal law at the University of Lwów.[30] At the beginning of the 20th century the Lwów faculty was one of the most important law research centres in Europe.[31] Lemkin worked on genocide in the 1930s, though he first used this expression in his book Axis Rule in Occupied Europe published in the US in 1944. Lemkin stood behind the UNGA resolution on genocide in December 1946, and subsequently behind the 1948 Genocide Convention.

K Skubiszewski published a book on money in occupied territories in 1960. This unique study was based on the experience of the occupations of World War I, the occupation of Poland by the Nazis, and the occupation of Germany by the Allied powers. Skubiszewski also published important studies on the law-making activities of international organizations, on the international use of force, and on the relationship between domestic and international law (including implementation of international human rights). He also wrote several studies on Polish-German relations, defending the Polish legal position.

M Lachs influenced the concept and development of international law of outer space (the cosmos). In his book: Law of Outer Space—An Experience in Contemporary Law-making (1972) he formulated the principles of outer space treaties and space activities. He also published a treatise on multilateral treaties, in which he presented his whole experience as a diplomat, and The Teacher in International Law: Teachings and Teaching (1982), a story of the history of international law.

Finally, K Wolfke's Custom in Present International Law continues to be one of the classic works on sources of international law. Wolfke supported the voluntarist theory of custom. He was cautious as to factors objectively verifiable as evidence of custom. Wolfke also discussed the relationship between custom and other sources of international law, and was highly sceptical as to the importance of opinio iuris.

7. Conclusion: Poland's Unique Contribution to International Law

Poland has never developed specific 'Polish international law'. Polish authors have supported general international law, regardless of whether they wrote at home or abroad.[32] Successive generations of lawyers have consistently proved that Polish doctrine of international law is part of Western legal science. Even under communist rule, Poland managed to maintain its distinctiveness, rejecting the influence of Soviet doctrine (like the concept of socialist international law). Border regions, where the influences of different cultures combine, usually produce a very rich heritage. Poland was a typical State at the crossroads of Europe. Influences from local tradition, Austrian, Russian, and, to a lesser extent, German, clashed here. After World War I, the study of international law in Poland brought all these elements together.

Notes

1. This expression was very popular in Poland, as it reflected the allegedly special position of the country within Christian Europe (and in that way a link between Poland and the Western world).
2. *Cancellarius sive de dignitas et officio Cancellarii Regni Poloniae.*
3. The Sovereign should send: to Turkey—the brave and generous; to Moscow—the prudent, because without long bargains nothing can be obtained from the Russians; to Rome—the pious, but secular, because the clergy succumb to the Pope; to Spain—people of a calm disposition, devoid of any desire for adventure, as life there is modest; to Italy—those who are polite and of good manners, because in this country politeness and etiquette are highly valued; to France—people of quick mind; to England—handsome and serious diplomats, because it is only those types that English people respect; and those of a stubborn disposition to Germany. Krzysztof Warszewicki, *O pośle i poselstwach*, translated from Polish Edition of 1887 by the Author 192–194.
4. Mowy o głośniejszych materiach politycznych (Speeches on Important Political Matters).
5. F Kasperek, *Udział Polaków w uprawie prawa międzynarodowego* (Lwów 1885) 8.
6. Judgments of 18 May 1970, case I CR 58/70; and 5 October 1974, case IIICZP 71/73.
7. On 10 November 1980, the Supreme Court invoked ILO conventions Nos 87 and 98 on the freedom of trade unions and workers' rights.
8. Dziennik Ustaw (official journal) 2000 No 39 Item 443.
9. PolYBIL.30 (2010), 232–236.
10. Case 18/04, judgment of 1 May 2005, OTK-A 2005/5/49, paragraph 2.2.
11. For a review of the international legal aspects of the creation of the Polish State after 1918 see L Antonowicz, *Status prawnomiędzynarodowy Polski (1918–2018)* (Wydawnictwo Wyższej Szkoły Ekonomii I Innowacji 2018); J Kolasa, *Odzyskanie przez Polskę niepodległości w 1918 r. w świetle prawa międzynarodowego*, 5(88) Przegląd Sejmowy 2008, 9 ff; J Crawford, *The Creation of States in International Law* (OUP 2007); K Marek, *The Identity and Continuity of States in Public International Law* (Librairie Droz 1968) 417 ff. As to judicial practice, cf A Wyrozumska, 'The Role of Polish Courts in the Development of International Law after Regaining Independence by Poland in 1918', 9(1) Polish Review of International and European Law 2020, 73 ff.
12. The traditional name of the State, *Rzeczpospolita Polska*, referred to the Latin expression res publica, and had a different meaning from 'Republic of Poland' but corresponded more closely with the name 'Polish Commonwealth'.
13. W Komarnicki, *Polskie prawo polityczne* (Nakł. F. Hoesicka 1922) 40.

14. St Hubert, *Rozbiory i odrodzenie Rzeczypospolitej Polskiej. Zagadnienie prawa międzynarodowego* (Zakład Prawa Politycznego i Prawa Narodów 1937) 281–284.
15. The only State which constantly and consistently protested against the partitions of Poland was Turkey. It is said that official events at the Turkish court could not begin until a Polish legation was present. The usage was that the Grand Vizier of the Sultan had to declare officially that the representative of the Kingdom of Poland could not arrive on time because of extraordinary obstacles.
16. C Berezowski, *Powstanie państwa polskiego w świetle prawa narodów* (Kasa im.Mianowskiego 1934) 78–108.
17. K Dembski, 'Polonia Restituta—kontynuacja czy państwo nowe?' 2 Czasopismo Prawno-Historyczne 1974, 167–191.
18. S Krukowski, 'Polska odrodzona czy państwo nowe?', 1 Czasopismo Prawno-Historyczne 1977, 105–129.
19. The existence of the protocol was denied by the USSR, as its text was allegedly not available in the Soviet archives—however, the protocol was found by the American military in the archive of the German Ministry of Foreign Affairs and published by the US government. This approach is typical of authoritarian regimes: namely, if we do not talk about something, it does not exist.
20. The same model was applied by Putin's Russian Federation after the invasion of the Crimea in 2014 and with respect to Eastern Ukraine during the war of 2022.
21. Then Soviet ambassador to the UK.
22. The Polski Komitet Wyzwolenia Narodowego (Polish Committee on National Liberation, PKWN) was recognized exclusively by the USSR. It was unlawful and was unable to represent Poland in international relations.
23. Recognized by the Western States.
24. On Polish-German legal disputes see, eg, K Skubiszewski, 'Poland's Western Frontier and the 1970 Polish-German Treaties', 67 The American Journal of International Law 1973, 23; L Gelberg, 'The Warsaw Treaty of 1970 and the Western Boundary of Poland', 76 The American Journal of International Law 1982, 119; W Czapliński, 'The New Polish-German Treaties and Changing Political Structure in Europe', 86(1) The American Journal of International Law 1992, 163; J Kranz, 'Polish-German Legal Controversies—An Attempt at Synthesis' in WM Góralski (ed), *Breakthrough and Challenges. 20 Years of the Polish-German Treaty on Good Neighbourliness and Friendly Relations* (Warsaw 2011) 419; JA Frowein, 'Legal Problems on the German Ostpolitik', 23 International and Comparative Law Quarterly 1974, 105; JA Frowein, 'The Reunification of Germany', 86 The American Journal of International Law 1992, 152; C Arndt, 'Legal Problems of the German Eastern Treaties', 74(1) The American Journal of International Law 1980, 122; K Hailbronner, 'Legal Aspects of Unification of the Two German States', 2 European Journal of International Law 1991, 18.
25. W Czapliński, 'State Boundaries and Third States—Issues of Opposability. Remarks on the Polish-West German Normalization Treaty', Polish Yearbook of International Law 2021, and authors quoted therein.
26. Article 13(2): '[P]ersons belonging to the Polish minority in the Republic of Lithuania, i.e., persons possessing Lithuanian citizenship being of Polish nationality or declaring their attachment to Polish nationality, culture or tradition, and recognizing Polish as native language.'

27. Reorientation of foreign policy took place, in particular resulting in a critical approach to the EU, relations with neighbouring States, and the Council of Europe. International legal issues, omitting problems of European law, are briefly discussed.
28. Joined cases C-643, 647/15 *Slovakia and Hungary v Council*, ECLI:EU:C:2017:631; Joined cases C-715/17, C-718/17, and C-719/17 *European Commission v Poland, Hungary and Czech Republic*, ECLI:EU:C:2020:257.
29. The first pushback case was communicated to the Polish government in 2022, Case 54862/21 *F.A. and S.H. v Poland*; see also interim measures in R.A. and Others v Poland (App no 42120/21).
30. The story of the Law faculty was described in a brilliant book by Phillippe Sands, *East-West Street* (Weidenfeld & Nicolson 2016).
31. The quality of researchers was so high that Hersch Lauterpacht could not be appointed to the chair of the law of nations, as his competitor Ludwik Ehrlich was found to be a better candidate for the vacancy. Disappointed, Lauterpacht left Lwów and started his career at Cambridge.
32. Numerous Polish lawyers (eg Krystyna Marek and Jerzy Sztucki) emigrated during communist rule and worked at Western universities.

CHAPTER 34

RUSSIA

VERA RUSINOVA

1. Introduction—Unpacking Russia's Approach to International Law

Russia, as one of the main architects of the existing post-World War II international legal order, a 'P5' member, a nuclear power, and a State with one of the biggest armies, rich natural resources, and the largest territory, situated in both Europe and Asia, has a multi-layered relationship with international law, in both its universal and European dimensions.

In addition to being one of the principal founders of the post-World War II international legal order, Russia was a creator and co-creator of several projects conceived as European: the Russian Tsar Nicholas II initiated both Hague peace conferences that gave the world the first codified rules of international law and the Soviet Union stood at the roots of creation of the Conference (and later - Organization) on Security and Cooperation in Europe. Russia has joined some keystone European projects: for two-and-a-half decades it was a member of the Council of Europe (CoE) and a party to the Convention on Protection of Human Rights and Fundamental Freedoms (ECHR). Some European doctrines, approaches, and institutions were transplanted into the Russian legal system or strongly influenced it, such as the strong French and German models of constitutional review or the Scandinavian model of the ombudsperson. The European Union (EU) has served as an example for economic integration for post-Soviet space, in particular the Eurasian Economic Union (EAEU).[1] At the same time, Russia also contests or resists the 'European concept' of international law. This contestation is primarily linked to upholding 'traditional values' in contrast to (European) 'liberal' values. Direct resistance to the implementation of judgments of the European Court of Human Rights (ECtHR) is revealed in two judgments of the Constitutional Court of the Russian Federation and found its heyday in the constitutional reform of 2020. Competitiveness with the 'European project' can be seen in the development of regional and sub-regional integration led by Russia and creation of regional organizations such as the

EAEU, the Collective Security Treaty Organisation (CSTO), the Shanghai Cooperation Organisation (SCO), or the club of major emerging economies, such as the BRICS.

The special military operation, launched on 24 February 2022 in Ukraine with a reference to self-defence under Article 51 of the UN Charter, but qualified by the UN General Assembly as a violation of Article 2(4) of the Charter,[2] has provoked unprecedented consequences with the number, intensity, and volume of unilateral and multilateral coercive measures, international isolation, and the termination of Russia's membership in the CoE, qualified by Russia as a withdrawal and by the CoE as a cessation,[3] and, consequently, the termination of participation in the European Convention on Protection of Human Rights and Fundamental Freedoms (ECHR).[4] These epochal changes marked a new stage in Russia's geopolitical standing and also in national approaches to international law, and some features of this new period can be identified already.

All research on a national approach to international law inevitably faces the difficulty of coexistence of many different views on two intertwined issues of methodology and the definition of what counts as such an approach. The positivistic stance on international law has very limited explanatory capacities[5] and all authoritative authors who have addressed the Russian approach to international law have stepped away from this stance and drawn a broader and deeper picture, finding the necessary instruments and tools in the disciplines of history, sociology, and international relations and representing a complex of a 'historically oriented "constructivism" ' combined with the theory of international relations.[6] This chapter will methodologically follow that path, although the results will differ from previous research because both its premises and the conclusions are not only a result of access to relevant sources, the standpoint of the author as an insider, or outsider of the system.

In this chapter the State's approach to international law will be represented as a complexity of recognizable trends, repeatable and typical stands, conceived from behaviour (from what the State says and, more importantly, does), disclosing its attitude towards international law as a normative order.

Conceptualization of the methodological way of analysing the national approach to international law also presupposes designation of the subject, whose attitude will be taken into account or preferred. Searching for an 'official view' will shrink the circle to State officials and State bodies participating in the creation of *opinio juris*, and will be, first, elite and, secondly, political in the sense that it is formed by the politicians, not lawyers. The role of professionals specializing in international law (namely, State servants, privately practising lawyers, and academics)—in shaping a national approach should be assessed with the view that it is in all states rather modest per se, allowing, at best, such professionals to influence to some extent the normative and institutional outcomes which are a result of international political and economic—not legal—bargaining and, more realistically, to shape 'the structure and interpretation of numerous legal doctrines and institutional frameworks'.[7] Therefore, in order to study a 'national approach' one should trace the content, ideology, and conceptual basis of the political stance of the State with respect to international law, secondly, the specificity of the lawyers' layer, and, thirdly, the relationships between two professional 'worlds', namely, lawyers and the foreign policy establishment.[8]

2. What Shapes the 'Russian Approach' to International Law?

2.1 The political layer of the Russian approach to international law

2.1.1 *The turn to Realpolitik*

The contemporary Russian approach to foreign politics, and thus also the role and place of international law as a normative system, is underpinned by Realpolitik. Besides the classic features of this widespread international relations concept, consisting of the preference of State interests, which are relevant for all realistic politics, it has some specific traits typical of Russia.

2.1.1.1 *Promotion of the multipolar system and contestation of US hegemony*

Should we take the period following the fall of the Soviet system, then the shift of Russia to Realpolitik with a subsequent attitude towards international law was hardly visible in the first years of the presidency of Boris Nikolayevich Yeltsin, a time when Russia was opening its doors to international law, starting from the adoption in 1993 of a new Constitution with an unprecedentedly open approach to international law, then in 1996 joining the CoE and acceding two years later to the ECHR, lifting reservations to compromissory clauses in human rights treaties. Very soon, Mikhail Sergeevich Gorbachev's idea of a 'common European home',[9] as well as the subsequent 'Kozyrev doctrine' based on the involvement of Russia in a real partnership with the 'collective West' were replaced by bitter disappointment, heated by the slow realization that Russia's efforts to build a partnership and be treated as an equal subject are 'unilateral'[10] and that the 'West' was not willing to seriously take into consideration Russia seen by them as an enemy defeated in the 'Cold War'.

The switch from early Russian values politics to political realism was connected with the turn from pro-Western (and strictly speaking, pro-US) politics in the beginning of 90s, when Russia was even considering joining NATO,[11] to the more independent politics based on protection of national interests. This switch was symbolized by a turn over the Atlantic in March 1999, when Minister of Foreign Affairs Evgeniy Maksimovich Primakov cancelled the Russia-US negotiations in response to the NATO bombardment of the Federal Republic of Yugoslavia and his aircraft returned to Moscow.[12] Hopes for a 'reboot' were then linked with Russia's support for the US after the terror acts of September 11, 2001. However, these hopes remained unfulfilled.

In 2002, the US withdrew from the ABM Treaty that had been curbing the arms race since 1972. In 2004, seven Central and East European States (among them the three Baltic States) were accepted as members of NATO. In 2007, missile defence systems were stationed outside the territory of the US and aimed against Russia, thus changing the parity between the two States and for the first time since the dissolution of the USSR, Russia was officially designated as a 'threat'.[13] Later, in 2008, NATO officially promised membership to Georgia and Ukraine. Degradation of the relations between Russia and the US was progressing (with only a small attempt at 'rebooting') from a deficit of trust in the 2010s to open hostility at the beginning of the 2020s[14] and an indirect clash[15] in Ukraine in 2022. One of the reasons for the launch of the special military operation in Ukraine was officially articulated by President Vladimir Vladimirovich Putin as disrespect for the security interests of Russia (the militarization of Ukraine in cooperation with NATO[16]) and resentment over the 'politics of exclusion'. However, alongside a desire to be accepted, the driving force of Russian foreign policy was based on the requirement to be treated as one of the leaders.[17] The elements of contestation of the unipolarity of the world order and US hegemony include political and military rivalry, mutual attempts to interfere in domestic affairs by indirect means, and building new blocs and coalitions without (and against) competitors.

2.1.1.2 *Power politics*

The three decades since the early 1990s have highlighted the more frequent resort of Russia to the use of force. Chronologically, this period starts with the 2008 operation to enforce Georgia to peace as a response to the Georgian attack on Tskhinval, which resulted in Russia's subsequent recognition of the independence of both South Ossetia and Abkhazia; the 2014 reunification with Crimea; the 2015 'intervention by invitation' in Syria; the 2022 sending of a military contingent to Kazakhstan following its request to the CSTO; and, finally, the launch of the special military operation in Ukraine. Participation in the Syrian armed conflict showcases that Russia uses power politics not only in the sphere of post-Soviet space as a zone of its regional strategic interests.[18]

The resort to force in foreign policy can be explained in identity terms as status-seeking:[19] for most of the post-Soviet era, Russia has perceived itself as a 'status-underachiever' with its security interests being disrespected by the US or more generally by the West, the State 'is compelled to follow a more power-based foreign policy to seek and maintain status'.[20]

At the same time, the official State rhetoric of the Russian Federation with respect to international law has been pro-normative and highlighted the centrality of the international rule of law.[21] Alongside pledges of commitment, Russia has always relied on international law to justify its actions in inter-state relations. In the list of different situations, the case of Ukraine stands apart. In 2014 the set of arguments was based on the historical mistake in the State affiliation of Crimea, the illegitimacy of the Maidan coup d'état, remedial secession or secession on the grounds of referendum in the course of realization of the right to self-determination,[22] and in 2022 the reference was made to collective self-defence.[23] At the same time both were qualified by the General Assembly as breaching the UN Charter.[24]

2.1.2 *Traditional values, conservatism and critique of liberalism*

The state policy of Russia is self-presented[25] and assessed as conservative: a 'conservative turn' in foreign and domestic policy has been traced from 2012.[26] However, we should be careful not to read too much into use of conservative ideology, as it should be distinguished from state policy: 'state/official conservatism is closer to a natural attitude, favouring stability and gradual change over revolutionary shocks … the driving force of Russian actions on the international scene remains a pragmatic understanding of Russian interests rather than any passing ideological considerations'.[27] Moreover, official conservatism is only weakly linked to Orthodox/Slavophil or Eurasian philosophical ideas.[28]

One of the recognizable traits of official 'Russian conservatism' consists in protection of 'traditional values'. Among these 'traditional Russian values' the National Security Strategy of 2021 enumerates 'life, dignity, human rights and freedoms, patriotism, citizenship, service to the Fatherland and the responsibility for its destiny, high moral ideals, a strong family, creative work, the priority of the spiritual over the material, humanism, mercy, justice, collectivism, mutual assistance and mutual respect, historical memory and the continuity of generations, the unity of the peoples of Russia'.[29] Notably, this list contains some remnants of the Soviet doctrine of human rights, which can be recognized in the considerable weight given to communal—as opposed to individual—values, and the linkage between rights and duties. At the same time, the 'traditional values' approach differs from the Soviet concept by not presupposing the fulfillment of the same level of economic and social protection.

The key issue is how the terms 'human rights and freedoms' and 'dignity' are to be interpreted, and state policy makes it clear that these liberal notions are filled in by 'etatist' content. In contrast to political articulation, sociological study of the individual values of Russians carried out in 2006–2016 reveals a complex heterogeneous picture of what is appreciated by the population. The main priority for Russians is security (albeit the importance of this value has decreased since the early 2010s), with the next group formed of universalism and benevolence, and the third group consisting of tradition, self-direction, conformity, achievement, and power.[30] According to a world value survey that distinguishes two major dimensions of cross-cultural variation in the world: 'traditional values versus secular-rational values' and 'survival values versus self-expression values', Russia—together with Bulgaria, Ukraine, and Estonia—belongs to societies with high scores in secular-rational and survival values, while Nordic and West European States demonstrate high scores in secular-rational and self-expression values.[31] It should not be overlooked that Russia is itself subnationally diverse (see Bílková, this volume)—and like all other States possesses its own unique cultural identity. However, from the value-based perspective, Russians do not possess a distinct list of characteristics but remain very close to a number of other European peoples (specifically, Slavonic and/or Orthodox).

The implications of traditional values-oriented policy can be traced in different registers, both international and domestic. At the international level, the Russian

Federation speaks out against the 'politicisation of democracy and human rights problems and forcible export of non-universally recognised standards as global', as protecting human rights involves 'taking into account the traditional values of societies, their level of development, economic, social, cultural and historical peculiarities'.[32] UN human rights bodies' recommendations to States—except the universal periodic review of the UN Human Rights Council (at least, before Russia's rights of membership in this body were suspended in 2022[33])—have been criticized as 'superficial' and 'often politicised'.[34] It is also symptomatic that in the 2022 Joint Statement by Russia and China the emphasis is notably put on inter-state relations ('the pretext of protecting democracy and human rights' should not be used to interfere in the internal affairs of sovereign States) and on cultural relativism in the application of universal human rights.[35]

At the domestic level, the implications of protection of traditional values are concentrated on traditional family values and can be traced to the extension of administrative responsibility for propaganda of non-traditional sexual relations among minors[36] to a general ban.[37] In the 2020 reform—albeit it was already set in force in the Family Code—the Constitution of the Russian Federation was amended to include the phrase 'the family as a union of a man and a woman'.[38] Draft laws on domestic violence and harassment in the workplace have not been adopted. However, other examples indicate a more liberal direction. Russia has implemented the UN CEDAW views and significantly shortened the list of professions forbidden for women.[39]

In general, the often-used division between 'westernisers' and 'slavophiles' (zapadniki and slavjanofily) and a discussion of the proximity of Russia to Europe or Asia, the East or the West, does not go beyond the metaphorical meaning, and does not reflect 'political consciousness', which is to be designated by the terms 'étatism' and 'liberalism'.[40] Indeed, Russian political consciousness from the beginning of the 1990s a combination of both.[41]

2.2 The legal layer of the 'Russian approach' to international law

Giving a holistic answer to what constitutes the legal layer of the Russian approach to international law requires a shift in the analytical perspective from the paradigm of searching for evidence of what constitutes 'doing international law' to the paradigm of what 'thinking about international law' looks like.

Starting from the first known legal writing on international law by Peter the Great's lawyer Piotr Pavlovich Shafirov, published in 1717, the literature shifts from being practice-oriented towards more abstract natural law writings.[42] Research during this period was rather scarce, as invited German professors teaching international law in Russia were not specialists in it[43] and served as mere 'glossators'.[44] The seeds of positivism, visible by the end of the 18th century, were gone by the beginning of the next century with the invitation of a new wave of German scholars expounding natural law to Russian universities.[45] This period lasted until the beginning of the 'reaction', a conservative backlash in Russian politics, that followed the rise of liberal and revolutionary ideas with its apogee in the Decembrist revolt in 1825 after the defeat of Napoleonic France and the triumphal European march of the Russian army. The reaction led to the fall of—and even cleansing of universities from—natural legal thought. However, though predominant at the end of the 19th century to the beginning of the 20th century, positivism did not have a monopoly in Russia. This was a period of the golden age in legal thought in Russia when international legal theory was also thriving.

A new stage began with the October Revolution of 1917, which launched a 'new way of thinking' about international law[46]—a critical one. The problem, however, was connected with the standpoint of the critics, as it was non-critical of itself. Though the appearance of 'Soviet international law' can be qualified as a 'first fragmentation' and a challenge to universality,[47] what should not be overlooked is that it was a critique[48] (and to some extent a contestation), and also partly a development, but not a 'divorce'. Soviet doctrine was built on the existing international normative framework and made profound use of its topoi (doctrines of sources and of interpretation) and norms of 'general' international law.

One of the central roles in the intellectual embedding of Soviet international law into the canvas of existing normative structures and theoretical constructs was played by Professor Grigory Ivanovich Tunkin.[49] His works were accepted by the 'capitalist' camp as a 'leading statement of Soviet views concerning theoretical problems of international law',[50] albeit with the reservation that they were 'less hostile to the easing of international tension than those of many other colleagues, less doctrinaire and more realistic'.[51] He has often been presented as an intelligent and erudite 'spokesman' for the Soviet doctrine of international law.[52] Nonetheless, the real contribution of Tunkin was misunderstood. His theory of 'coordination of wills' as a means of norm creation—the North Star both for Soviet and post-Soviet research in Russia—was 'not much' different from Western approaches to international law.[53] From the universalist and normativist positions, Tunkin's linkage of the Soviet approach with the grand theoretical discourse of international law was opposed to centrifugal forces, and, therefore, was not a weakness, but was indeed the strength of his contribution. Tunkin's theory allowed the bypassing of straightforward application of the alpha and omega of 'Marxist-Leninist' doctrine and consideration of international law as a 'superstructure' over the economic 'base'. A straightforward application of this approach would have precluded the possibility for 'Soviet doctrine' to acknowledge the existence of a part of international law as general or common for States with capitalist and socialist economic systems. By arguing that the need for peaceful co-existence prompts States with different economic 'bases' to enter into international relations and conclude agreements, using as a bridge the necessity for 'coordination of wills' of States, Tunkin justified the existence of a general part of international law applicable to all States.[54]

Being obliged to follow the course of the State in the Soviet period, post-Soviet scholarship experiencing perestroika immediately not only got rid of the ideological burden, but also rushed to disassociate itself from the elements of the critical (Marxist) stance, which were embedded in Soviet doctrine, and came back to the realm of pure positivism. Not without inertia, and encountering strong forces of self-preservation and dominance of the national academic school, teaching and research found themselves in a catching-up stage. This was exacerbated not by political factors but by economically-rooted problems of restricted access to foreign literature and instruments of academic mobility, which had prolonged the life of the already phantom 'iron curtain' for decades, strengthening self-preservation forces in Russian academia.

The 'political self-marginalisation' of international lawyers in the post-Soviet period took place due to tradition and was also a product of the methodological features of positivism.[55] Having served Marxism-Leninism, Russian international legal scholarship knowingly or unknowingly continued to serve realism, which by definition treats legal advice as, at best, belonging to the periphery of the political process. Russian academia is just at the beginning of its way from discovery and acknowledgement of the heterogeneity of methodologies and theories of international law[56] and more frequent citation of critical stances of foreign scholars,[57] to their own non-positivist research[58] (see Shany and Varaki, this volume).

3. Russia's Contribution to the Evolution of International Law

However complicated and complex the task might be of indicating and assessing the intellectual input of Russia to the evolution of international law, taking into account the conscious or unconscious widespread silencing of the Russian (Soviet) contribution from the side of foreign scholarship, on the one hand, and non-critical self-representation of domestic scholarship, on the other hand, some ideas and projects have nevertheless been advanced by Russian scholars and practitioners that belong to the world intellectual heritage of the discipline.

3.1 First codifications of international law

The first codifications of international law are closely linked with the name of the brilliant Russian diplomat, lawyer, arbitrator,[59] and the father not only of the 'Hague Tradition'[60] but also of the 'European tradition of international law',[61] namely Fyodor Fyodorovich Martens.[62] Among others, he authored and promoted the idea of compulsory arbitration, and (fact-finding) commissions of enquiry.[63] Although the authorship of Martens with respect to the clause[64] under his name was challenged a century after the First Peace Conference,[65] what has remained uncontested is his dedication, charisma, and authority, all of which helped to overcome the diplomatic deadlock that divided the small and 'Great Power' States since the first attempt in Brussels[66] with respect to the status and rights of a population under occupation, in particular the right to resist. Irrespective of the ongoing debates on the content of the clause,[67] its impact has reached far beyond its historical origin.[68] Not all of Martens' ideas were successful, like obligatory arbitration, which was ahead of its time, and some were adjusted to 'political realities', like a restriction for inquiry commissions' applicability only to disputes 'involving neither honour nor vital interests' and a dubious combination of both pure fact-finding and facilitation of a solution.[69]

3.2 Self-determination of peoples

Whereas in Soviet literature the history of the normative rise of the principle of self-determination of peoples was written from the Revolution's Decree on Peace and the Declaration of the Rights of the Peoples of Russia, which reflected Vladimir Ilyich Lenin's works on it, in foreign literature—until recently[70] it was commonplace to stick to Woodrow Wilson's Fourteen Points. The reasons for this division of views stem from the different evaluation of Soviet practice related to self-determination.

After proclamation of the principle of self-determination, dozens of the former parts of the Russian Empire declared their independence and in 1920–1921 explicitly mentioned the principle of self-determination. Russia concluded international peace treaties with Estonia, Georgia, Latvia, and Lithuania. Notably, Latvia and Estonia were recognized as independent States for the first time in history. The subsequent implementation of this principle by the Soviet government was, indeed, ambivalent, for the application of this doctrine was restricted with respect to the Socialist bloc, among others, in the framework of the 'Brezhnev doctrine'[71] and the concept was consistently applied by the USSR only in the part concerning decolonizsation.[72] However, it is also true that the USSR did much to ensure that self-determination 'became one of the fundamental principles of international law'.[73]

3.3 Definition of aggression and the concept of national liberation wars

The Russian (Soviet) contribution to the development of the *jus contra bellum* can be traced to promotion of the definition of aggression and the concept of national liberation wars. The definition of aggression was first presented in 1933 by the Soviet delegation at the Disarmament Conference in Geneva. Albeit being expelled from the League of Nations for the Soviet-Finnish war in 1939, after World War II the USSR consistently insisted on adoption of a definition of aggression. In 1950 it submitted the 1933 proposal in an almost unchanged version to the General Assembly.[74] The definition was finally adopted by the General Assembly only in 1974.[75]

The Marxist-Leninist concept of wars of national liberation, legitimizing resort to force by national liberation movements seeking their independence from the colonial or occupying power or racist regime as 'just wars', was first brought to the international normative agenda by the USSR only in the 1960s. Efforts by the Soviet government and its allies resulted in a number of General Assembly resolutions adopted in the 1960s and 1970s[76] and expansion of the scope of international armed conflicts to national liberation wars in the First Additional Protocol to the 1949 Geneva conventions.[77] Thus, the concept of national liberation wars challenging the scope of exception from the prohibition on use of force obtained legal significance in the framework of *jus in bello*. The intellectual influence of the concept was not fully overcome by the end of the decolonization process and its proponents can be found not only in Russia.[78]

3.4 International human rights law

The story of the creation of international human rights law was not solely a liberal or Western one.[79] The USSR—although its policy was not always free of human rights violations and the human rights movement of the 1960s was strongly repressed—with its non-Western allies 'added many new angles and panes to the multistoried, fragile glass house of human rights'.[80] The USSR's contribution included not only decolonization and self-determination issues, but the introduction and development of economic and social rights, as well as advocacy of elimination of racial discrimination[81] and—in strong competition with the US[82]—of women's rights. Soviet ideas—among them collective rights, the necessity for human rights guarantees and obligations of States—were initially rejected in the course of the drafting of the Universal Declaration of Human Rights (UDHR),[83] but were then realized in the work on the Covenants and the thematic UN human rights conventions. The USSR was a proponent of a single treaty, while a split into two Covenants was supported by the Western States (see Çalı, this volume).

3.5 International criminal law

Soviet lawyers played a foundational role in establishing the first international criminal tribunal and in conceptualizing international criminal law.[84] The intellectual behind the Soviet position was Professor Aron Naumovich Trainin.[85] He advanced the idea of establishing an international court for war crimes before it became a matter of negotiations between the allies, introduced the concept of 'crimes against peace', and developed the legal concept of complicity (it should not be overlooked that this concept was used for Stalin's 'show trials'). Trainin's ideas were used during the Nuremberg trials, by the UN War Crimes Commission (in which the USSR did not participate), and later by the International Law Commission.

Not only for the Soviet Union but also for the other allies, the Nuremberg and Tokyo trials were a challenge and they were balancing in order to exclude any attempts to apply the same material and procedural rules to the victors' side. Whilst the allies did not deny the shelling of cities and the bombing of Hiroshima and Nagasaki by the US army, they have never officially given excuses,[86] while for Russia the separate Molotov-Ribbentrop pact, was officially acknowledged as an 'act of personal authority' that 'did not reflect the will of the Soviet people, who were not responsible for this conspiracy'.[87]

3.6 International space law

A Soviet international lawyer, Evgeniy Alexandrovich Korovin, stood at the origins of international space law. This was back in 1934, when he published the article 'La conquête de la stratosphère et le droit international' in the Revue Générale de Droit International Public.[88] Negotiating the Treaty on Principles Governing the Activities of States in the Exploration and Use of Outer Space, Including the Moon and Other Celestial Bodies,[89] the Soviet delegations also relied on the theses of Yuriy Mikhailovich Kolosov and Gennady Petrovich Zhukov.[90]

After adoption of the five outer space treaties, the USSR continued its efforts to constrain the arms race in outer space and in 1981 presented the first draft of the treaty on the prohibition of placement of weapons of any kind in outer space.[91] A new proposal was made in 1991 to prepare an international agreement on comprehensive prohibition of weapons specially designed to destroy satellites. In 2004, Russia launched a political pledge not to be the first to place weapons in outer space, which was supported by thirty States.[92] In 2008 Russia and China sponsored an initiative to impose on States obligations to refrain from placing objects carrying any type of weapon into orbit, installing weapons on celestial bodies, and threatening to use force against objects in outer space.[93] In 2015, the UN General Assembly adopted a Russian-led resolution denouncing the placement of weapons in outer space.[94] These initiatives were met with strong resistance by States favouring 'non-aggressive' or 'non-hostile' placement of weapons, supported by a critique that Russia, as the sponsoring State, was itself developing and testing various counter-space capabilities.[95]

4. Characteristics of Contemporary Russian Approaches to International Law

4.1 Objection to the US-led 'rules-based international order'

A strong objection to the concept of the 'rules-based international order' has sharply separated Russia from those foreign States that share this frame of reference (notably, not only the 'West'). According to Russia's foreign policy, this concept seeks 'to replace the term and the concept of international law with some rules-based order', it substitutes universality by closed groupings and formats, or (the EU) 'effective multilateralism', and is a framework legitimizing US hegemony.[96]

It is clear that both sides of this political dispute espouse different views on the relationship between the 'rules-based international order' and international law. The exchange of critique comes down to mutual allegations on the building of a power-based order. For the adherents of the concept, its appearance is a response to the shortcomings of the liberal order based on the framework of universal international law. This order allowed for power politics of others—pre-eminently Russia—albeit it was not always directly against international law. The indeterminacy of norms bound to their universality, and the shortcomings of the UN architecture were being exploited and played against the liberal democracies themselves. For Russia, a shift in the fundamental rules of the international order from unanimity to the majority that produces binding effects for all, and deformalization (introduction and legitimization of alternative regulators) showcase the establishment of an order based on the power of the West with a hegemonic role played by the US.

In the programmatic article of Russian scholars from Moscow State Institute of International Relations (MGIMO), to be able to produce positive effects the concept of 'rules-based order' 'should correspond to International Law', namely it should not question the legitimacy of 'international law-making procedures' or 'distort' 'universal legal rules'; it should not assign binding legal character to non-binding norms; it should be concrete, not abstract, and it should not overcome the will of third States by extending to them the effects of those rules.[97] Albeit processes labelled as 'global governance' with the rise of an international bureaucracy (or administration), diversification of the forms and formats of their institutions (network-based, hybrid, private, and the like) with subsequent deformalization actually started long before collective articulation of the conceptual shift,[98] this turn was not a spontaneous, unintended development. The question might arise as to how this shift correlates with the international 'rule of law' concept (see van Aaken, this volume). With no changes, this concept seems to be incompatible with the 'rules-based' approach. If not to extend the notion of (international) 'law' to non-binding 'rules' and accept the legality of the shift from (at least, relative) unanimity to a majority, the 'rules-based' approach will resist the 'rule of law'.[99] If the latter is to be respectfully transformed, then substituting consent by the majority by means of a majority decision will be a breach of the international rule of law (even in its thinnest (formal) version) and will mean the self-destruction of this very concept.

4.2 Étatist sovereignty

Legal discourse on the concept of sovereignty in international law is drawing a picture of the shift from the Westphalian absolute to a modern view, underpinned by notions of responsibility and human rights protection. In this process Russia is often represented as being among conservative forces, sticking to the étatist sovereignty model.

In 2016 the purpose to 'counter attempts to interfere in the domestic affairs of States with the aim of unconstitutional change of regime, including by supporting non-State actors, such as terrorist and extremist groups'[100] was officially set up in the foreign policy concept. The normative reflection of this purpose can also be found in the Collective Rapid Reaction Forces agreement, signed in 2009 in the framework of the CSTO. This agreement not only extended the use of force and threat of use of force beyond armed attack—as is provided in the 1992 Collective Security Treaty—to 'challenges and threats' to the member States' security, but also left the list of grounds open and up to the decision of the Collective Security Council.[101]

Portrayal of Russian resistance to the new, humanitarian reading of sovereignty is often also supported by its opposition to the 'responsibility to protect' (R2P) doctrine in its broad sense and its objection to the remedial secession of Kosovo. However, the Russian State's position is not as categorical as it might seem. Russia did not object to use of the 'responsibility to protect' concept in its 'thin' sense, reflected in the 2005 World Summit Outcome,[102] where the first pillar reflects sovereignty as responsibility and, thus, a humanitarian concept, and also supported a number of relevant UN Security Council resolutions.[103] Moreover, in at least three cases Russia relied on the R2P in its broad sense as providing a ground for military operation in case of grave and massive human rights violations. For the first time, this was expressed with respect of the use of force in South Ossetia in 2008.[104] The second time that Russia relied on the R2P concept was in 2014 with respect to Crimea.[105]

In the Advisory proceedings on the unilateral declaration of Kosovo, the Russian Federation did not contest remedial secession per se, but subjected its legitimacy to the existence of 'truly extreme circumstances, such as an outright armed attack by the parent State, threatening the very existence of the people in question'[106] and argued that the situation in Kosovo does not meet this threshold.[107] Grave human rights violations ('genocide') were relied on by Russia in the cases of its recognition of South Ossetia and Abkhazia in 2008.[108] With regard to Crimea and Sevastopol, the emphasis was placed on the permissibility of unilateral secession under international law. Violations of basic rights were also mentioned, though as an additional argument, but its quantitative threshold was lowered by questioning the legitimacy of 'counting human lives'.[109]

All these examples point to the non-absolutist character of Russia's otherwise étatist conception of sovereignty. At the same time, application of the humanitarian concept of sovereignty was connected with the territory of post-Soviet States, which Russia has regarded as a zone of its national—first and foremost, security—interests. This reveals Russia's 'instrumentalisation' of the principle of sovereignty[110] for the realism-driven protection of national security interests (ie non-enlargement of NATO eastwards), continued rivalry with the US, recovery of Russia's great-power status, and a struggle for multipolarity.

4.3 International court decisions on Russia: execution, non-execution, and resistance

The attitude of Russia towards international court decisions can be assessed through the binary of execution—non-execution, with specific reference to 'resistance', taken in the narrow sense as refusal to implement a binding decision of an international judicial body shaped in legal form by Russia's national courts.[111] Russia's 'execution rate' looks non-homogeneous with regard to the different fora, is far from amounting to a denial of the binding force of international jurisprudence.

Russia's stance on the execution of international court decisions should be assessed in the light of several factors. First, for a State participating in rivalry for 'great power' status, Russia has rather an advanced profile in accepting the compulsory jurisdiction of international courts and quasi-judicial bodies in comparison with the US and China. Russia accepted the jurisdiction of the ECtHR (until 2022),[112] the EAEU court, the WTO's DSB, the ITLOS, and four UN human rights committees (the UN HR Committee, the Committee against Torture, the Committee on the Elimination of Discrimination against Women, and the Committee on the Elimination of Racial Discrimination). Reservations made by the USSR to international treaties on human rights with respect to the ICJ's jurisdiction were waived by Russia at the beginning of the 1990s. Secondly, no other State in the world (except Turkey) has been confronted with such a large number of ECtHR judgments.[113] Thirdly, transformation of Russian law and its application in accordance with the 'law of the ECtHR' was objectively a gradual process, albeit with a visible resistance to implementation of some types of judgments. Fourthly, it should be taken into account that 'operationalising' the supremacy of the Constitution took place against the background of a very broad monistic approach of the Russian basic law to international law enshrined in a 'protected' Article 15(4) and a 'green light' to direct application of self-executing provisions of international treaties at the domestic level.[114]

Statistics show that in the majority of cases just compensation (albeit not always timely) was paid and measures of an individual character prescribed by the ECtHR have been taken. However, it would be unfair to calculate the rate of enforcement in absolute numbers and in terms of paying compensation. The bulk of the ECtHR's judgments pointed at systemic (clone) violations and failure to adopt general measures, which also erupted into six pilot judgments and one 'semi-pilot' judgment. At the same time, some systemic problems have been gradually and partly resolved, among them: several shortcomings of civil, criminal, and administrative procedure; excessive length of proceedings or non-execution of final judgments; and conditions for the use of lethal force by security agencies.[115] Some previously rendered judgments pointing at systemic problems could have been executed gradually, but the termination of the ECHR with respect of Russia and the adoption of Federal Law on non-execution of the ECtHR's decisions taken after 15 March 2022 leaves no possibility for that.[116] The situation with the International Tribunal for the Law of the Sea (ITLOS) decisions is different: in one of three relevant cases the judgment was enforced,[117] and in two others the factual release of the crew and vessels, as required by the tribunal, were not in line with ITLOS orders on provisional measures.[118] By contrast, the rate of execution of the Would Trade Organization's Dispute Settlement Body (WTO's DSB) reports is 100 per cent: out of eleven disputes with Russia as a respondent, four decisions required implementation and were fully executed.[119]

Russia's stance on resisting enforcement of international court decisions is still a relatively recent one: it started in 2015 by extending the competence of the Constitutional Court to decide upon the enforceability of 'decisions of international interstate human rights bodies' at variance with the Constitution. This competence has been used twice so far,[120] but gained momentum with the 2020 constitutional reform, which enlarged the scope of potentially non-enforceable decisions by lifting the restriction on human rights and changing the circle of judicial bodies to embrace the courts and arbitrage, and added the 'basics of public order' to the list of grounds for non-enforceability.[121]

The grounds for non-execution of international court decisions that have already officially been used or reserved in Russia were not new for doctrine and included counter-limits,[122] formal inconsistency with the Constitution or its interpretations (domestic hierarchy),[123] and public order.[124] At the same time, the grounds for non-enforcement in the publicly articulated part also comprise lack of financial resources, protection of traditional values,[125] or are based on contestation of jurisdiction as in the ITLOS cases and the arbitrage involving former shareholders of Yukos.[126] The non-enforcement trend could have been partly chilled by Russia's slowly growing desire to initiate disputes as the applicant and not remain in the status of the victim of 'lawfare'.[127] However, with a tsunami of new cases against Russia related to its actions in Ukraine it is clear that the domestic 'defensive shield' against decisions by international courts will be used to the maximum.

5. Conclusions—Realpolitik and Civilizational Forces

Russian approaches to international law have evolved throughout history. In contrast to many other European States, these changes were of a revolutionary nature, in the shape of both the October Revolution of 1917 and the official birth of the democratic, liberal, and rule-of-law-oriented Russian Federation at the beginning of the 1990s. Axiologically, they were a farewell and a return to the European legal fold. A new wave of alienation erupted into the termination of Russia's membership in the CoE and in the ECHR—once again a revolution, but this time a 'creeping' one. Russia articulated it as a 'divorce' from *l'ordre public européen* that was caused by both 'security and values conflict' between Russia and the 'West' (see Mälksoo, this volume).

Albeit it looks like a civilizational rupture, there is much more realpolitik behind it. As highlighted in this chapter, the Russian approach to international law is predominantly formed by the elite political layer. Hence the problem, and at the same time a solution, can be found in the relationship between the political regime and civilizational development. Politics can stick with, deviate, or even for decades distort the civilizational development of the State—be it values, goals, and even the identity of society. But inner civilizational forces will gravitate to true values, which are by their nature neither volatile nor elitist.

Notes

1. See Maksim Karliuk, 'The Influence of CJEU Judgments on the Legal Order of the Eurasian Economic Union' in Arie Reich and Hans-W Micklitz (eds), *The Impact of the European Court of Justice on Neighbouring Countries* (OUP 2020) 54–77.
2. UNGA Res (ES-11) 'Aggression against Ukraine' (2 March 2022).
3. On 15 March 2022, by a letter from the Minister of Foreign Affairs S.V. Lavrov to the Secretary General of the CoE, Russia notified of its withdrawal from the organization under Article 7 of the Statute. In accordance with this article, the membership of Russia should have been terminated from 1 January 2023. However, the Committee of Ministers of the CoE adopted on 16 March 2022, referring to Article 8 of the Charter, a resolution on the immediate cessation of Russia's membership in the Council of Europe from 16 March 2022 (CoE Committee of Ministers Res (CM/ Res/ 2022/ 2) (16 March 2022)). The Russian Ministry of Foreign Affairs emphasizes that in doing so, Article 7 and Article 8 of the Statute have been fragrantly violated: 'The CoE [Committee of Ministers of the CoE] is first obliged to invite a State to leave the Organisation on its own and only in case of refusal has the right to expel it forcibly' (On the Withdrawal of Russia from the Council of Europe (O vykhode Rossii iz Soveta Evropy) (spravochnyi material) (14 March 2023) https://www.mid.ru/ru/foreign_policy/rso/).
4. Russia's position is that on 23 March 2022, the Committee of Ministers of the CoE adopted resolution CM/Res(2022)3 on legal and financial consequences of the cessation of membership of the Russian Federation in the CoE, which determined that the Statute and the treaties ratified by Russia, which are open only to CoE members, 'automatically' ceased to be in force for Russia as of 16 March 2022. Accordingly, no formal denunciation of these conventions (ie withdrawal in accordance with the procedures provided for in them) was required, as their effect on Russia ceased in fact upon termination of its membership in the CoE. In order to take this fait accompli into account in Russian domestic legislation, on 28 February 2023 the President of the Russian Federation signed Federal Law No. 43-FZ 'On the Termination of the International Treaties of the Council of Europe with Respect to the Russian Federation'. The exception made in Resolution CM/Res(2022)3 for the ECHR, the validity of which for Russia (hence the jurisdiction of the European Court of Human Rights) has been extended for another six months, until 16 September 2022, is voluntaristic (On the Withdrawal of Russia from the Council of Europe (O vykhode Rossii iz Soveta Evropy) (spravochnyi material) (14 March 2023) https://www.mid.ru/ru/foreign_policy/rso/1834254/). The position of the Council of Europe is that Russia ceased to be a High Contracting Party to the ECHR on 16 September 2022 and the ECtHR remains

competent to deal with applications directed against the Russian Federation in relation to acts or omissions capable of constituting a violation of the Convention provided that they occurred until 16 September 2022. (Resolution of the ECtHR on the consequences of the cessation of membership of the Russian Federation to the Council of Europe in light of Article 58 of the European Convention on Human Rights (22 March 2022) (Res ECtHR (22 March 2022)); Resolution CM/Res(2022)3 on legal and financial consequences of the cessation of membership of the Russian Federation in the Council of Europe (23 March 2022)).

5. See, eg, the article by Tolstykh and Kudinov, who, having taken a strict positivistic standpoint to assessment of the Russian approach to international law, encountered its limits: Vladislav Tolstykh and Aleksey Kudinov, 'Russia and International Law in 2000–2020: 100 Theses about Facts and Trends', 9 Russian Law Journal 2021, 4–32.
6. Anthea Roberts, *Is International Law International?* (OUP 2017); Lauri Mälksoo, *Russian Approaches to International Law* (OUP 2015); Lauri Mälksoo, 'Case Law in Russian Approaches to International Law: Sovereign Cautiousness of a Semi-Peripheral Great Power' in Anthea Roberts, Paul B Stephan, Pierre-Hugues Verdier, and Mila Versteeg (eds), *Comparative International Law* (OUP 2018) 338.
7. David Kennedy, 'The Disciplines of International Law and Policy', 12 Leiden Journal of International Law 1999, 10.
8. ibid, 18.
9. See Neil Malcolm, 'The "Common European Home" and Soviet European Policy', 65 International Affairs 1989, 659–676.
10. Address by the President of the Russian Federation to the Federal Assembly on Strengthening the Russian State [Poslanie Presidenta Rossijskoj Federatsii Federalnomy Sobraniu ob ukreplenii Rossijskogo Gosudarstva] // Rossijskaja gazeta (25 February 1994).
11. The Washington Declaration, signed and issued by the Heads of State and Government participating in the meeting of the North Atlantic Council in Washington DC (23 April 1999), https://www.nato.int/cps/en/natohq/official_texts_27445.htm?mode=pressrelease (12 December 2022); address by the President of the Russian Federation (24 February 2022), http://en.kremlin.ru/events/president/news/67843
12. Dmitry Novikov, 'The Knight of Russian Realism', 1 Russia in Global Affairs 2017, 35–48, https://eng.globalaffairs.ru/articles/the-knight-of-russian-realism/
13. Rose Gottemoeller, 'Bob Gates and the New Russia Threat' (15 February 2007), https://carnegieendowment.org/publications/19030
14. Dmitry Trenin, '"Reissue" of the Russian Federation' ['"Pereizdanie" Rossijskoj Federatsii'], 2 Russia in Global Affairs [Rossia v globalnoj politike] 2022 https://globalaffairs.ru/articles/pereizdanie-rossijskoj-federaczii/
15. Address by the President of the Russian Federation (9 May 2022), http://en.kremlin.ru/events/president/news/68366.
16. Address by the President of the Russian Federation (24 February 2022).
17. Sergey Lavrov, *Between the Past and the Future. Russian Diplomacy in a Changing World* [Mezhdu proshlym i budushchim. Rossijskaja diplomatija v menyaushchemsja mire] (Prosviashchenie 2011) 67–68.
18. Address by the President of the Russian Federation, 18 March 2014, http://kremlin.ru/events/president/news/20603; The Foreign Policy Concept of the Russian Federation, adopted by Decree of the President of the Russian Federation (30 November 2016) No 640 [Kontseptsiya vneshnei politiki Rossiiskoi Federatsii, utverzhdennaja Ukazom Prezidenta

Rossijskoi Federatsii 30.11.2016 No 640], http://kremlin.ru/acts/bank/41451 (The Foreign Policy Concept 2016).

19. See also Ian Johnstone, 'Status as a Reward', 115 American Journal of International Law Unbound 2021, 227–231.
20. Maria Raquel Freire and Regina Heller, 'Russia's Power Politics in Ukraine and Syria: Status-seeking between Identity, Opportunity and Costs', 70 Europe-Asia Studies 2018, 1189.
21. The Foreign Policy Concept of the Russian Federation (12 January 2008), http://en.kremlin.ru/supplement/4116; paragraphs 2, 3a, 3e, 8, 21, 23, 26, 28, 74 of the Foreign Policy Concept 2016.
22. Address by the President of the Russian Federation (18 March 2014), http://en.kremlin.ru/events/president/news/20603; Legal Grounds of Russia's Position on Crimea and Ukraine (2014) [Pravovye obosnovaniya pozicii Rossii po Krymu i Ukraine], https://telaviv.kdmid.ru/content/doc/JustificationPositionCrimea.pdf
23. Address by the President of the Russian Federation (24 February 2022).
24. UNGA Res (68/262) (27 March 2014) and (ES-11/3) (7 April 2022).
25. See, eg, Valdai Discussion Club meeting (21 October 2021), http://en.kremlin.ru/events/president/news/66975
26. See Alfred Evans, 'Ideological Change under Vladimir Putin in the Perspective of Social Identity Theory', 23(4) Demokratizatsiya: The Journal of Post-Soviet Democratisation 2015, 401–402; Interview of President Vladimir Putin with The Financial Times (27 June 2019), http://en.kremlin.ru/events/president/news/60836
27. Paul Robinson, 'Russia's Emergence as an International Conservative Power. Russian Conservatism: An Ideology or a Natural Attitude?', 1 Russia in Global Policy 2020, 32.
28. ibid.
29. Paragraph 91 of the National Security Strategy of the Russian Federation, approved by Decree of the President of the Russian Federation (2 July 2021) No 400 [Strategija Natsionalnoj bezopasnosti Rossijskoj Federatsii, utverzhdena Ukazom Presidenta Rossijskoj Federatsii 02.07.2021] No 400, http://publication.pravo.gov.ru/Document/View/0001202107030001
30. Nadezhda Lebedeva and Alexander Tatarko, 'Basic Values in Russia: Their Dynamics, Ethnocultural Differences, and Relation to Economic Attitudes', 11(3) Psychology in Russia: State of the Art 2018, 36, 42.
31. https://www.worldvaluessurvey.org/WVSContents.jsp
32. https://www.mid.ru/ru/foreign_policy/vnesnepoliticeskoe-dos-e/mezdunarodnye-organizacii-i-forumy/rossijskie-podhody-k-pravozasitnoj-problematike-v-oon/
33. UNGA Res (ES-11/3) (7 April 2022).
34. https://www.mid.ru/ru/foreign_policy/vnesnepoliticeskoe-dos-e/mezdunarodnye-organizacii-i-forumy/rossijskie-podhody-k-pravozasitnoj-problematike-v-oon/
35. Part 1 of the Joint Statement of the Russian Federation and the People's Republic of China on the International Relations Entering a New Era and the Global Sustainable Development (4 February 2022), http://en.kremlin.ru/supplement/5770
36. Article 6.21 of the Code of Administrative Offences of the Russian Federation [Kodeks ob administrativnykh pravonarushenijakh Rossijskoj Federatsii] (introduced by Federal Law (29 June 2013) No135-FZ, http://pravo.gov.ru/proxy/ips/?docbody=&nd=102166334&rdk=&backlink=1). It was found constitutional by the Constitutional Court of the Russian Federation (Case of N.A. Alekseeva, Ya.N. Evtushenko and D.I. Isakova, Judgment

(23 September 2014) [Postanovlenie Konstitutsionnogo Suda Rossijskoj Federatsii po delu o proverke konstitutsionnosti chasti 1 stat'i 6.21 Kodeksa ob administrativnykh pravonarushenijakh Rossijskoj Federatsii v svyzi s zhaloboj grazhdan N A Alekseeva, YaN Evtushenko i D.I. Isakova] Rossijskaja Gazeta (3 October 2014) No 226) and strongly criticized by the ECtHR (*Baye and Others v Russia* (App nos 67667/09 and others) (ECtHR, 20 June 2017) paragraphs 61–92).

37. Article 6.21 of the Code of Administrative Offences of the Russian Federation [Kodeks ob administrativnykh pravonarushenijakh Rossijskoj Federatsii] (introduced by Federal Law (24 November 2022) No 47-FZ).
38. Article 72(1)(zh1) of the Constitution of the Russian Federation (Law on the Amendment to the Constitution of the Russian Federation) [Zakon o popravke k Konstitutsii Rossijskoj Federatsii] (14 March 2020) No 1-FKZ Rossijskaya gazeta (4 July 2020) No 144.
39. *Svetlana Medvedeva v Russian Federation* (Comm no 60/2013) (CEDAW, 25 February 2016); Order of the Ministry for Labour and Social Security of the Russian Federation 'On Approval of the List of Industries, Jobs and Occupations with Harmful and (or) Dangerous Labour Conditions with Restricted Application of Women's Labour' (18 July 2019) No 512n [Prikaz Ministerstva truda i sotsial'noj zashchity Rossijskoj Federatsii 'Ob utverzhdenii perechnja proizvodstv, rabot i dolzhnostej s vrednymi i (ili) opasnymi usloviami truda, na kotorykh ogranichivaetsja primenenie truda zhenshchin'], http://publication.pravo.gov.ru/Document/View/0001201908150010
40. A V Ryabov and E Sh Kurbangaleyeva (eds), *Basic Values of Russians: Social Attitudes. Life Strategies* [Bazovye tsennosti rossijan: Sozialnye ustanovki, Zhiznennye strategii. Mify] (Dom intellectualnoj knigi 2003) 113.
41. ibid.
42. eg Vladimir T Zolotnitskij (See V E Grabar, *Materials on History of the Literature on International Law in Russia (1647–1917) [Matrerialy k istorii literatury mezhdunarodnogo prava v Rossii (1647–1917)]* (Zertsalo 2003) 161); Vasilij F Malinovsky, *Razsuzhdenia o vojne i mire [Thoughts on Peace and War]* (Pri Gubernskom pravlenii 1803).
43. The first Chair for International law was created at Moscow University in 1863.
44. Vladislav Tolstykh, *A Treatise on International Law* [Kurs mezhdunarodnogo Prava] (Wolters Kluwer 2009) 96.
45. Grabar (n 42) 176.
46. Kathryn Greenman, Anne Orford, Anna Saunders, and Ntina Tzouvala, 'International Law and Revolution: 1917 and Beyond' in Kathryn Greenman, Anne Orford, Anna Saunders, and Ntina Tzouvala (eds), *Revolutions in International Law: The Legacies of 1917* (CUP 2021) 1–24.
47. Lauri Mälksoo, 'The Soviet Approach to the Right of Peoples to Self-determination: Russia's Farewell to jus publicum europaeum', 19 Journal of the History of International Law 2017, 204.
48. Greenman, Orford, Saunders, and Tzouvala (n 46) 1–24.
49. His main writings comprise: *Fundamentals of Contemporary International Law* (in Russian, 1956; in English, 1969); *Questions of the Theory of International Law* (in Russian, 1962); *Ideological Struggle and International Law* (in Russian, 1967); *Theory of International Law* (in Russian, 1970; in English, 1974).
50. Akehurst Michael, '*Theory of International Law. By G I Tunkin (translated from the Russian, with an introduction, by William E Butler)* (George Allen & Unwin 1974)', 47(1) British Yearbook of International Law 1975, 496.

51. Walter Butler, 'The Learned Writings of Professor G I Tunkin', 4 Journal of History of International Law 2002, 394.
52. Anne Peters, 'Introduction. A Century After the Russian Revolution: Its Legacy in International Law', 19 Journal of the History of International Law 2017, 134.
53. Rein Müllerson, 'The Tunkin Diary and Lectures: The Diary and Collected Lectures of G I Tunkin at the Hague Academy of International Law. Edited by William E Butler and Vladimir G Tunkin. The Hague: Eleven International Publishing, 2012', 107(3) The American Journal of International Law 2013, 713.
54. Rein Müllerson, 'The Formation and Development of the Soviet Doctrine of International Law' [Stanovlenie i razvitie sotsialisticheskoj doktriny mezhdunarodnogo prava. K 80-letiu G.I. Tunkina], Soviet Yearbook of International Law [Sovetskij ezhegodnik mezhdunarodnogo prava] 1986, 110–111.
55. See Vladislav Tolstykh, 'The Current State of the Russian Doctrine of International Law: An Essay' [Ocherk sovremennogo sostojanija rossijskoj doktriny mezhdunarodnogo prava], 3 Electronic Annex to the Russian Legal Journal [Elektronnoe prilozhenie k Rossijskomu juridicheskomu zhurnalu] 2016, 50–58.
56. Yury Yumashev, 'The Western Doctrine of International Law of the Beginning of XXI Century. A Brief Overview' [Zapadnaja doktrina mezhdunarodnogo prava nachala XXI veka. Kratkij obzor], 2 Law Journal of the Higher School of Economics [Pravo. Zhurnal Vysshej Shkoly Economiki] 2009, 3–9.
57. The first attempt to apply a non-positivist reading of international law was by Sergey Rogoshin (Sergey Rogozhin, 'Myths of Law. An Experience of the Paradox Analysis of Public International Law' [Mify prava. Opyt paradoksal'nogo analiza mezhdunarodnogo publichnogo prava], 3 Moscow Journal of International Law [Moskovskij zhurnal mezhdunarodnogo prava] 2003, 16–33). The critical stances of foreign scholars on different international norms, principles, and institutions were summarized by Tolstykh (Vladislav Tolstykh, 'The Five Levels of the International Legal Mythology' [Pjat urovnej mezhdunarodno-pravovoj mifologii], 3 Electronic Annex to the Russian Legal Journal [Elektronnoe prilozhenie k Rossijskomu juridicheskomu zhurnalu] 2019, 5–18).
58. International law and economics approaches and critical legal studies are slowly finding followers among Russian scholars and young researchers. The first Ph D thesis applying a critical legal approach was defended in Russia in 2018 by Grigory Vaypan ('The Principle of Proportionality in Contemporary International Law', A dissertation submitted for the degree of Doctor of Philosophy (Ph D) in Law (2017) https://disser.spbu.ru/files/phd_spsu/vaipan_g_v_disser.pdf). See also Anita Soboleva, 'Judges as Readers, Authors and Dialecticians: Legal Interpretation in ECtHR Cases on Mental Disability', 29(3) International Journal for the Semiotics of Law 2016, 557–575; Vera Rusinova, 'Privacy and the Legalisation of Mass Surveillance: In Search of a Second Wind for International Human Rights Law', 26(4) International Journal of Human Rights 2022, 740–756.
59. One of the awards rendered under the Presidency of Fyodor Fyodorovich Martens—the Arbitral award of 3 October 1899 in the Venezuela-British Guiana dispute—is being contested before the ICJ (https://www.icj-cij.org/en/case/171) on the ground of Martens' alleged partiality. This allegation is based on a posthumously published letter from Severo Mallet-Prevost (Otto Schoenrich, 'The Venezuela-British Guiana Boundary Dispute', 43 American Journal of International Law 1949, 523). Martens' diaries refute this version (see 'A Fragment from Fyodor Fyodorovich Martens Diary for 1899' [Vyderzhka iz dnevnikov Fyodora Fyodorovicha za 1899 god] 12(1) Mezhdunarodnoe pravosudie 2022, 122–137; see

Ilya Rachkov and Elizaveta Rachkova, 'Guyana vs. Venezuela: How the Past Prevents Us from Living in the Present. Instead of a Foreword' [Delo Gayana protiv Venesuelly: o tom, kak proshloe ne dajet zhit v nastojashchem: Vmesto predislovija], 12(1) Mezhdunarodnoe pravosudie 2022, 113–121).

60. Arthur Eyffinger, 'Friedrich Martens: A Founding Father of The Hague Tradition. The Fourth Friedrich Martens Memorial Lecture', 15 ENDC Proceedings 2012, 13–43.
61. See Lauri Mälksoo, 'F.F. Martens and His Time: When Russia Was an Integral Part of the European Tradition of International Law', 25(3) European Journal of International Law 2014, 811–813.
62. Friedrich Fromhold (he later changed his name to Fyodor Fyodorovich) Martens was born in Parnu in Livland (now Estonia), which was a province of the Russian Empire. At the age of nine he moved to Saint Petersburg for his studies and after graduating from the Saint-Petersburg University, started to teach and was later accepted into the diplomatic service. See Vladimir Pustogarov, *Our Martens. F.F. Martens: International Lawyer and Architect of Peace*, ed and trans with an Introduction by WE Butler (Kluwer Law International 2000).
63. See Larissa J van den Herik, 'An Inquiry into the Role of Commissions of Inquiry in International Law: Navigating the Tensions between Fact-Finding and Application of International Law', 13 Chinese Journal of International Law 2014, 510–512.
64. Paragraph 9 of the preamble to the Convention with Respect to the Laws and Customs of War by Land, 1899.
65. Rotem Giladi, 'The Enactment of Irony: Reflections on the Origins of the Martens Clause', 25(3) European Journal of International Law 2014, 847–869.
66. Brussels Declaration concerning the Laws and Customs of War (27 August 1874). (D Schindler and J Toman, *The Laws of Armed Conflicts* (Martinus Nijhoff Publishers 1988) 22–34).
67. See, eg, Vladimir Pustogarov, 'The Martens Clause in International Law', 1 Journal of the History of International Law 1999, 125–135; Antonio Cassese, 'The Martens Clause, Half a Loaf or Simply Pie in the Sky', 11 European Journal of International Law 2000, 187–216; Meron Teodor, 'The Martens Clause, Principles of Humanity, and Dictates of Public Conscience', 94 American Journal of International Law 2000, 78–89.
68. See *Trial of Alfried Felix Alwyn Krupp von Bohlen und Halbach and Eleven Others*, United States Military Tribunal, Nuremberg, 17 November 1947–30 June 1948 (1949) X The United Nations War Crimes Commission, Law Reports of Trials of War Criminals 130–159; ICTY, *Prosecutor v Martic*, Trial Chamber (8 March 1996) paragraph 13; Legality of the Threat or Use of Nuclear Weapons. Advisory Opinion. ICJ Reports 1996, 226, §§ 259–260.
69. See Larissa van den Herik, 'An Inquiry into the Role of Commissions of Inquiry in International Law: Navigating the Tensions between Fact-Finding and Application of International Law', 13 Chinese Journal of International Law 2014, 507–537, at 510–512.
70. Bill Bowring, *Law, Rights and Ideology in Russia: Landmarks in the Destiny of a Great Power* (Routledge 2013); Johannes Socher, *Russia and the Right to Self-Determination in the Post-Soviet Space* (OUP 2021) 14–56.
71. See Stephen Schwebel, 'The Brezhnev Doctrine Repealed and Peaceful Co-Existence Enacted', 66(4) American Journal of International Law 1972, 816–819.
72. Lauri Mälksoo, 'The Soviet Approach to the Right of Peoples to Self-determination: Russia's Farewell to jus publicum europaeum', 19 Journal of the History of International Law 2017, 210–216.
73. Bowring (n 70) 85.

74. Benjamin Ferencz, 'The United Nations Consensus Definition of Aggression: Sieve or Substance', 10 The International Journal of Law and Economics 1975, 704.
75. UNGA Res 3314 (XXIX) (14 December 1974).
76. UNGA Res 1514 (XV) (14 December 1960); Res 2105 (XX) (20 December 1965), paragraph 10; Res 2621 (XXV) (25 October 1970); Res 3103 (XXVIII), (12 December 1973), paragraphs 1, 3; Res 3314 (14 December 1974), paragraphs 6, 7 (preamble).
77. Article 1(4) Protocol Additional to the Geneva Conventions of 12 August 1949, and relating to the Protection of Victims of International Armed Conflicts (8 June 1977).
78. See an overview in Johannes Socher, 'Lenin, (Just) Wars of National Liberation, and the Soviet Doctrine on the Use of Force', 19(2) Journal of the History of International Law / Revue d'histoire du droit international 2017, 240–245.
79. See Eric D Weitz, *A World Divided: The Global Struggle for Human Rights in the Age of Nation-States* (Princeton UP 2019).
80. ibid, 283.
81. Richard F Rosser, 'Soviet Opposition to Racial Discrimination in the United Nations', 21(1) The Russian Review 1962, 25–37; Egon Schwelb, 'The International Convention on the Elimination of All Forms of Racial Discrimination', 15(4) The International and Comparative Law Quarterly 1966, 996–1068.
82. See Lisa Baldez, 'Geopolitics and Drafting the UN Treaty on Women's Rights', American Political Science Association Annual Meeting Paper (31 August–2 September 2012), https://ssrn.com/abstract=2108725
83. Anna Lukina, 'The Soviet Legacy and Current Human Rights Debates', OxHRH Blog (21 January 2018) https://ohrh.law.ox.ac.uk/the-soviet-legacy-and-current-human-rights-debates
84. This role of the USSR was not seriously contested, but rather glossed over in foreign literature. The works of Aron Trainin were first mentioned in E van Sliedregt, *Individual Criminal Responsibility in International Law* (OUP 2012) 21, 25 and several recent publications in English pay tribute to his role for international criminal law (see Francine Hirsch, *Soviet Judgment at Nuremberg: A New History of the International Military Tribunal After World War II* (OUP 2020); Thomas Earl Porter 'In Defense of Peace: Aron Trainin's Contributions to International Jurisprudence', 13(1) Genocide Studies and Prevention: An International Journal 2019, 98–112; Gleb Bogush, 'Aron Trainin: The Legal Mind Behind a Soviet International Criminal Law Project' in Frédéric Mégret and Immi Tallgren (eds), *The Dawn of a Discipline: International Criminal Justice and Its Early Exponents* (CUP 2020) 260–279.
85. See Aaron Trajnin, *Criminal Intervention. The Movement on Unification of Criminal Legislation of Capitalistic States* [Ugolovnaja interventsija. Dvizhenie po unifikatsii ugolovnogo zakonodatelstva kapitalisticheskikh stran] (Sovetskoe zakonodatelstvo 1935); Aaron Trajnin, *Protection of Peace and Criminal Law* [Zashchita mira i ugolovny zakon] (Juridicheskoe izdatelstvo NKYu SSSR 1937); Aaron Trajnin, *Criminal Responsibility of Hitlerites* [Ugolovnaja zashchita gitlerovtsev] (Juridicheskoe izdatelstvo NKYu SSSR 1944); Aaron Trainin, *Hitlerite Responsibility under International Law* (Hutchinson & Co. 1944).
86. The US has never officially apologized for the nuclear bombing of Hiroshima and Nagasaki (See Do Hiroshima Residents Even Want an Apology? BBC (26 May 2016) https://www.bbc.com/news/world-asia-36366018)
87. Decision of the Congress of People's Deputies of the USSR on Political and Legal Assessment of the Soviet-German Non-Intervention Treaty [Postanovlenie Soveta

narodnykh deputatov SSSR o poloticheskoj i pravovoj otsenke sovetsko-germanskogo dogovora o nenapadenii] (24 December 1989) http://docs.historyrussia.org/ru/nodes/183748-postanovlenie-sezda-narodnyh-deputatov-soyuza-sovetskih-sotsialisticheskih-respublik-o-politicheskoy-i-pravovoy-otsenke-sovetsko-germanskogo-dogovora-o-nenapadenii-1939-g-24-dekabrya-1989-g#mode/inspect/page/3/zoom/4.

88. Eugène Korovine, 'La conquête de la stratosphère et le droit international', XLI Revue Générale de Droit International Public 1934, 675–686.
89. 610 UNTS 205.
90. Jury Kolosov, *Critique of the Reactionary International Legal Conceptions in the Sphere of International Space Law* [Kritika reaktsionnykh mezhdunarodno-pravovykh konzeptsij v oblasti mezhdunarodnogo kosmicheskogo prava] Thesis (1966); Gennadij Zhukov, *International Legal Problems of Space Exploration* [Mezhdunarodno-pravovye problemy issledovanija kosmosa] Thesis (1966).
91. 'Conclusion of a Treaty on the Prohibition of the Stationing of Weapons of Any Kind in Outer Space', Official Records of the General Assembly (A/RES/36/99) (9 December 1981).
92. https://mid.ru/ru/foreign_policy/news/1786138/?lang=en
93. The draft was initially submitted to the Conference on Disarmament in 2008 and a revised version in 2014.
94. UNGA Res (70/27) (7 December 2015).
95. See Stefan Talmon, 'Germany Opposes Russian Initiatives on the Prevention of the Placement of Weapons in Outer Space' (28 October 2021) https://gpil.jura.uni-bonn.de/2021/10/germany-opposes-russian-initiatives-on-the-prevention-of-the-placement-of-weapons-in-outer-space/
96. Press conference of Sergey Lavrov (16 January 2019) https://mid.ru/en/press_service/minister_speeches/1451497/; Sergey Lavrov, 'On Law, Rights and Rules', 3 Russia in Global Affairs 2021, 228–240; Alexander Vylegzhanin, Boris Nefedov, Evgeny Voronin, Olga Magomedova, and Polina Zotova, 'The Concept 'Rules-Based Order' in International Legal Discourses', 2 Moscow Journal of International Law 2021, 57.
97. Alexander Vylegzhanin, Boris Nefedov, Evgeny Voronin, Olga Magomedova, and Polina Zotova, 'The Concept "Rules-Based Order" in International Legal Discourses', 2 Moscow Journal of International Law 2021, 57.
98. Benedict Kingsbury, Nico Krisch, and Richard Stewart, 'The Emergence of Global Administrative Law', 68 Law and Contemporary Problems 2005, 17.
99. Stefan Talmon, 'Rules-based Order v. International Law?' https://gpil.jura.uni-bonn.de/2019/01/rules-based-order-v-international-law/. 20 January 2019, 2.
100. The Foreign Policy Concept 2016, paragraph 26(b).
101. Collective Rapid Reaction Forces Agreement [Soglashenie o kollektivnykh silakh operativnogo reagirovanija Organizatsii Dogovora o kollektivnoj bezopasnosti] (14 June 2009) Bulleten' mezhdunarodnykh dogovorov (2011) No 7.
102. 2005 World Summit Outcome, UN Doc A/RES/60/1 (16 September 2005), paragraphs 138, 139.
103. UN SC Res 1674 (28 April 2006); 1706 (31 August 2006); 1970 (26 February 2011), 1973 (17 March 2011), 1975 (30 March 2011), 2014 (21 October 2011); 1996 (8 July 2011) 2121 (10 October 2013).
104. See http://www.un.org/press/en/2008/sc9419.doc.htm
105. Address by the President of the Russian Federation (18 March 2014), http://en.kremlin.ru/events/president/news/20603

106. Accordance with International Law of the Unilateral Declaration of Independence by the Provisional Institutions of Self-Government of Kosovo (Request for Advisory Opinion), Written Statement by the Russian Federation (16 April 2009) 31–32, https://www.icj-cij.org/public/files/case-related/141/15628.pdf
107. ibid, 32–38.
108. Statement of the President of the Russian Federation (26 August 2008), http://kremlin.ru/events/president/transcripts/1222
109. Address by the President of the Russian Federation (18 March 2014), http://kremlin.ru/events/president/news/20603
110. Ruth Deyermond, 'The Uses of Sovereignty in Twenty-first Century Russian Foreign Policy', 68(6) Europe-Asia Studies 2016, 958–959.
111. Marten Breuer, '"Principled Resistance" to ECtHR Judgments: Dogmatic Framework and Conceptual Meaning' in Marten Breuer (ed), *Principled Resistance to ECtHR Judgments—A New Paradigm?* (Springer 2019) 18.
112. The Russian Federation ceased to be a party to the ECHR on 16 September 2022 (see Res ECtHR (22 March 2022)).
113. Since Russia's accession to the ECHR in 1998 to the end of 2021 the ECtHR issued 3,116 judgments with respect to Russia (https://echr.coe.int/Documents/Overview_19592021_ENG.pdf).
114. Federal Law 'On International Treaties of the Russian Federation' (15 July 1995) No 101-FZ, Article 5.
115. Execution of the European Court of Human Rights' Judgments, Main Achievements in Member States, Russian Federation, https://rm.coe.int/ma-russia-eng/1680a186c0
116. Federal Law 'On Changes in Particular Legislative Acts of the Russian Federation and Repealing Particular Legislative Acts of the Russian Federation' (11 June 2022) No 183-FZ.
117. The 'Hoshinmaru' case (*Japan v Russian Federation*) (Judgment of the ITLOS, 6 August 2007).
118. The 'Arctic Sunrise' case (*Kingdom of the Netherlands v Russian Federation*) (Order of the ITLOS of 22 November 2013); Case Concerning the Detention of Three Ukrainian Naval Vessels (*Ukraine v Russian Federation*) (Order of the ITLOS, 25 May 2019).
119. https://docs.wto.org/dol2fe/Pages/SS/directdoc.aspx?filename=q:/WT/DS/475-16.pdf&Open=True; https://docs.wto.org/dol2fe/Pages/SS/directdoc.aspx?filename=q:/WT/DS/479-12.pdf&Open=True; https://docs.wto.org/dol2fe/Pages/SS/directdoc.aspx?filename=q:/WT/DS/485-11.pdf&Open=True; https://docs.wto.org/dol2fe/Pages/SS/directdoc.aspx?filename=q:/WT/DS/499-11.pdf&Open=True
120. Enforceability of the Anchugov and Gladkov v Russia Judgment of the ECtHR of 4 July 2013 (Judgment of the Constitutional Court of the Russian Federation, 19 April 2016); Enforceability of the OAO Neftyanaya Kompaniya Yukos v Russia Judgment of the ECtHR of 31 July 2014 (Judgment of the Constitutional Court of the Russian Federation of 19 January 2017).
121. Law of the Russian Federation on Amendment to the Constitution of the Russian Federation (14 March 2020) No 1-FKZ 'On Improvement of Regulation of Particular Questions of Organization and Fuctioning of Public Power' [Zakon Rossijskoj Federatsii 'O sovershenstvovanii otdelnykh voprosov organizatsii i funktsionirovanija publichnoj vlasti'] Sobranie Zakonodatel'stva Rossijskoj Federatsii (16 March 2020) No 11.
122. Constitutional Review of Sec. 4 of the Order of Application of the Exemption from Customs Duties during the Import of Selected Products Categories to the Single Customs

Territory of the Customs Union (Decision of the Constitutional Court of the Russian Federation, 3 March 2015), paragraph 2.2.

123. Judgments of the Constitutional Court of the Russian Federation of 19 April 2016 and of 19 January 2017 (n 120).
124. Article 125(5.1)(b) Constitution of the Russian Federation.
125. On the reasons not to enforce the 'Fedotova and Others v Russia' ECtHR Judgment of 13 July 2021 on legalization of same-sex relationships see Same-sex offer [Odnopoloe predlozhenie], Kommersant (13 July 2021), https://www.kommersant.ru/doc/4899710
126. The 'Arctic Sunrise' case (*Kingdom of the Netherlands v Russian Federation*), Provisional Measures, Note Verbale No 3838/H from the Embassy of the Russian Federation in Germany to the Tribunal (22 October 2013) https://www.itlos.org/en/main/cases/list-of-cases/case-no-22/; Case Concerning the Detention of Three Ukrainian Naval Vessels (*Ukraine v The Russian Federation*), Provisional Measures, Memorandum of the Government of the Russian Federation (7 May 2019), 9–15.
127. In the WTO Dispute Settlement Body Russia figures as the applicant in eight cases against the US, the EU, and Ukraine; in 2017 Russia won a case against Belarus in the EAEU Court; in 2021 Russia lodged with the ECtHR the first inter-state application (against Ukraine); in 2002 the ITLOS upheld Russia's application against Australia in the 'Volga' case.

CHAPTER 35

SPAIN AND PORTUGAL

CARLOS ESPÓSITO AND PATRÍCIA GALVÃO TELES

1. Introduction

Spain and Portugal are countries with centuries of history, yet they are relatively young democracies that emerged after decades of isolated dictatorial regimes during the 20th century, with minimal involvement in international and European affairs and institutions. Nowadays, Spain and Portugal are committed to upholding international law, practising multilateralism, and safeguarding human rights. This commitment was fostered through the development of new constitutions in the 1970s, where international law, especially human rights law, was enshrined as paramount and seamlessly integrated into their domestic legal frameworks. Moreover, particularly their integration into the European Union (EU) in 1986 and their active participation in various international co-operation and defence organizations underscore their dedication to upholding global norms. In this chapter we offer a study of the features that best describe each country's contemporary concept of international law, both in theory and practice, which are deeply indebted to the process of 'internationalization by democratization' of Portugal and Spain.

2. Spain and International Law

During the Francoist period (1939–1975), Spain was not characterized by a profound commitment for international law or full cooperation with international institutions. Although it was admitted as a member of the United Nations (UN) in 1955, Spain remained rather isolated during these decades, with a poor record of compliance with international human rights and limited participation in international treaties or organizations. It was only with the transition to democracy that Spain was able to fully reintegrate into the international community and actively engage with international law and organizations.

The advent of democracy in the 1970s ushered in a new legal and institutional structure centred around the Spanish Constitution of 1978.[1] The Constitution accorded international law a paramount position among the sources of law in Spain, underscoring the country's commitment to the international rule of law, particularly emphasizing the incorporation of international human rights law. Simultaneously, there was a broad political consensus and a strong dedication to joining the EU while maintaining a multilateralist stance in international relations, fostering a special connection with Latin American countries.

2.1 International law is part of Spanish law

The Spanish Constitution falls short of offering a comprehensive, coherent, and organized response to the challenges posed by the State's external activities within the constitutional framework. Instead, it presents a collection of disconnected provisions and allusions.[2] To describe its relationship with international law, this section explains how treaties and general international law are considered an integral part of the Spanish domestic legal system. This explanation is completed by referencing the obligation of Spanish judges to interpret domestic rights and liberties in conformity with international law.

One crucial aspect addressed by the Constitution is the integration of 'validly concluded treaties' into the Spanish legal system.[3] These treaties become an integral part of the domestic legal order and can only be repealed, amended, or suspended following the procedures specified within the treaties themselves or in accordance with general principles of international law.[4]

The Spanish Constitutional Court frequently relies on Article 96.1 of the Constitution as a legal foundation when applying international treaties as domestic law in its judgments.[5] This article serves as a reference point for justifying the application of treaty provisions within the national legal context as it recognizes treaties as the law of the land. This provision is also decisive to determine the supremacy of international treaties over domestic law, except for the Constitution itself. Indeed, Article 96 provides that international treaties 'may only be repealed, amended or suspended in the manner provided in the treaties themselves or in accordance with the general rules of international law'.[6]

The conformity of treaties with the Constitution may be reviewed by the Constitutional Court prior to the Spanish government's expression of consent to abide by the treaty.[7] Subsequently, the judiciary may review them after the treaties are validly concluded by Spain and published in the official bulletin. A determination by the judiciary that treaty provisions are unconstitutional would logically have only domestic implications regarding their conformity with the Constitution.

In the event of a contradiction between a treaty norm and a domestic norm other than the Constitution, due to the supremacy of the treaty, the domestic norm is superseded by the treaty norm. The judge cannot declare the domestic rule null and void but can only set aside provisions of national law which are in contradiction or incompatible with self-executing obligations of a binding treaty.[8] This understanding has been generally accepted over the years, and the Constitutional Court itself has often referred to the work of the ordinary judge as responsible for selecting the treaty rule applicable to the specific case. However, recently, in a judgment where it was considering the constitutionality of a law reforming and restricting universal jurisdiction, the Constitutional Court referred to the 'control of conventionality'[9] in one of the meanings used by the Interamerican Court of Human Rights (IACtHR),[10] introducing a concept which has produced a significant scholarly debate as the concept may be associated with a diffuse control of constitutionality conducted by common judges, which in principle is alien to the Spanish system of constitutional review.[11]

While the Constitutional Court has not necessarily changed its way of understanding constitutional review, which leaves the selection of applicable treaty norms to the ordinary judge, it has certainly prompted an important doctrinal debate on the meaning of conventionality control in Spanish law.[12]

Regarding general international law, it also forms an integral part of Spanish law. Unlike other constitutions, including the Portuguese Constitution,[13] the Spanish Constitution does not expressly state that general international law is part of Spanish law. Some have wanted to interpret the reference to general international law in Article 96 of the Constitution as an implicit acceptance that these norms belong to the Spanish legal order.[14] Be that as it may, a principle of coherence between the internal and external activity of the State indicates that general international law is an integral part of the Spanish legal order, for if the State is internationally bound by customary rules, these must be equally relevant in the domestic order.[15] This has been the view of the Spanish courts, including the Supreme Court and the Constitutional Court. It suffices to refer to the early judgments on jurisdictional immunities of foreign States and their property where both the Supreme Court and the Constitutional Court correctly applied customary international law to cases involving immunity from execution of foreign States' assets.[16] A caveat is necessary: the Constitutional Court has limited the effects of customary international law as a source of domestic criminal law.[17]

Binding resolutions from international organizations are applicable in Spanish law, but they are not explicitly mentioned in the Spanish Constitution.[18] Spanish courts and tribunals address this issue by respecting the rules of the organs issuing the resolutions and by applying an analogy with the regulations governing treaties.[19]

To complete the Spanish commitment to international law, Article 10.2 states that 'the principles relating to the fundamental rights and liberties recognized by the Constitution *shall be interpreted in conformity with* the Universal Declaration of Human Rights and the international treaties and agreements thereon ratified by Spain'.[20] The Portuguese Constitution of 1976 has a similar provision which was a relevant precedent for the Spanish Constitution.[21] This provision has been of fundamental importance in the evolution of human rights and liberties for the new Spanish democracy. The Constitutional Court has made it clear in its judgments on the matter: this mandate of interpretation in conformity with the Universal Declaration of Human Rights (UDHR) and the international treaties and agreements ratified by Spain 'expresses the recognition of our coincidence with the sphere of values and interests that these instruments protect, as well as our will as a Nation to join an international legal order that advocates the defence and protection of human rights as a fundamental basis for the organisation of the State'.[22]

2.2 Spain in international organizations

A key priority in Spain's foreign policy is to foster robust and legitimate multilateral and regional international institutions.[23] This vision encompasses safeguarding fundamental human rights, promoting development, upholding environmental protection, and maintaining regional and international security. Spain's full participation in the UN epitomizes this pledge.

Spain was unable to join the UN at the time of its creation in 1945. Initially, there was a consensus among UN founding members to exclude countries that were not, in the words of Article 4.1 of the UN Charter, 'peace-loving states', that is, States which had sympathized with the Axis during World War II. The isolation of Spain, supported by Latin American countries such as Mexico, is known as 'the Spanish question'.[24] It was only in 1955, with a change in the world's geopolitical conditions that started early in that decade, that Spain was admitted to the Organization.[25]

UN membership, however, had no significant effect on the authoritarian system of government in Spain, which remained a dictatorship for several decades. Therefore, Spain's participation in the UN must be distinguished in at least two periods: before and after the transition to democracy.[26] Indeed, during the Francoist era, Spain maintained a low profile, was severely limited in its activities, and held a marginal position within the overall context of the UN.[27] Since the beginning of the democratic transition in the mid-1970s, Spain has deepened its commitment to the principles and objectives of the UN, actively participating in their activities, and embracing democratic values and respect for human rights. Regarding the commitment to respect human rights, Spain ratified all the core treaties on human rights in the years of democratic transition, and the example of the ratification on 27 April 1977 of the International Covenant on Civil and Political Rights (ICCPR) and the International Covenant on Economic, Social and Cultural Rights of 1966 (ICESCR) stands out.[28] Two years later, on 4 October 1979, Spain ratified the Convention for the Protection of Human Rights and Fundamental Freedoms (ECHR), signed in Rome on 4 November 1950.

Spain committed itself to the system of peaceful settlement of disputes and to the International Court of Justice (ICJ), the principal judicial organ of the United Nations. On 29 October 1990 Spain deposited its declaration recognizing the jurisdiction of the ICJ as compulsory.[29] Spain has been brought before the Court by Belgium in the *Barcelona Traction* case,[30] and by Yugoslavia together with another nine member States of the North Atlantic Treaty Organization (NATO) in a case concerning the breach of the prohibition to use force under international law.[31] Spain filed a complaint against Canada in 1995 in the fisheries case.[32] In all three cases the Court declared that it lacked jurisdiction to entertain the applications.

Spain has participated in several cases in the advisory jurisdiction, including of course the case of its former colony in Western Sahara.[33] This case is still very controversial. Everything seems to indicate that the Spanish government now takes a more favourable approach to Morocco's legal position as the administering power of Western Sahara, that is, the autonomous integration of the territory into Morocco, a stance that has generated much criticism from numerous international law scholars.[34] Spain also participated actively in the advisory opinion on Kosovo,[35] in which it took a strong position against the legality of the unilateral declaration of independence under international law.[36]

In brief, Spain has been an active member of the UN. It has served as an elected member of the Security Council on five separate occasions[37] and is an important and respectful net contributor to both the regular budget[38] of the Organization and the Peace Operations budget.[39]

With democracy also came the opportunity to join two other international organizations that are key to fulfilling the commitments of a policy of effective multilateralism: NATO and the EU.

NATO membership was attained on 30 May 1982 during President Calvo Sotelo's term of office.[40] In those early years of democracy, Spanish popular support for NATO was negligible. The opposition was initially against NATO membership. When President Felipe González came to power, he called a referendum on Spain's continued membership in the defence organization. The referendum was held on 31 January 1986.[41] The YES vote won with 56.85 per cent of the valid votes in favour of remaining in NATO, with a turnout of 59.4 per cent. In 1995, former Foreign Minister Javier Solana was elected NATO Secretary General, and since 1999, Spain has been a fully integrated member of NATO's military structure.

EU membership was the most cherished goal of Spain's new democracy.[42] Spain had integrated into international economic institutions at an early stage with a certain degree of normality.[43] However, despite its attempts, Spain was not accepted into the European Communities until it established its democracy.[44] The negotiations took several years and the Accession Treaty to the European Community was signed in Lisbon and Madrid on 12 June 1986.[45]

The EU's contribution to the consolidation of Spain's democracy and prosperity is difficult to measure. It transformed the social, economic, and, above all, legal structure of Spain, which had to accept the *acquis communautaire* to become a member of the European Communities. The legal revolution was total. It changed the laws, the institutions, and even the way of thinking of lawyers, judges, and all kind of legal practitioners. It also changed the way of learning and teaching law in Spain's law schools both by creating specific subjects of European law and by introducing a European law perspective in general courses of law. Initially, voluntary courses in EU law were taught by professors of international law at various universities. The subject was then incorporated into law school curricula. The first handbooks in Spanish published during that time were useful in the task of teaching EU law,[46] as were the specialized academic journals,[47] and learned societies of European law.[48]

Spain became a loyal and important member of the Union, leaving its mark on significant measures such as European citizenship, promoted by the Spanish government during the Maastricht reform, and the Erasmus programme, strongly advocated by Commissioner Manuel Marín. This influence persists to this day. EU membership also brought Spain closer to its Portuguese neighbours in a new and unique way.

It is worth mentioning Spain's continuous efforts to cultivate its special relationship with Latin American countries. The Ibero-American summits, initiated in 1991, and the establishment of an international organization—the Ibero-American General Secretariat—aimed at fostering dialogue and cooperation among the community of Ibero-American countries, serve as compelling evidence of this commitment.[49]

2.3 The practice of international law within Spain

The practice of international law in Spain has undergone significant changes since the beginning of democracy. These changes have been driven by the country's deepened commitment to international law, as well as its opening up to the world at a time when information became more available to all kind of legal practitioners and scholars. Spain has numerous laws related to foreign affairs and the practice of international law,[50] and its application does not appear to be inherently controversial. Today, it is normal to find Spanish court rulings applying international law in all its variety and ambivalence.[51]

The most well-known instance of judicial practice related to international law in Spain pertains to a series of cases concerning the principle of universal jurisdiction, which had substantial global ramifications, notably demonstrated in the renowned *Pinochet* case. The original Spanish model of universal jurisdiction, as outlined in Article 23(4) of the 1986 law governing the judiciary, was solely based on the nature of the crimes under persecution, devoid of any limitations or prerequisites. This framework facilitated the notion that universal jurisdiction was not exclusive to 'low-cost defendants',[52] but could indeed serve as an effective tool to combat worldwide impunity. This broad interpretation was affirmed by the Constitutional Court in its verdict on the *Mayan genocide* case,[53] asserting that the concept of universal jurisdiction, as originally conceived in 1986, possessed an 'absolute' character, founded solely on the exceptionally severe nature of the crimes subject to its prosecution. Consequently, the only means to restrict the application of universal jurisdiction was through an amendment to the law itself.

That is what happened next. In 2009, the government introduced restrictions that proved ineffective, and in 2014, it significantly curtailed the scope of universal jurisdiction, marking what was referred to as 'the demise of the Spanish model of universal jurisdiction'.[54] This reform, prompted by external pressure from influential foreign nations reacting against judicial investigations by Spanish courts, imposed new prerequisites concerning the alleged perpetrators of the crimes, who must now be Spanish citizens or residents of Spain. Furthermore, it imposed a stringent adherence to the principle of subsidiarity and the constraint of *actio popularis*. The Supreme Court ruled that the restricted interpretation of the principle of universal jurisdiction, as amended in 2014,[55] was compliant with both international law and constitutional law. This was determined through a lengthy and exhaustively researched judgment concerning China's alleged genocide and crimes against humanity directed at the Tibetan people.[56]

Another example of judicial practice is the recent case law concerning the State's obligation to provide legal grounds for refusing to exercise diplomatic protection of its nationals in cases of grave violations of international law. The Audiencia Nacional[57] and the Supreme Court[58] have taken a rather liberal interpretation of the law of diplomatic protection in favour of the rights of individuals vis à vis the State. According to the Supreme Court, the State's discretion involved in diplomatic protection must be understood as the freedom to choose how to exercise protection, rather than deciding whether to exercise it or not. The Supreme Court, upholding the decision of the Audiencia Nacional, ruled that the State owed compensation to the family of José Couso for not having responded at all to his family's request to exercise diplomatic protection vis-à-vis the US.[59] These Courts could have avoided inaccuracies in its interpretation of international law[60] by simply deciding, exclusively under domestic law,[61] that the State has an obligation to provide a reasoned response to petitioners seeking diplomatic protection for its omission to provide such protection. In any case, it seems that in the future the government will be required to provide a reasoned legal response to petitioners seeking diplomatic protection if it wishes to avoid having to pay compensation for failing to exercise diplomatic protection.

Obviously, there are entrenched Spanish issues in international law. Some are very well-known, such as the Gibraltar claim.[62] Some are controversial within Spain, such as the way in which Spain should deal with transitional justice.[63] What is crucial is that all these positions are argued taking into account international law and a commitment to upholding it. This is also applicable to the so-called 'right to decide' that advocates of Catalan independence aim to align with the right to self-determination according to international law. There is a broad consensus among international law scholars and practitioners in Spain that this 'right to decide' does not stem from international law, and that the issue of Catalonia must be resolved within the framework of domestic law.[64]

2.4 The Spanish doctrine of international law

International law scholarship has undergone a significant evolution in recent decades. Arguably, it has transitioned from a majority focus on natural law to a prevalence of various types of positivism, particularly inclusive positivism.[65] Today, the number of international law scholars working in Spain and the diversity of their research projects are quite impressive. One only need look at the Spanish Association of Professors of International Law and International Relations (AEPDIRI), which was founded in 1978. The scope of AEPDIRI is very broad. It aims to promote the study and advancement of public and private international law, EU law, and international relations. Its first president was Antonio Truyol y Serra and it has been chaired by distinguished Spanish professors throughout its history.[66] AEPDIRI now has around 800 members, more than 50 per cent of whom are women, with a huge variety of interests and projects. This is reflected in the activities of the research teams and their publications, which are mostly published in journals and books supported by AEPDIRI.

Indeed, AEPDIRI is associated with three international law journals and a significant number of books generated by its regular or special conferences.[67] The flagship publication of AEPDIRI is the Revista Española de Derecho Internacional (REDI). REDI, founded in 1948,[68] has a long history that reflects the Spanish reality of those decades, including the ostracism of its early years until the transition to democracy.[69] REDI is now a prestigious *Open Journal Systems* publication, with a considerable scientific and academic impact. Its chief editors and editorial board are influential scholars in the fields of international law and international relations.[70]

The other two journals associated with the AEPDIRI are the Spanish Yearbook of International Law (SYbIL), founded in 1991 as the only publication of the Association published in English,[71] and the Revista Electrónica de Estudios Internacionales (REEI), founded in 2000 as the first fully online publication of the AEPDIRI.[72] Both publications represented innovations and significant challenges for Spanish academics. Reflecting upon three decades of publication, it is evident that these challenges have been successfully overcome, and the optimistic belief can be held that these publications will carry on making substantial contributions.

We cannot discuss the Spanish doctrine of international law without mentioning the contributions of the Asesoría Jurídica Internacional (AJI). Established in 1938, the AJI has been led by diplomats[73] with distinguished legal careers as well as by esteemed professors[74] of international law. The AJI plays a pivotal role in providing counsel to the government on matters of international law, representing Spain before international organizations, and advocating for Spain in international courts and tribunals.[75]

Of course, Spanish jurists have distinguished themselves in international tribunals as judges[76] and lawyers.[77] And there have been many Spaniards who have taught courses at the Hague Academy of International Law, including the general courses on public international law of Professors Juan Antonio Carrillo Salcedo and José Antonio Pastor Ridruejo.[78]

3. Portugal and International Law

3.1 Portugal joins the United Nations: first steps towards decolonization and the transition to democracy

During the Salazar dictatorship and after being neutral during World War II, Portugal joined the United Nations (UN) in 1955, at a time when the UN Charter, including the principles of self-determination and the promotion and protection of human rights, was not particularly favourable to the domestic and foreign policy of the regime of that time.

However, due to geopolitical considerations between the two blocs in the context of the Cold War, which are beyond the scope of this contribution, Portugal decided to join the UN and was accepted by the UN, together with a number of other countries, through UNGA Resolution 995(X) of 14 December 1955.[79]

During the initial period of its membership, and until the transition to democracy and the beginning of the decolonization process in 1974, as will be discussed below, Portugal was an outcast member of the Organization, with several General Assembly (GA) resolutions condemning its colonial policies.[80]

Just after Portugal joined the UN, it received a letter from the Secretary-General inquiring about its Non-Self-Governing Territories for the purposes of the reporting obligations under paragraph e) of Article 73 of the UN Charter. It reportedly took the government of the time one year to respond and to briefly state that Portugal had no Non-Self-Governing Territories.[81]

In 1960, just after it adopted Resolution 1514 on the Granting of Independence to Colonial Counties and Peoples and Resolution 1541 on the Principles which should guide members in determining whether or not an obligation exists to transmit the information called for under Article 73e of the Charter, the General Assembly adopted Resolution 1542, clearly listing the Non-Self-Governing Territories under the administration of Portugal.

The accession of Portugal to the UN and the rapid evolution of the stance of the Organization on the issue of decolonization were undoubtedly instrumental in the regime change in the mid-1970s and the transition to democracy, with the 'Carnation Revolution' being led by young members of the military who were against the colonial wars being fought in Africa. The April 1974 Revolution opened the way for decolonization,[82] with the exception of East Timor which, due to the Indonesian occupation in 1975, only became independent in 2002, after a UN-led referendum in 1999 and a period of UNs transitional administration.[83]

3.2 Portugal and the International Court of Justice

It may come as no surprise that it is also colonization/decolonization issues that have been central in the cases that Portugal has brought before the ICJ, but with some interesting twists.

Just five days after Portugal joined the UN, on 19 December 1955, it delivered to the Secretary-General of the UN in New York a declaration of acceptance of the ICJ's jurisdiction. Three days later, on 22 December 1955, it initiated litigation against India in The Hague over the right of passage between Goa and the remaining Portuguese enclaves in Indian territory, in what became known as the 'Right of Passage' case.[84]

In a perfectly choreographed diplomatic move, Portugal had just joined the UN which advocated decolonization while bringing an action—which was successful with the decision later obtained affirming such right of passage in 1960,[85] and before the invasion and annexation of Goa—aimed at defending its rights as a colonizing power.

However, two decades after 25 April, known as the Carnation Revolution which ended the authoritarian regime and started the transition to democracy, Portugal asked the ICJ to decide a dispute in precisely the opposite situation: to defend the self-determination of East Timor, in the famous case of the Timor Gap Treaty against Australia, decided by the Court in 1995,[86] which it lost on procedural grounds due to the 'Monetary Gold' principle, that is, the absence of an indispensable third party (Indonesia).

Overall, it can be said that Portugal has made good use of the generous declaration of acceptance of the ICJ's jurisdiction. Such declaration was drafted in a very open manner in 1955 under Article 36 of the Statute, at the time for a very specific purpose of bringing the Right of Passage case against India. It was, however, the same declaration that enabled Portugal to bring the Timor Gap Treaty case against Australia. The optional clause declaration was only revised in 2005,[87] after the single instance so far in which Portugal was a defendant, in the case regarding the legality of the use of force in Kosovo in 1999.[88] Some adjustments were made, but Portugal's spirit of great openness and support for the ICJ remained.[89]

Portugal has also had the tradition of accepting compromissory clauses that confer jurisdiction to the ICJ contained in treaties, including in multilateral treaties such as, for instance, the 1948 Genocide Convention, regarding which it has exercised its right under Article 63 of the Statute to intervene in the *Ukraine v Russia* case concerning allegations of genocide.[90]

3.3 Participation in multilateral treaties after joining the United Nations

Due to the political circumstances of the time and until the democratic transition, Portugal remained relatively discreet on the international scene as regards the progressive development and codification of international law.[91]

Until 1974, the key accessions of Portugal are those in 1963 to the Geneva Conventions of 1958 on the Law of the Sea (Territorial Sea and Contiguous Zone, Continental Shelf and High Seas) and the Vienna Conventions on Diplomatic Relations of 1961,[92] in 1968, and Consular Relations of 1963, in 1972. Regarding the 1958 Geneva Conventions on the Law of the Sea, Portugal also became a party to the Optional Protocol on Dispute Settlement, however that was not the case with regard to the similar optional protocols regarding the Vienna Conventions on Diplomatic and Consular Relations.

Amongst the most important multilateral conventions negotiated in the 1960s, following a preparatory process by the International Law Commission, as those mentioned in the previous paragraph, others such as the 1969 Vienna Convention on the Law of Treaties were not identified by Portugal as a priority, and Portugal only acceded to it in 2004. However, it was widely used by the Portuguese State even before the accession, since a large part of its content was considered as codifying customary law at the time or at least to be evolving in that direction.

It was only after the democratic revolution of 25 April 1974, and as a way of integrating with the UN and the international community, that Portugal became more active in ratifying and acceding to international conventions negotiated within the scope of the UN, with great emphasis on the area of human rights.[93]

Not only did Portugal hasten to accede to the main human rights conventions negotiated in the meantime under the auspices of the UN, but since then it has also shown a commitment to ratify with considerable speed the main international instruments in this area, as well as several others, such as those concerning the law of the sea or environmental law.

With regard to the instruments that compose the UN human rights universal protection system,[94] the UDHR was adopted in 1948 at a time when Portugal was not yet a member of the UN.

For those instruments that were adopted in the 1960s, when Portugal was already a member of the UN, but in the period before the transition to democracy, Portugal chose to stay out of them until the period after 25 April 1974. There was, however, the notable exception of the 1951 Convention relating to the Status of Refugees, which Portugal ratified in 1968.

The 1965 Convention on the Elimination of Racial Discrimination and the very important 1966 International Covenant on Civil and Political Rights (ICCPR) were only ratified by Portugal in 1982 and 1978 respectively. Regarding the optional protocols to these covenants, Portugal became a party to the First Optional Protocol to the ICCPR of 1966 (submission of individual communications) in 1983, the Second Protocol of 1989 (abolition of the death penalty) in 1999, and the Optional Protocol to the ICESCR of 2008 (submission of individual communications) in 2013.

Noticeably, the new regime that emerged after 1974 and the new Constitution of the Portuguese Republic of 1976 were great engines for this change. In fact, the 1976 Constitution not only considers in its Article 16 that its own precepts on fundamental rights shall be interpreted and integrated in accordance with the UDHR, but also contains one of the most advanced and comprehensive catalogues in the world on civil and political rights and economic, social, and cultural rights.

It is with this constitutional architecture, also reflected in terms of positioning and foreign policy priorities concerning the respect and promotion of human rights at the international level, that Portugal has progressively become an assiduous and expeditious participant in nearly all the international conventions on human rights adopted by the UN.

By way of example, Portugal ratified the 1979 Convention on the Elimination of All Forms of Discrimination against Women (CEDAW) in 1980, the 1984 Convention for the Prohibition of Torture in 1989, the 1989 Convention on the Rights of the Child in 1990, its two Optional Protocols of 2000 (on children in armed conflicts and on the trade of children, child pornography, and child prostitution) in 2003, the 2006 Convention on the Rights of Persons with Disabilities in 2009, and the 2006 Convention on Enforced Disappearances in 2014.

In 2002, Portugal also ratified the 1998 Statute of the International Criminal Court,[95] an important mechanism for dealing with the most serious violations of human rights, such as international crimes. Portugal has also ratified the Kampala amendment on the Crime of Aggression. In 1999, it ratified the Genocide Convention of 1948, being also a party to the Geneva Conventions of 1949 (since 1961) and their Additional Protocols of 1977 (since 1992). The only major exception is the fact that Portugal is not a party to the 1990 International Convention on the Protection of the Rights of All Migrant Workers and Members of Their Families.

In other areas that are central to Portugal's foreign policy and in which the UN has been a pivotal point in the development of international law through treaty law, Portugal has also shown itself to be an active participant, both in the negotiating phase and afterwards in accepting the resulting international treaties.

For example, in matters of the law of the sea and oceans, Portugal actively participated in the negotiations of the 1982 United Nations Convention on the Law of the Sea,[96] became a party in 1997, and has also ratified the agreements implementing this important convention. It was fully committed to the negotiation of the new legally binding agreement, which was negotiated in the framework of the United Nations Convention on the Law of the Sea (UNCLOS), on the conservation and sustainable use of marine biodiversity in areas beyond national jurisdiction, known as the BBNJ agreement, which Portugal signed on the date it the treaty was opened for signature.[97]

In matters of environmental law, Portugal is party to the main international conventions negotiated within the framework of the UN; the same applies to the more specific issue of climate change, including the 1992 Framework Convention and the 2015 Paris Agreement, and in both cases Portugal ratified these instruments promptly. In the case of the Paris Agreement, Portugal was one of the first EU member States to ratify this important international treaty.

3.4 The 1976 Constitution and the full integration in the international community, including through the European Union and the Council of Europe

Differently than Spain, Portugal was a founding member of NATO. Thus, the post-revolution integration in the international community since 1974 was mainly through the shifting position within the UN as discussed above, and also through accession to the then European Economic Community (EEC) (now EU) together with Spain in 1986 and accession to the Council of Europe (CoE) in 1976.

This was possible with the transition to democracy by the 1974 Revolution and consolidated in the 1976 Constitution, but the accession to the CoE and to the EEC also had as its purpose the need to protect and make the transition to democracy half a century ago a lasting one.

The fundamental values and foreign policy goals that were inscribed in the 1976 Constitution were totally in line with the purposes and principles of the UN, the CoE, and (what is now) the EU.[98] The Constitution also gives great prominence to international law.[99]

Article 7 of the Constitution, 'International Relations', highlights, for example, that in its international relations, Portugal shall be governed by the respect for human rights, the right to self-determination of peoples, the peaceful settlement of disputes, and international cooperation. Additionally, Portugal shall advocate the abolition of imperialism, colonialism, and all other forms of aggression, dominion, and exploitation in relations between peoples, as well as simultaneous and controlled general disarmament, the dissolution of the political-military blocs, and the setting up of a collective security system, all with a view to the creation of an international order which can ensure peace and justice in relations between peoples. At a later constitutional revision, a paragraph was added which stated that, with a view to achieving an international justice that promotes respect for the rights of both individual human persons and peoples, and subject to the provisions governing complementarity and the other terms laid down in the Rome Statute, Portugal may accept the jurisdiction of the International Criminal Court.

Article 8 of the Constitution on 'International Law' states in its four paragraphs that:

- the rules and principles of general or common international law shall form an integral part of Portuguese law;
- the rules set out in duly ratified or passed international agreements shall come into force in Portuguese domestic law once they have been officially published, and shall remain so for as long as they are internationally binding on the Portuguese State;
- rules issued by the competent bodies of international organizations to which Portugal belongs shall enter directly into force in Portuguese domestic law, on condition that this is laid down in the respective constituent treaties;
- the provisions of the treaties that govern the EU and the rules issued by its institutions in the exercise of their respective responsibilities shall apply in Portuguese domestic law in accordance with Union law and with respect for the fundamental principles of a democratic State based on the rule of law.

3.5 Brief appraisal

It can therefore be said without much doubt, after this brief examination of Portugal's concept of international law, that it rapidly integrated into the process of development of international law after 25 April 1974, and on the basis of the 1976 Constitution. Portugal's ratification of, and accession to, various multilateral treaties drawn up within the United Nations can be seen as a form of participation and integration of Portugal into the

Organization and the international community, as was its accession to the Council of Europe and the European Union, of which it is now a respected and active member. Certainly, as a consequence of this and its recognition, it is worth noting that António Guterres was elected Secretary-General of the United Nations in 2016 and Miguel de Serpa Soares has been the Organization's Legal Counsel since 2013. Portugal has also been a non-permanent member of the Security Council on three occasions and has announced its candidacy for the 2027–2028 term.[100]

The relevance that Portugal has given to the process of development of international law by the UN can also be evidenced by the importance it attaches to its active participation—ensured by the Department of Legal Affairs in the Ministry of Foreign Affairs and by the Permanent Mission of Portugal to the UN in New York—in the 6th Committee (Legal Affairs) of the General Assembly,[101] as well as to the work of the International Law Commission, which has already counted with two Portuguese members—in fact, two of the ten women who have served on the Commission in its seventy-five years of existence, one of them being the author of the present contribution regarding Portugal.[102]

4. Concluding Remarks

This chapter has presented a survey of the features that best describe Spain and Portugal's conceptions and approaches to the theory and practice of international law. It has maintained that the commitment to international law and the involvement of both countries in international affairs and institutions have been defined by their democratization and 'Europeanization' which was made possible by their embracing of democracy. In the decades since the 1970s, Spain and Portugal have committed to upholding international law, practising multilateralism, and safeguarding human rights. Both countries have profited from new constitutions that regard international law, particularly human rights law, as supreme and incorporate it appropriately into domestic law. They have also benefitted from membership of the European Union since 1986 and in several other international cooperation and defence organizations, as well as their commitment to accepting the compulsory jurisdiction of international courts such as the International Court of Justice and the European Court of Human Rights.

Acknowledgements

Professor Espósito thanks Ángel Rodrigo Hernando, Antonio Remiro Brotóns, Ignacio Perotti, Irene Blázquez Navarro, and Ignacio Alvárez Arcá for their helpful comments.
Professor Galvão Teles thanks Flávia Cabaço for her assistance.

Notes

1. See Antonio Remiro Brotóns, 'The Spanish Constitution and International Law', 9 Spanish Yearbook of International Law 2003, 27.
2. ibid.
3. For a brief account of the treaty-making power and the Constitution, see Carlos Espósito, 'Spanish Foreign Relations Law and the Process for Making Treaties and Other International Agreements' in Curtis A Bradley (ed), *The Oxford Handbook of Comparative Foreign Relations Law* (OUP 2019) 205, at 210–212.
4. Article 96.1 Spanish Constitution: 'Validly concluded international treaties, once officially published in Spain, shall form part of the internal legal order. Their provisions may only be repealed, amended or suspended in the manner provided in the treaties themselves or in accordance with the general rules of international law.' See the commentary by Paz Andrés Sáenz de Santa María, 'Artículo 96' in Miguel Rodríguez-Piñero y Bravo-Ferrer and María Emilia Casas Baamonde (eds), *Comentarios a la Constitución Española* (Fundación Wolters Kluwer, Boletín Oficial del Estado, Tribunal Constitucional y Ministerio de Justicia 2018).
5. See, eg, the judgments of the Constitutional Tribunal 71/1988 (legal reasoning no 2, referring to human rights treaties) or 58/2004 (legal reasoning no 10, referring to the Treaty of the European Community (TEC)).
6. See also Article 30, Ley 25/2014, 27 November 2014, of Treaties and Other International Agreements. See commentary by Javier Díez-Hochleitner in Paz Andrés Sáenz de Santa María, Javier Díez-Hochleitner, and José Martín y Pérez de Nanclares, *Comentarios a la Ley de Tratados y Otros Acuerdos Internacionales* (Cizur Menor, Civitas, 2015) 530.
7. See Article 95 of the Constitution: '1. The conclusion of any international treaty containing stipulations contrary to the Constitution shall require prior Constitutional amendment. 2. The Government, or either of the Houses may request the Constitutional Court to declare whether or not there is a contradiction.' This article was applied twice. In 1992, the Constitutional Court ruled that the ratification of the Treaty of Maastricht required an amendment to the Constitution to incorporate the right of EU citizens to be eligible in municipal elections (Declaration 1/1992, 1 July 1992). In 2004, the Constitutional Court held that the proposed Treaty establishing a Constitution for Europe was not in contradiction with the Constitution (Declaration 1/2004,13 December 2004).
8. See Díez-Hochleitner (n 6). A similar situation applies to EU law. cf C-106/77, *Simmenthal* [1978] ECR 629, where the Court upheld the duty to set aside provisions of national law that are incompatible with Union law.
9. Judgment of the Constitutional Court 140/2018, 20 December 2018, particularly legal reasoning no 6.
10. Sergio García Ramírez, 'The Relationship between Inter-American Jurisdiction and States (National Systems): Some Pertinent Questions', 5(1) Notre Dame Journal of International & Comparative Law 2015, 115–152.
11. Eduardo Ferrer Mac-Gregor, 'Interpretación conforme y control difuso de constitucionalidad', 9(2) Revista de Estudios Constitucionales 2011, 531–622.
12. See Ricardo Alonso García, 'El Control de Convencionalidad: Cinco Interrogantes', 119 Revista Española de Derecho Constitucional 2020, 11; Cristina Izquierdo Sans, 'En torno al control de convencionalidad: la aplicación de los tratados internacionales en España' in Enrique Jesús Martínez Pérez (ed), *Cuestiones actuales en torno a la aplicación de normas*

y obligaciones en materia de derechos humanos: diálogos interdisciplinares con la práctica (Tirant lo Blanch 2022) 223; Ignacio G Perotti Pinciroli, 'El Control de Convencionalidad en el Derecho Español: ¿una Importación Defectuosa?', 5(1) Revista Electrónica de Estudios Internacionales 2021 <http://www.reei.org/index.php/revista/num41/articulos/control-convencionalidad-derecho-espanol-una-importacion-defectuosa> accessed 7 November 2023.

13. Article 8.1 Constitution of Portugal: 'The rules and principles of general or common international law shall form an integral part of Portuguese law.'
14. See n 7.
15. Julio D González Campos and Luis Ignacio Sánchez Rodríguez y Paz Andrés Saénz de Santa María, *Curso de Derecho Internacional Público* (6th edn, Civitas 1998) 266.
16. See eg, judgment 107/1992, 1 July 1992, upholding the impossibility of seizing a foreign State's bank accounts in Spanish territory when they are intended for the operation of its diplomatic or consular representation. From 2015, Spain has a law regulating jurisdictional immunities: Ley 16/2015, of 27 October 2015, on privileges and immunities of foreign States, international organizations with headquarters or offices in Spain, and international conferences and meetings.
17. Constitutional Court, Decision 80/2021, of 15 September 2021 ('International customary law as an insufficient criminal source because it does not respond to the principles of *lex scripta*, *praevia* and *certa*').
18. cf Article 8.3 Constitution of Portugal: 'Rules issued by the competent bodies of international organizations to which Portugal belongs shall come directly into force in Portuguese internal law, on condition that this is laid down in the respective constituent treaties.'
19. Angel J Rodrigo Hernández, *Las Resoluciones Obligatorias de las Organizaciones Internacionales de Cooperación: Su recepción en el ordenamiento jurídico español* (Tecnos 1997).
20. Emphasis added. See Alejandro Saiz Arnaiz, 'La interpretación de los derechos fundamentales y los tratados internacionales sobre derechos humanos (art. 10.2)' in Rodríguez-Piñero y Bravo-Ferrer and Casas Baamonde (n 4) 230.
21. Article 16.2 Portuguese Constitution: 'The constitutional and legal precepts concerning fundamental rights must be interpreted and completed in harmony with the Universal Declaration of Human Rights.'
22. Judgment of the Constitutional Court 91/2000, 30 March 2000, legal reasoning no 3.
23. For a recent expression of this enduring commitment, see *Estrategia de Acción Exterior 2021–2014* (Spanish Foreign Policy Strategy) <https://www.lamoncloa.gob.es/consejodeministros/resumenes/Documents/2021/270421-estrategia_de_accion_exterior_2021-2024.pdf> accessed 7 November 2023.
24. Alberto J Lleonart Amsélem, 'El Ingreso de España En La ONU Obstáculos e Impulsos', 17 Cuadernos de Historia Contemporánea 1995, 101; Florentino Portero, *Franco Aislado: La Cuestión Española (1945–1950)* (Aguilar 1989).
25. UN General Assembly Res 995(X), 14 Dec 1955. Previously, Spain was admitted to other organizations since the early 1950s, including UNESCO on 12 December 1952; Spain signed a Concordat with the Vatican in 1953; and concluded three executive agreements known as the Pact of Madrid with the US on 23 September 1953. These executive agreements gave the US the right to construct and use air and naval facilities on Spanish territory.

26. Xavier Pons Rafols, 'Spain in the United Nations: Sixtieth Anniversary', 19 Spanish Yearbook of International Law 2015, 101. Pons Rafols proposes three periods of analysis in his excellent account of Spain in the UN, as he distinguishes between the period of transition to democracy and the democratic era. While his approach is accurate, a two-period approach is sufficient for our explanation.
27. Ibid, 103.
28. There is currently much debate in Spain about the effects of the decisions of UN bodies. See Cristina Izquierdo Sans, 'Los Efectos de Las Decisiones de Los Comités de Derechos Humanos Resolviendo Comunicaciones Individuales. El Caso de España' in Cristina Izquierdo Sans and María García Casas (eds), *Litigación internacional para la defensa de los derechos humanos* (Colex 2022) 203; Eduardo Jiménez, 'A Commentary on the Supreme Court's Judgment of 17 July 2018 (Sts 1263/2018) and its Supposed Impact for a Legally Binding Value of the Decisions Adopted by the Committee on the Elimination of Discrimination Against Women (Cedaw)', 23 Spanish Yearbook of International Law 2019, 129; Jorge Cardona, 'The Legal Value of the Views and Interim Measures Adopted by United Nations Treaty Bodies (A Response to the Opinions of E. Jimenez Pineda, C. Jiménez Sánchez and B. Vázquez Rodríguez)', 23 Spanish Yearbook of International Law 2019, 146; Concepción Escobar Hernández, 'Sobre la problemática determinación de los efectos jurídicos internos de los «dictámenes» adoptados por Comités de Derechos Humanos. Algunas Reflexiones a la luz de la STS 1263/2018, de 17 de Julio', 71 Revista Española de Derecho Internacional 2019, 241.
29. Available at https://www.icj-cij.org/declarations/es accessed 7 November 2023.
30. *Barcelona Traction, Light and Power Company, Limited*, Judgment, ICJ Reports 1970, 3.
31. *Legality of Use of Force (Yugoslavia v Spain), Provisional Measures, Order of 2 June 1999*, ICJ Reports 1999, 761.
32. *Fisheries Jurisdiction (Spain v Canada)*, Jurisdiction of the Court, Judgment, ICJ Reports 1998, 432.
33. *Western Sahara, Advisory Opinion*, ICJ Reports 1975, 12.
34. See the discussion in 'El Gobierno español y la propuesta de autonomía para el Sáhara Occidental', 74 Revista española de derecho internacional 2022, 427, with articles by Javier A González Vega, José Antonio Yturriaga Barberán, Juan Soroeta Liceras, and Mariano Aznar Gómez.
35. *Accordance with international law of the unilateral declaration of independence in respect of Kosovo*, Advisory Opinion, ICJ Reports 2010, 403.
36. See 63 Revista Española de Derecho Internacional 2011, with articles by Paz Andrés Sáenz de Santa María, Jorge Cardona Llorenz, Concepción Escobar Hernández, Carlos Jiménez Piernas, Araceli Mangas Martín, and Carlos Espósito.
37. Spain has been elected as a non-permanent member of the UN Security Council in the following terms: 1969–1970; 1981–1982; 1993–1994; 2003–2004; 2015–2016. The data can be consulted in the Security Council Membership Dashboard https://www.un.org/security council/content/repertoire/research-tools/scmd accessed 7 November 2023.
38. As can be seen from the table prepared by the UN, Spain is one of the largest net contributors to the budget of the international organization: United Nations, Contributions Committee, 'Contributions received for 2023 for the United Nations Regular Budget' https://www.un.org/en/ga/contributions/honourroll.shtml accessed 7 November 2023.

39. Contributions to the UN Peacekeeping budget are calculated on the basis of contributions to the regular budget. The latest available data covers the period 2019–2021. They reveal that Spain is also one of the largest contributors to this budget. See United Nations General Assembly Resolution, 'Implementation of General Assembly resolutions 55/235 and 55/236', *A/73/350/Add.1*, 24 December 2018 <https://documents-dds-ny.un.org/doc/UNDOC/GEN/N18/461/91/PDF/N1846191.pdf?OpenElement>.
40. Angel Viñas, 'Spain and NATO: Internal Debate and External Challenges' in John Chipman (ed), *NATO's Southern Allies* (Routledge 2004) 152–206.
41. Anthony Gooch, 'A Surrealistic Referendum: Spain and NATO', 21(3) Government and Opposition 1986, 300–316.
42. Article 93 of the Spanish Constitution may be interpreted in that vein, as it requires a mere absolute majority of the *Cortes Generales* (Congress and Senate) to authorize the executive to conclude treaties through which powers derived from the Constitution shall be transferred to an international organization.
43. It has been a member of the International Monetary Fund (IMF) and the International Bank for Reconstruction and Development since 1958, the OECD since 1959, and signed up for the GATT in 1963.
44. Powell points out that the proof of this is that, due to the timid reform attempts of the first Arias Navarro government, the Parliamentary Assembly of the European Community adopted a report in 1976 linking Spain's future membership to the establishment of full and true democracy. Charles Powell, 'The Long Road to Europe: Spain and the European Community, 1957–1986', *Real Instituto Elcano Working Paper*, June 2015, 12 <https://www.realinstitutoelcano.org/wp-content/uploads/2021/11/dt9-2015-powell-long-road-europe-spain-european-community-1957-1986.pdf> accessed 7 November 2023.
45. Instrumento de Ratificación del Tratado hecho en Lisboa y Madrid el día 12 de junio de 1985, relativo a la adhesión del Reino de España y de la República Portuguesa a la Comunidad Económica Europea y a la Comunidad Europea de la Energía Atómica, BOE núm. 1, de 1 de enero de 1986 (Instrument of Ratification of the Treaty signed at Lisbon and Madrid on 12 June 1985, concerning the accession of the Kingdom of Spain and the Portuguese Republic to the European Economic Community and the European Atomic Energy Community, BOE No 1 of 1 January 1986) <https://www.boe.es/buscar/doc.php?id=BOE-A-1986-1> accessed 7 November 2023.
46. For example, the handbook by Araceli Mangas Martín and Diego J Liñán Nogueras, first published in 1996 and now in its 10th edition, was crucial in the study of European law. See Araceli Mangas Martín and Diego J Liñán Nogueras, *Instituciones y derecho de la Unión Europea* (10th edn, Tecnos 2020). Also the helpful commentary of the EU Treaties first published in 1996 by Javier Díez-Hochleitner and Carmen Martínez Capdevila: *Derecho de la Unión Europea: textos y comentarios* (McGraw-Hill 2001). For a recent handbook on EU law, see the excellent book by Daniel Sarmiento, *El Derecho de La Unión Europea* (4th edn, Marcial Pons 2022).
47. For instance, the Revista de Derecho Comunitario Europeo, which has published articles on European law since 1974.
48. The creation of the Spanish Society for the Study of European Law (AEDEUR) in 1982 was also instrumental in the study of European law. It was founded with the impetus of prestigious jurists such as Manuel Díez de Velasco, Eduardo García de Enterría, Joaquín Garrigues y Díaz Cañabate, Araceli Mangas Martín, Gil Carlos Rodríguez Iglesias, and Antonio Truyol y Serra. The Association, whose current president is Professor Javier

Díez-Hochleitner, has previously been presided over by Joaquín Garrigues y Díaz Cañabate, Eduardo García de Enterría, Gil Carlos Rodríguez Iglesias, and Pedro Cruz Villalón.

49. Celestino del Arenal (ed), *España y América Latina 200 años después de la independencia: valoración y perspectivas* (Marcial Pons 2009).
50. For example, Ley 25/2014, 27 November 2014 on the law of treaties and other international agreements; and Ley 16/2015, of 27 October 2015, on privileges and immunities of foreign States, international organizations with headquarters or offices in Spain, and international conferences and meetings. See Espósito (n 3).
51. Although there is still sometimes a certain caution and even mistrust of international law in the highest courts See, eg, judgment of the Supreme Court 3026/2021, 9 July 2021 (legal reasoning no 3: 'Diplomatic protection is the fruit of internationalist doctrine and, as with almost everything that comprises international law, it is entangled in a configuration that is not free of conceptual difficulties').
52. Máximo Langer, 'The Diplomacy of Universal Jurisdiction: The Political Branches and the Transnational Prosecution of International Crimes', 105 American Journal of International Law 2011, 1, 2–3.
53. Judgment of the Constitutional Court 237/2005, 26 September 2005.
54. Angel Sánchez Legido, 'El fin del modelo español de jurisdicción universal', 27 Revista Electrónica de Estudios Internacionales 2014 <http://www.reei.org/index.php/revista/num27/articulos/fin-modelo-espanol-jurisdiccion-universal> accessed 7 November 2023. See also Agora on Universal Jurisdiction after the entry into force of the Organic Law 1/2014, 13 March 2014, 18 Spanish Yearbook of International Law 223 (2013–2014) <https://www.sybil.es/sybil/issue/view/109 accessed 17 November 2023.
55. Organic Law 1/2014, 13 March 2014, amending Organic Law 6/1985 on the Judicial Power in relation to universal justice.
56. Judgment of the Supreme Court 296/2015, 6 May 2015.
57. Judgment of the Audiencia Nacional 4391/2019, 11 December 2019.
58. Judgment of the Supreme Court 998/2021, 9 July 2021.
59. Cameraman José Couso was killed on 8 April 2003 by US tank fire while standing on the balcony of his hotel in Baghdad during the Gulf War.
60. For commentary, see Elena Crespo Navarro, 'La sentencia de 9 de julio de 2021 del Tribunal Supremo en el caso Couso. Una interpretación errónea de la discrecionalidad estatal en el ejercicio de la protección diplomática', 74 Revista Española de Derecho Internacional 2022, 241.
61. Article 2.10 of the State Action and Foreign Service Act (Ley 2/2014, 25 March 2014) provides that one of the objectives of Spain's foreign policy is 'to assist and protect its citizens'.
62. See Antonio Remiro Brotóns, 'Gibraltar', 1 Cuadernos de Gibraltar – Gibraltar Reports 2015, 13, with a helpful bibliography. See also Alejandro Valle Gálvez and Inmaculada González García, *España y Gibraltar tras el Brexit: nuevo tratado y marco de relación con la Unión Europea* (Marcial Pons 2022).
63. Compare different views in the chapters by Alicia Gil Gil, 'Spain as an Example of Total Oblivion with Partial Rehabilitation', and Javier Chinchón Alvárez, 'The Challenges Posed to the Recent Investigation of Crimes Committed during the Spanish Civil War and Francoism',both in Jessica Almqvist and Carlos Espósito (eds), *The Role of Courts in Transitional Justice: Voices from Latin America and Spain* (Routledge 2012) 103 and 132, respectively.

64. See Xavier Pons Rafols, *Cataluña: Derecho a Decidir y Derecho Internacional* (Editorial Reus 2015); Robert Kolb and Tarcisio Gazzini, 'Catalonia Independence Claim: An Analysis from the Standpoint of International Law', 25 Spanish Yearbook of International Law 2021, 3; 'Declaración sobre la falta de fundamentación en el Derecho Internacional del referéndum de independencia en Cataluña', 70 Revista Española de Derecho Internacional 2018, 295.
65. See Oriol Casanovas y La Rosa, 'Setenta y cinco años de Derecho internacional público en la Revista Española de Derecho Internacional', 75 Revista Española de Derecho Internacional (forthcoming 2023).
66. AEPDIRI is currently chaired by Professor Ana Salinas de Frías, and its previous presidents were: Antonio Truyol y Serra, Manuel Díez de Velasco Vallejo, Juan Antonio Carrillo Salcedo, Antonio Marín López, Julio D González Campos, Elisa Pérez Vera, Roberto Mesa Garrido, Diego J Liñán Nogueras, Francisco Aldecoa Luzárraga, José Manuel Sobrino Heredia, Carlos Esplugues Mota, and Caterina García Segura.
67. There are well-recognized journals which are not associated with AEPDIRI. Worthy of mentioning is the Anuario Español de Derecho Internacional, which was founded in 1974. The current editors-in-chief are Eugenia López Jacoiste and María José Cervell Hortal.
68. REDI was founded by Fernando María Castiella, who served as the Minister of Foreign Affairs from 1957 to 1969, Antonio de Luna, the Legal Advisor to the Ministry of Foreign Affairs from 1957 to 1963, and Federico De Castro, a professor of civil law and judge at the ICJ from 1970 to 1979.
69. Except for the years during which Professor Mariano Aguilar Navarro served as the chief editor (1964–1968). For a brilliant assessment of the first four decades of the REDI, see Antonio Remiro Brotóns, 'El Discreto Encanto—y Desencanto—de La Revista Española de Derecho Internacional (1948–1978)' in *Estudios de Derecho Internacional. Libro Homenaje al Profesor A. Miaja de la Muela*, vol I (Tecnos 1979). See also Ignacio de la Rasilla del Moral, *In the Shadow of Vitoria: A History of International Law in Spain (1770–1953)* (Brill/Nijhoff 2017)who has made a great contribution to this field with his study of a period which was 'mysteriously neglected by both Spanish international law scholars and foreigners alike'.
70. The current editor-in-chief of the REDI is professor Joaquín Alcaide and since 1975 the editors-in-chief have included Antonio Truyol y Serra, Julio D González Campos, Luis I Sánchez Rodríguez, Paz Andrés Sáenz de Santa María, Alegría Borrás, Araceli Mangas Martín y Jorge Cardona Llorens. For a full list of members of the board and other organs of the REDI, see https://www.revista-redi.es/redi/about#organos accessed 7 November 2023.
71. The SYBIL (<https://www.sybil.es>) was founded under the leadership of its first editor-in-chief, professor Carlos Fernández Piernas. The current editor-in-chief is Professor Ángel Rodrigo Hernández, and his predecessors were Alejandro Rodríguez Carrión, Maribel Torres Cazorla, and Mariano J Aznar Gómez.
72. REEI's first editor-in-chief was Professor Carlos Espósito. The current editor-in-chief is Professor Guillermo Palao Moreno and his predecessors were Professors Luis Pérez-Prat Durbán, Andreu Olesti Rayo, and Pedro De Miguel Asencio. REEI is available at <htttps://www.reei.org> accessed 7 November 2023.
73. Including José Manuel Lacleta Múñoz (a former member of the International Law Commission), José Antonio Yturriaga Barberán, and Juan Antonio Yáñez Barnuevo.
74. The current legal adviser is Professor Santiago Ripol Carulla. His predecessors were Professors José Antonio Pastor Ridruejo, Concepción Escobar Hernández (a former member of the International Law Commission), José Martín Pérez de Nanclares, and Carlos Jiménez Piernas.

75. For an extensive assessment, see José Martín y Pérez de Nanclares, 'La Labor de Asesoramiento Jurídico Internacional al Gobierno: El Papel de La AJI' in *España y la práctica del Derecho internacional: LXXV Aniversario de la Asesoría Jurídica Internacional del MAEC* (Ministerio de Asuntos Exteriores 2014) 11. See also Aurelio Pérez Giralda, 'Advising Governments from the Inside: The Legal Adviser of the Ministry of Foreign Affairs' in Carlos Jiménez Piernas (ed), *The Legal Practice in International Law and European Community Law: A Spanish Perspective* (Martinus Nijhoff Publishers 2007) 461.
76. Particularly, the former Registrar and judge ad hoc of the ICJ, Mr Santiago Torres Bernárdez, who is also a renowned member of the *Institut de Droit International.*
77. Notably, Professor Antonio Remiro Brotóns, who has reflected on this matter in his chapter 'The International Legal Consultancy of Governments from the outside' in Jiménez Piernas (n 75).
78. Juan-Antonio Carrillo-Salcedo, 'Droit International et Souveraineté Des États Cours Général de Droit International Public. Cours Général de Droit International Public' in *Collected Courses of the Hague Academy of International Law* (Brill 1996) 257; José Antonio Pastor Ridruejo, 'Le Droit International à La Veille Du Vingt et Unième Siècle: Normes, Faits et Valeurs Cours Général de Droit International Public. Cours Général de Droit International Public' in *Collected Courses of the Hague Academy of International Law* (Brill 1998) 274. It is also worth mentioning two excellent general courses by Spanish academics in the Bancaja Euromediterranean Courses on International Law: Antorio Remiro Brotóns, 'Desvertebración del Derecho Internacional en la Sociedad Globalizada' in Jorge Cardona Llorens (ed), *Cursos euromediterráneos Bancaja de Derecho Internacional* (Tirant lo Blanch 2002) 45; Oriol Casanovas y La Rosa, 'Unidad y Pluralismo en Derecho Internacional Público' in Jorge Cardona Llorens (ed), *Cursos euromediterráneos Bancaja de Derecho Internacional* (Tirant lo Blanch 1999) 35.
79. For a general overview of Portugal's accession to the UN and its first sixty-five years of membership see J Freitas Ferraz and R Duque, *Portugal nas Nações Unidas: 65 Anos de História* (Instituto Diplomático e Tinta da China 2021).
80. See, for instance, Bruno Cardoso Reis, 'Portugal and the UN: A Rogue State Resisting the Norm of Decolonization (1956–1974)', 29 Portuguese Studies 2013, 251.
81. ibid.
82. See, among others, Miguel Galvão Teles and Paulo Canelas de Castro, 'Portugal and the Right of Peoples to Self-determination', 34 Archiv des Volkerrechts 1996, 3.
83. See, among others, Patrícia Galvão Teles, 'Autodeterminação em Timor-Leste: Dos Acordos de Nova Iorque à consulta popular de 30 de Agosto de 1999', 79/80 Boletim do Ministério da Justiça – Documentação e Direito Comparado 1999, 381.
84. Regarding this case, see Inocêncio Galvão Telles, 'Direito de passagem por território indiano', Themis – Edição especial 2004.
85. *Case concerning Right of Passage over Indian Territory* (Merits), Judgement, ICJ Reports 1960, 6.
86. *East Timor (Portugal v Australia)*, Judgment, ICJ Reports 1995, 90. cf, among others, Miguel Galvão Teles, 'Timor Leste' in *Dicionário Jurídico da Administração Pública — 2.º Suplemento*, Lisboa, Gráfica do Areeiro Lda., 2001, 583; and Patrícia Galvão Teles, 'Timor e o direito internacional' in *Tributo a Miguel Galvão Teles por ocasião dos 15 anos da independência de Timor-Leste* (IMGT 2017) 43. See also Carlos Espósito, 'El Asunto Timor Oriental Ante La Corte Internacional de Justicia', 12 Anuario Español de Derecho Internacional 2018, 617.
87. Available at <https://www.icj-cij.org/declarations/pt> accessed 7 November 2023.

88. Legality of Use of Force (*Serbia and Montenegro v Portugal*), Preliminary Objections, Judgment, ICJ Reports 2004, 1160. On this case, see Luís Serradas Tavares and Patrícia Galvão Teles, 'Alice no País das Maravilhas ou breve história de um processo no Tribunal Internacional de Justiça: Sérvia e Montengro c. Portugal e outros Membros da NATO sobre a legalidade do Uso da Força', 8 Negócios Estrangeiros 2005, 31.
89. cf Patrícia Galvão Teles, 'Portugal e o Tribunal Internacional de Justiça' (2004) Janus OnLine <https://www.janusonline.pt/arquivo/2004/2004_3_2_2.html>.
90. Allegations of Genocide under the Convention on the Prevention and Punishment of the Crime of Genocide (*Ukraine v Russian Federation*: 32 States intervening).
91. On this issue see Patrícia Galvão Teles, 'Portugal, a ONU e o Direito Internacional: adesão a convenções, pactos e protocolos' in Jose de Freitas Ferraz and Raquel Duque (eds), *Portugal nas Nações Unidas: 65 Anos de História* (Instituto Diplomático e Tinta da China 2021) 137.
92. cf Patrícia Galvão Teles (ed), *A Convenção de Viena sobre Relações Diplomáticas de 1961 Comentada* (Instituto Diplomático/Ministério dos Negócios Estrangeiros 2020).
93. cf Ana H Marques et al (eds), *Portugal e os Direitos Humanos nas Nações Unidas* (Instituto Diplomático/Ministério dos Negócios Estrangeiros 2017).
94. On the 'System of protection of human rights at the United Nations', see the text from the author of this contribution relating to Portugal in ibid.
95. See Paula Escarameia, 'Portugal e o Tribunal Penal Internacional' (2004) Janus OnLine <https://repositorio.ual.pt/handle/11144/1579>.
96. See, among others, Fausto Quadros, Paulo Otero, and Jorge Bacelar Gouveia, *Portugal e Direito do Mar* (Ministério dos Negócios Estrangeiros 2004); Tiago Pitta e Cunha and Nuno Marques Antunes, 'Portugal e os oceanos: importância estratégica e definição especial' (2004) Janus OnLine; and Maria Eduarda Gonçalves, 'Portugal e a Convenção das Nações Unidas sobre o Direito do Mar' (2008) Janus OnLine.
97. See Marta Chantal Ribeiro et al, 'O direito português do mar: perspetivas para o século XXI', Revista Eletrónica de Direito 2019 <https://repositorio-aberto.up.pt/bitstream/10216/123355/2/322743.pdf>; and Vasco Becker-Weinberg, 'Marine Spatial Planning and Conservation and Sustainable Use of Marine Biological Diversity in Areas Beyond National Jurisdiction' in André Paiva Toledo and Virginie JM Tassin (eds), *Biodiversity Beyond National Jurisdiction: The Challenges of the next implementing agreement of UNCLOS* (D'Plácido 2018) 193–217.
98. See, among others, Paulo Canelas de Castro, 'Portugal's World Outlook in the Constitution of 1976', 71 Boletim da Faculdade de Direito da Universidade de Coimbra 1995, 469.
99. See, among others, Francisco Ferreira de Almeida, 'Portugal' in Dinah Shelton (ed), *International Law and Domestic Legal Systems: Incorporation, Transformation, and Persuasion* (OUP 2011) <https://www.parlamento.pt/sites/EN/Parliament/Documents/Constitution7th.pdf>.
100. See SusanaVaz Patto, João Madureira, and Mateus Kowalski (eds), *A Participação de Portugal no Conselho de Segurança* (Instituto Diplomático 2015).
101. For Portugal's participation in the 6th Committee of the General Assembly in recent years, see *Anuário de Direito Internacional*, published by the Portuguese Ministry of Foreign Affairs.
102. Including the co-author, who is honoured to be the second Portuguese woman in the International Law Commission, Co-Chair of the Study Group on Sea-Level Rise in relation to International Law, the first female Chair of the Drafting Committee and Chair of the second part of the 74th Session of the ILC.

CHAPTER 36

SWITZERLAND

HELEN KELLER, NICOLE LÜTHI, AND VIOLETTA SEFKOW-WERNER

1. Introduction

The role of international law in Switzerland illustrates well the country's balancing act between its image as a global diplomatic hub and proud defender of national sovereignty and particularity. Switzerland is home to a multitude of international organizations and institutions and takes an active role in strengthening international law and cooperation. Its Constitution is drafted and applied in a way as to effectively integrate public international law into the domestic legal order (*Völkerrechtsfreundlichkeit* of the Swiss Constitution).[1] Switzerland's legal system follows the monistic model, thus public international law is automatically and directly part of Swiss law[2] and relevant for its interpretation.[3] While not part of the European Union (EU),[4] Switzerland is a strong advocate of human rights and the rule of law as a loyal member of the Council of Europe (CoE).[5] Both on the legislative[6] and judicial[7] levels, it has a well-established practice of giving special weight to the European Convention on Human Rights (ECHR) and the European Court of Human Rights (ECtHR) jurisprudence. Moreover, the Strasbourg Court's case law shows that Switzerland does not struggle with systematic human rights deficiencies. Judgments by the ECtHR that do find a human rights violation by Switzerland[8] are taken seriously and are reliably complied with. Overall, Switzerland displays a positive track record of safeguarding human rights within its domestic legal order and blends in well with Europe's efforts for peace, security, and the rule of law.

One of the core aspects, however, that defines Switzerland's place in the international order is its long-standing tradition of neutrality. Swiss neutrality has become particularly visible in the context of the international reaction to the 2022 Ukraine war. However, on closer inspection, its complex historical, political, and legal dimensions unfold, which is why this chapter seeks to explore Switzerland's relationship with international law with a special focus on Swiss neutrality as a unique feature of Switzerland's role within Europe.

Swiss neutrality is held in high esteem by the Swiss people. According to a security study conducted by the Swiss Federal Institute of Technology *(Eidgenössische Technische Hochschule Zürich*, ETH) in the beginning of 2022, 97 per cent of the population are in favour of maintaining neutrality. Even younger generations (18–30 year-olds) who did not experience World War II or the Cold War support neutrality.[9] In surveys on identity features, neutrality takes the top position, placing even higher than direct democracy.[10] However, current events such as the Russian invasion of Ukraine in 2022 have raised the question of whether Swiss neutrality should be redefined or reshaped. A follow-up survey in mid-2022 shows that the Swiss population has rarely before questioned and discussed neutrality as critically as in the context of this event. Although a clear majority (89 per cent) is still in favour of maintaining neutrality, this widespread view has dropped by 8 per cent within only six months.[11]

This chapter discusses the Swiss practice of neutrality in light of international law. To understand the role of neutrality in Switzerland, it first explains the concept of neutrality (Section 2) and then illustrates its evolution throughout history (Section 3). The following section turns to the transformation of the meaning of neutrality in the current framework of international law and international relations (Section 4). After addressing the challenges and opportunities of neutrality (Section 5), the chapter summarizes the most important points and provides an outlook on potential future issues in neutrality practice (Section 6).

2. The Concept of Neutrality

As a permanently neutral State, Switzerland differentiates between neutrality law and neutrality policy. Neutrality law refers to a particular status, defined by international law, of a State not party to an armed conflict.[12] In essence, it obliges the neutral State to refrain from supporting the parties to an international armed conflict through military means; in return, it retains the right to remain unaffected by the conflict.[13] Following that, a neutral State cannot join military alliances (such as the North Atlantic Treaty Organization (NATO)), since membership would entail an obligation to provide military assistance in case of an attack on another member.[14] Neutrality law developed through custom and was later codified to a large extent in the 1907 Hague Conventions,[15] which remain the legal basis of neutrality law until today.[16] The Hague Conventions regulate the rights and obligations of neutral States. They entail the right to remain apart from and not to be adversely affected by the conflict.[17] Another core aspect is the duty of non-participation, which requires the neutral State to abstain from military involvement in an armed conflict between States. Moreover, the neutral State must not support any party to the conflict and is prohibited from allowing one party to the conflict to use its resources (such as troops, arms and munition, war material) and territory against the will of the opponent.[18] Finally, neutrality imposes a duty of impartiality in the sense of a prohibition of discrimination in the treatment of the belligerents, while permitting the continuation of existing commercial relations (*courant normal*).[19] The Hague Conventions do not prescribe economic neutrality.[20] In Switzerland, the domestic legal framework for the implementation of economic sanctions is laid out in the Swiss Embargo Act.[21] The Embargo Act stipulates in its Article 1 that Switzerland may—subject to its discretion—enforce sanctions imposed by the United Nations (UN), the Organization for Security and Co-operation in Europe or Switzerland's major trade partners and that serve compliance with public international law, particularly human rights. Furthermore, neutrality law is domestically flanked by the Swiss War Material Act[22] of 1972, which regulates the manufacture and transfer of war material, for example by subjecting imports and exports to authorization by the Swiss Confederation.

The scope of this legal framework shows that neutrality law in the strict sense only applies during an international armed conflict and to actions directly related to warfare. It therefore only determines the conduct of States in a specific and narrow context. Permanent neutrality, as chosen by Switzerland, goes beyond this setting and reflects a State's general approach in defining its role within the international community that may be deployed as an instrument to fulfil central purposes of international law, namely peaceful relations between States and stability. A permanently neutral State commits itself to remaining neutral in any future war. Neither the Hague Conventions nor any other international treaties address the concept of permanent neutrality.[23] Consequently, the precise legal obligations in peacetime remain vague and need to be supplemented by a neutrality policy, which is left to the State's discretion.[24]

The Federal Council defines neutrality policy as all measures taken by a State to ensure the credibility and effectiveness of its neutrality during times of conflict.[25] While neutrality law has remained mostly unchanged since its codification in 1907, neutrality policy has undergone various adaptations, shifts, and transformations. As shown by its historical development, which will be mapped out in the following, neutrality policy is a flexible concept that can take various forms.

3. Evolution of Swiss Neutrality

The precise origins of Swiss neutrality are disputed. Older literature claims that Swiss neutrality dates to 1515, after the defeat of the Confederates at the battle of Marignano.[26] Some allege that this defeat prevented the Swiss Confederates from pursuing their policy of expansion, whereupon they took refuge in neutrality. However, there is evidence of further attempts at expansion after the Marignano battle.[27] Others claim that neutrality originated in 1647, when the *Tagsatzung* declared that the Swiss Confederation would remain neutral and not interfere in battles in the context of the Thirty Years' War (1618–1648).[28] According to more recent historiography, Swiss neutrality did not emerge until the 19th century.[29] In any event, neutrality remained an internal concept until then, primarily aimed at securing the inner coherence ('common denominator') and security of the Swiss Confederation.

It is generally agreed that Switzerland's neutrality was first recognized under international law at the Congress of Vienna in 1815.[30] This Congress established a new and lasting peace order in Europe. Because Switzerland's neutrality was in the interest of all European States, the Congress of Vienna and the Treaty of Paris granted Switzerland formal and legally binding recognition of its perpetual neutrality. The rationale behind this was to use Switzerland as a buffer zone between France and Austria with the aim to balance and stabilize Europe,[31] revealing the pacifying potential of neutrality as an instrument of international law and politics. Hence, at that time, neutrality was a well-established component of international relations because it provided States with an alternative to war, which was considered a legitimate means of conducting politics. The Treaty of Paris conferred an external dimension on Swiss neutrality and cemented the country's neutral position within the international community.[32] Based on this, the evolution of Swiss neutrality over the last 200 years can be roughly divided into the following three phases.

3.1 Swiss practice of neutrality from 1815 to 1945

In the first Federal Constitution of 1848, neutrality was intentionally not mentioned among the objectives of the Confederation. The political establishment understood neutrality as a means to an end and as a political instrument that seemed appropriate at the time to secure Switzerland's independence.[33] Thus, the Confederates left open the option to abandon neutrality if it no longer served Switzerland's sovereignty. However, to strengthen the policy of neutral independence, the Constitution prohibited the cantons from forming alliances with other countries.[34] The Constitution also prescribed universal military service for men. Thus, Swiss neutrality evolved into armed neutrality, so that its neutral status could be secured and therefore appear credible.[35] Switzerland still understands neutrality as an obligation to defend its territory by means of adequately armed forces.[36] By contrast, other neutral States, such as Costa Rica, do not have an army.[37] The question of whether a neutral State needs military forces to defend its neutrality is less a question of law than of credibility, which is an essential element of neutrality policy.[38]

Throughout the second half of the 19th century, and against the background of devastating wars across Europe, Switzerland developed a humanitarian focus in its foreign policy and used its neutrality to promote international peace and cooperation, thus dedicating itself to key features of international law. The establishment of important international organizations, such as the International Committee of the Red Cross (1863), the adoption of the First Geneva Convention (1864), and the exercise of protective power mandates for many countries illustrate that development alongside an increase in Swiss diplomatic services.[39] This period marked a time in which Switzerland was actively involved with the international community. In 1907, Switzerland adopted the Hague Conventions on the rights and obligations of neutral powers. Today's neutrality law is still based on these Conventions, supplemented by customary international law.[40]

Swiss neutrality was put to the test in both world wars. Due to the increasing use of economic warfare and the nature of these conflicts, neutrality was called into question as a concept and could not always be maintained. Switzerland officially upheld its neutrality, and its territorial integrity was principally respected in both wars. Neutrality during World War I was especially important for Switzerland's internal stability since the sympathies of many German-speaking Swiss were directed towards Germany at the beginning of the war, while most French-speaking Swiss sympathized with France.[41] In World War II, not all measures taken by the federal authorities complied with the imperatives of a neutral State. Practices such as exporting weapons to Germany with generous loans or receiving gold from the German Reichsbank were tricky in view of Switzerland's neutral status.[42] Consequently, Switzerland faced strong pressure and criticism from the Allies. In addition, there were border closures which, although permitted under neutrality law, raised questions about morality since neutrality is traditionally associated with and legitimized by the principle of humanitarianism.[43] The fact that Switzerland was spared in both world wars, especially in the second, led the Swiss people to glorify neutrality. They were convinced that neutrality was the only policy that could guarantee Switzerland's independence and safety.[44]

Switzerland placed high hopes in the notion of a collective security system when it joined the League of Nations in 1920.[45] The Treaty of Versailles recognized Switzerland's neutrality and simultaneously allowed for membership in the League of Nations, as both were considered to serve the same goal, that is, securing peace. The League of Nations confirmed the recognition of Swiss neutrality in the 1920 London Declaration.[46] To uphold neutrality, Switzerland was exempt from participating in military but not in economic sanctions.[47] This was understood as 'differential neutrality'[48] and marked a turning point in the practice of Swiss neutrality.

The League of Nations and the 1928 Kellogg-Briand Pact were the first, albeit unsuccessful, attempts to create a system of collective security and strengthen the notion of solidarity in the international community. Due to the lack of universal application and legal gaps in its legal regime, the League of Nations could not achieve its goals, and a more conservative understanding of neutrality ('integral neutrality') experienced a revival at the beginning of the 1930s.[49]

3.2 Swiss practice of neutrality post-World War II

The idea of a system of collective security was revisited in 1945 with the establishment of the UN. While other neutral States, such as Austria, Sweden, and Finland (Wrange & Kjeldgaard-Pedersen, this volume), joined the UN rather soon after its establishment, Switzerland remained sceptical and insisted that its permanent neutrality was not compatible with UN membership.[50] By this time, Switzerland had elevated neutrality to an overarching state doctrine pursuant to which every foreign policy measure was placed under reserve. This attitude was expressed in the *Bindschedler* doctrine of 1954,[51] which was drawn up by the Federal Department of Foreign Affairs under Professor Rudolf Bindschedler. Although never endorsed by the responsible authorities, it shaped the Swiss concept of neutrality.[52] According to this doctrine, neutrality meant that Switzerland should not participate in international conferences or join political or military alliances. On this understanding, neutrality was no longer a means to an end, that is, to assure Swiss independence, but a goal in itself.[53] This made it difficult for Switzerland to find its place in the European integration process, showing the distinct role of Switzerland within Europe in a very visible way.[54] However, it tried to uphold the maxims of neutrality and solidarity. As a result, Switzerland was entrusted with several international mandates, such as representing the United States' interests in Cuba from 1961 and in Iran from 1979.[55]

Due to Switzerland's actions during World War II, namely its continuing economic ties with Nazi Germany while officially proclaiming to be neutral, neutrality was perceived rather critically in the international arena during the post-war period. It was not until the 1950s that Swiss neutrality regained international recognition and legitimacy.[56] In a polarized world, and given the resulting blockages in the UN Security Council (UNSC), the UN's collective security system failed to fulfil its purpose. The increased demand for good offices in the Cold War provided neutral States with the opportunity to fill this gap and deploy neutrality to foster peace and dialogue between States, thereby strengthening the idea of international law in a unique way.[57] Consequently, Switzerland took on a prominent role as a mediator and in providing 'good offices'. For example, along with Sweden, it supervised peace agreement processes and actively participated in the 1953 armistice agreement in Korea.[58] As an appointed member of the Neutral Nations Repatriation Commission as well as the Neutral Nations Supervisory Commission, Switzerland took on a role as a 'Western Neutral' alongside Sweden and in contrast to the 'Eastern Neutrals', Poland and Czechoslovakia.[59] Switzerland did not always strictly adhere to its concept of neutrality during the Cold War. While Switzerland officially remained neutral and advocated diplomacy, in reality, it identified more strongly with Western than with Eastern values. As a result of its sympathies with the West, Switzerland gave in to pressure from the United States in 1951 and participated in embargo measures against communist States.[60]

The Crypto affair illustrates Switzerland's controversial role in the Cold War. During the Cold War, the Swiss company Crypto AG produced encryption machines. From 1970, the US Central Intelligence Agency (CIA) and the German Federal Intelligence Agency (BND) owned the company. Crypto AG sold its encryption devices for the transmission of sensitive—and particularly military—data to 130 States, including Iraq, Iran, Libya, Argentina, and Chile. The devices were intentionally manipulated so that the CIA and BND had access to this data.[61] Whether the Swiss government already had knowledge of this during the Cold War, and whether it was able to intercept messages during this time period, has not been fully established. Officially,

Switzerland has been aware of the Crypto affair since 1993[62] and able to read encrypted messages since 2002.[63] However, there were earlier indications that Crypto AG was cooperating with foreign intelligence agencies.[64] If this were the case, there are strong arguments in favour of a violation of neutrality law. In any event, the Crypto affair marks a serious rupture of neutrality policy and severely undermined the credibility of Swiss neutrality.[65]

Another controversial chapter in the evolution of Swiss neutrality is Switzerland's cooperation with the apartheid regime in South Africa. Switzerland maintained strong economic relations with South Africa after the end of World War II. While South Africa relied on foreign investment to finance its development, Swiss banks were particularly interested in the gold found in South African mines. Finally, in 1963, increasing international pressure forced Switzerland to ban the import of war material into South Africa under the apartheid regime. However, the ban did not include war material produced under licence abroad and could therefore be easily circumvented. This rather reserved policy allowed economic activities to be continued and expanded between the two countries.[66] The apartheid regime became gradually isolated and, in 1985/86, the UN decided to impose strict economic sanctions. Although Switzerland publicly condemned the system of apartheid at several UN human rights conferences,[67] it refrained from adopting the sanctions and even increased its investments in South Africa. As a result, Switzerland again faced severe criticism at the international level. Therefore, at the beginning of 1974, the Federal Council decided to cap capital exports to South Africa.[68] However, the cap contained several exceptions and loopholes, and was by no means complete.[69] Initially, the Federal Council justified this reservation to its South Africa policy by claiming that participating in sanctions against South Africa would be incompatible with its neutrality policy. Then, at the end of the 1980s, the Federal Council allowed arguments concerning the universality of sanctions to prevail over the neutrality argument. This led to an incongruous combination of the two concepts.[70] Switzerland's actions during apartheid in South Africa show that the Federal Council only took measures (albeit insufficient) as a result of intense international pressure.[71] These instances led to Swiss neutrality losing integrity during the Cold War. The fact that the Swiss government endeavored to define its neutrality policy vaguely in order to provide as little room as possible for criticisms concerning its (in)consistency only diminished its credibility.[72]

With regard to participation in economic sanctions, the Federal Council made a different choice in the 1990 Gulf War, which marked a turning point in Switzerland's neutrality policy. In response to Iraq's annexation of Kuwait on 2 August 1990, the UN imposed a comprehensive sanctions regime, which Switzerland followed.[73] For the first time since World War II, Switzerland fully adopted an economic sanctions regime, and held this to be compatible with neutrality. Since then, Switzerland has opted for an autonomous application of UNSC resolutions regarding non-military sanctions as well as sanctions independent of a UN resolution, notably those by the EU.[74] Switzerland hence returned to a more active neutrality policy after the Cold War.[75]

3.3 Swiss practice of neutrality in light of the 1993 Neutrality Report

The 1993 Neutrality Report was the first written document by the Swiss government dedicated to outlining the concept of neutrality within the context of Swiss foreign policy. It reinterprets neutrality to be less restrictive and sets out neutrality's core content under international law, allowing for participation in UN sanctions (including authorized military measures) and non-UN economic sanctions, meaning economic sanctions imposed by the EU, regional organizations or groups of States.[76] As for the latter, the 1993 Neutrality Report states the following:

> [T]he Federal Council is principally willing to join in non-UN economic sanctions as well. After carefully assessing the situation, it will decide on a case-by-case basis whether abstention or participation is in Switzerland's interest and which course will most effectively serve to re-establish a situation which conforms with international law. The Federal Council will also take into account the security policy risks participation would bring, such as Switzerland being drawn into a military conflict.[77]

Additionally, the Report addressed how neutrality could be preserved even if Switzerland were to join the EU. A year before the report was released, the Federal Council had stated that it was primarily up to the neutral State itself to decide whether EU membership was compatible with the status of neutrality or not.[78] In its 1993 Report, Switzerland considered maintaining neutrality in case of EU membership to be legally possible since membership would not preclude neutrality in future armed conflicts.[79]

In 1996, Switzerland agreed to cooperate with NATO within the Partnership for Peace (PfP). Switzerland considers the PfP an instrument for cooperating with NATO on security policy on a selective basis. Such cooperation is voluntary and determined by the respective partner State itself.[80] While the PfP is compatible with neutrality law because it does not entail any obligation to provide military assistance, it raises questions in the context of neutrality policy. For this reason, the Federal Council explicitly stated that Switzerland is and will remain neutral throughout its participation in the PfP.[81] Additionally, the Federal Council has already emphasized in several statements that NATO membership is not an option for Switzerland since neutral States must not favour any warring party in an international armed conflict.[82]

During the Kosovo conflict in 1998/99, the Federal Council was confronted with a difficult decision regarding Swiss neutrality practice. NATO's air strikes against Yugoslavia were carried out without authorization by the UN. Switzerland, relying on its neutrality, decided not to authorize NATO overflights for combat missions, but only for humanitarian purposes. In this regard, one may wonder whether this distinction is actually feasible in practice. In addition, Switzerland participated in the UN arms embargo and most of the EU sanctions against Yugoslavia. This participation in EU sanctions marked the first time that Switzerland imposed economic sanctions absent a decision by the UNSC.[83] With regard to the relations between Kosovo and Switzerland, it is also noteworthy that Switzerland recognized Kosovo as an independent State only ten days after its declaration of independence was made.[84] In terms of neutrality law, the recognition of Kosovo did not cause any problems. Nonetheless, in terms of neutrality policy, the recognition was controversial because it was considered premature by some.[85] With its decision, the Federal Council made use of the flexibility it had chosen in the 1993 Neutrality Report. This shows that Switzerland's neutrality did not prevent it from taking a stand within the international community.[86]

The possibility of UN membership also raised questions in terms of Swiss neutrality. After several unsuccessful votes, a majority of Swiss citizens (55 per cent) voted in favour of Switzerland joining the UN in 2002.[87] In its application for membership, the Federal Council insisted that Switzerland would maintain its neutrality as a UN member State. International law leaves open the question of whether UN membership and neutrality are compatible. The Hague Conventions of 1907 stem from a time when there was no system of collective security.[88] However, like the UN itself, Switzerland and all other neutral States consider UN membership to be in line with neutrality (see Wrange and Kjeldgaard-Pedersen, this volume).[89] Twenty years after Swiss accession to the UN, the limits of Switzerland's neutrality policy have been tested in a new way. For the first time ever, the UN General Assembly (UNGA) elected Switzerland to the UNSC. Switzerland has assumed its role as a non-permanent member in 2023/2024.[90] The Federal Council already stated in 2015 that this undertaking is compatible with neutrality.[91]

As a UN member, Switzerland continued to invoke its neutrality. Even before the Iraq conflict escalated in 2003, the Federal Council decided not to allow US aircraft to fly over Swiss territory for military purposes. Overflights for medical and humanitarian purposes were declared permissible. This decision was maintained throughout the conflict. Additionally, the Federal Council prohibited the Confederation from supplying war materials to the States involved in the conflict.[92] When Russia annexed the Crimean peninsula in 2014, the Federal Council decided to take measures to ensure that the sanctions imposed by the EU could not be circumvented on Swiss territory. However, Switzerland did not adopt the sanctions themselves.[93]

At the end of February 2022, Russia attacked Ukraine, which was universally characterized as an act of aggression.[94] After brief hesitation, the Federal Council adopted the EU sanctions against Russia.[95] The Federal Council explicitly stated that Switzerland's neutrality would remain intact despite the implementation of EU sanctions and that this decision does not imply that EU sanctions will be automatically adopted in the future.[96] In a later decision, the Federal Council vetoed the planned delivery of Swiss ammunition from Germany to Ukraine, invoking neutrality law.[97] Switzerland received heavy criticism for this decision from Germany and the EU.[98] The Federal Council's decisions in the Ukraine conflict revived the debate on neutrality. While right-wing politicians predicted the end of neutrality given the adoption of EU sanctions,[99] others saw this situation as an opportunity to rethink or reshape Swiss neutrality.[100] In light of these circumstances, the Federal Council ordered the drafting of a new neutrality report. In the preliminary draft, the concept of 'cooperative neutrality' is outlined as a moderate development of the one in the 1993 Report. Among other aspects, this concept aims to expand the scope for action in foreign policy and foresees closer cooperation with other States that share democratic values as well as the EU and NATO.[101]

Overall, Switzerland's practice of neutrality has changed since it was first recognized under international law in 1815. Although neutrality law has not undergone changes since that time, neutrality policy continues to be adapted to political circumstances and Switzerland's interests. With the implementation of a ban on the use of force in international law and the establishment of international organizations such as the UN, NATO, and EU, the understanding of neutrality has further changed.[102] The next section of this chapter will turn to this transformation of the meaning of neutrality in the framework of international law and international relations.

4. The Changing Meaning of Neutrality

4.1 Ambivalence of Swiss neutrality

The above historical account shows that Switzerland has applied neutrality in various ways. The development of its practice on neutrality has neither been linear, nor free of ruptures. In the decades following the end of the Cold War, Switzerland has opened up to the international community and indicated that it considers itself part of that community, although its exact role remains to be defined.

The 1990 Gulf War was a turning point for Swiss neutrality. For the first time, Switzerland participated in comprehensive economic sanctions even beyond those adopted by the UN. The 1993 Neutrality Report then codified the idea that Switzerland's foreign policy will be guided by the majority opinion of the international community. In 1999, Switzerland's recognition of Kosovo shortly after its declaration of independence appears to have been driven by the desire for universal action with other European States[103] despite ongoing controversies about Kosovo's statehood.[104] Likewise, the 2002 Swiss Embargo Act entails the notion of universal action as a yardstick for Switzerland's foreign policy. It enables the Swiss government to join economic sanctions and cites in particular those that have been adopted by the UN, the EU or other important economic trade partners and that serve compliance with international law.[105]

Switzerland's reaction to the Russian invasion of Ukraine in 2022 represents both a continuity and a singularity in its application of neutrality. Switzerland fully participated in the EU sanctions regime against Russia. As in the case of the Iraq-Kuwait conflict or Kosovo,[106] Switzerland grounded its decision on another State's brute violation of elementary norms of international law and, albeit less explicitly, the unified response by Western States. Using this momentum, Federal Councillor and head of the Swiss Federal Department of Foreign Affairs *Ignazio Cassis* introduced the notion of 'cooperative neutrality'.[107] However, the impact of this new term should not be overestimated. It confirms what had already been laid out in the 1993 Neutrality Report: Switzerland is embedded in an interdependent system of peace and security that requires multilateral efforts.[108] The novelty lies in the fact that increasing polarization between Western democratic States and authoritarian regimes, and obvious grave breaches of fundamental norms of international law, make it difficult for Switzerland to maintain good relationships with all major powers. Switzerland was seemingly forced to realize that, politically, it could no longer afford to take the middle ground between Russia and the EU, as this would alienate Western partners. Its former practice of only preventing the circumvention of sanctions would likely have been interpreted as support for Russia and would have carried the risk of sparking negative backlash against Switzerland itself.

Neutrality has always been an integral part of Swiss foreign policy. Throughout history, Switzerland has officially maintained and insisted on its neutral status. While the legal core of neutrality, that is, non-involvement in any military action during an ongoing international armed conflict, has been upheld fairly consistently, Swiss practice with regards to economic sanctions is shaped by reluctance and contradiction. Whenever Switzerland has joined economic sanctions, it has typically done so under increasing political pressure by other States. This was the case, for instance, during World War I and World War II, the 1990 Gulf War, the Cold War, and the 2022 Ukraine war. In other instances, such as its collaboration with the South African apartheid regime or in the 2014 Crimea crisis, Switzerland, relying on neutrality, has refused to take part in sanctions and confined its contribution to preventing the circumvention of sanctions. Considering that both instances involved severe and clear violations of international law and that—at least in the latter case—the (European) international community was unified in its assessment of the situation, it is difficult to identify a clear-cut course in Switzerland's neutrality policy.

4.2 Neutrality in the UN Charter system

4.2.1 *Normative perspective*

From a normative perspective, the UN Charter system leaves little to no room for neutrality. One of the cornerstones of the UN Charter is its general ban of the use of force (Article 2(4) UN Charter) with only two expressly stipulated exceptions, namely measures ordered by the UNSC under Chapter VII and self-defence under Article 51 UN Charter. The Charter thereby establishes two categories of force, namely lawful and unlawful force, and predefines a State's position when another State resorts to force.[109] Moreover, there is a substantive hierarchy in place as the prohibition of force is considered a *ius cogens* norm[110] with *erga omnes* effect, and thus calls for discriminatory conduct against the perpetrator, which appears impossible to reconcile with the core principles of neutrality.[111]

In light of the UN Charter's aim of maintaining peace, the fact that it outlaws war, and its establishment of a collective security system, some consider the UN Charter and the legal system it stands for as part of a development towards a global public order with fundamental norms that require collective protection (see Wiener, this volume).[112] In particular with regard to peremptory norms, one can argue that the obligations stemming from these rules supersede neutrality law.[113] This view strengthens the idea of a European unification process, which seems to exclude national extra paths such as neutrality. To what extent this holds true will be shown further below.

Looking at the notion of collective responsibility entailed in the UN Charter system and its emphasis on unified and joint action against a peace breaker also raises the question of how a neutral position fits into this conception. Without UN membership, neutral States would not generally[114] be obliged to respond to another State's violation of international law or to participate in UN sanctions.[115] Some, however, rely on a general duty of cooperation and suggest that States are thereby obliged not to frustrate or decisively impede sanctions concerning evident, grave violations of international law.[116] This duty is also enshrined in Article 2(5) UN Charter.[117] The obligations under Article 2(5) UN Charter, in any case, apply to Chapter VII measures[118] and do not impose any further obligations than those resulting from a UNSC resolution.[119] Confined to that scope of application, this precludes neutrality.[120]

Finally, neutrality law and collective security differ in their approach towards securing peace: The former is indifferent as to whether an act of force is justified, individual and defensive. The latter is value-based, collective and action-oriented.[121] This shows that, also from a conceptual point of view, neutrality and the UN Charter system are difficult to reconcile.[122]

4.2.2 *Legal perspective*

From a legal perspective, the UN Charter narrows the scope of application of neutrality law. Neutrality law does not apply to measures ordered by the UNSC acting under Chapter VII. For other lawful acts of force, in particular self-defence cases, recourse to neutrality law is controversial.

4.2.2.1 *Measures under Chapter VII of the UN Charter*

By becoming a member of the UN, Switzerland committed itself, according to Article 25 UN Charter, to implement UNSC decisions under Chapter VII. Pursuant to Article 103 UN Charter, it cannot invoke neutrality law in such cases.[123] Non-military measures ordered by the UNSC must be carried out by member States according to Articles 25, 48, and 2(5) UN Charter. As these measures call for discriminatory treatment, they entail a deviation from impartiality under neutrality law.[124] With regards to military measures, active participation is not mandatory except for States that have concluded a special agreement under Article 43 UN Charter. For every other member State, Article 49 UN Charter imposes a general duty not to obstruct measures by the UNSC,[125] and Article 2(5) UN Charter provides the bottom-line of solidarity member States have to display.[126] Obligations such as the furnishing of troops, facilities, and transit rights thus generally only arise when there is an agreement under Article 43 UN Charter in place.[127] However, especially with regards to transit rights, there is some legal controversy as to whether they fall under Article 43 or Article 49 UN Charter.[128]

There is general agreement in legal scholarship that the UN Charter's provisions supersede or modify neutrality law to the effect that neutrality law does not apply to military action authorized or ordered by the UNSC under Chapter VII.[129] This corresponds to Austrian and Swiss State practice.[130] The underlying rationale is that UNSC military measures do not constitute an inter-state conflict but are legalized under the UN Charter; States accordingly act as enforcement agents of international law on behalf of the international community.[131]

Even as a non-member to the UN, Switzerland implemented economic sanctions adopted by the UNSC on many occasions,[132] and sometimes even took part in UN-authorized military operations by granting overflight and transit rights to foreign troops.[133] While, as a non-member, Switzerland could rely on political discretion in its decision to support UN measures,[134] since 2002, it is obliged to do so under Article 25 UN Charter. With regards to military operations, the extent of assistance owed is not defined precisely and depends on the individual circumstances of the case. Other neutral States, such as Austria, Ireland, or Sweden, participate in UN peace operations by providing troops or aircrafts. In Switzerland, the Military Act has, since 2000, stipulated that Swiss troops may participate in UN operations for peace enforcement as long as they do not engage in combat action.[135] With regards to transit and overflight rights for foreign troops that carry out military operations, Switzerland requires a UNSC mandate.[136] This shows that while committing itself to a seemingly universal legal order as reflected in the UN Charter, Switzerland has partially adhered to national specificities in an attempt to establish its own approach to implementing international law.

Thus, generally, Switzerland has taken a rather formal position and required a UNSC mandate when departing from its neutral position.[137] This is in conformity with the UN Charter's concept of collective security, which implies a joint responsibility of the international community to secure peace. Institutionally, this responsibility is bundled at the UNSC. It acts as the voice of the international community and has the power to provide an authoritative assessment on the lawfulness of forcible action (Article 39 UN Charter). The 2000 Neutrality Report, however, raised the question of whether Switzerland should apply neutrality law to situations where the international community acts in lieu of the UNSC in response to grave violations of fundamental norms of international law.[138] Such universal[139] and (quasi-)authoritative[140] assessments may also be found in resolutions by the UNGA when invoking its residual power of recommendation[141] or even in decisions by an international court or tribunal.[142]

4.2.2.2 *Lawful use of force without UNSC authorization*

While the law and practice on the application of neutrality law to formally legalized uses of force are rather instructive, it is less clear for other instances of the lawful use of force (in particular self-defence). Switzerland has not taken a clear stance on this matter. The 2000 Neutrality Report indicated that Switzerland might consider not applying neutrality law even absent a UNSC resolution provided a recourse to force is consistent with international law.[143] Subsequent statements suggested a more reserved position. Namely, the 2005 Neutrality Report left open the question of whether a State's recourse to self-defence justifies a departure from Swiss neutrality.[144] The practical problem is that, in most instances, there is no agreement in the international community on whether the conditions for self-defence are met. Cases where an aggressor is clearly and universally identified are rare, if not unique, in State practice.[145] Moreover, factual and evidentiary uncertainties make these determinations difficult, especially during an ongoing conflict.

4.2.3 *Practical perspective*

Neutrality then provides a viable position whenever the UNSC has not (yet) made a decision on the role of the aggressor and the victim in a given conflict, or where the international community is in disagreement.[146] Although the UN Charter lays out the theoretical framework for that substantive assessment, in practice, the formal aspect of an authoritative decision on that question renders it unapplied, mainly due to the veto power of the UNSC's permanent members. Put differently, in practice, there is room for neutrality because the theoretically clear distinction between lawful and unlawful force under the UN Charter does not hold up in practice.[147] In this regard, Switzerland has adopted a rather pragmatic approach by keeping neutrality in place for when the UN's collective security system cannot fulfil its purpose.[148] Instead of this rather restrictive approach, Switzerland could, for example, also implement sanctions if the UNGA acts on the basis of the resolution 'Uniting for Peace'.[149] Furthermore, Switzerland could make use of another more recent resolution in this respect, according to which the members of the UNSC who have exercised their right of veto must provide an explanation for this action in front of the UNGA.[150] Switzerland could ground its decision to support possible sanctions on the existence of such an explanation.[151]

The practice of other States, courts, and the ILC also shows that neutrality is still considered a valid principle of law.[152] Furthermore, neutrality law remains applicable in cases when the UNSC or UNGA adopt only non-binding recommendations, the UNSC does not call upon member States to carry out decisions (Article 48 UN Charter), or measures are taken against a State outside of an international armed conflict.[153]

Thus, practice has shown that there is still room for neutrality, both from a legal and political standpoint, due to controversies on the law or facts of an ongoing conflict and the absence of a binding decision by the UNSC. This may show the possibilities of a neutral status, namely the potential to de-escalate, provide a political buffer zone, and keep diplomatic doors open. A neutral power is most likely to be able to launch relief operations and pave the path to peace.[154] In that way, neutrality and the UN Charter are no contradiction. In this context, neutrality simply means defending the international legal order by purely non-military means. Furthermore, State practice includes unilateral applications of force beyond the UN Charter[155] that States deem 'legitimate'. Thus, many military operations are carried out without a UNSC mandate outside the collective security system, which may give neutrality a right to exist after all.[156]

4.3 Neutrality as a security concept

Neutrality has been used and is—domestically—perceived and communicated as an instrument to protect Switzerland's national security interests. Neutrality originates in the context of warfare and was motivated by the desire to shield the State, that is, its territory, population, and economy, from the adverse consequences of a nearby armed conflict.[157] In that way, its pacifying role unfolds rather internally. However, this initial function of neutrality has lost significance in today's geopolitical environment.[158]

Neutrality is historically rooted in sovereignty, and served to secure independence.[159] However, the practical value and achievability of independence is increasingly called into question, as many problems can only be solved globally through combined transnational efforts rather than by one State alone.[160] This shift from independence to interdependence as the new safeguard for peace and stability may require increasing cooperation and solidarity.[161] The UNSC embodies that vision by acting as the guardian of the legal order. Hence, a more active involvement in the UN, for example through a non-permanent seat in the UNSC, would not limit neutrality and, in the end, serve Switzerland's own security interests.[162] Withholding participation could, in turn, eventually harm one's own security and scope of action.[163] The introduction of the notion of 'cooperative neutrality' by the Swiss government might indicate some degree of acknowledgement in that regard, although its primary purpose more likely lies in making a political statement.

Today, Switzerland is surrounded by peacefully co-existing States that enjoy close cooperation.[164] It profits from Europe's security architecture, which is largely supported by NATO and supplemented by the EU's cohesion and peacebuilding efforts. Neutrality as a safety plan is increasingly being replaced by a collective security system and strong military alliances within organizations such as NATO.[165] The more international solidarity is fortified, the more neutrality becomes dispensable.[166]

Finally, neutrality does not protect against modern threats to peace, such as cyberattacks, civil wars, hybrid warfare, or terrorism.[167] At the same time, inter-state wars have become less frequent.[168] And, in practice, indirect economic or financial support of warring parties still takes place under the application of neutrality.[169]

4.4 Switzerland and the EU

Neutrality has also been submitted in the context of the relationship between the EU and Switzerland. Yet, this line of argument is another reflection of how neutrality is used as a blanket shield to justify political decisions rather than providing a substantial and compelling reason.[170] Although neutrality serves as a protection mechanism for State sovereignty, it is more State sovereignty than neutrality that has been argued against EU membership. In that regard, Switzerland resembles Denmark, a EU member State, who has opted out of the EU defence cooperation for reasons of national sovereignty until July 2022. Other EU member States, such as Austria, Finland, Ireland, or Malta, however, have acceded to the EU without (formally) forfeiting their neutral status.[171] This has become particularly relevant with regard to the mutual defence clause under Article 42(7) of the Lisbon Treaty (TEU).[172] Similar to Article 5 of the NATO Treaty,[173] this clause stipulates an 'obligation of aid and assistance' by member States in case of an aggression against another EU member. While this initially raises concerns in terms of neutrality, Article 42(7) TEU does not pose an obstacle to EU membership for several reasons. First, the assistance owed does not have to be military aid but is up to the discretion of each member State.[174] Second, the Treaty provides an opt-out by giving way to 'the specific character of the security and defence policy' of (neutral) member States.[175] Third, neutral member States have shown to have varying understandings of neutrality, the specific requirements of Article 42(7) TEU, and the character of the EU itself, that is, to what extent it is an economic project or a security and defence alliance.[176] This shows how international unification efforts inevitably still leave room for individual national approaches towards the adoption of shared European ideas, projects, and institutions.

Ever since the Swiss population rejected the accession to the European Economic Area (EEA) in 1992, the relationship between the EU and Switzerland has been designed through bilateral agreements.[177] The agreements between Switzerland and the EU are, in principle, static. Except for the Schengen/Dublin treaty, Switzerland cannot partake in the formation of EU law[178] and is not obliged to automatically adopt EU law.[179] However, EU law does shape Swiss law considerably.[180] The practice of '*autonomer Nachvollzug*' strongly resembles the application of Switzerland's neutrality policy: Switzerland maintains a reserve regarding the protection of its own interests.[181] This illustrates and solidifies division and to some extent fragmentation within Europe that is essentially rooted in diverse and well-guarded national traditions.

The Swiss-EU relationship is characterized by a concept of sovereignty that has not changed much since the 1992 EEA vote. This understanding of sovereignty grounds on the Swiss values of direct democracy, federalism, and neutrality in Switzerland.[182] Switzerland's European policy also reflects this by targeting a participation in the EU's internal market and cooperation in selected areas of interest while preserving the greatest possible political autonomy.[183] In the negotiations on the institutional framework agreement, Switzerland insisted that its sovereignty must not be restricted.[184] This ultimately led, among other factors, to the Federal Council's decision to end the negotiations on the institutional framework agreement in May 2021.[185]

4.5 Neutrality policy compared

A look abroad shows that the security argument no longer fully speaks in favour of neutrality. Other States, such as Finland, Sweden,[186] or Austria, have developed a different understanding of neutrality, which increasingly allows for institutionalized cooperation and formal alliances and has resulted in a looser concept of neutrality.

In Sweden and Finland, neutrality is more of a political choice than a legal concept. Finland's neutrality is based on rather pragmatic reasons and grew out of geopolitical necessities, namely, a shared border with Russia.[187] Both Finland and Sweden have a record of active and engaged foreign policy as UN[188] and EU[189] members and saw their role and advantage in acting as a mediator and de-escalator between East and West.[190] Until today, their concept of neutrality has taken the form of a military non-alliance policy. Nevertheless, transnational cooperation is largely institutionalized. Sweden in particular holds close ties with NATO, for example in the form of secret intelligence and technical alliances, the establishment of infrastructure for the delivery of military material, and participation in NATO operations. The Russian invasion of Ukraine in 2022 brought a dramatic shift in perception.[191] Finland and Sweden decided to provide direct military support to Ukraine and clearly sided with Western countries against Russia. Shortly after, they applied for NATO membership. Finland has officially joined NATO on 4 April 2023 and Sweden on 7 March 2024.

Austria's neutrality initially followed the Swiss model, but, over the course of time, placed a stronger focus on solidarity and integration in Europe.[192] Austria simultaneously reconciled its neutral status with UN membership and an active participation ever since,[193] as well as with membership of the EU,[194] in particular, the EU's Common Foreign and Security Policy is integrated into Austria's foreign policy.[195] After the Cold War, Austria opted for automatic implementation of UNSC Resolutions and granted transit rights for the anti-Iraq coalition during the First Gulf War[196] (which Switzerland refused to do).[197] While Austria's neutral status is to a certain degree still being upheld, it has largely evolved into a concept of non-alliance.[198] This comparison illustrates the variety of meanings that the political dimension of neutrality can take—reaching from the image of an isolated or indifferent State towards an internationally engaged one—and highlights diverse approaches within the international community.[199]

5. Challenges and Responsibilities of a Neutral Switzerland

Neutrality is a changeable and changing concept. Its content and significance depend on the circumstances at hand: historical momentum, the security architecture in place, the political atmosphere, and public opinion. Considering the changeability of neutrality as a concept, one might ask what then neutrality means. The recent decline in neutrality approval ratings in light of the 2022 Ukraine war,[200] for instance, reflects this spectrum of meanings given to neutrality. Its flexible application in practice shows that neutrality itself is an intangible concept that provides few guidelines. Switzerland has mainly used it as an instrument to maintain a maximum scope of action.

Nevertheless, neutrality is part of the Swiss national identity and deeply rooted in society. A critical look at history reveals, however, that the domestic perception and understanding of neutrality do not correspond to its actual meaning.

First, in public perception, neutrality is understood in a much broader sense, by parts of the population as an obstacle to UN or EU membership, participation in economic sanctions, or even any kind of positioning regarding international conflicts, and generally considered as a final value in itself regardless of actual benefits.[201] Some have viewed Switzerland's—albeit delayed—response to the Russian invasion of Ukraine, and specifically Switzerland's alignment with the EU, as a farewell to neutrality and a danger to Switzerland's national security.[202] The national-conservative Swiss People's Party's (SVP) initiative to enshrine perpetual and armed neutrality in the Swiss Constitution, which aims to prevent the taking of economic sanctions outside the UN as a foreign policy response,[203] shows the vehemence with which some parts of the Swiss population defend (their understanding of) neutrality. This view disregards both the legal framework and political practice. In its 1993 Neutrality Report, the Swiss government communicated that economic sanctions within and outside the UN framework are compatible with Switzerland's neutrality. This understanding reflects Swiss practice. In the same vein, other States proclaimed as neutral, such as Austria, Finland, and Sweden (regardless of and before their NATO application), have demonstrated the extent of cooperation and participation that neutrality allows for if the political will to act in such a manner exists.

Second, neutrality is considered indispensable for Switzerland's protection. This fails to recognize Europe's changed security architecture and the increasing significance of cooperation as well as the fact that neutrality cannot protect from unconventional threats (see Section 4.3 above). These developments call for a reinterpretation of neutrality.[204]

Third, while the Swiss government has consistently officially relied on neutrality, its practice has not been consistently neutral. Foreign policy decisions are made on a case-by-case basis and are primarily motivated by the aim to protect Switzerland's own interests. This aim is often misconstrued as preventing Switzerland from taking any sides in a dispute, which has sometimes failed to reflect reality. Switzerland did and does—discreetly—take sides. Neutrality thus appears to be a fraudulent label that is used internally to sugarcoat foreign policy decisions.

Both domestically and in terms of its role internationally, Switzerland must face the question of whether it uses neutrality as a pretext to maintain profitable relations with the largest possible number of States. Does the fact that Switzerland profits economically and financially from its foreign policy decisions based on neutrality call its neutral status into question? Or, in a nutshell, are neutrality and economic profit at odds with each other? Two perspectives can be taken here: one is to say that neutrality does not mean that no profit may be made from a neutral stance. Another would be to think of neutrality as an expression of Switzerland putting its own interests above those of the international community (see Shany and Varaki, this volume).

Switzerland has mostly turned a blind eye to the potential nexus between its economic and financial relations with other countries and neutrality. This did not strengthen credibility and trust in a coherent foreign policy strategy. During the South African apartheid regime, for instance, the political position of the Swiss government did not correspond with its economic practice. While officially condemning the apartheid regime, no further action followed that would corroborate such statements. Switzerland's lax and half-hearted restrictions allowed UN sanctions to be easily circumvented and brought large profits for Switzerland.[205] Being primarily driven by economic interests, neutrality was considered not to stand in the way although this practice strengthened the South African regime.[206] Neutrality has also been used as a pretext to protect prosperous economic activities.[207] For instance, Swiss banking secrecy was construed as a corollary of neutrality when it really shielded the financial sector from transparency and regulatory requirements, helped to keep Switzerland attractive as a financial hub, and ultimately hindered the effective enforcement of financial sanctions.[208] Finally, the Crypto affair casts serious doubts on the integrity of Swiss neutrality. Not only does it nourish suspicions that Switzerland is not particularly invested in putting a stop to profitable economic activities that also benefit certain other States. It is particularly problematic because the Swiss secret service itself enabled other States to gain a military advantage by taking part in the use of the manipulated devices.[209]

Yet, the issue of whether foreign policy and economic relations must be aligned does not arise exclusively for neutral States. While this may put fundamental criticism of neutrality into perspective, Switzerland would still be well advised to reflect upon its economic policies when priding itself on (political) neutrality. If Switzerland succeeds in establishing an honest, credible, and transparent practice of neutrality, the true potential of that concept may unfold. Neutrality is also an image than can be deployed to fill a gap in the current international peacekeeping system. A permanently neutral State may use its neutrality to ease or prevent international conflicts. In this way, neutrality can be used as a means to promote peace.[210] Whereas neutrality originally created a territorial buffer, it may now serve as a political buffer with the potential to enable inter-state dialogue. This could become the Swiss way of strengthening international law in its fundamental aims, namely peace, stability, and cooperation.

Promoted by domestic sacralization and constant invocation by the government, neutrality has become Switzerland's trademark. This image has been cultivated by an extensive practice of good offices[211] and enhances Switzerland's credibility.[212] Today, this is no longer a function exclusively provided by neutral States, as good offices are increasingly being taken over by international organizations or other States (major powers, groups of States, or other non-neutral States such as Norway).[213] Nevertheless, Switzerland has kept its standing in the international community as a diplomatic agent and international focal point. Switzerland's international reputation and credibility have the potential to open doors and offer a place to bring States together. Especially in the current political environment, Switzerland may use its neutrality to mediate between conflicting parties. As has been shown above, neutrality does offer the potential for such a contribution. However, it is not enough to simply label oneself as 'neutral'. After all, neutrality alone does not ensure the successful promotion of peace.[214] A neutral State must take concrete action.[215] Switzerland is asked to put its well-groomed label to good use and embody diplomacy in a fruitful way.

6. Conclusion

This chapter has aimed to shed light on the concept of neutrality as it is understood and applied in Switzerland, and how it defines the country's role in the international community. While neutrality law provides the legal framework of neutrality, its legal and practical relevance has diminished. Although clear and simple at its core, neutrality law provides guidelines for only a limited number of political decisions. This is because of its narrow scope of application, fortified by superseding UN Charter law, lack of answers to contemporary security threats, and a certain amount of leeway in its interpretation.[216] This produces a wide range of options for Switzerland's neutrality policy but does not discharge Switzerland from having to specify and explain this policy. Switzerland has succeeded in making neutrality a label but has failed to substantiate it with effective action and concrete content. A close look at Switzerland's practice throughout history reveals the ambivalence of Switzerland's neutrality. On the one hand, Switzerland insists on its role as a small State caught in the middle and refusing to take sides. On the other hand, it communicates a clear commitment to international law, shares European values, seeks cooperation with the rest of Europe, and uses neutrality as a means to promote peace. Over the course of these developments, Switzerland's neutrality has been given many names: from integral neutrality to differential neutrality, then active neutrality and, most recently, cooperative neutrality. This 'labelling of the label' draws attention away from the question of neutrality's precise meaning and reinforces the impression that Switzerland hides behind a concept that is ultimately empty of content. Official statements either paraphrase the term or rely on Switzerland's discretion to decide on a case-by-case basis, which simply preserves maximum flexibility covered by the image of neutrality.

In order to turn this image into a credible and accountable foreign policy concept, Switzerland needs to strengthen its communication on the law and policy of neutrality. Both on the international and the domestic fronts, it needs to clarify which guidelines it draws from its neutral status that result in concrete decisions being made. Only then can Switzerland be a reliable member of the international community, counter deceptive understandings of neutrality, and prevent the conflation of legal requirements with political discretion. Switzerland may legitimately rely on the aim of best protecting its own interests, but this does not absolve it from explaining how and why neutrality serves as a basis for its decisions. Either way, an interest-based foreign policy must carefully weigh short-term and long-term interests, bearing in mind which values Switzerland wants to promote externally and which partnerships it wants to prioritize. A seat on the UNSC could be an opportunity for Switzerland to strengthen its credibility and actively take part in shaping a legal order based on the rule of law, human rights, and peace. In any event, Switzerland should not duck away from the responsibility to stand up for and defend its own values. Whether or how Switzerland will seize this opportunity remains to be seen.

Notes

1. Matthias Oesch, 'Verfassungswandel durch Globalisierung und Europäisierung' in Oliver Diggelmann et al (eds), *Verfassungsrecht der Schweiz, vol I: Grundlagen* (10th edn, Schulthess 2020) ch 6 [10–12]. Regarding the tension and potential conflicts between Switzerland's direct democracy and the European Convention on Human Rights (ECHR) guarantees, see Regina Kiener, 'Grundrechte in der Bundesverfassung' in Oliver Diggelmann et al (eds), *Verfassungsrecht der Schweiz, vol II: Rechtsstaatlichkeit, Grund- und Menschenrechte* (10th edn, Schulthess 2020) ch 2 [19]; and Jörg P Müller, 'Entstehung und Entwicklung der Grundrechte in der Schweiz' in Diggelmann et al (eds), *Verfassungsrecht der Schweiz, vol II*, ch 1 [13], as well as BGE 139 I 16 [E.5.2.1]. For a critical account regarding the interplay between the ECHR and the Swiss Constitution, see Helen Keller and Anja Dillena, 'EMRK-Freundlichkeit der Bundesverfassung kritisch beleuchtet, Heidelberg Journal of International Law 2023, 847; see also in the same volume Oliver Diggelmann, 'Die "Völkerrechtsfreundlichkeit" der Bundesverfassung: Zum Zusammenspiel von Erzeugungs- und Aufnahmeebene', 647; Maria Stemmler, 'Völkerrechtsfreundlichkeit im schweizerischen Recht: Das Beispiel der unmittelbaren Anwendbarkeit von Völkerrecht', 717; Evelyne Schmidt, 'Völkerrechtskonforme Auslegung aus schweizerischer Sicht: Ein Randphänomen', 783; Martin Wyss, 'Die schweizerische Bundesversammlung und das Völkerrecht - Spurensuche zwischen Verfassungsrecht und politischer Praxis', 903.
2. Articles 5(4), 139, 190, 193, and 194 of the Swiss Constitution address how international law is relevant in Switzerland's domestic legal order. Accordingly, public international law supersedes cantonal law and federal directives. On the constitutional level, (only) 'mandatory provisions of international law' bar the emergence of contradicting constitutional norms. In terms of the relationship between international law and federal (constitutional) law, the hierarchy is less clear-cut and guided by nuanced jurisprudence. Broadly speaking and in principle, international law and the ECHR in particular take precedence over Swiss federal law, however with room for exceptions. See landmark decisions by the Swiss Federal Supreme Court: BGE 99 Ib 39 (1973) [E.3 and E.4] (*Schubert*); BGE 125 II 417 (1999) [E.4d and E.7] (*PKK*); BGE 139 I 16 [E.5.1-5-2]; BGE 144 I 126 [E.3]; and most recently BGE 148 II 169 (2022) [E.5.2]. For an overview, see Ulrich Häfelin et al (eds), *Schweizerisches Bundesstaatsrecht* (10th edn, Schulthess 2020) [1917–1928].
3. Häfelin et al (n 2) [162–167]; for a detailed empirical study of the Swiss Federal Supreme Court's jurisprudence, see Odile Ammann, 'International Law in Domestic Courts Through an Empirical Lens: The Swiss Federal Tribunal's Practice of International Law in Figures', Swiss Review of International and European Law 2018, 489.
4. Much can be said about the distinct and complicated relationship between Switzerland and the EU. As this chapter aims to take a broader view of Switzerland's approach to public international law, we will only briefly address this issue (see Section 4 and, for further reading, the references provided therein). For an overview, see also Häfelin et al (n 2) [192–199a].
5. Switzerland joined the Council of Europe on 6 May 1963, the ECHR entered into force on 28 November 1974.

6. For instance, the reformulation of fundamental rights in the Swiss Constitution in 1999 considerably relied on the ECHR and ECtHR jurisprudence, see Jörg Künzli, 'Internationaler Menschenrechtsschutz und die Schweiz' in Diggelmann et al (eds), *Verfassungsrecht der Schweiz, vol II* (n 1) ch 4, in particular [18 and 24].
7. Matthias Oesch, 'Verfassungswandel durch Globalisierung und Europäisierung' in Diggelmann et al (eds), *Verfassungsrecht der Schweiz, vol I* (n 1) ch 6, [12]; Häfelin et al (n 2) [165–167]; Ammann (n 3); but see Keller and Dillena (n 1).
8. Since the ECHR's entry into force, around 8,000 applications against Switzerland have been lodged. 206 of these reached the merits stage, in 59 per cent of them, the Court found a violation of the ECHR, see Swiss Federal Department of Foreign Affairs, 'New Trends Influencing Human Rights Protection' (15 February 2022) <https://www.eda.admin.ch/eda/en/fdfa/fdfa/aktuell/newsuebersicht/2022/02/neuorientierung-europaeischer-gerichtshof-menschenrechte.html> accessed 24 October 2022; and the ECtHR's statistics on violations by Article and by State 1959–2021 <https://www.echr.coe.int/Documents/Stats_violation_1959_2021_ENG.pdf> accessed 31 October 2022. See also list of ECtHR judgments against Switzerland by Human Rights Watch at <https://www.humanrights.ch/de/ipf/rechtsprechung-empfehlungen/europ-gerichtshof-fuer-menschenrechte-egmr/liste-aller-schweizer-faelle/> accessed 21 October 2022. For the impact of ECtHR judgments on Swiss legislation, see Department for the Execution of Judgments of the European Court of Human Rights, Switzerland 'Main Achievements' <https://rm.coe.int/ma-switzerland-eng/1680a186c8> accessed 24 October 2022, and for comprehensive information on the implementation process the Department's database at <https://hudoc.exec.coe.int> accessed 24 October 2022.
9. Tibor Szvircsev Tresch et al (eds), 'Sicherheit 2023 – Aussen-, Sicherheits- und Verteidigungspolitische Meinungsbildung im Trend' (Militärakademie and Center for Security Studies, ETH Zurich) 185.
10. Micheline Calmy-Rey, 'Vorwort' in Georg Kreis (ed), *Die Schweizer Neutralität* (Weber 2007) 7, 8.
11. Tresch et al (n 9) 185. In 2023, the number increased slightly to 91 per cent.
12. Michael Bothe, 'Neutrality, Concept and General Rules' in Rüdiger Wolfrum (ed), *Max Planck Encyclopedia of Public International Law* (online edn, October 2015) para 1.
13. Paul Seger, 'The Law of Neutrality' in Andrew Clapham and Paola Gaeta (eds), *The Oxford Handbook of International Law in Armed Conflict* (OUP 2014) 248, 249; for an extensive overview of the rights and obligations of neutrals, see Michael Bothe, 'The Law of Neutrality' in Dieter Fleck (ed), *The Handbook of International Humanitarian Law* (3rd edn, OUP 2013) 549, 559–580.
14. Seger (n 13) 248, 260; Bothe, 'The Law of Neutrality' (n 13) 549, 554.
15. Convention (V) respecting the Rights and Duties of Neutral Powers and Persons in Case of War on Land, The Hague, 18 October 1907; Convention (XIII) concerning the Rights and Duties of Neutral Powers in Naval War, The Hague, 18 October 1907.
16. René Rhinow, 'Neutralität als Deckmantel für eine aktive oder restriktive Aussenpolitik? Anmerkungen zu einer Phantomdiskussion' in Georg Kreis (ed), *Die Schweizer Neutralität* (Weber 2007) 19, 23.
17. Bothe, 'Neutrality, Concept and General Rules' (n 12) paras 1–2.
18. Seger (n 13) 248, 249.
19. Bothe, 'Neutrality, Concept and General Rules' (n 12) paras 1, 3–4.
20. ibid, para 4; this principle applies equally to political and other relations, see Seger (n 13) 248, 249.

21. Federal Act on the Implementation of International Sanctions of 22 March 2002 (SR 946.231), Article 1 [1]:
'The Confederation may enact compulsory measures in order to implement sanctions that have been ordered by the United Nations Organisation, by the Organisation for Security and Cooperation in Europe or by Switzerland's most significant trading partners and which serve to secure compliance with international law, and in particular the respect of human rights.'
22. Federal Act on War Material of 13 December 1996 (SR 514.51).
23. Seger (n 13) 248, 259.
24. Swiss Federal Department of Foreign Affairs (FDFA), 'White Paper on Neutrality, Annex to the Report on Swiss Foreign Policy for the Nineties of 29 November 1993' (White Paper 1993 on Neutrality, here: '1993 Neutrality Report') para 13 <https://www.eda.admin.ch/eda/en/fdfa/foreign-policy/international-law/neutrality.html> accessed 30 May 2022.
25. Federal Council, 'Aussenpolitischer Bericht, Juni 2007, Appendix 1 Neutralität' (BBl 2007 5557) 5557, 5558 <https://www.fedlex.admin.ch/eli/fga/2007/769/de> accessed 28 May 2022.
26. Mathieu van Berchem, 'Schlacht von Marignano scheidet die Geister' (*SWI swissinfo.ch*, 6 January 2015) <https://www.swissinfo.ch/ger/ursprung-der-neutralitaet-_schlacht-von-marignano-scheidet-die-geister/41157770> accessed 24 May 2022; see Thomas Maissen, 'Seit wann ist die Schweiz "neutral seit Marignano"?: Zu den Wurzeln eines nationalpädagogischen Topos', 68 Schweizerische Zeitschrift für Geschichte 2018, 214.
27. Edgar Bonjour, *Die Schweizerische Neutralität* (Herbert Lang & Cie 1943) 11.
28. ibid, 10; Calmy-Rey (n 10) 7, 9.
29. Georg Kreis, 'Die Neutralität – eine historische Kategorie für eine künftige Politik?' in Georg Kreis (ed), *Die Schweizer Neutralität* (Weber 2007) 35–36.
30. Rolf C Ribi, 'Neutralität—Mythos oder Chance?' in Georg Kreis (ed), *Die Schweizer Neutralität* (Weber 2007) 125, 128; Alois Riklin, 'Neutralität' (HLS *hls-dhs-dss.ch*, 9 November 2010) <https://hls-dhs-dss.ch/de/articles/016572/2010-11-09/#_hls_referenceshttps://hls-dhs-dss.ch/de/articles/016572/2010-11-09/#_hls_references> accessed 23 May 2022.
31. Thomas Maissen, 'Fakten und Fiktionen, Mythen und Lektionen' (*Neue Zürcher Zeitung*, 4 January 2015) <https://www.nzz.ch/feuilleton/fakten-und-fiktionen-mythen-und-lektionen-ld.1047584?reduced=true> accessed 25 May 2022; Olivier Pauchard, 'Der Tag, an dem die Schweiz neutral wurde' (*SWI swissinfo.ch*, 20 March 2015) <https://www.swissinfo.ch/ger/wiener-kongress_der-tag--an-dem-die-schweiz-neutral-wurde/41322772?utm_campaign=teaser-in-focusmeta&utm_source=swissinfoch&utm_content=0&utm_medium=display> accessed 6 June 2022.
32. Alexander Spring, *The International Law Concept of Neutrality in the 21st Century* (Dike 2014) 56.
33. Riklin, 'Neutralität' (n 30).
34. ibid.
35. 1993 Neutrality Report, para 13.
36. ibid.
37. André Tinoco, *Völkerrechtliche Grundlagen dauernder Neutralität. Die dauernde aktive und demilitarisierte Neutralität Costa Ricas unter der Satzung der Vereinten Nationen* (Nomos 1989) 170.
38. Seger (n 13) 248, 256; Bothe, 'The Law of Neutrality' (n 13) 549, 560–561.

39. Dietrich Schindler, 'Neutrality and Morality: Developments in Switzerland and in the International Community', 14(1) American University International Law Review 1998, 155, 156; Riklin, 'Neutralität' (n 30).
40. Rhinow (n 16) 19, 23.
41. Riklin, 'Neutralität' (n 30).
42. ibid.
43. See Unabhängige Expertenkommission Schweiz (Independent Commission of Experts Switzerland)—Zweiter Weltkrieg, *Die Schweiz, der Nationalsozialismus und der Zweite Weltkrieg* (Pendo 2002); Daniel Thürer, 'Neutralität – ein Verbrechen?' (*Neue Zürcher Zeitung*, 14 February 2005) <https://www.nzz.ch/articleCL9OA-ld.332555> accessed 24 May 2022.
44. Schindler, 'Neutrality and Morality' (n 39) 160.
45. ibid, 160 et seq.
46. Antoine Fleury, 'Völkerbund' (*HLS hls-dhs-dss.ch*, 15 April 2015) <https://hls-dhs-dss.ch/de/articles/026468/2015-04-15/> accessed 26 May 2022.
47. 1993 Neutrality Report, para 12.
48. Tresch et al (n 9) 180.
49. Fleury (n 46).
50. Armando Mombelli, 'UNO-Beitritt: das Ende des Schweizer Paradoxes' (*SWI swissinfo.ch*, 2 March 2012) <https://www.swissinfo.ch/ger/uno-beitritt--das-ende-des-schweizer-paradoxes/32197544> accessed 5 June 2022.
51. Rudolf Bindschedler, 'Der Begriff der Neutralität' (26 November 1954) <https://dodis.ch/9564> accessed 14 June 2022.
52. Riklin, 'Neutralität' (n 30).
53. Andreas Wenger and Jon Fanzun, 'Schweiz in der Krise—Krisenfall Schweiz' in Kurt Spillmann (ed), *Bulletin 1997/98 zur schweizerischen Sicherheitspolitik* (Center for Security Studies 1998) 12, 20.
54. Andreas Wenger, Christoph Breitenmoser, and Marcel Gerber, 'Vermächtnisse des Kalten Kriegs—Sechs Thesen zum schwierigen Wandel der schweizerischen Sicherheitspolitik' in Kurt R Spillmann and Andreas Wenger (eds), *Bulletin 2000 zur schweizerischen Sicherheitspolitik* (Center for Security Studies 2000) 109, 126.
55. Riklin, 'Neutralität' (n 30).
56. Thomas Fischer and Daniel Moeckli, 'The Limits of Compensation, Swiss Neutrality Policy in the Cold War', 18 Journal of Cold War Studies 2016, 12, 22–23; Schindler, 'Neutrality and Morality' (n 39) 161.
57. Standing outside the UN, Switzerland seemed predestined for the fulfilment of good offices during the Cold War, see Wenger, Breitenmoser, and Gerber (n 54) 109, 115.
58. Riklin, 'Neutralität' (n 30).
59. The 'Western Neutrals' were appointed by the United Nations Commander, while the 'Eastern Neutrals' were appointed by the Supreme Commander of the Koran People's Army and the Commander of the Chinese People's Volunteers. The term 'neutral nations' as used in the armistice agreement is 'defined as those nations whose combatant forces have not participated in the hostilities in Korea', see 'Agreement Concerning a Military Armistice in Korea' (27 July 1953) <https://peacemaker.un.org/koreadprk-militaryarmistice53> accessed 14 July 2022.
60. Riklin, 'Neutralität' (n 30); see also Hotz-Linder-Agreement of 1951.

61. Dominik Landwehr, 'Die Crypto-AG: Ein Spionage-Thriller aus dem Kalten Krieg' (*SWI swissinfo.ch*, 15 December 2020) <https://www.swissinfo.ch/ger/crypto-ag-schweiz-usa-spionage-kryptografie-kalter-krieg_die-crypto-ag--ein-spionage-thriller-aus-dem-kalten-krieg/46216566> accessed 7 June 2022.
62. Swiss Confederation, 'Fall Crypto AG' (2 November 2020) 20 <https://www.parlament.ch/centers/documents/de/bericht-gpdel-2020-11-10-d.pdf> accessed 21 May 2022.
63. ibid, 25.
64. Landwehr (n 61).
65. Marco Sassòli, 'Die schweizerische Neutralität und der Fall Crypto AG', Swiss Review of International and European Law 2021, 523.
66. Sébastien Guex and Bouda Etemad, 'Die wirtschaftlichen Beziehungen zwischen der Schweiz und Südafrika, 1945–1990' Summary of the Study NFP 42+ (Swiss National Science Foundation 2005) 3 <https://www.snf.ch/media/de/6SfskXAzNq6FUwz9/nfp42p_guex-d.pdf> accessed 30 June 2022.
67. 'Final Act of the International Conference on Human Rights' (13 May 1968) UN Doc A/CONF.32/41, 28; 'Diplomatische Dokumente der Schweiz (1.1.1967–31.12.1969)' (Chronos 2012) 184 et seq; Jörg Künzli, *Zwischen Recht und Politik, Der rechtliche Handlungsspielraum der schweizerischen Südafrikapolitik* (Chronos 2005) 62–63.
68. Guex and Etemad (n 66) 5.
69. Künzli (n 67) 172–173.
70. ibid, 134–135.
71. ibid, 137.
72. Eric Flury-Dasen, 'Kalter Krieg' (*HLS hls-dhs-dss.ch*, 14 January 2021) <https://hls-dhs-dss.ch/de/articles/017344/2021-01-14/> accessed 26 May 2022.
73. Calmy-Rey (n 10) 7, 13.
74. UNSC Resolutions: Yugoslavia 1992, Libya 1992, Haiti 1993, Sierra Leone 1997, Angola/Unita 1998, Afghanistan/Taliban 2000; EU sanctions: Yugoslavia 1998, Myanmar 2000. See Swiss Federal Department of Foreign Affairs (FDFA), 'Swiss Neutrality in Practice—Current Aspects', Report of the Interdepartmental Working Group of 30 August 2000 (Report 2000 on the Swiss Neutrality Practice in Kosovo, here: '2000 Neutrality Report') para 2.2.2.a <https://www.eda.admin.ch/eda/en/fdfa/foreign-policy/international-law/neutrality.html> accessed 31 May 2022.
75. Alois Riklin, 'Verwirrung um die Neutralität' in Georg Kreis (ed), *Die Schweizer Neutralität* (Weber 2007) 111, 113.
76. 1993 Neutrality Report, para 42.
77. ibid.
78. 1992 Bericht über einen Beitritt der Schweiz zur Europäischen Gemeinschaft, BBl 1992 III 1185, 1305–1306 <https://www.fedlex.admin.ch/eli/fga/1992/3_1185__/de> accessed 7 July 2024.
79. 1993 Neutrality Report, para 531.
80. Swiss Federal Department of Foreign Affairs (FDFA), 'Die Schweiz und die Partnerschaft für den Frieden: Warum die Schweiz in der Partnerschaft für den Frieden mitmacht' (*Admin.ch*) <https://www.pfp.admin.ch/de/ueber-uns.html> accessed 7 June 2022.
81. Präsentationsdokument der Schweiz für die Partnerschaft für den Frieden of 30 October 1996.
82. Swiss Federal Department of Foreign Affairs (FDFA), 'Swiss neutrality' (Brochure 'Switzerland's Neutrality', here: '2022 Neutrality Brochure') 13, <https://www.eda.admin.

ch/eda/de/home/das-eda/publikationen.html/content/publikationen/de/eda/schweizer-aussenpolitik/Neutralitaet_Schweiz> accessed 31 May 2022; Tresch et al (n 9) 182 and 200–201.

83. Rolf C Ribi, 'Neutralität—Mythos oder Chance?' in Georg Kreis (ed), *Die Schweizer Neutralität* (Weber 2007) 125, 130; 2000 Neutrality Report.
84. Swiss Federal Department of Home Affairs (FDHA), 'Erklärung von Bundespräsident Pascal Couchepin' (*Admin.ch*, 27 February 2008) <https://www.admin.ch/gov/de/start/dokumentation/medienmitteilungen.msg-id-17497.html> accessed 20 May 2022.
85. Simon Gemperli, 'Calmy-Rey will direkt mit Kosovo verhandeln' (*Neue Zürcher Zeitung*, 29 March 2008) <https://www.nzz.ch/calmy-rey_will_direkt_mit_kosovo_verhandeln-ld.474267> accessed 12 June 2022; SWI, 'Anerkennung Kosovos: "Ein diplomatischer Fehler?"', (*SWI swissinfo.ch*, 16 December 2010) <https://www.swissinfo.ch/ger/anerkennung-kosovos---ein-diplomatischer-fehler--/29043928> accessed 12 June 2022.
86. David Hofmann, 'Die Anerkennung Kosovos durch die dauernd neutrale Schweiz' (*Jusletter*, 7 July 2008) paras 45–50 <https://jusletter.weblaw.ch/juslissues/2008/477/_6656.html__ONCE#section7c020763-55c8-4192-be97-a89500e08880> accessed 30 May 2022.
87. People's vote of 3 March 2002, <https://www.bk.admin.ch/ch/d/pore/va/20020303/index.html> accessed 20 May 2022.
88. Seger (n 13) 248, 261.
89. Riklin, 'Neutralität' (n 30).
90. Swiss Federal Department of Foreign Affairs (FDFA), 'Die Schweiz im UNO-Sicherheitsrat' (*Admin.ch*, 28 June 2022) <https://www.eda.admin.ch/eda/de/home/aussenpolitik/internationale-organisationen/vereinte-nationen/schweizer-engagement/UNO-Sicherheitsrat.html> accessed 5 July 2022.
91. Swiss Federal Department of Foreign Affairs (FDFA), 'Switzerland's candidature for a non-permanent seat on the United Nations Security Council for the 2023–2024 term', Report of the Federal Council in response to Parliamentary postulate 13.3005, submitted by the Foreign Affairs Committee of the National Council on 15 January 2013 (5 June 2015) <https://www.newsd.admin.ch/newsd/message/attachments/39662.pdf> accessed 7 June 2022.
92. Swiss Federal Department of Foreign Affairs (FDFA), 'Neutrality under Scrutiny in the Iraq Conflict. Summary of Switzerland's Neutrality Policy During the Iraq Conflict in Response to the Reimann Postulate (03.3066) and to the Motion by the SVP Parliamentary Group (03.3050)' of 2 December 2005 (Abstract 2005 of Swiss Neutrality Practice During the War in Iraq, here: '2005 Neutrality Report), <https://www.eda.admin.ch/eda/en/fdfa/foreign-policy/international-law/neutrality.html> accessed 31 May 2022.
93. 2022 Neutrality Brochure, 15.
94. UNGA Res No ES-11/1 (1 March 2022); Peter A Fischer, 'Neutral, aber mit einer klaren Haltung' (*Neue Zürcher Zeitung*, 23 February 2022) <https://www.nzz.ch/meinung/schweiz-im-ukraine-konflikt-neutralitaet-mit-sanktionen-ld.1671202> accessed 31 May 2022.
95. 2022 Neutrality Brochure, 15.
96. Swiss Federal Department of Foreign Affairs, 'Fragen und Antworten zur Neutralität der Schweiz' (*Admin.ch*, 18 May 2022) <https://www.eda.admin.ch/eda/de/home/das-eda/aktuell/newsuebersicht/2022/03/neutralitaet.html> accessed 23 May 2022.
97. Daniel Gerny, 'Völkerrechtsprofessor Sassòli: "Die Schweiz darf wegen des Ukraine-Kriegs nicht unüberlegt Neutralitätsprinzipien über Bord werfen"' (*Neue Zürcher*

Zeitung, 25 April 2022) <https://www.nzz.ch/schweiz/voelkerrechtsprofessor-sassoli-schweiz-braucht-eine-debatte-ueber-den-sinn-der-staendigen-neutralitaet-ld.1680945> accessed 24 May 2022.

98. Fabian Schäfer, 'Harte Kritik am Bundesrat, weil er Waffenexporte in die Ukraine verhindert—doch das Parlamanet hat ihm ganz bewusst die Hände gebunden' (*Neue Zürcher Zeitung*, 25 April 2022) <https://www.nzz.ch/schweiz/harte-kritik-am-bundesrat-weil-er-waffenexporte-in-die-ukraine-verhindert-doch-das-parlament-hat-ihm-ganz-bewusst-die-haende-gebunden-ld.1680980> accessed 24 May 2022.

99. Yvette Estermann, 'Sich positionieren ist Gift für die Neutralität' (SWI swissinfo.ch, 11 February 2021) <https://www.swissinfo.ch/ger/-sich-positionieren-ist-gift-fuer-die-neutralitaet-/46099322> accessed 26 May 2022; Barbara Steinemann, 'Die Neutralität begünstigt die humanitäre Rolle der Schweiz' (*SWI swissinfo.ch*, 16 March 2022) <https://www.swissinfo.ch/ger/-die-neutralitaet-beguenstigt-die-humanitaere-rolle-der-schweiz-/47437376> accessed 20 May 2022.

100. Thomas Beschorner, 'Warum die Schweiz ihre Neutralität jetzt neu definieren sollte' (*SWI swissinfo.ch*, 11 March 2022) <https://www.swissinfo.ch/ger/schweiz-neutralitaet-ukraine/47409684> accessed 26 May 2022; Kaspar Villiger, 'Neutralität ist nicht heilig: drei Leitlinien, an denen die Schweiz ihre Aussenpolitik orientieren sollte' (*Neue Zürcher Zeitung*, 4 March 2022) <https://www.nzz.ch/feuilleton/neutralitaet-die-schweiz-muss-den-begriff-neu-denken-ld.1672742> accessed 28 May 2022; Georg Häsler, 'Die Schweiz soll ihre bewaffnete Neutralität in den Dienst des Völkerrechts stellen' (*Neue Zürcher Zeitung*, 25 March 2022) <https://www.nzz.ch/meinung/sicherheitspolitik-solidarische-neutralitaet-ld.1675748> accessed 25 March 2022. For a critical, constructive outlook on Swiss neutrality in light of recent developments, see also Marco Jori, *Die Schweiz und ihre Neutralität* (Hier und Jetzt 2023) 466–473.

101. eg Switzerland could conduct joint military exercises with NATO—even on Swiss soil, see Adrian Schmid, 'Cassis will Schweizer Neutralität neu ausrichten' (*Tagesanzeiger*, 16 June 2022) <https://www.tagesanzeiger.ch/cassis-will-schweizer-neutralitaet-neu-ausrichten-139411358539> accessed 26 June 2022; the 2022 Neutrality Report was adopted by the Federal Council on 26 October 2022.

102. Rhinow (n 63) 19, 30. For a recent and comprehensive account of Swiss neutrality, see Mark E Villiger, Handbuch der schweizerischen Neutralität (Schulthess 2023).

103. Conseil National, Interpellation Graber Jean-Pierre. Problématique reconnaissance du Kosovo, 08.3010, Avis du Conseil Fédéral du 14 Mai 2008, para 3 <https://www.parlament.ch/de/ratsbetrieb/suche-curia-vista/geschaeft?AffairId=20083010> accessed 31 May 2022.

104. Hofmann (n 86); Stefan Oeter, 'Yugoslavia, Dissolution of' in Rüdiger Wolfrum (ed), *Max Planck Encyclopedia of Public International Law* (online edn, May 2011) paras 85–86.

105. Federal Act on the Implementation of International Sanctions (Embargo Act) of 22 March 2002, SR 946.231, Article 1 (see full text in n 21).

106. 2000 Neutrality Report, paras 3.2 and 2.2.2.a (although regarding the first case, the Report highlights that it was of central importance that there was no risk for Switzerland to be drawn into the conflict and abstention from the sanctions would have harmed its credibility and reputation).

107. Oliver Washington, '"Kooperative Neutralität": Cassis überrascht mit neuem Begriff' (*SRF HeuteMorgen*, 24 May 2022) <https://www.srf.ch/news/schweiz/neue-neutralitaetsdefinition-kooperative-neutralitaet-cassis-ueberrascht-mit-neuem-begriff> accessed 31 May 2022.

108. 1993 Neutrality Report, paras 3.3, 6.3, 6.6. In fact, the Report uses the wording 'security through co-operation' (para 3.3).
109. Dietrich Schindler, 'Transformations in the Law of Neutrality since 1945' in Astrid JM Delissen and Gerard J Tanja (eds), *Humanitarian Law of Armed Conflict—Challenges Ahead: Essays in Honour of Frits Kalshoven* (Nijhoff 1991) 367, 371; Jörg Künzli, *Vom Umgang des Rechtsstaats mit Unrechtregimes* (Staempfli 2008) 116; cf Seger (n 13) 248, 261–262.
110. Jochen A Frowein, 'Ius Cogens' in Rüdiger Wolfrum (ed), *Max Planck Encyclopedia of Public International Law* (online edn, March 2013) para 8.
111. Seger (n 13) 248, 261 (already in times of the Briand-Kellogg-Pact of 1829); Patricia Egli, 'Aktuelle Leitsätze zur Neutralität' (*Jusletter*, 21 August 2006) para 15 <https://www.weblaw.ch/jusletter/juslissues/2006/385/_4935.html__ONCE> accessed 2 May 2022.
112. See, eg, Daniel Thürer, 'Comment: UN Enforcement Measures and Neutrality. The Case of Switzerland', 30(1) Archiv des Völkerrechts 1992, 63, 78–80 who lists the concept of *ius cogens*, the principle of universality, and the *erga omnes* effect of certain obligations as manifestations of such a system.
113. Künzli (n 109) 117–118.
114. Exceptions (to the extent that they require non-forcible reactions) must be considered for breaches of *erga omnes* or *ius cogens* obligations.
115. *A fortiori*, if a non-UN member State does not participate in sanctions and thereby renders their implementation less effective, this neither constitutes an offence in itself, nor does it amount to participation in the offence that the sanction addresses, see Thürer (n 112) 75–76 and 82.
116. ibid, 82.
117. Article 2(5) UN Charter reads as follows: 'All Members shall give the United Nations every assistance in any action it takes in accordance with the present Charter, and shall refrain from giving assistance to any state against which the United Nations is taking preventive or enforcement action.'
118. Helmut Aust, 'Article 2(5)' in Bruno Simma et al (eds), *The Charter of the United Nations. A Commentary. Vol I* (3rd edn, OUP 2012) 235, paras 16 and 24. With regards to the duty to assist in 'any action' the UN takes, there is limited State practice of an application beyond Chapter VII measures. With regards to the duty to refrain from assisting the State that is the target of UN action, reference by the UNGA to such a duty outside of Chapter VII measures must be understood as a political argument to remind member States of a broader obligation not to contradict or impede UN efforts.
119. ibid, para 4.
120. Seger (n 13) 248, 262.
121. Thürer (n 112) 67.
122. Künzli (n 109) 116–117.
123. ibid, 117–118; Seger (n 13) 248, 262.
124. Schindler (n 109) 367, 372; Bothe, 'The Law of Neutrality' (n 13) 549, 553.
125. August Reinisch and Gregor Novak, 'Article 49' in Bruno Simma et al (eds), *The Charter of the United Nations. A Commentary. Volume II* (3rd edn, OUP 2012) 1385, para 9.
126. Aust (n 118) 235, para 27.
127. Reinisch and Novak (n 125) 1385, para 8; Nico Krisch, 'Article 43' in Simma et al (eds), *The Charter of the United Nations. A Commentary. Volume I* (3rd edn, OUP 2012) 1351, paras 6–7.

128. Reinisch and Novak (n 125) 1385, para 10 (also distinguishing between air, land and sea passage).
129. See, eg, Künzli (n 109) 119–120 with further references; Peter Hostettler and Olivia Danai, 'Neutrality in Land Warfare' in Rüdiger Wolfrum (ed), *Max Planck Encyclopedia of Public International Law* (online edn, November 2015) para 21; Spring (n 32) 137–139 with further references.
130. 1993 Neutrality Report, para 4.1.2; 2000 Neutrality Report, para 4.2; 2005 Neutrality Report, para 4.1; Austrian Parliament, 'Bericht betreffend Sicherheits- und Verteidigungsdoktrin: Analyse-Teil' (22 January 2001) III-87 d.B. XXI GP para 4.4.1 <https://www.parlament.gv.at/PAKT/VHG/XXI/III/III_00087/imfname_522643.pdf> accessed 31 May 2022.
131. Spring (n 132) 138–139; but see Aust (n 118) 235, para 26 (arguing that, for the purposes of ad hoc neutrality, military enforcement action under Chapter VII UN Charter leads to an armed conflict).
132. Mathias-Charles Krafft, Daniel Thürer, and Julie-Antoinette Stadelhofer, 'Switzerland' in Vera Gowland-Debbas (ed), *National Implementation of UN Sanctions* (Brill 2004) 523, 573, for a detailed account of the implementation of the non-military sanctions by Switzerland, see 540–559. As a non-member of the UN, the implementation took place autonomously, meaning without legal obligation (*autonomer Nachvollzug*). The 1993 Neutrality Report mentions as reasons for this decision the fact that non-participation might be construed as taking sides with the lawbreaker by providing moral and *de facto* support and thus be detrimental to Switzerland's image throughout the world, see 1993 Neutrality Report, para 4.1.2.
133. Such as for the UN protection forces for Yugoslavia (UNPROFOR 1993), the OSCE Mission in Kosovo (Kosovo Verification Mission 1998), or the IFOR/SFOR (Bosnia-Herzegovina 1995) and KFOR (Kosovo 1999), see 2000 Neutrality Report, para 2.2.2.b.
134. For non-military measures, Switzerland's official position was that, as a matter of principle and solidarity, it will participate in collective efforts that are based on a UNSC resolution and supported by the overwhelming majority of States, see 1993 Neutrality Report, para 4.1.2.

   Regarding military measures, Switzerland's position is a bit more reserved: As the 1993 Neutrality Report States, Switzerland will decide on a case-by-case basis, carefully weighing Swiss interests against its solidarity obligations. As a general rule, Switzerland will not obstruct military operations authorized or ordered by the UNSC, see 1993 Neutrality Report, para 4.1.3.
135. Loi fédérale sur l'armée et l'administration militaire du 3 février 1995 (SR 510.10), Article 66a.
136. 2005 Neutrality Report, paras 4.2.1 and 4.2.2. In regard of the military actions taken by the US and UK in 2003, it was unclear whether they were covered by a UNSC resolution. Switzerland took the position that there was no authorization and invoked neutrality law. This implies that, given a respective mandate, Switzerland would have granted those rights. For that reading, see Aust (n 118) 235, para 17. See also Krafft, Thürer, and Stadelhofer (n 132) 523, 528 with regards to the 1999 NATO intervention in Kosovo.
137. Künzli (n 109) 126–128.
138. 2000 Neutrality Report, para 5.1 in fine.
139. Stefan Talmon, 'Waffenlieferungen an die Ukraine als Ausdruck eines wertebasierten Völkerrechts' (*Verfassungsblog*, 9 March 2022) <https://verfassungsblog.de/waffenlief

erungen-an-die-ukraine-als-ausdruck-eines-wertebasierten-volkerrechts/> accessed 9 May 2022: UNGA resolutions reflect the international community's legal opinion; a two-thirds majority is deemed sufficient to provide a credible and legitimate identification of the aggressor. A two-thirds majority is also the quorum required by Article 18(2) UN Charter for decisions on 'important questions', including 'recommendations with respect to the maintenance of international peace and security'.

140. Kai Ambos, 'Will a State Supplying Weapons to Ukraine Become a Party to the Conflict and Thus Be Exposed to Countermeasures?' (*EJIL:Talk!*, 2 March 2022) <https://www.ejiltalk.org/will-a-State-supplying-weapons-to-ukraine-become-a-party-to-the-confl ict-and-thus-be-exposed-to-countermeasures/> accessed 9 May 2022.
141. Originating in the *Uniting for peace*-Resolution UNGA Res No 377 (V) (3 November 1950); also made use of regarding the Russian invasion in Ukraine in 2022: UNGA Res No ES-11/1 (1 March 2022).
142. For instance, *Allegations of Genocide under the Convention on the Prevention and Punishment of the Crime of Genocide (Ukraine v Russian Federation)* Request for the Indication of Provisional Measures: Order General List No 182 [2022] ICJ 1; see also ECtHR, 'Decision of the Court on requests for interim measures in individual applications concerning Russian military operations on Ukrainian territory' Press Release ECHR 073 (2022) (4 March 2022).
143. 2000 Neutrality Report, para 5.1 (raising the question of application of neutrality law for cases of hypothetically lawful humanitarian interventions). However, as there is no universal agreement on the legality of a humanitarian intervention, the decision could be left open.
144. 2005 Neutrality Report, para 4.1. According to the Report, the material conditions for the right to self-defence were not met, nor was this invoked by the intervening States. The Report thus only addressed the question of whether the UNSC had authorized the US and UK military operation.
145. See, for instance, Kuwait's annexation of Iraq in 1990 and Russia's invasion of Ukraine in 2022.
146. Bothe, 'The Law of Neutrality' (n 13) 549, 552–553. According to Künzli (n 109) 124–125, however, the fact that the applicability of neutrality law depends on the impossibility of a legal assessment (legality of the use of force) only highlights the incompatibility of both legal systems and advocates for resolving legal conflicts based on objective legal rules rather than ad hoc decisions by the neutral State.
147. Seger (n 13) 248, 261–262; Talmon (n 139), also referring to this phenomenon as a 'construction error' (*Konstruktionsfehler*) of the UN Charter.
148. As the 1993 Neutrality Report (para 4.1.2) puts it: The collective security system requires unity among states. When there is no unity, neutrality comes into play.
149. UNGA Res No 377 (V) (3 November 1950); see Section 4.2.2.1 in fine.
150. UNGA (26 April 2022) UN Doc A/RES/76/262.
151. See Helen Keller, 'Vor einer vorschnellen Aufgabe der Neutralität muss gewarnt werden' (*Neue Zürcher Zeitung*, 6 July 2022) <https://www.nzz.ch/meinung/keine-zeitenwende-fuer-die-neutralitaet-ld.1690292> accessed 27 July 2022.
152. Schindler (n 109) 367, 368–371; *Legality of the Threat or Use of Nuclear Weapons* (Advisory Opinion) (1999) ICJ Rep 66, paras 88–89; ILC, 'Report of the International Law Commission on the Work of its 63rd Session' (26 April–3 June and 4 July–12 August 2011) UN Doc A/CN.4/SER.A/2011/add.1 (Part 2) 119.

153. Schindler (n 109) 367, 372.
154. Bothe, 'Neutrality, Concept and General Rules' (n 12) para 4.
155. Such as preventive self-defence or counter-terrorism operations against non-State actors.
156. Samantha Besson, 'Souveränität, Verantwortung und Neutralität: Damit aus der aktiven Neutralität kein Prokrustesbett wird' in Georg Kreis (ed), *Die Schweizer Neutralität* (Werd 2007) 95, 101.
157. Seger (n 13) 248, 250.
158. Laurent Goetschel, 'Neutralität: Handicap oder Branding der Schweizer Aussenpolitik?' in Georg Kreis (ed), *Die Schweizer Neutralität* (Weber 2007) 81, 82–84.
159. Thürer (n 112) 78.
160. Tresch et al (n 9) 147–148; Daniel Thürer, 'Aktive Neutralität? Ein Beobachter und seine (naiven) Fragen' in Georg Kreis (ed), *Die Schweizer Neutralität* (Werd 2007) 137, 143–144 (arguing for a redefined concept of neutrality in light of current developments and shifts in the international legal order and world politics that have led to a changed content and meaning of State sovereignty—however in the sense of a supplement to a general global peace policy with the positive aim to strengthen peace, solidarity, and cooperation).
161. Besson (n 156) 95, 99–100.
162. Micheline Calmy-Rey, *Die Neutralität* (NZZ Libro 2020) 30–31; Alois Riklin, 'Verwirrung um die Neutralität' in Georg Kreis (ed), *Die Schweizer Neutralität* (Weber 2007) 111, 120–121: If independence is understood in the sense of autonomy, this may, in an interdependent world, best be achieved through participation in international decision-making processes, the effects of which Switzerland cannot escape, rather than adhering to an anachronistic understanding of State sovereignty.
163. Dietrich Schindler, quoted in Georg Kreis, *Kleine Neutralitätsgeschichte der Gegenwart* (Haupt 2004) 290.
164. Goetschel (n 158) 81, 83; 2000 Neutrality Report, para 6.1.3.
165. Working Group Aussenpolitische Vision Schweiz 2028, 'Die Schweiz in der Welt 2028', Report (2 July 2019) 16 <https://www.eda.admin.ch/dam/eda/de/documents/aktuell/dossiers/avis28-bericht-190619_DE.pdf> accessed 2 May 2022: As long as Switzerland is surrounded by the EU and NATO, the security function of neutrality steps back. However, neutrality is defended as a concept serving Switzerland's credibility as a peace mediator and problem solver without its own power political agenda. Nevertheless, Switzerland plans to deepen its cooperation with NATO as far as possible without becoming a member; see Thomas Stephens, 'Switzerland and NATO: Just Flirting or the Start of a Wild Marriage?' (SWI swissinfo, 2 February 2024) <https://www.swissinfo.ch/eng/politics/switzerland-and-nato-just-flirting-or-the-start-of-a-wild-marriage/49181146> accessed 5 July 2024.
166. Daniel Thürer, quoted in Georg Kreis, *Kleine Neutralitätsgeschichte der Gegenwart* (Haupt 2004) 295: Neutrality is no longer a useful basis for Switzerland's foreign policy but rather a supplement to a concept with stronger focus on international solidarity and collective peace efforts.
167. Riklin, 'Verwirrung um die Neutralität' (n 162) 111, 121.
168. ibid; Seger (n 13) 248, 267–268, although noting that in light of climate change and competition over resources, armed conflicts between States may resurface in the future.
169. Riklin, 'Verwirrung um die Neutralität' (n 162) 111, 121.
170. René Schwok and Stephan Bloetzer, 'Annäherung statt Mitgliedschaft? Die Schweiz und die EU nach den zweiten bilateralen Abkommen', 28(3) Integration 2005, 201, 203.

171. Clara Sophia Cramer and Ulrike Franke (eds), 'Ambiguous Alliance: Neutrality, Opt-Outs, and European Defence' (European Council on Foreign Relations, Essay Collection, June 2021) <https://ecfr.eu/wp-content/uploads/Ambiguous-alliance-Neutrality-opt-outs-and-European-defence.pdf> accessed 12 August 2022.
172. Article 42(7) TEU reads as follows: 'If a Member State is the victim of armed aggression on its territory, the other Member States shall have towards it an obligation of aid and assistance by all the means in their power, in accordance with Article 51 of the United Nations Charter. This shall not prejudice the specific character of the security and defence policy of certain Member States.'
173. For a comparative analysis, see Aistė Mickonytė, 'The Mutual Assistance Clause under Article 42(7) TEU. Considerations in Light of the Ukraine's Quest for Membership' Graz Law Working Paper No 04-2022 (29 April 2022) 6–14 <https://papers.ssrn.com/sol3/papers.cfm?abstract_id=4097998> accessed 12 August 2022.
174. European Parliament, 'The EU's Mutual Assistance Clause. First ever activation of Article 42(7) TEU' (Briefing, November 2015) 3 <https://www.europarl.europa.eu/thinktank/en/document/EPRS_BRI(2015)572799> accessed 12 August 2022; Jasper Kamradt, 'Was wird aus der Beistandsklausel der EU?: Zum Stand der EU-Beistandsklausel nach dem NATO-Beitritt Finnlands und Schwedens' (*Völkerrechtsblog*, 8 August 2022) <https://voelkerrechtsblog.org/was-wird-aus-der-beistandsklausel-der-eu/> accessed 12 August 2022.
175. Mickonytė (n 173); Cramer and Franke (n 171).
176. Cramer and Franke (n 171).
177. Matthias Oesch, *Schweiz—Europäische Union* (EIZ 2020) 20–24.
178. Matthias Oesch, 'Die bilateralen Abkommen Schweiz—EU und die Übernahme von EU-Recht' (2017) 5 Pratique Juridique Actuelle 638, 639; Thomas Cottier, 'Das Rahmenabkommen und die Souveränität' (2019) 11 Revue Suisse de Jurisprudence 345, 346.
179. Oesch, 'Die bilateralen Abkommen Schweiz' (n 178) 639.
180. Matthias Oesch, 'Die Europäisierung des schweizerischen Rechts' in Thomas Cottier (ed), *Die Europakompatibilität des schweizerischen Wirtschaftsrechts: Konvergenz und Divergenz* (Helbing Lichtenhahn 2012) 13, 17; Matthias Oesch, 'The Swiss Model of European Integration' in Andrea Biondi, Patrick J Birksinshaw, and Maria Kendrick (eds), *Brexit: The Legal Implications* (Kluwer Law International 2018) 35, 36 and 43.
181. Oesch, 'Die Europäisierung des schweizerischen Rechts' (n 180) 13, 29.
182. Thomas Cottier, 'Das Rahmenabkommen und die Souveränität' (29 October 2020) <https://suisse-en-europe.ch/wp-content/uploads/2020/10/Cottier-Rahmenabkommen-und-die-Souver%C3%A4nit%C3%A4t-1020.pdf> accessed 26 June 2022.
183. Federal Council, 'Bericht betreffend die Verhandlungen über ein institutionelles Abkommen zwischen der Schweiz und der EU' 25 (26 May 2021) <https://www.newsd.admin.ch/newsd/message/attachments/66828.pdf> accessed 27 July 2022.
184. See ibid, 6. Meaning no automatic adoption of EU law.
185. FDFA, 'Das Institutionelle Abkommen Schweiz-EU wird nicht abgeschlossen' (26 May 2021) <https://www.eda.admin.ch/eda/de/home/das-eda/aktuell/news.html/content/eda/de/meta/news/2021/5/26/83705.html> accessed 27 July 2022. However, on 8 March 2024, the Federal Council approved a negotiating mandate with the EU with negotiatings to begin in the same month; see Federal Council, 'Swiss-EU Relations: Federal Council Approves Definitive Negotiating Mandate' (8 March 2024) <https://www.admin.ch/gov/en/start/documentation/media-releases.msg-id-100342.html> accessed 5 July 2024.

186. See Chapter on Nordic States in this volume.
187. Avenir Suisse (ed), 'Perspektiven der Sicherheitspolitik' (March 2022) 50 <https://www.avenir-suisse.ch/publication/perspektiven-der-schweizer-sicherheitspolitik/> accessed 24 May 2022.
188. Sweden joined the UN in 1946, Finland in 1955. Both have held non-permanent seats in the UNSC multiple times (Sweden in 1957/58, 1975/76, 1997/98, and 2017/18; Finland in 1969/70 and 1989/90, <https://www.un.org/securitycouncil/search/country?field_member_state_value=SWE > and <https://www.un.org/securitycouncil/search/country?field_member_state_value=FIN> both accessed 30 October 2023) and participated in UN peacekeeping operations.
189. Finland and Sweden acceded to the EU in 1995.
190. Rudolf Hermann, 'Russland treibt Finnland und Schweden unter den Schutz der Nato—deren Bevölkerung hat die Zeitenwende rasch erkannt' (*Neue Zürcher Zeitung*, 5 May 2022) <https://www.nzz.ch/meinung/der-ukraine-krieg-treibt-finnland-und-schweden-in-richtung-nato-ld.1680435> accessed 31 May 2022.
191. Avenir Suisse (n 187) 51–53.
192. Austrian Parliament, 'Bericht betreffend Sicherheits- und Verteidigungsdoktrin: Analyse-Teil' (n 130) para 5.3.
193. Austria joined the UN in 1955 and has been a non-permanent member of the UNSC three times so far; namely in 1973/74, 1991/92 and 2009/10, see <https://www.un.org/securitycouncil/search/country?field_member_state_value=AUT> accessed 30 October 2023.
194. After applying for membership in the European Communities in 1989, Austria acceded to the EU in 1995.
195. Avenir Suisse (n 187) 55.
196. Austrian Parliament, 'Bericht betreffend Sicherheits- und Verteidigungsdoktrin: Analyse-Teil' (n 130) para 5.3.
197. 2000 Neutrality Report, para 2.2.2.b.
198. Austrian Parliament, 'Security and Defence Doctrine' (Vienna, 12 December 2001) 7 <https://www.files.ethz.ch/isn/155910/Austria-2001.pdf> accessed 31 May 2022.
199. Seger (n 13) 248, 268.
200. See ETH mid-2022 survey above, Section 1 (n 9).
201. Tresch et al (n 9) 181–182, 185–188, and 193.
202. David Vonplon, 'Christoph Blocher prüft die Lancierung einer Volksinitiative für Neutralität' (*Neue Zürcher Zeitung*, 12 March 2022) <https://www.nzz.ch/schweiz/christoph-blocher-prueft-die-lancierung-einer-volksinitiative-fuer-neutralitaet-ld.1674256> accessed 24 May 2022; Christina Neuhaus, 'Christoph Blocher: "Je schlimmer es in der Welt zugeht, desto wichtiger ist die Neutralität"' (*Neue Zürcher Zeitung*, 7 March 2022) <https://www.nzz.ch/schweiz/christoph-blocher-neutralitaet-ist-nicht-nur-selbstzweck-ld.1672984> accessed 31 May 2022.
203. The initiative proposes a new Article 54a of the Swiss Constitution incorporating permanent armed neutrality into the Swiss Constitution as well as to supplement Article 58 of the Swiss Constitution with a new paragraph confining foreign deployment of the Swiss army exclusively to emergency relief operations. The Federal Council however has recommended to reject the initiative; see Swiss Federal Council, Press Release of 26 June 2024 <https://www.admin.ch/gov/en/start/documentation/media-releases.msg-id-101632.html> accessed 5 July 2024. Other politicians have proposed a counter model to the initiative that aims at reshaping neutrality in a ten points plan;

see '"Neutralität überdenken" - 87 Persönlichkeiten unterzeichnen Manifest gegen Blocher' (Watson, 29 May 2024) <https://www.watson.ch/schweiz/russland/142147571-schweizer-neutralitaet-neu-denken-87-persoenlichkeiten-gegen-blocher> accessed 5 July 2024.

204. Avenir Suisse (n 187) 57–64.

205. See Section 3.2.

206. Guex and Etemad (n 66); Jean-Michel Berthoud, 'Comment la Suisse a soutenu l'apartheid' (*SWI swissinfo.ch*, 27 October 2005) <https://www.swissinfo.ch/fre/comment-la-suisse-a-soutenu-l-apartheid/4811948> accessed 24 May 2022.

207. Hans-Ulrich Jost, 'Die von der Schweiz praktizierte Neutralität ist ein rein politisches Mittel' (*SWI swissinfo.ch*, 17 February 2021) <https://www.swissinfo.ch/ger/-die-von-der-schweiz-praktizierte-neutralitaet-ist-ein-rein-politisches-mittel-/46121122> accessed 24 May 2022.

208. Although Switzerland was forced under international pressure to tighten some of its laws regarding banking secrecy and confidentiality, it is still criticized for being too lax and leaving too many loopholes. Recently, the US Commission on Security and Cooperation in Europe ('Helsinki Commission') raised allegations that Switzerland's secrecy laws undermine the international sanctions against Russia in response to the invasion of Ukraine: Commission on Security and Cooperation in Europe, 'Helsinki Commission Briefing to Examine Swiss Enabling of Russian Oligarchs' Press Release, 29 April 2022 <https://www.csce.gov/international-impact/press-and-media/press-releases/helsinki-commission-briefing-examine-swiss> accessed 31 May 2022; Matthew Allen, 'US commission accuses Switzerland of hiding Russian assets' (*SWI swissinfo.ch*, 5 May 2022) <https://www.swissinfo.ch/eng/us-commission-accuses-switzerland-of-hiding-russian-assets/47570650> accessed 31 May 2022.

209. Katrin Ammann, '"Crypto-Leaks" stellen Schweizer Neutralität unter Stresstest' (*SWI swissinfo.ch*, 13 February 2020) <https://www.swissinfo.ch/ger/geheimdienst-affaere_-crypto-leaks--stellen-schweizer-neutralitaet-unter-stresstest/45556920?utm_campaign=teaser-in-article&utm_source=swissinfoch&utm_medium=display&utm_content=o> accessed 24 May 2022; Landwehr (n 61). Fiona Endres and Nicole Vögele, 'Geheimdienstaffäre Cryptoleaks—Weltweite Spionage-Operation mit Schweizer Firma aufgedeckt' (*SRF*, 11 February 2020) <https://www.srf.ch/news/schweiz/geheimdienstaffaere-cryptoleaks-weltweite-spionage-operation-mit-schweizer-firma-aufgedeckt> accessed 24 May 2022.

210. Seger (n 13) 248, 269.

211. ibid, 248, 269; Département fédéral des affaires étrangères (Suisse), 'Rapport de politique étrangère, juin 2007' (15 June 2007) 07.058 Annexe 1, para 4 <https://www.fedlex.admin.ch/filestore/fedlex.data.admin.ch/eli/fga/2007/768/fr/pdf-a/fedlex-data-admin-ch-eli-fga-2007-768-fr-pdf-a.pdf> accessed 30 June 2022.

212. Pascale Baeriswyl, 'Bei Völkerrechts-Verletzungen ist die Schweiz nicht neutral' (*SWI swissinfo.ch*, 18 March 2021) <https://www.swissinfo.ch/ger/-bei-voelkerrechtsverletzungen-ist-die-schweiz-nicht-neutral-/46448494> accessed 8 June 2022.

213. 2000 Neutrality Report, para 3.3; Riklin, 'Verwirrung um die Neutralität' (n 162) 111, 122; Switzerland currently holds six protective power mandates; this number peaked during World War II (219 mandates for thirty-five States) and has continuously dropped, see Center for Security Studies, 'Schutzmacht Schweiz: Rennaissance einer Tradition' in CSS Analysen zur Sicherheitspolitik, No 108 (February 2012) 3 <https://css.ethz.ch/content/

dam/ethz/special-interest/gess/cis/center-for-securities-studies/pdfs/CSS-Analysen-108-DE.pdf> accessed 31 May 2022.

214. Baeriswyl (n 212).

215. Seger (n 13) 248, 269–270; Daniel Trachsler, 'Gute Dienste—Mythen, Fakten, Perspektiven' in Andreas Wenger (ed), *Bulletin 2004 zur schweizerischen Sicherheitspolitik* (Center for Security Studies 2004) 33, 64.

216. Peter Hostettler and Olivia Danai, 'Neutrality in Land Warfare' in Rüdiger Wolfrum (ed), *Max Planck Encyclopedia of Public International Law* (online edn, November 2015) paras 22–25; 1993 Neutrality Report, para 1.3; for the legal difficulties of the application of neutrality law, see Bothe, 'The Law of Neutrality' (n 13) 549, 556–580; cf Künzli (n 109) 106–115.

CHAPTER 37

TURKEY

OLGUN AKBULUT AND IŞIL ERGÜVENÇ KARAKAŞ

1. Introduction: An Overview of Turkey's Engagement with International Law

This chapter sheds some light on the relationship of the Republic of Turkey with general international law and human rights law throughout the 20th and first quarter of the 21st centuries. The chapter first explores early engagements with international law during the founding years. Secondly, post-World War I peace negotiations with the young State and its membership in the League of Nations are explained, with historical cornerstones. Turkey's post-World War II engagement with the newly emerged international law forms the third focus of the chapter. Finally, the chapter discusses the current policy of Turkey vis-à-vis international law and institutions in order to test its historic bid to be 'an equal sovereign partner'.

2. Early International Law Policies of Modern Turkey

2.1 First international law engagement: the emerging State as sole representative of the peoples of Turkey

The first roots of the Turkish Republic go back to 1920. On 23 April of that year, the parliament of modern Turkey held its first meeting. The critical factor that created this new movement, centred in Ankara, was the occupation of Istanbul in order to give effect to the severe terms of the Armistice of Mudros brokered between the Ottoman government and the principal Allied and associated powers.[1] While the Ottoman government was under the complete political control of the Allied powers, national liberation movements across the country put the full enforcement of the armistice at risk. As a response, on 16 March 1920, the Allied powers occupied Istanbul; depriving the country of its capital of the last 500 years. On 10 August 1920, the Ottoman government signed the Treaty of Sèvres, a peace Treaty prepared as part of the Versailles treaty system following the Paris Peace Conference. The Treaty created a tiny 'semi-colonized agrarian state'[2] in Anatolia as Turkey and left the throne of the Sultan untouched.[3] The leadership of the national liberation movement declared these instruments as degrading to the whole nation and condemned those who signed them as traitors.[4]

In early 1921 the new Turkish parliament prepared and accepted its first constitution, which provided legal personality to the new State. Even before this, a military confrontation with Armenian forces on the eastern front resulted in an agreement between the government of the Grand National Assembly of Turkey and the Armenian Republic. With this Treaty, the Armenian side not only recognized the emerging government in Ankara but also promised to consider international treaties harmful to Turkey's interest null and void.[5] Soon after the signing of this Treaty, the Armenian Republic was annexed by Soviet Russia. The Moscow government forced both sides to agree on a new deal and redraw the borders.

The first rapprochement between the leadership of emerging Turkey and the Soviet leadership goes back to the spring of 1919. As soon as the Soviet leadership realized that these two countries could act together, they did not hesitate to recognize the international legal personality of the Ankara government.[6] Since Western States were still maintaining diplomatic relations only with the Ottoman government in Istanbul, the Soviet rapprochement was seen as a life jacket by Ankara. A delegation from Turkey met with Lenin's foreign minister to sign a friendship and brotherhood treaty (known as the Treaty of Moscow).[7] The Soviet side recognized the international legality of the Ankara government and promised not to accept any international instrument jeopardizing Turkey's interests. Ankara achieved its key aim: international recognition and amicable resolution of border problems in the East. In return, the Soviets gained a great partner in confronting the West, especially concerning the future legal status of the straits of Marmara and Istanbul.

The next deal was brokered by the Soviets seven months later. This time the Soviet republics of Armenia, Georgia, and Azerbaijan signed a friendship treaty with Turkey.[8] The Treaty of Kars declared all other treaties in contradiction with its provisions null and void. The only exception to this rule was the Treaty of Moscow.

Last but not least, the government in Ankara also managed to sign a treaty with a European power. The Treaty of Ankara, signed with France, formalized the evacuation of the occupying French troops in Turkey and fixed and determined the border with Syria.[9] In addition, France had to recognize the Ankara government as the sovereign power in Turkey.

During the negotiations and the final authoring of the terms of these instruments, the government in Ankara pursued the aim of being recognized as the only representative of Turkey's peoples by the State parties to the instruments mentioned.

2.2 The emergence of the 'equal sovereign partner' doctrine at Lausanne

The Ankara government's signing of the above-mentioned international instruments could be seen as a rehearsal for the approaching symphony. Following the liberation of the occupied territories in Anatolia with victorious military movements against enemy troops, the Allied powers, this time, had to invite the Ankara government to ceasefire negotiations. Representatives of the Grand National Assembly of Turkey and the allied powers signed the armistice and agreed to negotiate a new peace treaty for an international settlement of the post-war situation.[10]

Before departing for peace negotiations, the parliament in Ankara terminated the political power of the throne.[11] This made them legally the sole representative of the nation, at least for the time being, internally. This capacity would now be approved at Lausanne internationally.

The parties convened in Lausanne had difficulties agreeing with the Turkish insistence on equality on procedural issues such as rotation of the presidency, election of the secretary-general of the conference, and representation in working commissions.[12] As to the merits, while the Allied powers expected to reach a deal very similar to those signed by the defeated Ottoman State, the Turkish delegation firmly insisted on being the representative of the nation that won a national liberation war. These two opposite approaches of the parties dominated all stages of peacemaking in Lausanne.

There were complicated issues that needed to be resolved: Turkey's border with Greece, the Turkey-Iraqi border, the regime of the straits of the Sea of Marmara and Istanbul, Ottoman debts, capitulations, war reparations, demilitarization, and the status of minorities in Turkey. Each topic dealt with during the conference came with intense negotiations. Although initially scheduled by the Allied powers for a couple of weeks, due to Turkish resistance against imposed provisions, the conference lasted eight months in two sessions with an interval of two and a half months (20 November 1922 to 4 February 1923 and then 23 April 1923 to 24 July 1923).

Elaborating on the multidimensional issue of minorities in Lausanne may provide significant elements for Turkey's bid to be accepted as a sovereign partner by its Western adversaries.

According to the chief British delegate, Lord Curzon, the minority issue was a topic of international concern and delegations should realize that the eyes of the world were upon them as they discussd the question.[13] The Allied powers demanded that Turkey accept minority provisions very similar to the Polish Minority Treaty of 28 June 1919 with the argument that such an international concert would also be a good experience for Turkey. This was seen as 'the minimum which Turkey should accept if she really desires to take her place among modern States'.[14] The minimum was that a new regime for minorities politically evolved in the post-war period and was legally placed in the peace treaties with provisions together with a guarantee system under the League of Nations.

Under the Turkish approach, two principal factors were important regarding the minority question in Turkey: interference by certain powers in the internal affairs of the country under the pretext of protecting minorities, and the desire of minorities thus encouraged to liberate themselves in order to constitute independent States.[15] Long and arduous negotiations yielded minority rights similar to other treaties but for only one subject: non-Muslims. Kurds, who are mainly Muslim with distinct cultural and linguistic characteristics, and Alevis, who are non-Sunni Muslims with distinct cultural differences, were left outside.[16] The Allied powers had chosen to spend their energy in exhaustive negotiations for their economic and strategic interests instead of the rights of others.

In the end, the Lausanne Treaty gave birth to the international personality of the new State of Turkey in the eyes of the world. For the Allied powers, the Lausanne Treaty was the last peace treaty that ended World War I and closed the file on the centuries-old Eastern question.

2.3 Doubts about equal membership in the League of Nations

Throughout the Lausanne conference, the British delegation and the representatives of other Allied powers constantly invited Turkey to apply for membership of the League of Nations. The Turkish delegation had never turned this invitation down. They were aware that being recognized as a sovereign State in the eyes of the Western powers necessitated membership in this newly established international organization. However, they had some doubts. First, the Turkish delegation had difficulty in accepting the role of the League of Nations as a guarantor of minorities. For them, although the ulterior examination of questions concerning minorities might be within the jurisdiction of the Permanent Court of International Justice, every member of the Council of the League of Nations would have the power to raise minority questions.[17] Nothing would prevent powers having designs on Turkey from secretly inciting minorities and profiting, as had happened in the past. The British delegation considered Turkish suspicions not only ill-founded but most unwise. They had also advised that the time had come for Turkey to decide its future attitude towards the League.[18] From time to time, British suggestions reached the level of threat.[19]

Secondly, Turkey hesitated to transfer the issues under discussion at the Lausanne table to the League of Nations, due to British and French hegemony at the League. Therefore, they responded to the Allied powers' invitation based on their 'equal sovereign partner' doctrine: Turkey was willing to apply for membership of the League only after the Allied powers recognized a newly-emerged Turkey's sovereignty by signing the Lausanne Treaty.[20]

Due to these concerns, twelve years after its establishment, Turkey accepted the invitation, and was admitted to the League on 18 July 1932 with a unanimous vote at the

League of Nations Assembly.[21] Two years later, Turkey's ally in the 1920s, the USSR, joined the League, following a more controversial membership process.[22]

In the years following membership, Turkey stood firmly behind the rules of international law. In 1943, at the opening ceremony of the Turkish Institute of International Law, the then foreign minister, Numan Menemencioglu, without any legal basis at the national level, stated that 'Turkey was not a country where international law merely took shelter but one in which it reigned supreme'.[23] At the same ceremony, American legal scholar and diplomat Philip Marshall Brown declared Turkey as a country that had 'not only attained a position of equality among the nations of the earth but [one that had] also attained a wise and powerful leadership'.[24]

Starting during the Lausanne years, throughout the 1930s and onwards, Turkey implemented extensive legal reforms in order to harmonize its civil, criminal, and administrative law with continental European legal systems. This transformation aimed at taking part in the Western world, which reached its peak following the emergence of international human rights law in the post-World War II era.

3. Post-World War II Approach to International Law: Positioning with the Western World

Turkey stayed neutral during World War II. As a result, it had no wounds to direct itself negatively while constructing relationships with the new world order during the post-war period. When the United Nations (UN) was established, Turkey displayed no hesitation in becoming a member and gave its full support to the success of the organization. Speaking before the General Assembly in 1946, the Turkish representative stated: 'Turkey is not among the pessimists who harbour doubts as to the future of this organization. With courage, with determination and with faith, we look forward to the predestined success of the United Nations.' In the eyes of the Turkish State, 'Turkey has done her share in the endeavour to attain the United Nations ideal, which is the highest manifestation of civilization. She will continue to do her part.'[25]

Turkey held its first multi-party general elections in 1946. Paving the way for a pluralist democracy helped the country to abide by international rules in the areas of democracy and human rights. So Turkey stood with the countries that voted to adopt the Universal Declaration of Human Rights (UDHR) on 10 December 1948 at the UN General Assembly (also referred to as UNGA). Since then, Turkey has signed and ratified almost all international and regional human rights instruments with the same motivation, namely that of of aligning itself with the Western world.[26]

Early UN membership was followed by membership in the Council of Europe (also referred to as the CoE). Turkey was the thirteenth member of the Council of Europe in 1950, and the eleventh country to sign the European Convention on Human Rights (ECHR) the same year. The ECHR was ratified in 1954. These attempts aimed at bringing the country further into line with European legal standards.[27] Indeed, being part of common European standards is seen as *a sine qua non* in constructing the country's European identity.

Turkey had also seen the UN Charter rules on sovereignty and use of force as a first step towards entering the common security umbrella. For completion of its position within Western international legal space—this time in the area of security—Turkey became the thirteenth member of the North Atlantic Treaty Organization (NATO) in 1952, together with Greece.[28] A threat from Stalin directed against the existing status and security of the Bosphorus Straits, together with some territorial demands, had also been a driving force to move quickly towards membership of European and international institutions.[29] Since 1952, Turkey has taken an active part in dozens of NATO operations. Both NATO and Turkey seem mutually satisfied with the partnership. It is only in recent years that Turkey has had some problems with some individual NATO members. Purchasing Russian S400 missile systems triggered US CAATSA (Countering America's Adversaries Through Sanctions Act) sanctions and exclusion of Turkey from the F35 fighter jet programme. And Turkey complicated Finnish and Swedish applications for membership in NATO, not as a rule but due to their arms embargo on Turkey, alleged support for the PYD/YPG (Democratic Union Party/People's Protection Units) in Syria, and Sweden's hosting of PKK members. Interestingly, Sweden and Finland lifted their long-standing neutral status and moved towards NATO in 2022 with the same motive that Turkey had expressed in the 1950s: safety against the Russian threat.

It should also be underlined that the Russian war of aggression against Ukraine was recognized by Turkey as a state of war, and Turkey condemned Russian aggression. Turkey enforced the Montreux Convention, whereby the passage of warships was limited to those returning to their bases. Turkey has aimed to facilitate talks between Ukraine and Russia and to work on de-escalation and bringing about a ceasefire. It also undertook a diplomatic initiative to facilitate the export of Ukrainian grain. The deal agreed upon by Ukraine and Russia on 22 July 2022 in Istanbul, facilitated by the UN, would not have been possible without the constructive role of Turkey, which was involved in implementing the deal. Nevertheless, Turkey refrained from aligning with EU sanctions against Russia.[30]

While Turkey supports the strategic partnership between NATO and the EU,[31] the future role of NATO in European security[32] and Turkey's potential role in this security architecture remains to be seen.

In addition to its ambition to be within European public law space, Turkey also aimed to take part in the European economic area. With this in mind, Turkey applied for full membership in the European Economic Community (EEC) in 1959, just after establishment of the organization. Partnership negotiations led to a partnership treaty being signed in 1963. In other words, Turkey's current bid to be a full member of the EU started six decades ago.

4. Being a Part of European Public Law

The Association Agreement (Ankara Agreement) between the EC and Turkey was signed on 12 September 1963. Its aim was to establish a customs union with a transitional stage and to provide economic cohesion via common policies in order to prepare Turkey for full membership. The Additional Protocol signed in 1970 laid down a timetable and envisaged a period of twenty-two years for the realization of free movements of goods, persons, and services.

However, Turkey could not assume its obligations, especially those relating to political criteria, due to human rights problems caused by the coup d'état of 12 September 1980, which led to formal suspension of relations. After 1986, relations were gradually normalized with the restoration of democratic institutions, the Association Council (in 1986) and the Mixed Parliamentary Commission (in 1989).

Following Turkey's application for membership in 1987, the Commission issued an Opinion on 20 December 1989, stressing that 'although there have been developments in recent years in the human rights situation and in respect for the identity of minorities, these have not yet reached the level required in a democracy'.[33]

In conclusion, the Commission recommended a series of substantial measures on the road to interdependence and integration. These cover completion of the customs union, intensification of financial cooperation, promotion of industrial and technological cooperation, and strengthening of political and cultural links.

Turkey should implement universal human rights standards in its internal system in order to integrate with the EU.[34] There exists an undeniable parallelism between the bilateral human rights policies individually pursued by Western countries and European policies as a whole.

Although the Commission notes some positive changes in its human rights situation,[35] Turkey is still far from being a liberal democracy.[36]

Turkey's bid to join the EU took on new momentum in the 1990s. The first step taken by the government was to recognize the jurisdiction of the European Court of Human Rights (ECtHR) in 1990. Turkey had been sending judges to the Strasbourg Court since 1969, but the original version of the ECHR allowed State parties not to accept individual applications to the ECtHR for individuals living within their jurisdiction.[37]

During the 1990s, Turkey launched widescale anti-terror operations in southeast Turkey. Planning and implementation of these operations did not take into account the government's human rights commitments under international law. As a result, when the first applications reached the ECtHR in the 1990s, Turkey had to meet its international human rights obligations under the ECHR, which it had ratified four decades earlier. Moreover, now unlike a political guarantee, the country's responsibility was examined before an international court: the ECtHR.

In several resolutions, the European Parliament has taken the view that financial aid is linked to the human rights situation[38] and has blocked it due to Turkey's failure to embrace human rights and democratization,[39] as well as the Cyprus and Kurdish issues.[40]

After the 1997 Luxembourg Summit crisis, which put Turkey in a special category[41] on its own and was strongly condemned by the Turkish authorities, the 1999 Helsinki European Council qualified Turkey as 'a candidate state destined to join the Union on the basis of the same criteria as applied to other candidate states'.[42]

As a response, during the 2000s, Turkey aimed to resolve the disharmony between its domestic legal system and the country's obligations under international law. For this purpose, the legislature and the executive launched legal reform campaigns. Judgments against Turkey from the ECtHR and criticism from the EU shaped the content of new laws in almost all fields.

In that respect, according to the Commission 2000 Regular Report, an Accession Partnership for Turkey, by unanimous political agreement at the Council on 4 December 2000, was approved by the Council on 8 March 2001 and Turkey, as a response, announced its National Programme on 19 March 2001. Consequently, a new era had begun in Turkey-EU relations, including voluntary conditionality, on an equal basis with other candidate States.[43] Accession negotiations were opened in October 2005. This, a new stage began for the up-and-down relationship between Turkey and the EU.[44]

Through the first judgments of the ECtHR, Turkey entered a new phase in its relations with international law. Serious, and widespread human rights violations found by the Strasbourg Court against Turkey led to doubts over the country's equal partnership bid vis-à-vis international law and international institutions. After decades-long enjoyment of an equal partnership role built heavily on Turkey's neutral stance during World War II and the early Republican legal reforms, the time had again come for the country to prove its belief in the fundamental values of democracy, the rule of law, and human rights.

According to the Accession Partnership (2001), Turkey's 'short-term' priorities concerning human rights were as follows: to strengthen legal and constitutional guarantees for the right of freedom of expression in line with Article 10 ECHR and for the right of freedom of association and peaceful assembly and to encourage the development of civil society, to align its legal procedures concerning pre-trial detention with the provisions of the ECHR. It can simply be observed that, after twenty years, the same problems continue to exist.

The accession Partnership document was revised by the EU in 2003, 2005, 2006, and 2008, whilst the National Programme was updated in 2003, 2005, and 2008.[45] Turkey began to take significant steps in order to comply with the political criteria, and harmonization packages entered into force. This reform process strengthened existing regulations on democracy, the rule of law, and human rights, particularly on freedom of expression. Within this framework, between 2002 and 2004, eight harmonization packages, and between 2001 and 2004, two constitutional amendments were accepted.

At the constitutional level, Article 90 of the Turkish Constitution of 1982 stipulates that 'international agreements duly put into effect have the force of law'. That is to say, treaties are situated on the same level as laws in the Turkish normative hierarchy. The validity of international treaties in the Turkish legal order depends on the legislature's approval by a law approving ratification.

In order to improve implementation of the ECHR, the Constitution was amended in 2004, giving international human rights conventions precedence over ordinary legislation. The last paragraph of Article 90 states that 'in the case of a conflict between international agreements, duly put into effect, concerning fundamental rights and freedoms and the laws due to differences in provisions on the same matter, the provisions of international agreements shall prevail'. Theoretically, the 2004 amendment emphasizes that international human rights agreements enjoy precedence over domestic laws.

In 2010 (entered into force in 2012), an amendment to the constitution empowered the Turkish Constitutional Court (TCC) to accept individual applications from the victims of human rights violations. One can consider that Turkey created its own European Court of Human Rights but, in terms of the decisions handed down, it is difficult to see any strong engagement by the TCC with European human rights law.

Following the General Affairs Council's conclusions of June 2018—namely, that Turkey's accession negotiations had effectively come to a standstill—no further chapters are being considered for opening or closing. During this period, the EU's serious concerns about the continued deterioration of democracy, the rule of law, fundamental rights, and the independence of the judiciary have not been addressed. Further backsliding has occurred in many areas. Following the 2015 refugee crisis, the EU has prioritized maintaining functional cooperation with Turkey over firmly applying conditionality. The EU-Turkey relationship changed in nature, becoming functional and non-membership-oriented in this period.[46] Despite this new functional relationship, Commission reports on Turkey continue to assert a lack of democracy, rule of law, and human rights.

The EU Commission's Turkey Report 2021[47] states that the legal framework includes general guarantees of respect for human and fundamental rights, but that legislation and practice still need to be brought into line with the ECHR and ECtHR case law. Turkey's refusal to implement ECtHR rulings[48] increased concerns regarding the judiciary's adherence to international and European standards. Turkey's withdrawal from the Istanbul Convention[49] also raised questions about its commitment to such standards.

According to the latest Report by the EU Commission on 12 October 2022,[50] severe deficiencies are affecting the functioning of Turkey's democratic institutions, and democratic backsliding continues. Structural problems in the presidential system remain in place. Key recommendations from the Council of Europe and its bodies have yet to be addressed, and the serious backsliding observed in the judicial system since 2016 has continued. Concerns remain, in particular over the systemic lack of independence of the judiciary and undue pressure on judges and prosecutors.

The 2022 Report, like previous reports, also notes serious deficiencies in freedom of expression. Legislation and its implementation, especially national security and anti-terrorism provisions, continue to contravene the ECHR and other international standards and to diverge from ECtHR case law. Criminal cases and convictions of journalists, human rights activists, writers, opposition politicians, and social media users continue. Further serious backsliding occurred in the area of freedom of assembly and association in light of recurrent bans, disproportionate interventions, and excessive use of force in peaceful demonstrations. Legislation and its implementation are not in line with the Turkish Constitution, European standards, or international conventions. Regular reports by the EU Commission testify to the pressing power of the Union on candidate countries concerning human rights, referring to ECtHR case law.

Unfortunately, even after many constitutional and legal amendments, the Turkish judiciary is far from applying ECtHR decisions or indeed any reference to other international legal materials. While the Turkish lower courts almost never make use of international law, the trajectory of the TCC's decisions demonstrates another grave disconnect: international commitments by ratification of human rights treaties have remained on paper but are not matched in practice.[51] The infringement procedure before the Council of Europe and the ECtHR judgment on Article 46/4 is the latest testimony.[52]

5. Direct Conflicts with International Law in Two Respects

Turkey has displayed full respect for the norms of post-World War II international law except in two instances. The first is the status of the administration in Northern Cyprus. In the summer of 1974, the Turkish military occupied the northern part of Cyprus, resulting in the island's territorial division into two parts, Northern and Southern Cyprus. Subsequently, a local administration was established in the North. Since then, only the South has remained under the sovereignty of the Republic of Cyprus.

Further, in 1983, the Northern administration proclaimed the independence of the 'Turkish Republic of Northern Cyprus' (TRNC). As a response, the UN Security Council (UNSC) declared the proclamation of the establishment of the TRNC to be legally invalid.[53] Additionally, the Committee of Ministers of the CoE decided to continue recognizing the government of the Republic of Cyprus as the sole legitimate government.[54] In 2004, the EU accepted the territorially divided Republic of Cyprus as a full member with suspension of EU law in the North.[55] So far, only Turkey has recognized the TRNC as a sovereign, independent State.

The leadership of the Turkish Cypriot community argued the need for statehood as a response to the events of the past twenty years, during which they were deprived of their rights, ignored, ridiculed, and treated with contempt by the Greek Cypriot leaders.[56] Parenthetically, for Turkey, the TRNC is set up by the Turkish Cypriot people to exercise its right to self-determination—but not by Turkey.[57] The Cyprus question has remained unresolved for almost five decades as one of the longest-lasting international disputes of the post-UN era. In the eyes of the international community, Turkey is an occupying power, in other words, a rule-breaking country. However, the whole problem was left to possible negotiation that would take place under the good offices of the Secretary-General of the UN.

The Commission's 2021 Report underlined that relations with the EU deteriorated until December 2020, primarily due to action taken by Turkey in the Eastern Mediterranean, directly challenging the rights of the Republic of Cyprus in its maritime zones. The EU has stressed the need for Turkey to respect the sovereign rights of EU member States, which includes entering into bilateral agreements and exploring and exploiting their natural resources in line with the EU *acquis* and international law, including the UN Convention on the Law of the Sea (UNCLOS).[58]

The second objection by Turkey to the international law created during the post-World War II era came after the adoption of UNCLOS in 1982. This Treaty, in its Article 3, provided that every State has the right to establish the breadth of its territorial sea up to a limit not exceeding twelve nautical miles. Turkey has been one of the few countries that have not signed and ratified the Convention. Turkey's argument was obvious: when Article 3 is applied comprehensively, due to the existence of the Greek islands and islets, many of which are in close proximity to the Turkish coastline, Greece will acquire approximately 71.5 per cent—currently 43.5 per cent under the six miles rule—of the Aegean sea, while Turkey's share would increase by only 8.8 per cent. And the Aegean high seas would diminish from 49 to 19.7 per cent. Therefore, for Turkey, the impact of such a Greek extension of its territorial waters would be to deprive Turkey, one of the two coastal States of the Aegean, of its fundamental right of access to the high seas from its territorial waters, the economic benefits derived from the Aegean, and scientific research. As a result, for Turkey, the extension by Greece of its territorial waters beyond the present six miles in the semi-enclosed Aegean Sea constitutes an abuse of rights.[59]

Since the entry into force of the Convention in 1994, Article 3 has become a cause for dispute between Turkey and Greece. While Greece, as a party to the Convention, argues that its territorial sea around the Aegean islands is as long as twelve miles, Turkey declares that the Article 3 rule is not binding on Turkey as a non-State party. It remains open to question whether one State's rejection of an international instrument would deplore the right of others under the same instrument. In other words, do the rules in UNCLOS constitute customary international law?

The answer in international law circles was clear: the Law of the Sea presents a codification of customary law. In this case, Turkey based its argument on the concept of 'persistent objector state'. Turkey does not object to the twelve-mile rule altogether; rather, its objection is limited to applying the rule in the Aegean Sea.[60] Finally, Turkey declared that the Greek extension of its territorial sea to twelve miles would be regarded as a *casus belli*.[61]

The dispute over territorial waters unavoidably created another controversy for air space. Article 2 of the 1944 Chicago Convention on International Civil Aviation reads: 'For the purposes of this Convention the territory of a State shall be deemed to be the land areas and territorial waters adjacent thereto under the sovereignty, suzerainty, protection or mandate of such State.'[62] Since the Convention links the breadth of national airspace to the breadth of the territorial sea, Turkey and Greece continue a legal dispute through the Flight Information Region arrangement on Aegean Airspace.

Due to historical hostility and current problems, these two countries have come to the edge of war on many occasions. A matter of cotinued debate is whether American pressure over these two countries or their NATO membership has prevented them from entering into a full-scale war.[63]

6. New Approaches to the Equal Sovereign Partner Bid

Except in the two cases described above, Turkey has been respectful of the rules of post-World War II international law, decisions of international organizations, and ECtHR judgments. In addition to the crisis it created between Turkey and the UNSC and the entire world, the Cyprus problem has also affected Turkey's commitments under international human rights law. Until recently, Turkey has clearly rejected implementation of ECtHR judgments in only one area: the Cyprus cases. Already in 1996, in *Loizidou v Turkey*,[64] the ECtHR declared Turkey's responsibility for human rights violations that occurred in the northern part of the island of Cyprus.

According to the ECtHR, the concept of jurisdiction is not restricted to the national territory of the Contracting States.[65] The Court further noted that:

> the responsibility of Contracting States can be involved by acts and omissions of their authorities which produce effects outside their own territory ... the responsibility of a Contracting Party could also arise when as a consequence of military action—whether lawful or unlawful—it exercises effective control of an area outside its national territory. The obligation to secure, in such an area, the rights and freedoms set out in the Convention, derives from the fact of such control whether it be exercised directly, through its armed forces, or through a subordinate local administration.[66]

For Turkey, the TRNC is an independent state and Turkey should have no responsibility for human rights violations that occur on its territory.[67] In addition, Turkey has repeatedly argued for decades that the Cyprus problem can only be resolved under UN peaceful solution mechanisms. Until a final solution is reached, no other international organization, no matter whether it is a political body or a judicial authority, should interfere.

Turkey's attitude towards international human rights monitoring started to change in 2013, when the government faced nationwide protests at Gezi Park in Turkey. Until that time, the government had been enjoying the results of liberal reforms, which were mainly used to criticize democracy and justice problems of the past. For the first time during Gezi, collective freedom of expression was directed against the same government which was behind enlargement of the scope of fundamental rights and freedoms. The government's reaction was harsh. Since 2013, step by step, Turkey has lost its enthusiasm vis-à-vis any norms and principles of international human rights. In the eyes of the government, the supranational monitoring organs are no longer implementing human rights conventions objectively and independently.[68]

Decades after the Cyprus judgment mentioned earlier, Turkey clearly rejected implementation of another group of judgments from the ECtHR. These judgments are known as 'Article 18' judgments in reference to Article 18 ECHR, which prohibits States parties from applying the restrictions permitted for Convention rights for any purpose other than those prescribed. The founding fathers of the European human rights machinery described the crucial role of Article 18 as follows:

> In all the countries of the world the exercise of freedom has to be organized ... The limitation imposed will be valid only if it has as its aim the public interest and the common good ... In a totalitarian regime ... the State arrogates to itself the right to limit individual freedom not in the sole name of a higher freedom, not in order to permit the exercise of the freedom of all, but simply to defend its own dictatorship, its justification for its interference.[69]

In recent years, journalists, academics, human rights activists, political figures, and any other individuals who find a way to express a critical opinion against the government in power are likely to be jailed, stripped of fair trial rights, and convicted on vague charges. Before Turkey, only five States among the forty-seven members of the CoE were found guilty by the ECtHR of violating Article 18.

These States (or 'Article 18 countries': Azerbaijan, Georgia, Moldova, Russia, Ukraine) were member States of the CoE which were not known for their adherence to democracy. In almost all cases decided by the ECtHR under Article 18, the victims have somehow raised a dissenting voice. Turkey entered the club of Article 18 countries in 2018 as the sixth member.[70] In the case of *Demirtas v Turkey*,[71] the ECtHR concluded that 'national authorities have repeatedly ordered the applicant's continued detention on insufficient grounds consisting simply of a formulaic enumeration of the grounds for detention provided for by law, the Court finds that it has been established beyond reasonable doubt that the extensions of the applicant's detention, especially during two crucial campaigns, namely the referendum and the presidential election, pursued the predominant ulterior purpose of stifling pluralism and limiting freedom of political debate, which is at the very core of the concept of a democratic society'.[72] When the judgment was declared, both the President and the Turkish foreign minister announced that the judgment was not binding, and illegal.[73] One week later, a Turkish court defied the ruling of the ECtHR, which demanded the applicant's release.[74]

One year later, in another case, the ECtHR found that Turkey had violated Article 18 by detaining a businessman who was financially supporting human rights nongovernmental organizations (NGOs) in the country.[75] The ECtHR underlined the correlation between accusations of helping terrorists, which were made openly by the

President, and the wording of the charges used by the prosecutors against the applicant in the bill of indictment.[76] When finding Turkey guilty of violating Article 18, the ECtHR demanded the applicant's release; but neither political figures in power nor the judiciary have taken any action to implement the judgment. As a response, the Secretary General of the Council of Europe stated that despite a final ruling from the ECtHR, the Turkish authorities' attitude is utterly wrong. She further recalled that compliance with the rulings of the ECtHR is not a 'kind request' but a 'binding legal requirement'.[77]

Almost two decades after the first ruling in the Cyprus group of cases, Turkey now directly rejects judgments from the ECtHR in Article 18-related cases. In recent years, the country's reaction to other rulings, if not a direct rejection, has also been questionable.

As far as Turkey has stepped into a disengagement policy with international human rights law, the country's attitude towards Greece is hardening regarding the above-mentioned problems under international law. Furthermore, the UN General Assembly witnessed Turkey's direct criticism against the existing post-World War II international legal system. President Erdoğan made the following statement before the UNGA in 2020: 'Globalization, a rules-based international system and multilateralism, which were already the subject of discussions, are now even more questioned under the impact of the pandemic.' Criticism against a 'rules-based international system' is worth underlining. He continued as follows:

> When we look at the picture in front of us, we need to accurately and sincerely evaluate the full and empty parts of the glass. In the empty part of the glass, there is the need of reform for multilateral organizations, in particular the United Nations ... it took weeks, even months, for the Security Council, the most fundamental decision-making body of the United Nations, to include the pandemic on its agenda. We have once again seen the rightfulness of the 'The World is bigger than Five' thesis, which I have been advocating for years from this rostrum. The fate of humanity cannot be left at the mercy of a limited number of countries.[78]

In recent years, the Turkish official sector, as well as government-backed think tanks and media, have elaborated on this criticism under the rubric 'the world is bigger than five', a reference to the five permanent members of the UNSC. Turkish arguments can be summarized as follows: UNSC decisions are made behind closed doors, especially by the five permanent members. The UN in general and the Security Council in particular only decide matters in line with the interests of the five. Thus the world's fate is left in the hands of five countries. Further, the concept of permanent membership goes against the principle of sovereign equality, the founding principle upon which the UN was built, and Turkey suggests abolishing the decision-making power of the Security Council, stating that binding decisions should be made by the UNGA and executed by a more representative Security Council with no member having the power of veto.[79]

7. Conclusion: Turkey's Evolving International Concerns

The founding principles of modern Turkey are aimed at the country's being an equal sovereign partner before international law and its institutions. This bid is not only interested in equal representation at the international level but also in Turkey's undertaking equal collective responsibilities as well. Until almost a decade ago, Turkey had seen international law-based obligations as the other side of the equal representation coin. This had specifically been the case when Turkey underwent extensive domestic legal reforms to abide by international human rights law and Turkey's military contribution to NATO operations. However, the latest approach by Turkey vis-à-vis international institutions conveys another policy, which cannot simply be explained under its 'equal partnership bid'.

While human rights are no longer in the 'domaine réservé' of sovereign States and constitute a part of the legitimate international concern of the international community, Turkey has difficulty in adapting to these new standards. The level of rights constraints and violations are deepening in Turkey's illiberal democracy. Illiberalism and the perpetuation of illiberal power necessitate restrictions on speech, assembly, and association as well as demanding regulation of moral behaviour.[80] This practice can be seen quite clearly in newly adopted laws on the media, withdrawal from the Istanbul Convention, and 'serious backsliding' marking the independence of the Turkish judiciary and fundamental freedoms since 2016.[81]

Turkey also positions itself as a justice seeker at the UN and wishes to be involved in reforming the UN. Indeed all the criticism directed against the UN focuses on the status and role of the Security Council. Moreover, when targeting the structure of the Security Council, Turkey's criticism is directed against Western representation. Turkey underlines the importance of the Chinese and Russian presence among the five. However, this is not seen as going far enough. Turkey also argues that the existing system ignores the one and a half billion Muslims worldwide, as not a single country from the Muslim world appears among the permanent members.[82]

Additionally, despite NATO's focus on the Eastern/Russian front, Turkey argues the need to strengthen NATO operations in the Mediterranean.[83]

The big question over these policies is whether UN and NATO members will sympathize with Turkey's new position, or question the continued impediments to the country's adoption of the universal principles of human rights, democracy, and the rule of law.

Notes

1. Armistice of Mudros, 30 October 1918. British and Foreign State papers at HeinOnline; see also Gwynne Dyer, 'The Turkish Armistice of 1918: 1: The Turkish Decision for a Separate Peace, Autumn 1918', 8(2) Middle Eastern Studies 1918, 143–178.
2. This new Turkey was left with no freedom to maintain an army, tailor its budget, or enjoy spending powers. See Bulent Tanor, Kurtulus-Kurulus [Independence-Establishment], Cumhuriyet pub, Istanbul 2000, 37.
3. The Treaty of Peace between the Allied Powers and Turkey, signed at Sèvres, 10 August 1920. For the text, see 15 American Journal of International Law 1921, 179–181. This Treaty has never been ratified by any State parties to it.
4. The terms of the Treaty were far stricter than those imposed on Germany. See Bernard Lewis, *The Emergence of Modern Turkey* (OUP 1968) 247 (hereafter Lewis, *The Emergence of Modern Turkey*).
5. Article 14 Treaty of Alexandropol: 2 December 1920, https://western-armenia.org/history/treaty-of-alexandropol/ accessed 9 March 2022.
6. Tsvetelina Tsvetkova, 'Turkish National Movement and Soviet Russia in Caucasus (1919–1922)', 1(1) Journal of Balkan and Black Sea Studies 1921, 78, 81.
7. See Traité d'Union et de Fraternité of 16 mars 1921, Martens, NRG 3rd Series, vol 16, 37.
8. Traité de Kars: Traité d'union et de fraternité, signed at Kars, 13 October 1921. See https://mjp.univ-perp.fr/traites/1921kars.htm accessed 23 March 2022.
9. Agreement signed at Angora on 20 October 1921, between M Franklin-Bouillon, Former Minister, and Youssouf Kemal Bey, Minister for Foreign Affairs of the Government of the Grand National Assembly of Angora, LIV(1284) League of Nations Treaty Series 1926–1927, 177–193.
10. Armistice of Mudanya, signed on 11 October 1922 by the Allied Powers of WWI and the Grand National Assembly of Turkey. See Martens, NRG 3rd Series, vol 13, 336.
11. Lewis, *The Emergence of Modern Turkey* (n 4) 257. The Ottoman State had been legally terminated step by step by the new government in Ankara. The following are the cornerstones of this process: establishment of a new parliament in Ankara in April 1920; adoption of a new constitution in 1921; elimination of the title of Ottoman Sultan in 1922; ratification of the Lausanne Treaty in August 1923; and finally the proclamation of the Republic in October 1923.
12. Lausanne Conference on Near Eastern Affairs (1922–1923) Records of Proceedings and Draft Terms of Peace (HMSO 1923) 4, 7–9, 16–17 (hereafter 'Lausanne Records and Proceedings'). See also 'Conférence de Lausanne. Le Matinée de Lundi', Journal de Géneve, Mardi 21 Novembre 1922, 4.
13. Lausanne Records and Proceedings, 175.
14. Statement by the representative of the Kingdom of Serbs, Croats and Slovenes. See Lausanne Records and Proceedings, 177, 188.

    Treaty Between the Principal Allied and Associated Powers and Poland, signed at Versailles, 28 June 1919 known as the 'Polish Minority Treaty'. For the full text of the Treaty, see Manley O Hudson, *International Legislation*, vol I, (Oceana Publications 1919–1921) 283–298.
15. Lausanne Records and Proceedings, 201–202. In fact, foreign political and military intervention in the case of violence against religious and ethnic groups had been considered moral and lawful at the time. See Martti Koskenniemi, *The Gentle Civilizer of Nations: The*

Rise and Fall of International Law 1870–1960 (CUP 2009) 95, fn 386, 134; Davide Rodogno, 'European Legal Doctrines on Intervention and the Status of the Ottoman Empire within the "Family of Nations" Throughout the Nineteenth Century', 18 Journal of the History of International Law 2016, 5–41.

16. Alevis also comprise the second-largest minority group in Turkey. For more details of minority negotiations at Lausanne, see Olgun Akbulut, 'TBMM Tarihinde Özerklik Düzenlemeleri [Autonomy Discussions in the History of TGNA]', in *In Memory of the Centennial of the Turkish Grand National Assembly* (Tekin Publishing 2022) 599–604, 618–622.
17. For the other side of the token, see André Nicolayévitch Mandelstam, 'La Société des Nations et les Puissances devant le Problème Arménien', Édition spéciale de la Revue Générale de Droit International Public, A Pedone, Paris 1926.
18. Lausanne Records and Proceedings, 202. The British delegation had also expected the Turkish side to show respect towards the League.
19. As the head of the British delegation, Lord Curzon stated: 'Many arrangements now under discussion with the Turks would be easier to carry out if the League of Nations were involved, and the protection afforded to Turkey in the future would certainly be greater. If, on the other hand, the Turkish delegation refused to have any contact with the League of Nations, there would be a very marked change, not only as regards the feeling of his own country and some others, but also as regards the solution of the problems now before the conference.' See Lausanne Records and Proceedings, 213.
20. See ibid, 219, 221.
21. M Alice Matthews, 'Chronicle of International Events', 26(4) American Journal of International Law 1932, 827. Before Turkey's admission, the League of Nations Assembly with original members elected new members only upon application. See Manley O Hudson, 'Membership in the League of Nations', 18 American Journal of International Law 1924, 436–449.
22. See H L, 'The U.S.S.R. and the League of Nations', 11 Bulletin of International News (27 September 1934), 3–12.
23. Cemil Bilsel, 'International Law in Turkey', 38(4) American Journal of International Law 1944, 549.
24. ibid, 546–547.
25. UNGA, 1st Sess, 38th plen Mtg, A/PV.38, 762–763 (26 October 1946) available from https://digitallibrary.un.org/record/731267/files/A_PV-38-EN.pdf accessed 6 July 2022.
26. The status of ratification of major human rights instruments by Turkey is available at http://hrlibrary.umn.edu/research/ratification-turkey.html accessed 6 July 2022.
27. For details of this process see Olgun Akbulut, 'Turkey: The European Convention on Human Rights as a Tool for Modernisation', in Patricia Popelier, Koen Lemmens, and Sarah Lambrecht (eds), *Criticism of the European Court of Human Rights. Shifting the Convention System: Counter-Dynamics at the National and EU-Level* (Intersentia 2016) Ch 16, 413–414 (hereafter Akbulut, 'Turkey: The European Convention on Human Rights as a Tool for Modernisation').
28. Currently, NATO has thirty members. See https://www.nato.int/nato-welcome/index.html accessed 6 July 2022. For more information see the chapter on NATO by Tom Grant in this volume.

29. For the so-called 'Stalin's Demands' see Kıvanç Coş and Pınar Bilgin, 'Stalin's Demands: Constructions of the "Soviet Other" in Turkey's Foreign Policy, 1919–1945', 6 Foreign Policy Analysis 2010, 43–60.
30. See the EU Commission Report 2022, https://neighbourhood-enlargement.ec.europa.eu/turkiye-report-2022_en accessed 27 December 2022.
31. Republic of Turkey Ministry of Foreign Affairs, 'Türkiye's Relations with NATO', https://www.mfa.gov.tr/nato.en.mfa accessed 6 December 2022 (hereafter Republic of Turkey Ministry of Foreign Affairs, 'Türkiye's Relations with NATO').
32. See the chapter on NATO by Tom Grant in this volume.
33. Commission Opinion on Turkey's Request for Accession to the Community, SEC (89) 2290 final/2.
34. For admission requirements, see the chapter by Justus Vasel in this volume.
35. Recognition of individual application to the European Commission on Human Rights in 1987, ratification of the European convention for the prevention of torture and inhuman and degrading treatment or punishment in 1988.
36. See the chapter on the rule of law by Anne van Aaken in this volume.
37. See the chapter on human rights by Başak Çalı in this volume.
38. See, eg, Bull EU 12/95, OJ C 17, 22 January 1996.
39. Many resolutions concern different cases such as the arrest of DEP deputies (Bull EU 3/94, 12/94), peaceful settlement of the Kurdish problem, freedom of the press, and release of arrested journalists (Bull EU 5/97).
40. See Section 5.
41. The decisions of the Luxembourg Summit gave Turkey a special status with a long lead time to full membership. Turkey was included in the enlargement process but not given a pre-accession strategy like the other eleven candidate countries. The Union formulated a special 'European Strategy' that would prepare Turkey for accession. See Atila Eralp, 'Turkey in the Enlargement Process: From Luxembourg to Helsinki', 8 Private View Spring 2000, 1–9.
42. Helsinki European Council, 10–11 December 1999.
43. See Işıl Karakaş, 'La Turquie et l'Union européenne: une adhésion à long terme' in L Beurdeley, R de la Brosse, and F Maron (eds), *L'Union européenne et ses espaces de proximité* (Bruylant 2007) 93–102.
44. See Birol Yeşilada, *EU-Turkey Relations in the 21st Century* (Routledge 2013).
45. Until today, in the Turkey-EU accession negotiations, sixteen chapters have been opened and remain open. See the official web page http://www.ab.gov.tr
46. Beken Saatçioğlu, 'The European Union's Refugee Crisis and Rising Functionalism in EU-Turkey Relations', 21 Turkish Studies 2020, 169–187.
47. SWD(2021) 290.
48. Notably in *Selahattin Demirtaş v Turkey* (No 2), 14305/17, 22 December 2020 and *Kavala v Turkey*, 28749/18, GC Judgment of 11 July 2022.
49. 'Council of Europe Convention on preventing and combating violence against women and domestic violence', adopted in Istanbul on 11 May 2011 and entered into force on 1 August 2014, CETS No 210.
50. SWD(2022) 333.
51. Ikboljon Qoraboyev and Emre Turkut, 'International Law in the Turkish Legal Order: Transnational Judicial Dialogue and the Turkish Constitutional Court', The Italian Yearbook of International Law Online October 2017, 56.

52. The Court concluded that Turkey has failed to fulfil its obligation under Article 46(1) to abide by the *Kavala v Turkey* judgment of 10 December 2019. See *Kavala v Turkey*, 11 July 2022, para 174.
53. UNSC Resolution no 541 (1983) http://unscr.com/en/resolutions/541 accessed 17 July 2022.
54. COE COM Resolution No: (83)13 on Cyprus, 73rd Session on 24 November 1983 <https://search.coe.int/cm/pages/result_details.aspx?objectid = 09000016805365a4> accessed 17 July 2022.
55. See https://europa.eu/european-union/about-eu/countries/member-countries/cyprus_en accessed 17 July 2022.
56. Rauf Denktas's statement before the UNSC S/PV.2498, 17 November 1983, 4–5, https://undocs.org/en/S/PV.2498(OR) accessed 17 July 2022.
57. *Cyprus v Turkey*, 25781/94, 10 May 2001, para 15.
58. EU Commission 2021 Report https://neighbourhood-enlargement.ec.europa.eu/turkiye-report-2021_en accessed 27 December 2022. Similarly, see EU Commission Report 2022 (n 30).
59. 'Background Note on the Aegean Dispute', prepared by the Foreign Ministry of the Republic of Turkey, available from https://www.mfa.gov.tr/background-note-on-aegean-dispute.en.mfa accessed 18 July 2022.
60. For details of the Turkish position, see Rıza Türmen, 'Whose Sea? A Turkish International Law Perspective on the Greek-Turkish Disputes', available from https://www.institutmontaigne.org/en/blog/whose-sea-turkish-international-law-perspective-greek-turkish-disputes accessed 28 July 2022.
61. For details of the Greek position, see Anastasia Strati, 'Greece and the Law of the Sea: A Greek Perspective' in Aldo Chircop, André Gerolymatos, and John O Iatrides (eds), *The Aegean Sea after the Cold War—Security and Law of the Issues* (Macmillan Press 2000) 89–103 (hereafter Chircop, Gerolymatos, and Iatrides, *The Aegean Sea after the Cold War*).
62. No 102. Convention on International Civil Aviation, signed at Chicago, on 7 December 1944 (came into force on 4 April 1947), 15 UNTS 295–374.
63. For details of this discussion, see John O Iatrides, 'NATO and Aegean Disputes: The Cold War and After', in Chircop, Gerolymatos, and Iatrides, *The Aegean Sea after the Cold War* (n 61) 32–46.
64. *Loizidou v Turkey*, 15318/89, 18 December 1996 GC.
65. See Işıl Karakaş and Hasan Bakırcı 'Extraterritorial Application of the ECHR: Evolution of the Court's Jurisprudence on the Notions of Extraterritorial Jurisdiction and State Responsibility', in Anne van Aaken and Iulia Motoc (eds), *The ECHR and General International Law* (OUP 2018) 112–134 (hereafter van Aaken and Motoc, *The ECHR and General International Law*).
66. *Loizidou v Turkey* (n 64) para 52.
67. Compare with the Russian approach in the Case of *Ilaşcu and Others v Moldova and Russia*, 48787/99, 8 July 2004, paras 353–358; and the Armenian arguments in *Chiragov and Others v Armenia*, 13216/05, Grand Chamber Judgment of 16 June 2015, paras 158–164. See also Ganna Yudkivska, 'Territorial Jurisdiction and Positive Obligations of an Occupied State: Some Reflections on Evolving Issues under Article 1 of the Convention', in van Aaken and Motoc, *The ECHR and General International Law* (n 65) 138.
68. During the hearing at the Grand Chamber of the ECtHR in the Case of *Perinçek v Switzerland*, the Turkish Minister of Justice was heard to say to journalists in Strasbourg: 'A decision on the contrary means bankruptcy. This also means that it is not a court

that delivers justice but a court that has a political stance; it would then not be a human rights court that examines cases objectively and independently, but a biased and independent court that rules in line with countries' political interests. I believe that the Grand Chamber of the ECtHR will not make such a mistake.' See Akbulut, 'Turkey: The European Convention on Human Rights as a Tool for Modernisation' (n 27) 422. The *Perinçek* case was about a Turkish politican's freedom of expression since he denied calling the '1915 Events' 'genocide' at a speech delivered in Switzerland. See *Perinçek v Switzerland* (27510/08), Grand Chamber Judgment of 15 October 2015.

69. Speech by Mr Henry Teitgen on 16 August 1950 during the Preparatory Works for the ECHR. See CoE, Information document prepared by the Registry, CDH (75) 11 Confidentiel, Preparatory Work on Article 18 of the European Convention on Human Rights, 18.
70. In 2021, Bulgaria and, in 2022, also Poland entered the club as the seventh and eight members. See ECtHR, *Miroslava Todorova v. Bulgaria*, 40072/13, 19 October 2021; *Juszczyszyn v Poland*, 35599/20, 6 October 2022.
71. ECtHR, *Demirtas v Turkey (No 2)*, 14305/17, 20 November 2018. The findings in this judgment by the second section of the ECtHR were further approved by the Grand Chamber on 22 December 2020.
72. *Demirtas v Turkey (No 2)*, Chamber Judgment, para 273.
73. 'EU, Turkey face off over jailed Kurdish politician', *Al Monitor*, 23 November 2018, available from https://www.al-monitor.com/originals/2018/11/eu-turkey-face-off-demirtas-erdogan.html accessed 25 July 2021; 'Minister Çavuşoğlu: We Will Appeal Against ECtHR Ruling on Demirtaş', *Bianet*, available from https://m.bianet.org/english/politics/202974-minister-cavusoglu-we-will-appeal-against-ecthr-ruling-on-demirtas accessed 25 July 2022.
74. 'Turkish court rejects European rights court ruling to release top Kurdish politician', *Deutche Welle*, 30 November 2018, available from https://www.dw.com/en/turkish-court-rejects-european-rights-court-ruling-to-release-top-kurdish-politician/a-46532769 accessed 25 July 2022.
75. ECtHR, *Kavala v Turkey*, 28749/18, 10 December 2019.
76. ibid, para 229.
77. 'Human rights conventions are the "soul" of modern Europe: Secretary General tells PACE', 25 January 2021, available from https://www.coe.int/en/web/secretary-general/speeches-20211/-/asset_publisher/XKVJFrFkkWVr/content/opening-of-the-first-part-session-of-the-parliamentary-assembly?inheritRedirect=false&redirect=https%3A%2F%2Fwww.coe.int%2Fen%2Fweb%2Fsecretary-general%2Fspeeches-20211%3Fp_p_id%3D101_INSTANCE_XKVJFrFkkWVr%26p_p_lifecycle%3D0%26p_p_state%3Dnormal%26p_p_mode%3Dview%26p_p_col_id%3Dcolumn-1%26p_p_col_count%3D1 accessed 26 July 2022. At the time of the writing the ECtHR released more judgments finding Turkey guilty of violating Article 18. See *Yüksekdağ Şenoğlu and Others v. Türkiye*, 14332/17 et al., 8 November 2022.
78. UNGA, 4th plenary meeting, 22 September 2020, New York, Annex III to A/75/PV.4, available from https://undocs.org/en/A/75/PV.4, 19–20.
79. Republic of Turkey Ministry of Foreign Affairs, 'Turkey's Priorities for the 60th Session of the United Nations General Assembly: The Current International Security Environment

and the Role of the UN', available from https://www.mfa.gov.tr/turkey_s-priorities-for-the-60th-session-of-the-united-nations-general-assembly.en.mfa accessed 15 October 2022; 'UN Security Council requires serious reform, says Turkish foreign minister', *Anadolu Agency*, 19 March 2022, available from https://www.aa.com.tr/en/asia-pacific/un-security-council-requires-serious-reform-says-turkish-foreign-minister/2540181# accessed 15 October 2022; Yücel Acer, Reforming the United Nations and Türkiye's Approach, SETA Report, 2022, 36–43.

80. Andras Sajo, *Ruling by Cheating Governance in Illiberal Democracy* (CUP 2021) 229.
81. EU Commission Report 2022 (n 30).
82. See SETA Report (n 79) 39.
83. Republic of Turkey Ministry of Foreign Affairs, 'Türkiye's Relations with NATO' (n 31).

CHAPTER 38

UKRAINE

MYKOLA GNATOVSKYY

1. Introduction

On the last day of the fifteenth month of his country's large-scale invasion in Ukraine, Russia's leader, Vladimir Putin, received the President of Russia's Constitutional Court, Valery Zorkin. In a widely broadcast video fragment, Zorkin is showing Putin a copy of an old map. The following conversation ensued:

> ZORKIN: We found in the Constitutional Court a copy of a 17th century map made under Louis XIV. That is the middle of the 17th century, made by the French themselves. Why did I bring it, Vladimir Vladimirovich: there is no Ukraine there!
>
> PUTIN: Well, of course.
>
> ZORKIN: Indeed, there is no Ukraine. There is an area in two places. The land of the Rzeczpospolita, south there to Frankovsk [city of Ivano-Frankivsk], and Cossackia [the land of the Cossacks].
>
> PUTIN: Well, yes.
>
> ZORKIN: And the Great Kingdom of Russia.
>
> PUTIN: Of course.
>
> ZORKIN: Why I will still venture to show you, because there has been a lot of speculation about where the origins are, where and what and how all this was formed.
>
> PUTIN: Well, we know that these lands were simply part of the Rzeczpospolita, and then they asked to be part of the Kingdom of Muscovy. That is all. And they ended up as part of the Kingdom of Muscovy. And then, after the October Revolution, all sorts of quasi-state configurations started to form, and the Soviet authorities created the Soviet Ukraine.[1]

This surrealistic conversation between two persons educated as Soviet lawyers has nothing to do with legal arguments of any sort. Yet it gives perhaps the clearest idea of what Russia's war against Ukraine—the biggest ground war in Europe since the end of

World War II—is about: the massive use of armed force to prove the most reactionary and absurd 'historical' argument that Ukraine has never existed. This type of argument is a reiteration of what Putin said in his speeches on the eve of his country's large-scale invasion into Ukraine of 24 February 2022. It had been tested in his political manifesto 'On the Historical Unity of Russians and Ukrainians' published in July 2021,[2] where wild pseudohistorical speculations were used openly to question the legitimacy of Ukraine's contemporary borders and ultimately to refuse the Ukrainian nation the right to sovereignty and to determining its own future.[3] The article, often compared to Hitler's *Sudetenland* speech,[4] could also be seen as 'laying the groundwork for incitement to genocide: denying the existence of the Ukrainian group'.[5] Leaving aside the genocide discussion, it was the basis for Putin's further statements that 'Modern Ukraine was entirely created by Russia' and 'Ukraine never had a tradition of genuine statehood'.[6]

This sort of imperialist narrative[7] is paradoxically both a stark departure from the highly elaborated treaty framework of relations between Ukraine and Russia as sovereign States with mutually recognized borders that had been formed prior to the 2014 Russia's annexation of Ukraine's Crimea and the armed conflict in Donetsk and Luhansk regions, and a logical continuation of the revived imperialist policies against Ukraine. Among many examples, anyone who has studied Ukraine's history would immediately recall the infamous Valuev Circular, issued by the Russian Empire's Minister of Interior in 1863, 160 years prior to the conversation between Putin and Zorkin about the alleged non-existence of Ukraine on the map, which ordered censorship committees to ban the publication of books (at least those for a broad readership) in Ukrainian by stating, *inter alia*, the following: 'a separate Little Russian ['*malorosiyskiy*', ie Ukrainian—MG] language never existed, does not exist, and shall not exist, and the dialect used by the common herd is nothing but Russian corrupted by the influence of Poland'.[8]

Ironically though, one might state that the presence of Ukraine on the 'international law map' of Europe had not been so evident either. Being a founding member of the United Nations (UN) and a fully-fledged independent State since 1991 has hardly placed Ukraine at the forefront of the attention of international lawyers, at least until the beginning of Russia's war of aggression against it in 2014. Even then, serious studies by Western scholars, such as a monograph by Thomas D Grant,[9] were rather exceptional, and the flagrant case of Crimea's annexation, let alone the armed conflict in the eastern part of Ukraine, deserved at best a cursory mention in leading courses on international law. A good illustration of such a mention can be found in the eighth edition of a popular textbook by Malcolm N Shaw, where obviously correct statements about the illegality of Crimea's annexation by Russia were accompanied, no doubt with the best academic intentions (such as objectivity), by references to Russian authors trying to justify the unjustifiable.[10] Ukrainian voices were not to be heard in what could have been perceived as an attempt to continue the 'business as usual' of seeing former parts of the Soviet Union (perhaps with the exception of the Baltic States) exclusively through the Russian lens.

Now, as Ukraine in its resistance to Russia's neocolonial war of territorial conquest has defined, quite likely for many years to come, one of the recurrent points on the agenda of international lawyers, we are faced with a difficult question of how Ukraine should be painted on the 'international law map'. The answer appears to be positioned somewhere between two diametrically opposed approaches. The first would be simply to enter into a discussion with the big lies of Putinist propaganda by trying to offer a correct historical discourse about how the Ukrainian State has come into being, providing a basic fact-checking of claims made by Russian propaganda in justification of the theory that Ukraine has never existed as a sovereign nation. The second approach would be to leave history, pseudohistory, and propaganda to scholars of humanities and social science and concentrate instead on how Ukraine has manifested itself in international law and how it has seen international law itself.

This chapter will attempt to combine these two approaches. It will begin with an overview of various stages of development of Ukraine's international legal personality (Section 2), before going on to highlight some of the key features of Ukraine's vision of international law and the development of its own scholarship of the field (Section 3). Section 4 concludes.

2. Ukraine's International Legal Identity

Answering the question about Ukraine's identity, including its international legal aspect, is not exactly a straightforward matter. Here, substantive and formal issues are tightly intertwined and mixed with certain preconceptions and stereotypes existing both inside and outside the country. Furthermore, the wide and wild use of 'historical' (or one might say pseudohistorical) arguments by the Russian Federation to justify its war against Ukraine, compels the author—admittedly reluctantly—to go deeper in history that would be habitual for an international lawyer simply wishing to provide a very broad framework useful for looking into issues related to international law and Ukraine.

Providing an historical framework might help us to paint a sufficiently broad picture of what Ukraine is as a sovereign State today and not to engage in any sort of academic discussion with Putin who, as Fuad Zarbiyev put it with utmost clarity, 'tried ... not to persuade the international audience that Russia had legal grounds to launch a war against Ukraine, but to convey his contempt to that audience. If this is so, taking Putin as offering international legal justifications would be adding insult to injury.'[11]

Interestingly, the origins and development of Ukraine's statehood have been studied not only by numerous historians but also by Ukraine's leading international lawyers, such as Volodymyr Butkevych,[12] Olga Butkevych,[13] and Volodymyr Vassylenko,[14] and, in an attempt to comprehensively study the origins of Ukraine's international legal personality throughout the entire known history, Oleksandr Zadorozhniy.[15]

Based on historic studies, Zadorozhniy traced various forms in which Ukraine appeared on the international arena in different epochs. In the preface to his voluminous study,[16] he notes that the name 'Ukraine' appears first in 1187 in the Ipatiev

Chronicle. Its subsequent mentions in this and other chronicles in 1189, 1213, 1280, 1282, and so on make it clear that the name is applied to various lands of Kyivan Rus, such as Kyiv, Galicia, and Volyn. The name 'Ukraine' was in use in parallel with the word 'Rus' and its derivatives. Zadorozhniy also notes that the decision of Peter the First to rebrand the Grand Duchy of Moscow into Russian Empire accelerated the changes in the self-naming of peoples: Rusins (Rusians) became Ukrainians while Muscovites renamed themselves as Russians. He quotes a Ukrainian historian who came up with an analogy both loose and trivial but anyway memorable: 'this is like Romans became Italians while Vlachs became Romanians'.[17] Zadorozhniy, following his academic mentor V Butkevych, gives credit to the most ancient periods of the land's history, mentioning discussions about concrete periods of existence and ethnic roots of the Trypillian tribes (VI–IV millennia BC), the Cimmerians (II–early I millennium BC), the Scythians (III century BC), the Vistula (or Baltic) Venetians (I–III centuries AD), as well of the associations of Slavic tribes (IV century). He also notes that the ethnic roots as such are generally immaterial to such studies and notes that it would be wise to abstain both from any attempt to extend artificially the continuity of Ukraine's statehood and from limiting its roots to a proper State organization, that is, to the creation of the (Kyivan) Rus. Like most present-day Ukrainian historians, Zadorozhniy was in favour of considering the State-like organizations of the Union of Antes (VI–VII centuries) and to the later (VII–IX centuries) unions other Slavic tribes in the pre-Rus period.

The traditional sequence of Ukrainian States presented by Zadorozhniy starts with the Kyivan Rus, followed by the Grand Duchy of Lithuania and Ruthenia. He describes both States as 'influential' and stresses the key role of the 'Rusian element' in the functioning of the Grand Duchy. As the next stage in the development of Ukraine's statehood he marks the Cossack State or the Hetmanate with its policy of polyvassalage, most importantly during the reign of Bohdan Khmelnytsky (mid-XVII century). The polyvassalage essentially meant operating under simultaneous protectorates from Rzeczpospolita, Transylvania, the Ottoman Empire, and Muscovy and trying to remain independent in the sense of guaranteeing the 'rights and privileges' of the Cossack State.[18] One of several such agreements, the 1654 Pereiaslav Agreement on the protectorate between Khmelnytsky and the Muscovite tsar Alexey Mikhaylovich, one of typical manifestations of the Cossacks' polyvassalage policy, was used as a basis for one of the most persistently defended legends of the Russian Empire, that of the so-called 'reunification' of 'Russian' and 'Little Russian' peoples. This legend—which has very little to do with the actual contents and context of the agreement which was in no way perceived in ethnic terms[19]—has been reiterated a countless number of times, including in Putin's 'historical unity' essay and in the justifications for the 2022 'special military operation' of Russia against Ukraine.[20]

After the demise of the Hetmanate in the late XVIII century, the vast majority of Ukrainian lands was annexed to the Russian Empire, which ruled them through the so-called governorates-general. Interestingly, Zadorozhniy's comprehensive monograph pays very little attention to discussing the status of Ukrainian territories within other empires, most importantly Austro-Hungary.[21] It is noteworthy that despite the efforts to suppress the Ukrainian national movement in the Russian Empire, such as the already mentioned Valuev Circular (which was one of many efforts of the kind), the Ukrainian nation appeared to be intellectually and emotionally (but not necessarily logistically or otherwise practically) ready for restoring its statehood once the empires started to crumble.

During the period of national liberation struggle in 1917–1921, often referred to as the Ukrainian Revolution, Ukraine was a sovereign State, which took the forms of the Ukrainian People's Republic under the leadership of a parliament named the Central Rada (Central Council), the Ukrainian State ruled by the Hetman Pavlo Skoropadsky, and the Ukrainian People's Republic ruled by a government called 'the Directory'. During that period Ukraine was recognized *de jure* or *de facto* by some thirty States (a very significant number compared, eg, with the forty-two founding States of the League of Nations in 1919)[22] and established diplomatic and consular relations with many of them.[23] In January 1919, the act of unification between the Ukrainian People's Republic and the West Ukrainian People's Republic, established in part of the country that belonged to the Austro-Hungarian Empire, was declared.

Soviet Russia's military invasion in Ukraine resulted in the creation, in 1920, of the Ukrainian Socialist Soviet Republic (SSR), still a formally sovereign State, although fully controlled by the Moscow-run Bolsheviks. On 30 December 1922, the Treaty on the Establishment of the Union of Soviet Socialist Republics was signed, and in accordance with the Constitutions (of the USSR and the Ukrainian SSR) adopted, respectively, in 1924 and 1925, the Ukrainian Soviet State became a part of the Union as a decentralized federation. In Zadorozhniy's view, Ukrainian SSR actually retained its own international legal personality. He further states, somewhat overly optimistically, that Ukraine's international legal status within the Soviet Union, despite periodic changes caused by internal political events, was preserved until the collapse of the USSR in 1991, when Ukraine regained its full State sovereignty.[24]

Even if Zadorozhniy's statement about the preservation of Ukraine's international legal personality within the Soviet Union might be taken with a pinch of salt, one cannot fail to notice the important connection between the Ukrainian SSR and modern Ukraine.

The consolidation of the population and territory of contemporary Ukraine in its existing internationally recognized borders after World War II coincided with the construction of a curious international legal personality of the Ukrainian SSR (as well as that of the Byelorussian SSR inherited by today's Belarus), which could be explained, depending on one's perspective, either in a more high-style mode or in a pragmatic, if not cynical way. Symbolically and officially, it is frequently mentioned that Soviet Ukraine and Soviet Belarus were admitted to become UN member States in their own right as a tribute to the input of those two Soviet republics to the defeat of Nazi Germany as well as to the enormous numbers of victims of World War II from those lands. More pragmatically though, their incomplete international legal personality could be seen as a compromise reached by the collective West with Joseph Stalin who had initially wanted as many votes in the UN as the total number of all Soviet republics but was eventually satisfied with three: for the Soviet Union as a whole (not independently for the Soviet Russia though) as well as for the Belarussian and Ukrainian Soviet Socialist Republics.

Indeed, even if one might question the degree to which Ukraine retained its status under international law in the first two decades following the creation of the Soviet Union, the situation clearly changed with the end of World War II, following which the Ukrainian SSR was listed among founding members of the UN in 1945. Whilst remaining part of the Soviet Union, the Ukrainian SSR became, at least nominatively, an international actor with independent membership in international organizations of the UN system and an independent treaty-making capacity. With the restoration of its full independence in 1991, Ukraine entered the field of international law as a new actor while formally continuing the international legal personality of the Ukrainian SSR in terms of its UN membership and participation in treaties. Unlike Estonia, Latvia, and Lithuania, which restored their independence with the end of their occupation by the Soviet Union and afterwards never claimed their 'share' of legacy left by the communist empire, Ukraine was also simultaneously one of the States succeeding the Soviet Union.

The slow and peaceful gradual approach of pulling away from its Soviet past, chosen by Ukraine at the time of the breakup of the Soviet Union, was based on the 'multi-vector' foreign policy which was simultaneously geared towards modernization and integrating into the European community, while remaining friendly and preserving various ties with its former ruler and the biggest neighbour, Russia, as well as with other former parts of the Soviet Union, both bilaterally and through participation in the Commonwealth of Independent States (CIS), simultaneously a loose multilateral arrangement and an intergovernmental organization seen as a way for a 'peaceful divorce' of its participants.

On the formal side, as a subject of international law, Ukraine is a continuator of the Ukrainian SSR, which was both a constituent part of the Soviet Union and a founding member of the UN, and one of the successor States to the USSR. This dual status was both convenient and problematic.

The convenience could easily be seen in the fact that, like its closest neighbour Belarus, Ukraine did not need to be admitted to the UN after its independence in 1991 as it had already been a member of the organization.[25] At various times it had been a member of the Security Council (for the first time, 1947–1949) and of the Economic and Social Council. The Ukrainian SSR had been a member of UNESCO since 1954 and had permanent representations at the UN and other international organizations in New York, Paris, and Geneva.

In the same fashion, there was hardly any question about the continuation of Ukraine's participation in the treaties to which Ukrainian SSR had been a party. By its independence, Ukraine had been a party to over 120 treaties. Its capital, Kyiv, also hosted consulates-general (but never embassies) of several countries, mostly from the 'socialist camp', such as Bulgaria, Czechoslovakia, the German Democratic Republic, Hungary, Poland, Romania, and Yugoslavia, and Odesa accommodated consulates of Bulgaria, Cuba, India, and Egypt.

Interestingly, the right of the Ukrainian SSR to enter into direct relations with foreign States, conclude agreements with them, and exchange diplomatic and consular representatives was only introduced in its Constitution in 1973[26]. Soon afterwards, Article 74 of the 1978 Constitution of the Ukrainian SSR similarly stipulated that it 'has the right to enter into relations with foreign states, to conclude treaties with them and to exchange diplomatic and consular representatives, and to participate in in the activities of international organisations'.

The breakup of the Soviet Union in 1991 meant in practice that Ukraine emerged as a fully independent State. However, it was not a brand-new subject of international law. Ukraine's dual status was reflected in its domestic legislation. In particular, Article 7 of the Law of Ukraine 'On Succession of Ukraine' of 12 September 1991 stated that 'Ukraine is the successor to the rights and obligations under international treaties of the USSR that do not contradict the Constitution of Ukraine and the interests of the republic'. At the same time, in Article 6 of the same legislative act, Ukraine reaffirmed its obligations under 'international treaties concluded by the Ukrainian SSR before the proclamation of Ukraine's independence' without any restrictions, that is, there was full continuity. This reflected the approach whereby Ukraine's independence did not mean the creation of an international legal person but rather a change in the status of an existing one, which was also recognized by some contemporaneous authors.[27]

The vast majority of issues related to the legal succession to the Soviet Union were handled through various agreements reached within the CIS, a multilateral political arrangement established in 1991 and was commonly understood as a way to a 'civilised divorce' between the ex-Soviet nations. Ukraine has always had a 'separate opinion', for example refusing to accede to the 1993 Statute of the CIS (thereby remaining a party to the 1991 political arrangement but not of the 1993 international intergovernmental organization under the same name) or to ratify the so-called 'zero option agreement', ceding its share of the USSR's assets to the Russian Federation in exchange for the latter's obligation to pay the respective share of the Soviet debts. The official reason cited by the Ukrainian Parliament in its decision not to ratify that treaty was the lack of audit of such assets and debts—Ukraine did not want to ratify such a deal without being fully informed about its implications. Ultimately the question of State succession with respect to debts and assets has never been resolved between Ukraine and Russia—as all other successors to the USSR did ratify the 'zero option' proposed by Moscow.

Ukraine's borders with the former Soviet republics became its State bodies in application of the '*uti possidetis*' principle. In particular, borders between Ukraine and Russia were clearly and unequivocally determined in a series of bilateral treaties between 1990 and 2003, with some peculiarities relating to the status of the Sea of Azov as 'shared internal waters' of the two countries. Notwithstanding the existence of a clear treaty basis, in reality one could nevertheless agree with the view that Russia has been reluctant to recognize Ukraine's borders and its territorial integrity.[28] This is generally indicative of Russia's sustained policy vis-à-vis Ukraine not to attach real importance to international law and its instruments as well as to the fundamental principles of international law stemming from the Charter of the United Nations and the 1975 Helsinki Final Act.[29]

Following the collapse of the Soviet Union, Ukraine became the third-largest holder of nuclear weapons globally, with a substantial arsenal including intercontinental ballistic missiles and nuclear warheads. As early as in 1991, an agreement was reached among the member States of the CIS who aimed to establish unified control over nuclear weapons, with Belarus, Kazakhstan, Russia, and Ukraine committing not to transfer nuclear weapons or related technologies. The agreement also outlined the gradual transfer of rights and obligations of the Soviet Union as a 'nuclear' State to Russia, the accession of Belarus and Ukraine as 'non-nuclear' States to the Treaty on the Non-Proliferation of Nuclear Weapons (NPT), and the dismantling and destruction of nuclear weapons.

Another agreement, signed in 1991, emphasized the need for unified control over nuclear weapons and other weapons of mass destruction in the Armed Forces of the former Soviet Union. Ukraine had set a deadline of the end of 1994 for the complete destruction of nuclear weapons on its territory. In May 1992, during the signing of the Lisbon Protocol, Belarus, Kazakhstan, Russia, and Ukraine reaffirmed their commitment to keeping the nuclear weapons of the former Soviet Union under unified command and expressed their intention to join the NPT as non-nuclear-weapon States. Subsequently, in January 1994, Ukraine signed a trilateral statement with Russia and the US, committing to eliminate all nuclear weapons on its territory in exchange for security guarantees from the nuclear weapon States. In November 1994, Ukraine's parliament ratified the NPT Treaty. On 5 December 1994, the (in)famous Budapest Memorandum on security assurances was signed between Ukraine, Russia, the US, and the UK. China and France provided such assurances by means of unilateral declarations. By August 1996, all nuclear warheads had been removed from Ukraine's territory.

Under such strong pressure from the leading world powers, Ukraine thus unilaterally gave up the nuclear arsenal it inherited as a successor to the Soviet Union in exchange for vague security assurances in the so-called 'Budapest Memorandum' and several other interrelated documents—a step bitterly regretted by Ukrainians in 2014 with the beginning of Russia's armed aggression against their country, and even more so in 2022. Occasional discussions about the legal nature of the Budapest Memorandum (a treaty, a series of binding unilateral declarations, a non-binding political arrangement), regardless of their outcome, cannot conceal the bitter disappointment of Ukraine being betrayed not only by Russia but also by other nuclear States who had provided assurances of its independence and territorial integrity.[30]

Two events appear to have played the decisive role in the further development of Ukraine's attitude to international law. Both have a European component and both of them have defined Ukraine as a European nation striving to be fully integrated in the regional political, economic, and legal space. Ukraine was the first post-Soviet State (after the three Baltic States, if the 'post-Soviet' label is applicable to them at all) to join the Council of Europe (CoE) (in 1995) and to conclude a Partnership and Cooperation Agreement with the European Communities and their member States (in 1998).

The accession to the CoE brought about tectonic changes in Ukraine's legal system. These developments also prompted Ukraine's international law scholars to enter the previously unexplored fields of international human rights law and law of the European Union (EU). Following the tumultuous events of 2013–2014, Ukraine signed an Association Agreement with the EU, which was a major step in its European integration both practically and symbolically, and reflected its strong desire to become a fully-fledged part of the Euro-Atlantic and European community. Amendments to that effect were, in 2019, even directly introduced in the country's Constitution by an overwhelming majority in the Parliament. The next step, EU candidate status was granted to Ukraine in 2022, in what has generally been perceived as part of the Europe's response to Russia's large-scale invasion.

Unlike the Soviet Union and its continuator, the Russian Federation, Ukraine has demonstrated a much more positive attitude to the idea of third-party dispute settlement, including international courts. This could be best illustrated by Ukraine's giving consent in a 1997 bilateral treaty with Romania to the jurisdiction of the International Court of Justice (ICJ) on the issue of maritime delimitation in the Black Sea. Romania instituted proceedings in that case in 2004, and in 2009 the Court unanimously adopted its judgment,[31] which was positively received by both parties concerned[32] and laid a solid foundation for their positive relations ever since. However, until 2014 international courts were not seen by Ukraine as a crucial element in its policy. It did not go as far as recognizing the compulsory jurisdiction of the ICJ, and the ratification of the Rome Statute of the International Criminal Court, signed by Ukraine in January 2000, was hampered by an unfortunate opinion of the Constitutional Court adopted in 2001,[33] in which the constitutional judges apparently misunderstood—in any case, (mis)interpreted—the principle of complementarity as being incompatible with Ukraine's 1996 Constitution.

Russia's aggression pushed Ukraine into turning to international law for help. Already in 2014, unable to liberate its territories by force and restore constitutional order there, Ukraine sought assistance from international institutions. It quickly became clear that the UN Security Council was unlikely to be able to offer any solution to the situation, since Russia, as one of its permanent members, was directly involved in the conflict. International courts, although much less promising in terms of speed and specificity of judgment, seemed to be a worthy alternative. Since 2014, the task of achieving justice through law as well as what has sometimes been referred to as 'lawfare', has been among the main objectives of Ukraine's foreign policy. Ukraine turned to the ICJ, the International Tribunal for the Law of the Sea (ITLOS), and the European Court of Human Rights (ECtHR), and initiated numerous arbitrations and consented to the jurisdiction of the International Criminal Court (ICC) by making two declarations under Article 12(3) of the Rome Statute.[34] From the first days of the large-scale invasion by the Russian Federation on 24 February 2022, Ukraine has pursued the idea of creating a special tribunal for the crime of aggression committed against this country—and the list is not exhaustive. The expectations and belief in the potential of international law are high. It is of course another matter whether these expectations will be met, when, and to what extent.

3. International Legal Scholarship in Ukraine

Studying and teaching international law in Ukraine has been paradoxical in many ways. While the modern independent State of Ukraine is a little over thirty years old, one would have to admit that international law doctrine has been developed by various scholars working in its present-day territory as well as by Ukrainians outside of Ukraine.

In fact, studying the works of the 19th-century international lawyers who worked in the universities located in what is now Ukraine has been an important topic for the contemporary Ukrainian scholars. In most cases their studies were fully in line with the Russian tradition of studying the so-called 'native' doctrine of international law, as explained by Lauri Mälksoo (see Rusinova, this volume).[35]

Professors like Dmitriy Kachenovsky,[36] Petr Kazansky, or Vassili Nezabitovsky from Kharkov (today's Kharkiv), Odessa (Odesa), and Kiev (Kyiv) respectively, to name but a few, were important figures of international law academia in the Russian Empire. Universities in those three major centres had their departments of the law of nations ('all-nations law' in the terminology of that period) which were important parts of the international law scholarship in the Russian Empire. International legal thought was also present in the part of Ukraine that was part of the Austro-Hungarian Empire. Suffice it to mention academics like Ludwik Ehrlich or Hersch Lauterpacht who graduated from the University of Lemberg (today's Lviv) were formed in the Austrian tradition, whereas Rafał (Rafael) Lemkin, another alumnus from Lviv (which for him was rather 'Lwów'), was, in his turn, a Polish lawyer by training.[37]

While the legacy of all these scholars, as well as their somewhat lesser-known colleagues, were subject to numerous studies by the Ukrainian historians of international legal thought, there is no denying that hardly any of them felt anywhere near being Ukrainian or appeared to care about Ukraine as a possible independent international actor (or at least a vast majority of them felt this way). Among notable exceptions would be Otto (Otton) Eichelmann who, after obtaining master's degree at the University of Derpt (Tartu) with a thesis about prisoners of war in the context of international law, began his career at St Vladimir's University of Kiev as a typical Russian (albeit of a German origin) professor of the law of nations ('all-nations law' in the terminology of that period) but then actively supported the short-lived Ukrainian People's Republic in 1918–1920 as assistant (ie deputy) Minister for Foreign Affairs and, following his emigration to Prague, joined the Ukrainian emigrant academic community.[38]

The international legal personality of the Ukrainian SSR, even in the limited form that emerged after World War II, objectively required that it be represented not just by any Soviet diplomats but of those working for the toy-size Ministry of Foreign Affairs of the Ukrainian SSR. This resulted in the creation of a school of international relations ('The Faculty of International Relations') at the University of Kiev in 1944 followed by re-establishing the Department of International Law and Foreign Legislation first within the Faculty of Law and then within the Faculty of International Relations and International Law.

This school's rapid development can be traced to 1960s, when it was led by Professor Igor Lukashuk, a prominent Soviet international lawyer of Ukrainian origin trained in Kharkov, a successor of Professor Vladimir Koretskiy (Volodymyr Koretskyi), arguably the most successful Soviet Ukrainian international lawyer, a judge, and Vice-President of the ICJ. The Koretskiy/Lukashuk line of the development of international law schools gave Ukraine a department of international law at Taras Shevchenko University of Kyiv with Professors Volodymyr Butkevych, Volodymyr Vassylenko, Kostiantyn Zabihaylo, Kostiantyn Sandrovsky, and others. The department of international law at this university was alma mater to many foreign students, including, notably, the ICJ's Judge Abdul Koroma from Sierra Leone. In 1982, it also hosted another future ICJ Judge and President, Peter Tomka.

The two other schools of international law in the Soviet Ukraine included the department of international law and foreign 'State' (ie constitutional) law at Kharkiv Law Institute/Law Academy with Professors Mykhaylo Yanovsky, Volodymyr Semenov, and Mykhailo Buromenskyi, and, last but not least, the department of international and comparative law at the Institute of State and Law established in Kyiv by Judge Koretskiy himself and developed by his successors such as Professors Volodymyr Denysov and Volodymyr Yevintov.

However, until 1991, none of them had worked under the conditions of an independent Ukrainian State. Their scholarship developed in a rather peculiar situation when any kind of international law doctrine existing outside of Moscow and Leningrad (St Petersburg) had to respect the 'division of labour' within the Soviet 'science' ('наука') of international law. Being excessively abstract and deeply theoretical in general, it quite categorically banned 'peripheric' universities from developing any controversial topics of practical international significance. Hence, any doctoral (including habilitation) theses produced in the Soviet Ukraine had better deal with the theory (in the Soviet understanding of the term) of international law (the more obscure and abstract the better) and its history (preferably far distant in time).

Things did not change immediately with the independence of Ukraine in 1991. During the first decade of living in the new, sovereign reality, Ukrainian scholars of international law were mostly rather passive, and their occasional writings remained within the (post-) Soviet discourse. This may be explained by several factors.

First of all, account must be taken of a certain 'limbo' in Ukraine's international legal doctrine in the first years of independence which coincided with a deep economic crisis and exodus of the most productive academics from universities to private legal practice or any other business which could provide for the income that would exceed that of a university professor by ten if not a hundred times. For the same reason, talented younger lawyers had, until the last years of 1990s, very little incentive to dedicate themselves to public international law. It would not be an overstatement to talk about a 'lost generation' of Ukraine's international lawyers as those who graduated with a specialization in international law between late 1980s and late 1990s hardly ever found themselves researching or teaching the subject. Nor was there much incentive to practise international law as members of staff of the foreign ministry, such positions being ridiculously unattractive from a financial point of view.

Secondly, there was very little integration of the older-generation international lawyers into the 'global college of international lawyers'. While individual contacts of leading Ukrainian international lawyers with their Western counterparts were of course happening, the 'old connections' with post-Soviet peers remained far more extensive.

Thirdly, while the Soviet system might have fallen and there was no longer any need to resort to long meaningless quotations from the resolutions of the most recent Congress of the Communist Party of the USSR, fresh speeches or articles by the Secretary General of that party, or from 'Marxist-Leninist philosophy', most Ukrainian lawyers perpetuated the idiosyncratic view of international law they had formed under the 'old regime': State-oriented, suspicious of human rights (even though they had to pay lip service to something like 'humanistic nature of modern international law'), and, for the most part, uncomfortable with the idea that individual should be seen as a 'subject' of international law[39] (with the notable exception of Volodymyr Butkevych[40]).

Fourthly, Ukrainian international lawyers of the 1990s continued to follow the Soviet paradigm of being apologetic of their State and avoiding any sort of criticism. The State, however, did not rush to provide guidance on how exactly they might help it. The officially proclaimed goal of becoming a leading regional power had never materialized, nor had any meaningful international law ideas backing that ambition been advanced by Ukrainian international law scholars who generally did not seem to take such an ambitious goal seriously. Even though the Ukrainian Association of International Law (UAIL) was formed in 1993 (chaired by Volodymyr Butkevych), and the *Ukrainian Journal of International Law* published (predominantly in Ukrainian), most activities of the Association took place almost exclusively thanks to the individual enthusiasm of its first President as well as his former student and successor in the UAIL, Oleksandr Zadorozhniy.

When Ukraine joined the Council of Europe and became party to the European Convention on Human Rights (ECHR), Volodymyr Butkevych became, in 1996, the first Ukrainian judge of the ECtHR. His successor, Ganna Yudkivska, who served in this position from 2010 to 2022, despite her background of being predominantly a legal practitioner, has worked hard to integrate Ukraine's international law scholarship in the European context, most notably via her active role as a Board member at the European Society of International Law. She has also published widely on, *inter alia*, how participation in the ECHR has changed Ukraine's legal system.[41]

Many other lawyers—not necessarily with a strong background in international law—have researched the legal regime created by the ECHR. While there have been little, if any, critical accounts of European human rights law produced by Ukraine's academia, the more educational if not promotional accounts of the subject were fairly important in bringing Ukraine's lawyers into the contemporary context. In parallel, the gradual movement of Ukraine in the direction of European integration—from the 1998 Partnership and Cooperation Agreement to the 2022 EU candidate country status—also meant that EU law became a discipline which attracted many lawyers in Ukraine, including those who started as specialists in public international law.

While the level of integration of Ukrainian international lawyers into the European discourse had remained extremely low for the best part of the last thirty years, the situation started to improve with more Ukrainians studying and teaching abroad. Russia's large-scale invasion of 2022 forced a number of Ukrainian international lawyers to find temporary positions at various foreign, predominantly European, universities. The long-term consequences of these events have yet to be seen but it is already evident that Ukrainian voices in international law are gradually becoming louder and clearer.

4. Conclusion

This brief chapter was written while the biggest continental war in Europe was still raging in Ukraine's territory. The country is defending itself, with the limited but still absolutely vital help from many other States, from the aggression by a nuclear power and a permanent member of the UN Security Council. No matter when and how exactly that war will end, it is clear that Ukraine's place on the world map is not going to disappear. Nor will it disappear from the 'international law map of Europe'.

International law is one of Ukraine's best allies. It must rely on it to survive. It puts its hopes in international law and the institutions it created to achieve peace and justice. The new generation of Ukrainian international lawyers is becoming ever more deeply integrated with the European community of international lawyers. All of this gives some reason to be optimistic. However, when expectations are high, disappointment and frustrations, big and small, can become increasingly dangerous. In any case, while Ukraine and Ukrainians see a huge value in international law, they call for its further development, but they also understand that it has to be backed up with the required military, political, and economic power as well as with resolute action.

Notes

1. Glava Konstitutsionnogo suda «risknul» pokazat' Putinu kartu, sostavlennuyu pri Lyudovike XIV (President of the Constitutional Court 'ventured' to show Putin a map compiled in the times of Loius XIV), 23 May 2023 <https://meduza.io/feature/2023/05/23/glava-konstitutsionnogo-suda-risknul-pokazat-putinu-kartu-sostavlennuyu-pri-lyudovike-xiv> accessed 26 June 2023.
2. Article by Vladimir Putin 'On the Historical Unity of Russians and Ukrainians', 12 July 2021 <http://en.kremlin.ru/events/president/news/66181> accessed 26 June 2023.
3. Vidhuk ukrainskykh istorykiv na stattiu V.Putina 'Pro istorychnu yednist rosiian ta ukraintsiv' (Review of Vladimir Putin's article 'On historical unity of Russians and Ukrainians' by Ukrainian historians)/Instytut istorii Ukrainy NAN Ukrainy; Hromadskyi prosvitnytskyi proekt 'Likbez. Istorychnyi front', 2021. <https://archive.org/details/vidguk_ukrainskikh_istorikiv> accessed 26 June 2023.

4. See, eg, Toomas H Ilves, 'Putin kasutas Hitleri retoorikat' (Putin used Hitler's rhetoric) <https://www.err.ee/1608276348/ilves-putin-kasutas-hitleri-retoorikat> accessed 26 June 2023; Timothy Snyder, 'Putin's Hitler-like tricks and tactics in Ukraine', 24 February 2022 <https://www.bostonglobe.com/2022/02/24/opinion/putins-hitler-like-tricks-tactics-ukraine/> accessed 26 June 2023.
5. 'Independent Legal Analysis of the Russian Federation's Breaches of the Genocide Convention in Ukraine and the Duty to Prevent'//New Lines Institute for Strategy and Policy; Raoul Wallenberg Centre for Human Rights, 27 May 2022 <https://newlinesinstitute.org/wp-content/uploads/English-Report.pdf> accessed 26 June 2023.
6. Extracts from Putin's speech on Ukraine. Reuters, 21 February 2022 <https://www.reuters.com/world/europe/extracts-putins-speech-ukraine-2022-02-21/> accessed 26 June 2023.
7. This perception of nations bordering Russia as not subjects of history but objects, has been persistent. In 2016, eg, Putin expressed a view regarding the three Baltic States: in 1918, Russia gave them to Germany with Brest-Litovsk Peace Treaty and in 1939, with the Molotov-Ribbentrop Pact, (Nazi) Germany gave them back to the Soviet Union (or its sphere of influence) <https://www.youtube.com/watch?v=wfosguuwTF4> accessed 26 June 2023.
8. *Tsirkulyar ministra vnutrennikh del P. A. Valueva Kievskomu, Moskovskomu i Peterburgskomu tsenzurnym komitetam ot 18 iyulya 1863 g* (Circular letter by the Minister of Internal Affrairs P.A.Valuev addressed to the censorship committees in Kiev, Moscow and Saint-Petersburg, 18 July 1863) in Mikhail Lemke, *Epokha tsenzurnykh reform 1859–1865 gg* (Herold 1904) 302–304.
9. Thomas D Grant, *Aggression against Ukraine: Territory, Responsibility, and International Law* (Palgrave Macmillan 2015).
10. Malcolm N Shaw, *International Law* (8th edn, CUP 2017) 389–390.
11. Fuad Zarbiyev, *Of Bullshit, Lies and 'Demonstrably Rubbish' Justifications in International Law*, Völkerrechtsblog, 18 March 2022, doi: 10.17176/20220319-000933-0.
12. Volodymyr Butkevych, *Mizhnarodno-pravova ideolohiia slovianskykh vozhdivstv—poperednykiv ukrainskoho etnosu (International Law Ideology of Slavic chiefdoms—Predecessors of Ukrainians as an Ethnic Group)*//Ukrainskyi shchorichnyk mizhnarodnoho prava (Ukrainian Yearbook of International Law 2008) 172–261.
13. Among many other publications, see Olga Butkevych, *Teoretychni aspekty pokhozhdennia i stanovlennia mizhnarodnoho prava* (*Theoretical Aspects of Origins and Development of International Law*) (Ukrayina 2003); Olga Butkevych, *U istokov mezhdunarodnogo prava* (*At the Origins of International Law*) (Yuridicheskiy Tsentr Press 2008); Olga Butkevych, *Teoriia i praktyka doklasychnoho mizhnarodnoho prava* (*Theory and Practice of Preclassic International Law*) (Habilitation thesis, Taras Shevchenko National University of Kyiv 2009).
14. V A Vasylenko, *Pravovi aspekty uchasti Ukrainskoi RSR u mizhnarodnykh vidnosynakh* (*Legal Aspects of the Participation of the Ukrainian SSR in International Relations*) (Politvydav Ukrayiny 1984).
15. O V Zadorozhniy, *Geneza mizhnarodnoyi pravosubiektnosti Ukrainy* (*Genesis of Ukraine's International Legal Personality*) (K.I.S. 2014).
16. ibid, 8–12.
17. ibid, 10.
18. Taras Chukhlib, *Sekrety ukrajinskoho polivasalitetu. Khmelnytsky-Doroshenko-Mazepa* (*The Secrets of Ukrainian Polyvassalage*) (Kyiv Mohyla Academy 2011) 13–21.

19. Among English-language sources see, eg, John Basarab, *Pereiaslav 1654: A Historiographical Study* (Canadian Institute of Ukrainian Studies, University of Alberta 1982) or, for a shorter recent summary, Sergii Plokhy, *The Gates of Europe. A History of Ukraine* (Penguin 2015) 103–107.
20. See, among many others, Sergii Plokhy, *Ukraine and Russia. Representations of the Past* (University of Toronto Press 2008) 90–112.
21. Zadorozhniy (n 15) 276.
22. Christian J Tams, 'League of Nations' (last updated in 2006) in A Peters and R Wolfrum (eds), The Max Planck Encyclopedia of Public International Law (Oxford University Press 2008) <www.mpepil.com> accessed 26 June 2023.
23. Zadorozhniy (n 15) 406.
24. ibid, 11–12.
25. Alexander J Motyl, 'The Foreign Relations of the Ukrainian SSR', 6(1) Harvard Ukrainian Studies 1982, 62–78.
26. New Article 15-b on this subject was added then to the 1937 ('Stalin's') Constitution.
27. Konrad G Bühler, 'State Succession, Identity/Continuity and Membership in the United Nations. Final Report' in *State Succession: Codification Tested against Facts* (The Hague 1996) 82. See also, on Russia's claim to be the continuator of the entire Soviet Union (while also being one of its successors), Guido Acquaviva, 'Russia as the State Continuing the Legal Personality of the USSR – An Inquiry into State Identity or Succession', 23(2) Journal of the History of International Law/Revue d'histoire du droit international 2019, 310–353.
28. Kataryna Wolczuk and Rilka Dragneva, *Russia's Longstanding Problem with Ukraine's Borders* (Chatham House 2023) <https://www.chathamhouse.org/2022/08/russias-longstanding-problem-ukraines-borders> accessed 26 June 2023.
29. Oleksandr Zadorozhniy, *Porushennia ahresyvnoiu viinoiu Rosiiskoi Federatsii proty Ukrainy osnovnykh pryntsypiv mizhnarodnoho prava* (*Violation of the Fundamental Principles of International Law by the Aggressive War of the Russian Federation against Ukraine*) (K.I.S. 2015).
30. For a recent summary of such discussions, see Mykhailo Soldatenko, *Constructive Ambiguity of the Budapest Memorandum at 28: Making Sense of the Controversial Agreement*, Lawfare, 7 February 2023 <https://www.lawfareblog.com/constructive-ambiguity-budapest-memorandum-28-making-sense-controversial-agreement> accessed 26 June 2023.
31. *Maritime Delimitation in the Black Sea (Romania v Ukraine), Judgment*, ICJ Reports 2009, 61.
32. World Court Decides Ukraine-Romania Sea Border Dispute. Radio Liberty/Radio Free Europe, 3 February 2009 <https://www.rferl.org/a/World_Court_Decides_Ukraine_Romania_Sea_Border_Dispute_/1378615.html> accessed 26 June 2023. Interestingly, Serpent Island (also referred to as Snake Island) in the Black Sea, the legal characterisation of which was at the heart of the delimitation dispute, in 2022 became one of the key symbols of Ukraine's resistance to Russia's war of aggression (Ukraine reveals 'Russian warship, go f*** yourself!' postage stamp, *The Guardian*, 12 March 2022 <https://www.theguardian.com/world/2022/mar/12/ukraine-reveals-russian-warship-go-fuck-yourself-postage-stamp> accessed 26 June 2023.
33. *Vysnovok Konstytutsiinoho Sudu Ukrainy u spravi za konstytutsiinym podanniam Prezydenta Ukrainy pro nadannia vysnovku shchodo vidpovidnosti Konstytutsii Ukrainy Rymskoho Statutu Mizhnarodnoho kryminalnoho sudu (sprava pro Rymskyi Statut)*

(Opinion of the Constitutional Court of Ukraine in the case on the constitutional petition of the President of Ukraine on giving an opinion on the compliance of the Constitution of Ukraine to the Rome Statute of the International Criminal Court (the *Rome Statute* case)), 11 July 2001, No 3-B/2001 <https://zakon.rada.gov.ua/laws/show/v003v710-01/conv#Text> accessed 26 June 2023. For an analysis see Mykola Gnatovskyy, *Ukraine and the International Criminal Court: a Constitutional Matter* (Vox Ukraine 2016) <https://voxukraine.org/en/ukraine-and-the-international-criminal-court-a-constitutional-matter-en> accessed 26 June 2023.

34. Mykola Gnatovskyy, 'Litigating War: Ukraine's Quest for Justice at the "World Court"', 2(12) Ukraine Analityca 2018, 20–26 <https://ukraine-analytica.org/litigating-war-ukraines-quest-for-justice-at-the-world-court/> accessed 17 November 2023; Iryna Marchuk, *Application of the International Convention for the Suppression of the Financing of Terrorism and of the International Convention on the Elimination of all Forms of Racial Discrimination (Ukraine v. Russian Federation)(Preliminary Objections) (ICJ)* (International Legal Materials 2020); Iryna Marchuk, 'From Warfare to "Lawfare": Increased Litigation and Rise of Parallel Proceedings in International Courts. A Case Study of Ukraine's and Georgia's Action against the Russian Federation' in Avidan Kent, Nikos Skoutaris, and Jamie Trinidad (eds), *The Future of International Courts* (London 2019) 217–234.
35. Lauri Mälksoo, *Russian Approaches to International Law* (OUP 2015) 87–92.
36. See, eg, Kostiantyn Savchuk, '*Dmytro Ivanovych Kachenovskyi—odyn iz fundatoriv vitchyznianoi nauky mizhnarodnoho prava*' ('Dmytro Kachenovskyi— A Founder of the Native International Law Scholarship'), 2 *Mizhnarodne pravo* 2013, 219–229.
37. Philippe Sands, *East West Street. On the Origins of 'Genocide' and 'Crimes against Humanity'* (New York 2016) 231–232.
38. For an overview see Olga Butkevych, *Ukrainian Legal Scholarship on the History of Ancient and Medieval International Law* in *Baltic Yearbook of International Law*, vol 7(1) (2007) 187–223; Olga Butkevych, *Istoriia mizhnarodnoho prava (History of International Law)* (2019) 29–34.
39. A comprehensive analysis of the issue from such a position has been provided, most notably, by Professor Vsevolod Mitsik, who in 2017 succeeded Oleksandr Zadorozhniy as the head of international law at the Taras Shevchenko University of Kyiv: Vsevolod Mitsik, *Pytannia pro mizhnarodnu pravosubiektnist fizychnoi osoby u mizhnarodnomu pravi prav liudyny* ('The question of international legal personality of individuals in international human rights law'). Paper presented at the readings of the Ukrainian Association of International Law, Kyiv, 23 November 2011.
40. Volodymyr Butkevych, '*Mizhnarodna pravosubiektnist fizychnoi osoby*' ('International Legal Personality of Individuals) in Volodymyr Butkevych (ed.) *Mizhnarodne pravo. Osnovy teorii* (*International Law. Principles of Theory*) (Lybid 2002) 333–334.
41. See, eg, Ganna Yudkivska, 'Ukraine on the Way to Democracy: Role and Achievements of the European Court of Human Rights' in Iulia Motoc and Ineta Ziemele (eds), *The Impact of the ECHR on Democratic Change in Central and Eastern Europe. Judicial Perspectives* (CUP 2016) 457–490; Ganna Yudkivska, '*Ex Aequo et Bono*—Some Post-Mandate Reflections', 3(4) European Convention on Human Rights Law Review 2022, 435–442.

CHAPTER 39

THE UNITED KINGDOM

JAMES HARRISON AND MICHAEL WOOD

1. Introduction

THERE is little doubt that the United Kingdom of Great Britain and Northern Ireland (UK) has played a central role in the development of international law. The UK participated in most major diplomatic conferences of the 19th and 20th centuries and was closely involved in the establishment of the new global order after the two World Wars. This chapter examines the scope and character of British engagement with international law.

As a prominent supporter of multilateralism, the UK has been active in promoting core values of the international system, such as international peace and security, human rights, and the rule of law. Section 2 of this chapter will elaborate some of the principal contributions of the UK to international law, as well as noting some of the controversies surrounding UK practice. The purpose is not to engage in a critical evaluation of a recent series of exceptional events in which the then British government seemed to show limited respect for international law, or sought to justify the unjustifiable. Rather, the chapter focuses on whether the UK approach to international law is distinct from that found in other parts of the European continent. To this end, Section 3 revisits the debate about the possible existence of a 'British school' of international law, considering the influence of legal culture on the approach to international law in the UK. Section 4 then examines how international law has been 'domesticated' within the UK, highlighting the dynamic character of the incorporation process, as well as how respect for international law became entwined in ongoing constitutional debates arising as a result of British withdrawal from the European Union (EU) (Brexit).

2. The Influence of the United Kingdom on International Law

The UK has long been a leading player in international law. This influence reflects both the UK's role in international affairs, and the range and quality of its practitioners and teachers. A good deal has already been written about the UK and international law[1] and the purpose of the current section is not to summarize what has been said before, but to contextualize the contribution of the UK within the broader themes highlighted in this volume. To this end, this section will consider the main contributions of the UK to the international legal system, acknowledging that there are different perspectives on this question.

Whilst the influence of the UK on international law has varied over the years, it is generally accepted that the UK has made, and continues to make, a prominent contribution.[2] Indeed, the UK has occupied a privileged position within the international legal system, which one author has characterized as embedding a 'legalised hegemony' that perpetuates the dominance of a small number of powerful States over the rest of the international community.[3] This status is particularly reflected in the UK's permanent membership of the United Nations Security Council,[4] but it is also evidenced by the fact that, since 1921, there has usually been a UK judge on the International Court of Justice (ICJ)[5] and since 1948 a UK member of the International Law Commission (ILC).[6]

On the whole, the UK has used its standing in the international community to support multilateralism, both within Europe and beyond.[7] The UK was pivotal in the establishment of both the League of Nations and the United Nations (UN). The latter was born out of the Atlantic Charter issued on 14 August 1941 by Franklin D Roosevelt, President of the United States, and Prime Minister Winston Churchill.[8] The Charter set out a vision for a new international order based upon eight common principles, many of which are reflected in the modern multilateral framework, including territorial integrity, self-determination, liberalization of international trade, and the pursuit of minimum labour, economic, and welfare standards.

Within Europe, the UK has been at the forefront of promoting these values, cementing the place of international law in European affairs. In particular, the UK was influential in the Nuremberg trials, as well as in the drafting of the European Convention on Human Rights (ECHR). In terms of its broader commitment to international law, the UK was an early advocate of arbitration as a peaceful means for the settlement of international disputes[9] and today it is the only permanent member of the Security Council with an optional clause declaration under the Statute of the ICJ, albeit one with very extensive reservations.[10] Moreover, it is also one of only fourteen parties to the European Convention on the Peaceful Settlement of Disputes, concluded under the auspices of the Council of Europe and committing parties to settlement of disputes before the ICJ, arbitration, or conciliation.[11] These examples are testament to UK support for the pacifying role of international law (see van Aaken, this volume). Indeed, regardless of its recent exit from the EU, the UK continues to be very active in other 'European' institutions, including the Council of Europe, the United Nations Economic Commission for Europe, and the Organisation for Security and Cooperation in Europe.

Viewed from further afield, however, the UK's contribution to international law may be perceived differently. As noted elsewhere in this volume, the role of Europe has been widely criticized in part because it tends to ignore European oppression and abuses in the history of international law (see Mälksoo, this volume on the role of European States and lawyers in the history of international law). The UK's colonial past inevitably has implications for how its contribution to international law is seen (see Anghie, this volume).

At the height of the British Empire, the UK was responsible for the international relations of a large number of territories around the globe, many of them of considerable size. It is a matter of historical record that the UK gained wealth and power from this relationship. The reach of the UK diminished throughout the 20th century, at first through the gradual transfer of powers to the self-governing dominions[12] and later through the decolonization process. The transfer of power was in many cases peaceful and the UK retains important links with former parts of the British Empire through the Commonwealth,[13] an informal association of States[14] which seeks to promote 'consultation, discussion and co-operation'[15] in furtherance of common principles of democracy, human rights, international peace and security, the rule of law, good governance, and sustainable development.[16] Furthermore, the Commonwealth has had an influence on UK international legal practice,[17] which, though less prevalent today, continues to be reflected in part by the exclusion from the UK declaration accepting the jurisdiction of the ICJ of 'any dispute with the government of any other country which is or has been a Member of the Commonwealth'.[18] The continuing justification for the exclusion was once described as 'very tenuous',[19] and in any event disputes between the UK and Commonwealth members may subject to compulsory settlement, either before the ICJ or other international courts and tribunals, on other jurisdictional grounds.[20]

The UK's colonial legacy has received increasing attention in legal writings[21] and it has even prompted litigation in the case of the dispute with Mauritius over the status of the Chagos Archipelago.[22] In 2019, the ICJ held that, 'having found that the decolonization of Mauritius was not conducted in a manner consistent with the right of peoples to self-determination, it follows that the United Kingdom's continued administration of the Chagos Archipelago constitutes a wrongful act entailing the international responsibility of that State'.[23] Following this opinion, the UN General Assembly, by a vote of 116 votes to six (with fifty-six abstentions), demanded that the UK 'withdraw its colonial administration from the Chagos Archipelago unconditionally within a period of no more than six months from the adoption of the present resolution, thereby enabling Mauritius to complete the decolonization of its territory as rapidly as possible'.[24] Several EU Member States (namely Cyprus, Finland, Greece, Ireland, Liechtenstein, and Sweden) voted in favour of the resolution, with others abstaining, demonstrating the isolation of the UK on the question. Nevertheless, the UK official response was to underline the non-binding nature of the advisory opinion and to criticize the approach of the Court for 'fail[ing] to give due regard to material facts and legal issues that the UK Government explained in detail in our submissions to the ICJ'.[25] The issue continued to be debated in a number of international institutions (eg Universal Postal Union, Indian Ocean Tuna Commission) and, more than three and a half years after the advisory opinion was delivered, the UK Government opened negotiations with Mauritius on the exercise of sovereignty over the Chagos Archipelago with a view to securing 'an agreement on the basis of international law to resolve the outstanding issues'.[26]

This is not the only example where the UK's commitment to multilateralism has come under close and critical scrutiny in recent times. The invasion of Iraq in 2003 stands out as a major example in which the UK's stance on international law was criticized, both internationally and domestically.[27] Whilst there was no formal legal judgment on the matter, there has been clear reputational damage to the standing and influence of the States involved in the military action, including the UK.[28]

It is not the purpose of this chapter to take a position on these individual issues. No nation, whether in Europe or beyond, has an impeccable record on compliance with international law. Indeed, the whole purpose of international law is to reconcile competing claims of States, and the UK has generally sought to justify its conduct in many of these cases through legal argument, rather than ignore or repudiate the relevant rules. With this in mind, the following section will consider a more general question as to whether it is possible to discern a particular British approach to international law that distinguishes it from other nations of Europe. To address that question, we must return to a long-standing debate about international law in Europe and the existence of different 'approaches' based in different countries, regions or legal systems.

3. A 'British School' of International Law?

Whilst the UK has been a key actor in European affairs for many centuries, it has often been observed that the UK does not fully embrace the culture and traditions of other legal systems on the European continent, for a variety of geographical and historical reasons. To this effect, the literature in this area tends to highlight possible distinctions between 'common law' and 'civil law' approaches to international law, or between 'Anglo-Saxon' and 'Continental' schools.[29] It was with such distinctions in mind that, in 1920, representation of 'the principal legal systems of the world' found its way into Article 9 of the Statute of the Permanent Court of International Justice (PCIJ)[30] and was carried over into the corresponding provision of the ICJ Statute[31] and into the Statute of the ILC.[32]

In its most prominent form, such a distinction draws attention to an overarching difference in legal technique and philosophy as applied at the international level.[33] The general caricature of the two systems adopted by most writings in this vein would describe common lawyers as taking a pragmatic approach to the development of the law,[34] whereas civil lawyers are apt to turn to general overarching principles as a guide for deciding individual cases. Yet, the distinction was not merely theoretical but played out in debates relating to a range of topics, including the judicial settlement of disputes[35] and codification.[36]

It is distinctions such as this that provide the foundation for what some have claimed to be an 'English school of international law' with 'a strong predilection for the development of the law through decided cases and specific instances; suspicious if not impatient, of abstract theories and doctrine; but realizing to the full the crucial importance of history and not just of "legal" history—to the understanding, practice, and future development of international law.'[37] As such, practitioners of this so-called English approach drew a strong distinction between legal and moral questions,[38] with an emphasis on law being 'the child of custom, of practice, and of human political development, and not the result of any scientific formulation'.[39] Some English lawyers have been known to assert the history of their own legal system—based upon the gradual development of rules and practice, rather than revolutionary change and the assertion of overarching principles—as an appropriate analogy for the development of international law.[40]

The idea of an 'English school' was by no means parochial. English writers on international law frequently acknowledged the intellectual debt owed to their continental cousins engaged in the field.[41] Rather the emphasis was on a different way of approaching legal problems. The source of this difference is sometimes ascribed to national legal training and culture,[42] sometimes to language itself.[43] Whatever form it takes, such a conception of an 'English school of international law' emphasized the detachment between the UK and the rest of Europe where different traditions were thought to prevail.

Of course, within the UK, generalizations based upon legal culture should be treated with care, as the UK itself consists of three separate jurisdictions: England and Wales (with Wales in some respects forming a distinct jurisdiction[44]); Scotland; and Northern Ireland.[45] In addition, the UK is responsible for the international relations of the three Crown Dependencies[46] (the Bailiwick of Guernsey and the Bailiwick of Jersey, known collectively as 'the Channel Islands', and the Isle of Man), as well as some fourteen British overseas territories, although these territories are not constitutionally part of the UK[47] and when making decisions on behalf of the territories, UK Ministers are acting on behalf of Her Majesty in right of the territory and not of the UK.[48] Each of these jurisdictions has its own characteristics and identity, not all of which necessarily align with the English common law.

Amongst the four nations of the UK, Scotland stands out, since its legal system exhibits characteristics of both common law and civil law. As a 'mixed' legal system, Scots law places much greater emphasis on the works of institutional writers and the exposition of general principles as a basis for the development of the law.[49] This has led some commentators to speculate that a distinct 'Scottish tradition of international law' could be identified, rooted much more closely to the traditions of European countries and drawing inspiration from the values of the Scottish Enlightenment.[50] James Lorimer (1818–1890) perhaps represents the epitome of any such tradition, with his embrace of moral philosophy and his willingness to engage in the process of deduction from general principles as the basis for his writings on the international legal system. Lorimer's approach has been described as 'essentially European, not British, in its composition',[51] something that led to criticism from contemporaneous English scholars.[52] However, Lorimer has also been described as 'an outlier even in his own time'[53] and thus may provide a dubious basis on which to build a Scottish tradition of international law. Following his death, it is difficult to discern any continuation of this tradition and the approach to international law in Scotland would appear to have aligned with that of England, as have other jurisdictions of the UK.

While there are some differences between British and European approaches to international law, the extent of these differences should not be overstated.[54] Even at the height of the debate, there were sceptical voices about how significant this distinction was. For his part, Hersch Lauterpacht forcefully argued that 'statements on the alleged contrast between Anglo-American and Continental schools of thought in international law ... find no support either in the existing rules of international law, or in the practice of international tribunals, or in the general jurisprudential considerations on which they profess to be based'[55] and he urged the 'abandonment of this deeply-rooted belief'.[56] Such beliefs may not have been completely discarded, but it is likely that the scale of any difference has further diminished over time. There are ever more opportunities for international lawyers to practise at the international level before courts and tribunals that are disconnected from any national legal system. In this context, practising international lawyers regularly work in multinational teams, in which national differences must be put aside in order to achieve a common position.[57] Furthermore, international legal education in the UK has become somewhat detached from national legal culture, with international law being taught in many British law schools by academics from a variety of nationalities and backgrounds—though it was ever so, Gentili, Oppenheim, and Lauterpacht being among the greatest of 'British' international lawyers. That is not to say that practising international lawyers may not be influenced by their national systems, but at the end of the day, '[d]espite differences in style and education, [common lawyers and civil lawyers] are dealing with the same subject matter ... there is just international law'.[58]

4. The Influence of International Law within the United Kingdom

If there is no particular British approach to international law at a conceptual level, what about the treatment of international law within the legal systems of the UK? In contrast to all other European nations, the UK does not have a written constitution based upon a 'single coherent code of fundamental law which prevails over all other sources of law', but rather the constitutional arrangements of the UK 'have developed over time in a pragmatic as much as in a principled way'.[59] Thus, it is to legislation, judicial decisions, and institutional practice that we must look in order to understand how international law is received in UK law.

Traditionally, though with separate legal systems, the UK was understood as a unitary State with power concentrated in a sovereign and a sovereign Parliament in Westminster. Yet, constitutional arrangements have evolved significantly in past decades as power has been devolved from the UK institutions to 'national' seats of government in Scotland, Wales, and Northern Ireland.[60] Under devolution, the conduct of international relations and international trade are reserved or excepted matters.[61] It does not follow, however, that the devolved institutions have no interest or role in the development or implementation of international law. Firstly, the devolution legislation makes clear that representatives of the devolved governments may 'assist Ministers of the Crown' in relation to any matter falling within the scope of international relations or international trade[62] and it has been argued on behalf of the devolved institutions that they should have a stronger voice in international negotiations.[63] Secondly, the devolved legislatures may adopt legislation giving effect to the international obligations of the UK where the matters covered by international law fall within their devolved competence. It is necessary to understand how international law is incorporated into the legal systems of the UK and what role international law plays in constraining the powers of governmental bodies within the UK.

The UK is often considered a dualist State, in large part because of its approach to the incorporation of treaties. Indeed, it has been said that 'the dualist system is a necessary corollary of Parliamentary sovereignty'.[64] The characterization of the UK as a dualist State is, however, simplistic and understates the influence that international law has had on UK law and practice.[65] Even though treaties are not binding without some act of incorporation[66] and courts have been traditionally unwilling to scrutinize the prerogative powers of the UK government to enter into treaties,[67] it has long been recognized that this doctrine 'does not preclude the decision of justiciable issues which arise against the background of an unincorporated treaty in a way which renders it necessary or convenient to refer to, and consider, the contents of the treaty'.[68] In practice, the UK courts have adopted a 'presumption of compatibility' with international treaties, meaning that 'the words of a statute passed after [a treaty] has been signed and dealing with the subject matter of the international obligation of the [UK] are to be construed, if they are reasonably capable of bearing such a meaning, as intended to carry out the obligation and not to be inconsistent with it'.[69] When interpreting treaties, the UK courts are clear that they are construing an international instrument and they must therefore follow the international rules on interpretation because 'the text of an international convention is intended to be given the same meaning by all the states which become parties to it'.[70] It follows that it will be just as relevant to have regard to judicial decisions from other jurisdictions, as well as from international courts and tribunals.[71]

By and large, the principles discussed above have been followed in all of the jurisdictions of the UK. Whilst there was for some time doubt as to whether Scottish courts would have regard to unincorporated (human rights) treaties when interpreting domestic statutes if there was no clear intention of Parliament to implement the treaty,[72] it now seems to be accepted that 'drawing of a distinction between the law of Scotland and that of the rest of the [UK] on this matter can no longer be justified'.[73] However, a major area of distinction does relate to compatibility between devolved legislation and international law. There is nothing that generally demands that the devolved institutions adhere to international law as a condition of legality of their enactments. In other words, the devolution settlements are based upon a dualist model of international law similar to that applied more generally in the UK. Two exceptions apply. Firstly, the devolution legislation permits the UK Government to intervene and prevent Bills passed by the devolved administrations from being submitted for Royal Assent where there are 'reasonable grounds to believe [the Bill] would be incompatible with any international obligations or the interests of defence or national security'.[74] This power has not been utilized to date and it raises some interesting questions of what threshold must be met to intervene. Secondly, and more significantly, all of the devolved institutions must comply with the ECHR in order for their actions to be lawful.[75] These provisions go significantly further than the demands placed by the Human Rights Act 1998 on the UK Parliament, by which courts are limited to making a declaration of incompatibility if an Act of the UK Parliament is considered to be incompatible with Convention rights.[76]

Whilst the presumption of compatibility goes some way to increasing the currency of international treaties in domestic law, two important aspects of the doctrine must be highlighted, both of which potentially limit the influence of international law on decisions by UK courts. Firstly, it is always necessary to identify a relevant provision of domestic law requiring interpretation and it has been emphatically held that 'our courts will not interpret or give rulings under instruments of international law unless there is a question of domestic law directly involved'.[77] Indeed, there must be sufficient ambiguity in the legal text that justifies recourse to the treaty. Secondly, as the doctrine operates as a presumption, it is still open to a court to construe legislation or some other legal act in a manner in which does not give effect to international law, particularly if there is evidence of an intention to legislate without regard to international law.

In practice, the role of international law as a source of interpretation may also depend upon the nature of the legal instruments in question. Thus, in the case of human rights treaties, there is perhaps a greater willingness of courts to ensure that international obligations are complied with.[78] Indeed, the Human Rights Act 1998 deviates from the basic presumption of compatibility described above, instead requiring that 'so far as it is possible to do so, primary legislation and subordinate legislation must be read and given effect in a way which is compatible with the Convention rights',[79] and in doing so must take into account any judgment of the European Court of Human Rights (ECtHR).[80] This requirement has been described as 'imposing a remarkably powerful interpretative obligation, which goes well beyond the normal canons of statutory construction'.[81] This obligation has been controversial and there have been proposals to abolish it, although no such proposal has (yet) been implemented.[82] At the same time, attempts by the Scottish Parliament to extend human rights protections in Scotland by introducing a stricter presumption of compatibility in relation to other human rights treaties (namely the United Nations Convention on the Rights of the Child) have run afoul of limitations on their devolved competence.[83] There is an ongoing debate in the UK about the reception of international human rights law into domestic law, which has broader implications for the UK's reputation at the international level.

The position of customary international law in the UK legal systems is as equally nuanced as that of treaties. The bare statement that 'the rules of [customary] international law, as existing from time to time, do form part of our English law'[84] is today 'more accurately understood as a doctrine of judicial transformation or judicial adoption' according to which 'customary international law is a source, and not as such a part, of the common law'.[85] This area of law also tends to operate by way of presumptions. As expressed by Lord Sumption in *R (Keyu) v Secretary of State for Foreign and Commonwealth Affairs*, 'the presumption ... is that [customary international law], once established, can and should shape the common law, whenever it can do so consistently with domestic constitutional principles, statutory law and common law rules which the courts can themselves sensibly adapt without it being, for example, necessary to invite Parliamentary intervention or consideration'.[86] This gives considerable leeway to the courts to determine the precise circumstances in which customary international law should be applied and it underlines the flexible nature of the rules in this area of law.

Ultimately, there is no clear constitutional guarantee that the UK must abide by its international legal commitments as a matter of domestic law. The UK Ministerial Code refers to 'the overarching duty on Ministers to comply with the law',[87] after an explicit reference to international law was removed in 2015.[88] Comparable texts in Scotland and Wales still make reference to a duty to comply with international law and treaty obligations.[89] What is interesting for present purposes is that this duty has been invoked by devolved administrations when laying legislative consent memorandums in relation to UK legislation covering devolved matters. According to constitutional convention, the UK Parliament must seek the consent of a devolved legislature before it adopts measures within devolved competence.[90] Yet when the UK Parliament sought the consent of the Scottish Parliament and the Senedd (formerly the Welsh Assembly) for the proposed United Kingdom Internal Market Bill, both the Scottish Government and the Welsh Government objected to the Bill, in part because it granted a power to UK Ministers to override the terms of the EU-UK Withdrawal Agreement.[91] In particular, the Scottish Government noted that 'the fundamental principle, reflected in the Ministerial Code, that Ministers do not knowingly break the law requires that the Scottish Government recommend that consent is withheld to a bill that, by UK Ministers' own admission, is in breach of international law'.[92] A similar position was taken in relation to the Northern Ireland Protocol Bill published in June 2022.[93] These statements have no legal effect[94] and the question of compatibility of the proposed legislation with international law is itself contested. Nevertheless, the examples illustrate how respect for international law has become part of broader debates about the future constitutional arrangements of the UK following Brexit.

5. Conclusion

Overall, this survey has revealed a strong engagement with international law by and within the UK, which sees itself as playing a central role on the global stage and contributing to an international order based upon the rule of law.[95] In the past, it has pursued this agenda both on its own behalf, but also as a member of the EU. In this respect, the place of the UK in European affairs has radically changed in recent years. UK withdrawal from the EU has not only led to a significant reshaping of legal relationships within Europe, but has also prompted a resurgence in thinking about the identity of the UK on the international stage. The objective of Brexit was not only to take back control of domestic matters, but also to ensure a stronger voice for the UK at the international level, allowing it to pursue its own foreign policy priorities independently from the EU. The term 'Global Britain' has been coined to capture these ambitions, although the concept has been criticized in some quarters for its ambiguity and lack of substance.[96] Indeed, the UK Foreign and Commonwealth Office has itself stressed that strategic foreign policy objectives have not fundamentally changed as a result of Brexit.[97]

At the same time, it is undeniable that Brexit has brought to the fore key policy divergences between the UK and other parts of Europe. Such differences should not be allowed to overshadow the agreement that remains on a number of core values, as is apparent from the EU-UK Trade and Cooperation Agreement. The preamble to the Agreement begins by reaffirming the commitment of the parties 'to democratic principles, to the rule of law, to human rights, to countering proliferation of weapons of mass destruction and to the fight against climate change, which constitute essential elements of this and supplementing agreements' and the Agreement goes on to impose obligations on both parties to 'cooperate in promoting those values and principles, including with or in third countries'.[98] The coordinated response of the UK and the EU to the Ukraine crisis underlines that continuing agreement on core values. Moreover, as discussed in this chapter, the UK remains engaged with many other European institutions.

Beyond policy divergences between the UK and the EU, the existence of a distinctive British approach to international law should not be overemphasized. Such thoughts run counter to international law's aspiration to be a universal legal system. That having been said, the reception of international law into the national legal systems of the UK does have certain unique features. The lack of a written constitution means that the relationship between international law and national law in the UK is particularly dynamic. International law is arguably more prominent in post-Brexit Britain, given that many international commitments were previously given effect through EU law, but now have to be implemented directly. The chapter has illustrated that respect for international law has featured prominently in ongoing debates about the UK's international role following Brexit, as well as how international law is implemented in the different legal systems of the UK. These debates are ongoing, but the clear message from the UK is that it intends to continue to play a leading role in promoting international peace and security, human rights and democracy.[99] The challenge is to make sure that its practice, at home and abroad, matches the rhetoric.

NOTES

1. See, eg, Michael Wood, 'British Contributions to Public International Law' in Peter Hilpold (ed), *European International Law Traditions* (Springer 2021) 191–215.
2. See, eg, the four-volume compilation: Jill Barrett and Jean-Pierre Gauci (eds), *British Contributions to International Law, 1915–2015* (Brill/Nijhoff 2020).
3. Gerry Simpson, *Great Powers and Outlaw States: Unequal Sovereigns in the International Legal Order* (CUP 2004) 67.
4. United Nations Charter (adopted 26 June 1945, entered into force 24 October 1945) 1 UNTS xvi, Article 23(1).
5. Until February 2018. For analysis of the non-election of a British judge in 2017, see House of Commons Foreign Affairs Committee, *2017 Elections to the International Court of Justice: Fourth Report of Session 2017–19* (27 February 2018).
6. With the exception of the quinquennium 1997–2001.
7. See House of Commons Foreign Affairs Committee, *Global Britain: Sixth Report of Session 2017–19* (6 March 2018) para 10.
8. See Mohamed Bennouna, 'Atlantic Charter (1941)' in Rüdiger Wolfrum (ed), *Max Planck Encyclopedia of Public International Law* (OUP 2007).
9. eg the 1794 Treaty of Amity, Commerce and Navigation between his Britannic Majesty and the United States of America.
10. Michael Wood, 'The United Kingdom's Acceptance of the Compulsory Jurisdiction of the International Court of Justice' in Jean-Pierre Gauci and Jill Barrett (eds), *Anthology of British Contributions to International Law 1915–2015* (Brill/Nijhoff 2020) 3261–3284. This article was written before the two most recent declarations introducing far-reaching reservations were made in 2014 and 2017.
11. European Convention for the Peaceful Settlement of Disputes (adopted 29 April 1957, entered into force 30 April 1958) 320 UNTS 243.
12. Whilst the early practice of the British Empire was to conclude treaties on behalf of all of the British possessions, the position changed from the late 1800s when it was established that the self-governing colonies (namely Canada, Australia, Newfoundland, South Africa, and New Zealand) would not be bound by certain treaties unless they had consented. In 1919, most of the self-governing colonies became members of the League of Nations in their own right and the independence of these territories from the UK was recognized in the Statute of Westminster 1931.
13. Not all current members of the Commonwealth are former British colonies: Gabon, Rwanda, Mozambique.
14. See, eg, Charlotte Steinorth, 'Commonwealth' in Rüdiger Wolfrum (ed), *Max Planck Encyclopedia of Public International Law* (OUP 2017)paras 29–31.
15. Declaration of Commonwealth Principles (adopted at the Commonwealth Heads of Government Meeting, Singapore, 14–22 January 1971).
16. See Charter of the Commonwealth (adopted 19 December 2012).

17. See James Fawcett, *The British Commonwealth in International Law* (Stevens & Sons 1963); Arthur Watts, 'The Commonwealth and International Law', 15 *Journal of the Commonwealth Lawyers Association* 2006, 21–26.
18. See UK Declaration recognizing the jurisdiction of the Court as compulsory, 22 February 2017 <https://www.icj-cij.org/en/declarations/gb> accessed 14 July 2022.
19. Robert Jennings, 'The Commonwealth and International Law', 30 *British Yearbook of International Law* 1953, 320–351, 329. A wish to avoid compulsory jurisdiction over matters arising from a different age is, however, understandable.
20. eg *Award in the Arbitration regarding the Chagos Marine Protected Area between Mauritius and the United Kingdom* (2015) 31 Report of International Arbitral Awards 359.
21. See, eg, Surabhi Ranganathan, 'The "English School" of International Law: Soundings via the 1972 Jubilee Essays', 80 *Cambridge Law Journal* 2021, 126–153.
22. Alongside inter-state litigation discussed here, the Chagos Archipelago has inspired numerous claims in the national courts, as well as before the European Court of Human Rights (ECtHR); *Chagos Islanders v the United Kingdom*, App no 35622/04, Decision of the Fourth Section of the European Court of Human Rights, 11 December 2012.
23. *Legal Consequences of the Separation of the Chagos Archipelago from Mauritius in 1965 (Advisory Opinion)* [2019] ICJ Rep 95, [177]. See Niko Pavlopoulos, 'Chagos (Advisory Opinion)' in Anne Peters (ed), *Max Planck Encyclopedia of Public International Law* (OUP 2021).
24. Advisory opinion of the International Court of Justice on the legal consequences of the separation of the Chagos Archipelago from Mauritius in 1965, UNGA Res 73/295 (22 May 2019) UN Doc A/RES/73/295, para 3.
25. See statement of Sir Alan Duncan (Minister for Europe and the Americas), 3 July 2019, Hansard, vol 662, col 584WH. See also Philippa Webb, 'The United Kingdom and the Chagos Archipelago Advisory Opinion: Engagement and Resistance', 21 *Melbourne Journal of International Law* 2021, 726–748.
26. Statement by James Cleverly (Secretary of State for Foreign, Commonwealth and Development Affairs) 3 November 2022 <https://questions-statements.parliament.uk/written-statements/detail/2022-11-03/hcws354> accessed 12 December 2022.
27. The invasion led to huge protests in the UK, as well as to the departure of Elizabeth Wilmshurst, deputy legal adviser at the Foreign and Commonwealth Office. More generally, see Sean Murphy, 'Assessing the Legality of Invading Iraq', 92 *The Georgetown Law Journal* 2004, 173.
28. See Report of the Iraq Inquiry (the 'Chilcot' Inquiry) (2016) <https://www.gov.uk/government/publications/the-report-of-the-iraq-inquiry> accessed 19 July 2022.
29. eg Hersch Lauterpacht, 'The So-Called Anglo-American and Continental Schools of Thought in International Law', 12 *British Yearbook of International Law* 1931, 31; James Crawford and Alain Pellet, 'Anglo Saxon and Continental Approaches to Pleading before the ICJ' in Isabelle Buffard et al (eds), *International Law between Universalism and Fragmentation: Festschrift in Honour of Gerhard Hafner* (Martinus Nijhoff Publishers 2008) 831–868.
30. Article 9 PCIJ Statute.
31. Article 9 ICJ Statute.
32. Statute of the International Law Commission, UNGA Res 174 (II) (21 November 1947), Article 8. The ILC itself has very recently used a rather different expression, 'the various legal systems of the world' in draft conclusion 4 on General Principles of Law as adopted

on first reading in 2023. The commentary explains that '[t]he use of the term "the various legal systems of the world" is aimed at highlighting the requirement that a principle must be found in legal systems of the world generally. It is an inclusive and broad term, covering the variety and diversity of national legal systems of the world'; ILC, Report of the International Law Commission on the Work of its 74th session (2023) UN Doc A/78/10, 17.

33. Lauterpacht (n 29) 32. See also Alexander Pearce Higgins, *International Law and Relations* (CUP 1928) 30.
34. For an emphasis on pragmatism in a British approach see Stephen Samuel, 'British Influences on the Ideals of International Lawyers' in Robert McCorquodale and Jean-Pierre Gauci (eds), *British Influences on International Law, 1915–2015* (BIICL 2016) 77; Philippe Sands and Arman Sarvarian, 'The Contribution of the British Bar to International Law', in ibid, 519.
35. See, eg, Lauterpacht (n 29) 31.
36. See, eg, Cecil Hurst, 'A Plea for the Codification of International Law on New Lines', 32 *Transactions of the Grotius Society* 1946, 135, 146.
37. Address by Professor Robert Jennings at the Memorial Service to Professor Clive Parry on 16 October 1982 in Great St Mary's Church, Cambridge in Anthony Parry (ed), *Collected Papers of Professor Clive Parry* (2 vols) (Wildy, Simmonds and Hill Publishing 2012) xxxvii. See also Douglas Johnson, 'The English Tradition in International Law', 11 *International and Comparative Law Quarterly* 1962, 416–445.
38. eg John Fischer Williams, *Aspects of Modern International Law: An Essay* (OUP 1939) 8–9.
39. ibid, 107.
40. eg ibid, 107.
41. See, eg, James Brierly, *The Law of Nations* (Clarendon Press 1928) 18–33; Sir Arnold McNair, 'The Debt of International Law in Britain to the Civil Law and the Civilians', 39 *Transactions of the Grotius Society* 1953, 183.
42. See, eg, James Crawford et al, 'Anglo-American and Continental Traditions in International Advocacy before International Court and Tribunals', 2 *Cambridge International Law Journal* 2013, 715, 717.
43. See eg Brierly (n 41) 43; Fischer Williams (n 38) 9–10. See also Hugh Thirlway, 'International and Municipal Legal Reasoning', 294 *Receuil des Cours* 2002, 267, 286–287.
44. Historically, the law of England and Wales has been treated as a single jurisdiction (as a matter of law it was said that 'England includes Wales'). England and Wales still share a common judicial system (which is a reserved matter under the Government of Wales Act 2006, Sch 7A), but legislative and executive powers in many areas have been devolved to the Senedd and Welsh government respectively; Government of Wales Act 2006, s A2 recognizes that 'the law that applies in Wales includes a body of Welsh law'.
45. The authors initially considered extending this chapter to include a section on Ireland, with the assistance of James Kingston, the much admired Legal Adviser to Ireland's Department of Foreign Affairs. Very sadly, James passed away, all too young, in April 2022.
46. David Anderson, 'Channel Islands and Isle of Man' in Rüdiger Wolfrum (ed), *Max Planck Encyclopedia of Public International Law* (OUP 2013).
47. Ian Hendry and Susan Dickson, *British Overseas Territories Law* (2nd edn, Hart Publishing 2018)14.
48. See *R (Quark Fisheries Ltd) v Secretary of State of Foreign and Commonwealth Affairs* [2005] UKHL 57.

49. See, eg, Thomas B Smith, *British Justice: The Scottish Contribution* (Stevens & Sons 1961) 8–9.
50. See Douglas Johnston, 'The Scottish Tradition of International Law', 16 *Canadian Yearbook of International Law* 1978, 3–45.
51. ibid, 33. See also Alexander Pearce Higgins, 'James Lorimer (1818–1890)', 45 *Juridical Review* 1933, 239, 240.
52. See Sir Frederick Pollock, *An Introduction to the History of the Science of Politics* (Macmillan & Co 1890) 123–124.
53. Stephen Tierney and Neil Walker, 'Through a Glass, Darkly: Reflections on James Lorimer's International Law', 27 *European Journal of International Law* 2016, 409, 412.
54. See Wood (n 1) 193.
55. Lauterpacht (n 29) 32.
56. ibid, 61.
57. See Crawford and Pellet (n 29) 856.
58. Crawford et al (n 42) 725.
59. *R (Miller and another) v Secretary of State for Exiting the European Union* [2017] UKSC 5, [40] (hereafter *Miller*).
60. Legislative devolution in Scotland and Wales can be traced to the late 1990s, although the extent of devolution has differed in each jurisdiction. Devolution has a longer, albeit troubled, history in Northern Ireland. There are no equivalent devolution arrangements for England. Nevertheless, in a sense there are four 'nations', including England; health being a devolved matter, the response to Covid-19 made this clear to everyone.
61. Scotland Act 1998, Sch 5; Government of Wales Act 2006, Sch 7A; Northern Ireland Act, Sch 2. A key exception in the context of Northern Ireland is the participation of Ministers of the Northern Ireland Executive in meetings of the North-South Ministerial Council and the British Irish Council.
62. See Scotland Act 1998, Sch 5; Government of Wales Act 2006, Sch 7A.
63. See, eg, Scottish Government, *Scotland's role in the development of future UK trade arrangements* (2018). A more recent proposal from the Labour Party suggests that 'the Foreign Affairs reservation should be amended to permit the Scottish Government, with the agreement of the Scottish Parliament, to enter into international agreements and join international bodies in relation to devolved matters'; *Report on the Commission on the UK's Future, A New Britain: Renewing our democracy and rebuilding our economy* (Labour Party 2022) 104.
64. *Miller*, [57].
65. See generally Joanne Foakes et al, 'International Law and Foreign Relations' in *Halsbury's Laws*, vol 61 (6th edn, Lexis Nexis 2018) paras 12–30; Jacqueline Fordyce, 'Public International Law (2nd Reissue)' in *Stair Memorial Encyclopedia* (Lexis Nexis 2021) paras 55–64.
66. eg *JH Rayner (Mincing Lane) Ltd v Department of Trade and Industry* [1990] 2 AC 418 (HL) 499F–500C (hereafter *JH Rayner*): 'Quite simply a treaty is not part of English law unless and until it has been incorporated into the law by legislation.' On ratification of treaties, see the Constitutional Reform and Governance Act 2010, Part 2. Incorporation may take different forms and the courts have emphasized that 'there is no rule specifying the precise legislative method of incorporation'; *R v Immigration Officer at Prague Airport ex parte European Roma Rights Centre and others* [2004] UKHL 55, [42] (hereafter *ERRC*).

67. eg *Miller*, [55]; *Blackburn v Attorney-General* [1971] 1 WLR 1037 (CA) 1040B; *R v Secretary of State for Foreign Affairs, ex parte Rees-Mogg* [1994] QB 552.
68. *JH Rayner*, 164B–D.
69. *Garland v British Rail Engineering Ltd* [1983] 2 AC 751, 771; see also *R v Secretary of State for the Home Department Ex p Brind* [1991] 1 AC 696, 747. For recent confirmation of a 'strong presumption in favour of interpreting our domestic law in a way which does not place the United Kingdom in breach of its obligations in international law', see *Reference by the Lord Advocate of devolution issues under paragraph 34 of Schedule 6 to the Scotland Act 1998* [2022] UKSC 31, [87].
70. *Basfar v Wong* [2022] UKSC 20, [16].
71. See eg *Reyes v Al-Malki and another* [2017] UKSC 61, [22] where Lord Sumption describes decisions of the US courts as 'a valuable source of law in [the area of diplomatic immunities] because of the long-standing engagement of the US courts with international law and the existence of a highly developed body of domestic foreign relations law belonging to the same tradition as our own'. Lord Sumption also refers to various decisions of the ICJ, as well as decisions of Portuguese and French courts. In *Reference by the Lord Advocate of devolution issues under paragraph 34 of Schedule 6 to the Scotland Act 1998* [2022] UKSC 31, the Supreme Court make reliance upon the decision of the Supreme Court of Canada in the *Reference re Secession of Quebec* [1998] 2 SCR 217.
72. See *Kaur v Lord Advocate* 1980 SC 319, 328.
73. *T, Petitioner* 1996 SCLR 897, 910.
74. Scotland Act 1998, s 35(1). See also Government of Wales Act 2006, s 101; Northern Ireland Act 1998, s 14(5). Similar powers exist to prevent executive acts with might be incompatible with international law or the interests of defence or national security.
75. See Government of Wales Act 2006, s 94(6); Scotland Act 1998, s 29(2); Northern Ireland Act 1998, s 6(2)(c).
76. Human Rights Act 1998, s 4(4).
77. *Coverdale v Tony Blair PM* [2003] EWCA Civ 436. See also *R (CND) v The Prime Minister* [2002] EWHC 2777 (Admin).
78. See, eg, *R v Secretary of State for the Home Department ex p Simms* [2000] 2 AC 115, 131: 'Parliamentary sovereignty means that Parliament can, if it chooses, legislate contrary to fundamental principles of human rights.... But the principle of legality means that Parliament must squarely confront what it is doing and accept the political cost. Fundamental rights cannot be overridden by general or ambiguous words.... In the absence of express language or necessary implication to the contrary, the courts therefore presume that even the most general words were intended to be subject to the basic rights of the individual.'
79. Human Rights Act 1998, s 3(1). It has been pointed out that this duty 'may require a court to depart from the unambiguous meaning the legislation would otherwise bear'; *Ghaidan v Godin-Mendoza* [2004] UKHL 30, [30]. See also *R (Friends of the Earth and others) v Secretary of State for Business, Energy and Industrial Strategy* [2022] EWHC 1841 (Admin), [265]: 'If the court does have to rely on s. 3(1), it should limit the extent to which the ordinary interpretation of the provision is modified to that which is necessary to achieve compatibility.'
80. Human Rights Act 1998, s 2(1). See *R (Alconbury Developments Ltd) v Secretary of State for the Environment, Transport and the Regions* [2001] UKHL 23, [26], where it was explained that although a national court is not bound by these decisions, 'it is obliged to take account

of them so far as they are relevant' and 'in the absence of some special circumstances, ... the court should follow any clear and constant jurisprudence of the European Court of Human Rights [because] if it does not do so there is at least a possibility that the case will go to that court which is likely in the ordinary case to follow its own constant jurisprudence'.

81. *Reference by the Attorney General and the Advocate General for Scotland – United Nations Convention on the Rights of the Child (Incorporation) (Scotland) Bill* [2021] UKSC 42, [25] (hereafter *UNCRC Incorporation*).
82. See, eg, British Bill of Rights (as introduced), clause 3(3) <https://www.gov.uk/government/publications/bill-of-rights-bill-documents> accessed 14 July 2022. For the view that this approach is liable to lead to the UK becoming out of step with its obligations under the ECHR, see Michael Wood and Elizabeth Wilmshurst, Response to the Ministry of Justice's 2021 Bill of Rights consultation, submitted on 2 March 2022. The Bill was withdrawn on 27 June 2023.
83. *UNCRC Incorporation*, [30].
84. *Trendtex Trading Corporation v Central Bank of Nigeria* [1977] 1 QB 529; [1977] 1 All E R 881, 889–890. The reception of customary international law into Scots law has been recognized in similar terms; *Lord Advocate's Reference No 1 of 2000* 2001 JC 143, [23].
85. Roger O'Keefe, 'The Doctrine of Incorporation Revisited', 79 *British Yearbook of International Law* 2009, 7, 85.
86. *Keyu and others v Secretary of State for Foreign and Commonwealth Affairs and another* [2015] UKSC 69, [150]. See also *R (Freedom and Justice Party) v Secretary of State for Foreign and Commonwealth Affairs* [2016] EWHC 2010 (Admin), [166]–[179]. On the identification of customary international law by British courts see, eg, *ERRC*, [23]. The High Court of Justiciary in Scotland overturned the decision of the Sheriff at first instance that customary international law was a question of fact to be examined and cross-examined in front of the jury; see Stephen Neff, 'Idealism in Action: International Law and Nuclear Weapons in Greenock Sheriff Court', 4 *Edinburgh Law Review* 2000, 74–86.
87. Cabinet Office, Ministerial Code (May 2022) para 1.3.
88. The omission was challenged in the courts (see *R (Gulf Centre for Human Rights) v Prime Minister* [2018] EWCA Civ 1855), and has been the subject of conflicting statements by successive British governments.
89. Welsh Government, Ministerial Code (August 2021) para 1.3; Scottish government, Ministerial Code (February 2018) para 1.3.
90. See Scotland Act 1998, s 28(8); Government of Wales Act 2006, s 107(6).
91. Welsh Government, Legislative Consent Memorandum: United Kingdom Internal Market Bill (25 September 2020), para 77; Scottish Government, Legislative Consent Memorandum: United Kingdom Internal Market Bill (28 September 2020) para 18.
92. Scottish Government (n 91) para 117. In a parliamentary debate, the then Northern Ireland Secretary, Brandon Lewis, had admitted that the proposed legislation could have been used to 'break international law in a very specific and limited way'; Hansard, HC Deb, vol 679, 8 September 2020, col 509.
93. Scottish Government, Northern Ireland Protocol Bill: Ministerial Statement <https://www.gov.scot/publications/ministerial-statement-northern-ireland-protocol-bill/> accessed 14 July 2022; see also Welsh Government, Written Statement: The Northern Ireland Protocol Bill <https://gov.wales/written-statement-northern-ireland-protocol-bill-nip-bill> accessed 14 July 2022.
94. The requirement for consent is political rather than legal; see *Miller*, [146]–[148].

95. See, eg, HM Government, Global Britain in a Competitive Age: The Integrated Review of Security, Defence, Development and Foreign Policy (March 2021).
96. House of Commons Foreign Affairs Select Committee (n 7) paras 18–21. See however HM Government (n 95).
97. See Foreign and Commonwealth Office, Memorandum on Global Britain, para 8, reproduced in House of Commons Foreign Affairs Select Committee (n 7).
98. Trade and Cooperation Agreement (adopted 30 December 2020, entered into force 1 May 2021) UKTS No 8 (2021), Article 763(2).
99. See HM Government (n 95).

CHAPTER 40

THE VISEGRÁD (V4) COUNTRIES

PAVEL ŠTURMA

1. Introduction

COMPARATIVE international law reflects the fact that international law, despite its quest for universalism (both in terms of values and application), is largely influenced by, and depends on, national and regional approaches.[1] Since the 1980s, it has been noted that international law is different in different places.[2] However, academic interest in those approaches has increased considerably during the recent years.[3] This gives rise to the question of whether the four Visegrád (V4) countries have enough important common features to justify the joint treatment of theory and practice of international law in those countries that are east of the West and west of Eastern Europe.

Those neighbouring countries in Central Europe have a long common but still diverse history. Nevertheless, the lack of knowledge of that history may also contribute to misunderstandings in the current approaches to various issues of international law. The four decades of Europe's division by the 'Iron curtain' contributed significantly to this situation.

On the one hand, there is a clear and growing trend to recognize, along with Europe's undeniable contribution to the development of universal international law,[4] also some of the shortcomings of the Eurocentric approach in the history of international law.[5] Moreover, the concepts of 'centre' and 'periphery' found their place in the discussion on the role of lawyers in countries other than the traditional Western countries.[6] On the other hand, while the long neglect of the contribution of non-European countries and lawyers to the shaping of general international law has largely been acknowledged, it is not always the case when it comes to the 'semi-peripheral' lawyers from the outskirts of the very European centre. A telling example can be found in a recently published textbook where all the contributions, with one exception, deal with international law traditions in the 'old' Europe.[7]

This is the reason why this chapter opens with a section that aims to briefly describe the history and traditions of international law in the V4 countries, that is Poland, Czech Republic, Hungary, and Slovakia with a focus on the latter three (Section 2). The next section will address some issues of practice of international law in the V4 countries (Section 3). It then offers the view on the academia in those countries (Section 4). The chapter closes by offering some conclusions and perspectives.

Given that Poland is the largest of the V4, it will be given more attention in a separate chapter in this book.[8] The Czech Republic and Slovak Republic, on the other hand, have over seventy years of common modern history (1918–1992), which facilitates their joint treatment.

2. International Law Traditions in the V4 Countries

The V4 have a 1000-year history in the centre of Europe. The three of them, namely the Czech Republic, Hungary, and Poland, emerged from the early medieval principalities and the kingdoms of Bohemia, Hungary, and Poland. Slovakia was a part of the Hungarian kingdom. The newly acquired statehood of Czechoslovakia and Poland is closely connected with the Fourteen Points of President W Wilson, the end of World War I (with the defeat of the Central Powers), and the Versailles Treaty.

Both Czechoslovakia and Poland were among the first victims of the expansion of Nazi Germany (in 1938 and 1939 respectively).

Unlike Czechoslovakia and Poland, who were on the side of the victorious Powers in World War I and World War II, Hungary lost in both wars. As a result, Hungary lost major parts of its pre-1914 territory to Czechoslovakia, Romania, and the Kingdom SHS (later known as Yugoslavia). This was confirmed by the Trianon Treaty of 1920, which remains one of the most traumatic events in Hungarian memory.

This short historical survey shows that at the end of World War II (1945), the countries of today's V4 remained in an unstable political, legal, and economic situation, including territorial changes and transfers or exchanges of population, mainly Germans transferring from Czechoslovakia and Poland (also connected with the major territorial changes), but there was also an exchange of Hungarian and Slovak minorities.

On balance, the subsequent period of the communist regime in those countries (between 1947–1948 and 1989) seems to contribute to a certain rebalancing of the earlier inequalities in economic and political terms. The 'socialist internationalism' imposed by the Soviet Union also moderated the burden of historical resentments and territorial disputes among the 'ally' countries.

The intensification of the economic, political, and military but also cultural and economic relations between the European socialist countries, which were satellites of the Soviet Union, was also reflected in international legal instruments. They were not limited just to the network of bilateral treaties but gave rise to regional organizations in economic and defence areas, namely the COMECON[9] and the Warsaw Treaty Organization.[10] They were a product of the Cold War, starting from the refusal of these countries to join the Marshall Plan in 1947 (under pressure from Stalin).

This situation also led to the isolation of international lawyers in both practice and academia of these Central European countries (now V4 countries) from international law developments in Europe. Not only was the ongoing political and economic integration in Western Europe absent from the political agenda of lawyers and diplomats of these countries, the newly emerging regional organizations, such as the Council of Europe and the European Communities, were largely neglected even in academia, including universities. After a short period of increasing liberalization in the second half of 1960s (a period of opening-up which ended in the 1970s), this started to change again, albeit slowly, during the 1980s. In addition, while the main international law textbooks included some older, classic works by Western authors, in addition to the Soviet doctrine,[11] the more up-to-date international legal literature was not always easily accessible.

Generally speaking, this situation, as well as the challenges arising from economic and political changes and the efforts being made to integrate the V4 countries into the Western European organizations (NATO and the European Union (EU)) in the 1990s, support the main argument of this chapter, namely that the development of international law in the V4 countries was *diachronic* rather than *synchronic* with the developments in Western Europe, resulting in a gap (and misunderstanding) between the V4 and Western Europe.

3. Practice of International Law in the V4 Countries

In spite of different starting positions after World War I (and partly also after World War II), all the countries, which today form the V4, have been interested in the issues of statehood, sovereignty, and security, with particular emphasis on the delimitation and stability of borders.

In addition, the dissolution of some multinational empires (such as the Austro-Hungarian and Russian empires), and the territorial changes affecting Germany, gave rise to new nation-States with significant national minorities. There were several bilateral minorities treaties signed between one of the countries in question and the League of Nations. In particular, Czechoslovakia and Poland were not only beneficiaries of the Versailles system but also subject to the treaty obligations for the protection of minorities. The obligation to sign a minorities treaty, as a condition for their recognition, arose from Articles 83 and 93 respectively of the Treaty of Versailles.[12] Hungary was also a signatory of such a treaty.[13]

The system of minority protection also gave rise to a number of complaints discussed in the organs of the League of Nations[14] and to some cases before the Permanent Court of International Justice. While the advisory opinion in *Jaworzina*[15] concerns rather delimitation of the disputed part of frontier between Czechoslovakia and Poland rather than minorities, other decisions deal with the minority protection.[16]

Generally speaking, the minorities treaties were subject to criticism,[17] as they only bound some European countries, namely the newly re-established, and some of the defeated, nations. In addition, they protected only certain national minorities, but not all (eg Jews). Increasingly, in the 1930s, the system of the League of Nations proved to be inefficient and began to be misused by some countries. The system of minorities treaties suffered an apparent death blow with Poland's rejection of its treaty in 1934.

However, the main concern of these Central European countries in the 1930s was their security. While Czechoslovakia relied mostly on the League of Nations and bilateral treaties with some major Powers (France (1925) and the Soviet Union (1935)), other countries were less enthusiastic about the League and preferred instead bilateral relations with their neighbours. In spite of that difference, both Czechoslovakia and Poland became the first victims of Nazi aggression in 1938 and 1939 and the Western Allies did not help them. At the same time, Poland and Hungary also benefitted from the breakdown of Czechoslovakia and took some parts of its territory. Although the fate of the Czech lands and Poland during World War II was different from that of Hungary and the so-called independent Slovak State, this did not play too important a role in the post-war period.

In 1947–1948, internal political developments and the strong influence of the Soviet Union—the Soviet army having liberated all the countries mentioned (with the exception of a small part of Southwestern Bohemia)—led to the instalment of communist governments. The following period (until 1989–1990) was thus characterized by the Cold War, several unsuccessful periods of unrest or reform; all suppressed by the Soviet Union and/or its Warsaw Treaty allies. It was the period of limited sovereignty of those countries (under the so-called Brezhnev doctrine).

This fact may explain why sovereignty has never been viewed as something self-evident and to be taken for granted. Therefore, the V4 countries generally consider their newly restored sovereignty as something important and not an obsolete concept. Although they aimed to become members of the EU and NATO, on some occasions, they still assert their residual sovereignty in the sense of competences that have not (yet) been transferred to the supranational institutions.

The different concerns of the V4 countries (in comparison with most West European countries) may be demonstrated with two relatively recent examples. One concerns the migration crisis in Europe and the attitude to the UN Global Compact on Migration. The prevailing view of these countries is that they have the right to distinguish between legal and illegal migrants and, consequently, the right not to allow the latter to enter their territory and to enjoy the same status or benefits there as nationals. The other refers to relations with Israel and Palestine. In particular, Czechoslovakia (in 1948) and the Czech Republic (from the 1990s) has been one of the closest allies of the State of

Israel. This often leads to the Czech Republic taking positions or voting in the universal organizations (typically the UN General Assembly or Human Rights Council) in ways that depart from the majority, more pro-Palestinian, position of the EU.

When it comes to the Global Compact for Safe, Orderly and Regular Migration, adopted by the majority of UN member States at an Intergovernmental Conference in Marrakesh (10 December 2018)[18] and endorsed by General Assembly resolution (19 December 2018), the Czech Republic, Hungary, and Poland voted against the proposal (together with Israel and the US).[19] Eleven other member States abstained, many delegations made statements explaining their positions regarding this document that may be seen as controversial. In particular, it was stated that the Compact did not make a clear distinction between legal and illegal migration.

Czechoslovakia was established as an independent State after the dissolution of the existing State, Austria-Hungary. At that time, recognition still played a constitutive role. Therefore, at the beginning, Czechoslovak diplomacy aimed at securing the recognition and frontiers of the new State.[20] The recognition by the Allied powers, namely France, Great Britain, Italy, and the US, was key. As a result, Czechoslovakia was invited to attend the Paris Peace Conference. Its frontiers with Germany, Austria, and Hungary were guaranteed by the Treaty of Versailles (1919), the Treaty of Saint-Germain (1919), and the Treaty of Trianon (1920). This was one of the Czechoslovak diplomatic mission's priorities in the 1920s. At the same time, like other countries under scrutiny, Czechoslovakia was also bound by the minority treaties. In addition to the provisions of the Saint-Germain Treaty,[21] Czechoslovakia also concluded bilateral treaties with its neighbouring countries, namely the treaty with Austria (1920),[22] the treaty with Germany (1920),[23] and that with Poland (1920), non-ratified and replaced by the treaty of 1925.[24] Czechoslovakia was also bound by the decision of the Conference of Ambassadors of the Principal Allied and Associated Powers (28 July 1920) concerning the division of Těšín/Cieszyn Silesia between Poland and Czechoslovakia.

However, Czechoslovak practice and doctrine were equally concerned with general issues of international law and multilateral treaty regimes, in particular in relation to the newly established League of Nations. Czechoslovakia was one of the most ardent supporters of the League of Nations and participated fully in the activities of this international organization. This was also because Czechoslovakia realized that, due to its location in the middle of the continent, its security would always depend on the overall political situation in Europe.[25]

The League of Nations was also quite often analysed and commented on in the writings of Czechoslovakia's contemporary international lawyers. For example, Professor Hobza, the leading scholar of Czech international law at that time, pointed to the unaccomplished supranational aspirations of the organization.[26] He also wrote about the nature of the Covenant of the League of Nations, stating that it had the nature of both a legal and political act, in particular with respect to the system of collective security.[27] The particular features of the system of collective security, namely Article 16 of the Covenant, were also commented on by Professor Zimmermann, a Russian émigré who established himself in Czechoslovakia.[28] Quite logically, Czechoslovakia also supported and signed the Treaty of Paris (also known as the Kellogg-Briand Pact).[29]

However, the failure of the system of the League of Nations and, in particular, the German threats against the territorial integrity and independence of Czechoslovakia that, together with the 'appeasement policy' of European Powers (France and Great Britain), led to the Munich Agreement and Vienna Arbitration (1938), meant that Czechoslovakia lost large parts of its territory to Germany and Hungary. The occupation of the residual part and the establishment of the Protectorate Bohemia and Moravia in March 1939 only completed the tragic failure of the security system and became one of the first acts of World War II in Europe.

Moreover, far from being just a part of modern history, the Munich trauma has had a lasting impact on the collective memory of nations of the former Czechoslovakia, including its post-war political orientation to its Eastern neighbour (the USSR) and the prioritization of certain topics in the practice and doctrine of international law.

During the post-World War II period, Czechoslovakia first continued in its pre-war tradition of multilateral diplomacy and cooperation. It was thanks to its exile government in London which, during the war had sought and obtained recognition from both the Western Allies and the Soviet Union, that Czechoslovak representatives attended all the major conferences and negotiations (such as at Bretton-Woods or San Francisco) that gave rise to the creation of new universal organizations. Thus, Czechoslovakia was one of the original members of the United Nations (UN), the International Monetary Fund (IMF), and the International Bank for Reconstruction and Development. The fact that it later left the Bretton-Woods institutions is quite another story that took place in the midst of the Cold War (1954). Additionally, Czechoslovakia was an original contracting party to the GATT (1947) and maintained this status, in spite of some problems, over the entire period of the communist regime. Czechoslovakia also actively cooperated with the UN War Crimes Commission established in 1943.[30]

The 'Iron Curtain' in Europe explains why Czechoslovakia, like other Eastern bloc countries in Europe, did not join any regional economic, political, or defence organizations emerging in the Western part of Europe from 1949.

On the whole, Czechoslovakia retained its interest in diplomatic and law-making activities in the UN and other universal international organizations. It also attended major codification conferences convoked by the UN.

International law topics on which Czechoslovak practice focused included, in addition to diplomatic and consular law, the law of treaties, in particular the grounds of invalidity or voidness of treaties imposed by the threats of force. On the one hand, it welcomed the concept of *jus cogens*, confirmed in the Vienna Convention on the Law of Treaties (VCLT). Another issue that was supported by Czechoslovak diplomacy in the 1960s and 1970s related to the drafting and adoption of the Declaration on Principles of International Law concerning Friendly Relations and Cooperation among States in accordance with the Charter of the United Nations.[31]

On the other hand, the Czechoslovak practice before 1990 took a much more ambivalent position when it comes to the developing branch of international law of human rights. Similarly, prior to 1990, the relationship between international and domestic law and the implementation of international law is an issue which is rarely explored. The traditional dualistic approach, which had prevailed since the beginning of the 20th century, was largely adopted and developed by the socialist legal doctrine.[32]

This changed radically in the 1990s. The federal Constitutional Act No 23/1991 included not only the text of the Charter of Fundamental Rights and Freedoms, that later became a part of the constitutional order of the Czech Republic, but also some other (introductory) provisions. According to section 2 of that Act, '[i]nternational conventions on human rights and fundamental freedoms, ratified and promulgated by the Czech and Slovak Federal Republic, shall be generally binding on its territory and take precedence over laws'. This clause was later taken over into Article 10 of the Czech Constitution (Act No 1/1993). The current version of Article 10 provides for direct effect and priority of all ratified and promulgated international treaties. Similar, but slightly different, is Article 7(5) of the Slovak Constitution that provides that human rights treaties, international treaties which do not need to be implemented by law, and international treaties that set direct rights or obligations to natural or legal persons, ratified and promulgated, shall take precedence over domestic laws.

The Conference for Security and Cooperation in Europe (later transformed in the Organization for Security and Cooperation in Europe) played important role already during the communist regime in Czechoslovakia, after the suppression of the Prague Spring. While the then government accepted reluctantly some commitments regarding the 'human dimension' (ie human rights), the Helsinki Final Act was an important document to which the opposition could refer. An unequivocally positive attitude towards the Helsinki process was one of the elements of post-November 1989 Czechoslovak foreign policy. However, the Czech Republic (after 1993) adopted a less enthusiastic and more pragmatic approach, giving priority to speedy integration into the Western organizations (NATO and EU).[33] The Czech Republic is also active in the Council of Europe, including its Committee of Legal Advisors on Public International Law (CAHDI). It initiated the Czech-Austrian Declaration on Jurisdictional Immunities of State-Owned Cultural Property.[34]

There are three notable issues to discuss regarding the Hungarian attitude (or approach) to international law. First, according to its Constitution (Fundamental Law), the relations between international and domestic law present a combination of monistic and dualistic approach. Article Q(3) provides that 'Hungary shall accept the generally recognized rules of international law. Other sources of international law shall be incorporated into Hungarian law upon their promulgation by laws'. The term 'generally recognized rules of international law' only covers the peremptory norms of international law, general principles, and customary international law. Otherwise, Hungary follows the dualistic approach with transformation regarding international treaties and certain decisions of international courts.[35]

Second, Hungary pays great attention to the protection of ethnic Hungarians living abroad. The 2001 Act on Hungarians Living in Neighbouring Countries (the Hungarian Status Law),[36] grants, *inter alia*, Hungarian work permits and subsidized travel to ethnic

Hungarians living in Slovakia, Ukraine, Romania, Yugoslavia, Croatia, and Slovenia. This Law provoked protests from neighbouring countries, in particular Romania and Slovakia. From the point of view of international law, bilateral treaties (eg Hungary–Romania, Hungary–Slovakia) are preferable to the protection of Hungarian minority by a unilateral act.[37]

Third, Hungary has problems with the European institutions concerning the respecting of the rule of law. This is not limited to the Hungarian backlash against refugees and migrants that seems to be even stronger in comparison with other V4 countries.[38] Recent Hungarian policy displays serious shortcomings regarding the rule of law and democracy. According to the report adopted by the European Parliament in September 2022, four years after the report that started the process under Article 7 of the Treaty on the European Union (TEU), MEPs remain concerned about democracy and fundamental rights in Hungary, specifically: the functioning of its constitutional and electoral system; the independence of the judiciary; corruption and conflicts of interest; and freedom of expression, including media pluralism. The European Parliament also called on the European Commission to refrain from approving the Hungarian national recovery plan until Hungary has fully complied with all relevant European recommendations and implemented all the relevant judgments of the EU Court of Justice (CJEU) and the European Court of Human Rights (ECtHR).[39]

4. Academia (Doctrine) of International Law in the V4 Countries

This section briefly presents some leading scholars of international legal doctrine in the V4 countries (except of Poland), mostly during the 20th century and at the beginning of this century. The section will be structured according to two main axes or questions that are presented throughout this volume: (1) the pacifying role of international law in Europe; and (2) the diversity of international law traditions.

4.1 Contribution of the V4 academia to the pacifying role of international law in Europe

It is the fate of 20th-century international lawyers in this region that they were often born in one country but later lived in another State or, even if they did not emigrate, under a different political regime. For example, the first generation of scholars noted below were not only born in the Austro-Hungarian Empire, they also studied and started their professional life there. The following generation spent much of their working life in Czechoslovakia, irrespective of their Czech or Slovak origins. Most of them had personal experience of World War I or World War II, an experience which impressed upon them the importance of international law for the maintenance of peace.

The most important Czech writer in international law in the first half of the 20th century was Antonín Hobza (1876–1954), who started his career at the Czech-language Law Faculty in Prague (since 1911), having been an ordinary professor of international law since 1917. During the first years of the Czechoslovak Republic, Hobza also worked at the Ministry of Foreign Affairs as head of the Legal Section (1920–1921). He represented Czechoslovakia in several international negotiations (including at the Paris peace conference). He was a member of the Institut de Droit International and contributed to creation of the Czechoslovak branch of the International Law Association. His main work, *Introduction to International Law of Peace*, was published in two parts, in 1933 and 1935 respectively.[40] After World War II, he published a *Survey of International Law of War*, with an annex on the punishment of war criminals (1946).[41] Hobza's pacificist views were influenced by his personal experience of World War I. He firmly supported the settlement of disputes by peaceful means and the role of the League of Nations.

Another Czechoslovak lawyer who contributed to the protection of peace through the prosecution of war criminals was Bohuslav Ečer. Dr Ečer (1893–1954) was an officer (with the rank of general) of military justice. During the World War II, he became a member of the London International Assembly and its committee on war crimes. In this capacity, he first set out his solution to the problem of retroactivity of crime against peace (aggression) in a memo dated 10 October 1942.[42] He also represented the Czechoslovak government at the International Military Tribunal in Nuremberg. Later, he became Professor of International Law at the Masaryk University in Brno. He was appointed a judge ad hoc in the *Corfu Channel* case before the International Court of Justice (ICJ).[43] He is known for his dissenting opinion in which he criticized the Court for failing to apply the general principle *in dubio pro reo*.[44]

The pre-war trend in Czech scholarship continued, to some extent, even after 1948. Although some professors chose to, or had to, leave the Czechoslovak universities, new members of teaching staff joined the faculties of law. The emigration was also the fate of many other Czech international lawyers who left the country after the suppression of the Prague spring in 1968. They include Professor Jaroslav Žourek (1908–1979) who, after 1945, lectured at the Faculty of Law of the Charles University in Prague and later joined the Institute of Law of the Czechoslovak Academy of Science. In 1950s, he was the first Czechoslovak member of the UN International Law Commission and the Special Rapporteur for the codification of the law of consular relations. He was interested in various areas of international law, in particular the definition of aggression and consular law.[45]

However, the *prima facie* discontinuity of the new textbooks and other writings with the pre-war scholarship was not total. Hobza's successor as Chair of International Law in Prague was Professor Vladimír Outrata (1909–1970). During World War II, he worked at the Ministry of Foreign Affairs of the Czechoslovak exile government in London and at the Embassy in Moscow. His activities after 1945 included work with the Ministry of

Foreign Affairs in Prague and the post of US Ambassador. In 1951, he became Professor of International Law at the Charles University in Prague. His most notable work includes *Public International Law*,[46] a textbook that influenced subsequent generations of international lawyers and future textbooks in the area. This textbook presents a moderate, compromise-oriented view of international law, based on consent of States and principles of peaceful co-existence. It also stresses the general and absolute relevance of the principle of non-intervention as a necessary basis for a peaceful co-existence of States and the economic and cultural development of peoples.[47]

The Slovak doctrine of international law followed a similar path. The general conditions in Slovakia before 1918 (including the lack of Slovak-language university), which is younger than the other countries under scrutiny, were not favourable to the academic and cultural life in general, including the research and teaching of international law.

One of the internationally renowned Slovak lawyers was Ivan Krno (1891–1961), who, after his studies at the universities in Budapest and Paris (Sorbonne), joined the diplomatic service of the new Czechoslovak Republic. He held diplomatic posts in Paris, Geneva, and The Hague. In 1938–1939, Krno held high-level positions at the Czechoslovak MFA and was also a member of the Commission on Delimitation of Frontiers with Hungary following the Vienna Arbitration. Next, he emigrated to France. He represented the government in exile at the San Francisco Conference (1945). In 1946, Dr Krno became the first Legal Counsel and Under-Secretary-General of the United Nations.

The development of Slovak academic work on international law is connected with the period after 1945, when the doctrine was developed mainly at two law faculties (Comenius University in Bratislava and, later, University of Košice) and the Institute of Law of the Slovak Academy of Sciences. The most significant names of that period are Professors Juraj Cúth, Ján Tomko, and Ján Azud. Juraj Cúth (1926–2006) graduated from Comenius University in Bratislava. He became professor at that Faculty of Law, teaching international law[48] and the law of international trade.[49] He was also Dean of that faculty and, for a short time, Dean of the new faculty in Košice. Ján Tomko (1922–1991) was also Professor of International Law and Dean of the Comenius University Faculty of Law.[50] Last but not least, Ján Azud (1928–2014) worked as a research fellow at the Institute of Law of the Slovak Academy of Sciences in Bratislava and Professor of International Law at the University of Banská Bystrica. He published work focusing on many areas of international law.[51]

Probably the most renowned Slovak internationalist is Dr Peter Tomka (1956) who was born in Banská Bystrica (Slovakia) but studied at, and graduated from, Charles University in Prague. From 1979–1986, he was assistant professor in the Department of International Law of the Prague Law Faculty. In 1986, Dr Tomka joined the Ministry of Foreign Affairs. From 1993, he became deputy permanent representative of the Slovak Mission to the UN in New York and later Ambassador (1999–2003). In the mid-1990s, he worked at the Slovak MFA in Bratislava and represented his country as co-agent before the ICJ in *Gabčíkovo-Nagymaros*. Dr Tomka was member of the International Law

Commission (1999–2002) prior to his election to the ICJ. He has been an ICJ judge since 2003 and has also served as the Court's president (2012–2015).

Hungary has a long tradition of university education, including law, due to its non-interrupted statehood. However, for the purpose of this chapter, the list includes just some of the leading academic figures in the 20th century who contributed to the pacifying role of international law. Most of these are connected either to the oldest public university Eötvös Loránd University (ELTE) in Budapest or the Hungarian Academy of Sciences.

The ELTE is represented by László Valki (1941), who was an expert in the theory of international law and international relations. After graduating from the ELTE, he taught international law in his capacity as lecturer, associate professor, and professor. He was head of the Department of International Law (1981–2006) and published mainly on international security issues.[52] He also ran the Centre for Peace and Conflicts Research of the Hungarian Academy of Sciences (1982–1999). Professor Valki represented Hungary before the ICJ in the *Gabčíkovo-Nagymaros* case.

Regarding the Academy of Sciences and its Institute for Legal Studies, a notable name is Hanna Bokor-Szegö (1925–2006). She graduated from Péter Pázmány University in Budapest before going on to work at the Ministry of Foreign Affairs, and then (in 1960) becoming a research fellow at this Institute and head of Department of International Law (till 1997) and professor at University of Economy. She was also a member of the UN Committee on Elimination of Discrimination against Women. Her research and publications cover a wide range of topics, including the succession of States, the law of treaties, and the UN.[53]

However, the Institute is mainly connected with Vanda Lamm (1945). After graduation from the University of Budapest, she became research fellow and later director of the Institute (1991–2011). She was also Professor of International Law at the University of Miscolc and at the University of Györ. Professor Lamm was also a member of the UN Committee on Elimination of Discrimination against Women. She is, *inter alia*, president of ILA Hungarian Branch, honorary president of the International Nuclear Law Association, and a member of the Institut de Droit International. She is the author of many publications, focusing mainly on international nuclear law, human rights, and international dispute settlement.[54]

4.2 Differences and similarities of international law traditions in the V4 countries

A comparison of international law traditions in the Czech Republic, Slovakia, and Hungary reveals both differences and similarities across the approaches and themes of the leading academic figures.

The above mentioned Professor Hobza belonged to the positivist school of legal thought. He developed his ideas in dissension with the pure theory of law (normativism), as represented mainly by Kelsen, Verdross, and Weyr. He strongly criticized the pure theory of law as speculative and even called it the new emergence of natural law. On the other hand, he was more sympathetic to other contemporary schools, including the solidarism of Georges Scelles.[55]

His main Czech opponent, Professor František Weyr (1879–1951) was the leading figure and co-founder of the pure theory of law. He was present at the establishment of Masaryk University in Brno and became the first dean of its Faculty of Law. Professor Weyr was interested mainly in legal theory and constitutional law but he also wrote on the topic of international law. His main work in this area, *The Contemporary Struggle for a New International Law*, was written as early as 1918, that is, before the end of World War I, but was published in 1919.[56]

Like his friend Hans Kelsen,[57] Weyr constructed his view of international law on the foundations of his general theory of law. The basic elements of the social development of mankind are States, viewed as being some kind of social union. States stand out from other kinds of unions because of their sovereignty. They subject all individuals within their territory to their power. The status of sovereign States puts them in a position of natural hostility vis-à-vis other unions.[58] The concept of a legal order is based on norms which do not stipulate 'what is' but rather, 'what ought to be'. Norms regulating relations between States fall within the realm of international law. These norms are similar to norms of national law but they differ in some aspects.[59] Weyr made a distinction between heteronomous and autonomous norms. The former are set up by an external authority, whilst the latter are adopted by their subjects themselves.[60] While in national law, the legal order occupies a position above all subjects, there is no single legal order in the field of international law. International law is created by sovereign States, its norms are autonomous. There is no enforcement of international obligations in the sense of national law enforcement. In order to become similar to national law, international law would require the existence of a supra-State which would include all (or most) States.[61]

Although the differences in opinion and approach between the representatives of two schools was interrupted first by the Nazi regime (all Czech universities were closed during the German occupation) and then by the communist regime after 1948, certain plurality and diversity re-emerged within the Czech and Slovak academia of international law in the 1970s and 1980s. To some extent, this resembles the rivalry between Prague and Brno from the pre-war period.

In spite of the new wave of emigration after 1968, some Czech and Slovak international lawyers remained in Czechoslovakia. Teaching and research in international law were influenced by two leading figures. Professor Miroslav Potočný (1925–2001), a disciple of Professor Outrata and later, his successor as Chair of International Law, continued with the scheme of the textbook, *Public International Law* (1973, 1978), later writing a *Special Section* in the textbook (1996). He also maintained the tradition of editing *Documents of International Law*, thus continuing in the footsteps of Hobza and Outrata. In his work, Professor Potočný focused mainly on the law of international organizations[62] and on the principles of international law.[63]

His main adversary, Professor Čestmír Čepelka (1927–2022), another disciple of Professor Outrata, developed his own critical method rather than further developing the scheme of Outrata's textbook. He had been a leading figure and the most original scholar in international law at the Prague law school. Together with Vladislav David (1927–2014), who was Professor of International Law at the Faculty of Law in Brno, he wrote an *Introduction to International Law* in 1978[64] as well as the updated second edition in 1983.[65] This theoretical publication also became a textbook at the Brno law school and an alternative textbook in Prague. It passed on much historical and theoretical information on international law, including foreign sources, which would have not been otherwise accessible to law students in the 1970s and 1980s. In contrast to the prevailing positivist approach of the Prague school of law, Čepelka's *Introduction* presented an original combination of the influence of both normativism (pure theory of law) and the sociological approach to international law. Dissenting from the Soviet doctrine (particularly that of Grigory Tunkin) and the mainstream Czech and Slovak scholars who favoured treaty, he stressed the role of international custom and rejected a consensual interpretation of customary law.[66] He wrote on various theoretical issues of international law, in particular *jus cogens*, the responsibility of States,[67] and the law of treaties.[68] In turn, Professor David published extensively on sanctions, State responsibility, and international crimes.[69]

For their part, the above mentioned Slovak professors shared rather the approach of Potočný and other lawyers of the mainstream positivism with the 'socialist flavour'.

At the same time, there are some parallel or similar themes shared by scholars from the countries under scrutiny. In the field of international humanitarian law, three important figures should be mentioned. The older generation is represented by Dr Gejza Mencer (1910–1992), Slovak lawyer, senior research fellow of the Institute of Law of the Czechoslovak Academy of Sciences. He published in various areas of international law.[70] Next is his Hungarian colleague and friend Géza Herczegh (1928–2010) who was born in Nagykapos (in Slovak Veľké Kapušany) in the former Czechoslovakia and graduated from the University of Szeged. Later, he became Professor of International Law at the University of Pécs and Dean of its Faculty of Law (1981–1987). He also represented the Hungarian Red Cross at international conferences. Between 1990 and 1993, Professor Herczegh was judge and vice-president of the Hungarian Constitutional Court and then the first Hungarian judge of the ICJ (1993–2003). He was also appointed a full member of the Academy of Sciences.[71] Last but not least, Jiří Toman (1938–2020), a Czech who, after his studies at the Charles University in Prague and the Graduate Institute of International Studies in Geneva, worked at the Institute Henry-Dunant in Geneva (as researcher, deputy director, and later director 1992–1998) and then became professor at Santa Clara University, California, as well as at Danube University Krems, Austria. His specialization was international humanitarian law and the protection of cultural property.[72]

More recently, the relationship between international law and other legal orders became the research focus of two important Czech and Slovak lawyers. The Brno law school is also represented by Professor Jiří Malenovský (1950). Later, he became ambassador to the Council of Europe, Constitutional Court judge, and CJEU judge. He retired from the CJEU in 2020 and resumed teaching and research activities in Brno. In addition to several editions of his textbook,[73] he also published on the relationship between international, European, and domestic law,[74] as well as on the international and European judiciary.[75]

His Slovak counterpart, Ján Klučka (1951) is professor at the Institute of International and European Law of the Faculty of Law in Košice. During his career, he was also a Slovak Constitutional Court judge (1993–2004) and CJEU judge (2004–2009). His rich publishing history includes publications across various areas of public international law and relations between international and constitutional law.[76]

5. Conclusions

The difficult historical developments of three of the V4 countries, namely the Czech Republic, Slovakia, and Hungary, influenced the role of international lawyers, both in academia and practice. Indeed, international law and its scholarship cannot be dissociated from politics, which is also true in this part of Europe. Their legal systems and academia had the roots in the (West) European traditions. However, almost six decades of totalitarian regimes (Nazi and communist) between 1939 and 1989 caused a break in the development of these traditions, with just short periods of relaxation in the aftermath of World War II and at the end of 1960s.

Even though they are now part of the European structures, the long relative isolation of these countries is probably why they are viewed as semi-peripheral, from the point of view of the West. At the same time, the experience of these countries contributes to a higher sensitivity to the issues of peace, statehood, and sovereignty. Since these values have not been present for a long time, they are not taken for granted and need to be protected.

The community of international lawyers in these countries has been relatively small, which accounts for the fact that there is relatively little division between academics and practitioners of international law. Indeed, sometimes, individuals have experience of both areas which may contribute to the focus on more practice-oriented topics rather than the theory. Nevertheless, in the case some eminent lawyers, they have contributed not only practical efforts to the pacifying role of international law in Europe, but also to theoretical debates.

Historical events in these countries also meant that a significant number academics emigrated, first during the Nazi occupation and then during the communist regime (mainly in the case of Czechoslovakia). However, it is to the credit of those professors who remained that they educated subsequent generations of international lawyers and kept pace, to the extent possible, with the development of international law in Europe and contributed to it.

NOTES

1. See Anthea Roberts, *Is International Law International?* (OUP 2019).
2. William E Buttler (ed.), *International Law in Comparative Perspective* (Sijthoff 1980); David Kennedy, 'The Disciplines of International Law and Policy', 12 Leiden Journal of International Law 1999, 19; Mark W Janis, 'Comparative Approaches to the Theory of International Law, 80 ASIL Proceedings of the Annual Meeting 1986, 152.
3. See, eg, Peter Hipold (ed), *European International Law Traditions* (Springer 2021) hereafter Hipold (ed), *European International Law Traditions.*
4. Martti Koskenniemi, 'International Law in Europe: Between Tradition and Renewal', 16 European Journal of International Law 2005, 113–114.
5. Arnulf Becker-Lorca, 'Eurocentrism in the History of International Law' in Bardo Fassbender and Anne Peters (eds), *The Oxford Handbook of the History of International Law* (OUP 2012) 1034–1057.
6. See Arnulf Becker-Lorca, *Mestizo International Law: A Global Intellectual History (1842–1933)* (CUP 2014).
7. Hipold (ed), *European International Law Traditions* (n 3). For the exception see Lauri Malksoo, 'The Russian Concept of International Law as Imperial Legacy' in ibid, 261–268.
8. See the chapter, 'Poland' by Czapliński in this volume.
9. The Council for Mutual Economic Assistance was a Soviet-led economic and trade organization, established in 1949. It was dissolved at the meeting in Budapest in June 1991.
10. Warsaw Treaty of Friendship, Cooperation and Mutual Assistance (1955) was a treaty establishing a mutual-defence organization. It was terminated at the meeting in Prague on 1 July 1991, <https://www.britannica.com/event/Warsaw-Pact> (last visited on 20 April 2023).
11. See, eg, V Outrata, *Mezinárodní právo veřejné* (Public International Law) (Orbis 1960); G Haraszti, G Herczegh, and K Nagy, *Nemzetközi Jog* (International Law) (Tankönyvkiadó 1976); Č Čepelka and V David, *Úvod do mezinárodního práva* (Introduction to International Law) (AUB 1978); Ján Tomko and Juraj Cúth, *Medzinárodné verejné právo* (Public International Law) (Obzor 1988).
12. Treaty of Peace between the Allied and Associated Powers and Germany (Treaty of Versailles) 1919, 225 CTS 188. The Polish minorities treaty, called the Little Treaty of Versailles, was signed the same day (28 June 1919). The treaty with Czechoslovakia is referred to as the Treaty between the Principal Allied and Associated Powers and Czechoslovakia (Saint Germain-en-Laye, 10 September 1919). See also Carole Fink, 'The Minorities Question at the Paris Peace Conference' in Manfred Franz Boemeke, Gerald D Feldman, and Elisabeth Gläser (eds), *The Treaty of Versailles: A Reassessment after 75 Years* (CUP 1998) 249 ff.
13. Section VI (Protection of minorities), Treaty of Peace between the Allied and Associated Powers and Hungary and Protocol and Declaration, signed at Trianon on 4 June 1920, <https://wwi.lib.byu.edu/index.php/Treaty of Trianon>
14. See, eg, Jennifer Jackson Preece, *National Minorities and the European Nation-States System* (OUP 2008); Péter Kovács, 'The Protection of Minorities under the Auspices of the League of Nations' in Dinah Shelton (ed), *The Oxford Handbook of International Human Rights Law* (OUP 2013), 325–342; Ján Klučka, 'Protection of Minorities', 9 Czech Yearbook of Public & Private International Law 2018, 17 ff.
15. Question of Jaworzina (Polish-Czechoslovakian Frontier), PCIJ, Series B, No 8, 1923.

16. See, eg, Rights of Minorities in Upper Silesia (Minority Schools), PCIJ, Series A, No 15, 1928; Treatment of Polish Nationals and Other Persons of Polish Origin or Speech in the Danzig Territory, PCIJ, Series A/B, No 44, 1932.
17. eg by Hersch Lauterpacht, cf Philip Sands, *East West Street. On the Origins of 'Genocide' and 'Crimes against Humanity'* (Knopf 2016) 109.
18. See UN doc. A/CONF.231/3, and UN doc. A/73/L.66.
19. UN Press Release, doc. GA/12113 (2018).
20. See Jan Kuklík, 'The Establishment of the Independent Czechoslovak State and Its Frontiers in the Light of International Law and Politics of 1918–1920', 9 Czech Yearbook of Public & Private International Law 2018, 3 ff.
21. Consolidated Treaty Series, New York, 1919, pp 9–167.
22. Treaty published under No 107/1921 Coll. (Czechoslavak).
23. Treaty published under No 308/1922 Coll. (Czechoslovak).
24. Treaty published under No 33/1926 Coll. (Czechoslovak).
25. See Alexandr Ort, *Edvard Beneš diplomat a politik* (*Edvard Beneš, Diplomat and Politician*) (IRMA 1994) 19; Jan Ondřej and Magda Uxová, 'The Contribution of the League of Nations to the Development of International Law, Especially in the Area of International Peace and Security', 11 Czech Yearbook of Public & Private International Law 2020, 90.
26. Antonín Hobza, *Úvod do mezinárodního práva mírového. Část I.* (*Introduction to International Law of Peace. Part I*) (Typus 1933) 248.
27. ibid, 219–220.
28. See M A Zimmermann, *Společnost národů* (*League of Nations*) (Orbis 1931) 270–271, 290.
29. Treaty between the United States and other Powers providing for the renunciation of war as an instrument of national policy (Kellogg-Briand Pact), signed in Paris, 27 August 1928, <htttps://avalon.law.yale.edu/20th_century/kbpact.asp>
30. See Petr Válek, 'The United Nations War Crimes Commission and the Czechoslovak Charges in Relation to Auschwitz and Birkenau', 7 Czech Yearbook of Public & Private International Law 2016, 301 ff.
31. UN GA res. 2625 (XXV) of 24 October 1970.
32. See Jiří Malenovský, *Poměr mezinárodního a vnitrostátního práva obecně a v českém právu zvláště* (Relationship between International and Internal Law in General and in particular in Czech Law) (Brno 2000).
33. See Jan Pechácek, 'The Czech Republic and the OSCE' in IFSH (ed), *OSCE-Yearbook 1995/1996* (Nomos 1997) 105–110.
34. See Petr Válek, 'Czech-Austrian Declaration on Jurisdictional Immunities of State-Owned Cultural Property' 6 Czech Yearbook of Public & Private International Law 2015, 387–399.
35. See Erszébet Csatlós, 'The Application of International Law as an Instrument of Interpretation in Hungary—The Practice of the Constitutional Court and Ordinary Courts in a Comparative Approach' in Attila Badó, Detlev W Belling, János Bóka, and Péter Mezei (eds), *Internationale Konferenz zum zehnjährigen Bestehen des Instituts für Rechtsvergleichung der Universität Szeged* (International conference marking the tenth anniversary of the Institute for Comparative Law at the University of Szeged) (Universitätsverlag Potsdam 2014) 127 ff.
36. Act LXII of 2001; 'On Hungarians Living in Neighboring Countries', 40 International Legal Materials 2001, 1242.
37. Christin J Albertie, 'The Act of Hungarians Living Abroad: A Misguided Approach to Minority Protection', 24 Michigan Journal of International Law 2003, 961–1007.

38. OHCHR, Press release 'Hungary violating international law in response to migration crisis' (17 September 2015). See also Tamás Hoffmann, 'Illegal Legality and the Façade of Good Faith—Migration and Law in Populist Hungary', 47 Review of Central and East European Law 2022, 139–165.
39. EP Press release, 'Hungary can no longer be considered a full democracy' (15 September 2022); cf also the chapter by van Aaken, 'Rule of Law: A Multi-layered Network' in this volume.
40. See A Hobza, *Úvod do mezinárodního práva mírového* (Introduction to International Law of Peace) Part I (Praha 1933); Part II (Typos 1935).
41. See A Hobza, *Přehled mezinárodního práva válečného. Dodatek: Trestání válečných zločinců* (Survey of International Law of War. Annex: Punishment of War Criminals) (Všehrd 1946).
42. 'The Punishment of War Criminals' in London International Assembly's Reports on Punishment of War Crimes (Report of Commission I) 56–58. See also O A Hathaway and S J Shapiro, *The Internationalists. How a Radical Plan to Outlaw War Remade the World* (Simon & Schuster 2017) 252–253.
43. *Corfu Channel* case, Judgment of 9 April 1949, ICJ Reports 1949, 4.
44. ibid, 124. See Monika Novotná, *Život a dílo prof. JUDr. Bohuslava Ečera* (Life and Work of Prof. JUDr. Bohuslav Eče) (Masaryk University Press 1993). See also Jaroslav Fenyk, 'Gen. Prof. Bohuslav Ečer', 41(3) Universitas 2008, 62–64.
45. cf, eg J Žourek, Le statut et les fonctions des consuls. Académie de droit international. Recueil des cours. 1962, T. 106, 357–497; J Žourek, *L 'Interdiction de l'Emploi de la Force en Droit international* (Sijthof 1974).
46. V Outrata, *Mezinárodní právo veřejné* (Orbis 1960).
47. ibid, 69.
48. See, eg, Juraj Cúth, *Medzinárodné rieky* (International Rivers) (Slovenská akadémia vied 1964).
49. Juraj Cúth, Otto Kunz, and Zdeněk Kučera, *Medzinárodné obchodné právo* (International Trade Law) (Obzor 1983).
50. See, eg, Ján Tomko, *Vnútorná právomoc štátov a OSN* (Internal Powers of Sattes and the UN) (Slovenská akadémia vied 1961); Ján Tomko, *Medzinárodné verejné právo* (Public International Law) (Obzor 1988).
51. Ján Azud, *Diplomatické imunity a výsady* (Diplomatic Immunities and Priviledges) (Slovenská akadémia vied 1959); *The Peaceful Settlement of Disputes and the United Nations* (Slovak Academy of Sciences 1970); *Medzinárodné problémy kozmického priestoru* (International Problems of Outer Space) (Veda 1989); *Medzinárodné právo* (International Law) (Veda 2003).
52. László Valki and Joseph Rotblat (eds), *Coexistence, Cooperation, and Common Security* (Macmillan 1988); László Valki (ed), *Changing Threat Perceptions and Military Doctrines* (Macmillan 1992).
53. Hanna Bokor-Szegö, *New States and International Law* (Akadémiai Kiadó 1970); Hanna Bokor-Szegö, *The Role of the United Nations in International Legislation* (North-Holland 1978); Hanna Bokor-Szegö, *Államazonosság-államutódlás* (State Identity–State Succession) (Akadémiai Kiadó 1984).
54. Vanda Lamm, *The Utilization of Nuclear Energy and International Law* (Akadémiai Kiadó 1984); Vanda Lamm, 'Quatre nouvelle déclarations d'acceptation de la juridiction obligatoire de la CIJ', Révue Générale de Droit International Public 1996, 335–365; Vanda

Lamm, 'The Protocol Amending the 1963 Vienna Convention', 61 Nuclear Law Bulletin 1998, 7–24.

55. See Hobza. *Úvod do mezinárodního práva mírového. Část I.* (*Introduction to International Law of Peace. Part I*)
56. See F Weyr, *Soudobý zápas o nové mezinárodní právo* (Contemporary Struggle for a New International Law) (A. Píša 1919).
57. Kelsen and Weyr met for the first time in 1912 and became close friends, with Weyr acknowledging Kelsen's great influence on his academic development. See F Weyr, *Paměti* (Memoires) vol I: 1879–1918 (Atlantis 1999) 414–415.
58. Weyr, *Soudobý zápas o nové mezinárodní právo* (n 56) 3–4.
59. ibid, 12–13.
60. ibid, 1–2.
61. ibid, 16–17.
62. cf, eg M Potočný, *Mezinárodní organizace* (International Organizations) (Svoboda 1971, 2nd edn, 1980); M Potočný and E A Šibajeva, *Právo mezinárodních organizací* (Law of International Organizations) (Panorama 1984).
63. cf M Potočný, *Deklarace zásad mírového soužití* (The Declaration of Principles of Peaceful Coexistence) (Acta Universitatis Carolinae–Iuridica 1972).
64. Č Čepelka and V David, *Úvod do mezinárodního práva* (Introduction to International Law) (Acta Universitatis Brunensis 1978).
65. Č Čepelka and V David, *Úvod do teorie mezinárodního práva* (Introduction to the Theory of International Law) (Acta Universitatis Brunensis 1983).
66. Čestmír Čepelka, *Smlouva a obyčej v mezinárodním právu* (Treaty and Custom in International Law) Acta Universitatis Carolinae–Iuridica (Charles University Press 1984).
67. Čestmír Čepelka, *Les conséquences juridiques du délit en droit international contemporain.* Acta Universitatis Carolinae–Iuridica, Monographia (Charles University Press 1965).
68. Čestmír Čepelka, *Právo mezinárodních smluv* (Law of International Treaties) (SPN 1986, 2nd edn, 1999).
69. See, eg, Vladislav David, *Sankce v mezinárodním právu* (Sanctions in International Law) (Acta Universitatis Brunensis 1976); *Odpovědnost státu za mezinárodně protiprávní chování* (State Responsibility for Internationally Wrongful Acts) (Acta Universitatis Brunensis 1980); Vladislav David, *Mezinárodní zločiny a jejich právní následky* (International Crimes and Their Legal Consequences) (Acta Universitatis Brunensis 1988).
70. Gejza Mencer, *Mezinárodní právní problémy Antarktidy* (International Legal Problems of Antarctica) (ČSAV 1963); Gejza Mencer, *Co je intervence?* (What Is Intervention?) (NPL 1964); Gejza Mencer, *Nové mezinárodní humanitární právo* (New International Humanitarian Law) (Academia 1983).
71. Géza Herczegh, *General Principles of Law and the International Legal Order* (Akadémiai Kiadó 1969); Géza Herczegh, *Development of International Humanitarian Law* (Akadémiai Kiadó 1984).
72. See Jiří Toman, *Les biens culturels en temps de guerre: quel progrès en faveur de leur protection ? Commentaire article-par-article du Deuxième Protocole de 1999 relatif à la Convention de La Haye de 1954 pour la protection des biens culturels en cas de conflit armé* (UNESCO 2015).
73. Jiří Malenovský, *Mezinárodní právo veřejné. Obecná část* (Public International Law. General Part) (7th edn, Masaryk University 2020).

74. Jiří Malenovský, *Poměr mezinárodního a vnitrostátního práva obecně a v českém právu zvláště* (Relationship between International and Internal Law in General and in particular in Czech Law) (Doplněk 2000).
75. Jiří Malenovský, 'L'indépendence des juges internationaux' in *Recueil des Cours de l'Académie de droit international*, vol 349 (Nijhoff 2011) 9–276.
76. See, eg, Ján Klučka, *Regionalism and International Law* (Routledge 2018); Ján Klučka, *Medzinárodné právo veřejné (všeobecná a osobitná časť)* (Public International Law. General and special part) (Wolters Kluwer 2017).

CHAPTER 41

THE COUNTRIES OF THE FORMER YUGOSLAVIA

MARKO MILANOVIĆ AND TATJANA PAPIĆ*

1. Introduction

This chapter takes one of the three major themes (see Mälksoo, this volume)[1] of the handbook—diversity within Europe—to describe and discuss the international legal tradition in (some of) the countries of the former Yugoslavia, the tradition in which both authors of this chapter were initially socialized as lawyers and scholars. Specifically, we want to grasp the understanding of international law and its relevant international law debates, if any, in this part of Europe, to provide a possibility for broader assessment of diversity within Europe that this handbook strives to unpack.

Yugoslavia was always a relatively peripheral country in the international (legal) system, yet many modern developments of that system, for example with regard to statehood, international humanitarian law, and international criminal law, grew out of the system's engagement with Yugoslavia. Yugoslav and post-Yugoslav academics made substantial contributions to international legal scholarship, although not really as part of a cohesive school of thought. Their conceptual or theoretical approaches are not particularly distinctive and, in line with most of Eastern Europe, can mainly be described as positivist and doctrinal. But Yugoslavia's painful break-up meant that international law and institutions became more directly relevant to its peoples (and lawyers) than in most other societies. As with war-torn Ukraine today, questions of international law ranging from statehood and self-determination to individual and State responsibility for genocide and war crimes assumed near-existential importance for professional lawyers, for elites, and for the general public in Yugoslav States.

Now, there are many possible approaches to studying any legal tradition. Bearing in mind the theme of the diversity within Europe and purposes of this handbook, the one we have decided to take here is to first give a brief socio-legal overview of the development of the international legal profession in the former Yugoslavia. Then we engage in a comparative study of the textbooks used at prominent universities in the post-Yugoslav States, following Anthea Roberts' lead,[2] in a kind of sociology of international law of the region of the former Yugoslavia. Our main goal is to expose the underlying values and ideologies promoted by the authors of these textbooks, which may be indicative of the understanding and the effect of international law in this part of the world.[3] Namely, textbooks are, what Bianchi and Hirsch call, 'invisible frames',[4] which set both the borders and the substance of what and how to think (or not to think about),[5] influencing not only the articulation of international law issues, but also a process of discursive socialization.[6] Textbooks shape 'the vocabulary, identity, and perception' of their authors and readers,[7] revealing how international law is understood by the current generation and passed on to the next.[8]

We are focusing on textbooks for two additional reasons. First, textbooks are (still) considered to be the apex, most prestigious, and influential form of legal scholarship in the countries of the former Yugoslavia and have the widest audience and reach. Second, in this part of the world international law is taught and studied entirely through textbooks. University syllabi that assign articles, documents, and/or cases are rare, certainly at the undergraduate level. In other words, in this part of the world, the knowledge of and attitudes towards international law amongst generations of students are almost exclusively shaped by textbooks (in addition to their lecturers), at least for those students who have studied abroad. Moreover, the way in which future practitioners will view, comprehend, and resort to international law is almost exclusively contingent on how the textbooks instructed them.[9]

Consequently, analysing textbooks can provide insights into the narratives and values embedded into the many thousands of young lawyers churned through universities in Yugoslavia and the Yugoslav successor States, with consequences for how they see and use international law professionally.[10] Hopefully, this will provide a basis for some future analysis and explanations on effects of international law and how it is applied in practice in the former Yugoslavia, which is beyond the scope of this chapter.

2. Historical and Social Background

First for a bit of history, which is necessary to understand the context.[11] Yugoslavia was born out of World War I and the demise of the two empires that historically controlled much of the territory—Austria-Hungary and Ottoman Turkey—following the relative success, consolidation, and expansion of the Kingdom of Serbia before World War I. The Yugoslav State was first formed and styled as the Kingdom of Serbs, Croats and Slovenes in 1918, and then renamed as the Kingdom of Yugoslavia in 1929. Like the two predecessor empires, Yugoslavia was a multi-ethnic State. From its inception it was in a perpetual state of tension between competing ideologies and national projects, between centripetal and centrifugal forces. And, like the two empires, it had its own internal centres and peripheries, political, economic, religious, and linguistic. While most of the population spoke and was educated in some variant of Serbo-Croatian, the Slovenes, Macedonians, and Albanians spoke their own languages. The politics of the country tended to be dominated by the relationship between its two most numerous constituent peoples, the Serbs and the Croats, although Slovenia had always been the richest and most developed part of the country.

Yugoslavia was invaded, occupied, and partitioned by the Axis powers during World War II, resulting in the creation of quisling regimes and intercommunal violence. The Jewish population of the country was destroyed almost entirely, while the puppet Independent State of Croatia committed mass atrocities against the Serbs in particular. Communist resistance, led by Josip Broz Tito, emerged victorious at the end of the war and overthrew the monarchy, establishing the Democratic Federative Yugoslavia and shortly thereafter the Federal People's Republic of Yugoslavia in 1945, renamed as the Socialist Federal Republic of Yugoslavia in 1963. Yugoslavia thus became the only Eastern European country in which communism was largely autochthonous and not imposed by the occupying Soviet forces. Indeed, in 1948 Tito famously and decisively broke away from Stalin, and initiated Yugoslavia's central Cold War policy of balancing between the two blocs. In 1961 Yugoslavia was one of the founders of the Non-Aligned Movement and tended to play an outsized role in international relations when taking into account its economic and military capacities.

After Tito's death in 1980, due to the impact of parallel social and economic crises that the country's leadership was unable to manage, coupled with ethnic tensions and growing nationalism, the country fell apart, followed by a succession of conflicts characterized by mass atrocities (see Mälksoo, this volume).[12] Before its dissolution in 1990 Yugoslavia was divided into six republics—Bosnia and Herzegovina, Croatia, Macedonia, Montenegro, Serbia, Slovenia—while there were two further autonomous provinces, Kosovo and Vojvodina, within Serbia. All of the republics eventually declared independence, except for Serbia and Montenegro, which for a time persisted in a joint State called the Federal Republic of Yugoslavia (FRY), that claimed to have been the sole continuator of the SFRY (a claim rejected by the other successor States, and ultimately abandoned after the fall of the Milošević regime in the FRY/Serbia). Montenegro consensually became independent in 2006, while Kosovo contentiously declared independence from Serbia in 2008. Today, Slovenia and Croatia are European Union (EU) member States, while the rest are in the process of the accession to the EU, albeit at different stages.[13]

The legacy of the conflicts within the former Yugoslav States remains strong, and poisonous; nationalist parties have dominated most of Yugoslavia's successor States, and Bosnia in particular is highly dysfunctional. The 1999 NATO bombing of the FRY,[14] which precipitated the withdrawal of Serbian forces from Kosovo and Kosovo's subsequent independence, continues to exert a strong influence within the Serbian public in particular and generates anti-Western sentiment, with ample help from nationalist elites. The bombing and the unresolved dispute over Kosovo's independence have also been used instrumentally by Vladimir Putin in justifying Russia's invasion of Ukraine and support of various separatist entities.

For our purposes we can thus divide the history of Yugoslavia into three main periods—the monarchical, between the two world wars; the communist, between 1945 and 1990; and the post break-up period from 1990 to the present day. These three periods are essential for understanding developments in legal doctrine in Yugoslavia, their ideological underpinnings, and the preoccupations of Yugoslav scholars. They similarly shaped the views of Yugoslav or successor State officials on various matters of international law.

3. A General Overview of the Yugoslav (International) Legal Tradition

The academic study of law in the former Yugoslavia largely follows positivist orthodoxy (see d'Aspremont, this volume) in all areas of the law, including international law, and has historically been influenced by Austrian, German, and French scholars. There is no unique 'school' here, such as Scandinavian realism, nor has there generally been much engagement with newer conceptual approaches such as critical legal studies or law and economics. In the SFRY the dominant communist/socialist ideology meant that, at least for internal publications, Yugoslav academics had to integrate Marxist theories into their work, even if this was only skin deep and they remained doctrinal positivists at heart, with the Marxism quickly getting discarded as communism fell (see Tzanakopoulos, this volume).

The SFRY's position as a leader of the Non-Aligned Movement also meant that Yugoslav scholars felt the need to write about topics such as peaceful co-existence and non-intervention, mainly for internal consumption. Some of them were very active on the international plane, taking part in the preparation of the relevant international law instruments, such as the UN General Assembly 1970 Declaration on Principles of International Law Concerning Friendly Relations and Co-operation Among States and the 1974 Definition of Aggression, as well as the 1975 Helsinki Final Act and the 1977 Additional Protocols to the Geneva Conventions.[15] Previously, Yugoslavia had its judges in the World Court, who were not academics; at the International Court of Justice (ICJ), Dr Milovan Zoričić from Zagreb (1946–1958),[16] and Mihajlo Jovanović from Belgrade (1920–1930) at the Permanent Court of International Justice (PCIJ).

The Yugoslav university system was entirely State-owned, with the most prestigious universities concentrated in Serbia (Belgrade, Novi Sad), Croatia (Zagreb, Rijeka, Split), and Slovenia (Ljubljana). Serbo-Croatian was the dominant language of scholarship even for academics working in non-Serbo-Croat-speaking parts of Yugoslavia. As a general matter there was little mobility in the academic market—it was rare, for example, for a professor from Belgrade to move to Zagreb and vice versa—but there was a common space for publication, conferences, and other kinds of academic engagement. There was the Yugoslav Association of International Law, established between the two world wars, that published the only dedicated international law journal, the *Yugoslav Review of International Law* (*Jugoslovenska revija za međunarodno pravo*), in which scholars from all regions of the country normally published. More generalist journals came out under the auspices of the most important universities. The *Yugoslav Review* published articles in Serbo-Croat, but also in English and in French. But as the country broke apart, so did this common academic space. The *Yugoslav Review* ceased publishing,[17] and it has generally become rare for scholars from the successor States to write in the journals of the other successor States, despite the common *lingua franca*.

In all successor States, except in Croatia, private law schools were established after Yugoslavia's break-up, sometimes with their own journals. One of us (Papić) teaches at one such institution, the Union University Law School Belgrade, which was established in 2002 by a group of professors who were purged by the Milošević regime in 1998 from the University of Belgrade Faculty of Law. In very broad strokes the break-up of Yugoslavia had detrimental effects on higher education in many of the successor States, with a decrease in available resources, causing diminished meritocracy and numerous scandals involving plagiarism and corruption, particularly in the awards of degrees to politicians, and a substantial amount of 'brain drain' and emigration.

In the SFRY and its successor States, universities have generally remained more teaching- than research-oriented. In common with many other countries, the vast majority of Yugoslav international law academics have published purely for internal audiences, in domestic journals and writing in Serbo-Croatian or other local languages.[18] During the SFRY's existence only a handful of Yugoslav academics regularly published for international audiences, writing in English or in French and gaining international recognition—among them Juraj Andrassy, Milan Bartoš, Vojin Dimitrijević, Vladimir-Djuro Degan, Vladimir Ibler, Konstantin Obradović, Miloš Radojković, Milan Šahović, and Danilo Türk.[19] Some of these academics were also well-respected members of the UN expert bodies—the UN International Law Commission, Milan Bartoš (1957–1973) and Milan Šahović (1974–1981),[20] and the UN Human Rights Committee, Dejan Janča and Vojin Dimitrijević[21] (the latter also served as its Vice-President).

Today there is an increasing number of academics working at local universities who have had some of their legal education outside Yugoslavia; there is also increasing pressure to publish internationally for the purpose of career progression in particular. But again inward-oriented scholarship remains very much the norm. As in many other countries there are dozens of colleagues in the post-Yugoslav States teaching and researching in international law who do so primarily in the local languages and who, despite their rank and influence domestically, have little international reputation and recognition.

In terms of the practice of international law in the former Yugoslavia, outside a very small circle of government lawyers it has generally been quite limited. This is despite the fact that the constitutional orders of the SFRY and its successor States are formally very open to the application of international law.[22] Ratified treaties are considered to be a part of the respective domestic legal order,[23] with supremacy over other laws.[24] However, in reality, issues of public international law are rarely litigated before national courts in the former Yugoslavia, with a few exceptions. The membership of the SRFY successor States in the Council of Europe (see Ziemele, this volume) and consequential accession to the European Convention of Human Rights (ECHR) (see Çalı, this volume), submitted the SFRY successor States to the compulsory jurisdiction of the European Court of Human Rights (ECtHR), which contributed to their domestic courts gradually starting to refer and apply[25] international human rights law in domestic proceedings, though not without inconsistencies.[26] Similarly, war crimes proceedings before general or specialized courts in some of the successor States have required reliance on international criminal law and international humanitarian law. But the circle of lawyers practising in these areas remains quite small, although it is worth mentioning that a number of practising lawyers have also been exposed to international practice in the field of international commercial and investment arbitration. That said, some Yugoslav international law academics themselves became practitioners in disputes before international courts and arbitral tribunals, such as the ICJ, many of which have arisen in the context of the SFRY's dissolution—for example, Vukas, Kreća, and Dimitrijević became ICJ judges ad hoc. Some academics and attorneys have also practised before the International Criminal Tribunal for the former Yugoslavia (ICTY). These proceedings have tended to be politically charged, and have generated a lot of media attention and general public interest.

4. Study Design

We will now turn to the main portion of our study, which will try to paint a general picture of international law doctrine in the former Yugoslavia by surveying some of the leading textbooks used in local universities. Due to space constraints, but also due to the fact that we speak Serbo-Croatian and not any of the other local languages (again bearing in mind the local centre-periphery dynamics), we will analyse a sample of leading textbooks from Bosnia and Herzegovina, Croatia, Montenegro, and Serbia. For Bosnia and Herzegovina, these include textbooks used at the law faculties of the University of Sarajevo[27] and the University of Banja Luka,[28] for Croatia textbooks used at the University of Zagreb[29] and the University of Rijeka,[30] for Montenegro textbook used at the Law Faculty of the University of Montenegro,[31] and for Serbia the textbooks at the University of Belgrade[32] and the Union University Belgrade.[33] All universities are public, except for the Union University Belgrade, which is private.

We have therefore selected five textbooks, whose single or principal authors are:

Juraj Andrassy et al[34] (required at Zagreb, recommended at Sarajevo),
Vladimir Đuro Degan[35] (required at Rijeka and Sarajevo),
Miljenko Kreća[36] (required at Belgrade and Montenegro),
Vojin Dimitrijević and Obrad Račić et al[37] (required at Union Belgrade, additional at Banja Luka), and
Ljiljana Mijović[38] (required at Banja Luka).

To this selection we have added the textbook by Smilja Avramov and Miljenko Kreća (Avramov-Kreća),[39] which is currently out of curricular use but is still representative. This textbook was a required reading at the University Belgrade[40] for almost a quarter of a century, from 1983 until 2007, and it may be the most influential textbook in Serbia in the past. Today it remains a recommended text in Banja Luka.

Most of the selected textbooks were published only after the dissolution of Yugoslavia (Degan in 2000, Dimitrijević-Račić et al in 2005, Kreća in 2007, and Mijović in 2019); all, except for Mijović, have at least two editions. So, we have compared the first[41] and the last editions to see if, and to what extent, authors changed their stance on certain issues and/or presented relevant developments in international law. On the other hand, Andrassy et al and Avramov-Kreća, date from before the dissolution of Yugoslavia, so they would allow for exploration and interpretation of ideology of international law promoted during socialist times, but this is beyond the scope of this chapter.

It is also worth noting that all institutions included in the study, expect for Sarajevo, use textbooks authored or principally authored by their professors. Additionally, the University of Sarajevo Law Faculty appears to be the most inclusive, as it assigns books authored by professors from Croatia and Serbia in its recommended material.[42]

Our comparative analysis of the textbooks looks at how they deal with those parts of international law that are most directly relevant to the experience of the former Yugoslavia and where its pacifying influence can be most felt (or not). We will therefore focus on questions of statehood, including the creation, dissolution, recognition, and continuity of States, and the position of the individual in international law, including international human rights law and international criminal law. In the context of higher legal education exclusively based on studying textbooks, international law scholarship is not only formative in a value sense, but also in a sense of practical application of and attitude to international law. That is to say that the way future practitioners will view, comprehend, and resort to international law is contingent on the way the textbooks instructed them to do so. We have, therefore, also studied how selected textbooks describe and discuss the topic of relation between domestic and international law, particularly the application of international law domestically.

5. Statehood

Because all the successor States emerged into statehood from the crucible of Yugoslavia's dissolution, the creation, recognition, extinction, and succession of States are inevitably going to be topics that the textbook authors will regard as especially important, even if we took aside the centrality of statehood in international law more generally. While all of the textbooks discuss the Montevideo criteria for statehood,[43] they differ in conceptualizing the creation (or extinction) of a State as a question of fact or a question of law. The first camp of authors (Dimitrijević-Račić et al, Degan and Mijović) take the position that statehood is a question of fact (effectiveness) to which international law attaches consequences.[44] The second camp (Andrassy et al, Avramov-Kreća, and Kreća) regard the creation of States as a process subject to international legal rules.[45]

This is not a trivial divide. It substantially impacts the narrative given in each textbook of the dissolution of the SFRY and the creation of new States on its territory. Namely, the statehood-as-fact camp does not frame the creation of new Yugoslav States as either legal or illegal. It is just a fact. The second camp, however, sees Yugoslavia's dissolution and the creation of successor States as a legal question, but they differ in how they apply the law to the facts. For Andrassy et al, the most-used Croatian textbook, the international community confirmed that Croatia 'was created in accordance with fundamental principles of international law, the UN Charter, especially in accordance with the principle of self-determination of peoples'.[46] But in the counterpart Serbian textbook authored by Avramov and Kreća, the authors reach the opposite conclusion: for them the secession of the federal units of Yugoslavia was contrary to international law.[47]

Both camps also apply their described approach to Kosovo's secession from Serbia. The first camp treats this as essentially a question of fact.[48] As for the second camp, as can be expected the Serbian textbook (Kreća[49]) sees Kosovo's secession from Serbia as illegal,[50] but interestingly Andrassy et al do not argue that it is legal. Rather, it points to the lack of the fulfilment of statehood criteria embodied in the effective authority in the time of the declaration of independence (which was in the hands of UNMIK) but ultimately remains inconclusive on the legality of Kosovo's secession.[51]

When it comes to recognition, the textbooks by and large adopt the declaratory theory of recognition[52] and agree that the grant of recognition is invariably influenced by political considerations.[53] But they differ again as to whether legality plays any role in recognition. The authors in the statehood-as-fact camp do not dwell on the legality of recognition and see it as a political act. For example, on the basis on the practice related to Bosnia-Herzegovina and Croatia, Mijović maintains that there are no firm legal criteria for recognition. And even if there were, they are often neglected in practice, which indicates that the recognition of State is a purely discretionary act.[54] Degan mentions the examples of the recognition of Bosnia and Herzegovina and Croatia, without fulfilling all statehood criteria, that is, effectiveness over the whole territory, as proof that recognition is a discretionary political act.[55] He explains that in these cases legitimacy prevailed over effectiveness, as recognitions were a political compromise reached not to reward the aggression against these States committed by the Yugoslav National Army.[56]

As for the authors from the second camp, who argue that the creation of States needs to be subjected to international law (Andrassy et al, Avramov and Kreća), they test the legality of recognitions exclusively on the new States of the former Yugoslavia, and again reach opposite conclusions. For Andrassy et al, Croatia was created legally and the process of its recognition was also legal.[57] But Avramov-Kreća views the recognitions of the independence of the secessionist Yugoslav federal units as an illegal act, because they did not possess any of the attributes of statehood and used force to gain independence.[58] Accordingly, they claim that the admittance to the SFRY secessionist States to the United Nations (UN) was 'a collective legitimization of an illegal act', which was a result of the pressure exercised by the US and Germany.[59] Avramov-Kreća also continuously promote the mainstream narrative of Milošević's Serbia that the dissolution of Yugoslavia was a project of the West, the then-European Community (especially, Germany[60]) and the US, which pressured other States to follow their lead in recognizing secessionist States in 1992, leading to 'tragic consequences: escalation of civil war and discreditation of the system of the UN'.[61]

In his independent textbook, Kreća has a similar overarching narrative regarding the dissolution of the SFRY. But then he veers into rather exotic departures from his textbook co-authored with Avramov, ranging from an argument that in the case of the successor States of the former Yugoslavia recognition had a constitutive rather than declaratory effect[62] (a point he shares with Degan),[63] to a proposal to adopt some sort of registration process for new States with the UN Secretariat, coupling it with the idea that 'if someone opposed this registration, there would be an international dispute before the independent court, under Art. 33 UN Charter'.[64]

Another interesting point of comparison between the textbooks is on issues of State continuity and succession. The official State position of the FRY was that it was the continuator of the SFRY, with the same legal personality and continuing the SFRY original membership as a founder of the UN. The other republics consistently rejected this claim, arguing that the FRY was a successor State just like them, and that the dissolution of the SFRY did not produce a continuator, as was the case with Russia and the USSR. When it comes to the textbooks we surveyed, the only one to support the FRY's continuity claim is Avramov-Kreća.[65] Mijović is silent on this issue,[66] and generally entirely ignores Yugoslavia when discussing statehood issues. Dimtrijević-Račić points out the different views on this question and inconsistencies in the relevant practice of the UN to discreetly oppose the claim on continuity (which again was abandoned by the FRY after the fall of Milošević),[67] while Degan and Andrassy et al strongly oppose this claim,[68] relying on the opinions of the Badinter Commission.[69]

The bottom line here is that some of the textbook authors unsurprisingly sell particular narratives to their audiences ('Croatia was lawfully created' versus 'Yugoslavia was unlawfully dissolved'; the FRY was or was not the SFRY's continuator). Others attempt to provide more neutral, less political but at times evasive, reflections on the end of Yugoslavia, but the price for doing so is to deny the normative role of international law in the process of the creation and dissolution of States.

6. Status of the Individual

All of the surveyed textbooks agree that, while States remain the main subject of international law, contemporary international law endows individuals with certain capacities.[70] They differ, however, in how they conceptualize this position and its importance for international law.[71] Dimitrijević-Račić et al, Degan, and Mijović[72] adopt a progressive or liberal stance—while admitting the limitations on individual subjecthood under international law, they insist on its importance for contemporary international law.[73] Degan goes as far as to expressly claim that 'individual is the ultimate addressee of any law, including international law'.[74] Andrassy et al's stance, on the other hand, has over successive revised editions gradually moved from the more conservative towards the more liberal understanding of the status.[75] But Avramov and Kreća are unmoved by contemporary developments. They continued to hold the most conservative position, exclusively assessing the status of individuals through the formal lens of States consenting to their limited capacities,[76] viewing individuals as marginal if not irrelevant for international law.[77] Kreća continues to subscribe to this view to this day.[78]

The discussion on international human rights and international criminal law, to which we now turn, is a natural extension of the views presented on the status of the individual under international law.

6.1 International human rights

While all textbooks include specific chapters dedicated to international human rights law, they do not invariably promote a view of sovereignty tempered by human rights. Again, we have two camps: human rights enthusiasts (Andrassy et al,[79] Dimitrijević-Račić et al, Degan, and Mijović) and human rights cynics (Avramov and Kreća).

Human rights enthusiasts view human rights as a matter of international concern not an internal affair of a State.[80] They advance the relevance and effects of the international protection mechanisms, especially the ECtHR,[81] to the domestic protection of human rights. Even the position towards the concept of humanitarian intervention, a controversial issue in the doctrine and in the practice of States, towards which all authors of this camp are sceptical (Degan somewhat less than others),[82] discloses their strong preference towards the protection of individuals. Specifically, while exercising extreme caution due to the wide possibilities for abuse (admitting that these abuses happen at the hands of powerful States), all raise the question of whether international community can be an innocent by-stander in the face of such atrocities.[83]

The human rights cynics, on the other hand, present arguments that frequently equate sovereignty with an absolutist version of the principle of non-interference in domestic matters, counting human rights as such domestic matters. A particularly striking example of this is Avramov and Kreća's notional acknowledgement that 'human rights give civilising physiognomy to a state' while promoting anti-American narratives that argue that a foreign policy with human rights as its main goal

> aim[s] to undermine the power of a state and interfere with domestic affairs for achieving political ends, which were once acquired by war. Geostrategic and hegemonistic ambitions are frequently disguised by human rights. Planetary order is pure fiction or, at best, a project of far future. Human rights require certain type of institutions to be protected and implemented, and ... a moral vision of community.

> The international community does not have the infrastructure for applying and protecting human rights.[84]

Thus, Avramov-Kreća does not, like the other textbooks, engage in a reasonable criticism of the idea of using human rights violations for justifying humanitarian intervention (Kreća does that in his independent textbook),[85] but treat international human rights protection as such with suspicion.

Moreover, this textbook incorporates conspiracy theories, especially pertaining to the dissolution of SFRY,[86] standing out from all other textbooks surveyed in this regard. The editions written after the 1999 illegal use of force by NATO against Serbia (we have studied the one from 2003), took these positions to their most radical and irrational extent. Here is a quote to illustrate what we mean:

> [Some theorists and politicians] emphasize the superiority of the 'Western culture', which puts other cultures in an inferior position. In the name of this, there is 'a brain wash' under the label of 'global human rights'. The development of science enabled new techniques of repression, which can have catastrophic consequences on physical and mental integrity of individuals. This is especially evident in the work of some religious sects, which use different kind of 'light' drugs and modern methods of changing physical and mental structure of humans.[87]

One can ascribe these most radical and irrational positions to Avramov, as she has written the relevant chapters.[88] Kreća's textbooks, which he single-authored since 2007 (we have studied 2010 and 2020 editions), when read after the previous quote seem almost balanced.[89]

To an outsider, Avramov and Kreća would undoubtedly seem like looney outliers, the kind of which exist in every corner of the world. But our main point is that, in their context, they are *not* outliers. Generations of students have been instructed in international law and relations from their textbook, which mainstreams political narratives of the Milošević era, heavily coloured with anti-Western sentiment (the SFRY was illegally broken apart by Western States, human rights are a disguise for hegemonistic interests,[90] war crimes prosecutions (as we will soon see) are yet another tool for victimizing Serbs, etc), dressed up in international law doctrines and rules. Such narratives still govern the hearts and minds of a great majority of people in Serbia. This is arguably one of the reasons why the majority of Serbian political elites and people found it difficult in 2022 to condemn Russia's unlawful war against Ukraine, despite themselves being victims of an unlawful use of force by NATO in 1999.

6.2 International criminal law

This brings us to international criminal law (ICL), a particularly acute and sensitive topic in the former Yugoslavia. The International Criminal Tribunal for the Former

Yugoslavia (ICTY), the first modern international criminal court, was established by the UN Security Council in 1993, and ceased operating in 2017. During its mandate it convicted some ninety individuals for international crimes committed in the Yugoslav wars, including much of the Serb political and military leadership in particular. The ICTY is still reviled among ethnic Serbs and Croats, whereas more positive attitudes towards the Tribunal exist within the Bosniak (Muslim) and Albanian communities, in more or less perfect proportion to the number of defendants from each community.[91] Serb and Croat legal scholars were also, for the most part, highly critical of the ICTY, arguing for example that it was unlawfully established, applied theories of responsibility not grounded in the law, or was generally biased against their own community.

In Croatia (or among ethnic Croats) the ICTY was most controversial for the cases it brought against Croatian generals for the ethnic cleansing of Croatian Serbs in the 1995 Operation Storm, whereby Croatia defeated the separatist Serb forces and recovered control over all of its territory. The Prosecutor filed indictments against three generals in 2001 and 2004; two of them were convicted by a unanimous Trial Chamber in 2011; they were then both acquitted by a divided Appeals Chamber, by 3 votes to 2, in 2012.[92] Only somewhat less controversial were the proceedings brought in 2004 against the leadership of Croat forces in Bosnia,[93] which resulted in convictions for all of the accused in 2017.[94]

A particularly remarkable feature of Croatia's engagement with the ICTY was the rejection of any finding that crimes against Serbs were committed as part of a 'joint criminal enterprise' (JCE), a theory of liability that by the labels it used ran counter to the official just war narrative. In other words, the mainstream Croatian opinion was that it was unacceptable for the military operations that resulted in the consolidation of Croatia's statehood to be regarded as being commanded by officers engaged in joint criminality. In 2007 the Croatian government thus commissioned the Croatian Academy of Sciences and Arts to produce a study critiquing the JCE theory, which it did (at almost 200 pages), which was then sent to the ICTY in a strange and futile effort at persuading it to overturn a key part of its jurisprudence.[95]

How then is the ICTY presented in the two textbooks from Croatia that we have examined? The 1995 edition of Andrassy et al—published before the major controversies regarding the ICTY in Croatia began—contains an objective description of the development of ICL and in particular of the establishment of the ICTY by the UN Security Council. No doubts are expressed about the legality of the establishment of the Tribunal (which again at the time of this edition was yet to try any defendants), nor about the appropriateness and fairness of this accountability mechanism. The chapter concludes with the authors stating that the Tribunal's establishment 'inspires hope that the international community will not subvert the activity of that Tribunal to an attempt to find a political solution to the consequences of Serbian aggression',[96] calling against impunity for atrocities committed. In the 2010 edition of Andrassy et al, however, there is no additional examination of the work of the ICTY at all, even though fifteen years had passed, and despite the controversies now running rampant in the Croatian public. Yet Andrassy et al now carefully omits any kind of normative evaluation of the Tribunal (even in terms of expressing hope that there will be no impunity).[97] There is, however, a more extensive analysis of the ICJ's *Bosnian Genocide* judgment and of how ethnic cleansing legally differs from genocide.[98]

As for Degan, in both 2000 and 2011 he is broadly supportive of the Tribunal and does not echo any of the criticisms levied against it from within Croatia. Both editions of the textbook are written in an objective, dispassionate tone, save for a brief passage in which he laments the 'aggression of the former "Yugoslav National Army" against the legally and democratically elected authorities' in Slovenia, Croatia, and Bosnia and Herzegovina, as well as the atrocities committed during the wars.[99] But while clearly positioning himself in arguing that Croatia and the other successor States had the right to establish their independence from the SFRY, Degan is quite careful to avoid Croat nationalist narratives. He also expressly mentions crimes committed against Serb victims[100] and harshly criticizes the decision of the ICTY Prosecutor not to investigate the use of cluster bombs and depleted uranium munitions by NATO forces during the 1999 Kosovo war.[101] Yet Degan is also careful to avoid discussing any of the controversies regarding the ICTY in Croatia, such as the prosecutions of the Croatian generals or the notion of joint criminal enterprise.

Turning now to Serbia, Avramov and Kreća are notable in their treatment of war crimes committed in the Yugoslav conflicts—which essentially go unmentioned—and of the ICTY, which very much is mentioned, as the International Criminal 'Tribunal' for the Former Yugoslavia (scare quotes theirs).[102] It is a 'Tribunal' because it was, according to the authors, unlawfully established by the Security Council, which is an executive and not a legislative organ, and had acted outside its powers and in violation of the Charter.[103] Again, according to the authors, the establishment of the ICTY and the ICTR provoked 'stormy debates in the world' with 'the most eminent experts' advocating against ad hoc tribunals and in favour of a permanent one.[104] Recall that this is a textbook, designed for, and for many years required for, thousands of students at the University of Belgrade, and it is these students whom Avramov and Kreća essentially systematically misled.[105] Their view on the illegality of the Tribunal is presented as the singular, correct one. No consideration is given to the views of those who argued that the Tribunal was established lawfully, nor to the *Tadic* decision of the Tribunal, which extensively dealt with its establishment.[106] And global scholarly consensus was misrepresented as somehow arguing against the legality of the ad hoc tribunals, when the converse is true—that most scholars sensibly think that a permanent international court is better than having many ad hoc tribunals does not entail that they consider the latter to have been unlawfully established.

As for Kreća's independent textbook, which is currently in use at the University of Belgrade, it is much milder in tone. It also does not engage with the issue of the ICTY's legality, while criticizing it and other ad hoc tribunals for dispensing 'selective, and partly vengeful justice' and for relying on extra-legal considerations in making their decisions.[107] Dimitrijević-Račić et al, on the other hand, is broadly supportive of the ICTY and examines its creation and work in substantial detail, while relying extensively on its decisions when discussing substantive crimes.[108] To anyone even remotely familiar with the Serbian context it would be apparent that the Dimitrijević-Račić et al textbook was conceived, in a sense, to be an antidote to the misrepresentations of the ICTY in the other textbooks in the country.

Finally, turning to Mijović, the textbook used at the University of Banja Luka, in the Bosnian Serb entity of Republika Srpska, its most notable feature is that in the eleven pages it devotes to international criminal law it says virtually nothing about prosecutions before the ICTY or before Bosnian domestic courts,[109] even though these were issues that completely preoccupied the public consciousness in Bosnia, and still do. The textbook's presentation is entirely abstract and acontextual—for an uninformed reader, it could have been written literally anywhere. But for readers from the region—that is, all of them—it is manifest that Mijović's avoidance of all the controversies regarding war crimes in Bosnia and the rest of the former Yugoslavia was entirely deliberate.

To conclude, the Croatian and Bosnian textbooks are particularly interesting for their silences, for the topics that they deliberately avoided—even though their readers would inevitably be aware of them. In Serbia, on the other hand, there is an open conflict between more nationalist and more liberal textbooks. Topics that are idiosyncratic and are hardly discussed at all in international textbooks, such as the legality of the establishment of the ICTY, have a central place here. And each textbook, either openly or cautiously, pushes the reader towards its own worldview, nationalist or cosmopolitan.

7. The Application of International Law in Domestic Legal Orders

The selected textbooks are chiefly absorbed with the grand themes of international law. The matter of its application in their respective domestic legal orders does not seem to particularly occupy their attention, again despite the nominal direct internal applicability of international law under the constitutions of former Yugoslav States.

While all of the textbooks include a chapter on the relationship between international and domestic law, they generally discuss it theoretically, by contrasting monist and dualist paradigms,[110] rather than as a question of daily practical relevance. None of the textbooks, except for Dimitrijević-Račić et al, engage in a discussion on the status and application of international law in their respective national legal system.[111] On this point, they could have been written anywhere in the world.[112] Dimitrijević-Račić et al, by contrast, dedicates a whole subchapter to the provisions of the Constitution of Serbia pertaining to the incorporation, application, and hierarchy of international law in the Serbian legal system.[113] Furthermore, this is the only textbook that addresses the practical application of the international law domestically in some of its substantive chapters.[114]

Again with the exception of Dimitrijević-Račić et al, the textbooks do not address the issue of how any conflicts between national and international law should be addressed.

And even Dimitrijević-Račić et al only sends a general message that such conflicts should be addressed by reference to the principle that national law cannot be used to absolve a State from violation of its international obligation.[115]

To sum up, the discussion on the application of international law domestically in the former Yugoslav textbooks is so abstract that it leaves the reader—including legions of students—with an impression of the complete irrelevance of international law in the national legal system of their State. And this impression is strengthened by the absence of any discussion of the national constitutions or of examples in their domestic judicial practice of the application of international law before national courts (again, except for Dimitrijević-Račić et al).

Hence, despite constitutional rules providing that international law is an integral part of their domestic legal orders[116] and is hierarchically superior to regular laws in these countries,[117] students in Bosnia and Herzegovina, Croatia, and Serbia graduate with the impression that international law is completely immaterial for the daily application of law. International law is presented as something elusive, dealing with grand themes that they can neither influence nor apply in their daily practice of law. The singular exception of Dimitrijević-Račić et al does not change this conclusion, as only a small portion of law students have studied international law using this textbook.[118] This undoubtedly influences how international law is perceived by the legal profession in all of these countries, including by casting doubts on its properly legal character.

8. Conclusion

What can we learn from examining the international legal tradition in the former Yugoslavia? Putting aside the skin-deep flirtation with Marxism during the SFRY, Yugoslav and post-Yugoslav international law scholars remain committed positivists. Some of them have published internationally, but most have published only domestically, writing in local languages. And domestically the textbook remains the most prestigious form of scholarship and the primary method of instruction, influencing generations of students. From those textbooks we have seen how their authors, despite their avowed positivism, fill their descriptions of, and arguments about, international law with extra-legal considerations, many of which relate to the trauma of the dissolution of the former Yugoslavia and its continuing after-effects.

The textbooks are shaped by the ideologies of their authors, as can only be expected, from the more conservative or nationalist to the more liberal or cosmopolitan. Some directly endorse mainstream positions within their respective societies, for example with regard to the legality or illegality of the creation of new States on Yugoslavia's ruins. Others are more cautious and evasive, especially in their silences. Some seem to be permeated by a Westphalian conception of State sovereignty, under which the State will decide what it pleases on questions such as war crimes prosecutions; most at least superficially endorse more modern, progressive conceptions of sovereignty. Some are rabidly partisan, others attempt to be as neutral or objective as possible. But, as is only natural, none can escape their context.

Still, the international legal tradition of the former Yugoslav countries resembles the international legal tradition of most other countries, certainly those of Eastern Europe, particularly in embracing positivism as the overarching theoretical framework for understanding the nature of international law. Also, divides between conservatives or nationals and liberals or cosmopolitans found in the international law scholarship in the former Yugoslavia exist elsewhere. For example, they are present in Russian international law scholarship, as shown by Lauri Mälksoo in the part of his study on international law in Russia,[119] where academia is occupied by similar debates we have found in the former Yugoslavia. Specifically, there are strong parallels in the approach to international law between the former Yugoslav conservative scholars (Avramov and Kreća), and conservative Russian scholars.[120] Interestingly, however, unlike Russian conservatives,[121] the conservatives of the former Yugoslavia do not expressly support constructing the relationship between domestic and international law in a dualistic fashion. Peculiarly, only Andrassy, the least liberal of the liberal authors, is of that view.[122] Be that as it may, our examination confirms that the former Yugoslav international law scholarship, most certainly, is not an isolated island. The countries of the former Yugoslavia have directly experienced the operation of international law in ways that most other societies have not—from wars, sanctions, and arm embargoes, to international courts deciding on the criminal responsibility of their political and military leaders, or on State responsibility for genocide, or on their borders. The textbooks we have surveyed have shaped the views of many thousands of law students on these issues. Having examined the textbooks' treatment of some of the topics that were inescapably important in the Yugoslav context, it is hard to say that upon completing their legal education the average student in the former Yugoslavia will have absorbed a vision of a cosmopolitan legal order that pacifies the worst urges of States. Perhaps most disappointing is how almost all of the textbooks surveyed convey an academic, abstract picture of international law—again along the lines of Russian international law scholarship[123]—that has little relevance for the daily practice of law in their societies. And this is a strange paradox, because again international law has in fact been more relevant in these societies than elsewhere.

Notes

*. We would like to thank the editorial team of the *Handbook* for insightful comments. We are especially grateful to the librarians—Ms. Vanja Eror of the University of Belgrade Faculty of Law, and Ms. Ksenija Mitrović, of the Union University Law School Belgrade—who have helped us acquire all relevant textbooks for this study. The research for this chapter conducted by Papić was supported by the Science Fund of the Republic of Serbia, grant no. 7744512, Monitoring and Indexing Peace and Security in the Western Balkans—MIND.

1. Yugoslavia is also an instructive case for exploring the other two themes of this handbook. The violent breakup of the former Yugoslavia and its aftermath could serve to explore the pacifying role of international law (or the lack thereof), the Non-Aligned Movement

established partly under Yugoslav leadership, which had its founding conference in Belgrade, can be used to test the universality of European ideas and practices. However, due to limited space, we have decided to concentrate on only one theme: diversity of legal traditions.

2. See Anthea Roberts, *Is International Law International?* (OUP, 2017) for the groundbreaking work on comparative international law, ie on how international law is understood and applied in different parts of the world.
3. ibid, 32, 129.
4. Andrea Bianchi and Moshe Hirsch, *International Law's Invisible Frames: Social Cognition and Knowledge Production in International Legal Process* (OUP, 2021).
5. Ana Luísa Bernardino, 'Going by the Book: What International Law Textbooks Teach Us Not to Know' in Bianchi and Hirsch (n 4) 293–307.
6. ibid, 294.
7. ibid.
8. Roberts 2017, 32.
9. Roberts, *Is International Law International?* (n 2) 32; Bernardino 2021, p 294.
10. Roberts 2017 (n 8) 32, 129.
11. For a good introductory text in English, see John R Lampe, *Yugoslavia as History* (CUP, 2nd edn, 2008).
12. As claimed by Lauri Mälksoo, these wars were 'waged around civilizational ideas of distinctness of culture and religion and which piece of land belonged to which people'.
13. Serbia and North Macedonia are candidate countries, while Bosnia and Herzegovina and Kosovo are recognized as potential candidates.
14. On the NATO bombing and unilateral humanitarian intervention as an arguable failure of international law's pacifying mission, see Mälksoo, this volume.
15. Vladimir-Djuro Degan, 'An Essay on the Doctrine of International Law in Croatia and the Former Yugoslavia' in *Baltic Yearbook of International Law*, vol 7 (2007) 181. For more on that see Milan Šahović, 'The Former Yugoslav Federation and International Law' in Ronald St John Macdonald (ed), *Essays in Honour of Wang Tieya* (Brill, 1994) 619–629.
16. He was claimed to be one of the architects of the judgment in the *Fisheries* case. See Degan (n 15) 181.
17. This was in 1996. It is worth noting that issues published in Belgrade after the break-up of the country were very critical of the regime of Slobodan Milošević in Serbia. See ibid.
18. For an extensive overview of the Yugoslav international doctrine until 1980, see Slobodan Milenković, 'Razvoj doktrine međunarodnog prava u Jugoslaviji', 21 Zbornik Pravnog fakulteta u Nišu 1981, 121–143.
19. Andrassy, Bartoš, and Šahović were also members of the prestigious Institut de Droit International, the first also serving as its President from 1969–1971 https://www.idi-iil.org/fr/histoire/presidents-precedents/, accessed 7 November 2021. After the dissolution of the SFRY, Dimitrijević (Serbia), Vukas (Croatia), and Dražen Petrović (Bosnia and Herzegovina) became associate member of the Institute https://www.idi-iil.org/en/membres-par-categorie/associes/, accessed 7 November 2021.
20. https://legal.un.org/ilc/guide/annex2.shtml
21. Rosalyn Higgins, 'On Vojin Dimitrijevic' in *Themes and Theories: Selected Essays, Speeches, and Writings in International Law* (OUP, 2009) 990–991.
22. The last SRFY Constitution (1974) stipulated that published international treaties are to be directly applied by domestic courts. SRFY Constitution 1974, Article 210(2).

23. See Croatian Constitution, Article 134; Montenegrin Constitution, Article 9; Serbian Constitution, Article 16(1); North Macedonian Constitution, Article 118. The Slovenian Constitution provides for their direct applicability (Article 8), while the Constitution of Bosnia and Herzegovina sets this only for 'general principles of international law' (see Article III(3b)).
24. See Croatian Constitution, Article 134 (for ratified treaties); Montenegrin Constitution, Article 9 (ratified treaties and generally accepted rules of international law); Serbian Constitution Articles 16(1) and 194(5) (ratified treaties and generally accepted rules of international law); North Macedonian Constitution, Article 118 (ratified treaties); and Slovenian Constitution, Article 8 (ratified treaties and 'generally accepted principles of international law'). In Bosnia and Herzegovina this status is given to the ECHR, see Constitution of Bosnia and Herzegovina, Article II(2).
25. Thus, this was not due to the same reasons described in Eyal Benvenisti, 'Reclaiming Democracy: The Strategic Uses of Foreign and International Law by National Courts', 102 *American Journal of International Law* 2008, 241.
26. For Serbia see Tatjana Papić and Vladimir Djerić, 'On the Margins of Consolidation: The Constitutional Court of Serbia', 10 *Hague Journal on the Rule of Law* 2018, 59–82. For Croatia, see Maša Marochini Zrinski, 'Izazovi u primjeni i tumačenju Konvencije u Republici Hrvatskoj', 55(2) *Zbornik radova Pravnog fakulteta u Splitu* 2018, 423–446.
27. See https://www.pfsa.unsa.ba/pf/wp-content/uploads/2021/04/STUDIJSKI-PROGRAM-DODIPLOMSKI-UNIVERZITETSKI-STUDIJ-PRAVA.pdf accessed 22 October 2021, 135.
28. See https://pf.unibl.org/medjunarodno-javno-pravo/?script=lat%22%20\l%20%221526734721693-946b4a2b-cf7e#1526734721693-946b4a2b-cf7e accessed 22 October 2021.
29. See https://www.pravo.unizg.hr/mp/predmet/mjpis accessed 22 October 2021.
30. On file with authors.
31. See https://www.ucg.ac.me/objava/blog/41568/objava/53098-ects-medjunarodno-javno-pravo-2021
32. On file with authors.
33. See http://pravnifakultet.rs/wp-content/uploads/2021/09/Informator-III-godina-2021-2021.pdf, 12–13.
34. Juraj Andrassy, Božidar Bakotić, Budislav Vukas, Međunarodno pravo 1 (Školska knjiga 1995), Juraj Andrassy, Božidar Bakotić, Maja Seršić, Budislav Vukas, Međunarodno pravo 1 (2nd rev edn, Školska knjiga 2010), id., Međunarodno pravo 3 (Školska knjiga 2006). Hereinafter this textbook will referred as Andrassy et al.
35. Vladimir Đ Degan, Međunarodno pravo (Pravni fakultet Sveučilišta u Rijeci 2000), Vladimir Đ Degan, Međunarodno pravo (Školska knjiga 2011).
36. Milenko Kreća, Međunarodno javno pravo (Pravni fakultet Univerziteta u Beogradu, 4th edn, 2010), Milenko Kreća, Međunarodno javno pravo (12th edn, Pravni fakultet Univerziteta u Beogradu 2020). As of 2007 Kreća independently authored his textbook on international law, and as of 1983 he co-authored the textbook with Avramov (n 39).
37. Vojin Dimitrijević, Obrad Račić, Vladimir Djerić, Tatjana Papić, Vesna Petrović, Saša Obradović, Osnovi međunarodnog javnog prava (1st edn, Beogradski centar za ljudska prava 2005), Dimitrijević-Račić et al., Osnovi međunarodnog javnog prava (3rd edn, Beogradski centar za ljudska prava 2012). One of us (Papić) is one of the authors of this book. Hereinafter this textbook will be referred as Dimitrijević-Račić et al.
38. Ljiljana Mijović, Osnove međunarodnog javnog prava, I i II dio (Comesgrafika 2019).

39. First edition of this book is from 1983: Smilja Avramov, Miljenko Kreća, Međunarodno javno pravo (Savremena administracija 1983). Here we have analysed Smilja Avramov, Miljenko Kreća, Međunarodno javno pravo (15th edn, Savremena administracija 1997), Smilja Avramov, Miljenko Kreća, Međunarodno javno pravo (18th edn, Savremena administracija 2003).
40. Not only at the Faculty of Law but also at the Faculty of Political Science.
41. We have departed from this in the case of Kreća's textbook, taking the edition from 2010 as that we wanted to take into consideration the author's approach to Kosovo's declaration of independence, which took place after the first edition of the textbook, ie in 2008.
42. See n 27.
43. Andrassy et al (1995) 66; Andrassy et al (2010) 81; Degan (2000) 226–229; Degan (2011) 210–214;, Avramov-Kreća (1997) 65–67, Avramov-Kreća (2003) 75–79; Dimitrijević-Račić et al (2005) 75, Dimitrijević-Račić et al (2012) 73; Mijović (2019) 48; Kreća (2010) 132–135, Kreća (2020) 135–138.
44. Dimitrijević-Račić et al (2005) 75, Dimitrijević-Račić et al (2012) 73; Degan (2000) 226, Degan (2011) 211; Mijović (2019) 49.
45. Andrassy et al (1995) 66, Andrassy et al (2010) 81; Avramov-Kreća (1997) 67–71, Avramov-Kreća (2003) 79–83; Kreća (2010) 138–142, Kreća (2020) 142–146.
46. Our translation. Andrassy et al (1995) 66, Andrassy et al (2010) 82.
47. Avramov-Kreća (1997) 70–71, Avramov-Kreća (2003) 82–83; Kreća (2010) 142, Kreća (2020) 146.
48. See Degan (2011) 216; Dimitrijević-Račić et al (2012) 266–267; and Mijović (2019) 53. Dimitrijević-Račić et al does not mention Kosovo in the section on the creation of States and recognition, but does so in the one which discusses advisory jurisdiction of the ICJ, giving a short and balanced overview of the case without any comment on the position of the Court. Mijović mentions Kosovo when raising issue of the compliance of the creation of a new State with international legal order but continues with arguing on the importance of effectiveness regardless of whether a State was created in accordance with domestic or international law, to never come back to Kosovo. Mijović (2019) 53.
49. Avramov-Kreća textbook last edition was of 2007, so no views on Kosovo's 2008 declaration of independence could have been expressed.
50. Kreća (2020) 147–150, 158.
51. Andrassy et al (2010) 85. Furthermore, this textbook says that 'it remains to be seen if the USA and the part of EU members states will succeed in their attempt to make Kosovo an independent state' which is at odds with the starting position that the creation of States is subject to international legal rules. ibid.
52. Andrassy et al (1995) 74, Andrassy et al (2010) 96; Degan (2000) 277, Degan (2011) 263; Avramov-Kreća (1997) 72, Avramov-Kreća (2003) 85; Dimitrijević-Račić et al (2005) 82, Dimitrijević-Račić et al (2012) 79; Mijović (2019) 52; Kreća (2010) 162–163, Kreća (2020) 170–171. Degan shows more nuance in respect to exploring the effects of recognition then others. Moreover, he sees the case of recognition of SRFY secessionist States on the basis of the opinions of the Badinter Commission to be of constitutive effect. Degan (2000) 282; Degan (2011) 266.
53. Andrassy et al (1995) 76–77, Andrassy et al (2010) 94; Avramov-Kreća (1997) 74, Avramov-Kreća (2003) 86; Dimitrijević-Račić et al (2005) 82, Dimitrijević-Račić et al (2012) 79; Degan (2000) 280; Degan (2011) 265; Kreća (2010) 164–165, Kreća (2020) 172–173.
54. Mijović (2019) 51.

55. Degan (2000) 280, Degan (2010) 265.
56. ibid.
57. Andrassy et al (2010) 95.
58. Avramov-Kreća (1997) 74, Avramov-Kreća (2003) 87.
59. Avramov-Kreća (1997) 71, Avramov-Kreća (2003) 83.
60. ibid.
61. Avramov-Kreća (1997) 71, Avramov-Kreća (2003) 87.
62. Kreća (2010) 164, Kreća (2020) 172.
63. See n 53.
64. Kreća (2010) 171, Kreća (2020) 179.
65. Avramov-Kreća (1997) 75, Avramov-Kreća (2003) 88. Kreća holds similar view but presents it to look more balanced. Kreća (2010) 230, Kreća (2020) 244.
66. Mijović (2019) 85–87.
67. Dimitrijević-Račić et al (2005) 89–90, Dimitrijević-Račić et al (2012) 83–84.
68. Andrassy et al (1995) 274–277, Andrassy et al (2010) 342–345; Degan (2001) 787, Degan (2011) 217–218, 761.
69. Andrassy et al (1995) 274–277, Andrassy et al (2010) 342–345; Degan (2001) 232–233, Degan (2011) 217–218.
70. Andrassy et al (1995) 58, Andrassy et al (2010) 371; Degan (2000) 476–778, Degan (2011) 462–464; Avramov-Kreća (1997) 63–64, 267–268, Avramov-Kreća (2003) 74, 326–327; Dimitrijević-Račić et al (2005) 148, Dimitrijević-Račić et al (2012) 128; Mijović (2019) 43–44; Kreća (2010) 127, Kreća (2020) 132.
71. The same divide on the status of an individual under international law is identical in Russian textbooks. See Lauri Mälksoo, *Russian Approaches to International Law* (OUP, 2015) 104–110.
72. Claiming that individuals are subject of international law, Mijović (2019) 44.
73. Degan (2000) 477–480, Degan (2011) 463–465; Dimitrijević-Račić et al (2005) 148–149, Dimitrijević-Račić et al (2012) 128; Mijović (2019) 162–164.
74. Degan (2000) 473; Degan (2011) 460. His later claim that 'for the sake of clarity, it is the best to deny the attribute of subject of international law to the individual' is rectified and put in accordance with the initial position by the statement that 'would not prevent further development of law to her advantage'.
75. Deleting references and quotes denying an individual the status of subject of international law as of 1995 edition. cf 1990 edition (at 54), 1995 edition (at 60), and 2012 edition (at 70–80).
76. Avramov-Kreća (1997) 266–268, Avramov-Kreća (2003) 325–327; Kreća (2010) 127–128, Kreća (2020) 131–132.
77. In Avramov-Kreća, an abundance of space is wasted on presenting theories which claim individuals are not subjects of international law. Avramov-Kreća (1997) 266–267, Avramov-Kreća (2003) 325–326. Kreća seems particularly keen to stress that the individual is not a subject of international law. Kreća (2010) 125–129, Kreća (2020) 129–133.
78. Kreća (2010) 125–129, Kreća (2020) 129–133.
79. While one does not get an impression of Andrassy at al as a fully-fledged human rights enthusiast, this textbook is far from being the human rights cynic that Avramov-Kreća is.
80. Andrassy et al (1995) 298, Andrassy et al (2010) 371, 402; Degan (2000) 246, 501, Degan (2011) 231; Mijović (2019) 169.

81. Andrassy et al (1995) 297–326, Andrassy et al (2010) 370–403; Dimitrijević-Račić et al (2005) 195–210, Dimitrijević-Račić et al (2012) 202–217; Degan (2000) 501–522, Degan (2011) 484–506; Mijović (2019) 167–179.
82. He does not address the possibility of abuse head-on but argues that the issue of gross human rights violations against the background of the UNSC paralysis to decide on the matter is sensitive. See Degan (2000) 246–247, fn 14, Degan (2011) 232, fn 18. Neither he nor Andrassy specifically discuss the legality of the 1999 NATO bombing of the FRY. Andrassy et al (2006) 81–82. Predictably, all Serbian textbooks do so and agree on the NATO intervention's illegality. Avramov-Kreća (2003) 232–234; Dimitrijević-Račić et al (2005) 275–276, Dimitrijević-Račić et al (2012) 290–291; Kreća (2010) 189–191, Kreća (2020) 198–199. Avramov-Kreća refer to it as 'aggression', while Dimitrijević avoids this term, depicting the 1999 NATO bombing as an illegal 'intervention'. Avramov-Kreća even view the 1999 NATO action against FRY 'as the gravest crime in Europe after the Holocaust'—see Avramov-Kreća (2003) 233.
83. Andrassy et al (2010) 402–403; Dimitrijević-Račić et al (2005) 275–277, Dimitrijević-Račić et al (2012) 290–291; Degan (2000) 10, fn 6, 246–247, fn 14, Degan (2011) 10, fn 6, 232, fn 18.
84. Avramov-Kreća (2003) 316–317.
85. Kreća (2010) 189–191, Kreća (2020) 197–200.
86. This textbook even manages to emanate anti-American sentiment when presenting the theory of critical legal studies, claiming it is 'authentically American construction, which supposes to serve as theoretical umbrella to policy of this country, the policy of double standards'. Avramov-Kreća (2003) 37.
87. Avramov-Kreća (2003) 315.
88. See the note in Avramov-Kreća (2003) xviii.
89. Kreća (2010) 47–48, Kreća (2020) 50.
90. This is also widespread in the Russian international law scholarship, which argues that international law is manipulated by the US as global hegemon, see Mälksoo (n 71) 103, 134.
91. For more on attitudes towards the ICTY and the facts that it established in the former Yugoslavia, see M Milanovic, 'The Impact of the ICTY on the Former Yugoslavia: An Anticipatory Post-Mortem', 110 *American Journal of International Law* 2016, 233.
92. *Prosecutor v Gotovina et al*, IT-06-90.
93. One of them, Slobodan Praljak, committed suicide by cyanide in the ICTY courtroom as the Appeals Chamber affirmed his conviction.
94. *Prosecutor v Prlić et al*, IT-04-74.
95. Available in English at https://www.pravo.unizg.hr/_download/repository/Studija_o_zajednickom_zlocinackom_pothvatu_engleska_verzija.pdf.
96. Andrassy et al (1995) 348.
97. Andrassy et al (2010) 436–437.
98. ibid, 427–430.
99. Degan (2000) 547–548, Degan (2011) 532–533.
100. Degan (2000) 548.
101. Degan (2011) 536.
102. Avramov-Kreća (1997) 285, Avramov-Kreća (2003) 355.
103. ibid.
104. Avramov-Kreća (2003) 356.

105. The same stands for the 1991 'Desert Storm' operation against Iraq, which this textbook depicts as the abuse of the UN. Avramov-Kreća (1997) 185–186, Avramov-Kreća (2003) 229–230.
106. *Prosecutor v Tadic*, IT-94-1, Decision on the Defence Motion for Interlocutory Appeal on Jurisdiction, 2 October 1995.
107. Kreća (2020) 632–633.
108. Dimitrijević-Račič et al (2005) 221–241, Dimitrijević-Račič et al (2012) 226–249.
109. Mijović (2019) 192–202.
110. Andrassy et al (1995) 4–6, Andrassy et al (2010) 4–7; Degan (2000) 15–32, Degan (2011) 14–30, Avramov-Kreća (1997) 32–35, Avramov-Kreća (2003) 37–42; Mijović (2019) 17–20; Kreća (2010) 67–79, Kreća (2020) 69–83; Dimitrijević-Račić et al (2005) 68–70, Dimitrijević-Račić et al (2012).
111. Kreća does not even mention this issue, while Andrassy et al, Avramov-Kreća, Mijović, and Degan deal with it in a paragraph or two. Andrassy et al (1995) 6, Andrassy et al (2010) 7; Avramov-Kreća (1997) 35, Avramov-Kreća (2003) 41–42; Degan (2000) 27; Degan (2011) 25–26, Kreća (2010) 67–79, Kreća (2020) 69–83; Mijović (2019) 18–20.
112. This is especially true for Kreća (2020).
113. Dimitrijević-Račić et al (2005) 68–70, Dimitrijević-Račić et al (2012) 66–68.
114. See, eg, the chapter on privileges and immunities, Dimitrijević-Račić et al (2012) 160–161, 165–166, 174–175.
115. Dimitrijević-Račić et al (2005) 68, Dimitrijević-Račić et al (2012) 65–66.
116. See n 23.
117. For Bosnia and Herzegovina this is only the case for the ECHR. See n 24.
118. It is a required reading only at the Faculty of Law of the Union University Belgrade, a small private law school, which enrols ten to fifteen times fewer students than the State-owned Faculty of Law of the University of Belgrade. In Banja Luka, it is only recommended reading.
119. Mälksoo (n 71) 77–146.
120. See ibid.
121. ibid, 112–121.
122. Andrassy et al (1995) 3; Andrassy et al (2010) 3, 6.
123. Mälksoo (n 71) 94–95.

Index

For the benefit of digital users, indexed terms that span two pages (e.g., 52–53) may, on occasion, appear on only one of those pages.